World Literature
and Its Times

VOLUME **6**

Middle Eastern
Literatures and
Their Times

World Literature
and Its Times

Profiles of Notable Literary Works and the
Historical Events That Influenced Them

Joyce Moss

THOMSON

GALE

Detroit • New York • San Francisco • San Diego • New Haven, Conn. • Waterville, Maine • London • Munich

World Literature and Its Times
Profiles of Notable Literary Works and the Historical Events That Influenced Them
Volume 6
Middle Eastern Literatures and Their Times

Joyce Moss

Product Manager
Carol DeKane Nagel

Editorial
Michelle Kazensky, Julie Keppen, Dan Marowski, Ira Mark Milne, Lemma Shomali, Maikue Vang

Rights Acquisition and Management
Mari Masalin-Cooper, Shalice Shah-Caldwell

Imaging and Multimedia
Lezlie Light, Michael Logusz, Daniel Newell, Christine O'Bryan, Denay Wilding

Manufacturing
Lori Kessler

Copyright © 2004
Joyce Moss
ISBN 0-7876-3731-9
Printed in the United States of America
10 9 8 7 6 5 4 3 2 1

Library of Congress Control Number: 2004108151

Contents

Preface. . . . . *vii*

Acknowledgements . . . . *xi*

Introduction. . . . . *xv*

Chronology of Relevant Events . . . . *xxi*

Contents by Title . . . . *xlv*

Contents by Author . . . . *xlvii*

Contents by Language . . . . *xlvix*

Text and Image Credits. . . . . *li*

Entries *1*

Index. 559

General Preface

The world at the dawn of the twenty-first century is a shrinking sphere. Innovative modes of transmission make communication from one continent to another virtually instantaneous, quickening the development of a global society, heightening the urgency of the need for mutual understanding. At the foundation of *World Literature and Its Times* is the belief that within a people's literature are keys to the perspectives, emotions, and formative events that have brought the people to the present point. As manifested in their literary works, societies experience phenomena that are in some respects universal and in other respects tied to time and place.

Kahlil Gibran's *Broken Wings*, for example, concerns the repression of women in Lebanon in the early twentieth century; Virginia Woolf's *Mrs. Dalloway* concerns their repression in England during the same time period. The two novels, though generated continents apart, evince a general similarity of experience. The specific nature of the two experiences diverges sharply, however, depending on place, and when time is also a variable, the divergences only multiply. Contextualizing the works in their respective places and times helps illuminate the differences as well as the similarities between such experiences.

World Literature and Its Times regards both fiction and nonfiction as rich mediums for understanding individuals and societies. In its view, full understanding of a literary work demands attention to events and attitudes of the period in which it takes place and the one in which it is written. Therefore, the series contextualizes a given work within both time periods. Each volume covers some 50 literary works spanning a mix of societies, centuries, and genres, from novels and short stories to biographies, essays, speeches, poems, and plays. The literary work itself takes center stage, with its contents determining the types of history—social, political, psychological, economic, and/or cultural—that are covered within a particular entry. Every entry discusses the relevant historical issues apart from the literary work, making connections to the literature when merited, and allowing for comparisons between the artistic and the historical realities. Also discussed is the literary work itself, in the interest of extracting historical understandings from it. Of course, the function of literature is not necessarily to represent history accurately. Nevertheless, the images and ideas promoted by a powerful literary work—be it Isak Dinesen's memoir *Out of Africa* (set in Kenya), William Shakespeare's play *Macbeth* (Scotland), or José Hernandez's poem "The Gaucho Martín Fierro" (Argentina)—leave impressions commonly taken to be historical.

In taking literature as fact, one risks acquiring a mistaken notion of history. A case in point is the gaucho of Argentina, who inspired poetry by non-gauchos that conveys a highly romanticized image of these cowboy-like nomads, albeit one that includes some realistic details. Exposing such discrepancies, this series distinguishes historical fact from its literary reworkings. On the other hand, literary works can broaden and deepen our understanding of history. They are able to convey more than the cut-and-dried record by portraying events in a way that captures the fears and challenges of a period or that draws attention to groups left out of or marginalized by standard histories. Many of the literary works covered in this series—from Miguel de Cervantes's *Don Quixote* (Spain) to Nelson Mandela's "The Rivonia Trial Speech" (South Africa), to Abd al-Rahman Munif's *Cities of Salt* (Arabian Peninsula)—draw attention to such groups. Featured in *Cities of Salt* are the Bedouin and the impact of Western-controlled development of the oil industry on their lives in the Arabian Peninsula.

Featured in other works (e.g., Yehuda Amichai's *Songs of the Land of Zion, Jerusalem;* Najib Mahfuz's *Miramar*) are views and characters that point to the complexity of the associated societies, defying the existence of stereotypes. Taken together, the entries in a volume present a cross-section of perspectives and experiences in a given society in a manner that begins to do justice to its complexity. Nonfiction too must be anchored in its place and time to derive its full value. While fictional works can defy stereotypes through characters and plot twists that are contrary to preconceptions, nonfiction may attack stereotypic ideas directly, as some of the world's most pivotal essays do. In *Plagued by the West,* the Persian writer Jalal Al-i Ahmad seeks to stop in its tracks a notion gaining ground in 1960s Iran that Western values and customs should be elevated over those of the East; covered in the entry on his essay are the political and social conditions that gave rise to it. Another entry, on Charles Darwin's *On the Origin of Species,* links his essay to scientific and religious developments in nineteenth-century Britain, and to challenges to its empire abroad. From Africa, the *Wretched of the Earth* by Frantz Fanon reaches a conclusion about the value of violent revolution that the entry on this work relates to Algeria's war of liberation and to Fanon's involvement in it.

The task of reconstructing the historical context of a literary work can be problematic. The work may be so ancient that understanding its context involves a degree of conjecture (e.g., The Dead Sea Scrolls). Or perhaps the work features a legendary hero who defies attempts to fit him into a strict time slot (such as Gilgamesh of ancient Mesopotamia, or the Danish hero Beowulf of medieval British epic). Or maybe a novelist has presented events out of chronological order, as Carlos Fuentes does in *The Death of Artemio*

Cruz (twentieth-century Mexico). *World Literature and Its Times* adapts to these changing circumstances, contextualizing ancient texts according to the most recent scholarship, or profiling relevant customs of the culture that gave rise to an epic hero, or, in the third instance, unscrambling the plot and providing a linear rendering of events. Invariably the effort sheds light on the relationship between fact and fiction, both of which are shown to provide insight into the people who generated the writing.

And always the approach is taken with a warm appreciation for the beauty of a literary work independent of historical facts, but also in the belief that ultimate regard for the work is shown by placing it in the context of pertinent events. Beyond this underlying belief, the series is founded on the notion that a command of world literature bolsters knowledge of the writings produced by one's own society. Long before the present century, writers from different locations affected one another through trends and strategies in their literatures. In our own age, such cross-fertilization has intensified. Latin American literature, having been influenced by French and Spanish trends, itself influences Chinese writers of today. Likewise, Africa's literary works have affected and been affected by France's, and the same holds true for India and Great Britain, and various Middle Eastern countries and the United States. In the process, world literature and its landmark texts gain even greater significance, attaining the potential to promote a fundamental understanding, not only of others but also of ourselves.

The Selection of Literary Works

The works chosen for inclusion in *World Literature and Its Times,* Volume 6: *Middle Eastern Literatures and Their Times* have been carefully selected by the university professors listed in Acknowledgments. Keeping the literature-history connection in mind, the team made its selections based on a combination of factors: how frequently a literary work is studied, how closely it is tied to pivotal events in the past or present, how strong and enduring its appeal has been to readers in and out of the society that produced it, and how well it helps represent the breadth of the four major literatures of the region (Arabic, Hebrew, Persian, and Turkish) over the centuries.

Attention has been paid to modern as well as classic works that have met with critical and/or popular acclaim and to foundational literary and scriptural texts of the region. There has also been a careful effort to represent female and other minority voices and to cover a mix of genres while at the same time acknowledging that for centuries poetry was the most celebrated medium in the Middle East. Please see *World Literature and Its Times 2: African Literature and Its Times* for a number of additional literary works with overlapping geographical ties (e.g., Taha Husayn's *An Egyptian Childhood*).

Many literary works in the Arabic, Persian, Turkish, and Hebrew traditions of the Middle East fall outside the purview of this volume, including works in the colloquial dialects and very anecdotal or episodic works (for example, in Persian literature, the "Mirror for Princes" parables; in Arabic, the *zajal* ballads of al-Andalus; in Hebrew, the ancient rabbinic teachings [stories, legends, witticisms] known as *aggadah*, and in Turkish, *asik* minstrel poetry). Works conceived in other languages of the region, such as Armenian or Kurdish, lie outside the scope of the titles included too. The volume in no way professes complete coverage of Middle Eastern literatures. Rather it focuses on a core set of works for each of the four literatures, making sure to include a representative sampling from the inception of the tradition to the present. Along with meeting the criteria identified above, the selection has been limited to those titles presently available in English translation. There are, of course, many more pivotal works by Middle Eastern writers than could be included. The inclusion of the selected titles was achieved by keeping the above-detailed concerns in mind.

Transliteration Practices

Middle Eastern Literatures and Their Times has adopted transliteration policies with utmost regard for the needs of its readers when representing the letters of a foreign alphabet by those in the English alphabet. In determining the policies to adopt, the editors kept in mind two primary goals: 1) making foreign words as approachable as possible for those unfamiliar with a given language and 2) providing readers with spellings used in library catalogs to facilitate additional research. Of the four languages covered, only Turkish is written in a Latin alphabet. *Middle Eastern Literatures and Their Times* spells both modern and Ottoman Turkish words according to modern Turkish spelling to eliminate confusion that would otherwise arise from variant spellings of the same word. The use of Turkish

diacritics has been retained, except for the breve over the *g* and the undotted *i*.

For Arabic, Persian, and Hebrew, the volume uses the transliterations found in the Library of Congress Romanization tables at http://lcweb. loc.gov/catdir/cpso/roman.html with the exclusion of diacritical marks. *Middle Eastern Literatures and Their Times* retains the letter ayn (indicated by `) and the letter hamza (indicated by ´) in the middle of a word when either is necessary to explain the word's root or for scansion in poetry. To pronounce words, readers without knowledge of Arabic can ignore both signs. The forms of proper names established by the Library of Congress are frequently used. For some prominent individuals, the Library of Congress prefers popular spellings in Western publications rather than those that conform to transliteration tables, and *Middle Eastern Literatures and Their Times* has followed suit. At times the volume uses the most common form of a name rather than the Library of Congress form and generally the volume uses a shortened Library of Congress form, as publications on the Middle East frequently do. An example from Arabic is Muhammad ibn Abd al-Malik ibn Tufayl; initially the volume identifies him by the common form of his name, Abu Bakr ibn Tufayl, and thereafter simply as Ibn Tufayl. In such cases, *Middle Eastern Literatures and Their Times* includes both the shortened form and the Library of Congress form in the index. For names or words used primarily in speech, the volume invokes the colloquial rather than standard Arabic spellings. In keeping with the individual Middle Eastern literatures, it refers to the collected works or corpus of a given poet by a standard term: the spelling *diwan* indicates the pronunciation in Arabic (in which the term originated); the spelling *divan*, the pronunciation in Persian or Turkish.

Format and Arrangement of Entries

The volumes in *World Literature and Its Times* are arranged geographically. Within each volume, the collection is arranged alphabetically by title of the literary work. An additional contents page at the beginning of *World Literature and Its Times*, Volume 6: *Middle Eastern Literatures and Their Times*, provides a breakdown of the titles covered by the language in which they were generated.

Each entry is organized as follows:

1. **Introduction—provides identifying information in three parts:**

   The literary work—specifies genre of a work, place and time period in which it is set, when it was written and/or first published, and when it was first translated into English; also provided is the title of the work in its original language.

Synopsis—summarizes the storyline or contents of the work.

Introductory paragraph—introduces the literary work in relation to the author's life.

2. **Events in History at the Time the Literary Work Takes Place**—describes social and political events that relate to the plot or contents of the literary work. The section may discuss background information as well as relevant events during the period in which the work is set. The subsections in this section vary, depending on the particular literary work. In general, the section takes a deductive approach, starting with events in history and telescoping inward to events in the literary work.

3. **The Literary Work in Focus**—summarizes in detail the plot or contents of the literary work, describes how it illuminates history, and identifies sources used to generate the work as well as the literary context that surrounds it. First comes a *plot summary* of the highlighted work. The next subsection focuses on a specific aspect of the work to show how it illuminates our understanding of events or attitudes of the period; taking an inductive approach, this subsection starts with the literary work and broadens outward to events in history. Lastly, a third subsection identifies sources that inspired elements of the work and discusses its literary context, or relation to other works in the region.

4. **Events in History at the Time the Literary Work Was Written**—describes social, political, and/or literary events in the au-

thor's lifetime that relate to the plot or contents of a work. Also discussed in this section is the initial reception accorded the literary work.

5. **For More Information**—provides a list of all sources that have been cited in the entry as well as sources for further reading about the different issues or personalities featured in the entry.

If the literary work is set and written in the same time period, sections 2 and 4 of the entry on that work ("Events in History at the Time the Literary Work Takes Place" and "Events in History at the Time the Literary Work Was Written") are combined into the single section "Events in History at the Time of the Literary Work."

Additional Features

Whenever possible, primary-source material is provided through quotations in the text and material in sidebars. Other sidebars feature historical details that amplify issues raised in the text, or anecdotes that promote understanding of the temporal context. At the front of the volume is a set of timelines that provides a historical overview of the societies highlighted; each of the timelines correlates the events in its historical overview to the literary works covered for that society in this volume. Additional timelines appear within entries when needed to summarize chains of events. Finally, historically relevant illustrations enrich and further clarify information in the entries.

Comments and Suggestions

Your comments on this series and suggestions for future editions are welcome. Please write: Product Manager, *World Literature and Its Times,* Thomson Gale 27500 Drake Road, Farmington Hills, Michigan 48331-3535.

Acknowledgments

World Literature and Its Times, Volume 6: Middle Eastern Literatures and Their Times is a collaborative effort that progressed through several stages of development, each monitored by a team of outstanding experts in Arabic, Persian, Turkish, or Hebrew literature and history. A special thank you goes to Professors Roger Allen (Arabic), Ahmad Karimi-Hakkak (Persian), Arnold J. Band (Hebrew), and Bill Hickman (Turkish) for overseeing each stage, from the inception to the end of the development process. Warm gratitude is extended also to professors who, along with the above-named experts, provided continuous guidance in their respective fields: Terri DeYoung, for Arabic; Raymond P. Sheindlin, for Hebrew, and Sarah G. Moment Atis, for Turkish. Middle Eastern Studies is replete with conflicting views and innovative perspectives; negotiating the information to produce the most objective coverage possible was, in the end, achievable because of the exceptional consultants, writers, and librarians involved, and their joint commitment to fidelity with respect to the historical and cultural experiences in their given fields.

For their incisive participation in selecting the literary works to cover, the editors extend deep appreciation to the following professors:

Roger Allen, University of Pennsylvania, Department of Asian and Middle Eastern Studies (Arabic)

Terri DeYoung, Associate Professor, University of Washington, Seattle, Department of Near Eastern Languages and Civilizations (Arabic)

Ahmad Karimi-Hakkak, University of Washington, Seattle, Department of Near Eastern Languages and Civilizations (Persian)

Arnold J. Band, University of California at Los Angeles, Department of Near Eastern Studies (Hebrew)

Barbara Harshav, Yale University, Department of Comparative Literature (Hebrew)

Bill Hickman, formerly University of California at Berkeley, Department of Near Eastern Studies (Turkish)

Sincere gratitude is extended to the following professors and subject-matter specialists for their careful review of the entries to insure accuracy and completeness of information:

Roger Allen, University of Pennsylvania, Department of Asian and Middle Eastern Studies

Russ Arnold, Ph.D. candidate, University of California at Los Angeles, Department of Near Eastern Languages and Cultures

Sarah G. Moment Atis, University of Wisconsin, Department of Languages and Cultures of Asia

Arnold J. Band, University of California at Los Angeles, Department of Near Eastern Languages and Cultures

Scott Bartchy, University of California at Los Angeles, Department of History

Acknowledgments

Nancy E. Berg, Washington University St. Louis, Department of Asian and Near Eastern Languages and Literatures

Terri DeYoung, University of Washington, Seattle, Department of Near Eastern Languages and Civilizations

Nili Scharf Gold, University of Pennsylvania, Department of Asian and Middle Eastern Studies

Barbara Harshav, Yale University, Department of Comparative Literature

Todd Hasak-Lowy, University of Florida, Department of African and Asian Languages and Literatures

Bill Hickman, formerly University of California at Berkeley, Department of Near Eastern Studies

Richard Kalmin, Jewish Theological Seminary, Department of Talmud and Rabbinics

Ahmad Karimi-Hakkak, University of Washington, Seattle, Department of Near Eastern Languages and Civilizations

Kenneth Moss, University of Pennsylvania, Center for Judaic Studies

Adam Michael Rubin, Hebrew Union College, Los Angeles, Department of Jewish History

Raymond P. Scheindlin, Jewish Theological Seminary, Department of Jewish Literature

Benjamin D. Sommer, University of Chicago, Department of Religion

Suzanne Pinckney Stetkevych, Indiana University, Department of Near Eastern Languages and Cultures

For their painstaking research and composition, the editors thank the writers whose names appear at the close of the entries that they contributed. A complete listing follows:

Glenda Abramson, Cowley Lecturer, Oxford University, England

Wali Ahmadi, Assistant Professor, University of California at Berkeley

Dina Amin, Lecturer, University of Pennsylvania

Walter G. Andrews, Professor, University of Washington, Seattle

Russell C. D. Arnold, Finkelstein Fellow, University of Judaism

Carol Bakhos, Assistant Professor, University of California at Los Angeles

Zekeriya Baskal, Ph.D., University of Wisconsin

Michael Beard, Professor, University Of North Dakota

Nancy E. Berg, Assistant Professor, Washington University, St. Louis

John K. Bragg, Ph.D. candidate, University of Wisconsin at Madison

Warren Carter, Pherigo Professor of New Testament, St. Paul School of Theology

Ipek Azime Çelik, Ph.D. candidate, New York University

Miriam Cooke, Professor, Duke University

Jonathan P. Decter, Assistant Professor, Brandeis University

Terri DeYoung, Associate Professor, University of Washington, Seattle

Ellen Ervin, Ph.D., Columbia University; professional writer

Stephen Geller, Professor, Chair of the Department of Bible, Jewish Theological Seminary

Todd Hasak-Lowy, Assistant Professor, University of Florida

Persis M. Karim, Assistant Professor, San Jose State University

Ahmad Karimi-Hakkak, Professor, University of Washington, Seattle

Trevor LeGassick, Professor, University of Michigan

Pamela S. Loy, Ph.D., University of California at Santa Barbara; professional writer

Majd Al-Mallah, Assistant Professor, Grand Valley State University

Caroline Sawyer, Assistant Professor, State University of New York, College at Old Westbury

Raymond P. Scheindlin, Professor, Jewish Theological Seminary

Samah Selim, Assistant Professor, Princeton University

Anna Oldfield Senarslan, Ph.D. candidate, University of Wisconsin at Madison

Irfan Shahîd, Professor, Georgetown University

Benjamin D. Sommer, Visiting Associate Professor, University of Chicago

Paul Sprachman, Assistant Extension Specialist, Rutgers University

Suzanne Pinckney Stetkevych, Professor, Indiana University

Christopher R. Stone, Assistant Professor, Middlebury College

Kamran Talattof, Associate Professor, University of Arizona

Barry Tharaud, Professor Emeritus, Mesa State College, Colorado

Mark Wagner, Ph.D. candidate, New York University

Nadiya Yakub, Assistant Professor, University of North Carolina at Chapel Hill

Douglas C. Young, Lecturer, Stanford University

Joseph Zeidan, Associate Professor, Ohio State University

For determining the transliteration strategy and reviewing the Arabic-, Persian-, and Turkish-related entries to insure consistency of spelling of foreign words across the volume and with Library of Congress format, the editors thank Mary St. Germain of the Suzzallo Library at the University of Washington in Seattle. For the Hebrew-related entries, they thank David Hirsch of the Young Research Library at the University of California at Los Angeles.

Deep appreciation is extended to Michael L. LaBlanc of Thomson Gale for his editorial refinements. Anne Leach indexed the volume with great sensitivity to readers and content. An additional thank you goes to Mary St. Germain for facilitating the indexing of foreign names in ways that promote future research. Lastly warm gratitude is extended to Danielle E. Price for editing, to Lorraine Valestuk for editing and proofreading, and to Monica Riordan and Lisa Granados for proofreading and organizational management.

Introduction

Romeo and Juliet may be the world's most celebrated lovers, but the couple could learn a thing or two from Khusraw and Shirin, a star-crossed pair from Persian literature who lived far longer lives and ended up happily united for a time before meeting their own tragic fates. Of course, this Persian twosome, penned into posterity by Nizami of Ganja, "lived" some seven centuries before Shakespeare's duo and contended with issues pertinent to their own environs.

Still, the two plots, whose similarities are as striking as their differences, form just one of a host of parallels between the East and West that emerges from a close look at some of the finest literature generated in the Middle East. Another is the set of functions served by literature itself, from origin tales, to scripture, historical and realistic fiction, social criticism, philosophical introspection, moral edification, and ribald entertainment. In the Middle East, the rich storehouse of literary works that achieves these ends is especially revealing because of its longevity, stretching from the world's earliest recorded poem (*The Epic of Gilgamesh*, 1700-1000 B.C.E.), composed in Akkadian, to a present-day mix of writings in multiple genres and languages.

Most notable for *Middle Eastern Literatures and Their Times* are the works in Arabic, Persian, Turkish, and Hebrew, the four major languages of the societies that people the region, each of them multifaceted in its own way. In the beginning, before there was scripture, man—or more

exactly, a Sumerian king by the name of Gilgamesh—wrestled in story with the already timeless issues of his own mortality and the dynamics of human relations. Several centuries later, there appeared the Torah, the first five books of the Hebrew Bible, a scriptural compendium of narration, beliefs, and laws (in biblical Hebrew) that accounts for the origins of the ancient Israelites and includes prescriptions for personal and social behavior. This and subsequent texts testified early in history to the factious nature of humankind, a point well-illustrated by the lately discovered Dead Sea Scrolls, the writings of a separatist group committed to Judaism, the religion of the mainstream population in ancient Israel.

While the separatists extracted themselves from this mainstream, others, also deeply disturbed by the direction it was taking, set out to transform it from within, most notably the artisan-peasant Jesus. Jesus' struggle gave rise to a second scriptural work (in ancient Greek), the Christian Bible, which became the basis for a new but related faith, Christianity. Composed five centuries after the Torah, the Christian Bible would not, however, be the last word in major scripture conceived in the Middle East. That word would come six centuries later from the Arabs in the form of the Quran, believed to be a record of all the Divine revelations delivered (in Arabic) to the Prophet Muhammad. Regarded by his followers as a true prophet in the line that began with the Hebrew Bible's Abraham, Muhammad inspired a third faith—Islam.

Thus, over the span of a millennium, the same wellspring gave rise to three major faiths and their associated scriptures, a line of sacred texts that were intimately interconnected indeed. For the Arabs, however, literary tradition did not start with scripture. Already a pre-Islamic literature existed that testified to the lifeways and values of the pagan Arabs, as demonstrated by the poem commonly known as *The Mu`allaqah of Imru al-Qays*—an ode concerned with the capricious desert environment, personal renewal, the hunt, and sexual conquest.

Poetry would continue to dominate Arabic literature for a dozen centuries, and within this genre, the ode—in Arabic, the *qasidah*—remained a pre-eminent form. After the advent of Islam, a special type of ode gained new importance, the praise poem. A panegyric celebration of a patron's victories or military prowess, the praise poem could be considered a type of historical document, with the understanding that it originated as a complimentary work of art by a poet in a patron's employ (see al-Mutanabbi's "Ode on the Reconquest of al-Hadath," for example). Such odes sometimes functioned as ancient tools of self-promotion on the part of a patron-ruler, as advertisements for his virtues; in today's world, they would easily qualify as public relations. A number of these also reached poetic heights in content and technique (see Abu Tammam's "Ode on the Conquest of Amorium").

In time, Islam spread through Asia and Africa; in the Middle East, it became a driving force not only in Arabic but also in Persian and Turkish writings. The Quran proved to be a fountainhead of poetic and aesthetic output in the three Middle East literatures. Politically their societies dominated the region in waves, during which the separate literatures came to the fore, the spotlight shifting from one to another over a few roughly delineable periods. First came an era of Arabic literary predominance (500-1100s C.E.), then Persian (900s-1500), and finally Turkish (1400s-1800s) before each of the three literatures moved into a modern phase in the nineteenth century.

This was the last in a progression of phases often ascribed to the three literatures, starting with the *ancient* or pre-Islamic phase, advancing to the *classical* phase (from the rise of Islam in the seventh century to the nineteenth century) and culminating with the *modern* phase (nineteenth century to the present). The terms that designate the different phases, though familiar to many, are not to be confused with their altogether different meanings in the West. While the three literatures share some key elements, such as the profound influence of the Quran on their later works, each also maintains its own traditions, the pre-Islamic Arabic ode being a case in point.

Both the Persian and Turkish literatures likewise hark back to works featuring characters and values at the root of their societies (see the *Shahnamah* for the Persian, the *Book of Dede Korkut* for the Turkish).

Meanwhile, Hebrew literature in the Middle East experienced a separate trajectory, ruptured by unique ethno-historical developments—of conquest, exile, and return—during which Hebrew mostly fell into disuse as an everyday language. Its proponents nevertheless employed Hebrew to produce or help produce notable works in the biblical (e.g., the Torah), rabbinic (e.g., the Talmud), and medieval (e.g., *The Book of Tahkemoni*) periods before a concerted effort to revive the language and its literature was initiated in the late nineteenth century. The effort grew, despite formidable obstacles for writers and readers, propelling Hebrew literature in the Middle East into its own distinctly modern period in the twentieth century.

In Arabic letters, not all poetry was stately or deadly serious; there were poetic lampoons and irreverent verses, the poet exemplar in this last tradition being Abu Nuwas. Aiming probably to entertain the elite in Baghdad in the 900s, this literary rebel gained distinction for his erotic verse and his verse about the pleasures of wine drinking, despite the Islamic prohibition against it. Open to sacred as well as profane interpretations, the poems of Abu Nuwas reached literary heights and left audiences thirsting for more. But other rebels of the age met with a less happy fate, among them, the Islamic mystic al-Hallaj, whose martyrdom was documented a thousand years later in the verse play *Murder in Baghdad*. While poetry won the highest esteem in the classical era, prose forms flourished then too. There were assorted genres—the didactic animal fable (*Kalilah and Dimnah*), the popular narrative (*Arabian Nights*), and the anecdotal *maqamah,* a mixture of poetry and prose unique to the Middle East (*Maqamat*).

The tendency of the region's different literatures to feed on and into one another becomes readily apparent in the various prose forms. From India, the animal fable identified above found its way first into Persian, then into Arabic letters, its plot gaining significant new features at each incarnation. All this cross-cultural literary interaction continued the type of exchange demonstrated earlier by the scriptural line that began with the Torah and ended with the Quran, and the exchange transpired in both directions. So charmed were medieval Hebrew writers by the Arabic *maqamah* that they adopted and adapted the genre to their own milieu; in the far-flung reaches of the Islamic Empire, in al-Andalus (today's Spain), writers such as Judah al-Harizi generated Hebrew *maqamat* (most famously, his *Book of Tahkemoni*).

That the Arabs of al-Andalus had their own richly developed intellectual traditions, in philosophy among other fields, comes to the fore in a fanciful twelfth-century tale (*Hayy ibn Yaqzan*) about a boy raised on a deserted island; the boy's experiences lead to some intense existential soul-searching eight centuries before the coining of the term *existential* for a set of philosophies popular in France and other parts of the Western world in the mid-1900s. A child of Arabic literature, Hayy grows up to shun human society and to evince a deep spiritual connection to his patch of earth, his "home" land, so to speak.

In medieval Hebrew literature, a real-life poet of al-Andalus shows parallel inclinations. Only the poet is a Jew and his homeland, Palestine, is elusive, because his people have for centuries lived in exile, a situation that leaves him achingly bereft and that he tries to remedy, at least for himself, with results as pathos-laden as his spiritual longing (*The Diwan of Judah Halevi*).

During the twelfth and thirteenth centuries, some Persian masters added significant works to the line of mystical poetry that had begun to convey Sufi ideas, making these ideas newly accessibly to many Muslim readers (*Conference of the Birds* by Farid al-Din Attar and *Spiritual Couplets* by Jalaladdin Rumi). Other Persian poets waxed more generally philosophic (the *Ruba`iyat of Omar Khayyam*), returning to the issue of human mortality raised over two thousand years earlier in *Gilgamesh* and reaching a hedonistic conclusion that struck a chord in Westerners during the 1800s, when the *Ruba`iyat* first appeared in a landmark English translation that remains vital today. The ode, the couplet, the quatrain—the Persian poets mastered them all, along with the sonnet-like *ghazal*. It is this last genre that dominates the corpus of Hafiz, a Persian master of the fourteenth century whose subjects range from mystical and philosophical insights to love and social criticism.

When Turkish letters entered its period of predominance under the Ottoman Empire in the late fifteenth and the sixteenth century, poets such as Necati and Baki adopted and adapted the *ghazal* to their own stylistic and imaginative needs. The result was *Ottoman Lyric Poetry*, which reflects the thoughts and practices of a society that would continue to dominate politics as well as culture in the Middle East from the classical into the modern era. Aside from the *ghazal*, the Ottomans contributed to another tradition common to Arabic, Persian, and Turkish literatures—the love story in verse. Such stories carried multiple, interwoven meanings, amenable to interpretations of earthly physical love or divinely spiritual love, as demonstrated by *Leyla and Mejnun*, which centers on the love between a maiden and a "madman." The Ottoman poet Fuzuli, who was fluent in all three languages, produced a landmark Turkish version of the tale, achieving a seamless blend of the literal and the metaphoric in the process. Along with the vigorous exchange among its own societies, the Middle East became subject to Western influences in the sixteenth century. Innovations such as Italian portraiture—Europe was fully engaged in the Renaissance at the time—began to infiltrate Ottoman court society, threatening the persistence of traditional ways long before the modern era, as intimated by Orhan Pamuk in his art-related mystery *My Name Is Red*. Given the wide expanse of the Ottoman Empire then and later, such influences threatened the status quo not only in Turkish-speaking areas but also in the areas that would come to comprise modern-day Iran and more than twenty contemporary Arab countries.

During the twentieth century, the already well-established tradition of storytelling in the Middle East took a decisive turn when Western genres, the short story and then the novel, gained currency in the region. Along with these genres came stylistic influences. In Persian fiction, Sadiq Hidayat took cues from the European modernists and from America's Edgar Allan Poe, mixing them with elements of his own Iranian heritage to produce a mysterious masterpiece (*The Blind Owl*), a novella written in a style that itself forms part of the puzzle.

The acceptance of Western influences by Middle Eastern writers at this juncture can be attributed to several factors: the translation of Western works into Middle Eastern languages; the travel or migration of major authors from the Middle East to the West; and the rise in Western universities of an intellectual tradition—Orientalism—that popularized an image of the East (and Middle East) as exotic but inferior. The literature itself counters such a mistaken notion. Across time, the works written in the Middle East convey an image of a region that is both different and rich with its own sophisticated network of complexities. Some of the early-twentieth-century novels are virtual social documents in their depiction of the lives of peasants, the working class, and the urban poor. A Turkish novel, *Memed, My Hawk,* portrays the adventures of a Robin Hood-style bandit, whose story exposes the conditions of oppressed peasants in rural twentieth-century Anatolia. Behind such tales often lurks a voice critical of the status quo, a dimension of the "fictions" produced here as elsewhere in the world.

Many of the twentieth-century novels held up a mirror to the peoples of the Middle East, exposing the disastrous consequences that time-worn traditions could have (as in Kahlil Gibran's *Broken Wings*—Lebanese), or that the infusion of Westerners into a country's economy could have (as in Abd al-Rahman Munif's *Cities of Salt*—Saudi Arabian), or that self-preoccupation within a dispossessed society could have (as in Ghassan Kanafani's *Men Under the Sun*—Palestinian Arab). Early-twentieth-century fiction assailed the aping of Western ways in different areas (*Once Upon a Time*—Iran; "The Secret Shrine"—Ottoman Turkey); late in the century, nonfiction attacked the same, now more prevalent tendency (*Plagued by the West*—Iran).

Meanwhile, Arab, Persian, Turkish, and Hebrew writers produced novels that penetrated beyond the idealistic rhetoric of the century to depict their changing societies with sobering realism. Egypt's Nobel laureate Najib Mahfuz, one of the first to concentrate on middle-class Arabs, wrote fiction of this kind for five decades before winning his coveted award (see *Miramar*). During that same half-century volatile events in Palestine led to the emergence of the modern State of Israel, home to a polyglot society with self-critical writers of its own.

A number of Arab Israeli writers took the new state to task, sometimes through satire, as Emile Habiby does in a novel (*The Secret Life of Saeed the Ill-Fated Pessoptimist*) that features both the dispossession of the Palestinian Arabs and the subsequent experience of his own subpopulation—the minority of Palestinian Arabs who remained in the land after statehood was declared.

All four Middle Eastern literatures generated works on the repression of women in the twentieth century. In Arabic literature, Egypt's Mahmud Taymur wrote fiction ("Am Mutwalli") that raised the issue as early as the 1920s. At mid-century, the nearly identical titles of a modern Persian and a modern Hebrew poem suggest some common experiences for women in two otherwise very different lands ("Mechanical Doll"—Persian; "Clockwork Doll"—Hebrew). A novel of the late

twentieth century (*Curfew*) depicts both the painful psychological awakening of Turkish women to the limits long imposed on them, and their attempts to reconcile this awakening with their provincial or urban circumstances.

While modern Hebrew literature resembles the other three Middle Eastern literatures in conspicuous ways, there is a significant difference: many of Israel's renowned writers have not only been influenced by Europeans but have been Europeans themselves. Born and often bred on the Continent, they moved to Palestine before the founding of Israel and were joined by other writers from elsewhere in the Middle East and from North Africa. In fact, the writer regarded as the national Jewish poet, Hayyim Nahman Bialik, generated most of his celebrated Hebrew verse in Russia before immigrating to Israel. One of the poems, "In the City of Slaughter," helped galvanize a movement for self-defense among his people and a form of activism that led ultimately to the founding of Israel. Bialik was not alone in his concentration on life in Europe; some of the key Hebrew literature of Israel treats the people's pre-statehood experience, including the attempt to annihilate European Jewry during World War II (*Badenheim 1939*; *See Under: Love*). Innovations in style figure in these works, becoming part of the authors' struggle to understand and portray the unspeakable and still unfathomable horror of the Holocaust. Other Hebrew literature centers on experiences in the land of Israel before and after statehood. Often these works take a self-critical approach, submitting Israeli society to intense self-scrutiny through story.

In his magnum opus (*Only Yesterday*) Shmuel Yosef Agnon penetrates Zionistic rhetoric to expose the dissonance between the ideal and the real for pioneering Jews of the pre-statehood days; Amos Oz reveals some of the nerve-wracking stresses of living in a divided Jerusalem in the days of early statehood (*My Michael*). Fittingly for a region in which poetry has been so celebrated, some of the most anguished self-scrutiny has come in verse, for example, that of Dalia Ravikovitch about the invasion of Lebanon in 1982 ("You Can't Kill a Baby Twice") and an agonizingly soul-searching cycle (*Songs of the Land of Zion, Jerusalem*) by the nationally and internationally acclaimed Yehuda Amichai, generated in response to another Arab Israeli conflict, the October or Yom Kippur War.

Modern Hebrew poetry has no monopoly on self-scrutiny. Late-twentieth-century Arabic poetry used the genre for this same purpose in an elegy ("Introduction to the History of the Petty

Kings") on the death of the Egyptian leader Gamal Abdel Nassar in 1970, a few years after the Arabs' devastating loss of yet another conflict with Israel, the Six-Day War. The elegy reflects vast changes in the Middle East in the three millennia since the region produced *Gilgamesh.* By the late twentieth century, there was a relatively new factor to contend with—nationalism, which took root in the Middle East, as in Europe, in the nineteenth century. The impulse grew, at first haltingly, then unrestrainably, becoming the cause, implies one of the modern Hebrew novels (*Mr. Mani*), of much divisiveness in the region.

Meanwhile, the nature of the literary protagonists in the Middle East changed too. *Gilgamesh* centers on a king with little reference to the people he governs; in the elegy, Nasser's connection to his people takes precedence, and in another modern Arabic work (the play *The King Is the King*) a commoner even replaces the king. No longer are all heroes cut from the same old cloth. Not divine, not royal, sometimes they are leaders but often just ordinary women and men, much like Halil in *Human Landscapes,* a modern-day epic that is Turkish in origin, socially inclusive in scope, and universal in relevance.

Chronology of Relevant Events

Middle Eastern Literatures and Their Times

MESOPOTAMIAN SOCIETY:
EARLY MIDDLE EASTERN CIVILIZATIONS

Note: Ancient dates in the Mesopotamian and subsequent timelines represent a degree of consensus among scholars but are subject to ongoing debate and are necessarily approximations.

Often called the "cradle of civilization," the Mesopotamian crescent—which corresponds roughly to modern-day Iraq—was settled around 5000 B.C.E. by migrating farmers from the north. More than a thousand years later, with the advent of the Sumerians, Mesopotamia witnessed the rise of one of the world's earliest civilizations. The Sumerians established the first cities in the region, founded the first ruling dynasties, and introduced a system of writing that transformed countless aspects of economic, social, and intellectual life. One of the Sumerian kings, Gilgamesh, inspired multiple legends, which led to the composition of *The Epic of Gilgamesh,*. thought to be the oldest surviving epic poem in world history. Although the Sumerians were eventually supplanted by later Mesopotamian peoples, such as the Akkadians, Assyrians, and Babylonians, many Sumerian ideas, inventions, and practices left a lasting impression on the civilizations that followed. During the sixth century B.C.E., Mesopotamia fell to the forces of Cyrus the Great of Persia and was thereafter ruled as a Persian province, after which it would fall to the Greeks, later to the Persians again, and then, most lastingly, to the Arabs.

	Historical Events	Related Literary Works in *WLAIT 6*
5000 B.C.E.	Agricultural settlements are founded in region that extends from Babylon to the Persian gulf	
4000–3500 B.C.E.	Obeid period in Mesopotamia—Semitic nomads from Syria and the Arabian peninsula invade Mesopotamia and intermingle with Obeidian population	

Historical Events	Related Literary Works in *WLAIT 6*
3500–3200 B.C.E. Uruk period—Sumerians migrate to the region, possibly from Central Asia through Iran, settling on the banks of the Euphrates River; their arrival leads to the founding of urban communities	
3000–2750 B.C.E. Democratic assemblies develop into kingships of limited authority, which, in turn, evolve into hereditary monarchies; Kish becomes leading Sumerian city; Meskiagger founds Sumerian dynasty of Erech	
2800–2360 B.C.E. Sumerian city-states vie for dominance over a period of several centuries; during the reign of King Eannatum, the city of Lagash gains power through military conquests	
2700 B.C.E. Supposed reign of Gilgamesh, king of Erech, who becomes a source of Sumerian legends	*The Epic of Gilgamesh.*
2300s B.C.E. Sargon the Great of Akkad rises to power, conquering Kish and eventually the rest of Sumer	
2100–2000 B.C.E. Resurgence of the Sumerians in the neo-Sumerian Period; composition and editing of major works of Sumerian literature, including the earliest known written versions of *Gilgamesh*.	
1800 B.C.E. Babylonian ruler of West Semitic (Amorite) descent, named Hammurabi, creates empire encompassing all of Mesopotamia with its capital in Babylon; empire crumbles not long after his death	
1200 B.C.E. Nebuchadnezzar expels Elamites from Babylon	
1100–1078 B.C.E. Tiglath-Pileser of Assyria captures Babylon, extends his influence over Asia Minor, and exacts tribute from Mediterranean coastal cities; after his death, Aramean tribes and Zagros mountain dwellers break up the Assyrian empire	
721–725 B.C.E. Sargon II of Assyria subdues an empire in revolt, destroys Samaria and conquers (northern) kingdom of Israel	
704–681 B.C.E. Reign of Sargon's son, Sennacherib, who destroys Babylon	
668–27 B.C.E. Flourishing of culture during the reign of Assyrian king Ashurbanipal, who collects literature and texts, especially from Babylon, creating perhaps the finest library of Mesopotamian civilization; located in his capital, Nineveh, and later discovered by archaeologists, the library will become the greatest source for knowledge of Sumerian and Akkadian literature	
604–562 B.C.E. Reign of Nebuchadnezzar II of Babylon; he razes Jerusalem and takes Jews into captivity in Babylon	
539–330 B.C.E. Cyrus the Great of Persia conquers Babylon; the Mesopotamian region becomes a Persian province	

ARAB SOCIETY: THE PRE-ISLAMIC AND CLASSICAL PERIODS

For centuries the Arabian Peninsula was home to nomadic peoples known collectively as Arabs. The Arab peoples, a Semitic group whose origins are unclear, lived in tribes and concerned themselves almost exclusively with supporting the immediate family or the small clan in their harsh desert environment. Despite being divided into small, self-contained groups, Arab society of the pre-Islamic period gave rise to a rich culture, which relied on a shared language and on oral transmission of poems and legends. Some of the tribesmen traded extensively with ancient empires, including those of the Persians, Greeks, Romans, and Byzantines. The rise of Islam in the seventh century transformed the Arab world, moving it from the pre-

Islamic period into what is often called the classical era (which coincides with and extends beyond the medieval era in the West). The teachings of Muhammad, Islam's Prophet, won followers across the peninsula, which became the center of an expanding Arab-Islamic Empire. From the deserts as well as the cities, zealous converts emerged to conquer territories for Islam in Byzantium, Persia, and North Africa. Under dynasties such as the Umayyads and Abbasids, the Arab-Islamic Empire grew quickly, its boundaries expanding to include parts of Spain and India. In the process, the Arabs attained cultural pre-eminence in the Middle East, becoming famous for their patronage of science, medicine, and the arts. In the 1100s, however, weakened by invasions and internal conflicts, the Arab-Islamic Empire started to disintegrate. The next few centuries saw the achievement in Europe of scientific, technological, and military advances, which promoted European imperial ambitions, leading to later challenges to power relations in the Middle East. More immediate, however, was the challenge posed by the nearby Ottoman Empire, which would ultimately extend its dominion over the entire Middle East.

Historical Events	Related Literary Works in *WLAIT 6*
c. 4000 B.C.E. Beginnings of settlement in the Tigris-Euphrates Valley and along the Nile River—the future Arab heartlands	
c. 3500 B.C.E. Establishment of city states in Mesopotamia/Iraq	
c. 2500 B.C.E. Domestication of the camel; settlement begins in the interior of the Arabian Peninsula	
c. 2400 B.C.E. Growth of empires—Babylonian, Akkadian, and Assyrian—in Tigris-Euphrates Valleys; in the fertile Nile Valley, the civilization of the Pharaohs emerges	
c. 750–275 B.C.E. Assyrian, Persian, and Greek empires successively absorb the Middle East	
550 B.C.E. Emergence of the Achaemenid Empire in today's Iran	
331 B.C.E. Alexander the Great conquers the Achaemenid Empire; Greek culture starts to influence the Middle East	
c. 200 B.C.E. Initiation of long-distance trade using the Silk Route and the Spice Route, which takes traders across the heartlands of the future Islamic empires	
64 B.C.E. Roman Empire begins to divide the Middle East into provinces	
20 B.C.E. Encompassing Egypt, Palestine, and Syria, the Roman Empire reaches as far as the Euphrates River in Iraq	
306–37 C.E. Reign of Emperor Constantine, who makes Christianity the official religion of the Roman Empire and divides it administratively into western and eastern halves	
328 First dated inscription in northern Arabic (which eventually becomes the "Arabic" language)	
476 Fall of the western half of the Roman Empire; eastern half is reorganized as the Byzantine Empire	
c. 500 Semi-settled Arab tribes like the Ghassanids and Lakhmids thrive along the borders of the Byzantine and Sasanian empires	"Stop and We Will Weep: The Mu'allaqah" by Imru al-Qays
c. 570 The Prophet Muhammad is born in the western Arabian city of Mecca	

	Historical Events	Related Literary Works in *WLAIT 6*
c. 610	Beginnings of the revelation of the Quran, the sacred text of Islam; Muhammad wins converts to the new religion through public preaching	The Quran, or Koran
622	Muhammad's new religious ideas provoke opposition from the leading families in Mecca; his flight north (the *Hijra*) to Medina marks the beginning of the Islamic calendar	
622–32	Muhammad turns Medina into the center of a religious and political struggle, winning supporters across the Arabian Peninsula; Muhammad's forces recapture Mecca, and the existing shrine (the *Ka'bah*) becomes a center for Islamic devotion; the Quran continues to be revealed orally to Muhammad; the Arabian Peninsula is now the center of an expanding religious state	
632	Muhammad dies, revered as the Prophet; his father-in-law and closest companion, Abu Bakr, is chosen as the first caliph, or leader of the Islamic community	
632–61	The rule of the Rashidun (righteous) caliphs	
633–44	Converts to Islam emerge from the Arabian deserts, conquering Byzantine and Persian territories	
655–61	A struggle over succession to the caliphate results in civil war; after the murder of Ali, Muhammad's son-in-law, Mu'awiyah of the Umayyad family (one of the leading families of Mecca) takes office; his succession is opposed by Ali's followers, who become the Shi'ites; ultimately the struggle gives rise to the rival Sunni and Shi'ite branches of Islam	
661–750	The Umayyad dynasty rules the Islamic empire from Damascus, Syria; the empire expands across North Africa and eastward toward the Indus River; Westerners lose direct access to the Spice Route	
680	The murder of Husayn, a grandson of the Prophet, and of his followers in Karbala (Iraq) becomes a definitive tragedy for the Shi'ites	
711	Victory in the battle of Guadalete begins the Muslim conquest and occupation of Spain, which lasts until 1492	
732	A small Arab force marches across the Pyrenees Mountains to conquer France but is defeated by Charles Martel in the battle of Poitiers	
740s–50	Descendents of the Prophet's uncle Abbas, the Abbasid family, win supporters (Arabs, Persians, and Muslim converts); the supporters rebel, overthrowing the Umayyad dynasty	
750–1258	After ruthlessly eliminating Umayyad claimants to the caliphate, the Abbasid dynasty governs the Islamic empire from Baghdad, Iraq, a settlement founded in 756	*Kalilah and Dimnah* as translated by Ibn al-Muqaffa'
786–809	Reign of Harun al-Rashid, fifth Abbasid caliph; court society flourishes	*The Arabian Nights; The Diwan of Abu Nuwas*
800s	Islamic mystical tradition (Sufism) grows	
838	The caliph al-Mu'tasim leads a successful campaign against the Byzantine Empire, capturing the city of Amorium	"Ode on the Conquest of Amorium" by Abu Tammam
868–905	Under Ahmad ibn Tulun, a military leader and former slave, Egypt breaks away from Abbasid rule	
900s	Start of the "Shi'ite century," during which mostly Shi'ite local dynasties become powerful; caliphate described—a successor to the Prophet, the caliph directs Muslim community affairs and guards the faith, may appoint another leader to run military affairs	

Historical Events	Related Literary Works in *WLAIT 6*
922 Execution by the Abbasids of Ibn Mansur al-Hallaj, mystic, poet, preacher, and political agitator	*Murder in Baghdad* by Salah Abd al-Sabur
945 Buwayhid clan seizes control of weakening Abbasid Empire, but allows Abbasids to remain as figureheads	
954 Participating in the long conflict between Arabs and Byzantines, Sayf al-Dawlah al-Hamdani, emir of Aleppo, defeats the Byzantine army at the battle of al-Hadath	"Ode on the Reconquest of al-Hadath" by al-Mutanabbi
969 The Fatimids, a Shi'ite dynasty from North Africa, conquer Egypt and found Cairo, which becomes their capital	
late 900s Prose genres—*adab* (moral tale), treatises, essays, and *maqamat* (entertaining tales in rhymed prose) grow increasingly popular	*Maqamat* by al-Hamadhani
1000s Growth of the madrasahs, Islamic schools devoted largely to legal reasoning	
1050s Arabic literary dominance in poetry fades, begins to give way to Persian masters	
1070-80 The Seljuk Turks—converts to Sunni Islam from central Asia—join and dominate the Arab armies; defeating the Byzantines in Asia Minor and then moving to Syria and Palestine, the Seljuks reverse the trend toward Shi'ite pre-eminence	
1095 Pope Urban II calls for Europeans to join a "crusade," or holy war, to return control of Jerusalem to Christian rule	
1140s The Almoravid dynasty of Muslim Spain is conquered by the Almohads, another Muslim dynasty from North Africa	*Hayy ibn Yaqzan* by Ibn Tufayl
1171 Saladin, a general in the Syrian army, deposes the Fatimids, founding a Sunnite dynasty in Egypt and Syria	
1187 Saladin defeats the Crusaders near Jerusalem	
1221 Mongol troops led by Genghis Khan invade eastern regions of the Muslim world	
1250–1500 Founding of the Mamluk (slave) dynasty in Egypt and Syria	
1258–60 Mongolian invaders destroy Baghdad and execute the Abbasid caliph; they are finally defeated in Palestine by Egypt's armies	
c. 1300 Rise of Osman, a Turkish military leader, after whom the Ottoman Empire is named	
1320–30 Rise of *ghazi* warriors increases Turkish military prowess	
1400 The Asian conqueror Tamerlane (Timur the Lame) attacks Iraq and Syria	
1453 Constantinople falls to the Ottoman armies, is renamed Istanbul; Westerners lose direct access to the Silk Route, which provides impetus for their subsequent explorations	
1492 The fall of Granada, the last Muslim kingdom in Spain; Christians expel Jews from Spain	
1501–1722 The Safavid family establishes a dynasty based in Persia, becomes a powerful promoter of the Shi'ite branch of Islam, challenging the Sunni Ottoman Empire for domination of the Middle East	
1502 Muslims must choose between converting to Christianity or leaving Spain	
1517 Ottoman forces capture Cairo, defeating the Egyptian Mamluks	

Historical Events		Related Literary Works in *WLAIT 6*
1517–early 1800s	Arab literary tradition continues shift from classical (standard) Arabic to colloquial Arabic that began in the 1100s; focus in standard Arabic literature turns from poetry to religious tracts, local history, and biography	
1534	Ottoman forces capture Baghdad, defeating the Iraqi Mamluks and bringing the Arab world under their control	
1609	Spain expels the Moriscos, the Christians of Muslim descent	
c. 1750	In central Arabia, Muhammad ibn Abd al-Wahhab launches a fundamentalist reform campaign, mainly against Sufism (Islamic mysticism); his movement seeks to return Islamic practice to its roots, leads to the formation of the Saudi state	

ARAB SOCIETY: THE MODERN PERIOD

While the Turkish Ottoman Empire remained the dominant power in the Middle East until the early twentieth century, intellectual movements in Egypt, Syria, and Lebanon worked to foster a renewed sense of Arab cultural identity during the nineteenth century. At the same time, European nations, such as France and England, carved out spheres of influence in various Arab countries, sometimes annexing them outright. The First World War permanently broke the Ottoman Empire's hold over the Middle East, and in the 1920s and 1930s individual Arab nations began to emerge. Several (such as Syria, Lebanon, Iraq, and Palestine) were governed under mandates granted by the League of Nations to two European colonial powers— Great Britain and France. In the years between the First and the Second World Wars, much of the conflict in the Arab sphere was concentrated in the disputed region of Palestine, governed under a British mandate and claimed separately by Palestine's Arabs and Jews. In the wake of World War II and the discovery of the Nazi genocide suffered by European Jews, support for a Jewish state in Palestine increased dramatically. Subsequent events led to the declaration of the State of Israel in 1948, fueling internal and external hostilities that persist to the present day. Meanwhile, other Arab nations realized their own ambitions for independence as Europe's colonial powers withdrew from the Middle East. In the economic sphere, various Arab nations were transformed by the discovery of oil, a valuable commodity to the Western powers of Europe and United States; the United States in particular increased its presence and influence in the region. In the 1960s and after, relations became more volatile between various Arab nations and the Western powers, with a rising number of Islamic fundamentalists expressing resentment and suspicion of Western influences, at times through terrorist attacks.

Historical Events		Related Literary Works in *WLAIT 6*
1798–1801	French troops led by Napoleon Bonaparte invade Egypt, but are later driven out by the British and Turks	
1811–82	Egypt attains semi-independence from the Ottomans	
1830	The French occupy Algeria and make it a colony	
1840–70	*Tanzimat* ("Reorganization") occurs: Ottoman Empire modernizes structures and policies as a result of increased contact with Western powers	
1860–1900	An Arabic artistic renaissance unfolds in Beirut and Cairo; groups such as the Syrian Scientific Society advance education in the region and raise self-respect, nurturing the idea of a pan-Arabic cultural identity that could unite Christian and Muslim Arabs	*The Broken Wings* by Kahlil Gibran

Historical Events	Related Literary Works in *WLAIT 6*
1861 Under pressure from European powers, the Ottoman Empire acknowledges an autonomous Lebanon	
1866 American missionaries in Lebanon found the Syrian Protestant College, the future American University of Beirut	
1869 The Suez Canal is completed	
1881–83 France conquers Tunisia; in Egypt, Ahmad Urabi Pasha leads an unsuccessful army rebellion against the British under the banner "Egypt for the Egyptians"; Britain occupies Egypt and takes charge of the Suez Canal	
1912 France and Spain occupy and control Morocco; the Ottoman Empire passes control over Libya to Italy	
1914 Outbreak of World War I; the Ottoman Empire becomes Germany's ally; the Ottomans discover oil in Iraq	
1915–16 Correspondence between A. H. McMahon, British High Commissioner in Egypt, and Husayn ibn Ali, Sharif of Mecca: British agree to an independent Arab kingdom in return for Arab support in fighting the Ottoman Empire during World War I	
1917–18 "Arab Revolt" against the Ottoman sultan; after fighting across the Arabian desert, forces under Husayn's son Amir Faysal, accompanied by British liaison officer T. E. Lawrence (Lawrence of Arabia), occupy Damascus, Syria; Germany surrenders; World War I ends November 11, 1918	
1919–20 Faysal's Syrian kingdom collapses after two years; the postwar Versailles conference places Egypt, Transjordan, and Palestine under British control, Syria and Lebanon under French control; Egyptians mount 1919 revolution for independence; from his base in Mecca, Husayn becomes involved in a civil war with Abd al-Aziz ibn Sa'ud, a rival leader whom the British support	"Amm Mutwalli" and "Hagg Shalabi" by Mahmud Taymur
1920 San Remo conference awards mandates over Syria and Lebanon to France; over Palestine, Transjordan, and Iraq to Britain under the League of Nations Mandate System	
1921–32 Abd al-Aziz ibn Sa'ud consolidates north and central Arabia to form the kingdom of Saudi Arabia	
1924 Ibn Sa'ud rejects Husayn's right to rule Arabia; Ibn Sa'ud's forces invade the Hejaz region and capture Mecca; Wahhabism becomes the official version of Islam in Saudi Arabia	
1930s Discovery of oil in Saudi Arabia leads to sweeping economic changes	*Cities of Salt* by Abd al-Rahman Munif
1932–46 League of Nations mandates end; Syria and Lebanon become republics; heirs of Husayn—Faysal in Iraq, Abdullah in Transjordan—come to power	
1933 King Ibn Sa'ud grants the first oil concession in Saudi Arabia to Standard Oil of California	
1936 British occupation of Egypt formally ends, though Britain keeps some troops around the Suez Canal; Persia is officially renamed Iran	
1939–45 During World War II, Allied powers (including Britain, France, and America) and Axis powers (including Nazi Germany and Fascist Italy) battle each other in campaigns in North Africa and the Middle East	
1945 Arab League is formed by Egypt, Lebanon, Iraq, Syria, Transjordan, Yemen, and Saudi Arabia; France relinquishes control of Syria and Lebanon	

Historical Events	Related Literary Works in *WLAIT 6*
1947 The newly formed United Nations proposes dividing Palestine into separate Jewish and Arab states	
1948 Jewish leader David Ben-Gurion proclaims the State of Israel; military intervention by neighboring Arab states fails to prevent Israel from establishing national borders	*The Secret Life of Saeed the Ill-fated Pessoptimist* by Emile Habiby
1949 Arab-Israeli war of 1948–49 ends with armistice agreements that lead to official incorporation of West Bank into Transjordan (today's Jordan) and Gaza Strip into Egypt; displaced by the State of Israel, Palestinian refugees flee to Transjordan, Lebanon, Syria, Egypt, Kuwait, and elsewhere	*Men in the Sun* by Ghassan Kanafani
1952 King Farouk of Egypt is ousted by a military coup led by Gamal Abdel Nasser and others of the Free Officers group	
1955–57 The discovery of oil fields in the southern part of the Arabian peninsula leads to conflict between forces from the Gulf emirates (allied with Britain) and Saudi Arabia	
1956 In the Suez Crisis, Egyptian president Nasser assumes control over the Canal Zone, provoking military intervention by Britain, Israel, and France	
1958 Egypt and Syria form the United Arab Republic; the Iraqi monarchy is toppled by a military revolt	
1960s Period of turmoil in the Arab world: tensions rise between Syria and Egypt; civil war in Yemen pits Egypt against Saudi Arabia; civil war in Jordan pits Palestinians against non-Palestinians; Nasser adopts "Arab Socialism" and land-reform policies in Egypt	*Miramar* by Najib Mahfuz
1961 Syria withdraws from the United Arab Republic	
1962 Algeria achieves independence from France after a bloody eight-year rebellion	
1967 The Six-Day War: Israel captures East Jerusalem, the West Bank of the Jordan River, the Sinai Peninsula, and the Gaza Strip; the U.N. Security Council passes Resolution 242, prescribing the trading of land for peace: declares that Israel must return captured territory and that Israel's right to exist must be acknowledged by surrounding Arab states; declaration fails to elicit hoped-for responses	*The King Is the King* by Sa'dallah Wannus
1970 Civil war between Palestinians and non-Palestinians in Jordan; Jordan's King Hussein expels Palestinian militants connected with Yasser Arafat's Palestine Liberation Organization (PLO); Egyptian president and Arab nationalist Gamal Abdel Nasser dies in the midst of negotiations to prevent civil war in Jordan	"Introduction to the History of the Petty Kings" by Adunis
1973 The October War (Yom Kippur War): Egypt and Syria stage coordinated surprise attacks against Israel; the United States reinforces Israeli military with arms supplies; after three weeks, U.S. Secretary of State Henry Kissinger brokers a cease-fire; for the first time, Arab oil-producing countries jointly attempt to use their oil supply as a political tool	
1975–90 The Lebanese Civil War, involving the (Christian) Phalangists, Muslim Lebanese National Movement, and Palestinian resistance, claims an estimated 150,000 lives	*The Story of Zahra* by Hanan al-Shaykh
1979 In Iraq, an army faction led by Saddam Hussein assumes control of government; second oil embargo is imposed on the West by OPEC (Organization of Petroleum Exporting Countries); after the fall of the shah in Iran, an Islamic Republic is established under Ayatollah Khomeini	
1980–88 Iran-Iraq War is fought over border disputes and religious/ethnic divisions	

Historical Events	Related Literary Works in *WLAIT 6*
1981	Egyptian president Anwar Sadat is assassinated	
1982	Israeli army invades Lebanon; Beirut is besieged and Yasser Arafat's PLO is forced to leave for Tunisia; Lebanese poet Khalil Hawi, a Christian, commits suicide to protest three developments—Israel's invasion of a country that it is not at war with, Israel's bombardment of Beirut (thousands die), and the failure of other Arab nations to rally around the victims; suicide note protests the death of Arab nationalism	
1987	The "Intifada," the popular uprising against Israeli rule, begins in the Palestinian West Bank and Gaza Strip	
1989	Palestinian leader Yasser Arafat addresses U.N. General Assembly, stating that the PLO accepts U.N. Resolution 242 (Israel's right to exist) and renounces terrorism	
1990s	Numerous unsuccessful attempts are made to forge a lasting peace between Israel and the Arab nations	
2001	Close to 3,000 die and Saudi Arabian-U.S. relations grow newly complicated when hijackers linked to al-Qaidah terrorist group crash two U.S. commercial planes into World Trade Center and a third into the Pentagon in the United States; a fourth hijacked plane crashes in Somerset County, Pennsylvania; Americans pursue al-Qaidah leader Osama bin Laden, a former Saudi citizen who claims credit for the attack	
2003–04	Iraq is invaded by U.S. and British forces, whose troops topple the government of Saddam Hussein; all parties grapple with Iraq's future	

PERSIAN SOCIETY: THE ANCIENT AND CLASSICAL PERIODS

Over several thousand years the area that comprises present-day Iran (the heartland of a former Greater Iran) witnessed a series of migrations and conquests, each of which left a particular impression. The Sumerian, Elamite, Assyrian, Medean, Achaemenian, Macedonian, Parthian, and Sasanian empires all added elements to the civilization developing in the region. Bounded by the Tigris and Oxus rivers and by the Caspian Sea and Persian Gulf, the area was known to its early inhabitants as "Iran," but the Greeks and other outsiders named it "Persia," after a smaller area—Persis—in southern Iran, near modern-day Shiraz. The name would endure for centuries, during which outsiders wielded considerable power over the region. In the seventh century, Iran fell to the Arabs and became part of their Islamic empire, transitioning from the ancient (pre-Islamic) into the classical era. More political upheaval followed when Arab rule devolved from the Umayyad caliphate to semi-independent dynasties. Ultimately the Seljuks, a family of Turkish tribes from central Asia, wrested control. Meanwhile, from the ninth through twelfth centuries, Iran enjoyed a scientific and cultural renaissance, and Islam experienced the growth of Sufism, a mystical form of the faith that would become an institutionalized orientation. Subsequent centuries witnessed invasions by the Mongols and Tartars under Genghis Khan and Tamerlane, who both laid claim to Iran. In 1501 the Safavids rose to power, beginning a dynasty that survived for two centuries, until 1722, when Afghan tribesmen seized the Iranian capital of Isfahan. The Afghans, in turn, were driven out by Nadir Shah, chief of the Afshar tribe, who was later murdered. Afterwards, rivalry between factions ushered in decades of political instability that finally ended in 1797, when the Qajar dynasty assumed power. It was with the rise of this dynasty and the regularization of cultural and diplomatic contact between Europe and Iran that the millennial-long classical period was brought to an end.

Historical Events	Related Literary Works in *WLAIT 6*
c. 4000 B.C.E. Bronze Age settlements in Iran (Sialk, Hasanlu, Hissar)	
2700–1600 B.C.E. Elamite Kingdom	
c. 728 B.C.E. Deioces establishes Median Kingdom	
c. 600 B.C.E. Zoroastrian religion is founded in Iran by the legendary priest Zoroaster, entails monotheism and belief in a dualistic universe of good and evil	
550 B.C.E. Cyrus the Great unites the Persians and Medes into a regional superpower that dominates the Middle East under the Achaemenian dynasty	
331 B.C.E. Greek leader Alexander the Great defeats Persian ruler Darius III, the last Achaemenid King, at Gaugamela; Iran falls to the Greeks, is influenced by the pre-eminence of Hellenistic cultural practices until Iranians regain control under the Sasanians	
226–641 C.E. Reign of the Sasanid dynasty of Persia; Zoroastrianism is adopted as the state religion; Iranian society becomes highly stratified, allows for little social mobility	*The Shahnamah,* or *Book of Kings* by Abu al-Qasim Firdawsi
642 C.E. Sasanian Empire collapses; Iran falls to Arabs; conversion of non-Arabs to Islam begins; Iran becomes part of Islamic empire	"Khusraw and Shirin" by Nizami of Ganja
c. 750–1000 Abbasid caliphate moves the center of Islam to Baghdad, Iraq, and adopts much of the administrative system of ancient Iran; a vibrant intellectual, commercial, and governmental network connects parts of the Islamic empire	
819–1005 Samanid dynasty, the first Islamic Persian dynasty, takes root in Khurasan, in northeastern Iran, and begins to nurture the Persian language and Persian culture	
c. 930–1400 Persian literature spreads over the Iranian heartland, Central Asia, Anatolia, and the Indian subcontinent	
977–1186 Ghaznavid dynasty defeats the Samanid dynasty in the late 900s, continues royal patronage of Persian poetry	
1055–1157 Seljuk confederation grows, wrests western half of the empire from the Ghaznavids	
1072–92 Reign of Seljuk sultan Malik-Shah and his Persian vizier Nizam al-Mulk marks zenith of Seljuk sultanate; social, economic, and intellectual reforms are implemented; astronomers are hired to remake Iranian calendar	*Ruba'iyat of Omar Khayyam*
c. 1100s– 1300s Followers of Sufism—a mystical form of Islam—organize into brotherly orders, founding lodges throughout the Islamic world; by 1300s Sufism has become an institutionalized approach to Islam	*The Conference of the Birds* by Farid al-Din Attar; *The Spiritual Couplets* by Jalal al-Din Rumi; *The Divan of Hafiz*
1220s Mongols (nomadic tribes from western China) merge into a conquering force under Genghis Khan; invading Iran, they annihilate many of its inhabitants and dismantle the political system; Iran becomes a Mongol province	
1380–93 After Mongol rule disintegrates or dissolves into local tribal administrations, a Tartar chieftain, Tamerlane, invades Islamic lands	
1501–1722 A young warrior, Isma'il, claims the Persian throne, starting the Safavid dynasty; Isma'il declares the Shi'ite branch of Islam the official state religion, begins building a powerful Iran	
1580s–1620s Safavid shah Abbas the Great moves capital from Qazvin to Isfahan	

Historical Events	Related Literary Works in *WLAIT 6*
1722 A revolt led by Afghans brings Safavid rule to an end	
1736–47 Nadir Shah, an Afshar tribal chief, defeats the Afghan revolt and restores Iranian rule over Afghanistan; after he is murdered by chiefs of his own tribe, rival factions foster political instability	
1750–79 Karim Khan Zand unifies most of the country under a loose form of central control	
1797–1925 Ascension of Qajar dynasty ends protracted period of political instability; Qajars revive the concept of "shah" as absolute ruler and move the capital from Isfahan to Tehran	

PERSIAN SOCIETY: THE BIRTH OF MODERN IRAN

Despite its antiquity and rich heritage, in certain respects, Iran found itself eclipsed by European nations during the seventeenth and eighteenth centuries. The inventions and ideas that transformed life in Europe—inspired by exploration, scientific experimentation, and humanism (which focused on the individual and the secular rather than on the religious)—were virtually absent from Iran and other Middle Eastern societies at the time. During the early nineteenth century, Iran engaged in two devastating wars with the Russians; defeated both times, it was forced to cede several disputed territories and to pay daunting war reparations. The Iranians meanwhile struggled to fend off British colonial ambitions, particularly menacing because of the control Britain exerted in nearby India and over much of the southern coast of the Persian Gulf. An Anglo-Russian rivalry for control of Iran continued for more than 150 years, leaving the contested land weak and virtually helpless. Neither Britain nor Russia would ever formally colonize Iran, but especially in the nineteenth century the two powers continued to meddle in its affairs, with Britain exerting control in the south of Iran and Russia in the north. The two powers and the native intelligentsia introduced a number of innovations into Iranian society. These innovations met with a divided response—a degree of acceptance from the ruling classes but strong opposition from others, as demonstrated in the "Tobacco Rebellion" of the 1890s. In the early twentieth century, Iran gave rise to a Constitutional movement (1906–11) that culminated in the establishment of the country's first parliament and the transformation of the government into a constitutional monarchy after the model of European kingdoms. The more than 100-year-old Qajar dynasty collapsed, Reza Shah assumed power, and still Britain and Russia (which became known as the Soviet Union) tried to exert control over Iran, invading it during the two world wars. Equally cataclysmic developments marked the second half of the century, from sweeping efforts to Westernize the country, to the rise of Islamic fundamentalism, the abolition of the monarchy, and the founding of the Islamic Republic of Iran. A year-long confrontation between Iran and the United States, involving American hostages, initiated a crisis in international relations, the repercussions of which are still observable in the early twenty-first century. Meanwhile, after two decades of strict Islamic rule, a new generation of activists began voicing a desire for democracy in Iran.

Historical Events	Related Literary Works in *WLAIT 6*
1804–28 Iran is defeated in the First and Second Russo-Persian Wars (1804–13 and 1826–28), loses disputed lands, is forced to pay high war reparations	

Historical Events	Related Literary Works in *WLAIT 6*
1850s–1900s The shah sells newly discovered mineral and petroleum resources to Britain and Russia to fund the opulence of the royal court	
1856–57 Anglo-Persian war removes disputed territory of Herat from Iranian control; Iran gives up other Afghan territories, recognizes Afghan independence	
1872–73 Iranian government weakens; royal concessions to foreigners breed resentment among Iranians; Reuter Concession allows Britain to undertake railroad construction; opposition forces the shah to cancel the concession a year later	
1891–92 Tobacco Rebellion—Iranians resist concession that allows British-owned corporation exclusive rights to produce, sell, and export all tobacco in Iran for 50 years	
1906–11 Constitutional movement leads to the founding of a parliament (the Majlis); Russian and British influences persist	
1911 Russian troops invade Iran after it refuses to comply with a Russian ultimatum to dismiss U.S. administrator Morgan Shuster as treasurer general; the second Majlis collapses; Iran is forced to accept the Russian ultimatum	
1914–18 World War I; British and Russians move to secure their interests in Iran	*Once Upon a Time* by Muhammad Ali Jamalzadah
1921–25 Reza Khan, a former officer in the Persian Cossack Brigade, ousts the Qajar dynasty and takes the name Reza Shah Pahlavi; Cossack Brigade, formerly under command of the Russians, turns into an autonomous Iranian force	
1925–41 Reza Shah becomes king, beginning Pahlavi dynasty; his regime enacts ambitious Westernizing project (in education, banking, dress), creating ruptures in ongoing society; the king ignores constitution, turns parliament into a rubber stamp, and establishes a strong autocracy	*The Blind Owl* by Sadiq Hidayat
1935 Attracted to the ideology of Adolf Hitler, Reza Shah asks the League of Nations to refer to the country by its native name, *Iran*, which means "home of the Aryans"	
1936 Reza Shah's regime outlaws the veiling of women in Iran, brutally enforces the decree	
1941–45 Iran is occupied as part of the Allied efforts during World War II; Reza Shah abdicates in favor of his son, Mohammad Reza	*Savushun (A Persian Requiem)* by Simin Danishvar
1945–53 A nationalist movement forms; Mohammad Mossadeq rises to its head; appointed prime minister in 1950, he nationalizes Iranian oil, challenging British claims; the United States, Britain, and the shah stage a coup that ousts Mossadeq	
1954 The shah gradually aligns Iran with the West in the Cold War (U.S.-Soviet competition for world leadership)	
1958 Iranian government establishes a secret police administration, known by its Persian acronym as the SAVAK	
1963–79 Shah conducts "White Revolution," initiating land reform and Literacy Corps; women gain the right to vote; religious protests ensue; Ayatollah Khomeini is exiled	"Mechanical Doll" and Other Poems by Furugh Farrukhzad; *Plagued by the West (Gharbzadigi)* by Jalal Al-i Ahmad
1970s Public dissatisfaction grows; Islamic movement is revived	
1975 Mohammed Reza Shah openly abandons his role as a constitutional monarch to rule as dictator, establishes a one-party system that gives him total control of the state	

1978–79	Riots and demonstrations lead to "Black Friday" massacre of those who protest state repression; in September 1978 crippling strikes in the oil and heavy industries leave Iran at the brink of revolution; shah flees Iran on January 16, 1979; Ayatollah Khomeini returns from exile; Islamic Revolution abolishes the monarchy February 22, 1979; popular referendum transforms Iran into an Islamic republic	
1979	On November 4, U.S. embassy in Tehran is invaded; 54 U.S. diplomats are taken hostage; standoff lasts for 444 days, souring relations between Iran and the United States	
1980–88	In September 1980, Saddam Hussein's Iraqi army invades Iran; eight-year war weakens both countries; hostilities end after Iran's Ayatollah Khomeini accepts a cease-fire	
1989	Khomeini pronounces a death sentence against Salman Rushdie for his novel *Satanic Verses*; Rushdie is forced into hiding; Khomeini dies shortly thereafter	
1997	In a landslide election, Muhammad Khatami becomes president of Iran, an event widely interpreted as a deep national desire for reform	

TURKISH SOCIETY: THE ANCIENT AND CLASSICAL PERIOD

According to existing records, the early history of the territory now known as Turkey begins with the Hittites, who ruled the region for nearly a millennium. They were eclipsed after 1000 B.C.E. by the Assyrians, who remained a significant force in the region for much of the next thousand years. Assyrian control of Anatolia (as much of present-day Turkey was called) gave way toward the end of the millennium, when the land was absorbed into the Macedonian empire of Alexander the Great. Beginning about 200 C.E., waves of nomads thought to be related to the Turks migrated from Central to Western Asia, their religious beliefs undergoing a significant change during the centuries of migration. Soon after its emergence in Arabia in the 600s C.E., the new faith of Islam was carried into Central Asia, where the efforts of missionaries and military conquest led to conversions among Turkish-speaking peoples. By the tenth century, Turkish horse-mounted warrior bands had begun making incursions from Central Asia into Anatolia (an area then under Byzantine rule) and larger Turkish forces exercised political power in Iran. By the early thirteenth century, the Turks had established themselves as a powerful force throughout the Middle East. The Arabs continued to exercise religious authority. Their caliphate in Baghdad and the *ulama* (guardians of Islam) governed alongside the Turkish military leadership. Culturally the Turks proved to be patrons of the arts wherever they wielded power. When the Mongols invaded the Middle East, they overthrew the Turkish as well as other Muslim dynasties and institutions of the region. In the wake of this destruction, numerous Turkish chiefdoms emerged in Anatolia, most notably that of the Ottomans, whose dynasty finally defeated the Christian-oriented Byzantine Empire. In 1453 Constantinople, the seat of the Byzantine Eastern Orthodox Church for more than a thousand years, fell to the Ottoman Sultan Mehmed II. Shortly thereafter much of the Islamic world to the east also fell under Ottoman sway. More territorial conquests followed until under Suleyman I (r. 1520–66), known as "the Magnificent" and "the Lawgiver," the Ottomans reached the apogee of world power.

Historical Events		Related Literary Works in *WLAIT 6*
1700–1200 B.C.E.	Hittite Kingdom establishes itself in region that will become modern-day Turkey	
c. 1000 B.C.E.	Assyrians become significant force in region	
750–600 B.C.E.	Phrygian state in central Anatolia; state of Urartu in eastern Anatolia	
334–33 B.C.E.	Alexander the Great absorbs Anatolia into his Macedonian empire	
c. 200 C.E.	Turkish-speaking peoples begin several centuries of migration from Central Asia, settling in regions east and west of the Caspian Sea, from present-day Turkmenistan to Asia Minor and the eastern Mediterranean Sea	
c. 300–1300	Breakup of the Roman Empire; Byzantine emperor sets up court in Constantinople, establishing an Eastern empire of Christendom that lasts about 1,000 years; Eastern Orthodox Church develops independently of the Roman papacy	
c. 312–14	Emperor Constantine converts to Christianity	
453	Attila the Hun, leader of what may have been a Turkic people, dies after extending his empire deep into Central and Western Europe	
600s	First written evidence of Turkish language appears in Inner Asia, in today's Mongolia	
640	Arab invasion of Armenia	
700–800	Muslims make contact with the Turkish-speaking communities in Iran and surrounding areas; wandering preachers, inspired mystics, and traveling merchants all contribute to the gradual conversion of the Turks	*The Book of Dede Korkut*
1000–1100	Various Turkish kingdoms and tribal powers establish themselves in Anatolia and eastern Turkey; kingdoms become home to a multiethnic, multilingual society of Turks, Arabs, Greeks, Kurds, Armenians, Assyrians, Jews	
1055	Seljuk Turks take power in Baghdad, emerging as defenders of the Abbasid (Sunni) caliphs, who exercise religious authority	
1071	Seljuks defeat Byzantine army in the battle of Manzikert, effectively destroying Byzantine resistance to incursions of Turkish nomads and warriors into central and western Anatolia	*The Book of Dede Korkut*
1095	Christian armies of the First Crusade reach Constantinople, intending in part to defend the Byzantine emperors against the growing Muslim Turkish presence in Anatolia	
1204	In the Fourth Crusade, Constantinople is sacked by Western Roman Catholics, who rule in place of Byzantine emperors (Eastern Orthodox Christians) until 1261	
1204–61	Byzantine resistance to Turks increases, with ousted emperors operating from Asia Minor	
1219–36	Reign of Ala al-Din Kaykubad, Seljuk Turkish ruler in Konya, the dynastic capital; Seljuk Turkish state of Anatolia reaches its zenith	
1243–90	Major defeat of the Seljuk army by Mongols near the city of Sivas; rule of the Mongols; their withdrawal gives rise to small chiefdoms in Anatolia	
1290–1325	Osman, a Turkish tribal leader, expands holdings, defeats Byzantine forces, becomes eponymous founder of Ottoman (or *Osmanli*) state and dynasty; Sufism—mystical Islam—continues to spread throughout territory	Mystical Poetry of Yunus Emre

Historical Events		Related Literary Works in *WLAIT 6*
1361	Ottomans cross into Europe, capture Edime (Adrianople) and make it their capital; "janissaries"(from *yeni çeri,* new troops) are conscripted from conquered Christians	
1389	Ottoman forces defeat the Serbs at battle of Kosovo; death of Serb king weakens resistance, contributes to Ottomans gaining a hold over southeastern Europe	
1402	Tamerlane (Timur the Lame) defeats Ottoman sultan Bayezid at battle of Ankara	
1402–11	Ottoman interregnum, civil war as Bayezid's sons struggle for power; Mehmed I triumphs, reunifies Anatolia	
1453	Ottoman forces under Sultan Mehmed II lay siege to Constantinople, enter city on May 30; city becomes new Ottoman capital, is renamed Istanbul; Byzantium disappears from world stage	
1453–1520	Period of conquest as Ottoman Empire continues to expand	Ottoman Lyric Poetry by Necati and Bakiwest into Albania and \ Hungary
1517	Ottoman forces defeat the Egyptian Mamluks, seize Cairo, Egypt, and gain control of much of the Arab world	
1520–66	Süleyman the Magnificent continues to expand Ottoman Empire, annexes the island of Rhodes as well as Hungary and parts of North Africa	
1534	Ottoman conquest of Baghdad	*Leyla and Mejnun* by Fuzuli
1570	Spanish-led naval forces unexpectedly defeat the Ottoman navy at the battle of Lepanto, near Greece	
1590s	Ottoman Empire is embroiled in military campaigns to protect its borders; empire is beset by economic problems, including a devaluation of currency	
1590s–1826	Ottomans continue to come into contact with cultural innovations from the West; growing Austrian and Russian empires block Ottoman influence; Shi'ite branch of Islam challenges Sunni Ottoman Empire for domination of the Middle East; conservative Janissary Corps continues to resist reforms	*My Name Is Red* by Orhan Pamuk
1683	Ottoman Turks fail for a second time to capture Vienna	
1699	According to the Treaty of Karlowitz, Ottomans cede Hungary to Habsburg Empire and other territories to Venice and Poland	
1768–74	War between Ottoman Empire and Russia; the Ottomans lose the Crimea peninsula while Russia wins navigational rights in Ottoman waters and right to protect Orthodox Christians in the Ottoman Empire	

TURKISH SOCIETY: THE MODERN PERIOD

During the nineteenth century, Greece, Serbia, and Romania all fought successful wars of independence against the Ottoman Empire. Weakened by its losses, the once nearly invincible empire retreated further into stagnation and intellectual isolation. Meanwhile, Ottoman politics seesawed between liberal and ultraconservative control. Although a new constitution and the first Turkish parliament were implemented in the late 1800s, the former was abrogated and the latter dissolved by the autocratic sultan Abdülhamid II. In the 1880s, military cadets and medical students formed the Young Turks movement, which promoted modern reforms and an end to foreign interference in imperial affairs. The First World War saw the Ottoman Empire fighting on the side of Germany and incurring a mortal wound with that country's defeat. While the victor nations planned to divvy up Ottoman lands according to the punitive Treaty of Sèvres, a group of army officers under Mustafa Kemal formed a separatist government in Ankara that resisted the terms of the treaty. Further complicating the situation, Greek forces invaded Anatolia, prompting the Turkish War of Independence (1919–22). The Turkish rebels triumphed, which led to the expulsion of the Greeks, the abolition of the sultanate, and success in overturning the Treaty of Sèvres. In the subsequent Treaty of Lausanne, Kemal and his fellow nationalists recovered Turkish sovereignty and territory. In 1923 the Republic of Turkey was declared into existence, with Kemal as its first president. Determined to ensure Turkey's place among modern nations, Kemal implemented numerous reforms—the closing of religious schools, the replacement of the Arabic script by a new Latin-based Turkish alphabet, the use of a Turkish instead of an Arabic call to prayer. The reforms pleased progressives, angered conservatives, and earned Kemal the nickname *Atatürk* ("father of the Turk"). Atatürk's death in 1938 left a void in Turkish politics. Westernization continued, and the related liberal-conservative tensions resulted in military coups in 1960 and 1980, both of which were reversed by restorations of the republic.

	Historical Events	Related Literary Works in *WLAIT 6*
1810–78	Nationalism inspires wars of independence in Greece, Serbia, and Romania; in all three provinces the Ottoman Empire loses control; seeds of nationalism take root among Armenians, Macedonians, Arabs, and others	
1821–30	With the aid of France, Russia, and Britain, Greeks win independence from the Ottomans	
1826	Sultan Mahmud II abolishes the Janissary Corps	
1839–76	Sultan Abdülmecit proclaims equality of all Ottoman subjects, begins period of *Tanzimat* ("Reorganization"); influenced by contact between Ottomans and the West, the sultan modernizes political and civil structures	
1853–56	Crimean War pits Russia against the Ottoman Empire, France, and Britain; the empire regains the Crimea and Russia relinquishes claim of protection over Turkish Christians	
1876	The Grand Vizier, Midhat Paşa, promulgates the empire's first modern constitution; the sultan reserves considerable power nonetheless	
1878–1909	Despite constitutional reforms, Sultan Abdülhamid II rules autocratically for 30 years, dissolves the recently formed Ottoman parliament and abrogates the 1876 constitution; new emphasis on Islam and resistance to Western European influence	
1889	Military cadets and medical students form Committee of Union and Progress (CUP), often called the Young Turks movement, which favors modern reforms and an end to foreign interference	
1908	Pan-Turkism, a parallel to pan-Arabism, emerges; Young Turks Revolution begins with the mutiny of the Ottoman Third Army in Macedonia; Abdülhamid II is forced to restore the constitution	"The Secret Shrine" and "The Frog Prayer" by Ömer Seyfettin
1909	Abdülhamid II is deposed and a new representative government takes over under Sultan Mehmet V; the CUP now exercises considerable power, but is also autocratic	

Historical Events	Related Literary Works in *WLAIT 6*
1912–13 First and Second Balkan Wars—the Turks lose most of their remaining European territories	
1913 Enver Paşa leads CUP coup in Istanbul	
1914–18 During World War I, the Ottoman Empire sides with Germany; Allied forces of France, Britain, and Russia declare war on the Ottomans	
1915 Turkish troops, including Mustafa Kemal, successfully defend the Dardanelles against Allied attack	
1915–16 Correspondence between A. H. McMahon, the British High Commissioner in Egypt, and Husayn, the Sharif of the Hejaz, indicates British agreement to an independent Arab kingdom in return for Arab support in fighting the Ottoman Empire	
1916–18 In Anatolia mass deportations of Armenians, seen as pro-Russian, lead to loss of hundreds of thousands of Armenian lives; Britain captures Ottoman provinces in the Middle East; Allied forces occupy Istanbul and parts of Anatolia	
1917–18 The "Arab Revolt"—after fighting across the Arabian desert, forces under Husayn's son Amir Faysal, accompanied by British liaison officer T. E. Lawrence (Lawrence of Arabia), enter Damascus, Syria, on October 1, 1918; World War I ends on November 11 with Germany's surrender	
1919 Greek forces invade Anatolia at Smyrna (Izmir); Turkish nationalists under Mustafa Kemal fight the Allies and resist the partition of Turkey	
1919–20 The Treaty of Sèvres strips away Ottoman territory and power; an independent Kurdistan and an autonomous Armenia appear on the maps of Anatolia	
1919–22 Turkish War of Independence; nationalists rout the Greek army, taking Smyrna; the Ottoman sultanate is abolished	*Human Landscapes from My Country* by Nazim Hikmet
1922 The last sultan, Mehmed VI, flees Istanbul, marking the end of the Ottoman Empire and the birth of modern Turkey	
1923 At Lausanne Conference in July, Kemal's diplomats win back Turkish sovereignty and territory; Armenia and Kurdistan cease to exist as autonomous entities; Ankara becomes the new capital of the Turkish Republic and Kemal, its first president; Arabic script is replaced by a new Turkish alphabet based on the Latin alphabet	
1923–38 Government enacts measures to create a Turkish national consciousness and to modernize law, education, and public administration; Islam is abolished as the state religion, the fez is outlawed, and most areas of public life and employment are open to women, who are encouraged to abandon veils; reforms are resisted by Muslim clerics and some constitutional nationalists	*Memed, My Hawk* by Yaşar Kemal
1934 Kemal is officially honored by the National Assembly with the name Atatürk, "father of the Turk"	
1938 Atatürk dies	
1940 Village Institutes open throughout nation, train young villagers as primary-school teachers and teach them modern technical and agricultural skills	
1945 Neutral throughout most of World War II, Turkey declares war on Germany and Japan, and becomes a charter member of the United Nations (U.N.)	
1947 The United States begins assistance program to Turkey	

Historical Events	Related Literary Works in *WLAIT 6*
1950–52 After World War II, Atatürk's People's Party loses public support while the Democrat Party wins the first free, two-party election in Turkish history; U.S.-Soviet competition and the strategic situation in the Near East leads to Turkey's joining NATO	
1955 On the island of Cyprus, violence erupts between Greek and Turkish communities	
1959 Republic of Cyprus is declared an independent state	
1960–61 Junior army officers seize power in Turkey's first military coup, forming the National Unity Committee; several members of the former Democrat government are tried and executed, including Prime Minister Adnan Menderes; civilian rule is restored the following year, and the Second Republic begins	
1963–64 First Cyprus War between Turkish and Greek Cypriots; U.N. forces occupy Cyprus	
1967–68 Second Cyprus War; Turkey and Greece agree to withdraw troops from Cyprus	
1970s–80s Left-wing extremism (often directed against the U.S. and its military presence), the rise of political Islam, and the resurgence of Kurdish separatism in Anatolia keep political tensions high	
1974 Coup in Cyprus; Turkish military invades, protects Turkish minority but prompts international censure	
1980 Turkish military stages a coup, seizing control of the government, suspending the constitution, and closing parliament	*Curfew* by Adalet Agaoglu
1982 National referendum on new constitution; Kenan Evren is elected seventh president of the Republic; beginning of Third Republic	
1989–91 Reforms are gradually introduced, reduce time detainees can be held by police without being charged (from 15 days to 24 hours)	
1989–93 Prime Minister Turgut Özal becomes eighth president; upon Özal's death, Süleyman Demirel becomes president	
1991 Turkey supports American-led U.N. military campaign against Iraq's occupation of Kuwait; Turkey asks to be admitted to the European Union, indicating its claim to be a European as well as a Near Eastern nation	
1994–95 Welfare Party wins local elections in Istanbul and Ankara, then wins national elections the following year	
1996 Necmettin Erbakan becomes prime minister	
1997 Pressured by the military, Prime Minister Erbakan agrees to measures limiting influence of Islam in public life; European Union rejects Turkish bid for membership	
1998 Prime Minister M. Yilmaz resigns from office amid charges of corruption; Bülent Ecevit becomes prime minister	
1999 Democratic Left Party wins national elections; over 17,000 people die in a massive earthquake in northwestern Turkey; European Union reconsiders Turkey as candidate for membership	
2000 Ahmet Necdet Sezer becomes tenth president of the republic	

HEBREW SOCIETY IN THE MIDDLE EAST: FROM THE TORAH TO THE JEWISH DIASPORA

The society of the ancient Israelites is traditionally believed to have originated with the settlement in Canaan of seminomads after their migration from the Tigris and Euphrates valley, events that are chronicled in the Torah, the first five books of the Hebrew Bible. Later enslaved by the Egyptian pharaohs, the society conducted a mass exodus out of bondage in Egypt. The year was around 1400 B.C.E. according to the Torah, between 1250 and 1300 B.C.E. according to modern scholarship. Scholars disagree not only about when but also about how and even if such biblical events occurred. It is commonly held that after great travail the Israelites reached the "Promised Land," the land of Canaan, then conquered it under the leadership of Joshua. Subsequently they founded the Israelite kingdom under King Saul and renamed the land Israel. Saul's successor, King David, is credited with the consolidation and expansion of the kingdom, and David's son, King Solomon, with the construction of the First Temple in Jerusalem. During Solomon's reign, trade and commerce brought prosperity to the Israelite kingdom. His death, however, ushered in divisive times. The kingdom split into a northern half (Israel) and a southern half (Judah), both of which ultimately fell victim to foreign invaders. The Assyrians conquered and dispersed the people of Israel in 722 B.C.E.; the Babylonians exiled the people of Judah in 586 B.C.E., destroying the Temple in Jerusalem in the process. Cyrus the Great of Persia reversed this ill fortune around 539 B.C.E., when, after conquering Babylon, he allowed the Israelites to return to Jerusalem, the capital of the province now called Judea. They proceeded to build the Second Temple, which was completed c. 515 B.C.E. In succeeding centuries, various invaders—including the Greeks and Syrians—laid claim to Judea, and communities of Judeans (now also called Jews) developed outside the home province, in Mesopotamia, Egypt, and Asia Minor. The revolt of the Maccabees led to a brief period of independence, after which Judea fell under Roman control in 63 B.C.E. Then came the Great Jewish Revolt of 66–70 C.E., which tried but failed to throw off Roman rule, ending in the destruction of Jerusalem and the Second Temple. The crushing of the last Jewish revolt around 135 C.E. destroyed all hopes of a restored independence and initiated many centuries of prohibitions against Jewish settlement in Jerusalem. These developments Contributed to the spread of Jewish communities throughout the Roman Empire, a phenomenon that, as noted, began centuries earlier and that became known as the Diaspora. Meanwhile, the Romans renamed Judea after the Latin word *Palestina,* derived from the Greek for "Philistine Syria," the Philistines being an ancient people of the region. The Diaspora continued, as did struggles for control of Palestine, which remained a hotly contested area for many invaders over succeeding centuries as the majority of Jews dispersed into countries around the world.

2000–1250 B.C.E.	Events of the Torah—the first five books of the Old Testament—including the accounts of Abraham and Moses The Torah
c. 1800 B.C.E.	Hebrews migrate from Tigris and Euphrates Valleys, settle in Canaan until they migrate to Egypt

Historical Events		Related Literary Works in *WLAIT 6*
c. 1440– 1400 B.C.E.	According to biblical chronology, Hebrews leave Egypt in a mass exodus, wander for four decades, conquer Canaan	
c. 1250 B.C.E.	According to historical scholarship, Hebrews leave Egypt in a mass exodus	
c. 1020– 1000 B.C.E.	Reign of King Saul, under whom Israelite kingdom is established	
c. 1000–960 B.C.E.	After Saul's death in battle with Philistines, David becomes king, consolidating and expanding the kingdom	
c. 960–20 B.C.E.	Reign of King Solomon, construction of First Temple in Jerusalem	
920s B.C.E.	Israel is divided into two kingdoms: Judah in the south; Israel (Samaria) in the north	
c. 722 B.C.E.	Assyrian conquest of northern kingdom leads to exile of large number of Jews	
586 B.C.E.	Babylon conquers Judah, destroying Jerusalem and the First Temple; a third of the Jewish population is deported to Babylon; another third flees to Egypt; the final third remains in Judah	
538 B.C.E.	Cyrus the Great of Persia conquers Babylon and grants Jews permission to return to Jerusalem and rebuild the Temple	
515 B.C.E.	Second Temple is completed in Jerusalem, marking restoration of the city	
c. 458- 400 B.C.E.	New wave of Jews returns to Judea from Babylonia; Ezra the Scribe restores Torah law and expels pagan interlopers	
334–31 B.C.E.	Armies of Alexander the Great annex Judea, beginning an era of Greek dominance over Middle East	
c. 250 B.C.E.	Translation of Hebrew Bible into Greek begins in Alexandria, Egypt	
c. 200 B.C.E.	Of Greek descent, Antiochus III, Seleucid king of Syria, assumes control of Judea	
168 B.C.E.	Antiochus IV attempts to wipe out Judaism, desecrating the Temple in Jerusalem; Judah Maccabee leads Maccabean revolt against Antiochus	
167–64 B.C.E.	Maccabean revolt brings about liberation of Jerusalem and rededication of Temple; Maccabean family assumes kingship	
c. 150 B.C.E.-C.E.	Flourishing of Jewish sectarianism and religious and political factionalism	The Dead Sea Scrolls from Qumram
63–39 B.C.E.	Roman generals assert dominance in Judea, including the right to choose the Maccabean king	
37–4 B.C.E.	Herod, sponsored by Rome, becomes "King of the Jews"; he enlarges and beautifies the Temple; later he suffers from insanity, killing his wife and three of his sons and persecuting the rabbis of the Pharisees	
6–67 C.E.	Roman procurators govern Judea; Herod's descendants rule as puppet princes; emergence of Jesus of Nazareth, an artisan and preacher who, along with a group of followers, challenges the ruling elite	
c. 30	Jesus of Nazareth is crucified at Golgotha	
c. 50-c. 100	Composition of the New Testament gospels in Greek The Gospel According to Matthew	
66–73	Jews revolt against Roman rule; rabbinic school is established at Yavneh to insure continuity of tradition	

Historical Events		Related Literary Works in *WLAIT 6*
70	Under their commander Titus, Romans besiege, recapture, and destroy Jerusalem, including the Second Temple; Roman rule continues for three centuries	
73	Jewish resistance is stamped out at Masada	
132–35	Simon Bar Kokhba leads Jewish revolt that is crushed by Romans; Jewish rebels are sold as slaves, which leads to spread of Jewish communities throughout Roman empire; Romans adopt the name "Palestine" to indicate Judea is again Philistine	
c. 200s–700s	Jewish communities in Babylon-Parthia establish rabbinic academies that become the center of Jewish religious thought as Jewish community in Palestine diminishes	The Talmud
311–13	Constantine the Great makes Constantinople the center of Roman Empire, promotes Christianity, which results in a marked decline in Jews' social and religious security	
395–638	Byzantine rule over the Middle East	
c. 637	Arab Muslims conquer Palestine; Jews are allowed to return to Jerusalem	
750–1300	Jewish population thrives throughout the Islamic world, especially in al-Andalus (Islamic Spain), with Jews serving as doctors, diplomats, tax-collectors; many ultimately migrate to Christian Spain; anti-Jewish violence erupts sporadically in both Islamic and Christian Spain	*The Diwan of Judah Halevi; The Book of Tahkemoni* by Judah al-Harizi
1096–99	First Crusade marks European Christian conquest of Palestine; Jerusalem falls to the Crusaders; Jewish community of Jerusalem is slaughtered (Muslim and Christian communities as well)	
1187	Jerusalem is captured by Egyptian king Saladin, who is tolerant of Jews; Jewish residence in Palestine increases	
1291–1516	Mamluk rules Arab world in the Middle East; Jews as well as Christians are subject to restrictive laws	
1453	Ottomans conquer Constantinople, initiating dominance of Ottoman Turks over the Middle East	
1517–1917	Ottomans conquer Palestine, Egypt, and Mecca in the Arabian Peninsula in 1517; Ottoman Empire rules the Middle East; Jewish resettlement in Galilee and in Jerusalem increases; nationalist movement to establish a modern Jewish homeland in Palestine emerges in the late 1800s	

HEBREW SOCIETY IN THE MIDDLE EAST: ZIONISM AND THE STATE OF ISRAEL

During the nineteenth century, in keeping with the rise of modern nationalism and in response to the virulent anti-Semitism in Europe, Jewish voices began to call for the establishment of a homeland for the Jews in Palestine. Their ambition led to the formation of the modern Zionist movement, a drive to found just such a homeland. From the late 1800s to the mid-1900s, Jews left Europe for Palestine by the thousands, immigrating in waves, a phenomenon known as *aliyot* ("going up"). Each aliyah would contribute to the Yishuv (Jewish community in Palestine) in a distinctive way, beginning with the Jewish pioneers of the First Aliyah, who aspired to establish themselves as successful farmers. By contrast, many pioneers of the Second Aliyah showed more psychological and political orientations, intending to re-build not only "the land of Israel," but to remake themselves, to recreate the private and public image of the Jew. From the growth of collective farms (kibbutzim) and agricultural settlements to the emergence of urban centers, the Yishuv matured into an eclectic society of people from divergent backgrounds who spoke various languages. Outside the Middle East, in Europe political support for the establishment of a Jewish homeland wavered. At times the European powers demonstrated support for the Zionist drive; at times they showed sympathy for the Palestinian Arabs, who deeply resented the mounting influx of Jews into a region the Arabs had occupied for centuries. The horrors of World War II, which included the annihilation of 6 million European Jews during what became known as the Holocaust, lent a renewed urgency to the Zionist drive and a more favorable global disposition to it than ever before. On May 14, 1948, in a portion of Palestine, Israel declared itself an independent state. There ensued decades of warfare and bitter Arab-Israeli hostility, with the situation remaining volatile and unresolved to this day, despite peacemaking attempts by both parties and the mediation of outsiders.

Date	Historical Events	Related Literary Works in *WLAIT 6*
1878	Jewish agricultural settlement of Petah Tikvah is founded in Palestine	
1882	Dr. Leo Pinsker publishes *Auto-Emancipation*, urging the creation of a Jewish national homeland	
1882–1903	The First Aliyah—thousands of European Jews immigrate to Palestine after the assassination of Tsar Alexander II of Russia in 1881 and the ensuing anti-Semitic pogroms; in 1893, Nathan Birnbaum coins the term *Zionism*	
1896	Theodor Herzl publishes *The Jewish State*, urging the establishment of a Jewish state by international agreement	
1897	First World Zionist Congress—organized by Herzl, father of the political Zionist movement—is held in Basel, Switzerland; 21 more Zionist congresses will follow	
1903–05	Kishinev Pogrom kills and injures hundreds of Jews in Russia, shocking the world; two years later, another wave of pogroms and a failed revolution cause more European Jews to flee to Palestine and America	"In the City of Slaughter" by Hayyim Nahman Bialik
1904–14	The Second Aliyah—anti-Semitic violence in Europe drives another influx of Jews into Palestine	*Only Yesterday* by Shmuel Yosef Agnon
1909	Founding of first kibbutz (Degania) in Palestine	
1917	Britain's Balfour Declaration announces sympathy for Zionism and promises to assist in the establishment of a Jewish homeland in Palestine	*Mr. Mani* by A. B. Yehoshua
1919–23	Third Aliyah	
1922	League of Nations ratifies mandatory charter that grants Great Britain control over Palestine; territory becomes a British Mandate until 1948	
1923–31	Fourth Aliyah	
1932–38	Fifth Aliyah	
1933	Adolf Hitler becomes chancellor of Germany and initiates viciously anti-Semitic policies	
1936–39	Series of Arab rebellions in Palestine	

Historical Events	Related Literary Works in *WLAIT 6*
1938–39 Austria is annexed to Germany; several thousand Austrian Jews are sent to Nazi concentration camps	*Badenheim 1939* by Aharon Appelfeld
1939 Attempting to win Arab support for the impending world war, Britain abandons the pledges to Zionism, proposing in the "White Paper" to drastically reduce the number of Jews permitted to immigrate to Palestine	
1939–45 World War II; the Nazis implement the "Final Solution," interning Jews in concentration camps and killing 6 million Jews; the immigration of Jews to Palestine is restricted by quotas	*See Under: Love* by David Grossman
1946 Final (22nd) Zionist congress is held in Basel	
1947–48 Britain announces its intent to abandon its mandate and withdraw from Palestine	
1948 Establishment of the State of Israel; Arab-Israeli hostilities increase as Egypt, Transjordan, Iraq, Lebanon, and Syria invade the new nation	
1948–49 First Arab-Israeli War (War of Independence); several hundred thousand Palestinian Arabs flee or are pushed out of Israel, becoming refugees	
1948–56 Number of Jewish immigrants from Muslim lands climbs from 14 percent of Israel's immigrants in 1948 to 87 percent in 1956	
1949 Election of First Knesset (Israeli parliament); Israel becomes member of the United Nations	
1956–57 Sinai-Suez War; Israel agrees to withdraw from the Sinai only if major world powers issue assurances that Egyptians will be barred from aggression against Israel	*My Michael* by Amos Oz
1967 The Six-Day War: Egyptian forces enter the Sinai Peninsula, block Straits of Tiran to Israeli shipping; Israeli military attacks Egypt; war ends with Israel in possession of the Sinai, the Gaza Strip, the Jordanian West Bank, and the Syrian Golan Heights; U.N. Resolution 242 calls for withdrawal from territories, the trading of land for peace	
1968 Palestine Liberation Organization (PLO) endorses a charter pledging destruction of Israel through terror and war	
1970 King Hussein of Jordan expels the PLO; most of the leadership flees to Lebanon	
1971 Israel and Jordan open trade and tourist passages across the Jordan River and cooperate against terrorist attacks along the border	
1973 The October (Yom Kippur) War—Egypt and Syria effect a surprise attack on Israel; U.N. Resolution 338 calls for cease-fire in the October War and implementation of U.N. Security Council Resolution 242	*Songs of Zion, Jerusalem* by Yehuda Amichai
1978–79 Camp David Accords, overseen by U.S. President Jimmy Carter, lead to Israeli-Egyptian peace treaty; Israel agrees to return the Sinai fully to Egypt, while Egypt relegates the fates of Gaza and the West Bank to future negotiations	
1982 June—Israeli Army invades Lebanon; September—Phalangists (group of Lebanese Christians) massacre Palestinians in Sabra and Shatila refugee camps in Lebanon with tacit consent of Israeli military authorities	*Mr. Mani* by A. B. Yehoshua; "The Clockwork Doll" and Other Poems by Dalia Ravikovitch
1983 Prime Minister Menachem Begin resigns in wake of Lebanon War; Ariel Sharon resigns as Defense Minister; Israel and Lebanon sign an agreement with the help of U.S. Secretary of State George Schultz	

Historical Events		Related Literary Works in *WLAIT 6*
1987	Palestinian Arab uprising (Intifada) in the West Bank and Gaza Strip threatens Israeli authority in the territories	
1991	Israel and Soviet Union restore diplomatic relations	
1992–96	Prime Minister Yitzhak Rabin accepts Oslo peace agreements with the PLO	
1993	Palestinian and Israeli leaderships negotiate at Oslo; Palestinian leader Yasir Arafat recognizes right of State of Israel to exist in peace and security, accepts U.N. Security Council Resolutions 242 and 338, renounces use of terrorism; Israeli leader Rabin recognizes PLO as representative of the Palestinians; nearly two-thirds of Israelis and Palestinians in West Bank and Gaza support agreement; terrorist opponents attack to derail peace process	
1995	Rabin and Arafat reach agreement (called Oslo II) on West Bank and Gaza Strip, calling for elections in the territories, and the redeployment of Israel Defense Forces out of populated centers of the West Bank; Yitzhak Rabin is assassinated	
1996	Likud Party victory results in election of Binyamin Netanyahu as Israeli prime minister	
1996–98	Netanyahu upholds some of the Oslo agreement but does not continue the process of trading parts of the West Bank for peace; multiple suicide bombings by Palestinian terrorists kill and injure Israeli citizens	
2000	Complete withdrawal of Israeli Defense Force from Lebanon; peace talks between Israelis and Palestinians break down; Second Intifada begins	

Contents by Title

"Amm Mutwalli" and "Hagg Shalabi"
Mahmud Taymur 1

Arabian Nights, The
Husain Haddawy (as translated by) 13

Badenheim 1939
Aharon Appelfeld 25

Blind Owl, The
Sadiq Hidayat 37

Book of Dede Korkut, The 47

Book of Tahkemoni, The (Hebrew Maqamat)
Judah al-Harizi. 57

Broken Wings, The
Kahlil Gibran. 65

Cities of Salt
Abd al-Rahman Munif. 75

"Clockwork Doll, The" and Other Poems
Dalia Ravikovitch 85

Conference of the Birds, The
Farid al-Din Attar 93

Curfew
Adalet Agaoglu. 101

Dead Sea Scrolls from Qumram, The 111

Divan of Hafiz, The
Hafiz. 121

Diwan of Abu Nuwas, The
Abu Nuwas 131

Diwan of Judah Halevi, The
Judah Halevi 141

Epic of Gilgamesh, The 153
Gospel According to Matthew, The. . . . 165

Hayy ibn Yaqzan
Ibn Tufayl 177

Human Landscapes from My Country
Nazim Hikmet 187

"In the City of Slaughter"
Hayyim Nahman Bialik 197

"Introduction to the History of the Petty Kings"
Adunis 209

Kalilah and Dimnah
Abd Allah Ibn al-Muqaffa` (as
translated by). 221

"Khusraw and Shirin"
Nizami of Ganja. 229

King Is the King, The
Sa`dallah Wannus. 237

Leyla and Mejnun
Fuzuli. 247

Maqamat
al-Hamadhani 257

Contents by Title

"Mechanical Doll, The" and Other Poems
Furugh Farrukhzad. 267

Memed, My Hawk
Yasar Kemal. 275

Men in the Sun
Ghassan Kanafani. 285

Miramar
Najib Mahfuz. 295

Mr. Mani
A. B. Yehoshua. 305

Murder in Baghdad
Salah Abd al-Sabur. 315

My Michael
Amos Oz. 327

My Name Is Red
Orhan Pamuk 337

Mystical Poetry of Yunus Emre, The
Yunus Emre. 347

"Ode on the Conquest of Amorium"
Abu Tammam 355

"Ode on the Reconquest of al-Hadath"
al-Mutanabbi. 367

Once Upon a Time
Muhammad Ali Jamalzadah. 377

Only Yesterday
Shmuel Yosef Agnon. 387

Ottoman Lyric Poetry: "Those Tulip-
Cheeked Ones" and "Row by Row"
Necati and Baki 397

Plagued by the West (Gharbzadigi)
Jalal Al-i Ahmad. 407

Quran (Koran), The 415

Ruba`iyat of Omar Khayyam
Omar Khayyam 429

Savushun (A Persian Requiem)
Simin Danishvar. 441

Secret Life of Saeed the Ill-fated
Pessoptimist, The
Emile Habiby. 449

"Secret Shrine, The" and "The Frog Prayer"
Ömer Seyfettin. 461

See Under: Love
David Grossman. 471

Shahnamah, or The Book of Kings
Abu al-Qasim Firdawsi 481

Songs of the Land of Zion, Jerusalem
Yehuda Amichai. 493

Spiritual Couplets, The
Jalal al-Din Muhammad Balkhi Rumi . . 505

"Stop and We Will Weep: The
Mu`allaqah"
Imru al-Qays 515

Story of Zahra, The
Hanan al-Shaykh 527

Talmud, The 535

Torah, The 545

Contents by Author

Abd al-Sabur, Salah
Murder in Baghdad 315

Abu Nuwas
Diwan of Abu Nuwas, The 131

Adunis
"Introduction to the History of the Petty
Kings" 209

Agaoglu, Adalet
Curfew 101

Agnon, Shmuel Yosef
Only Yesterday 387

Ahmad, Jalal Al-i
Plagued by the West (Gharbzadigi) 407

Amichai, Yehuda
Songs of the Land of Zion, Jerusalem. . . . 493

Appelfeld, Aharon
Badenheim 1939 25

Attar, Farid al-Din
Conference of the Birds, The 93

Baki and Necati
Ottoman Lyric Poetry: "Those Tulip-
Cheeked Ones" and "Row by Row" 397

Bialik, Hayyim Nahman
"In the City of Slaughter" 197

Danishvar, Simin
Savushun (A Persian Requiem)

Farrukhzad, Furugh
"Mechanical Doll, The" and Other
Poems 267

Firdawsi, Abu al-Qasim
Shahnamah, The, or Book of Kings 481

Fuzuli
Leyla and Mejnun 247

Gibran, Kahlil
Broken Wings, The 65

Grossman, David
See Under: Love 471

Habiby, Emile
The Secret Life of Saeed the Ill-fated
Pessoptimist 449

Hafiz
Divan of Hafiz, The 121

Halevi, Judah
Diwan of Judah Halevi, The 141

al-Hamadhani
Maqamat 257

al-Harizi, Judah
Book of Tahkemoni, The (Hebrew
Maqamat) 57

Hidayat, Sadiq
Blind Owl, The 37

Ibn al-Muqaffa`, Abd Allah
Kalilah and Dimna 221

Contents by Author

Ibn Tufayl
Hayy ibn Yaqzan 177

Imru al-Qays
"Stop and We Will Weep: The
Mu`allaqah" 515

Jamalzadah, Muhammad Ali
Once Upon a Time 377

Kanafani, Ghassan
Men in the Sun 285

Khayyam, Omar
Ruba`iyat of Omar Khayyam 429

Mahfuz, Najib
Miramar 295

Munif, Abd al-Rahman
Cities of Salt 75

al-Mutanabbi
"Ode on the Reconquest of
al-Hadath" 367

Nazim Hikmet
Human Landscapes from My Country . . . 187

Necati and Baki
Ottoman Lyric Poetry: "Those Tulip-
Cheeked Ones" and "Row by Row" 397

Nizami of Ganja
"Khusraw and Shirin" 229

Ömer Seyfettin
"Secret Shrine, The" and "The Frog
Prayer" 461

Oz, Amos
My Michael 327

Pamuk, Orhan
My Name Is Red 337

Ravikovitch, Dalia
"Clockwork Doll, The" and Other
Poems 85

Rumi, Jalal al-Din Muhammad Balkhi
The Spiritual Couplets 505

al-Shaykh, Hanan
Story of Zahra, The 527

Tammam, Abu
"Ode on the Conquest of Amorium" . . . 355

Taymur, Mahmud
"Amm Mutwalli" and "Hagg Shalabi" 1

Wannus, Sa`dallah
King Is the King, The 237

Yasar Kemal,
Memed, My Hawk 275

Yehoshua, A. B.
Mr. Mani 305

Yunus Emre
Mystical Poetry of Yunus Emre, The . . . 347

Contents by Language

Akkadian

Epic of Gilgamesh, The 153

Ancient Greek

Gospel According to Matthew, The 165

Arabic

"Amm Mutwalli" and "Hagg Shalabi"
   Mahmud Taymur 1

Arabian Nights, The
   Husain Haddawy (as translated by) 13

Broken Wings, The
   Kahlil Gibran 65

Cities of Salt
   Abd al-Rahman Munif 75

Diwan of Abu Nuwas, The
   Abu Nuwas 131

Hayy ibn Yaqzan
   Ibn Tufayl 177

"Introduction to the History of the
   Petty Kings"
   Adunis 209

Kalilah and Dimnah
   Abd Allah Ibn al-Muqaffa`
   (as translated by) 221

King Is the King, The
   Sa`dallah Wannus 237

Maqamat
   al-Hamadhani 257

Men in the Sun
   Ghassan Kanafani 285

Miramar
   Najib Mahfuz 295

Murder in Baghdad
   Salah Abd al-Sabur 315

"Ode on the Conquest of Amorium"
   Abu Tammam 355

"Ode on the Reconquest of al-Hadath"
   al-Mutanabbi 367

Quran, The (Koran) 415

Secret Life of Saeed the Ill-fated
   Pessoptimist, The
   Emile Habiby 449

Contents by Language

"Stop and We Will Weep: The Mu`allaqah"
Imru al-Qays 515

Story of Zahra, The
Hanan al-Shaykh 527

Hebrew

Badenheim 1939
Aharon Appelfeld 25

Book of Tahkemoni, The
Judah al-Harizi 57

"Clockwork Doll, The" and Other Poems
Dalia Ravikovitch 85

Dead Sea Scrolls from Qumram, The 111

Diwan of Judah Halevi, The
Judah Halevi 141

"In the City of Slaughter"
Hayyim Nahman Bialik 197

Mr. Mani
A. B. Yehoshua 305

My Michael
Amos Oz 327

Only Yesterday
Shmuel Yosef Agnon 387

See Under: Love
David Grossman 471

Songs of the Land of Zion, Jerusalem
Yehuda Amichai 493

Talmud, The 535

Torah, The 545

Persian

Blind Owl, The
Sadiq Hidayat 37

Conference of the Birds, The
Farid al-Din Attar 93

Divan of Hafiz, The
Hafiz 121

"Khusraw and Shirin"
Nizami of Ganja 229

"Mechanical Doll, The" and Other Poems
Furugh Farrukhzad 267

Once Upon a Time
Muhammad Ali Jamalzadah 377

Plagued by the West (Gharbzadigi)
Jalal Al-i Ahmad 407

Ruba`iyat of Omar Khayyam
Omar Khayyam 429

Savushun (A Persian Requiem)
Simin Daneshvar 441

Shahnamah, or The Book of Kings
Abu al-Qasim Firdawsi 481

Spiritual Couplets, The
Jalal al-Din Muhammad Balkhi Rumi . . . 505

Turkish

Book of Dede Korkut, The 47

Curfew
Adalet Agaoglu 101

Human Landscapes from My Country
Nazim Hikmet 187

Leyla and Mejnun
Fuzuli 247

Memed, My Hawk
Yasar Kemal 275

My Name Is Red
Orhan Pamuk 337

Mystical Poetry of Yunus Emre, The
Yunus Emre 347

Ottoman Lyric Poetry: "Those Tulip-Cheeked Ones" and "Row by Row"
Necati and Baki 397

"Secret Shrine, The" and "The Frog Prayer"
Ömer Seyfettin 461

Text and Image Credits

Curfew: Agaoglu, Adalet, photograph. Reproduced by permission of Adalet Agaoglu, photograph. Reproduced by permission of Adalet Agaoglu.—Family tree for the cast of characters in the novel *Curfew,* by Adalet Agaoglu. Courtesy of Joyce Moss and Thomson Gale.—Book jacket illustration from *Curfew,* by Adalet Agaoglu. © Yapi Kredi Cultural Activities Arts and Publishing. Reproduced by permission.

Dead Sea Scrolls from Qumran, The: Dead Sea Scrolls, on display at the Special Museum, House of the Book in Jerusalem, photograph. Corbis-Bettmann. Reproduced by permission.—Caves of Essenes, Qumran, Israel, photograph. ©Richard T. Nowitz/Corbis. Reproduced by permission.—"The Scroll of the Rule," Dead Sea Scroll, photograph by Bruce E. Zuckerman. © West Semitic Research/Dead Sea Scrolls Foundation/Corbis. Reproduced by permission.

Divan of Hafiz, The: Hafiz ash Shirazi, manuscript painting, folio 1R, part of a collection of poems by Hafiz ash Shirazi, in the collection of the National Museum, Damascus, Syria, photograph. The Art Archive / National Museum Damascus, Syria / Dagli Orti. Reproduced by permission.—Miniature painting, folio 103R of manuscript "Poetry of Hafez," Persian, 1554, photograph. The Art Archive / Real biblioteca de lo Escorial / Dagli Orti. Reproduced by permission.

Diwan of Abu Nuwas, The: Mughal Prince and his courtiers drinking wine and eating in a garden, painting by Philip Spruyt. Corbis. Reproduced by permission.

Diwan of Judah Halevi, The: "Crusaders Take Jerusalem," engraving by Lechard after a painting by Schnetz. Mary Evans Picture Library. Reproduced by permission.

Epic of Gilgamesh, The: Gilgamesh, from sculpture in alabaster found in Khorsabad, Louvre, Paris. Corbis-Bettmann. Reproduced by permission.—Sumerian ruins of the city of Uruk, photograph by Nik Wheeler. Corbis. Reproduced by permission.

Gospel According to Matthew, The: Parable from the Gospel of St. Matthew, photograph by Grabriel Bodmear. © Historical Picture Archive/Corbis. Reproduced by permission.

Hayy ibn Yaqzan: "Vizir Who was Punished," illustration. Mary Evans Picture Library. Reproduced by permission.

Human Landscapes from My Country: Hikmet, Nazim, Istanbul, Turkey, 1950, photograph. AP/Wide World Photos. Reproduced by permission.—Haydarpass train station, on the eastern shore of the Bosphorus River, Istanbul, Turkey, photograph. © Chris Hellier/Corbis. Reproduced by permission.

"In the City of Slaughter": Bialik, Hayyim N., photograph. The Library of Congress.

"Introduction to the History of the Petty Kings": Nasser, Abdel, United Arab Republic President, addressing a crowd in Algiers, Algeria, on May 7, 1963, photograph. © Bettmann/Corbis. Reproduced by permission.—Mourners reaching out to touch the flag-draped coffin of President Gamal Abdel Nasser, October 1, 1970, Cairo, Egypt, photograph. © Bettmann/Corbis. Reproduced by permission.

Kalilah and Dimnah: "Sultan Overseeing Justice Administered to Culprits," illustration from *Kalila and Dimna.* © Archivo Iconografico, S.A./Corbis. Reproduced by permission.

Khusraw and Shirin: Ganjavi, Nizami, illustrated portrait, photograph. © Azerbaijan International. Reproduced by permission.—"Khosroe Surprising Shirin in the Bath," miniature painting. © Archivo Iconografico, S.A./Corbis. Reproduced by permission.

Memed, My Hawk: Koprulu Canyon National Park, in Toros Daglari, Turkey, photograph. © O. Alamany & E. Vicens/Corbis. Reproduced by permission.

Men in the Sun: Kanafani, Ghassan, photograph. © 2003 Courtesy of the Palestinian Academic Society for the Study of International Affairs. Reproduced by permission.—Refugee camp in Beirut, photograph. © Bettmann/Corbis. Reproduced by permission.

Miramar: Mahfouz, Naguib, 1984, photograph. AP/Wide World Photos. Reproduced by permission.—Multi-story buildings lining the city streets in Alexandria, Egypt, in November 1963, photograph. © Roger Wood/Corbis. Reproduced by permission.

Mr. Mani: Yehoshua, Abraham, smiling, photograph by Dina Guna. Reproduced by permission.—Allenby, General Edmund Henry Hynman, riding through the Jaffa Gate as part of his formal entry into the city of Jerusalem. © Hulton-Deutsch/Corbis. Reproduced by permission.

My Michael: Oz, Amos, photograph. © David Rubinger/Corbis. Reproduced by permission.

My Name is Red: Pamuk, Orhan, photograph by Sophie Bassouls. © Corbis. Reproduced by permission.—"Magum all Ka'ba," from the *Khamsa,* written by Nizami, illustration by Bihzad, 15th Century. The Bridgeman Art Library. Reproduced by permission.

Ode on the Conquest of Amorium: Spiraling tower in Samrra, Iraq, October, 1963, photo-

Ode on the Reconquest al-Hadath: Camel caravan passing by the city of Aleppo, Syria, photograph. © Bettmann/Corbis. Reproduced by permission.

Once Upon a Time: Persian constitutionalists fighting in a trench, Tabriz, Iran, photograph. © Underwood & Underwood/Corbis. Reproduced by permission.

Only Yesterday: Agnon, Shay, photograph. © David Rubinger/Corbis. Reproduced by permission.

Ottoman Lyric Poetry: Sultan and his court in the Divan Room, Topkapi Palace, Constantinople, from "Turkish Memoirs," a 17th century Turkish manuscript. The Art Archive / Museo Correr Venice / Dagli Orti. Reproduced by permission.—Map of the Turkish Empire, from the Mercator Atlas, engraving. The Stapleton Collection. Reproduced by permission.

Quran, The: Pilgrimage to Mecca, Saudi Arabia, photograph. The Library of Congress.—Two pages from a Koran, dated 1510, photograph. The Art Archive / Private Collection / Eileen Tweedy. Reproduced by permission.

Ruba'iyat: Khayyam, Omar, photograph. © Bettmann/Corbis. Reproduced by permission.— Scene from "Rubaiyat of Omar Khayyam," illustration by Gilbert James. The Art Archive. Reproduced by permission.

Savushun (Persian Requiem): A small group of nomads and heavily laden horses, traveling from Chatt-el-Arabe towards the higher plateau of Sultanabad, Iran, photograph. © Paul Almasy/Corbis. Reproduced by permission.

Secret Life of Saeed the Ill-fated Pessoptimist, The: Habibi, Emile, Tel Aviv, Israel, photograph. AP/Wide World Photos. Reproduced by permission.—Palestinian mother and her two children at a refugee camp, formerly the ruins of a Roman amphitheater, in Amman, Jordan, 1949, photograph. © Hulton-Deutsch Collection/Corbis. Reproduced by permission.

"Secret Shrine, The": "Balkan War. Bombardment of Adrianoplis, Turkey 1913," photograph. The Art Archive / Dagli Orti. Reproduced by permission.

See Under: Love: Grossman, David, New York City, March 11, 2002, photograph. AP/Wide World Photos. Reproduced by permission.—Eisenhower, Dwight D., touring a German concentration camp at Gotha, April, 1945, photograph. © Bettmann/Corbis. Reproduced by permission.

Shanamah, The, or Book of Kings: Zoroaster, illustration. The Granger Collection. Reproduced by permission.—Page from the *Shah Nameh* (Book of Kings), written by the Persian poet Firdausi, 16th-century manuscript, photograph. The Art Archive / Musee Conde Chantilly / Dagli Orti. Reproduced by permission.

Songs of the Land of Zion, Jerusalem: Amichai, Yehuda, photograph. © AFP/Corbis. Reproduced by permission.—Fumes and smoke fill the air and Israeli artillerymen hold their ears while laying down a barrage on Syrian positions, Syrian-Israeli border, October 12, 1973, photograph. © Bettmann/Corbis. Reproduced by permission.

Spiritual Couplets, The: Jalal al-Din Rumi, Persian poet and sage, outside a blacksmith's shop, Shiraz style miniature from "Majalis al-Ushshaq (The Assemblies of the Lovers)" manuscript commissioned by Sultan Husayn Mirza, 1552, from Ouseley Add 24 folio 78v. The Art Archive / Bodleian Library, Oxford University. Reproduced by permission.

"Stop and We Will Weep": The Mu'allaqah: Male oryx at Buffalo Springs Wildlife Reserve, Kenya, Africa, photograph. © Darrell Gulin/Corbis. Reproduced by permission.

Story of Zahra, The: Tank with Arabic writing on it turning a corner on a street in Beirut, Lebanon, photograph by Francoise de Mulder. Corbis. Reproduced by permission.

Talmud, The: First page of commentary on the Pentateuch, by Rashi, written by Meir ben Samuel, Italy, 1396, photograph. The Art Archive / Bodleian Library Oxford / The Bodleian Library. Reproduced by permission.

Torah, The: "Moses Breaking the Tablets of the Law," engraving by Chris Hellier. Corbis. Reproduced by permission.

"Amm Mutwalli" and "Hagg Shalabi"

by

Mahmud Taymur

M ahmud Taymur (1894-1973) grew up in Cairo, in an aristocratic literary family of Kurdish origin. His father, Ahmad Taymur Pasha, was a philologist and a bibliophile whose personal library numbered among the largest and most important in Egypt. Mahmud's paternal aunt, A'isha al-Taymuriyah (1840-1920), was a respected poetess and essayist. His older brother Muhammad (1892-1921) was a dramatist and short-story writer and a leading light in modern Arabic literature in his own right. As a youth, Mahmud was deeply influenced by his older brother's literary activities as well as by the famous salons regularly held at the Taymur residence and attended by the intellectual luminaries of the day. Muhammad introduced his younger brother to the work of the French author Guy de Maupassant, who was to exercise an important influence on Mahmud Taymur's writing (the source of Taymur's sobriquet, "Egypt's Maupassant"). While attending college, Taymur contracted typhus, and the illness left him a semi-invalid for most of his life. He dropped out of college, then worked briefly at various government ministries, but soon retired to devote himself full-time to his literary career. Taymur traveled extensively in Europe over a 17-year period and lived there between 1925 and 1927, indulging his passion for modern French and Russian fiction during this period. An immensely prolific writer, he published more than 80 books, including novels, literary criticism, drama, travel literature, biography, and short-story collections. Taymur is considered a founding father of the modern

THE LITERARY WORKS

Two short stories set in Cairo, Egypt, in the 1920s; first published in Arabic in 1925 ("Amm Mutwalli") and 1930 ("Hagg Shalabi"), in English in 1947.

SYNOPSIS

In "Amm Mutwalli," a poor hawker who moved to Cairo from the Sudan becomes convinced he is the promised Mahdi and goes insane. "Hagg Shalabi" features a brutal neighborhood thug who marries and impregnates women so that he can hire them out as wet nurses for wealthy families.

Arabic short story, having written 29 collections over his lifetime; many would become available in English, French, and Russian translations. His best-known works are the two volumes of short stories entitled *Hagg Shalabi* (1930) and *Abu Ali amil artist wa-qisas ukhra* (1934, Abu Ali Pretends To Be an Artist) as well as his novella *Rajab Afandi* (1928) and his novel *Nida al-majhul* (1934, The Call of the Unknown). In his early fiction especially, Taymur built his plots around a single, somehow representative yet often quite unusual or shady Egyptian character. His most famous characters—of which Amm Mutwalli and Hagg Shalabi are just two examples—are individual studies in the mental and social eccentricities of a certain segment of Egyptian society. The stories are groundbreaking not only for their style, but also for their focus on Egypt's lower classes.

Events in History at the Time of the Short Stories

The *Nahdah* and Arabic literature. The novel and the short story are relatively recent genres in Arabic literature. For centuries, poetry reigned supreme in the Arabic literary canon, and the highly formalized classical *qasidah,* or ode, remained the dominant and most respected cultural and literary form in Arab society (see, for example, ***Ode on the Conquest of Amorium,*** also in *WLAIT 6: Middle Eastern Literatures and Their Times*). Prose writing, though not as prestigious as poetry, had its own rich tradition throughout the classical and medieval periods of Arab history and included a wide variety of genres such as the essay, the epistle, the biography, the chronicle, and the *maqamah*—a short, rhymed prose narrative that features the adventures of a picaresque hero (see ***Maqamat,*** also in *WLAIT 6: Middle Eastern Literatures and Their Times*). These genres collectively constituted a body of belles-lettres that, strictly speaking, did not include quasi-oral fictional genres like the romance, the epic, and the famous collection of stories known in English as ***The Arabian Nights*** (also in *WLAIT 6: Middle Eastern Literatures and Their Times*). While tremendously popular—especially among the illiterate urban lower classes—this type of oral narrative was, until quite recently, considered by Arab writers and scholars to be a vulgar and debased form of literature, unworthy of serious attention or study. Sometime around the middle of the nineteenth century, this state of affairs began to change.

Back in the eighteenth century, the Arab world experienced significant social and economic ferment. Important shifts in international trade patterns and political institutions contributed to a gradual transformation in late medieval social structures—the urban guild system, the religious establishment, and the political and economic relationship between the city and the countryside. During this period, literary production and scholarship began to change as well, emphasizing a new utilitarian approach to language and the human sciences associated with it. For example, philology and lexicography began to focus on living linguistic usage rather than ideal word forms associated with the Quran or with classical poetry. This transformation was further accelerated by the introduction of the modern European sciences and humanities onto the Arab intellectual stage following the French conqueror Napoleon's occupation of Egypt in 1798.

Some Arab writers and intellectuals were impressed by the scientific and technological superiority of Europe and attracted to its Enlightenment culture. More exactly, they were attracted to the "secular rationalism" of this culture—that is, its attempts to improve the human condition by focusing on knowledge and on the ability of people to reason. Though the French occupation of Egypt was short-lived, the cultural and intellectual ferment that it introduced became an important factor in the history of the nineteenth century, most notably in Egypt and Syria. Recognizing the importance of acquiring the secrets of European military technology, Egypt's ruler, Muhammad Ali (reigned 1804-49) sent numerous educational missions to study in France and established a School of Languages in Cairo, at which the concerted translation of European texts into Arabic was conducted. Christian missionary schools in Syria were also important centers of translation activity.

The process of literary and scientific translation into Arabic contributed to the simplification and revitalization of the medieval Arabic language and stimulated writers to experiment with older Arabic prose genres. Writers in Syria rediscovered the finest examples of classical prose and used them as a model for a modern revival of narrative genres like the *maqamah.* Other European genres like drama and the novel were introduced into the Arab world around the middle of the nineteenth century. Numerous literary magazines dedicated to fiction, both original and in translation, sprang up around the turn of the twentieth century. The novel and the short story became immensely popular among Arab audiences during this period, which is broadly referred to as the *Nahdah,* or the Awakening—a term that is used to denote a seminal era of cultural and political change in the nineteenth and twentieth centuries.

Egyptian intellectuals, colonialism, and social reform. French and then British financial, political, and cultural influence continued to grow throughout the nineteenth century. Between 1860 and 1867, the number of Europeans who settled in Egypt increased from a few thousand to over 100,000. By 1876 Egypt's reigning monarch, the Khedive Ismail, had plunged the country into a major financial crisis through his extravagant expenditure of public monies. Both the British and the French, their eyes long

NAPOLEON IN EGYPT (1798-1801)

~

The rivalry over trade and imperial possessions between Britain and France—the two great powers of the eighteenth century—came to a head in 1798, when Napoleon Bonaparte decided to lead an expeditionary force to Egypt. Britain was anxious to safeguard its Red Sea trade routes to India—then a British colonial possession. France meanwhile wished to limit English supremacy in the East. Wise to the international competition, Egypt's eighteenth-century Mamluk rulers played the two powers against each other by granting trading privileges to one or the other, depending on Egyptian interests. When one such Franco-Egyptian treaty was abrogated by the Mamluks in favor of Britain, Napoleon decided to invade Egypt. The short-lived French military occupation was accompanied by an extensive academic mission that included scientists, historians, and men of letters. This mission formed the nucleus of the Institute of Egypt, founded by Napoleon in the year of the invasion to "(1) work for the advancement of science and knowledge in and about Egypt; (2) to study the natural, industrial and historical sciences relevant to Egypt; and (3) to consult with, and advise, the government on specific matters relating to policy" (Vatikiotis, p. 41). Though scholars disagree as to the overall significance of the French expedition for modern Egyptian and Arab history and culture, there is no doubt that the Institute provided the occasion for important encounters between French and Egyptian intellectuals as well as an impetus for the dissemination of European technologies and cultural texts in the Arab world.

fastened on the strategic and economic potentials of Egypt, had already established a presence in the area. They owned controlling stakes in the newly built Suez Canal and held consular authority over both the resident European populations and a substantial segment of Egypt's religious minorities. Using Ismail's incompetence as an excuse, the two powers took over the country's crumbling finances and began to actively interfere in its domestic affairs. Not long afterwards, the British used a domestic Egyptian conflict—a nationalist army rebellion led by Colonel Ahmad Urabi Pasha—as an excuse to occupy Egypt. This occupation was to last nearly three-quarters of a century, during which the British insinuated themselves into Egyptian government. They ruled Egypt in a shifting, uneasy alliance with the king and the country's landowning elite. British politicians and administrators introduced a particular kind of reformist colonial discourse into Egypt, one that emphasized the need to slowly "modernize" what they deemed to be the country's culturally backward and racially inferior population. At the turn of the twentieth century, reformers appropriated this discourse and used it to push for limited changes in Egyptian society.

Many of the intellectual luminaries of the Nahdah came from the upper echelons of Egyptian society. They were members of the landowning urban elite, educated in Europe and engaged in Egyptian politics and in the law. Also they were prolific writers and dedicated reformers whose ideas were heavily influenced by nineteenth-century European positivist social theory disseminated through Arabic translations of writers like Jeremy Bentham, Herbert Spencer, and Gustave Le Bon. Social Darwinism—the concept that the fittest rise to the top in society and therefore deserve their position—was extremely influential in Egyptian intellectual circles. Just as powerful individuals occupied their high-level positions for good reason, argued some of the social Darwinists, powerful nations held their political positions because they were inherently superior to less powerful ones. Le Bon's description of a "collective mind" or "mental constitution" evolving over many generations of a nation's history was intended to demonstrate the difference between advanced and backward nations. Many Egyptian intellectuals adopted this idea of a collective mind and applied it to Egypt, often in very negative ways. Egypt's liberal reformers wholeheartedly admired and identified with Western liberal culture and saw themselves as the elite vanguard of Egypt's social and political renaissance and the natural leaders of the degraded Egyptian masses. They believed that the key to this renaissance lay in the radical reform of Islam and the adoption of the secular, rationalist values espoused by Europeans. With these values in mind, they identified a variety of pressing issues in their society. Muhammad Al-Muwaylihi criticized the chaos and injustice of the legal system and the decadence of the religious establishment in Egypt. Qasim Amin championed the education of women, while Ahmad Fathi Zaghlul and Ahmad Lutfi al-Sayyid wrote extensively about the need to foster a liberal political culture amongst the emergent Egyptian middle classes. However, a deep sense of suspicion of and disdain for the masses lay at the root of their reformist project.

IMPERIALIST STEREOTYPES

British administrative manuals, ethnographies, and travel guides of the nineteenth century circulated racist views of "the Egyptian character," reflecting a general cultural arrogance on the part of the British. An English schoolmistress who taught in Cairo for many years recollects Egyptians' being regarded by her compatriots as "a cut above camels" (Rodenbeck, pp. 178-79). Colonial manuals described the Egyptian as intellectually limited, congenitally lazy, and spitefully recalcitrant. British writer Edward Lane's *Manners and Customs of the Modern Egyptians* devoted entire chapters to the "indolence," "obstinancy," "libidinous" sensuality, and invariable drug addiction of Egypt's lower classes (Mitchell, pp. 105-106). Later, this type of racism would find its way into pseudo-scientific discourse about the relationship between the "character" and historical destiny of nations.

For the most part, turn-of-the-century liberal Egyptian intellectuals harbored an ambivalent attitude towards the peasants, the poor, the working classes, and their popular culture. While believing that Egypt as a whole needed to modernize in order to be admitted to the ranks of sovereign and independent nations, they blamed the masses for Egypt's backwardness and dependence. The "common" Egyptian man was in fact often the target of their polemic. They described

him in all sorts of negative ways—cunning, lazy, ignorant, superstitious, and addicted to vice— and blamed him for the ills of the Egyptian nation, its corruption, and, ultimately, its political weakness on the international stage. This disdain for the Egyptian masses and for Egyptian popular culture (as yet untouched by the cultural values of the invading West) manifested itself especially in the reformist attack on popular religious practice. In the words of one Muslim reformer writing in Egypt at this time: "Faith has deteriorated into a negation of reason. [Muslims] call indolence trust in God and the search for truth heresy. For them, this is religion, and anyone who holds different views is exposed to abuse. . . . Unquestioning acceptance of everything old is the heart of wisdom" (Ahmad, p. 45). The corrupted and archaic doctrine of the existing religious establishment, the hypocrisy and opportunism of popular preachers and mystics, and the superstition and gullibility of the pious masses were repeatedly criticized by secular liberals and Muslim reformers alike. In this context, a stock character begins to appear in the literature of the Nahdah—that of the dishonest and ignorant *shaykh* or preacher who at best is an incompetent fool and at worst, a hypocritical and treacherous knave. On the other hand, the simple folk who willingly participated in this type of religious hocus-pocus were deemed equally if not more to blame for the decadence of Egyptian society. In short, during this period, popular Islam was viewed by the educated upper and middle classes as a potentially dangerous social pathology that had to be reformed before Egypt could become a truly modern and independent nation.

Another important target for reform was the status of women in Egyptian society. This was a more controversial issue, though—one on which Muslim and secular reformers strongly differed. Between 1889 and 1891, Qasim Amin published two seminal books, *Kitab tahrir al-mar'a* (The Liberation of Women) and *al-Mar'ah al-jadidah* (The New Woman), in which he forcefully argued against the practice of female seclusion and for the reform of polygamy and divorce laws. In Egypt, both personal status laws and the customary interpretation of these laws were heavily weighted towards male authority and interests. Men had the exclusive right to divorce and to engage in a limited form of polygamy. Though the spirit of the law required extenuating circumstances for both divorce and multiple marriages, in practice abuses were widespread and legally sanctioned. Qasim Amin's book argued too for

Cairo in the mid-1920s.

increased educational opportunities for women, an issue hotly debated by contemporary Egyptian intellectuals around the turn of the century. For secular reformers, the attempt to educate women and integrate them more fully into public life was part and parcel of an urgent social and intellectual revolution. The more conservative Muslim and nationalist intellectuals, on the other hand, viewed this project as a dangerous capitulation to Western imperialism that would undermine the very basis of Egyptian culture and society. Acceptance of a woman's right to an education, however, was one of the earliest social reforms to gain wide currency. By the end of the 1920s, even very conservative intellectuals believed women should be educated, if only because they were the mothers of the next generation and illiterate mothers meant uneducated and ignorant children.

Nonetheless, the cause of women's rights in Egyptian society continued to gain momentum throughout the 1910s, '20s, and '30s. Women themselves began to agitate on behalf of feminist issues. Many participated in the massive demonstrations for independence that took place in 1919. Some, like the celebrated Mayy Ziyadah and Fatma al-Yusuf, hosted important literary salons and founded political journals. In 1923, an upper-class political activist, Huda Sha`rawi,

founded the Egyptian Feminist Union, the first feminist union in Egypt. Its activities focused on reform of the legal and customary conditions of marriage and divorce and on women's education. In response to feminist demands, the Egyptian parliament enacted legislation between 1921 and 1931 that restricted polygamy, divorce, and the widespread practice of child-marriage. These restrictions did not reach the bulk of the Egyptian population, however. Not until a quarter of a century after Taymur's stories take place would women gain the right to vote. It was only in the 1950s that all women won this right and that universal free education further integrated middle- and lower-class women into public intellectual and political life in Egypt.

The Mahdist Revolt in the Sudan (1881-98). In 1820, well before the arrival of the British, Egypt's first independent ruler, Muhammad Ali (1769-1849), initiated the conquest of the Sudan and installed a centralized civil and military bureaucracy in Khartoum. Egypt was part of the Ottoman Empire at the time, so the bureaucracy operated under the authority of Ottoman governors, who taxed the local population heavily and instituted a system of forced labor. Moreover, the government attempted to interfere with Sudanese religious beliefs and practices. Sufism or Islamic mysticism held sway in the region, an unacceptable state of affairs to Ottoman rule. Its agents set out to replace the powerful Sufi institutions of the region with a more orthodox version of Islam, which served only to further alienate the local population from the regime. Later on, the disaffection intensified because of Egyptian attempts to abolish the slave trade—from which certain Sudanese tribes had profited greatly over the nineteenth century. These heavy-handed and unwelcome policies, in addition to the general local unhappiness with Egyptian rule, contributed to the rise of the Mahdist revolt that would bring an end to Egyptian rule of the Sudan.

In 1881 a popular Sudanese religious leader named Muhammad Ahmad declared himself to be the Mahdi—a divinely guided leader and successor of the Prophet Muhammad. Not only did Muhammad Ahmad al-Mahdi found an Islamic revivalist movement; he also spearheaded a successful military revolt against Turco-Egyptian rule. The religious movement he founded was based on the eschatology or teaching in popular Islamic mysticism about the coming of the divinely guided Savior. A conviction about the coming of the Mahdi was widespread in nineteenth-century Sudan, where Islam was characterized by the dominance of a series of powerful, tightly knit Sufi orders (such as that to which Muhammad Ahmad belonged—the Sammaniyah Order). For the most part, these orders practiced a popular, syncretic form of Islam, combining local beliefs and superstitions with elements of more orthodox Islamic doctrine. The arrival of the Mahdi was expected to "fill the world with justice, even as it has been filled with injustice" (Voll, p. 64). Stepping into this role, Muhammad Ahmad set out to cleanse the Muslim community of what he and his followers saw as the corruption and immorality of the authorities of the day, be they Turks, Egyptians, or Europeans. For inspiration, the Mahdists turned to the original example of the Prophet and his followers: "This [initial] period was regarded as the only one in Islamic history in which the umma [Islamic Community] was undivided and followed a path leading to the establishment of a just community of believers" (Warburg, p. 9). Mahdism had tremendous popular appeal among the Sudanese Sufi Orders precisely because it was viewed as a direct political and theological challenge to the rigid orthodoxy imported into the Sudan by the Egyptian government. It was even viewed sympathetically by the masses back in Egypt; many identified with its syncretic version of Islam and

with its powerful messianic message of popular revival and resistance to a corrupt social and political establishment.

A British officer, Charles Gordon Pasha, was sent to quell the rebellion, but his men were defeated and he was killed in battle in 1885. Khartoum and most of northern Sudan were taken by the Mahdi's armies. Soon after this major victory, Muhammad Ahmad al-Mahdi died. His successor, the Khalifah Abd-Allah, consolidated the movement against internal division and outside threats. Finally, in 1898, an Anglo-Egyptian army, led by Lord Kitchener, won a decisive battle outside Omdurman and defeated the Mahdist forces. In 1899 an agreement between Britain and Egypt redefined the structure of the post-Mahdist Sudanese government. Although, in theory, Egypt was supposed to share in the rule of the Sudan, in practice the condominium gave full control over the country to Britain, an arrangement that lasted until Sudanese independence in 1953. Meanwhile, the 1920s witnessed the rise of Sudanese nationalism and increasing anticolonial activity against the British. Some of the new nationalist organizations advocated independence for Sudan, while others, like the popular White Flag League, called for union with Egypt. Events came to a head in 1924, when a military uprising against the British was quashed, its leaders jailed, the nationalist parties outlawed, and most Egyptian officials expelled from the country.

The Wafd Party and the 1919 revolution. Meanwhile, in Egypt, anticolonial nationalism also came to a head in the 1920s. At the beginning of the First World War, the British declared Egypt a protectorate and imposed martial law on the country, sending in thousands of new British troops. Food shortages caused prices to skyrocket, and thousands of Egyptian peasants found themselves being conscripted into massive rural and military labor gangs by the British authorities. Over a quarter of these peasants-turned-laborers died from disease and malnutrition. Egyptians from all walks of life grew increasingly resentful of the occupation, and the movement for independence gained momentum. In 1918 a group of Egyptian politicians headed by Saad Zaghloul formed a national delegation (Wafd) to demand independence for Egypt at the Versailles Peace Conference. The British authorities in Cairo refused to let the delegation travel to the conference, however, and after almost a year of growing popular anger, on March 8, 1919, they arrested Zaghloul and exiled him and two colleagues to Malta. The massive nationwide demonstrations of 1919 immediately broke out, and popular agitation continued until Zaghloul was allowed to return. Three years later, on February 22, 1922, the British government finally granted Egypt limited independence, and a constitution was drawn up. In 1924, the Wafd—by now the most popular political party in the country—came to power in national elections. It would continue to dominate Egyptian political life through the time of the short stories until 1936, when a second treaty with the British, negotiated by the Wafd, met with popular condemnation.

The Short Stories in Focus

Plot summaries. "Amm Mutwalli." The title of this story is also the name of its main character, a poor Sudanese vendor of nuts and melon seeds who, we learn, moved to Cairo 15 years ago after having fought as a Divisional Commander in the Mahdist revolt in the Sudan. Amm Mutwalli lives in a small, dark room that contains nothing but his bedding and a box in which he keeps his old sword. During the day, he follows his usual route, making two regular stops—the first at a small mosque where he eats his lunch, prays, and takes a nap, and the second outside the mansion of Nur al-Din Bey, a wealthy Cairo notable. At night, he returns home exhausted, his sole entertainment being to take out and caress his old sword, losing himself in memories of the glorious old battles and the heroic Mahdi—"the Bearer of the Standard of Islam" (Taymur, "Amm Mutwalli," p. 89). Amm Mutwalli dreams of the Mahdi's return and the end of sin and worldly corruption. At dawn, before he shoulders his basket of wares and begins his long day, the vendor reads a few pages of pious or mystical religious tracts. He is furthermore in the habit of giving daily religious discourses and reminiscences about the great Mahdi to an assembled audience of gatekeepers and servants in the fancy neighborhood where Nur al-Din Bey lives: "They would talk about Islam during its days of glory, and how it had fallen a prey to misfortunes" ("Amm Mutwalli," p. 90). The crowd listens to him in ecstasy, and Amm Mutwalli generally finishes by talking of the Mahdi's promised return.

One day, Nur al-Din Bey's irreverent young son—who buys a penny's worth of nuts from Amm Mutwalli from time to time, but only after poking a little fun at him and his heroic claims—informs him that the father wishes to speak to him. Nur al-Din Bey tells Amm Mutwalli that his elderly mother has heard of his stories and would

like to meet him in person. Amm Mutwalli is astonished. He feels honored. When taken into the august lady's magnificent presence, he proceeds to narrate, with his usual eloquence, his stories and anecdotes of the past, "completely captivating the old lady's heart" ("Amm Mutwalli," p. 93). In parting, she gives him an unexpectedly handsome gift and makes many gestures of respect and gratitude, which confounds and embarrasses him. Moreover, as he leaves the mansion, a group of female servants crowd round him and try to touch his garment in order to acquire his blessing. Then they buy his entire stock. Amm Mutwalli hurries off to his little mosque and performs 40 prostrations in thanks for God's bounty.

A major change of fortunes now commences in Amm Mutwalli's life. He becomes a regular visitor at Nur al-Din Bey's house and is able to give up his trade as a hawker while significantly improving his lifestyle. He can now afford to eat meat twice a week and wear the clothes of a well-off *shaykh*. He moves into larger and more comfortable lodgings and devotes his time to helping the poor, visiting mosques, and listening to religious discourses that he can then rework for his new patroness's edification. Consequently his reputation as a great *shaykh* and a blessed man grows in the neighborhood until one day, a small group of his servant-followers engages in a fatal discussion while waiting for his arrival outside Nur al-Din Bey's house. In furtive whispers, they decide that he is, first, one of God's saints and, finally, that he is none other than the Mahdi himself, returned in secret to redeem Islam and vanquish its foes. As proof, one of them swears that Amm Mutwalli's sword—"the sword of prophethood"—has cured his son of a fatal disease ("Amm Mutwalli," p. 96). When the men confront Amm Mutwalli with his "true" identity, he is shocked and confused to the point of silence, unable to resist the onslaught of their certainty. The next day, a sick man arrives at his door and begs to touch "the sword of prophethood." The man spends the night clutching the sword and wakes up cured. People now begin to come from far and wide to be cured by Amm Mutwalli—the Awaited Mahdi—or to be blessed by his touch. Amm Mutwalli begins to lock himself up in his room more and more frequently, taking out his sword and losing himself in feverish, distracted reveries. When one day his patroness, Nur al-Din's mother herself, arrives at his door with her rich train of attendants and meekly begs for a blessing from the successor of the Prophet, Amm Mutwalli finally cracks. For several weeks he shuts himself up in his room and begins to have fits where he imagines he is fighting an invisible enemy with his sword. A man possessed, Amm Mutwalli jumps about and shouts until he drops unconscious to the floor. Then one day he rushes outside, "his eyes burning like hot embers," and brandishes his sword at the customers of a nearby café, calling them "corrupt heathens"; as the police drag him off, he brokenly murmurs, "thanks be to God . . . I have performed my mission and brought my holy war to its conclusion" ("Amm Mutwalli," p. 99).

"Hagg Shalabi." Once again, this story takes its title from the main character's name. Hagg Shalabi is a powerful and menacing figure in the popular quarter of Cairo where he lives. When the story opens, he has just been released from jail and, dressed in his finest clothes, is preparing to pay a visit to his old friend, the matchmaker Umm al-Khayr (her name literally means "Mother of Goodness"), who regularly provides him with young brides. Umm al-Khayr receives Hagg Shalabi warmly, and from their conversation we learn that this man makes a living by exploiting the wives that the matchmaker finds for him. He marries a girl and waits for her to give birth. Once she has done so, and hence has ample quantities of breast-milk, he forces her to abandon her child and to work instead as a wet nurse for a wealthy family. When he tells Umm al-Khayr that he is looking for a new bride, she asks him about his other two wives. He replies that one is off at work and the other "has gone away—she was barren and gave me no children"—a roundabout way of saying that he has divorced her (Mahmud Taymur, "Hagg Shalabi," p. 106). Umm al-Khayr then shows him a young girl called Farh who is not yet 17. They strike a bargain and cheerfully proceed to negotiate the terms of their agreement.

After the marriage, Farh gives birth to a baby girl, and Hagg Shalabi promptly gets her a job as a wet nurse in the family of a rich pasha, or Ottoman-era nobleman. Her own baby remains with Hagg Shalabi. Unhappy about abandoning her infant daughter, Farh seeks and is given permission to visit her husband and child once a month. On her first visit, she finds the child emaciated and pale. When her husband returns and finds her there playing with the baby, he scolds her and sends her off to the pasha's house. On her next two visits home, Farh finds her daughter in worse and worse condition and finally on the verge of death. When she reproaches her husband and attempts to stay with her child, he

strikes her, heaps threats and curses upon her, and throws her bodily out of the house. Farh returns to the house secretly the next day, but her child is no longer there. She searches frantically for Hagg Shalabi and finds him carousing with a group of his shiftless friends. When she confronts him, he defiantly tells her that the child is indeed dead and strikes her again, threatening to kill her if she does not return to her job. A week later, a haggard, broken Farh reappears and tells Hagg Shalabi that she has been fired because her milk has dried up. He promptly divorces her and throws her out for good. The story ends with Hagg Shalabi cheerfully preparing to make his next visit to Umm al-Khayr.

Millenarianism, madness, and the oppression of women. As previously noted, early-twentieth-century Egyptian reformers targeted popular culture as the source of the country's backwardness and decay. The superstitious religious beliefs and practices of the uneducated masses as well as the prevailing popular attitudes towards women were two ways in which this backwardness seemed to manifest itself.

In "Amm Mutwalli," the very recent history of Mahdism in the Sudan and its either real or perceived popularity among the Egyptian lower classes is intertwined with the liberal elite's suspicion of Islamic mysticism and millenarianism. The liberals regarded these two phenomena as pathological social developments and as potentially destabilizing political movements. The story itself is clearly a kind of parody of Sudanese Mahdism, which was unfavorably viewed by Taymur's nationalist contemporaries as a tool of British imperialism in the region. In their view, the Mahdists' challenge to Egyptian rule in the Sudan directly threatened Egypt's strategic geopolitical interests vis-à-vis Britain. "Amm Mutwalli" is a caricature of the historical Muhammad Ahmad al-Mahdi and his rise to fame and power. The tragicomic ending, in which a thoroughly mad Amm Mutwalli attempts to wage holy war on a bunch of peaceable café customers, declaring that he has "brought my holy war to its conclusion" as he is led off by the police, represents a damning indictment of Mahdism and its champions.

Taymur uses Amm Mutwalli's strange story to illustrate and criticize the ignorance and superstition of the Egyptian masses, who are conceived of as a menace to progressive society. Their representatives in the story are the servants and hangers-on who first declare the hapless hawker to be the new manifestation of the Mahdi. This rabblelike crowd, which freely indulges in saint-worship, miracle cures, exorcism, and other popular religious rituals, is portrayed as a potentially destabilizing political force. It is the illiterate and credulous crowd that pushes Amm Mutwalli into megalomania and madness—much, the story implies, like the dangerous forces of demagoguery and insurrection attached to the followers of the real Mahdi. Amm Mutwalli himself has a history as a Mahdist officer. His piety and devotionalism have been rendered harmless enough by defeat, poverty, and middle age, but he is easily seduced by the popular delusion that grows up around him. Gradually he too becomes convinced that he is the awaited Mahdi, after his fortunes take a turn for the better and he is able to acquire the means and habit of an affluent and powerful religious authority. A supposedly spiritual and selfless sense of mission, the story shows us, has been infected by the acquisition of wealth and power, and the infection grows until the ailing party succumbs to self-delusion. Mutwalli's newfound power is his downfall. The story's message is that religion and politics—especially when leavened with a good dose of "ignorance"—are an explosive mix.

Similarly the liberal literati saw gender roles in popular culture as a symptom of national backwardness and decay. Hagg Shalabi, the brutal lower-class thug—a thoroughly disagreeable, even sinister, character—makes no bones about living off his wives' sweat while maintaining the violent prerogatives of an oppressive patriarchal society. He is able to marry and divorce at will and with total disregard for the rights and responsibilities attached to the ideal Islamic laws governing polygamy and divorce. A man without honor or compassion, Hagg Shalabi regards women as chattel to be bought and sold. Even his own child is nothing but an unfortunate encumbrance on his wife's ability to work for his own selfish profit. Women are portrayed as complicit in this corrupt social order. The matchmaker, Umm al-Khayr, is an unsavory merchant of flesh who, like Hagg Shalabi himself, makes a living by trading in women. Even Hagg Shalabi's unfortunate young wife is shown as partly complicit in her own oppression. Ignorant and weak, she complacently allows her husband to separate her from her child and proves unable to stand up to his beating and bullying. Even after the child has died and Farh has lost her job as a wet nurse, she humbly returns to Hagg Shalabi's doorstep, only to be thrown out for the last time.

Literary contexts. Throughout the first three decades of the twentieth century, Egyptian writers and critics were struggling to define Egypt's national identity. The idea of "national character"—in both a sociological sense and a literary one—was one of the focal points of this project. As far back as 1906, the critic Ahmad Dayf was already declaring that

> We wish to have an Egyptian literature that will reflect our social state, our intellectual movements, and the region in which we live; reflect the cultivator in his field, the merchant in his stall, the ruler in his palace, the teacher among his students and his books, the Shaykh among his people, the worshipper in his mosque or his monk's cell, and the youth in his amorous play. In sum, we want to have a personality in our literature.
> (Gershoni & Jankowski, p. 192)

The birth of the short story in Egypt was closely linked to this urgent need to understand and realistically represent authentic Egyptian characters and settings.

PLAYING WITH NAMES

In "Hagg Shalabi," Taymur plays on the names of his characters to make some ironic jabs at the social hypocrisy of his age. The honorific title "Hagg," which refers to a pious person who has performed his religious duty to make the pilgrimage to Mecca, is used here for a ruthless cad. Similarly the complicit matchmaker Umm al-Khayr has a name that means "the mother of goodness," but she is clearly the opposite, though she does provide Hagg Shalabi with a steady stream of what he sees as "good things" in the form of unsuspecting wives.

The Revolution of 1919 represented an important moment in this project. It unleashed "a movement to express the new awareness of a national identity, to shape the dreams and aspirations of the nation, and to purge Egypt of the distortions which had resulted from the occupation" (Hafez, p. 158). "Egypt for the Egyptians" became the rallying cry of this movement, and writers and intellectuals set out to define and celebrate the Egyptian national genius in books and articles as well as through the arts. Artists like the composer Sayyid Darwish, the painter Ahmad Sabri, and the sculptor Mahmud Mukhtar created works inspired by Egyptian folklore, landscapes, and character types. This urgent focus on national identity manifested itself in letters as well. Writers called for a new

Egyptian literature that would break with the conventions of the classical Arabic canon as well as blind imitation of fashionable European literature, since both of these were judged to be alien to the Egyptian spirit and character. This impetus, called the "National Literature" movement, gave birth, in turn, to the "New School" group of authors (1925-27), who began to write realistic short stories about everyday Egyptians. According to Taymur, who was loosely affiliated with the New School group,

> The outline and specificity of the Egyptian character were obscure, lost amongst foreign currents, and so all intellectual effort turned towards the reform and foregrounding of this Egyptian character and to the exploration of its strengths and capabilities in life. . . . The new writers responded to the calls for modernization that demanded the creation of a properly Egyptian literature that would express Egyptian feelings and experiences in a narrative form modeled on western literature. . . . And when Egypt's national revolution of 1919 ignited and the Egyptian character burst forth . . . the modern artistic story immediately responded, representing, describing and analyzing this authentic popular character.
>
> (Taymur in Badr, p. 206-207; trans. S. Selim)

Rather than the heroic exploits of legendary Arab heroes or the aristocratic intrigues of foreign European characters, the new national literature sought to depict "real people in plausible situations" (Hafez, p. 182). The writer came to be seen as a kind of surgeon and the process of observation and writing as a surgical dissection of "the obscure human heart"—a metaphor that Isa Ubayd, another of the New School writers, used in 1921 in the preface to his first collection of short stories:

> The purpose of fiction must be the investigation of life and its sincere portrayal as it appears to us. . . . The writer [must study] . . . the hidden recesses of the obscure human heart, as well as the moral and social development [of people] and the role of civilization, environment and heredity [in that development]. . . . For the function of the writer is to dissect the human soul and to record his discoveries [in writing].
>
> (Ubayd, p. 9; trans. S. Selim)

This emphasis on environment and heredity in the formation of character was significant because it meant that personality was determined by factors beyond an individual's control, such as class and family history. Taymur believed that an individual's psychological makeup was largely predetermined in this way. His ideas about char-

acter were influenced by his readings in the new science of psychoanalysis and by the fiction of French naturalist writers such as Emile Zola and Guy de Maupassant. This is one of the reasons why Taymur was fascinated by the Egyptian lower classes. To him, these classes provided striking examples of a specifically Egyptian social pathology.

Reviews. In the 1930s and '40s, Taymur was universally acclaimed by critics as the voice of a new literary generation. Reviewers praised him as "one of the few contemporary writers who have injected new blood into Arabic literature by writing fascinating Egyptian short stories that analyze the various aspects of the Egyptian psychology and describe Egyptian customs and traditions in a realistic and creative manner" (Shadah, p. 500; trans. S. Selim). A contemporary German Orientalist, or scholar of Arabic language and culture, claimed that would-be European tourists wishing to discover the real Egypt could just as well stay at home and read Taymur's stories instead—so accurate and subtle were their portrayal of "the inner life of the Egyptian people" (Shadah, p. 501; trans. S. Selim). Another Egyptian critic praised Taymur's "living portraits" of everyday people and his illumination of a national mentality still rooted in the Middle Ages ("Abu Ali amil artist," p. 320; trans. S. Selim). A decade later, Taha Husayn, the twentieth-century doyen of Arabic letters, described Taymur's 1942 collection of stories, *Qala al-rawi* (The Storyteller Said)—which included newly edited versions of both "Amm Mutwalli" and "Hagg Shalabi"—as "a wonderful and moving description of some aspect or condition of life, or of some particular Egyptian landscape, character or emotion" (Husayn in Taymur, *Qala al-rawi*, p. m; trans. S. Selim). However, Husayn suggested that there was a veiled element of "moralizing" or "preaching" in Taymur's style, which certainly served a healthy didactic purpose, but which also constituted a certain kind of "deception" on the part of the writer. This insight was picked up again in the 1960s and '70s. These later critics argued that rather than creating truly representative and realistic Egyptian characters, Taymur's obsession with the violence and pathological psychology of extremely eccentric individuals and singular events actually distorted the realities of Egyptian society in all its vitality and complexity and produced unconvincing, one-dimensional characters. The late critic Abd al-Muhsin Taha Badr suggested that this flaw in Taymur's writing was rooted in the social prejudices belonging to his elite background—prejudices that produced a morbid fascination with the poor and their culture (Badr, p. 252). In spite of this increasingly critical reception, Taymur is still considered a great figure of modern Arabic literature whose works figured prominently in the invention and refinement of the modern Arabic short story.

—Samah Selim

For More Information

"Abu Ali amil artist." *al-Muqtataf*, 1 April 1934, p. 320.

Ahmad, Jamal Muhammad. *The Intellectual Origins of Egyptian Nationalism.* London: Oxford University Press, 1960.

Badr, Abd al-Muhsin Taha. *Tatawwur al-riwayah al-Arabiyah al-hadithah fi Misr.* Cairo: Dar al-Ma`arif, 1992.

Gershoni, Israel, and James P. Jankowski. *Egypt, Islam, and the Arabs.* New York: Oxford University Press, 1987.

Hafez, Sabry. *The Genesis of Arabic Narrative Discourse.* London: Saqi Books, 1993.

Mitchell, Timothy. *Colonising Egypt.* Cambridge: Cambridge University Press, 1991.

Rodenbeck, Max. *Cairo: The City Victorious.* New York: Knopf, 1999.

Shadah, Dr. "Adab Mahmud Taymur lil-mustashriq al-almani." *al-Muqtataf*, 1 April 1931, pp. 500-501.

Taymur, Mahmud. "Amm Mutwalli" and "Hagg Shalabi." In *Tales From Egyptian Life.* Trans. Denys Johnson Davies. Cairo: The Renaissance Bookshop, 1947.

———. *Qala al-rawi.* Cairo: al-Maktabah al-Tijariyah al-Kubrah, 1942.

Ubayd, Isa. *Ihsan Hanim.* Cairo: Matba`at Ramses, 1964.

Vatikiotis, P. J. *The History of Modern Egypt.* London: Weidenfeld and Nicolson, 1991.

Voll, John Obert. *Historical Dictionary of the Sudan.* London: Scarecrow Press, 1978.

Warburg, Gabriel R. *Historical Discord in the Nile Valley.* London: Hurst and Company, 1992.

The Arabian Nights:
The Frame Tale

The tales and even the frame story of *The Arabian Nights* have their roots in many countries: India, China, Persia, the Arabian Peninsula, Egypt, and Greece. Scholars contend that the stories circulated orally from the ninth century onward. Corroborating their contention, during the 1940s an Arab papyrus that dates back to the ninth century and apparently contains a fragment of *The Arabian Nights* was discovered in Egypt and acquired by the University of Chicago in the United States. Many of the work's tales, however, do not appear to have been transcribed until the latter half of the thirteenth century, in either Syria or Egypt, forming the first more-or-less complete version. This earliest version of a complete manuscript was lost, but it served as a prototype for others, including the fourteenth-century Syrian manuscript that scholars consider the purest rendition of *The Arabian Nights*, despite its lack of completeness. Other manuscripts, dating between the eighteenth and nineteenth centuries, surfaced in Egypt, containing stories not in the Syrian version. Arabic scholars have questioned the authenticity of this additional material, which includes characters—such as Sinbad—who would become famously associated with the work. It was not until the early eighteenth century that *The Arabian Nights* first appeared in Europe, proving immediately popular there. The scholar Antoine Galland translated and edited the Syrian manuscript into French as *Mille et une nuits* (1704-06), dividing the material into 282 nights (Mahdi, p. 23). In 1706, Grub Street publishers hurriedly produced an English translation of Gal-

THE LITERARY WORK

A frame narrative set in India and Indochina in the legendary past links a series of inner tales from Persia, Arabia, and China; in circulation since the ninth century, transcribed into Arabic in a thirteenth-century version that survives in the fourteenth-century Syrian manuscript *Alf laylah wa-laylah* (*The Thousand and One Nights*); published in English in 1706.

SYNOPSIS

Betrayed by his unfaithful queen, a king takes a new bride every day and, to prevent her betrayal, executes her the next morning. One bride, determined to put a stop to this, diverts him from his plan with stories for 1001 nights until he is convinced of her fidelity.

land's work, calling it *The Arabian Nights' Entertainments*. By 1800, more than 80 editions had been printed, captivating such writers as Alexander Pope, William Wordsworth, and Samuel Taylor Coleridge. Late in the twentieth century (1984), Muhsin Mahdi published what many scholars consider the definitive edition of the Syrian manuscript; Husain Haddawy translated Mahdi's version into English in 1990. Critics praised both efforts, commending them for introducing readers to an *Arabian Nights* such as the public had never yet known: violent, vigorous, and sensual.

The Sasanid period. Determining the exact setting of *The Arabian Nights* presents the reader with a conundrum; although the frame story is said to take place "long ago, during the time of the Sasanid dynasty"—between 226 and 641 C.E.—many of the tales are set much later, in the 700s or 800s. Indeed, Harun al-Rashid, the fifth Abbasid caliph, who reigned from 786 to 809, appears as a character in several stories. It is possible to argue that the frame story's ostensible setting is not intended to be historically accurate, but rather is meant to suggest antiquity, a conceit of "long ago and far away."

However directly they figure in *The Arabian Nights*, the Sasanids certainly played a major role in the development of Persia. This dynasty of Persian kings acceded to power early in the third century, overthrowing the Parthians who had ruled the region from 250 B.C.E. to 226 C.E. Once in power, the Sasanids—so called because their first king, Ardashir I, claimed descent from the legendary hero Sasan—quickly set their own mark upon the area, amassing an extensive empire that included not only present-day Iran and Iraq but also parts of the Arabian Peninsula (Bahrain, Yamamah, and Yemen). Many historians credit the Sasanid dynasty with Persia's development as a world power between the third and seventh centuries, its influence rivaled only by Rome and Byzantium.

The Sasanid dynasty boasted a strong centralized administration, a rigid social hierarchy, and a unifying religious faith. Sasanid rulers took the title of *shahanshah* (king of kings) and enjoyed absolute sovereignty over numerous lesser rulers, known as *shahrdars*. Shahanshahs and *shahrdars*, along with great landlords and priests, occupied the topmost rank of what historians hypothesize was a four-level hierarchy. Below them, in descending order, came the warriors, the secretaries, and the commoners. The royal family's attempts to maintain a centralized monarchy was a frequent source of tension within the Sasanian Empire, especially as the lesser kings and the aristocracy were no less determined to retain their own rights and independence. Over the centuries, the Sasanian house withstood various threats to its authority, mainly because other contenders for the Persian throne could not command prestige comparable to that of the ruling family.

In another major development, the Sasanids established Zoroastrianism as the state religion of Persia. During the sixth century, Zoroaster had held that two forces—Ahura Mazda, creator of the world and source of light and order, and Ahriman, god of darkness and disorder—were locked in an eternal struggle, in which Ahura Mazda would ultimately prevail. All people, however, were free to choose between good and evil, light and darkness, truth and lies. The Zoroastrian priesthood acquired great power during the Sasanids' reign. Meanwhile, to reinforce their hold on the Persian throne, the Sasanids claimed the support of Ahura Mazda and that they themselves were divine. They also exercised religious tolerance. The Sasanids encouraged scholarship, too, dispatching scholars to other countries to collect books, which were then translated into the Pahlavi (Middle Persian) language, along with scientific and technical lore. Many foreign scholars came to Persia to teach and study, finding the country remarkably accepting of differences in faith and race.

By the seventh century, however, the Sasanid Empire was in decline, weakened by years of warfare with Byzantium and riddled with internal problems, including heavy taxation, religious unrest, and overall economic decline. In 633 Bedouin (tribal) Arabs, newly converted to Islam, organized a campaign against the crumbling Byzantine and Sasanid Empires; by 637 Arab forces were occupying the Sasanid capital of Ctesiphon, and by 650 Persian resistance to the invaders had been quelled. Soon Persian customs would be too. The Muslim conquerors imposed their religion and language upon their Persian subjects and integrated the former Sasanian territories into the core of their realm under the rule of a caliph (the Arabic term for "successor"), who succeeded the Prophet Muhammad as temporal, but not spiritual, leader of the Muslim community. Some aspects of Sasanid life remained, however. The Muslims retained the Sasanid coinage system and several Sasanid administrative practices, including the office of vizier (minister) and the divan, an organization that controlled state revenues and expenditures.

In *The Arabian Nights*, few elements of the Sasanid legacy are visible, despite the frame story's purported setting. Those few, however, include the absolute authority of King Shahrayar, whose power enables him to take a bride every night and execute her the following morning, and the presence of a vizier who unquestioningly carries out Shahrayar's commands (Muslim rulers would later adopt the use of viziers in their government).

Rise of the Abbasid caliphate. Although the connection between *The Arabian Nights* and the

Sasanid period remains tenuous at best, the same cannot be said of a subsequent era. Individual tales strongly evoke historical events of the Abbasid caliphate, which lasted from 750 to 1258 C.E. Previously the Umayyad dynasty had governed the Islamic dominions, which included present-day Iran, Iraq, and Syria. The Umayyads were supported predominantly by troops from Syria and by Arab tribesmen from the southern Arabian Peninsula (modern-day Yemen). The Abbasids, by contrast, relied on Persians, Iraqis and other Arabs, and various followers of the Shi'ite branch of Islam. Led by Abu al-Abbas, who based his claim to the caliphate on his descent from an uncle of the Prophet Mohammed, this eclectic group formed a coalition that successfully toppled the Umayyad regime, crushing the Umayyad army at the battle of the Great Zab in 750.

With all the Umayyad claimants to the caliphate dead or exiled, the victors appointed Abu al-Abbas as the first Abbasid caliph. Known as al-Saffah (the Bloodshedder), Abu al-Abbas transferred the capital of the empire from Syria to the city of Baghdad in Iraq. During his reign and those of his first six successors, Baghdad developed into "a center of power where Arab and Iranian [Persian] cultures mingled to produce a blaze of philosophical, scientific, and literary glory" (Metz, p. 21). Fortifications and canals were constructed to make Baghdad more defensible against invaders, while surrounding swamps were drained to reduce the spread of fever and malaria. Canals also linked the various rivers, helping to establish Baghdad as a trading base between Asia and the Mediterranean, which contributed to an increase in population and prosperity there. By the eighth century, only Constantinople rivaled Baghdad in size within the Islamic Empire.

Besides the transformation of Baghdad into a major metropolis, Abbasid achievements included the maintenance of a standing professional army, the development of an effective taxation system and the formation of a stable bureaucracy to control it, the construction of mosques and palaces, and the support of intellectual pursuits. What some considered the golden age of the Abbasid caliphate coincided with the reign of Harun al-Rashid, the fifth Abbasid caliph, who has become strongly identified with *The Arabian Nights*, not least because he appears as a character in several tales.

The caliphate of Harun al-Rashid. Of the 37 caliphs of the Abbasid dynasty, the fifth caliph, Harun al-Rashid, is probably the most famous. Succeeding to the caliphate upon the death of his brother al-Hadi, who occupied the office for no more than a year, Harun ruled from 786 to 809 over a prosperous, thriving empire. For the most part, his reign coincided with a long period of peace, although he did lead several successful military expeditions against the encroaching Byzantines. In the end, the once-proud empire of Byzantium paid tribute to Harun al-Rashid, the "Commander of the Faithful." Other moments of strife during Harun's caliphate consisted of small-scale insurrections in the provinces, which resented the administration's increasingly exploitative taxation policies.

Historians have divided the reign of Harun al-Rashid into three phases. During the first phase, he relied on the advice and counsel of the Barmakids, a Persian family who had helped to bring him to power. During the second, he distanced himself from the Barmakids, choosing instead to rely upon his chief minister, al-Fadl al-Barmaki, and the military leaders who had supported his brother. During the third phase, Harun exiled or executed several members of the Barmakid family and, in the absence of a single powerful minister, took a more active part in political life. Throughout his reign, the caliph remained consistent in his tendency to delegate day-to-day affairs to his various ministers, a policy that was to create problems, especially in his dealings with the provinces.

Whatever the shortcomings of Harun's administration, his court was among the most splendid in the world: wealthy to the point of opulence and highly cultured. The caliph patronized the arts, taking special pleasure in poets and singers, and encouraged scholarship. The historian Rom Landau describes the caliph's Baghdad palace as "the hub of a giant wheel with spokes radiating to all parts of the empire. A continuous stream of scientists, theologians, musicians, poets and merchants walked these spokes to pay homage to the Abbasid caliph; he in turn listened, learned and patronized. The golden age of Arab arts and letters, the zenith of Arab sciences, was at hand" (Landau, p. 54).

It is this world that *The Arabian Nights* continually evokes in its inner tales. Several stories featuring Harun al-Rashid, which were probably composed during the ninth or tenth century, allude to his splendid palace and gardens, along with his love of the arts. In "The Story of the Slave Girl and Nur Al-Din Ali Ibn Khaqan," the main characters find themselves in a garden.

[The garden] that had no equal in all of Baghdad, for it belonged to the caliph Harun al-Rashid and was called the Garden of Delight, and in it there stood a palace called the Palace of Statues, to which he came when he was depressed. The palace was surrounded by eighty windows and eighty hanging lamps, each pair flanking a candelabra holding a large candle. When the caliph entered the palace, he used to order all the windows opened and the lamps and candelabras lighted and order Ishak al-Nadim [a famous musician and lute player] to sing for him, while he sat surrounded by concubines of all races until his care left him and he felt merry.

(Haddawy, *Arabian Nights*, p. 364)

Other tales allude not only to Harun's taste for luxury but also to his difficult relationship with the Barmakid family, especially Ja'far al-Barmaki, who was his vizier, his companion, and, finally, his victim. In "The Story of the Three Apples," the caliph continually orders Ja'far to investigate several crimes, threatening him with death should he fail to produce results. Although events conspire to prevent this sentence from being carried out within the story, listeners would probably have been aware that, historically, Harun al-Rashid did execute Ja'far in 803, seeing in him and his family a threat to his own authority as caliph.

The Frame Tale in Focus

Plot summary. *The Arabian Nights* consists of a frame narrative that connects a series of tales and tales within tales, ostensibly told by a queen to her sister but really intended to capture the attention of a jealous king.

The frame narrative opens with an account of two royal brothers. The elder brother, Shahrayar, rules India and Indochina and gives the land of Samarkand to the younger brother, Shahzaman. Ten years later, Shahrayar wishes to see his brother again and sends his vizier to Samarkand to invite Shahzaman for a visit. Pleased by the invitation, Shahzaman begins travel preparations. The night before his departure, however, he discovers his wife lying in the arms of a kitchen boy. Furious, Shahzaman kills the lovers, throws the bodies into a trench, and sets off on his journey.

Although Shahzaman receives a warm welcome from his brother, the cuckolded husband remains morose and distracted by his queen's infidelity but refuses to confide in Shahrayar. One day, while Shahrayar is on a hunting expedition, Shahzaman, who remains behind at court, sees his brother's wife and her ladies lying with black slaves, who

have disguised themselves as women. Concluding that it is the nature of all women to be unfaithful and to betray their husbands, Shahzaman begins to recover his spirits. On his return from hunting, Shahrayar notices his brother's improved health and asks the reason. Shahzaman tries to avoid answering, but finally admits that he was betrayed by his wife and adds that Shahrayar has been cuckolded as well.

Enraged, Shahrayar insists on having proof. Giving out a false report that he means to go hunting again, he and Shahzaman sneak back into the palace and witness the queen's infidelity with her black slave. Out of his mind with anger, Shahrayar, accompanied by his brother, leaves his kingdom, determined not to return unless he finds someone whose misfortune is greater than his. While on the road, the two kings see a black demon carrying a large glass chest, which the demon unlocks, revealing a beautiful woman inside. The demon lies down with his head in the woman's lap and falls asleep. Spying the two kings, the woman beckons to them and demands that they lie with her, or she will wake the demon and have them killed. Cowed by her threat, Shahrayar and Shahzaman ultimately comply. The woman then orders them to give her their rings. She reveals that, despite the demon's vigilance and determination to keep her pure and chaste, she has managed to sleep with 98 men, each of whom gave her a ring afterwards. Shahrayar and Shahzaman give her their rings as well, rejoicing that the demon's plight is worse than their own.

On returning to his kingdom and parting from his brother, who goes home to Samarkand, Shahrayar exacts a terrible vengeance. He orders his vizier to have the queen put to death and to slay all the slave girls in the palace. Reasoning that there is no such thing on earth as a chaste woman, the king decides to take a new wife every day, then have her executed the next morning before she can betray him.

Learning of this tragic development and the grief of the brides' families, Shahrazad, the vizier's learned elder daughter, asks her father to marry her to Shahrayar so she can try to save the women of the kingdom. The horrified vizier refuses, trying to dissuade his daughter with cautionary tales, but she remains adamant. Reluctantly, the vizier offers Shahrazad to the king, who consents to marry her. Meanwhile, Shahrazad and her younger sister, Dinarzad (or Dunyazad), concoct a plan by which Dinarzad will be summoned to the palace the night of the marriage and will ask her sister to tell a story before daybreak. Their

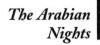

King Shahrayar holding Queen Shahrazad's hand as she regales him with stories.

life at her request and retains her as his queen and consort.

> By Allah, O Shahrazad, I pardoned thee before the coming of these children, for that I found thee chaste, pure, ingenuous, and pious! Allah bless thee and thy father and thy mother and thy root and thy branch! I take the Almighty to witness against me that I exempt thee from aught that can harm thee.
> (Burton, *Arabian Nights*, p. 722)

Research has shown that this ending, neatly providing a resolution to the tales, was added by the French translator, Antoine Galland (Mahdi, p. 48). The fact that it was, nevertheless, adopted by all subsequent versions of the *Arabian Nights,* even those composed in Arabic, testifies to the truly international scope of contributions to the tales.

The inner tales. In the Syrian manuscript of *The Arabian Nights,* the stories told by Shahrazad involve themes that reflect her own situation in the frame tale. Several of the stories, for example, deal with issues of gratitude, loyalty, and the abuse of power: protagonists find themselves at the mercy of cruel monarchs or capricious demons but manage to win a more favorable destiny through acts of wit, kindness, or charity. Other tales address betrayal and sexual infidelity, especially between white women and black men—a sore point with Shahrayar, whose queen betrayed him with a black slave. In such stories as "The Tale of the Enchanted King" and "The Story of the Three Apples," Shahrazad elicits sympathy for the husbands wronged by their unfaithful wives but, at the same time, subtly conveys the message that not all women are false and some are even cruelly misjudged.

In "The Fisherman and the Demon," a poor fisherman casts his net after three unsuccessful attempts and brings in a sealed brass jar. Curious, the fisherman unstops the jar, only to find himself confronted by a huge demon. Furious over his long captivity, the demon has decided not to reward whoever frees him but rather to give that person only the choice of his manner of death. The fisherman pleads for his life, saying that he performed an act of kindness, but the demon remains adamant. All is not lost, for the fisherman tricks the demon into showing how he became small enough to fit into the jar. Then the fisherman promptly reseals the jar and threatens to return it to the sea and warn all other fisherman not to open it if they should ever bring it back up. Relenting, the demon rescinds his earlier vow and eventually persuades the fisherman to free him again, this time promising him a reward.

plan is successful. After Shahrayar consummates the marriage, he allows Shahrazad to receive a visit from Dinarzad, who promptly asks her to tell a tale to while away the night. With the king's consent, Shahrazad begins a story but deliberately stops before morning.

> But morning overtook Shahrazad, and she lapsed into silence, leaving King Shahrayar burning with curiosity to hear the rest of the story. Then Dinarzad said to her sister Shahrazad, "What a strange and lovely story!" Shahrazad replied, "What is this compared with what I shall tell you tomorrow night if the king spares me and lets me live? It will be even better and more entertaining."
> (Haddawy, *Arabian Nights*, p. 18)

Curious about the tale's outcome, Shahrayar decides to spare his bride's life until the tale is finished.

Over succeeding nights, Shahrazad spins out the tales, beginning a new one immediately after the old one is finished and always pausing before morning to gain another day of life. This process continues for a thousand and one nights, at which time Shahrazad points out to Shahrayar that she has borne him three children and proven her fidelity beyond question. Having learned to love and trust Shahrazad, Shahrayar spares her

Once liberated, the demon takes the fisherman to a lake full of rare-colored fish—white, red, blue, and yellow—and tells him to cast his net there once a day and bring whatever he finds to the king. The fisherman obeys, snaring one fish of each color, and takes the catch to the royal palace, starting a chain of events that eventually leads into "The Tale of the Enchanted King."

Amazed, the king pays the fisherman handsomely, and the fish are taken to the kitchen to be prepared for the king's dinner. While the cook is frying the fish, however, a beautiful maiden appears through the kitchen wall, speaks to the fish, then overturns the frying pan and disappears, leaving the fish too scorched to eat. The shocked cook tells the vizier what she sees, and the vizier orders the fisherman to fetch four more fish from wherever he found the others. The same sequence of events takes place, only this time the vizier witnesses the maiden's apparition as well and decides to tell the king. Again, the fisherman is ordered to bring his catch to the palace. On the third night, the fish are fried in the king's presence, but this time a huge black slave appears, speaks to the fish, and overturns the frying pan.

At the king's command, the fisherman takes the monarch and several members of the court to the mysterious lake, surrounded by four hills, which no one in the kingdom has ever visited before. Intrigued, the king decides to explore the region alone that night and comes upon an apparently deserted palace. On entering, the king discovers another, younger monarch. This monarch has been enchanted: his lower half turned to stone by a curse. The helpless monarch, otherwise known as the enchanted king of the Black Islands, reveals that his beloved queen betrayed him by taking a black lover. Discovering the two together, the king attacked his rival, inflicting a serious wound that deprived the latter of speech. Bent on vengeance, the queen turned the king to stone below the waist, whipped him daily, and forced him to wear a coarse hair shirt under his fine garments. She also cast a spell on the realm and the king's subjects, turning them into a lake full of colored fish, each color signifying the faiths of the different inhabitants. Meanwhile, she arranged for her wounded lover to be taken to a mausoleum where she could visit and tend him every day.

Upon hearing all this, the first king vows to help the second and goes to the mausoleum. There, the first king kills the black lover, disposes of the body, then assumes the lover's clothes and

Illustration from a tale that Queen Shahrazad tells King Shahrayar, in which a ruler's fish dinner is ruined.

place in the tomb. In this guise, he successfully dupes the queen into restoring her husband, his subjects, and the realm to their proper form: "Damn you, cursed woman, it is the inhabitants of this city and its four islands, for every night at midnight, the fish raise their heads from the lake to implore and invoke God against me, and this is why I do not recover. Go to them and deliver them at once" (Haddawy, *Arabian Nights*, p. 64). After the queen has performed these deeds, the still-disguised king lures her into the mausoleum and kills her. The enchanted king, restored to full capacity, expresses eternal gratitude to his rescuer, and they travel together to the first king's realm. To reward the fisherman, the first king takes one of the fisherman's daughters as a bride and marries off the other to the enchanted king. He blesses the fisherman's son with good fortune too, making the son one of his own attendants.

The themes of race and infidelity play a major part in another tale also, "The Story of the Three Apples," one of the episodes that connects *The Arabian Nights* to the Abbasid period, especially to the caliphate of Harun al-Rashid, who makes an appearance. The tale begins as the caliph and his vizier, Ja'far al-Barmaki, walk through the royal city to assess the conduct and competence of the caliph's administrators. Encountering a poor fisherman in need, the caliph offers to buy for a handsome price whatever the fisherman next catches. Casting his net, the fisherman draws up a locked, heavy chest, which the caliph purchases and has brought to his palace. To his horror, the chest contains the decapitated body of a young girl. Concluding that the girl has been murdered, Harun commands Ja`far to find the killer within three days or forfeit his own life. Not knowing how to proceed, Ja`far does nothing, and on the third day, he is arrested and sentenced to death by hanging.

Before the execution can take place, however, two men—one young, one old—come forward to take responsibility for the murder. The young man, who is the old man's nephew and son-in-law, proves that he is the culprit by describing in detail how he disposed of the victim's body. Astonished, the caliph demands to know the entire story. The young man reveals that the dead girl was his wife. They had been happy together for 11 years until she fell ill. During her long convalescence, she developed a craving for apples, which proved hard to find in the city; her husband finally located some in an orchard in Basra. The husband traveled for several weeks before reaching his destination and obtaining three apples from the orchard's gardener. The wife, however, lost interest in the apples once they were brought to her and remained in poor health. One day, the husband saw a black slave walking through the street, carrying one of the apples he had brought from Basra, and asked the slave where he had obtained the fruit. The slave answered that he had received the apple from his mistress, who had mentioned that her husband had journeyed half a month to get them for her. Going home, the husband confronted his wife about the missing apple, but she was unable to account for its absence. In a jealous rage, the husband cut off his wife's head, put her body into the chest, and threw the chest into the river.

On returning home again, the husband learned from his eldest son that the boy had taken one of the apples from his mother's room, which had, in turn, been stolen from him by a black slave who refused to give it back, even after the boy mentioned how his father had made a long journey to get the fruit for the boy's mother. Realizing he had murdered his wife unjustly, the husband was overcome with remorse and blamed the slanders of that unknown slave, who claimed to have obtained the apple from his mistress, for the tragedy. Before the caliph, the husband again reiterates his own guilt and offers up his own life for his crime.

The caliph, however, vows to hang no one but the slave and again commands Ja`far to find this person on pain of his own death. Still not knowing where to look for the culprit, Ja`far instead decides to trust in God's will and do nothing. In the nick of time, he discovers the apple in the possession of his own daughter, who bought it from one of his slaves. Astonished, Ja`far has the slave brought before him and learns that he was indeed the one who took the apple from the boy who had taken it from his mother. Ja`far brings the slave before the caliph, who is amazed by the coincidences in the whole situation. Initially disposed to hang the slave, the caliph reconsiders after Ja`far tells him another story about two viziers that is even more fraught with coincidences. Ultimately, the caliph decides to free the slave and confer a choice concubine, a substantial income, and a position at court upon the husband. The tale illustrates the value of compassion and forbearance in judging others, but the question of justice for the murdered girl goes unasked and unsettled.

Women in pre-Islamic and Islamic society. Given the widely held view of Islam as a thoroughly patriarchal religion, the figure of Shahrazad, the intelligent, resourceful queen who literally manages to talk her way out of a deadly situation, may seem like an anomaly to Western readers. Placing limitations on the role of women in public life and viewing them as inferior to men was a ubiquitous feature of societies surrounding the Mediterranean Basin. We find traces of these attitudes in ancient Greece and Israel as well as in the Byzantine Empire, which was Islam's greatest rival for most of its history. However, both Islamic and pre-Islamic societies included learned, capable women who, like Shahrazad, managed to wield a surprising amount of power.

During the Sasanid period—the ostensible setting of *The Arabian Nights*—women were considered the spiritual equals of men according to the tenets of Zoroastrianism. Granted, in practice, women remained largely under the tutelage of men: first their fathers or brothers, then their husbands. The *Madigan i hazar dadistan*—"Book of 1,000 Legal Judgments"—partially clarified the rights and status of women in Sasanian law. With regard to marriage, for example, fathers generally sought suitable husbands for their daughters once the girls reached the age of 15; however, a daughter could refuse to marry. She would not be punished for her refusal, nor would she be required to forfeit whatever allowance her

SLAVERY AND THE ARABS

A recurring event in *The Arabian Nights* tales is adultery between white women and black slaves, who then conspire against the women's husbands. Historically, Arabs are considered among the first slave traders. During the eighth century Arabs from the Arabian peninsula began colonization of the east African coast; large numbers of black Africans were captured and carried by ship to Arabia, India, Europe, and even to distant China. This practice continued intermittently until the nineteenth century, when the slave trade was abolished, accounting for the presence of black slaves in Arab countries. Within medieval Islamic society, slaves of all colors ranked at the bottom of the social scale and then were ranked within this bottom according to their skills and attributes, their market value, and even the social position and personal character of their owners. History indicates, "Some [slaves] labored in the harshest conditions on large-scale construction schemes or estate agriculture. Some were pampered favorites of kings or highly prized artists in the homes of great merchants. Some were nurses, housemaids, cooks, or porters. Some became generals. In their own differences, they reflected the social system, its mobilities and rigidities" (Segal, pp. 27-28). There has been much speculation about the frequency of the black slave as the cuckolder in *The Arabian Nights.* Subscribing to widely held racial notions of his day, the nineteenth-century translator Richard Burton ascribed it to "the size of their parts" (Burton, p. 732). Others have argued that black-white racial prejudice of the sort familiar to the modern world does not apply. Slaves within the Islamic Empire could be white, black, or Asiatic. Significantly, say these others, the slave dynasty that rose to power in Egypt and Syria, overthrowing an Arabic caliphate, consisted of Turkish Mamluks, not black Africans. In view of this fact, anxiety about any slave's betraying his master may account for the theme's frequent occurrence in the Arabian Nights' tales.

father had settled upon her. Similarly, if a father failed to find a husband for his daughter and she subsequently entered a "love-match" of her own choosing, the father would still support her and she would retain her inheritance, though it might be reduced, depending on how severely the father disapproved of the relationship.

Within marriage a Sasanian woman, especially one known as the *zan-i padikhshayih* (wife in authority), had full authority over the internal running of the house, the organization of other members of the household, and the upbringing of the children. With regard to the last, sons remained in the care of their mother until they were five, at which point their formal schooling began. Boys belonging to the upper ranks of society might receive an education similar to that described in the Pahlavi text "King Khusraw and the Page," which included such diverse subjects as "writing, hunting, polo-playing, chess, music, games, apparel,

food, wines, perfumes, and women" (Rose in Hambly, p. 36).

Comparatively little is known of the formal education of Sasanian girls beyond the acquisition of domestic skills. However, an incident mentioned in the *Madigan i hazar dadistan*—during which a learned lawyer and five women discuss several cases involving loans—suggests that some women may have been instructed in scholarly reasoning and the study of law. The education of Shahrazad, who had read "books of literature, philosophy, and medicine" and "was acquainted with the sayings of men and the maxims of sages and kings" was clearly exceptional, although perhaps not as unprecedented as it first appears (Haddawy, *Arabian Nights*, p. 13).

The displacement of Zoroastrianism by Islam during the seventh century had few radical effects upon the status of upper-class women. Generally Islam presupposed and supported a sexually polarized society in which men occupied the public, economic sphere; women, the private, domestic one. In Islam's sacred text, the **Quran** (also in *WLAIT 6: Middle Eastern Literatures and Their Times*), women are spiritual equals to men, with the same rights and duties (Quran 33:35). Elsewhere, however, the Quran says the man is head of the family and that his wife should obey him. One verse states,

> The men are overseers over the women by reason of what Allah (God) hath bestowed in bounty upon one more than another, and of the property which they have contributed. Upright women are therefore submissive, guarding what is hidden in return for Allah's guarding (them); those on whose part ye fear refractoriness, admonish, avoid in bed, and beat if they then obey you, seek no (further) way against them.
> (Quran in Walther, p. 48)

Although there was more freedom in the early Islamic period and in the lower classes, by Abbasid times the sexes were rigorously segregated. Girls like Shahrazad, from the upper classes, grew up in the harim (harem), the women's quarters of the household, which were off-limits to every man except the master of the house, his sons, and perhaps a physician should the services of one be required. Segregation continued when the children were old enough to be educated. Sons might be taught reading, writing, and the basics of arithmetic. Most daughters, by contrast, were trained as future housewives, schooled in domestic activities such as needlework and cooking. In some aristocratic families, daughters might have the opportunity to receive the same education as their brothers; however, in that case, girls were entrusted to female teachers only.

Despite these conservative dictates, some women, especially those of the ruling elite, managed to establish themselves successfully outside the household, in certain sectors of Islamic society, including the religious and scholastic. With regard to the former, women helped to maintain folk cults and pilgrimages to local shrines, and some founded convents dedicated to Sufism, a branch of Islam emphasizing mysticism and spirituality. A few female mystics became famous in their own right, including Rabi`ah al-Adawiyah (713-801), who was one of the earliest women Sufis.

Women also served as scholars, teachers, and transmitters of knowledge—most notably in the form of *hadiths*, traditions based on Muhammad's non-divinely-revealed words that served as a source of Islamic law. Even within the domestic sphere, some women contrived to improve their education, establishing study circles in private homes, in which women delivered lectures to other women. Moreover, despite one pervasive tenet of Islamic thought that advocated the total exclusion of women from public life, some managed to transcend the domestic sphere through a combination of wealth, social circumstances, and individual strength of character. Gavin R. G. Hambly writes, "In reality, well-placed women in traditional Islamic societies always had the opportunity to influence public affairs, even if that influence was used inconspicuously. There was always the possibility of a strong female personality determining the actions of a less forceful husband, son, or brother, or of a ruler becoming infatuated with one of the women in his harem" (Hambly, p. 10). The character of Shahrazad, a strong-willed queen who uses her wit and education to influence and redeem a king whose bitterness has led him to commit cruel and barbarous acts, may thus be regarded as a viable role model for women of pre-Islamic and Islamic society.

Sources and literary context. Scholars tend to agree that most of the tales that comprise *The Arabian Nights* were drawn from Persian story collections. Of these, *Hazar afsanah* (Thousand Tales) is considered the most immediate source. Other tales originated in China, India, Egypt, and even Greece. It was centuries, however, before *The Arabian Nights* achieved anything that resembled a "fixed" form. Despite the existence of thirteenth- and fourteenth-century manuscripts, the collection continued to grow until the late eighteenth and early nineteenth centuries. A common core does exist, however, a nucleus of eleven stories:

1) "King Shahrayar and Shahrazad, His Vizier's Daughter"
2) "The Merchant and the Demon"
3) "The Fisherman and the Demon"
4) "The Porter and the Three Ladies"
5) "The Three Apples"
6) "The Two Viziers, Nur al-Din Ali al-Misri and Badr al-Din Hasan al-Basri"
7) "The Hunchback"
8) "Nur al-Din Ali ibn Bakkar and the Slave-Girl Shams al-Nahaar"
9) "The Slave-Girl Anis al-Jalis and Nur al-Din Ali ibn Khagan"
10) "Jullanar of the Sea"
11) "Qamar al-Zaman and His Two Sons, Amjad and As`ad"

Significantly, some of the tales with which *The Arabian Nights* has become most closely associated—not only "The Story of Sindbad the

Sailor," but also "The Story of Ali-Baba and the Forty Thieves" and "The Story of Ala al-Din (Aladdin) and the Magic Lamp"—were late additions to the collection, composed some time between the fifteenth and nineteenth centuries.

As a work, *The Arabian Nights* is most often described as a story cycle and has evoked comparison with such staples of world literature as Geoffrey Chaucer's *Canterbury Tales* and Boccaccio's *Decameron*. All three works consist of tales told by the main characters and embedded in a framing narrative. *The Arabian Nights* is distinctive in having really only one storyteller, Shahrazad, at the heart of the work, although many characters within Shahrazad's tales are storytellers themselves.

Events in History at the
Time the Tales Were Written

Decline of Arab civilization. Even at the height of its power, the Islamic empire of the Abbasids carried the seeds of its eventual dissolution, a process that occurred over several hundred years. Initially, much of the strife was internal; political unity within the empire began to break down during the ninth and tenth centuries. Religious sects and splinter groups emerged from the provinces to challenge the supremacy of the Abbasid caliphate, including the Aghlabids of Tunisia, the Fatimids of Egypt, and the Hamdanids of Syria. An increasing number of new states sprang up after declaring independence from Baghdad. Meanwhile, the Abbasid caliphate itself went into a gradual decline, partly because of an increased reliance on Turkish military slaves to maintain its armies and serve as bodyguards. Known as Mamluks ("owned ones"), the slaves were strong, well-disciplined fighters. Gaining the confidence of their masters, they managed to manipulate the caliphate from within, and their influence spread to other parts of the empire as well. In 1250 a Mamluk seized power as sultan in Egypt. The Mamluks proceeded to form a military elite that would rule Egypt and Syria for some 250 years.

Internal strife within the empire was more than matched by outside threats. During the eleventh century, various invaders overran parts of the empire. Seljuk Turks, newly converted to Islam, infiltrated the Arab kingdom from Central Asia, defeating the Byzantines and occupying Syria and Palestine. Meanwhile, the first Crusaders descended on the Near East from western Europe in 1096, intent on wresting control of the Holy Land from the Muslims. On June 7, 1099,

the Crusaders laid siege to Jerusalem, which fell to them little more than a month later. The Crusaders proceeded to enter the city, slaughtering Egyptian soldiers as well as Muslim and Jewish civilians along the way. After their victory, the Crusaders established a chain of principalities along the eastern Mediterranean coast.

A far worse threat overtook the Arab world in 1221 when Mongol troops led by famed warrior Genghis Khan invaded the eastern frontiers of the Islamic Empire, advancing into Persia and Afghanistan. In 1258 Hulagu Khan, grandson of Genghis, invaded Asia Minor and Iraq, captured Baghdad, and ordered that all of its 600,000 inhabitants be put to death. His army caught Musta`sim, the last Abbasid caliph, and kicked him to death on Hulagu's orders. The Mongols invoked a policy of all-out destruction, leveling cities and massacring people as they marched through the Near East. Poised to invade Egypt, they were finally driven back by a Mamluk army consisting of combined Syrian and Egyptian troops.

From the fourteenth century onward, however, an even greater threat emerged as the powerful Ottoman Empire—based in Turkey—launched a series of expeditions against the crumbling Islamic kingdoms. In 1516 Ottoman forces advanced into Syria, crushing Mamluk forces at the battle of Marj Dabiq; the following year Egypt also fell to the Turks, ending Mamluk rule in the region. Ultimately, all the states that had made up the Arab Empire fell under the control of the Turks. Arab civilization became a casualty of the Ottoman conquests. Scholarly pursuits, such as the study of the arts and sciences, fell into decline; the once-rich cultural heritage of the Arabs was absorbed and overshadowed by the priority their Turkish conquerors gave to administrative and military matters.

Not surprisingly, the Ottoman conquest evoked nostalgia for a bygone age among the conquered. This nostalgia forms part of the appeal of *The Arabian Nights*, which was most likely set down in manuscript form during the thirteenth and fourteenth centuries. Robert Irwin, author of *The Arabian Nights: A Companion*, observes,

> When one finds stories set in Baghdad during the caliphate of Harun al-Rashid, the notional setting should be read as an expression of nostalgia for a lost golden age, located in the early ninth century, when Arabs still controlled their own destiny, before the Turks took control over the army and administration, and when almost all the Islamic lands were united under one ruler, the Abbasid caliph.
>
> (Irwin, p. 124)

Reception. Although the Western world has long counted *The Arabian Nights* among the classics of literature, this collection of tales occupied a less exalted position in the Arabic-speaking world, at least until the twentieth century. For many centuries, Arab scholars and intellectuals looked down upon *The Arabian Nights* as intended for the marketplace and common people rather than for the more sophisticated audience of the court. The continued admiration of the West for these tales, however, has inspired modern Arab scholars to re-evaluate this part of their literary heritage.

Revival of interest in *The Arabian Nights* inspired new translations of the available manuscripts, among them Haddawy's recent English version. His translation has received considerable acclaim. Working from Muhsin Mahdi's critical edition in Arabic of the oldest surviving Syrian manuscript, Haddawy retained the original shape and order of the stories. Sophia Grotzfeld wrote in *Middle East Journal* that Haddawy's is a "sensitive translation," adding that he succeeds at "conveying to the English-language reader the full narrative variety of the Arabic text and transmitting the true impression of the original" (Grotzfeld in Mooney, p. 68). Geoffrey O'Brien, writing for *Voice Literary Supplement*, was likewise enthusiastic, calling Haddawy's version "indispensable. He has given us not a new version of an old favorite, but a work we've never known. . . . The real and unacknowledged legacy of the *Nights* . . . lies in the qualities that Haddawy's version brings out: their spareness, their harshness, the high-speed complexity of their storytelling mechanisms" (O'Brien in Mooney, p. 68).

—Pamela S. Loy

For More Information

Burton, Sir Richard F., trans. *The Arabian Nights*. New York: Modern Library, 2001.

Clot, Andre. *Harun al-Rashid and the World of the Thousand and One Nights*. Trans. John Howe. London: Saqi, 1989.

Haddawy, Husain, trans. *The Arabian Nights*. New York: W. W. Norton, 1990.

Hambly, Gavin R. G., ed. *Women in the Medieval Islamic World: Power, Patronage and Piety*. New York: St. Martin's Press, 1998.

Irwin, Robert. *The Arabian Nights: A Companion*. London: Allen Lane, 1994.

Kennedy, Hugh. *The Prophet and the Age of the Caliphates*. London: Longman, 1986.

Landau, Rom. *Islam and the Arabs*. New York: Macmillan, 1959.

Mahdi, Muhsin. *The Thousand and One Nights*. Leiden: E. J. Brill, 1995.

Metz, Helen Chapin, ed. *Iraq: A Country Study*. Washington, D.C.: Federal Research Division, Library of Congress, 1990.

Mooney, Martha T., ed. *Book Review Digest*. New York: H. W. Wilson, 1992.

Segal, Ronald. *Islam's Black Slaves*. New York: Farrar, Straus and Giroux, 2001.

Walther, Wiebke. *Women in Islam*. Princeton: Markus Wiener, 1993.

Badenheim 1939

by

Aharon Appelfeld

THE LITERARY WORK

A novel set in Austria in 1939; published in Hebrew (as *Badenheim `ir nofesh*) in 1975, in English in 1980.

SYNOPSIS

On the eve of the Holocaust, a group of Jews in an Austrian resort town goes blindly on with life as some mysterious authorities prepare to deport the group to Poland.

Aharon Appelfeld (also spelled Aron Appelfeld) was born in 1932 in Czernowitz, the capital of Bukovina, a largely German-speaking region of central Europe that was under Romanian rule. His hometown was a commercial and intellectual center, including highly assimilated Jews, who spoke German and identified with German culture. In 1941, two years after the outbreak of World War II, Bukovina was caught up in Germany's invasion of Russia and the Bukovinan Jews were rounded up for deportation. Like many others, Appelfeld's mother was shot on the spot; the boy and his father were separated and imprisoned in the concentration and labor camps. Appelfeld escaped, lived on farms and in villages of the Ukraine for a few years, then joined the Russian army as a kitchen boy and made his way to Italy. From there, at age 14, he boarded a ship of Jewish refugees bound for Palestine. Appelfeld settled in Palestine in 1946 and reunited with his father there after the state of Israel was established. From 1950-52 Appelfeld served in the Israeli army, and he served repeatedly in the Arab-Israeli wars. At the Hebrew University Appelfeld studied under a number of Jewish intellectuals who, like him, had escaped from central Europe and whose works became highly influential on his own works. While Appelfeld's fiction and nonfiction addresses various topics, he has become best known for his writings that concern the Holocaust, the systematic attempt to exterminate European Jewry during World War II. Among his translated novels are *The Immortal Bartfuss* (1988), *For Every Sin* (1989), and *The Iron Tracks* (1998). His first novel to be translated into English (and the second one he wrote), *Badenheim 1939* established him as one of Israel's foremost literary voices. Crafted in his distinctive style, the novel addresses the Holocaust indirectly. The story ends before the genocide begins, grappling in an innovative, almost surrealistic way with the inability of a largely assimilated group of Jews to grasp the calamity about to befall them.

Events in History at the Time the Novel Takes Place

Liberalism, anti-Semitism, and Hitler's rise to power. Austria's history makes it an especially apt setting for an allegorical novel in the ominous days before the Holocaust. Over the course of the nineteenth century, Austrian Jews had assimilated into the Austro-Hungarian Empire's

Aharon Appelfeld

dominant Christian culture to a higher degree than in many other parts of Europe. Along with Austria and Hungary, the empire, which lasted from 1867-1918, encompassed ten other lands, including Appelfeld's birthplace, Bukovina. The empire's assimilated Jews contributed significantly to the cultural flowering in Vienna, Austria, a major center of European art, literature, music, and science at the turn of the twentieth century. Appelfeld's hometown of Czernowitz was culturally tied to Vienna, as were other areas that had formerly been part of the Austro-Hungarian Empire. Popular cafés in Czernowitz named themselves after Viennese cafés, and Jews, like other residents, conversed and took university courses in German. From throughout the empire, Jews migrated to Austria, the empire's German core, with an eye toward Vienna as a locus of Jewish modernization and intellectual creativity, evidenced by, for example, the theories of Sigmund Freud (1856-1939). The characters in *Badenheim 1939* form a representative array of assimilated Austro-Hungarian Jews, from musicians to doctors, businessmen, historians, and working-class waiters and prostitutes.

The success of Austria's Jewish community in the nineteenth century was enhanced by the liberal tradition, which played an influential part in the political life of the multiethnic Austro-Hungarian Empire. Jews identified with the largely German-speaking liberal leadership and its championship of individual freedom. Under the liberal ascendancy of the 1860s, Austria's Jews had been awarded equal rights with Christians (1867) and Jewish communities had received official recognition by the state. By the early twentieth century, however, Austrian liberalism—like liberalism elsewhere in Europe—was in decline. Along with this decline came growing anti-Semitism, the intensifying nature of which some of the assimilated failed to glean. In Austria, the long tenure of a right-wing demagogue, Karl Lueger, as mayor of Vienna, showed how deep-seated anti-Semitism was in the land. From 1897 until his death in 1910, Lueger won repeated elections on a strongly anti-Semitic and nationalistic platform that exploited lower-middle-class anxieties and hostility to both the Jews and the socialists.

In 1907 an aimless young Austrian named Adolf Hitler drifted into Lueger's Vienna and became involved in right-wing politics. It was in Vienna that Hitler conceived the fearful and obsessive hatred of Jews that would remain for him a driving force of his ideological worldview. Moving to Germany in 1913, Hitler served in the German army during the First World War. When Germany and its ally Austria met with defeat in 1918, Hitler blamed it on an international Jewish conspiracy (and on the socialists and communists), accusing German and Austrian Jews of betraying their countries to the enemy. In 1921 Hitler became the leader of a small right-wing party called the National Socialist German Workers party, later known as the Nazis. By the early 1930s, Hitler had built a fringe group of malcontents into a major political force. In January 1933—amid the economic turmoil of the Great Depression—he was appointed chancellor of a new coalition government in Germany, despite the fact that his Nazi party had won substantially less (33 percent) than a majority of the votes cast. Soon after, the German parliament granted him dictatorial power.

Anschluss—from Germany into Austria. For decades the right wing in Austria and Germany had called for the unification of the two nations. Yet such a unification, or *Anschluss,* was expressly forbidden by the Treaty of Versailles, which had ended World War I. Furthermore, Austria's two authoritarian leaders of the 1930s, Engelbert Dollfuss and Kurt von Schuschnigg, were both conservative in their political orientation. Austrian Jews reassured themselves that while neither Dollfuss nor Schuschnigg could be considered friendly to Jews, at least both leaders vowed to keep Austria independent from Germany. In

THE VANISHED WORLD OF AUSTRIAN JEWRY

Austrian culture was centered in Vienna, where 170,000 of Austria's 185,000 Jews lived in 1938. They formed less than 3 percent of the country's population at the time, yet occupied a conspicuous place in Austrian society. Jews comprised more than half the country's doctors and lawyers, and three-quarters of Vienna's banks, newspapers, and textile companies were owned by the city's Jews (Bukey, p. 131). Not everything about their successful assimilation into Austrian lifeways was positive, however. It exacerbated the anti-Semitism of the larger populace.

Austria's often poverty-ridden Christian public imagined the Austrian Jews to be a unified, powerful force, an image that was unfounded but nevertheless promoted by anti-Semitic propaganda. In truth, a number of social and religious divisions fragmented the Austrian Jews, most importantly the divide between the culturally assimilated central European Jews and the *Ostjuden,* the mostly less well-educated, still Orthodox eastern European Jews. The *Ostjuden* (represented in *Badenheim 1939* by Dr. Pappenheim and others) retained cultural ties to Poland, whereas the assimilated Jews looked to Austria's German-oriented Christian society for their cultural norms. Mirroring a real-life attitude, the central European Jews of Appelfeld's novel express resentment against the *Ostjuden,* blaming them for the troubles inflicted on all the Jews.

March 1938, however, this hope was shattered when Hitler's army marched into Austria, Schuschnigg resigned, and the formal Anschluss (annexation) of Austria to Germany was announced, resulting in the creation of a so-called Greater Germany.

The success of the Anschluss emboldened Hitler to pursue more open persecution of the Jews within Greater Germany. In retrospect, a series of grim signposts marks the road from the Anschluss in 1938 to the mass murder of Jews that began three years later, in 1941. But these signposts were not so visible to many at the time. The attempt to solve the so-called Jewish question in Austria evolved through three stages, the first being emigration (1938-39). From August 1938, when Nazi officer Adolf Eichmann opened the Central Office for Jewish Emigration in Vienna, officials employed discrimination, confiscation, torture, imprisonment, and other measures to encourage Jews to leave Greater Germany. Next came the stage of deportation (1939-40), during which Jews were arrested and forcibly removed to parts of Poland and other areas under German control. While many were shot, starved, or beaten to death, there was no systematic attempt as yet to exterminate them. Austrian Jews began to be deported to Poland on October 18, 1939, on a train bound for the newly established ghetto in the Lublin area of eastern Poland. At the end of *Badenheim 1939* the town's Jews are about to be deported this way. Their fictional experience can be seen as representing the actual deportations of October 1939 and after. The final stage, genocide (1941-45), is one the novel only alludes to; like a specter, it lurks behind the action. In this stage the Nazis and their accomplices attempted to murder all the Jews in German-controlled lands through starvation, mobile extermination squads (*Einsatzgruppen*), and deportation to the six extermination camps in Poland.

Austria and the Holocaust. In various European countries, non-Jews risked their lives to help Jewish neighbors and strangers escape the storm of hatred, by concealing them or assisting their flight. Those brave few, however, were a minority. The vast majority simply stood by, while another minority joined in the genocide. From France to Russia, from Sweden to Croatia, Germany's Nazi conquerors encountered inhabitants who voluntarily—in some cases eagerly—helped the Germans murder or otherwise persecute Jews. In some places, such as the Baltic states and the Ukraine, on occasion the Nazis found significant numbers of local people whose anti-Semitic brutality surprised even them. The Nazis utilized such anti-Semites effectively, organizing

THE GERMAN CAMP SYSTEM

On March 20, 1933, Germany's first concentration camp opened at Dachau. The camps, guarded compounds, "concentrated" and imprisoned undesirables, mostly so the Nazis could exploit their labor and, in the end, kill them as efficiently as possible. The earliest inmates were political enemies (communists, socialists, labor union leaders) of the Nazis. Other undesirables soon followed—hardened criminals, the homeless, prostitutes, Gypsies, and homosexuals. At the same time, the German government began to implement anti-Semitic policies aimed at "cleansing" Germany of its Jewish population by encouraging Jews to emigrate. By the end of 1933, a series of laws banned Jews in Germany from accepting jobs in civil service, law, the arts, and the media. Books written by Jews and other undesirables were publicly burned. In 1934 the S.S. (*Schutzstaffel*), originally Hitler's personal bodyguard, now an elite military police force, was put in charge of the concentration camps. Over the next decade, Austrians would form a substantial minority of the officers in the S.S. and the system would grow into a vast network, stretching from France in the west to the Ukraine in the east and including three kinds of camps:

- **Concentration camps,** such as Dachau (est. 1933) and Buchenwald (est. 1937) in Germany, where "undesirables" were imprisoned; forced labor became a key feature of their internment. "Particularly notorious was the quarry at Mauthausen (est. 1938) in Austria, where thousands met their death (Yahil, p. 133). Exterminations occurred here too.
- **Labor camps,** where millions of able-bodied Jews, Slavs, and other "undesirables" were used as expendable slave labor, essentially worked to death. Many labor camps were located in the Ukraine, such as the one that Aharon Appelfeld and his father were sent to in 1941.
- **Extermination camps,** where industrial mass-killing techniques were adopted to exterminate mainly Jews but also others. Six extermination camps were built starting in late 1941, all in Poland: Chelmno, Auschwitz, Majdanek, Belzec, Sobibór, and Treblinka. About half of the 6 million Jews killed in the Holocaust perished in these six camps from 1941-44, many of them in gas chambers disguised as shower rooms.

In addition, hundreds of transit camps were established to aid in the transport of the millions imprisoned from 1933 to 1945. The extermination camps have been called "death camps," but scholars caution that this term is misleading. Conditions in all the camps were brutal. While the extermination camps set out to achieve the systematic killing of the Jews, those in concentration and labor camps died from beatings, shootings, starvation, and neglect. In truth, all the camps were "death camps."

them into paramilitary battalions and calling them *Hiwis* (short for *Hilfswillige* or "willing helpers").

> Eventually they came to number in the hundreds of thousands. . . . The Germans found that they could usually rely on the Hiwis to perform the least pleasant tasks, such as flushing Jews out of ghetto hiding places and shooting on the spot those too frail to walk to deportation vehicles. Other volunteers became guards at camps and ghettos all over Eastern Europe. More than three-quarters of the guards at Treblinka, Belzec, and Sobibór [three of the six extermination camps] were Hiwis.
>
> (Niewyk and Nicosia, pp. 86-87)

Prior to 1939, Germany's Nazis had found similarly enthusiastic assistance in Austria. It is thus possible that the characters in *Badenheim 1939* are headed into the hands of the Hiwis and their S.S. teachers at the end of the novel.

Austria's Nazi Party, in existence long before the Anschluss of 1938, had already done significant damage. It was responsible for the assassination of Prime Minister Dollfuss in 1934 during an attempted coup. The coup failed, but as his successor, Prime Minister Schuschnigg, discovered after four years of political turbulence in Austria, its Nazi Party enjoyed broad public support. The single most important factor in marshaling this support was anti-Semitism. Long a major theme in Austrian politics, anti-Semitism unified public support for the Nazis in Austria much more than in Germany, where other factors (such as the economy) were more important. As historian Evan Burr Bukey explains, "The collective phobia may not have envisaged mass murder, but subsequent events suggest that thousands of Austrians, especially in Vienna, yearned to strip the Jews of their rights and property, to segregate them from society, to eliminate them from their midst. In 1938 the spontaneous anti-Semitic riots accompanying the Anschluss were so violent that they shocked even the Germans" (Bukey, p. 131).

On March 12, 1938, the day after Schuschnigg's radio broadcast announcing the annexation of Austria to Germany, Austrian mobs manhandled Jews at will, looting Jewish stores and domiciles while the police looked the other way. Vienna passed a succession of anti-Semitic laws that year. Jews were forbidden to enter parks, attend the opera or theater, or sit on benches marked for Aryans. The authorities made Jewish students drop out of the schools and Jewish entrepreneurs turn their businesses over to Aryans. Jewish residents had to move out of the suburbs and concentrate in Jewish districts. "The optimists," reports one eyewitness historian, "thought it would get better" (Schneider, p. 39). Bringing to mind an attitude in *Badenheim 1939,* the historian's father was such an optimist:

> [My father] obtained a position where his job consisted of building and repairing bridges. He showed great aptitude and was soon assisting one of the architects; in a curious way, he seemed happy, especially when he received a coveted stamp on his identity card, which made him a *Wirtschafts-Wichtiger Jude* (a Jew important to the economy), and therefore thought to be a valuable commodity. His older brother Nachman, being head bookkeeper of a clothing firm, which now started to produce uniforms, received the same classification. Both brothers thus felt safe; both preferred the known to the unknown; both had served in the imperial forces of the Great War and therefore felt less vulnerable; and both were to pay a terrible price for their optimism and their never-ending affection for Austria.
>
> (Schneider, p. 23)

A major signpost of impending doom was the wave of anti-Jewish riots on Kristallnacht (means "Night of the Broken Glass"), an episode of anti-Semitic violence that reverberated through Jewish communities of Germany and Austria on November 9-10, 1938. Of all municipalities, only in Vienna did the Nazi Storm Troopers (*Sturmabteilung*), who perpetrated the violence, find a large share of the public willing to join them. Almost everywhere else in Greater Germany, the public stood by while the uniformed Storm Troopers wrecked Jewish synagogues, businesses, and homes, and killed 91 people. Some 4,600 Viennese Jews were sent to Dachau at this time (Gutman, vol. 2, p. 838). Close to 8,000 Austrian Jews would be sent to Dachau and Buchenwald between April 1938 and September 1939; of this total, nearly 5,000 were released during the spring and summer of 1939 if they had a visa or a permit to emigrate (Schneider, p. 40). Most of these ex-inmates went into voluntary exile. Roughly a third of Austria's Jews was sucked into the Nazi death mill.

Some non-Jewish Austrians protested all the anti-Jewish violence—finding fault not with the victimization, but with the random destruction of valuable property. The Jewish property, they reasoned, should be put to good use: it should enrich the Aryan Germans and Austrians, the non-Jewish Caucasian members of the self-appointed "master race." Random violence was considered a mistake, one that those in control were careful not to repeat. Kristallnacht taught them that bureaucratic, legal measures would be more effective and more popular than random violence. It is this quiet, nonviolent but remorseless bureaucratic approach that *Badenheim 1939* reflects. In the novel such an approach is represented allegorically by the Sanitation Department, whose powers are mysteriously expanded to include authority over the Jews.

The imaginary Sanitation Department's real-life counterpart was Adolf Eichmann's Central Office for Jewish Emigration in Vienna, where assembly-line efficiency reduced the number of Jews in Austria from 185,000 in 1938 to fewer than 82,000 by May 1939. Subsequently a similar office was set up under Reinhard Heydrich in Berlin, Germany. Eichmann was promoted and later put in charge of implementing the Final Solution, the attempt to wipe out European Jewry by mass extermination. Their experience

German soldiers in Austria around the time Appelfeld's story takes place.

in Austria thus offered the Germans key lessons that sealed the fate of millions.

The Novel in Focus

Plot overview. As the novel opens, Badenheim, a small resort town in Austria, is preparing for the upcoming spring cultural festival. At the same time, inspectors from the Sanitation Department are making a different set of preparations, suggested by posters hanging in their office that rave about how fresh the air is in Poland and how labor is the crux of life, messages ominous to the reader more than to the vacationers or resort dwellers. Two realities co-exist—the first is life through the lens of the resident and vacationing Jews, the second is life as viewed by the Sanitation officials. Privy to all these goings on, the reader merges the two, a jarring experience that creates an altogether fantastic effect. The fictional world appears as double-edged; its inhabitants proceed unhurriedly along parallel but disjunctive tracks of expectation. Self-delusion sets in, along with tension and an eerie sense of foreboding.

Plot summary. The novel opens in spring, as sun and warmth return to the small, attractive Austrian resort town of Badenheim after a par-

ticularly stormy winter: "It was a moment of transition. The town was about to be invaded by vacationers" (Appelfeld, *Badenheim 1939*, p. 1). The town's pharmacist, Martin, has resigned himself to the illness of his wife, Trude, who is beset by disturbing hallucinations that make the world seem "poisoned and diseased" (*Badenheim 1939*, p. 3). They watch as the first guests of the season arrive and the town's hotel becomes a beehive of activity.

First to appear is Dr. Pappenheim, the impresario in charge of arranging the town's famous annual music festival, which brings many visitors back each spring. Other guests include the historian Dr. Fussholdt; his pretty young wife; an escaped mental patient named Frau Zauberblit; and the youthful, handsome mathematician Dr. Shutz. The town's two prostitutes, Sally and Gertie, don summer dresses and parade down the avenue. Dr. Pappenheim's musicians arrive and energize the audience with their evening's performance. Pappenheim has also secured the services of a *yanuka*, or child prodigy, and of twin brothers who recite poetry aloud in beautiful voices. Later, after two days of eating nothing, the twins will perform a reading about death. Their passion is the poet Rainer Maria Rilke ("Who, if I cried, would hear me . . . / . . . Not angels, not men," Rilke, p. 79).

The morning after the musicians perform, Martin is visited by an inspector from the Sanitation Department:

> He wanted to know all kinds of peculiar details. The ownership of the business, if Martin had inherited it, when and from whom he had acquired it, and how much it was worth. Martin, surprised, explained that everything had been whitewashed and thoroughly disinfected. The inspector took out a yardstick and measured. He left abruptly without apologizing or explaining.
>
> Martin was upset by the visit. He believed in the authorities and blamed himself as a matter of course. Perhaps the back entrance had been neglected. He stood on the lawn. A morning like any other.
>
> (*Badenheim 1939*, pp. 8-9)

The following day an announcement informs the town "that the jurisdiction of the Sanitation Department [has] been extended, and that it [has] been authorized to conduct independent investigations" (*Badenheim 1939*, p. 11). As the inspectors spread out and begin their investigations, the townspeople gossip speculatively about the inspectors' intentions. Soon the inspectors are busy all over town: "They took measurements, put up fences, and planted flags. Porters unloaded rolls of barbed wire, cement pillars, and all kinds of appliances suggestive of preparations for a public celebration" (*Badenheim 1939*, p. 15). The mostly Jewish population figures that the activity is in aid of the upcoming music festival.

Preoccupied with their own lives, the people barely notice when, in mid-May, the Sanitation Department announces that all Jews are required to register with the department by the end of the month. Rumors spread, and Samitzky, a Jewish musician who is proud of his Polish heritage, declares happily that they will be going to Poland soon. His statement seems confirmed when posters go up in the Sanitation Department office, with slogans proclaiming the pleasures of Poland: "LABOR IS OUR LIFE . . . THE AIR IN POLAND IS FRESHER . . . SAIL ON THE VISTULA. . . . GET TO KNOW SLAVIC CULTURE" (*Badenheim 1939*, pp. 29-30). Soon the townspeople and visitors find themselves barricaded inside town, cut off from the outside world: "Life was now confined to the hotel, the pastry shop and the swimming pool" (*Badenheim 1939*, p. 39). Yet despite the confinement, a relaxed atmosphere prevails as the festival continues. Only a visitor named Dr. Langmann objects: "I still consider myself a free Austrian citizen. Let them send the Polish Jews to Poland; they de-serve their country" (*Badenheim 1939*, p. 45). But Dr. Pappenheim says, "There are wonderful places in Poland" (*Badenheim 1939*, p. 49).

The characters interact, sometimes happily, sometimes not. Pappenheim is overjoyed when the famous musician Mandelbaum arrives after escaping the authorities in another quarantined resort town. Pappenheim has been trying for years to entice the great Mandelbaum to the festival, so the maestro's arrival is a wonderful victory for him. Despite this coup, another guest, Princess Milbaum, an aristocrat of high culture, looks down on Pappenheim. She calls him "an international criminal" and complains about the *Ostjuden*, who, she says, have "taken over Badenheim and [are] dragging every bit of true culture through the mud" (*Badenheim 1939*, p. 80). When food supplies are cut off, the hotel owner opens his food stores to everyone, and the people enjoy fine delicacies. The musicians practice, filling the hotel with music. Dr. Fussholdt, the historian, works singlemindedly on the proofs of his new book while his young wife, Mitzi, grows bored.

Mitzi is frightened by the prospect of their impending journey. Dr. Pappenheim tells her that there is nothing to fear: "There are many Jews living in Poland. In the last analysis, a man has to return to his roots" (*Badenheim 1939*, p. 89). Others have begun complaining about their enforced isolation, and outside the hotel, frustrated people now prowl "the streets and cast their angry shadows" (*Badenheim 1939*, p. 92). Only the formerly pessimistic Trude seems happy. She was born in a small town in Poland and is eager to return. She praises Poland's beauty, declaring that the Yiddish language (spoken by many Polish Jews) is beautiful and easy to learn. Meanwhile, her husband, Martin, has "absorbed her sickness," feeling an inexplicable desolation that grips him "like a vise" (*Badenheim 1939*, pp. 95, 96). More people arrive, and the town is now full of strangers who have been uprooted from their homes. Dr. Pappenheim continues to assure everybody that things will be better in Poland:

> He would tell them about Poland. About the wonderful world to which they were going. "Here we have no life left," he would say. "Here everything has become empty." Only a few days before, they had been sitting in their warm houses, busy with their flourishing practices. Now they were sitting here, without shelter. Everything had been taken from them; it was like a bad dream.
>
> (*Badenheim 1939*, p. 97)

A stranger loses his temper, telling everyone that there has been a mistake. He was brought to Badenheim because he is a Jew, he says, but he is an Austrian, not one of the *Ostjuden*. And anyway what does it matter who his ancestors were? The man apologizes for his outburst.

"Gray days settled on the town. In the hotel they stopped serving meals. Everyone stood in line to get their lunch—barley soup and dry bread," daily fare foreshadowing the crumbs doled out to death-camp inmates (*Badenheim 1939*, p. 100). An old rabbi appears, confused and disoriented from long isolation in an empty synagogue, which was once filled with old men, all of whom are now dead. New arrivals are brought to Badenheim daily because their ancestors had once come from the town. Martin's pharmacy is looted, and all his drugs are stolen. "The last days of Badenheim were illuminated by a dull, yellow light. There were no more cigarettes. People fed in secret on the stolen drugs. Some were gay and others sunk in depression" (*Badenheim 1939*, p. 106). More newcomers flood into Badenheim, frail people who die silently. The pastry cook buries them calmly in the town's formal gardens.

On the last day the people assemble in a group and walk to the train station, escorted by policemen. They await the train, enjoying refreshments and chatting about the new life ahead. Finally the train appears—"four filthy freight cars" that pull up to the station as the novel concludes:

> "Get in," yelled invisible voices. And the people were sucked in. Even those who were standing with a bottle of lemonade in their hands, a bar of chocolate, the headwaiter with his dog— they were all sucked in as easily as grains of wheat poured into a funnel. Nevertheless Dr. Pappenheim found time to make the following remark: "If the coaches are so dirty it must mean that we have not far to go."
> (*Badenheim 1939*, pp. 147-48)

Rendering the inconceivable. About halfway through *Badenheim 1939*, one of the musicians asks a friend why they are being sent to Poland:

> The friend sought an impressive formula. "Historical necessity," he said.
> "Kill me, I don't understand it. Ordinary common sense can't comprehend it."
> "In that case, kill your ordinary common sense and maybe you'll begin to understand."
> (*Badenheim 1939*, p. 70)

Rich in meanings that are hidden from the characters but accessible to the reader, this passage exemplifies Appelfeld's essentially ironic lit-

erary technique. The words "historical necessity," for instance, echo Nazi propaganda, while the joking expression "kill me" foreshadows the speaker's probable fate. But this brief exchange also suggests something more profound about the Holocaust: its fundamental incomprehensibility.

While *Badenheim 1939* is an allegorical fable rather than a realistic reconstruction, many real-life Austrian Jews in the 1930s shared the inability of the novel's characters to comprehend what was coming. In 1937, when the Austrian expatriate writer Stefan Zweig, living in London, warned Jewish friends in Vienna of approaching disaster, he was met with skeptical mockery. Even after the violence of Kristallnacht, many Austrian Jews believed that the persecution had reached its peak and would soon subside.

Attempting to account for such beliefs, historians have pointed out that while genocide has been all too common in human history, the Holocaust was unprecedented and remains unique. In the first place, its uniqueness is quantitative, since no other genocide has come close in sheer scale. But the Holocaust is also qualitatively unique. At no other time have the full available resources of an advanced bureaucratic and industrial state been dedicated to genocide. Nor has any other genocidal campaign exhibited such gruesome determination to wring every ounce of financial gain from its victims, from legally expropriating their homes and bank accounts to recovering the gold fillings in their teeth, even their hair and skin, for economic benefit. None has built entire industrial infrastructures devoted to death. The Holocaust stands alone as the darkest edifice of the industrial age, from the gas chambers and crematoria—death factories essentially—to the rail networks that delivered the raw material, living human beings. In this mass production of death, profound human suffering became no more than a byproduct. "Ordinary common sense" must be killed in order to envision it, for how could any sensible person have seen the Holocaust coming? Such a horror-ridden system of death requires an incredible flight of the imagination, in sync with the macabre atmosphere of Appelfeld's story. His techniques— metaphorical language, the omission of cause-and-effect, juxtaposition, and the evocation of relatively "flat" characters—lend a "mythic, timeless quality" to the Holocaust that begins to do justice to the horror of it (Ramras-Rauch, p. 494).

Sources and literary context. Like much of Appelfeld's other fiction, the world of *Badenheim 1939* is based in large part on the author's own childhood memories as a young boy in Czernowitz, Bukovina. Before 1918, Bukovina was, as noted, part of the Austro-Hungarian Empire, and even after the land changed hands (it was ceded to Romania) Czernowitz remained under the spell of Viennese high culture. Appelfeld's family was middle class—his father owned property and sold flour-milling machinery—and, like other middle-class Jewish families of Czernowitz, was assimilated into the Austrian cultural milieu. Appelfeld grew up speaking German as his first language. The fate of Czernowitz likely provided a partial model for Badenheim, since parts of the city were briefly turned into a Jewish ghetto after the German advance into Romania of July 1941. Before being deported to a labor camp in the Ukraine, Appelfeld and his father were held there with other Jews from the area.

Czernowitz in the 1930s was the home of other Jewish authors, who emerged as such in the postwar era, including novelist Paul Celan (1920-70) and poet Dan Pagis (1930-86). As with their works, the literary influences that helped inspire *Badenheim 1939* largely came from the interwar German-speaking culture of central Europe. Those influences gave rise to a number of novels that, like *Badenheim 1939*, take place in spa or resort towns, most notably Thomas Mann's earlier masterpiece *The Magic Mountain* (1924). The writer whose work played the most important role in shaping Appelfeld's own was Franz Kafka (1883-1924), who like Appelfeld came from an assimilated middle-class Austrian Jewish family. Kafka's fiction is allegorical, and often evokes human impotence in the face of dark, vaguely defined forces. In Kafka's *The Trial* (1925), for example, a man is prosecuted for an unspecified crime by an arbitrary, mysterious, and remorseless court. His *The Castle* (1926) depicts a village ruled by inscrutable and omnipotent authorities from a nearby castle. In Israel in the 1950s, Appelfeld met and studied with intellectuals who had known Kafka, including Kafka's biographer Max Brod.

Events in History at the Time the Novel Was Written

A lukewarm reception, an unpopular subject. Little Holocaust literature was published in Israel until nearly a generation had passed. In the early dates of statehood, the Holocaust was a topic rarely addressed, despite the influx of survivors: "At the time people in Israel weren't interested in the Holocaust. It was a heroic age, and people said, 'Don't speak about the Holo-

caust. Forget it. We are making a new Jew here, a blunt and blond Jew. We are remaking ourselves'" (Appelfeld in Wolfe, p. 358). The very idea of being a victim was repugnant to many; reminders of the Holocaust seemed to undermine the robust strength of the new Jew, the heroic antithesis of the European ghetto-dwelling and concentration-camp victim. The refugees themselves, brought to Israel from Displaced Persons camps in Cyprus and elsewhere, met with a mixed reception in the recently established homeland. To some degree, this was the plight of most newcomers, due to the fledgling nation's limited resources in the face of mass immigration. Refugees from the Holocaust, however, experienced a reception that was even less warm and welcoming, because of the focus on the "new" Jew and, in some cases, because of lingering suspicions. There were those who wondered what the victims had done to survive the Holocaust—had they collaborated with the Nazis? did the women compromise their honor? One survivor recalls the unsympathetic atmosphere that she experienced:

> Most painful to me was the denigration of the Holocaust and pre-state Jewish life by many of my Israeli friends. From them, those times of shame when Jews were weak and passive, inferior and unworthy, deserving not of our respect but of our disdain. "We will never allow ourselves to be slaughtered again or go so willingly to our slaughter," they would say. There was little need to understand those millions who perished or the lives they lived. There was even less need to honor them [at the time].
>
> (Roy, p. 8)

Until the 1960s the Holocaust was not a popular subject in Hebrew literature. The trial of Adolf Eichmann (1961) for the most part, but also the first payments of German war reparations and Israel's decisive victory in the 1967 Six-Day War, contributed to its becoming a key theme in Israeli fiction. In addition to Appelfeld's own *Ashan* (1962, Smoke), Yehudah Amichai's *Lo me-akhshav lo mi-kan* (1963; *Not of This Time, Not of This Place,* 1968), Haim Guri's *Iskat ha-shokolad* (1965; *The Chocolate Deal,* 1968), and Ben-Tsiyon Tomer's *Yalde ha-tsel* (1963; *Children of the Shadows,* 1973) were among the first works to address the subject. While Appelfeld belongs to this wave of writers chronologically, his lyrical style and hauntingly Kafkaesque sensibility, as well as his personal experience with the Holocaust, set him apart. The next wave of writers would include those of the second generation (such as Savyon Liebrecht), whose parents were survivors, as well as those without personal connection to the Holocaust, who have nevertheless invoked it in their writings (see, for example, Grossman's *See Under: Love,* also in *WLAIT 6: Middle Eastern Literatures and Their Times*). The immensity of the subject and its ineffability have led to some of the most creative writing in Israel, as demonstrated by *Badenheim 39.*

From extermination to survival. By the spring of 1945, as Allied armies closed in on the German capital of Berlin, the European continent lay in ruins. Starting the previous summer, several hundred thousand Jews had perished in so-called death marches, as the Germans shoved them away from the camps ahead of the advancing Allied troops. Others were slaughtered as the Allies approached. As they liberated the camps, Allied soldiers encountered numerous mass graves of the recent dead in addition to the living skeletons that were the survivors. Numbering an estimated 600,000, survivors were discovered in groups of perhaps 5,000 to 50,000, as appalled Allied soldiers liberated camp after camp.

When the Germans surrendered on May 8, 1945, tens of millions of people who had been swept up by the storm of war found themselves far from home. All of these Displaced Persons had been uprooted, all were deeply traumatized, but no group was more physically and psychologically devastated than the emaciated, numbed survivors of the Nazi camps. The Allies established a network of temporary camps for Europe's Displaced Persons, supplying medical care, food, and shelter until repatriation could be effected. But while many Europeans wished to make their way home, others had strong reasons not to do so. By September 1945 nearly 3 million remained in the camps. Among them were the surviving remnants of Europe's Jews, few of whom wanted to return to their places of origin. Of Austria's 185,000 Jews in 1938, only about 1,000 remained in Austria in 1945, and fewer than 2,000 refugees returned to join them after the war. More than 65,000 Austrian Jews died in the Holocaust.

As Zionists and other Jewish agencies worked to bring Jews to Palestine, they gave special priority to the children. Like Aharon Appelfeld, thousands of young Jews were shepherded onto ships that left European ports filled with hopeful emigrants to Palestine, the Jews' ancient holy land.

Riddled with guilt at its own inadequate response to the Holocaust, the international community supported the foundation in 1948 of the independent Jewish state of Israel. The new state was bolstered by a continuing influx of European Jewish immigrants, its population more than doubling from 1948 to nearly 2 million in 1961. By 1980 Israel had fought several successful wars against the hostile Arab countries that surrounded it. All the while the Holocaust has had a continuing effect on Israeli politics and foreign and security policies.

Publication and reception. *Badenheim 1939* was first published in 1975 under the Hebrew title "Badenheim `ir nofesh" (Badenheim, Resort Town), as one of two short works in the volume *Shanim ve-sha`ot* (Years and Hours). The Hebrew version appeared on its own as *Badenheim `ir nofesh* in 1979, followed the highly praised English translation (by Dalya Bilu) in the United States in 1980. The English version changes the title in a way that emphasizes the historical context, although the text itself does not reveal any precise year in which the events are purported to take place.

Both Hebrew editions of the story were praised by Israeli reviewers, and the English translation garnered immediate attention from English-language critics. One critic compared the novel favorably with those of Kafka, and several observed that its stylized presentation helps lend the narrative a universal significance. By slightly blurring the specific historical circumstances of the Holocaust, they said, Appelfeld suggests that it was a catastrophe for all humanity, rather than one limited to Jews alone. At the same time these critics recognized the centrality of the Jewish experience to the narrative itself. Some of them attacked the novel for representing assimilated Jews as unattractive—the implication being that they themselves were somehow partly to blame for their fate. Others countered that a negative portrayal of literary characters does not add up to the author's blaming them for their fate.

A number of critics singled out the novel's darkly ironic humor, praising the stylistic mastery with which Appelfeld evokes both laughter and horror even while describing the most trivial scenes in the blandest language. Writing in *The New York Times Book Review*, Irving Howe captured the reactions of many critics. Calling *Badenheim 1939* "a small masterpiece," Howe wondered rhetorically how its author could "achieve so unnerving an aura of anxiety even though his story is simply an accumulation of banal incidents" (Howe, p. 1). One possible answer is that this powerful but indirect tale relies for its full impact upon the reader's own historical knowledge of what comes next.

—Colin Wells

For More Information

Appelfeld, Aharon. *Badenheim 1939.* Trans. Dalya Bilu. Boston: David R. Godine, 1980.

Bukey, Evan Burr. *Hitler's Austria: Popular Sentiment in the Nazi Era, 1938-1945.* Chapel Hill: University of North Carolina Press, 2000.

Flanagan, Thomas. Review of *Badenheim 1939. The Nation* 232 (31 January 1981): 122.

Friedlander, Saul. *Memory, History, and the Extermination of the Jews of Europe.* Bloomington: Indiana University Press, 1993.

Gutman, Israel, ed. *Encyclopedia of the Holocaust.* New York: Macmillan, 1990.

Howe, Irving. "Novels of Other Times and Places." *The New York Times Book Review,* 23 November 1980, p. 1.

Niewyk, Donald, and Francis Nicosia. *The Columbia Guide to the Holocaust.* New York: Columbia University Press, 2000.

Ramras-Rauch, Gila. "Aharon Appelfeld: A Hundred Years of Jewish Solitude." *World Literature Today* 72, no. 3 (summer 1998): 493-551.

Rilke, Rainer Maria. "Duino Elegies: The First Elegy." In *Possibility of Being: A Selection of Poems by Rainer Maria Rilke.* Trans. J.B. Leishman. New York: New Directions, 1977.

Roy, Sara. "Living with the Holocaust: The Journey of a Child of Holocaust Survivors." *Journal of Palestine Studies* 32, no. 1 (autumn 2002): 5-12.

Schneider, Gertrude. *Exile and Destruction: The Fate of Austrian Jews, 1938-1945.* Westport, Conn.: Praeger, 1995.

Wolfe, Linda. "Aharon Applefeld: Re-telling the Unimaginable." *Publishers Weekly* 245, no. 3 (19 January 1998): 358-59.

Wyman, Mark. *DP: Europe's Displaced Persons, 1945-1951.* Philadelphia: Balch Institute Press, 1989.

Yahil, Leni. *The Holocaust: The Fate of European Jewry, 1932-1945.* Oxford: Oxford University Press, 1990.

The Blind Owl

by

Sadiq Hidayat

Sadiq Hidayat (1903-51; also spelled Sadegh Hedayat) spent most of his career at the periphery, exerting only an indirect influence on Iranian culture, but he ended up the most powerful literary voice of his generation. Hidayat grew up in a prominent family that had been at the center of intellectual life since the nineteenth century. His great-grandfather, Reza-Quli Khan (1800-72), was a tutor at the Qajar court and the author of a memoir describing Persian poets. (Reza-Quli Khan's pen-name, Hidayat or "guide," was the origin of the family name.) Technocrats and advisors to the government were numerous in the Hidayat family. His grandfather was Minister of Sciences; an uncle was director of the college of science and European languages Dar al-Funun; another was the Shah's physician. Hidayat himself received a secondary education at the exclusive French high school École St.-Louis in Tehran, and later he studied at the Dar al-Funun. In 1926 Hidayat traveled to Europe with a government-sponsored group of young Iranians to earn a professional degree in Belgium, but he abandoned his studies early to paint and write in France for four years. The short stories of his first collection, *Zindah bi-gur* (1930, Buried Alive), are dated and identified by city—Paris or Tehran. His return to Iran initiated a period of prolific publishing, during which Hidayat produced one series of short stories after another. Never earning enough from writing to support himself, he took bureaucratic positions in government. Meanwhile he lived alone, remaining unmarried throughout his life. Hidayat spent 1936-37 in India, studying Pahlavi, a pre-Islamic language of Iran (more

THE LITERARY WORK

A novella set in Iran in the city of Rayy (south of today's Tehran) at an undefined historical moment; published in Persian (as *Buf-i kur´*) in 1936-37, in English in 1957.

SYNOPSIS

Narrated sometimes in realistic terms, sometimes in dreamlike fantasy, the two-part novella centers on two accounts of a woman's death. In one account the narrator is a painter; in the other, an invalid with an estranged wife.

exactly, a dialect of Middle Persian) with the scholar Behramgore Anklesaria. In 1951, on his second trip to Paris, Hidayat committed suicide by leaving on the gas in his rented Paris flat. His suicide was later interpreted as an act of nobility, a withdrawal from a corrupt world, after which his stature grew until he became one of the most influential figures in contemporary letters. Hidayat's harsh realism and elegant pessimism contrast sharply with the often brittle optimism and hyperbolic praise that typified Iranian letters at the time. Frequently he showed a forthright skepticism about religion. After the 1979 revolution, this skepticism would make Hidayat a problematic figure in the eyes of government censors. Regardless of his status, *The Blind Owl* would continue to be regarded as his masterpiece, the work in which the issues raised in his other writings coalesce in a powerful condensed form.

Reza Shah Pahlavi

Events in History at the Time of the Novella

Reza Shah and Iran's intelligentsia. During the Constitutional revolution—a period of agitation in Iran that began in 1906—groups of disaffected citizens tried to restrict the power of the Qajar monarchy (1796-1925). This attempt was the defining event of Hidayat's childhood. In his early twenties, the writer saw his country undergo another pivotal political change. An officer in the Iranian Cossack brigade came to power in 1921, an event that marked the end of the Qajar dynasty and set the pattern for a new Iran. The officer, Reza Khan, called himself Reza Shah and took the title of "Pahlavi" for his dynasty. Until he was deposed in 1941 (by the Allies, during World War II) his innovations would be carried out forcefully and heavy-handedly, by intimidation. It is often said that Reza Shah Pahlavi aspired to modernize Iran in the way that Atatürk was remodeling neighboring Turkey in the wake of the Ottoman empire, except Reza Shah never established the same kind of trust or efficiency.

Under Reza Shah's rule, modernization accelerated in Iran. The government introduced paper currency alongside metal coinage in 1932; in 1935 the University of Tehran was founded. Meanwhile, Reza Shah made symbolic gestures that smacked of pre-Islamic Persian patriotism, taking the title "Pahlavi," the name of the final dynasty before the advent of Islam, and adopting a new type of calendar that invoked old, pre-Islamic Persian names for the months of the year.

For secular intellectuals, the response to Reza Shah's government was nuanced and often vexed. On one hand, they supported his projects of education and secularization; on the other hand, they were profoundly suspicious of and they fell victim to his heavy-handed methods. Intellectuals of all kinds were regularly censored and often imprisoned. The political poet Muhammad-Riza Mirzadah Ishqi, after writing critically of Reza Khan's rise to power, was assassinated in 1924. The writer Buzurg Alavi, a friend of Hidayat's, was imprisoned from 1937 to 1941. The story that the poet Farrukhi Yazdi's lips were sewn together in Reza Shah's prisons is no longer accepted as true, but he did die in prison, probably by a lethal injection, in 1939.

Many readers have seen Hidayat's political surroundings as crucial to his composition. As explained by writer Al-i Ahmad,

> [Hidayat] is a child of the Constitutional period and a writer of the dictatorial period. . . . During his life he witnessed either political chaos or suffocating dictatorship. The reality which held sway over Iran during the forty-some odd years of his life was nothing but trivialities, deceit, *poverty* and *misery* [italics added], anarchy and, at the end, tyranny: a constitution which had no meaning and durability and did not bring happiness with it; and then a central government which, under the guise of its "Brilliant Progress," had nothing but arrests and seizures and nothing but strangulating death.
>
> (Al-i Ahmad in Hillmann, p. 35)

In Persian, "poverty" and "misery" are *faqr* and *maskinat*, the same two words Hidayat uses in a famous passage from *The Blind Owl*: "In this mean world of wretchedness and misery (*faqr va maskinat*) I thought that for once a ray of sunlight had broken upon my life" (Hidayat, *Blind Owl*, p. 4). Al-i Ahmad suggests that the emphasis on solitude and reclusion in the *The Blind Owl* can be read in political terms: "When a person is afraid to talk to his friends, his wife, his colleagues, or . . . [anyone] else, ultimately 'he can talk [only] to his shadow'" (Al-i Ahmad in Hillmann, p. 36). Certainly there was "an atmosphere of insecurity" in Iran in the late 1930s; the shah himself "became increasingly insecure," attacking former friends in the process, killing "by the end of his reign . . . not only his former enemies, but the people who helped him in his rise to power" (Ghods, p. 110). Al-i Ahmad's vision of an Iran

A TIMELY COMPROMISE

The national calendar of Iran is a compromise characteristic of the culture, in that it pays deference to Islam but at the same time retains pre-Islamic elements. In most of the Islamic world, the common calendar is the lunar calendar, which dates from 622 C.E., the year the Prophet Muhammad's community emigrated from Mecca to Medina, and ends up being 11 days shorter than the solar reckoning used by the pre-Islamic Iranians. A Europeanized Iranian at the turn of the twentieth century would be aware of two calendars—the lunar Islamic calendar and the Western calendar. But starting in 1925 there was a third option: the solar Islamic calendar, a cultural compromise. Taking the names of its months from Zoroastrian tradition, this solar calendar, as in the days of the pre-Islamic Iranians, began the new year on March 21—the vernal equinox. At the same time, this third calendar dated back to 622 C.E., the date from which the Muslim era is reckoned, which made it Islamic as well as indigenously Iranian. Thus, the year on Hidayat's handwritten edition of *The Blind Owl* was 1315. (In the Islamic lunar calendar it would have been 1354 or 1355; in the Western calendar, between March 21 of 1936 and 1937.)

with government spies everywhere may or may not explain the reclusion and suspicion of Hidayat's narrator. In any case, it suggests that social contexts exert their force even in a story that perceives the outside world in a distorted fashion.

Hidayat and Khayyam. Today the most renowned Persian literary figure in the English-speaking world is probably the mystical poet Jalal al-Din Rumi (1207-73). In the nineteenth century, the most famous figure was Omar Khayyam (1048-1131), and his popularity has since endured. (See Rumi's *The Spiritual Couplets* and Khayyam's *The Ruba`iyat,* both also in *WLAIT 6: Middle Eastern Literatures and Their Times*). Omar Khayyam was in fact one of most respected mathematicians and astronomers of his time, part of a committee of scientists hired by the ruler Malik Shah to draft a new calendar. In later generations Khayyam became known for an extensive corpus of quatrains (called in Persian, as in English, by the Arabic term *ruba`i*—plural *ruba`iyat*) that expressed a skeptical, epicurean philosophy, devoted to the pursuit of pleasure in life. The poems attributed to Khayyam have grown in number over the generations, fueling debate about which ones he really wrote. According to scholars today, almost any sardonic quatrain from that era of Persian letters is likely to be attributed to Khayyam, regardless of actual authorship. In the anglophone world, the name Omar Khayyam became almost synonymous with Persian culture because of the popular

translations of his quatrains by poet Edward FitzGerald (1809-83). FitzGerald's collection of just over 100 quatrains (*The Ruba`iyat of Omar Khayyam* [1859]) became so well known that a particular style of melancholic skepticism and a stoic, carpe diem approach to experience came to be synonymous with the word "Persian."

Omar Khayyam was not a particularly famous poet in Iran before Hidayat's time, but Hidayat took the trouble to research him thoroughly and obviously considered him a kind of predecessor. He published an edition of Khayyam's quatrains, complete with extensive commentary, under the title *Taranah'ha-yi Khayyam* (roughly "Khayyam's songs," 1934), which sorted through the quatrains attributed to Omar Khayyam and chose those Hidayat felt to be most authentic. In an elaborate preface he shows a personal fascination with Khayyam as a figure of open-mindedness and skepticism, nonetheless able to make his mark in a strict religious society.

Familiarity with the poetry of Omar Khayyam is useful to an understanding of motifs in *The Blind Owl*. Khayyam's work is well known for its praise of wine and its skepticism about religion. Sometimes these two currents are combined, as in the quatrain that begins "The grape that can with logic absolute / the Two and Seventy jarring sects confute" (Quatrain 43 in the first edition; see FitzGerald, p. 54). Among the quatrains attributed to Khayyam is a series that might be a model for elements in *The Blind Owl* (the sketch on the pen cases or the scenes by the river); the series presents erotic scenes in natural settings—a garden or the bank of a river, for example—and proceeds to consider the remains of former lovers now buried in the same spot (Quatrains 18 and 19 in FitzGerald's 1859 edition). Another series, which FitzGerald calls the *kuza-namah* (the story of the vase) features a potter. The potter is compared to God in this series of quatrains, and the pots or vases discuss their fate. In the edition he published of Khayyam's quatrains, Hidayat discusses this "story of the vase." The fact that a vase is a central element in *The Blind Owl,* written two years later, suggests that the two works share a common worldview.

OPIUM—FROM TRADITIONAL ANTIDOTE TO "EVIL" HABIT

A time-honored medicine, opium has been prescribed as a remedy in Iran since at least the 200s B.C.E., having been in use by then for millennia (as far back as the Sumerians—c. 3400 B.C.E.). Muslim physicians used it extensively, as did philosophers, among them Ibn Sina (otherwise known as Avicenna; b. 980). By the sixteenth century the remedy had become entrenched in western European medicine. The nineteenth century saw a huge boost in production and an associated boost in consumption. "In Iran, supply created its own demand leading to wide-spread addiction to opium-smoking . . . as an evil habit . . . touching all strata of the society" (Poroy, pp. 1, 5).

The Novella in Focus

Plot overview. *The Blind Owl* can be understood as either a fantasy or the tale of an insane narrator, describing hallucinations. It is a tale told in the first person, by an eccentric male narrator, a character who turns out gradually to be at odds with his reality. His voice suggests a dependable observer, without ornament or verbal embroidery, but there are two incompatible components to the narration. On the one hand the speaker is a close observer who seems to inspire trust. His avowed project is to understand a very unusual experience ("I shall try to set down what I can remember, what has remained in my mind") and he describes it in sparse narrative, marked by visual intensity, with a minimum of rhetorical ornament (*The Blind Owl,* p. 2). On the other hand, the events he describes are so dreamlike that the reader must de-

cide whether to trust the persuasive authority of his voice or the supernatural aura generated by elements of the narrative. There are two sections, with a transitional passage between them and an epilogue at the end. Current scholarship regards the first section of the novella as a fantasy version of the second. The mysterious death of the ethereal woman in Part One is seen as the speaker's attempt to justify the murder of his wife in Part Two, which, although realistic, itself includes hallucinations and questionable judgments. In the handwritten, mimeographed version of *The Blind Owl* that Hidayat prepared in India, the entire second part appears in quotation marks. These quotation marks begin every paragraph of the second part up to the coda, intimating that this is the text in which the narrator committed his experience to writing as stated at the end of Part One.

Plot summary—Part One. The unnamed narrator introduces himself as a recluse living outside an unnamed town. An opium addict and a painter, he practices a kind of folk art, producing designs that resemble Persian miniatures on papier-mâché pen cases. The description of his pen cases is one of the most famous passages in the book:

> I would mention a strange, an incredible thing. For some reason unknown to me the subject of all my painting was from the very beginning one and the same. It consisted always of a cypress tree at the foot of which was squatting a bent old man like an Indian fakir [actually *misl-i jukiyan-i Hind*, like Indian yogis]. He had a long cloak wrapped about him and wore a turban on his head. The index finger of his left hand was pressed to his lips in a gesture of surprise. Before him stood a girl in a long black dress, leaning towards him and offering him a flower of morning glory [*gul-i nilufar*, also translated as "lotus" or "water lily"]. Between them ran a little stream. Had I seen the subject of this picture at some time in the past, or had it been revealed to me in a dream?
>
> (*The Blind Owl,* p. 6)

The painting offers up a palette of images and ideas that will recur throughout the novella. The first event of the narrative, a visit from an old man, identified tentatively as the narrator's uncle ("That is, he said he was my uncle"), replicates parts of the painting: "At all events my uncle was a bent old man with an Indian turban on his head and a ragged yellow cloak on his back" (*The Blind Owl,* p. 7). Even the morning glories recur regularly throughout the story.

The episodes that begin with the uncle's visit unfold with surprising speed. First the narrator notices a shelf. On the shelf sits a bottle of wine, which, he remembers, has been there all his life. Through a little window above the shelf, he glimpses the scene of his paintings. He describes a woman, sometimes identified as a "girl," in a long black dress in sensuous terms that make her seem otherworldly and ethereal. Fainting at the sight of her, he wakes to find no trace of the vision. The old man has left and, in an evocative inexplicable detail, there is no longer a window above the shelf.

In telling the tale, the narrator repeats and paraphrases passages in a manner unprecedented for its day. Uncannily he recounts—as if seeing them for the first time—scenes, phrases, and details used in previous descriptions. Infatuated with the sight of the ethereal woman, the narrator searches the wasteland around his house. After days of his searching, she appears on his doorstep, proceeds into his house, and lies on his bed. He gives her the same wine he planned to offer his uncle/the old man. She dies. His response is to paint a portrait of her face, for once a work of art instead of the folk craft that for him has become automatic, mechanical, and "ludicrous" (The Blind Owl, p. 6).

In the most explicitly supernatural moment (one of Hidayat's borrowings from Edgar Allan Poe's short story "Ligeia"), the dead woman's eyes open for an instant, presumably so he can draw them perfectly. This moment is a variation on the same odd plot device used by Poe.

From "Ligeia" by Edgar Allan Poe

The greater part of the fearful night had worn away, and she who had been dead, once again stirred. . . . The corpse . . . stirred, and now more vigorously than before. The hues of life flushed up with unwonted energy into the countenance . . . and, save that the eyelids were yet pressed heavily together . . . I might have dreamed that Rowena had indeed shaken off, utterly, the fetters of Death. And now slowly opened the eyes of the figure which stood before me.

(Poe, p. 328)

Hidayat's version of the scene is quiet, even gentle: "Her feverish, reproachful eyes, shining with a hectic brilliance, slowly opened and gazed fixedly at my face. It was the first time she had been conscious of my presence" (The Blind Owl, p. 25).

In a series of episodes, the narrator dismembers the body, places it in a suitcase, and receives a visit from an old man with a funeral carriage: "Suddenly, I caught sight of a bent old man sitting at the foot of a cypress tree. His face could not be seen for a wide scarf which he wore wrapped around his neck. I had still not uttered a word when the old man burst into a hollow, grating, sinister laugh which made the hairs on my body stand on end" (The Blind Owl, p. 28). The old man, described in the same terms as the uncle and old man in the painting, takes him to a deserted cemetery and digs a grave. In the grave they find an ancient vase, presumably pre-Islamic, and the narrator takes it home. There he discovers a portrait on the vase, identical to the one he painted when the dead woman opened her eyes. He smokes all of his stock of opium and descends into a dream, which brings the opening sequence to an end.

Transitional passage. Between the opening sequence and the longer narrative that follows is a transitional passage that describes an opium dream-state with great intensity. The passage includes what might be called a rebirth image:

With each moment that passed I grew smaller and more like a child. Then suddenly my mind became blank and dark and it seemed to me that I was suspended from a slender hook in the shaft of a dark well. Then I broke free of the hook and dropped through space. . . . When I came to myself, I found myself in a small room and in a peculiar posture which struck me as strange and at the same time natural to me.
(The Blind Owl, pp. 42-43)

On waking, the narrator speaks of waiting for the police to come and arrest him (a fear explained only later). He plans to commit suicide by drinking the poisoned wine that he keeps on the shelf (a detail that allows us to reinterpret the two references to the same wine in the opening sequence), and he decides to write down his experiences:

The source of my excitement was the need to write, which I felt as a kind of obligation imposed on me. I hoped by this means to expel the demon which had long been lacerating my vitals, to vent onto paper the horrors of my mind. Finally, after some hesitation, I drew the oil-lamp towards me and began as follows . . .
(The Blind Owl, p. 45)

The reader may expect that what he is about to write will be the series of events we have just read. In fact, the longer episode he now composes is much more realistic.

Part Two. The speaker reintroduces himself. This time he is an invalid rather than an artist, living in a house on a busy city street in the town of Rayy, south of contemporary Tehran. The sense of mystery in the opening sequence has given way to a tone of realism, even of mundanity. The relation between the two narratives becomes problematic because the more realistic lies within the less realistic, dreamlike account. It makes a considerable difference whether the opening sequence is regarded as a frame for the realistic narrative or whether the imbedded, realistic narrative is itself considered the frame. The latter reading, first suggested by Al-i Ahmad and Hassan Kamshad, has a paradoxical element, since it means that the dream encloses the frame or waking vision. On the other hand, it forces the reader to examine consciously the relationship between the two accounts.

In a brief lyrical episode, the narrator of the realistic version tells a story about his birth: "I have heard several different accounts of my father and mother. Only one of them, the one Nanny gave me, can, I imagine, be true" (*The Blind Owl,* p. 54). This story takes the form of a classical folktale. His mother, a temple attendant in India, was seduced by an Iranian merchant, or perhaps by the twin brother traveling with him, and the result was a child—the narrator— sent to Iran to be raised in the household of the Iranian branch of the family. There is confusion over the identities of the uncle and father, which is a common literary device and adds to the folkloric style. The story of the parents also features a "trial by cobra." In this trial, the twin brothers are placed in a pit with the temple snake; one is bitten, the other driven crazy. The whole ordeal is recounted with hallucinatory intensity.

Returning to the present, the narrator describes a tormented love-hate relationship with an unfaithful wife, the daughter of his adopted household in Iran, who resembles the ethereal woman of Part One. In the narrator's account, this woman has seduced him into marriage. She afterwards refused to consummate the marriage and has proven repeatedly unfaithful to him. He plans to kill his errant wife, then during an intense scene of lovemaking kills her accidentally, or at least professes to plunging the knife into her by mistake. The climactic ending shows him visiting her in disguise, forgetting he has a knife in hand, killing her by accident during a vividly articulated scene of lovemaking. ("I involuntarily jerked my hand. I felt the knife, which I was still holding, sink somewhere into her flesh" [*The Blind Owl,* pp. 126-27]). After the folkloric subplot of the parents and the emotional intensity of his anger at his wife, the reader is likely to distrust the narrator's account and to see the conclusion as a murder rather than an accident.

The realistic version includes a walk outside town, to a landscape that resembles the scene at the end of Part One, in which the narrator visited a cemetery with an old man who dug a grave and discovered a vase (*The Blind Owl,* pp. 71-79). The symmetry between the two scenes is not complete, since in this instance his excursion precedes the murder of his wife, whereas in the former instance the trip to the graveyard explains how he disposes of the body. As indicated by this example, events in the dreamlike first part are repeated in the realistic section, with variations.

In the realistic account, a figure described in much the same way as the uncle and gravedigger reappears as an old man selling odds and ends across the street from the narrator's house.

> He looked at me over the folds of the scarf that muffled his face. Two decayed teeth emerged from under the hare-lip and he burst into laughter. It was a grating, hollow laugh, of a quality to make the hairs on one's body stand on end.
> (*The Blind Owl,* p. 108)

A vase resembling the vase in Part One shows up for sale among the old man's wares, and the narrator buys it. A character described in much the same way as the ethereal woman turns out to be the narrator's wife.

The identities continue to intertwine in the scenes leading up to the murder, when the narrator decides that one of the people with whom his wife has had an affair is this odds-and-ends man. The narrator disguises himself to look like the old man and goes to her room, and the resulting sex scene is described with unusual candor. It is then that the murder occurs: "For some reason I kept the bone-handled knife in my hand. . . . As we struggled, I involuntarily jerked my hand. I felt the knife, which I was still holding, sink somewhere into her flesh" (*The Blind Owl,* pp. 125, 127). Afterwards, the narrator sees himself in the mirror and utters the final words of the realistic section: "I had become the old odds and ends man" (*The Blind Owl,* p. 128).

The epilogue returns us to the world of Part One. In this brief coda, the old man, seen once more as a character apart from the narrator, steals the vase that was earlier purchased from him and disappears down the street. It is possible to read the realistic segment as a reality the speaker can acknowledge only intermittently, like a repressed memory that becomes conscious during analysis (the concept of writing for one's shadow can be read as exploring one's darker or unacknowledged self). In the event of such a reading, the coda suggests a return into fantasy.

The Blind Owl and religion. One of the reasons that Hidayat did not publish *The Blind Owl* in Iran until the 1940s is the narrator's attitude towards religion. In reacting to his nurse's gift to him of a prayer book, for example, the narrator adopts a clearly anti-religious tone:

> As for mosques, the muezzin's call to prayer, the ceremonial washing of the body and rinsing of the mouth, not to mention the pious practice of bobbing up and down in honour of a high and mighty Being, the omnipotent Lord of all things, with whom it was impossible to have a chat except in the Arabic language—these things left me completely cold.
>
> (*The Blind Owl*, p. 88)

Religion has long been an important component in the complex process of forging an Iranian national identity, and the narrator's skepticism can be seen as a way to redefine the Iranian mentality by suggesting that Islam is not a universal revelation but is rather tailored to the culture.

In Iran, a division within Islam shaped Iran's sense of itself over the course of the sixteenth century, when a Shi`ite dynasty, the Safavids, came to power. Sunnism is the majority branch of Islam and the one that dominates in most countries of the Middle East. Shi`ism, which emphasizes the importance of religious authority as passed down through a succession of descendants in the family of the Prophet Muhammad, is the minority branch. In non-Arab Iran, Shi`ites are an overwhelming majority, about 98 percent of the population, and Shi`ism is a major component of the Iranian self-definition.

Even within Shi`ism there are potential divisions. A person can be for or against the clerical community. A person can be more or less amicable towards the practices and beliefs of Sufism (mysticism). A person can be more or less secular in habits. Reza Shah's project of modernizing Iran aimed at secularization; a 1928 edict, for example, demanded that the fez be replaced by a brimmed hat.

Hidayat was in many ways in tune with the secularization and Europeanization of Iran. But his critique of the Shi`ite clergy went beyond the focus on surface details such as clothing. In his short story "Seeking Absolution," pilgrims to the Shi`ite holy city of Karbala tell stories, each revealing a horrific sin he or she plans to have expunged by paying a donation to a religious authority once the pilgrim gets there. In "The Man Who Lost His Self," a Sufi (Islamic mystical) leader is exposed as a hypocrite; so thoroughly does he disillusion a disciple that the disciple commits suicide. To Hidayat's mind, not only religion but Arab culture in general had been too thoroughly absorbed during the period of conversion to Islam. He saw both Islam and the Arab influence as inimical to the Persian character; they were a corruption, he felt, of an earlier, purer culture. In "The Last Smile," for example, Arabized Persians in eighth-century Baghdad mock the Abbasid court as simple-minded and unrefined.

Sources. Genuine elements of Persian life find their way into *The Blind Owl*. The novella makes allusions to actual artifacts, such as the mosque of Shah Abd al-Azim (near which the narrator buries the ethereal woman's corpse), but these references pass without historical resonance. As Elton Daniel has demonstrated in an essay on Hidayat's use of history in the story, its references are frequently anachronistic, but Part One appears to take place sometime between 1800 and 1930. The city of Rayy as described in the story seems to be the site in its days as a great metropolis, before its destruction during the Mongol invasions in the thirteenth century. Also in the novella are references to coins (*qiran* and *Abbasi, pishiz* and *dirham*) used at different times in history. The narrator visits a river called *Suran*—a stream named occasionally in early sources. The anachronisms may be intended to establish a specific effect:

> It may be argued that . . . the deliberate evocations of the medieval period are designed to tell the reader about the narrator's psychological aberrations, about his belligerent insistence that time has no meaning, and about his assertion that the past is more real for him than the present. . . . They are expressions of the narrator's overwhelming desire to believe that his situation is of universal as well as personal significance.
>
> (Daniel in Hillmann, pp. 81-82)

Motifs from Iranian folklore emerge from time to time in *The Blind Owl*. The image the speaker paints on pen cases in Part One, with the stream dividing the two figures and the cypress tree in the background, reaches deep into Persian iconography. (Indeed, papier-mâché pen cases, a common piece of folk art in pre-twentieth-century Iran, remain popular among collectors today.) When the speaker first resolves to murder his wife in Part Two, he abandons the project because he hears a sneeze, a reaction that is in keeping with a common Iranian superstition that a sneeze is sent as a warning. In Hidayat's writing about folklore one sometimes gets the impression

THE BLIND OWL AND PSYCHOANALYSIS

Sigmund Freud was a controversial figure in Iran, as in Europe. Freud's *Interpretation of Dreams* was translated into Persian by Muhammad Hijazi (in 1933, as *Ru'ya*); he apparently benefited from Hidayat's advice about how to translate difficult terms. An interest in psychoanalysis developed among intellectuals in Iran during the generation after Hidayat. If the relation between the two narratives of *The Blind Owl* is understood to be a system of transformations, in which the speaker takes events from his reality and presents them in altered, fantasy form, Hidayat's interest in psychoanalysis becomes immediately visible. It is furthermore known that Hidayat was familiar with two books by a member of Freud's early circle, Otto Rank. Rank's study *The Double* explains the transformation of the narrator into the old man at the end of the book. In such a transformation a person finds another self committing crimes in his name. Such a fantasy, suggests Rank, is generated by the feeling of guilt. The guilty party invents a fantasy self in order to disclaim activities that are difficult or painful to own up to having committed. Another book by Rank, *The Myth of the Birth of the Hero* (1909), may have had a direct impact on the narrator's legend about his family history in *The Blind Owl*. *The Myth of the Birth of the Hero* discusses a story type (visible everywhere in world folklore) in which the hero, by birth an exalted or noble individual, is abandoned and raised by humble substitute parents. In sum, Hidayat, whether consciously or not, seems to combine two archetypes discussed by Rank—that of the double and that of the myth of the birth of the hero.

that he was most drawn to Iranian folklore when it echoed widely distributed motifs or conventions. A superstition alluded to in Part Two, that a person about to die would cast a headless shadow, is also a European tradition that Otto Rank lists in his study *The Double* (*The Blind Owl*, p. 79; Rank, pp. 49-50).

Literary context. *The Blind Owl* becomes more interesting still if seen as part of the evolution of the novel in Iran. At the turn of the twentieth century Iran boasted a tradition of historical romances set in pre-Islamic times, most notably by San`atizadah Kirmani. The new century saw the rise of a more realistic line of Persian fiction, influenced by a burgeoning field of translations that began in the nineteenth century and featured works from European languages by Jules Verne, Arthur Conan Doyle, and Alexandre Dumas, to name a few. Recent Persian literature exerted an influence too. Most significant in the new Persian fiction for later writers was the collection of short stories by Muhammad Ali Jamalzadah titled ***Once Upon a Time*** (1922; also in *WLAIT 6: Middle Eastern Literatures and Their Times*). What set Jamalzadah apart particularly was his linguistic exuberance. All but one of these stories are recounted in the

first person, and this allows him to explore personalized and regional vocabularies. Hidayat's short stories often explored what a narrative could gain by including characters who spoke in dialect, but his first-person narrators tended to sound like him—precise, neutral, clear—even those who seem out of touch with reality. What sets *The Blind Owl* apart is not just his engagement with psychology, but the strategy of a narrative voice that strives to sound like a neutral observer. At the time Hidayat was writing, most Persian prose featured mannered, rhetorically balanced and static text or a colloquial voice, usually comic, personalized as an agent of local color. Jamalzadah preferred the latter. Hidayat contributed a third type of voice, neither rhetorically elevated nor regional, as noted by Al-i Ahmad: *The Blind Owl* proves that "Persian, simple Persian, is capable of describing the most novel sensual states of a writer and can be employed for introspection" (Al-i Ahmad in Hillmann, p. 30). Hidayat developed a plain style, something close to what Roland Barthes has dubbed (in reference to the French writer Albert Camus) a "degree zero" style—colorless, unmarked, impersonal, objective (Barthes, pp. 76-78).

HIDAYAT AND POE

It is uncertain at what point in his career Hidayat read Edgar Allan Poe (1809-49), no doubt in the French translation by Charles Baudelaire (1821-67). However, the resemblances between their stories are clear. There is a distinctive pattern to Poe's most famous tales, in which the conclusion presents a revelation that inspires terror, usually involving an act of violence or unveiling a hidden motive. Hidayat seems to have been interested in Poe's scenes of claustrophobia and enclosure (as in "The Black Cat" or "The Cask of Amontillado"), his characters dominated by fetishes (as in "The Telltale Heart" or "Berenice"), and the sense of panic that characterizes many of his plots. Facets of *The Blind Owl* echo elements in Poe's short stories. For example, the character Egaeus in Poe's "Berenice" also fails to remember violence he has committed against his wife. The narrator of Poe's story "The Black Cat" kills his wife and opens his testament with the phrase "I neither expect nor solicit belief," much like the speaker in *The Blind Owl*, who prefaces his account saying, "for after all, it does not matter to me whether others believe me or not" (Poe, vol. 3, p. 849; *The Blind Owl*, p. 2). In Poe's "Ligeia," when the narrator's second wife, Rowena, dies, the spirit of Ligeia (his dead first wife) takes over the body. Poe's story ends with a Gothic sense of horror, as does Part Two in *The Blind Owl*.

Translations of *The Blind Owl* into French (1953) and English (1958) established Hidayat's international reputation. Iranian readers, always very aware of the world scene, valued this fact as evidence that Hidayat was not simply a proponent of Iranian culture but also a master of European modernist styles. The persistence of his reputation abroad has catapulted *The Blind Owl* to the context of world literature, in which Hidayat has been compared to European writers from Fyodor Dostoevsky to Jean-Paul Sartre.

In Italo Calvino's *If On a Winter's Night a Traveler* (1979), there is a scene in which a reader (addressed as "you") finds a passage repeated in a novel: "you [the reader] remark 'This sentence sounds somehow familiar. In fact, this whole passage reads like something I've read before.' . . . just when you were beginning to grow truly interested, at this very point the author feels called upon to display one of those virtuoso tricks so customary in modern writing, repeating a paragraph word for word" (Calvino, p. 25). Had *The Blind Owl* come out in 1979, many of its devices would have seemed commonplace. (In fact, the French writer Alain Robbe-Grillet, who is credited with pioneering the repeated passage in the 1950s, may have been influenced by the 1953 French translation of *The Blind Owl*.)

Publication and reception. Hidayat knew full well that *The Blind Owl* could not be published in Iran, because of both its outspoken skepticism about religion and the erotic scene that closes the book. The first publication was in fact a kind of *samizdat*, a hand-written text (with two illustrations by the author) copied on a mimeograph machine and clearly marked *tab va furush dar Iran mamnu ast* on the back of the title page: "Printing and sale in Iran are prohibited." The novella was not published in Iran until the period of relaxed censorship after Reza Shah's abdication in 1941.

Hidayat remained a respected writer during his lifetime, but it was after his suicide in 1951 that his reputation reached the dimensions of a cult figure, and *The Blind Owl* became his defining work. People began to think of him as a mythical figure, an observer who saw further than anyone else, a soul too sensitive to remain in a fallen world. Supporters have often approached *The Blind Owl* as a repository of hidden meanings and symbols, a tendency encouraged by the psychoanalytical framework that organizes the novella. Conversely, with his suicide in mind, one could see his pessimism as pathology, and in fact his writings have attracted attacks from conservatives who point to Hidayat's eccentricities as a key to the difficulties of his writing.

The French version, *La chouette aveugle*, translated by Roger Lescot (assisted by Hidayat), appeared in 1953, two years after Hidayat's suicide.

A positive review by one of the early voices of surrealist poetry, André Breton, helped build the novella's reputation among European readers, particularly among aficionados of Gothic and existentialist fiction.

In the quarter-century following Hidayat's death, Reza Shah's son (Mohammed Reza Pahlavi) attempted to control the intellectual world in Iran as his father had done, but even when the most confrontational works were banned, *The Blind Owl* continued to be read and reread, perhaps because its hermetic qualities made it seem personal and apolitical. After the revolution of 1979, when the Pahlavi reign ended and the Islamic Republic came to power, there was little tolerance for a skeptical and secular writer, though many of Hidayat's works remained in print in bowdlerized versions. Among Iranian writers themselves, he remains an essential source, the predecessor with whom everyone must come to terms.

—Michael Beard

For More Information

Barthes, Roland. *Writing Degree Zero.* Trans. Annette Lavers and Colin Smith. New York: Hill and Wang, 1968.

Beard, Michael. *Hedayat's* Blind Owl *As a Western Novel.* Princeton: Princeton University Press, 1990.

Browne, E. G. *A Literary History of Persia.* 4 vols. Cambridge: The University Press, 1969.

Calvino, Italo. *If On a Winter's Night a Traveler.* Trans. William Weaver. New York: Harvest, 1981.

FitzGerald, Edward. *Rubáiyát of Omar Khayyám.* Ed. Dick Davis. New York: Penguin, 1989.

Ghods, M. Reza. *Iran in the Twentieth Century: A Political History.* Boulder: Lynne Rienner, 1989.

Hedayat, Sadegh. *The Blind Owl.* Trans. B. P. Costello. New York: Grove Press, 1957.

Hillmann, Michael, ed. *Hedayat's `The Blind Owl' Forty Years After.* Austin: Center for Middle Eastern Studies, University of Texas at Austin, 1978.

Kamshad, Hasan. *Modern Persian Prose Literature.* Cambridge: Cambridge University Press, 1966.

Katouzian, Homa. *Sadeq Hedayat: The Life and Legend of an Iranian Writer.* London: I. B. Tauris, 1991.

Poe, Edgar Allan. *The Collected Works of Edgar Allan Poe.* Ed. Thomas Olive Mabbot. Vol. 2. Cambridge: Harvard University Press, 1978.

Poroy, Ibrahim I. *An Economic Model of Opium Consumption in Iran and Turkey during the Nineteenth Century.* San Diego: San Diego State University Center for Research in Economic Development, 1981.

Rank, Otto. *The Double.* Trans. and ed. Harry Tucker, Jr. Chapel Hill: University of North Carolina Press, 1971.

———. *The Myth of the Birth of the Hero.* Trans. F. Robbins and Smith Ely Jelliffe. New York: Robert Brunner, 1952.

The Book of Dede Korkut

The Book of Dede Korkut tells the stories of Bayindir Khan, leader of the Oghuz Turks, and his circle of lords and ladies as they battle enemies, free captives, and fall in love. The Oghuz were a federation of Turkic tribes who would become the ancestors of the modern Turks, as well as other Turkic peoples (such as the Azeri and the Turkmen who settled in the regions of Azerbaijan, Northern Iran, Iraq, and Turkmenistan). The Book of Dede Korkut differs from a typical epic and in some ways defies classification. Instead of following the adventures of one hero or one family though a number of different trials, the episodes each focus on one of several different families of the Oghuz nobility, giving the work a collective (rather than an individual) hero. In addition, the narrative uses a combined form of verse and prose typical in Turkic oral narrative but rare in the Western epic. The episodes, although each a distinct story, are united by a common framework and a consistency of tone. Like all heroic epics, this one describes a legendary age populated by larger-than-life-characters. The text looks nostalgically back on the heroic days of the nomadic warrior Oghuz, when "the nobles' blessings were blessings and their curses were curses, and their prayers used to be answered" (The Book of Dede Korkut, p. 59). Originally the tales would have been told and sung by a minstrel (ozan) accompanied by a stringed instrument called a kopuz. Sometime in the fourteenth or fifteenth century the stories were collected and written down by an anonymous scribe. The manuscript subsequently disappeared from the annals of history. Lost for hundreds of years, one version was

---

THE LITERARY WORK

A heroic epic set in Central Asia and Asia Minor in the eighth to the thirteenth centuries; probably written down in the fourteenth or fifteenth century; published in Turkish (as *Kitab-i Dede Korkut*) in 1916, in English in 1972.

SYNOPSIS

Twelve tales depict chivalry, daring, and heroism among the noble men and women of the Oghuz Turks.

---

found in the Dresden library in 1815, while a shorter manuscript with only half of the stories was found later in the Vatican library. First published in Turkish in 1916, The Book of Dede Korkut is considered by many to be a national epic of the Turkish people. The work is accepted worldwide as a masterpiece of folklore and has been honored by UNESCO (United Nations Educational, Scientific, and Cultural Organization) as one of the world's cultural treasures. It has furthermore been recognized as a repository of ethnic history and foundational values and customs of the Turkish people.

Events in History at the Time the Epic Takes Place

Layers of history. Originally oral tales, sung for hundreds of years before being written down, the stories in *The Book of Dede Korkut* refer to two distinct periods in the history of the Oghuz. The first period covers approximately the eighth to the eleventh centuries, when the Oghuz lived in Central Asia, in the region of the Syr Darya and Amu Darya Rivers (in present-day Kazakhstan, Uzbekistan, and Turkmenistan). At that time their enemies were other Turkic tribes, such as the Kipchaks and the Pechenegs. The second period is set during the eleventh to the thirteenth centuries, after the Oghuz had migrated westward to a region that includes today's Azerbaijan, Northern Iran, and Eastern Turkey. There they fought against local enemies such as the Byzantine Greeks, the Georgians, and the Abkhazians. In the stories, this second layer of historical context is superimposed on the first: the reader thus finds Georgian kings with Turkic names from the earlier period (such as the evil King Shökli) and Central Asian rivers (such as the Emet) flowing through the plains of Turkish Anatolia. The stories represent life in an imaginary Oghuz homeland, which combines various elements from the real places that the Oghuz lived.

After leaving Central Asia, the Oghuz federation divided into several branches, such as the Turcoman, the Seljuk (who led the way into Anatolia in the eleventh to twelfth centuries), and the Osmanli (who founded the Ottoman empire at the end of the thirteenth century). As the influence of Persian and Arabic literature grew, emerging literary forms, such as Ottoman lyric and religious poetry, became increasingly prominent (see **Leyla and Mejnun**, also in *WLAIT 6: Middle Eastern Liter atures and Their Times,* for an example of a Turkish adaptation of a traditional Arabic tale). The Turks developed a sedentary culture, and heroic oral narrative, presumably connected to former nomadic social forms, became associated with the legendary past.

The written version of the epic adds two more layers of historical context. Although the stories were taken from oral narrative, the scribe who selected these specific tales and wrote them down left his own traces in the manuscript as well. Numerous quotes from the text show that the scribe comes from a culture that considers the Oghuz customs antiquated. For example: "In the days of the Oghuz the rule was that when a young man married he would shoot an arrow and wherever the arrow fell he would set up his marriage-tent" (*The Book of Dede Korkut*, p. 68). Place names, vocabulary, and cultural references help narrow the time of the work's composition. Although no one knows the exact date that the

stories were first recorded, from clues in the text, Geoffrey Lewis and other scholars have argued that the manuscript was written down in the sphere of the Turcoman White Sheep (*Ak-koyunlu*) Empire, which ruled in Northern Iran, Northern Iraq, Azerbaijan, and Eastern Anatolia from 1378-1508. The White Sheep dynasty claimed Bayinder Khan as their ancestor, and thus would have had particular reason to tell the heroic adventures of these Oghuz leaders. The manuscript found in Germany has references to the Ottoman Empire that place the existing copy in the sixteenth century, most likely recopied from a fourteenth- or fifteenth-century version. In retrospect, *The Book of Dede Korkut*, retold and rewritten over hundreds of years, reflects Turkic culture as it changed and developed.

The Oghuz way of life. The Oghuz lived nomadically, traveling on horseback as they moved their sheep from summer to winter pastures. They housed themselves in tents made of thick felt on a collapsible wooden frame, portable quarters that were easy to disassemble and carry. Although there were several hundred thousand Oghuz, *The Book of Dede Korkut*, like most heroic epics, describes only the aristocratic few who lived in sumptuous tents with "golden smoke holes" (*The Book of Dede Korkut*, p. 53). The Oghuz not only herded sheep, horses, and camels but also carried out raids against their enemies, taking both plunder and captives. At times they also acted as paid mercenary guards for Arab and Persian merchants. Such a way of life was fraught with danger; consequently values such as bravery, loyalty to family and tribe, and the ability to fight were highly esteemed.

Although constantly on the move, Oghuz society had a well-organized structure to it. The people were a confederation of 24 tribes divided into two branches, which the text refers to as the "Inner" and "Outer" Oghuz. Each tribe had a territory (*yurt*), which was ruled over by a lord called a Bey. A council led by a head Bey administered each of the branches, and a joint council led by a grand Bey, or Beylerbeyi, administered a confederation of the two branches. A Great Khan, or king, presided over the entire structure. In *The Book of Dede Korkut*, Bayindir is the Khan of all the Oghuz, and his son-in-law, Salur Kazan, is the Beylerbey.

Originally the Central Asian Oghuz subscribed to a religion with a strong reverence for nature. The religion is often classified as shamanist, a faith whose adherents believe nature is a gateway to the spiritual realm and whose shaman-priests use music and other devices to communicate with that realm. Over time the Oghuz encountered Islamic societies to the south and by the eleventh century the Oghuz had converted to Islam, although they infused into their practice of the new faith many elements of their pre-Islamic past, such as ceremonially giving a young man his name only after he had performed a valiant act: "In those days, my lords, until a boy cut off heads and spilt blood they used to not give him a name" (*The Book of Dede Korkut*, p. 60). Contrary to the beliefs of many about Islamic societies, the one featured in *The Book of Dede Korkut* allows the drinking of wine and *kumis* (fermented mare's milk). If the stories are an indication, drinking wine was a common pastime in Oghuz culture, although then, as now, it often led to foolish acts. The Oghuz were monogamous, and Oghuz women were very active; in *The Book of Dede Korkut* they are shown riding, wrestling, and even taking part in battle.

The Epic in Focus

Plot summaries. Each of the stories in Dede Korkut focuses on an individual hero and his family. The first story, "Boghach Khan Son of Dirse Khan," begins with Dirse Khan and his wife praying and doing good works in hopes that they will be blessed with a child. They have a son who grows up so strong that he can wrestle a bull and who is given the name Boghach (means "bull") by Dede Korkut. Dirse Khan's private warriors become jealous of Boghach and slander him, prompting Dirse Khan to shoot his son in the back with an arrow and leave him for dead. When her son does not return home, his mother goes out looking for him, finds him, and heals his wounds with flowers and breast milk. The 40 warriors, worried that they will be punished when Dirse Khan finds out the truth, kidnap Dirse Khan and take him to enemy territory as a captive. Boghach's mother implores him: "My lord, my son, arise! Take your [own] forty warriors, and deliver your father from those forty cowards. Bestir yourself, son; if your father showed no mercy to you, Do you show mercy to your father" (*The Book of Dede Korkut*, p. 38). Boghach bravely rescues his father and after a tearful embrace they return home. A great feast is held where Dede Korkut sings a tale of the heroes of this adventure, and Bayindir Khan grants Boghach a principality.

"How Salur Kazan's House Was Pillaged" describes how Salur Kazan, the Beylerbey of the Oghuz, drinks too much wine and takes the Oghuz out on a hunting trip, leaving his family at home unprotected. The evil King Shökli takes advantage of the situation, pillaging Salur Kazan's house, stealing his property, and kidnapping his mother; his wife, Lady Burla the Tall; and his son, Uruz. The infidel army also tries to steal his sheep, but is repelled by a brave shepherd, Karajuk, who destroys the infidels by shooting goats at them with his giant slingshot. When Salur Kazan returns, Karajuk informs him of the tragedy. Salur Kazan gathers a huge army of Oghuz and attacks the infidels, killing the evil King Shökli in a bloody battle and saving Lady Burla, Uruz, and his mother. After they return home, Salur Kazan holds a great feast where Dede Korkut sings a tale of the heroes of this adventure.

"Bamsi Beyrek of the Grey Horse" is a longer tale that combines a number of different subplots. The story begins when one childless couple is granted a son and another a daughter, and the babies are betrothed in the cradle. The boy reaches 15 and proves his valor by protecting a merchant caravan from an infidel raid. He is given the name Bamsi Beyrek by Dede Korkut, who sings,

> May God Most High give him good fortune.
> Your pet-name for your son is Bamsa
> Let his name be Bamsi Beyrek of the grey horse.
> I have given him his name; may God give him his years.
> (*The Book of Dede Korkut*, p. 63)

One day while out hunting, Bamsi Beyrek comes to the camp of Lady Chichek, his betrothed. She tells him that "Lady Chichek is not the kind of person to show herself to you . . . but I am her serving woman. Come, let us ride out together. We shall shoot our bows and race our horses and wrestle. If you beat me in these three, you will beat her too" (*The Book of Dede Korkut*, p. 64). After the competition, she reveals her identity and they pledge themselves to each other. Bamsi Beyrek goes to his father and asks to marry her, but it turns out that she has an insane brother named Crazy Karchar who kills all her suitors. Dede Korkut is sent to negotiate, which he does, taming the wild brother with a host of fleas. On the eve of his wedding, Bamsi Beyrek and his soldiers are captured by enemies and whisked away for 16 years. Meanwhile, the unscrupulous Yaltajuk falsely reports Beyrek's death and becomes engaged to Lady Chichek. Hearing about the wedding, Beyrek escapes with the help of an infidel

THE FIGURE OF DEDE KORKUT

Although almost certainly not the author of these stories, the character Dede Korkut is one of the most interesting figures in them. Combining the attributes of seer, wise man, tribal elder, and religious leader, he gives young men their names, advises the Oghuz, and intercedes in difficult situations (such as bargaining with the Cyclops). At the end of each story he is depicted as the minstrel who chronicles the tale, playing on a three-stringed instrument called a *kopuz*.

The figure of Dede Korkut (or "Korkut Ata") is known throughout Central Asia and seems to have been a real person. Historian Rashid al-Din (d. 1318) describes a Dede Korkut who was a ninth-to-tenth-century statesman and diplomat, noting that he gave advice to the Great Khan of the Oghuz, that he gave names to the Oghuz children, and that he lived for 295 years (the historian considered legend to be a historical source). Dede Korkut is known, in his religious or shamanic role, as protector of epic singers and inventor of the *kopuz*. People also came to see him as a popular saint who could be called on for assistance. Synthesizing attributes of a shaman and Muslim saint, the figure of Dede Korkut achieved near cult status in Central Asia, where tales about him abound. His legendary tomb is situated on the banks of the Syr Darya river in Kazakhstan.

princess, who makes him promise that he will return and marry her. Returning home in the disguise of a minstrel, he is recognized by Lady Chichek and prevents the wedding from taking place. However, he cannot marry his betrothed, for he must return to the enemy kingdom, free his captive warriors, and honor his promise to marry the infidel princess. All this he does. The story ends with a huge wedding feast where Dede Korkut sings a tale of the heroes of this adventure.

In "How Prince Uruz, Son of Prince Kazan, Was Taken Prisoner," Salur Kazan laments to his son Uruz that "You have not drawn bow, shot arrow, cut off head, [or] spilled blood" (*The Book of Dede Korkut*, p. 89). Uruz retorts, "When have you ever taken me to the infidel frontier, brandished your sword and cut off heads? What have I seen you do? What am I supposed to learn?" (*The Book of Dede Korkut*, p. 90). Salur Kazan agrees and takes his son off on an educational hunting trip. On the trip they are attacked by a huge infidel army and become separated. Uruz fights bravely but is taken captive. Angrily thinking that his son had run off to his mother, Salur Kazan returns home to Lady Burla, who furiously demands to know what happened to her son. Trying to avoid the wrath of his wife, Salur Kazan tells her that the boy is out hunting. He then goes to raise an army to rescue him. Realizing her husband is lying, Lady Burla and her 40 maidens ride out to help free Uruz by joining

Salur Kazan in the battle. Lady Burla strikes down the enemy standard and Salur Kazan's army defeats 15,000 infidels in a huge battle. Uruz is freed; husband, wife, and son embrace; and the Oghuz go home with their plunder. After they return, Salur Kazan holds a huge feast where Dede Korkut sings a tale of these heroes.

"Wild Dumrul, Son of Dukha Koja" diverges from the typical plot to center on a religious mother. The tale features a man named Wild Dumrul, who will fight anybody. When a warrior falls ill and dies, the man, Wild Dumrul, asks who the murderer was—Azrael (the angel of death in Islamic belief), he learns. Not realizing that his adversary is Death, Wild Dumrul naively asks, "And who is this person you call Azrael, who takes men's lives? Almighty God, I conjure you by Your Unity and Your Being to show me Azrael, that I may fight and struggle and wrestle with him and save that fine warrior's life" (*The Book of Dede Korkut*, p. 108). God is not pleased and sends Azrael to take Wild Dumrul's soul. Wild Dumrul begins to fight, but then realizes Azrael's power. Claiming that he was drunk and knew not what he was saying, he begs Azrael not to take his soul. Azrael tells him to ask God, since it is God who takes souls, and he is only God's servant. Wild Dumrul retorts, "Then what good are you, you pest? Get out of the way and let me talk to God Most High" (*The Book of Dede Korkut*,

p. 111). Thereafter, Wild Dumrul asks God to take his soul directly, without involving Azrael. God is pleased, and tells Wild Dumrul that he can live if he can find someone to die in his place. Wild Dumrul first asks his father, who refuses and tells him to ask his mother. His mother also refuses. Giving up, Wild Dumrul finds his wife, bequeaths her all the property, and tells her that if she loves anybody, she should marry him. She refuses the offer and asks to give her life as sacrifice in place of his. Wild Dumrul asks God to either take both him and his wife together or to leave them both alive. God then orders Azrael to take the lives of Wild Dumrul's parents, and Wild Dumrul and his wife live another 140 years. Thus, Wild Dumrul's parents are punished for not being willing to sacrifice themselves for their son, while he and his wife are rewarded for their devotion to each other.

"Kan Turali Son of Kanli Koja" is the most romantic story of the collection. Kanli Koja wants to marry off his son, but his son has very high standards for a wife:

> Before I rise to my feet she must rise; before I mount my well-trained horse she must be on horseback; before I reach the bloody infidels' land she must already have got there and brought back a few heads.
>
> (The Book of Dede Korkut, p. 117)

After much searching, a suitable girl is found, the daughter of the infidel king of Trebizond. Kan Turali rides off to the infidel Byzantine castle, where he has to defeat a lion, a bull, and a savage black camel to win the hand of Princess Saljan. Refusing to go to the bridal tent before he has received his parent's blessing, Kan Turali heads for the land of the Oghuz with his betrothed. The infidel king regrets giving away his daughter and sends an army to attack the betrothed couple while Kan Turali is sleeping. Caught off guard, Kan Turali fares badly in the fight and Princess Saljan saves him, which leaves him furious that he has been shown up by a woman. He threatens to kill her, whereupon she promises not to boast about saving him, but still he is furious. Annoyed, she proposes they settle the matter with their bows. She shoots first and fails to kill him only because she does not remove the tip from her arrow. Realizing that they really love each other and do not want to kill each other, they embrace and reconcile. Returning to the land of the Oghuz, they hold a grand wedding feast where Dede Korkut sings a tale of these heroes.

"Yigenek Son of Kazilik Koja" returns to the subject of capture and rescue. One day when Bayindir Khan has a feast, Kazilik Koja drinks some wine and decides to raid an infidel castle, leaving a baby son, named Yigenek, at home. Kazilik Koja is captured and imprisoned by the infidel King Direk, who wields a half-ton mace, a war club with a spiked metal head. When he is 15, Yigenek sallies forth with an army of Oghuz nobles to rescue his father, but all are defeated by the half-ton mace. Yigenek prays to God, and then is able to withstand the mace and kill King Direk. When Kazilik Koja asks who freed him, Yigenek reveals himself as his son and they joyously embrace. The Oghuz plunder the king's castle and return home to have a great feast where Dede Korkut sings a tale of the heroes of this adventure.

The next story, "How Basat Killed Tepegöz," is a variation on a familiar theme of the world's epics. The first part of the tale concerns a baby who is lost and raised by a lioness. When the child is found, he is returned to his father, Uruz Koja (not to be confused with Salur Kazan's son Uruz), but the boy attacks horses and sucks their blood. Dede Korkut explains to the boy that he needs to act like a human and gives him the name Basat (means "attack-horse"). Sometime later, a shepherd traveling with flocks of sheep happens upon a peri (a flying supernatural being) and rapes her. A year later she comes back and leaves a baby with only one eye on the top of its head, a Cyclops. Calling it Tepegöz ("eye on top"), Uruz Koja brings the child home, but the baby Cyclops bites the noses and ears off his playmates and is driven out of the house. Because Tepegöz, the Cyclops, starts attacking and eating many people, Dede Korkut strikes a deal to provide Tepegöz with two men and 500 sheep daily. Returning from a military campaign, Basat learns of the monstrous behavior of his "brother" and goes to his cave to fight him. Basat blinds Tepegöz with a spit and tricks him, finally beheading him. The Oghuz rejoice and have a great feast where Dede Korkut sings a tale of this hero.

In "Emren Son of Begil," the warrior Begil falls off his horse and breaks his leg, but in his embarrassment tells no one. Finally, his wife hears him groaning in his sleep and begs him to let her know what the matter is. He tells her, and she tells her slave-girl, who tells the gate keeper, and thus, "what came out past thirty-two teeth [is] broadcast to the whole encampment" (The Book of Dede Korkut, p. 155). Soon the evil King Shökli finds out and orders his army to attack and plunder Begil's lands. Getting wind of the plan, Begil tells his son, Emren. Emren dons his father's huge suit of armor, jumps on his father's horse, and sallies forth to defeat the invaders. The infidels recognize Begil's horse and Begil's armor, but see that the person in the armor is much smaller than Begil. Realizing that it is a boy, the infidel warriors taunt him, but he bravely taunts them back. Emren falls into hand-to-hand combat with King Shökli, who is much stronger than he, so the boy calls on God to help him. God orders Gabriel to give Emren the strength of 40 men and he defeats King Shökli. "Mercy, warrior! What do you call your religion? I accept it," says Shökli, who converts to Islam (*The Book of Dede Korkut*, p. 160). After witnessing this, the infidel army flees, and Emren and his father return home to a sumptuous feast where Dede Korkut sings a tale of this hero.

"Segrek Son of Ushun Koja" is another capture-and-rescue story. Caught during a raid, Egrek, the older son of Ushun Koja, is thrown into a dungeon. His younger brother, Segrek, finds out that Egrek is captive, then vows to go and save him. Wanting to keep Segrek home, his parents get him a lovely bride, but he refuses to enter the bridal tent without having freed his brother. Finally his parents give Segrek their blessing, and he rides off to rescue his brother. On the way, he falls asleep in a park that belongs to the enemy king. The king sends 60 men after him and he drives them off, after which he is again overcome by sleep. The king sends 100 men after him and he drives them off, after which he again falls asleep. The infidel king summons the captive Egrek and tells him that if he kills this crazy warrior, he will win his freedom. Seeing the young man asleep, Egrek recognizes that he is an Oghuz and asks him to identify his clan and his parents. Segrek reveals his name, and they realize they are brothers and embrace. Together they defeat the enemy soldiers and then round up all of the horses and drive them home. Their parents rejoice, and Dede Korkut sings a tale of these heroes at their double wedding.

"How Salur Kazan Was Taken Prisoner and How His Son Uruz Freed Him" describes how Salur Kazan is tricked by a falcon sent to him by the Byzantine king of Trebizond. The falcon flies away and leads Salur Kazan to the land of the enemy, where he is captured and thrown into a pit. His son Uruz grows up and, upon discovering that his father is a captive, sets off with an army of Oghuz nobles to free him. On their way, they capture a citadel. The infidel king decides to give Kazan an army and sends him to kill the invaders. Not recognizing him, Uruz charges his father, Kazan, and wounds him in the shoulder, at which point Kazan declaims:

> Summit of my black mountain, my son!
> Light of my dark eyes, My son!
> My hero Uruz, my lion Uruz, Spare your white-bearded father, son!
>
> (*The Book of Dede Korkut*, p. 180)

Uruz recognizes him, and kisses his father's hand. Together with the nobles they rout the infidel army and return home to a sumptuous feast where Dede Korkut sings a tale of these heroes.

"How the Outer Oghuz Rebelled Against the Inner Oghuz and How Beyrek Died" describes a breakdown of relations within the Oghuz. Once every three years Kazan lets both branches of the Oghuz nobles pillage his tent and take anything they wish. One year, he lets the Inner Oghuz pillage his tent before the Outer Oghuz arrive. The Outer Oghuz nobles are outraged at being slighted, and they swear enmity to Prince Kazan. Uruz Koja (the Bey of the Outer Oghuz) invites Bamsi Beyrek, his son-in-law, to join the rebels in an effort to test his loyalty. Beyrek refuses to rebel against Kazan, and Uruz kills him. Kazan and the Inner Oghuz come to the Outer Oghuz to avenge Beyrek's death. In the ensuing fight, Kazan kills Uruz Koja. The Outer Oguz nobles beg Kazan's forgiveness, which he grants, and Uruz Koja's house and lands are pillaged, after which there is a feast where Dede Korkut sings a tale of the heroes.

The final chapter, "The Wisdom of Dede Korkut," does not fit thematically or culturally with the rest of the stories. Probably it was added by the Turcomen White Sheep and Ottoman authors. The chapter lists sayings attributed to Dede Korkut, including a prophecy that the Ottoman Empire will rule until the resurrection. Most of the sayings are proverbs, such as "unless one calls on God, no work prospers; unless God grants, no man grows rich" (*The Book of Dede Korkut*, p. 190). Ending the section is a satirical description of "the four types of wife"— the pillar, the withering scourge, the ever-rolling ball, and the one who does not listen— figures that have no relation to the heroic females portrayed in the epic (*The Book of Dede Korkut*, p. 191).

Cultural values in *The Book of Dede Korkut*.
The Book of Dede Korkut promotes such healthy ideals as loyalty and self-sacrifice, respect and love between family members, and bravery and heroism. Considerable space in the individual narratives is actually devoted to the transgression of these values, particularly the pitting of father against son, husband against wife, brother against brother, and even a bloody civil war in

which the hero, Bamsi Beyrek, is murdered by his own father-in-law. What is remarkable about the epic is the stability, confidence, and adaptability of the social order it describes. The Oghuz heroes are able to express and resolve transgressions of highly cherished values such as family loyalty and to preserve the whole.

Many of the conflicts involve families and their children. Sometimes fathers do not fulfill their duties to safeguard their families but make poor decisions that lead to the families' capture (as in "How Salur Kazan's House Was Pillaged"); other times, fathers make poor decisions and themselves are captured (as in "Yigenek Son of Kazilik Koja"). In most of the stories the self-sacrificing heroism of a husband, wife, son, mother, or brother leads to the happy reunion of the members of the family and the festive reintegration of the family into society. Some of the stories relate very serious betrayals, such as when Dirse Khan shoots his son in the back and leaves him for dead ("Boghach Khan Son of Dirse Khan"). However, the conflicts are all successfully resolved. Voluntary self-control, seen as the overcoming of such harmful passions as rage or vengeance against a member of one's family (Boghach Khan and his mother must overcome any feelings of anger against Dirse Khan), helps the Oghuz overcome their familial conflicts. So does conscious re-channeling of aggression (such as when Lady Burla transforms her anger against her husband—for losing track of their son—to anger used productively to help free her son in "How Prince Uruz Son of Prince Kazan Was Taken Prisoner"). Strong and enduring bonds of love between family members help them to understand and forgive, and family harmony is seen as the greatest happiness. In similar fashion, bonds of loyalty and affection in larger society overcome anger, as when the Inner and Outer Oghuz are able to reunite without damage to the social structure, even after many on both sides have been killed.

As a cultural narrative, Dede Korkut can be seen as a set of directions for behavior, showcasing challenging situations that place stress on family and social relations but give examples of ways to repair them. There is an underlying assumption that all people, even Oghuz nobles, make mistakes, but mistakes are forgivable if everyone shares a common belief in the importance of family and social bonds. It is perhaps the very use of oral narrative as a way to continuously tell this society about itself—integrating the past and the present, and resolving contradictions in the varieties of experience encountered—that kept the integrity of Oghuz culture whole even as it moved through time and space. Unsurprisingly the narratives changed as they were retold, but importantly the newer and older elements (such as Islamic and pre-Islamic beliefs) are blended rather than set against each other, showing a strong tendency to synthesize differences, adapt to new situations, and resolve conflicts. It may be this ability to adapt and forgive, rather than the perceived warrior ethic of riding into battle, "cutting off heads, and spilling blood," that is the real heritage of The Book of Dede Korkut (The Book of Dede Korkut, p. 161).

The women of Dede Korkut. Although the Turkish intellectual Ziya Gökalp wrote optimistically that "the ancient Turkish women were all amazons," the image of the woman in Dede Korkut is more complicated (Gökalp, p. 8). In the epic, the female figures are highly individual, perhaps even more so than the men, but they are not all "amazons." While it is true that Princess Saljan bravely cuts down enemy soldiers to save her husband (in "Kan Turali Son of Kanli Koja"), it is Begil's wife in "Emren Son of Begil" who foolishly leaks the information that her husband's leg is broken, prompting an attack by an enemy king. More often, though, women show extreme loyalty to and a willingness to sacrifice for their husbands, such as Wild Dumrul's wife, who offers to die in his place. Additionally, it is important to note that although wives are loyal to their husbands they are not dominated by them. The women in The Book of Dede Korkut freely confront their husbands, as Lady Burla does when Salur Kazan returns without Uruz. In no case is a woman ever punished for speaking her mind or chastising her husband. Although no historical documents describing the position of women in this society have been found, the similar treatment of women in other Turkic epics and tales, as well as the high status of women in traditionally pastoral nomadic societies of today's Central Asia, testify to the legitimacy of the descriptions in The Book of Dede Korkut.

Often giving good advice or getting their husbands out of trouble, women are clearly respected in Dede Korkut. The majority of the women depicted are wiser than their husbands and have an equal capacity for heroic and self-sacrificing behavior, although they do not act in all the same spheres. Women, for example, do not go hunting with the men, nor do they go on raids to pillage the infidel, or take part in the men's wine-drinking parties, which inevitably lead to disaster. But, as far as we know, they are free to drink wine at the feasts that follow the heroic acts. Also it seems that, like Lady Chichek, they can hold their own in shooting, racing, and wrestling. It is doubtful that all Oghuz women were such able sportsmen, but given the Oghuz way of life, they probably needed to be able to ride and to defend themselves against enemy raiders.

Sources and literary context. *The Book of Dede Korkut* is only one example of a vast oral tradition still alive in Turkic regions of China, Central Asia, Siberia, Northern Iran, Northern Iraq, Turkey, and Azerbaijan. Oral literature of many varieties continues to be performed throughout the Turkic world. Huge epic cycles such as the Kyrgyz *Manas* (with over a million verses), as well as romantic minstrel tales sung in Anatolia, are only two examples of this living tradition. Like *Dede Korkut,* many of these narratives are comprised of mixed prose and verse forms, and employ the same themes, legends, and characters. Other adventures of characters from the epic—including Bamsi Beyrek, Salur Kazan, and Dede Korkut—appear in songs, folktales, and legends of several Turkish-speaking peoples of Central Asia and the Middle East. Moreover, this set of Oghuz stories (*Oghuzname*) was apparently not the only one of its kind. A fourteenth-century historian refers to another such work, indicating that there were more written collections of Oghuz legends at the time. However, *The Book of Dede Korkut* is the only one that has survived into the present.

The Book of Dede Korkut also fits into the broader epic tradition, which includes heroic tales from all over the world, such as the Anglo-Saxon *Beowulf,* the Indian *Ramayana,* and the Finnish *Kalevala.* Heroic epics share many qualities: they all refer to a legendary past age; they all recount feats of strength and daring in battle; and they all champion moral goodness and self-sacrifice. Many epics share common themes, such as the fight against a monster. Scholars have been especially intrigued by the close relation of the story of Tepegöz to the story of Odysseus and the Cyclops in Homer's *Odyssey.* Some scholars argue that the Homeric story somehow found its way into the Turkic version; others argue that Homer took the story from an earlier tradition circulating in Asia Minor.

Impact of the epic. Although *The Book of Dede Korkut* was discovered in Germany in 1815, it was lost to the Turks until 1916, when the first edition of it was published in Istanbul. Its timing could not have been better. Dropped into a vigorous intellectual climate surrounding the demise of the Ottoman empire and the birth of the Turkish Republic, *The Book of Dede Korkut* had an enormous impact. In 1920, sociologist Ziya Gökalp published *The Principles of Turkism,* a small volume which was vital in shaping and defining a new concept of Turkish nationalism as it was being formulated by the emerging Republic. Seeking to overcome the devaluation of Turkish culture during the Ottoman era, Gökalp urged intellectuals to read *The Book of Dede Korkut,* the "Iliad of the Oghuz," as a source for pure Turkish language, culture, and values (Gökalp, p. 90). Citing especially their show of Turkic strength, optimism, and family ties, and their active, unveiled women, Gökalp held up the Oghuz as models for modern Turks. His emphasis on the oral narratives of the Turks (such as *The Book of Dede Korkut*) stressed the importance of their pre-Islamic heritage in Central Asia over that of the acquired Islamic culture of the Persian and Arab peoples.

Since the early twentieth century, *The Book of Dede Korkut* has been reprinted in Turkey in many scholarly and popular editions. Noted twentieth-century writers, such as Yaşar Kemal and Latife Tekin, have incorporated themes and motifs from *The Book of Dede Korkut* into their novels (see Kemal's **Memed, My Hawk**, also in WLAIT 6: *Middle Eastern Literatures and Their Times*). A recent essay ("Women Who Save Their Husbands From Difficult Situations in *The Book of Dede Korkut*") in a Turkish women's-studies journal shows the enduring interest of the epic for Turkish women. Folklorists in Turkey and abroad are still debating and discussing aspects of the epic. In Soviet and post-Soviet Azerbaijan, many scholars have used studies of it to rediscover and discuss Azeri culture. More than five centuries after it was written down, in the year 2000, the Director General of UNESCO declared *The Book of Dede Korkut* a protected Masterpiece of the Intangible Heritage of Humanity (a reference to oral lore), confirming the work's importance to both Turkey and the world.

—Anna Oldfield Şenarslan

For More Information

Başgöz, Ilhan. "The Epic Tradition among Turkic Peoples." In *Heroic Epic and Saga.* Ed. F. Oinas. Bloomington: Indiana University Press,

1978.

The Book of Dede Korkut. Trans. Geoffrey Lewis. Middlesex, U.K.: Penguin, 1974.

Chadwick, Nora, and Victor Zhirmunsky. *Oral Epics of Central Asia.* Cambridge: Cambridge University Press, 1969.

Gökalp, Ziya. *The Principles of Turkism.* Trans. Robert Devereux. Leiden, Netherlands: E. J. Brill, 1968.

Güneli, Gün. "World Literature in Review: Turkey." *World Literature Today* 57, no. 4 (autumn 1993): 886-87.

Güngör, Seyma. "Women Who Save Their Husbands From Difficult Situations in *The Book of Dede Korkut.*" *Kadin Araştirmalari-Dergisi/Journal For Woman Studies* 2, no. 2 (2000): 25-47.

Hasluck, Frederick William, *Christianity and Islam under the Sultans.* Oxford, U.K.: Clarendon Press, 1929.

Hickman, William. "Traditional Themes in the Work of Yaşar Kemal: *Ince Memed.*" *Edebiyat* 5, no. 1: 55-68.

Lewis, Geoffery. "Heroines and Others in the Heroic Age of the Turks." *Women in the Medieval Islamic World.* Ed. Gavin Hambly. New York: St. Martin's Press, 1998.

Matsuura, Koichiro. "Speech to the United Nations Educational, Scientific and Cultural Organization (UNESCO)." *Special Collections Library, Texas Tech University, Lubbock.* 5 May 2000. http://aton. ttu.edu/unesco_dede_korkut.asp (30 May 2002).

Sümer, Faruk, Ahmet Uysal, and Warren Walker.

The Book of Tahkemoni
(Hebrew Maqamat)

by

Judah al-Harizi

For more than 700 years Islamic dynasties ruled over a swath of the Iberian Peninsula designated as al-Andalus, which, though dominated by Muslims, was also peopled by minority groups. Christian Spain meanwhile engaged in a gradual conquest of al-Andalus (commonly called the Reconquest), during which the centers of Jewish life moved from areas under Islamic domination to areas under Christian control. Even after the Arabic-inspired Golden Age of Hebrew poetry in al-Andalus (c. 960-1147), Arabic currents continued to be felt in the Hebrew literature written in Christian Spain. Hebrew fictional narratives were grounded in the Arabic *maqamah*, an anecdotal short story in rhymed prose. Most famous among the collection of Hebrew *maqamat* is the *Book of Tahkemoni* by Judah al-Harizi (1166?-1225), an author who composed works in Hebrew and Arabic and ultimately left Christian Spain to settle in the Islamic lands to the east. Born in Toledo, Spain, al-Harizi grew into an accomplished writer. He created his *maqamat* in the tradition of the Arabic masters Badi` al-Zaman al-Hamadhani (967-1007) and al-Hariri (d. 1122). Writing in Hebrew, al-Harizi spun 50 short pieces, many of them stories centering on the encounters of a narrator and a protagonist rogue. He had begun his career as a translator of Arabic and Judeo-Arabic legal, philosophical, and belletristic works into Hebrew. He composed a fluid translation into Hebrew of *Dalalat al-ha'irin (The Guide for the Perplexed)*, which had been written in Judeo-Arabic by the Jewish philosopher Maimonides (1135-1204). Commissioned by the notables of Provence

---

THE LITERARY WORK

Three of 50 tales set in Middle Eastern cities, primarily during the early thirteenth century; completed between 1216 and 1225; published in Hebrew (as *Sefer Tahkemoni*) in 1952, in English from 1965 to 1973.

SYNOPSIS

A rogue swindles an unsuspecting country bumpkin in the "Maqamah of Rehovot," upbraids Iraqi Jewish aristocrats in the "Maqamah of Babylonia," and is the object of a mob's scorn in the "Maqamah of the Astrologer."

---

to write the translation in simple and clear language, al-Harizi complied. He also composed an artful Hebrew translation of al-Hariri's Arabic *Maqamat*, probably a response, as he claims, to a challenge that their perfection could not be imitated. For reasons that are not altogether clear, al-Harizi left Spain to wander the Islamic East, ultimately settling in Aleppo, Syria, where he died. He produced an account of his Eastern journeys in Arabic rhymed prose and spent his final years composing Arabic poetry in honor of Muslim patrons. It was during his travels in the East that he composed the *Tahkemoni*. Although not the first of the Hebrew *maqamat*, it became the rhetorical model to which all subsequent narratives would have to conform.

Events in History at the Time of the Tales

The Jews in Christian Spain. Throughout the medieval period, the Iberian Peninsula stood at the crossroads between the Islamic and Christian worlds, between the Middle East and Europe. Toledo was a premier city of al-Andalus, or Islamic Spain, from the time of the Islamic conquest of 711 until 1085 when the city fell to Christian forces. Significantly the establishment of Christian hegemony did not entail the immediate dissolution of Arabic intellectual and literary culture in the city. Arabic literature retained its prestige, and great works of Arabic philosophy, mathematics, and medicine were translated into Latin for Christians (sometimes through a collaborative effort of Jews and Christians).

Although scholars of medieval history generally view Jewish life under Islam as better than under Christendom, Christian Toledo remained a leading Jewish intellectual center after the Christian takeover. In the twelfth century, the city served as a surrogate soil for the regeneration of the Jewish courtier class of al-Andalus once Jewish life there became untenable because a new set of intolerant rulers, the Almohads, established hegemony (1146-47). After centuries of Jewish culture flourishing under Islamic aegis in al-Andalus, the Almohad invasion forced many Jews to convert to Islam or flee to Christian Spain, to other parts of Europe, or to the Islamic East.

Wherever they settled, these Jews and their descendants maintained the intellectual traditions of al-Andalus and often viewed their contemporaries as culturally inferior. The issue of the regeneration of Andalusian Jewish culture is at the heart of al-Harizi's *Tahkemoni*.

The Jews in the Islamic East. Before al-Andalus became a significant intellectual center, the intellectual jewel of the Islamic world (both for Muslims and for Jews) was the Iraqi city of Baghdad. In the pre-Islamic period, ancient Babylonia had been home to two great Jewish learning academies (*yeshivot*) in Sura and Pumbeditha, both in modern-day Iraq. About a century after the Abbasid dynasty moved the capital to the new city of Baghdad (in 751), these two yeshivot relocated there. In the mid-tenth century, the Abbasid empire began to crumble, yielding to local dynasties (in Persia, Egypt, Syria, Morocco, Tunisia, and Spain), yet Baghdad remained an important intellectual center for Jews as well as Muslims.

Although Jewish culture in the Islamic East during the eleventh to thirteenth centuries did not compare in general brilliance with that of al-Andalus, the East was home to a successful and stable Jewish community. Throughout the Islamic world, Jews retained a status that was relatively secure, if second-class, thanks to protections inherent in *The Quran* and Islamic doctrine (also in *WLAIT 6: Middle Eastern Literatures and Their Times*). After the Almohad conquest of al-Andalus, numerous Jewish (and Muslim) intellectuals chose the East for resettlement, likely in search of linguistic and cultural continuity. For example, Abraham ibn Ezra's son Isaac went to Baghdad (though his father went to Europe) to study with the philosophical teacher Abu al-Barakat. Both teacher and student participated in Baghdad's interconfessional intellectual culture and, for reasons of conviction, ultimately converted to Islam. Although Jews were tolerated in the Islamic East, religious difference remained significant; the masses of Muslims, if not the elite, viewed Jews with suspicion as a potential subversive element, a people whose beliefs stood at odds with the Islamic worldview.

In al-Harizi's day Iraq continued to decline while Syria and Palestine were contested territories, both among competing Muslim dynasties and between Muslims and Christians. Earlier, in 1099, Latin kingdoms were established from the Sinai Peninsula to Syria, and Jerusalem was captured by the Christian Crusaders after a five-week siege. In the mid-twelfth century, the Islamic Ayyubid dynasty arose in Egypt under the leadership of Salah al-Din ibn Ayyub (known in the West as Saladin [1138-93]), who supplanted the Fatimid dynasty in 1171. Saladin extended his power from Egypt to Syria, fighting numerous wars against competing Muslim dynasties and wresting Jerusalem from the Crusaders in 1187.

Several generations of Ayyubid rulers fostered an environment of economic prosperity and intellectual openness. Trade was established with distant (including European) kingdoms, schools (called *madrasahs*) were founded to educate the masses, and poets found ample patronage at the royal court. Numbering among them, al-Harizi dedicated Arabic panegyric poetry to the Ayyubid ruler al-Malik al-Ashraf ibn Abu Bakr Ayyub (d. 1237). All the while, Ayyubid territories continued to be threatened by Christian advances. Al-Harizi was undoubtedly aware of the skirmishes that ensued. He was probably less aware that he was living during the final years of Ayyubid reign; Aleppo (and Damascus) would fall to the Mongols only five years after al-Harizi's death.

ELEGY FOR JEWISH ANDALUS

The fall of Jewish centers in cities such as Lucena, Seville, and Cordoba is commemorated in a moving lament by Abraham ibn Ezra (1089-1164):

> Woe for calamity has descended upon Spain from the heavens!
> My eyes, my eyes flow with water.
>
> . . . .
>
> Without guilt, the Exile dwelled there untroubled,
> Undisturbed for one thousand and seventy years.
>
> . . . .
>
> I shave my head and cry bitterly over the exile from Seville,
> Over noble ones, now fallen ones, their sons in captivity,
> Over refined girls gone over to the strange faith.
> How the city of Cordoba was abandoned
>
> . . . .
>
> (Levin, pp. 101-03; trans. J. Decter)

The Tales in Focus

Plot overview. The *Tahkemoni* is the collection of Hebrew *maqamat* most faithful to the classical Arabic *maqamat*. Suggesting might and wisdom, the collection's title derives from the tribe to which a warrior of the biblical King David belonged (II Samuel 23:8); the root (*hkm*) signifies "wisdom." The collection conforms to the *maqamah* form—a loose rhymed prose with rhymed, metered poems interspersed. As in the classical *maqamat,* each of the 50 episodes involves an encounter between a narrator (named Heman the Ezrahite) and a rogue protagonist (named Hever the Qenite). The episodes often incorporate fine rhetoric, the ruse motif, and a conclusion in which the narrator recognizes the protagonist through a disguise. As in the Arabic *maqamat,* the narrator is traveling in search of learning, culture, and rhetorical excellence. The protagonist is a mercurial master of eloquence. A sort of anti-hero, his disregard for social convention makes him entertaining. He is a master of disguise and chicanery who earns a living through petty scams, duping unsuspecting citizens with his eloquent tongue as he secretly flouts social mores.

In the introduction to the *Tahkemoni*, al-Harizi relates a near-prophetic experience in which his intellect charges him to fight zealously on behalf of the Hebrew language:

> Open the eyes of your thought, marshal the troops of your intellect and the warriors of your tongue . . . for the Holy Tongue, the language of prophecy that has *declined appallingly.*
> (al-Harizi, *Sefer Tahkemoni*, p. 8; trans. J. Decter)

Once the author pursues this vocation, the Hebrew Tongue itself appears to him in the form of a lovely maiden who further petitions al-Harizi to restore her lost luster. Al-Harizi states explicitly that he wrote the book to restore the status of the Hebrew language, which had been eclipsed ever since the appearance of al-Hariri's Arabic *maqamat.*

> Now I will tell you what moved me to compose this book: A certain Arab sage, the pride of his age, master of incision, who turned rivals to a mockery and derision, whose mouth was an open vision, one known as al-Hariri, who left all rivals panting and weary, composed a stunning work in Arabic, rhymed prose wed with metric stich. . . . Hence I wrote this book to raise Hebrew's holy tower, to show our holy folk her suppleness and power.
> (al-Harizi, *Book of Tahkemoni*, p. 14)

As the collection progresses, al-Harizi undertakes many literary feats, such as the inclusion of an epistle that read forward is panegyric but read backward is invective (Maqamah 8), or a trilingual poem (Hebrew, Aramaic, and Arabic) in a single rhyme and meter (Maqamah 11), or the *maqamah* that has two speeches structured such that every word in the first speech includes the Hebrew letter *resh* but every word in the second omits the same letter (Maqamah 11). In didactic episodes, the learned protagonist imparts practical information, such as the rules for the composition of poetry (Maqamah 18), and serves as a mouthpiece for the author's diatribes, such as a diatribe against the Karaites (a non-Rabbinic Jewish sect, Maqamah 17). At other times, particularly in episodes of deceit, the protagonist's speech is meant to mislead; a dissembling swindler out to make a profit, he cannot be trusted.

The narrator, who reveals his native land to be Spain, is Heman the Ezrahite, a name that appears in the Bible as the author of Psalm 88. There is also a wise Heman in the Bible to whom King Solomon is compared (1 Kings 5:11) and another Heman called "Heman the poet" (1 Chronicles 6:18). The protagonist, Hever the Qenite from Alon Tza'ananim, has the name of a character from the biblical text Judges 4. The place Tza'ananim derives from a root signifying "wandering," which befits the protagonist's itinerant spirit.

"Maqamah of the Astrologer." At the beginning of the *maqamah*, Heman the Ezrahite encounters an undisguised Hever the Qenite. Hever relates a story in which he and a band of Hebrew youths come to the gate of an unnamed city. A throng of people has gathered there around an Arab astrologer, a master interpreter of the stars, planets, and constellations and their influence on individuals' lives. The astrologer predicts the future with the aid of an astrolabe (used for studying the movement of heavenly bodies).

Doubting the efficacy of the astrologer's predictions, Hever and his friends conspire to test him, saying "Let us see what will become of his dreams!"—words that echo those of Joseph's brothers (Genesis 37:20) just before casting Joseph into the pit (*Sefer Tahkemoni*, p. 216; trans. J. Decter). Like Joseph's dreams, the astrologer's predictions turn out to be true. The youths challenge the astrologer to guess a certain question that they are keeping hidden in their minds. Their question is perhaps the most enduring question of the Jewish people in exile, concerning when the Messiah will come to inaugurate an age of Jewish autonomy: "When shall Salvation come to the sons of our scattered nation?" (*Book of Tahkemoni*, pp. 207-08).

Without so much as a hint, the astrologer makes calculations in the sand, tinkers with his astrolabe, and finally declares,

I swear, he said, by Him who fashioned the earth and air, moon and sun, the planets every one, who set the Zodiac turning and the whirling constellations burning, yes, who put

each star in place: you be not of us nor do you the Nazarene embrace; no—you are of the accursed Jewish race. . . . You ask if a scattered folk, laughed to scorn, can be ingathered in a world reborn? You seek the dead's rejuvenation and the nation's devastation; by God and His revelation, you ask Earth's ruination! Sons of death, you would see our kingdom destroyed; you would hurl us to the void!
(*Book of Tahkemoni*, pp. 208-09)

Assuming that Jewish salvation would entail Islamic downfall, the angry mob seizes and beats the youths, then drags them bloodied through the streets to stand before the city's magistrate. Rather than punishing them, the magistrate, who himself is a "righteous man among the gentiles," offers them asylum, promises their security, and lets them spend the night in the protection of a cell (*Book of Tahkemoni*, p. 209).

The youths' initial disbelief in the astrologer's ability reflects a broad debate in medieval Islamic and Jewish society concerning the efficacy of astrology, which was accepted by some as a hard science, condemned by others as superstition and idolatry. Another dimension of medieval reality the story conveys is that the Jewish minority risked maltreatment at the hands of the Muslim populace for even thinking of subversion in medieval Islamic society. At the same time, as suggested in the tale, the guarantee of protection by Muslim authorities remained a stabilizing force for Jews.

"Maqamah of Babylonia." Another of the *Tahkemoni's maqamat* is known for its literary history of the Hebrew poets of al-Andalus. While traveling in Iraq, Heman the Ezrahite is invited to a feast where aristocrats consume wine and delicacies.

Around that courtyard sprang golden towers myriad as flowers, housing frescoed chambers rich with streams. . . . And the banquet—a dream, a fable: table upon groaning table whose wealth I would describe if I were able. And round about—rugs plush and spacious, lush and capacious.
(*Book of Tahkemoni*, p. 39)

Glad to stumble upon such abundance, Heman rejoices and recites a Hebrew wine poem in the traditional Arabic style. Among the well-mannered guests is a gluttonous old man in tattered clothes, whose eating habits shock the other guests.

He honoured the cup like his father and mother, smothered it with kisses like a long-lost brother. Slavering, slurping, belching, burping, he careened like a mad sloop through salads, vegetables and soup. On, on he raced: before him lay like Eden; after him a waste.

(*Book of Tahkemoni*, p. 41)

While the other guests discuss the history of Hebrew poetry in al-Andalus, the glutton inhales every morsel in sight as he glares at the aristocrats with a disapproving eye. Finally he speaks up, upbraiding the aristocrats for scorning his appearance and dismissing their conversation as uncultured banter. He rebukes them for their ignorance in matters of poetry: "As for the poets you have mentioned, I was there when they fought their battles; I am come from the battlefield. My heart is a scroll for their themes, I am a book of remembrance for their poems" (*Sefer Tahkemoni*, p. 43; trans. J. Decter). After waxing eloquent about the poetry of the former age, he identifies himself (as Hever the Qenite) and storms out in frustration at these second-rate "connoisseurs" of poetry.

From this *maqamah*, modern scholars have recovered important information about the history of Hebrew poetry including the names of otherwise unknown poets.

"**Maqamah of Rehovot.**" This tale is based entirely on al-Hamadhani's "Maqamah of Baghdad" (see **Maqamat**, also in *WLAIT 6: Middle Eastern Literatures and Their Times*). In both stories, the main character swindles an unsuspecting country bumpkin by inviting him to a meal at a public place, consuming succulent meats and other viands, then sneaking off and leaving the rustic to settle the bill. In the parent text, the narrator rather than the rogue plays the trickster, an unusual turn of events for a *maqamah*. But the Hebrew *maqamah* normalizes the structure by making Hever the Qenite the trickster.

Apart from the difference in the frame narrative, the plot of the "Maqamah of Rehovot" is virtually identical to that of the "Maqamah of Baghdad." Heman the Ezrahite encounters Hever the Qenite, who is laughing with self-congratulation after having pulled off his latest scam. While cruising the marketplace in a state of hunger and penury, Hever encountered a country "Arab," whom he duped into becoming an unsuspecting victim. As in Arabic, "Arab" is used to signify his rustic, non-cosmopolitan background more than his ethnicity. Feigning friendliness, Hever pretends the rustic is a long-lost friend and calls him by an invented name, which he continues to use despite the bumpkin's protestations that the name is wrong. At the inn, Hever orders a sumptuous feast for himself and the rustic, who thinks that he is dining at Hever's gracious expense. After gorging himself, Hever takes leave of the rustic, on the excuse that he will fetch some ice-cold water and return shortly. Of course, the swindler does not return, leaving the moneyless rustic to suffer a beating inflicted by the angry innkeeper. The account of Hever's cunning impresses Heman the Ezrahite.

Al-Harizi translates from one cultural discourse into another, coloring the text with witty biblical references. When acting as if the bumpkin is his long-lost friend, Hever addresses him as "Abidan son of Gideoni" instead of his real name, which Hever could not possibly know since in truth he has never seen this "friend" before. The name strikes a humorous chord through biblical allusion; a generous character, the biblical Abidan, son of Gideoni, brings a bountiful offering to the Tabernacle in Numbers 7:60-65:

> One silver bowl weighing 130 shekels and one silver basin of 70 shekels . . . both filled with choice flowers . . . for a meal offering . . . one goat for a sin offering; and for his sacrifice of well-being: two oxen, five rams, five he-goats, and five yearling lambs. That was the offering of Abidan son of Gideoni.

For the educated Hebrew reader, the name immediately brings to mind this long list of valuable vessels with expensive contents and, most importantly, meat. It is as though Hever walks up to the bumpkin and says, "Hello, sucker!" through an allusion that goes right over the head of his unlettered victim, an Abidan who is about to contribute a great "offering" to the rogue's appetite rather than the Tabernacle. In this way, al-Harizi adds a level of humor that is not present in the Arabic original.

No place like home. The *Tahkemoni* is remarkable for its ironic exploitation of traditional texts, including the Bible, the Talmud, and the traditional prayer book. In Maqamah 24, Hever the Qenite relates that he attended a synagogue of imbeciles where the cantor distorted the traditional liturgy into a blasphemous garble by mispronouncing select words:

> Lo, the cantor entered and took his honoured seat, and in tones dulcet sweet began the daily blessings, as is meet. According to the practice of our nation, he begged God's lumination, thundering, *Make the words of Thy Torah pheasant in our mouth*, rather than *pleasant in our mouth*; and *May the Lord flavour you and grant you peas*, instead of *May the Lord favour you and grant you peace*.

(*Book of Tahkemoni*, pp. 216-17)

A FRUSTRATED ARTIST

If one assumes that the "Maqamah of Babylonia" takes place during the author's lifetime, one must conclude that Hever the Qenite, who plays the part of the glutton-critic, has been alive for more than a century because he claims to have encountered Hebrew poets such as Judah Halevi and Moses ibn Ezra, who were active in the late eleventh and early twelfth centuries. A relic from a bygone age, he is condemned to wander the earth without an equal. His knowledge of that age makes him a conduit of a lost, idyllic culture. The present, in his view, is lacking a refined circle of luminaries as once existed in al-Andalus.

While Heman the Ezrahite is grateful to happen upon a gathering of intellectuals conversant in matters of poetry, reflecting, perhaps, al-Harizi's longing for literary peers, Hever the Qenite's rebuke at the same gathering may reflect the author's frustration at and disdain for the available intellectual culture. Although it is impossible to confirm, al-Harizi may have left Spain for the Islamic East in search of a Hebrew literary scene set within an Arabic-Islamic context similar to that which formerly existed in al-Andalus; his parody of intellectual life in the East is likely an expression of disappointment.

Although the scene is certainly intended to be humorous, its setting in a real city of the Islamic East, Mosul of Iraq, suggests that al-Harizi, the wanderer, may have found Jewish learning to be substandard in the lands of his journey.

Nostalgia for the refined literary culture of Spain is a recurring theme of the *Tahkemoni*. Already in the book's introduction, the author is introduced as one whose "land was the garden of God though he was banished, exiled from its dwellings. . . . His name is Judah son of Solomon and the name of his homeland is Spain" (*Sefer Tahkemoni*, p. 3; trans. J. Decter). In one episode, Hever the Qenite recalls that in former days "Spain was a delight to the eyes, her light was like the sun in heaven, her air was the life of souls, the flowers of her gardens were like the stars in the heavens" (*Sefer Tahkemoni*, p. 345; trans. J. Decter). As already noted, the "Maqamah of Babylonia" also suggests nostalgia for the past.

Literary context. It has been established that al-Harizi's first Hebrew compositions were not original creations but were translations of renowned Arabic texts. In his translation of al-Hariri's *Maqamat*, which he titled *Mahberot Iti'el* (Iti'el's Notebooks, after a wise man in Proverbs 30:1), al-Harizi strives to capture the sense of the original but also to create a new work that is fine literature in its own right. Al-Harizi transforms the *maqamat* into a thoroughly Jewish text. Arabic names are changed to biblical names, cities around the Islamic world are replaced with biblical place names, and ironic uses of biblical allusions abound at every turn. For example, in al-Hariri's twelfth *maqamah*, set in Ghutah (the plain near Damascus), a (drunk) preacher in the guise of a Sufi mendicant teaches a prayer for protection that opens with the first surah of the Quran and includes blessings for the Prophet Muhammad. In al-Harizi's rewriting, the story is set in the "Heights of Naphtali and Asher" in the land of Israel, praise for Muhammad is replaced with praise for Moses, and the Quranic Surah is replaced with Psalm 91, which appropriately is a prayer for protection.

When possible, al-Harizi preserves the literary, sometimes orthographic, conceit around which al-Hariri structures a *maqamah*. For example, al-Hariri builds his seventeenth *maqamah* around an epistle that can be read either forwards or in reverse. Rather than translating the story literally, al-Harizi creates a reversible epistle of his own, thus translating its central conceit rather than its precise meaning.

In retrospect, al-Harizi felt a certain amount of remorse for having translated al-Hariri into Hebrew because *Mahberot Iti'el* was a derivative work that promoted the Arabic author's celebrity as much as it advanced the cause of Hebrew revival. In the introduction to the *Tahkemoni*, al-Harizi writes,

> But after I had translated the treasure of this all-but-prophet to my readers pleasure and profit, I left the west, dared mountain peaks and the wave's curled crest, and eastward came—where I was struck with shame. Forgive me, Lord, I

AL-HARIZI, THE ARABIC POET

Although al-Harizi was an unflagging champion of the Hebrew language, he also remained a dedicated author of Arabic literature. In 1996, Joseph Sadan published a remarkable eight-page section from the Arabic biographical dictionary by Ibn al-Sha`ar al-Mawsili (1197-1256) that shed new light on the life and work of al-Harizi. The section begins:

> Yahya ibn Suleiman ibn Sha'ul Abu Zakariya al-Harizi the Jew from the people of Toledo. He was a poet of great talent and prolific creation who composed poems in the area of panegyric and invective. He composed numerous works in the Hebrew language such as the "Book of *Maqamat*" (i.e. the *Tahkemoni*); (he also composed) a single *maqamah* in the Arabic language that he titled "The Elegant Garden."
>
> (Sadan, p. 52; trans. J. Decter)

From this document, we learn vital information about the author, such as the place and year of his death, and curious facts, such as his uncommon height, his inability to grow a beard, and his *Maghrebi* accent. Importantly the dictionary preserves six Arabic poems by al-Harizi that adhere to the literary tastes of his day. The following example, describing a lover's secret visit to his beloved beneath the gaze of her disapproving family, is based on a verse by the Andalusian poet and prince al-Mu`tamid ibn Abbad (d. 1095):

> A night when I visited the tribe in a garment of gloom,
> When the garments of the horizon were adorned with bright stars,
> I came to her in stealth when her family dozed off
> (around her) like bubbles around a wine cup.
> Surrounding her were cutting swords and lances,
> Heroic lions with their bloodied claws,
> While the mouth of Fate laughed (showing) its teeth,
> Unveiling the cheek of a reddened sword.
> I emerged in golden vestments as the flowers
> Of the stars became entwined with the full moon.
> I picked her flowers in the garden of beauty.
> She is fertile in the behind but barren at the waist.
> I kissed her: thin of body, a long-necked young gazelle,
> Lips blood-red and a mouth (white) with saliva.
>
> (Sadan, pp. 53-54; trans. J. Decter)

cried, for I am much to blame! Alas my name and my father's name, that I diverted the Bible's crystal brook to fructify a foreign book. I mistook my purpose. Look: I tended strangers' vineyards and my own forsook [from Song of Songs 1:6]. (*Book of Tahkemoni*, p. 18)

It was, in part, because of al-Harizi's compunctions over his earlier work that he composed the *Tahkemoni*.

Al-Harizi claims that his book is entirely original: "I took nothing from the book of the Ishmaelite [al-Hariri]" (*Sefer Tahkemoni*, p. 14; trans. J. Decter). However, it is well known that he borrowed plots liberally from al-Hamadhani, al-Hariri, and other Arabic sources, as illustrated by the "Maqamah of Rehovot." These he rewrote with allusions pulled from Hebrew sources over which he had a command, creating new texts that were also, in a sense, "original." Other plots are indeed of al-Harizi's own design, such as the "Maqamah of the Astrologer" and the "Maqamah of Babylonia" (though the later has parallels in al-Hariri's *maqamat*).

Al-Harizi, as noted, laments what he sees as the appalling decline of the Hebrew language. He is probably concerned here with the decline of poetic writing in the style of the great Andalusian poets. This low estimation of the state of Hebrew letters in the early thirteenth century is somewhat exaggerated. The twelfth and thirteenth centuries, even before the composition of al-Harizi's *tour de force,* were extremely fruitful for Hebrew writing, continuing the poetic tradition of al-Andalus and expanding into several areas of prose writing. Hebrew was used for writing expositions on topics previously treated in Arabic only, such as philosophy, science, mathematics, and biblical exegesis.

The first Hebrew fictional narrative in rhymed prose was Judah ibn Tzakbel's *Asher Son of Judah Spoke* (c. 1100-50), the story of a bumbling lover's humiliating quest for his beloved. Not sophisticated enough to play the game of courtly love, Asher is led to a veiled figure he believes to be his beloved only to discover "a long beard and a face like death" when the veil is lifted (Ibn Tzakbel, pp. 266-67). Other Hebrew narratives that precede the *Tahkemoni* include Joseph ibn Zabara's *Sefer sha`ashu`im* (Book of Delights) and Judah ibn Shabbetai's *Minhat Yehudah sone ha-nashim* (Gift of Judah the Misogynist). Of all the early Hebrew rhymed prose narratives, only *Asher Son of Judah Spoke* merits mention in al-Harizi's review of literary history in the "Maqamah of Babylonia."

Reception. The *Tahkemoni* was popular among patrons and survives in many manuscripts. In Christian Spain, the collection was followed by several original works in rhymed prose including the *Book of Stories* (thirteenth century) by al-Harizi's younger contemporary Jacob ben Eleazar, *The Tale of the Ancient One* (thirteenth century) by Isaac ibn Sahula, *The Debate Between the Pen and the Scissors* (fourteenth century) by Shem Tov ibn Ardutiel, and the allegorical love story *The Eloquent Tale of Efer and Dinah* (fifteenth century) by Don Vidal Benveniste. Hebrew authors in Italy, Egypt, Yemen, Turkey, and Greece continued to utilize the rhymed prose form for centuries to come. The *Tahkemoni's* influence reached as far as India, where a verse from the book adorned the dedication plaque of an ornate synagogue in Cochin (built 1544). More than any other rhymed prose author, al-Harizi has been recognized by modern readers as a literary genius whose verve and wit have transcended the ephemeral.

—Jonathan P. Decter

For More Information

Brann, Ross. "Power in the Portrayal: Representations of Muslims and Jews in Judah al-Harizi's *Tahkemoni*." Princeton Papers in Near Eastern Studies, no. 1. Princeton, N.J.: Darwin Press, 1992.

Cohen, Gerson D. *Sefer ha-Qabbalah: The Book of Tradition by Abraham Ibn Daud: A Critical Edition with Translation and Notes*. New York: Jewish Publication Society, 1967.

Drory, Rina. "Al-Harizi's *Maqamat*: A Tricultural Literary Product?" *Medieval Translator* 4 (1994): 66-85.

————. "Literary Contacts and Where to Find Them: On Arabic Literary Models in Medieval Jewish Culture." *Poetics Today* 14, no. 2 (1993): 277-302.

————. "Maqama." In *The Literature of al-Andalus*. Ed. Maria Rosa Menocal, Raymond P. Scheindlin, and Michael Sells. Cambridge: Cambridge University Press, 2000.

al-Hariri, al-Qasim ibn Ali. *Mahberot Iti'el*. Trans. Judah al-Harizi. Ed. Yitshak Perets. Tel Aviv: Mosad ha-Rav Kuk, 1955.

al-Harizi, Judah Ben Solomon. *The Book of Tahkemoni: Jewish Tales from Medieval Spain*. Trans. David Simha Segal. Portland, Ore.: The Littman Library of Jewish Civilization, 2001.

————. *Sefer Tahkemoni*. Ed. J. Toporovsky. Tel Aviv: Mosad ha-Rav Kuk, 1952.

Ibn Tzakbel, Solomon. "Asher in the Harem." Trans. Raymond P. Scheindlin. In *Rabbinic Fantasies: Imaginative Narratives from Classical Hebrew Literature*. Ed. David Stern and Mark J. Mirsky. New Haven: Yale University Press, 1990.

Lavi, Abraham. "A Comparative Study of al-Hariri's Maqamat and Their Hebrew Translation by al-Harizi." PhD diss., University of Michigan, 1979.

Levin, Israel. *Yalkut Avraham ibn Ezra* (Gleanings from Abraham ibn Ezra). New York: Keren Yisrael Mats, 1985.

Maimonides, Moses. *Hakdamot le-ferush ha-Mishnah* (Introductions to the Commentary on the Mishnah). Ed. M. D. Rabinovitz. Jerusalem: Mosad ha-Rav Kook, 1960.

Sadan, Joseph. "Rabi Yehudah al-Harizi ke-tsomet tarbuti." ("Rabbi Judah al-Harizi as a Cultural Crossroads"). *Pe`amim* 68 (1996): 18-67.

The Broken Wings

by

Kahlil Gibran

THE LITERARY WORK

An Arabic novella set in the village of Bsharri, Lebanon, around 1900; written between 1903 and 1908; published in Arabic (as *al-Ajnihah al-mutakassirah*) in 1912, in English in 1957.

SYNOPSIS

A young man falls in love with a rich heiress who reciprocates his passion, but the local bishop interferes, ensnaring the heiress in a loveless match. Its tragic ending turns the story into both a scathing denunciation of clerical corruption and a spirited defense of women's rights.

Gibran Kahlil Gibran was born January 6, 1883, in Bsharri, Lebanon. Part of a wave of several hundred thousand emigrants from Syria and Lebanon, his mother moved with her four children to Boston, Massachusetts, in 1895. Gibran met his first mentor here, the photographer Fred Holland Day, who recognized the budding artist in the young man. Three years after his arrival, Gibran returned to Lebanon to attend the secondary school Madrasat al-Hikmah in Beirut. He read voraciously here, consuming the Arabic literary classics during his four-year stay in Lebanon and developing an intimate connection with his homeland and its problems. Gibran returned to Boston to spend the next half-dozen years in artistic pursuits, including the writing of stories and short "prose poems" in a biblical style. In 1904 the aspiring young writer had a fateful meeting with Amin al-Ghurayyib, editor of *al-Muhajir* (The Immigrant), the journal that published his early works. Soon after, Gibran published two short-story collections: *Ara'is al-muruj* (1906; *Nymphs of the Valley,* 1948) and *al-Arwah al-mutamarridah* (1908; *Spirits Rebellious,* 1947). The two collections, along with the prose poems, would establish him as an innovative man of letters. But first, also in 1904, Gibran met Mary Haskell. The headmistress of the School for Girls in Boston, Haskell became something of a guardian angel to Gibran until the end of his life, supporting him in his careers as both a writer and a painter (five of his canvases would later grace the walls of the Metropolitan Museum of Art). Gibran finished *Broken Wings* in 1908 but did not publish it. That same year, on a trip financed by Haskell, he set sail for Paris, France, where he spent two years studying art and meeting distinguished artists and men of letters. Gibran returned to Boston for a couple of years, then, in 1912, moved to his final home, New York. There he continued his artistic and literary pursuits, publishing in 1918 a long philosophical Arabic poem, *al-Mawakib* (The Processions), and also his first work in English, *The Madman.* In 1923 Gibran published his English-language masterpiece, *The Prophet,* which made him a household name in the United States and a well-known author globally. In the Arab and Muslim world, however, *The Prophet* did not have the same impact. There the most widely read and

Kahlil Gibran

beloved of his writings is *Broken Wings*—a Romeo and Juliet-type romance about a love thwarted by social realities that are daringly exposed in this groundbreaking work.

Events in History at the Time the Novella Takes Place

Beirut at the turn of the twentieth century. *Broken Wings* is set between 1898 and 1902, a period Gibran spent in Lebanon, mostly in Beirut, where the action unfolds. Beirut in this era was directly ruled by the Turks, or more exactly by the Ottoman sultan Abdülhamid II (1876-1909), whose regime was well known for its suppression of constitutional government and freedom of speech, its imposition of censorship, and its pervasive practice of espionage. Turkish as well as Arab nationalists wrote and otherwise protested against the regime. A victim of the regime's policies, Madrasat al-Hikmah, the school Gibran attended at the time, suffered from Ottoman opposition to its founding and construction. Gibran became a diehard enemy of Ottoman rule and of the social inequity that plagued his Arab surroundings.

In Beirut, as elsewhere in Lebanon, the Arab social structure consisted of rigid, widely disparate categories. The rich were exceedingly rich, and the poor were exceedingly poor. Lebanese society was run by notables, *al-Zu'ama*, whose wealth or high social status gave them authority over a particular set of relatives and followers. "In league" with these notables were "religious leaders who themselves control[led] and own[ed] large areas of land" (Zuwiyya Yamak in Binder, p. 149). Arab writers speak of feudal-like relations being rampant in the Lebanon of this period, not only in secular but also ecclesiastical circles. They speak too of the fact that corruption, especially bribery, became plainly visible at the end of the nineteenth century (under the rule of Wasa Pasha [1883-92]), followed by "ceaseless squabbling for place and power" and by the "interventions of religious dignitaries in the political fray" (Longrigg in Kisirwani, p. 3). It was the presence of notables and groups of followers that gave rise to these feudal-like relations. In exchange for their support, a notable would protect or advance his followers' interests, which perpetuated social inequity. The situation was changing somewhat at the time of the novel, because large-scale emigration led to some money being funneled back to family members left in Lebanon, but inequity remained rampant in the country. Gibran, who found its persistence even more oppressive than the Ottoman policies, which were in many cases innovations not yet consistently implemented, made social inequity a main theme in *Broken Wings*. At the same time, there was fierce competition in Lebanon for high social status and wealth (or at least the appearance of wealth), which is another primary factor in the novella.

Beirut was the hub of intellectual life in Lebanon. By the end of the nineteenth century, it could boast two major academies of learning—the American Protestant and French Jesuit Universities—and other schools where distinguished men of the Arab Renaissance taught, such as the Yazijis and the Bustanis. It was a city in which the East met the West, in which Islam met Christianity. One of the most significant literary cultural events of this period was the translation of the Christian Bible into Arabic. A feat sponsored by the Protestant American missionaries, it entailed the work of three distinguished men of letters: Butrus al-Bustani, Nasif al-Yaziji, and Yusuf al-Asir. Then came another translation sponsored by the French Jesuits and perfected by other distinguished scholars, such as Ibrahim al-Yaziji.

The school Gibran attended—Madrasat al-Hikmah—had a profound influence on his work. A Maronite secondary school, it was founded in

Kahlil Gibran as a young man.

Bsharri at the turn of the twentieth century. The setting in *Broken Wings* is a fictional environment for a personal drama that really unfolded in Gibran's own village of Bsharri. Bsharri sits in Mount Lebanon, which was politically in the *mutasarrifiyah*, that is, the part of present-day Lebanon that, after tragic denominational strife in 1860, witnessed the intervention of the Western powers, especially France, to determine its future. In 1861, the mountain, al-Jabal, became autonomous and no longer had a Turkish garrison. Its governors were Catholics, and each was called a *mutasarrif*, giving rise to the name *mutasarrifiyah* for the region as a whole. The independent province would flourish until the outbreak of the First World War, at which point it was abolished by the Turks. But before then, in this relatively autonomous Christian atmosphere, Gibran was born and bred.

1875 by Yusuf al-Dibs (1833-1907), a bishop and an author of some important historical works such as the eight-volume *Tarikh Suriya* (The History of Syria). The school was celebrated for its excellence in the teaching of the Arabic language by such distinguished instructors as Sa'id al-Shartuni and Sulayman al-Bustani, who translated the *Iliad* into Arabic verse.

Gibran himself had as a teacher at the school an inspiring tutor, a priest, Father Yusuf al-Haddad, who recommended to his precocious student a series of influential Arabic books. First, there was *Kitab al-aghani* of al-Isfahani, a text on Arabic poetry, music, and song that would have acquainted Gibran with Arabic love poetry and with many accounts of Arab lover-poets, such as the legendary Majnun of Layla and Majnun. Next the instructor recommended the Bible, whose impact is evident in the many biblical references that abound in Gibran's work (such as a reference to the "immortal songs of Solomon" in *Broken Wings* [p. 175]). Father Haddad also advised Gibran to read the works of Adib Ishaq, a fiery reformer and patriot, whose vigorous style and bold ejaculations no doubt appealed to the rebel in Gibran. Perhaps even more influential was the philosophy of universal love touted by Fransis Marrash of Aleppo; to express his philosophy, he coined innovative Arabic phrases, which became precursors of many others that Gibran himself would coin.

FRANSIS MARRASH OF ALEPPO

A forerunner of the early Arabic novelists, Fransis Marrash of Aleppo (1836-73) lost his sight at about the age of 30 yet went on to write fiction as well as poetry and articles. His *Ghabat al-haqq* (The Forest of Truth) is an allegory about human freedom, hampered by the arbitrary social systems of civilization. Another title by him, *Durr al-sadaf fi ghara'ib al-sudaf* (Pearl Shells in Relating Strange Coincidences), which, as the title implies, is the narration of a series of events, paved the way for the more sophisticated narrative of later novelists. It includes a romance as well as Marrash's own ideas about compassion, respect, and love for humankind. The romance ends happily in the marriage of lovers, but the fiction includes ideas that serve as objections or protests to common behaviors of the day, and so was as daring for its time as Gibran's own novella would be later.

Bsharri and the region in which it was located, which overlooked the Valley of Qadisha (Wadi Qadisha), was the center of the Maronite Church in Lebanon. The followers of St. Maron (d. 410) had emigrated here from Apamea on the Orontes in Syria in the second half of the seventh century. A Christian sect—the most populous in Lebanon—the Maronites saw their highest authority as the Pope in Rome, but their practice differed from the Roman Catholics'—Maronite clergy could marry, and they used a Syriac liturgy.

If Maron was the saint of the new sect, Yuhanna Marun (Joannes Maro, d. ca. 707) was the hero and founder of the new nation cradled on the banks of the Qadisha and in the shades of the cedars. . . . Since then, the Maronites have isolated themselves and developed the individualistic traits characteristic of mountaineers. . . . For centuries, beginning with the fifteenth, Qannubin, carved and sheltered in the solid rock of the rugged Qadisha valley, provided a seat for the Maronite patriarchate which now uses Bakirki in winter.

(Hitti, p. 249)

The Bsharri region was dotted with monasteries such as Mar Sarkis (Sergius), Mar Alisha (Elijah) and Qazhayah, well-known to Gibran. Both they and their members would figure in Gibran's life and writings.

A LEBANESE CAPITAL OUTSIDE LEBANON

Increasing denominational strife in the early nineteenth century climaxed in a bloody civil war between the Maronite Christians and the Druzes in 1860. Pivotal in this war was the tragic massacre of some 12,000 Maronites, which prompted the intervention of European powers and the creation of Mount Lebanon as a primarily Christian province of the Ottoman Empire in 1861. Strictly speaking, the city of Beirut sat outside the province's borders, but culturally and commercially it functioned as the capital anyway, playing host to Lebanon's Christian merchants and to its Christian schools. Later, in 1920, Mount Lebanon would be enlarged to include Beirut along with other additional areas, forming Lebanon as we know it today.

Most relevant for understanding *Broken Wings* is the social structure prevalent in Bsharri and, more generally, in Mount Lebanon at the time. Society was stratified into levels that had long remained strictly divided. If a lover from a poor working class were to court a maiden from a well-to-do, established family, the suitor would be contemptuously rejected. Such is the case in *Broken Wings,* which draws from Gibran's personal life to tell a tragic, if dramatic, love story.

Marriage—strictly a family matter. Before the First World War, marriage in the Maronite communities of Mount Lebanon was a family affair. Marriage preferences followed a scheme

of choices for a partner ranked in the following order:

1. A cousin on the father's side of the family
2. A cousin on the mother's side of the family
3. A member of another family in the village
4. A member of a family in a neighboring village

At age 14 or 15 the family would assemble to choose a suitable wife for a boy. The young woman was usually 12 or 13, the initial marriageable age. Selection of the spouse was based mainly on the needs and interests of the family. If an outsider wanted to marry a girl, his family would ask her father's permission, and only if no one in his family wanted her for himself would the permission be granted. In the novel, the protagonist is an outsider—his father now lives a "great distance" away—compared to the bishop's nephew, who both seek the hand of Salma (Gibran, *Broken Wings,* p. 15). Not only is the nephew a local resident, but in comparison to the poor protagonist, he is a man of status, derived largely from that of his uncle the bishop.

Whether or not the match was appealing to Salma had little to do with the matter. It was common for these arranged marriages to be devoid of feeling. Typically a young man and woman who barely knew each other would become engaged, as reflected by lyrics from a late-nineteenth-century love song: "Oh dear: it has been one or two years since I got engaged to you (and) / I still do not know your name / Oh dear: Your name is the golden chain in the jewelry box / Oh dear; win the one who buys you and lose the one who sells you" (Tohme-Tabet, p. 44). In the novella Salma's father feels he has little choice in the matter, and for her, ignoring or defying his wishes is out of the question: "children [like Salma] who had great respect for their parents were compelled to abide by their desires" (Tohme-Tabet, p. 44). Some families required the fiancé to be of the same social status. Others with money but little status made a match that would help their family climb the social ladder, and by the same token, the opposite could occur: those with social status might make a match that brought the family money. A young person who refused to comply would be isolated or expelled from the family. There was, in any case, little opportunity for young men and women, whatever their religious affiliation, to meet in turn-of-the-century Lebanon. Society practiced a strict separation of the sexes in both public and private places. Village celebrations were for men only, and it was forbidden for women to dance

An overview of Bsharri, Gibran's birthplace and home, overlooking the Valley of Qadisha.

with men. At church, women sat on the back benches; at home they were not supposed to appear before a foreign visitor. The protagonist in *Broken Wings,* son of an old chum of Salma's father, is more friend than foreigner.

Since the appearance of Mikhail Naimy's life story of Gibran in the 1930s, research has established that the love affair in *Broken Wings* is autobiographical, based on Gibran's love for a maiden from Bsharri, identified as Hala al-Dahir. According to his biographer-relatives, "there is little doubt . . . that in portraying [Salma] he tenderly recalled Hala Dahir" (Gibran, Jean, and Kahlil Gibran, p. 86). Gibran's father, also named Kahlil Gibran, was a simple shepherd and tax collector. Gibran's mother, Kamila, was a widow when his father married her. There was a local *shaykh* (sheikh) in Bsharri called Tannous, sometimes referred to as Raji. The patriarch of a family named Dahir, this shaykh had a son called Iskandar (Alexander) and two daughters, Sa'ida and Hala. Apparently, Gibran and his father visited the Dahirs before emigrating, and the shaykh behaved contemptuously toward the son of the goat herder. When Gibran returned to Lebanon in 1898, this attitude of condescension on the part of the father persisted. But it was the brother, Iskandar, who decided that no marriage between Gibran and his sister Hala would take place. His

other sister, Sa'ida, became important to scholars as an informant about this love affair between Gibran and Hala. Apparently when Gibran bade Hala farewell, he gave her a ring, a lock of his hair, a vial (in which there were some drops of his tears), and his cane. Hala never married and died a blind woman in 1955.

It is clear that opposition to a marriage between Gibran and Hala came more from the family than from the bishop. In *Broken Wings,* however, the bishop is the villain, thereby serving as a vehicle for a violent attack on clerical corruption. In fact, there was a real-life churchman who seconded the family's opposition to the match, a priest of the Bsharri parish who chided Gibran for his cheekiness in aspiring to marry a Dahir. No doubt the priest's opposition helped stimulate the novella's anti-clerical stance, but the priest's voice was the only ecclesiastical one to involve itself in the love affair, and it was not the decisive factor. The vehemence of the novella's attack on the church is better explained as a reaction to the tragic events surrounding the death of As'ad al-Shidyak, a Maronite who had converted to Protestantism around that time. After all attempts to retrieve him to the fold of Maronite Catholicism failed, As'ad al-Shidyak was confined to a cell, where he died of starvation and neglect. Qannubin in Wadi Qadisha, where

Gibran's village Bsharri was located, was the seat of the Maronite Patriarchate to which As`ad had been summoned, and the case would have been well known to Gibran. His outrage at the fate of the convert seems to have surfaced in other tales by Gibran too. The same As`ad is thought to be the hero of his short stories "Yuhanna al-Majnun" (John the Madman), and "Khalil al-Kafir" (Khalil the Infidel).

The Novella in Focus

Plot summary. *Broken Wings* tells the story of two star-crossed lovers. The maiden, Salma, daughter to Faris Karama, lives in a stately mansion in a suburb of Beirut. It is here that the narrator, of lower social status than she but son to an old friend of her father's, falls in love with Salma at first sight. Her father, an aging gentleman, adores his lovely and lovable daughter and would happily see her married to an eligible and dependable young man worthy of her. Future meetings between the young man and Salma only deepen his chaste love and allow her to return it in kind. But any hopes for a match are dashed by the bishop of the region, Bulus Ghalib, who persuades the father to have his daughter betrothed to the bishop's nephew, Mansur Ghalib.

This bishop is a man of "malicious cunning"; he chooses Salma to be his nephew's wife "not for the beauty of her features or the nobility of her spirit, but because she [is] moneyed; her substantial fortune [will] guarantee the future of Mansur Bey and help establish his high status among the elite" (*Broken Wings,* p. 50). For his part, the adoring father has met the bishop's nephew. He knows of the young man's "coarseness, greed and corrupt morals" but feels trapped, for what "man in the East can decline to obey the leader of his religion and retain his honor among the people?" (*Broken Wings,* p. 50). "Is this your will, Papa?" asks Salma, dutiful daughter that she is, ready to forfeit her happiness (*Broken Wings,* p. 44). Salma cannot, in this society, disobey her father, just as he cannot disobey the bishop. Her predicament is far from unusual in her country; there are in Lebanon during this time "many girls of her kind who are sacrificed at the altars of their fathers' fortunes and of their grooms' ambitions" (*Broken Wings,* p. 51).

Unsurprisingly, Salma's marriage to Mansur is full of unhappiness and hardships. Her one comfort comes from her secret monthly meetings with the protagonist, in which the two lovers embrace, kiss, and bare their innermost thoughts. The bishop, becoming wise to Salma's monthly disappearances but not yet knowing where to, has her followed, whereupon she insists on stopping the monthly assignations, overpowering her lover's desire to emigrate, determined for him to "remain honorable in the eyes of the people" (*Broken Wings,* p. 99).

Meanwhile, in her loveless marriage, Salma fails to give birth to a child for five years. Then hope stirs in her, for she does bear one, but the baby dies almost immediately after birth, and she soon follows. Mother and child are buried in the same spot. The tragic love story ends with the lover speaking to the gravedigger and then mourning at his beloved's grave. At the end, he remains anonymous, as he has been throughout. Told in his first-person voice, the narration suggests that the story has autobiographical origins.

The plight of women, a literary issue. While *Broken Wings* deals with various problems that plagued early-twentieth-century Lebanon—outworn social conventions, clerical corruption, and the status of women—Gibran's main issue in the novella is this last one. "Writers and poets try to perceive the reality of woman," says Salma, "but at present they have not understood the secrets of [my] heart" (*Broken Wings,* p. 86). The writer Gibran tried. His efforts, in the context of his fiction, made him one of the most powerful defenders of women's rights in his day. Gibran's previously published short-story collections, *Nymphs of the Valley* and *Spirits Rebellious,* include other tales that depict the plight of Lebanese women. In the first collection is the story "Marta al-Baniyah," which features a poor, innocent village girl. Seduced by a rich man from Beirut, she gives birth to a child by him, then is haplessly discarded. She must therefore find work as a prostitute to earn enough money to feed her baby and herself. "Rose al-Hani," in the second collection, features a young woman who is married off to a wealthy and kindly enough old man. A caretaker, he fails to rouse in her feelings that allow for a full relationship. So she lives a duplicitous life, married to one man and in love with another, until the young heroine finally braves the disdain of society by leaving her husband for her beloved.

Gibran was not the only male writer to champion women's rights in Arab society; another such writer in the Muslim world was Egypt's Qasim Amin (d. 1908), author of *Tahrir al-mar'ah* (1899; The Emancipation of Women) and *al-Mar'ah al-jadidah* (1900; Modern Woman), who urged his society to educate women, not just for their benefit but for its own. But the global fame that

Gibran achieved made him more effectual than most writers in the defense of women's rights.

Arabic female writers of the era (e.g., Zaynab Fawwaz) raised issues on their own behalf, too, but it was not until later in the century that such women would attract a sizable readership. Indeed, the second half of the twentieth century saw the emergence of distinctive female writers, including Nawal al-Sa`dawi in Egypt, Fatima Mernissi in Morocco, Ghadah al-Samman in Syria, and Hanan al-Shaykh in Lebanon (whose *The Story of Zahra* is also in *WLAIT 6: Middle Eastern Literatures and Their Times*). Centering on feminist issues, these later writers can be seen as Gibran's descendants in spirit.

Sources. Stylistically the most important influence on Gibran's writing was that of the Bible— its straightforward prose; its employment of parables and allegories; its modes of expression. Taking the Bible as his cue, Gibran cultivated what might be termed the "prose poem," modeled on the Psalms of David instead of the traditional *qasidah,* the polythematic ode of classical Arabic poetry. Inventing new literary forms (generally referred to as Gibranesque), he wrote poetic prose as well as the prose poem. In his essays (published in 1914 under the title *Dam`ah wa ibtisamah* [Tear and a Smile]), as well as his two previously mentioned short-story collections (*Ara'is al-muruj,* 1906, and *al-Arwah al-mutamarridah,* 1908), Gibran appears to be the implacable enemy of outworn social conventions, of clerical and secular corruption, and of feudalism. The climax to all these literary endeavors was *Broken Wings,* composed in 1908 but published in 1912. The novella is genetically related to his previous short stories, specifically to "Ara'is al-muruj," which features both the setting of Bsharri and the character Yuhanna al-Majnun, who foreshadows the hero in *Broken Wings.* Another forerunner is the character Khalil al-Kafir in "al-Arwah al-mutamarridah," a story that again takes place in Bsharri, this time in a monastery. The two semiautobiographical stories "Yuhanna al-Majnun" and "Khalil al-Kafir" are virtual rehearsals for the composition of *Broken Wings.* Clearly Gibran considered it the most intensely personal, as signified by his shift from third- to first-person singular in composing the narrative.

The model for Salma, Hala al-Dahir, survives in the literary consciousness of the modern Arab world together with Gibran as the Romeo and Juliet of modern Arabic literature and a revivification of the classical Arab lovers Qays and Layla. That Gibran dedicated his novella to Mary Haskell does not negate the probable autobiographical element. Hala is the inspiration for the novella's heroine. Gibran's dedication of *Broken Wings* to Haskell and his further elaboration on the matter to her (he said the story was *not* autobiographical) were undoubtedly motivated by various considerations: she was his patron and he needed to neutralize any jealousy she might harbor towards the real heroine by pretending that no one real inspired the female protagonist. Exercising foresight, Gibran apparently took the precaution of massaging egos before they were bruised.

Reception and impact. Immediately after its publication, *Broken Wings* received a torrent of reviews by critics in the Arab world, especially in Egypt, and in the United States. Most of these reviews were favorable, although critics found *Broken Wings* wanting in some of the novella's conventional elements. What genre does it conform to, then? In truth, the work has defied categorization. It is perhaps most aptly described as a "love-poem-in-prose," unified by the force of its universal theme of love, though critics have regarded it from the traditional perspective of the novella.

The Arab American writer Mikhail Naimy reviewed *Broken Wings* in an article in Arabic titled "Fajr al-amal ba`da layl al-ya's" (The Dawn of Hope after the Night of Despair), published in the journal *al-Funun* (1913; The Arts). Naimy's article expressed concern about the state of his homeland's literature and then heralded Gibran as the star of a new dawn in Arabic letters (Naimy, pp. 57-70). The critic praised the Arab setting of *Broken Wings,* regarding this as the first sign of a genuine contribution to a vigorous new Arab literature. But the review found fault with the novella, too, saying it lacked realism and criticizing its heroine, Salma, in ways that distinguished Naimy as an even greater champion of women's rights than Gibran. The critic expressed reservations over the characterization of the father, Faris Karami; the bishop, Bulus Ghalib; and his nephew, Mansur, as well, yet ended the review with a salute to Gibran.

Naimy's own forte was the short story, a genre new to Arabic literature, and he soon distinguished himself as the Arab American writer who perfected composition in this genre in Arabic. Indeed, his critique of *Broken Wings* may have been an important stimulant that led Naimy in that direction, as he attempted to avoid mistakes ascribed to Gibran. More specifically, an element in *Broken Wings* may have inspired

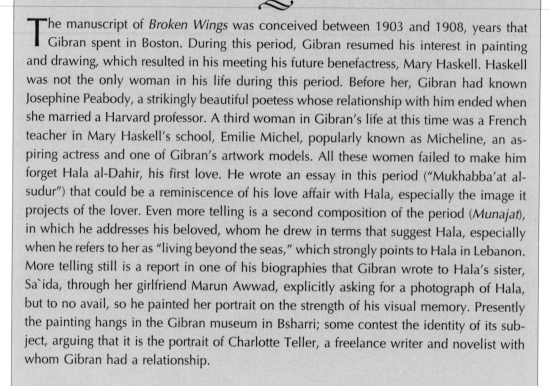

BEHIND THE ARTISTIC MAN—GIBRAN'S INSPIRATIONAL WOMEN

The manuscript of *Broken Wings* was conceived between 1903 and 1908, years that Gibran spent in Boston. During this period, Gibran resumed his interest in painting and drawing, which resulted in his meeting his future benefactress, Mary Haskell. Haskell was not the only woman in his life during this period. Before her, Gibran had known Josephine Peabody, a strikingly beautiful poetess whose relationship with him ended when she married a Harvard professor. A third woman in Gibran's life at this time was a French teacher in Mary Haskell's school, Emilie Michel, popularly known as Micheline, an aspiring actress and one of Gibran's artwork models. All these women failed to make him forget Hala al-Dahir, his first love. He wrote an essay in this period ("Mukhabba'at al-sudur") that could be a reminiscence of his love affair with Hala, especially the image it projects of the lover. Even more telling is a second composition of the period (*Munajat*), in which he addresses his beloved, whom he drew in terms that suggest Hala, especially when he refers to her as "living beyond the seas," which strongly points to Hala in Lebanon. More telling still is a report in one of his biographies that Gibran wrote to Hala's sister, Sa`ida, through her girlfriend Marun Awwad, explicitly asking for a photograph of Hala, but to no avail, so he painted her portrait on the strength of his visual memory. Presently the painting hangs in the Gibran museum in Bsharri; some contest the identity of its subject, arguing that it is the portrait of Charlotte Teller, a freelance writer and novelist with whom Gibran had a relationship.

what is considered Naimy's finest short story, "al-Aqir" (The Sterile Woman). In *Broken Wings*, Gibran treated the subject of sterility when discussing how the misery of Salma's arranged marriage was compounded by her failure to conceive a child for five years. *Broken Wings* thus has additional significance because of its influence on the writer who won renown as the master of the short story in Arab American literature.

As one might predict, *Broken Wings* elicited adverse criticism from conservative circles, both Christian and Muslim, in view of its violent attack on clerical corruption and ecclesiastical feudalism. The writer Mayy Ziadah, Gibran's female counterpart in Egypt, took him to task, again for his characterization of Salma, but this time because she thought it leveled a blow at family life and the sanctity of the marriage bond. However, Naimy's praise was reiterated and expanded upon by Muhammad Najm, a well-known critic in the Arab world. A century after the novella appeared in Arabic, the high regard accorded it in the Arab world endures. The American reader used to Gibran's *Prophet*, which was composed in English, may not fully appreciate this love-poem-in-prose in translation, since its power is

so closely bound up with the language in which it was originally written. Yet despite the lapse of a hundred years, *Broken Wings* continues to grip readers as in 1912, when it first took the literary Arab world by storm. So enduringly popular is the novella that in 1962 it was adapted into an Arabic film with English subtitles, and in 2003 a reviewer waxed rhapsodic about the film and the story (Hall). Eliciting praise for close to a century, *Broken Wings* is thus a testament to Ezra Pound's observations not only that fine literature is language infused with meaning to the highest possible degree but also that it is "news that stays news" (Pound, pp. 28-29).

—Irfan Shahîd

For More Information

Antonius, George. *The Arab Awakening: The Story of the Arab National Movement.* Philadelphia: J. B. Lippincott, 1939.

Binder, Leonard, ed. *Politics in Lebanon.* New York: John Wiley, 1966.

Bushrui, Suheil, and Joe Jenkins. *Kahlil Gibran: Man and Poet.* Oxford: One World, 1998.

Gibran, Jean, and Kahlil Gibran. *Kahlil Gibran: His Life and World.* New York: Interlink, 1974.

Gibran, Kahlil. *Broken Wings*. Trans. J. R. I. Cole. New York: Penguin, 1998.

Hall, Phil. "The Broken Wings." *Film Threat Reviews*. 7 February 2003. http://www.filmthreat.com/Reviews.asp?Id=4223. (9 May 2003).

Hitti, Philip K. "Gibran's Place and Influence in Modern Arabic Literature." *Syrian World* 3 (February 1929): 3032.

———. *Lebanon in History*. New York: St. Martin's Press, 1967.

Jayyusi, Salma K. *Trends and Movements in Modern Arabic Poetry*. Vols. 1-2. Leiden: E. J. Brill, 1977.

Kisirwani, Marun Y. "Attitudes and Behavior of Lebanese Bureaucrats." Ph.D. diss., Indiana University, 1971.

Naimy, Mikhail. *Kahlil Gibran: A Biography*. New York: Interlink, 1974.

Pound, Ezra. *ABC of Reading*. New York: New Directions, 1960.

Shahid, Irfan. "Gibran and the American Literary Canon: The Problem of *The Prophet*." In *Tradition, Modernity and Postmodernity in Arabic Literature: Essays in Honor of Professor Issa J. Boullata*. Ed. Kamal Abdel-Malek and Wael Hallaq. Leiden: E. J. Brill, 2000.

Tohme-Tabet, Annie. "Selection of the Spouse and the Network of Matrimonial Alliances among the Maronites in Mount Lebanon between 1830 and 1940: A Study of Three Cases." al-*Raida* 18-19, nos. 93-94 (spring/summer 2001): 43-46.

Cities of Salt

by
Abd al-Rahman Munif

THE LITERARY WORK

The first in a five-part series of novels set in an unnamed kingdom in the Arabian Peninsula in the 1930s; published in Arabic (as *Mudun al-milh: al-tih*) in 1984, in English in 1987.

SYNOPSIS

The discovery and exploitation of oil by an American company results in the destruction of two traditional villages and the creation of a new coastal city fraught with economic, social, and political problems.

Abd al-Rahman Munif was born in Amman, Jordan, in 1933 to a Saudi father and an Iraqi mother. Munif grew up in the Jordanian capital and went on to study law in universities in the Iraqi city of Baghdad and the Egyptian city of Cairo. He completed his doctorate in petroleum economics at the University of Belgrade in Yugoslavia, then worked as a petroleum economist in Syria and later for OPEC (Organization of Petroleum Exporting Countries). While in Baghdad, he edited the monthly journal *al-Naft wa al-tanmiyah* (Oil and Development). Munif began writing fiction in the early 1970s and in 1973 published his first novel, *al-Ashjar wa ightiyal marzuq* (The Trees and the Assassination of Marzuq), about an Arab intellectual psychologically damaged by political despotism. In 1977 he published *Nihayat* (1977; *Endings*, 1988), his first novel about the Bedouin of the Arabian Peninsula. By 1981 Munif, who had moved to France—only five years later would he settle in Damascus, Syria—was devoting himself full time to his writing. He wrote his five-volume series *Mudun al-milh* (Cities of Salt) between 1984-89, the first three volumes of which have been translated into English as *Cities of Salt, The Trench,* and *Variations on Night and Day*. Munif continues to write prolifically. Most recently, he has published the quintet *Ard al-sawad* (1999; The Fertile Land), about rural Iraq during the nineteenth century. With Libyan writer Ibrahim al-Kuni, Munif is widely regarded as the preeminent Arab writer who has made the desert and its people a major theme of his work. His novels allude to and borrow from Arab classical and popular traditions while experimenting with structure and voice. In *Cities of Salt*, Munif experiments with literary elements as he traces the impact of modern technology on desert society.

Events in History at the Time the Novel Takes Place

Saudi Arabia before oil—a fateful alliance. Although set in an imaginary oil kingdom, *Cities of Salt* is widely regarded as a *roman à clef*—a fictional account of real events, in this case the oil industry's impact on the Arabian Peninsula. The novel portrays in particular the impact on the Eastern Province of present-day Saudi Arabia, where the first oil exploration began. Events stretch from the 1930s, when oil was first discovered, to the workers' strike at Aramco, Saudi Arabia, in 1953.

The discovery and exploitation of oil fundamentally altered pre-existing social, political, and economic structures in Arabia. One often thinks of Arabia before oil as a country of deserts and nomadic tribes. Actually, the part of the Arabian Peninsula that currently comprises Saudi Arabia has been home to many ancient civilizations. For centuries before the discovery of oil, Arabian society was a complex mix of agrarian, pastoral, and mercantile sectors. In addition to pastoral Bedouin raising camels and sheep, the peninsula boasted the holy cities of Mecca and Medina, which since the seventh century C.E. have attracted thousands and later millions of Muslim pilgrims every year from around the world. The annual pilgrimage served as an important source of income not only for residents of these two towns but for the young Saudi state as well. From at least the sixteenth century, the port city of Jiddah served as the most prosperous commercial center on the Red Sea. Fishing and pearling villages dotted the Persian Gulf coast. Large oases, such as al-Hasa in what is now the Eastern Province of the country, supported orchards of dates, which served not only as a staple in the local diet but also as an important export commodity.

The relationship among the cities, agrarian villages, and pastoral nomads was complex. The nomadic tribes have traditionally been characterized as a destabilizing force on the peninsula, charged with limiting the development of trade by their attacks on caravans and with endangering the viability of agrarian villages through raids. Scholars have also noted their role as a fickle military force for the various princes of the peninsula who sought to widen their realms. However, anthropological studies have shown that the relationship between nomadic and settled peoples in Arabia was not purely antagonistic. Villages included settled Bedouin who maintained personal ties with nomadic groups. In addition, productive political and economic interaction between nomads and settled oasis-dwellers made it hard at times to draw a clear distinction between the two.

As is true of most countries of the Middle East, the Kingdom of Saudi Arabia did not come into being in its present political form until well into the twentieth century. Before that time, the Arabian Peninsula was characterized by the absence of a unified state. The Hejaz, the mountainous area along the west coast of the peninsula and home to the cities of Mecca, Medina, and Jiddah, was under Ottoman rule. Meanwhile, the eastern and central regions (al-Hasa and al-Najd), although nominally territories of the Ottoman Empire, were in fact governed almost entirely by local rulers. Nonetheless, the roots of present-day Saudi Arabia, which comprises most of the peninsula, reach back to the 1700s.

The birth of the modern state of Saudi Arabia began with an alliance between Muhammad ibn Sa`ud (1744), a minor ruler of the Najd region of central Arabia, and Muhammad ibn Abd al-Wahhab, a religious reformer from the same region. An Islamic scholar who had studied in Mecca and Medina, Abd al-Wahhab sought to stamp out what he regarded as superstition, ostentation in religious practice, and saint worship in Islam. His uncompromising reaffirmation of the basic tenets of Islam attracted followers who called themselves *al-muwahhidun*, or the Unitarians. His activities also gave rise to Wahhabism, an austere form of Islam which has been inexorably linked to the royal House of Saud and continues to be practiced in much of the Arabian Peninsula today. In the Najd region, Abd al-Wahhab attracted the attention of Muhammad ibn Sa`ud, at that time a minor prince of the area. Ibn Sa`ud and his tribe adopted Abd al-Wahhab's doctrines and in 1763 set out to conquer their Arabian neighbors. By 1811, a decade after the death of Abd al-Wahhab, the rule of Muhammad ibn Sa`ud's grandson (Saud ibn Abd al-Aziz) extended over much of the Arabian Peninsula, including parts of present-day Yemen and Oman.

The Ottoman sultan, nominal ruler of the peninsula, sought to crush the Saudis and in 1818 succeeded in driving them back to the deserts of Najd. Less than a decade later, the House of Saud succeeded once more in regaining control over the eastern part of the peninsula, but its power steadily weakened over the course of the nineteenth century, and by 1889 the family was forced to seek refuge in neighboring Kuwait.

The House of Saud rose to prominence for a third time in 1902 when Abd al-Aziz ibn Sa`ud (often referred to as Ibn Sa`ud), a fifth-generation descendant of Muhammad ibn Sa`ud, emerged from exile in Kuwait to reclaim his position as a ruler in the Najd and eventually over the rest of Arabia.

Saudi Arabia before oil—the House of Saud asserts itself. Abd al-Aziz employed a number of shrewd tactics to achieve his goals. A difficulty that had plagued previous rulers, including those he sought to overthrow in his current campaign, was the shifting loyalty of the mobile Bedouin or nomadic population. At the time of Abd al-Aziz's ascendancy, a serious drought threatened the livelihood of Bedouin in the Najd. Abd al-Aziz managed to secure the continued loyalty of dispossessed Bedouin by settling them in agricultural communities (*hujar*) and educating them in Wahhabi Islam. These settlements, called *ikhwan*, or brotherhood settlements, began in 1912. Though not all Bedouin settled in them, they quickly grew to include several thousand elite troops loyal to Abd al-Aziz.

As World War I approached, Abd al-Aziz signed a treaty with Great Britain, which promised British recognition of Abd al-Aziz as the hereditary ruler of the Najd and the eastern parts of the peninsula in return for his supporting the British in World War I. At the same time, the British negotiated with Husayn ibn Ali, Sharif of the Hejaz, a province to the west. In a secret agreement, the British agreed that once World War I ended, they would recognize Husayn as the ruler of an Arab state to the east of Egypt, including Arabia as well as Syria and Iraq, in exchange for Husayn's support during the war. However, the British reneged on that agreement, granting Husayn suzerainty over the Hejaz only. Conflict between Abd al-Aziz and Husayn over who should rule in the peninsula continued after the end of the war. By 1925 Abd al-Aziz had consolidated control over the realm. In 1932 he named it the Kingdom of Saudi Arabia.

Although Abd al-Aziz's conflict with Husayn ended in 1925, his control of the peninsula was threatened by other incidents. By the late 1920s, differences began to surface between Abd al-Aziz and the *ikhwan*, or Wahhabi Bedouin communities, who had been instrumental in bringing him to power. The *ikhwan* were suspicious of the modern technology imported and used by the Saudi rulers. Also they refused to recognize the sovereignty of nearby non-Wahhabi countries, such as Iraq. In 1928 the *ikhwan* attacked Iraq against the orders of Abd al-Aziz. Abd al-Aziz responded by crushing his erstwhile supporters. Nonetheless, in later years, members of the *ikhwan* and in some cases their descendants continued to be rewarded with state subsidies in recognition of their earlier role in establishing the Saudi dynasty in Arabia.

Abd al-Aziz ruled Saudi Arabia until his death in 1953, at which time he was succeeded by his son, Saud, who ruled until 1964. *Cities of Salt* bases the character of Crown Prince Khazael, who visits Harran to celebrate the completion of the oil pipeline, on this successor, Saud. Saud's reign was, in turn, followed by that of his brothers Faysal (1964-75), Khalid (1975-82), and the present king, Fahd (1982-).

Oil and social change in Saudi Arabia. Instability in political leadership was the general rule in the Arabian Peninsula before the rise of the House of Saud in the early twentieth century. Dynasties came and went, toppled by up-and-coming members of the elite who vied for power. In fact, this instability had its advantages, in that it allowed for the overthrow of dictators and served as a check on the absolute power of any one ruler. Were it not for the discovery and exploitation of oil in the 1930s and '40s, the House of Saud might well have been like the many other dynasties the peninsula has known, rising to power and quickly fading when challenged by another political family. Oil wealth, however, provided Abd al-Aziz and his descendants with an income that enabled them both to placate tribal leaders, who might have otherwise challenged Saudi authority, and to control the general population through the creation of a National Guard and other police forces.

Oil exploration began in the Middle East in the late nineteenth century in Persia. The first concession for oil exploration in the Arabian Peninsula was granted in 1923 to the British. In 1933, that concession was transferred to Standard Oil of California (SOCAL), whose Arabian oil enterprise would eventually evolve into the Arabian American Oil Company (Aramco) in consortia with other American oil companies. SOCAL discovered oil in commercial quantities in 1938. *Cities of Salt* presumably begins sometime in the 1930s when American geologists would have been prospecting in the Eastern Province.

Oil was not pumped in Saudi Arabia in significant quantities until the late 1940s, but even before then, SOCAL had a significant impact on the communities of the Eastern Province. In previous centuries, only a handful of Westerners had traveled through this sparsely populated area, so the presence of increasing numbers of Americans was conspicuous. Also, the consumer goods brought to the Eastern Province by the early oil geologists and engineers impressed local leaders and notables, who then sought such goods themselves. Moreover, it was in the 1930s that construction started on the town of Dhahran, whose history closely mirrors that of Munif's fictional coastal town of Harran in the novel.

Aramco began to quickly expand its operations in the Eastern Province after World War II by building new wells and refineries. The construction of Tapline, the Trans-Arabian Pipeline (also chronicled in *Cities of Salt*), a huge project to move oil across the peninsula to the Mediterranean Sea and thereby increase the efficiency of oil production, was completed in 1950.

In these early years, American engineers and geologists were brought to Arabia by SOCAL and then Aramco to work in the oil fields. These specialists provided the skilled labor, while manual labor was performed by indigenous Arabs, mostly from the Eastern Province. Much of the literature on the oil industry describes these manual laborers as peripatetic nomads for whom work in the oil fields was simply another way to earn a living. But in *Cities of Salt*, Munif furnishes another perspective, one of Arab Bedouin and village dwellers who saw their world transformed at a bewildering speed and found themselves unwittingly sucked into the oil economy.

THE FOUNDING OF DHAHRAN

Dhahran began in 1935 as a small tent camp of American wildcatters who had come to drill for oil in the Damman Dome. In 1936 six air-conditioned portable cottages were imported and the first group of wives of American oil workers came to live in Dhahran. By 1938, when oil was first struck in commercial quantities, the compound boasted a movie theater and recreation hall, and the next year the community was officially named Dhahran. By 1940, it housed 371 American oil employees, 38 wives, 16 children, and 3,300 Arab and South Asian oil employees. The American population shrank considerably during World War II but grew at a frenetic pace when the war ended and commercial exploitation of Saudi Arabia's oil began in earnest. Today Dhahran, whose own population is 60,000, has merged with the nearby towns of Damman and al-Khobar to form a metropolitan area of more than one million.

Until the late 1940s, oil revenue was relatively modest, and what wealth there was found itself being channeled into cities such as Riyadh, Jiddah, Mecca, and Medina. Thus, traditional structures in the Eastern Province were not substantially affected until later. Still, oil production brought far more wealth to Saudi Arabia than it had previously known. By the late 1940s, 65 percent of the Saudi government's income came from the petroleum industry, a number that rose to 90 percent in the 1960s. Through the 1940s and '50s, this revenue concentrated wealth and power in the hands of those who were already in positions of authority at the expense of the general population. The government spent oil revenue on luxury projects such as royal palaces and on increased subsidies to tribal leaders, rather than on an infrastructure and public institutions to benefit the populace. These expenditures only aggravated pre-existing economic inequities. Meanwhile, traditional handicrafts diminished, as did the agricultural and pastoral sectors, whose products were replaced with imports. Landowners and merchants profited from these developments, but they also brought significant inflation, which, in effect, lowered the standard of living for wage earners in the oil industry.

The petroleum industry brought other difficult social changes to the region as well, particularly to the Eastern Province. Large segments of what had once been a subsistence agrarian and pastoral economy became transformed into a pool of wage earners in the oil economy. There were concomitant population shifts from villages and oases to the workers' camps of the new oil towns. At the same time, Aramco began to import foreign workers—not only the trained engineers and administrators but also low-cost manual laborers—who brought with them differing values and codes of behavior. Many of these workers came from other Arab countries and, along with Saudis sent abroad for training, brought with them the pan-Arabist and socialist ideologies on the rise throughout the Arab world at the time. By 1952, Aramco employed 9,187 foreign workers and 14,819 Saudis, but the Saudis were virtually unrepresented in senior and intermediate staff positions. Indigenous Arabs began to feel they were being discriminated against in their own country (Abir, p. 71).

The Aramco strike of 1953. Workers' dissatisfaction culminated in a general strike in 1953, similar in many ways to the strike that ends *Cities of Salt*. Although the strike in *Cities of Salt* is portrayed as a spontaneous reaction to the laying off of workers, that which actually took place at Aramco was probably the manifestation of a number of social and political problems, including Aramco management's insensitivity to the grievances of its Saudi workforce, uncertainty about the stability of the Saudi regime due to the failing health of the king, and a growing anti-Western sentiment in the region. Calls for a strike began to circulate among workers in early 1953, and in June of that year, a workers' committee presented a formal demand for wage increases, improved working conditions, and the right to

An oil refinery in Saudi Arabia.

unionize. The government responded by arresting 12 members of the committee, which sparked a strike in which 13,000 out of 15,000 Aramco workers participated. The National Guard was sent to Dhahran to crush the strike. Shortly thereafter, King Abd al-Aziz died and was succeeded by King Saud, who immediately granted the workers a 20 percent pay increase as well as other concessions.

Some leaders of the 1953 strike went on to join political movements whose agendas reflected discontent with the Saudi regime. The government's response to such political activity was generally repressive. Movement leaders were imprisoned or forced into exile. In 1954, King Saud issued a royal decree banning all strikes and demonstrations. The government sent extra elite military units to the Eastern Province and tightened its control of all media, vigorously hunting down socialists, communists, and Arab nationalists.

The Novel in Focus

Plot summary. *Cities of Salt* is unusual in that it takes as its main characters two towns: the oasis village of Wadi al-Uyoun and the coastal fishing village of Harran, which is later transformed into a coastal center for the growing petroleum industry. The novel opens with a loving description of Wadi al-Uyoun, a desert oasis, "one of those rare cases of nature expressing its genius and willfulness," a welcome miracle to caravans crossing the harsh desert (Munif, *Cities of Salt,* p. 1). But Wadi al-Uyoun is hardly an Eden. Although it supports a subsistence agrarian economy, frequent droughts make life in the oasis difficult. Its inhabitants suffer from malnutrition, and the fragile ecology can support only a limited population. Passing caravans lure away young men, who leave the village to seek their fortunes for years or even decades in other towns and cities.

Wadi al-Uyoun is described as supporting two peoples: the farmers of Wadi al-Uyoun itself, who live off the produce of their land and the goods they can trade with passing caravans, and the Atoum, a Bedouin tribe settled on hills on the outskirts of the oasis. Camel herders, the Atoum, though poor, are disdainful of material possessions and proud of their independence. The patriarch of this second group is Miteb al-Hathal, whereas the de facto headman of Wadi al-Uyoun is Ibn Rashed.

The pace of life in Wadi al-Uyoun is disrupted by the arrival of three Americans, who come in search of oil. Although welcomed, and indeed hosted, by Ibn Rashed, their presence and activities are mysterious to the people of the oasis.

The Bedouin patriarch Miteb al-Hathal is particularly suspicious of this visit. When the Americans return the following year and stay longer, Miteb, Ibn Rashed, and other village leaders visit the emir, the local government authority, to inform him of the situation. Miteb's concerns are rebuffed, and the others in the delegation agree to support the oil exploration when they are told that it is in their economic interest to do so. Miteb returns to Wadi al-Uyoun, consumed by fever and guilt at his inability to stop the encroaching Americans. His worst fears are realized as bulldozers are brought in to destroy the orchards.

> For anyone who remembers those long-ago days, when a place called Wadi al-Uyoun used to exist, and a man named Miteb al-Hathal, and a brook, and trees, and a community of people used to exist, the three things that still break his heart in recalling those days are the tractors[,] which attacked the orchards like ravenous wolves, tearing up the trees and throwing them to the earth one after another, and leveled all the orchards between the brook and the fields. . . .
>
> (*Cities of Salt*, p. 106)

During the destruction of Wadi al-Uyoun, Miteb al-Hathal leaves his family and the oasis for the desert, whence his forefathers had emerged decades before.

The town of Wadi al-Uyoun is completely destroyed to make way for the industrial complex that will be built in its place, and the people of the village find themselves evicted from their homes. One of Miteb's sons, Shaalan, remains in the oasis to work as a laborer for the oil company, but the rest of his family is forced to move. On the road, Miteb's wife, Wadha, is struck by a fever that leaves her mute.

At this point, the focus of the novel switches to another of Miteb's sons, Fawaz. Though still a boy, Fawaz feels the need to leave his family in the town of al-Hadra, where they are staying with relatives, in search of jobs. He and his cousin, Suweyleh, are denied work on the oil rigs of Wadi al-Uyoun, but Ibn Rashed, who now works for the American oil company recruiting laborers, directs them to Harran, a sleepy fishing village on the Persian Gulf that is to become the headquarters for the Americans' oil operations. In Harran, Fawaz and Suweyleh, like other workers, are required to sell their camels, symbols of independence and familial and cultural ties to the life they have left behind, and take up residence in work camps. Like Wadi al-Uyoun, the village of Harran is destroyed, and in its place, three

communities are built: a comparatively luxurious American compound, outfitted with air-conditioned buildings and swimming pools but off-limits to Arabs; a new Arab Harran, built quickly from the construction scraps of the American compound; and a workers' camp, first of tents, then of sheet-metal barracks.

The remainder of the novel describes the painful development, from these inauspicious beginnings, of the very human town of Harran. Through a series of interwoven vignettes and characters, the narrative describes how Ibn Rashed supplies the company with additional workers from other regions, as well as specialized merchants (a butcher, baker, grocer, and so on) to serve the growing town. The economic activity in Harran attracts entrepreneurs and specialists from as far away as Syria and Egypt. A road is paved to connect Harran to the inland trading town of Ujra in the interior. Also regular bus service comes to Harran. A café opens and serves as the first secular public meeting place for Harrani residents. A school, as well as medical and dental clinics, appears. As the town develops, the value of the real estate there increases. And a business class savvy enough to profit from these developments emerges.

The transformation of Harran is accompanied by both physical and psychological violence. In an incident that eventually causes the downfall of Ibn Rashed, a worker is killed in an industrial accident. The accident pits the American oil company and its rules of legal liability against the Arabian custom of payment in blood money— that is, avoiding a blood feud by paying a sum to compensate for the death of a family member. A feud ending in death arises between al-Mufaddi, an irascible character and traditional healer, and Subhi al-Mahmalji, a Western-trained doctor who sets up a clinic in Harran and eventually comes to serve as the emir's physician. At several other points in the novel smoldering tensions threaten to erupt into uncontrolled violence. These tensions are palpable, for example, when new workers arrive and receive better accommodations than older workers during the construction of the pipeline and when Crown Prince Khazael visits Harran.

Next to Arab Harran, American Harran stands as a constant reminder of the economic and cultural divide that separates the two communities. A fantastic ship brings beautiful women to entertain the Americans while Arab Harran watches. Barred from entering the compound, the Arabs grieve for the ties of intimacy they gave up when they left their homes to pursue economic opportunities in the oil industry. Interactions between the Americans and Arabs seem only to underscore the differences between them. On one occasion, the Americans cause an uproar among the Arab workers by conducting a sociological survey. The Arabs are bewildered and outraged by the personal questions they are asked (about their wives, female relatives, and religious practices). When the Americans are invited to a wedding in Arab Harran, they are delighted and take numerous photos but describe the music as uncouth.

Told from the point of view of the Arab community, the novel portrays the Americans as utterly alien masters of Harran's destiny, while for most of the novel the Arabs are generally childlike in their incomplete understanding of what is taking place around them and their inability to control the political and economic developments that shape their lives. Even at its best, the relationship between the Americans and Arabs is marred by the cultural and economic distance that separates them. When the Arabs and Americans celebrate the completion of the pipeline, the Arabs are amazed: "the Americans were so friendly that the Arabs wondered if these were the same people they knew" (*Cities of Salt*, p. 519). However, once the party is over, the workers are made to feel their social inferiority with a curt order to report to the administration authorities in the morning.

The novel describes Harran's political and economic developments in considerable detail. Shortly after the construction of the transformed Harran, Emir Khaled comes to rule, presumably sent by a centralized government with which the ordinary citizens of Harran have no dealings. Savvy characters like Ibn Rashed set out immediately to curry favor with Emir Khaled, whereas workers and city residents wait and judge from the sidelines. Emir Khaled emerges as a completely ineffective, self-absorbed ruler, preoccupied with hunting, building his personal residence, and playing with the technological toys he is given (radio, telephone, automobile, telescope, and more). His interest in the workers and residents is awakened only when political unrest forces him to act.

Cities of Salt also details the transformation of the subsistence economies of Wadi al-Uyoun and Old Harran into the stratified, capitalist society of New Harran. In Wadi al-Uyoun before its destruction, it was possible for the Atoum, the poorest residents of the oasis, to be proud of their independence from material needs. In New Harran, however, a consumer society develops in which the emir and his cronies ostentatiously flaunt their wealth, a growing middle class provides a widening array of goods and services, and a working class is increasingly dependent on its wages for bare survival. While some men manage to expand their businesses and become quite wealthy in this new Harran, others are forced to sell their lands to pay medical bills for illnesses that in the past were treated by a traditional healer.

The people of Harran experience a gradual political awakening. For much of the novel, the workers seem to have little if any control over their lives. They feel they have no choice but to live where Ibn Rashed or the company tells them to live, or to perform the jobs assigned to them—the backbreaking labor that the Americans refuse to do. But gradually they learn to assert control. Early in the novel, after the visit of the fantastic, female-laden ship, three workers decide they no longer wish to work in Harran. They steal back the camels they had sold to Ibn Rashed and flee the camp, never to be found again. In time, the other workers begin to question the differences between themselves and the Americans. During the construction of the pipeline, outside the compound and in a desert environment familiar to the Arabs but strange and hostile to the Americans, the workers play practical jokes on the foreigners, teasing them with lizards and snakes. A mysterious fire has the Americans on edge but energizes the Arabs, who wonder if this might have been an act of defiance by one of their own.

The culmination of this awakening occurs at the end of the novel. For unknown reasons, several workers are laid off, sparking a general strike, in which workers and residents of Arab Harran unite in their demands that the workers be reinstated and that there be an investigation into the mysterious death of al-Mufaddi, a local healer who has had a longstanding conflict with the emir's bodyguard. The strike is forcibly ended by the emir's guards, but the emir accedes to the strikers' demands before having to leave Harran, presumably because he has been stricken with mental illness.

At the end of the novel, in marked contrast to the bewilderment that characterized the Arabs' response to changes in Harran at the beginning, the workers and residents are able to discuss the causes of violence and distress in their society. One senses that the people of Harran will no longer serve as passive and naïve pawns of either the government or the oil company.

Tradition, modernity, and the character of Miteb al-Hathal. Because *Cities of* Salt takes two towns, rather than people, as its main focus, the novel moves episodically from character to character. One exception to this rule is the character of Miteb al-Hathal, the Bedouin patriarch of Wadi al-Uyoun, who upon the destruction of the oasis disappears into the desert with his camel, waterskin, and rifle. His disappearance is far from final, however. At key points during the novel, Miteb reappears. He resurfaces first as a vision to his sons, on the outskirts of the transformed Wadi al-Uyoun, where his eldest boy works, and on the road out of Wadi al-Uyoun, when the second eldest is denied work by Ibn Rashed. Miteb reappears too in Harran during times of unrest, most notably during fires that break out when the oil pipeline is constructed and during the strike that ends the novel.

That Miteb should appear at times of great stress is not surprising, for he embodies a past that has been violently destroyed by the petroleum industry. The author himself describes the character as "the symbol of the great heroism of the past and also the hope for the future" (*Middle East Times*). Indeed, Miteb embodies both Wadi al-Uyoun, the archetypical traditional Arabian community, and the ethos of the ideal Arabian man. He is a tribal leader by virtue of his age, experience, and aptitude, a proud Bedouin who eschews worldly comforts in favor of independence, but who is nonetheless deeply attached to Wadi al-Uyoun. He is generous to a fault and a virtuous Muslim. When faced with the destruction of Wadi al-Uyoun, he chooses not to serve the emir and the Americans but rather to return to his roots in the desert. Miteb, then, is the classic Arabian hero celebrated in poetry and folklore since pre-Islamic times. His reappearance at times of crisis and stress represents the continuation of that ancient Arabian ethos in the souls of those who see him. In a literary work dominated by the melancholy tone appropriate to the violent transformation that is the subject of the novel, the reappearance of Miteb al-Hathal at critical junctures is a sign of optimism on the part of the author. As Munif himself observed, "Miteb had children and his children will have children, meaning that hope is always there" (*Middle East Times*).

In contrast to Miteb, his descendants and other compatriots struggle to live in the modern society that has come to their corner of the world. Gradually they evolve into modern citizens—who replace close ties to family and community with mobility and a new type of independence. The workers of Harran, for example, create a new community for themselves based not on blood ties but on their shared experience as employees of the company. But their break with tradition does not occur without violence. For many of them, the violence is manifested in psychosomatic illness. Miteb sickens with a fever after the Americans visit Wadi al-Uyoun. His wife, Wadha, is stricken with an illness that leaves her mute when she is forced to quit the oasis. Similarly, a worker whose brother dies in an industrial accident is struck dumb by the incident. Ibn Rashed suffers from a mental illness when his own actions as well as the machinations of other ambitious Harranis leave him isolated from the community. Even the emir, divorced from his people and completely caught up in his technological devices and dependency on the Americans, suffers a mental breakdown.

Literary context. Munif has been widely recognized in the Arab world as a politically committed novelist who regularly treats the issues of freedom and human rights in his works. As he sees it, the novel is an opportunity to write an alternative historiography—what some critics have called a counter to the master narrative of historical events put forth by the Saudi state (Siddiq, p. 651). Munif's works are especially important in that he is the first major Arab novelist to emerge from the Arabian Peninsula and hence the first to take oil development and its effect on indigenous desert communities as the central theme of a fictional work. Although no other writer has dealt as exhaustively with this theme, the oil industry and its sociopolitical effect on the Arabian Peninsula have inspired other writers as well. Egyptian writer Ibrahim Abd al-Majid, for instance, has written about the communities of foreign workers in Saudi Arabia in his novel *The Other Place* (1999).

Events in History at the Time the Novel Was Written

Saudi Arabia 50 years later. *Cities of Salt* was published in 1985, approximately 50 years after the discovery of oil in Saudi Arabia. By then oil had brought tremendous prosperity to the region but had also become the source of considerable anxiety and social unrest. The industry attracted so many foreign workers that by the early 1980s noncitizen residents numbered approximately 5 million, a very large percentage in a country whose citizen population was approximately 8 million. Western influence in the country, from

THE REMAINING VOLUMES IN ABD AL-RAHMAN'S QUINTET

The five novels (three of which have been translated into English) that comprise *Cities of Salt* share characters and themes but are not ordered chronologically. The first novel, *Cities of Salt: The Wilderness,* is only tangentially related to the other novels in the series, which chronicle the rise to power of the Hudayyibi family. In this first novel, Crown Prince Khazael, who is a major character in the later works, visits Harran to celebrate the completion of the oil pipeline. The second novel, *al-Ukhdud* (*The Trench*), recounts the rule of Khazael after he succeeds to the throne. The novel details the founding of a modern state and the creation of transportation, communication, and military infrastructure, ending with Khazael's dethroning while he is abroad. The third novel, *Taqasim al-layl wa-al-nahar* (*Variations on Night and Day,* 1993), is actually a prequel to *The Trench.* It takes us back to the time of Khazael's father, Khuraybit, who with a small band of men regains the throne that had been seized from his family previously and proceeds to extend his rule throughout the Arabian Peninsula. Novel Four, *al-Munbatt* (The Isolated One*),* returns to the life of Khazael, this time in exile in Germany, and ends with his death. Novel Five, *Badiyat al-zulumat* (The Desert of Darkness*),* focuses on two different historical periods. First, the novel recounts the upbringing of Khuraybit's sons, Khazael and Fanar, ending with Khazael's ascension to the throne. Next, the novel describes the dethronement of Khazael and the assassination of Fanar. Though set in a fictional Arabian kingdom, the series of novels parallels closely the history of Saudi Arabia and together are generally understood to be a biting commentary on the Saudi regime.

both the influx of foreigners and the Western education of many Saudis, led to a yearning for traditional Arabian culture. Meanwhile, Saudi princes argued about oil-related matters, from Saudi Arabia's role in OPEC, to the quantity of oil to pump, to how the oil revenues ought to be spent. These debates were sharpened by a significant reduction in oil revenues at this time. (Revenues dropped from a high of $109 billion in 1981 to $17 billion in 1987). By the mid 1980s Saudi Arabia had fallen into a recession and its inhabitants had begun to suffer unemployment. Support for the regime continued to be strong among the lower classes, especially in the Najd and Hejaz, but the new middle class, consisting largely of technocrats, was less content. This group had done well financially under the Saudis, but it had no voice in the government and remained completely dependent on the regime and its whims for continued prosperity.

Meanwhile, Saudi Arabia's Eastern Province suffered from the recession with the rest of the country. There was unrest in the oil fields and oil towns of the province in late 1979 and early 1980, sparked in part by the 1979 revolution in Iran, whose residents, like the Eastern Saudis, are largely Shi'ite Muslims. The Saudi government reacted by increasing both security in the area and investment in the infrastructure of the long-neglected region. Thus, nearly three decades after the general strike that ends *Cities of Salt,* the Eastern Province continued to challenge the Saudi regime.

An uprising in Mecca that year by 200 armed fundamentalists, some of whom were descendants of the *ikhwan* warriors originally nurtured by King Abd al-Aziz, was also brutally crushed, and its leaders were publicly beheaded.

Reception. Abd al-Rahman Munif's writings have been well received in the Arab intellectual world, both because of the saliency of the themes he treats and because of his literary innovations. *Cities of Salt* has been acclaimed for its voice, which narrates from the standpoint not of a character or narrator but of an entire city or community. However, the implicit criticism of the Saudi regime and its oil policy reflected in his fiction has not gone unnoticed by Arab governments. The five novels that comprise the *Cities of Salt* series were banned

POPULATION SHIFTS IN SAUDI ARABIA

Because Saudi Arabia has no official population census, most figures relating to population movement and growth are estimates. We do know, however, that the population has increased dramatically. While 1959 population estimates range from 3 to 7 million, those for the early 1980s fall between 6 and 12 million. Since the advent of the petroleum industry, the country has also played host to a large number of foreigners. In 1952, 38.2 percent of Aramco employees were non-Saudis. The percentage of all foreign workers in Saudi Arabia in 1980 was 47.4. Because the population of the major cities (Riyadh, Jiddah, Mecca, and Medina) has increased dramatically since the founding of the Saudi state in the early twentieth century, we know that there has been a pronounced shift from rural to urban centers. There are no figures on the numbers of Bedouin and rural Saudis who, like those in *Cities of Salt,* moved into the oil sector. However, company records show a substantial increase (from 3,000 in 1938 to 19,600 in 1956) in number of employees at Aramco as the century wore on and indicate that most of these employees were indigenous Saudis.

upon publication in several Persian Gulf countries, including Saudi Arabia, and Munif was stripped of his Saudi citizenship. The English translation of the novel is banned in Egypt, although the Arabic version is not.

Palestinian novelist Jabra Ibrahim Jabra has said of Munif, "I do not know of any other Arab novelist who relishes, and indeed, even suffers from, such a fierce and passionate sensitivity to nature" (Jabra in Allen, p. 266).

—Nadia Yakub

For More Information

Abd al-Ghani. *al-Khuruj min al-tarikh: Abd al-Rahman Munif wa Mudun al-milh.* Cairo: al-Hay'ah al-Misriyah al-Ammah lil-Kitab, 1993.

Abir, Mordechai. *Saudi Arabia in the Oil Era: Regime and Elites; Conflict and Collaboration.* Boulder, Colo.: Westview Press, 1988.

Allen, Roger, ed. *Modern Arabic Literature.* New York: Ungar, 1987.

Habib, John. *Ibn Sa'ud's Warriors of Islam.* Leiden: E. J. Brill, 1978.

Middle East Times. "Changing the World with His Pen." 3 December 1999. http://www.metimes .com/issue99-49/cultent/ changing_the_world .htm (26 May 2003).

Munif, Abd al-Rahman. *Cities of Salt.* Trans. Peter Theroux. New York: Random House, 1987.

Netton, Ian Richard, ed. *Arabia and the Gulf: From Traditional Society to Modern States: Essays in Honor of M. A. Shaban's 60th Birthday.* London: Croom Helm, 1986.

Niblock, Tim. *State, Society and Economy in Saudi Arabia.* New York: St. Martin's Press, 1982.

Nixon, Rob. "The Hidden Lives of Oil." *The Chronicle of Higher Education* 48 (5 April 2002): B7-B9.

Quandt, William. *Saudi Arabia in the 1980s: Foreign Policy, Security, and Oil.* Washington, D.C.: The Brookings Institute, 1981.

al-Rasheed, Madawi. *Politics in an Arabian Oasis: The Rashidi Tribal Dynasty.* London: I. B. Tauris, 1991.

Siddiq, Muhammad. "The Making of a Counter-Narrative: Two Examples from Contemporary Arabic and Hebrew Fiction." *Michigan Quarterly Review* 31, no. 4 (fall 1992): 649-62.

Stegner, Wallace. *Discovery!: The Search for Arabian Oil.* Beirut, Lebanon: Middle East Export Press, 1971.

"The Clockwork Doll" and Other Poems

by

Dalia Ravikovitch

<table>
<tr><td>

THE LITERARY WORK

Poems set mainly in Israel and Lebanon in the mid- to late-twentieth century; published in Hebrew from the 1950s to the 1980s, in English in 1989.

SYNOPSIS

The collection explores war, racial and religious conflict, and women's place in Israeli society.

</td></tr>
</table>

Dalia Ravikovitch was born in 1936 in the suburb of Tel Aviv known as Ramat Gan; after the death of her father in a hit-and-run accident, she and her family went to live on a kibbutz. Ravikovitch later attended high school in Haifa and the Hebrew University of Jerusalem. She also served in the Israeli army, and it was during this period that her poems first appeared in newspapers and journals. In 1959 Ravikovitch published her debut collection of verse, *Ahavat tapuah ha-zahav* (The Love of an Orange), which established her as one of Israel's foremost poets. Other volumes—*Horef kasheh* (1964; A Hard Winter), *ha-Sefer ha-shelishi* (1969; The Third Book), *Tehum koreh* (1974; Deep Calleth Unto Deep)—consolidated her reputation. In 1978 Ravikovitch's poetry was first translated from Hebrew into English by American poet Chana Bloch in *A Dress of Fire* (1976). *The Window*, a second collection, with translations by Chana Bloch and Ariel Bloch, appeared in 1989. Spanning several decades, it builds from such poems as "The Clockwork Doll" and "Marionette" ("Bubah memukhenet," 1959, and "Maryonetah," 1969) to poems that deal with other topical concerns. In "You Can't Kill a Baby Twice" and "Hovering at Low Altitude" ("Tinok lo horgim pa`amayim," 1986, and "Rehifah be-govah namukh," 1986), Ravikovitch explores such concerns as war, cruelty, and the devastation in the wake of the Israeli invasion of Lebanon in 1982.

Events in History at the Time of the Poems

The status of women in modern Israeli society. During Ravikovitch's lifetime, the role of women in Israeli society has been redefined. During the 1900s the first women who emigrated from Eastern Europe to Palestine—often called the *halutsot* (women pioneers)—showed dedication to a dream of socialism, equality, and justice in their reclaimed homeland. They expected to find fulfillment working the earth and toiling in the fields beside their male counterparts. The harsh climate, arduous working conditions, and ingrained male prejudices, however, undermined those expectations; most *halutsot* found themselves working in the kitchen and laundry instead, once again relegated to traditional domestic roles and duties.

Between the 1920s and 1940s, however, Jewish women in Palestine achieved some progress, mainly through the efforts of separate organizations, such as the Working Women's Council. Golda Meir, the future prime minister, describes their struggle "not as one for 'civic' rights, which they had in abundance, but for equal burdens. They wanted to be given whatever work their male comrades were given—paving roads, building houses, or standing guard duty—not to be treated as though they were different and automatically relegated to the kitchen" (Meir in Hazleton, p. 19).

One major result of this campaign for "equal burdens" was the inclusion of women in the armed forces, beginning with the Haganah, or Jewish defense organization, which existed from 1920 until Israel's statehood in 1948 and was the precursor to the Israel Defense Forces (IDF). Although the responsibilities of Haganah women most often involved nursing the wounded and keeping the weaponry in fit condition, they were trained to use guns as well and some served in the fighting arm of the Haganah, the Palmach, during its seven years from 1941 to 1948. During the first stages of the War of Independence (1948-1949), women soldiers also carried out convoy duties, secretly transporting guns and grenades to Israeli troops. For the most part, however, Israeli women worked as nurses, wireless operators, and quartermasters, much as British women had done during World War II.

During the decades that followed, the status of Israeli women became increasingly ambiguous. From the formation of the state of Israel, even in provisional pre-state "governments," women had the right to vote. Israel's Declaration of Independence, issued in 1948, announced "The State of Israel will maintain equal social and political rights for all citizens, irrespective of religion, race, or sex" while the new Israeli government maintained that women would enjoy "equality in rights and duties, in the life of the country, society and economy, and throughout the entire legal system" (Hazleton, pp. 22-23). Laws passed during the 1950s, however, seemed to compromise or contradict those sentiments. For example, the Women's Equal Rights Law of 1951 and the Rabbinical Courts Jurisdiction (Marriage and Divorce) Law of 1953 upheld the monopolistic and paternalistic control of the religious establishment over marriage and divorce for all Jewish citizens. According to rabbinic law, for example, the husband must grant his wife a divorce (known as a *get*); without his authorization, she is an "*agunah*," or "chained woman," whose future marriages will be considered invalid, and future children illegitimate. In 1954 the Employment of Women Law forbade women from working at night on the grounds that it was injurious to their health. The existence and passage of such legislation undermined the statements in the Scroll of Independence, revealing that true social and political equality was still more a myth than a reality for Israeli women. Several of Ravikovitch's

Dalia Ravikovitch

early poems, including "Clockwork Doll" and "The Marionette," explore the contradiction between the promise of full equality for women and their lack of it in everyday Israeli society.

Israeli involvement in Lebanon—an overview. In its first years of statehood, Israel made a point of cultivating friendly relations with Lebanon, an Arab country that might conceivably become an ally to the new nation. As early as 1954, David Ben-Gurion proposed that Israel support the Maronite Christians, who had held power in Lebanon. But internal rivalries in Lebanon complicated matters. The population of Shi'ite Muslims had by this time outstripped that of the Maronites and other groups and controversy raged over who should hold political posts. Civil war broke out in Lebanon in 1975. In keeping with Ben-Gurion's earlier advice, Israel sold $118.5 million worth of arms to the Lebanese Christians in the first six years of war (Morris, p. 504).

Israel's involvement in Lebanese affairs increased during the late 1970s after the Palestine Liberation Organization (PLO)—expelled from Jordan in September 1970—set up its major base of operations in southern Lebanon, from which it launched attacks on northern Israel. In March 1978, after a PLO guerrilla attack on the Tel Aviv-Haifa road killed 37 people, Israel retaliated with Operation Litani, a military offensive that led to the Israeli occupation of southern Lebanon up to the Litani River. By June, however, under pressure from the United States, Israeli troops withdrew from the region, leaving the PLO stronghold in southern Lebanon essentially untouched. This development caused major embarrassment for the administration of Prime Minister Menachem Begin, which had come to power partly because of its hard-line security policy.

The Begin government endured similar embarrassment in 1981 when Maronite forces, known as the Phalangists, clashed with Syrian forces in Zahlah, a city in eastern Lebanon. Leading the Phalangists was Bashir Gemayel (also spelled Jumayyil). After Syrian troops drove his forces from Zahlah, Israel came to its ally's defense by having its aircraft destroy two Syrian helicopters over Lebanon. In retaliation, Syrian president Hafez al-Assad moved Soviet missiles into Lebanon. Israel threatened to destroy the missiles but again was persuaded to back down by the American government.

After a narrow victory in the Knesset elections of June 1981, the Begin administration adopted a more aggressive defense policy, especially against the PLO presence in Lebanon. Ariel Sharon, an Israeli war hero, became Begin's new minister of defense; he found an ally in General Raphael Eitan, another military man and the chief of staff under Begin. Together, Sharon and Eitan became the major arbiters of Israel's defense policy. In July 1981, a month after the Knesset elections, Israel bombed PLO encampments in southern Lebanon in retaliation for PLO rocket attacks on northern Israeli settlements; with the help of U.S. envoy Philip Habib, a tentative cease-fire was eventually achieved.

Hostilities resumed in early June of 1982 after another Palestinian group, Abu Nidal, attacked Israel's ambassador in London, Shlomo Argov. He was shot in the head and permanently paralyzed. Blame was mistakenly assigned to the PLO for the incident. On June 4, the Israeli air force bombed a sports stadium in the Lebanese capital of Beirut; the stadium was reportedly being used as a PLO ammunition depot. In response, the PLO shelled Israeli towns in Galilee. The following day, the Israeli government formally accused the PLO of violating the cease-fire and, on June 6, Israeli ground troops marched into southern Lebanon in a military campaign known as Operation Peace for the Galilee. The campaign sought to eliminate the large PLO presence in southern Lebanon and insure that Israel's allies, the Maronite Christians, would hold power in Beirut. From mid-June to mid-August, Israel laid siege to Beirut; U.S. intervention eventually lifted the siege and PLO guerrillas were evacuated from the city.

Significantly, the Israeli invasion of Lebanon occurred without a domestic consensus; far from unilaterally supporting their government's actions, the Israeli public was divided on the issue. Many, including Dalia Ravikovitch, did not view the operation as necessary or essential to Israel's survival as a nation and were emboldened to speak out against the invasion. Israeli public protests became even more heated after the massacres in the Sabra and Shatila refugee camps in September 1982.

The Sabra-Shatila massacres. In September 1982 violence in Lebanon erupted once again. On September 14, the Maronite leader Bashir Gemayel, newly elected president of Lebanon, showed up at a party branch office to deliver his weekly lecture. He was speaking to a Maronite women's group when a bomb, planted by a pro-Syrian dissident, exploded, killing dozens of people, Bashir included. Shocked by the death of one of their prominent allies, the Israeli government prepared to retaliate against the Palestinians, whom they held responsible for the bombing.

The day after Bashir's assassination, Israeli defense minister Ariel Sharon and General Eitan authorized both the seizure of key junctions commanding West Beirut and the entrance of Phalangist militiamen into the Palestinian refugee camps of Sabra and Shatila to search for PLO operatives. Sharon himself gave the Phalangists permission to destroy PLO installations and personnel, declaring, "I don't want a single one of the terrorists left" (Sharon in Sachar, p. 914). Accompanied by the Israel Defense Forces (IDF), about 300 to 400 Christian militiamen—most of them Phalangists, some members of the Israeli-sponsored South Lebanon Army—proceeded to the camps on September 16. Once in the vicinity, all the troops dropped out of the Israelis' sight. However, Israeli intelligence officers watching the camps from the nearby roofs overheard fragments of radio conversation among the Christian militiamen and began to suspect that indiscriminate violence was taking place inside. Although the Israeli officers relayed their suspicions to army headquarters, it was several hours before they received a response. A directive ordered them to remove the Phalangists from the camps, but it was not until September 18, after Sharon himself visited them, that the order was carried out. Over a period of two days the Christian militiamen had massacred scores of Palestinian men, women, and children in the camps. There is contention over approximately how many were killed—Israeli intelligence estimated a total of 700 to 800 people (Morris, p. 547).

Outrage over the Sabra and Shatila massacres was vocal and widespread. Although the Israeli government insisted that the Phalangist officers had lost control of their men, it appeared that Israeli troops had done little to stop the killings, even turning back some groups of escaping refugees because of orders to block the exits (Butler in Shahid, p. 40). On September 29, some 400,000 Israelis demonstrated in Tel Aviv, demanding that those even partly to blame be punished, whereupon a commission of inquiry was established (the Kahan Commission). It became clear that various Israeli soldiers had reported the killings to their superiors. In the wake of the investigation, Ariel Sharon was forced to resign as defense minister, though he remained in the cabinet. The massacres at the camps inspired Ravikovitch's "You Can't Kill a Baby Twice," one of her most overtly political poems.

AN EYEWITNESS ACCOUNT OF THE MASSACRE

One eyewitness, a Palestinian from the Haifa region who was born and raised in the Shatila camp, offered the following account of what he saw on the first evening of the Phalangists' attacks: "I saw a group of women and children screaming in terror and running towards us. I saw one woman trying to support her body against the shoulder of another woman. Her hand pressed against her stomach and blood gushed between her fingers. Another woman screamed as she saw us: 'They are butchering us, they are butchering us'" (al-Shaikh, p. 3). On September 20, the witness reported, "The killers had gone, but the results of their bloody work had stayed. Most of the corpses were piled up one over another or covered by the rubble of houses brought down on top of them. The dead were indistinguishable" (al-Shaikh, p. 14).

The Poems in Focus

The contents. Selected from several volumes of Ravikovitch's poetry, spanning the years 1959 to 1986, the poems in *The Window* range in content from the status of women, to nature, family life, and ancient history, to war and violence. The poems related to this last issue, war and violence,

were prompted by the 1982 Israeli invasion of Lebanon. Along with the first issue, the status of women, it is a topic treated in the poems that are covered here.

"Clockwork Doll" and "Marionette." In "Clockwork Doll" and "Marionette," Ravikovitch explores the ambiguous roles modern Israeli women are expected to play. The first poem describes a dream vision in which the speaker becomes "a clockwork doll," whirling in various directions, until "I fell on my face and shattered to bits / and they tried to fix me with all their skill" (Ravikovitch, "Clockwork Doll," lines 1, 3-4). Patched up (or corrected) by these unidentified experts, she becomes "a proper doll again," doing whatever she is told, but she is still not quite as she was before—"an injured twig that dangles from a stem" ("Clockwork Doll," lines 5, 8). The doll attends a ball, meaning to dance, but despite her "measured and rhythmical" steps, she is still left alone "with the dogs and the cats," creatures who are less than human yet more alive in their way than she is. By the following verse, the doll no longer moves or acts but merely sits there while her beauty is admired: "And I had blue eyes and golden hair / and a dress all the colors of garden flowers, / and a trimming of cherries on my straw hat" ("Clockwork Doll," lines 12-14). She has been transformed from an autonomous being to a controlled object, to something that is finally abandoned and observed.

"The Marionette" contains imagery reminiscent of the earlier "Clockwork Doll." But this later poem draws a stronger parallel between a living woman and a puppet. "The threads that bind my whole life," says its speaker, "are pure silk" ("The Marionette," lines 8-9). Women throughout history, she continues, have found themselves enacting the role of a marionette, beautiful, helpless, unable to act but deftly manipulated by others:

> Four hundred years ago
> she was Dona Elvira, Contessa of Seville,
> with three hundred chambermaids.
> The moment she glanced at her fine
> silk handkerchief,
> she knew her fate: she'd be a wax doll
> or a porcelain marionette.
> ("The Marionette," lines 14-20)

Fragile and malleable, Dona Elvira is treated with deference by her courtiers but wields no real power or authority, her death as gentle and ineffectual as her life. In the last verse, however, the speaker's tone becomes ironic as she examines the situation of modern women who find themselves equally helpless and constrained: "In the twentieth century, on a precious gray dawn, / how fortunate to be / a marionette" ("The Marionette," lines 29-31). Like their spiritual ancestress, modern women are denied true power or autonomy. "This woman is not responsible for her actions, / say the judges. / Her fragile heart is gray as dawn, / her body hangs by a thread" ("The Marionette," lines 32-36).

"You Can't Kill a Baby Twice" and "Hovering at Low Altitude." The first poem refers at the outset to the massacres at the Sabra and Shatila refugee camps in June 1982. The opening stanza ironically notes how, among "the sewage puddles of Sabra and Shatila," the prisoners were transported "from the world of the living to the world / of eternal light" ("You Can't Kill a Baby Twice," lines 1, 4-5). This pious image is immediately undercut by the stark description of just how those prisoners met their fate:

First they shot,
they hanged,
then they slaughtered with their knives.
Terrified women climbed up on a ramp of
    earth, frantic:
"They're slaughtering us there,
in Shatila."
    ("You Can't Kill a Baby Twice," lines 7-12)

Israeli soldiers turn on searchlights, rendering the camp "bright as day," then yell at the screaming women to return to the camp ("You Can't Kill a Baby Twice," line 16). The narrator notes that such a soldier "was following orders" and goes on to describe, almost dispassionately, the ghastly sight of the camp's slaughtered children, who at least cannot be harmed further because "You can't kill a baby twice" ("You Can't Kill a Baby Twice," lines 20, 25). The poem concludes with further irony as the narrator echoes lines from a popular 1967 song about a war hero: "Our sweet soldiers / wanted nothing for themselves. / All they ever asked / was to come home / safe" ("You Can't Kill a Baby Twice," lines 28-32).

While "You Can't Kill a Baby Twice" is grounded in the context of a specific historical event, "Hovering at Low Altitude" explores the horrors of an unspecific, seemingly random event—the rape and murder of an Arab shepherdess. An ominous note is sounded in the first stanza as the narrator—who strives to distance herself from the action by repeatedly stating "I am not here"—observes the girl leading her herd of goats to pasture and remarks, "She won't live out the day, / that girl" ("Hovering at Low Altitude," lines 9-10). From this point onward, descriptions of the girl and her activities are interspersed with descriptions of the narrator's whereabouts as she queasily tries to protect herself from emotional involvement with the tragedy about to unfold:

I am not here
I've been in the mountains many days now.
The light will not burn me, the frost
Won't touch me.
Why be astonished now?
I've seen worse things in my life.
    ("Hovering at Low Altitude," lines 21-26)

> ### FROM *THE BEIRUT MASSACRE: THE COMPLETE KAHAN COMMISSION REPORT*
>
> ~
>
> "Following a quite lengthy debate, Brigadier General Yaron responded to the remarks of the participants by stating 'the mistake, as I see it, the mistake is everyone's. The entire system showed insensitivity. I am speaking now of the military system. . . . On this point everyone showed insensitivity, pure and simple. Nothing else. So you start asking me, what exactly did you feel in your gut on Friday. . . . I did badly, I admit it. I did badly. I cannot, how is it possible that a divisional commander—and I think this applies to the Division Commander on up—how is it possible that a Division Commander is in the field and does not know that 300, 400, 500 or a thousand, I don't know how many, are being murdered here? If he's like that, let him go. How can such a thing be? But why didn't he know? Why was he oblivious? That's why he didn't know and that's why he didn't stop it . . . but I take myself to task. . . .'"
>   (*The Beirut Massacre,* p. 49)

Despite her attempts to continue "hovering at low altitude," the narrator still cannot help looking at the girl and speculating as to what her thoughts might be during the last hours of her life. At noon a man, looking "innocent enough," proceeds up the mountains and the narrator hurriedly absents herself as he launches his murderous attack upon the shepherd girl: "With one strong push I can hover and whirl around / with the speed of the wind. / I can get away and say to myself: / I haven't seen a thing" ("Hovering at Low Altitude," lines 46, 55-58). Even as the narrator hastens to escape from the scene, however, her thoughts linger on the shepherdess, eyes bulging in terror as the man's hand "closes over her hair, grasping it / without a shard of pity" ("Hovering at Low Altitude," lines 61-62). In this poem, the shepherdess is doubly a victim by virtue of being both an Arab and a woman; and the guilt is widespread, falling both on the actual rapist and the complicit narrator.

Dolls, puppets, and Israeli women. Much of Ravikovitch's early poetry is individual and subjective, focusing on such events as her childhood, the loss of her father, and her experiences as a modern Israeli woman. This last condition is explored in two poems originally published ten years apart—"Clockwork Doll" (1959) and "The Marionette" (1969). In the two poems, which use similar imagery and language, women are presented as fragile, doll-like creatures, whose seeming autonomy masks a deeper dependency. Both poems reflect the ambiguous social and political position in which Israeli women found themselves in the first decades of statehood. Although the new nation's Declaration of Independence proclaimed that all its citizens were equal regardless of race, religion, or sex, laws passed during the 1950s restricting women's working hours and control over their marital status seemed to belie that proclamation.

In 1959, the same year "Clockwork Doll" was published, the Defense Service Act decreed that women would undergo a shorter period of compulsory military service than men and also exempted from military service all women who were married, pregnant, or had children. The unspoken implications of such legislation appeared to be that the most important function of an Israeli woman was still to be a wife and mother. According to one psychologist, "None of these laws encourage[d] women to take a full and equal part in Israel's public life"; in the 1970s, "Israeli women tend[ed] to work from the time they [left] school or graduate[d] from the army until their marriage or first pregnancy, and then drop out" (Hazleton, pp. 29-30). Moreover, many women in the more affluent classes did not work at all, serving as a status symbol in Israeli society, demonstrating that the husband earned enough to support the family without help. "The wealthier of such wives may engage in volunteer activities . . . but most of their time is spent around the pool, at the hairdresser's, dressing up to stroll through the shops or linger in a café with friends" (Hazleton, p. 30). Such a woman might easily be depicted as "a wax doll / or a porcelain marionette," devoid of real power or purpose.

Although many Israeli women accepted their ambivalent status—that of being theoretically but not socially, economically, or professionally equal to men—a new women's movement began to form during the 1970s. Lectures and seminars at such institutions as Haifa University raised women's consciousness of their situation and inspired the founding of feminist groups in such cities as Tel Aviv and Jerusalem. The Tel Aviv group, which eventually called itself "The Israel Feminist Movement," bore a resemblance to both the National Organization for Women in the United States and Choisir in France. Women's centers were also set up in Haifa and Tel Aviv, and their personnel lectured in schools and on army bases and kibbutzim, although the centers did not attract many women. In 1978 the first women's conference was held in Beer Sheba; some 150 women attended. Representatives were able to report such encouraging developments as the establishment of the first shelter for battered women (1977) and the first rape crisis intervention center (1977)—in Haifa and Tel Aviv, respectively. Feminism also infiltrated Israeli politics; in 1975 Prime Minister Yitzhak Rabin appointed a committee to examine the status of Israeli women, which became the main feminist issue during the 1980s. Israeli feminists also became more active in their country's peace movement, protesting the 1982 invasion of Lebanon by forming Women Against Occupation. During the Intifada—Palestinian uprising—of 1987, feminists organized women's peace groups to demand both an end to the occupation and negotiation with the PLO.

Sources. Ravikovitch's body of work draws upon many sources for inspiration, including her own experiences as an Israeli woman and a variety of religious and mythological texts. Her early poems especially integrate language, metaphors, and images from sources as diverse as the Jewish prayer book, the Bible, the Midrash, and Greek mythology. By contrast, Ravikovitch's later poems became more public, less internal or visionary in scope, and more focused on current events, such as the Lebanon War and the escalating hostilities between Israelis and Palestinians.

As a poet, Ravikovitch has elicited comparisons with Adrienne Rich, on the basis of the formal, tightly structured poems written during her early years. In 1977 one critic, Shimon Sandback, described those early works as an exploration of "the exotic geography of the unconscious" (Sandbank in Glazer, p. 256). By 1989, however, Robert Alter, in a foreword to *The Window*, noted a shift "from the visionary to the quotidian" in

Ravikovitch's work, observing that her more recent poems seemed to express a "desire to achieve a kind of naked verbal engagement with what is seen as the awfulness of everyday reality" (Alter in Ravikovitch, p. xi).

Literary context—protest poetry. While the Lebanon War in 1982 served as a catalyst for the writing of protest poetry, there was already a strong tradition of both self-criticism and political poetry in Israeli letters. Among the most famous precedents are H. N. Bialik's **"In the City of Slaughter"** (also in *WLAIT 6: Middle Eastern Literatures and Their Times*) and "Upon the Slaughter." Both poems were written in the diaspora, in the wake of the Kishinev pogrom in 1903 Russia. While the first poem is replete with self-criticism, the poetic voice in the second poem reverberates with prophet-like anger, raging not only against the perpetrators of the horror but also against those who would seek vengeance: "Fit vengeance for the spilt blood of a child / The devil has not yet compiled . . ." (Bialik, p. 113). The poems were patently political in that they were connected to a concrete historical event. Ravikovitch's poem "You Can't Kill a Baby Twice" is a near direct descendent of Bialik's shorter poem "Upon the Slaughter," which expressed outrage at the death of children in the 1903 Kishinev pogrom.

In Israel, *political* is often narrowly defined as dealing with the security situation and relations with neighboring Arab countries and the Palestinians. Sometimes the term is connected to religious and ethnic fissures, only rarely to so-called women's issues, which is Ravikovitch's original concern. In any case, she is drawing not only on the modern tradition of Bialik but also on a more recent tradition of political protest poetry in Israel. In these poems, it is not unusual to encounter references to biblical stories and characters. Perhaps most prominent is the story of the *akedah*, the binding of Isaac (Genesis 22), which has served as a creative source to protest the sending of the younger generation to battle and even to express empathy for the Palestinians. In *The Window*, in keeping with her original focus on women, Ravikovitch's "Like Rachel" turns the spotlight on a biblical matriarch and how she died, relating it to the poet's personal present. The most powerful examples mine the past to comment on the current situation, in personal and broader terms. These commentaries are characterized by an honest self-examination and an unflinchingly critical tone.

Reviews. On its publication in 1989 *The Window* received mainly positive reviews. Rochelle Owens, writing for the *American Book Review*, deemed Ravikovitch's poetry "unquestionable in its values for it yields a spectrum of important themes from Jewish history and contemporary events. She creates with dramatic power the poignancy of deprivation, the horror and cruel intentions and inevitabilities of war" (Owens in Riviello, p. 1496). The pertinence of these words to "Hovering at Low Altitude" and "You Can't Kill a Baby Twice" is clear. Falling into the category of "important themes from contemporary events," the status-of-women poems are singled out for their important themes. Elsewhere, called a "classic Israeli text," the "Clockwork Doll" has been described as the "literary proof text of the female condition" (Feldman, p. 133). That the poems share a general tone is something observed by a third critic: "The poet's vision is always gripping," L. Berk observes, "however grim and terrible it often is" (Berk in Riviello, p. 1496).

—Pamela S. Loy

For More Information

The Beirut Massacre: The Complete Kahan Commission Report. New York: Karz-Cohl, 1983.

Bialik, Hayyim Nahman. *Selected Poems of Hayyim Nahman Bialik.* Trans. Israel Efros. New York: Bloch, 1948.

Feldman, Yael S. *No Room of Their Own: Gender and Nation in Israeli Women's Fiction.* New York: Columbia University Press, 1999.

Glazer, Miriyam, ed. *Dreaming the Actual: Contemporary Fiction and Poetry by Israeli Women Writers.* New York: State University of New York Press, 2000.

Hazleton, Lesley. *Israeli Women: The Reality Behind the Myths.* New York: Simon and Schuster, 1977.

Morris, Benny. *Righteous Victims: A History of the Zionist-Arab Conflict, 1881-2001.* New York: Vintage, 2001.

Petran, Tabitha. *The Struggle Over Lebanon.* New York: Monthly Review Press, 1987.

Ravikovitch, Dalia. *The Window: New and Selected Poems.* Trans. Chana Bloch and Ariel Bloch. Riverdale-on-Hudson, New York: The Sheep Meadow Press, 1989.

Riviello, Barbara Jo, ed. *Book Review Digest.* New York: The H. W. Wilson Company, 1991.

Sachar, Howard M. *A History of Israel from the Rise of Zionism to Our Time.* New York: Alfred A. Knopf, 2000.

Shahid, Leila. "The Sabra and Shatila Massacres: Eye-Witness Reports." *Journal of Palestine Studies* 32, no. 1 (autumn 2002): 36-58.

al-Shaikh, Zakaria. *Sabra and Shatila 1982: Resisting the Massacre.* London: PLO London Office, Information Dept., 1982.

Swirski, Barbara, and Marilyn P. Safir, eds. *Calling the Equality Bluff.* New York: Pergamon Press, 1991

The Conference of the Birds

by

Farid al-Din Attar

Farid al-Din Attar of Nishapur, Iran, is one of the three greatest mystical poets in Persian literature. His life spanned the period between that of the other two master poets of the Islamic mystical tradition—Sana'i of Ghaznavi (d. 1130) and Jalal al-Din Rumi (1207-73). Attar's birth and death dates remain unknown, though he is thought to have perished in his nineties around 1229, when the Mongols invaded Nishapur in northeastern Iran. During his lifetime, the Seljuqs, a Turkish-speaking dynasty from Central Asia, ruled the northeastern Iranian province of Khurasan, where Nishapur is located. To administer their empire in Iran and collect its lucrative tax revenues, the Seljuqs employed other Turkic tribes, who formed dynasties of their own that competed, often brutally, for the revenues. These upheavals did not prevent Attar from following his father into the apothecary trade (*attar* means "perfumer" or "druggist" in Persian). It was a profession that put him in the patrician class, along with religious scholars, judges, physicians, landed gentry, Christian monks, philosophers, food wholesalers, and farmers (Ravandi, p. 423). Doubling as a physician and an apothecary, he examined patients (as many as 50 per day) and prescribed and prepared remedies for their ailments (Nafisi, p. 34). His busy days financed Attar's first love: expressing in nightly poetry writing what he encountered in the world of ideas. In his own words, "there is so much meaning in my mind that, God knows, I am wholly captive to its expression" (Attar in Nafisi, p. 37; trans. P. Sprachman). His literary career could have followed the servile path of the

THE LITERARY WORK

A twelfth-century allegorical poem set in mythical Iran about a journey to the fabled Mount Qaf; completed in Persian (as *Mantiq al-tayr*) in 1188; first published in its entirety in English in 1984.

SYNOPSIS

A number of birds set out on a pilgrimage. Along the way, many fall prey to worldly distractions, but 30 reach the source of spiritual enlightenment—the phoenix, or Simurgh, whose identity comes as a complete surprise to them.

court poet, which began with exaggerated praise of the many petty tyrants who ruled Nishapur, then proceeded to flattery of the ministers close to imperial power, and, if the poet was very fortunate, culminated in panegyrics (praise poetry) for the great Seljuq himself. Bits of praise poetry tell us that Attar traveled this path briefly, but the rest of his voluminous writing shows that he "repented," for his "heart was sickened by praise poetry and absurdity" (Attar, *Divan*, p. 49). Instead of squandering his genius on self-promotion and advancement through the ranks of court poets, he devoted himself to the two main goals of Islamic mysticism: self-denial and union with God. His works are filled with exemplary stories about the great mystics, both male and female, who scaled the heights of spiritual understanding. One of his prose works, *Tazkirat al-awliya* (The Lives of the Saints), is a compendium of such tales, many of which also appear in verse form in *The Conference of the Birds*. Altogether Attar composed at least eight poetical works as well as shorter works in prose, some of his best-known titles being *Ilahi-namah* (The Book of God), *Musibat-namah* (The Book of Affliction), and *Asrar-namah* (The Book of Secrets). Attar's most renowned work, *The Conference of the Birds,* is about the difficult journey to spiritual enlightenment and the excuses that people make to avoid taking it.

DIVINE WORDPLAY

Attar did not consider his poetry merely a means of expressing the ideas that teemed in his head. He also treated it as hallowed ground, innocent of the religious prejudices (*ta`assubat*) that historians tell us poisoned the social climate of Nishapur. To express the transcendent nature of true poetry, he often uses puns that exploit the fact that Persian writing is a string of consonants written without short vowels. In Persian, for example, the three consonants that form *shi`r*, "poetry," are not written with short vowels but appear as *sh`r*. Instead of "poetry," the consonants can be rearranged to produce *shar`*, "divine law," or *`arsh*, "the throne of God" (Ritter, pp. 156-57). To the Sufi imagination this accident of orthography is proof enough of the sacred nature of literature.

Events in History at the Time of the Poem

Caliphs and pilgrims. In Attar's time, centuries-old differences of opinion about who should have been caliph or "successor" to the Prophet Muhammad when he died in 632 often caused strife between the two main sects of Islam. On one hand, the Sunni majority to which the poet belonged favored succession by election. This resulted in the following line of leaders: Abu Bakr (caliph 632-34), Umar (caliph 634-44), and Uthman (caliph 644-56). On the other hand, the Shi`ite minority championed a hereditary succession, which would have made the Prophet's cousin and son-in-law, Ali, the first caliph. Ali finally became caliph in 656, but Shi`ites have always resented the usurpation of his right by the other three caliphs. Part of the prologue to *The Conference of*

the Birds attacks these ancient prejudices. Attar accuses the Shi`ites of rejecting the incontestable truth (*haqq*) that the companions (*sahabah*) of the Prophet would never have chosen an unworthy or unlawful candidate to take his place, as could happen if one relied on heredity (Attar, *Mantiq al-tayr*, original, pp. 27-28; this part is not in the English translation).

There was less contention about another aspect of Muslim life, the hajj, which caliphs, like all Muslims, were obligated to take if they had the means to do so. The hajj is the principal pilgrimage in Islam. During the month set aside for it, pilgrims (hajjis) of all ages and from all social classes and ethnic groups visit the holy cities of Mecca and Medina in today's Saudi Arabia. Since the hajj occurs during a lunar month, the pilgrimage takes place at various times during the solar year. All hajjis don the simple white robes of a pilgrim, which are designed to erase class and national distinctions. Among the rites they perform is the circumambulating of the Ka`bah, the black stone that stands in the middle of the Grand Mosque of Mecca and is associated in the Quran (2:125) with Ibrahim (Abraham of the Bible).

Shi`ites become hajjis along with all other Muslims; however, they have also traditionally performed other pilgrimages (*ziyarat*) that are closer to home (principally in Iraq and Iran). These local visitations, which unlike the hajj happen any time of year, take the hajjis to shrines that honor the 12 imams and their families, the holiest figures in Shi`ism. (The imams, direct descendants of Ali, are regarded as intermediaries to the divine in Iran.) The most important Shi`ite pilgrimage sites are in Iraq: Najaf (the shrine of Ali, cousin and son-in-law of the Prophet Muhammad) and Karbala (the shrine of Ali's martyred son, Husayn). Shi`ite pilgrims also visit the shrine of the eighth of the Shi`ite leaders, Imam Reza, in Mashhad in northeastern Iran. As in the Hajj, during Shi`ite visitation it is customary to circumambulate—only in the case of visitation one goes around the sepulchers of the imams, intoning prayers and imploring their spirits to intervene in matters of wealth, health, fertility, and so forth. In addition to these main sites, there are hundreds of sub-shrines that honor Shi`ite saints, who are typically descendants of the imams or members of their families. Pilgrims make their way to these sub-shrines as well.

Sufis also visit the shrines (*zawiyah*) dedicated to the saints venerated by their individual orders. During these pilgrimages, which like the Shi`ite

THE SEVEN STAGES ON THE SUFI PATH TOWARD ENLIGHTENMENT

There are seven stages—known in Arabic as *maqamah*—on the path to spiritual enlightenment and union with God. These stages become progressively more difficult as the wayfarer passes from one to the next. The seven *maqamah*s are:

Maqamah 1: The struggle (*jihad*) against the Imperious Self (*al-nafs al-ammarah*). In this stage the Sufi learns to overcome those feelings that place the self above other considerations: e.g., lust, anger, greed, etc.

Maqamah 2: The struggle against the Blaming Self (*al-nafs al-lawwamah*). In this stage the Sufi grapples with envy and the urge to scheme and to make invidious comparisons.

Maqamah 3: The acquisition of the Enlightening Self (*al-nafs al-mulhamah*). At this point the wayfarer attains such good qualities as contentment, humility, gentleness, etc.

Maqamah 4: The attainment of the Tranquil Self (*al-nafs al-mutma'innah*). In this stage Sufis learn complete acceptance of their lots in life and patience in the face of hardship.

Maqamah 5: The evolution of the Satisfied Self (*al-nafs al-radiyah*). The renunciation of every thought but the contemplation of God. So entrancing is divine beauty at this stage that all other sights become illusory by comparison.

Maqamah 6: Achieving the Approved Self (*al-nafs al-mardiyah*). Here love between the Creator and creation enters the soul, and the Sufi learns to view the reality of this world with knowledge of the next.

Maqamah 7: The stage of the Perfect Soul (*an-nafs al-kamilah*). This phase encompasses all the good qualities of the previous stages. Here the Sufi no longer needs physical exercises or stimulants to achieve a spiritual state—it comes naturally.

(Adapted from Trimingham, pp. 155-57)

---

visitations do not take place at any particular time of year, they perform spiritual exercises (repeating the names of God, chanting, dancing) and pray to the saints for guidance on how to become better devotees to their orders. Sufis often sleep at these shrines in hopes of dreaming of the saints buried in them. Such spiritual odysseys take them all over the world of Islamic mysticism, from Mauritania in West Africa to India and Indonesia in South Asia.

Sufism. Sufism is Islamic mysticism. This simple definition masks the dizzying complexity of the subject. At least one scholar asserts that a proper description is impossible because Sufism includes a wide variety of beliefs and practices (Schimmel, p. 3). The word itself derives from the Arabic *suf* or "wool," the rough fabric composing a cloak (*dalq*, *zhindah*), which, like the Christian mystic's hair shirt, was the badge of the Sufi's penance and poverty. The original Muslim mystics denied themselves the comforts of clothing, food, and shelter so as not to be distracted from the true way

(*tariqah*) toward knowledge (*ma`rifah*) of and, ultimately, union (*wusul*) with God. Like the poem's Shaykh Noughani, real-life mystics often appeared in "tattered clothes, alone and weak" (Attar, *The Conference of the Birds,* line 1770). Some bragged that their cloaks became oppressively heavy because of all the patches they had to sew onto them.

In addition to self-deprivation, the Sufis of Attar's day relied on intuition, inspiration, and a range of physical exercises to progress from stage (*maqamah*) to stage along the true way.

Early in the spread of Islam, the Sufis began to read the revelations of the Quran allegorically, finding hidden meanings behind practically every expression in the Arabic text. These readings eventually became the standard Sufi learning that informs large parts of mystical poems like Attar's *Conference of the Birds* and Rumi's *Masnavi*.

A mystical understanding of part of the Quran dealing with Sulayman (biblical Solomon) is essential to an informed reading of *The Conference of the Birds*. At the beginning of the narrative,

Attar writes that Solomon understood the language of the birds:

> Dear hoopoe, welcome! You will be our
>   guide:
> It was on you King Solomon relied
> To carry secret messages between
> His court and distant Sheba's lovely queen.
> He knew your language and you knew his
>   heart.

(Conference of the Birds, lines 616-20)

This is a Sufi interpretation of Quran 27:16, which says that Solomon knew the language of the Tayr, the name of a tribe of people over whom he and his father David had dominion. The Sufis chose to read *Tayr* as "birds," which is possible in Arabic but not supported by the Quran, where, as explained, it denotes a specific tribe of people. The reading of *Tayr* as "birds" turns Solomon into a Sufi at the highest level of enlightenment, privy to the language of the birds. Because birds commonly symbolized the soul in Sufi literature, Sufi Solomon becomes aware of humanity's inner spiritual musings.

Other Sufi methods were and are less contemplative, at times verging—from the point of view of non-Sufis—on "excessive" or "wild" behaviors. Expressing the rapture (*wajd*) associated with closeness to God, these behaviors include singing, dancing or whirling (the practice of the Mevlevi dervishes of Konya), and listening to music, all of which were and are condemned in orthodox Islam. These behaviors, say the orthodox, distract the devout from the prescribed means of reaching God—the five daily prayers.

By Attar's time Sufi methods and beliefs had become standardized and many orders had emerged throughout Western and Central Asia. The general route from initiation to graduation was uniform across the orders. One entered the path as a novice (*murid*) and followed the instructions of an adept or guide (*murshid*) at a retreat (*khanaqah*). Attar's order was named the "Kubrawiyah," after the great Khivan scholar and mystic Najm al-Din Kubra (1145-1221). His teacher was Majd al-Din al-Baghdadi, who also perished in the Mongol invasion of Iran.

The Kubrawiyah used a form of spiritual exercise called *dhikr* or "remembrance." The practice grows out of the prayer ritual in Islam during which certain Arabic phrases like *Allah akbar* ("God is great") are intoned several times. In *dhikr* the names of God (in Islam there are 99) or the names of revered Imams (saints and martyrs) are repeated, mantra-like, several thousand times so

that the Sufi reaches a state of spiritual understanding (*hal*) unavailable to the intellect. These repetitions are accompanied by hyperventilation, which leads to a dizziness conducive to alternate views of reality.

Another important feature of Sufi life is a practiced indifference to the opinions of society. The Sufis of Attar's day often went out of their way to be disreputable, either affecting or actually engaging in activities designed to repel the vast majority of the devout. In an Islamic context these activities included frequenting taverns and using intoxicants, openly carrying on love affairs with non-Muslim males and females, uttering obscenities and blasphemies, and similar violations of religious practice. The Sufis behaved this way to drive a point home to the orthodox, to counter what seemed to be excessive control in the name of religion. Reminding others that God looks into people's hearts, not their actions, they promoted tolerance for individual ways of worship. They also practiced such deviant behavior to show how much the mystic wayfarer was willing to forgo the self. Only if Sufis abandoned worldly attachment could they annihilate love of self, the main barrier to knowing God.

In *The Conference of the Birds*, Attar often uses forbidden love as a metaphor for the abandonment of worldly attachments. The longest tale in the poem (lines 1185-1593) tells how one of the most pious and learned Muslims of his time, Shaykh Sam`an (or San`an), falls in love with a Christian girl whose "mouth was tiny as a needle's eye" and whose breath "as quickening as Jesus' sigh" (*Conference of the Birds,* lines 1221-22). The shaykh's infatuation forces him to do things Islam strictly forbids. First, he begins to worship the girl (idolatry violates monotheism, the first principle of Islam); second, he drinks wine (prohibited so one can fix one's total consciousness on God, without any of the senses being dulled); and, third, he becomes a Christian (leaving Islam is a mortal sin, punishable in some places by death). Shaykh Sam`an completes the process of self-abasement by becoming the girl's swineherd (Muslims abhor pork). Finally the angels take pity on the shaykh, and the Prophet himself intervenes through a dream to cure him of his infatuation.

The Sufi ideal of selfless love can also take the form of a king's affection for his slave boy (*ghulam*). Typically there were many such slaves at the royal court, and the sultan had life-and-death power over them. He could give his slaves as presents to courtiers or use them however he wished. The relationship between the sultan and the slave thus became metaphorical for the tie between the Creator and His creatures. The great disparity between the status of the king (the highest) and the place of the slave (abject) suits the ideal perfectly. Like the Sufi wayfarer, the king abandons all wealth, power, and position to attain the ultimate joy of divine enlightenment, typically symbolized by the beauty of the slave boy. In the lover's eyes, the perfect beauty of the slave is an earthly replica of the perfection of the divine visage. Both are objects of absolute adoration.

Sufi poets often use the story, which is in part supported by history, of Mahmud, sultan of Ghazni (reigned 998-1030), and Ayaz, his stunning servant, to express this theme. In *The Conference of the Birds* (lines 3078-80), Attar writes:

Shah Mahmoud called Ayaz to him and gave
His crown and throne to this bewitching slave,
Then said: "You are the sovereign of these
    lands;
I place my mighty army in your hands—
I wish for you unrivaled majesty,
That you enslave the very sky and sea.

These lines capture the paradoxical character of Islamic mysticism. It is a world in which a slave enslaves and a king becomes sovereign by giving up his kingdom.

Dispensing with gender. The quest for eternity, or union with God, also changes the fundamental natures of those who embark on it. It can, for example, make women of men and men of women. This is not accidental. The blurring of gender is important to the quest because it gives the Sufi license to engage in activities that are outlawed in "normal" society. The life of Rabi`ah al-Adawiyah (d. 801), perhaps the most celebrated woman among the great Sufis, typifies the gender switch. Attar devotes part of his *Lives of the Saints* to Rabi`ah. In the beginning of the entry, he anticipates objections to including a woman among the "men of the path." His justification is based on a saying (*hadith*) of the Prophet Muhammad: "Verily God does not look at your faces [rather He reads what is in your hearts]" (Attar, *Guzidah-'i tazkirat al-awliya*, p. 61). To Sufis, this means that once a woman enters the path, she becomes a "man," as she acquires the male traits of initiative and daring, which are needed to become one with God. Moreover, writes Attar, since unity (*tawhid*) is the ultimate goal of the quest, grammatical and other distinctions disappear: the pronouns "you" and "I" and the separate genders male and female cannot have any meaning.

A story in *The Conference of the Birds* illustrates the opposite case: how the quest feminizes a man. It seems that in Baghdad where he spent most of his life, the great mystic Abu Bakr Shibli (d. 945) would disappear from public view from time to time. When one of his followers finds him in a house of prostitution that features boys and creatures of "questionable" gender (*mukhannath khanah*, i.e. transvestites), he explains (lines 1926-28):

In the world's way these you see
Aren't men or women; so it is with me—
For in the way of Faith I'm neither man
Nor woman, but ambiguous courtesan—
Unmanliness reproaches me, then blame
For my virility fills me with shame.

A MEDIEVAL FEMINIST?

In most medieval Islamic societies, the sexes were strictly segregated. Men and women attended separate shrines or partitioned parts of the same shrine. Women's religious activities could also take place within the confines of the inner home, far from the prying eyes of men not allowed to see their faces. Women were not expected to speak in public, let alone express themselves on sexual matters. A notable exception is the poetess Mahsati (b. 1141) from Ganjah (in modern Azerbaijan). Poetic chronicles report that she had the temerity to write of her desire in, for example, the following quatrain, which she recited.

I'm Mahsati, the fairest of the flock,
For beauty famed from Mashhad to Iraq;
O preacher's boy, you good-for-nothing bum,
We're through if I've no bread or meat or cock!
    (Mahsati in Sprachman, p. 3)

Whether Mahsati indeed wrote all the quatrains attributed to her is a matter of some debate. In any case, she is representative of those women who performed and served at taverns and other public places. Many were the entertainers and prostitutes that inhabited the *kharabat*, or "ruins"—disreputable places that existed on the outskirts of every proper town.

By frequenting such a disgraceful place, Shibli not only loses his reputation but his gender as well. His story serves the same paradox found in the sultan/slave-boy tales mentioned above: namely, seekers must debase themselves—unsex themselves, in fact—before they can become pure and one with divine Truth.

The hoopoe bird

The Poem in Focus

Plot summary. Because most of *The Conference of the Birds* is composed of parables and exemplary tales that do not advance the plot, the poem's basic story line is quite spare.

The poem begins with customary praise of God, the Prophet Muhammad, and the four caliphs: Abu Bakr, Umar, Uthman, and Ali. It then launches into the strong criticism of the Shi`ite religious prejudices described above. These preliminary sections do not appear in the English translation.

The actual story begins at verse 617 with greetings to the hoopoe (*hudhud*), the leader of the pilgrim flock. The birds agree in principle to seek the Simurgh, the source of all divine enlightenment, but when it comes to actually going, a number of them try to avoid the journey with excuses that reflect their particular avian natures. For example, love of the rose threatens to stop the nightingale (*bulbul*); a cage prevents the parrot (*tuti*); the duck (*batt*) cannot live without water; the partridge (*kabk*) likewise cannot do without mountains, and so on. The hoopoe responds to each objection with anecdotes drawn from the vast body of Islamic and Sufi learning. He eventually manages to convince a number of birds to make the pilgrimage.

The pattern of defection from the quest and the leader's artful recourse—using the Quran and Sufi anecdotes to bring the birds back into line—continues. For example, when one of the birds is unable to go on the journey because of a love of gold (lines 2079-82), the hoopoe tells the story of the novice and his master (lines 2101-11). The novice had a hidden stash of gold that the master knew about. While on a journey with a decisive fork in the road, the novice asked his master which way they were to go. The master replied that the way to know is to rid oneself of all hidden things.

The hoopoe then describes the seven valleys that they must cross before they can reach the Simurgh: the Valley of the Quest (*talab*); the Valley of Love (*ishq*); the Valley of Insight into Mystery (*ma`rifat*); the Valley of Detachment (*istighna*); the Valley of Unity (*tawhid*); the Valley of Bewilderment (*hayrat*); and the Valley of Poverty and Nothingness (*faqr*). Because each valley is more difficult to cross than the one before it, more and more of the birds fall prey to fatigue or temptation as the journey proceeds. By the last stage only 30 pilgrims, who have been fully cured of their worldliness, remain. When the birds finally meet the Simurgh, the significance of the number 30 becomes clear. Attar reveals the pun that governs the entire poem in the following lines:

> Their souls rose free of all they'd been before;
> The past and all its actions were no more.
> Their life came from that close, insistent sun
> And in its vivid rays they shone as one.
> There in the Simurgh's radiant face they saw
> Themselves, the Simurgh of the world—with awe
> They gazed, and dared at last to comprehend
> They were the Simurgh and the journey's end.
> They see the Simurgh—at themselves they stare,
> And see a second Simurgh standing there;
> They look at both and see the two are one,
> That this is that, that this, the goal is won.
> (*Conference of the Birds*, lines 4232-37)

In Persian "thirty" is *si* and "bird" is *murgh*; thus "Simurgh" literally means "thirty birds." At the end of the quest, the flock realizes that together they compose the Simurgh, their final destination. Ultimately the quest of the birds amounts to a circle; the pun brings home the message that they themselves were actually the enlightenment that they sought.

Mystical use of history. A great deal of language in *The Conference of the Birds* is borrowed from the world of the royal court. The Simurgh is the "king" of the birds that holds "court." The birds approach his royal threshold as "suppliants." The "blaze of his majesty reduces their souls to unreality" (*Conference of the Birds,* line 4186). Several bird pilgrims boast of their proximity to royalty. For example, the *huma,* biologically the bearded vulture, but in mythology a phoenix-like creature associated with kingship, asks

> . . . Who can look down
> On one whose shadow brings the royal
> crown?
> The world should bask in my magnificence—
> Let Khosroe's [the Sasanian king Khusraw's]
> glory stand in my defense.
> (*Conference of the Birds,* lines 922-23)

This language is typical of the refined discourse of a courtier, which was necessary in the presence of the king.

Aside from the courtly language, real sultans and monarchs figure prominently in many of the exemplary tales, where history is recast to suit the Sufi message. As noted, Sultan Mahmud, the ruler of the Ghaznavid Empire from 998-1030, is celebrated in mystical Persian literature for his relationship to his slave Ayaz. To Muslim historians, the sultan was the perfect *ghazi,* or warrior, for Islam because his expeditions into northern India (known as Hindustan) brought vast territories into the Islamic empire. The spoils from his raids on the temples in India, which were coated in layers of gold leaf and filled with jewel-encrusted statues of the many Hindu gods, financed a standing army of some 50,000 troops (Boyle, p. 13). Needless to say, the Hindu historians of India do not see Mahmud the way the Muslims do. To them, the sultan was a bloodthirsty conqueror who converted millions of non-Muslims by the sword.

One of Mahmud's most famous exploits in India was the taking of the temple at Somnath (in Persian the word is *Sumanat*). Before the Islamic conquest, the temple was the richest Hindu shrine in the region of Gujrat. A thousand Brahmin priests resided at the temple and spent their lives in continuous worship of its idol. Some 500 dancing and singing girls and 200 musicians devoted themselves to serving this idol (Habib, pp. 52-53). Mahmud left Ghazni on October 18, 1025, and took the temple in November of the same year. He stripped the shrine of its gold and gems and, true to the Islamic iconoclastic ideal, smashed the idol. The shattered pieces were installed in the entryway to Ghazni's great mosque, where believers wiped their feet.

The Conference of the Birds includes a retelling of the Somnath story. In this version the idol, which was actually a Hindu focus of worship carved from solid rock, becomes Lat, one of three pre-Islamic goddesses shaped like female cranes that the Prophet Muhammad destroyed when he brought monotheism to the Arabian peninsula:

> When Mahmoud's army had attacked Somnat
> They found an idol there that men called
> "Lat."
> Its worshippers flung treasure on the ground
> And as a ransom gave the glittering mound;
> But Mahmoud would not cede to their desire
> And burnt the idol in a raging fire.
> A courtier said: "Now if it had been sold
> We'd have what's better than an idol—gold!"
> Shah Mahmoud said: "I feared God's
> Judgement Day;
> I was afraid that I should hear Him say
> 'Here two—Azar and Mahmoud—stand and
> behold!
> One carved idols, one had idols sold!'"
> And as the idol burned, bright jewels fell
> out—
> So Mahmoud was enriched but stayed devout;
> He said: "This idol Lat has her reward,
> And here is mine, provided by the Lord."
> Destroy the idols in your heart, or you
> Will one day be a broken idol too—
> First burn the Self, and as its fate is sealed
> The gems this idol hides will be revealed.
> (*Conference of the Birds,* lines 3121-31)

Though, as historians point out, this story is a fabrication, it is useful because it shows how Sufis interpret history (Habib, p. 57). Instead of being a great Muslim conqueror, Mahmud is a mystic more concerned with his soul than gaining the riches of India and expanding the sweep of Islam. The idols become the worldly preoccupations that keep the Sufi from destroying the self—killing the self to become selfless and reach God. The gems, like the beauty of the slave boy, symbolize the enlightenment that comes from union with God.

Sources and literary context. The title *The Conference of the Birds* (*Mantiq al-tayr*—literally "the speech of birds") is a reference to a verse in the Quran (27:16). In this verse Solomon (corresponding to the Jewish king in the Bible) proclaims, "O ye people! We have been taught the speech of the Tayr." This is usually interpreted to mean that God distinguished Solomon by granting him knowledge denied to other men and prophets. In one of Attar's poems (*Divan,* p. 81), this secret language is the medium of communication of the "bird of the soul." In other words, Solomon had the pure knowledge of mysticism. Such Sufi interpretations begin with the Quran and the Hadith (sayings of the Prophet

Muhammad) and, in some cases, with Islamic folklore.

Attar was not the first writer to use this title. Another work that describes the pilgrimage of a group of birds toward God is Ibn Sina's (also known as Avicenna, 980-1037) *Risalat al-tayr* ("Treatise of the Birds"). This treatise describes the eight stages that the birds must traverse before they can reach God. The influential Iranian theologian Abu Hamid al-Ghazzali (1058-1111) also wrote a "Treatise of the Birds," which seems to have been Attar's model.

Impact. Since its completion in February of 1188, *The Conference of the Birds* has been considered Attar's masterpiece. It is one of two or three basic texts of Persian literature and Sufism that is still taught in the original and in translation throughout the world. Revered Persian mystics who follow Attar, such as Jalal al-Din Rumi (also in *WLAIT 6: Middle Eastern Literature and Its Times*) and Abd al-Rahman Jami (1414-92), praise both the quality of the poetry and the poet's encyclopedic knowledge of religion and Sufi traditions. All scholars of Persian mysticism agree that next to Rumi's *Masnavi*, Attar's *Conference of the Birds* is the most important Sufi text (Schimmel, p. 304). Since its publication, the work has achieved the status of a handbook of mystical knowledge. For many Sufis it is the work that most clearly and concisely captures the essence of the mystical quest.

—Paul Sprachman

For More Information

Attar, Farid al-Din. *The Conference of the Birds.* Trans. Afkham Darbandi and Dick Davis. New York: Penguin, 1984.

———. *Divan.* Ed. Sa'id Nafisi. Tehran: Sana'i, 1961.

———. *Guzidah-'i tazkirat al-awliya* [*The Lives of the Saints*]. Ed. Muhammad Isti'lami. Tehran: Jibi, 1973.

———. *Mantiq al-tayr.* Ed. Sayyid Sadiq Gawharin. Tehran: Bungah-i Tarjumah va Nashr-i Kitab, 1969.

Boyle, J. A., ed. *The Seljuq and Mongol Periods.* Vol. 5 of *The Cambridge History of Iran.* Cambridge, England: Cambridge University, 1968.

Habib, Mohammad. *Sultan Mahmud of Ghaznin.* Delhi: S. Chand, 1951.

Nafisi, Sa'id. *Justuju dar ahval va athar-i Farid al-Din Attar.* Tehran: Iqbal, 1941.

Quran. *The Glorious Kur'an.* Trans. Abdallah Yousuf Ali. Riyadh, Saudi Arabia: Muhammad ibn Sa'ud Islamic University, n.d.

Ravandi, Muhammad. *Rahat al-sudur.* Ed. Muhammad Iqbal. London: E. J. Gibb Memorial Series, 1921.

Ritter, Hellmut. *Das Meer der Seele: Mensch, Welt und Gott in den Geschichten des Fariduddin Attar.* Leiden: E. J. Brill, 1955.

Schimmel, Annemarie. *Mystical Dimensions of Islam.* Chapel Hill, N.C.: University of North Carolina, 1975.

Sprachman, Paul, ed. *Suppressed Persian: An Anthology of Forbidden Literature.* Trans. Paul Sprachman. Costa Mesa, Calif.: Mazda, 1995.

Trimingham, J. Spencer. *The Sufi Orders in Islam.* Oxford: Oxford University, 1973.

Curfew

by

Adalet Agaoglu

THE LITERARY WORK

A novel set in Istanbul and a provincial Turkish city in the violent days just before the September 1980 military coup; published in Turkish (as *Üç beş kişi*) in 1984, in English in 1997.

SYNOPSIS

An unhappy love affair links the fall of old aristocratic families in Turkey with the rise of a new provincial business class and the liberation of women.

By 1984, the year *Curfew* first appeared in Turkey, Adalet Agaoglu was already an admired and widely discussed author. Although preferring not to identify herself as a feminist (she declares that she is writing about human beings), Agaoglu is a prominent spokesperson for women and deals extensively with women's issues in her writing. She was born as Adalet Sümer in 1929 to a shopkeeper's family in a small town not far from Ankara, the newly designated capital of Turkey. After graduating from Ankara University with a degree in French literature, Adalet worked for the State Radio-TV organization, wrote several radio plays, and saw some of her stage plays performed. In 1983 she and her husband, Halim Agaoglu (pronounced *A-ah*-oh-lu), moved permanently to Istanbul. Adalet Agaoglu is part of the second generation to attend school after Atatürk's revolutionary changes in Turkey and her work reflects this revolutionary atmosphere. Her first novel *Ölmeye yatmak* (1973; Lying Down to Die) tells the story of a woman's graduating from primary school with the first co-ed classes. Beginning a trilogy, the novel initiated Agaoglu's dominant theme of conflict in a rapidly modernizing society and the ensuing difficulties for those who aspire to the status of modern, Western women. In addition to eight novels, Agaoglu has published several volumes of plays, short stories, an autobiography, a book of dreams, and essays. The novels' dark themes—murder, rape, and flirtation with suicide—are relieved by flashes of humor. In 1996 Agaoglu was severely injured by a speeding automobile, which hurled her into the Bosporus Strait and left her in a temporary coma. Her long, slow recovery involved more than 18 operations, yet she continued an active public life, running (unsuccessfully) for parliament in hopes of forging a truly democratic constitution. By then her political and social voice had already found its way into her fictional writings. *Curfew*, Agaoglu's fifth novel and the first to be translated into English, typifies her complex narrative style and reflects her concerns about the changing status of women as well as the effects of politics and society on private lives.

Events in History at the Time of the Novel

The military presence in Turkish political life. After the First World War, military officers, led

Adalet Agaoglu

by Mustafa Kemal, founded the modern Turkish state, and they continue to play a crucial role in Turkey today. The military has stepped in on several occasions to restore constitutional government or to quell disorder, and it stands ready to do so whenever it deems necessary. Its officers see themselves, and are widely seen, as the guarantors of the legacy of Mustafa Kemal (also known as Atatürk), particularly of his commitment to a secular state and a Turkish national identity.

A charismatic leader, Mustafa Kemal commanded the defense forces that fought off the Allied troops at the Dardanelles (a strait between Europe and Turkey), in 1915 during World War I. He also repelled the postwar Greek invasion, rescuing Turkey from domination by the Allied powers in what became known as the War of Independence, taking over the government and then forcing the deposition and exile of the last Ottoman sultan. After moving the capital from the seat of Ottoman power to Ankara, then a village close to the geographic center of modern Turkey, Mustafa Kemal proclaimed the Republic of Turkey in 1923 and became its first president. The surname Atatürk ("father Turk"), which stresses his pride in his Turkish ancestry, was officially bestowed on him by the Grand National Assembly in 1934.

As president, Mustafa Kemal Atatürk made a clear division between military and civilian rule by insisting that officers who wished to go into politics resign their commissions. Despite this proviso, the military would remain a strong presence in the political life of the Republic. Through periods of quasi-dictatorship and corruption, or perceived threats to the state by radical leftist groups and Islamic or fascistic right-wing nationalists, the Turkish military has stood ready to suspend civilian rule until things are set right and order is restored once again.

Under Atatürk's leadership, which can be characterized as a dictatorship despite its parliamentary trappings, radical and symbolic changes in society took place almost overnight. Revolutionary policies such as the adoption of the Latin alphabet, the emancipation of women, the adoption of the Swiss Civil Code, and the abolition of the office of caliph, were swiftly introduced by the single-party government. The government also experimented with opposition parties, at first encouraged by Atatürk but dissolved as soon as they caused difficulty for his ruling faction, the Republican People's Party (RPP). In November 1938, after a period of increasingly repressive rule, Atatürk died and was succeeded by a close associate, Ismet Inönü, another career soldier and War of Independence hero. Inönü tried to maintain the same tight hold over military and parliamentary power.

In the post-World War II era, in 1946, the Democratic Party was founded by several former RPP members. Initially Inönü and the RPP welcomed the new party as the "loyal opposition" and a logical development on the gradual road to a multiparty system. But RPP members were entirely unprepared for the fierce, unrelenting attacks hurled at them by their erstwhile colleagues. The RPP tried to retain power through various repressive tactics of dubious legality, such as holding elections before the Democrats were ready to compete.

Toward a capitalist economy. In 1950 the Democratic Party assumed control. Its members, like the RPP, had no understanding of multiparty democracy and continued to rule in the highhanded manner of their predecessors. But they differed in one important respect: at their helm was a business-oriented wealthy landowner, Adnan Menderes, who believed that prosperity and modernization could be achieved by freeing the economy from government controls and modeling the country on their idea of Western capitalism. The Democrats thus adopted a strongly proAmerican foreign policy and early in 1952 joined the NATO (North Atlantic Treaty Organization)

WOMEN'S RIGHTS IN MODERN TURKEY

Atatürk's reforms were crucial in the history of women's rights, but they did not include all the elements we have come to think of as essential to women's equality with men. In its desire to put Turkey on a par with secular Europe, Atatürk's government adopted a Civil Code in 1926 that was based on the Swiss Civil Code, and Switzerland is a country where women would not have the right to vote in federal elections until 1971. Some landmark legislation on the road to equality for Turkish women shows that some key advances came as late as the 1990s and 2002:

1923 Declaration of the Turkish Republic.

1926 Adoption of the Civil Code—only monogamous marriages are recognized, and women gain equal rights in divorce, child custody, and inheritance.

1930 Women gain right to vote and be elected to local governments.

1933 Women gain right to vote and be elected to village administrations.

1934 Women gain right to vote and be elected in parliamentary elections.

1935 First elections are held in which women have the right to vote and be elected to parliament.

1971 First woman is appointed minister (extra-parliamentary).

1986 First woman member of parliament becomes part of the ministerial cabinet.

1990 Constitutional Court annuls the law requiring women to have spousal permission to work outside the home.

1990 General Directorate on the Status and Problems of Women is set up (affiliated directly to the prime ministry in 1999).

1993-95 First woman prime minister (Tansu Çiller).

1995 Turkey signs without reservations the Beijing Declaration at Fourth World Conference on Women.

1996 Adultery is no longer a crime for men.

1998 Adultery is no longer a crime for women; Law on Protection of the Family contains regulations for protection against domestic violence; requirement that income must be declared by head of the family for taxation purposes is abolished: women and men can declare income separately.

2002 Civil Code law on protection of the family is amended to declare equality of spouses rather than identify the man as "head of the family."

alliance of Western nations. The Democrats also attempted to attract foreign capital. Unfortunately the capitalist approach ushered in adverse developments: new wealth led to shortages of goods; profiteering abounded; and Turkey incurred a huge debt, due to loans that enabled it to obtain agricultural machinery. These developments led to inflation and unrest. So dire was the economic situation that the champions of free enterprise had to reintroduce severe economic controls that had been used in the Second World War.

Despite zigzags in economic policy, the decade of the 1950s saw the emergence in smaller cities of a newly wealthy Turkish business class. In Ottoman times Turks had preferred careers in the bureaucracy and the military to careers in business, which they left mostly in the hands of Greeks, Armenians, and Jews. Economic activity, along with politics and cultural affairs, had been centered not in smaller cities but in Istanbul. The rise of smaller cities in the provinces and the creation of a successful provincial Turkish business elite became an economic legacy of the 1950s, although Menderes, the leader whose policy inspired this legacy, was executed for subverting the constitution.

With the rise of Menderes's Democratic Party, a prosperous business class developed in provincial cities like Eskişehir, which Agaoglu makes the center of her novel. The wealthy farmers and newly rich entrepreneurs of this business class began to build factories, hotels, and office blocks. Intimidated by Istanbul society, they formed a gentry class of their own and began to look toward Ankara and the Asiatic, predominantly rural heart of the country. In *Curfew* a member of this gentry has a heart attack—so devastated is he by the ignominious way in which his hero, Menderes, is hunted down, arrested, tried, and executed. His reaction reflects a real-life reverence for the leader. Many of his provincial supporters considered Menderes specially chosen by God and therefore invincible. It was a notion they acquired when he walked away unscathed from a plane crash at Gatwick Airport in England in 1959 after 14 members of his group had been killed. This seemingly miraculous event was exploited to encourage expression of religious fervor and for political gain. Democrats accused the opposition of being anti-Islam.

As the economic situation worsened, the Menderes group became more repressive, clamping down on the press and the universities, restricting the activities of the opposition party and the National Assembly itself, and flouting the constitution along the way. On various pretexts, they declared martial law in the larger cities, a tactic that became part of the governing party's repertoire for suppressing unruly opposition. On May 27, 1960, members of the military intervened to overthrow the regime. They were exasperated by the inflation that was eroding their salaries, by the lack of improvement in the lives of the peasantry from which the military was drawn, by the vacillating economic policies, and by the apparent trampling on Atatürk's legacy of a secular state. Junior officers carried out the coup, but the top brass soon co-opted it. Its members appointed a committee to draft a new constitution, whereupon the May 27 coup took on some trappings of a revolution. Menderes and his Ministers of Finance and Foreign Affairs were put to death and other Democratic Party leaders were sentenced to long prison terms. The Democratic Party itself was dissolved.

In their haste to give back control of government to the feuding political parties and thus scotch the radical plans of junior officers, who hoped for a social transformation, the top brass returned Turkey to the pre-coup status quo. As before, there was endless squabbling. Government consisted of confrontational, embittered party politics; nothing much got done and unlikely coalitions had to be pieced together to form a majority. From the ashes of the old Democratic Party there arose a new Justice Party that took over the mantle of opposition against the old RPP. Prior political conditions were reasserting themselves, but before handing back power to the civilians, the military insisted that Atatürk's old colleague, the soldier Inönü, be prime minister once again.

The new constitution was written by a committee of professors. While not making any fundamental changes in the organization of society, the document gave individuals greater rights, at least on paper. The military took a direct role in government in the form of a National Security Council, a mix of high-ranking officers and some civilians whose function was to assist the cabinet. Also the military joined the capitalists by going into business for itself, setting up a compulsory fund that invested in various industries and joint ventures, making loans to army officers and getting them discounted goods. The constitution explicitly guaranteed new freedoms, such as the right of workers to strike and of people to organize, which led to the formation of socialist, non-communist leftist groups (such as the Turkish Workers Party). A new election law gave small parties more seats in parliament than they would otherwise have had. Thus, the left grew more powerful, but its rising influence, far beyond its actual numbers, provoked a reaction in the generally conservative government. Its leaders would use the activities and influence of the left as a pretext to continue the repressive martial law for years to come.

The Justice Party took the lead in opposing political groups that championed the workers, putting the RPP on the defensive as being "soft on communism." Led by Süleyman Demirel, an American-trained engineer from a small-town background, the Justice Party managed to oust Inönü and take over the reins of government from the Republican Party. Demirel served repeatedly as prime minister (1965-71 with two short gaps and several times more, ending 1991-93). Under Demirel the government stepped up its repressive policies against the left, while attempting to fend off complaints from some of its own adherents, who, as small businessmen and craftspeople, suffered economically because of intensifying capitalism. The push to industrialization and foreign investment, successful in the short run, kept wages low and thus harmed the workers and small farmers. Massive worker migration to Germany,

Belgium, and other European countries with labor shortages only postponed the day of reckoning. Meanwhile, polarization increased between the political parties and among university students and other youth groups. Since 1968, when Europe and even the United States exploded in student-led protests and riots, Turkey had experienced increasing violence among its own young people, both extreme leftist factions and fascistic right-wing nationalists. Already in 1970, with a Justice Party severely weakened by internal factions and Demirel unable to control it, the military was waiting impatiently for its chance to intervene. Strikes, paralyzing demonstrations, kidnappings, and acts of violence gave the military leaders an excuse to again declare martial law. On March 12, 1971, they pressured Demirel to resign and once more assumed control over the government.

Repression and terror. The period between March 12, 1971, and September 12, 1980, provided little respite from the escalating violence that was becoming a way of life in Turkey. The military was dedicated to restoring law and order but went about it by repressing only the left, while fascist groups, both nationalist and Islamist, continued carrying out assassinations and fire bombings. A group of technocrats governed for a relatively brief period, with the military acting as overseer. Almost immediately, however, martial law was declared in much of Turkey because of leftist kidnappings. The military disbanded the Turkish Workers Party and other leftist organizations. On the flimsiest of pretexts, newspapers were closed down or censored while writers had their books suppressed. University professors, journalists, and many prominent writers found themselves being arrested and jailed. Students and faculty alike were placed under surveillance, and the liberal constitution was amended. In response, the RPP swung to the left. Bülent Ecevit replaced Inönü as its leader. The rejuvenated party won the 1973 elections. Despite a strong showing, Ecevit could only form a government with the aid of the leading Islamist party (National Salvation Party), with which a secular politician had very little in common. Ecevit was riding a wave of popularity following the Turkish invasion of Cyprus in the summer of 1974, leading to a partition of the island between its Turkish and Greek communities (still in effect in 2004). He, however, made a disastrous miscalculation, deciding to resign in order to force early elections, which, he thought, would return him to power with an absolute majority

for his party. He was stymied, though, by Justice Party leader Demirel's strategy of accommodation with the National Salvation Party, extreme fascists whose street thugs were known as the Grey Wolves. It was a member of this party, Mehmet Ali Agca, who assassinated one of Turkey's most liberal journalists (Abdi Ipekçi) and later made an attempt on the life of Pope John Paul II.

Ecevit returned to power in the next elections, but only with a coalition government. He had to impose martial law in 1978 when the Grey Wolves set out to destroy entire communities of Alevis (a sect of Shi'ite Muslims) and harassed RPP gatherings. He also had to impose severe economic restrictions because of an ultimatum from the International Monetary Fund (IMF), which was concerned about Turkey's worsening economy and inability to make payments on loans. In light of the economic belt tightening and measures such as martial law, the RPP and Ecevit were voted out of office. Demirel returned to power and implemented the IMF program while giving free reign to the fascist gangs.

The military finally intervened when concern over the Islamic revolution in Iran and Soviet invasion of Afghanistan made Turkey's strategic role critically important to NATO, of which Turkey was a staunch member. Many felt the military had waited far too long, given the fact that there were some 20 killings a day. In June 1980, martial law imposed a curfew; many were probably relieved when the military assumed control of the government in September that year (it would retain power for two years). Certainly, after two decades of political anarchy, another military takeover was no surprise.

The Novel in Focus

Plot summary. The novel begins with a conversation echoing in the head of one of the main characters, Murat. It takes us a while to understand who he is and where he is. The novel is told mainly in the third person, but each character also "thinks" out loud. Murat relives his past, comments on the present, and imagines the future—several versions of the future, in fact. The present is one night in June 1980 in Istanbul, close to the start of curfew, which demands everyone be indoors by 2:00 A.M. We are gradually let in on the story. Murat is a young man who regards himself as a failure, and indeed his friends and upper-class family agree. He hopes to recover his self-esteem by an act of courage and responsibility. Murat plans to meet his sister, who has sent him a telegram announcing her arrival in Istanbul by train, but first he must seek out a young man to bring along. The young man, Ufuk, is in love with her. To find Ufuk, Murat must travel across town late at night and risk being attacked by vigilantes or arrested for curfew violation. He also senses his sister is asking him to take some responsibility for her and is unhappy about being forced to apprise her of his total lack of success.

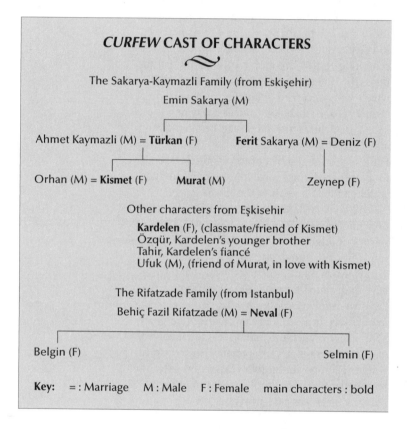

CURFEW CAST OF CHARACTERS

The Sakarya-Kaymazli Family (from Eskişehir)

Emin Sakarya (M)

Ahmet Kaymazli (M) = **Türkan** (F)   **Ferit** Sakarya (M) = Deniz (F)

Orhan (M) = **Kismet** (F)   **Murat** (M)   Zeynep (F)

Other characters from Eşkisehir

Kardelen (F), (classmate/friend of Kismet)
Özgür, Kardelen's younger brother
Tahir, Kardelen's fiancé
Ufuk (M), (friend of Murat, in love with Kismet)

The Rifatzade Family (from Istanbul)

Behiç Fazil Rifatzade (M) = **Neval** (F)

Belgin (F)   Selmin (F)

Key: = : Marriage   M : Male   F : Female   main characters : bold

Looking for Ufuk and clutching only a slip of paper with an unfamiliar address, he stumbles about a newly built part of the city—a stretch with vacant lots and no street lights—desperately trying to find the right apartment. It is dangerous for a young man to wander these darkened, unfamiliar streets and fields at a time when vigilantes roam freely and police may mistake a passerby for a terrorist.

The imagined future is told in the present, as a fantasy of Murat's that is not identified as fantasy. The alternate versions are all intensely real to him, as he "tries on" one vision after another—finding Ufuk, not finding him, finding his sister, not finding her—as if the vision were actually happening at that moment.

The past that Murat recalls includes troubled family relationships, failing friendships with radicalized young men who harshly judge his lifestyle to be self-indulgent, and an unhappy love affair, which began in the city of his birth, Eskişehir, located between Ankara and Istanbul. While still a spoiled mother's boy, dabbling in song writing, he fell in love with a nightclub singer from Istanbul named Selmin. This relationship was completely unsuitable for the scion of two prominent families in Eskişehir. Possibly to help destroy his nephew's obsession or just to satisfy his own curiosity, Murat's uncle, Ferit, commits an unforgivable act of betrayal. He seduces Selmin, whom he treats contemptuously, as if she were a high-class prostitute.

Murat has abandoned his family—and his prospects, through the family, for a secure future—to follow Selmin to Istanbul. Now, jealous and possessive, he finds himself deprived of even the grudging company she had been keeping with him. Selmin, who became enamored of Ferit, drinks ever more heavily and turns into a sloven who can no longer support herself, much less her family. She has relatives in Istanbul, an older sister and a widowed, aristocratic mother, who spent all her money on extravagant living. The mother has encouraged her two daughters to form sexual relationships without the promise of marriage, schooling neither of them in how to convince a member of the new business class to propose. The mother is finally reduced to filching meals from her drug-addicted elder daughter.

We last see the soft and sentimental Murat in an open-ended situation that is typical of Agaoglu's novels. He is either dead or severely wounded and left for dead by vigilantes who mistake him for a leftist terrorist. Perhaps he will survive. One simply does not know.

Murat is only one of seven main characters. After him we meet Kardelen, a young woman of "the people," the child of a peddler but, owing to the small-city school system, a classmate and close friend of Murat's sister, Kismet. Kardelen is proud and unashamed of her humble origins. She is also openly in love with Murat, who seems too class-bound to reciprocate. The one who does esteem her, and hires her as his private secretary, is Murat's uncle, Ferit. Except for his behavior toward Selmin, Murat's girlfriend, Ferit seems to be an admirable man—an exemplar of the rising business class, but with superior cultural as well as technical education and interests. He has many ideas about how to modernize industry in Eskişehir and is comfortable in a variety of circles. He would like to help his nephew Murat establish himself, and shows respect for his niece's friend Kardelen.

Ferit attends a party in Ankara one evening, where he encounters former classmates, who are long on emotional speechifying and short on logic and nonacademic experience. These former schoolmates are mostly academics with leftist attitudes that have become a matter of habit, now with an overlay of cynicism. Light banter and sexual insinuations abound at this gathering, but there is no true dialogue. Ferit tries to communicate his ideas on how best to industrialize Turkey. However, most of the conversation takes place in his own head, since his old friends are not interested in pursuing anything related to business, even in conversation. Ferit would like to see Turkey build factories that produce materials to make the country more self sufficient and not dependent on Europe. The shortsighted businessmen with "shopkeeper mentality," whom he struggles to interest in his long-range plans, want only to produce soft drinks and pretzels for immediate profit, not concrete pilings and other building materials for long-term gain on a national scale. Although Ferit spent several years studying in Paris, he is not at all taken with the Common Market as the solution to Turkey's economic difficulties; he sees Europe as interested in exploiting Turkey, not welcoming it as a genuine partner. (In 2004 Turkey has still not been given a definite date when it might be asked to join.) Throughout this section, Ferit's thoughts wander from his sexual feelings for his wife, to his experience with Selmin and his troubled relations with members of his family, for which he feels responsible: his betrayal of Murat, his misunderstanding of Kismet, and his inability to break through his father's opposition to an industrial park on family farmland.

Except for Ferit's wife, a minor character, all of the women in the novel are troubled. Murat's mother, Türkan, is lonely and bored. She lives out her widowhood with little to occupy herself apart from bathing, shopping, running her household, and worrying about her two children. Kismet, her daughter, is unhappily married to a coarse man, who caused the death of their only child by driving while drunk. So circumscribed has Türkan's own life been that she does not have the imagination or empathy to think that her daughter could even leave her spouse. Meanwhile, Selmin sinks into alcoholic self-pity with little care for her own relatives. Her mother, Neval, terrorized by her other daughter, lives in squalid conditions. As for Kardelen, socially she is subjected to the snobbery of Kismet's family; politically she serves a prison term for her leftist political views; and physically she suffers rape by prison guards.

There is, however, movement in the novel toward a brighter future for two sturdy young women. During the few pre-curfew hours in which the novel occurs, Kardelen (the name means "snowdrop," suggestive of her staunch innocence) sews her wedding dress, looks back on her infatuation with Murat without regret, and looks forward to a loving marriage to a worthy man from a similar background. She also waits and worries about her younger brother, who hasn't come home yet and is just as spoiled and pampered as Murat. Kismet, in her mother's house, awaits the right moment to evade her mother's watchful eyes and flee her marriage before her husband returns from a business trip. She intends to travel alone by train to Istanbul to meet Murat. Never having lived on her own, she plans to take refuge with her brother.

In the final section, open-ended like the one about Murat, Kismet reveals her former unduly close relationship with her brother and her unhappy marital life and walks away from both. She originally intends to join Murat but changes her mind during the train ride. As the train approaches Istanbul, she decides to step off at a suburb. So even though Murat, because of his misfortune, would never have shown up to meet her at the station, Kismet courageously takes charge of her future (Kismet means "fate") and strikes out on her own to begin a new life. On the often quoted final page, she "turns and looks back with an apologetic smile at the handful of people she's leaving behind, far behind her. I wanted every novel I have ever read to end with a true beginning" (Agaoglu, *Curfew*, p. 247).

The dream and the reality: women's plight and men's pressures. In the final scenes on the train to Istanbul, Kismet is traveling alone, without male escort. Not only is she defenseless, she is also guilty of being a woman. She must search on the train for a toilet, and is so unused to being out in the world on her own that she feels acutely embarrassed about calling attention to her bodily functions. This small detail dramatizes the huge leap she is taking into her "true beginning." Kismet stands at the other end of the spectrum from Selmin, a Europeanized woman of Istanbul who attracts awkward provincial young men at the Hilton Hotel, men who are intimidated by her and yet applaud her for "every form of behavior they condemned back home in their sisters, mothers and wives" (*Curfew*, p. 137).

Agaoglu has spoken about the guilty feelings that are deeply ingrained in Turkish girls and women, just by virtue of their being female. As the sociologist Deniz Kandiyoti pointed out in 1987, "Women [in Muslim societies] are vested with immense negative power because any misbehavior on their part can bring shame and dishonor to the male members of a whole community, lineage, or family" (Kandiyoti, p. 322). While Agaoglu's first novel, *Lying Down to Die*, dealt with a woman whose family moved from a village to the capital city, much of *Curfew* is set in a small provincial city midway between Istanbul and Ankara. Agaoglu has observed that the lives of young women are often far less constricted in both villages and large cities than in provincial cities. In these provincial centers, close relatives and distant acquaintances alike censor their movements and keep watch over their contacts with men. On the other hand, the anonymity of large cities and the requirements for village women to work in the fields without direct supervision can provide more freedom.

Curfew depicts a society in flux. The aristocratic values with which Selmin's mother was raised no longer serve her among the newly rich, who have few scruples and certainly do not see impoverished aristocrats as deserving of respect. In the social upheaval of Turkish society, uneducated rough men are able to dictate terms to the kind of young women who would not previously have even looked at them. There is no great value attached to the aristocratic name of Selmin's mother so she cannot negotiate a marriage for one of her daughters that would trade her name for an upstart's wealth. In this society in flux, formerly aristocratic women with scant material resources must shift for themselves. The Turkish constitution has given women equal rights, but, as shown by the lives of the characters in *Curfew*, there is a huge difference between legal ideals and day-to-day realities. The extended family, particularly in provincial cities, still watches over women and regulates their conduct.

Men, on the other hand, carry the burden of upholding male superiority in a society that still endorses it. Murat is clearly unequal to the task, perhaps because he has been pampered by his widowed mother; in any event, he abdicates entirely by running away and refusing to return to take up a position in the family businesses.

Sources and literary context. Agaoglu wrote *Curfew* to illuminate the birth pangs of modern Turkish society and to highlight its inherent conflicts. None of the characters is based on anyone living or dead, according to Agaoglu, although the author's personal experience is certainly reflected in many individual portraits. Interestingly, after the book appeared, Ferit Sakarya was likened to a member of the real-life provincial elite, the Zeytinoglu family from Eskişehir, because they too were enlightened and concerned with the idea of a national economy. Another person from real life, the engineer and later prime minister Turgut Özal, was pointed to as exemplifying the rightness of Agaoglu's predictions about the rise of a modern business class.

The Turkish novel had not previously focused on provincial cities. Most pre-World War II novels were set in Istanbul. If they dealt with provincial life at all, it was from the viewpoint of the Istanbul elite. After the war enthusiasm steadily grew for works written by or about the small farmers in physically or psychologically remote areas. These farmers' crises revolved around feuds over water or women and the unbearably harsh conditions of raising crops and livestock. Their traditional social relationships began slowly to change only with the introduction of mechanized agriculture and the migration of the unemployed to Germany or to the large cities in Turkey. Agaoglu chose the provincial city of Eskişehir as the primary setting for *Curfew* because it maintained close ties with Istanbul in the Ottoman period but then, from 1980 on, turned toward Ankara, and in so doing underscored the transformation of Turkish society as a whole.

Another innovation in Agaoglu's novel is the strategy of having a character project into the future via his or her thoughts, without any transition to warn the reader. For example, in this passage from the novel, Murat is stumbling around in the dark looking for Ufuk's apartment. Without any warning to the reader, his thoughts shift into the future, fixing on the arrival of his sister, Kismet, after he has failed to meet her train. He internalizes her fears, especially her sexual fears.

> The same Kismet tried out a few smiles from the compartment window and stepped down from the train. . . . She stood there on the station steps, her little bag trailing at her feet, unable to decide what transport to take or where to go: Should I take a taxi? But heaven knows where the driver would take me! Better perhaps to take the ferry that's about to leave. But where and how to buy a ticket? And I don't know where on earth I'm supposed to be going! . . . The best thing is to get out of this crowd and find a quiet corner. Wrap myself in anonymity. But

that man with the black mustache. Why is he walking towards me in that way? What's he going to do? Heavens, what does he want from me? "Please, Mr. Gendarme, Mr. Policeman, Mr. Soldier, friend." What's he doing? Why is he grinning like that? Why's he pressing into me? I'm a decent woman. . . . Kismet felt herself being pressed from all sides. . . . One of those harassing her said "Here's a nice bit of stuff." The other added "She's drunk." Two police came up. They took hold of Kismet. "Better search her. All over. Find out what drugs she's high on." Kismet struggled. . . . She thrashed about. Why so many eyes staring at her, when she had hardly taken a step out of the house? So many men's hands touching her all over.

Murat . . . tries to rid himself of these thoughts. . . .

(*Curfew*, pp. 12-13)

Agaoglu explored this technique further in two later novels, *Hayir* (1987; No) and *Romantik: bir Viyana yazi* (1993; Romantic: A Viennese Journal). This last novel was much praised and has been referred to in Turkey as the most important work of Turkish fiction in several years.

Reception. *Curfew* occupies a special place among Agaoglu's novels because one of its main characters (Ferit) is a successful and powerful businessman. At the time of publication, in 1984, the sympathetic treatment of a businessman was considered an act of betrayal among left-leaning readers and critics who influenced this readership.

Like the majority of important Turkish writers in the early 1980s, Agaoglu herself was pro-left. Although not a member of the Turkish Workers Party, she never hid her sympathy with their socialist aims. The party was banned in 1971, and its leaders were jailed. Because of her political sympathies, she and her husband Halim suffered economic and political pressures, ranging from the loss of his state job as a highway engineer to the suppression for about a year (1981-82) of another of Agaoglu's novels, the apolitical work *Fikrimin ince gülü* (1976; Slender Rose of My Desire).

Nevertheless, the distaste among leftists for *Curfew*'s portrayal of Ferit Sakarya as a highly trained and cultivated businessman able to prevail in discussions with committed leftists, who actually looked up to him, affected the book's sales and its critical reception. By the rigid code of leftist critics, Agaoglu had "betrayed the cause" and changed her beliefs. What Agaoglu showed, in fact, was the need for and impor-

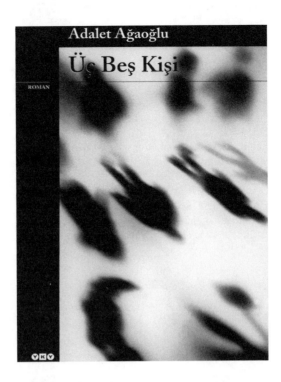

Cover from *Üç Beş Kişi,* translated into English as *Curfew.*

tance of such people, who would turn out to be responsible for Turkey's progress in the next generation.

Other Turkish critics received the book favorably. They especially liked Agaoglu's unflinching descriptions of the severe conflicts in a society in transition, her skillful depictions of a range of characters, and the interesting introduction of future-as-present into her narrative style.

In the words of these critics, the novel succeeds on multiple levels: "The history of our recent past will, I think, be written several times and perhaps many times, but as an analysis of a period of history and society in writing . . . 'Curfew' will never lose its distinction and power," prophesied one of these critics. "With her latest novel 'Curfew,'" observed another such critic, "Adalet Agaoglu continues to perfect the qualities of her narrative art and with expert portraits brings to life Time as the seal of modern form" (Cemal, p. 15; Aytaç, p. 74; trans. E. Ervin).

—Ellen Ervin

For More Information

Agaoglu, Adalet. *Curfew.* Trans. John Goulden. Center for Middle Eastern Studies. Austin: The University of Texas at Austin, 1997.

Ahmad, Feroz. *The Making of Modern Turkey*. New York: Routledge, 1993.

Arat, Zehra F., ed. *Deconstructing Images of "The Turkish Woman."* New York: St. Martin's Press, 1998.

Aytaç, Gürsel. Review of *Curfew,* by Adalet Agaoglu. *Cagdaş Eleştiri* [Criticism Today], Mayis 1984, 16-18.

Bugra, Ayşe. *State and Business in Modern Turkey. A Comparative Study.* State University of New York Press: Albany, 1994.

Cemal, Ahmet. Review of *Curfew,* by Adalet Agaoglu. *Cumhuriyet* [Republic], 14 Haziran 1984, 5.

Cosar, Fatma Mansur. "Women in Turkish Society." In *Women in the Muslim World.* Ed. Lois Beck and Nikki Keddie. Cambridge, Harvard University Press, 1978.

Ervin, Ellen W. "The Novels of Adalet Agaoglu: Narrative Complexity and Feminist Social Consciousness in Modern Turkey." Ph.D. diss., Columbia University, 1988.

Kandiyoti, Deniz A. "Emancipated But Un-liberated? Reflections on the Turkish Case." *Feminist Studies* 13, no. 2 (summer 1987): 317-38.

Mango, Andrew. *Ataturk: The Biography of the Founder of Modern Turkey.* Woodstock, N.Y.: Overlook, 2000.

Tekeli, Şirin, ed. *Women in Modern Turkish Society: a Reader.* London: Zed Books, 1995.

The Dead Sea Scrolls from Qumran

In early 1947 Bedouin shepherds investigating a cave in the cliffs northwest of the Dead Sea discovered the first of the scrolls that would be considered the greatest archaeological find of the twentieth century. Within a decade, ten nearby caves were found to contain more scrolls. Scholars soon recognized that these scrolls were 2,000-year-old manuscripts written or collected by an ancient sect, probably the Essenes, living at a site known today as Qumran. These Qumran scrolls form a subset of the Dead Sea Scrolls, which include ancient texts discovered at other locations, such as Masada, Murabba'at, and Nahal Hever. Included among the Qumran manuscripts were sectarian texts describing a community that broke away from the Jewish temple in Jerusalem and lived a pietistic, communal life as they awaited the final battle when God would destroy the wicked and restore the righteous to a place of honor. Excavations indicated that the site itself was likely a community center that supported up to 200 people from before 100 B.C.E. until 68 C.E. The Qumran site contained communal dining facilities, an elaborate water system with as many as ten ritual baths, an assembly room, kilns for making pottery, and possibly a room for copying scrolls. Types of pottery within the settlement were also found in the nearby scroll caves, thus connecting the site with the scrolls. By combining the information from the scrolls with accounts from other ancient sources, scholars have begun to flesh out theories about the nature and history of this group. They posit that a group of pious Jews, some of

THE LITERARY WORK

A collection of more than 900 Hebrew and Aramaic texts dated between 350 B.C.E. and 70 C.E., from caves near the Dead Sea; first discovered in 1947, published 1950-2002.

SYNOPSIS

Including the oldest manuscripts of the Hebrew Bible and other ancient Jewish texts, as well as previously unknown texts, the collection is most likely the library of a separatist religious group that inhabited the site known as Qumran from around 150 B.C.E. until 68 C.E.

whom were priests, separated from the temple in Jerusalem because of concerns about the legitimacy and purity of the mainstream high priests. At some later point a priest, called in some of the scrolls the Teacher of Righteousness, established a community of his followers at Qumran that focused on ritual purity, interpretation of Scripture, and preparation for the time when God would bring final judgement on the wicked and restore the Qumran community to control over a pure temple. In addition to collecting and copying many Hebrew and Aramaic texts commonly used by other Jewish groups (some are now part of the Hebrew Bible and some are not), the members of this community developed a rich literature of their own. They wrote prayers and hymns, legal codes, commentaries on biblical texts, wisdom texts (texts similar to Proverbs, Job, and Ecclesiastes that deal with philosophical issues such as the meaning of life and the best way to live), and eschatological texts describing the last days. Among the first group of texts discovered, *The Community Rule* and *The Commentary on Habakkuk* express the unique worldview of the Qumran sectarians and provide evidence of religious and political diversity that has affected our understanding of the historical circumstances of the late Second Temple period (200 B.C.E.-70 C.E.) in and around Jerusalem.

Events in History at the Time of the Scrolls

Hellenization. After the conquest of Alexander the Great in 333 B.C.E., the entire population of the area known today as the State of Israel and the Palestinian territories was confronted with increasing tension between the religious and social traditions of Israel and those of the Greeks. Many Jews, attracted to the new ways of the Greeks, left behind their Jewish traditions and joined the dominant culture. This process, called Hellenization, accelerated after 200 B.C.E. when control of the region transferred from the Ptolemies based in Egypt to the Seleucids based in Syria. Significant segments of the Jewish population reacted against such assimilation and committed themselves to holding fast to their Jewish ways.

During the reign of the Seleucid king Antiochus IV Epiphanes (176-64 B.C.E.), the Jewish high priests presiding in the temple in Jerusalem adopted a Greek way of life and transformed Jerusalem into a Greek-style *polis* with a gymnasium and amphitheater. They were joined by many of the elite urban Jews who mingled easily with the Greeks among them. In 167 B.C.E. Antiochus, for reasons not totally clear from historical sources, outlawed practices of the Jewish religion, such as circumcision, and required, on penalty of death, that sacrifices be offered to the Greek gods. The Jewish temple in Jerusalem was rededicated to the chief Greek god Zeus Olympus, and swine and other animals forbidden to Jews were offered on the altar.

The Maccabean revolt and the Hasmonean Dynasty. The religious persecution by Antiochus sparked a revolt led by Mattathias, a rural priest from Modi'in, and his sons, John, Simon, Judah (called the Maccabee [Hammer]), Eleazar, and Jonathan. They were joined by other groups of pious Jews "zealous for the law," among them the

Asideans, also called the Hasidim (1 Maccabees 2:27). Together the groups waged a guerrilla war to restore religious freedom. In 164 B.C.E., the Maccabees, led by Judah, regained control of the temple in Jerusalem, purified it and rededicated it to the worship of Israel's God. Even after this victory, Judah and his brothers continued fighting to gain political independence from the Seleucids. The Hasidim and perhaps others who were satisfied with religious freedom split from the Maccabees to make peace with the newly appointed Jewish high priest, Alcimus.

The Maccabees, also called by their family name Hasmoneans, eventually gained political independence from the Seleucids, and in 152 B.C.E. Jonathan, Judah's brother, accepted the dual role of high priest and governor of Judea. From about 152 B.C.E. until 63 B.C.E., a Hasmonean representative ruled Israel as king and high priest in Jerusalem. Although the Maccabees' military victories gave them authority to continue to lead the people, Israel's tradition was clear that any king over Israel must be from the royal family of David, and that the high priest must be a descendent of Zadok, David's high priest. Maccabee rule spelled a departure from Israel's ancient traditions. This departure certainly attracted protest from the disaffected members of Zadok's high priestly family and from the traditionalists that had originally supported the Maccabees and their revolt.

Another source of friction was the fact that the Hasmoneans' access to power led to increased interaction with the Hellenized elite around them. In the end, the leaders of the traditionalist revolt against Hellenism became significantly Hellenized themselves, evidenced by their taking on Greek names.

Sectarianism. The period of the rise of the Maccabees also saw the rise of a number of Jewish groups that competed for control of the Jerusalem temple and for influence on the people. Already brought to light is evidence of the disagreements between the Maccabees, the Hasidim, and the high priests. The first century C.E. Jewish historian Josephus provides more detailed information about three other groups: the Pharisees, the Sadducees, and the Essenes. These groups differed from one another on issues of religious law, biblical interpretation, oral tradition, beliefs about predestination and the afterlife, and the degree that their community encouraged interaction with those around them.

Josephus described the Pharisees as excellent expositors of the Law, who passed down laws from their ancestors not recorded in the Bible. They believed in bodily resurrection and that fate and free will both influence human actions. They seem to have been a popular group that vied for political influence with the Hasmonean priest-kings. After a dispute, the priest-king John Hyrcanus (reigned 134-104 B.C.E.) rejected the Pharisees and allied himself with rivals, the Sadducees. The subsequent priest-king, Alexander Jannaeus (reigned 104-76 B.C.E.), dealt harshly with the Pharisees who opposed him. When he began waging war against them, they invited the Seleucid king Demetrius to come to their aid. In response, Alexander executed 800 Pharisees by hanging them alive. When Alexander died and his wife, Salome Alexandra, took the throne, she reversed his policies and restored the Pharisees to a position of influence. The New Testament mentions that the Pharisees often disputed with Jesus over matters of law and justice, but they also shared many common views. The Pharisaic approach to oral tradition and interpretation was eventually taken up by the rabbis and forms the foundations of rabbinic Judaism even today.

Unlike the Pharisees, very little is known about the Sadducees, since no writings clearly associated with them have been preserved. Josephus describes them as a group more popular among the wealthy. They were highly influential among the Hasmonean rulers from the time of John Hyrcanus until the reign of Salome Alexandra (reigned 76-67 B.C.E.), when the Pharisees were favored. The name Sadducee, which most likely is equivalent to the Hebrew *Zadokim*, probably indicates a connection with the priestly class. The Sadducees rejected the idea of an afterlife and the Pharisees' oral traditions as well as God's determination of human activity. In cases where specific legal rulings are discussed, the Sadducees seem to have held a stricter position than the Pharisees. For example, they believed ritual impurity could be transferred from one vessel to another, even if the two were connected only by an unbroken stream of water poured from the pure vessel to the impure one. The Pharisees only considered impurity transferable if the water traveled from the impure vessel to the pure one.

The third major group, the Essenes, to which the Qumran community was probably connected, is described in more detail by Josephus and also by Philo of Alexandria. Mostly living in communities of celibate men, the Essenes were extremely pious. They formed communal groups that shared property and in most cases did not marry or seek wealth. Not enamoured of power either, they seem to have avoided the struggle for political influence and to have cared for their own communities. They relied on fate and on a strictly observant life. The Essenes emphasized purity, immersing themselves in water before sharing communal meals. Also, says Josephus, they engaged in a lengthy, highly selective admission process for new members that ended with the initiate swearing "tremendous oaths" to the community (Josephus, 2.139).

These groups, as well as others, most likely emerged as reactions to the social and political conditions of the Hellenistic period. The influence and attractiveness of Greek culture, philosophy, literary traditions, athletic contests, and political ideals engendered a variety of responses from Jews intent on preserving their ancestral traditions. Some rejected all forms of interaction with the Greeks, while others sought a middle way that would allow them to maintain their identity as Jews within a Greek world. Even those who desired to maintain the ancestral traditions fragmented over who had the authority to interpret those traditions and over the correct interpretation of them.

As the central Jewish institution, the temple in Jerusalem was often a lightning rod for provoking opposition. As we have seen, the Maccabean revolt against the Seleucids was ignited by Antiochus's defiling of the temple. The Hasmoneans, in turn, stirred up opposition when they accepted for themselves the role of high priest, dismissing the rightful heirs to that post. The temple also served as the national treasury, regularly imposing and collecting taxes, often to pay the Greek and Roman rulers. Consequently, many people saw the priesthood as corrupt and sought other ways to identify themselves.

Roman occupation. In 63 B.C.E. the Romans removed the Hasmonean rulers and once again subjected Judea to foreign control. They appointed procurators to govern the region on behalf of the Roman emperor. Contrary to the Greeks, who through their ideology and culture had mainly exerted an indirect influence on the people they dominated, the Romans influenced their subjects by force. For the Jews this was most difficult to bear with respect to the temple in Jerusalem. The Romans allowed the practice of Judaism but stationed an army garrison in the tower overlooking the temple courts and assumed control of the high priestly garments, thereby controlling the priests' activity. Josephus describes a number of occasions in which

Caves where the Dead Sea Scrolls were discovered, located near Qumran, south of Jericho.

Contents overview. Found in 11 caves near the Dead Sea, the Dead Sea Scrolls from Qumran represent more than 900 texts. They can be divided into three categories: biblical, extrabiblical, and sectarian.

Texts categorized as biblical are versions of books that were later to be considered part of the Hebrew Bible (Old Testament) by Judaism and Christianity. While it seems that the Qumran community considered these books sacred, it is possible that they also considered some other books as having similar authority. The Old Testament books of Psalms, Deuteronomy, and Isaiah were found in multiple copies, and there was at least one copy for every book except for Esther. In all, more than 200 texts comprise the biblical category. These manuscripts are nearly 1,000 years older than those used as the basis for all modern translations of the Bible. Scholars have been able to better understand, on the basis of these ancient Qumran biblical manuscripts, a much earlier stage in the process by which the Bible became standardized and copied from generation to generation. These manuscripts show evidence that various Hebrew textual traditions existed before the "official" version was chosen to become today's Bible. They attest to significant variations in some of the texts at a time before the books of the Bible were selected and standardized.

"Extrabiblical" is a catchall category that includes any texts not now considered biblical but also not written by the Qumran community. The category includes books long known in translation in Greek or Ethiopic, such as 1 Enoch, Tobit, Jubilees, and others. Also in this category are texts not found elsewhere but surmised to have been generated outside the Qumran community.

The final category, sectarian, includes all those texts considered to have been composed by the Qumran community. They consist of many types, from laws to hymns and prayers, Bible commentaries and translations, wisdom literature, and texts about the last days. From these texts comes the most information regarding the nature of the community at Qumran. Many of them are highly fragmentary and difficult to read. But two important sectarian texts, *The Community Rule* and *The Commentary on Habakkuk*, were found in jars in Cave One that kept them well preserved.

The Community Rule. Originally called *The Manual of Discipline*, *The Community Rule* was

symbols of Roman might, such as banners or standards, were introduced into the temple area, causing great distress and protest from the Jewish people.

From 36-34 B.C.E. the Romans appointed Herod the Great as King of Judea. Herod, who was considered a half-Jew in the eyes of the Jews, was notorious for his extravagant building projects and his ruthless hold on the throne. While Herod enlarged and beautified the temple area in Jerusalem, he also built cities and temples in honor of Rome and its emperor. Soon after Herod died, Rome once again took direct control over Jerusalem.

Resistance to Roman rule eventually led to the First Jewish Revolt for independence from Rome, which began in 66 C.E. but was plagued by fighting among the many Jewish factions. When the Romans laid siege to Jerusalem, there was so much internal strife that the Romans waited while the Jews within the city fought and killed one another. The revolt ended with the destruction of the temple by the Romans in 70 C.E. and the dispersal of the surviving Jewish communities out of Judea. The temple's destruction initiated the decline of Jewish sectarianism, giving rise in succeeding generations to rabbinic Judaism and early Christianity.

one of the first texts removed from Cave One. Multiple copies of it, with some variations indicating editorial activity, were also found in Cave Four. The manuscript, which dates to around 100 B.C.E., probably served as the community's constitution, providing a basis for the hierarchical structure of the group and governing the behavior of its members. The text divides into three main sections: a description of the initiation ceremony with an exhortation regarding two spirits; a set of laws to govern behavior; and instructions for the Master, along with the Master's hymn.

The text begins by describing the role of the Master, perhaps a priest, who is responsible for using *The Community Rule* to prepare potential members for the initiation ceremony. The Master is to determine who among the would-be initiates has "freely devoted" themselves to follow God's truth according to what has been revealed to the community; these are the ones who can be "joined to the counsel of God and may live perfectly before Him," loving the sons of light (the community) and hating the sons of darkness (its opponents) (Vermes, *The Community Rule* in *The Complete Dead Sea Scrolls*, pp. 98-99). The priests pronounce blessings on all those who have accepted the rule of the community and are being accepted into the covenant. The Levites, a secondary class of priests responsible for the upkeep of the temple, then pronounce curses on "the lot of Belial [personification of evil]"—all those who reject or oppose the community and are therefore considered agents of evil. Additional curses are spoken against those who might enter the covenant while secretly "walking in the stubbornness of their heart," or who decide at a later time to leave the community to follow their own way (*The Community Rule*, p. 100). At a later point in the text we learn that initiates undergo a two-year probation period before they can participate in the communal meal and their property can be joined together with that of the community.

The text continues with the Master's instructions for the community regarding some of the basic principles of its belief. First, all things were created and predetermined by God, even the tasks of humanity. Second, God created humankind and "has appointed for him two spirits in which to walk until the time of His visitation: the spirits of truth and injustice" (*The Community Rule*, p. 101). Those who continually choose to walk in the spirit of truth are worthy to be called sons of light and shall receive rewards of healing, peace, long life, blessing, and "eternal

Section of the Dead Sea Scrolls, in exhibition at the Shrine of the Book in Jerusalem.

joy in life without end, a crown of glory and a garment of majesty in unending light" (*The Community Rule*, p. 102). In contrast, the spirit of injustice produces all sorts of cruelty and destruction and is rewarded by plagues and eternal torment. These two spirits are constantly battling within each person, as well as throughout the spiritual world of the angels. God has created the two spirits in equal measure for now, but in the end He will come and destroy the spirit of injustice forever and cleanse the people with waters of holiness and pour upon the people the spirit of truth. The teaching concludes with a reminder that each person's eternal destiny is determined by the spirit within him or her at the time of God's visitation.

The middle section of the text lists the rules governing the behavior of all those who "have freely pledged themselves to be converted from all evil and to cling to all His commandments according to His will" (*The Community Rule*, p. 103). The first part establishes the organizational structure of the community and grants complete authority to its leaders, the sons of Zadok, to determine doctrine, property issues, and justice. Each member must swear an oath before the community to return to the Law of Moses as interpreted by the divinely inspired Teacher of Righteousness and to separate from all men of injustice. All members are ranked according to their wisdom and understanding and are required to obey all those of higher rank. Whenever members of the community come together to eat, pray, or study the Law, they are to sit according to rank and participate in order, beginning with the priest. Murmuring against the authority of the community carries a penalty of expulsion from the community.

The next set of laws governs behavior during an assembly of the congregation. Members are not to interrupt one another nor speak out of turn. Punishments, typically in the form of exclusion from the pure Meal of the Congregation (presumably the communal covenant meal) for a period, are also described for other acts related to speech, such as lying, addressing a companion impatiently, speaking God's name, speaking in anger against a priest, insulting someone, speaking foolishly, slandering someone, and so forth. Other punishable deeds include falling asleep during the assembly, spitting, and walking naked unnecessarily. This second section concludes with an admonition to "be ruled by the primitive precepts in which the men of the Community were first instructed until there shall come the Prophet and the Messiahs of Aaron and Israel" (*The Community Rule*, p. 110). This designation of two awaited Messianic figures retains the traditional separation between the offices of the high priest (designated by the term "Aaron") and the king (designated by the term "Israel"), in stark contrast to the Hasmonean rulers who had merged these offices.

The final section begins with instructions for the Master regarding the education and evaluation of the members of the community according to their piety and their capacity for understanding. The Master is to reveal the true knowledge only to those he determines to be worthy, concealing the truth from men of injustice. The Master himself is to be perfectly obedient to the will of God, giving praise to God for all things at all the times ordained by God. There follows a lengthy hymn, first recounting the times of day and seasons of the year that require praise.

> I will sing with knowledge and all my music
> shall be for the glory of God.
> (My) lyre (and) my harp shall sound
> for His holy order
> and I will tune the pipe of my lips
> to His right measure.
> With the coming of day and night
> I will enter the Covenant of God,
> and when evening and morning depart
> I will recite His decrees.
> (*The Community Rule*, p. 112)

The rest of the hymn reinforces God's complete sovereignty and humanity's need for God.

The Commentary on Habakkuk. Also found in Cave One, *The Commentary on Habakkuk* dates to the period when Herod ruled Judea for the Romans. This writing is the best preserved of the group of biblical commentaries found at Qumran called *Pesher* texts, which present a biblical prophetic book, interrupted periodically by commentary connecting the words of the prophet with the life and history of the Qumran community. (Found among these texts was a commentary on Psalms as well, which was read like a book of prophecy.) *The Commentary on Habakkuk* claims that the real meaning of the words of Habakkuk has been hidden to all prior generations but is now being revealed and understood. The text calls this new prophet, "to whom God made known all the mysteries of the words of His servants the Prophets," the Teacher of Righteousness (Vermes, *The Commentary on Habakkuk* in *The Complete Dead Sea Scrolls*, p. 481). This Teacher of Righteousness is understood to be the founder of the community at Qumran. Habakkuk 2:4, "the righteous shall live by his faith," is interpreted to refer to "those who observe the Law," who will be delivered from judgement "because of their faith in the Teacher of Righteousness" (*The Commentary on Habakkuk*, p. 482).

The Commentary on Habakkuk also interprets phrases in Habakkuk as referring to the enemies of the Teacher and his group of followers. Habakkuk 2:5-11 is interpreted as describing the Wicked Priest, the main opponent of the Teacher, who, "when he ruled over Israel his heart became proud, and he forsook God and betrayed the precepts for the sake of riches. . . . [H]e took the wealth of the peoples, heaping sinful iniquity upon himself. And he lived in the ways of abominations amidst every unclean defilement" (*The Commentary on Habakkuk,* p. 482). The Wicked Priest is also accused of defiling the temple of God by his deeds and of pursuing the Teacher of Righteousness to confuse the community on Yom Kippur, called the Day of Fasting. This event highlights the fact that the Wicked Priest was not using the strict solar calendar observed at Qumran, for he would not have been permitted to travel on a holy day. Rather he must have been using a lunar calendar closer to the variety now used in Jewish life. Given the great emphasis within the scrolls on the importance of following a strictly solar calendar, the Qumran community would have considered this to be a significant failure on the part

THE CASE FOR THE ESSENE HYPOTHESIS

A connection between the scrolls and the Essenes was made by scholars very soon after the texts were discovered. This connection is based on a comparison of a number of ancient sources:

1) According to Josephus, a Jewish historian of the first century C.E., the Essenes were one of the philosophies or sects of Jews at the end of the Second Temple period (100 B.C.E.– 70 C.E.). They are distinguished by belief in determinism and an afterlife, a long initiation process, celibacy (at least among some members), piety, and communal living.
2) The Roman geographer Pliny the Elder in his *Natural History,* published in 77 C.E., mentions that a group of solitary, celibate Essenes lived near the Dead Sea between Jericho and En Gedi.
3) The Qumran Scrolls themselves show evidence of isolation, celibacy, determinism, and a long rigorous initiation procedure.

Challengers have lodged protests to the Essene connection:

1) The term "sons of Zadok" in the scrolls and a number of similarities in legal rulings suggest connections with the Sadducees. Not enough is known about the Sadducees to determine whether these similarities are not just cases of shared traditions among different groups.
2) Josephus describes a total of 4,000 Essenes living in all the towns and cities, and of there being some who married and had families.

Since this second challenge raises issues about which there are differences among the Qumran scrolls, most conclude that the Qumran community represents one part of the broader Essene movement.

---

of the Wicked Priest. In the end, God finally delivered the Wicked Priest into the hands of his foreign enemies as punishment for his wicked treatment of the Teacher of Righteousness and his council.

The Commentary on Habakkuk also mentions a character it calls the Spouter of Lies, who led many astray and founded a community based on deceit. In other Qumran texts, this character has a number of other names related to lying and deception and seems to be connected with a group called the Seekers of Smooth Things (VanderKam and Flint, p. 287). Understanding that "smooth things" in the Bible refers to flattery and deceit, the Teacher of Righteousness is accusing this group of faulty interpretation of the Law in order to find an easy way out. Once again the Qumran community is claiming for itself the true interpretation of God's Law and castigating those who do not accept Qumran legal authority. *The Commentary on Habakkuk* ends with the promise that "on the Day of Judgment, God will destroy from the earth all idolatrous and wicked men" (*The Commentary on Habakkuk*, p. 485).

The historical identities of those mentioned in the texts. One of the most intriguing and frustrating things about the Qumran texts is their use of code terminology to describe themselves and their opponents. Very seldom is a term used that corresponds well with designations given by other historical sources of the period. For example, the texts use descriptive titles such as Teacher of Righteousness, Wicked Priest, the Seekers of Smooth Things and so on, rather than names of historical figures or groups, like Jonathan or the Pharisees. This ambiguity has made it possible for scholars to propose many different identifications between the descriptive titles and historical figures; consensus has been reached in some cases.

First, there is the question of how to identify the group responsible for the texts. Based on comparisons between the scrolls and other historical sources, most scholars have agreed that they were connected to a group called the Essenes. The name's precise meaning and its Hebrew or Aramaic equivalent has long been debated, so it is impossible to determine whether or not the community used this name for themselves. Their most common self-designations are "The Community" or "the sons of light," but some scholars have proposed a connection with the term "doers" (*osim*) found in the phrase "doers of the Torah." Others have argued for some connection with the Hasidim, who split with the Maccabees after achieving religious freedom.

After identifying the group, there is the question of who is the group's founder, the Teacher of Righteousness. He was responsible for uniting the community, formulating their religious practice, and moving them to Qumran. Most importantly, he was considered by his followers to have received divinely inspired understanding of how the words of all the prophets applied to the life and future of the community. Although a few scholars have tried to identify the Teacher with key figures of early Christianity, these connections are impossible considering the texts were composed nearly a century before Jesus lived. Since we have no information about leaders of the Essene movement, the most we can say is that the Teacher of Righteousness was probably a priest, perhaps even acting as high priest when the Hasmoneans took over that office in 152 B.C.E.

The main opponent of the Teacher of Righteousness is somewhat more identifiable. The Wicked Priest was certainly a priest of high standing and power in the Jerusalem temple, likely the high priest. According to *The Commentary on Habakkuk*, he began his term favorably but grew prideful, amassing wealth and power when he became ruler over Israel. This description almost certainly identifies the Wicked Priest as one of the Hasmoneans, from whose dynasty came the leader that served as both the king and high priest of Israel from 152 to 76 B.C.E. The description of his amassed wealth and his death at the hands of his foreign enemies probably best fits the first Hasmonean ruler, Jonathan (reigned 152-42 B.C.E.).

The Spouter of Lies mentioned in *The Commentary on Habakkuk* has been identified as a leader of the group designated in other texts as the Seekers of Smooth Things. *The Commentary on Nahum* gives additional information that can help us identify this group. This text indicates that the Seekers of Smooth Things invited Demetrius, king of Greece, into Jerusalem but that God saved the city from him. Someone referred to as the "furious young lion" then exacted revenge on the Seekers of Smooth Things, hanging them alive (Vermes, *The Commentary on Nahum* in *The Complete Dead Sea Scrolls*, p. 474).

Josephus describes these events during the reign of the Hasmonean ruler Alexander Jannaeus in his conflicts with the Pharisees. According to the Qumran community, these Pharisees, especially their leaders, were deceiving the people and were being much too lenient regarding the faithful obedience to God's Law.

Many Qumran texts also refer to a group called the Kittim. In *The Commentary on Habakkuk* they are great warriors who "inspire all the nations to fear and dread" (*The Commentary on Habakkuk*, p. 479). They come from afar to devour the peoples and lay waste to the earth. They also are described as making sacrifices to their standards and worshipping their weapons. It is clear from these descriptions that the Kittim are the Romans, who were known for their military capabilities and were perceived as a constant threat that stood ready to destroy Judea and the Jewish way of life. The Qumran community saw this impending destruction as a sign of the final judgement that would befall the wicked in Israel, the ones who had rejected the True Way taught by the Teacher of Righteousness.

Sources and literary context. As a group claiming to be the true remnant of Israel, the Qumran community and its writings were completely dependent upon the literature that became the Hebrew Bible. Frequently biblical language permeated even the sectarian texts. For example, *The Community Rule* describes the blessing of the righteous and the cursing of the wicked based on a blessing that Aaron and his sons, the priests, spoke to the people:

From the Hebrew Bible

Blessing of Aaron to the people:
The LORD bless you and keep you; the LORD make his face to shine upon you, and be gracious to you; the LORD lift up his countenance upon you, and give you peace.
(Numbers 6:24-26)

From *The Community Rule*

Blessing of the righteous (members of the community)
May He bless you with all good and preserve you from all evil! May he lighten your heart with life giving wisdom and grant you eternal knowledge! May He raise His merciful face towards you for everlasting bliss!

Curse of the wicked (opponents of the community)
. . . Be cursed without mercy because of the darkness of your deeds! Be damned in the shadowy place of everlasting fire! May God not heed you when you call on Him, nor pardon

Dead Sea Scroll manuscripts as they look today.

you by blotting out your sin! May He raise His angry face towards you for vengeance! May there be no "Peace" for you in the mouth of those who hold fast to the Fathers!

(*The Community Rule*, pp. 99-100)

The Qumran authors also drew from other texts not considered biblical that were circulating in contemporary Jewish communities. Examples are the books of Enoch, which describe the sin of the angels, whose interaction with the daughters of men caused the flood in the time of Noah and began the cosmic battle between good and evil, and Jubilees, which recast Israel's history with an emphasis on the use of a solar calendar.

In addition, similarities between the scrolls and later New Testament and early Christian texts have helped scholars better understand Jesus and his early followers within the context of Second Temple Judaism. Early Christian texts seem to have been influenced, if not by the scrolls themselves, at least by the ideas that were circulating at Qumran and elsewhere at the time about communal life, the dualism of light and darkness, and the low worth of humans without God. It seems clear, however, that there is no direct link between the Qumran community and the early Christians.

Events in History at the Time of Discovery and Publication

Discovery of the scrolls. The scrolls from Cave One were discovered by Bedouin (nomadic shepherds) in 1946-47, just before the end of the British Mandate in Palestine. The period of British control of Palestine, which lasted from 1918-48, was a period of increasing tension and violence between the Jewish and Arab populations, with both sides claiming that the British were unfairly partial to the other. As the British were withdrawing and the United Nations was attempting to define a plan to partition the land into two states, one Jewish and one Palestinian, antiquities dealers were attempting to determine the nature and worth of the scrolls. The tumultuous political climate made collaboration between Jewish scholars at the Hebrew University, European and American scholars in East Jerusalem, the Arab antiquities dealers in Bethlehem, and the Bedouin very difficult indeed. In fact, it was some time before any scholars knew that the scrolls, which had been separated into two groups, were found together in a cave, and it was not until early 1949 that the cave itself was identified and excavated.

After the conclusion of the 1948 war that established the modern state of Israel and divided Jerusalem, the newly formed Kingdom of Jordan acquired the caves and the rest of the scrolls and therefore controlled the appointment of a team to excavate the subsequent caves and publish the remaining scrolls. Because of the political tensions between Israel and Jordan, no Israeli scholars were selected for the team, which was made up of European and American scholars from the Ecole Biblique and the American School of Oriental Research, both in East Jerusalem. After the 1967 War, Israel gained control over the caves as well as the Palestine Archaeological Museum (renamed the Rockefeller Museum), which housed all the scrolls in East Jerusalem. However, out of respect for the original group of scholars, additional members, including Israeli scholars, were not added to the team until 1987.

Publication and reception. The discovery of the scrolls initiated a frenzy of excitement among scholars certain that these manuscripts would mark a major turning point in our understanding of Second Temple Judaism and early Christianity. The authenticity and antiquity of the scrolls was established originally by handwriting analysis, which was later corroborated by carbon-14 dating. Very early in the post-discovery period, scholars posited the theory connecting the Qumran community with the Essenes, which has since been modified but not discarded.

Of the 11 caves found containing scrolls, Cave 1 and Cave 11 contained the longest and best preserved texts. Cave 4 held by far the greatest number of manuscripts, but they were badly preserved and very fragmentary. The other caves produced relatively small fragments of relatively few texts. The texts from Cave 1 were all published within ten years or so, and the texts from the minor Caves 2-3 and 5-10 were also published quickly in the official series *Discoveries in the Judaean Desert* (vols. 1-3, 1955-62). The Cave 4 texts, and a few of the Cave 11 texts, however, remained unpublished and unavailable to the public. These texts numbered more than 600 and were very fragmentary and difficult to assemble. A team of seven scholars was given the daunting task of preparing them for publication. This work proved to be so slow that very few texts were published over the next 20 years.

Increased impatience and frustration led to public outcry for the release of the manuscripts. The mysterious delay of the publication of the texts opened the door for all kinds of sensationalized claims regarding the contents of those unpublished texts. The team of scholars was accused of either purposely covering up, on behalf of the Vatican, findings that would undermine Christianity or withholding evidence that the manuscripts were in fact Christian texts themselves. In the early 1990s, unauthorized editions began to appear based on computer reconstructions and on photographs released by the Huntington Library in San Marino, California. Many scholars were therefore added to the official team to speed along publication. Since 1990, more than 20 additional volumes of the official DJD series, covering the rest of the Cave 4 texts, have been published, and photographs of all the texts are readily available to all. The discovery and publication of the Dead Sea Scrolls has by all accounts been a major turning point in the study of the Bible, Second Temple Judaism, and early Christianity. Scholars in these fields now have abundant evidence of the variety of beliefs and religious practices behind the emergence of Christianity and rabbinic Judaism. This variety provides a context for understanding as Jewish many elements of early Christianity that had previously been considered non-Jewish in origin. The rise and success of rabbinic Judaism has also come to be regarded as a much more complex process than previously seen. All future discussions of this important period in world history will have to consider the evidence of the Dead Sea Scrolls from Qumran.

—Russell C. D. Arnold

For More Information

Cohen, Shaye J. D. *From the Maccabees to the Mishnah.* Library of Early Christianity. Ed. Wayne A. Meeks. Philadelphia: Westminster Press, 1987.

Discoveries in the Judaean Desert. Vols. 1-39. Oxford: Clarendon Press, 1955-2002.

Josephus, Flavius. *The Works of Josephus.* Trans. William Whiston. Peabody, Mass.: Hendrickson, 1987.

Schiffman, Lawrence H., and James C. VanderKam, eds. *Encyclopedia of the Dead Sea Scrolls.* 2 vols. Oxford: Oxford University Press, 2000.

———. *Reclaiming the Dead Sea Scrolls: Their True Meaning for Judaism and Christianity.* New York: Doubleday, 1994.

VanderKam, James. *The Dead Sea Scrolls Today.* Grand Rapids: Eerdmans, 1994.

———. *An Introduction to Early Judaism.* Grand Rapids: Eerdmans, 2001.

VanderKam, James, and Peter Flint. *The Meaning of the Dead Sea Scrolls: Their Significance for Understanding the Bible, Judaism, Jesus, and Christianity.* San Francisco: Harper San Francisco, 2002.

Vermes, Geza, ed. *The Complete Dead Sea Scrolls in English.* New York: Penguin, 1997.

The Divan
of Hafiz

Shams al-Din Muhammad Hafiz (nickname: *Khwaja*, or nobleman; surname: *Hafiz*, or the one who has memorized the Holy Quran) was born in the city of Shiraz (in the present-day province of Fars in Iran), probably in 1326 or 1327. He died there in 1389 or 1390. In his youth, the future poet received specialized training from the leading teachers and scholars of the city. A superb student, he concentrated on Quranic studies and theology, philosophy, music, the natural sciences, and poetics. Hafiz won the support of powerful characters at successive local courts in Shiraz and wrote a number of panegyrics in praise of regional rulers. In his *divan*, or collected poems, (spelled with a *v* for Persian pronunciation) are a number of allusions and references to historical figures and incidents. An acknowledged master of the intricacies of the Persian language, Hafiz produced harmonic melodies that demonstrate the subtlety and sophistication of his thoughts and sensibilities and that have few, if any, rivals in the entire tradition of Persian poetry. His poetry also shows that Hafiz had a strong predilection for philosophy. He was well informed about the intellectual trends of his day, and his own ideas challenge the contours of conventional thought about the essence of love, life, society, justice, and the purpose of human existence. Hafiz mainly wrote *ghazals* (sonnet-like poems of between five and fifteen couplets, in which each couplet is composed of two lines with a rhyme pattern *aa, ba, ca,* and so forth). It has been argued that each individual verse in a *ghazal* should convey a complete thought, and that just as the string of pearls on a thread makes a neck-

> ### THE LITERARY WORK
> The collected poems of Hafiz of Shiraz compiled in the alphabetical order of the final letters of the various end-rhymes; composed in fourteenth-century Persia; published in English in 1891.
>
> ### SYNOPSIS
> A collection of numerous multilayered poems, the *Divan* consists primarily of sonnet-like verses (*ghazals*), quatrains (*ruba`is*), and a few miscellaneous odes (*qasidas*) and fragments (*qit`as*). Strong mystical themes abound, along with social criticism and philosophical and intellectual insights.

lace, the combination of independent verses produces a *ghazal*. Conventionally, as in Hafiz's poems, the poet mentions his penname (*takhallus*) in the final verse (*maqta*). Many individual couplets of Hafiz's *ghazals* have become notable aphorisms over time, leading to the contention that Hafiz's *ghazals* possess some disparate couplets with independent meaning and thus lack coherence and overall thematic unity. A closer look at his divan indicates some truth to this assertion, yet often there is also a loose thematic unity that binds the individual couplets of each of Hafiz's *ghazals*. We know almost nothing of his life outside his poetry, which has given rise to the tendency to extract biographical information from his *ghazals*.

Hafiz, an imaginative rendering.

Events in History at the Time of the Divan

The Mongol/Il-Khan invasion of Persia. During his lifetime, Hafiz witnessed some momentous events in the long history of Persia. Except for a couple of brief trips, the poet lived and wrote exclusively in Shiraz, a city fortunate enough to escape the first and most destructive Mongol onslaught a century earlier. Persia was less than a priority to the Mongol chief Genghis Khan (d. 1227), whose attention was transfixed instead by China and central Asia. However, Persia became a focus of the Mongols when Ghenghis's grandson Möngke entrusted the expedition into western Asia to his brother Hulegu. Hulegu's army encountered two potent adversaries: the Isma`ilis (a militant Shi`ite sect, later known in the West as the Order of the Assassins) in Persia proper and the Abbasid Caliphate in Baghdad. In 1256, the Assassins' fortress of Alamut "offered a desperate resistance to the onslaughts of the Central Asian hordes and only succumbed after a prolonged siege. The leader of the sect, known as 'The Old Man of the Mountain' (*Shaykh al-Jabal*), was executed forthwith" (Spuler, p. 18). After breaking the power of the Isma`ilis in Persia and subduing the resistance of a few fiefdoms on his way, Hulegu marched straight to the city of Baghdad. His men seized and destroyed the city in February 1258, and he executed the caliph. For all practical purposes, Abbasid power evaporated, though it continued nominally for some time to come. The Arabic rulers of Egypt, the Mamluks, successfully checked Hulegu's invasions, though it was primarily internal rivalries among the Mongol leaders that stopped their western expansion. Hulegu finally settled in northwestern Persia and was given the title of Il-Khan (viceroy) by his brother Kublai Khan, the new Great Khan. The kingdom he established in western Asia (with Persia as its center) was called the Il-Khanate.

The Il-Khans were originally adverse to Islam, the faith of most of their Persian subjects at the time. Nonetheless, within a few decades, Islam had spread widely among the Mongols, especially the ruling elites. When Ghazan Khan acceded to the throne in November 1295, he acknowledged Islam to be the official religion of the state. Many ordinary Mongols who had remained on Persian soil since the first wave of invasions followed their king and converted to Islam. With little knowledge of the basic tenets of the religion, the erstwhile shamanistic Mongols were drawn to the mystical (Sufi) forms of Islam rather than its more legalistic (*shari`ah*) forms. The last great Il-Khan, Abu Sa`id, ruled until 1335, relying for assistance on prominent Persian viziers (ministers). He left no heir, and upon his death, the house of Hulegu fell into rapid decline.

From the disintegration of the Il-Khans to the appearance of the conqueror Timur in the 1380s, Persia witnessed the rule of various rival princely houses—from the Jalayirids, the Muzaffarids, and the Injuids in western Persia to the Karts and Sarbadars in the Khurasan region in the East. In this period of sociopolitical confusion and disorder, "the tyranny of petty princes, bloody conflicts between local powers, and devastating invasions were a constant menace, not only to the general well-being, but to people's very existence" (Roemer, p. 2). There are a number of direct and indirect references to these contemporary realities in Hafiz's work. The following verses, for example, clearly refer to the state of affairs in his time:

> In these times, the only perfect friend
> Is a vessel of pure wine and a book of *ghazals*
>
> . . .
>
> To reason's eye, in this tumultuous pathway
> The world and all its affairs are groundless
>   and volatile.
>   (Hafiz, *Divan*, pp. 113-14; trans. W. Ahmadi)

In another poem Hafiz writes, "I said to a clever one, 'Observe this state of affairs!' / 'A harsh day,' he laughed and said, 'an odd matter, a troubled world!'" (*Divan*, p. 350; trans. W. Ahmadi).

Social commentary, the poetic way. In marked contrast to the political and social state of affairs, the fourteenth century proved to be an especially dynamic and productive period of literary activity in Persia. A reason for the flourishing of poetry was "the existence of numerous small courts that competed with each other in attracting literati" (Schimmel, "Hafiz and His Contemporaries," p. 930). Hafiz was one of the major figures on the literary scene during this period. A close reading of his *ghazals,* with particular attention to his allusions and references to political figures and events, sheds important light on the history of his time. Hafiz was very young when the Il-Khan rule disintegrated. The province of Fars (with Shiraz as its capital) and its neighboring areas fell into the hands of the Inju dynasty. The poet himself was quite favorably inclined towards the last of the Injuid rulers, Shah Shaykh Abu Ishaq. In a number of famous *ghazals,* Hafiz praises him (along with his vizier Qivam al-Din Hasan). A man of letters and a patron of poets, Abu Ishaq was quite tolerant regarding religious requisites and practices. Prompted by the liberal atmosphere of the times, Sufi lodges (*khanaqahs*) flourished in and around Shiraz.

The Inju rule was threatened by the rival dynasty of Muzaffarids, centered in Yazd. In 1353, when Hafiz was in his late twenties, the Muzaffarid chief, Mubariz al-Din, invaded the poet's hometown of Shiraz. A ruthless, dogmatic Muslim, he prohibited *sama* (Sufi dancing), closed down all the taverns and brothels, and harshly prosecuted those who breached social and moral edicts, like wine drinkers. His austere interpretation of Islam made him detestable to many residents of Shiraz. In several poems, Hafiz criticizes Mubariz al-Din's rule and decries his hypocrisy:

> Will they ever unlock the doors of taverns
> And undo the knot from our muddled affairs?
> . . .
> They have closed down the tavern door, O
>   God,
> Do not allow them to open the door of
>   insincerity and duplicity.
>   (*Divan*, p. 196; trans. W. Ahmadi)

In 1358 the austere ruler's oldest son, Shah Shuja, in collaboration with some of his brothers, overthrew his father and subsequently blinded him. He relaxed his father's policies, es-

pecially with regard to religious requirements and practices. Hafiz did not approve the manner in which the son replaced the father, but the poet welcomed the termination of Mubariz al-Din's reign and the new, more liberal atmosphere in his hometown:

> At daybreak, the guardian angel chanted the
>   good news into my ear:
> "It is the reign of Shah Shuja`. Drink wine
>   valiantly!"
> Gone are the times when men of insight were
>   shunned,
> A thousand words in their mouths but their
>   lips tied.
>   (*Divan*, p. 238; trans. W. Ahmadi)

Hafiz wrote many songs of praise to Shah Shuja, who, himself being a poet, appreciated Hafiz's work. Shah Shuja died in 1384. Thereafter, internecine struggles resurfaced among his descendants and facilitated the occupation of Persia by the next conqueror, Timur, who eventually executed some 70 Muzaffarid princes in Shiraz. Legend has it that Hafiz met the new conqueror, but the legend, in the words of E. G. Browne, is "more celebrated than authentic" (Browne, p. 282).

Sufism in fourteenth-century Persia. Sufism refers to mystical consciousness derived from the principle of inner knowledge whereby intuitive revelation (*kashf*) becomes the highest and the best source of cognition. According to a prominent scholar of Islamic mysticism,

> The reality that is the goal of the mystic, and is ineffable, cannot be understood or explained by any normal mode of perception; neither philosophy nor reason can reveal it. Only the wisdom of the heart, *gnosis*, may give insight into some of its aspects. A spiritual experience that depends upon neither sensual nor rational methods is needed. Once the seeker has set forth upon the way to this Last Reality, he will be led by an inner light.
>   (Schimmel, *Mystical Dimensions*, p. 4)

Contributing to the development of Sufism were such diverse influences as the pre-Islamic religions, Manichean doctrines, Christian monasticism, Indian asceticism, Gnosticism, Greek neo-Platonism, even Central Asian shamanism. But the main formative components came from Islam, the Quran, and the Prophet's sayings and deeds. Part of the reason for this development was that "Muhammad's Prophetic consciousness . . . was founded upon very definite, vivid, and powerful mystic experiences" (Rahman, p. 138).

By the fourteenth century, in much of the Islamic world, Sufism had become institutional-

A subject central to Hafiz's poems is love, illustrated here in a Persian miniature.

ized as a discipline, just like philosophy and theology. Scattered throughout Persia in Hafiz's day were numerous Sufi lodges, signifying how important a social and cultural force Sufism had become. Even people with no clear Sufi affiliation who were discontent with the strict interpretation of Islamic doctrines inclined towards the *khanaqahs*. There is some evidence that "Hafiz used to attend the meetings of a Sufi master, and was seen by an Indian Sufi visitor as an *Uwaysi*, that is to say a mystic who obtains guidance from absent or dead teachers" (Baldick, p. 100). Based on a number of references in his divan, it is probably true that Hafiz was attached to one of the Sufi orders (*tariqahs*) in Shiraz, at least at some point in his life.

Religious commentary, or not? In the context of Persian poetry, Sufism is essentially connected with a complete and often ingenious frame of reference whereby sensuous words and images convey hidden, mystical thought. For instance, wine represents spiritual ecstasy, the beloved refers to the Divinity, the tavern is the Sufi lodge, and the Magi (in the person of the tavern keeper) is the spiritual guide who introduces the seeker to the arduous Sufi path. Using the conventional Sufi code book, one could interpret Hafiz's divan mystically, and many scholars of classical Persian poetry have studied it in terms of the mystical meanings and allu-

sions. Yet, although Sufi phrases, symbolism, imagery, and metaphors abound in his compositions, Hafiz's relation with Sufism was essentially an ambivalent one. His Sufi terminology, to take one aspect, "may easily be interpreted as non-mystical and allude to actual rather than spiritual matters" (Meisami, p. 25). While many scholars see only a purely mystical meaning in Hafiz's *ghazals,* others find in his work only sensual love, profane sentiments, and sheer hedonism. The complexity of Hafiz's poetic universe in the *Divan* evades either a clear mystical interpretation or a purely earthly reading. This is directly related to the texture of Persian lyrics, where "poetry provides almost unlimited possibilities for creating new relations between worldly and otherworldly images, between religious and profane ideas; the talented poet may reach a perfect interplay of both levels and make even the most profane poem bear a distinct 'religious' flavor" (Schimmel, *Mystical Dimensions,* p. 288). Given this overall tendency, ambiguity laces the work of many classical poets, but "the ambiguity is certainly much stronger, and intentionally so, in the poetry of Hafiz than in that of others" (Bürgel, p. 27). The multifaceted quality of his work endows any given image with diverse meanings and invites the reader to interpret Hafiz in a variety of ways. As Bürgel maintains, "in the poetical universe of Hafiz, one verse contradicts the other, one interpretation is belied by another and this by a third one, all of which can point to a number of verses in their support" (Bürgel, p. 35).

It follows that reducing the poetic language of Hafiz to the usual stock-in-trade Sufi connotations does it a grave injustice. Furthermore, the designation of the poet himself as a Sufi becomes problematic when one considers his many trenchant and sarcastic references to the conduct and deeds of "deceitful" Sufis, "fraudulent" mystics, and "hypocritical" ascetics.

The Divan in Focus

Contents overview. *The Divan of Hafiz* contains about 500 *ghazals* on a variety of themes and topics, both mystical and profane. In addition to poems of a profound philosophical and mystical nature, Hafiz wrote several panegyrics to rulers and leaders of Shiraz, poems describing nature, poems with ethical and moral themes, and poems that reveal his significant social awareness. A few of the poems do not belong to any conventional genre of Persian verse.

A central theme that affects all other themes and assumes an unusually prominent place in the poetic universe of Hafiz is love. According to the Sufi doctrine, *ishq* or love (the word is hardly an exact translation) refers to an intuitive process that entails the unwavering and creative striving of the human individual towards self-realization. The process occurs through the essential oneness of the lover (*ashiq*) and the beloved (*ma`shuq*), culminating in the annihilation (*fana*) of the former in the latter. Through the arduous achievement of annihilation, the lover attains attributes of the beloved and eventually realizes eternity (*baqa*). In other words, the path to eternity lies through annihilation.

Who is this beloved? Is the beloved ethereal or earthly? Scholars have long debated whether Hafiz's beloved is divine or human, a prince or a commoner, a man or a woman. By Hafiz's time, the secular, earthly love and the mystical, heavenly love had become symbolically indistinguishable. This is especially the case in Hafiz's *ghazals,* where strong erotic expressions that characterize human love are often used to define the divine beloved (*ma`bud*), the object of worship. In some poems, Hafiz clearly praises the secular ruler or the prince by using expressions that are similar to the divine beloved, on the one hand, and the earthly beloved, on the other hand.

Contents summary. The following *ghazal*—one of the few poems in the *Divan* that employs a narrative structure from start to end—contains some of the essential elements that preoccupied Hafiz's poetic discourse. Here Hafiz privileges love and considers it to have been molded along with human substance since pre-eternity. The intuitive moment of the manifestation of the beloved (in this instance, the moment the divine beloved stirs emotions in the heart of the seeker) coincides with the appearance of an all-consuming love that sets the entire universe on fire.

> In Pre-Eternity [when] the ray of your beauty
>   manifested itself
> Love appeared and set aflame the whole
>   world.
> Your face showed its splendor: it found that
>   angels lacked love
> It became like pure fire from fury and
>   decided [instead] on Adam.
> Reason wanted to ignite a lantern from that
>   raging flame
> [But] the radiance of fury flashed out and
>   brought turmoil to the world.
> [When] the pretender [profaner] wished to
>   come to the arena of the secret
> The hand of the Unseen struck the stranger.
> All others cast the lot of their destiny with
>   pleasure

> But our afflicted heart drew only sorrow.
> My noble spirit had fancied your dimple
> So it placed its hand on the chains of your
>   coiled and curled tresses.
> Hafiz wrote the delightful book of your love
> On the day when he erased the reasons for
>   contentment.
>   (*Divan*, p. 170; trans. W. Ahmadi)

As the poem suggests, the manifestation of the creator of the world in the pre-eternity was an instance of intense illumination derived from love. Precisely because of the power of love, Adam, the epitome of humanity, deserves to share God's splendor while angels (who are devoid of love) do not. After all, as Hafiz writes in another *ghazal*, it was love that constituted the essence of humankind on the day God created Adam: "Praise God at the door of love's tavern, o angel / For they ferment there the clay of Adam" (*Divan*, p. 195; trans. W. Ahmadi). More specifically, in the *ghazal* under consideration, Hafiz makes a reference to the constant opposition between love and reason. He privileges love and describes reason as a mere "pretender" and "stranger" utterly incapable of disentangling the "secret" of life.

As in many other instances in the *Divan*, a significant element in Hafiz's concept of love can be found in the contrast between *ishq* (love) and *aql* (reason/intellect) whereby he points to the efficacy of the former and the futility of the latter. In another *ghazal* Hafiz maintains: "By way of analogy, the prudence of reason on the path of love / Is like a dew drop drawn on the surface of a sea" (*Divan*, p. 351; trans. W. Ahmadi). Hafiz especially reproves those who seek the "subtlety" of love through the "certainty" of reason: "O you who seek the sign of love in the book of reason / I fear you will never learn this subtlety with certainty" (*Divan*, p. 115; trans. W. Ahmadi). This is so because love is hardly an easy undertaking: while it is ultimately a most rewarding destination, its arduous path involves formidable challenges, including a great degree of anguish, sorrow, and pain. In numerous couplets, the *Divan* maintains that you must "Endure pain if you are our companion / For continuous pleasure and ease are not the way of love" (*Divan*, p. 351; trans. W. Ahmadi). Love is the fountain of human life, and whoever is not in love is merely a living dead: "Whosoever in this congregation is not alive by power of love / By my edict, recite his death prayer before his death" (*Divan*, p. 217; trans. W. Ahmadi). Elsewhere, Hafiz insists that love is the guarantor of permanence and immortality for the lover: "Never shall die he whose heart is animated with love / Our immortality is imprinted in the register of time" (*Divan*, p. 95; trans. W. Ahmadi). In what may sound paradoxical, despite the predominance of the theme of love in the *Divan*, Hafiz argues that the nature of love makes it virtually inexpressible and incommunicable. He also notes that language, given its nature as a system of communication, fails to encompass love in its entirety: "O' you who take pride in love through discourse and speech / We have nothing to talk about, farewell!" (*Divan*, p. 138; trans. W. Ahmadi). This he shared with such Sufi poets as Rumi (Jalal al-Din Balkhi Rumi) and Farid al-Din Attar, who, finding language inadequate, expressed their desire to transcend it by privileging irony and paradoxes.

Transcending the contours of established Sufi discourse at this time, the poems in the *Divan* express social criticisms pertaining to the turbulent era in which Hafiz lived. In the following *ghazal*, Hafiz criticizes the hypocrisy, insincerity, and duplicity of the upholders of morality in his age:

> Preachers who make an appearance on the
>   pulpit
> Do other than what they sermonize when
>   they go into retreat.
> I have a query for the learned man of the
>   congregation:
> Why do those prescribing repentance,
>   themselves rarely repent?
> I suppose they do not believe in the
>   Judgment Day
> For they so slip and swindle in the work of
>   the Judge.
> I am the slave of the old tavern keeper
> Whose dervishes slight treasure for they are
>   so rich in hearts.
> His unlimited beauty kills so many devotees
> Still, from the Unseen, multitudes rise in love.
>   (*Divan*, pp. 194-95; trans. W. Ahmadi)

As much as Hafiz praises the "old tavern keeper," he criticizes the indignant official representatives of the religious establishment. The elder (*shaykh*), the ascetic (*zahid*), the preacher (*wa`iz*), the theologian (*faqih*), the judge (*qazi*), the *mufti* (one who gives *fatwas*, or religious opinions, on legal and moral issues), the public inspector (*muhtasib*), and the sermonizer (*imam*) are objects of his derision. Hafiz insists that these authorities may adhere to the legalistic strictures of faith, but they lack love. The duplicitous nature of the official upholders of public morality is what Hafiz especially despises and attempts to reveal in his poetry. Proponents of dry, religious legalisms are no more than "surface-adorers," with no sub-

stance of their own, precisely because they have shut their eyes to the magnitude and grandeur of love: "From Hafiz hear love's tale, not from the preacher / Even if the preacher is very crafty in the use of words" (*Divan*, p. 195; trans. W. Ahmadi). Hafiz warns his readers, "Remember, love is the marker of the people of God / I see not this sign in the clergy of the town" (*Divan*, p. 282; trans. W. Ahmadi). The officially recognized Sufi is especially the object of sarcasm: "The Sufi devised a trap and opened his bag of tricks / He started to play with the deceptive trickster of the universe" (*Divan*, p. 160; trans. W. Ahmadi). Hafiz even recommends that the *khirqah* (patched frock) and *dalq* (coat) of the trite Sufi should be either burned to ashes or at least cleansed with pure wine: "A Sufi's gold is not always lucid and clear / So many *khirqahs* deserve to be put on fire!"; and, "No scent of candor comes from the present tablet / Rise up and cleanse the Sufi's tarnished *dalq* with pure wine" (*Divan*, pp. 174, 361; trans. W. Ahmadi). Neither does the *zahid* escape his mockery.

> The ostentatious ascetic knows not our plight
> Whatever he says about us, we do not deny
>
>   . . .
>
> I am the slave of the old tavern keeper, whose
>   courtesy is constant
> whereas the good will of the *shaykh* and *wa`iz*
>   is ephemeral.
>   (*Divan*, p. 361; trans. W. Ahmadi)

Against those who condemn him for being anti-religion, Hafiz does not seem to mount a defense. He accepts his human imperfections but ingeniously insists on the principle of God's unlimited forgiveness and leniency (since in Islam, God is, first and foremost, "benevolent" and "merciful"): "Go away, o' man of devotion: my destination is paradise! / For it is the sinners who surely deserve forgiveness!" (*Divan*, p. 192; trans. W. Ahmadi). In another *ghazal* Hafiz declares with much confidence, "Last night the grace of God conveyed to me the good news: / 'Come back, for I vouch that your sins will be forgiven'" (*Divan*, p. 192; trans. W. Ahmadi).

Human nature: free will and predestination. Hafiz's sense of faith is essentially a philosophical and reflective one. Drawing upon his deep grasp of the ambiguity in theological discourse, he ponders human existence: "Our being is an enigma, O Hafiz, / Whose explication is a fiction and a fable" (*Divan*, p. 192; trans. W. Ahmadi). By insisting that human existence is an "enigma," Hafiz questions the certainty with which proponents of religious dogma seem to address the human condition. In the meantime, despite his profoundly philosophical approach, his stance is characteristically speculative and suspicious of systematic philosophical investigation. In a few instances, especially concerning the order (or disorder) of the universe, the instability of the world, the role of religion, hedonistic life, and the destiny of the individual human, Hafiz seems to have been influenced by the Khayyamite worldview. As shown by most of the extant quatrains in the famous *Ruba`iyat* (also in *WLAIT 6: Middle Eastern Literatures and Their Times*), for Omar Khayyam (d. 1122), life is full of challenges, and the human being is accountable for his/her actions in this life. To pursue life after death is illusory, for nothing awaits the human being after the transitory world of the living passes. Therefore, the best course of action is to live as happily as one can and truly enjoy worldly delights. Khayyam regards the attempt to unfold the mysteries of the enigmatic present futile and ineffective. Hafiz, too, in a manner that resembles Khayyam's "resolution" of human existential quandaries, writes, "Do not irritate the mind about being and nonbeing. Rejoice! / For all perfection culminates in nothingness" (*Divan*, p. 103; trans. W. Ahmadi). Or, in a reference to the mystifying work of the universe, he says, "What is this lofty, lucid, many patterned ceiling? / No wise person in the world can solve this puzzle" (*Divan*, p. 127; trans. W. Ahmadi). And, consequently, he proposes the following, "Tell the story of the minstrel and wine, seek not the secret of the world / For no one has unraveled this conundrum by wisdom, nor ever will" (*Divan*, p. 90; trans. W. Ahmadi). Hafiz castigates the ascetic who supposes that he can puzzle out the conundrum: "Leave, o egotistical ascetic, for the secret behind this veil / Is concealed from our eyes, and will remain so" (*Divan*, p. 198; trans. W. Ahmadi).

Since the world of being is unknowable, is the knowing human being, then, incapable of discovering its mysteries? Is human destiny fixed, irrevocable, and unalterable? Does the human being have the capacity of free self-actualization, a process that would run counter to the conventional notion of destiny (as predetermined by God)? The questions call for a determination of Hafiz's stance vis-à-vis free will and predestination. As his writings indicate, his stance in this respect is not always systematic and coherent. He sometimes comes close to the predominantly determinist point of view of Ash`arism (after the

name of its chief advocate Abu al-Hasan al-Ash`ari [883-941 C.E.]).

The following couplets from one of his *ghazals* demonstrate Hafiz's affinity with certain Ash`arite doctrines:

I have said many times before and here reiterate:
Bewildered, I do not tred this path by my own will.
I have been held like a parrot behind the mirror
I only utter whatever the Supreme Master of Pre-Eternity
orders me.
(*Divan*, p. 294; trans. W. Ahmadi)

THE CONCEPT OF *RINDI* IN HAFIZ'S *DIVAN*

For Hafiz, a life with love is best when it is complemented with *rindi*. The *rind* is a person who is free from worldly attachments and ordinary desires and wishes. A *rind* intentionally behaves improperly and in a socially objectionable manner in order to avoid hypocrisy and insincerity associated with everyday life. The word, which literally means "rogue" or "scoundrel," is turned into an honorable epithet in the *Divan*: "Your consummate joy lies in the attainment of love, youth, and *rindi*" (*Divan*, p. 172; trans. W. Ahmadi). Hafiz praises the *rind* for his breach of all bounds of conventional social and moral dictates and speaks of his own commitment to pursue *rindi*: "Since we laid claim to *rindi* and love on the Day of Creation / We must not adopt a path other than this" (*Divan*, p. 290; trans. W. Ahmadi). He further declares, "My vocation has always been love and *rindi* / From now on, I will keep up with my profession" (*Divan*, p. 270; trans. W. Ahmadi).

Yet in the following verses Hafiz strongly advocates free will and insists on the transformative human capacity to change one's own destiny and even to bring about a new humanity. With a measure of defiance he writes, "I will wreck the wheel [of destiny] if it spins against my will / I shall not be disgraced by the wheel of destiny" (*Divan*, p. 249; trans. W. Ahmadi). Here Hafiz is registering an impossibility. He wishes to do that which cannot be done, given one's human limitations. Nonetheless, he maintains that "In this earthly world no humanity may be found / One must create a new world and a new humanity" (*Divan*, p. 350; trans. W. Ahmadi).

ASH`ARISM

During the reign of the Abbasid caliph al-Ma'mun (d. 833), the proponents of ratio-nalist thought (the Mu`tazilites) had dominated discussions of scholastic theology in Islam. Less than a century later, due to the transformation of the political atmosphere as well as the persistence of literal-minded jurists and exegetes, the traditionalists succeeded in repressing the Mu`tazilites. The notion of upholding the supremacy of revelation over reason was forcefully rearticulated, and the Muslim intellectual scene soon became dom-inated by the Ash`arites, whose founder, Abu al-Hasan al-Ash`ari (d. 935), was a former Mu`tazilite from the city of Basra.

Considering the issue of free-will versus predestination, in opposition to the libertarian doctrines of the Mu`tazilites (who insisted on human agency, moral freedom, and re-sponsibility) and the fatalistic views of the orthodoxy (who saw human decision and ac-tion as determined by the undisputed power of God), the Ash`arites chose a somewhat middle ground. Since God is omnipotent, the creature cannot be the creator of his/her own deeds. To say otherwise would be tantamount to questioning God's absolute power and assuming that human being is a co-creator with God. In a subtle manner, the Ash`arites introduced the concept of acquisition (*kasb*), which refers to the merit or demerit of the human action. God has eternal power but creates in the human being the ability to per-form an act and take responsibility for it. Since the human being is intuitively conscious of his actions, he/she has the choice (*ikhtiyar*) between two alternatives—right and wrong—even though the initiation and completion of the human act is the work of God alone. Human freedom, then, consists of deciding (or intending to decide) between these two al-ternatives. The Ash`arites clearly intended to formulate a systematic Islamic theology that would draw, to some degree, from independent reasoning (associated with the Mu`tazilites) without disavowing the literalist strictures fundamental to the faith.

Sources and literary context. Hafiz was not a Sufi poet in the sense that such other leading Persian poets as Attar, author of ***The Conference of the Birds***, or Rumi, the celebrated author of ***The Spiritual Couplets***, were (both also in *WLAIT 6: Middle Eastern Literatures and Their Times*). Hafiz was certainly schooled in the Sufi tradition, but his views regarding some of the Sufi doctrines were more reflective, philosophi-cal, and, at times, ambivalent. While Attar and Rumi inherited and contributed to a relatively cohesive Sufi institution that maintained a sem-blance of legitimacy and independence from political affairs, Hafiz saw the institutionalized Sufism of his time (i.e., post-Mongol invasion Persia) enmeshed in the ideology of conservative religious functionaries, who were, in turn, ma-nipulated by the competing centers of power. It is largely for this reason that even Hafiz's clearly Sufi poems differ distinctively from the work of his great Sufi predecessors. Nonetheless, schol-ars of classical Persian poetry have traditionally studied the *Divan of Hafiz* almost exclusively in terms of the mystical meanings and allusions that are supposedly hidden behind his *ghazals*.

While many scholars only see a purely mys-tical meaning in Hafiz's *ghazals,* others find only sensual love, profane joyousness, sheer hedo-nism, or simple playfulness. Again the complex-ity of Hafiz's poetic universe in the *Divan* evades either a clear mystical interpretation or a purely earthly reading. For instance, images of "wine" (whose prohibition is advocated by the *ulama* [re-ligious authorities] and enforced by the uphold-ers of public morality) recur throughout the *Divan.* One may suggest that Hafiz's wine refers only to "divine intoxication" in such couplets as: "There is no compassion in anyone, and time for happiness fast passes / The remedy is to sell the prayer-mat for wine" (*Divan*, p. 292; trans. W.

Ahmadi). Or: "The wine-seller may take the frock and the prayer-rug of Hafiz / If the wine is from the hand of that moon-faced cup-bearer" (*Divan*, p. 174; trans. W. Ahmadi). But a more literal interpretation of such couplets is equally possible.

Publication and reception. Literary historians and critics regard Hafiz as perhaps the greatest of all lyric poets in the Persian language. Hafiz has enjoyed fame throughout Persian-speaking lands, where he is called *lisan al-ghayb* ("the tongue of the Unseen World") and *tarjuman al-asrar* ("the interpreter of mysteries"). It is now established that Hafiz himself did not collect his own poems. Thus, reconstructing an unquestionably sound compilation of his collected poems has always posed a serious textual problem for scholars. The earliest edition of Hafiz's was prepared, allegedly, by his friend and disciple Muhammad Gulandam, soon after the poet's death. Numerous manuscripts of the *Divan* have been reproduced ever since. A sign of people's love and admiration for Hafiz's poetry is the existence of many manuscripts of his work, often written in splendid calligraphy, ornate with elegant miniature drawings.

Although it was the British translator Sir William Jones who first introduced the poetry of Hafiz in Europe, it was Johann Wolfgang Goethe's influential *West-öestlicher Divan* (1819)—in which the German poet declares that "Hafiz has no peer"—that brought fame to the Persian poet in the West (Goethe, p. 37). In the words of the American writer Ralph Waldo Emerson, Hafiz "was a poet for poets," one who "adds to . . . Pindar, Anacreon, Horace, and Burns, the insight of a mystic, that sometimes affords a deeper glance at Nature than belongs to either of these bards" (Emerson, p. 244).

Numerous fragments of Hafiz's poetry have appeared in translation in histories of Persian literature and anthologies of Eastern poetry. Generally there have been three types of translations of Hafiz's work: literal prose translations; translations that reproduce either the meter or the mono-rhyme; and, finally, the numerous translations executed with a freer hand, not bound by literal exigencies. While the methods employed differ, the recognition that the verse itself deserves a wide audience does not.

—Wali Ahmadi

For More Information

Baldick, Julian. *Mystical Islam: An Introduction to Sufism.* New York: New York University Press, 1989.

Browne, Edward G. *A Literary History of Persia.* Vol. 3. London: Cambridge University Press, 1964.

Bürgel, J. Christoph. "Ambiguity: A Study in the Use of Religious Terminology in the Poetry of Hafiz." In *Intoxication: Earthly and Heavenly.* Ed. Michael Glünz and J. Christoph Bürgel. Bern: Peter Lang, 1991.

Emerson, Ralph Waldo. *Works, Volume 8: Letters and Social Aims.* New York: Houghton Mifflin, 1904.

Goethe, Johann Wolfgang von. *West-Eastern Divan: West-Oestlicher Divan.* Trans. J. Whaley. London: Oswald Wolff, 1974.

Gray, Elizabeth T. *The Green Sea of Heaven: Fifty Ghazals from the Divan of Hafiz.* Ashland, Oreg.: White Cloud Press, 1995.

Hafiz, Shams al-Din Muhammad. *Divan.* Ed. Qasim Ghani and Muhammad Qazvini. Tehran: Ququns, 1998.

Meisami, Julie Scott. "Allegorical Techniques in the *Ghazals* of Hafez." *Edebiyat* 4, no. 1 (1979): 1-40.

Rahman, Fazlur. *Islam.* Chicago: University of Chicago Press, 1979.

Roemer, H. R. "The Jalayirids, Muzzafarids and Sarbadars." In *The Cambridge History of Iran.* Vol. 6. Ed. Peter Jackson and Laurence Lockhart. London: Cambridge University Press, 1986.

Schimmel, Annemarie. "The Genius of Shiraz: Sa`di and Hafez." In *Persian Literature.* Ed. Ehsan Yarshater. New York: Persian Heritage Foundation, 1988.

———. "Hafiz and His Contemporaries." In *The Cambridge History of Iran.* Vol. 6. Ed. Peter Jackson and Laurence Lockhart. London: Cambridge University Press, 1986.

———. *Mystical Dimensions of Islam.* Chapel Hill: University of North Carolina Press, 1975.

Spuler, Bertold. *The Mongol Period: History of the Muslim World.* Leiden: E. J. Brill, 1969.

The Diwan of
Abu Nuwas

Al-Hasan ibn Hani Abu Nuwas (d. 814 or 815) is widely considered one of the greatest Arab poets of all time, largely because of his wine poems. He was born around 760 to a Persian seamstress, probably in Ahwaz province. His father, a Damascene, died while he was a child and his mother moved with him to Basra. There Abu Nuwas memorized the Quran at school and studied Islamic law and prophetic traditions (*hadith*). In Basra, and later in Kufa, Abu Nuwas continued his education in Arabic poetry, Arabian lore, and tribal genealogy with some of the renowned intellectual luminaries of the day. In Kufa, he fell under the sway of the reprobate poet Walibah ibn al-Hubab, who taught him poetry and with whom he had a sexual relationship. In 786 Abu Nuwas moved to Baghdad in search of his fortune. That year, Harun al-Rashid, immortalized in Islamic tradition for his asceticism and wisdom, and in the world's imagination for ruling the stylized Baghdad of *The Arabian Nights* (also in *WLAIT 6: Middle Eastern Literatures and Their Times*), was installed as caliph. The pious caliph probably held Abu Nuwas at arm's length. Nor did the poet find favor among Harun al-Rashid's viziers, the Barmakids, members of a clan descended from the high priests of the Buddhist shrine in the Central Asian city of Balkh, themselves responsible for the upkeep of a number of poets. In 803 the Barmakids were suddenly and inexplicably slaughtered on orders from Harun al-Rashid. No one knows why they were wiped out, but the most popular reason that contemporaries supplied was an illicit love affair between the vizier Ja`far al-Barmaki and the caliph's sister Abbasah. Abu Nuwas wrote an elegy on the dis-

> ## THE LITERARY WORK
> The collected poems of Abu Nuwas set in Iraq in the late eighth century C.E.; first compiled in Arabic (as *Diwan Abi Nuwas*) in the mid-tenth century, translated into English in 1974.
>
> ## SYNOPSIS
> Though Abu Nuwas wrote various kinds of verse, he is most famous for his wine poems, likely written to entertain the Baghdad elite. The poems celebrate the physical and metaphysical experiences of wine drinking in a uniquely rebellious tone.

graced clan. His poems are generally full of rebellious and often shocking content, which has shaped the poet's biographical representation; in works ranging from highbrow Arabic literary anthologies to Swahili folktales, Abu Nuwas is typically portrayed as the most compelling drunk, fornicator, and blasphemer who ever lived. He would become most known for his wine poems, which embody and proclaim the bohemian mores of the elite citizens of Baghdad, then the cosmopolitan center of the medieval Islamic world. These poems reflect many of the intellectual and literary currents of Abu Nuwas's day.

Events in History at the Time of the Diwan

Cosmopolitan Baghdad. In 752 the caliph al-Mansur decided to build his capital in the center of Iraq, where the Tigris and Euphrates Rivers come closest to each other, at a confluence of trade routes that had a healthy climate and fertile soil. Al-Mansur dubbed his capital "The City of Peace," but most people called it by the old name of the village that had been there: Baghdad. According to an apocryphal story, on al-Mansur's orders, builders used bricks from the palace of Ctesiphon, the nearby capital of the vanquished Iranian Sasanian empire, foreshadowing a vision of cosmopolitan grandeur intended to outstrip the Persian court. At the center of the so-called Round City was the Abbasid caliph's palace, crowned by the Green Dome and the Great Mosque. Baghdad's quarters were divided by geographical origin and occupation, with separate housing for Arabs, Persians, and, for example, for water-carriers.

THE MOCK-HEROIC SPEAKER

The poem "Many a Nagging Shrew" is mock-heroic. For the Arab listener, the protagonist's brave disregard for the rebuking woman and his indulgence in costly wine may well have called to mind a famous ode by Tarafah ibn al-Abd, a poet of pre-Islamic Arabia. In his and other ancient poems, the hero, a warrior-tribesman, defied his nagging wife by squandering the family savings at the wine shop. He courageously demonstrated his lack of attachment to money and challenged fate. Abu Nuwas took such rebellion further than any poet before him. In many of his most original poems he adopted the pose of the *majin* ("he who cares not"). Although the stance of the *majin* permeates Abu Nuwas's wine poems, it also generated its own genre of poetry, *mujun,* distinguished by its offensive sexual explicitness and scatalogical lines. Such poems, often detailing the sexual conquest of a young man, were not merely crude humor. In their vulgarity and their homoeroticism, they parodied the chaste longing for an idealized woman characteristic of contemporary Arabic courtly love poetry (see Meisami).

The city soon became a center of trade in goods and in learning, the core of what the historian Adam Mez famously called "the Renaissance of Islam." Its mosques and homes hosted meetings of the most influential thinkers of the age. When Arab Muslim scholars became curious about the Greek treatises in the libraries of their Christian neighbors, Islamic philosophy

and theology was born. Those who sought to bend Islam to fit Aristotelian metaphysics and natural science became the first Muslim philosophers. Those who sought to bend Greek thought, on, for example, the eternity of the world, to fit Islamic beliefs became the first Muslim theologians. Scholars in Abbasid Baghdad played critical roles in shaping Islam itself, collecting and organizing traditions on the meaning of the Quran and compiling the authoritative biography of the Prophet Muhammad. Grammarians, lexicographers, and philologists took stock of the Arab heritage and arrived at new and systematic formulations of Arabic language and authoritative anthologies of literature. For the first time, historians viewed the rise of the Islamic empire in the global light of past and contemporary empires, East and West.

Although Arab armies defeated the Sasanians, some of the conquered continued to practice Zoroastrianism, the Persian Empire's state religion. There is an image of a triumphant and universal Islam offering new converts equal footing, but the image is not accurate. In its first two centuries Islam was the religion of a ruling Arab elite. Non-Arabs (mainly Persians) who converted became clients of Arab tribes (*mawali*). Their attempts to move upwards in society stimulated cultural life. Intellectuals of Persian origin quickly became some of the most eloquent spokesmen for and shapers of Arab culture. Arabs were accorded special privileges and this rankled non-Arabs, some of whom, under the aegis of a movement called the *shu'ubiyah*, championed the superiority of non-Arab, especially Persian, culture. But Persian was not Baghdad's only non-Arab culture. Some Christians, holdouts for the Nestorian Christianity that most Iraqis practiced before the Arab conquests, were drawn to the new Muslim polis. Also, leaders of the ancient Jewish community of Iraq, recognizing the value of an education in Baghdad, had moved their main rabbinical academies there by the late ninth century.

Courtly culture and Abu Nuwas's place in it. During their leisure time, the Abbasid family, their coterie, viziers, high-ranking agents in the imperial chancery, and the wealthy merchants of Baghdad enjoyed polite entertainment in opulent quarters, manicured gardens, and estates outside the city. Groups of such people might have embarked on pleasure cruises down the Tigris (Abu Nuwas describes three ornately carved touring boats commissioned by the caliph al-Amin),

ISLAMIC VITICULTURE

Itinerant merchants, usually Jews or Christians, brought wine to the oasis towns of central Arabia before the rise of Islam. There, they hoisted flags above their tents to show that they had a supply of the costly product. The Arabic poetry of the pre-Islamic period refers to wines from Iraq, Persia (the Shiraz grape is familiar to Western wine lovers), the Golan Heights, and Yemen, the fertile southern tip of the Arabian Peninsula. In his delineation of the tenets of Islam, the Prophet Muhammad forbade wine (though his court poet, Hassan ibn Thabit, was the generation's greatest wine bard). While some jurists wrangled over precisely which alcoholic beverages fell under the ban, Islamic law affirmed the ban on drinking alcohol by a broad consensus. Nevertheless, after the rise of Islam, wine was surreptitiously sold to Muslim libertines by Christians and Jews. Medieval Muslim legal discussions on the (il)legality of drinking make clear that the alcoholic beverages, both fermented and distilled, were made from a number of grains, honey, grapes, fresh or raisins, or other fruit. Grape wine, however, stood as the alcoholic beverage *par excellence*. At a tavern, whether free-standing or attached to a monastery or royal residence, grapes were trod on by a person standing in a "press" and the juice was collected. The juice was either cooked down or allowed to ferment in the sun or in vaults in a large clay wine jar or amphora, lined with bitumen to make it watertight and sealed with clay or aromatic plaster. Its pointed base enabled it to be stood upright in loose soil, presumably during the aging process, or set on a tripod once it was brought forth ready to drink. Examples of such jars, discovered by a German archaeological team in Iraq, measure about 32 by 8 inches. On each jar was a painted figure (a singing-girl, monk, or hunter). The painted figure is relevant to Abu Nuwas's poetry, which sometimes describes the wine cask as a body (the wine being its soul), or as a person in general.

played polo, watched horse races, hunted antelope, with trained falcons, saluki hounds, or cheetahs in tow. Returning home, assembled guests might have played sophisticated literary games displaying their detailed knowledge of the Arabic language, listened to songs of unrequited love performed by singing slave girls and their accompanists, and drank wine. Literary accounts and miniatures suggest that wine was brought forth with great ceremony. In festive clothing, the vintner, his assistants, and guests were surrounded by candles and sweet-smelling herbs. The vintner broached the amphora with a special tool and strained it into smaller vessels. Guests were offered small samples before the drinking began in earnest. One particularly fastidious vintner of the Umayyad period is said to have washed his hands every time he opened a jar and to have given everyone a fresh napkin after each drink. Such reports, along with Abu Nuwas's odes, point to a sophisticated appreciation of wine, despite the prohibition. In an atmosphere given also to a refined philological taste, lyricism, and eroticism, a good poet, particularly one as unburdened by conventional pieties as Abu Nuwas, could be the life of the party.

Poets and other men of letters enabled this courtly culture to exist. Philologists tutored youthful caliphs, teaching them to savor novel usages of obscure Arabic words. Anthologists collected entertaining and astonishing anecdotes illustrating the machinations of fate, providing rich conversation pieces for elite soirées. Writers of ornate prose (mainly non-Arabs) honed their skills through their work as secretaries in the imperial chancery. Poets composed grand odes in praise of the caliphs' piety, bravery, and generosity, in praise of their subordinates, and in praise of prominent members of society. Such poetry was only prudent on the poet's part, since courtly culture enabled the poet to subsist. If the addressee appreciated an ode composed on his behalf,

An Eastern prince and his courtiers gather to drink wine in the gardens.

a poet could garner prestige and a substantial monetary reward. A patron brazen enough to refuse a poet payment might find himself, his tribe, and his mother the subject of witty and obscene lines of invective. The efflorescence of literary life that took place in this period depended on the desire and ability of wealthy individuals to patronize writers.

For Abu Nuwas (like most professional poets of his time), composing panegyric poems for patrons was his bread and butter. After the fall of the Barmakids in 803 he found work in the entourage of the Inspector of Land Taxes. He had to accompany his new employer to Cairo, Egypt (in 805 and 807).

When the caliph Harun al-Rashid died in 809, Abu Nuwas proved to be a boon companion to his shiftless and hedonistic son, the caliph al-Amin. Al-Amin's mother, Zubaydah, who wanted to ensure the continuation of the dynasty, noted her son's lack of interest in the opposite sex with concern. Zubaydah is said to have devised a strategem whereby young women sought the caliph's favor by wearing boys' clothing and painting moustaches on their faces with aromatics. Abu Nuwas described them in an often excised line of a famous poem, as girls "who had two lovers, a sodomite and an adulterer" (Abu

Nuwas, *Diwan Abi Nuwas*, vol. 3, p. 3; trans. M. Wagner). Such cross-dressing became the rage in Baghdad, as evident from Abu Nuwas's collected poetry (*diwan*; spelled with a *w* for Arabic pronunciation). There is a section in it devoted to *ghulamiyat* ("poems on girls dressed like boys"). An impending civil war cast a shadow over al-Amin's frivolity. While al-Amin's brother, al-Ma'mun, believing that his sibling had usurped his rightful place, mustered an army in the volatile eastern province of Khwarazm, al-Amin affixed jeweled earrings to a fish in his private pond. Al-Amin is said to have sat in a lean-to made of fragrant wood, draped with silk and red gold, drinking wine from an oversized goblet while his brother besieged the capital. Among the particulars of al-Amin's debauchery used by al-Ma'mun to rally his troops was his brother's association with the poet Abu Nuwas.

Al-Mas'udi provided a gripping account of the civil war that erupted in 813 between the brothers al-Amin and al-Ma'mun in his history *Muruj al-dhahab wa-ma'adin al-jawhar* (The Meadows of Gold). According to this history, al-Amin was defended by tens of thousands of "rowdies" (*ayyarun*), who wore nothing but loincloths and palm-fiber helmets, rode other rowdies as steeds, and defended Baghdad with stones, spears, and similarly crude weapons. The siege devastated Baghdad and al-Amin was killed. Despite al-Ma'mun's earlier rhetoric against Abu Nuwas, the poet apparently survived the regime change. He probably died in Baghdad a few years later as a result of an illness.

This represents what is known about the life of Abu Nuwas with some degree of certainty. A much larger corpus of stories about Abu Nuwas revolves around his poems. Drawing on the poems, the Egyptian literary critics Abbas Mahmud al-Aqqad and Muhammad al-Nuwayhi developed psychological portraits of the poet. Al-Aqqad concluded that Abu Nuwas's obsession with wine resulted from his narcissism and al-Nuwayhi diagnosed Abu Nuwas as having an Oedipal complex that led to homosexuality. A poet who became caliph for one day, Ibn al-Mu'tazz (d. 908), judged Abu Nuwas's celebration of sodomy as a literary affectation, arguing that he was "more heterosexual than an ape" (Ibn al-Mu'tazz, p. 308). More recently, John Mattock found some of the sexual and alcoholic images in Abu Nuwas's wine poetry so inherently improbable that he saw the poems as the imaginings of a celibate teetotaler. Another scholar, James Montgomery, saw in Abu Nuwas's obsession with wine and his guilty poems of contrition the symptoms of alcoholism. Therefore, the question of whether or not Abu Nuwas was a drunken and debauched homosexual or simply the author of many poems treating such themes resembles the proverbial chicken and egg. In any case, these stories were clever and entertaining, ensuring Abu Nuwas's place in posterity.

The Diwan in Focus

Contents overview. Most collections of Arabic poetry (*diwans*) were originally organized alphabetically by the letter that ended each verse of a poem. In contrast, Abu Nuwas's *diwan* was divided by genre: panegyric poems, elegies, invective, courtly love poems on men and women, poems of penitence, hunting poems, wine poems, and salacious poems. Abu Nuwas's innovations were primarily in the last three genres. Within these, most aficionados of Arabic poetry would point to Abu Nuwas's wine poems (*khamriyat*) as the source for his mighty reputation. While wine and its consumption might play a small part in a number of poetic genres, wine poems devote their undivided attention to this subject.

Contents summary—the wine poems. The centerpiece in a wine poem is often its finely chiseled and vivid description of wine. A patterned narrative repeats itself with variations in Abu Nuwas's wine poems: brief description of the revelers, arrival at the drinking venue, conversation with the proprietor, bringing the wine cask, breaking it open, pouring the wine, mixing it with water, drinking, and drunkenness. The dynamic narrative contrasts with the description of the wine, a moment when time nearly stands still. A number of Abu Nuwas's wine poems paint a vivid picture of the drinkers, the setting (often a verdant garden), the cup (finely chiseled with scenes from ancient history), and the beautiful sight of the deep red wine's admixture with water.

Featured in the following poem is an extended description of wine, which likens the intoxicant to a woman:

> What a wonderful night I spent, sleepless
>   until dawn broke.
> We were given a wine, the "daughter" of a
>   monastery, unblemished
> By excessive sediment, stored in earthen jugs.
> Her pourer picked the grapes that made her:
>   red and black, like irises and pupils,
> When she is decanted, it looks as though
>   saffron and blood mingled together,
> Her pourer protected her in amphorae so that
>   she had nothing to fear . . .

> . . . for fifty years, until she aged, her color
>   having become darker than grape leaves.
> Noble men, hawks, fought over her, their
>   faces as red as anemones,
> Her pourer brought her forth and she was
>   like saffron-infused perfume,
> Flashing like lightning bolts that shone from
>   the decanter's hollow,
> She was as white as glittering swords and the
>   drinkers gave her a position of
>   responsibility,
> She was brought forward, bubbling, spurred
>   on by a fickle youth who walked gingerly.
> The drinkers hurried to break her hymen
>   with a sharp-edged implement,
> Blood flowed from it like a nosebleed from a
>   shell-shocked man.
> It looked like a solitary flame blazing in mid-
>   air, when the wine touched the water,
> And the foam that gathered around the rims
>   of the goblets was like chokers of purest
>   white snakeskin.
> What a night spent in the company of a
>   group of people who committed no sin
>   other than telling stories and speaking
>   eloquently,
> Who were given drink from a vintage wine
>   that stalks the brain and takes it by force,
> The sound of the decanter, poured into the
>   cup, was like an old man's cackling and
>   choking.
>   (*Diwan Abi Nuwas*, vol. 3, pp. 218-19; trans.
>   M. Wagner)

The poem begins with the narrator promising to provide an account of a night out with his friends. He focuses on describing the wine they were served. There is a sequence to this description: grapes are picked, the wine is aged, brought forth in an amphora, the amphora is pierced, the wine is poured off into a decanter, then into cups containing some water, then drunk. The narrator also praises his drinking companions.

Likening the wine to a woman is a signature technique of Abu Nuwas's wine poems, characterized as the "erotic-in-bacchic" (Kennedy, pp. 26-36). According to this poetic logic, buying the wine turns into paying a young bride's dowry and breaking open the wine jug becomes defloweration. This current of sexual violence recurs in the poem when the wine takes the drinkers' brain by force, figuratively raping them. This poem is replete with blood-red imagery, ranging from the flushed faces of the drinkers to spilled blood, breaking the hymen, and a nosebleed. When considered in conjunction with the wine's own electric luminescence, heat, and aggression, such images inject a note of mock-heroism into the poem, the drinkers calling to mind warriors, the poem invoking a variety of dangers to life and limb. There is a serious undertone to the imagery of combat. Together the images and language effect a relatively dark tone, suggesting that for Abu Nuwas, the world of wine was, while festive on its surface, a deadly serious realm, fraught with implications for man's confrontations with the vicissitudes of fate.

Another example of a wine poem follows. This time the wine acquires a quasi-religious aura: it is exceedingly old, perhaps having witnessed great events of prophetic and profane history. It is luminous and monks might serve as its attendants.

HOMOSEXUALITY IN THE MEDIEVAL MUSLIM WORLD

Islam forbids homosexual sex (*liwatah*). Nevertheless, by the ninth century, Islam's strict separation of the sexes and the burgeoning traffic in "youths" created the social circumstances for a considerable loosening of these strictures. (Singing girls—concubines similar to the *hetairai* of ancient Greece—were also bought and sold.) Male heterosexuality extended to taking the active role in sex with an effeminate and socially inferior male adolescent. This proclivity is amply documented in premodern Arabic literature, a vast corpus that contains the most voluminous and frank treatment of male homoeroticism in all of world literature. This is not to say that Islam's ban on homosexuality was overturned. Most sources insisted that a young man who had sprouted a beard could no longer have sex with an older man. In addition, a stigma attached to the passive partner in homosexual sex. Abu Nuwas, who described his love of young chancery secretaries, sons of respectable Baghdadis, and monastic novices in his poetry, probably expressed his genuine sexual preference. Yet he cannot be said to have been "homosexual" or "gay" in a modern sense, as his was a predilection not uncommon among (usually married) heterosexual men of his time, place, and social status. Among Sufis (Muslim mystics) the singing of homoerotic lyric poetry and "gazing upon a beardless youth" (*al-nazar bi 'l-murd*) figured prominently in their sacred concerts (*sama*).

Many a nagging shrew, full of good advice,
    seeks this impious rebel's repentance.
One such woman hurried to set me on the
    right path but my nature, my personality,
    and my chosen course are thoroughly
    crooked.

When she harangued me, I shooed her away
    and she left with her heart a-flutter.
Know that I have diligently conditioned my
    heart to find following the right path
    unacceptable.
I have devoted many mornings to an ancient
    wine like saffron-infused perfume, secreted
    away for ages in the churches of Dabiq [a
    village near Aleppo],
Boasting myriad colors when it spreads out in
    the glass, silencing all tongues,
Showing off her body, golden, like a pearl on
    a tailor's string,
In the hand of a lithe young man who speaks
    beautifully in response to a lover's request,
With a curl on each temple and a look in his
    eye that spells disaster.
He is a Christian, he wears clothing from
    Khurasan and his tunic bares his upper
    chest and neck.
Were you to speak to this elegant beauty, you
    would fling Islam from the top of a tall
    mountain.
If I were not afraid of the depredations of He
    who leads all sinners into transgression,
I would convert to his religion, entering it
    knowingly and with love,
For I know that the Lord would not have
    distinguished this youth so unless his was
    the true religion.
          (Abu Nuwas, *al-Nusus al-muharramah*,
          pp. 173-74; trans. M. Wagner)

The poem's outrageous and carefully cultivated rebelliousness is striking—a fact that was not lost on the pious Caliph Harun al-Rashid, who is said to have ordered the poet jailed upon hearing it.

The poem begins with the speaker shooing off a woman concerned for his soul. He then accounts for some of his sins: mornings spent served fine wine (described in detail) by a Christian youth, whose beauty testified that Christianity was the one true faith (an ironic ascription).

This poem successively thumbs its nose at heterosexual propriety, Islam's ban on alcohol consumption, its condemnation of homosexual sex, and Islam itself. Abu Nuwas's wine poems, like this one, often describe the physical charms and coquettish behavior of serving boys or singing girls. In the conclusions of some poems, the poet-reveler boasts of having penetrated the server, with or without his consent.

Flirting with the Devil. Non-Muslims were not subject to the Islamic ban on wine production and drinking. Though expressly forbidden from selling wine to Muslims, the Christian, Jewish, or Zoroastrian tavern-keeper is a stock character in Abu Nuwas's wine poems. One poem expresses a degree of empathy for the restrictions under which Jews lived in his time. However, for Abu Nuwas, of religions other than Islam, Christianity is the most richly associative. In his poems (and, broadly speaking, in medieval Arabic literature), the monastery serves as the scene for debauchery, the crack of its wooden clapper sounding a call not to ascetic devotion but to the cup. Scattered throughout his wine poems are the names of many monasteries and out-of-the-way taverns in Iraq, particularly around Baghdad, and in Syria, where a Muslim could find wine. In "Many a Nagging Shrew," as in other poems by Abu Nuwas, the young monastic novice who serves the wine to the speaker appears to arouse his carnal interest. Abu Nuwas also seems to have reveled in the sheer impiety of a Muslim drinking the day away in a monastery. One of his poetic vignettes alludes to the significance of wine in the sacrament of the Eucharist, the consumption of wine and bread to remember Jesus' death, when the poet drinks the winelike saliva from a Christian boy's mouth. (Drinking saliva is a stock metaphor for kissing in Arabic poetry.) While in this instance Abu Nuwas showed some familiarity with Christian practices, in general he saw Christianity negatively as all that was contrary to Muslim piety.

In an ironic line, the drinker explains that his reluctance to apostasize stems from his fear of the depredations of "He who leads all sinners into transgression." The leader of all sinners into transgression is Satan (called Iblis in the Islamic tradition). As in Christianity, the Satan of Islam tempts man to sin. This role assured Satan a supporting role in Abu Nuwas's poetry. The most remarkable of such poems is a dialogue between Abu Nuwas and the Devil, in which Satan tries to entice the poet to "repent" of his (temporarily) upright behavior. In a different poem, Abu Nuwas threatens Satan that if the Devil does not make a lovely young man fall in love with the poet, he will give his undivided attention to studying the Quran. Such witty dialogues were highly ironic (and probably very funny) in a society where Satan was not thought to have had any redeeming qualities.

Poetry as protest The great Islamicist Ignaz Goldziher, contemplating Abu Nuwas's poetry, concluded that "In Islam we find the phenomenon of a people's poetry being for centuries a living protest against its religion" (Goldziher, p. 35). While one might argue that this scholar threw too wide a net in including *all* Islamic poetry, his question remains: why was Abu Nuwas em-

braced by a civilization whose social and religious norms he took pleasure in flaunting? The Quran heaps opprobrium upon poets for being people "who say what they do not do" (Quran 26:226). For poets like Abu Nuwas, this statement of God's became a defense. (Abu Nuwas is said to have won release from a jail term with this verse.)

Abu Nuwas's scatalogical compositions can be explained with reference to the place of humor in classical Islamic civilization. Al-Tha`alibi (d. 1038) offered something of an explanation of why his poetry anthology, *The Unique Pearl of the Age,* contained so many salacious poems by quoting a verse that said every house needs a toilet. Yet Abu Nuwas's wine poems, shot through with the grave and hoary themes of heroic struggle in the face of death, honor, violence, and beauty, as well as allusions to Muslim theology and scripture, present a more serious challenge to Muslim society. The scholar Andras Hamori perhaps offered the best explanation for the paradox when he defined Abu Nuwas as a ritual clown. This may also explain Abu Nuwas's appearance in *The Arabian Nights* as a kind of court jester and his guises as an eloquent trickster in folktales from Morocco to Zanzibar. Abu Nuwas reminds modern readers, familiar to one extent or another with the severe and puritanical aspect of contemporary Islam, of the following historical truth: a variety of intellectual trends, including strong elements of humor and self-criticism, once flourished in the metropolitan center of an exuberantly self-confidant Islamic empire.

Sources and literary context. The poets of pre-Islamic Arabia, eloquent spokesmen for the experiences and tensions of a nomadic life, lived in an extraordinarily harsh physical environment. For these distant predecessors of Abu Nuwas, wine served as a potent symbol for man's struggle against death. A poet might liken the singular taste of wine, an imported luxury, to his beloved's mouth. More often, however, spending money on wine represented a heroic thumbing of his nose at fate, a dramatization of *muruwwah,* the tribal code of manliness.

Abu Nuwas, having studied the ancient poets with the top scholars of his day, would surely have known such ancient poems. His wine poems digested and synthesized poems on wine by many poets who lived before him. To take one major example, Abu Nuwas reproduced the antithesis between wine and Islamic values articulated by Abu Mihjan al-Thaqafi, a poet who lived before but also after the emergence of Islam (died in the mid-seventh century). Abu Nuwas even concluded one of his poems by quoting a famous line of Abu Mihjan—"If I die, bury me next to a vine whose roots will give my bones a drink" (Abu Mihjan al-Thaqafi, p. 14; trans. M. Wagner).

ARAB-PERSIAN RELATIONS

Arab-Persian relations in the Iraq of Abu Nuwas's day were considerably more complex than a division into two camps. Many of the most eloquent defenders of the Arab heritage from its *shu`ubi* critics, such as the great essayist al-Jahiz, Ibn Qutaybah, the poet Abu Tammam, and Abu Nuwas himself, were not pure Arabs. Typically, new non-Arab converts to Islam became clients of Arab tribes. These Arab tribes were divided into two main branches, northern and southern. Already by the late seventh century, enmity had developed between the northern and southern tribes, then ensconced in garrison cities across the Near East. Abu Nuwas took great pride in his southern Arab lineage and perhaps also in his mixed heritage. According to one story, he based his honorific title, Abu Nuwas, on the title of a Jewish king of ancient Yemen, Dhu Nuwas ("the one with dangling locks of hair").

Quotation was a favorite technique in Abu Nuwas's repertoire. He would place lines or fragments from famous or not-so-famous poems in a context that gave them a completely new, and often offensive, meaning. Such quotations were often placed in the mouths of singing girls or serving boys at the end of a poem. Abu Nuwas made frequent and sophisticated allusions to verses of the Quran and he showed more than a passing familiarity with the theological currents of his day. Occasionally he would give a verse of the Quran a shocking and scatalogical twist. The overall effect, however, of weaving Quranic language into his wine poems was the enhancement of their quasi-religious character.

From the Umayyad caliph al-Walid ibn Yazid (d. 743), who installed a private bath—to be filled with wine—at his palace near Jericho, Abu Nuwas inherited a sharply defiant attitude towards Islam as well as the portrayal of wine as a near-divine substance. The poet Abu al-Hindi (d. mid-eighth century) provided precedent for the wine poem's merging of bacchism with eroticism as well as the dramatic conversation with the tavern-keeper. A

descent from lyricism to obscenity, so prominent in the wine poems of Abu Nuwas that end in the seduction of the cup bearer, can be found in the poetry of Abu Nuwas's tutor (and lover), Walibah ibn Hubab (d. late eighth century). Satan shows his face in some of Walibah's poems too. Walibah was affiliated with a group of poets, "the libertines of Kufa" (*zurafa al-kufa*); of all Abu Nuwas's contemporaries, these libertines most influenced his work. Several of these poets wrote poems on wine and on sexual encounters with adolescent boys, two of Abu Nuwas's main poetic preoccupations. Other poets of his time may have influenced his work in different ways. A poem by the blind poet Bashshar ibn Burd begins as an ethereal ode to an honorable young woman and ends with the protagonist's groping her. Mock-heroism sets the tone for Abu al-Shamaqmaq's account of a flea's brave and bloody campaign against a human.

Abu al-Hindi and Walibah used themes associated with the *shu`ubiyah*, the anti-Arab, pro-Persian literary-political trend. If Abu Nuwas inserted *shu`ubi* elements in his wine poems, they merely added another hue to a broader picture of contrariness rather than making a discrete statement of political affiliation. A number of his poems poke fun at the desert Arabs (the Bedouin), whom cosmopolitan Arabs viewed as the fathers of culture and civilization. *Shu`ubis* portrayed them as rude denizens of hair tents and as lizard-eaters. Abu Nuwas's poems in this vein spoke to urban sophisticates of Persian stock with *shu`ubi* leanings, meanwhile challenging stock conventions of the ancient Arab ode, the *qasidah*, with a new paradigm—the wine poem.

In retrospect, literary historians speak of Abu Nuwas as standing at the vanguard of a contemporary trend in Arabic poetry, called "New" poetry (*muhdath*). New poetry emphasized rhetorical embellishment and metaphorical sophistication. The philologist Abu Ubaydah considered Abu Nuwas the greatest of New poets. Elite audiences, tutored by literary scholars, came to appreciate and even demand poems that used a wide variety of rhetorical figures, many of them rooted in the similarities between Arabic words, rare vocabulary, and striking metaphors.

Reception and impact. Despite his irreverent poetry (or perhaps because of it), and despite the release of a book called "Abu Nuwas's Plagiarisms," which took a stern view of his poems' liberal borrowings from other poets' work, Abu Nuwas fared well among later generations of scholars and continued to exert influence. He

A HUNTING POEM BY ABU NUWAS

Like many of the best medieval Arab poets, Abu Nuwas divided his attention between innovative poetic pursuits, like wine poetry and *mujun*, and more conservative poetry, like panegyric, elegiac, and hunting poems, that relied upon convention. In addition to his fame as the poet of wine, Abu Nuwas garnered praise for his poems on hunting. These are full of the obscure vocabulary dear to connoisseurs of ancient Arabic poetry. An example follows.

> I set out very early—the night was still full of dark clouds but morning (cut) through the
>   darkness quickly,
> Like a waving jeweled saber, with a wide-jawed and resolute
> [cheetah] in tow,
> Courageous, with sinewy back and muscled neck, its body sturdy and lean,
> A massive and frightening creature, its cheeks deeply lined, with black stripes on its throat,
> Thick-necked and mighty pawed, with an adamantine build, it has a chest like a Bactrian
>   camel and a leonine throat,
> A lion but for its leopard-like spots, ready for any fight.
> After gazing outwards for a long time, its forehead smooth and dry, it spotted two herds
>   of gazelles,
> It approached them, stalking at a languid pace,
> Burning with desire for them, it set a devious ambush, sliding by like a viper,
> Past every hillock and crevasse until it reached its goal,
> Then it burst into a sprint across the level plain, sending the gazelles in all directions and
>   shattering their tranquility with a racing attack.
> Between the way it bides its time and the way it nurses its will, hunting has no merit
>   without a cheetah.
>
>   (*Diwan Abi Nuwas*, vol. 2, pp. 662-63; trans. M. Wagner)

Of all the animals a medieval Arab gentleman might take to the hunt, the cheetah (*fahd*) was the most ostentatiously luxurious because it was difficult to catch and tame and maintain. Since the caliph al-Amin, Abu Nuwas's employer, was an avid hunter, the poet may have watched this predator in action while on the hunt with this caliph. His poem describes a cheetah approaching herds of gazelles, possibly riding into the field on a horse's saddle (teaching the big cat to ride on horseback was a tricky part of its training). It portrays the cheetah's creeping up on its prey and bursting into a run, concluding with a sententious maxim about hunting. Like hunting poems by earlier poets, this one was composed in an archaic form called *rajaz*, which many poets and critics of Abu Nuwas's day regarded with distaste. Although the essayist al-Jahiz quoted a substantially identical descriptive poem on a cheetah by the poet al-Raqashi (d. c. 815), with whom Abu Nuwas exchanged poetic verse, Abu Nuwas is thought to be the likely author of this poem.

himself was notoriously unconcerned with passing on his poetic legacy to posterity. An anecdote about his sojourn in Egypt illustrates the problems connected to the collection of his poetry. According to this story, Abu Nuwas, dead drunk, extemporized a sublime wine poem, passed water, and passed out in the resulting puddle. The next morning he did not remember it. Only the diligent notetaking of a bystander saved the poem. Abu Nuwas's powerful persona was detrimental in that it exercised a gravitational pull over diverse literary material. An unknown quantity of the poetry attributed to him may, in fact, have been composed by other poets, among them, Husayn ibn al-Dahhak, a poet who, like Abu Nuwas, sang of wine and homoeroticism in the court of the caliph al-Amin. Decades after his death, the poetry of Abu Nuwas was collected in three versions: that of al-Suli (d. c. 946); the lengthy version by the historian Hamzah al-Isfahani (d. c. 971); and that of Ibrahim ibn Ahmad al-Tabari (d. 966). Abu Hiffan al-Mihzami, a contemporary of Abu Nuwas designated as his "youth" (d. c. 870) and chosen by the poet himself to transmit his poetry, compiled a work entitled "Stories about Abu Nuwas" (*Akhbar Abi Nuwas*). Much later, the lexicographer Ibn Manzur (d. 1311) assembled a more expansive work by the same name.

Abu Nuwas appeared as a character in other literary works as well. In the eleventh century, for example, an Arab poet of Spain, Abu Amir ibn Shuhayd, wrote of a fictitious journey in which he visited some of the great Arab poets in the afterworld. Traversing Paradise, he came across a celestial version of the monastery of Dayr Hanna, a favorite haunt of Abu Nuwas's in life. He thought to look up Abu Nuwas and he found him in the midst of a bender. An Iraqi novelist, Safa Khulusi, wrote *Abu Nuwas in America*, about the adventures of Abu Nuwas in the United States during the 1950s.

Abu Nuwas probably died of an illness in Baghdad, leaving behind very little money for his aged mother, but his impact on succeeding generations has been enormous. Poems of wine-drinking and homoeroticism served important functions at the vigils of Islam's Sufi mystics. There poems inspired by Abu Nuwas, recited or sung by beardless youths, could bring individual mystics to heights of spiritual ecstasy for which drunkenness and sexual abandon served as profound metaphors. The poet Ibn al-Hajjaj, who lived a century after Abu Nuwas, made his reputation by writing salacious poetry in the mold of Abu Nuwas. This man (who worked, counterintuitively, as the supervisor of public morality) researched his craft by sitting on the roof of his father's house in Baghdad and writing down the words he heard emanating from the tavern below. Wine poetry, in both secular and mystical garb, enriched Persian poetry. The Arabic strophic poetry that emerged in Islamic Spain, both the "girdle poem" (*muwashshah*) with its characteristic closing line in the local Romance vernacular, and the licentious *zajals* of Ibn Quzman, owes much to Abu Nuwas. These earliest

examples of European lyric poetry often evoke wine, quote lines from the mouths of singing girls, and evince the descent into depravity characteristic of many poems by Abu Nuwas. Also in Spain, a Jewish poet, Samuel ha-Nagid, vizier to the Muslim ruler of Grenada, composed wine poems in biblical Hebrew that owe much to Abu Nuwas's wine poems.

—Mark Wagner

For More Information

Abu Mihjan al-Thaqafi. *Abū Mihgan poetae arabici carmina*. Ed. Ludwig Abel. Batavia: E. J. Brill, 1887.

Abu Nuwas, *Diwan Abi Nuwas*. 4 vols. Ed. Ewald Wagner and Gregor Schoeler. Weisbaden: Franz Steiner Verlag, 1958-.

———. *al-Nusus al-muharramah*. Ed. Jamal Jum`ah. London: Riyad al-Rayyis, 1994.

Goldziher, Ignaz. *Muslim Studies*. Vol. 1. Trans. S. M. Stern. London: George Allen & Unwin, 1966.

Hamori, Andras. *On the Art of Medieval Arabic Literature*. Princeton: Princeton University Press, 1974.

Ibn al-Mu`tazz, Abdallah. *Tabaqat al-shu`ara*. Ed. Abd al-Sattar Ahmad Faraj. Cairo: Dar al-Ma`arif, 1968.

Kennedy, Philip. "Abu Nuwas, Samuel and Levi." *Medieval and Modern Perspectives of Muslim-Jewish Relations*. Vol. 2. Ed. Ronald L. Nettler. Luxembourg: Harwood Academic Publishers in cooperation with the Oxford Centre for Postgraduate Hebrew Studies, 1995.

———. *The Wine Song in Classical Arabic Poetry: Abu Nuwas and the Literary Tradition*. Oxford: Clarendon, 1997.

Mattock, John. "Description and Genre in Abu Nuwas." *Quaderni di Studi Arabi* 5-6 (1987-88): 528-40.

Meisami, Julie Scott. "Arabic Mujun Poetry: The Literary Dimension." In *Verse and the Fair Sex: Studies in Arabic Poetry and the Representation of Women in Arabic Literature*. Utrecht: M.Th. Houtsma Stichting, 1993.

Montgomery, James. "Abu Nuwas the Alcoholic." In *Philosophy and the Arts in the Islamic World*. Ed. U. Vermeulen & D. DeSmet. Leuven: Uitgeverij Peeters, 1993.

———. "For the Love of a Christian Boy: A Song by Abu Nuwas." *Journal of Arabic Literature* 27 (1996): 115-24.

Rice, D. S. "Deacon or Drink: Some Paintings from Samarra Reexamined." *Arabica* 5 (1958): 15-33.

Rowson, Everett K. *Homosexuality in Traditional Islamic Culture*. Forthcoming. New York: Columbia University Press.

The Diwan of Judah Halevi

Judah Halevi, the best-known Hebrew poet of the Middle Ages, was born in the 1070s, probably in Tudela in what is now called Spain, where he lived for most of his life. At the time, Spain was predominantly an Arabic-speaking, Muslim territory known as al-Andalus and linked more tightly to North Africa and the rest of the Islamic world than to Europe. Halevi belonged to the Jewish social and intellectual aristocracy that flourished in al-Andalus during the age of the Islamic ascendancy (750-1300) in the Judeo-Arabic world. He was a physician, theologian, merchant, religious scholar, and prominent figure in public affairs. Sometime in his sixties, during the summer of 1140, after much debate within himself and with family and friends, Halevi sailed from al-Andalus with the intention of settling and dying in the original Jewish homeland of Palestine. Traveling by way of Alexandria, Egypt, he arrived in the Egyptian city in September 1140. Halevi, by then of wide renown, was acclaimed as a celebrity by its local Jewish community. He remained there for months and visited Cairo before boarding a ship for Palestine on May 14, 1141. Did his ship ever reach Palestine? According to a famous legend, Halevi reached the gates of Jerusalem and was kneeling there, reciting his "Ode to Zion," when an Arab horseman, enraged at this display of Jewish piety, trampled him under the hooves of his steed. All we know for certain is that Halevi died sometime that summer and that medieval travelers say his grave was pointed out to them when they reached Tiberias. Before his pilgrimage, Halevi had been one of the most fluent and

THE LITERARY WORK

The collected Hebrew poems of Judah Halevi; written between the 1080s and 1141 in the area now known as Spain and in the medieval Near East; first published in English in 1851.

SYNOPSIS

The poetic corpus includes secular verse (panegyrics, love poetry, descriptive poetry, wine poetry, wedding songs), liturgical verse, and personal verse. In the personal verse Halevi meditates about his religious vision, the fate of the Jewish people, and making a pilgrimage to Palestine.

productive of the Hebrew poets, writing for both liturgical functions and for entertainment, and exchanging complimentary poetry with some of the most important Jewish leaders of al-Andalus. (During the Islamic ascendancy, Jewish intellectuals wrote and sponsored the writing of poetry, a taste they to a great extent acquired from the Arabic culture that surrounded them.) In middle age, Halevi began to compose poetry of a more personal kind, exploring his own religious motivations, arguing his principles with imaginary interlocutors, and revealing his doubts and fears. Some of his liturgical poetry found its way into the prayer rites of various Jewish communities. His secular poetry was collected even in his lifetime by the Egyptian Jews and soon after his death, an Egyptian scholar assembled his *diwan*,

Engraving depicting the invasion of Jerusalem by Crusaders in 1099.

the corpus of his Hebrew poetry, both sacred and secular. Although the diwan has not reached us in its original form, several medieval recensions (revisions based on studying manuscripts of it) have survived. Thanks to these, we have access to one of the greatest Hebrew literary works of pre-modern times and to a magnificent record of Halevi's own mind and sensibilities.

Events in History at the Time of the Diwan

A religious crossroads. In Halevi's time, Islamdom was still the dominant force in the Mediterranean region, although it had long ago ceased to be a single political unit. Ruled by the Abbasid dynasty, the empire stretched, unmanageably, from Persia to the Atlantic Ocean. So unwieldy was it that individual territories had begun functioning more or less independently as early as the eighth century; al-Andalus, conquered for Islam in 711, had operated completely free of Abbasid control since the establishment of the Umayyad dynasty there in 756. In 929, at the high point of Umayyad rule, its emir had proclaimed himself *caliph* (a term for ruler that implies a claim to be the successor of Muhammad as head of the entire Islamic world). But unified Muslim rule of al-Andalus broke down early in the eleventh century and in its place there arose a number of miniature states. Generally referred to as the *taifa* kingdoms, these miniature states were continually making war on each other and on the rising Christian kingdoms of the North.

By the eleventh century, Christendom had begun encroaching on Islamic territories. The best known of these encroachments was the Crusades, a movement that led to the establishment of the Christian Kingdom of Jerusalem in 1099 on territory that had mostly been controlled by another independent dynasty, the Fatimid Kingdom, centered in Egypt. The entire territory would finally be retaken by Islam, but only after two centuries of intermittent warfare, during which Halevi made his journey. Christian pressure against Islam met with success as well in the central Mediterranean, where the Normans ended Arab rule over Sicily and southern Italy in 1071. Farther west, the Christian kingdoms of Castile and Aragon made headway in their so-called *Reconquista*, their campaign to clear Spain of Muslim rule. Spread over centuries, the campaign amounted to a gradual conquest of al-Andalus, which in fact led to the unification of most of the peninsula under Christian kingdoms in 1492.

Halevi was probably born shortly before one of the milestone events of the *Reconquista,* the conquest of the city of Toledo by Alfonso VI of Castile in 1085. Born either in Toledo or Tudela (the evidence is inconclusive), Halevi went south, to the heartland of Arabized Jewish culture, as a young man. He spent part of his adult life in Christian Toledo, several times moving within and between the Christian domain of Castile and the Muslim domain of al-Andalus. The following decades saw increasing Christian pressure on the rulers of the *taifa* kingdoms, as a result of which, they solicited the help of the Almoravids, a military-religious sect that ruled what is now Morocco. After a resounding victory over the Castilian troops in 1086, the Almoravids returned in 1091 to swallow up Seville, Granada, and the other remaining *taifa* kingdoms. They would dominate al-Andalus until the 1140s, when they would be replaced by the Almohads, another military Islamic sect from North Africa. The Almohads took over al-Andalus a few years after Halevi's departure for Palestine, which spared him the fate awaiting non-Muslims there. The arrival of the Almohads was disastrous for the monotheistic minorities, since this fanatical group abrogated the tolerance of mainstream Islam toward the minorities, forcing Judaism underground and resulting in the flight of most of the Jewish leadership to Christian territories, which, momentarily, were more hospitable.

The Jewish poet in al-Andalus. Jews had been present in the Iberian peninsula since Roman times (the oldest known synagogue to be excavated, in Elche, dates from the fourth century). Subject to intense persecution in the pre-Islamic period, while the peninsula was under Visigothic control, the Jews welcomed the arrival of the Muslim conquerors in 711. The Muslims were especially welcome to the Jews because mainstream Islam guaranteed the security of the minority monotheists—be they Jews or Christians—and their right to continue their ancestral ways. Al-Andalus experienced an economic and cultural efflorescence under the Umayyad caliphate and the period of the *taifa* kingdoms, which benefited the Jewish community along with the Muslim majority. During most of Muslim rule over al-Andalus, the Jews enjoyed freedom from persecution as well as communal autonomy, conditions that allowed some of its members to acquire real wealth. Members of the Jewish elite were able to obtain positions at court as physicians, tax and duty collectors, and all-purpose courtiers; others engaged in such lucrative businesses as silk manufacturing and international trade. This elite class produced a cadre of rabbis, philosophers, poets, and "men-of-many-parts," who simultaneously occupied positions in the independent Jewish community and the Islamic court, managing their businesses and, in a few cases, carrying on a literary career.

The intellectual horizons of these men were broad, for many of them were engaged in Jewish and in larger Islamic society. In their younger years, they had progressed through both the Jewish and the Arabic educational systems. First they studied the Jewish religious tradition—the Old Testament, the Talmud (or oral law), and the associated works of religious lore. Next they often studied the native Arabic intellectual tradition, especially its poetry, grammar and belles-lettres, sometimes even the Quran, or Muslim holy book, and other Islamic religious texts. Alongside the native Arabic tradition, the Arabic language furthermore permitted them access to the Greek scientific and philosophical tradition.

In this rarefied society, poetry was an important vehicle of social cohesion as well as a popular form of entertainment. The Jews acquired a taste for poetry from Muslim court life, in which panegyric, lampooning, and funeral odes were vital political tools. Comparable to today's promotional media, poems often served as a means of publicity for leaders, who would compensate individual poets with financial support in the form of patronage. Outside the political arena, poetry on love and wine-drinking were the most popular form of entertainment, and the improvisation of poetry was a much-relished amusement. Beginning in the tenth century, a Jewish courtier of the first Umayyad caliph of al-Andalus encouraged the development of poetry in Hebrew serving similar social functions as those served by poetry in Arabic and employing similar prosodic systems, rhetorical techniques, and thematic material. By Halevi's time, the taste for this kind of poetry had spread to other Jewish communities of the Arabic-speaking world and several Hebrew poets of genius had emerged, such as Samuel the Nagid (d. 1056) and Solomon ibn Gabirol (d. 1058).

Coming of age after a century and a half of this new form of Jewish literary productivity, Halevi contributed prolifically to all the themes and genres that were by now standard, writing panegyric odes to many of the leading members of the Jewish community and funeral odes on a number of them. He excelled in love poetry and expanded the repertoire of this popular genre by creating the subgenre of wedding songs, some of which are surprisingly sensuous considering their quasi-religious function:

> Fragrances from far away,
> riding on the breeze—
> fragrances the wind has stolen
> from this lovely maiden—
> fragrances that tell the world
> her time for love has come.
> Lover, go to her! Don't linger!
> Browse inside her garden.
> Hurry to her garden bed,
> there to pluck her roses.
> Touch the mandrakes of her breasts,
> when they yield their fragrance.
> Underneath her ornaments
> is fruit her sun has ripened.
> Only hold off one more day,
> till the moon is full;
> for tomorrow it will be
> one of her adornments;
> then her radiance will light you,
> guide you to her chamber.
> (Halevi, *Diwan*, vol. 2, pp. 29-30; trans R. P.
> Scheindlin)

The Arabized poet in the Jewish community.
The Arabization and secularization of Hebrew literature did not find complete acceptance within the Jewish community. Later in the twelfth century, Maimonides would object vigorously to the singing of such songs as the one just quoted on the ground that they created an atmosphere of lewdness and degraded the holy language. In the early eleventh century, Samuel the Nagid's son

felt it necessary to claim that his famous father's love poetry was never intended to be taken literally but only as an allegory of the Jewish people's love for God, in the tradition of the biblical Song of Songs. Here and there, Hebrew poetry itself hints at a certain degree of discomfort with its own subversiveness. To moralists, secular poetry was but the surface expression of the underlying illness of Jewish aristocrats: their love of luxury, power, and prestige; their aping of Arab ways, their worldliness; their inclination to forget that they were members of an exile community that by rights should be devoted not to pleasure but to penance for the sins that, it was generally assumed, had induced God to exile them from Palestine in the first place.

Even the intellectual pursuits of these Arabized poets were suspect, for Greek philosophy in its Arabic garb was seen by many as competing with Jewish religious teachings. The analogous problem had arisen in Islamic society, especially in the twelfth century, when the thought of Aristotle became more widely disseminated, especially in the Islamic west. Greek thinking, based on strict logic, applied to universally observable data, tended to level distinctions between religions and to relegate the revelations on which different faiths are based to mere principles of communal organization without any absolute claim to truth. As a pursuit common to intellectuals across the Jewish and Islamic communities, the very practice of philosophy threatened to blur communal distinctness.

Leaders of both religions reacted by laboring mightily to exploit the methods and materials of philosophical analysis in order to defend their revealed and traditional religious doctrines, thereby creating the disciplines of Islamic and Jewish theology. In the East, the Muslim thinker al-Ghazzali (d. 1111) had written a vehement polemic against philosophy to vindicate the absolute claims of Islam, and his work was quickly disseminated throughout the Muslim world. In the West, Halevi took a similar position in favor of Judaism by writing his theological treatise known as the *Kuzari* (*Kitab al-hujjah*). Echoes of this conflict resound in Halevi's poetry.

In fact, the Jewish aristocracy to a large extent did not deserve the reproaches heaped on it by the Jewish moralists. Whether rich and sensuous or philosophically relativistic, Jewish aristocrats were, on the whole, generous in their financial support to their community. They were also devoted to their synagogues; faithful in their

JUDAISM VS. PHILOSOPHY—THE *KUZARI*

~

Halevi's book is named for the Khazars, a kingdom of probably Turkic origin that inhabited the region of the lower Volga River in what is now southern Russia. One of the kings of the Khazars converted to Judaism in the eighth century, and the ruling class of the kingdom remained Jewish until the destruction of the kingdom in the tenth century.

Halevi's *Kuzari* is couched as a fictional dialogue between a rabbi and the Khazar king who converted. In response to the king's questions about religion, the rabbi demonstrates to the king the superiority of Judaism to Aristotelian philosophy, Christianity, and Islam. Convinced by the rabbi's arguments, the king converts, after which the rabbi discourses on many aspect of the Jewish religion as interpreted by Halevi. Halevi is not opposed to the application of reason to the understanding of religion, but he insists on the limitations of reason. Rather than philosophical speculation, he places prophetic revelation and personal experience of the divine at the center of his religious thought. At the end of the book, the rabbi takes leave of the king in order to make the pilgrimage to and settle in the land of Israel, Palestine. This is the place where, as he has asserted throughout the book, God reveals himself to man, and is therefore the place where one can live closest to Him.

The rabbi of the *Kuzari* takes a strict position in favor of authenticity in Jewish life, belittling the conventional piety of the Jewish aristocracy and even attacking poetry, as practiced by the Jewish aristocracy of the time, as an unworthy use of Hebrew. Thus, in the *Kuzari* we find Halevi at odds with himself and his own career, and aligned with the moralists.

observance of religious rituals, commands and prohibitions; and enthusiastic in their intellectual pursuits. Moreover, their poetry was not all secular. The synagogue service was continually embellished with new liturgical poetry, which the Jewish aristocrats patronized just as enthusiastically as they did panegyric, love, wine-drinking, and other secular poems. But worldly these aristocrats surely were, as the poetry they wrote, patronized, and devoured attests.

The Diwan in Focus

Contents overview. In the first part of his career, Halevi was a model representative of the aristocratic class in which he was raised. One recently discovered document permits us to glimpse him raising funds, via correspondence, for the communal project of ransoming a captive Jewish woman. In another document to Halevi in al-Andalus from a stranger in Castile, the stranger parades his knowledge of philosophy in the hope of gaining an audience with the great man. From the handful of existing documents comes a sketchy picture of a man who is well-connected, widely respected, and fully engaged

in the affairs of the Jewish community. It is a portrait amply confirmed and expanded by the poems in his own diwan. Here, in addition to official letters, we see Halevi's poetic laments on the death of Jewish dignitaries, including scholars, poets, and courtiers. The *diwan* contains his panegyrics on rabbinic and lay leaders of al-Andalus, North Africa, and Egypt—many of whom were his personal friends—and it contains his love poems to young beauties, both female and male, as was the custom in his day. Also in the *diwan* are wine-drinking poems, poems describing nature, wedding songs, epigrams, riddles in verse, and enormous quantities of poetry for the synagogue. A few of these synagogue poems have found their way into the traditional Jewish prayer book, and one is still sung at the midday meal every Sabbath by traditional Jews ("The Sabbath day, not to be forgotten"). Beyond these standard types, Halevi's diwan contains verse that does not belong to any common genre and verse that, while belonging to a standard genre, has a twist that is distinctly his own.

Contents summary. In Halevi's personal poems, he speaks about himself and about the change that began to overcome him in middle age:

Teach me your ways, O Lord, and turn
me back from being folly's captive.
Teach me while yet I have the strength
to bear my penance, one You will not scorn,
before I turn into a burden to myself,
my limbs too weak to hold each other up,
my bones like cloth moth-eaten,
too frayed to carry me—
> (*Diwan,* vol. 3, pp. 266-67; trans. R. P. Scheindlin)

We cannot tell if the poem with this passage was intended to be recited publicly as part of the liturgy, though it is so used by some Jewish communities. It sounds more like a personal prayer by someone who has become conscious not only that he will die, but also that the time will come when he will be too old to bear a reasonable penance for the sins of his youth, when there will be no merit in giving up worldly passions since they will have been dulled by frailty. The expression of this concern gives the standard moralizing about the need to repent before death a particular twist.

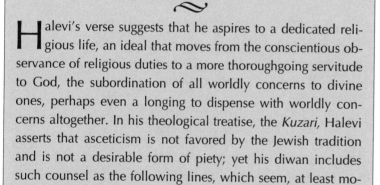

HALEVI AND THE ASCETIC LIFE

Halevi's verse suggests that he aspires to a dedicated religious life, an ideal that moves from the conscientious observance of religious duties to a more thoroughgoing servitude to God, the subordination of all worldly concerns to divine ones, perhaps even a longing to dispense with worldly concerns altogether. In his theological treatise, the *Kuzari,* Halevi asserts that asceticism is not favored by the Jewish tradition and is not a desirable form of piety; yet his diwan includes such counsel as the following lines, which seem, at least momentarily, to envision a kind of Jewish monasticism.

Go out in the middle of the night
to follow the way of the men of old,
whose mouths held praises,
whose souls held no deceit,
who spent their days in prayer
and their nights in fasting.
> (*Diwan,* vol. 3, p. 203; trans. R. P. Scheindlin)

From other poems, we learn of Halevi's frustrations with his daily life. He complains of being too busy to attend to the study of Torah, of being at the beck and call of others, and of being too dependent on the practice of medicine (which, in line with some pietists, he has come to believe does not really have the power to heal, since disease and health are the result of God's decree). Above all, he complains of being a slave to men rather than to God, a thought that recurs in his poetry, and to which he gives memorable expression in an epigram:

The slaves of Time are slaves of slaves;
the slave of God alone is free.
And so when others seek their lot,
God is lot enough for me.
> (*Diwan,* vol. 2, p. 300; trans. R. P. Scheindlin)

Halevi's diwan shows concern not only for personal spiritual welfare, but also for the tribulations of the Jewish people. All Hebrew liturgical poets complained about Israel's exile from Palestine and some even reproached God for delaying its end, but the grief over Israel's powerlessness and a concomitant rage are typically Halevi's. In one poem, he describes Israel, God's estranged beloved, as a dove no longer able to fly, fluttering around her lover's head in a desperate effort to get his attention; the verse ends with his begging God to send a storm of fire that will destroy the oppressor. In another poem, Halevi speaks of a dream in which he sees the Muslim domination broken; slipping into the voice of prophecy, he evokes the biblical vision of a huge statue (representing the nations that have subjugated Israel), overturned and smashed into fragments by a stone flung from heaven. A different poem unites the desire for national redemption with the desire for personal spiritual fulfillment. Halevi describes a dream in which he sees the Temple in Jerusalem as it was before the destruction, more than a thousand years earlier (in 70 C.E.). Priests are offering sacrifices, and Levites (members of the tribe that, in antiquity, was devoted to the maintenance of the Temple and its non-sacrificial rituals) are singing psalms. Halevi pictures himself, a Levite and a poet, among the Temple singers, using his gift of song to assist in the cult of this imaginary Temple.

Two poems, both probably written when he was around 50 years old, tell us more concretely about Halevi's thinking in relation to his pilgrimage. The first, "Your words are perfumed as with myrrh," purports to be his response to a friend with whom the poet has been arguing about the sanctity of the land of Israel. Halevi puts into the friend's mouth the claim that the sanctity of Jerusalem has been neutralized by the Christian occupation. In reply, Halevi points out that if this were true, it would turn the entire

Jewish people into sinners for turning to Jerusalem in each of the daily obligatory prayers. But beyond that, it would turn the biblical patriarchs' devotion to the land of Israel into nonsense, for they yearned for it even before it belonged to the Jews and offered sacrifices there even before the Temple was built. Even now, Halevi continues, with the city destroyed and the land in control of foreigners, its holiness is still present in the sites where prophets had visions of God, in the remains of the homes of prophets, priests, and kings, and in their graves. Even the Holy Ark, the tablets of the Ten Commandments, and the paraphernalia of the Temple, are still there, buried since the destruction and awaiting rediscovery at the time of the redemption that is to come.

It is one thing to venerate Jerusalem, face in its direction in prayer, and supplicate God for its restoration to the Jews, quite another to make it a central theme of religious meditation. That is what Halevi seems to have done, for in his writing about the land, he describes it with a concreteness and in a visionary style not paralleled in the writings of any other medieval Hebrew poet. In his usual concrete way, Halevi recalls again and again the trekking of patriarchs and pilgrims to and in the land.

> He promised it to us.
> Though only owls and jackals haunt it now,
> what was there then but thorns and thistles
> when God bestowed it on our fathers long ago?
> Yet they paced its length and breadth
> like people strolling in a flower-garden,
> lived in it as strangers, transients,
> each night seeking somewhere to put down
>   their heads,
> always on the lookout for some plot
> where, dead, they might be buried.
> There they learned to walk before the Lord,
> adopted ways of righteousness.
>   (*Diwan*, vol. 2, pp. 165-66; trans. R. P.
>   Scheindlin)

The friend with whom Halevi argues in "Your words are perfumed as with myrrh" protests Halevi's obsessive devotion to the land. Probably Halevi had expressed a desire to leave al-Andalus to make his pilgrimage and the friend had tried to dissuade him by saying that until the messianic redemption, the land's holiness is inaccessible, or in a state of suspension. The friend certainly argued that holiness is available even in al-Andalus, in synagogues and in the burial places of great rabbis, for Halevi says,

> What sense is there in honoring our dead,
> when we neglect the tablets and the ark?
> What sense in visiting the place of graves and
>   worms,
> when we neglect the sources of eternal life?
> Are synagogues our only sanctuaries?
> How can we forget the holy mountain?
> (*Diwan*, vol. 2, p. 165; trans. R. P. Scheindlin)

Above all, the friend must have argued that the land does not really matter because God is too removed from worldly concerns to be aware of any particularity—any individual prayer or any particular religious rite. (This would likely have been the position of Jews who were strongly touched by philosophy; it is the position put by Halevi in the mouth of the philosopher in the *Kuzari*'s opening dialogue.) Toward the end of "Your words are perfumed as with myrrh" Halevi implies that this kind of thinking is the unspoken foundation of his opponent's view and Halevi's real target:

> Look here, friend, use your judgment, think it
>   over,
> save yourself from mental traps;
> above all, don't let Greek philosophy seduce
>   you;
> it may have flowers, but it never will bear
>   fruit.
> Or if it does, it only comes to this:
> The world was not created;
> and no one stretched the heavens like a tent;
> and in the beginning there was no creation;
> the moon will wax and wane forevermore.
> Just hear the incoherence of their doctrines,
> constructed out of chaos and pretension;
> they only leave a hollow in your heart,
> and nothing in your mouth but syllogisms.
> Why should I go following such twisting
>   trails,
> abandoning the mother of all highways?
> (*Diwan*, vol. 2, p. 166; trans. R. P. Scheindlin)

By ending with the images of the crooked path and the highway, Halevi returns to the theme of pilgrimage—implicit throughout the poem—and states that neither the argument from philosophy nor the argument from recent history has dissuaded him from his plan to travel to the Holy Land.

Halevi's contemplation of the pilgrimage is explicit in the second long poem on this subject, where he is again in dialogue, but this time with himself. He is 50 years old: When is he going to leave off childish things and devote himself seriously to God? How long will he put off collecting provisions for the road? Moralizing poets had long used this image of "provisions" to represent the accumulation of good works that would improve one's chances for a favorable decision at the last judgment, but Halevi's path is the more immediate one of pilgrimage. He urges himself to boldly walk the road of true devotion, regardless of the dangers he imagines. He sees himself on a ship during a storm at sea. The masts crack and collapse; the ballast has no more weight than straw; the sailors are terrified and their officers helpless; some passengers faint, and others throw themselves to the deck to pray, each to his own god. But he, the imaginary pilgrim, is facing east, in the direction of the Temple, and remembering how God split the Red Sea and the Jordan River. God approves the pilgrim's intention: to reach the land of Israel and there renew the hymns of the ancient Levites with his own new poetry of praise. Instantly the storm subsides, and night falls:

> The sun now sets, the stars are rising,
> with the moon as captain, watching over them.
> The night is like a Moorish woman dancing,
> wearing an embroidered cloth with eyes,
> cloth of sky-blue set with crystals.
> Lost in the heart of the sea, the stars
> dart and wander, like men compelled
> to leave their homes as exiles
>
> . . . .
>
> Sea and sky, so like in color, seem to merge,
> while in between
> my heart makes yet another sea,
> as my new songs and praises upward surge.
> (*Diwan*, vol. 2, p. 163; trans. R. P. Scheindlin)

TAKING HIS CUE FROM THE BIBLE

~

Halevi's vision of himself in the Holy Land is summed up in a single biblical verse, which he alludes to in his "Ode to Zion" and other poems. The verse, quoted pointedly near the end of his *Kuzari*, seems to anticipate Halevi's legendary end, kneeling and finally crushed on the stony, holy soil: "For your servants delight in her stones, long for her soil" (Psalms 102:15).

In his great "Ode to Zion," Halevi's visionary spirit imagines himself walking up and down the Holy Land in the footsteps of the patriarchs Abraham, Isaac, and Jacob, seeking the divine spirit that, he is certain, still inheres in its ruins:

> I wish that I could wander
> where the Lord revealed Himself
> to visionaries, prophets,

> wish that somebody would make me wings
> so I could fly away to you, so far,
> and set the fragments of my broken heart
> among your jagged mountains,
> throw my face down to your ground,
> to fondle your gravel, caress your soil
>
> . . . .
>
> What joy my soul would have if I could walk
> naked, barefoot, on the ruins,
> on the rubble that your Temple has become,
> where once your covenant-tabernacle was.
> (*Diwan*, vol. 2, pp. 156-57; trans. R. P. Scheindlin)

Here, the asceticism, the identification of personal salvation with the fate of the nation, the visionary spirit, the concreteness of Halevi's vision, and the pilgrimage all unite in this climactic expression.

But Halevi's diwan does not end here. The poet wrenched himself away from his family and community and left al-Andalus. He turned his back on the comforts due an old man who had led a long life in service to God, community, and poetry and in effect cast in his wake a rebuke to those who still believed in the synthesis of Jewish learning and tradition with Arabic social and intellectual life. But it was far from easy for Halevi to leave behind this complex and engaging culture. In Egypt, he was eagerly awaited by Jews no less committed to the synthesis than his compatriots in al-Andalus. Friends and admirers wanted to host him, vied over him, boasted of their connection with him. He quickly reverted to the kind of life he had left, and even to the writing of secular poetry. Viewing the Nile in Cairo, he writes as sensuously as he had ever done back home:

> Nature is dressed in white and colored
>   garments,
> sits on mats of gold brocade,
> and every plot of planted ground along the
>   Nile
> is wearing checkered cloth
>
> . . . .
>
> Beside the Nile are girls
>
> . . . .
>
> their arms are weighed down with heavy
>   bracelets,
> their feet hobbled with their golden anklets.
> They steal your heart, make you forget your age.
> your mind goes back to youths and girls
> from other times and places.
>
> . . . .
>
> in this Eden that is Egypt.
> (*Diwan*, vol. 1, p. 112; trans. R. P. Scheindlin)

In writing this poem, a panegyric to a high official of the Egyptian Jewish community, Halevi not only reverted to love poetry; he also made an exception to his vow to stop writing panegyric poetry. In the *Kuzari*, he had complained that the fashion of writing Hebrew poetry in Arabic metrics, of which he was one of the greatest practitioners of all time, was an offense to the holy language; later it was reported that he had vowed to stop writing such poetry altogether. Yet Halevi continued to write this type of poetry profusely during his eight months in Egypt. Many of these poems are of the standard variety—panegyrics, descriptive poems, poems of entertainment. But others from this period are about the ocean voyage and pilgrimage, and they rank among his greatest lyrical works. Halevi is known to have waited five days on his ship in Alexandria's port for a shift of wind. Perhaps he wrote these lines during the five days. "So up, my ship," he urges in the poem, and "forward drive," though he quakes at what awaits him (*Diwan*, vol. 2, p. 186; trans. R. P. Scheindlin).

I tremble
for my early sins,
all recorded in God's book,
and even more for recent sins,
sins of my old age,
new sins every day.
No way
to repent my
waywardness—
what to do in this distress?
I put my life in my two hands,
and my soul and my blood
(all now thralls to sin),
put sin behind me,
throw myself in perfect trust
on One who forgives much,
One with power, One with might,
One who sets the bondsman free.
Let Him judge or chastise
with harshness or leniency;
whatever the outcome,
righteous is His decree.
              (*Diwan*, vol. 2, pp. 186-87; trans. R. P.
                                        Scheindlin)

A window into the state of the Jews in al-Andalus. The intensity of Halevi's poems dealing with the exiled state of the Jews could well have arisen from his meditations on the world situation at his time. Although life in al-Andalus and Castile went on in the accustomed, comfortable ways, the Jews of Halevi's era faced some dangers. Christendom and Islamdom were at war not only in distant Palestine but in Iberia also, and the Jews felt caught between the two forces:

Between the troops of Se'ir and Qedar
    (Christians and Muslims),
my own troops perish
. . . .
For they go out to battle each other,
but in their defeat, it is we who fall;
so it has always been for Israel.
(*Diwan*, vol. 4, p. 131; trans. R. P. Scheindlin)

For Halevi, the Jews' status as bystanders in the duel for power between the two other monotheistic religions turned at least one Jewish holiday into a moment for the following ironic reflection. The late spring festival of Shavuot (sometimes known as Pentecost) is one of three annual pilgrimage festivals, on which the Jews are obliged by the Torah to visit the Temple in Jerusalem. But in Halevi's day homage to the holy city is being performed by Christians, who have trooped from all over Europe to conquer Jerusalem for the sake of their religion, and by Muslims, who have died by the thousands defending the city and trying to recapture it for the sake of theirs. In the meantime, thinks Halevi, the Jews complacently gather in their synagogues in al-Andalus, perform what rites they can, and go home to their families feeling that they have done right by God.

Was there reason for the Jews to be concerned about the future? Since Halevi's own death in 1141 coincides with the rise of the intolerant Almohad dynasty, the Jews of al-Andalus did not yet suffer directly from its repression. But long before the actual Almohad invasion, word must have reached al-Andalus of the fanaticism of this new North African dynasty and its fighting zeal. Probably some observers were imagining the day when the Almohads would replace the decadent Almoravids. Castile too gave cause for concern; during the reign of Alfonso VII (1126-57), Christians rioted against the Jews of Toledo, a noticeable shift from the security the Jews had enjoyed under Alfonso VI (1065-1109). Seeing danger everywhere, Halevi wonders in verse, "Is there a place for us in East or West where we are safe"? (*Diwan*, vol. 2, p. 165; trans. R. P. Scheindlin).

Such doubts must have seemed unnecessarily extreme to his contemporaries. In Halevi's lifetime, there were occasional moments of unrest but the Jews of al-Andalus were not regularly troubled; their lives, property, and ancestral practices were protected by the government and by Islamic law. They were welcomed in the Christian kingdom of Castile for their business skills, as population for the newly conquered territories, and for their command of Arabic (still needed to

The Diwan of
Judah Halevi

administer those territories). There was a decided need among Castilian Christians for access to the higher learning of the Islamic world; thus, educated, multilingual Jews were hired by Christian lords to influential posts, and Jews participated in the translation of Arabic treatises on philosophy, mathematics, and physical science into Latin and Castilian. The few episodes of persecution during the reign of Alfonso VII, while violently lamented by Halevi, passed. Probably almost no Jewish leaders of the early twelfth century predicted the disasters that were to come. It is easy to imagine Halevi's peers both wondering about his new level of piety and irritated by his premonitions of danger.

Sources and literary context. Like the work of all the Hebrew poets of al-Andalus and the other parts of the Arabic-speaking world, Halevi's poetry of entertainment rests on Arabic precedents and models. The functions, themes, metrics, images, and stylistic devices that he shared with other contemporary Hebrew poets were all adapted from tenth-century Arabic poetry. Even his poetry written for the synagogue incorporates elements of meter and imagery adapted by Hebrew poets from secular and sacred Arabic verse. Halevi's diwan also includes a handful of short poems written by others in Arabic and translated by Halevi into Hebrew.

By Halevi's time, the Arabic poetic tradition had become so deeply rooted in Hebrew and so disseminated among Jews throughout the Arabic-speaking world that it no longer felt foreign. His poems were the finest flowering of a tradition that was already a century and a half old when he came to maturity. Furthermore, Hebrew poets had long since diverged from their Arabic models. In using poetry to lay out his personal religious vision and dilemmas, Halevi was following a distinctively Hebrew tradition. Arabic poets were more severely limited by traditional poetic practice and decorum than their Hebrew counterparts in verse that concerned personal experience. Rarely in the much larger corpus of Arabic poetry does one find an Arabic poet writing as openly about his own public position as Samuel the Nagid (d. 1056), about his intellectual and social ambitions as Solomon ibn Gabirol (d. 1058), or about his inner religious life as Halevi.

Reception. Halevi's pre-eminence as a liturgical poet and as the author of social and personal poetry was recognized in his lifetime, as numerous contemporary references to him attest. Literary works from al-Andalus, medieval Provence, and Italy, single him out for special praise. His poems were often imitated, notably by poets in thirteenth-century Egypt and fourteenth-century Aragon. Many of his liturgical poems were adopted by contemporary congregations, especially in al-Andalus and other Arabic-speaking territories. A few of his poems were even incorporated into the prayers of the Jews of Christian Europe, notably his "Ode to Zion" (quoted above), still recited by Ashkenazic Jews on Tish`a be-Av (the fast day commemorating the destruction of Jerusalem), and the Sabbath hymn mentioned above.

As noted, Halevi's host in Alexandria made an unauthorized copy of Halevi's poems while Halevi was out of town, creating jealousy within the Jewish elite of Alexandria and irritating the poet himself. This small and specialized collection may have been the nucleus of Halevi's diwan, for it is generally accepted that the first recension of the diwan was made by an Egyptian Jewish scholar not long after Halevi's death. This collection, like many Hebrew diwans, included Arabic headnotes to the poems, indicating, whenever possible, the circumstances under which the poems were composed. We are still unable to trace the later history of Halevi's diwan except to ascertain that at least four copies have come down to us from pre-modern times, none of them identical but all showing traces of their origin in this original Egyptian recension, drawn from medieval manuscripts. In fact, the myriad copies of his poems on separate leaves or in miscellaneous manuscripts are the best evidence for the popularity of Halevi's poetry in the Middle Ages.

—Raymond P. Scheindlin

For More Information

Brann, Ross. "Judah Halevi." In *The Literature of al-Andalus.* Ed. Maria Menocal et al. Cambridge: Cambridge University Press, 2000.

Halevi, Judah. *Diwan.* Ed. Heinrich Brody. 4 vols. Berlin, 1909-1930.

———. *Kuzari.* In *Three Jewish Philosophers.* Trans. Isaak Heinemann. New York: Atheneum, 1969.

———. *Poems from the Diwan.* Trans. Gabriel Levin. London: Anvil Press, 2002.

———. *Selected Poems.* Trans. Nina Salaman. Philadelphia: The Jewish Publication Society of America, 1929.

Scheindlin, Raymond P. *The Gazelle: Medieval Hebrew Poems on God, Israel, and the Soul.* New York: Oxford University Press, 1999.

———. "Merchants and Intellectuals, Rabbis and Poets: Judeo-Arabic Culture in the Golden Age of Islam." In *Cultures of the Jews: A New History*. Ed. David Biale. New York: Schocken, 2002.

———. *Wine, Women, and Death: Medieval Hebrew Poems on the Good Life*. New York: Oxford University Press, 1999.

The Diwan of Judah Halevi

The Epic of Gilgamesh

Generally held to be the earliest recorded epic poem in the world, *The Epic of Gilgamesh* is based on stories that first appeared around 4,000 years ago in the Near East, where tales of Gilgamesh were written down in various editions by generations of Mesopotamian scribes. Like many early epics, these written forms probably grew out of oral compositions, recited by communal storytellers for generations before scribes set them down on clay tablets, in an archaic form of writing known as "cuneiform." Any view of the world of the epic must take into account that it was not composed by a single author, but evolved over time, in four stages. First, a series of stories describing Gilgamesh's adventures was transcribed in the Sumerian language sometime between about 2200 and 1800 B.C.E. Second, around 1700 B.C.E. Babylonian scribes composed the earliest version of the epic, known to modern scholars as the Old Babylonian (OB) Version. Embarking from some of the older Sumerian stories about Gilgamesh, these scribes created a unified poetic narrative in the Akkadian language. Next, generations of scribes and poets copied and adapted the OB Version, altering both its phrasing and themes and at times introducing new episodes. An edition written on 11 tablets and known today as the Standard Version seems to have become standardized between roughly 1200 and 1000 B.C.E. Lastly, at some point, perhaps in the early first millennium, a twelfth tablet was added to the Standard Version. This tablet consisted of an Akkadian translation of a Sumerian tale (composed in Stage 1) that had not previously

THE LITERARY WORK

An epic poem, set in the city of Uruk (the biblical Erech), around 2700 B.C.E.; composed in stages between 1700 and 1000 B.C.E., translated into English in two volumes (1884, 1891).

SYNOPSIS

A king and his companion brave many dangers together; after his companion dies, the king seeks the secret of everlasting life from a man who became immortal.

been included in the epic. A copy of this 12-tablet version was kept in the city of Nineveh at the royal library of Ashurbanipal, king of Assyria during the seventh century B.C.E. English archaeologists discovered this copy in the nineteenth century and made the epic known to modern scholars and readers. Additional tablets from earlier stages were subsequently discovered. The epic's sensitive exploration of friendship, death, and the hope for immortality, along with its meditations on the nature of humanity, divinity, and community, give this ancient work an enduring appeal.

Events in History at the Time the Epic Takes Place

The real Gilgamesh and the evolution of the myth. Although little is known about the real

THE LANGUAGES OF *GILGAMESH*

The first stories about Gilgamesh were composed in the third and early-second millennia B.C.E. in Sumerian, the language of southern Mesopotamia, which was also the language spoken by the historical Gilgamesh. Sumerian, which is not related to any other known language, was gradually displaced by Akkadian in the early to mid-second millennium B.C.E. However, Mesopotamian scribes continued to study and copy Sumerian texts up until the first century C.E.

The various editions of *The Epic of Gilgamesh* itself are all written in Akkadian, a Semitic language distantly related to Arabic and Hebrew. Akkadian was spoken by Semites who lived in Mesopotamia, and from the early to mid-second millennium it was the main language of the region. There were two major dialects, Babylonian (spoken in the southern region) and Assyrian (spoken farther north); the epic is written in the former. Akkadian was gradually replaced by Aramaic (another Semitic language closely related to Hebrew) in the mid-first millennium B.C.E., but, as they did with Sumerian texts, Mesopotamian scholars continued to study and read Akkadian texts until the first century C.E.

Akkadian and Sumerian documents were discovered by European travelers and archaeologists starting in the early nineteenth century; because some inscriptions in Akkadian were written alongside translations into Persian (which was still understood), European scholars were able to decipher Akkadian by the mid-nineteenth century. Working from Akkadian translations of Sumerian texts, scholars also deciphered Sumerian in the late nineteenth century.

Gilgamesh, historical evidence seems to indicate that he did indeed exist. The Sumerian king list, which purports to trace the royal lineage from the time when kingship was conferred by the heavens through the defeat of Uruk itself, names Gilgamesh (therein called by his original Sumerian name, Bilgamesh) as fifth in line of the First Dynasty of the kingship of Uruk; his reign supposedly occurred in the latter half of the third millennium—around 2700 B.C.E.—and lasted 126 years. Other traditions identify him as a great warrior and the builder of the great wall of Uruk, and claim that he was partly divine, for his mother was the goddess Ninsun, and his father was a demon-man, who served as high priest in Uruk. About a century after his death, Gilgamesh appeared on a list of gods found in a Sumerian sacred text. As the myth of Gilgamesh grew, he was referred to as a judge of the underworld, and later as king of the underworld. Prayers to Gilgamesh as king of the underworld are known from later periods of Mesopotamian culture, for example in the mid-first millennium.

The Epic of Gilgamesh was the product of several ancient cultures, all of which inhabited the region called "Mesopotamia," the Greek term for "between two rivers" (namely the Tigris and the Euphrates rivers); Mesopotamia today is divided among Iraq, eastern Turkey, and northeastern Syria. The climate of Mesopotamia was often harsh, marked by periods of drought and flooding. Nonetheless, cultivation of the rich soil in the river valley contributed over time to successful crops and the spread of thriving cities.

The Gilgamesh legend originated in the part of Mesopotamia known as Sumer, which extended from the area south of Baghdad to the Persian Gulf. This area was home to one of the world's earliest civilizations. The Sumerian region consisted of a vast, water-laid plain: its soil was alluvial silt deposited by the seasonal flooding of the Tigris and Euphrates rivers. During the sixth millennium, the inhabitants of southern Mesopotamia began to irrigate their land, a process that eventually led to the successful production of foodstuffs, which in turn gave rise to cities. By around 5000 B.C.E., these southern Mesopotamians had established an extensive infrastructure of canals, ditches, and basins to accommodate their growing population. The abundant harvests enabled farmers to feed their families and barter the surplus to neighbors who could devote themselves to other pursuits: crafts like pottery and metalworking, administrative jobs in the earliest forms of governments, and worship of and service to the local deities. During the fourth millennium B.C.E. human settlements in the region underwent a rapid transformation: villages grew into cities with markets, palaces, and, most prominently, temples and ziggurats (stepped temple towers).

In Sumer, as in the rest of Mesopotamia, the temple structured the society, encouraging the development of writing, government, a judicial system, fine art, and architecture. Because, for example, temples were often the largest landowners in the cities, temple employees had to keep track of cattle and other temple property; so the people developed writing, originally to record business transactions in the temples. Temples played other administrative roles too, mediating and facilitating contact between the different groups populating the region. Despite the mediating influence of the religious centers, tensions frequently flared between the inhabitants of the new cities located in the fertile river valley and the nomadic and hill peoples who dwelt in the Mesopotamian hinterlands; moreover, the cities themselves also developed rivalries with one another.

Around 2800 B.C.E., territorial disputes between the various cities in southern Mesopotamia initiated a number of important changes throughout the region, including significant migration to the cities from the hinterlands; construction of massive fortifications; and the emergence of the palace, which became the second major urban institution (after the temples) and dominated the political and military arena.

The Epic of Gilgamesh illustrates this transformation of Mesopotamian society in the growth and might of Uruk (biblical Erech, modern Warka), the Sumerian city-state ruled by Gilgamesh around 2700 B.C.E.:

> See its wall, which is like a copper band, / Survey its battlements, which nobody else can match, / Take the threshold, which is from time immemorial. . . . Go up on to the wall of Uruk, and walk around! / Inspect the foundation platform and scrutinize the brickwork! Testify that its bricks are baked bricks! / One square mile is city, one square mile is orchards, one square mile is claypits, as well as the open ground of Ishtar's temple. / Three square miles and the open ground comprise Uruk.
>
> (Dalley, *The Epic of Gilgamesh*, p. 50)

The poem also explores the conflict between wilderness and civilization through the character of Enkidu, a wild but innocent man who is civilized by a prostitute and who eventually befriends Gilgamesh. Later in the poem the gods punish Enkidu; they strike him down with a fatal illness because in a feat of heroism during his journey with Gilgamesh he killed a heavenly bull. As he lies dying, Enkidu at first curses the harlot who brought him to Uruk. Had she never initiated him into human society, he would never have embarked on his fatal journey. He would furthermore have been better off remaining uncivilized, for then he would not mourn his own death, any more than the wild animals do.

But Enkidu relents from his imprecations against the harlot when the sun-god Shamash reminds him: "Enkidu, why are you cursing my harlot Shamhat, / Who fed you on food fit for gods, / Gave you ale to drink, fit for kings, / Clothed you with a great robe, / Then provided you with Gilgamesh for a fine partner?" (*The Epic of Gilgamesh*, p. 87). The pleasures of civilized life—not only food and clothing but most of all human companionship—trump the ignorant bliss of the wild.

The Epic in Focus

Plot summary. The following summary is based on the Standard Version, which among the several versions of the epic has been most faithfully preserved. The poem opens with a prologue describing Gilgamesh—king of the great city of Uruk, two-thirds a god, one-third a man—telling of his wisdom and his exploits. As a young man, Gilgamesh is wild and unrestrained, especially in his pursuit of women. His subjects ask the mother-goddess Aruru to make the king a fitting companion: "You, Aruru, you created [mankind (?)]! / Now create someone for him, to match (?) the ardour (?) of his energies! / Let them be regular rivals, and let Uruk be allowed peace!" (*The Epic of Gilgamesh*, p. 52). (A question mark in parenthesis is how the translator indicates scholars' uncertainty about the exact meaning of a word in the ancient text.)

In answer to this prayer, Aruru creates Enkidu, a hairy wild man destined to be Gilgamesh's companion. Enkidu lives on the grasslands with the wild beasts, running with them and eating grass himself. One day, a hunter sees Enkidu at a watering-hole and complains to his father that this wild man has been setting free the prey in the hunter's traps and snares. The hunter's father advises his son to go to Gilgamesh with his complaint and ask for a temple prostitute

Sumerian ruins at Uruk, where *The Epic of Gilgamesh* is set.

who can turn Enkidu from his wild ways. The hunter obeys; his request is granted; and he and the prostitute, Shamhat, return to the grasslands together. Shamhat seduces Enkidu, who lies with her for seven days, after which he can no longer run as fast as the wild beasts, who now shun his company. Bewildered by these changes, Enkidu is taken in hand by Shamhat, who persuades him to accompany her to Uruk. Hearing about the might of Gilgamesh, Enkidu declares his intent to challenge and defeat the king. Shamhat tells Enkidu that Gilgamesh had a dream that presaged Enkidu's coming, in which a meteorite fell to earth and Gilgamesh was strangely drawn to it.

On their journey, the prostitute teaches the former wild man about bathing, wearing fine clothes, and eating cooked food. After the travelers arrive in Uruk, Enkidu and Gilgamesh meet on the threshold of a bridal chamber and engage in a mighty wrestling match throughout the city. When they finish wrestling, Gilgamesh recognizes Enkidu as his long-desired companion; they kiss and take each other by the hand.

Seeking fame and honor, Gilgamesh and Enkidu decide (against the advice of the elders of Uruk) to go on a quest to slay Humbaba, a demon who guards the Cedar Forest. Gilgamesh's mother, the goddess Ninsun, is saddened by her son's restless heart, and she makes offerings to Shamash, the sun god, to ensure Gilgamesh's safety. Fully armed, Gilgamesh and Enkidu set out on their quest, the latter using his knowledge of the wilderness to find water and build shelter for them. Every night, they make offerings to Shamash, and Gilgamesh has disturbing dreams, which Enkidu interprets as fortunate. They reach the Cedar Forest and do battle with Humbaba. Despite their individual fears, together Gilgamesh and Enkidu—with some assistance from Shamash—prevail against Humbaba. The defeated demon offers his services as guardian if they spare his life, but Enkidu persuades Gilgamesh not to listen. The two companions slay Humbaba and return to Uruk in triumph.

Beholding Gilgamesh's beauty, the goddess Ishtar asks him to be her husband. The language of Ishtar's offer, however, is full of loaded terms; it seems that she is craftily offering him not only marriage but also death (Abusch, "Ishtar's Proposal," pp. 148-60). Gilgamesh flatly refuses, taunting her by listing her former lovers, each of whom suffered disaster after his encounter with the goddess. Offended, Ishtar asks her parents, the gods Anu and Antum, to give her a ferocious heavenly animal known as the Bull of Heaven to destroy Gilgamesh, threatening to release the dead from the Underworld if her request is

Sculptural portrayal of the epic warrior Gilgamesh.

Hoping to avoid death, Gilgamesh resolves to seek out Utnapishtim, the only mortal granted eternal life by the gods, and to learn his secret. After a long and perilous journey, Gilgamesh arrives at the mountain portal to the land of the gods, which is guarded by Scorpion Beings. Gaining entrance into the mountain, Gilgamesh travels for 12 leagues through the darkness until he emerges into an Edenic garden, where "brightness was everywhere. / All kinds of [thorny, prickly] spiky bushes were visible, blossoming with gemstones. / Hanging in clusters, lovely to look at, / Lapis lazuli bore foliage, / bore fruit, and was delightful to view" (*The Epic of Gilgamesh*, p. 99).

Continuing on his quest, Gilgamesh encounters Siduri, a divine tavernkeeper, who gives him food and shelter. On hearing Gilgamesh's tale, Siduri initially dissuades him from seeking Utnapishtim, but eventually she directs Gilgamesh to the boatman Urshanabi, the only one who can ferry him across the treacherous sea to the place where Utnapishtim and his wife dwell.

Arriving at Urshanabi's home, Gilgamesh breaks the Stone Things (unidentified in the poem) that the boatman guards. Urshanabi rebukes him for having made his journey to Utnapishtim more difficult by this act, but instructs him to cut down trees for punting poles to protect himself from the waters of death they are about to cross. After a long and perilous journey, Gilgamesh reaches the distant shore and at last meets Utnapishtim, who informs him that death is inevitable for all humans, for the king Gilgamesh as well as for a fool.

Utnapishtim then tells Gilgamesh his own story of how the god Enlil decided to destroy the world by sending a great flood to cover the earth. Thanks to the advice of the god Ea, Utnapishtim escaped death by building a great boat and stowing his family and instances of every living thing on board. The flood lasted for six days and nights and everything on earth was destroyed except for the creatures on Utnapishtim's boat. After seven more days, Utnapishtim freed, by turns, a dove, a swallow, and a raven; the first two returned to the boat, but the third did not, meaning that dry land had been found. Utnapishtim then released the other birds, went ashore himself, and offered a libation for the gods.

The gods, who had been deprived of sacrifice for more than a week, were famished. They gathered around Utnapishtim's sacrifice "like flies," but Enlil's presence at the ritual was forbidden (*The Epic of Gilgamesh*, p. 114). Enlil came nonetheless and was angered to see that some-

denied. Her father, Anu, consents, and the Bull of Heaven is released in Uruk, killing hundreds of people. Again working together, Gilgamesh and Enkidu slay the Bull. When an enraged Ishtar appears on the city wall and curses Gilgamesh, Enkidu throws one of the Bull's haunches at her and threatens her in turn.

That night, however, Enkidu has a dream in which the gods meet in council and decree that one of the men—Gilgamesh or Enkidu—must die for killing the Bull of Heaven. Enkidu is chosen. After awakening and informing Gilgamesh of his dream, he falls ill; bitter over his encroaching demise, Enkidu initially curses the hunter and harlot who introduced him to civilization, but repents his harsh words after Shamash reminds him of the pleasures he has known as a civilized human and as Gilgamesh's companion. After suffering nights of terrible dreams, Enkidu dies. A grief-stricken Gilgamesh mourns his companion for a week until a worm crawls out the corpse's nose. Donning the skins of wild animals (and thus, in some sense, becoming the wild man that Enkidu had originally been), Gilgamesh leaves Uruk and wanders through the wilderness, grieving for Enkidu's death and the fate all mortal beings must share.

one had escaped the flood. Ea rebuked Enlil for his cruelty and decreed that all humanity should never again be forced to suffer for the evil acts of a few. Enlil then conferred eternal life on Utnapishtim and his wife and led them to their present dwelling-place.

Concluding his tale, Utnapishtim scornfully asks Gilgamesh what he has done to merit eternal life but nonetheless offers him the chance to earn immortality by staying awake for six nights and seven days. Exhausted by his journey, however, Gilgamesh instantly falls asleep. Utnapishtim's wife bakes a loaf of bread for every day the king sleeps. On the seventh day, Gilgamesh wakes up. Seeing the seven loaves (some of which are already crumbling and moldy), he is devastated by his failure. Utnapishtim's wife pities Gilgamesh and persuades her husband to offer the king some compensation for his terrible journey. Utnapishtim then tells Gilgamesh about an underwater plant that will make an old man young again. Gilgamesh dives underwater and picks the plant, then, cleansed and clad in fine raiment, he sets off with his prize for Uruk, accompanied by Urshanabi. However, Gilgamesh stops to bathe along the way, and a serpent steals away with the magic plant, shedding its skin (and hence becoming young again). Weeping over this latest loss, Gilgamesh acknowledges that his journey has been in vain and he must abandon what he sought. The poem ends as Gilgamesh returns to Uruk and invites Urshanabi to view the high walls, mason work, fields, orchards, and temples of his great city.

The Standard Version originally ended here; however, in the version preserved, the text continues with a tale that does not fit the plot of the epic but continues its themes. In this tale, a cherished drum and drumsticks belonging to Gilgamesh fall into the Nether World, and his faithful servant Enkidu volunteers to go there to bring back his king's possessions. Gilgamesh gives Enkidu a list of provisos to follow to ensure his safe return, but Enkidu disregards them all and finds himself a prisoner in the Nether World. Gilgamesh appeals, in turn, to the gods Enlil, Sin, and Ea (three leading gods of the Mesopotamian pantheon) for help in attaining Enkidu's release. The first two ignore his plea, but Ea intercedes on Gilgamesh's behalf. Ukur (apparently another name for Nergal, the god of the underworld) releases Enkidu's spirit into the Upper World. Gilgamesh and Enkidu's spirit then engage in a question-and-answer dialogue about the arrangement of things in the Nether World.

The great flood. The *Epic of Gilgamesh* first attracted modern scholars and critics because of its flood narrative. Utnapishtim, the one mortal man to achieve immortality, is sometimes referred to by these scholars as the "Mesopotamian Noah."

The flood story does not seem to have been found in the OB Version of *The Epic of Gilgamesh*, but it has been added to the Standard Version from an older mythological text known as *Atrahasis*. The Standard Version follows *Atrahasis'* flood story with minor variations: for example, the name of the main human character in the older text was Atrahasis ("extra-wise"), but in the Standard Version of *The Epic of Gilgamesh* his name is usually "Utnapishtim" ("he found life"), which is an Akkadian translation of the Sumerian name for this character (Zi-Usudra). Written in Akkadian in southern Mesopotamia around 1700 B.C.E., *Atrahasis* is a creation epic in three tablets that focuses on the origin and lot of humanity. Before humanity existed, lower-ranking gods had to perform backbreaking work for the higher-ranking gods, and the former revolted. The god Ea proposed creating a slave race, thus obviating the need for divine labor altogether. Ea and the goddess Belet-Ili (also known as Aruru or Ninhursag) created humanity from the blood of the god executed for leading the revolt. Humans then began toiling on behalf of the gods, but as they became more numerous, their noise bothered the gods (especially the chief god, Enlil), who repeatedly attempted to destroy them. Ea, whether out of compassion for humans or (more likely) the realization that destroying this labor force was not in the gods' long-term interests, always saved them. The third tablet of the story describes the gods' final attempt to destroy humanity by means of a flood; this section of *Atrahasis* served as the basis for the flood story in the Standard Version of *The Epic of Gilgamesh*. After the flood, the gods decide to limit human population through stillbirths, diseases, sterility, and crib-deaths, rather than continuing their shortsighted plan of universal genocide. Striking parallels exist between these Akkadian flood stories and the biblical account of the flood in the Book of Genesis. In both traditions, a lone man and his family are singled out for salvation from the deluge that will destroy the rest of humanity. That man is divinely instructed to build a great boat that will carry specimens of all living things. The flood covers the earth, killing everything not safely on board a ship that, after the flood has ebbed, comes to rest upon a mountain.

Utnapishtim and Noah both send out birds—doves and ravens—to search for dry land. Finally both narratives conclude with the human race being renewed and the survivors of the flood receiving special blessings from the god who decreed the flood, along with the assurance that no such punishment will ever be visited upon humanity again. The setting and terminology of the Hebrew-language flood story in Genesis indicate that it is based on Mesopotamian stories similar to those found in *Atrahasis* and *The Epic of Gilgamesh*.

The differences between the two flood narratives, however, are no less remarkable. The capriciousness of the Mesopotamian gods is reflected by their sudden decision in council, prompted mainly by Enlil's dislike of loud noise, to obliterate mankind. In Genesis, God decrees the flood because mankind has grown sinful and wicked. Moreover, Atrahasis/Utnapishtim and Noah are spared for different reasons: the former because he is a favorite of another god, Ea; the latter because of his moral righteousness. Finally, Noah and his descendants are instructed merely to repopulate the earth after the flood, while in *The Epic of Gilgamesh* Utnapishtim and his wife are permitted to join the company of the gods.

Flood narratives also appear in Sumerian texts that predate *Atrahasis*. The prevalence of these narratives throughout the Middle East has inevitably fueled speculation about whether there was indeed a historical great deluge that obliterated humanity or, at least, one civilization. In 1929 one prominent British archaeologist, Sir Leonard Woolley, went so far as to surmise that the great flood had occurred near the region of Ur during the late Ubaid times (5000 B.C.E.), covering much of Sumer and destroying hundreds of towns. This disaster, Woolley contended, gave rise to Sumerian accounts of the deluge and thus to all the later versions of the story. Later archaeologists amended Woolley's theory, arguing that the deluge that inspired these later accounts of the flood might have taken place more recently. *The Epic of Gilgamesh*, for example, links the flood to the Sumerian king Utnapishtim, who reigned at Shurrupak, 70 miles north of Ur, during the third millennium (2000s) B.C.E. Archaeological excavations at Shurrupak did indeed reveal evidence of a flood around that time. It has also been argued that seasonal overflows from the Tigris and Euphrates Rivers led to frequent flooding in the Sumerian region and that any incident in which flooding was particularly severe might have found its way into history and then legend as an account of a great deluge.

Sources and literary context. The first Sumerian tales of Gilgamesh appeared to circulate not long after his death, becoming part of the oral tradition of storytelling. As is often the case when history shades into legend, the king's lineage and deeds became much embellished; his father was now identified as Lugalbanda, another divinized ruler of Uruk. Five such tales have been uncovered (they are translated in George, *The Epic of Gilgamesh: A New Translation,* pp. 141-208). In these tales, Gilgamesh embarks on various adventures, often accompanied by faithful retainers, who include Enkidu. These Sumerian tales stood alone as independent compositions, some focusing on Gilgamesh as heroic warrior and king, others on themes of the fate of humans after death.

The Sumerian tales were first transcribed upon clay tablets around 2500 B.C.E. Later scribes combined elements of some of these tales to create the Old Babylonian (OB) Version of *The Epic of Gilgamesh*. Written in Akkadian, the OB Version focused especially on the theme of Gilgamesh as Everyman grappling with mortality. Initially the hero disdained death and sought immortality through fame, but the death of Enkidu (now portrayed as Gilgamesh's trusted friend and almost his double) became the catalyst for a type of quest unknown in the original Sumerian tales. After wandering in frenzied pain and embarking on an unsuccessful search for eternal life, Gilgamesh accepts that death is the fate of all mortals, and that the brief pleasures of this life—companionship, food, clothing, sex, and family—are the most humans are permitted. The central theme of the OB epic is articulated by an alewife whom Gilgamesh meets on his journeys:

> Gilgamesh, whither do you rove? / The life that you pursue you shall not find. / When the gods created mankind, / Death they appointed for mankind. / Life in their own hands they held. / You, Gilgamesh, let your stomach be full. / Day and night keep on being festive. / Daily make a festival. / Day and night dance and play. / Let your clothes be clean, / Let your head be washed, in water may you bathe. / Look at the little one who holds your hand, / Let a wife ever be festive in your lap. / These things alone are the concern of man.
>
> (Abusch in Maier, p. 111)

The Standard Version of the poem expands considerably the OB Version. Its prologue adds material about Gilgamesh's wisdom, while the OB prologue concentrates on his heroism. The Standard Version adds the stories of Ishtar's rejection by Gilgamesh, the slaying of the Bull of Heaven, and, most significantly, the entire story of the flood. (The OB epic probably limited itself to Gilgamesh's journey to meet the man who saved humanity from the flood, without recounting the whole tale, though we cannot be sure of this since the OB tablets are incomplete.)

The thematic focus of the Standard Version differs radically from the OB Version. No longer is Gilgamesh grappling with the sad but inevitable fact of mortality—no longer is he Everyman. The Standard Version alludes to the fact that Gilgamesh came to be regarded in Mesopotamia as a god of the underworld. Of mixed human and divine parentage, Gilgamesh is a strange sort of deity, and his position is an odd form of immortality: for as god of the underworld, he spends eternity among the dead. As the Assyriologist Tzvi Abusch has shown, the Standard Version depicts Gilgamesh's attempts to avoid not his mortality but the peculiar nature of his divinity. When Ishtar subtly presents an offer of kingship in the underworld (disguising it as a proposal of marriage), Gilgamesh rejects her offer out of hand. By the end of the epic, however, he realizes that he will not achieve immortality among the gods in heaven. Rather, his fate is to rule a city—not merely Uruk on the earth, but ultimately the Land of No Return beneath it. The addition to the Standard Version of tablet 12, in which the dead Enkidu describes the underworld to Gilgamesh, underscores this theme. The tablet seems to make little sense in terms of plot, for Enkidu here is Gilgamesh's servant, not his friend, and his death is described quite differently from his death earlier in the Standard Version. But it makes perfect sense in terms of theme. Gilgamesh, having accepted his role as god of the dead, learns the ways of the realm he is destined to rule. Significantly, the alewife's speech in the OB Version (according to which death is the lot of all humanity) is cut out of the Standard Version, for the Standard Version is concerned not with a typical human but with a peculiar god. Thus a single story was used by different Akkadian writers to explore very different themes (the nature of humanity in the OB Version, the nature of a specific deity in the Standard Version). In this respect, the evolution of the Gilgamesh epics serves as an outstanding example of textuality in the ancient Near East: a text was ever in flux, ever usable and adaptable,

with no one author, no one historical context, and thus no one immutable theme.

Unlike such epics as *The Iliad* and *The Odyssey*, *The Epic of Gilgamesh* was introduced to modern readers comparatively recently. Indeed, the poem was lost for thousands of years until archaeologists discovered the ancient clay tablets during the nineteenth century. Moreover, some portions of the story are missing because sections from the tablets were broken off or obscured; modern scholars and linguists have had to reconstruct the narrative at such points. Owing to its age and incompleteness, *The Epic of Gilgamesh* can be difficult to analyze or classify. However, the poem is usually categorized as an epic, possibly the first composed in the known world.

Events in History at the Time the Epic Was Written

From the Sumerians to the Akkadians. Some three centuries after the purported reign of Gilgamesh, Sumer underwent dramatic changes. During the 2300s B.C.E., a ruler by the name of Sargon rose to power and amassed an army that conquered the city-state of Kish—Uruk's great rival—and eventually the rest of Sumer. Unlike earlier rulers of southern Mesopotamia, Sargon was not a Sumerian but a Semite (i.e., a member of an ethnic group speaking Akkadian, a language distantly related to Arabic and Hebrew). Sargon then led his troops to victories that extended his domain to what is now Iran in the east and to the cedar forests on the shore of the Mediterranean Sea and Asia Minor (now Turkey) in the west. (The journey Gilgamesh takes to the cedar forest in the epic probably echoes real expeditions to Lebanon in search of wood, which was less available in Mesopotamia.) Establishing his base of power in central Mesopotamia, Sargon built a great capital city called Agade (Akkad). He reigned for 56 years, during which period Semites replaced the Sumerians as the most powerful inhabitants of Mesopotamia. These Semites and their language became known as Akkadian, after Sargon's capital.

But while the Akkadians may have conquered the Sumerians, they did not eliminate Sumerian culture but, rather, absorbed it into their own. For example, the Akkadians worshipped not only the gods of their own cities but also Sumerian gods (some under slightly different names). The Akkadians were also quick to adopt cuneiform writing, invented by the Sumerians, and countless Sumerian tales, including those of Gilgamesh.

After Sargon's death, his empire endured for over 60 years before invaders overran it. Around 2100 B.C.E., Sumerian speakers from Ur seized control of southern Mesopotamia for about 100 years, then laid claim to neighboring Assyria and Elam. Their reign represents the final flowering of Sumerian culture. Many Sumerian texts known today were composed, edited, and copied during this period. After the fall of the dynasty of Ur, Akkadian speakers regained control of Mesopotamia, and the Sumerian language slowly ceased to be spoken. Nevertheless, Akkadian-speaking scribes throughout Mesopotamia continued to cultivate Sumerian as a learned and prestigious language; they studied and copied Sumerian texts, and priests continued to recite prayers in Sumerian as well. As late as the first century C.E., Sumerian prayers were still being recited in Mesopotamia.

Babylon was the center of the next major empire of southern Mesopotamia. A city located north of both the Sumerian area and of Akkad, Babylon's empire flourished from 1800 to 1600 B.C.E., during which the Old Babylonian Version of the Gilgamesh story came to be written. Other empires exerted control over Mesopotamia for the next millennium, including the Assyrians (who were dominant in the fourteenth through early twelfth centuries B.C.E. and again from the ninth through the seventh) and the neo-Babylonians in the seventh and sixth centuries B.C.E.; both groups extended their influence as far north as Asia minor and as far west as Egypt. Indeed, so important were the Mesopotamians that Akkadian became the diplomatic language of the entire Near East. Mesopotamian culture, religion, myths, and terminology spread throughout the entire region, as scribes in Canaan, Israel, Egypt, and the Hittite empire studied Akkadian texts. The influence of Mesopotamian culture on the Hebrew Bible is profound, as the flood story in Genesis attests, and early Greek writers such as Homer and Hesiod were clearly, though indirectly, influenced by Mesopotamian myths. In 539 B.C.E., the Persians invaded Mesopotamia, and the era of Mesopotamian hegemony came to an end.

Impact. *The Epic of Gilgamesh* had considerable literary impact in ancient times. Archaeologists have uncovered copies of the OB and Standard Versions (and some intermediary versions) not only throughout Mesopotamia itself but in Hattusas, the capital of the Hittite empire (located next to today's town of Boghazköy in Turkey), the Amorite city of Ugarit (on the coast of present-day Syria), and Megiddo (or Armegeddon, in present-day Israel). Further, Gilgamesh stories were translated into at least two other ancient Near Eastern languages, Hittite and Hurrian (both spoken in what is today Turkey). As late as the first century B.C.E. the Dead Sea Scrolls (Hebrew and Aramaic texts written by a Jewish sect roughly contemporaneous with Jesus) include the names Gilgames [sic] and Hobabish (apparently a corrupted form of Humbaba) on a list of ancient giants.

Even when the influence was indirect, the epic and its sources had a great impact on ancient literature. The flood story in Genesis is certainly based on Mesopotamian forebears; further, the Hebrew Bible contains a passage (Ecclesiastes 9:7-10) strikingly similar to the alewife's advice in the OB version. The many themes and narrative elements that the various versions of *The Epic of Gilgamesh* share with *The Iliad* and *The Odyssey* likely result from some form of indirect influence. Note the intimate friendship of Achilles and Patrocles (whose death is the crucial turning point in *The Iliad*), Odysseus's refusal to accept a role as the eternal lover of a goddess (first Circe, then Calypso, the latter of whom resembles not only Ishtar but also Sidduri), the visit to Odysseus by Achilles' shade from the underworld, as well as the monsters and giants that Odysseus encounters on the journey. Similarly, a medieval Arabic tale found in *The Arabian Nights* is strikingly similar to the Standard Version of the epic. A young king named Buluqiyah (the name itself may be an echo of the original, Sumerian, form of the name Bilgamesh) embarks with a close friend on a quest to find the secret of immortality, but after the friend dies, Buluqiyah wanders, ultimately meeting an ancient sage who has achieved immortality. From this sage the young king hears the early history of the world; he then returns to his native city.

Nonetheless, after the decline of classical Mesopotamian culture at the end of the first millennium B.C.E., both the texts describing Gilgamesh and the languages in which they were written were lost. The texts were rediscovered in the 1850s C.E., during archaeological excavations in which the library of the Assyrian king Ashurbanipal was unearthed. In 1872 George Smith, a young Assyriologist from England in charge of reading the tablets, reported with great excitement to the Biblical Archaeology Society his discovery of a partial flood narrative—the Utnapishtim story contained within *The Epic of*

CUNEIFORM WRITING

In the mid-fourth millennium B.C.E. the economy of southern Mesopotamia grew more complex, and it became necessary to keep records of surpluses and exchanges. A writing system was invented to allow scribes or accountants (they were in fact originally a single profession) to do so. This writing system consisted of picture-like symbols scratched on lumps of clay. These symbols were later modified to produce cuneiform writing, which was in use as late as about 75 C.E. The writing system was soon used not only for accounting purposes but to record other sorts of texts in Sumerian as well. Eventually cuneiform writing was adopted by speakers of Akkadian, Hittite, and other languages. Archaeologists have found thousands of cuneiform tablets throughout the ancient Near East. These include historical and legal documents; letters; economic records; literary and religious texts; and studies in mathematics, astronomy, medicine, and magic. Each of the cuneiform symbols (usually called *signs*) can represent a word or a syllable; in fact, most signs represent several different words and syllables depending on their context. This writing system needs many more symbols than an alphabetic system (in which each symbol stands for a vowel or a consonant, not a whole syllable or word). Standard neo-Assyrian cuneiform has 495 signs, most of which have several possible meanings. Not surprisingly, literacy in ancient Mesopotamia was a highly specialized and rare skill. Only two kings (Shulgi, a Sumerian who ruled Ur in the twenty-first century B.C.E., and Ashurbanipal, who ruled over the Assyrian empire in the seventh) claimed in their inscriptions that they knew how to read; these boasts, whether truthful or not, indicate that literacy was almost unheard of even among royalty.

Gilgamesh—that bore striking parallels to the version found in the Bible. The academic world was fascinated; Smith's discovery prompted the *Daily Telegraph* of London to sponsor an expedition to find the rest of the fragment. Smith recovered the fragment in 1873, publishing a translation of his findings in 1876. Further fragments were unearthed in other excavations during the next century. Enough of the poem was recovered to warrant an English translation—by Paul Haupt—which was published in two volumes (1884, 1891). Initially, modern scholars were most interested in the many parallels between the Gilgamesh epic and the Hebrew Bible, but readers quickly came to realize the depth and sensitivity of the epic itself.

Of the many fine modern translations, those of Stephanie Dalley and Andrew George are especially useful. They carefully distinguish among versions of the epic, whereas other translations mix and match to create a version that never really existed in the ancient world or translate only the Standard Version, thus missing many beautiful passages found only in the OB Version. Attention to the epic has grown considerably in recent years, as new translations, studies, and poetic paraphrases have multiplied. After spending centuries buried beneath the earth, the epic has again been granted new life.

—Benjamin D. Sommer and Pamela S. Loy

For More Information

Abusch, Tzvi. "The Development and Meaning of the *Epic of Gilgamesh*." *The Journal of the American Oriental Society* 121 (2001): 614-22.

———. "Ishtar's Proposal and Gilgamesh's Refusal: An Interpretation of the Gilgamesh Epic, Tablet 6, Lines 1-79." *The History of Religions* 26 (1986): 143-87.

Dalley, Stephanie, ed. *The Epic of Gilgamesh*. In *Myths from Mesopotamia: Creation, The Flood, Gilgamesh, and Others*. Trans. Stephanie Dalley. Oxford: Oxford University Press, 1989.

Foster, Benjamin, ed. *The Epic of Gilgamesh: A New Translation, Analogues, Criticism*. Trans. Benjamin Foster. London: W. W. Norton, 2001.

George, Andrew, ed. *The Epic of Gilgamesh: A New Translation*. Trans. George Andrew. London: Penguin, 1999.

Jacobsen, Thorkild. *The Treasures of Darkness: A History of Mesopotamian Religion*. New Haven: Yale University Press, 1976.

Kramer, Samuel Noah. *The Sumerians: Their History, Culture, and Character*. Chicago: University of Chicago Press, 1963.

Maier, John, ed. *Gilgamesh: A Reader*. Wauconda, Il.: Bolchazy-Carducci, 1997.

Oppenheim, A. Leo. *Ancient Mesopotamia*. Chicago: University of Chicago Press, 1977.

Postgate, J. N. *Early Mesopotamia: Society and Economy at the Dawn of History*. London: Routledge, 1992.

Roux, Georges. *Ancient Iraq*. London: Penguin, 1992.

Sasson, Jack M., ed. *Civilizations of the Ancient Near East*. Vols. 1-4. New York: Charles Scribner's Sons, 1995.

Tigay, Jeffrey. *The Evolution of the Gilgamesh Epic*. Philadelphia: University of Pennsylvania Press, 1982.

The Gospel According to Matthew

THE LITERARY WORK

A gospel, or ancient biography, set in the first 30 years or so of the first century C.E. in Roman-controlled Jerusalem and Galilee; written in Greek in the 80s C.E.; first translated into English in 1382.

SYNOPSIS

The words and actions of Jesus, an artisan-peasant from Nazareth in Galilee, attract a group of followers and challenge the ruling elite. The elite crucifies Jesus, but he rises from the dead.

A form of ancient biography, the gospel of Matthew proclaims the "good news" of God's salvation of the world manifested in Jesus. The gospel does not identify its author. Second-century Christian writers associate it with the name "Matthew," but their reason is unclear. Twice the gospel identifies a Matthew as one of Jesus' disciples (Matthew 9:9; 10:3); however, he is probably not the author since the gospel was likely written after his death. One theory proposes that the name symbolically evokes the similar Greek word for "disciple" or "learner" (*mathetes*) to suggest that the gospel's ideal reader is a disciple learning to follow the ways of Jesus. Another theory argues that indeed the name honors the disciple Matthew, who played an important role in teaching and leading the community of followers from which and for whom the gospel was written after Jesus' death. Similarly the gospel does not identify its place of writing. Most scholars locate its origins in Antioch, capital of the Roman province of Syria, though some suggest Galilee. Support for Antioch comes from references the gospel itself makes to Syria in Matthew 4:24; the prominence it gives to the disciple Peter, who was influential in the Antioch church (Galatians 1-2); and the gospel's influence on later Christian writings from Syria. Finally, the gospel does not state its date of writing. Two clues point to a likely window. First, a couple of Syrian Christian writings from around 100 C.E.—the letters of Ignatius and a teaching manual (*Didache*)—cite material that appears only in Matthew, which indicates that it was written *before* 100. Second, since Matthew refers to Rome's catastrophic burning of Jerusalem in 70 C.E. (22:7), it must have been written *after* 70. Supporting this last deduction, Matthew reworks the gospel of Mark, which was written around 70 C.E. Allowing time for Mark's gospel to circulate and to be rewritten, a date in the 80s C.E. seems likely. Given this date of composition, some 50-60 years separate Matthew's story about Jesus from the time in which Jesus lived.

Events in History at the Time the Gospel Takes Place

Roman imperial rule. Matthew's story of Jesus takes place in a world dominated by Roman rule. The Roman general Pompey took control of the community of Jerusalem and the surrounding territory of Judea in 63 B.C.E. Some three decades later (in 37 B.C.E.), after a series of conflicts, the local ruler Herod, fiercely loyal to Rome, emerged as king. As Rome's puppet king until his death in 4 B.C.E., Herod maintained power by allying himself with elite figures. He appointed the high priests to Jerusalem's Temple, exercised control over the army, ruthlessly eliminated opposition, and levied harsh taxes that, along with income from seized lands, financed an extensive building program in Jerusalem. Chapter 2 of Matthew narrates Herod's attempt to kill the newborn Jesus by murdering males under two years of age in Bethlehem. No other sources verify the historicity of this story but such murderous behavior is consistent with Herod's character. According to the Jewish historian Josephus, Herod used the death penalty extensively against opponents and his own family members, including his wife (Josephus, *Jewish Antiquities*, 15.231-36,284-91, 365-68).

When Herod died in 4 B.C.E. (an event referred to in Matthew 2:15, 19-20), his territory was, with the approval of the emperor Augustus, divided among Herod's three sons. One son, Archelaus, ruled Judea and Samaria until Rome replaced him in 6 C.E. with Rome-appointed governors. Matthew identifies fear of Archelaus as the reason for Jesus' family not settling in Judea but moving to Galilee (Matthew 2:21-24). Jesus' death by crucifixion, narrated in chapters 26-27 of Matthew, occurs around 30 C.E. in Jerusalem at the hands of the Jewish elite and their ally the Roman governor, Pontius Pilate, who governed from 26-36 C.E. Governors represented Roman interests and used the power of life and death against those who threatened them.

Herod's second son, Herod Antipas, ruled Galilee and Perea to the north until he was exiled in 39 C.E. His policies of urban expansion and taxation caused widespread hardship for peasants and provided the context for Jesus' ministry. In Matthew's gospel, Herod Antipas beheads John the Baptist after John criticizes Herod's relationship with Herodias, his brother's wife (Matthew 14:1-12). Earlier, John has the role of preparing for Jesus' ministry (Matthew 3:1-12).

Domination and resistance. Understanding Matthew's story of Jesus requires awareness of the dynamics of Roman rule, the type of society it created, and the forms of resistance that developed. The Roman empire was hierarchical and vertical in structure. A small governing elite in Rome and throughout the empire secured for itself great wealth, power, and status by exploiting the population, which consisted mostly of peasant farmers and artisans. The elite lived extravagantly at the expense of this peasant-artisan majority, to which Jesus belonged.

Rome established control in several ways. It exercised its military muscle—through acts of warfare, intimidation, and a reputation for ruthlessness that deterred antagonists. Also Rome formed alliances with local elites, such as Herod Antipas in Galilee or the high priestly families and the leading Pharisees (a Jewish group), scribes, and Sadducees (another Jewish group) based in Jerusalem. In Matthew all these groups conflict with Jesus. These elites shared a mutual interest in maintaining the status quo. Another way in which the Romans secured control was through taxation—on property, products, and people. Often paid in goods, taxation confiscated much of the peasant's output. Estimates of the percentage of peasant production removed by taxation range from 25 to 40 percent in Galilee, and the practice proved generally destructive. The taxes imposed by various levels of the elite—local landowners, the Jerusalem Temple, local kings such as Herod, Roman tribute—diverted resources from the rural Jewish populace to elite urban centers such as Rome and Antipas's cities of Sepphoris and Tiberias. Peasants suffered the consequences—food shortages, malnutrition, breakup of households, poor health, anxiety, and overwork. The gap between rich and poor grew wider. Large landowners, including high priestly families, amassed larger property holdings in first-century Judea and Galilee as subsistence peasant farmers defaulted on loans, rents, and taxes. Not just a material matter, the paying of taxes was seen as a test of loyalty. Matthew includes two scenes about paying taxes, including one in which elite figures try to trap Jesus into denouncing it (Matthew 22:15-22; 17:24-27). His response artfully seems to express both support and criticism: "Give to the emperor the things that are the emperor's and to God the things that are God's" (Matthew 22:21).

Aside from their material hold on the people, Rome and the local elites exerted ideological control. Rome promoted itself, through personnel, coins, buildings, and festivals, as the chosen agent of Jupiter—the chief Roman god. With divine legitimization for its domination, Rome claimed to manifest Jupiter's will and to be the channel through which various divinities bestowed blessings of victory, peace, social harmony, wellbeing, and abundance.

At the same time, residents of Judea and Galilee encountered another set of ideological claims elucidated by the Jewish elite. The priestly rulers, based in Jerusalem and allied to Rome (the chief priest was appointed by Rome's governor), described the tithes and offerings/taxes necessary to maintain the Jerusalem Temple, its personnel, and festivities, as religious obligations of Judaism. The fulfillment of these obligations, said the priests, procured divine favor. They furthermore taught observances that, although accepted as part of divinely ordained instructions from God to Moses, nevertheless hurt many of the peasants materially. One such practice was the offerings of animals to maintain Temple operations; a proviso allowed for the poor to bring in substitute offerings (e.g., smaller animals, grain), but the practice exacted a material toll nonetheless. Studies of peasant societies show the ideological justifications for such practices to be the "public transcript" that expresses an elite view of the world. For the Jewish elite, the justification was the survival of the Temple in Jerusalem, seen as crucial at this point in history, to the survival of the Jews as a people of God.

Typically, pervasive domination by the elite and its sustained exploitation of the majority arouse resentment, which, in turn, inspires resistance. Resistance in first-century Judea and Galilee was sometimes violent. Small bands of peasants led by self-anointed kings or bandits would attack elite property and personnel before succumbing to the inevitable elite retaliation and death. Wide-scale war broke out in 66 C.E. There was also nonviolent resistance. People acted in calculated and self-protective ways, committing anonymous acts of pilfering or sabotage, or hiding production to avoid taxation.

Resistance, as shown in the studies of peasant societies, can be expressed in dignity-restoring actions, such as those Jesus teaches (Matthew 5:38-42). Or it can be expressed in ambiguous sayings—such as Jesus' references to "the reign or empire of the heavens," whose seditious meaning is known only to insiders (Matthew 4:17; 13:24, 31, 33, 44, 45, 47). In their response to public transcripts, peasants develop a hidden transcript or a little tradition that describes the world in vastly different ways. It contests the elite's claims, imagining different societal structures and the end of the elite. Matthew's account of Jesus' teaching serves as a hidden transcript of this kind. Central to it is Jesus' assertion that Rome and its elite allies do not rightly claim sovereignty over the earth—God is asserting God's rule through Jesus' ministry, the empire or reign of God (Matthew 4:17).

Jesus also refers to the imminent "end times," when God's reign will eventually remove everything, including Rome, that resists God's pur-

poses and God will be established as supreme over all (Matthew 24:27-31). While the hidden transcript often remains invisible to the elite, direct confrontations occur in which the hidden and public transcripts collide. Jesus confronts the ruling elite based in the Jerusalem Temple, pitting his truth against their power, denouncing them, says Matthew, for acting contrary to God's will (chapter 21). Jesus predicts the downfall of the Temple and consequent eradication of the Jerusalem elite's power base and way of life (chapter 24). For this direct attack, he is put to death.

SOCIAL BANDITS OR INSURRECTIONISTS

The Jewish historian, Josephus, an ally of Rome, refers disparagingly to various insurrectionists or "social bandits" in the first century C.E. These figures are usually rural peasants severely impacted by deteriorating socio-economic circumstances. Leading small bands of peasants, they attack elite figures, steal property, and disrupt the social order. When such leaders are captured, they are executed. For instance, Josephus narrates the execution of a leading insurrectionist, Tholomaeus, and the efforts of the Roman governor Fadus (44-46 C.E.) to eliminate them all. Later, after some "bandits" rob one of the emperor's slaves traveling to Jerusalem, the Roman governor Cumanus (48 C.E.) orders retaliation by plundering villages and arresting leaders (Josephus, *Jewish Antiquities*, 20.5, 113-14).

The Gospel in Focus

Plot overview. The gospel story unfolds chronologically, from Jesus' conception to his death and resurrection. We must remember as we read that the gospel is not primarily a historical record of Jesus' life. We have no such record. Rather the gospel tells the story of Jesus from a particular theological perspective (what God is doing through Jesus) for a particular purpose (to help readers be better followers of Jesus). This is not to suggest that the story has no historical basis. Scholars have sifted the material in Matthew (as well as in the other gospels) to recognize a basic outline of Jesus' life, including

- His birth in the time of Herod
- His baptism by and association with John the Baptist
- A prophetic preaching ministry in Galilee
- Healings and exorcisms

- Followers
- A confrontation with the Jerusalem Temple-based authorities
- Crucifixion by the Roman governor Pilate around the year 30 C.E.

Written some 50 years after these events, Matthew was produced by employing various traditions and sources about Jesus, which had been developing in communities of Jesus' followers (see "Sources" below). The gospel keeps the story riveted on Jesus, but its structure is episodic, as is typical of ancient biography. Instead of covering every aspect of Jesus' life, the story includes selective episodes to instruct Jesus' followers about living faithfully with respect to his teaching. In the gospel are five major collections of Jesus' teaching (Chapters 5-7, 10, 13, 18, 24-25). These five collections not only instruct, they also contribute to Jesus' characterization by showing consistency between his teaching and actions. Throughout the gospel, God's perspective controls and evaluates the action. Indirectly, through an angel, God names Jesus at conception and gives him his life's work of saving from sin and manifesting God's presence (Matthew 1:21, 23). Twice in the story God speaks directly, expressing approval for Jesus (Matthew 3:17; 17:5). Matthew also sprinkles his story with references to Jesus' "fulfilling" or enacting the Jewish scriptures to show Jesus doing God's will (e.g., Matthew 8:17; 12:18-21; 21:4-5). Three groups of characters interact with Jesus in the text: elite figures who oppose his teaching; crowds who show interest and benefit from Jesus' actions; and disciples who follow him, albeit imperfectly. The story divides into six sections.

Plot summary. Section 1 defines Jesus' lifework within the purposes and will of Israel's God (Matthew 1:1-4:16). First, to review Israel's history with God, there is a genealogy or family tree organized around three major figures or events:

- Abraham (c. 1800 B.C.E.; receives promise from God that through him "all the nations of the earth shall be blessed"—Genesis 12:1-3)
- King David (c. 1000 B.C.E.; Israel's king chosen by God to represent God's reign in a line of descendents that will last forever—2 Samuel 7:13-14)
- The experience of exile in Babylon (587-39 B.C.E.; end of David's line of kings and of Israel's political independence)

God's purposes of blessing the world (Abraham) and establishing God's rule (David) continue in Jesus the *Christ*, a Greek word that means the same as the Hebrew-derived "Messiah." The term literally means "anointed" (usually with oil), an

act that designates someone is chosen and commissioned by God for a particular role. Kings were anointed to rule (Psalm 2); priests were anointed to offer sacrifices on the altar on behalf of the people (Leviticus 4); prophets were anointed to speak God's word (1 Kings 19:16); the Persian king Cyrus, God's anointed, was unknowingly selected to set Israel free from exile in Babylon (Isaiah 44:28-45:1). Matthew designates Jesus as "the Christ" to show that he is anointed or commissioned by God. The question to be answered is "anointed to do what?"

The narration of Jesus' conception answers this question by elaborating his commission (Matthew 1:18-25). Mary, betrothed to Joseph, becomes pregnant not by Joseph but by God's action through the Holy Spirit. An angel from God instructs Joseph to name the child "Jesus, for he will save his people from their sins" (Matthew 1:21). The name Jesus, a Greek form of the Hebrew name Joshua, means "God saves." With his naming, the baby Jesus is commissioned to his lifework, to carry out God's saving purposes. A citation from the prophet Isaiah (spoken centuries previously in a situation of danger from the Assyrian empire) adds a further name, "Emmanuel," a Hebrew phrase meaning "God with us" (Matthew 1:23). Thus, Matthew's gospel claims, God commissions Jesus to manifest God's saving presence in a world dominated by Roman power and its death-inducing effects. This commission, both Jesus' performance of it and the resistance to his performance of it, frames the whole story.

Chapter 2 narrates three contrasting responses to Jesus' birth. First, the magi, who are Eastern astrologers, priests, and political advisers, arrive in Jerusalem after following a star and asking where is the newborn "king of the Jews." They bring gifts to honor this baby king. Second, King Herod in Jerusalem, his center of power, is deeply troubled. He learns from his allies, the chief priests and scribes, that the Christ or Messiah is to be born in Bethlehem, where David had been anointed king. His power threatened, Herod plots to kill the baby Jesus. Herod's plans are frustrated, though, by God, who through a dream warns the magi not to tell Herod where Jesus is. Then an angel instructs Joseph to take the baby Jesus off to Egypt. Herod kills all male babies under two in Bethlehem, but fails to find Jesus. When Herod dies, the faithful, obedient, endangered Joseph, guided by an angel, returns with Mary and Jesus to Nazareth in Galilee in preparation for Jesus' adult ministry there.

The narrative ignores Jesus' childhood and early adulthood. Sometime during this period, the prophet John the Baptist warns people to repent and prepare for God's intervention (Matthew 3:1-12). John does not specify particular wrongdoing that needs to be changed. His language, though, indicates that generally the status quo under the Roman-Jerusalem leadership is not according to God's purposes. Jesus is baptized by John, an act that denotes Jesus' embracing of God's commission. When he is baptized by John, God sends the Holy Spirit and God speaks from heaven, "This is my Son, the beloved, with whom I am well pleased" (Matthew 3:17). The image of "son" denotes in Israel's traditions one whom God chooses for special tasks and who enjoys special relations with God.

Chapter 4 introduces a cosmic context. The devil tempts Jesus to carry out the devil's will, not God's. Jesus remains loyal to God. Interestingly, the devil offers Jesus control of "all the empires of the world" (Matthew 4:8). By implication, the devil identifies Rome's empire as his agent, opposed to what God aims to effect through Jesus. Jesus returns to Galilee to manifest God's saving presence. Galilee is dangerous since its ruler Herod Antipas, Rome's puppet, has imprisoned Jesus' ally, John.

In Section 2 (Matthew 4:17-11:1), Jesus performs his commission to manifest God's saving presence. "Repent," he declares, "for the kingdom (or empire) of heaven has come near" (Matthew 4:17). Jesus announces that the divine rule or will is present in his life, not in the current societal structures of the Roman/Jerusalem-controlled world. He proclaims God's saving presence on earth, as God commissioned him to do (Matthew 1:21-23).

Jesus carries out his commission in three ways. First, he disrupts people's lives, calling them to "follow me" as disciples and form a community living God's purposes in the elite-dominated world (Matthew 4:18-22: 9:9; 10:1-4). Second, he teaches his disciples to live disruptive and transforming lives, committed not to Rome's rule but to God's reign of justice (Matthew 5:20). In a sermon on an unidentified mountain in Galilee (called "The Sermon on the Mount," chapters 5-7), Jesus outlines what God's transforming reign looks like. It creates an alternative community, marked by justice, mercy, and the suffering of persecution by its proponents since they challenge Rome's societal order (Matthew 5:3-16). Against the teachings of elite scribes and Pharisees, Jesus elaborates a different social ex-

perience comprising authentic relationships, the end of male privilege and domination in matters of adultery and divorce, nonviolent resistance, love for enemies, fasting, justice, prayer, trust in God not goods, seeking another person's well-being, discerning false teachers, and hearing and performing God's will (Matthew 5:21-48, 6:1-18, 6:19-7:27). Third, in chapter 10 Jesus instructs disciples about their mission. They are to proclaim "the good news, 'The kingdom of heaven has come near.' Cure the sick, raise the dead, cleanse the lepers, cast out demons" (Matthew 10:7-8). Jesus himself has performed such actions (in Matthew 4:23-25 and chapters 8-9); his disciples are to continue his mission of manifesting God's saving presence.

Section 3 continues to describe Jesus' mission and identity (Matthew 11:2-16:20). He invites the powerless and vulnerable poor to participate in God's purposes (11:25-30). As God's servant, he renounces violence in accomplishing divine justice for the nations (Matthew 12:15-21). He reveals God's power in calming a storm and God's compassion by miraculously feeding large crowds (Matthew 14:22-33). These feedings, like his healings, evoke Isaiah's vision of the establishment of God's reign as a time of abundant food and wholeness (Matthew 14:22-33; 15:29-39).

Matthew 15:29-31, 37-38

Jesus went up a mountain. . . . Great crowds came to him, bringing with them the lame, the maimed, the blind, the mute, and many others. He put them at his feet, and he cured them, so that the crowd was amazed when they saw the mute speaking, the maimed whole, the lame walking, and the blind seeing. . . . And all of them ate and were filled, and they took up the broken pieces left over, seven baskets full. Those who had eaten were four thousand men, besides women and children.

Isaiah 35:5-6; 25:6

The eyes of the blind shall be opened, and the ears of the deaf unstopped; then the lame shall leap like a deer, and the tongue of the speechless sing for joy. . . . On this mountain the Lord of hosts will make for all people a feast of rich food, a feast of well-aged wines.

Of special importance in Section 3 is the litany of responses to Jesus. The section begins with Jesus' explaining to some disciples that his actions reveal his God-given commission to manifest God's saving presence (Matthew 11:2-6). Jesus quotes from a vision of the prophet Isaiah (Isaiah 35:5-6) in which wholeness and health result when God's reign orders the earth: "the blind

Referring to someone who has a log in his eye and tries to remove a spec from someone else's eye, Jesus wittily warns against judging others (Matthew 7:1-5).

receive their sight, the lame walk, the lepers are cleansed, the deaf hear, the dead are raised, the poor have good news brought to them" (Matthew 11:5). In Jesus' actions, God's reign transforms the destructive consequences of the imperial system in which food and adequate nutrition are denied to overworked and humiliated peasants. Jesus' ministry challenges people to recognize him as the one who manifests God's rule and saving presence.

There are many negative responses. People defame John and Jesus (Matthew 11:19). Some towns refuse to repent (Matthew 11:20-24). Jesus struggles against the authorities over the requirement to observe the Sabbath. They do not disagree that the Sabbath should be observed. Their disagreement is over *how* it is to be observed. Should it be honored by not working, as they insist, which harms peasants and so helps maintain the current unjust order? Or should the Sabbath be honored by doing good and merciful actions like producing food and healing others, as Jesus teaches (Matthew 12:1-14)? When Jesus heals a blind and mute person thought to be possessed by a demon, his opponents accuse him of being the devil's agent (Matthew 12:22-32). His teaching offends his hometown synagogue, or worship assembly (Matthew 13:53-58). He attacks the authorities' practice of encouraging people to donate money

to the Temple instead of caring for aged parents (Matthew 15:1-20). Jesus challenges representatives of the elite, the Pharisees and Sadducees, to discern his identity from his actions (Matthew 16:1-4). The stakes are high. The authorities respond to Jesus' disregard for their control of the Sabbath by planning to kill him (Matthew 12:14). Meanwhile, John the Baptist meets with a grisly fate as Herod Antipas executes him (Matthew 14:1-12). To challenge the power structure is to lose one's life.

There are also positive responses. Jesus' disciples comprise a new community or household that supersedes all birth relationships (Matthew 12:46-50). They receive his teaching and God's revelation even though, as Jesus explains in numerous parables, God's reign seems difficult to detect (Matthew 13:10-17). It is worth everything to participate in this reign. His disciples discern Jesus' identity when he walks on water, declaring, "Truly you are the Son of God" (Matthew 14:33). Their declaration agrees with God's description of Jesus when he was baptized, of being God's son, the one commissioned to manifest God's saving presence and rule (Matthew 3:17). A Canaanite woman overcomes gender and ethnic prejudices to secure Jesus' healing for her demon-possessed daughter (Matthew 15:21-28). In the final scene of this section (Matthew 16:13-20), Jesus asks his disciples the identity question: "Who do people say that the Son of Man is?" Peter declares, "You are the Messiah, the son of the living God." Jesus blesses him for receiving God's revelation and announces that this acknowledgment is foundational for the community of disciples. Strangely, Jesus instructs them not to tell anyone (Matthew 16:13-20). Why?

Section 4 provides an answer (Matthew 16:21-20:34). Jesus' commission has a further dimension. He announces that he "must" go to Jerusalem and die, but God will raise him back to life. This announcement summarizes the rest of the story. Its importance is seen in that not only does Jesus repeat it four times (Matthew 16:21; 17:11, 22-23; 20:17-19), he also travels south from Galilee to Jerusalem (chapters 19-20). God confirms Jesus' declaration of what will take place. Three disciples see Jesus transfigured with a shining face and dazzling clothes, an anticipatory glimpse of his resurrection glory. For the second time God speaks directly, "This is my Son, the beloved . . . listen to him" (Matthew 17:5; compare 3:17). God's exhortation is necessary because the disciples themselves struggle with Jesus' new teaching. Peter openly declares Jesus will not die on a cross, but Jesus calls him Satan's agent for opposing God's purposes (Matthew 16:22-23).

Jesus has more bad news for his disciples. Not only must he die, his disciples must walk the way of the cross (Matthew 16:24). Rome uses crucifixion as a humiliating way to execute violent criminals, rebellious provincials, and unruly slaves who do not conform to its norms and threaten its control. So walking the way of the cross means a life that challenges the elite's interests. In chapter 18 he instructs disciples about being a community that, in contrast to imperial society, does not exclude and humiliate but welcomes everyone. In chapters 19-20, as he travels to Jerusalem, he instructs them about households that embody God's reign not by means of domination but in mutual relationships. Instead of the "power over" strategy in imperial society, disciples are to serve one another, imitating Jesus' life and death (Matthew 20:25-28).

In Section 5 (chapters 21-27), Jesus enters Jerusalem and struggles with the elite's show of power. His entry on a donkey mocks the ostentatious displays of might in the parades and military triumphs of Roman imperial personnel. He condemns the leaders for making the Temple a "den for robbers" (Matthew 21:1-17). In a series of stories or parables, he condemns the leaders' violent rejection of God's just purposes and messengers, including himself (Matthew 21-22). He denounces the power mongers by attacking them with a series of woes or judgments for ignoring "justice, mercy and faith" (Matthew 23:23). For the last time, he instructs the disciples (Matthew 24-25). He warns them that a time of great distress will precede his powerful and glorious return to overcome Rome and establish God's just rule and world (Matthew 24:27-31). Disciples must remain faithful in readiness for the judgment of the nations based on whether people heeded Jesus' admonition to live lives of mercy and justice (Matthew 25:31-46).

JESUS' DEATH

Often the *necessity* of Jesus' death is interpreted as God's having predetermined his demise, that is, having sent him from heaven to die. In Matthew, God does not send Jesus from heaven, and his opponents first mention his death in 12:14. The question is why "must" Jesus' death happen? His death is inevitable because violence is the means by which the elite retains power and eliminates challengers. It "must" also happen to show that God overcomes the worst that the empire and its allies can do. Jesus' announcement about his death and resurrection predicts that they will not be able to keep him dead, anticipating the victory of God's purposes and a just way of life.

Chapters 26-27 narrate Jesus' death against the backdrop of Passover, the festival celebrating God's freeing the Israelites from captivity in Egypt. Amidst the conspiracies of the elite, the handing over of Jesus to the Jerusalem elite by the disciple Judas (Matthew 26:14-16, 47-56), and the flight of all the disciples (Matthew 26:56), a woman pours oil on Jesus' head to recognize his identity as God's commissioned one, and to prepare for his death (26:6-13). After eating the Passover meal with his disciples, Jesus is arrested. The Jerusalem elite rejects his claim to share in God's reign (26:57-67). They send him to their ally, the Roman governor Pilate, knowing Jesus will receive the death sentence (Matthew 27:1-27). Pilate understands Jesus to be claiming that he is king of the Jews, a capital offense, since only Rome determines provincial kings and leaders, thereby ensuring their loyalty and cooperation. Pilate condemns him to death after questioning the crowd to see whether Jesus' death will provoke any unrest. Roman soldiers humiliate Jesus with insults and whipping, and crucify him with two "bandits," either violent criminals or insurrectionists. His death is accompanied by darkness, the splitting of the curtain inside the Temple that divided the entrance forecourt from the Temple proper, and the raising of the dead from tombs in the city in what seems to be an anticipation of the general resurrection. Rumors of attempts to steal his body cause the authorities to guard his tomb.

In the sixth section, chapter 28, two followers of Jesus—Mary Magdalene and Mary—visit his tomb to witness Jesus' resurrection as he had taught. Instead, an angel tells them that he is already risen. The women are told to instruct the disciples to go to Galilee. The risen Jesus appears to them and repeats the instructions to tell the disciples to meet him in Galilee (Matthew 28:1-10). Meanwhile, the Jerusalem leaders bribe soldiers to say that Jesus' body was stolen from the tomb (28:11-15). The gospel's final scene occurs in Galilee where the risen Jesus meets the disciples (some worshipping, some doubting). He announces that he shares God's authority over heaven and earth. He commissions his disciples to a worldwide mission of making disciples who learn and obey Jesus' teaching. The gospel ends with his promise, "I am with you always to the ends of the age" (Matthew 28:20).

Jesus' death and resurrection. At first glance, Jesus' death seems to be another victory for the ruling elite, who protect their interests by removing a troublemaker. The empire always strikes back. But Jesus willingly and nonviolently goes to Jerusalem, giving himself up to die because he understands he is enacting God's saving purposes. In Matthew 20:28, he describes his death as a "ransom for many." The image of "ransom" appears in the Hebrew Bible when God frees the Israelites from slavery in Egypt (Deuteronomy 7:8) and from exile in Babylon (Isaiah 43:1). Since Jesus' death is a ransom "for many," the setting free does not only involve God's bringing Jesus back to life. Rather, Matthew (1:21) claims that God sets free or saves many people from sin, from that which is contrary to God's just purposes.

How does Jesus' death and resurrection set free or save when Rome is still in power? In part, Jesus' death reveals the lengths to which the unjust Rome-Jerusalem regime will go to protect its own interests. But his resurrection also reveals the limits of their power. They do not have to-

tal power. They cannot keep Jesus dead because, says Matthew, they cannot resist God's power and life-giving purpose—the achievement of a just world. For Matthew's readers, followers of Jesus in a world controlled by Rome and its elite, this understanding of Jesus' death empowers them to resist Rome's sinful system and live for God's just and merciful purpose.

Sources. Scholars have established several sources for Matthew's gospel. One source is the Hebrew Bible. Sometimes, Matthew explicitly cites Hebrew Bible texts to interpret events in Jesus' life, as shown, for example, in the references to Isaiah cited above. Constantly the story employs Hebrew Bible language and images such as the references to Passover and "ransom" noted above. It also borrows ways of thinking about how God uses and judges empires like Assyria and Babylon to interpret Rome's actions and fate. For example, the two citations from Isaiah 7-9 in Matthew 1:23 and 4:15-16 recall that God used Assyria to execute judgment on God's people, but God also judged Assyria for not continuing to honor God's purposes. So it will be for Rome (Matthew 22:7; 24:27-31).

Matthew's primary source about Jesus is Mark's gospel written around 70 C.E. Matthew includes most of Mark's gospel, omitting only about 50 verses. He leaves out some references that do not present Jesus in a very positive light. In Mark 6:5 Jesus is powerless to do a miracle ("he cannot do") whereas Matthew uses a more descriptive and positive "he did not do" (Matthew 13:58). Matthew shortens Mark's stories (compare Mark 2:1-12 with Matthew 9:1-8), reorders material, and improves Mark's style. He frequently omits "and immediately," a phrase that Mark often uses to join episodes. Significantly, since Matthew is nearly twice as long as Mark, Matthew adds material. He lengthens Mark's collection of parables (compare Mark 4 with Matthew 13) and Mark's teaching about the end times (Mark 13; Matthew 24-25). Matthew also adds long sections containing Jesus' teaching for his followers, such as the Sermon on the Mount (chapters 5-7) or the community discourse (chapter 18). These sections are not in Mark, so where does this material come from?

This material appears to come from two collections of material about Jesus. Scholars identify one of these as Q, short for the German word *Quelle,* meaning "source." This reconstructed source that developed through the 40s and 50s is not a narrative, but a collection of sayings of Jesus that both Matthew and Luke employ. Schol-

JESUS' RHETORIC AND ANTI-JUDAISM

Jesus' strong condemnation of the Jewish leaders has fed a long and tragic tradition of hostility toward Jews. Shaped by such scenes as the Jerusalem crowd calling for Jesus' crucifixion ("His blood be on us and our children," Matthew 27:25), Christians have at times labeled Jews as "Christ-killers." Awareness of the terrible history and consequences of religious violence is growing as people embrace a multi-religious world. This tragic and hateful legacy is currently being addressed in some Christian churches with the help of recent scholarship that is raising awareness of the issue. Readers of Matthew are coming to understand that Jesus, himself a Jew, is not talking about all Jews for all time, and does not mandate hateful actions from his followers. The attacks are specific to Jesus' criticism of an unjust imperial world and the Jewish leaders who were allies of Rome's agenda. Recognizing the gospel's anti-imperial dynamics acknowledges that Jesus is attacking unjust practices not any ethnic group. Moreover, Christian readers are beginning to understand that Matthew's account is not objective research, but exaggerated and invested polemical writing that reflects the emotional conflict and struggle between Matthew's group and other members of a synagogue in Antioch in the 80s. Studies of ancient polemical writing, including studies of how Jewish writers talk about Jewish opponents, show that Matthew uses conventional rhetorical strategies to identify and attack opponents.

arship has identified another collection of material that is exclusive to Matthew's gospel (from which, for example, the genealogy and birth stories in chapters 1-2 are drawn). Scholars have (imaginatively) identified this material with the letter "M."

Events in History at the Time the Gospel Was Written

Synagogue dispute. Written some 50-60 years after the time of Jesus, Matthew's gospel tells the story of Jesus in a way that addresses the situation of Matthew's largely Jewish audience. This audience consists of Jesus' followers, probably in Antioch. Two events in particular appear to shape Matthew's telling of the story.

The first event is a bitter dispute with a synagogue community in Antioch that seems to have erupted just prior to writing the story. Evidence for this dispute comes from detailed examination of the changes that Matthew consistently makes to his sources. Five times, Matthew distances Jesus from synagogues by adding the term "their synagogues" to material from Mark and Q. This addition often appears where Matthew presents synagogues as hostile to Jesus' disciples or unreceptive to his preaching (Matthew 10:17; 13:54-

58). Matthew furthermore omits positive references to synagogues that appear in Mark and Q and adds negative comments charging synagogues with hypocrisy (Matthew 6:2, 5; 23:6). He increases negative references to Jewish authorities, seven times adding the charge "hypocrite" to other terms of abuse (Matthew 23). Similarly he adds eleven references to scribes, ten of which are negative. He also adds verses to parables to emphasize God's punishment of the Jerusalem leaders.

For example, in the Q material that Matthew uses (Luke 14:16-24), there is a parable of a wealthy and important man who invites guests to a dinner party but they make excuses and cannot come. The host then invites many poor and physically impaired people to come instead. Matthew changes the story in a number of ways (Matthew 22:1-14). Especially important is the addition of a whole verse (22:7) that describes the host's response (Matthew has made him a king to be like God) to the refused invitations. "He sent his troops, destroyed those murderers and burned their city" (Matthew 22:7). This is probably a reference to Jerusalem burned by Rome in 70 C.E. Matthew, like a number of Jewish writers, presents this event as God's punishment on the elite's center of power for rejecting God's purposes as demonstrated in Jesus (compare also Mark 12:11 with Matthew 21:43).

How do we explain Matthew's consistent addition of these attacks against these opponents? Scholars suggest that they reflect a dispute with a synagogue community. Followers of Jesus had been part of a Jewish community (a synagogue) in Antioch, but conflict had increased and relationships were very strained. One of the reasons for writing Matthew's gospel is to explain the deteriorating relationships and to help the followers of Jesus remain loyal in difficult circumstances.

There were reasons for such a conflict. From 66 C.E., Rome and its elite allies in Jerusalem had faced a revolt. After a military campaign, Rome retook Jerusalem, burning the city and destroying the Temple. Some Jewish writers interpreted this event as God's punishment on the people or their leaders for their sins; Matthew agrees with this view (Matthew 22:7). Post-70 C.E. Jewish leaders and communities set about reconstructing Jewish faith and observance without the Temple and wrestling with important questions. How could people know how God wanted them to live? How could people be sure of God's presence? How could people make atonement for sin and find God's forgiveness?

In the debates about these questions, Matthew's community proposed one answer: Jesus. They claimed that Jesus accurately interpreted God's will, which had previously been revealed through Moses (Matthew 5:21-48). Jesus manifested God's reign and God's presence as Emmanuel, "God with us" (Matthew 1:23; 4:17; 18:20; 28:20). Jesus saves from sin in giving his life as a ransom and being raised from the dead (1:21; 9:1-8; 26:26). They claimed, after the Temple's destruction in 70 C.E., that Jesus is the new Temple (Matthew 12:6). Comparisons with Mark and Q show that Matthew adds or heightens these emphases in telling his story of Jesus. Other members of the Jewish community for whatever reasons—their side of the story is unknown—were not convinced. The debate became increasingly bitter. In this context, Matthew wrote the gospel to remind followers of Jesus that, whatever others might say, they are right and they must remain faithful. As Jesus was rejected, so are his followers (Matthew 10:24-25).

Roman power. Rome's military victory in 70 C.E. starkly reconfirmed its great power and unwillingness to tolerate those who would not submit to its rule. Matthew's community probably lived in Antioch, the Roman capital of Syria, where troops, the governor and his personnel, buildings, statues of imperial figures, coins, imperial festivals, temples, and taxes exhibited Roman power daily. The war in Judea against Jerusalem had a high profile in Antioch. Rome's commander (and future emperor) Vespasian assembled troops there. It was Syria that supplied the troops with grain and corn (no doubt at cost to peasants around Antioch). Non-Jewish residents of Antioch rioted against Jews in the city. The victorious general and future emperor Titus visited Antioch in 70-71 en route to celebrations in Rome, displaying captured troops and booty from Jerusalem. Rome minted *Judaea Capta* ("Captive Judea") coins that represented defeated Judea as a subdued woman to broadcast the message of Roman victory. The emperor Vespasian imposed an extra tax on Jews after the defeat to mark them as a conquered people. Rome's world, its power elite and a populace mired in misery, was firmly in place.

In such a world, the followers of Jesus were in a vulnerable position. They devoted themselves to one who had been crucified for criticizing the ruling powers and who had offered a very different vision of human society under God's rule. Matthew's gospel guides them to understand the empire: Rome is allied with the devil (Matthew 4:8), Rome serves currently as an agent of God's purposes to punish Jerusalem, but ultimately God will punish Rome (Matthew 22:7; 24:27-31). Its structures of domination are contrary to God's purposes (20:25-28). In this context, Matthew presents Jesus' teaching. His followers are to live an alternative social experience, nonviolently resisting the status quo, enacting mercy in their city, announcing and embodying God's reign, whatever the consequences (Matthew 5:38-48).

Reception. We have no evidence as to how Matthew's gospel was immediately received by Jesus' followers in Antioch. We can guess, though, that since it told a story already familiar to them and was addressed to their circumstances, it was well received. Also pointing to a positive reception is the widespread use of Matthew's gospel in Christian communities for nearly 2,000 years. In Christian writings from the early centuries of the Church's history, Matthew's gospel, especially Jesus' teaching in the Sermon on the Mount, is the most extensively quoted.

For much of the last 2,000 years, Matthew was read as an eyewitness historical account of Jesus' life written by one of Jesus' 12 disciples. This view has changed significantly since the eighteenth century. The recognition of Matthew's use of sources, of consistent and meaningful changes from Mark's gospel to Matthew's story, and of the specific circumstances of the community from which the gospel derives, has altered the perception of the author's role and identity. Now scholars view the author as an astute theological interpreter of traditions about Jesus. He is seen as a sophisticated storyteller whose account provides pastoral support and direction for his distressed community of Jesus' followers. How much historical information the story contains about Jesus, and how to identify that material from a theologically and pastorally shaped story are issues that scholars continue to debate.

—Warren Carter

For More Information

Blasi, Anthony, Jean Duhaime, and Paul-André Turcotte, eds. *Handbook of Early Christianity: Social Science Approaches.* Walnut Creek: Altamira Press, 2002.

Carter, Warren. *Matthew: Storyteller, Interpreter, Evangelist.* Peabody: Hendrickson, 1996.

———. *Matthew and Empire: Initial Explorations.* Harrisburg: Trinity Press International, 2001.

Crossan, John Dominic. *The Historical Jesus: The Life of a Mediterranean Jewish Peasant.* San Francisco: Harper San Francisco, 1991.

Hanson, K. C., and Douglas E. Oakman. *Palestine in the Time of Jesus: Social Structures and Social Conflicts.* Minneapolis: Fortress Press, 1998.

Harrington, Daniel. *The Gospel of Matthew.* Collegeville: Liturgical Press, 1991.

Johnson, Luke. "The New Testament's Anti-Jewish Slander and the Conventions of Ancient Rhetoric." *Journal of Biblical Literature* 108 (1989): 419-41.

Josephus, Flavius. *Jewish Antiquities.* Vols. 4-9 of *Josephus.* Loeb Classical Library. Trans. H. St. J. Thackeray, R. Marcus, and L. H. Feldman. London: Heinemann, 1926-65.

Lenski, Gerhard. *Power and Privilege: A Theory of Social Stratification.* Chapel Hill: University of North Carolina Press, 1984.

Levine, Amy-Jill. "Visions of Kingdoms: From Pompey to the First Jewish Revolt." In *The Oxford History of the Biblical World.* Ed. Michael Coogan. Oxford: Oxford University Press, 1998.

Matthew. In *The Holy Bible: New Revised Standard Version of the Bible.* Cambridge: Cambridge University Press, 1989.

Saldarini, Anthony J. *Matthew's Christian-Jewish Community.* Chicago: University of Chicago Press, 1994.

Scott, James C. *Domination and the Arts of Resistance: Hidden Transcripts.* New Haven: Yale University Press, 1990.

———. *Weapons of the Weak: Everyday Forms of Peasant Resistance.* New Haven: Yale University, 1985.

Hayy ibn Yaqzan

by

Ibn Tufayl

Although Ibn Tufayl's philosophical tale *Hayy ibn Yaqzan* is one of the most famous medieval Arabic stories to reach the West, precious little is known about the author's biography. Abu Bakr ibn Tufayl was born c. 1116 in Gaudix, 60 kilometers northeast of Granada in al-Andalus, then the Muslim controlled region of southern Spain and North Africa, and he died in 1185. In 1147, when he was about 30 or 31, Ibn Tufayl traveled to Marrakesh (in modern-day Morocco), where he pursued a political career in the Almohad court. After serving for a time as secretary to the governor of Ceuta, Morocco, and Tangier, Morocco, he became the personal physician of the ruling caliph Abu Ya`qub al-Mansur and continued to enjoy his patronage even after stepping down from this post. Apart from *Hayy ibn Yaqzan*, Ibn Tufayl's works include ascetic and mystical poems, political poems calling on Arab tribes to battle Christian invaders, and a "*Rajaz* Poem on Medicine" consisting of more than 7,700 verses on theoretical and practical aspects of medicine. In *Hayy ibn Yaqzan*, he explores some of the most pressing questions of his day about philosophy and religion through the medium of imaginative fiction.

Events in History at the Time of the Tale

Twelfth-century politics in North Africa. Along with the story of *Hayy ibn Yaqzan* comes a universal message—through a person's rational faculties, unaided by human instruction or even language, the person can discover the truths of the

---

THE LITERARY WORK

A philosophical tale set on a deserted island at an unspecified time; composed between 1169 and 1182; printed in Arabic with Latin translation in 1671, in English in 1674.

SYNOPSIS

Isolated from human civilization, the infant Hayy ibn Yaqzan is raised by a gazelle on a deserted island. Through observation, experimentation, and speculation, he develops profound understandings of the physical and celestial realms. He tries, after a fateful visit, to convey these insights to others, with disappointing results.

---

natural world, metaphysics, and divinity. Setting the story on a generic island at an unspecified time helps establish this universality. But despite its indefinite setting, the story features intellectual interests, assumptions, and conclusions that point quite clearly to its origins in twelfth-century Almohad North Africa.

At the time of Ibn Tufayl's birth, Muslim Spain and the Maghrib (North Africa) were under the control of the Almoravids. The dynasty had entered Spain from North Africa in the late eleventh century, coming in response to a petition from the prince of Seville, al-Mu`tamid, who wanted help in staving off the conquering forces of the Christian king Alfonso VI. Al-Mu`tamid got more than he bargained for when the Almoravid prince Tashfin ibn Ali came to his aid and then seized Seville for himself. Soon after, the Almoravids conquered the numerous petty states (*taifa* kingdoms) that made up Muslim Spain. Throughout the period of Almoravid rule, the dynasty fought to protect its holdings from the swelling military might of Christian forces from northern Spain. Ibn Tufayl was no doubt aware of the continually shrinking status of al-Andalus, or Muslim Spain, as the Christian armies advanced in their conquest (generally called the "Reconquest" by Christian historiography).

In the late 1140s, Muslim Spain was conquered by another Muslim dynasty from North Africa, the Almohads, whose origins hark back to the early twelfth-century spiritual leader Muhammad ibn Tumart. Proclaiming himself "Mahdi" ("Rightly Guided One," who, it was believed, would rise to power just before the end of time), Ibn Tumart led an unsuccessful revolt against the Almoravids. His successor Abd al-Mu'min, however, conquered the Almoravid capital of Marrakesh in North Africa in 1145 and then proceeded to topple the Almoravids in al-Andalus as well.

It was in 1147, the year of the Almohad conquest of al-Andalus, that Ibn Tufayl journeyed to Marrakesh to seek a career at the nascent Almohad court, becoming a secretary in 1152, then court physician a decade later. Like the Almoravid period, the years of Almohad rule in al-Andalus saw unrelenting conflict with Christian forces from the north. Perhaps in response to the persistent conflict, the Almohads adopted an intolerant form of Islam that led to the persecution of Jews and Christians, one of the rare episodes of widespread forced conversion in Islamic history.

It was Ibn Tufayl's good fortune to serve at the court of Abu Ya`qub al-Mansur, one of the few Almohad rulers sympathetic to the pursuit of philosophy. In general the anti-philosophical thought of al-Ghazzali (1058-1111) dominated Almohad ideology. According to the thirteenth-century author Ibn Sa`id al-Andalusi (died 1286), Andalusian intellectuals remained unaccomplished in the art of philosophy and astronomy because the suspicions of the masses kept creativity in check, "Both of these [philosophy and astronomy] are of great interest to the elite, but no work on these topics can be undertaken openly out of fear of the common folk" (Ibn Sa`id al-Andalusi in Conrad, p. 10). Because of the anti-philosophical trend that became particularly fierce after Ibn Tufayl's death, Ibn Rushd (more commonly known by his Latin name, Averroes;

1126-1198), Ibn Tufayl's successor as court physician and the most renowned Arab philosopher to reach the West, was exiled from the court of Cordoba, Spain, and remained relatively unknown in the Islamic world as a philosopher (though he did maintain a reputation as a jurist). Read against this background, *Hayy ibn Yaqzan* stands out as a bold contribution to philosophy in the Almohad period in that it contains a defense of the philosophical project and an admonition against its neglect.

Twelfth-century Islamic philosophy. Far more apparent in *Hayy ibn Yaqzan* than contemporary political events is the state of intellectual achievement in al-Andalus and the Maghrib in Ibn Tufayl's day. Ibn Tufayl was well-trained not only in traditional Islamic teaching but also in the philosophical tradition of Muslim thinkers who had expanded upon the works of classical philosophers and natural scientists (such as Plato, Aristotle, Galen, Plotinus) known to the Islamic world through Arabic translations. In fact, for the most part, Aristotelian and Neoplatonic physics and metaphysics informed Ibn Tufayl's worldview. The earth was a sphere surrounded by concentric spheres in which the planets were embedded. The heart was the seat of the human soul, which consisted of three parts, the "rational soul" (unique to humans), the "animal soul" (common to humans and animals), and the "vegetative soul" (common to humans, animals and plants). The human body was a microcosm, a model of the universe in miniature.

Muslim philosophers in the East (al-Farabi and Ibn Sina, known by his Latin name, Avicenna) and in Spain (Ibn Bajjah—in Latin, Avempace) speculated about the identity of God. With their help, Muslims developed a view of God as an incorporeal Being, despite the many references in the Quran to humanlike characteristics (similar discussions were held among Jews and Christians about anthropomorphic descriptions of God in the Bible). God was understood to be the First Mover of Aristotelian physics, the originator who brought about the world either through an act of Will or out of Necessity, as explained by Aristotle (in the fourth century B.C.E). To concur with the later (third century C.E.) Neoplatonic view of creation, the scriptural creation story was often interpreted allegorically as a chain of successive emanations from God (called the One). (All existence, said the Neoplatonic philosophers, emanated from the One, with whom the soul could be reunited.) One hotly debated topic (about which Ibn Tufayl remained uncertain) was whether the world was "created in time," as religious tradition maintained, or was "eternal," as Aristotle held.

Despite the numerous achievements in Islamic philosophy (yet to reach its apex with Ibn Rushd), Ibn Tufayl remained frustrated by the limits of these achievements and by the scarcity of sources. His dissatisfaction with intellectual progress in his day is apparent in the introduction to *Hayy ibn Yaqzan,*

> Do not suppose that the philosophy which has reached us in the books of Aristotle and or in Avicenna's *Healing* will satisfy you . . . or that any Andalusian has written anything adequate on this subject. . . . Our contemporaries are as yet at a developmental stage.
> (Ibn Tufayl, *Hayy ibn Yaqzan*, pp. 99-100)

Hayy ibn Yaqzan is more than a fictional tale that digests and popularizes the intellectual traditions of al-Andalus. Rather, it braids together various intellectual strains—philosophical and mystical—to produce a unique and original synthesis. The tale participates in the "developmental" process its writer ascribes to philosophy in his day.

Although Ibn Tufayl was recognized by scholars in the East and West primarily as a *faylasuf*, a philosopher, there are undeniable leanings toward Sufism (Islamic mysticism) throughout *Hayy ibn Yaqzan*. In general, Sufis (despite their variety) sought to achieve states of spiritual intimacy with the Divine through such practices as fasting, prayer, wearing simple garments of wool (Arabic, *suf*, hence "Sufi"), repetitive movements and chanting the name of God (called *dhikr*). According to some, the spiritual seeker could attain a state of intimacy with the Divine wherein the boundary between seeker and object (i.e., God) would become obliterated.

Ibn Tufayl has not been identified as a member of any of the specific Sufi orders of his day. Yet his writing shows an awareness of and appreciation for some of Sufism's general goals and motifs. He may have studied Sufism while residing in Marrakesh, a prominent Sufi center in the Almohad period. The introduction of *Hayy ibn Yaqzan* contains an apology for the ecstatic utterances of famous Sufis charged with blasphemy; their statements, according to Ibn Tufayl, have been misconstrued simply because it is impossible to explain mystical experience through language. His protagonist, Hayy, adopts habits reminiscent of Sufi practices (asceticism, leaving his cave only once a week to obtain food, moving in circular motions like the famous "whirling dervishes" of the Mawlawi [or Mevleviyeh] Sufi order). As noted, Ibn Tufayl was pri-

The renowned Eastern philosopher Ibn Sina (Avicenna), an imaginative rendering.

marily a philosopher; nevertheless, the author of one thirteenth-century Sufi biographical work (*Kitab al-tashawwuf ila rijal al-tasawuff* [Book of Longing for the Men of Sufism]), Ibn al-Zayyat, cites Ibn Tufayl as his own teacher's mentor (Cornell, p. 136).

The Tale in Focus

Plot summary. Early translations of *Hayy ibn Yaqzan* unfortunately omit the important introduction in which the author sets forth his reasons for composing the text and paints a picture of the state of intellectual achievement in his day. As is the case with many medieval Arabic texts, the author addresses his work to a petitioner who has asked for clarification on a particular point, in this case the philosophy of the renowned Eastern philosopher Ibn Sina.

Ibn Tufayl writes that the petitioner's questions stimulated him such that he was elevated to an indescribable state of sublimity. It is in such a state of sublimity, Ibn Tufayl writes, that certain Muslim mystics would utter radical, even blasphemous statements, such as the martyr al-Hallaj's (died 922) cry "I am the Truth!" (a name for God), seeming to identify himself with God (see **Murder in Baghdad,** also in *WLAIT 6: Middle Eastern Literatures and Their Times*). Ibn

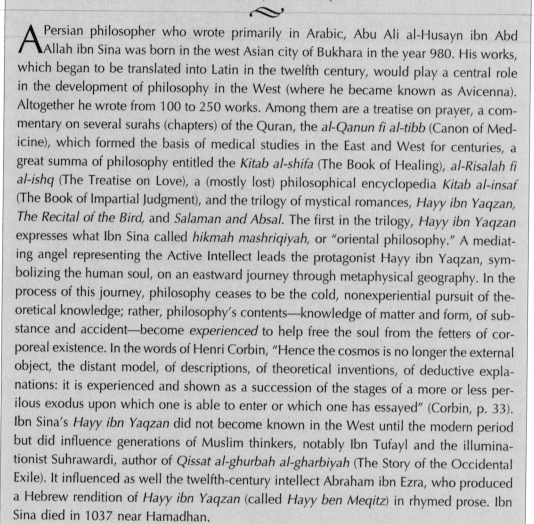

IBN SINA (AVICENNA)

A Persian philosopher who wrote primarily in Arabic, Abu Ali al-Husayn ibn Abd Allah ibn Sina was born in the west Asian city of Bukhara in the year 980. His works, which began to be translated into Latin in the twelfth century, would play a central role in the development of philosophy in the West (where he became known as Avicenna). Altogether he wrote from 100 to 250 works. Among them are a treatise on prayer, a commentary on several surahs (chapters) of the Quran, the *al-Qanun fi al-tibb* (Canon of Medicine), which formed the basis of medical studies in the East and West for centuries, a great summa of philosophy entitled the *Kitab al-shifa* (The Book of Healing), *al-Risalah fi al-ishq* (The Treatise on Love), a (mostly lost) philosophical encyclopedia *Kitab al-insaf* (The Book of Impartial Judgment), and the trilogy of mystical romances, *Hayy ibn Yaqzan, The Recital of the Bird,* and *Salaman and Absal.* The first in the trilogy, *Hayy ibn Yaqzan* expresses what Ibn Sina called *hikmah mashriqiyah,* or "oriental philosophy." A mediating angel representing the Active Intellect leads the protagonist Hayy ibn Yaqzan, symbolizing the human soul, on an eastward journey through metaphysical geography. In the process of this journey, philosophy ceases to be the cold, nonexperiential pursuit of theoretical knowledge; rather, philosophy's contents—knowledge of matter and form, of substance and accident—become *experienced* to help free the soul from the fetters of corporeal existence. In the words of Henri Corbin, "Hence the cosmos is no longer the external object, the distant model, of descriptions, of theoretical inventions, of deductive explanations: it is experienced and shown as a succession of the stages of a more or less perilous exodus upon which one is able to enter or which one has essayed" (Corbin, p. 33). Ibn Sina's *Hayy ibn Yaqzan* did not become known in the West until the modern period but did influence generations of Muslim thinkers, notably Ibn Tufayl and the illuminationist Suhrawardi, author of *Qissat al-ghurbah al-gharbiyah* (The Story of the Occidental Exile). It influenced as well the twelfth-century intellect Abraham ibn Ezra, who produced a Hebrew rendition of *Hayy ibn Yaqzan* (called *Hayy ben Meqitz*) in rhymed prose. Ibn Sina died in 1037 near Hamadhan.

Tufayl sympathizes with the dilemma of mystical experience—once one achieves a sublime state in which the distinction between self and God is obliterated, the experience becomes inexpressible through language. He illustrates this with a well-known verse by al-Ghazzali,

It *was*—what it was is harder to say.
Think the best, but don't make me describe it away.

(*Hayy ibn Yaqzan,* p. 96)

Any attempt to convey the sublime mystical experience only leads to misunderstanding. Thus, rather than offering a description of his own experience of ecstasy, Ibn Tufayl will present a fictional account, the tale of how one man achieved ecstasy using nothing but his faculties. That man is Hayy ibn Yaqzan, whose name literally means "Alive, son of Awake."

Hayy has been nursed, weaned, and raised by a gazelle on a "certain equatorial island lying off the coast of India," which, in medieval Arabic literature, is somewhat like setting a story in a "distant galaxy far far away" (*Hayy ibn Yaqzan,* p. 103). The author alerts the reader to the fictional nature of the narrative by presenting two alternate versions of how Hayy arrived on the island. In one version, Hayy came to life spontaneously out of clay, thanks to the superlative temperateness of the equatorial climate. In the second version, the sister of a tyrant king married a kinsman in secret, far from the eyes of her brother, who insisted on choosing her spouse himself. Soon she conceived and bore a child and, fearing her royal brother's wrath, cast the infant into the sea in a casket, praying for the baby's protection (a scene reminiscent of the Moses story in the Quran [20:39; 28:7]). A current carried the casket to a deserted island and lodged it in a thicket that protected it from inclement weather. When the baby grew hungry, his cries alerted a gazelle that nursed him from her udder.

By the age of two, Hayy learned to walk and went foraging with his gazelle-mother. He grew up among other gazelles, eating and sleeping with them and mimicking their various sounds. Soon Hayy discovered the physical differences between himself and the animals. At first he took these differences for his own deficiencies; he was naked because he lacked fur; he recognized too that he was physically weaker than the animals and unequipped with defensive attributes such as horns or claws. Later, at the age of seven, he realized he had an advantage over the other animals. He alone could use tools to clothe and protect himself. Hayy began to reason for practical purposes.

During Hayy's seventh year, his gazelle-mother grew ill and died, which led to perhaps the most transformative experience of Hayy's life. Hoping that he might heal the gazelle, using tools he himself had fashioned, he split open her chest and explored her organs. Reaching the same conclusion as Aristotle, Hayy reasoned that, that which renders the body without sensation or motion must be located in the heart. His mother was gone; only her lifeless body was left, low and worthless. Hayy was distinguishing between the being that had been his mother and the body she occupied.

Hayy soon fashioned himself a home and learned to control fire for warmth. He expanded his diet, learned to roast fish and meat and became a hunter. With great diligence, he pursued the questions his mind raised about the nature of life. He dissected and vivisected various animals, "improving the quality of his mind" until he reached "the level of the finest natural scientists" (Hayy ibn Yaqzan, p. 117).

At age 21, Hayy moved beyond this hands-on approach to the natural sciences and began to consider in his mind all entities that generate and decay in the world (plants, animals, minerals, water, steam, ice, snow, fire, smoke). He contemplated the qualities they share and those that differentiate one from the other. Considering collections of animals, he thought of them not only as individual beings but also as species and then of the entire animal kingdom as a unit. Next he

did the same with plants. And then he compared plants and animals, finding them to be alike in nutrition and growth but different in sense perception, locomotion, and sensation. He concluded that all bodies, whether animate or inanimate, share the quality of physicality. Hayy was thinking abstractly.

Recognizing that something apart from corporeality must distinguish animals from plants and inanimate objects, Hayy began to contemplate the spiritual world, which "cannot be apprehended by the senses, but only by reasoning" (Hayy ibn Yaqzan, p. 123). He discovered what philosophers call the "animal soul" and the "vegetative soul" and sought to understand the nature of the soul, much as he had sought to understand the nature of the body after the death of his gazelle-mother. Ultimately Hayy reached many of the same conclusions as the philosophers of Ibn Tufayl's day: all objects are composed of matter and form, everything that comes into being must have some cause, and so forth.

In his search for causes, Hayy postulated that there must be some Cause of all causes. Unable to find this Cause in the sensory world, he speculated further concerning the celestial realm and metaphysics. By way of experiments carried out through reason only, Hayy concluded (agreeing with Aristotle) that the physical universe is finite. By observing the motions of the heavenly bodies, he learned that the firmament is spherical.

Hayy also contemplated one of the most fiercely debated topics of Ibn Tufayl's day, whether, as religious tradition holds, the universe was created from nothing (ex nihilo) in time or whether, as Aristotle maintained, it is eternal. Neither solution seemed wholly satisfactory to him. Unable to resolve the issue, Hayy reached an astounding realization—both premises lead to a single conclusion. If the world was created in time, then it was created through the will of a Maker, the Cause of all causes, who cannot be apprehended by the senses. If the world is eternal, then the cause of its eternal motion must be an incorporeal Mover. Hayy in this way came to know what medieval philosophers understood to be God, the Unmoved Mover, the ontological cause of the world, whose eternal, unwavering existence, beneficence, and mercy sustain the world. The twelfth-century Jewish philosopher Maimonides would reach a similar conclusion.

Reaching the age of 35, Hayy becomes solely concerned with understanding this Being, believing that coming to know the Necessarily Existent before death is the key to everlasting joy and

HEPTADIC STAGES OF DEVELOPMENT

In the modern field of developmental psychology, Erik H. Erikson was influential for his epigenetic theory of personality development, which taught that critical elements of human personality unfold according to a hardwired plan, just as physical growth does. Like many aspects of modern thought, this system has ancient and medieval precursors, albeit with significant differences. The Greek poet Solon was probably the first to delineate the "ages of man," according to which the human being develops in ten distinguishable stages of seven years each (for this reason the system is called "septennial" or "heptadic"). In keeping with this scheme, Hayy ibn Yaqzan's cognitive and intellectual faculties develop according to a heptadic system. Each stage allows for achievements beyond Hayy's grasp at the previous stage. Up until age seven, Hayy is a child dependent upon his "mother" for nourishment and acts on the basis of instinct and imitation. From ages seven to 21, Hayy uses reason toward practical ends, creating tools and experiments to learn about the natural world. At 21, he begins to contemplate metaphysics and at 28, he uses pure reason to examine such abstract problems as the finite or infinite nature of the universe and whether the universe is created in time or is eternal. In the remaining seven-year stages (through age 49), Hayy seeks to know God through spiritual exercises that lead to his having the sublime experience of obliterating the distinctions between himself and the object of his contemplation.

delight. He quickly recognizes that his senses are of no use in this pursuit, since the Being is incorporeal. Encountering no other being on earth that pursues knowledge of the Being, he turns his attention toward the heavenly bodies, which he surmises must have knowledge of the Necessarily Existent since they are not subject to the hindrances of sensory distractions. Hayy believes that he is a species apart from the other animals, more akin to the celestial bodies. Even on the level of physical resemblance, he sees his body as a microcosm of the cosmos.

Hayy supposes that he can achieve understanding of the Necessarily Existent by imitating animals, celestial beings, and the Maker Himself in various ways. So he seeks to emulate the actions of the heavenly beings, even as he accepts that his body, like that of animals, requires sustenance and care. He swears to eat only the bare minimum of food, limiting his diet to only vegetables and fruits in order to preserve the work of the Creator. When he consumes fruits and vegetables, he is careful to disperse the seeds so that the species will not perish. He resorts to eating meat only when nourishing vegetables are unavailable and even then takes only from what is most abundant. He aids all plant and animal life, thereby imitating heavenly beings

(because they offer nourishment and protection). Also he keeps his body immaculately clean (because the stars are luminous and untainted), moves in Sufi-like circular motions (to imitate orbits), and fixes his mind on the Necessarily Existent Being. Soon afterward, Hayy tries to rid himself of his physical being entirely, sitting secluded in a meditative state without eating or moving. Ultimately the world of the senses melts away, even self-consciousness and identity, such that all that remains is the One, the True Being. Through nothing but his power of reason, Hayy has acquired the sum total of philosophical and theological teaching in Ibn Tufayl's day, mastering both physics and metaphysics.

However, the philosophical tale does not end here. One day, Hayy encounters Absal, a human from a nearby island who has come to Hayy's island in search of spiritual solitude. The guest, of course, baffles Hayy, who has never before set eyes on such a being. Absal hails from an island where all of the inhabitants adhere to an unnamed "true religion" that bears striking similarities to Islam. The religion is based on the teachings of a "certain ancient prophet" and has its own "Law" (called Shari`ah, the Arabic term for Islamic law proper); there are obligations to pray, fast, make pilgrimage and give charity (four of Islam's "Five Pillars"). Absal's practices of asceticism and spiritual solitude mimic the Sufi methods; having sworn off his worldly possessions, dressed in a woolen cloak (like Sufis), he spends his days in the service of God, eating little and contemplating His "most beautiful names and divine attributes" (*Hayy ibn Yaqzan*, p. 157).

Both Hayy and Absal refrain from their pursuit of sublimity in order to learn more about each other. Absal teaches Hayy to speak and Hayy recounts all he has experienced and learned. Absal listens attentively to Hayy's experiences beyond the sensory world, concluding that "all the traditions of his [Absal's] religion about God, His angels, bibles and prophets, Judgement Day, and Heaven are symbolic representations of these things that Hayy ibn Yaqzan had seen for himself" (*Hayy ibn Yaqzan*, p. 160). Absal then teaches Hayy about the deficiencies of human civilization, whereupon Hayy develops pity for humans and a desire to save them.

By God's command, a misguided ship finds Hayy and Absal on the shore and ferries them back to Absal's island. Recognizing (like many medieval philosphers) that the masses may not be amenable to his teachings, Hayy speaks only to an educated elite, headed by Absal's friend Salaman. Salaman and his circle, while steadfast in the practice of religion, are unfamiliar with the symbolic nature of the Law. Despite initial hopes, Hayy is unable to persuade even this group to think beyond the constraints of the physical world and the literal interpretation of their religion.

> Hayy ibn Yaqzan began to teach this group and explain some of his profound wisdom to them. But the moment he rose the slightest bit above the literal or began to portray things against which they were prejudiced, they recoiled in horror from his ideas and closed their minds . . . the more he taught, the more repugnance they felt, despite the fact that these were men who loved the good and sincerely yearned for the Truth. Their inborn infirmity simply would not allow them to seek Him as Hayy did, to grasp the true essence of His being and see Him in His own terms.
>
> (*Hayy ibn Yaqzan*, p. 163)

With resignation, Hayy accepts that these humans can do no better than continue on their present course of literal adherence to the Law and never achieve the "level of the blessed" (*Hayy ibn Yaqzan*, p. 165). Hayy and Absal return to the deserted island, again achieve states of spiritual ecstasy, and so serve God until death overtakes them.

The critique of orthodox Islam. Most of Western scholarship has stressed the philosophical dimension of *Hayy ibn Yaqzan*, focusing on the story up to the point of Hayy's sublime experience. However, it is from the tale's second part, following the appearance of Absal, that one can decipher Ibn Tufayl's attitudes toward contemporary religious belief and practice.

As noted, the religion of Absal's island bears a striking resemblance to Islamic practice. The Law of the island dwellers contains statements in favor of a life of solitude but other statements in favor of social integration and community involvement. Ibn Tufayl contrasts these two aspects of Islam through the characters of Absal and his friend Salaman.

> Absal devoted himself to the quest for solitude, preferring the words of the Law in its favor because he was naturally a thoughtful man, fond of contemplation and of probing for the deeper meaning of things; and he did find the most propitious time for seeking what he hoped for to be when he was alone. But Salaman preferred being among people and gave greater weight to the sayings of the Law in favor of society, since he was by nature chary of too much independent thinking or doing. In staying with the group he saw some means of fending off demonic promptings, dispelling distracting thoughts, and in general guarding against the goadings of the devil.
>
> (*Hayy ibn Yaqzan*, p. 157)

Prior to Absal's sojourn on Hayy's island, Absal and Salaman studied together, ardently maintaining the same beliefs about God, angels, resurrection, and reward and punishment. While both men were passionate adherents of the religion, Absal was a reflective and ascetic spiritualist who read the Law allegorically while Salaman was a political ruler concerned with the literal meaning of the Law and the outward performance of religious precepts. The story presents both paths as valid alternatives, but not equally so; in fact, there is a clear preference for the contemplative-allegorical approach and a rather unsubtle critique of an anti-philosophical orthodox Islam.

The critique is illustrated most strikingly through the ironic usage of a Quranic quotation in the text. As Absal teaches Hayy about the religious Law of his island, Hayy is dumbfounded by references to the corporeal existence of God, laws dealing with property and money, and the absence of general ethical teachings such as the curbing of wealth and of gluttony. Why did the prophet not describe God as an incorporeal entity and offer ethical prescriptions concerning moderation (like those of Aristotle and Plato)? According to Hayy, if people understood the truth as he had come to know it, they would not quibble over money or own personal property and would take only what was necessary to survive. Here the narrator inserts,

> What made him [Hayy] think so was his naïve belief that all men had outstanding character, brilliant minds and resolute spirits. He had no idea how stupid, inadequate, thoughtless, and weak willed they are, "like sheep gone astray, only worse."
>
> (*Hayy ibn Yaqzan*, p. 162)

The final part of the quotation is from the Quran (25:44), from a passage that censures the pagans of Mecca for not accepting Muhammad's revelation. By directing this charge against the believers on Absal's island who, after all, did follow the basic precepts of their "true religion," Ibn Tufayl is making a thinly veiled critique of institutional Islam in his day.

Like many of his contemporary philosophers, Ibn Tufayl held the uneducated masses in low regard. Yet, his critique is not leveled against the masses only. Also members of the elite, the men of learning and power under Salaman, are neither willing nor capable of grasping Hayy's teachings. They do not see that the teachings of their faith are merely symbols, garments for the truth that Hayy attained through his philosophical and spiritual engagement. In Ibn Tufayl's view, proper religious practice entailed speculation, meditation, and an allegorical approach toward law beyond what is required through the practice of precepts and literalist interpretation.

While Ibn Tufayl would not have advocated a renunciation of religious practice in favor of meditation and asceticism alone (even Hayy becomes a "believer" to some extent and adopts basic tenets of Absal's religion), his critique of the limits of orthodox Islam is striking. Ibn Tufayl insisted upon the equivalence of philosophy and religion. In contrast, the rising orthodox view in his day held in contempt speculation and the allegorical interpretation of the Quran. *Hayy Ibn Yaqzan* may be his way of advising the ruling Almohad dynasty, Ibn Tufayl's sometime patrons, to resist the growing orthodox trend. The disparaging portrayal of Salaman and his circle was certainly intended as an admonition to the ruling elite to not devalue the philosophical endeavor. Not long after Ibn Tufayl's death, an intolerant, orthodox form of Islam did predominate (partly as a unifying ideology to resist the Christian Reconquest), and it indeed stamped out the philosophical strain of theology.

Although not addressed explicitly, an important question grows out of Ibn Tufayl's narration with regard to the validity of other religious traditions. If the specific practices and teachings of Islam are really only metaphors for a truth that Hayy reached without instruction, then could not the practices and teachings of other religions (at least monotheistic ones) be equally valid metaphors for that same truth? There is no evidence that Ibn Tufayl saw this relativist suggestion as a logical corollary of his theory of the symbolic nature of revealed religion. That is, we do not know that he saw this conclusion as a necessary outcome of his theory that the tenets of revealed religion are only metaphors for truth. If he did, it may have been beyond the literary freedom of his time to espouse such a suggestion. In any case, the universal teaching of *Hayy ibn Yaqzan* attracted non-Muslims. There survives an anonymous medieval Hebrew translation, a Hebrew commentary by the fourteenth-century Jewish philosopher Moses of Narbonne, and a fifteenth-century Latin translation (from the Hebrew) by Giovanni Francesco Pico della Mirandola. *Hayy ibn Yaqzan* would enjoy an even warmer reception in late-seventeenth-century Europe.

Sources and literary context. *Hayy ibn Yaqzan* bears the imprint of diverse sources, including (among others) the Quran and *hadith* (sayings of and about the prophet Muhammad), Mu`tazilite theology, medical and mathematical works, al-Ghazzali's *Mishkat al-anwar* (The Niche of Lights), Sufi literature, and of course, the work's predecessor of the same name, *Hayy ibn Yaqzan* by Ibn Sina, the famous philosopher of the Islamic East about whom Ibn Tufayl's petitioner had inquired. Ibn Sina's work is a symbolic tale of an almost dreamlike quality in which a Sage named Hayy ibn Yaqzan (representing the Active Intellect) guides the narrator (representing the Human Soul) on a journey through metaphysical geography—through the realms of matter and form—ultimately to meet the Divine King. The names of Ibn Tufayl's other main characters are borrowed from another of Ibn Sina's allegorical tales, *Salaman and Absal.*

Perhaps the most surprising source of influence is an Alexander romance that is preserved fragmentarily in Arabic. In this story, the infant of a royal family is cast away at sea but is miraculously delivered to an island refuge where he is raised by a deer. Unlike Hayy, however, the youth begins to acquire knowledge only when encountered by another human being (who turns out to be his father). Despite the similarities, the stories lead to opposite conclusions. Knowledge in the Alexander romance comes through instruction and convention; in *Hayy ibn Yaqzan,* it is acquired naturally.

Publication and reception. Little is known concerning the reception of *Hayy ibn Yaqzan* in the medieval period apart from the survival of a handful of Arabic manuscripts and the Hebrew and Latin translations. The tale was first published in the West in 1671 by Edward Pococke with an introduction by his father, a renowned professor of Arabic and Hebrew at Oxford University. Translating it into Latin, Edward Pococke bestowed a title upon the work that betrays his own particular reading: *Philosophus autodidactus, sive epistola Abi Jaafar, Ebn Tophail de Hai Ebn Yokdhan. In qua Ostenditur, quomodo ex Inferiorum contemplatione ad Superiorum notitiam Ratio humana ascendere posit* (Self-taught philosopher: in which it is demonstrated by what means human reason can ascend from contemplation of the Inferior to knowledge of the Superior). By privileging the first part of the tale (up until Hayy's attainment of the sublime) over the second (Hayy's sojourn in the land of Absal), Pococke revealed the interests of his fellow late-seventeenth-century philosophers: Is religion natural or practiced only out of convention? Is the concept of God self-evident or derived through rational speculation? It has been suggested that the striking similarity between the self-taught philosopher and John Locke's famous claim that the human mind is a *tabula rasa* (blank slate) at birth is more than mere coincidence. Locke had personal connections to the Pocockes, both father and son, and began his drafts for his *Essay on Human Understanding* in the same year that Pococke's edition of *Hayy ibn Yaqzan* appeared. Pococke's Latin translation circulated among intellectuals throughout Europe and was soon retranslated into Dutch, German and English. First and foremost, *Hayy ibn Yaqzan* attained a reputation as a book of philosophy that espoused the natural philosophers' conviction that human reason, as long as it remained unhindered, was a reliable tool for learning the mysteries of the world, metaphysics, and God. There has been speculation that beyond this service,

Hayy ibn Yaqzan played a role in shaping Daniel Defoe's *Robinson Crusoe* (1717). Though this classic is likewise an adventure of isolation and fortitude set on a deserted island, significant plot differences allow for limited comparison only. In the modern Arab world, *Hayy ibn Yaqzan* continues to be reprinted frequently and to occupy a place in popular imagination through paintings, films, and television specials.

—Jonathan P. Decter

For More Information

Bürgel, J. C. "Ibn Tufayl and His *Hayy Ibn Yaqzan*: A Turning Point in Arabic Philosophical Writing." In *The Legacy of Muslim Spain.* Ed. Salma K. Jayyusi. Leiden: E. J. Brill, 1992.

Conrad, Lawrence I., ed. *The World of Ibn Tufayl: Interdisciplinary Perspectives on Hayy ibn Yaqzan.* Leiden: E. J. Brill, 1996.

Corbin, Henri. *History of Islamic Philosophy.* Trans. Liadain Sherrard. London: Kegan Paul, 1993.

Cornell, Vincent J. "Hayy in the Land of Absal: Ibn Tufayl and Sufism in the Western Maghrib during the Muwahhid Era." In *The World of Ibn Tufayl.* Ed. Lawrence I. Conrad. Leiden: E. J. Brill, 1996.

Hawi, Sami S. *Islamic Naturalism and Mysticism: A Philosophic Study of Ibn Tufayl's Hayy bin Yaqzan.* Leiden: E. J. Brill, 1974.

Hourani, George F. "The Principal Subject of Ibn Tufayl's *Hayy ibn Yaqzan*." *Journal of Near Eastern Studies* 15 (1956): 40-46.

Ibn Tufayl. *Ibn Tufayl's Hayy ibn Yaqzan: A Philosophical Tale.* Trans. Lenn Evan Goodman. New York: Twayne, 1972.

Malti-Douglas, Fedwa. "*Hayy ibn Yaqzan* as Male Utopia." In *The World of Ibn Tufayl.* Ed. Lawrence I. Conrad. Leiden: E. J. Brill, 1996.

Russell, G. A. "The Influence of *The Philosophus Autodidactus*: Pocockes, John Locke, and the Society of Friends." In *The "Arabick" Interest of the Natural Philosophers in Seventeenth-Century England.* Ed. G. A. Russell. Leiden: E. J. Brill, 1994.

Vajda, Georges. "Comment le philosophe juif Moïse de Narbonne, commentateur d'Ibn Tufayl comprenait-il les paroles extatiques (*satahat*) des soufis." In *Actas del primer congreso de estudios árabes e islámicos.* Madrid: Comité permanente del Congreso de estudios árabes e islámicos, 1964.

Human Landscapes from My Country

by

Nazim Hikmet

Nazim Hikmet (1902-63), the foremost poet of modern Turkish literature, had a turbulent life, full of prison sentences and exile because of his uncompromising commitment to freedom and justice. He was born in Salonica (now Thessalonica in Greece) in 1902 to a family of the cosmopolitan Ottoman elite. Hikmet studied French at a prestigious high school in Istanbul, then attended the Naval Academy, where he wrote his first poems. He traveled to Anatolia to join the anti-imperialist resistance against the occupation of Turkey after the First World War, and afterward to Russia. There he studied economics and sociology at the Communist University for the Workers of the East in Moscow and encountered revolutionary currents of thought. Hikmet was influenced by the ideology of Vladimir Ilich Lenin as well as the avant-garde artistic experiments of the poets Sergei Esenin and Vladimir Mayakovsky, and by the theatre director Vsevolod Meyerhold. His encounters with the effects of war and poverty inspired Hikmet to create a new poetry, innovative in language and form, written *for* the people and *about* the people. Returning to Turkey in 1928, he became the leader of an avant-garde movement in literature, publishing several collections of poems, essays, and plays that promoted his innovations. In 1938, after being arrested several times for his outspoken political views, Hikmet was sentenced to 28 years in prison by a military court on false charges of inciting revolt in the armed forces. In jail he encountered peasants, workers, the unemployed, and other common people whose lives became the collective

THE LITERARY WORK

An epic poem set mainly in Turkey between 1908 and 1950; complete version published in Turkish (as *Memleketimden insan manzaralari*) in 1966-67, in English in 2002.

SYNOPSIS

The epic highlights the struggles of ordinary heroes in the class conflict of the early-to-mid twentieth century.

source for his epic poetry. Released in 1950 and forced to live in exile thereafter, Hikmet died in 1963, the best-known poet of Turkey at the time but ironically a non-Turkish citizen banished from his homeland (his works would be banned in Turkey until the mid-1960s). Hikmet left behind more than 20 collections of poetry, three novels, two fairytale collections, 25 plays, and two collections of letters. His most ambitious project, *Human Landscapes from My Country* is an "episodic saga" that covers 42 years and includes dozens of "common" life stories not recorded in the official histories.

Events in History at the Time of the Epic

A war-torn age. *Human Landscapes* spans the years 1908 to 1950, nearly half a century. The era is a tumultuous one, encompassing two world wars, the Bolshevik and Chinese revolutions, and the anti-imperialist struggles in Turkey, as well as other occupied or colonized territories of the world.

Economic and territorial rivalries among Great Britain, Germany, France, Austria-Hungary, and Russia intensified at the end of the nineteenth century. Among the zones of contention was the decaying Ottoman Empire; the question of its partition, the "Eastern Question," was continuously being raised. The powers avoided serious conflict through a carefully balanced alliance system, which was upset by the assassination of Archduke Ferdinand after Austria annexed Bosnia Hercegovina. The assassination touched off the First World War (1914-18). After four grim years, the Allies (England, France, Russia, the United States, and others) defeated the Axis powers (Germany, Austria-Hungary, the Ottoman Empire, and others) at the cost of 10 million dead and 20 million wounded. Minimum estimates, these figures do not include all the deaths caused by starvation and epidemics once the war ended. Hikmet comments on the staggering toll in *Human Landscapes:* "Mehmets [common name for privates in the Turkish army] everywhere, everywhere troops on the move. / They leave hungry and thirsty, they come back crippled" (Hikmet, *Human Landscapes*, p. 37).

Postwar peace treaties radically changed the map of Europe and the Middle East. The Ottoman Empire disintegrated, and states such as Syria and Iraq were brought into existence. Meanwhile, Germany, held responsible for initiating the war, was burdened with huge reparations payments. Along with other factors, these payments led to an economic crisis that helped fuel the rise of Nazism—the German policy of racist nationalism, expansionism, and government economic control that led to World War II.

The October Revolution of 1917. In late 1917, after weathering successive internal revolutions (February 24-29 and October 24-25), Russia dropped out of the First World War. The Russian Revolution, which overthrew the imperial regime and brought to power the first Communist government, erupted after a long period of unrest under the autocratic rule of a tsar. Coming to Russia from Germany in 1917, Lenin galvanized the Bolshevik political party into action. He sallied forth with slogans such as "End the War," "All Land to the Peasants," and "All Power to the Soviets [workers' and soldiers' councils]"; the slogans attracted both intellectuals, who were either politically radical or romantically humanitarian, and the workers and peasants, who were tired of food shortages, military recruitments, and battlefront defeats.

Nazim Hikmet

Victorious, the Communists established a new government that aimed to construct a society on socialist premises. Peace remained elusive, however, as the Entente Powers (United States, Britain, France, and Japan) came to the aid of the anti-Bolshevik forces in Russia, attacking from all directions. The four-year civil war wreaked havoc on the country, crippling it with famine and casualties, which became the topic of "The Eyes of Hunger" (1922), one of Hikmet's early successful poems. At the same time, the revolution brought a dynamism to the environment that made Moscow a center of intellectual activity, especially until Lenin's death in 1924. Hikmet, thriving in this atmosphere from 1922 to 1928, carried back to Turkey the lively spirit, as evident in his poem "Optimism" (1930): "Believe in this: we'll see beautiful days my children / sunny days / we'll see / We'll sail our boats to the blue seas my children / to the bright blue seas / we'll sail" (Hikmet, *Şiirler 1*, p. 190; trans. I. Çelik). During Lenin's rule and after his death, however, the Soviet government developed increasingly into a totalitarian bureaucracy, culminating in the terror-ridden decades of Joseph Stalin's rule.

The Turkish War of Independence. Nazim Hikmet describes the conflicting moods of defeat and hope after World War I in his *Epic of Independence War* (which appears in part in *Human Landscapes*, Book 2). After the war, during the Paris Peace Conference in 1919, the triumphant Allied forces decided to settle the Eastern Question by partitioning the Ottoman Empire. In 1920, the Ottoman government signed the Treaty of Sèvres ceding all of eastern Thrace and western Asia Minor to Greece; a large part of the eastern territories to Armenia; and southern Asia Minor, Iraq, and Syria to Italian, British, and French rule. But even before 1920, an anti-imperialist resistance movement took shape in central Asia Minor. The movement, which went so far as to form a resistance government, defied the Ottoman sultan, who collaborated with the occupying forces. Its members initiated a fight for the sovereignty of the territories situated within a soon-to-be-born modern Turkey.

As relayed in Hikmet's verses, the timing was unfortunate.

Turkish War of Independence

We saw the flames, we saw betrayal.
Our spirits raged, our flesh endured.
Those who held out were not giants,
bereft of love and passion, but human beings
with their unbelievable weaknesses, scary
    power,

. . . .

The men wore long coats
  and went barefoot . . .
They had fur hats on their heads
  and in their hearts, grief
  and boundless hope . . .

Men were defeated, ungrieving and hopeless.
With bullet wounds in their flesh,
they were abandoned in village rooms.
    (*Human Landscapes*, pp. 157-58)

It took overwhelming energy, following the devastation of the First World War, to build up a resistance movement and equip it with the necessary resources (soldiers, ammunition, and food). Intense fighting broke out in the west between Turkish rebels, led by Mustafa Kemal (later called Atatürk), and a Greek army, which had been encouraged by the Allies to do battle against the national resistance movement. In 1922 the Turkish rebels scored a final victory over the Greek forces in Izmir, and in 1924 the Treaty of Lausanne was signed, confirming the independence of the new Turkish state under a National Assembly in Ankara. The last Ottoman sultan was sent into exile.

Rise of totalitarianism and World War II. To citizens in the new Republic of Turkey in 1923, the Ottoman past represented a backward and traditional society in contrast with the new modern

identity they were fashioning for themselves. After the triumphant War of Independence (1919-23), Turkey embarked on an intensive modernization process. A modified Swiss legal code replaced old religious laws and a modified Latin alphabet replaced the Arabic alphabet. Western units of measurement were adopted. The Western hat replaced the fez, which itself had been adopted barely a century before.

HIKMET ON MODERNIZATION

Hikmet's poetry rails against excessive reforms ["I think we've destroyed all we could, / and we should stop now: / it's gone far enough. / . . . We've had a revolution, but it's enough. / Now let's own up to our past and our roots" (*Human Landscapes*, p. 120)]. But his poetry also waxes enthusiastic for modernization and the economic, political, and social possibilities it engenders.

The destiny
  of iron
    coal
      and sugar
and red copper
and textiles
and love and cruelty and life
and the branches of industry
and the sky
  and the desert
    and the blue ocean,
of sad riverbeds
and plowed earth and cities
  will be changed one morning,
one sunrise when, at the edge of darkness,
  pushing against the earth with their heavy hands,
    they rise up.
      (*Human Landscapes*, pp. 150-51)

Meanwhile, in Germany, social unrest mounted in the midst of an economic depression dating from the Treaty of Versailles. The impotence shown by the rulers of its post-World War I Weimar Republic only aggravated the unrest, leading to political turmoil that culminated in Nazism's rise to power beginning in 1933. The ascendancy of totalitarian regimes in Germany, Italy, and Japan preceded a second world war brought on by these countries' ambitious military governments. While Italy seized Ethiopia and Albania, Germany occupied Czechoslovakia. Meanwhile, Britain and France watched and waited, finally declaring war on Germany after its invasion of Poland in 1939. Japan joined Germany and Italy on the Axis side; the Soviet Union and the United States joined Britain and France on the Allied side.

Allied victory in the six-year Second World War (1939-45) occurred only after the two sides had undergone some crucial junctures in the crisis: the Soviet counteroffensive in Stalingrad (1942), which led to the large-scale destruction of Hitler's eastern army, followed by uninterrupted Russian advances; the Japanese attack on Pearl Harbor in Hawaii (1941), which prompted U.S. involvement; and the U.S. use of the atomic bomb on the Japanese cities of Hiroshima and Nagasaki in 1945. After the largest and most costly war in world history, recovery was no easy process. There were long-lasting psychological and physical aftereffects from the Nazi attempts at ethnic, political, and religious extermination and from the American use of nuclear weapons on the Japanese cities. Hikmet protested the deaths in Hiroshima in his poem "Girl Child" (popularized by musician Pete Seeger in the tune "I Come and Stand at Every Door").

Weakened by the Second World War, Britain and France saw anti-imperialist struggles proliferate in their colonies in Asia and Africa. Meanwhile, the Soviet Union and the United States engaged in a competition for world leadership referred to as the Cold War (1945-89), which at times heated up into indirect but open combat around the globe. The two new superpowers, defined the world according to their competition, delineating separate power zones. On the side of the United States were Western capitalist nations; on the side of the Soviet Union, the Communist bloc nations.

Turkey had adopted a pragmatic foreign policy during World War II, refusing to side with either camp. Meanwhile, autocratic one-party rule by Ismet Inönü gave rise to an opportunistic domestic policy that paralleled the foreign policy, shifting between sympathy for fascist or communist factions, depending on German or Soviet victories throughout the war. Turkey adopted a multiparty system in 1946, and the newly formed Democratic Party came to power in 1950. It allied the country with the Western bloc nations, largely because of the financial support that was being provided by the United States through the Truman Doctrine (1947) and Marshall Plan (1948-52). Although a socialist party was quickly established and won Hikmet's allegiance, the party could hardly be effective, given the constant threat of American-style anti-communism that existed in Turkey at the time.

The Epic in Focus

Contents overview. As the title of the epic promises, the reader is invited into "human landscapes" from Turkey and the world. Highlighting love, suffering, treachery, and courage, the poem takes us on a journey through a gamut of human emotions and situations. The work resists categorization: it uses free verse and incorporates drama, social history, novel, song, and even cinema script. Its conversational tone of language, montage-like episodic structure, and huge canvas of themes and characters all contribute to its being considered a modern-day epic, or, as one scholar describes it, an "episodic saga of the twentieth century" (Halman, p. 63).

The narrative unfolds chronologically, but the sequence is oftentimes interrupted by a technique perhaps best described as cinematic montage. Hikmet, drawing on his experience as a screenwriter, inserts lives from the past into the narrative of the present by employing flashbacks, jump cuts, zooms, and different angles, all created through language. He moves through time and space by means of newspaper excerpts, radio transmissions, and letters that link Turkish history to international events.

Told in five books, the epic follows a circular path, starting with a journey by train from Istanbul to Anatolia and ending in a return to Istanbul. The main storyline centers on the political prisoner Halil, beginning with his transport to Ankara, then following him in his life in prison. The poem does not, however, spotlight him as hero. Instead Halil is an observer, sometimes the narrator, in a procession of "common" protagonists, such as Corporal Ahmet, worker Kerim, poet Jelal, partisan Zoe, and antagonists, such as submariner Hans Mueller, journalist Nuri Jemil, arms dealer Hikmet Alpersoy, and intellectual Osman Nejip. The epic is a patchwork of substories, recounted not only by an omniscient anonymous narrator but also by all these characters and many others, who relate events occurring around them through their dialogues with each other. The substories about the Soviet resistance, German aggression, modernization in Turkey, and the Turkish War of Independence, for instance, constitute an account of the twen-

Human Landscapes begins with two train journeys departing from Haydarpaşa Station, built in an Asian suburb of Istanbul, near the mouth of the Bosporus Strait.

tieth century as seen through the eyes of multiple Turkish observers.

Contents summary. Book 1 moves from a portrayal of Haydarpaşa, the central railroad station in Istanbul, to the heart of Anatolia. The narrative pans to the passengers of a lower-class train that carries peasants, workers, the unemployed, military privates, students, and prisoners out of the station. As the literary camera flits from people to incidents in the past and present, it finds a focus of sorts by centering mainly on the political prisoner Halil, who has been transported to the capital with three of his friends—the worker Fuat, the "underground fighter" Süleyman, and a comrade's wife, Melahat (*Human Landscape*, p. 55).

Halil (like Hikmet himself) is an intellectual activist who has been convicted for his ideology and writings. Though separated from his family, treated as a traitor (a spy for the Russians), and subjected to torture and the threat of blindness, he still believes it is the social responsibility of the intellectual to fight for a free, egalitarian, peaceful world and hopes for a better future:

> " . . . one of those sparkling nights
>   of Kalamish Bay
>   the stars and the rustle of water,
> or the boundless daylight

>   in the fields outside Topkapi
> or a woman's sweet face glimpsed on a
>   streetcar
> or even the yellow geranium I grew in a tin
>   can
>   in the Sivas prison—
> I mean, whenever I meet
>   with natural beauty,
> I know once again
>   human life today
>   must and will be
>   changed . . . "
>   (*Human Landscapes,* p. 44)

Optimism surfaces at the other end of the train too. The engineer Alaaddin, a representative of the proletariat, shares Halil's bright feelings and thoughts about the future, although "Whenever Aladdin looks back /—especially on inclines— he feels as if the cars were roped together / and harnessed to his shoulders" (*Human Landscapes,* pp. 18-19). Alaaddin converses with Ismail, the fireman of the steam train, about the ways of the world:

> . . . "Boss,
> I have another question.
> These rails here,
>   do they go around the whole world?"
> "They do."

"So if there's no war,
and not just no war
but if no questions are asked at borders,
and we let the engine loose on the rails,
it'll go from one end of the world to the
    other?"
"When you say 'sea,' it stops."
"You get on ships."
"Airplanes are better."

. . . .

"No problem, man,
we'll get on airplanes anyway—
not to kill people
but just for the fun
    of breezing through the sky."
                    (*Human Landscapes*, p. 20)

Book 1 ends with a suicide. The train is suddenly stopped when a 50-year-old man jumps off, leaving Alaaddin and Ismail sadly speechless as they witness a man defeated by outside forces.

Book 2 presents two simultaneous train rides. While it continues to follow the lower-class transport, it also introduces the wealthy industrialists, merchants, and civil servants who ride another train—the luxury Anatolian Express. In the alienating atmosphere of the luxury train's dining car, where the bourgeoisie sip their wine and discuss Nazi victories, the waiter and the cook recite an epic of the national liberation of Turkey that celebrates undocumented heroes, ignored by most historians:

"'They who are numberless
    like ants in the earth
        fish in the sea
            birds in the air,
who are cowardly
    brave
        ignorant
            wise
                and childlike,
and who destroy
    and create,
my epic tells only of their adventures.'"
                    (*Human Landscapes*, p. 150)

Such promising, revitalizing histories and the occasional glimpse of "a moon outside, and a sea, and a dream sailboat on the sea, / calling to mind / only big, beautiful, / loving thoughts" interrupt the passengers' unfeeling conversation (*Human Landscapes*, p. 127).

In Book 2, another intellectual, Doctor Faik, introduces us to the contaminated web of relations in the first-class dining car that gives rise to this unfeeling conversation. He describes the corrupt bureaucrats, the Turkish and foreign bourgeoisie who collaborate with the Nazis, and the authors and journalists who serve the imperialists. Doctor Faik acknowledges the dynamics of oppression within society, but unlike Halil, he is alienated from his people and does not nurture a belief in change. His tone is biting when his listener calls him a poet because of his elegant description of tyranny's victims:

These awful things build up inside you
you're sickened, horrified,
enraged.
and then you look and find your hands are tied.
You can't do anything.
Then come the words,
    the poeticizing,
        with a little irony
            and a touch of the lyrical-romantic.
                    (*Human Landscapes*, p. 137)

The luxury train keeps moving. As Book 2 closes, the first train arrives at its destination and the prisoners go their separate ways, bound for prisons in Ankara and further east.

The bustling flow of the narrative slows down in Book 3 to prepare the reader for the impassioned rhythm of Books 4 and 5. Book 3 takes us into a prison and a hospital to meet more "common heroes." Halil languishes in prison, Doctor Faik experiences suicidal alienation, and poor people struggle just to go on living. Everywhere people are constrained by ignorance, poverty, undereducation, and underdevelopment. Halil is taken to an isolated hospital in the Anatolian hinterland to be treated for a painful illness in his eyes by Doctor Faik, and Faik himself ends up committing suicide, frustrated at his inability to channel his intellectual energy into action against the injustices around him. In contrast, Halil feels invigorated by his interaction with the people for whom he will fight. Hamdi dies in the coal mines; Zeynep hoes the fields, rain or shine, to support her husband in prison; "the most hopeful man of the twentieth century," the factory worker Kerim, stands up to his father, who abuses his mother (*Human Landscapes*, p. 275); Dumel the peasant comprehends neither the reason for his wife's illness, nor the necessity of an operation, nor her death. Hikmet again overcomes the mood as he closes Book 3: deaths are followed by a birth, "the first victorious cry of the newborn" (*Human Landscapes*, p. 333). Halil's heart is filled with joy as he hears this "most beautiful sound in the world," reminding him of his own family and hope for renewal (*Human Landscapes*, p. 333).

Book 4, simulating radio transmission, visits the battlefields of World War II (from the Atlantic Ocean to Moscow). The anonymous narrator, like someone descending to Hades, speaks to the reader from among the dead at the bottom of the Atlantic Ocean. Hikmet's compassionate lyricism is mingled with powerful realism while he portrays the Second World War through the deaths of Hans, Thompson, Ivan, and Zoe. We come across a German and a British soldier, Hans and Thompson, lying side-by-side on the ocean floor, "little men" unquestioningly fighting for Fascism and imperialism respectively. Their fate portends the future of Nazi Germany and the British Empire:

> Together they swelled up,
> and together they rose to the top.
> The fish thoroughly enjoyed Thompson,
> but they wouldn't touch the other—
> scared, I guess, that Hans's flesh was poison.
>   (*Human Landscapes*, p. 368)

After some war news, the radio transmits the "Moscow Symphony" to three prisoners standing around it—among them, Halil. The music tells the story of Ivan, Ahmet, Yurchenko, and Sagamanian, soldiers of the Soviet Union's Red Army, who defended their homeland from "the German people [who] continued to be Hitler's hunting dogs" (*Human Landscapes*, p. 375). Then comes a lament for 18-year-old Zoe (the real-life Russian partisan Zoia Kosmodemianskaia [1923-41], code named *Tanya*); hanged by the Nazis, she "never got [her] share of the sun's warmth" (*Human Landscapes*, p. 397). A hymn follows for the French communist journalist and politician Gabriel Péri (1902-41), whose "head, like a beating heart, was ready everywhere: Ethiopia, Spain, China" and who died facing the Nazi firing squad with a song of revolution in his mouth (*Human Landscapes*, p. 401).

In the fifth book, prisoner Halil returns in his imagination to his beloved city and family through letters from his wife. Halil reads the letters sent by Aysha, which contain words of love and bitterness about the forced partition of 1920. His nostalgia for Istanbul and its multicultural environment emerges:

> "ah, Istanbul!
> *Que quieres, buenos?*
> Its water, air, fish, strawberries.
> Its Turks, Armenians, and Greeks,
>   plus Jews.
> I can almost taste it. *Ahparin girlas?*"
>   (*Human Landscapes*, p. 436)

The epic ends as modestly and as dialectically as it began, first describing young Fuat's optimistic return to Istanbul from prison and then lighting on a poor suicidal family during the years of deprivation in the Second World War. The juxtapositions posit first a better world, then a sobering reminder of the long, painful road to peace and freedom, which is nevertheless envisioned.

Poetry as revolution. Hikmet's poetic portraits are drawn in communal settings, such as a train or a prison. The vivid collage of biographies are based on real characters whose lives the poet witnessed in a Bursa prison; they are not "generals, sultans, distinguished scientists or artists, beauty queens, murderers and billionaires," but "workers, peasants and craftsmen, people whose fame had not spread beyond their factories, workshops, villages, or neighborhoods" (*Human Landscapes*, p. x). The hero of the Turkish War of Independence is not the publicly celebrated Atatürk, but Ismail from Arhave, who rows his boat to death on a mission to deliver a machine gun for the resistance army. The hero of the Russian resistance to the Nazis is not Joseph Stalin, but Zoia, an 18-year-old partisan executed by the Nazis. Moreover, this epic of "little people" is written in lifelike vernacular dialogue rather than the florid language of eulogies for great men.

In a time of intense nationalism, when traditionalist poets and authors chose to construct a modern Turkish literature based on heroic themes from official national histories and epics, Hikmet preferred international heroes and the solidarity of commoners in global society. The poet moves above the boundaries imposed by nationalisms, his epic attempting to establish a lingua franca. A reflection of his devotion to communism, the poem becomes an international verse, integrating social realist themes with a romantic, even utopian, tone. Ultimately Hikmet's revolutionary poetry cannot be separated from his political ideology, through which he envisions humanity fighting for a better tomorrow.

In fact, Hikmet's unique originality as a poet appears in every component of his poetics: technique, themes, and language. He is the first of the modern Turkish poets to introduce free verse and broken-off lines (or waves) to express details of mundane lives, and emphasize the fluent and conversational tone of language. Hikmet employs elements of spoken Turkish, such as vowel harmony (which endows the spoken language with a musical harmony) and inflection (which enables one to extend verbal repetition in sound while changing the meaning) to create resonance. His waves appear as a loose, one might say, an unordered or free-ranging typography that spreads in ladderlike style over the page, conveying an energetic spirit. The line breaks reflect the abruptness of street vernacular, supporting the use of ordinary people and their take on events as legitimate epic material.

In the late 1920s and 1930s Hikmet initiated a movement in literary criticism called "Demolishing the Idols," which attacked traditionalist poets for their thematic and structural stagnancy, and ethical irresponsibity. In *Human Lanscapes*, a soldier denounces the author of the national anthem, Mehmet Akif, for a mystical nationalism that ignores people's struggles:

> "There's something off about our national anthem,
> I don't know how to say it.
> The poet Akif is a believer.
> But I don't believe
> everything he does.
>
> . . . .
>
> For instance listen:
> 'The days God promised us will come.'
> No.
> No sign's descended from the sky
>   about the days to come.
> We've promised those days
>   to ourselves."
> (*Human Landscapes,* p. 195)

Then the poem criticizes Ahmet Haşim, a much praised icon of symbolist poetry, for being detached from social realities: "Ahmet Haşim doesn't have a single word—open, / amazing, / brave / just, or hopeful . . . " / "Is that what poetry is about, doctor?" / "Poetry is about the world. / And in today's world, those are the only things worth saying" (*Human Landscapes,* p. 168). Along with elitism, the poem attacks defeatism, "giving up hope in humanity," and "after-dinner philosophizing" in the belief that intellectuals must struggle against oppression (*Human Landscapes,* p. 218). The hopeful tone that pervades Hikmet's poetry only underscores his use of it for revolution. He aims to build an international community:

> I want my poems to address all my readers' problems. If a young man falls in love with a girl, he should be able to read my poems to his sweetheart, an old man in the grip of sadness about dying should read my poems, people on the way to a May Day demonstration should read my poems. When a bureaucrat is giving you a hard time, read my poems. A communist writer has to reflect all human feelings.
> (Hikmet in Göksu and Timms, p. 298)

Sources and literary context. Nazim Hikmet's most ambitious project, *Human Landscapes* was written in prison between 1938 and 1950. His prison experience brought his poetry closer to the spoken language and vastly broadened its scope, as measured by the social classes from which he drew his characters. Originally a much longer work, 17,000 lines survived after confiscations, burning by fearful relatives, and various forms of harassment. Originating as a biographical dictionary that would profile common people's lives, the epic resulted from Hikmet's dramatizing the individual heroes of the dictionary into a poetic whole. A subsection about the Turkish War of Independence in Volume 2 and another subsection on the Stalingrad resistance in Volume 5 are abridged versions of his poems "Epic of the National Militia," and "Moscow Symphony."

Hikmet had made use of "waves" and repetition to organize his poetry since his encounter with Vladimir Mayakovsky and Russian constructivism in the 1920s. He was consciously searching for a new structure to express contemporary social realities, a modern technique to revolutionize the rigid age-old forms of Ottoman poetry. In his view, the outmoded conventions of Ottoman verse had to be overthrown by a mix of street language and international trends in modern poetry. "How could anyone," the poet asked, "be called a national poet if he never marked any turning-point in the language of the people, if he never voiced the great struggles of his people?" (Hikmet in Göksu and Timms, p. 88).

In the 1940s Hikmet's defiance of traditional poetics, along with his search for a way to apply modern realism that would reach the masses, led him to embrace the formal structure of "encyclopedic fiction." Current events—Hitler's invasion of Russia and the Second World War—extended his project of recording the lives of ordinary Turkish people to an overview of the twentieth century from Turkey. Overall, Hikmet blended his personal fate—that of a communist poet in Turkey—with the fate of the Turkish people and humanity in the face of wars and economic hardships. His epic is the product of his own misfortunes, the hope he tries to preserve, and his love for homeland, family, and freedom.

Hikmet's readings of Friedrich Engels's ideas, of Denis Diderot's *Le Neveu de Rameau* (a French novel relating contrasting philosophical positions through vivid dialogue), and most importantly of William Langland's *Piers Ploughman* (a medieval English poem in which all sections of society appear in panoramic vision) influenced his creation of *Human Landscapes* too. Other readings influenced the poem as well. Written during a period of intense modernization in Turkey, *Human Landscapes* celebrates technological progress for enhancing the quality of life—railways and radios connect distances and eliminate borders. But, with the help of literary analogy, the poem notes some of the detrimental effects of technology too—airplanes kill people and people become half-beasts, "straight out of H. G. Wells's *Island of Dr. Moreau*" (*Human Landscapes*, p. 375).

Publication and reception. Though the publication of *Human Landscapes* was long awaited in Turkey, it received conflicting assessments. Most reviewers praised the poem for introducing a new form and historical consciousness to lyric poetics. But some criticized it for incoherency. In the view of Talat Sait Halman, "[*Human Landscapes*] lumps together scenes, faces, and minor occurrences which, superficial and repetitious, do not add up to a vast poetic panorama" (Halman, p. 63). A 1982 abridged translation of the poem into English elicited praise from Robert Hudzik: "Political, social, and historical themes are united by a common vision. Hikmet's ability to particularize the general helps make this a bold, remarkable work" (Hudzik, p. 1,991). Emily Grosholz raved, "Hikmet has an uncanny way of bringing characters to life in a few lines so vividly that, whether they are scurrilous or noble, one can't help but care about them" (Grosholz, p. 139). A complete translation of the work in 2002 prompted more commentary about cohesiveness: "The poem is structured as a series of vignettes of people and events, some short and telegraphic, others more discursive. Certain characters run through the whole poem, giving it a unifying thread" (Hanaway, p. 465). A final review refers to the innovative style as well as the content:

> Hikmet's poetic line is terse, staccato, conversational . . . while rhythmical variation and repetition create a narrative web and flow punctuated by moments of epiphany as someone finds his role, another his voice, to combat centuries of peonage. . . . Ultimately Hikmet's art suggests a spaciousness, a grandeur in the details of poor people seeking just

to breathe. . . . Finally available complete in English, Hikmet's hauntingly eloquent masterpiece never flags.

(Pinker, p. 142)

— Ipek Çelik

For More Information

Christie, Ruth, Richard McKane, and T. S. Halman. *Beyond the Walls: Selected Poems*. Istanbul: Yapi Kredi Yayinlari, 2002.

Fişekçi, Turgay. *Nazim Hikmet: yaşamöyküsü*. Istanbul: Kavram, 1997.

Fuat, Memed. *Nazim Hikmet üzerine yazilar*. Istanbul: Adam Yayinlari, 2001.

Göksu, Saime, and Edward Timms. *Romantic Communist: The Life and Work of Nazim Hikmet*. New York: St. Martin's Press, 1999.

Grosholz, Emily. "New Renderings." *The Hudson Review* 37, no. 1 (spring 1984): 132-42.

Halman, T. S. "Nazim Hikmet: Lyricist as Iconoclast." *Books Abroad* 43, no. 1 (winter 1969): 59-64.

Hanaway, W. L. Review of *Human Landscapes*. *Choice* 40, no. 3 (November 2002): 465.

Hikmet, Nazim. *Human Landscapes from My Country: An Epic Novel in Verse*. Trans. Randy Blasing and Mutlu Konuk. New York: Persea Books, 2002.

———. *Poems of Nazim Hikmet*. Trans. Randy Blasing and Mutlu Konuk. New York: Persea Books, 1994.

———. *Şiirler 1*. Istanbul: Yapi Kredi Yayinlari, 2002.

Hudzik, Robert. Review of *Human Landscapes*. *Library Journal* 107, no. 18 (October 1982): 1,991.

Kona, Prash Reddy. "Nazim Hikmet: Human Landscapes and the De-sentimentalization of History." *Literary Studies: Beginnings and Ends*. Ed. Nicholas O. Pagan and William S. Haney II. Lanham: University Press of America, 2001.

Pinker, Michael. Review of *Human Landscapes*. *Review of Contemporary Fiction* 23, no. 1 (spring 2003): 142.

"In the City of Slaughter"

by

Hayyim Nahman Bialik

THE LITERARY WORK

A poem set in Kishinev, Russia, in 1903; first published in Hebrew (as *Masa Nemerov*; later as *Be-ir ha-haregah*) in 1904, in English in 1906.

SYNOPSIS

Bialik's poem envisions the slaughter and devastation left in the wake of the Kishinev pogrom of 1903.

Born in the Russian village of Radi in 1873, Hayyim Nahman Bialik was the son of an innkeeper who died when the boy was just seven years old. Bialik's mother entrusted her youngest child to his paternal grandfather, who saw to it that the boy received rigorous instruction in Jewish law and tradition. At 16, Bialik entered a prestigious academy devoted to study of the **Talmud** (also in *WLAIT 6: Middle Eastern Literatures and Their Times*). A restless Bialik left the academy, which was located in Volozhin, in 1891. He traveled to Odessa, center of a burgeoning cultural movement in Hebrew letters and home to the Zionist thinker Ahad Ha`am. Bialik met the influential thinker and became one of several key disciples. The Jews, warned Ahad Ha`am, were headed for extinction unless they underwent a profound spiritual regeneration. In keeping with this conviction, Bialik and a few other intellectuals set out to effect a spiritual revival through teaching and writing. Bialik embarked on a project to compile, translate, and anthologize a canon of literature that would impart a sense of Jewish identity to the people of his day—especially to the young. Early in 1902 Bialik, Y. H. Ravnitski, and S. Ben-Tsiyon founded the publishing company Moriah. By this time Bialik was an accomplished poet, his reputation having begun with the publication of "El ha-Zippor" (1891; To the Bird), a poem of longing for Zion. News of his dying grandfather had drawn him away from Odessa for a time (1892-1900), during which he married Manya Averbuch, worked in the timber trade, taught, and wrote stories as well as poetry. In 1896, promoting the use of Hebrew as a modern written language, Ahad Ha`am launched the Hebrew journal *Ha-Shiloach* (The Dawn), which published several poems by Bialik. By the time he returned to Odessa in 1900, he was a renowned poet and his reputation would grow in the decade to come. Especially from 1903 to 1906, Bialik wrote emotionally charged poetic responses to a number of devastating Russian pogroms, or massacres of the Jews, consolidating his role as the "Jewish national poet." Reflecting on the condition of the Jews around him, he penned a series of prophetic poems, including "Upon the Slaughter," "In the City of Slaughter," and "This Too Is the Punishment of God." Shortly thereafter, Bialik experienced terrible doubts about his role as poet-prophet. His output slowed. Bialik produced little poetry after 1911, but continued as an essayist and critic, beyond his move from Odessa to Berlin, Germany,

Hayyim Nahman Bialik

in 1921, and to Palestine in 1924. His reputation as the Jewish national poet never faded, though, due in large part to his having written such consequential poems as "In the City of Slaughter."

Events in History at the Time of the Poem

Jews in tsarist Russia—waves of anti-Semitism. Early-twentieth-century Russian Jewry harked back to the community of Jews in the lands of medieval Poland. From the thirteenth to the fifteenth centuries, Polish Jewry multiplied into a substantial community as a result of a natural influx from central Europe into the economically expanding Polish kingdom. Large numbers of Jews settled not just in Poland but also in the Polish-held lands of Lithuania, the Ukraine, and Belorussia. By the late eighteenth century—when the Polish empire was lost to Russia, Austria, and Prussia (through divisions in 1772, 1793, and 1795)—the population included more than a million Jews. The majority of them lived in the lands that fell to Russia, whose ruler, Catherine the Great, quickly circumscribed the movement of her newly inherited Jewish population. In 1792, conceding to Moscow business leaders who wanted to keep out the Jews, she confined them to an area called the Pale of Settlement, extending their domain beyond the former Polish lands but restricting them from moving eastward into historical Russia. For the next hundred years, only a tiny minority of Jews, whose skills were deemed useful to Russia's empire, could travel or work beyond the Pale.

A fitful policy of repression and relaxed rule ensued for the Jews of nineteenth-century Russia, depending on the tsar in power. The first half of the century witnessed the highly conservative regimes of Alexander I (r. 1801-1825) and his brother, Nicholas I (r. 1825-1855). During Nicholas's reign, legislation related to the Jews reached a peak: over 600 edicts and regulations were passed. Besides setting the boundaries of the Pale into Russian law, Nicholas decreed that the Jews should pay double the taxes of other Russians. He forbade them from leasing land, running taverns, employing Christian servants, building a synagogue next to a church, or leaving Russia without permission (on pain of forfeiting their nationality). He tightened censorship laws, closing down all but two Hebrew printing presses. Finally he enforced a harsh conscription policy, requiring communities to supply soldiers for 25-year stints in the Russian army, which worked diligently to alienate Jewish conscripts from their faith.

The restrictions imposed by Nicholas I eased during the reign of his son, Alexander II (r. 1855-81). Although the new tsar shared his father's distrust of Jews—viewing them as a foreign element—he re-evaluated their presence with an eye to assimilating them more successfully into the larger population. To this end, Alexander shortened the army conscription of Jews and other groups to a two-year stint. He initiated other reforms too, repealing an 1844 regulation that banned Jews from government employment and relaxing settlement restrictions on where Jewish doctors and a few other professionals could live. The future seemed promising.

The promise proved illusory, however. Alexander II was assassinated in 1881 by a band of radical revolutionaries. Though only one of the revolutionaries was Jewish, the populace fixed on this detail, calling the assassination a Jewish plot. A wave of intense anti-Semitism swept the country. The next two tsars, Alexander III (r. 1881-1894) and Nicholas II (r. 1894-1917), considered Jews a disruptive, sinister element that should be excised from—not absorbed into—Russian society. The era began ominously with a wave of pogroms, or wholesale attacks, on the Jews in 1881-82, followed by occasional outbreaks and another wave in 1905-6. In community after community, Jews were beaten, raped, and killed, and their properties were destroyed. "In the City of Slaughter" concerns one such outbreak—the largest, most destructive pogrom since 1881-82—which erupted in 1903 in Kishinev, a city about 90 miles northwest of Odessa.

Pogroms—the Jewish response. It took more than 15 years for the Jews of Russia to mount an effective, consolidated response to the devastation wrought by the pogroms of 1881-82, but in the end they responded successfully and through more than one avenue. The pogroms helped spur a vigorous effort to infuse a strong current of Jewish nationalism into Russian society. Beginning in the 1890s, a small group of intellectuals set out to teach, write, and publish in ways that would impart a sense of Jewish identity, especially to the young. Members of the group founded innovative talmudic academies and schools and embarked on related endeavors. Y. L. Ben-David founded a society to promote speaking Hebrew; Ahad Ha'am introduced *ha-Shiloah*, his journal of new Hebrew thought and literature; Bialik generated modern Hebrew lyric poems; and other talents wrote landmark works in Russian (the historian Simon Dubonov) and in Yiddish (the storyteller Sholem Aleichem).

At the time, the sacred sources of Jewish literature were written in a format far removed from contemporary society. This format failed to speak to many of the highly assimilated Jews who lived in Odessa. Between 1903 and 1909 Bialik and his colleagues at Moriah assembled and initiated the publication of an authoritative national canon, including the sacred sources but in a modern format. They translated, updated, and published the classical Hebrew texts, compiled previously uncollected medieval Hebrew poetry (by such luminaries as Judah Halevi), and popularized new Hebrew poetry and prose, establishing a continuing tradition with which the Jewish nation could identify. Moriah released *Bible Stories*, *Words of the Prophets*, *The Poetry of Israel*, and more during these years. This feverish effort, on the heels of the pogrom in Kishinev, showed a devotion to biblical and post-biblical Jewish texts. For Bialik, this devotion existed uneasily alongside a distressing view of the Jews around him: "'Boorishness and indifference are increasing in every corner of the nation,' he complained" (Bialik in Rubin, pp. 136-37).

Meanwhile, another small minority of Jews was mounting a political response to the pogroms, most notably a drive, known as Zionism, to reestablish a Jewish homeland in Israel. Spearheaded by Theodor Herzl, the movement gathered steam in the 1890s, building to the founding of the World Zionist Organization in Basel, Switzerland, in 1897. Bialik looked skeptically on the timing of the Zionist movement, convinced that the first order of business was the people's spiritual regeneration. He would nevertheless become a central figure in international and Russian Zionism.

As Bialik saw it, spiritual regeneration called for a rejection of the notion that Jews should accept their sufferings like good martyrs and die dutifully in God's name. Out of the pogroms of 1881-82, there grew a momentum for self-defense, which would crystallize primarily in the pogroms of 1905-6, after the groundwork had been laid by Bialik and others. In the wake of the Kishinev pogrom, some of Odessa's writers, including Ahad Ha'am, Bialik, and Dubnov, issued

---

FROM ONE WAVE OF POGROMS TO THE NEXT: A 25-YEAR LEGACY OF HATE

1881-82 First wave of pogroms strikes Elizavetgrad, Kiev, Zhmerynka, Aleksandrovsk, Odessa, Warsaw, and Balta.

1884 Pogrom in Nizhnii-Novgorod is marked by extreme cruelty; victims are killed by axes or thrown from rooftops.

1897 Two days of rioting break out in Spola.

1899 Nikolaev pogrom erupts during the Passover holiday.

1903 Kishinev pogrom strikes at Passover and Easter; another pogrom in Homel meets with organized Jewish defense.

1904-1905 Pogroms erupt in Smila, Rovno, Aleksandria, and Mohilev-on-the-Dnieper.

1905 Second wave of pogroms ravages several hundred cities, including Kiev, Kishinev, Romi, Kremenchuk, and Odessa; in Odessa, 300 are killed, many more injured, and 40,000 financially ruined.

1906 Pogroms in Bialystok and Sedlets; second wave ends, bringing pogroms to a temporary halt.

---

a public statement urging the Jews to organize on their own behalf: "'It is degrading,'" the statement said, "'for five million people . . . to stretch out their necks to be slaughtered . . . without attempting to protect their property, dignity, and lives with their own hands'" (Harshav, p. 51). The Jews of Russia heeded the call. In defiance of hostile authorities, an illegal self-defense movement sprang up throughout the Pale, thanks partly to

Bialik's "In the City of Slaughter." Such a work, though critical of the people, was nevertheless "written from the inside" and therefore accorded legitimacy (Harshav, p. 64). Accepting the un-flattering parts of the self-image such writings conveyed, more and more readers responded by embracing Zionism and other new ideologies. They stopped trusting that redemption would come to the Jews through divine mercy and opted instead for redemption through self-improvement. It was a monumental transformation, one that most Jews had not yet experienced (and not everyone would) when, after viewing the ravages of the Kishinev, Bialik wrote "In the City of Slaughter."

The Kishinev pogrom. At the time of the 1903 pogrom, there were some 50,000 Jews living in Kishinev, alongside some 60,000 Christians (Baron, p. 57). Like Jews in other cities, the Kishinev community considered itself not just a religious but an ethnic-national grouping. Bound together by shared oppression and political as well as other interests, they had their own Jewish institutions of charity, defense, and education. But at the same time the community was deeply divided over such questions as how best to respond to the rampant anti-Semitism of the era.

Anti-Semitism had been smoldering for years in the Bessarabian city of Kishinev. Several prominent citizens fanned the flames of this hostility, including Pavolachi Krushevan, who published the local newspaper *Bessarabets* (Bessarabian); the businessman Georgii Alekseevich Pronin; and Vice-Governor V. G. Ustrugov, who oversaw the day-to-day administration of Bessarabia. To the proudly nationalistic Krushevan, Jews were "an evil force in the world, a well-organized, conspiratorial group seeking to subjugate the Christian masses" (Judge, p. 32). Pronin's attitude, by contrast, had as much to do with rival business interests as with racial and religious prejudice, while the ambitious Ustrugov hoped to advance his career by enforcing the anti-Semitic policies of the empire.

In 1903 the anti-Semitism in Kishinev escalated to a dangerous peak, partly because of an infamous blood-libel case. A 14-year-old Christian boy, Mikhail Rybachenko, was found stabbed to death in the nearby town of Dubossary. Although the murderer was later discovered to be a member of the boy's own family, a vicious rumor blamed the Jews for kidnapping and killing the boy. The rumor was an iteration of an age-old blood libel dating back to the Middle Ages in western Europe. The libel, which spread throughout the Christian world,

charged that Jews needed Christian blood to make the unleavened bread (matzos) that they ate during Passover. Though patently false, the charges cropped up several times in the early nineteenth century and after in Russia. This time, in 1903, they ignited an anti-Jewish riot in a town close to Kishinev—no lives were lost. In Kishinev itself, Krushevan, already well known for his anti-Jewish editorials, published the rumor as near-fact in *Bessarabets*. He was obliged to print a refutation when an autopsy was done on Rybachenko and new details came to the fore. But the damage had been done. An uneasy feeling settled on Kishinev's Jews, especially after they heard an attack was imminent over Easter. Alarmed, some of the community's most prominent Jews approached Ustrugov's superior, Governor Rudolf Samoilovich von Raaben. Well-meaning but ineffectual, von Raaben assured them there would be no violence, backing up his word with an increased police and army presence in Kishinev over the Easter holidays. But these measures proved inadequate.

Rioting broke out on Easter Sunday (April 6) in the late afternoon. The immediate cause is unknown, but it appears that an increasingly drunk and disorderly crowd broke into small groups, who then struck at Jewish property, throwing rocks and breaking the windows of homes and shops. More rioters followed, armed with canes and crowbars, after which looters and scavengers arrived to steal wares from the vandalized shops. The police were slow to intervene; from 6:00 to 10:00 P.M. the violence proceeded mostly unchecked, subsiding around 11:00 P.M. The damage that Sunday was mainly to property, though the head physician at the city hospital would report 22 injured and 4 dead—2 Christians and 2 Jews.

On Easter Monday, several Jewish merchants, alarmed by the lack of police protection, banded together at the New Marketplace in hopes of defending themselves against future assaults. Ironically the police—so ineffective the previous day—arrived and promptly dispersed the group, arresting several of its leaders. Meanwhile, small bands of Christians assembled throughout Kishinev, planning to mount more attacks upon the Jews. These bands, unlike the group of Jewish merchants, encountered no resistance from the police.

Initially the Easter Monday attacks resembled those of the previous day, with crowds vandalizing and looting Jewish businesses. But as new rioters joined in, the attacks grew ever more

FROM THE HISTORICAL RECORD

Testimony of Rivka Shif, rape victim:

"When the gentile kids broke into the attic through the roof, some of them jumped on Zaychik's daughter first and slapped her in the face and surrounded her. The slap knocked her down. They rolled up her dress, turned her on her face and began to beat her behind, then they turned her back over, pulled her legs open; they covered her eyes and her mouth so she wouldn't scream; one climbed on top of her and the rest stood around her and waited their turn. They all did what they did in front of all the people in the attic. Some of them jumped on me and my husband. We tried to run. They fell on him: 'Give us money!' And Mitya Krasilchik wanted to brutalize me and demanded money. I begged for mercy: 'Don't touch me, Mitya. Haven't I known you for years? I don't have any money.' Others tore my dress off, and one slapped me in the face, saying: 'If you don't have money, we'll get our pleasure from you another way.' . . . . I don't know how many were with me, but certainly no fewer than five, and maybe seven."

(Shif in Goren, p. 80; trans. K. Moss)

Testimony of Chana Sobelman, at the scene of a murder:

"Oshumirski, in his efforts to escape from his murderers and their sticks, ran into the alley behind the privy [a narrow place between the privy and the wall of one of the houses with no room to turn] and there he fell down and rolled in his blood. His killers chased him into this alley, thought he was dead, but then saw the ladder that was standing there—and there was a Jew also sitting up there. It was Yudl Krupnik, a man along in years, tutor to my children and an assistant to my husband in the loan business, who hid himself during the pogroms on the ladder while his son, who is about 28, hid near him in a corner between the dungheap and the privy. And the murderers turned away from Oshumirski and pulled Krupnik senior down from the ladder by his feet and killed him there, and they caught his fleeing son in the middle of the courtyard and began to hit him with their weapons."

(Sobelman in Goren, pp. 71-2; trans. K. Moss)

vicious. By the afternoon, the Jewish sector of Kishinev was overrun with hooligans, scavengers, and killers. The worst crimes took place in Jewish residential areas. Rioters broke into Jews' homes, ripped apart feather beds, smashed furnishings and utensils, then turned their rage on the Jews themselves, beating them with "clubs, canes, crowbars, and other such blunt instruments" (Judge, p. 57). In one of Kishinev's five police precincts, a 16-year-old Jewish youth found hiding in a closet was beaten to death in front of his family; an elderly woman was likewise killed before her grandson's eyes. In another neighborhood, three Jews hiding in an attic were found and beaten by rioters, then flung into the street, where a mob killed them with crowbars.

Elsewhere, several Jews, including an adolescent girl who was also raped, met grisly deaths in a carpenter's shed near the Skulianskii Turnpike in the Kishinev suburbs. Lacking clear directions from their superiors, the soldiers and local police—some of whom sympathized with the anti-Jewish crowds—made a few sporadic attempts to restore order. Only after von Raaben called for full-scale military force in putting down the riots did the violence at last subside. By 8:00 P.M. Monday night, more than 800 people had been arrested for rioting. Although some further disorder was reported the following morning, it was quickly quelled by the presence of military troops: the Kishinev pogrom was over. Figures released by the Ministry of Interior reported 51 dead—49 of them Jews—and 74 seriously wounded (Judge, p. 72). Other surveys reported extensive property damage: more than 1,500 shops and houses had been plundered or destroyed outright. Estimates placed the total cost at up to 2 million rubles.

The world reacted with outrage to the slaughter, which was perceived as all the more shocking because it was an isolated pogrom, one that had not been preceded by similar episodes (as in the string of 1881-1882 pogroms). Mass protests were held in England and the United States, while several prominent Russian intellectuals, including the novelist Leo Tolstoy, accused the government of complicity in the attacks. Most of the over 800 people arrested for rioting were charged only with minor crimes and misdemeanors. Although rioters accused of the more serious crimes were brought to trial, those convicted received relatively light sentences; no prison term exceeded seven years. Meanwhile, the government refused to make material amends to the victims, dismissing most of the Jewish civil suits. Tsarist officials reacted negatively only to the chaos, not to the suffering of the Jewish victims; some even opined that the Jews had gotten what they deserved. The culprits responsible for organizing the pogrom went unidentified and unpunished, remaining at large to conduct further damage in the future (a rash of even deadlier pogroms erupted in 1905).

Bialik never names the city featured in "The City of Slaughter," thereby circumventing the Russian censors and universalizing the horror of the event. His poem, however, is clearly a response to the Kishinev pogrom. Along with several other dignitaries, he had been dispatched to the city several days after it suffered the pogrom to collect eyewitness accounts of the violence, which he embeds in his verse:

> Proceed thence to the ruins, the split walls reach,
> Where wider grows the hollow, and greater grows the breach;
> Pass over the shattered hearth, attain the broken wall
> Whose burnt and barren brick, whose charred stones reveal
> The open mouths of such wounds that no mending
> Shall ever mend, nor healing ever heal.
> There will thy feet in feathers sink, and stumble
> On wreckage doubled wrecked, scroll heaped on manuscript.
> Fragments again fragmented—
>   (Bialik, "In the City of Slaughter," p. 114)

Significantly, Bialik directs his outrage not towards the attackers but towards the victims who seem to have passively accepted their fate. Although he was aware of Jewish attempts to defend themselves in Kishinev, including one instance of a Jewish sexton killed while trying to prevent the destruction of a Torah scroll, he deliberately ignored such instances in hopes of galvanizing his Jewish readers into taking more decisive, militant action against their oppression.

The Poem in Focus

The contents. "In the City of Slaughter" unfolds as a monologue. An unidentified speaker addresses a listener, who is called simply "man" or "son of man," which is the same epithet God uses to address the prophet Ezekiel in the Hebrew Bible. The man, a poet-prophet, is exhorted to "Arise and go now to the city of slaughter" ("In the City of Slaughter," p. 114). Leading him through the devastated city, the speaker shows him the blackened blood, smoldering ruins, and wreckage of elements that once formed a vital part of human lives.

As the journey progresses, the poet-prophet witnesses increasingly terrible sights: pigs rooting in the mingled blood of a Jew and his dog, both decapitated by their killers; a garret where victims were disemboweled and their cloven bellies stuffed with feathers or their heads beaten in with hammers; a baby finding rest on the cold and milkless breast of its dead mother; another child knifed into silence; a cellar where women were raped and murdered while their husbands and brothers hid behind barrels and made no attempt to defend them. From toilets, pigpens, and other filthy places, the men "saw it all; / They did not stir nor move" ("In the City of Slaughter," p. 119). "Concealed and cowering," the menfolk were discovered; the issue of brave ancestors of ages past, they "died liked dogs" ("In the City of Slaughter," p. 119). In somber silence, with their multitudinous eyes, the spirits of the martyrs ask a single, unanswerable question— "Why?" ("In the City of Slaughter," p. 117).

Next the speaker directs the poet-prophet to the graves of the martyred: "See, see, the slaughtered calves, so smitten and so laid; / Is there a price for their death? How shall that price be paid?" ("In the City of Slaughter," p. 122). Startlingly, the speaker reveals Himself to be God, who appears to have failed His people at their most desperate hour and has nothing to give the victims now either, no reward for their terrible sacrifice of life and limb. "Yours is a pauper-Lord! / Poor was He during your life, and poorer still of late . . . / See, I am fallen from My high estate" ("In the City of Slaughter," p. 122). The speaker feels pain for his people, pain and shame. Neither He nor they knows why they died. Their sacrifice is for nothing. And the Shekhina, the Divine Presence, hides Her head in a cloud of shame because of the pain inflicted upon the people and the disgrace of their reaction. (According to rabbinic teachings, God has a transcendent presence, identified as *He,* and an imminent, worldly presence, the Shekhina, associated with the Hebrew Bible and identified as *She.*) The shame His children have brought upon the Lord outweighs His pain. This is the message that must be engrained in their hearts, a task with which the poet-prophet is charged.

Next the speaker bids the poet-prophet turn his attention to the survivors, who lament their dead in the synagogue. It is Yom Kippur, the Jewish Day of Atonement, a day of fasting and confession. The survivors beg forgiveness for their sins, uttering the stock responses of ritual prayer: *"We have sinned! And Sinned have we!—* / Self-flagellative with confession's whips. / Their hearts, however, do not believe their lips" ("In the City of Slaughter," p. 124). The Almighty speaker wonders at the self-flagellation, the lack of rage.

Is it, then, possible for shattered limbs to sin?
Wherefore their cries imploring, their
    supplicating din?
Speak to them, bid them rage!
Let them against me raise the outraged
    hand;—
Let them demand!

. . . .
Let fists be flung like stone
Against the heavens and the heavenly Throne!
                    ("In the City of Slaughter," p. 124)

The poet-prophet must not join the people in their wailing, commands the speaker; it is a desecration of their tragedy. Should a cry issue forth from the poet-prophet, it will be stifled in his throat. Let the tragedy go unlamented, the speaker proclaims. Suppress your pity and your anger, let them fester, then loose them on the people "of thy love and hate" ("In the City of Slaughter," p. 125).

As the poem builds to a bitter conclusion, the broken survivors attempt to pray, but without conviction. The fast is over, the final prayers are said. But wait! A preacher mounts the pulpit to stammer out some parting thought; he does not comfort or rouse his flock: "The empty verses from his speaking flow. / And not a single mighty word is heard / To kindle in the hearts a single spark . . . / The mark of death is on their brows; their God / Has utterly forsaken every one" ("In the City of Slaughter," p. 126).

The Almighty speaker turns next to the mass of broken men sighing and groaning at the doors of the rich, "Proclaiming their sores, like so much peddler's wares," using their battered heads and fractured limbs for personal gain ("In the City of Slaughter," p. 127). In disgust, God bids these parasitical survivors to keep trading upon their people's misfortune and observes that their lives will continue unchanged. Let them dig up the bones of their fathers, pack them in their knapsacks, spread them on some filthy rags and do their business at all the country fairs, imploring sympathy from all the nations, as is their custom: "For you are now as you have been of yore / And as you stretched your hand / So will you stretch it, / And as you have been wretched / So are you wretched!" ("In the City of Slaughter," p. 128).

Forbidden from crying out in anguish or anger or pity, the poet-prophet has no more business here. The Almighty speaker dismisses him with a final directive: *"Rise, to the desert flee!"* with thy heavy heart. Unburden thyself to the elements, shed tears on the barren boulders and *"send thy bitter cry into the storm!"* ("In the City of Slaughter," p. 128).

A call to action. Perhaps one of the most striking aspects of Bialik's poem is that it spares nothing and nobody. The carnage of the Kishinev pogrom and its aftermath are presented in graphic, even nauseating, detail. The horrors are accentuated by juxtaposing them with the beauties of the natural world: "For God called up the slaughter and the spring together / The sun shone, the acacia bloomed, and the slaughterer slaughtered" ("In the City of Slaughter," p. 116). Similarly the outrages inflicted upon the Jews are enumerated, then accentuated by ending with pat statements about a return to normal life: "The matter ends; and nothing more. / And all is as it was before" ("In the City of Slaughter," p. 119).

While Bialik implicitly condemns the perpetrators of the pogrom by depicting their savagery, he reserves the greater share of rage for the passive victims. The poem denounces the Jews who hid behind casks while their women were raped—"the daughter in the presence of her mother and the mother in the presence of her daughter" ("In the City of Slaughter," p. 118). It chastises them for betraying their once-proud heritage by hiding instead of fighting back, for cowering, then dying in their ignominious hiding places. Most of all, Bialik's poem criticizes the broken, apathetic survivors who steep themselves in grief but do not stir.

> Thus groans a people which is lost.
> Look into their hearts—behold a dreary
>   waste,
> Where even vengeance can revive no growth,
> And yet upon their lips no mighty
>   malediction
> Rises, no blasphemous oath.
> ("In the City of Slaughter," p. 123)

Grief, lamentation, and self-reproach will not counteract the murderous deeds of one's enemies, the poem contends. Against such outrages, anger, resolve, and even hatred will stand the people in better stead than prayer and supplication.

Part of the team that collected eyewitness testimony after the pogrom, Bialik knew full well that a modicum of the resolve his poem advocates already existed. This can be substantiated by an excerpt from his own report:

> I was walking on Ismailskii Street and I saw a gang of pogromists, and at its head was an educated man running and gesturing excitedly "This way, come on!" But the gang was met by a big group of Jews from Ismailskii and Gostinnii armed with sticks—and the gang ran away [...]. Suddenly a police patrol showed up and dispersed the group of Jews. That's when I realized how terrible things were. The patrol was dispersing the Jews, not the murderers. I hurriedly ran home.
> (Oshumirski in Goren, p. 74; trans. K. Moss)

But such staunch resistance was the exception, not the rule. Bialik agonized over the common reaction, shown by, among others, the *Kohanim*, the descendants of priests. First they hid while their women were raped; then they sought out the rabbi to determine if it was religiously permissible to sleep with their ravaged wives. The poem excoriates such behavior.

The fact that others shared Bialik's sentiments is evident in the movement for self-defense that grew out of the pogrom. In April 1903 the Jewish Labor Bund of Russia and Poland, a workers' organization strongly influenced by socialist ideals, issued a statement condemning the attack and calling for Jews to confront their foes boldly: "We must answer violence with violence, no matter where it comes from. Not with sweet words but with arms in our hands can we prevail upon the frenzied pogromists. We mustn't hide in attics but must go out face to face, 'with a mighty arm,' to fight these beasts" (Bund in Roskies,

p. 156). In terms very similar to those in Bialik's poem, the statement declared, "Let not the Kishinev pogrom weaken our faith in our sacred ideal. With hatred and with a threefold curse on our lips let us sew the shrouds for the Russian autocratic regime" (Bund in Roskies, p. 156). Another statement, from the Union of Hebrew Writers to all the Jews of Russia, sent out an exhortation: "Brothers! The blood of our brethren in Kishinev cries out to us! Shake off the dust and become men! Stop weeping and pleading, stop lifting your hands for salvation to those who hate and exclude you! Look to your own hands for rescue!" (Union in Roskies, p. 158). The statement called for "a *permanent organization* . . . in all our communities, which would be standing guard and always prepared to face the enemy at the outset, to quickly gather to the place of riots any men who have the strength to face danger" (Union in Roskies, p. 158). There was a growing consensus that Russia's Jews could not depend on anyone but themselves for protection, a consensus that stems back to major agents of change, such as Bialik's poem. Future pogroms would not find the Jews similarly unprepared:

> Within weeks after the pogrom, in city after city within the Pale of Settlement, Jewish self-defense groups were formed. . . . By 1905, when the next major wave of pogroms swept through the Pale of Settlement, Jewish defense was conspicuous almost everywhere. . . . The Kishinev experience, and the shame it engendered, helped to transform the Jews from passive victims to active and militant resisters.
> (Judge, p. 144)

Sources and literary context. Bialik drew inspiration for his poem from the circumstances of the Kishinev pogrom of 1903. At the behest of the Jewish Historical Society of Odessa, he served as the central member of a three-person committee sent to Kishinev to report on the devastation. Bialik returned to Odessa five months later with a stack of notebooks in hand, including interviews with the survivors. His report was not published because of a dearth of funds in the Jewish Historical Society coffers, but his poems were printed. Within four months of his return to Odessa, he had composed "In the City of Slaughter," which differs from other poems that he wrote immediately after the pogrom. This one focuses not only on the distressing reaction of the survivors but also on "the futility of poetry as communication" (Mintz, p. 154). For a decade Bialik had been adopting the persona of the biblical

THE WORLD OBJECTS

While Bialik considered the victims and found them wanting, other dignitaries took the rioters to task. The Russian novelist Leo Tolstoy went so far as to implicate the tsarist regime in the pogrom, charging that it was "a direct consequence of lies and violence that the Russian government pursues with such energy" (Tolstoy in Judge, p. 89). Another writer, Vladimir Korolenko, traveled to Kishinev and then recounted some of the pogrom's worst atrocities in his short story "House Number 13," which blames Christian Russia as a whole for the pogrom.

Abroad, especially in Britain and the United States, the reaction was no less indignant. Newspapers reported on the pogrom and their editorials cast an increasingly harsh light on the Russian government's role in it. Two New York newspapers dispatched Michael Davit to Kishinev to investigate and report his findings. Davit confirmed the carnage, the failure on the part of the authorities to uphold Russian law and protect the victims, and the incendiary, anti-Semitic writing by Krushevan in *Bessarabets*. In dozens of American cities, from New York to Boston and San Francisco, protestors denounced Russia's policies towards the Jews.

prophet to express national concerns in verse. This time he takes the strategy further than ever before and "exhausts it"—"the insensibility of the listeners" discredits the model of prophet and people" (Mintz, p. 154).

Bialik lamented the lack of originality in the poetry of his day. "There is not talent," he complained, "and no new idea, no skill of language and no spark of God, but there is a spirit of fudging and pointless thoughts, a spirit of emptiness and wasted breath. . . . Lie and deceit . . . stands out in all their poems as [poets today] weep the destruction of their people" (Bialik in Miron, p. xix). Into this vacuum, Bialik introduced innovations in style and content. While most Hebrew poetry of his time centered on a collective *I*, he adopted a personal voice, an individual *I*. In his "poems of wrath" he adopted the voice of a prophet and used it unusually, to rage against the Lord and His people.

Other Russian poems about the pogroms waxed sentimental or philosophical. David Frishamn's "David in the Lion's Den" perceived the massacres as dashing hopes for a civilized world at the dawn of a new century. I. L. Baruch and Pesah Kaplan modeled their poems on accounts of the martyrs of 1096 (when the Crusaders attacked the Jews of Rhineland) and 1648 (at Nemirov, Kishinev, and other towns of the Ukraine). Finally, Bialik's poetry expressed a

degree of emotion and sense of inner turmoil largely lacking in most of the Hebrew poetry of his age but in keeping with **The Diwan of Judah Halevi** (also in *WLAIT 6: Middle Eastern Literatures and Their Times*), a comparsion made in his own day. "We studied by heart [Bialik's] poem[s]," explained one awestruck scholar in Odessa; "it was rumored that there were three hundred poems in his rucksack," he continued, and that they were "unmatched since the time of Yehudah ha-Levi" (Hillels in Rubin, p. 41).

Publication and reception. "In the City of Slaughter" was first published in *ha-Zeman*, a Hebrew quarterly of St. Petersburg, Russia, in 1904. To avoid government censorship, Bialik was forced to publish the poem under the title "Masa Nemirov" (translated as "The Nemirov March," "The Burden of Nemirov," or "The Oracle at Nemirov"), which disguised the poem's relevancy to the 1903 pogrom by linking it to a massacre of the Jews in 1648-49.

Early translations into Russian and Yiddish greatly expanded the potential impact of the poem. Although Hebrew was a key language of Jewish high culture at the time, the vast majority of Russian Jews did not know the language well enough to understand the verse in all its complexity. On the other hand, virtually all of Russia's Jews spoke and read Yiddish, and a significant minority had begun to find Russian more accessible than Hebrew. Thanks in no small part to the translations, the impact of the poem was indeed significant.

ANOTHER POET'S PERSPECTIVE

A more conventional, even sentimental view of the pogrom than Bialik's surfaces in Simon Frug's "Have Pity," which appeared on the front page of the St. Petersburg *Der Fraynd* in April 1903. If "In the City of Slaughter" aimed to inflame readers, Frug's poem intended to elicit pity for the victims and aid on their behalf.

Streams of blood and rivers of tears
Deep and wide they flow and roar . . . .
Our misfortune, great and timeless
Has laid hands on us once more.
Do you hear the mothers moan
And their little children cry?
In the streets the dead are lying;
The sick are fallen down nearby.
Brothers, sisters, please have mercy!
Great and awful is the need.
Bread is needed for the living,
Shrouds are needed for the dead.

. . . .

How weak our hand is to do battle,
How great and heavy is our woe—
Come and bring us love and comfort,
Jewish hearts, we need you so!
(Frug, pp. 149-150)

"In the City of Slaughter" became a rallying cry for Jews to fight back against their oppressors. The poem's anger towards the passivity of the victims of Kishinev had a galvanizing effect on Russia's Jews, who took the message to heart and resolved not to submit tamely to such atrocities again.

> Never before had one living hero of the Jewish people so bitterly chastised those he loved; and never before had one people taken such a message to heart and vowed never to let such a tragedy be repeated. "In the City of Slaughter" became, not a challenge to further introspection and lament, but a clarion call to militant action.
>
> (Jacobs, p. 124)

The clarion call rippled though Russia, and beyond. According to Vladimir Jabotinsky, founder of the Jewish Legion, "The revival of Maccabean tendencies in the Ghetto really dates from that poem; the self-defense organizations which sprang up everywhere in Russia to meet the new pogrom-wave two years later, the Shomrim (Yeomanry) movement in Palestine, even the Jewish Legion which fought for the Holy Land in 1918—they are all Bialik's children" (Jabotinsky in Jacobs, p. 124).

Besides spurring Bialik's Jewish compatriots to action, "In the City of Slaughter" further consolidated his reputation as national poet. The people lauded him as a prophet too, equating him with the persona he adopted in a number of his poems. In a comment of 1907, which brings this poem to mind, the critic B. Ibry described Bialik as "a prophet whose very love for his people causes him to burn with indignation at their weakness" (Ibry in Poupard, p. 49). Through the ages, critics would continue to acknowledge the distinct, invigorating place he holds in Hebrew letters: his was "a lone voice of defiance running counter to the general atmosphere of despondency," and, in the process, bringing to modern Hebrew poetry "a new sense of pride and vigor" (Gurevitch, p. 106).

—Pamela S. Loy

For More Information

Baron, Salo W. *The Russian Jew Under the Tsars and the Soviets.* New York: Macmillan, 1976.

Bialik, Hayyim Nahman, ed. "In the City of Slaughter." *Selected Poems of Hayyim Nahman Bialik.* Ed. Israel Efros. New York: Block, 1965.

Frug, Simon. "Have Pity!" In *The Literature of Destruction.* Ed. David G. Roskies. Philadelphia: The Jewish Publication Society, 1989.

Gassenschmidt, Christoph. *Jewish Liberal Politics in Tsarist Russia, 1900-14: The Modernization of Russian Jewry.* London: Macmillan, 1995.

Goren, Jacob, ed. *Eduyot nifge`e Kishinov, 1903 : kefi she-nigbu `al-yede H.N. Byalik va-haverav.* [Testimony of Victims of the 1903 Kishinev Pogrom as Written down by Ch. N. Bialik and Others]. Tel Aviv: Hakibbutz Hameuchad; Ramat Ef`al: Yad Tabenkin, 1991.

Gurevitch, Zali. "Eternal Loss: An Afterword." In *Revealment and Concealment,* by Haim Nahman Bialik. Jerusalem: Ibis, 2000.

Harshav, Benjamin. *Language in the Time of Revolution.* Berkley: University of California Press, 1993.

Jacobs, Steven L., ed. *Shirot Bialik: A New and Annotated Translation of Chaim Nachman Bialik's Epic Poems.* Columbus: Alpha, 1987.

Judge, Edward H. *Easter in Kishinev: Anatomy of a Pogrom*. New York: New York University Press, 1992.

Mintz, Alan. *Hurban: Responses to Catastrophe in Hebrew Literature*. New York: Columbia University Press, 1984.

Miron, Dan. Introduction to *Songs from Bialik*, by Hayyim Nahman Bialik. Trans. Atar Hadari. Syracuse, N.Y.: Syracuse University Press, 2000.

Poupard, Dennis, ed. *Twentieth-Century Literary Criticism*. Vol. 25. Detroit: Gale Research Company, 1988.

Roskies, David G., ed. Annotations to "In the City of the Slaughter." In *The Literature of Destruction: Jewish Responses to Catastrophe*. Philadelphia: The Jewish Publication Society, 1988.

Rubin, Adam. *From Torah to Tarbut: Hayim Nahman Bialik and the Nationalization of Judaism*. PhD diss. University of California at Los Angeles, 2000.

"Introduction to the History of the Petty Kings"

by

Adunis

Considered by many to be the most influential Arabic poet of the late twentieth century, Adunis was born Ali Ahmad Said in 1930 in Qassabayn, a small village near the Syrian coastal town of Latakia. His early education was frequently interrupted because his poverty-stricken family needed him to work in the fields and it was difficult to reach the schools. But his father urged Ali to study, encouraging him to learn Quran recitation in a local religious school and to memorize classical Arabic poetry. In early adolescence, young Ali had an opportunity to recite one of his own poems before the first president of republican Syria, Shukri al-Quwatli, who was so impressed that he awarded the boy an advanced secondary education at government expense in one of the best schools in the country, where he received rigorous intellectual training in both French and Arabic. It was also a center of political activism. The young Ali affiliated himself there with one of the smaller, but extremely well-organized nationalist factions, the Syrian Social National Party (SSNP). It was during this time (probably 1947 or 1948), that he took the pen name "Adunis," which is Arabic for the ancient Greek fertility spirit Adonis. An ancient center for worship of Adonis was in Lebanon, not too far from where the Arabic poet grew up. In taking the name, he was following the lead of SSNP members who aimed to show that many highly respected ideas and beliefs of the Greeks (long acclaimed, in the West, as the founders of their civilization) had actually originated farther east, in the "Syrian" lands. In 1949, the founder of the SSNP, Antun Saadah,

THE LITERARY WORK

A poem set in the Arab world around September 1970; published in Arabic (as "Muqaddimah li-tarikh al-muluk al-tawa'if") in 1970, in English in 1992.

SYNOPSIS

An elegy, the poem mourns the sudden passing of Gamal Abdel Nasser, whose death amplified a growing sense of frustration and despair among Arabs following their defeat in the 1967 Arab-Israeli war.

was executed for a coup attempt against the Syrian government, which inspired Adunis to compose a series of poems embracing extensive meditations on the nature of heroism and leadership (including "Qalat al-Ard" [1949-1950; The Earth Said] and "Al-Ba`th wa-al-Ramad" [1957; Resurrection and Ashes]). Within a decade, Adunis had begun to shift the object of his deliberations to another magnetic Arab leader, Gamal Abdel Nasser, who assumed power in Egypt in 1954. Over the next 15 years, Nasser became the foremost advocate for a revitalized vision of an all-embracing Arab nationalism transcending country boundaries. Adunis appears to have embraced a similar view at this time, as shown by his writing of two poems honoring Abd al-Rahman al-Dakhil, the founder of the Umayyad caliphate in Spain and a tenth-century hero of the Arab nationalist movement ("Ayyam al-Saqr" [Days of the

Eagle]; "Tahawwulat al-Saqr" [Transformations of the Eagle]). These poems have been interpreted as important expressions of Adunis's reaction to Nasser's leadership in the late 1950s and early 1960s. "Introduction to the History of the Petty Kings" laments Nasser's untimely death by heart attack at age 52, crowning the phase of Adunis's poetic career that preoccupies itself with defining political leadership and the nature of governance in the modern Arab world.

Events in History at the
Time the Poem Takes Place

The assassination of Ali. Though set in 1970, "History of the Petty Kings" covers an immense sweep of human history, touching on three major periods of political crisis in the Arab world. Decisive in its development, these three periods are related in that each of them shaped views on the role of leadership and the exercise of power among the Arabs as a new society emerged and matured under the influence of Islam. The first crisis occurred in the years immediately following the Prophet Muhammad's death. The second occurred in the tenth and eleventh centuries C.E., as the political structures that had allowed the caliphs to control the vast Islamic empire began to decay. The third crisis—at least for Adunis—emerges in modern times, as the powerful unifying message of Arab nationalism fails to be consistently translated into successful practice by Arab leaders.

In 632 C.E. the founder of the Islamic religion, Muhammad, died unexpectedly of natural causes. He had made no provisions for a successor and had no surviving male children to assume his now vacated position as leader of the Muslim community. This provoked a crisis among his followers. Through a combination of decisive action and persuasive power, Abu Bakr and Umar, two of Muhammad's closest friends and companions, who shared his vision of Islam as a religious orientation and blueprint for living a moral life, resolved the crisis, at least for the time being. Abu Bakr was proclaimed the *caliph* (Arabic for "successor") to Muhammad by an assembled group of leading Muslims. Soon he too died, whereupon Umar was chosen to assume the mantle of leadership.

When Umar died, the office of caliph was given to someone with a more problematic background. Uthman had been an early follower of Muhammad, and there was no doubt about his own personal piety and adherence to the ideals of Islam. But he also belonged to the powerful Umayyad clan in Mecca, which included some very vocal opponents to Islam's reformist message. So difficult had they made life for Muhammad that his followers sought refuge in Medina, a city that had offered protection to them in exchange for Muhammad's arbitrating among its feuding tribal groups.

Uthman's perceived favoritism toward his fellow Umayyads when he became caliph led eventually to his assassination at the hands of a group of disgruntled soldiers who may have had ties to Muhammad's cousin and son-in-law, Ali. Ali had married Fatimah, one of Muhammad's daughters, and they had two sons, Hasan and Husayn, who were the Prophet's only living male descendants. Now that Uthman had died, many saw Ali as the natural choice for the position and he agreed to take office. A feud followed, prompted by the Umayyad clan's belief that Ali had been somehow involved in Uthman's death. Publicly the clan leader, Mu`awiyah, called for Ali's removal if he did not find and punish the assassins, making demands that led to a virtual civil war. In the midst of this unrest, a disgruntled former supporter assassinated Ali, whereupon Mu`awiyah seized power for himself and the Umayyad clan. Ali's followers were unable to muster sufficient military power to overthrow Mu`awiyah, nor were Hasan and Husayn old enough to lead, so the Ali faction tacitly accepted the status quo. But Ali's followers never accepted the legitimacy of Umayyad rule. They simply bided their time, looking forward to the time when Muhammad's grandsons would assume power, either peacefully or through the military overthrow of the Umayyads.

Once in power, the Umayyad dynasty predictably moved in the direction of hereditary rule based on the support of a strong standing army. This trend was confirmed 19 years later when the Umayyads (now ruled by Mu`awiyah's son) killed Husayn, the last surviving male offspring of Ali, and massacred his men on the battlefield at Karbala (in contemporary Iraq). For the followers of Ali and his sons (later called "the Shi`ah" or "Shi`ites," from the Arabic term "shi`at Ali," or "party of Ali"), these murders were damning evidence that the rulers of the Muslim community had lost any claim to legitimacy. In their view, the sort of divine guidance that had inspired the Prophet Muhammad (and was presumably passed on to Ali and his sons) had been lost.

Adunis, who was raised in a Shi`ite family, would have been intimately familiar with this interpretation of Islamic history and with Shi`ite aspirations to fill the world "with justice as it is now filled with injustice" (Hodgson, p. 374). But the human failings of subsequent rulers made it unsurprising that political oppression, civil war, and internecine strife became more the norm than the exception in Islamic history. Early in his poem Adunis indicts the forces of authority collectively—"They piled up, they rent apart the face of Ali"—for the way they seem to single out one helpless individual as a target for their violence (Adunis, "Introduction to the History of the Petty Kings," lines 7-8).

Rise (and fall) of the petty kings. In 750 C.E., the Umayyads were overthrown by another clan, more closely related to Muhammad's family, the Abbasids. Although the Abbasids practiced more tolerant, inclusive policies than their predecessors, they were unable to sustain central authority. Their imperial rule entered a lengthy period of decentralization and growing ineffectualness, during which governors became semi-independent rulers, diverting taxes to local needs rather than sending them to the Abbasids in Baghdad. In time, these local rulers stopped paying anything more than lip service to the caliph, even setting up dynasties of their own in opposition to Abbasid rule.

One of these local dynasties was established in al-Andalus (Islamic Spain) by Abd al-Rahman al-Dakhil, a descendant of the older Ummayad dynasty. In power in the eighth century, this Ummayad ruler governed the Iberian peninsula as a state independent of the central Islamic empire. Al-Andalus was a flourishing province in this period and its loss weakened the Abbasid position considerably.

Even more damaging was the rule of another independent dynasty, that of the Fatimids, who claimed descent from Fatimah (Muhammad's daughter) through Husayn. By the late ninth century C.E. the Fatimids had welded together a rich North African and Levantine empire with its capital in Cairo. The loss of Egypt and its surroundings was particularly damaging to the Abbasids because this area was one of the richest sources of income in the world at that time.

In due course, these aspiring caliphates themselves lost power. By the early eleventh century C.E., many of their domains had been reduced to small principalities, consisting of just one city or fortress and its environs. The rulers of these small territories—especially in al-Andalus—became known as *muluk al-tawa'if* in Arabic, "the kings of the factions," otherwise known as "the party (or sometimes "petty") kings." The disintegration

was a slow, painful process. As the Fatimid dynasty grew weaker, army troops would seize first one member of the family, then another, temporarily elevating him to figurehead ruler, only to depose him weeks or even days later when another faction gained the upper hand.

THE PETTY KINGS AND THE CRUSADES

Pilgrims to the holy land spent relatively large amounts of money on their journeys and were thus a lucrative source of income to the local population. Therefore, the Fatimid caliphs had traditionally acted to protect the Christians travelling through their territories. One result of the disintegration of central authority was that the parties of Christian pilgrims coming from Europe to the Holy Land were left defenseless against Muslim marauders. The situation was used as justification for Christian knights from Europe to mount the First Crusade, an invasion of Arabic lands that was intent on capturing Jerusalem and controlling the surrounding territory. The weakness of the local petty kings, especially their inability to unite so they could drive out the European armies, has been widely seen as dooming the region to nearly a century of foreign rule by the Crusaders. Not until in the 1170s, did a leader by the name of Saladin (more precisely, "Salah al-Din") unite the local lords sufficiently to retake Jerusalem. Under Saladin's rule, the peace and prosperity of the Fatimid state at its height was at least partly reconstituted, only to be lost again in the decades following his death.

In Spain, the rise of many small, relatively peaceful kingdoms was in some ways beneficial, especially to the local intellectual and cultural life, for it led to friendly competition among the relatively prosperous and well-educated rulers to distribute patronage among their subjects. But the disintegration of central authority made the Muslim territories in Spain vulnerable to invasions by Christian rulers, who deposed its last Muslim ruler (in Granada) in 1492. Ferdinand and Isabella (known as the Catholic Monarchs) expelled the Jews in 1492, forced the Muslims to convert or leave in 1502, and then expelled the Muslim converts in 1609.

Among the Arabs, the view became widespread that if the Islamic world had been united at this time, and its leaders had all been as selfless and dedicated to the general welfare as Saladin, the

Christians would never have dared attack Muslim territory in the first place. As in the era of Ali's assassination and the rise of the Umayyads, the era of the petty kings exposed the dangers of Arab/Muslim disunity.

Arab nationalism and the rise of Nasser. Beginning in the 1300s, the Arabic-speaking territories of the old Abbasid empire were increasingly ruled over by outsiders. First these lands were gradually conquered by the Ottoman Turks, who controlled them for about 500 years (c. 1350-1918). The Ottomans saw themselves as fellow Muslims and did not discriminate against their Arab subjects the way future overlords would. But in retrospect Arab intellectuals have seen the centuries of Ottoman rule as a period of foreign, essentially colonial, occupation that led to backwardness and stagnation. There followed in the nineteenth and twentieth centuries a period of European colonial rule, especially British and French rule. In with the colonizers came modern forms of technology, industry, government, and education, but for the sake of the colonizers first, only secondarily for the Arab peoples. Finally, the colonial administrations (including the occupying armies) were expected to pay for themselves by levying local taxes on the colonized Arabs, who, much like the colonized Americans, then protested against "taxation without representation."

Throughout this period the Arabs retained a sense of mutual ties and group identification, fostered by a common language, history, and allegiance to the broadest ethical, moral, and social values of Islam as a monotheistic religion and a source of tolerant cultural attitudes. They were values that non-Muslims too could embrace. Encouragement for the sense of mutual Arab identity, which would eventually coalesce into the movement known as "Arab nationalism," came from political leaders who made pan-Arabism a cornerstone of the struggle for independence from foreign rule.

The enthusiasm generated by Arab nationalism rose and fell over the decades. Calling most immediately for throwing off foreign rule, it competed with other movements such as pan-Islamism and Pharaonism in Egypt. In the 1950s, however, Arab nationalism received a new lease on life from Gamal Abdel Nasser in the wake of his successful revolution in Egypt. Nasser had been one the first generation of native Egyptians who were allowed to rise to officer rank in the Egyptian army. Before that, most of the command positions had been held either by Englishmen or

Egyptian president Gamal Abdel Nasser.

members of the old Turko-Circassian elite who had ruled Egypt under the Ottomans. Possibly as early as 1938, while on his first garrison posting after graduation from the Military Academy, Nasser became involved with a secret group of army conspirators, the Free Officers, who sought to overthrow the corrupt and decrepit monarchy and expel the British army from Egypt. In 1952 the Free Officers seized power in a bloodless coup that abolished the monarchy. The peacefulness of the coup was spearheaded by Nasser, who prevailed against the arguments of his fellow conspirators that King Faruq should be tried and executed. The royal family was, instead, allowed to depart unmolested for exile in Italy. For the first years of Free Officer rule, Nasser stayed in the background but then in 1956 he was elected President (having run unopposed).

After his election, Nasser articulated a pair of twin goals: first, he sought freedom and independence for all Arabs, Egyptian and non-Egyptian, and second, he called for reform of Egyptian society founded on a policy of "Arab Socialism." Entailed in the policy, said Nasser, are land reforms, nationalization of key establishments, and redistribution of wealth but with provisions for individual investment and profit and with recognition of the import of the Islamic religion in Egypt. To attain freedom from foreign rule for all Arabs, Nasser supported the liberation struggles of revolutionary groups in the region, most notably those on the behalf of the Algerian Arabs and the Palestinian Arabs.

Nasser achieved some notable successes during his 14 years of rule—land reform, nationalization of the Suez Canal, construction of the Aswan High Dam, an anticorruption campaign, reforms in education, women's rights, and Egyptianization of the government bureaucracy and economy. But true democratic rule was never implemented. Revolutionary Egypt became an increasingly authoritarian state, in which censorship, jailing of the regime's opponents, and the imposition of martial law were common occurrences.

Nasser meanwhile had setbacks. In 1962 he entangled Egypt's troops in an indecisive civil war in Yemen, and in 1967 he lost a war to Israel, in which the West Bank (of the Jordan river) and Gaza Strip were occupied by the Israeli army. Another setback followed in the summer of 1970, when the Palestine Liberation Organization (PLO) and associated groups, which had sought refuge in Jordan after the 1967 defeat, attacked the monarchy of Jordan's King Hussein, deeming him insufficiently supportive of their aspirations to wage guerrilla warfare against Israel from his territory. The ensuing conflict threatened to turn into a civil war and, on September 27, 1970, in the midst of negotiations to resolve the conflict, Nasser suffered a fatal heart attack and died.

Nasser, Hussein, and the Palestinians. The growing Arab infighting after the defeat in 1967 and the resulting sense of impotence in the face of foreign aggression, clearly had parallels to what happened in the days of the petty kings. The sense of history repeating itself was heightened when Nasser died, for he had compared himself—and had often been compared by others—to the legendary Saladin. Nasser, like Saladin, seemed able to unite the Arabs by the sheer force of his personality when he first emerged. He had given them hope and confident optimism. His sudden death, coupled with a growing awareness of the failure of reforms associated with him, led to concerns about the future of Nasser's legacy, expressed by a number of Egyptians, including Adunis in his "Introduction to the History of the Petty Kings." The concern escalated now that the Palestinian cause was threatened by forces within the Arab world, and Nasser had identified himself closely with it. He had been instrumental in creating the PLO, the umbrella organization whose members would in the 1990s, establish institutions for state governance on the West Bank and in Gaza under the leadership of Yasir Arafat.

King Hussein of Jordan was another key player in the unfolding drama of Palestinian national aspirations. After World War I, under the auspices of the League of Nations, the victorious Allied nations had set up "mandates" in Syria, Lebanon, Palestine, Iraq, and Transjordan (the first two under French control; the last three under British control). When Transjordan (today's Jordan) became a mandate in 1920, it was a country of few resources, inhabited mostly by nomadic Bedouin tribes. Its composition would change radically in 1948, however, after the Palestine mandate was partitioned into Jewish and Arab states. The Transjordan mandate subsequently became a refuge for Palestinian Arabs, who fled the war and postwar upheavals in their homeland. After the war only two of its areas remained under Arab control: the west bank of the Jordan river (Transjordan occupied the East Bank) and a small coastal area around the city of Gaza known as the Gaza Strip. These two areas were to be the nucleus of a future Palestinian state. Egypt took control of the Gaza Strip; Jordan, of the West Bank. The population in Jordan had meanwhile been transformed; it now consisted mainly of Arab refugees from the former British mandate of Palestine, and it became King Hussein's job to mediate between them and the original Bedouin inhabitants. It was a precarious balancing act, and the difficulty of it increased after the Arab-Israeli war of 1967, in which the Jordanians lost control of the West Bank to Israel and a second exodus of refugees streamed into Jordan.

In "Introduction to the History of the Petty Kings" Adunis frequently evokes the Palestinian people through a line of metaphoric reference: "Jaffa's face is a child" ("Petty Kings," lines 1, 6-7, 115, 159, 186-90, 277). Jaffa was the Arab town that before 1948 dominated the region around Tel Aviv, and has since been largely engulfed by the growth of this much more economically vital Jewish Israeli city, just as the Palestinian inhabitants of the land have been displaced by new settlers. Since the first Arab Israeli war, especially since many in the first wave of refugees came from the area surrounding Jaffa, it has become a metaphor for the lost land of Palestine. Associating it with a "child's face" alludes to an idealized view of innocence that has been trampled upon and lost, an image seared into Arab consciousness by newspaper photographs and newsreel footage of frightened Arabs fleeing Palestine after the 1948 war.

The surface assertion of Jaffa's innocence in the poem, however, conceals the very different role

Palestinians had been playing on the stage of Arab politics shortly before it was written, a role that would have been in the forefront of every reader's mind. The image of the Palestinians in the post 1967 period changed from the suffering face of a Jaffa child into the confident, sometimes bullying figure of the fedayee (meaning "one who sacrifices himself for others"), the Palestinian militiaman trained in guerrilla warfare. Some of these fedayeen conceived of traditional leaders (like King Hussein), who, however tentatively, had sought some sort of accommodation with Israel, as their enemies. Under the pressure of such attitudes, a civil war erupted in Jordan in September 1970 between the early Palestinian refugees (allied to Hussein and the Bedouins) and the later refugees and leadership of the PLO. That this destructive internal warfare erupted at such a critical moment, in the wake of the 1967 war, only increased the sense of political disarray. Small wonder, given these conditions, that Adunis seizes on a comparison to the time of petty kings in his poem.

The Poem in Focus

Contents overview. The poem begins with a dedication to Nasser, hailing him as a leader "who worked toward ending the age of the petty kings and beginning another age" ("Petty Kings," lines ii-iv). Though there are no other formal divisions, the rest of the poem can be divided into four main sections. Each of the first three has a set of dominant motifs and a different mode of address (first person, second person, etc.). The last section attempts to synthesize all that has gone before.

In the first section ("Petty Kings," lines 1-62), the dominant motifs express a longing for rebirth or they center on self-sacrifice, ultimately on the part of the poet, who views himself, speaking in the first person, as a heroic figure attempting to rescue his fellow human beings through the power of his words. The second section ("Petty Kings," lines 65-115) tacitly acknowledges that an individual cannot effect change alone but must seek allies. Ali and another, unnamed, person (presumably Nasser) are examined as possible confederates and models for the poet in his quest to renew and change his world, and are evoked in the second person. Ultimately the unnamed model is chosen. But in the third section ("Petty Kings," lines 115-214), this individual (described mostly in the third person) is also rejected because his deeds as a person acting alone do not

result in change, but only reinforce the failures of the past. The poet seeks a way out of this impasse in the last part of the poem ("Petty Kings," lines 215-85) by searching for more collective models for action, especially one that involves children as representatives of a coming generation with the ability perhaps to transcend the mistakes of its predecessors.

Contents summary. In the first line, Jaffa is described as having the face of a child, an image that begins to characterize it as the helpless victim of outside violence over which it has no control. But suddenly the poem shifts to a mythical waiting for rebirth, much like T. S. Eliot's English poem *The Waste Land,* whose initial images carry a sense of bleakness and sterility related to the sense that World War I has dashed hopes for a more civilized world.

In Adunis's poem, the uncertainty about rebirth is reinforced by the constant use of questions. No one can answer these questions because no one knows when or if "the withered tree" (symbolizing the modern Arab world in crisis) shall "thrive." Likewise, no one can predict if the Virgin (almost certainly an allusion to Mary, the mother of Jesus, usually seen as a redemptive figure in Christianity) will become one with Mother Earth in the people's understanding, thereby gaining even more universal significance. This is an apt illustration of the cultural syncretism exhibited by Adunis's generation of poets who, like Anglo-American modernists in the West, were fascinated by the similarities they saw in symbols used by different cultures and blended these symbols in Arabic poetry. The poets sought thereby to achieve a greater emotional resonance for their work.

Line 4 makes references that can be tied to episodes in the decline of the Fatimid caliphate and the Andalusian Party (or Petty) Kings. Also in this section, Jaffa and Ali are linked by both being described as having "a face" ("They . . . prepared an ambush for the face of Ali / It was a child and it was white or black, Jaffa, its trees and its sons . . . / They piled up, they rent apart the face of Ali" ("Petty Kings," lines 5-8). The "face of Ali" becomes "a child," who then becomes Jaffa, with the political destruction of the man evolving into the political destruction of the city.

From a general search for rebirth, the focus shifts to the actions of the poet as redemptive figure. He declares himself powerless ("I ruptured and in the Arab greenness / I drowned my sun / Civilization is a stretcher"), but then makes a valiant attempt to reassert his power through his ability to manipulate words ("Petty Kings," lines 17-18). Every culture can point to examples in its history when stirring phrases, uttered in the right form at the proper moment, inspired people to believe in an ideal and act on that belief. Through his phrases, the poet wants to shape a new reality capable of inspiring his people to action, so "I wrote the city," he declares, meaning he has rewritten the history of the city so that it inspires people by giving them positive models to emulate and no longer just reproduces images of the Middle East such as dead "mummies" or "Constantinople[s]" ("Petty Kings," line 23).

The poet calls not for a return to Constantinople (today's Istanbul, capital of the last Muslim dynastic state in the region—the Ottoman Empire) but instead seeks something new. Unsure of what this new reality might be, he is reduced to inarticulate confusion by a succession of images of violent acts directed against children in his homeland, a violence he perceives as deadly to his own vision of future hope. At the end of the section, he addresses the unnamed violators, whom he identifies with his "country": "You [have] killed me you killed my songs / are you a carnage / or a revolution? / I am confused, every time I see you, my country, in a picture"("Petty Kings," lines 59-62).

The poet's initial optimism has been by this point completely undermined by a suspicion that all the killing around him reflects merely pointless mechanical bloodletting (carnage)—not a revolution that (for all its danger to individuals) might lead to productive social change. Anticipating this sense of helplessness is a passage whose words completely dissolve into their component letters. The poet's frustration at his lack of control over his own tools—words—leads him to fruitlessly order them over and over again to "perish, perish" ("Petty Kings," lines 37-44).

"And Ali requests the light, and leaves" ("Petty Kings," line 62).Having perceived by the end of the first section that his own individual initiative will not be sufficient to transform his reality, the poet begins in the second section to try to identify a partner who will help him. First, he looks to the martyred caliph Ali, who seems to have been for Adunis both a symbol of the unquestionably legitimate political leader and an inspiring example of a savior who is willing to put himself in danger and even die in an act of self-sacrifice to help his fellow human beings.

The Ali whom the poet encounters here diverges completely from the childlike individual portrayed earlier. Now he is a homeless wanderer

who seeks but cannot find a light to illuminate the darkness surrounding him and who carries "his murdered history from hut to hut" in a fruitless search for someone to infuse it with new life and relevance ("Petty Kings," line 65). When this Ali is confronted and forced to speak, his reply is a bitter denunciation of the most cherished slogans of Arab nationalism. He especially denounces the most famous one—that "the Arab nation extends from the Atlantic Ocean to the Arabian (Persian) Gulf":

> They notified me that I have a house
> —like my house—in Jericho
> that I have brothers in Cairo, that the limits
>   of Nazareth are Mecca.
> How can knowledge transform [itself] into a
>   shackle?
> Is it for this reason that history refuses my
>   face?
> Is it for this reason that I do not see
> an Arab sun on the horizon?
> ("Petty Kings," lines 66-74)

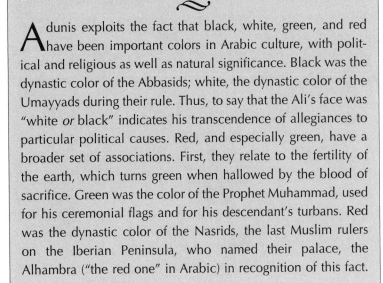

COLOR SYMBOLISM IN ARABIC

Adunis exploits the fact that black, white, green, and red have been important colors in Arabic culture, with political and religious as well as natural significance. Black was the dynastic color of the Abbasids; white, the dynastic color of the Umayyads during their rule. Thus, to say that the Ali's face was "white or black" indicates his transcendence of allegiances to particular political causes. Red, and especially green, have a broader set of associations. First, they relate to the fertility of the earth, which turns green when hallowed by the blood of sacrifice. Green was the color of the Prophet Muhammad, used for his ceremonial flags and for his descendant's turbans. Red was the dynastic color of the Nasrids, the last Muslim rulers on the Iberian Peninsula, who named their palace, the Alhambra ("the red one" in Arabic) in recognition of this fact.

For this Ali, the information that there is someone in Jericho who lives in a house like his, or that he has people he can think of as kin in Cairo, or that he can encounter lifestyles similar to his as far apart as Nazareth and Mecca has no enlightening consequences. It does not lead to greater insight about himself or infuse him with the strength to overcome adversity. The information merely chains him, limiting his ability to see from any new perspective, for it is an empty catch phrase used to whip up the enthusiasm of the crowd. The original principles of Arab nationalism have degenerated to the status of a formula, preventing history from recognizing Ali's potential and from supporting the aspirations of his people for freedom or a better life.

THE SCIENCE OF LETTERS

Throughout "Introduction to the History of the Petty Kings," Adunis makes extensive use of lore about the Arabic alphabet. The letter shapes themselves are frequently used as metaphors for parts of the human body or natural phenomena. For example, in line 120 ("*dal* is a frame that sorrow fractures . . . ") the success of the image depends on the reader's knowledge that in Arabic the letter *dal* (د) looks like a person seated in the bent-over posture of old age. Elsewhere the poem refers to other branches of the science of letters—the significance given them in the Quran, the numerical significance attached to them by pre-Islamic Arabs, and their connection with medieval medicine, which involved the recitation of words containing certain letters, and the mixing of potions, including words written in ink on paper and dissolved in water to produce a mixture to drink.

Disappointed in Ali's response, the poet appears to turn at this point to another individual, an unnamed "you." He still seems to nurture the hope that a savior can be found to rescue him from his despair. The "you" in this instance is not the country but a human. Like "others," including the human poet in section one, this "you" is in danger of dying a meaningless death. In fact, earlier in this section, the poet asserted that this "you" has already died. But later he reverses himself, saying even though it may be that "you have ended," "the thundering has not" ("Petty Kings," line 102). In the next lines the poet expands on this laconic statement by acknowledging that, after death, or after suffering through a misery that was like death-in-life, "You did not give up hope, you shook off the dust, you became the dream, / and the springs can be seen in the huts along the Jordan or in Gaza and / Jerusalem, they burst upon the street even though it is a funeral ceremony, / leaving it like a wedding feast" ("Petty Kings," lines 106-09). This "you" seems to have fulfilled the

promise of self-sacrifice for others and to have become a truly redemptive figure.

"The face of Jaffa is a child" (Petty Kings," line 115). In the third section, however, this promise of redemption proves illusory. This is underscored by the repetition of lines from the first section describing how "the withered tree" still waits for the rain-filled final storm that will revive it. The promise of renewal, so recently given, has already been betrayed, apparently by the "you" just glorified as a savior. As the poet says in lines 130-35,

> A master, you? You will remain
> A master. A slave? You will remain.
> It [he] changed the picture but the picture
>   shall remain.
> It [he] changed the flag but the flag shall
>   remain.

Though the faces may be different, the basic structures of control and oppression (embodied in the images of the official picture, presumably of the president, and the country's flag) remain in place exactly as before. There has been no real revolution.

That the "you" being criticized now has a more specific focus is indicated by the fact that the next line is a direct quotation from Gamal Abdel Nasser's most famous book, *The Philosophy of the Revolution*: "on a map that extends, . . . etc.," where he talks about the importance of physical proximity (shared space on a map) as a factor in shaping the Arab's consciousness of unity (Nasser, p. 54). The implication is that Nasser's promises of revolutionary change, made in the 1940s, at the height of support for his socialist reforms, were never fulfilled. The rest of this section provides a devastatingly detailed portrait of the corruption in this aborted revolutionary state, waiting for the apocalyptic deliverance that must destroy what has become rotten before something new and better can be born.

"In a map that extends . . . " ("Petty Kings," line 215). The poet realizes that this apocalyptic deliverance must occur before a way can be found out of his impasse, and it is this realization that inaugurates the final section of the poem:

> In a map that extends . . . etc.,
> the well-known history that cooks the sultan
>   on a fire refused to remember
> a poet . . . and the rest follows,
> in a map that extends . . . etc.,
>   A time between ashes and roses is coming
>   everything shall perish in it
>   everything shall begin in it.
>   ("Petty Kings," lines 256-62)

In order to effect revolutionary, cleansing change, the poet cannot rely on himself, nor can he put his faith in an "infallible" leader and sit back passively. He must work *with* others around him, including the leaders, but especially the children, who represent the hope for the future:

> Bring your axes let's carry God like an elder
> who has died, let's open a path for the sun
> other than minarets, for the child a book
> other than angels, for the dreamer a source
> other than Medina and Kufa / Bring your axes
> **I am not alone.**
> ("Petty Kings," lines 272-276)

No longer seeing himself as alone in his struggle, the poet advocates giving the children and the dreamers something to inspire them besides the religious discourse of a past tradition that, no matter how decorative or full of fine sentiments, he sees as irrelevant to the present and future. And it is in this context that he returns to the image of Jaffa as a child's face (which he repeats at the end of the poem). Now he sees it in a new light, as the child who will cast off the past to embrace a different and better future, who will reject evasions of the truth and see the world more clearly, as it really is. It is this vision of the power and potential of future generations to transcend old limitations that the poet offers as consolation for his own shortcomings, and for the loss of the "you" who inspired him, a loss that means "no prophet remains" ("Petty Kings," lines 269-70).

Nasser and the poets. In the period immediately following his death, Nasser was eulogized in extravagant terms by both ordinary people and intellectuals. Some compared him to the Biblical and Quranic prophets, as did Nizar Qabbani in his famous poem "Qatalnaka" (We Killed You). Its opening lines directly address the dead Egyptian president: "We killed you, last of the prophets / We killed you / This is nothing new for us, assassinating holy men and Muhammad's companions" (Qabbani, p. 3; trans. T. DeYoung). Such provocative lines associating contemporary conflicts and fighting among the Arabs with historical events like Ali's assassination clearly laid the ground for later works such as Adunis's poem.

Other writers, like the Egyptian literary critics Luwis Awad and Ghali Shukri, waxed more optimistic. Nasser's death, they thought, would lead to a reassessment by the Arab people of the role his nationalist ideas had played in their lives, and a stronger commitment to those goals. They celebrated this "rebirth" of idealistic commitment

by comparing Nasser to a wide range of religious figures, including those whose death led directly to the renewal/rejuvenation of the land (like the dying gods of ancient fertility myths) and less direct models such as Jesus, whose death on the cross inspired his followers to believe in the salvational promise of Christianity.

> During the time that Nasser lived among us . . . he . . . built for us a well-furnished nest . . . if the phoenix—as the myth goes—has burned itself up and become ashes, the divine fire will raise up a new phoenix to build a new nest. Indeed the resurrection of Christian Savior Jesus, the rise of the pagan Egyptian god Osiris and the return of the Babylonian god Tammuz have all been symbols of the return of the spirit to the burned-up ashes, they have become symbols of that minority of men whose lives after their death are transformed into a myth.
> (Shukri, p. 7; trans. T. DeYoung)

QAYS AND LAYLA

In the third section of the poem, allusion is made to Qays and Layla, characters from Arabic literature: "Call me Qays and call the earth Layla / in the name of Jaffa" ("Petty Kings," lines 191-92). Qays was one of the most famous Arabic love poets. He was called Majnun ("crazy" in Arabic) because his unfulfilled love for his cousin Layla drove him mad (see the Turkish adaptation **Leyla and Mejnun,** also in *WLAIT 6: Middle Eastern Literatures and Their Times*). Majnun wandered insane through the desert, befriending animals who protected him from harm, but eventually dying from exposure. Layla returned his love, but her father wed her to another. Adunis, it seems, uses Majnun to invoke the ideas of obsession (leading to madness) and self-sacrifice. The poet may have gone mad in a world in which violence and destruction are the norm but his willingness—even though he is not called to put that willingness into action—to sacrifice himself and die on behalf of his beloved Layla (here likened to an "earth mother") may ultimately make that death worthwhile.

But even more illuminating for Adunis's poem is how Nasser's role as the "prophet" of Arab nationalism devolves into a portrayal of him as the spokesman and "poet" of Arab nationalism. "Nasser converges with poetry in one thing," explains the Egyptian poet Abd al-Muti Hijazi, "both

Mourners surround Nasser's flag-draped coffin.

of them address themselves to the nation. Nasser has up to now been the single Arab leader who was able to . . . speak to the Arab people as whole and rouse within them a response to his sense of their unity" (Hijazi, p. 5; trans. T. DeYoung).

Traditionally the poet was the spokesman for his tribe. His poems were the records of the tribe's valorous deeds, their tribulations and sufferings, their responses to their environment in an age when few could read or write. Later the poet became spokesman for the ruler, governor, or whatever bureaucratic functionary happened to be his patron. With few exceptions, these patrons were not well-trained in the art of persuading people or publicly conveying their views. They needed a poet to serve as intermediary between themselves and their subordinates at court, or the populace at large, knowing full well that a fine poet could effectively sway a ruler's subjects by the almost hypnotic power of his words.

Nor were poets simply tools for their employers. They could, and often did, use their talent to call attention to the failings of those for whom they worked. The most famous medieval Arab poet, al-Mutanabbi, wrote biting satires that weakened—though they alone may not have destroyed—the careers of several patrons who displeased him. Certainly he fatally diminished these patrons in the eyes of posterity.

This attitude toward the Arab poet as both political spokesman and society's conscience continued into modern times. Gamal Abdel Nasser, at least in the perceptions of his contemporaries, was the first modern political leader who seriously challenged this ancient division of labor. Nasser's command of oratory left the contemporary poets in a very ambivalent situation. They admired him greatly for his personal traits, even when they criticized his policies sometimes overtly, but more often covertly, because Nasser's minions enforced censorship with a heavy hand, sometimes to the point of imprisonment. Several leading intellectuals, including the novelist and playwright Yusuf Idris, received harsh prison sentences because of their political views during Nasser's rule. Two years before writing his poem, Adunis had disassociated Nasser from this censorship and retribution, tying it instead to lesser functionaries in the Egyptian government, a plausible conviction since Nasser had progressively bureaucratized the regime's role in cultural activities. The power to censor was largely handed over to old-line establishment figures, who slowed revolutionary change while allowing Nasser to portray himself as standing above the fray.

Two years later Adunis's assessment of the relationship between poet and political leader was far less confident and optimistic about how closely the two could work together. Like many contemporaries, Adunis's approach to Nasser was mixed—full of profound respect and uneasiness borne of the recognition that he did not fit into conventional categories.

Sources and literary context. Like most twentieth-century Arab poets, Adunis was greatly influenced by modernist poetic movements originating in the English-speaking world and Europe. Anglo-American modernism, including poets like T. S. Eliot, had the strongest impact, but in Francophone areas (and Adunis was educated in a French-language school), French poets such as Charles Baudelaire, Arthur Rimbaud, Louis Aragon, and St. John Perse were also enormously popular.

In addition to direct influence from Western modernist writers, there was considerable interest in the kind of anthropological and comparative religion studies that helped inspire poems like Eliot's *The Waste Land*. Like Eliot, Adunis and his contemporaries saw in the elaborate, historical researches of James Frazer in *The Golden Bough* and Jessie Weston in *From Ritual to Romance* fruitful models for re-examining and reinterpreting their own cultural heritage to emphasize its importance on the world stage and to introduce alternative interpretations of the past in the interest of preparing the way for rejuvenation and rebirth. This impulse was aided by Frazer's examination of the persistence throughout Western history of images involving the dying and reborn gods of ancient fertility religions, with examples drawn from Arab rituals and customs. Part and parcel of this persistence, the language of Arab nationalism, with its emphasis on selfless devotion and sacrifice on behalf of others, can be seen in the portrayal of Nasser after his sudden death as prophet, poet, and mythically reborn god.

Literary context. "Introduction to the History of the Petty Kings" was first published the month following Nasser's death in the Beirut literary journal Adunis edited himself, *al-Mawaqif* (Situations). Soon after, it was re-published in an anthology of poems commemorating Nasser (called *Kitabat ala qabr Abd al-Nasir* [Some Writings on Nasser's Grave]. Produced in Lebanon, the anthology contained elegies by some of the most important young poets of the day (Adunis among them). These young poets mostly wrote in a style called *al-shi`r al-hurr* (sometimes translated as "free verse," although it is not exactly identical to Western *vers libre* or free verse, because it still employs meter and rhyme). The style gave them far more autonomy than in the past, because it

abandoned rigid rules of traditional Arab versification. There was meanwhile a parallel insistence on change in content: the freedom to treat new subject matter, to treat old subjects in new ways, to contradict entrenched political and cultural clichés, and to borrow from other world literatures that had not been heretofore accepted as legitimate influences on Arabic poetry. "Introduction to the Petty Kings" represented one of the most extreme examples of this trend.

"Introduction to the Petty Kings"

FROM THE "INTRODUCTION" TO SOME WRITINGS ON NASSER'S GRAVE

[The poets] had been the guardians of the revolution. And some of them persisted in keeping their distance [from those in power] and continued to show their hostility both to the power of the state and to the [1952 Egyptian] revolution. But now that Nasser has passed away, the tears of the Arab poets for him have been released, just as their songs about his victories flowed freely in earlier days.

(Hijazi, p. 10; trans. T. DeYoung)

Reception. In between the time "Introduction to the History of the Petty Kings" was first published in Adunis's magazine and its appearance in the anthology, it was printed as one of two poems by Adunis in a set called *Waqt bayn al-ramad wa-al-ward* (A Time Between Ashes and Roses). The other poem, "Hadha huwa ismi" (This Is My Name), is understood to be an expression of Adunis's reactions to the Arab defeat in the 1967 Arab-Israeli war. The two poems (with the addition of a third, "Qabr min ajli Niyu Yurk" [A Grave Because of New York], the fruit of a trip Adunis made there) were reprinted in 1971 and again in 1972. It is from this last publication of "Introduction to the History of the Petty Kings" that most critics became familiar with the poem, and their reviews usually deal with it as part of the three-poem suite.

The three poems were recognized as very difficult works, especially "Introduction to the History of the Petty Kings." It was felt that the challenge of decoding the many erudite and extremely technical references to a wide range of fields of knowledge would be beyond the resources of most readers, eliciting much the same reaction as T. S. Eliot's *The Waste Land* and Ezra Pound's *Cantos*. When confronted by these critical comments, Adunis himself is said to have quoted the reaction of the medieval Arab poet Abu Tammam, when a group of courtiers complained they could not make heads or tails of his poems and asked him to write more intelligibly: "Well, why don't you make the effort to understand what I compose, instead?" (Adunis in Faddul, p. 297).

The exception to these somewhat bemused but nevertheless admiring assessments of "Introduction to the History of the Petty Kings" has come from diehard political supporters of Nasserism, who read the poem as an unequivocal attack on Nasser himself. Abbud Kanju dismisses it as a weak poem that tarnishes the image of those who struggle on behalf of Arabism and a poem that disparages the struggle itself (Kanju, p. 53). More judicious assessments by Ahmad Yusuf Dawud and Ali Ahmad Shar concur on the importance but also the difficulty of the poem. Perhaps most telling is a comment by the eminent critic Kamal Abu Deeb about the three-poem set: "[Adunis presents himself as] a rebel and force of destruction . . . but also a force of positive rejection with a tormenting love for his culture and country, he is certainly one of the greatest poets in the history of the language" (Abu Deeb, p. 36).

—Terri DeYoung

For More Information

Abu Deeb, Kamal. "The Perplexity of the All-Knowing: A Study of Adonis." *Mundus Artium* 10, no. 1 (1977): 163-81.

Adonis (Adunis). "Introduction to the History of the Petty Kings by Adonis." Trans. Shawkat M. Toorawa. *Journal of Arabic Literature* 23, pt. 1 (March 1992): 27-35.

Bailey, Clinton. *Jordan's Palestinian Challenge 1948-1983: A Political History*. Boulder: Westview Press, 1984.

Boullata, Issa. "Adonis: Revolt in Modern Arabic Poetics." *Edebiyat* 2, no. 1 (1977): 1-13.

Faddul, Atif. *The Poetics of T. S. Eliot and Adunis: A Comparative Study*. Beirut: Alhamra, 1992.

Gabrieli, Frencesco. *Arab Historians of the Crusades*. Berkeley: University of California Press, 1957.

Hijazi, Abd al-Muti, ed. *Kitabat ala qabr Abd al-Nasir*. Beirut: Dar al-Awdah, 1971.

Hodgson, Marshall. *The Venture of Islam*. Vol. 1. Chicago: University of Chicago Press, 1974.

Kanju, Abbud. Jamal Abd Al-Nasir fi al-shi`r al-Arabi al-mu`asir. Cairo: n.p. 198?.

Nasser, Gamal Abdel. *The Philosophy of the Revolution*. Cairo: State Information Service, 1953.

Qabbani, Nizar. "Qatalnaka," al-Ahram, 10 October 1970, 3.

Shar, Ali Ahmad. "An Analytical Study of the Adonisian Poem." Ph.D. diss., University of Michigan, 1982.

Shukri, Ghali. "Awdat al-ruh ila al-ramad al-muhtariq," al-Ahram, 3 October 1970, 7.

Stephens, Robert. *Nasser: A Political Biography*. New York: Simon and Schuster, 1971.

Kalilah and Dimnah

THE LITERARY WORK

A series of fables, derived from India, set during an unspecified time; first translated into Arabic (as *Kalilah wa-Dimnah*) around 750 C.E.; published in English in 1569 or 1570.

SYNOPSIS

Upon the commands of his king, a philosopher relates a string of animal fables that feature a scheming pair of jackals.

Like *The Arabian Nights*, *Kalilah and Dimnah* boasts a mixed pedigree. Its stories originated in India, gathered by an unknown Brahmin during the third century C.E., then traveled to Persia where they were translated from the Sanskrit to Pahlavi (an old Persian language) during the reign of the Sasanian king, Khusraw Anushirvan (531-579). Nearly 200 years later, the Arab scholar Abd Allah ibn al-Muqaffa`, a Persian convert to Islam, translated the fables from Pahlavi into Arabic, under the title *Kalilah wa-Dimnah*. This version enjoyed great popularity throughout the Middle East and was itself translated into different languages, including late Syriac, Hebrew, modern Persian, and Turkish. During the thirteenth century Alfonso X of Spain set up a school of translators and chose *Kalilah wa Dimnah* as one of the Arabic texts to be rendered into Castilian. Scholars place the publication of this version, known as *Calila e Digna*, around 1251. The translation by Thomas Irving of this Spanish version, published in 1980, is the closest version available in English to the original Arabic. Throughout its various incarnations, *Kalilah and Dimnah* appealed to readers for its lively depiction of the animal kingdom as analogous to the human world and for its practical morality, originally intended to train princes in wise conduct. Their first translator into Arabic added a twist reflective of some harsh realities of his society.

Events in History at the Time of the Fables

The Umayyad dynasty—an overview. The introduction of *Kalilah and Dimnah* to the world of Arab letters coincided with a particularly tumultuous period in the Middle East: the fall of the Umayyads in 750 C.E. Religious and political problems had beset this ruling dynasty since its establishment in 661. The prophet Muhammad's death in 632 had left the Muslim community without a leader; several claimants vied for the position of caliph (Arabic for "successor"), the ruler of Islam within an empire that expanded to include present-day Iran, Iraq, and Syria. After Uthman (r. 644-656), the third caliph to reign since Muhammad's death, was killed in his home by Egyptian rebels, the caliphate was offered to Ali ibn Abi Talib, Muhammad's cousin and son-in-law (who had married Muhammad's daughter Fatimah). His assumption of office did not occur without difficulty, however.

Mu`awiyah, a kinsman of Uthman and the governor of Syria, contested Ali's right to the caliphate. Ali's and Mu`awiyah's forces engaged in several skirmishes, then finally met in a pivotal encounter at Siffin. Knowing themselves outnumbered, Mu`awiyah's forces, led by General Amr ibn al-As, proposed to settle the matter of Uthman's death and the question of succession through arbitration instead of battle. Ali consented to the proposal, angering some of his more extreme followers who felt he had bowed to the judgment of men instead of the judgment of God; these dissenters, who became known as Kharijites (seceders), deserted Ali's cause and harassed him mercilessly for the remainder of his rule. Meanwhile, the arbitrators ruled against Ali, calling for his removal from office; Ali protested the decision and hostilities resumed between his and Mu`awiyah's forces. Support for Ali's caliphate waned throughout the provinces and Ali himself was assassinated by a Kharijite rebel in 661. Mu`awiyah subsequently became caliph, founding the Umayyad Dynasty, which ruled from Damascus, Syria.

Ali's assassination was to have far-reaching consequences for the Islamic world, instigating a religious schism that persists to this day. Two opposing factions sprang up: the Shi`ites, who had favored Ali, and the Sunnis, who supported Mu`awiyah. Sunnis believed themselves the followers of orthodoxy, while Shi`ites considered the Sunni dynasty of the Umayyads to be usurpers, to whom they owed no allegiance. In 680 Ali's second son, Husayn, refused to pay homage to the caliph Yazid I, Mu`awiyah's son and successor, and fled to Mecca, where he amassed a band of perhaps 200 Shi`ites to revolt against the Umayyads. Umayyad troops defeated and killed the rebels at Karbala, in Iraq, cutting off Husayn's head and presenting it to Yazid as a trophy, deepening the animosity the Shi`ites felt toward the Sunnis.

Although the Umayyad government enjoyed relative stability and continuity during its first six caliphates, succession struggles began to plague the dynasty after Walid I died in 715 and his brother Sulayman seized the caliphate from Walid's son and heir. Thereafter, when a Umayyad caliph died, bloodshed usually ensued as various relatives claimed the right to succeed him. The relative who prevailed would commonly oust the prior administration and eliminate most of the people who supported it. The frequent interruptions in government, along with family feuds and warring factions, weakened the Umayyad caliphate, contributing to its collapse and overthrow in 750, at the hands of the Abbasids. Ibn al-Muqaffa` lived most of his life under the Umayyads, although it was under the Abbasids that he would meet his downfall.

The Abbasid revolution. Although the Umayyad regime had long had its detractors, a new threat began to emerge during the 720s, in the shape of a rival political faction. Called the Abbasids, because their leaders traced their descent from Abbas, an uncle of the Prophet Muhammad, this coalition included Arabs, Persians, Iraqis, and Shi`ite Muslims. Despite their internal national and religious differences, Abbasids were united on replacing the Umayyads' tribal aristocracy with what they saw as a more egalitarian government based more firmly on the principles of Islam.

The Abbasid movement gained momentum over the next two decades, breaking into open rebellion during the 740s; Abu Muslim, in charge of the rebellion's organizational side, attracted more followers to the cause by emphasizing the Abbasids' broad-based appeal to various religious and ethnic groups. In 747 the Abbasids raised black banners of revolution and the next year they successfully overthrew the Umayyad governor of Khurasan. In 749 Nahavand in Persia and Kufah in Iraq fell to the Abbasids; the commander-in-chief of the conquering army designated Abu al-Abbas, recently named head of the Abbasids, as caliph. Finding themselves outmaneuvered by this ploy, Shi`ite Muslims, who had hoped to choose a descendant of Ali as caliph, reluctantly pledged their allegiance. The new caliph promised a fresh start, an era of justice and pious living under the guidance of the Prophet's own family and the principles of Islam.

Not surprisingly, Marwan II, the Umayyad caliph, refused to recognize the Abbasid caliphate. In January 750, when the opposing armies at last met in the Battle of the Zab, Umayyad forces were decisively defeated and Marwan was forced to flee the battlefield. The Abbasid army pursued the former caliph into Egypt and killed him, sending his severed head to Abu al-Abbas, now firmly established as caliph. The Abbasid empire was to last from 750 to 1258 C.E.

One of the first tasks of the Abbasid regime, however, was to eliminate what remained of the Umayyad dynasty. This was undertaken with a ruthlessness bordering on savagery. Agents of the new government were sent all over the Muslim world to find and kill members of the deposed family. And in one notorious instance, Abd Allah ibn Ali, the caliph's uncle and governor of Syria, invited some 80 Umayyads to a banquet, at which the guests were to proclaim their loyalty to the new regime. Once all were assembled, a pre-arranged signal summoned to the fore a band of executioners, who massacred the Umayyads in cold blood. An unfazed Abd Allah and his high officials are said to have meanwhile partaken of their banquet, undisturbed by the victims' dying moans. In light of the violence and bloodshed that accompanied the deposition of one regime and the accession of another, the lessons contained in *Kalilah and Dimnah*—about kingship and the responsibilities of ruling wisely—became increasingly relevant to the Arab world, as Ibn al-Muqaffa` may have discerned when he first published his translation around 750.

**The rise and fall of Ibn al-Muqaffa`.** Although Ibn al-Muqaffa` was not the original author or collector of the *Kalilah and Dimnah* fables, his role should not be minimized, because his Arabic version—*Kalilah wa-Dimnah*—became the basis for all subsequent translations. Also, the life of Ibn al-Muqaffa`, no less than his work, reflected the volatile political situation of the eighth-century Islamic Empire.

The son of a tax collector known as al-Muqaffa` (the crippled), Ibn al-Muqaffa` was born around 720 in southern Iran and given the name of Ruzbah; it was after converting to Islam that he took the name Abd Allah. Fluent in Arabic and Persian, Ibn al-Muqaffa` served the Umayyad governors in the eastern provinces as a secretary and drafter of official correspondence. After the Abbasids came to power, Ibn al-Muqaffa` found employment under the new regime, becoming secretary to Isa ibn Ali, the nephew of Caliph al-Mansur. Scholars estimate that it was around this time that Ibn al-Muqaffa` translated *Kalilah and Dimnah*—to which he added a chapter of his own composition, dealing with Dimnah's trial (a reflection perhaps of his concern with government corruption and a related admonition that monarchs must investigate every particular before passing judgement and inflicting punishment). Ibn al-Muqaffa` also produced several original works, including the *al-Adab al-kabir* (The Comprehensive Book of Rules of Conduct), which offered advice to princes, and the *Risala fi al-sahabah* (Treatise on the Caliph's Entourage), an essay dealing with the political, religious, and social problems of his time.

Ironically, Ibn al-Muqaffa` fell into a trap he warned others to avoid; he ran afoul of the new regime, becoming caught up in political intrigue. After a relative of Caliph al-Mansur rebelled against the government, the caliph's nephew, patron to Ibn al-Muqaffa`, asked him to compose a letter to the caliph requesting pardon for the rebel. The resulting document essentially placed al-Mansur at the mercy of his uncle's goodwill. He was required to swear that "if I should injure my uncle Abd Allah ibn Ali, or any of those who accompanied him, in the smallest or greatest way, or cause some harm to befall them secretly or openly, and in any form, shape or manner, directly or indirectly, or through some deception, then I will declare myself disowned and illegitimate. All the community of the Prophet Muhammad will be permitted to cast me off, make war with me and kill me without any punishment" (Jahshiyari, p. 109; trans. T. DeYoung). Since the caliph's uncle would only have to make the accusation that his nephew had ill-treated him for the provisions of the document to come into force, and there was no requirement that he prove the charge, al-Mansur was naturally outraged at the presumption exhibited by Ibn al-Muqaffa`. He is reported to have remarked, upon reading the pardon, and hearing it had been written by Ibn al-Muqaffa`, "Who will save me from this man?" (Jahshiyari, p. 109; trans. T. DeYoung). The governor of Basra, Sufyan ibn Mu`awiyah al-Muhallabi, who had frequently been the target of Ibn al-Muqaffa`'s biting wit, was only too happy to oblige. Ibn al-Muqaffa` was last seen entering the governor's house in 755 or 756. It was later reported that he had been put to death there by a painful process of slow dismemberment. His untimely end only highlighted the significance of his works, especially those such as *Kalilah and Dimnah* that condemn tyrannical rulers and corrupt bureaucrats.

The Fables in Focus

Plot summary. In structure, *Kalilah and Dimnah* resembles episodic works, such as **The Arabian Nights** (also in WLAIT 6: *Middle Eastern Literatures and Their Times*), although it lacks a single framing narrative. Some versions include an account of how Burzoe, the royal physician to Khusraw Anushirvan, traveled to India and secretly copied the story of *Kalilah and Dimnah* into the medieval Persian language, Pahlavi, then presented the translation to the king. All versions relate how Dabshalim, the King of India, tells his chief philosopher, Bidpai, to make up a fable for him concerning a specific theme. Bidpai obliges, relating the fable, and other fables that are embedded within the main story. The fables associated with the characters *Kalilah and Dimnah*, represent the longest part of the narrative.

A sultan punishes the troublemakers in this fanciful rendering of an incident from *Kalilah and Dimnah*.

At the start of *Kalilah and Dimnah* Dabshalim commands Bidpai to tell him "a fable about two men who love each other, and how a swindling liar comes between them and incites them to be enemies" (*Kalilah and Dimnah*, p. 1). Bidpai complies, telling of a merchant who exhorted his four spendthrift sons to earn their living by working at a trade. The sons take his lesson to heart and the eldest sets off towards the land of Manud on business, in a cart pulled by two bulls, Shatrabah and Bandabah. The travelers encounter a great patch of mud, in which Shatrabah falls. The man and his servants work to free the bull, who is so fatigued afterwards that he cannot travel farther. Shatrabah's owner leaves a servant behind to look after the animal but the man becomes so bored that he abandons Shatrabah the next day and rejoins his master, saying that the bull has died.

Meanwhile, Shatrabah wanders off by himself until he finds a lush meadow in which to graze. Growing fat and healthy, the bull frequently roars and bellows to show his content. In that same region, however, a lion reigns as king over many beasts of prey, such as wolves, jackals, leopards, and foxes. One day, the lion hears Shatrabah bellow and becomes frightened by the noise and ceases to hunt.

The lion's court includes two wily jackals, Kalilah and Dimnah. The latter is especially ambitious and unscrupulous, "on the lookout for the main chance" (*Kalilah and Dimnah*, p. 4). Learning that the lion now fears to hunt, Dimnah determines to discover the cause and thus improve his own standing at court. On gaining an audience with the lion, the crafty Dimnah soon ingratiates himself with the king. Eventually, the lion confides to Dimnah that he no longer hunts because he fears the source of the powerful bellows coming from the nearby meadows. Dimnah offers to seek out whatever is making the noise, to which the lion consents, even as he fears the jackal might side with this unseen potential enemy against him. Dimnah returns and informs the lion that a bull was making the noise; he proposes that the bull be brought before the court as a humble and obedient servant, to which the lion agrees. Having ingratiated himself to Shatrabah as well, Dimnah tells the bull of the lion's willingness to receive him at court. Once Dimnah consents to grant him a safe-conduct, Shatrabah likewise agrees to meet the lion. After they are introduced, the lion takes a great fancy to the bull, who becomes one of his favorite companions. Envying Shatrabah's good fortune and feeling himself slighted, Dimnah resolves to drive a wedge between the lion and the bull.

Although Kalilah also dislikes Shatrabah's influence at court, he cautions Dimnah to undertake the bull's destruction only if he can do so without harming the lion. Dimnah tells the lion that Shatrabah has been plotting against him with the lion's army so that the bull may become king instead. Although the lion is initially reluctant to believe these reports, Dimnah's glib tongue and manipulation of various fables ultimately convince him of Shatrabah's treachery. In the fable of "The Three Fish," for example, Dimnah relates how a shrewd fish anticipates danger from two fishermen approaching her pool and swims away to another part of the river, a steady fish feigns death and also escapes capture, while a weakling fish swims back and forth in the pool until she is caught. The credulous lion is thus convinced to make the first move against the bull. Dimnah then visits Shatrabah and plays on his fears and doubts too, telling the bull that the lion intends to eat him. Thus, the two acquire a skewed perception of each other. When the fearful, suspicious lion and bull are brought face to face, a fierce battle ensues. Both combatants are seriously hurt, although the lion triumphs by killing the bull. Horrified by the carnage, Kalilah upbraids Dimnah for his evil nature and vows to quit his company.

Impressed by the first fable, Dabshalim orders Bidpai to relate what happened next and the

DABSHALIM AND BIDPAI

According to Ali ibn al-Shah al-Farisi, one of many Arabic adapters of the version of *Kalilah and Dimnah* by Ibn al-Muqaffa`, King Dabshalim and the court philosopher Bidpai were historical personages, who lived in India during the fourth century B.C.E. The translator relates how Alexander the Great appointed one of his officials to rule India after he conquered it. The people of India deposed the new ruler and choose Dabshalim, who was descended from one of their former kings. Initially, Dabshalim proved cruel and capricious; a philosopher of high caste, Bidpai, attempted to teach him moderation, wisdom, and justice. At first, the offended monarch imprisoned the philosopher; then, repenting of his actions, he released Bidpai and began to follow his advice. In time the reformed ruler won the loyalty and devotion of his subjects. Later, Dabshalim asked Bidpai to write a guide for rulers on how to reign wisely and earn the allegiance of their people. Within a year the philosopher produced *Bidpai's Fables*, or *Kalilah wa-Dimnah*, a book of 14 chapters, each containing a moral question and its answer. In the first chapter of *Kalilah and Dimnah*, for example, Dabshalim poses a question about "how a swindling liar comes between two men who love each other and incites them to be enemies"; Bidpai replies, "Whenever it happens that a lying swindler comes between two men who love each other, they then break up their friendship and are at odds with each other" and relates the fable illustrating that truth (*Kalilah and Dimnah*, p. 1). According to Ibn al-Muqaffa`, *Bidpai's Fables* came to Iran through the efforts of Burzoe, physician to the Sasanian king Khusraw Anushirvan (531-579), who had been sent to India by his royal master specifically to claim a copy of the book. Ibn al-Muqaffa` credits Burzoe with translating the fables from Sanskrit into Pahlavi (c. 570); Ibn al-Muqaffa` himself translated them from Pahlavi into Arabic nearly two centuries later, adding the trial scene.

philosopher resumes the story. Subsequently, the lion recovers his senses and begins to regret killing Shatrabah. He also starts to doubt that the bull conspired against him and decides to investigate the case further. Meanwhile, the leopard—another member of the court—overhears Kalilah and Dimnah arguing over the latter's plot against Shatrabah and reports what he has heard to the lion's mother but swears her to secrecy. The next day, finding her son despondent over Shatrabah's death, the lion's mother hints that she knows a secret that could shed some light on the subject. Commanded by the lion to tell what she knows, the lion's mother reveals Dimnah's treachery without disclosing the source of her knowledge.

The lion has Dimnah arrested, imprisoned, and put on trial. The wily jackal employs his skills of argument and manipulation to confound his accusers, including the lion's mother:

Judges should not judge according to their opinions or what people at large or in particular think. You know that thinking is not one whit

sufficient in the case of truth, even if all of you consider me the perpetrator of this crime. I know better about myself than you do, and my own knowledge is surer since it is quite free from doubt. My case only seems ugly to you since you are like that, for you think I have poked my nose into someone else's business.

(*Kalilah and Dimnah*, p. 68)

Even the lion is confused. While Dimnah is in prison, he receives a visit from the grief-stricken Kalilah, who again laments his friend's evil conspiracy against Shatrabah and his subsequent fall from grace. A wolf, imprisoned in the same jail, overhears the jackals' conversation, takes note of it, but chooses to keep his own counsel at present. Kalilah returns home so distressed in mind that "his stomach [is] upset and he [dies] before dawn" (*Kalilah and Dimnah*, p. 61). The trial of Dimnah resumes and the jackal continues to deny his guilt and to evade the traps set by his judges. The lion's mother, fearing that Dimnah will escape punishment and manage to stir up other animals against the lion, consults the leopard and at last persuades him to come forward and give evidence against Dimnah. Once he has done so, the jailed wolf also delivers his incriminating testimony. On the strength of both testimonies, the lion has Dimnah put in bonds and placed in solitary confinement until he dies of hunger and thirst. The fable of Dimnah's trial concludes with the moral "Such is the punishment of covetousness and what happens to envious and lying people" (*Kalilah and Dimnah*, p. 71).

Although not all fables in the collection are linked to the tale of *Kalilah and Dimnah*, they do form self-contained narratives of their own. Some are trickster tales, in which the protagonist escapes disaster through his own wits and cleverness, such as "The Monkey and the Tortoise." In other fables, the trickster outsmarts himself and

---

WHY TRANSLATE *KALILAH AND DIMNAH*?

The enduring appeal of *Kalilah and Dimnah* attests to the success of Ibn al-Muqaffa` in meeting the goals he set for it:

"The author of the book had four objectives in mind when he composed the work:

to render it attractive to the young reader by employing birds and animals in the stories

to capture the attention of rulers by the conduct of the animals who are faced with similar dilemmas and circumstances

to provide entertainment to all peoples and to arouse their curiosity, thereby enabling the book to be preserved through the ages

and to provide the philosophers of the future a forum for discussion and speculation."

(Ibn al Muqaffa` in Atil, p. 6)

---

is punished for his deceit ("The Pigeon, the Fox, and the Crane"). Most feature animals, while a few involve humans. All, however, are didactic in nature, in keeping with the fables' original intent of offering guidance to rulers. One fable—"The Ringdove"—offers lessons in friendship and loyalty, while another—"The Cat and the Mouse"—examines how natural enemies can form alliances in a common cause, even if they revert to enmity afterwards. Another long chapter—"Ayladh, Shadram, and Irakhat"—deals with the disastrous effects of hasty action. In the

first subsection of the chapter, King Shadram experiences a series of strange dreams and orders Brahman monks to interpret those dreams. Desiring revenge for the king's killing 12,000 members of their order, the monks falsely advise him that the dreams mean he should kill his queen Irakhat, his son Jawir, and his adviser Ayladh. The latter, however, persuades the king to seek a second interpretation before carrying out this bloody plan, which proves to be more benevolent and honest. Later, the king quarrels with Irakhat and rashly orders her execution, but Ayladh spirits the queen away to safety, waits for the king to repent, as he inevitably does, of his hasty decision, then reunites the royal couple.

A mirror for princes. Even in its earliest incarnations, *Kalilah and Dimnah* was intended to serve a very specific purpose—namely, to educate princes on the art of ruling wisely and well. Both the Persian and Arabic versions retained the major elements of the Sanskrit original, including the use of animals as the main characters. This had a deep significance in India, where people believed that animals possessed personalities and awareness, and inhabited a world very similar to that of human beings. The belief was preserved in the fables' various translations: animals exhibited the same passions, quirks, and flaws as humans and stood equally in need of guidance.

In the stories featuring the characters of *Kalilah and Dimnah*, the lion—represented as the king of beasts—learns a bitter lesson in how to distinguish loyalty from treachery. Duped by the ambitious jackal Dimnah, the lion hastily believes the worst about Shatrabah the bull and slays him, without attempting to discern the truth of the matter. Later, in a chapter written and appended by Arabic translator Ibn al-Muqaffa`, the lion orders an investigation into the bull's case; this time, having learned his lesson, he listens attentively to various bits of evidence and withholds judgment until he receives sufficient proof of Dimnah's guilt. Similarly, Dimnah learns the consequences of excessive ambition and of lying to further that ambition when his slanders of Shatrabah are exposed and he himself is sentenced to death for his crimes.

The many translations of *Kalilah and Dimnah* throughout the ages seem to underscore the timelessness of the fables and the practical lessons they offer. For Ibn al-Muqaffa`, whose eighth-century Arabic translation became the basis for all subsequent translations, *Kalilah and Dimnah* took on increased significance in light of the political upheaval during the last years of Umayyad rule

FROM *KALILAH AND DIMNAH* TO BRER RABBIT

~

The influence of *Kalilah and Dimnah* can be readily traced in the Brer Rabbit tales, the folklore of the American slaves, first published in the United States to popular acclaim in the late nineteenth century. In both versions of the story, a rabbit rids the neighborhood of a dangerous lion by tricking him into fighting his own reflection in the water:

[The rabbit] took the lion to a deep cistern full of clear water, and said: "This is the lion's place. I am going away unless you carry me in your arms so I won't be afraid when I point him out to you!"

The lion picked her up in his arms, and she brought him up to the clear water and said to him: "Here are the lion and the rabbit."

He put the rabbit down and jumped in to kill the [lion] in the cistern; and the rabbit escaped.

(*Kalilah and Dimnah*, p. 21)

***

Brer Rabbit creeped forward and looked in the lake. He screamed and jumped back. "He's in there, Brer Lion! Let's get out of here!"

Brer Lion walked up to the lake and peered in. Sure enough, there was a creature looking back at him. Brer Lion hollered at him. Creature in the lake didn't say a word. Brer Lion shook his mane; creature in the lake shook his. Brer Lion showed his teeth; creature showed his. Brer Lion got so mad that he jumped into the lake head first.

(Lester, p. 67)

and the first years of the new Abbasid regime: "Sporting a golden thread of diversion in a ground of edification [*Kalilah and Dimnah*] was intended to serve in Arabo-Muslim court circles the same purpose as it had served at the Sasanian court, whose values and political wisdom so dominated the secular thinking of Ibn al-Muqaffa` and others of the same secretarial class of the same era" (Ashtiany et al., pp. 12-13).

Sources and literary context. The fables comprising *Kalilah and Dimnah* appear to have originated in two Sanskrit texts, the *Panchatantra* and the *Mahabharata*. The former, a collection of Indian fables compiled around the third century C.E., contained five chapters—specifically, 1, 3, 4, 5, and 6—which were integrated into *Kalilah and Dimnah*. The latter, the *Mahabharata*, was an even more ancient Indian epic and three chapters of *Kalilah and Dimnah* were adapted from it. Arab and Spanish storytellers appear to have contributed still more tales to the cycle over the centuries. When Ibn al-Muqaffa` added the entire chapter dealing with Dimnah's trial and punishment, he infused into that episode a moral tone that is lacking in the earliest versions. In a sense, by doing this he was

bringing the work more closely into harmony with the Mediterranean tradition of the fable as found in Aesop (whose own fables were adapted into Arabic and attributed to Luqman, a legendary pre-Islamic sage). Although Aesop may be legendary himself, tradition speaks of him as a marginalized member of society, much like Ibn al-Muqaffa`, a sixth-century slave, who was cruelly put to death. Certainly Aesop's fables can be seen as "a form of covert political criticism" of the dominant social order (Lewis, p. 2).

During the mid-eighth century C.E., *Kalilah and Dimnah*'s popularity within the medieval Islamic world reflected a shift in Arab thought. As the Umayyad and Abbasid caliphates established themselves and the city of Baghdad developed into the Islamic empire's commercial and cultural center, a more secular literature—combining practical advice with entertainment—took hold as well. Examples of this literature—called *adab*—included manuals, romances, tales, and fables. As translated by Abd Allah ibn al-Muqaffa` around 750 C.E., *Kalilah and Dimnah* is considered to be the first example of *adab*, a guide offering entertainment and instruction to princes

Kalilah and Dimnah

and bureaucrats in the form of fables set in the animal kingdom. As rendered by Ibn al-Muqaffa`, *Kalilah and Dimnah* also represented a blending of Persian and Arabian cultures, inspiring countless imitators, poets, and artists, and thus enriching the Muslim intellectual world.

Impact. As translated by Ibn al-Muqaffa`, *Kalilah and Dimnah* was immensely popular and widely imitated, giving rise to similar works, such as Ibn Zafar al-Siqilli's *Sulwan al-Muta* (1159, *Prescription for Pleasure*) and Marzuban ibn Rustam's *Marzuban'namah* (The Book of Marzuban) in the thirteenth century. Over the centuries, the original prose was reworked several times into Arabic and Persian verse, as well as translated into countless other languages, including Greek, Syriac, Ethiopic, Persian, Hebrew, Spanish, English, French, and German. One translation—in Turkish—became famous in its own right: Ali ibn Salih's *Humayunname* was dedicated to Sultan Süleyman the Magnificent (1520-66). Many individual fables were to travel even farther, to Africa and thence to the United States, as tales told by African slaves, some of which were retold as the Brer Rabbit stories.

The impact of his work was no less important in educational circles. The two major architects of the medieval Islamic educational system in the next generation after the death of Ibn al-Muqaffa` were al-Jahiz (c. 776-869) and Ibn Qutaybah (828-889). Both were avid admirers of their predecessor and frequently quoted from *Kalilah and Dimnah* with great approval. As al-Jahiz says of him, "There was no one as good as he, not a great deal or even a little, and he was a master at arranging stories so that no one could figure out how the person deceived had been deceived, or how another had had his trust confirmed" (al-Jahiz, p. 44; trans. T. DeYoung).

This influence extended into modern times. *Kalilah and Dimnah* was one of the earliest texts chosen to be typeset and published on the first printing press imported into the Arab world, at Bulaq (near Cairo) Egypt in the 1830s. Later, at the end of the nineteenth century, when modern educational curricula were being developed in various Arabic-speaking countries, it became a staple school text.

—Pamela S. Loy

For More Information

Allen, Roger. *An Introduction to Arabic Literature.* Cambridge, U.K.: Cambridge University Press, 2000.

Ashtiany, Julia, T. M. Johnstone, J. D. Latham, R. B. Serjeant, and G. Rex Smith. *The Cambridge History of Arabic Literature: Abbasid Belles Lettres.* Cambridge, U.K.: Cambridge University Press, 1990.

Atil, Esin, trans. *Kalilah wa Dimnah.* Washington, D.C.: Smithsonian Institution Press, 1981.

Fariq, K. A. *A History of Arabic Literature.* Vol. 2. New Delhi: Vikas Publishing House, 1978.

Goldschmidt, Arthur, Jr. *A Concise History of the Middle East.* Boulder: Westview Press, 1988.

Hourani, Albert. *A History of the Arab Peoples.* New York: Times Warner, 1991.

Irving, Thomas Ballantine, trans. *Kalilah and Dimnah.* Newark, N.J.: Juan de la Cuesta, 1980.

al-Jahiz, Abu Uthman Amr ibn Bahr. "Risalat al-mu`allimin." In Vol. 3 of *Rasa'il al-Jahiz.* Ed. Abd al-Salam Muhammad Harun. Cairo: Matba`at al-Jahiz, 1979.

Jahshiyari, Abu Abd Allah Muhammad ibn Abdus. *Kitab al-wuzara wa-al-kuttab.* Ed. Mustafa al-Siqa et al. Cairo: Matba`at Mustafa al-Babi al-Halabi, 1938.

Lester, Julius. *The Tales of Uncle Remus.* New York: Dial, 1987.

Lewis, Jayne Elizabeth. *The English Fable: Aesop and Literary Culture, 1651-1740.* Cambridge, U.K.: Cambridge University Press, 1996.

Metz, Helen Chapin, ed. *Iraq: A Country Study.* Washington, D.C.: Federal Research Division, 1990.

Rahman, H. U. *A Chronology of Islamic History 570-1000 C.E.* London: Mansell, 1989.

"Khusraw and Shirin"

by

Nizami of Ganja

Nizami of Ganja (c.1140-c.1209) is the pen-name of Jamal al-Din Abu Muhammad Ilyas. ("Ganja" is the name of the town in Azerbaijan where the author spent most of his life.) In general, Nizami worked independently rather than forming an association with the court of any particular ruler. He did dedicate several of his works to local princes, for which he was compensated by a modest gift or fee. Nizami was orphaned in childhood, yet his poetry gives evidence of an excellent education in a wide range of subjects. He married three times, remaining monogamous each time, despite the allowance in Islam for simultaneous marriage to more than one wife. "Khusraw and Shirin" (also spelled "Khosrow and Shirin") is one of five romantic poems composed by Nizami for the collection *Khamsa* ("The Quintet"). Of the five, "The Treasury of Secrets" and "Seven Portraits" are original stories. The remaining three—"Layla and Majnun," "The Story of Alexander the Great," and "Khusraw and Shirin"—are tales adapted from the Arabic, Greek, and Persian traditions. Nizami wrote the most renowned account of the romance of Khusraw and Shirin, apparently to honor his beloved wife Afaq as well as his pre-Islamic heritage.

Events in History at the Time the Romance Takes Place

The Sasanian past. "Khusraw and Shirin" is set during the reign of the Sasanian kings of Persia, the last line of Persian kings (ruled 226-651 C.E.) before the Arabs conquered Persia in 640 C.E. At

---

THE LITERARY WORK

A romance set in Persia c. 600 C.E., completed in Persian (as *Khusraw va Shirin*) around 1180; the first surviving manuscript dates from 1362; first published in English in 1975.

SYNOPSIS

Khusraw, a Persian prince, dreams that his dead grandfather makes four predictions, all of which come true. The fulfillment of the last one, that he will marry Shirin, is delayed for years, during which the couple's personal qualities are tested.

---

the height of its power, the Sasanian empire stretched from Mesopotamia (the lands around the Tigris and Euphrates rivers in present-day Iraq), to modern Afghanistan, to the Persian Gulf and the Indian Ocean, and its armies made incursions as far west as Palestine and Egypt. For several centuries the Sasanians, whose official religion was Zoroastrianism, competed with the Christian Byzantine Empire to the west. The Sasanian-Byzantine rivalry broke into full-scale war at times, but there was also considerable cultural exchange between the two.

The Sasanians made their capital in Ctesiphon (Tisfun), at the mouth of the Tigris River, some 20 miles southeast of today's central Baghdad; Ctesiphon is now in ruins, but in Sasanian times it was a thriving cosmopolitan center. Along with a majority of Zoroastrians, the city had communities of Christians and Jews. Sasanian rulers took great care with the organization and smooth flow of goods, building and maintaining roads and bridges, and establishing networks of spies and guards for security. From the Achaemenids, the great Persian dynasty that rivaled the ancient Greeks, the Sasanians inherited a postal system centered on horses and riders. While most of what remains of Sasanian architecture is fairly modest, the people showed a love for fine crafts and elaborate decoration, producing especially high-quality metalware and textiles. Several Sasanian kings created large stone monuments to commemorate their achievements. It appears that culinary arts were highly developed in Sasanian times too, so one can easily imagine elaborate feasts.

Late Sasanian cultural life was dominated by royal courts, centered on a king believed to possess divine qualities. Elaborate ceremony marked the occasions on which the king met dignitaries from outside his domain, or lower-ranking people within it. The kings are known to have enjoyed music and the singing of minstrels. For exercise—and probably to escape the constraints of court life—they liked to hunt on horseback or with falcons. Otherwise the king tended to remain secluded. The seclusion of his wife—and royal women generally—was even more extreme. Sasanian women almost never showed themselves to anyone outside an inner circle of family and attendants. In principle the king was supposed to marry a sister, although this may not have always happened. Certainly it did not in "Khusraw and Shirin," which, while legendary, reflects at least some pre-Islamic practices.

In many ways the Sasanian Empire of the seventh C.E. was ripe for the fate that it suffered: invasion by the Muslim Arab army. While long, senseless wars with the Byzantine Empire had exhausted the energies of these two superpowers of the Near East, inroads by the Christians continued to present formidable challenges to the Persian state and to the official religion, Zoroastrianism. Internally, religion and politics had become closely intertwined, to the extent that high Zoroastrian priests often wielded more power than the Sasanian monarchs, at times dictating policies that served the interests of the upper classes at the expense of the general populace. Both state and religion had grown more opulent, more pompous, and far more ritual oriented, while the society had grown very rigid. Leaving little or no room for social mobility, the Sasanian caste system resulted in four distinct classes—royal princes and religious leaders, courtiers and

Nizami of Ganja—an imaginative rendering.

the nobility, artisans and craftsmen, and, at the bottom of the social pyramid, laborers and serfs. By the 600s, the division had created intense resentment in the lower strata of the society and a sense of estrangement between the people and their rulers that was unparalleled in the history of ancient Iran (Persia).

In the 620s and 630s, family and succession feuds aggravated this situation and led to chaotic relations between the rulers and the ruled, often to the detriment of the lower classes. The capital city of Ctesiphon had become the focal point of royal attention and the empire's wealth, leaving little to the outlying areas or faraway corners of the empire, such as Central Asia or the Caucasus. All this contributed to the downfall of the empire, so that when the Muslim Arab army poured over into its lands from Mesopotamia, many regions were left to fend for themselves. As it turned out, the invaders levied fewer taxes and proclaimed a faith that promoted the dignity of the individual and equality in the eyes of an omnipotent, omnipresent, and omniscient God. As such, they were more often welcomed than resisted. The result was that by the 650s, the empire that for centuries had vied for dominance over the ancient world with Greece, Rome, and Byzantium collapsed far more easily than later Persians, such as Nizami, could explain or even comprehend.

Khusraw II. Khusraw the Second, also known as Khusraw Parviz, was an actual Sasanid king of Persia (r. 590-628 C.E.). Little is known about his family life, but most historians concur that he had a wife named Shirin. Khusraw's reign was threatened by the ambitions of one of his late father's generals, Bahram Chubin. Taking an unusual measure, the threatened king fled to the Byzantine Empire and requested help from his longtime rivals, the Byzantines, from the emperor Maurice (ruled 582-602 C.E.). Khusraw promised Maurice land—most importantly, Armenia—if he would provide military aid against Bahram, which Maurice furnished in 591. The two appear to have become fast friends, for Maurice declared Khusraw to be his son. When Maurice was murdered by a Byzantine rival, Phocas, in 602, Khusraw declared war on the Byzantines, and the Sasanid army overran Byzantine holdings in Palestine, Syria, Egypt, northern Mesopotamia, and Anatolia. By 615 the Sasanids were approaching Constantinople, the Byzantine capital, but a new Byzantine emperor, Heraclius, reversed the losses in 623-28. The two empires continued their separate development thereafter. Meanwhile, Islam was gaining ground on the Arabian Peninsula.

With the rapid expansion of Islam beyond Arabia after the death of Prophet Muhammad (570-632), the Sasanian regime was swiftly overrun, and the Persian people adopted the new faith of Islam. They, however, retained high regard for their pre-Islamic heritage, especially for the Sasanian dynasty.

The Romance in Focus

Plot summary. In the sixth century B.C.E., in the kingdom of Persia, a noble son is born to a line of great kings. The boy is given his grandfather's name, Khusraw, with the title "Parviz," which means "victorious." Despite his promising name and an excellent upbringing, his path to greatness will not be an easy one.

Khusraw's father is the virtuous King Hurmuz, son of one of the greatest Persian kings of all time, Khusraw Anushirvan. His grandson Khusraw is his namesake. Despite this younger Khusraw's many talents and virtues, he disappoints his father. Concerned for all his subjects, King Hurmuz issues the following proclamation: "Woe to anyone who does violence against another person [or his property], whether to his horse grazing in the field or to the fruits that he cultivates" (Nizami, "Khusraw va Shirin," p. 43; trans. C.

Sawyer). When it comes to exacting justice, his stern edicts promise that everyone will be treated equally.

One evening, after hunting all day, Khusraw takes over a peasant's house for the night. There is much revelry during the night, replete with freely flowing wine and his minstrel's tunes. His senses dulled by drinking too much wine, Khusraw fails to notice when his servant sallies out to pick the peasant's grapes, which sets off a chain of unfortunate circumstances. The servant startles the prince's horse, and the horse then tramples and destroys a good part of the peasant's vineyard. So furious is King Hurmuz when he hears about the damage that he issues severe punishments: the servant who picked the grapes is made the peasant's slave; the horse that trampled the grapes has its hooves pared down; the minstrel's harp is unstrung and injury done to his hand; and Khusraw's princely throne is transferred to the peasant. Genuinely sorry, Khusraw pleads for forgiveness, whereupon Hurmuz relents and restores his son's position as crown prince.

That night Khusraw's grandfather, Khusraw Anushirvan, appears to him in a dream and predicts that his grandson will be rewarded for admitting the error of his ways:

> You will receive four things. . . . You shall ride Shabdiz, the world's swiftest and most fabled steed. . . . You shall sit on Taqdis, the throne of thrones . . . ; at your bidding Barbad the musician shall play and with the lightest touch will far surpass the broken notes of your lost minstrel. But beyond all these, you shall have Shirin, your destined love.
> ("Khosrow and Shirin," p. 22)

Khusraw has a loyal friend and confidante, a well-traveled painter named Shapur. The portraits painted by Shapur do not just represent a person's physical being; they capture the person's soul. Shapur's travels have taken him to Armenia, where he has learned of the beauty of Shirin, niece to Queen Mihin Banu. Not long after Khusraw's dream, Shapur speaks of the queen's exceptional horse, Shabdiz, and of the great beauty of her niece, Shirin. Khusraw, recalling his grandfather's predictions, dispatches Shapur to Armenia to bring back Shirin. The trusty Shapur arrives to discover that Shirin and her female companions often sip wine, sing and dance, and weave garlands of flowers in a meadow. He cleverly paints a lifelike portrait of Khusraw, hangs it on a tree at the edge of the meadow, and hides. When Shirin spots the picture, she nearly swoons with passion. Her companions, concerned that the painting might be the work of evil spirits, confiscate and destroy it. Undaunted, Shapur creates two more portraits; the companions refuse to bring the second one to Shirin, but she secures the third.

Desperate to know whose image it is, Shirin finds Shapur at the edge of the meadow, and he solves the mystery, explaining that Khusraw is a Persian prince who has already fallen in love with her. Next the ingenious painter devises a plan for her: on the pretext of going hunting, the princess should ride out on Shabdiz and flee to Persia. She acts on his counsel, receiving from him a signet ring of Khusraw's to take with her.

In all of legendary history, there cannot be many lovers who have traveled so far and long in search of each other as Khusraw and Shirin. While Shirin travels south to the Persian capital, Khusraw travels north to Armenia, his enemies once again making it impossible for him to tarry at home any longer. On the road between Ctesiphon and Armenia, Shirin and Khusraw have a chance meeting, which seals their love, though they do not recognize each other at the time. Shirin is bathing in a woodland pool when Khusraw happens upon her: "Beautiful was the whiteness of her skin against the blueness of the water. She loosed her braids and washed her long black hair, and the moon-like reflection of her face was caught in the shallows of the pool" ("Khosrow and Shirin," p. 25). So startled is she at being seen that she jumps on Shabdiz and speeds off, wondering if the handsome stranger might be Khusraw. He, on the other hand, travels on to Armenia, believing Shirin is there, doubtlessly wondering about the identity of the bathing beauty who has so recently filled him with desire.

Dreaming of the unattainable woman and her black horse, Khusraw weeps as he travels on to Armenia. He receives a royal welcome at court, but takes no pleasure in anything since Shirin is not there. Meanwhile, Shirin has arrived at the Persian capital and is equally miserable. Without news of Khusraw, she grows depressed and longs for the fresh green landscape of her homeland. Learning that Khusraw instructed his servants to build her a palace if she wishes, she asks them to erect one on a mountain plain. The workers comply, but, jealous of her privileges, build the palace in a hot, unhealthy place, not far from the capital. Shirin will spend far more time here than she could ever have imagined.

Khusraw has by now sent Shapur back to Persia to fetch Shirin. When she returns to her

A sixteenth-century miniature that shows Khusraw startling Shirin as she bathes.

mother's court, there is much rejoicing—without Khusraw, however. Before Shirin's arrival, King Hurmuz died suddenly, so Khusraw had to leave for home. He has returned to take the throne in Ctseiphon, which one of Hurmuz's generals, Bahram Chubin, covets for himself. The general has been spreading vicious rumors among the people, claiming that Khusraw is more devoted to wine than to his kingdom and so distracted by love for Shirin that he is unfit to rule. Losing his people's support, Khusraw must again flee. He reaches Armenia and is at long last united with Shirin.

Although she approves the match, Queen Mihin Banu counsels Shirin not to give herself to her beloved until she is his wife. The queen has heard that this crown prince has a thousand beauties: "Keep your jewel, and he will be addicted to you as to opium. Yield, and you will be a trampled flower before the world" ("Khosrow and Shirin," p. 31). Shirin remains true to this counsel. Khusraw tries to persuade her to meet him alone in an unwatched corner of the castle, but she resists. Remaining steadfast in her chastity, she schools him in the art of faithful love. When, on another occasion, Khusraw, flushed with wine, tries to overpower her by the palace garden, she again resists. Cleverly she urges him to uphold her reputation by establishing his own, by restoring his kingdom. Again Khusraw leaves

Armenia, this time to heed her advice. Entrusting care of Shirin to Shapur, he pursues a drastic but successful strategy. Khusraw appeals to the emperor of Byzantium for aid, which he receives, but in return, he must marry the emperor's daughter. When he wins back rule over Persia, Maryam, not Shirin, is his wife.

This news does not reach Shirin for some time, during which she herself is deeply occupied by affairs in her homeland. Her aunt, the beloved queen dies, and Shirin takes the throne of Armenia. Ruling justly becomes her primary concern. She does away with taxes, and the realm prospers. When the news of Khusraw's marriage reaches her, however, she grows so distracted she can think of nothing else. Finally she turns her rule over to a regent and retreats to the palace built for her near Khusraw's home in Persia. Khusraw learns of her arrival, but, because of his marriage, communicates with her only through messages. He learns that Shirin has given up her reign for love of him.

One night, after drinking too much wine, Khusraw informs Maryam of the forlorn Shirin and beseeches his wife to take her in as a slave. Maryam not only refuses but pledges to kill Shirin if she so much as catches a glimpse of her. Unable to prevail upon his wife, Khusraw urges Shirin to meet him in secret at his palace, but she refuses. If he wants to see her, he will have to saddle up Shabdiz and come himself.

During this lonely period of her life, Shirin gains the admiration of a renowned stonemason named Farhad, who falls desperately in love with her. News of his passion reaches Khusraw, who, failing to bribe Farhad to abandon Shirin, tries to occupy the mason with a supposedly impossible task. He is to carve a path for trade caravans through a towering mountain called Bisutun. Farhad consents to the task, but only on the condition that Shirin will be his if he succeeds. Khusraw finds no harm in agreeing to the request, since the job appears impossible. Then when it seems that Farhad is indeed about to succeed, Khusraw resorts to cruel deception, informing him that Shirin has died. Upon hearing this, Farhad throws himself off the mountain to his death. Shirin grieves deeply for his pure love, and Khusraw regrets the deception.

In time Queen Maryam grows ill and she too dies, leaving Khusraw with their son, Shiruya. Khusraw is free now to resume the match with Shirin, but impulsively he marries another woman, a Persian beauty named Shekar. So distraught is Shirin that she spends her nights praying for God to release her from her plight. In time

her prayers are answered. Khusraw tires of Shekar and arranges a pretext to travel to Shirin's palace; he goes on a great hunt with dignitaries from as far as China. One night Khusraw leaves them and ventures alone to Shirin's castle. Hearing of his arrival, she arranges for what appears to be the greatest of welcomes. On the palace grounds, "gold was showered, silks were spread; tents were raised and covered with jeweled canopies" ("Khosrow and

HORSES IN PERSIAN CIVILIZATION

Khusraw and Shabdiz form a hero-horse duo. The type is not unknown in Western culture—Alexander the Great had his Bucephalos ("Ox-Head"), for example. But such duos are far more common in Islamic and Persian lands. In the Persian epic the *Shahnamah* (also in *WLAIT 6: Middle Eastern Literatures and Their Times*), the hero Rustam is inseparable from his horse, Rakhsh. Horses were in fact important in northern Sasanian territory, where Azerbaijan in particular has well-watered grasslands. The Sasanian Persians cared greatly for their steeds and developed much skill in horse breeding, riding, and veterinary medicine. There were two favorite breeds: the Nisaean horse and the warhorse. The first was medium-sized, relatively slender, and preferably white or golden. Though the Sasanians sometimes used the Nisaean horse for battle, they especially prized it for hunting, pleasure riding, and ceremony. Khusraw's mount, Shabdiz, on the other hand, is a large, black muscular warhorse. The Persians were pioneers of full battle armor (the Romans adopted it from them), which required a sturdy mount to bear the outfitted soldiers. Aside from black, a choice warhorse might be white, dappled, or sorrel. Ceremonial trappings for the horses were often made of the most lavish and expensive materials available. When a hero died, the mane and tale of his horse would be clipped, presumably as a sign of the animal's mourning. Occasionally the ancient custom of killing and burying the horse with its rider was observed.

Shirin," p. 39). Shirin even has a special throne built for Khusraw. But when he arrives, she locks the palace doors, denying him entrance. From the roof, Shirin reproaches Khusraw, recounting her sufferings, insisting they can only be together if she becomes his wife.

Khusraw slinks back to his camp in the snow and rain, and Shirin, repenting of her severity, follows. In the camp, a curious scenario takes place between the lovers, whose desires have become so complicated over time. They do not speak to each other, but two minstrels, Barbad and Nikisa, voice the lovers' emotions, and Khusraw and Shirin commit themselves to each other at long last.

The lovers marry and live happily together for many years until Shiruya, Khusraw's son with Maryam, has his father imprisoned. Shirin, of her own free will, joins Khusraw in bondage. Exhausted one night, she falls asleep. An assassin sent by Shiruya stabs his father. Khusraw at this moment proves the depth of his devotion to her. Bleeding to death, thirsting for water, he refuses to waken his exhausted wife and dies of his wounds without a murmur.

Shiruya's wickedness continues. Although he was a mere child when Shirin married Khusraw, he lusts after her. At his entreaties, she promises to marry him, but on condition that Khusraw's possessions be distributed to the poor. That done, Shirin joins the funeral procession for her husband, not in mourning garments but in colorful robes, much to the astonishment of the people. There is, however, private cause for rejoicing. When they reach the vault, Shirin is granted a few moments alone with the body. She kisses Khusraw, draws a dagger from her robe, and stabs herself exactly where he was stabbed. And so the two lovers are joined in death.

Farhad the Mason and Taq-i Bustan. "Khusraw and Shirin" is a tale full of pathos and palace intrigue, not only because of the featured couple's passion for each other. For love of Shirin, the stonemason Farhad tackles the supposedly impossible task of carving a path for caravans through Mount Bisutun, a site that actually exists in west-central Iran. Located at the base of the mountain, about 10 kilometers northeast of Kermanshah is a famous Sasanian rock carving known as Taq-i Bustan ("Arch of the Grove"). Because this site lies by an ancient thoroughfare, Taq-i Bustan was visible to many travelers, who spread word of its beautiful carved grottoes and garden. The carvings and bas-reliefs represent scenes of hunting and coronation. (Some say that the rider depicted is Khusraw II, and that the carving commemorates a military victory, but the matter is far from settled.) Above the three-story arch is a relief carving of three figures: a man flanked by another man and a woman.

Sasanian monuments like Taq-i Bustan seem to have struck Persians of the Islamic period as mysterious, much as monuments with Egyptian hieroglyphics or American Indian rock carvings might strike us today. Although these monuments

were from a fairly recent, for them, pre-Islamic period, the early Muslim Persians did not know much about their ancestors. From the days of Khusraw II to those of Nizami, however, stories circulated about the monuments, especially about Taq-i Bustan. These stories spoke of the woman as a pre-Islamic water goddesss, Anahita, or alternatively as Khusraw II's wife, Shirin. They identified one of the men as Ahura Mazda, the Zoroastrian god of good, or else Farhad, Khusraw's rival.

According to some, a lower sculpture depicting the monument's craftsman once stood astride a stream that flowed from the spring at the base of the rock carving. This idea led to the notion that the carving itself represented the sculptor of the monument. It was Nizami's innovation to link Farhad, Shirin's legendary lover and the possible second man in the upper sculpture, to the craftsman who carved it. In Nizami's rendition of "Khusraw and Shirin," the stonemason creates the carving of Shirin and one of Khusraw riding on Shabdiz before starting to chisel through the mountain, so that the image can inspire him as he works: "He labored day and night," his legend spreading throughout Persia; he stopped only "to gaze upon the likeness of Shirin," "to kiss its feet" and "plead his love" ("Khosrow and Shirin," p. 37).

The stonemason character appears to be a product of Nizami's time, of people who contemplated a monument in their midst that had been created, from their point of view, in the remote and mysterious past. Part of what is interesting about Farhad's story is that he is not a nobleman or a warrior but a workman. In his heroic portrayal of this workman, Nizami takes an unusual, egalitarian approach. Few Persian poets of his time would have portrayed anyone but a king or warrior as a hero. In Nizami's story, love defies social status. The pure emotion of a stonemason fares well in competition with that of a king. Love eradicates distinctions between the high and low, between the common Farhad and the noble Khusraw.

Sources. While the rock carving of Taq-i Bustan served as one source for "Khusraw and Shirin," Nizami also drew inspiration from written works. One such work was a romance written by the Arab author Khalid ibn Fayyaz, who lived about 100 years after the historical Khusraw's death. Nizami also drew on the "Book of Government" (*Siyasat-namah*). Its author, Nizam al-Mulk, a Persian minister who between 1073-92 served two Seljuq (Turkish) sultans, wrote the book to instruct his patrons—military leaders who had risen quickly to high positions—how to rule a large, settled population. His approach was to present exemplary stories about prior Persian rulers. Although the vizier and his patrons were Muslims, most of the stories in "The Book of Government" are drawn from the Sasanian period, which Nizam al-Mulk regarded as an ideal one. The historical Khusraw II, though not without fault, is one of the rulers described as a model of leadership.

Nizami also drew inspiration from Firdawsi's *Shahnamah, or Book of Kings* (c. 1010 C.E.), a grand epic that relates the history of Khusraw Parviz, including a brief account of his love for Shirin. In Firdawsi's version, Shirin is not a particularly admirable character; she, for example, murders Khusraw's wife Maryam out of jealousy. Nizami, who knew and greatly admired the *Book of Kings*, did not want to duplicate it. In Firdawsi's time, enough people of his own class—traditional feudal landowners, or *dihqans*—felt attached to older ways to make writing an epic worthwhile. By Nizami's time, however, the *dihqans'* power had dwindled and the audience of educated readers had grown, providing an audience for shorter tales of love and adventure. Given the focus on love and the strength of Shirin's character, it seems possible that women figured among this broader reading audience, or at least that they possessed the leisure to listen to recitations of such tales.

Nizami wrote in the romance genre, which, though not entirely new to Persian literature (it had existed at least since the Parthian dynasty of 220 B.C.E.-226 C.E.), lapsed into disuse until about a century before Nizami was born. He may have drawn on a particular story in this genre: the ancient Persian romance "Vis and Ramin" (c. 1040-1054), by Fakhr al-Din Gurgani, tells of the illicit love between a prince and a princess destined for each other from birth but forced to marry others. Outside Persia, the story may have influenced European romances such as *Tristan and Isolde* and *Romeo and Juliet*. Closer to home, the dramatic and psychological elements of this ancient Persian romance may have also influenced Nizami's "Khusraw and Shirin."

Events in History at the Time the Romance Was Written

The Seljuq dynasty. Nizami lived in a time of transition in Persia, during the decline of the Seljuqs, before the invasion of the Mongols. The Seljuqs, Turkish military rulers, had taken over control of eastern Persia from the caliph (Muslim emperor) in Baghdad. Seljuq rule over Persia lasted almost exactly a century, from 1055-1157 C.E. To a significant extent, the period was one of peace and prosperity in which important and enduring institutions were established, notably the Islamic colleges known as madrasahs (from the Arabic for "place of study"). During Nizami's lifetime, however, Seljuq power diminished, and the caliphs in Baghdad regained some of their former power. However, a place as distant from Baghdad as Nizami's Azerbaijan needed strong local leadership if its diverse ethnic groups and social classes were to be kept in check. In the absence of such leadership, lawlessness reigned: ganglike factions disrupted city life and bandits wreaked havoc on trade and farming. Rough Turcomen tribesmen—the Seljuqs' kin—pushed farmers off the land to graze their own sheep, goats, and horses. The farmers fled for what protection they could get in the cities, while city

NIZAMI'S CHOICE OF LANGUAGE

Nizami's verse constitutes a model of Persian style. Since Persian is more restricted in vocabulary than Arabic, many early Persian authors employed Arabic vocabulary to sound more erudite. Nizami, however, did not reach for Arabic words; instead, he exploited to the fullest the inherent sophistication of Persian, which lies in its idioms. The brilliance of his writing derives not only from his linguistic skill but from the vividness of his characters and descriptions, images perhaps all the more fresh because, unlike most poets of his day, he was not working to please the tastes of a particular patron or ruler.

dwellers themselves sought out walled cities wherever they could find them. Nizami's depictions of palaces—both Khusraw's and Shirin's—may reflect some of the anxieties of the time, while the idealized scenes of hunts, polo games, and picnics set in the countryside may reflect nostalgia for a safer and more joyous time.

Finally around 1215 C.E. the Mongols began to sweep south and west from their homeland in northeast China. In 1258 they sacked Baghdad and killed the caliph, ending a line of rulers that had held power for more than 500 years. The fact that Persian literature survived—and even flourished—in the aftermath of the Mongol invasions probably has to do with the strong foundation laid by Nizami and other authors under Seljuq rule. Both the lingering optimism of the high Seljuq period and the mounting anxiety as leadership broke down seem to find their way into his work, leading to a style that is much more emotional and sensitive than anything that had graced Persian literature before. Yet "Khusraw and Shirin" is no fragile work; the tale endorses loyalty and commitment, even as it shows an increased appreciation for the importance of individuals, from noblemen to commoners.

Enlisting the Persians. As outsiders, the Seljuq sultans recognized that they required Persian help to rule effectively. They therefore enlisted numerous bureaucrats, and established the role of a top minister, called a *vizier*, who, as a Persian, could advise the Turkish sultan and implement his policies among the population. The Seljuqs also showed great interest in adopting elements of Persian culture that would prove their sophistication and authority in contrast to more rough-hewn kinsmen such as the Turcomen. To this end, they promoted Persian literature.

The madrasahs, or colleges, founded by the Seljuqs spread to almost every moderate-sized city and even to the smaller towns. Whether Nizami studied in such a madrasah is unknown, but he appears to have been part of a new social class created by these colleges and by the Seljuq administration, a category of urban intellectuals formed to meet the needs of the bureaucracy, such as record-keeping, accounting, educating princes, and so forth.

The decline of Seljuq power in the eastern domain after the mid-twelfth century left many members of this new category stranded. The Seljuqs had increased the size of what might be considered a "middle class"—lesser bureaucrats, merchants, artisans, and military officers. Now, in the period of decline, these urban dwellers were inclined to seek out associations of like-minded people to give their lives meaning and order. Young and restless men were especially attracted to these associations, which resembled professional guilds or social clubs. Closely related to them were the orders of Sufis (Muslim mystics), established about a century before Nizami's lifetime. It is quite likely that Nizami belonged to one or another of these groups. Some argue that he was a Sufi, or kept close contact with a Sufi order, others that he belonged to an association of professionals, perhaps artisans, a view supported by the role of Farhad the stonemason in "Khusraw and Shirin."

Composition and reception. The exact circumstances of the composition of "Khusraw and Shirin" are unknown but is speculated that Nizami probably wrote the tale as a memorial to his wife Afaq after she suffered an untimely death. Further speculation holds that she bore him a child, Muhammad, and that Nizami worked certain passages into his tales to instruct this son in the ways of virtuous living. Whatever truth there may be in these speculations, the romance became one of the most popular in Persian literature. Turkish literature too adopted (and adapted) the tale, going so far as to modify it, making Farhad and Shirin into a romance in its own right and relegating Khusraw to a minor role.

"Khusraw and Shirin" initiated a trend in Persian literature that would continue for centuries, inspiring other accounts of the tale and prompting Persian versions of the Arabic tale love story "Layla and Majnun" and of the Greek adventure-romance of Alexander the Great. The tale also affected the works produced in related arts. So rich in visual detail is Nizami's romance that several episodes constitute some of the most beloved subjects in Persian painting—for example, Khusraw's glimpse of Shirin at the woodland pool.

—Caroline Sawyer

For More Information

Boyle, J. A., ed. *The Cambridge History of Iran.* Vol. 5. Cambridge: Cambridge University Press, 1968.

Bürgel, Johann-Christoph. "The Romance." In *Persian Literature.* Ed. Ehsan Yarshater. New York: Bibliotheca Persica, 1988.

Chelkowski, Peter. "Nezami: Master Dramatist." In *Persian Literature.* Ed. Ehsan Yarshater. New York: Bibliotheca Persica, 1988.

Frye, Richard. *Golden Age of Persia.* New York: Barnes and Noble, 1996.

Nizami Ganjavi. *The Haft Paykar: A Medieval Persian Romance.* Trans. Julie Scott Meisami. Oxford, England: Oxford University Press, 1995.

———. "Khosrow and Shirin." In *Mirror of the Invisible World.* Trans. P. Chelkowski. New York: The Metropolitan Museum of Art, 1975.

———. *Khusraw va Shirin.* Ed. Vahid Dastgirdi. Tihran: 1333.

Soucek, Priscilla. "Farhad and Taq-i Bustan: The Growth of a Legend." In *Studies in Art and Literature of the Near East, in Honor of Richard Ettinghausen.* Ed. Peter Chelkowski. Salt Lake City, Utah: University of Utah, 1974.

Yarshater, Ehasan, ed. *The Cambridge History of Iran.* Vol. 3. Cambridge: Cambridge University Press, 1983.

The King Is the King

by

Sa`dallah Wannus

Sa`dallah Wannus, Syria's and perhaps the Arab world's best-known playwright of the late twentieth century, was born near the Syrian coastal city of Tartus in 1941. After receiving his primary and secondary education in Syria, he obtained an undergraduate degree in journalism from Cairo University in Egypt. Wannus subsequently received an advanced diploma in theater studies from the Sorbonne's Institute of Theater Studies in Paris in 1968. Throughout his life, he would balance critical with creative writing. He not only produced a large number of essays on his and others' theatrical works but for many years also edited the journal *al-Hayah al-masrahiyah* (Theater Life). In the late 1970s Wannus helped establish the High Institute for Theater Arts in Damascus and went on to teach there. He published two collections of short plays before leaving for Paris in 1966. It was upon his return from Europe and in the context of the defeat of the Arabs in the Arab-Israeli war of June 1967 that he wrote *Haflat samar min ajl khamsah haziran* (Soiree for the 5th of June), the play that catapulted him to fame. An experimental play within a play, the work concerns the causes of the defeat. The play marked the beginning of a period of great productivity for Wannus, whose literary highpoints include his writing of *The King Is the King*. With the 1982 Israeli invasion of Lebanon, Wannus went on an almost decade-long hiatus from play writing. The last decade of his life (he died in 1997), however, was nearly as productive as the pre-1982 era, despite a prolonged battle with liver cancer. Wannus wrote seven plays in eight years during the 1990s, in-

THE LITERARY WORK

A play set in an unnamed city in the pre-modern Arab world; published in Arabic (as *al-Malik huwa al-malik*) in 1977, in English in 1995.

SYNOPSIS

To allay his boredom, a king secretly places one of his subjects on the throne for a day. No one notices the change, and the original king goes mad when he realizes that he will never regain his throne.

cluding the highly acclaimed *Tuqus al-isharat wa-al-tahawwulat* (Rituals of Signs and Transformations), written in 1994 and first performed in 1996. His post-1967 body of work is characterized by the twin goals of breaking down the traditional barriers between stage and audience and spurring the audience into political action. Wannus also distinguished himself as a pioneer in infusing the historical and cultural heritage of the Arab world into his drama, a strategy that surfaces along with the others in *The King Is the King*.

Events in History at the Time of the Play

Syria in the context of the *Naksah*. Probably the most important historical event informing *The King Is the King* is the defeat of the Arabs in the Arab-Israeli war of June 1967, known in

Arabic as *al-Naksah* (the disaster). Syria was one of the Arab states to give up land in this conflict, losing its Golan Heights to the Israelis. While there is still a great deal of controversy surrounding the events that led to the start of this conflict, what is known for sure is that in May of that year, a period of escalating tension between Syria and Israel, the Soviet Union mistakenly informed Syria and Egypt that Israel was planning an imminent attack on Syria. This led to action by the Egyptians that the Israeli leadership interpreted as a direct threat to the country's sovereignty. Israel launched what it saw as a pre-emptive surprise attack on Egypt on June 5 and in a matter of six days (June 5-10) the Arab forces were routed and Israel occupied all of mandatory Palestine, the Sinai Peninsula, and the Golan Heights.

One of the reasons that this loss had such an impact on the societies of the Arab world was because many of the region's postcolonial governments had used the goal of the defeat of Israel to legitimize their regimes. The liberation of Palestine, the region's citizens were told on a daily basis, was imminent. Syria was no exception in this regard. Nor was it an exception to the fact that the defeat of the Arab armies in 1967 led to increased militarization of the region's countries. Under the leadership of Hafez al-Assad who came to power in Syria in 1971, the Syrian military forces grew from 60,500 in 1968 to 500,000 by 1986 (Yapp, p. 262).

The defeat of 1967 greatly compounded an already existing refugee problem, adding some 300,000 displaced Palestinians to the large number (500,000-900,000) of refugees from the Arab-Israeli conflict of 1948 (Yapp, pp. 301-302). These refugees added volatility to the region's already shaky postcolonial regimes, particularly in Jordan and Lebanon. The bloody expulsion of Palestinian leadership from Jordan to Lebanon in 1971 led to increased volatility in the latter country, where the minority Maronite Christian government was already having problems cementing its rule. This and other factors led to the outbreak of a civil and regional war in Lebanon in 1975, a conflict that would last until 1990. Over the years Syria became heavily involved in fighting for a variety of factions in Lebanon. In fact, Israel used the strong Syrian presence in Lebanon as justification for an Israeli invasion of Lebanon in 1982, an event that impacted Syrian and Lebanese intellectuals only slightly less than the defeat of 1967. Whereas 1967 had led to an outpouring of

artistic expression, the events of 1982 did not inspire increased artistic productivity. A case in point is Wannus. For him, 1982 marks the beginning of a multi-year hiatus from play authorship.

The haves and have-nots. In 1970, a few years after the *Naksah*, a military coup brought Hafez al-Assad to power in Syria. He would rule Syria continuously until his death in the summer of 2000. At first, Assad enjoyed considerable popularity. Paradoxically, his popularity did not decrease with Syria's failure to win back the Golan Heights from Israel in the "October War" of 1973. Though clearly a loss, Syrians were heartened by the fact that this time, unlike 1967, the Arab forces in both Syria and Egypt attacked and inflicted considerable damage on the Israeli forces in the first few days of the conflict. Despite the loss, the whole country remained united behind the struggle to reclaim the land given up in 1967. Also paradoxically, this loss resulted in an economic boom. The Arab oil embargo of 1973 led to a dramatic increase in world oil prices. Syria's revenue from oil skyrocketed from 70 million dollars in 1973 to 700 million the following year (Seale, p. 318). At the same time, increased oil revenue in the labor-poor Arabian Gulf states meant increased employment opportunities for Syrians willing to travel to those countries to work. Assad used the increased revenue to fund not only the Syrian military but also development projects in the country. Syria's five-year development plan for 1976-80, drawn up in the heady days after 1973, envisioned spending $13.5 billion, a considerable jump from the $2 billion of the prior five-year plan (Seale, p. 318).

As is often the case in such boom times, not everyone benefited equally from the improved economy. While the number of millionaires (in the local currency) climbed from 55 in 1963 to 3,500 in 1976, the gap between the rich and poor grew. Patrick Seale writes, "Instant millionaires constituted the core of a new bourgeoisie, many enriched by commissions, kickbacks, and even theft made possible by the dozens of government-financed projects" (Seale, p. 319). Almost simultaneously, the economy began to falter and migration from the countryside to the cities continued unabated.

The sputtering economy and increased gap between the rich and the poor clearly played a role in the rising tensions between Assad's largely secular regime and those who wanted a government shaped more centrally by the tenets of

Islam. What exacerbated the tension was the fact that Assad, like Wannus himself, came from the long oppressed and marginalized Alawite sector of Syrian society, whereas most of the Islamic fundamentalists were from the Sunni branch of Islam. Not only did many Sunnis consider the practices of the Alawites to be heretical to Islam, but they also felt, not without justification, that the Sunni majority had lost power at the expense of the Alawites under Assad. These are some of the factors that led to a rise in violent attacks on representatives of the government in the post-1975 years. The country slid into a brutal cycle of internal violence that culminated in the crushing of an uprising in the largely Sunni city of Hamah in 1982. Even before the tension reached this peak, however, Patrick Seale writes that Assad "looked weak indeed" (Seale, p. 317). His comment pertains to the years 1977-78, the very period Wannus was writing and publishing his *The King Is the King*.

The Play in Focus

Plot summary. In the Prologue, the reader (or viewer) not only meets all of the play's characters, but also is told repeatedly that they are just that—characters—and that what he or she is about to watch is nothing more than an elaborate game. This message is reinforced both in the script and the stage directions, which instruct the actors to enter "like a group of circus players" (Wannus, *The King Is the King*, p. 79).

The actors form two groups on stage. One group includes the poor nuclear family of Abu Izza (the father), Umm Izza (the mother), their daughter, Izza, and the family's servant, Urqub. The other group is composed of members of the royal court: the King, the Vizier, the Executioner, the Police Chief, and a courtier. These two groupings represent, we are told, the age-old war between rich and poor, between the proponents of the "allowed" and the supporters of the "forbidden," and indeed, this is the crux of the conflict between the two groups. In an exchange between the two factions, the poor are told that they are allowed to dream, as long as they do not dream collectively and as long as their dreams are not realized. Abu Izza dreams of becoming King and taking vengeance on those who have wronged him:

> Abu 'Izza (Spinning like someone in a swoon): I become Sultan of the realm. . . . I tighten my fist on my subjects, even if it's only for a day or two. (Singing:) There goes my seal, / Done is

my will. . . . Ah, Taha! That treacherous devious Shaykh. . . . He shall ride backwards on a donkey in the midst of everyone, and then shall be hanged in the unfurled cloth of his turban! And that great merchant [. . .] along with the silk dealers who control the markets and regulate goods and trade, they shall be flogged to my heart's content and then they shall hang, but not before I've taken over all they possess, money and land.

> (*The King Is the King*, p. 80)

His wife fantasizes about gaining an audience with the King to complain about the "bastards" who have ruined her husband's business. Their daughter, Izza, dreams of a knight in shining armor. Urqub, the servant, confesses that he only continues to work for Abu Izza because he dreams about winning Izza's hand. The King, being "the dream itself," dreams of nothing and is thus bored. It is this boredom that sets in motion events that lead to some of the above dreams being realized in a comi-tragic fashion. The play's other two main characters are the Head Merchant and the religious figure Shaykh Taha. Throughout the Prologue they are separate from the two groups mentioned above and stand in the corner manipulating actual puppet strings. At Prologue's end, they announce that with their puppet strings they control "the *souk* [the market]," "the rabble," and the King himself. The Prologue's events are hosted by Zahid and Ubayd, two characters who reappear later in a series of "Interludes" between the scenes.

Scene One takes place in the throne room of the King's palace. Aside from the King's ornate throne and elaborate vestments—in which he seems to be swimming—the room is empty and cold. The actors are instructed to move in a mechanical way to accentuate the coldness and constructedness of the setting. The King is bored and in no mood to listen to the praises of his royal band, his vizier's news report, or his sycophantic courtier Maymun. What he would rather do—to his vizier's consternation—is venture incognito into the city to have some fun at the expense of his subjects. In contrast to previous excursions, however, this time he wants his and his vizier's disguises to be complete, and he does not want them to be trailed by guards. They will tell no one of their plan.

Scene Two transports us to Abu Izza's house, where he is fantasizing about being King. Abu Izza is completely delusional. He believes that the sweat on his brow is a result of the physical effort it has taken him to ascend his throne. His servant, Urqub, himself seems to get caught up in the fantasy when Abu Izza says that he still has not made up his mind whom he will chose to be his vizier. After he selects his servant, Urqub, he calls for wine to celebrate. Not only does Abu Izza have no money to pay Urqub's wages, but he does not even have enough to buy himself wine. We learn that Urqub plans to exploit his master's impoverished straits to win Izza's hand—so indebted to him will his master become that he will not be able to refuse the match. Izza's clear disdain for the servant becomes readily apparent. When Umm Izza arrives home, she is enraged not only that her husband is drinking, but that he has borrowed even more money from his servant to do so. Toward the end of the scene, the King and the Vizier arrive disguised as Haj Mustafa and Haj Mahmoud respectively. It is made clear that these prominent citizens have visited Abu Izza before and are returning to take him out for a night on the town. To placate Umm Izza, they give her a card that will grant her an audience with the King.

Scene Three takes us back to the palace, where Abu Izza has been placed in the royal bed. At this point the King (Mustafa) conscripts Urqub for their plot, telling him they are courtiers and that for a bit of fun they are going to place Abu Izza on the throne for a day. To carry out their plans, they are going to have to dress both Abu Izza and Urqub in the King and Vizier's clothes respectively. This is the first time that the Vizier (Mahmoud) has heard that he will have to give up his clothes as well. Once they send Urqub off to bed, the Vizier spends the rest of the scene trying to dissuade the King from carrying out the plan. Left alone at the end of the scene the Vizier prophesizes, "The beginning of the end. . . . No King can afford to forget his ribbons, or to treat his robe and crown lightly" (*The King Is the King*, p. 101). He decides that he will have to devise a plan to save his own skin.

In the first part of Scene Four, Abu Izza—still in the King's bed—wakes up to find Maymun, the courtier, rubbing his feet. He thinks himself in a dream and rues the fact that he will soon have to awaken. When he sees his own servant, Urqub, dressed in fine robes, he begins to realize that he may not be dreaming. Urqub tells Abu Izza that he is King Fakhreddin and that Urqub is his loyal servant Barbir. In the second part of the scene, the King's valets dress Abu Izza while the royal band serenades him. Once robed as the King, Abu Izza is instantly transformed: he "holds the sceptre; his features assume a somber look;

his body becomes erect and his demeanor firm" (*The King Is the King*, p. 104).

Scene Five unfolds in five parts. In order to observe the playing out of their game, the King and the Vizier enter the court posing as new courtiers. The first sign of trouble comes when Maymun does not recognize his former master, the King, who suppresses his anger and continues in his new role of courtier. It is in this scene too that a slippage of names begins, when the Vizier (Mahmoud) refers to Abu Izza as the King and to the real king as Mustafa. In Part Two, Abu Izza slides even more completely into his role as King. His vizier Urqub, for example, reminds him that now would be a good time for him to take his revenge against enemies such as the Head Merchant and Shaykh Taha, the very figures responsible for his poverty. Urqub is baffled when Abu Izza defends them as upstanding citizens. (His reaction shows how easily he takes to his new role as King. Just as the former king held the merchant and the shaykh in high esteem, so does Abu Izza in his new role, highlighting the collusion between the wealthy and the privileged.) When it is announced that the day's first visitor is to be the Police Chief, the real king (Mustafa) is confident that the Chief will realize that something is amiss.

In Part Three of Scene Five, however, the Police Chief does not notice that he is not speaking to the "real" king. If anything, he senses that the man before him is even more of a king than the king to whom he is accustomed to report. It becomes clear, in fact, that the Police Chief is used to bullying the King in his daily reports. Abu Izza surprises the Chief by upbraiding him for not reporting to him that there had been a prison break that very night. The Police Chief leaves the throne room cowed, and the original king, who is beginning to realize that no one can tell that Abu Izza is not the real king, goes insane. The original vizier understands that he must look out for his own interests. In the meantime, Abu Izza has called the Executioner and asked for the blade of his ax to be held nearby so that "the King and his blade be one" (*The King Is the King*, p. 110). That the Executioner does not recognize Abu Izza as an imposter only drives the original king more deeply into insanity.

The farce reaches its apex in Part Four of the scene, with Abu Izza so consumed by his role as King that he sentences his former self to public embarrassment. This happens when his wife and daughter come to court with their petition card to complain about how the Head Merchant and

Shaykh Taha have conspired to ruin her husband. Umm Izza does not recognize her husband on the throne, nor does he recognize her. The only one who shows a glimmer of knowledge is Izza, but she becomes distracted when the King promises her in marriage to his vizier, none other than the very Urqub who has been unsuccessfully pursuing her for years. The King tells Umm Izza that he sympathizes with her complaints, but that the fault of her ruin is her husband's (i.e., his own) and thus sentences him (i.e., himself) to public humiliation. When he announces that he is going in to see the Queen, the original king has a last glimmer of hope and a final moment of sanity: he is sure that the Queen will recognize that something is amiss. When it is clear that she does not, the original king goes completely mad and ends up being leashed by the Queen and walked around the palace like a dog. In the meantime the original vizier has schemed to get his cloak (and thus post) back from Urqub.

In the fifth and final part of Scene Five, Abu Izza, in the role of King, informs the Executioner that the King is going to perform his own executions from now on. The original vizier goes to Abu Izza, having tricked Urqub into giving him his cloak back, and informs him that a mutiny has been crushed. Abu Izza orders the arrest of all suspects, but also puts the Vizier in charge of establishing a new security apparatus to keep an eye on the Police Chief's security organization. The scene ends with a meeting between the King, the Head Merchant, and Shaykh Taha, with the former reassuring the latter two that all is well in the kingdom. As the Merchant and the Shaykh exit, they note that the King has, in fact, "become more of a king" (*The King Is the King*, p. 119).

The play ends with an Epilogue that calls for all of the actors to appear on the stage. As in the Prologue, they talk about what just happened as having been a game, although this time several characters, such as Urqub, wonder if they have been both spectator and victim in this game. In his case, the money he was given in return for the Vizier's cloak turned out to be counterfeit. Zahid and Ubayd, our hosts in the Prologue, have the last spoken words of the play, talking about their always-deferred revolution: "We must wait for the right moment: not a second too early or too late" (*The King Is the King*, p. 119). The play ends with all of the actors taking off their costumes and singing alternate lines of a song about a group of people who, having become fed up with their king, slaughtered and then ate him:

> At first some had stomach
> Aches, others got sick,
> But after a while they
> Recovered, and sat down to
> Enjoy life without masks or disguises.
> (*The King Is the King*, p. 120)

These references at the end to revolution bring closure to a theme repeated through "Interludes" between each scene. These interludes usually feature the hosts of the Prologue, Ubayd and Zahid. In the First Interlude, these two meet on the street with Ubayd pretending to be a hunchbacked beggar. They speak in hushed tones about the coup they are plotting against the King. In the Second Interlude, we discover that Ubayd is living in Abu Izza's house, and that he and Izza are fond of each other. Izza tells him that she has noticed that he is not really hunchbacked, at which point he makes an indirect confession to being one of those plotting against the regime. The Third Interlude takes us back to the message of the Prologue, as the Executioner and Urqub remind the reader/spectator that he or she is witnessing nothing more than a game. The two argue over which sector of society the new King will favor once in power and when they come to blows, their fight is broken up by Ubayd, who tells them, "Let's watch, shall we? We'd better keep track of the story" (*The King Is The King*, p. 101). The Fourth—and final—Interlude comes between parts three and four of Scene Five, when the original king starts to go insane. The Interlude freezes everyone in his or her place, and only the original king continues to move about and to wonder how no one has noticed that the man on the throne is not actually their king. Ubayd and Zahid joke back and forth about how whoever wears the clothes of the King, or sits in the seat of the King, automatically becomes King.

A final element that figures into the plot and deserves mention are the signs to be held up or projected at the beginning of each scene. Usually they provide a short summary of the upcoming action. Here are some examples:

> "WHEN THE KING IS BORED HE REMEMBERS THAT HIS SUBJECTS ARE AN AMUSING LOT IN POSSESSION OF TREMENDOUS ENTERTAINMENT POTENTIAL."
> "REALITY AND ILLUSION CLASH IN THE HOUSE OF A SUBJECT CALLED ABU 'IZZA."
> "SUBJECT ABU 'IZZA EVAPORATES BIT BY BIT."

"LE ROI C'EST LE ROI [The King Is the King]: SUBJECT ABU 'IZZA FORGETS HIS ENEMIES."

(The King Is the King, pp. 82, 88, 103, 108)

The use of "heritage" in the play. The staging of this play in 1977 in Damascus stirred controversy. Several critics noted the close resemblance between Wannus's play and the German playwright Bertold Brecht's *Man Equals Man*. An examination of both texts confirms to some extent the validity of this observation. But, while there is no denying the influence of Brecht's work on Wannus, the main inspiration for this play lies elsewhere.

FROM "THE SLEEPER AND THE WAKER," A STORY IN *THE ARABIAN NIGHTS*

"And quoth Abu al-Hasan 'Would Heaven I might be Caliph for one day and avenge myself on my neighbors, for that in my vicinity is a mosque and therein four shaykhs, who hold it a grievance when there cometh a guest to me, and they trouble me with talk and worry me in words and menace me that they will complain of me to the Prince of True Believers [i.e. the Caliph], and indeed they oppress me exceedingly, and I crave of Allah the Most High power for one day, that I may beat each and every one of them with four hundred lashes . . . and parade them round the city of Baghdad. . . . This is what I wish and no more'."

(The Arabian Nights, p. 556)

Many of Wannus's plays, and *The King Is the King* is no exception, can be considered part of a trend in modern Arabic literature of borrowing form and content from classical Arabic history and literature, which is generally referred to as *turath* (heritage). In this vein, *The King Is the King* stands out for its use of not just medieval but also early modern *turath*. The basic plot of the play relies on a story from the medieval **The Arabian Nights** (also in *WLAIT 6: Middle Eastern Literature and Its Times*), and also on one of the first plays of modern Arabic literary history—Marun al-Naqqash's *Abu al-Hasan al-mughaffal aw-Harun al-Rashid* (Abu al-Hasan the Idiot or Harun al-Rashid, 1849)—which itself relies on *The Arabian Nights*. *The King Is the King*, in other words, not only uses *turath* itself, but is also a self-con-

scious comment on the trend of employing medieval *turath* in modern writing. Simultaneously, the reference to al-Naqqash is a nod to the importance of the nineteenth-century founders of modern Arab theater on the contemporary Arab theater movement.

The story of Abu al-Hasan appears in Sir Richard Francis Burton's translation of *The Arabian Nights* as "The Sleeper and the Waker." The story in the Burton translation is similar to that of Wannus's *The King Is the King* in many ways. One difference is that the King of Wannus's play is not a king but the Caliph Harun al-Rashid in *The Arabian Nights*. One group of tales in *The Arabian Nights* revolves around the fictional antics of this real-life caliph. Many of these stories, such as the one in question, involve the Caliph's disguising himself and going out at night among his people on the streets of Baghdad. In "The Sleeper and the Waker," disguised thus, the Caliph meets Abu al-Hasan, who invites him home and expresses his wish to be caliph for a day so that he can seek revenge against his oppressors. He is then drugged by the Caliph and placed on the throne. In *The Arabian Nights* version, however, the Caliph never loses control of his reign. The trick is played on Abu al-Hasan twice, and he is rewarded at story's end by being made the Caliph's chief companion. Another aspect of the story that Wannus changed is the outcome of Abu al-Hasan's desire for revenge. In *The Arabian Nights*, Abu al-Hasan demands that the religious figures who have been harassing him be flogged and publicly humiliated. His orders are duly carried out. In Wannus's play, on the other hand, those who have wronged Abu Izza not only remain unpunished but their high status in society is reinforced.

This *Arabian Nights* tale was the basis for one of the first works of modern Arab drama. Marun al-Naqqash, from present-day Lebanon, is often credited as founding modern Arab drama with his *al-Bakhil* (The Cheapskate) in 1847. His second play was the 1849 work whose title translates as "Abu al-Hasan the Idiot or Harun al-Rashid," cited in Arabic above. The similarities between this work and Wannus's play make it clear that Wannus was more directly indebted to this nineteenth-century drama than to *The Arabian Nights* itself. For example, al-Naqqash names his disguised caliph and his vizier Mustafa and Mahmoud, respectively. The character who is made the Caliph likewise has a servant named Urqub, who is in league with the real caliph, who becomes Abu al-Hasan's vizier, and who sells his position back to the original vizier at the end of the play.

In response to critics who accused Wannus of unacknowledged borrowing of the play's plot from Brecht, Wannus said that Brecht himself might have been influenced by *The Arabian Nights*. It is important to note that the text of the play *The King Is the King* does not explicitly state the borrowing either from *The Arabian Nights* or from al-Naqqash, though Wannus admitted his debt to these works in interviews and essays. More important than the similarities between all these texts, however, are the differences, which brings us to the crux of the issue of the use of *turath* by Wannus.

Wannus's writings were very much influenced by the defeat of the Arabs in the Six-Day War of 1967. His first play in reaction to that war was the smash-hit *Soiree for the Fifth of June*. The play, a direct critique of the outcome of the war, was originally banned when first performed in 1968 (Allen, *The Arabic Literary Heritage,* p. 351). Wannus seems to have learned his lesson by the time he wrote *The King Is the King,* which was written in the guise of heritage. One of the reasons often cited for writing in such a style is to avoid censorship, a strategy that seemed to work in view of the success and non-censorship of plays such as *The King Is the King.*

In addition to providing cover for direct criticism, another motivation for employing *turath* is to be able to locate the work's main message in the very contrast between the modern piece and the piece being quoted. A main difference between Wannus's work and that of al-Naqqash and *The Arabian Nights* story on which al-Naqqash's play is based is that in *The King Is the King* the original king, by simply giving up his royal cloak, loses his power. A further difference is that once on the throne Abu Izza does not seek revenge on those that were the root cause of his fantasies about becoming king, but instead treats them with the same honor and respect that his predecessor on the throne granted them. Thus, one of the key messages of the play—the corrupting nature of power and the dependence of that power on outward appearances—is highlighted by the differences between his and the original texts on which his play was based.

Wannus pays homage to pioneers such as al-Naqqash and al-Qabbani not simply to celebrate early modern Syrian theater, but also because he was very interested in the fact that the audiences of that day interacted freely with the players on the stage. This brings us back to the issue of Brecht and his influence on Wannus and his contemporaries. One of the goals of Wannus's post-1967 theater was to break down the traditional barrier between the stage and the auditorium and to involve the audience directly in his productions. This was one of Brecht's innovations. While Wannus accomplished the aim in more direct ways in his earlier plays, in *The King Is the King* he does so through the opening Prologue and the subsequent Interludes and Epilogue. Not satisfied with some of his earlier direct methods, such as encouraging conversation between the actors onstage and his audience members, or most famously having the whole audience arrested at the end of *Soiree*, Wannus returns here to a technique familiar to Arabic letters, that of a frame-story. In fact, the technique is a feature integral to *The Arabian Nights* itself, which is framed by the famous story of the king Shahrayar and the story-telling queen Shahrazad.

This, then, is one aspect of the genius of *The King Is the King*: it does not simply use the content of *turath*, with significant alterations, for very modern goals, but employs its form as well. By utilizing both the form—here the framing technique of *Arabian Nights*—and content of Arabic-language *turath*, Wannus is protecting himself from censorship and showing off the richness of Arab heritage. Beyond these two achievements, he is furthermore demonstrating that such works, whether they be the authorless medieval *The Arabian Nights* or the pioneering work of nineteenth-century Arab playwrights, have much to teach him and his contemporaries about artistic innovation. This brings us back to the importance of the debate about the close resemblance between *The King Is the King* and Brecht's *Man Equals Man*. While modern and contemporary Arab playwrights were unquestionably influenced by Western playwrights and theoreticians of theater such as Brecht, Wannus demonstrates that similar examples of the new can also be found in the older cultural texts of the region's past.

Literary context. The devastating military defeat of 1967 had the paradoxical effect of bringing about something of a literary renaissance throughout much of the Arab world. If the 1967 Arab-Israeli war had the short-term result of curtailing artistic activity all over the region, it was not long before writers of all genres and artists of all media began to express their individual and collective mix of grief, resolve, and disappoint-

WANNUS INTERPRETS *THE KING IS THE KING*

"At the beginning of the play *The King Is the King* Zahid announces an acting game in order to analyze the power structure in 'regimes of monarchy and disguise.' . . . What I mean by 'regimes of monarchy and disguise' are class societies, especially the contemporary bourgeois ones, military or not. He who has pointed to the external plot structure as proof that the play's target is Eastern dictatorial societies, and thus based his evaluation of the play on this assumption, is mistaken. The play, as I have said, is more inclusive in the regimes that it strives to treat. . . . The metaphor [I use to analyze these regimes] is the process of 'disguise.' The history of theater is full, especially the comedies of the seventeenth and eighteenth centuries, of works the plots of which are built on the exchange of roles through disguise. What catches one's attention in most if not all of these plays is that the 'disguise' is used to uphold the class structure, not to disturb it or to arouse suspicion as to its legitimacy. The prince would remain a prince even while in the clothes of the servant. And the servant would carry the characteristics of the servant despite the fact that he donned the clothes of the prince. . . . Class societies [are] but a complex chain of disguises which reach their apex in a pure abstraction . . . the ruler . . . this person . . . is made up of a series of symbols and signs: the clothes, the sepulcher, the throne, the customs, the retinue, etc. The tragedy of the ruler begins when he mistakenly believes that he has personal abilities separate from his symbols, i.e. when he forgets that his legitimacy is based precisely on these symbols. . . . the tragedy of the king in the play starts precisely when he becomes bored and believes that the throne has one size, i.e. his size."

(Wannus, "Hawla muqaranat," p. 105; trans. C. R. Stone)

ment over the devastating losses. As the Syrian novelist Hanna Minah has written, resistance literature "exploded after the [N]aksah of June 1967, especially through the pens of the Palestinian writers, but also generally by Arab writers. Its voice rose and rose until it drowned out all other literary voices, for the output was prolific, filling the pages of books, periodicals and magazines" (Minah, p. 221; trans. C. Stone).

Minah covers the impact of 1967's events on all of the major literary genres. He stresses the importance of the reaction of poetry to the defeat, singling out Palestinian poets such as Mahmud Darwish, Samih al-Qasim, and Tawfiq Ziyad. Of the poets outside Palestine, the Syrian poet Nizar Qabbani, in particular his collection of poetry *Hawamish ala daftar al-Naksah* (Notes on the Notebook of the *Naksah*, 1967), are often mentioned in this regard. One poem from that collection sums up succinctly and powerfully the effect that this event had on Arab poets in general: "Oh my sad nation. You transformed me in an instant from a poet who writes poetry of love

and nostalgia to a poet who writes with a dagger" (Qabbani, p. 9; trans. C. Stone).

Poetry was not the only genre to be shaped by the events of 1967. The fictional genres were greatly affected too, as demonstrated by Palestinian writer Ghassan Kanafani's novel **Men in the Sun** (also in *WLAIT 6: Middle Eastern Literatures and Their Times*). Next to poetry, however, concludes Minah, the genre most impacted by events of 1967 was theater. For example in Lebanon, works such as Isam Mahfuz's *al-Zanzalakht* (1968; The China Tree), Raymun Jabbara's *Latamat Dazdamuna* (1970; The Blows of Desdemona), Jalal Khuri's *Juha fi al-qura al-amamiyah* (Juha in the Front-Line Villages, 1971), and Faris Yawakim's *Akh ya biladna* (1971; Yikes, What a Country) can be seen in varying degrees as responses to the loss. In Egypt the reaction, due mostly to government censorship, was different. Though a clear leader in Arab theater in the decades preceding the defeat, Egypt experienced what has been called a "theater crisis" after the *Naksah* (Allen, "Arabic Drama," p. 124). This is not to say that there were no theatrical responses to the catastrophe of 1967 in that country. One example is Mahmud Diyab's 1970 *Rajul tayyib fi thalath hikayat* (A Good Man in Three Stories).

The threat of censorship is given as one reason for the trend of using *turath* (heritage) in literary works after 1967. Another reason, from the early 1960s on, was dissatisfaction with Western forms and content, as can be seen in the theatrical writing of Qasim Muhammad (Iraq) and al-Tayyib Siddiqi (Morocco) (al-Ra'i, p. 400). There is no doubt, however, that the use of *turath* increased after 1967. A favorite text employed in this trend is *The Arabian Nights*, as shown in Wannus's play and, for example, Alfrid Faraj's (Egypt) *Ali Janah al-Tabrizi wa-tabi'uhu Quffah* (1969; Ali Janah from Tabriz and His Henchman Quffah).

The events of 1967 seemed to speed up a process of experimentation in Arabic letters that was already underway, as evident in Egyptian works of the pre-*Naksah* period, such as Yusuf Idris's play *Farafir* (1964; The Farfurs) and Sonallah Ibrahim's novel *Tilka al-ra'ihah* (1966; *The Smell of It*, 1971), with its stripped down prose. After 1967, experimentalism became a more consistent feature of the region's literature, as shown in the corpus of plays generated by Wannus himself.

Sa'dallah Wannus is perhaps the most often mentioned writer of any genre in terms of reactions to the *Naksah* of 1967. Prior to that date he had published two collections of plays that can be characterized as "theater of ideas," thus placing him in a tradition of modern Arab playwrights such as the Egyptian Tawfiq al-Hakim, whose highly literary plays were very difficult if not impossible to produce on stage (Allen, "Arabic Drama," p. 97). It was the defeat of 1967 that led Wannus to strive for a more performable and political theater, or, as he sometimes called it, a "theater of politicization," a theater that provokes people to think critically and to strive for change. His first two post-1967 plays heralded the use of experimentation and heritage respectively. The first, *Soirée for the Fifth of June*, is "the most famous and notorious" of all reactions to the *Naksah* (Allen, "Arabic Drama," p. 99). The inner play within the play is a drama about the 1967 war that never gets staged because of arguments between the "director," the "author," and actors playing audience members about how best to depict the defeat. The play ends with the actual audience, which has been tense from the beginning because the play intentionally starts late, literally being placed under temporary arrest. Wannus's

second play, *Mughamarat ra's al-Mamluk Jabir* (The Adventures of the Mamluk Jabir's Head, 1970), no less experimental, has a traditional storyteller ignore his customers' requests for stories of past Abbasid-period glory and heroism. Instead, the storyteller weaves a macabre tale of grave injustice from that "golden age" of Islamic history. Wannus would continue to strive for ways to involve and impact his audiences as much as possible through the 1970s, his efforts culminating, say some, in *The King Is the King*.

THE NAME GAME

The reader may have noticed that Izza's parents names—Abu Izza and Umm Izza—contain her own name. Their literal meaning is "father of Izza" and "mother of Izza" respectively. This type of name is known in Arabic as the *kunya*. Traditionally the *kunya* takes the form of the Arabic words for father and mother, *abu* and *umm* plus the name of the parents' eldest male child. The use of the daughter's name in the *kunyas* in *The King Is the King*, however, demonstrates that the rules are flexible. The *kunya* can also be used as a nickname without any relation to the names of one's progeny. While there are some *kunyas* traditionally associated with certain names, such as Abu Ishaq or Abu Ya'qub for Ibrahim, other people may be assigned one or more *kunyas* less systematically. The *kunya* can also be used to refer to people by a physical trait, such as "Abu Kirsh," or "he of the paunch." A *kunya* can likewise be taken or given as a nom-de-guerre without any particular meaning—Palestinian leader Yasser Arafat, for example, acquired the *kunya* Abu Ammar. Finally a *kunya* can also be used to draw attention to peoples' negative qualities or be used as an insult (Wensinck, p. 396).

While his post-1990 plays would continue to be experimental in form and in the use of Arab heritage, they show a greater focus on the suffering of individuals than his earlier plays, which are more collective in their focus. Representative of this later group of plays is his 1994 (first performed in 1996) *Rituals of Signs and Transformations*, which is set in nineteenth-century Damascus and which portrays the way a woman's sexual and social liberation shakes a society to its core. The main text of reference for this female character is *The Arabian Nights*.

Reviews. Like much literary Arab drama, Wannus's written texts have generally been more highly acclaimed than their production on stage. Unlike much of the theater that preceded him, however, this is not so much because his texts were not written with live audiences in mind, but rather because he was always striving to reach, involve, and affect audiences in new ways. The performance of his first post-1967 work—*Soiree for the Fifth of June*—received rave reviews. It eventually became clear, though, that its high topicality made it difficult to perform as successfully five or six years after the *Naksah* itself. This perhaps explains why his plays became less historically specific over the years; his *The King Is the King,* for example, does not refer to any specific historical place or events. This timelessness earned the work accolades from the Syrian theater critic Riyad Ismat: it "is a theatrical work ambitious and advanced, and carries in its depths the value of eternality, and is full of comedic, visual and dramatic enjoyment" (Ismat, p. 76; trans. C. Stone).

Those who saw it on stage tended to find fault with it, although they disagree on where blame for its shortcomings should lie. The Syrian critic Zuhayr Hasan takes the director to task. "The production," he says summing up the problem, "was a midget compared to the giant of a text" (Hasan, p. 100; trans. C. Stone). Syrian critic Paul Shawul, on the other hand, praised the direction and production of the play, but found fault with the text itself:

> The viewer feels that he is in the presence of politicized and theatricized language that alienates him from reality more than it incites him against it. . . . For this reason Wannus, when he wanted to compensate for the absence of a rooted vision, falls into a kind of evangelical and direct preaching.
>
> (Shawul, p. 521; trans. C. R. Stone)

Generally, however, those evaluating the play in print rated it higher than those like Ismat who saw it performed live. Roger Allen saw it as something of a culmination of Wannus's theatrical talents, reckoning it to be "his last truly major contribution to Arabic drama" (Allen, *The Arabic Literary Heritage,* p. 354). There is general agreement on the pioneering work and significant contribution that Wannus has made to Arab theater. "It will be written for him," predicts Hasan, "that he was the first Arab writer to enter the realm of world playwrights" (Hasan, p. 95; trans. C. Stone).

—Christopher R. Stone

For More Information

Allen, Roger. "Arabic Drama in Theory and Practice: The Writings of Sa`dallah Wannus." *JAL* 15 (1984): 94-113.

———. *The Arabic Literary Heritage.* Cambridge: Cambridge University Press, 1998.

The Arabian Nights: Tales from a Thousand and One Nights. Trans. Sir Richard F. Burton. New York: The Modern Library, 2001.

Hasan, Zuhayr. "al-Malik huwa al-malik wa-masrah al-mir'ah." *al-Adab* 26, nos. 7-8 (1978): 92-103.

Ismat, Riyad. *al-Masrah al-Arabi: suqut al-aqni`ah al-ijtima`iyah.* Damascus: Maktabat al-Assad, 1995.

Minah, Hanna, and Najah al-Attar. *Adab al-harb.* Damascus: Manshurat Wizarat al-Thaqafah, 1976.

Qabbani, Nizar. *Hawamish ala daftar al-Naksah.* Bayrut: Manshurat Nizar Qabbani, 1970.

al-Ra`i, Ali. "Arabic Drama Since the Thirties." In *The Cambridge History of Arabic Literature: Modern Arabic Literature.* Ed. M. M. Badawi. Cambridge: Cambridge University Press, 1992.

Seale, Patrick. *Asad of Syria: The Struggle for the Middle East.* Berkeley: University of California Press, 1988.

Shawul, Paul. *al-Masrah al-Arabi al-hadith: (1976-1989).* London: Riyad al-Rayyis, 1989.

Wannus, Sa`dallah. "Hawla muqaranat al-Duktur al-Hamu bayna masrahiyatay 'al-Malik huwa al-malik' wa 'Rajul bi-rajul.'" *al-Mawqif al-adabi* 90 (1978): 93-110.

———. "The King is the King." In *Modern Arabic Drama: An Anthology.* Eds. Salma Khadra Jayyusi and Roger Allen. Trans. Ghassan Maleh and Thomas G. Ezzy. Bloomington: Indiana University Press, 1995.

Wensinck, A. J. "Kunya." In *Encylopaedia of Islam.* Vol. 5. Leiden: E. J. Brill, 1986.

Yapp, M. E. *The Near East Since the First World War.* New York: Longman, 1991.

Leyla and Mejnun

by

Fuzuli

The son of a clerical family, Muhammad ibn Sulayman (d. 1556) was born in Iraq c. 1480, probably near the Shi'ite holy city of Karbala. His pen name, Fuzuli, aptly describes his literary career. A Turkish derivation of the Arabic *fuduli*, the term *fuzuli* paradoxically denotes either "presumption" or "virtue." Fuzuli hoped to grow wealthy and win renown through his poetry, but he was never appointed to the lucrative position of court poet, despite his "countless invocations" and eulogies to "rulers ... begging for help and favors" (Bombaci in Fuzuli, p. 13). He followed the well-trodden path of medieval intellectuals—bureaucrats, who sought artistic achievement along with the comforts of patronage. However, in the end, Fuzuli's efforts earned him only a modest pension. Although he pandered to his clients' tastes, Fuzuli maintained the highest of artistic standards, and one can discern a sophisticated perspective on esoteric matters in his works. His compositions blend Turkish, Arabic, and Persian elements with grace and virtuosity and reveal a high level of erudition in the Islamic and rational sciences. In 1534, when the Ottoman sultan Süleyman the Magnificent occupied Baghdad and ushered in a period of sectarian tolerance, Fuzuli briskly switched his allegiance from the Safavids. He toned down his own Shi'ite tendencies to accommodate the sensitivities of the new regime, whose members belonged to the Sunni branch of Islam. In his greatest work, a verse rendition of the Arab story *Leyla and Mejnun*, Fuzuli complains that "his deeds have not been recompensed and that fate was protecting the dishonest and humiliating those like himself

---

THE LITERARY WORK

A Turkish reworking of a traditional Arab love story in verse, set in the northern Arabian Peninsula in the legendary past; composed in 1535-36; published in English in 1970.

SYNOPSIS

Kays, the son of a rich chieftain, falls in love with Leyla, and his infatuation leads to gossip that prompts her family to remove her from school. When Leyla marries another man, Kays becomes the madman Mejnun.

---

who were faithful and honest" (Bombaci in Fuzuli, p. 17). He thus identifies with Mejnun, the protagonist of the tragic love story, who wanders the desert a madman after society rejects his expressions of love for Leyla. Despite his frustrations, Mejnun produces fine poetry that the people not only appreciate but even recite.

Events in History at the Time of the Story

Madness and the malady of love. From early Abbasid times (750-1258), Muslim philosophers, theologians, doctors, and astrologers portrayed obsessive romantic feelings as a possible cause of madness. Therefore, they instructed members of the public to avoid undue attachments. Although the Quran has little to say about romantic love, it contains numerous verses that delineate the legal relationship between men and women and it admonishes believers to mistrust their carnal instincts in this regard: "God desires to turn towards you, but those who follow their lusts desire you to swerve away mightily; God desires to lighten things for you, for man was created a weakling" (Surah 4, lines 41-5).

Nonetheless, conceptions of romantic love (*ishq*) and divine love (*illahiyah*) frequently overlapped, both among the common people and scholars. Many thinkers characterized the believer's devotion to God, and vice versa, as a bond of overwhelming power. Sufis, or Muslim mystics, based their rituals on the intense relationship between the believer and God. If properly channeled, any form of earthly love, or for that matter, the senses' awareness of physical beauty, was a natural metaphor for the essential bond between God and the believer. In this sense, passionate but chaste romantic feelings could have an "ennobling power" (Dols, p. 314). Sufi poets invoked imagery to link earthly and divine love, imagery that non-Muslim Europeans drew on for their own explorations of chivalry and courtly love.

Romantic love taken to excess, however, was viewed as a moral lapse with grave consequences. Obsession with another to the exclusion of all other interests implied that the lover had replaced God with the false idol of the beloved. The lover's neglect of God led to madness, because in the Muslim theological understanding, the universe makes no sense without a central divine presence. The forlorn lover feels isolated, suffers intense melancholy, and exhibits a willingness to transgress social norms. Romantic love is thus not only a religious but also a psychological matter.

This conclusion, which grew out of the debate over Sufism, had important consequences for Muslim social science and medicine. Opponents of the Sufis contended that Sufi beliefs and practices led the faithful into idolatry and permissiveness. In reply, Sufi sympathizers pointed to "poetry . . . stories, pious traditions, and maxims" that illustrated cases where profane love enhanced awareness of the divine presence (Dols, p. 314). Ideologues from both sides reworked age-old love stories to support their views. Medical studies on love then consulted these stories.

Muslim doctors who treated the symptoms of love sickness generally followed the tenets of ancient Greek medicine. The malady was thought to stem from the disillusionment of the soul, which, the belief was, resided in the brain, the heart, and the liver. Among the symptoms were losses of appetite, creativity, and memory when the beloved departed. To diagnose the condition, doctors took a reading of the pulse. To treat the malady, they prescribed a permanent separation from the beloved.

Islam and the natural environment. As Mejnun dissolves into madness, he forsakes all social intercourse in favor of an ascetic's life of isolation in the desert. He establishes a special rapport with the creatures there, which console and protect him. In the story, as the space and time in which God immutably shaped the world and its objects, the wilderness reflects divine intent in its purity. Against this backdrop, Mejnun perfects the image of his beloved in his mind, and likens his love for Leyla to a more overpowering and essential bond, the reciprocal adoration of God and the believer.

Mejnun's flight to the desert is a skillful manipulation of the historical and evolving Islamic concepts of nature. The Quran teaches that the environment works in full concert with divine intent. Nature fulfills the beneficent aim to sustain all living creatures. God had appointed Adam and Hawwa (Eve), his "equal half," as the vice regents of Earth (Nomanul Haq, p. 147). As part of a primordial covenant (*mithaq*), human beings promise to praise God and uphold the measure (*qadr*) and balance (*nizam*) of the Earth.

Whereas the Quran encourages stewardship of nature, anecdotes of the lives of the Prophet Muhammad and his companions, collectively known as the traditions (*hadiths*), stipulate no such obligation. Although these traditions passed through a sophisticated process of authentication during their compilations in the ninth century, they inevitably reflected the attitudes of their transmitters. Incorporated into law (*fiqh*), the traditions performed a practical function—to supplement the rather modest social prescriptions of the Quran. They addressed human needs and relegated nature to a secondary role. Rather than worry about cosmic balance, jurists concerned themselves with how to exploit natural resources as a proprietary matter.

Given the conflicting view of nature from the Quran and the traditions, Muslims developed a complex view of nature. On the one hand, in keeping with the Quran, the environment was seen as a pure reflection of God's will. Creatures of the world held a privileged and sublime relationship to the divine that was inscrutable to human reason. On the other hand, in keeping with the traditions, the natural world was seen as subordinate to human needs. Accordingly, jurists designated land as either fruitful or wasted (*mawat*); humanity could tamper with nature in a unilateral manner. This second view reinforced popular conceptions of the wilderness as a hostile and antithetical domain.

Therefore, Mejnun's choice to wander the desert distinguishes him as atypical. In one sense, he is a romantic hero reminiscent of past prophets, such as Adam, who communed more directly with God and nature. In another sense, he is a transgressor of norms, who comes to disdain society's mandates when they obstruct his expression of love for Leyla. These dynamic contradictory readings animate the protagonist because they reflect a historical tension inherent to Islamic considerations of nature.

The pilgrimage (*hajj*) to Mecca and the Ka'bah Stone Sanctuary. In *Leyla and Mejnun* the king, beside himself about how to cure his son, resolves to help by performing a holy ritual—he makes a pilgrimage to Mecca. The Islamic faith requires every able-bodied Muslim with adequate financial resources to perform a pilgrimage to Mecca, and Muslims believe that the pilgrimage reinvigorates one's faith.

Mecca, located in the interior of west-central Saudi Arabia, is the holiest city of Islam and the focus of ritual prayers. It was here that the Prophet Muhammad established Islam as the triumphant seat of the monotheistic faith. In a sequence of ritual acts over the course of three days synchronized with the holy calendar, the pilgrim recommits his or her faith to God. In theory pilgrims express their devotion as individuals, but in practice the event brings together thousands of believers as a community.

The holy center of Mecca is the Ka'bah Stone Sanctuary and the monuments around it. The pilgrimage begins and ends with circumambulation and prayer around the sanctuary. The word *ka'bah* means cube in Arabic. Indeed, in the center of a large portico-lined sanctuary (*haram*), there is a cubical blue-gray stone structure. Inside the structure lies "a blackish stone of either lava or basalt" (Peters, p. 9). The stone is covered from view on all sides by a tapestry of black brocade. When Muhammad returned triumphantly from his exile in Medina, he instructed his followers to smash the pagan idols surrounding the sanctuary and rededicate it to the one God Allah. The Ka'bah shrine, in the eyes of Muslims, is therefore a dual symbol: it reminds believers both that Muhammad was the culmination of the Abrahamic line of prophets, who taught belief in a single god, and that Islam triumphed over paganism.

Around the Ka'bah Sanctuary, there are other potent symbols of the importance of monotheistic faith. Near the sanctuary a domed shrine called the Station of Abraham marks the place where the biblical Abraham is said to have stepped and left impressions in the stone. Also near the Ka'bah is the well of the Zamzam spring, where Abraham's son Ishmael reportedly found water to quench his thirst. Such monuments connect one of the first and most important prophets, Abraham, to Muhammad, and underscore that Mecca has long been a focal point of revelation and divine interest.

Muslims understand that the pilgrimage, incumbent on every able-bodied believer, provides an opportunity to reaffirm the faith. Upon completion of the hajj, the pilgrim is expected to return to the community and to behave with greater moral probity. The believer expects his or her pilgrimage, as an act that God not only sanctions but also enjoins, to merit spiritual blessings if conducted properly and in good faith. In Fuzuli's story, the king believes that by sending his son on pilgrimage, God will reward Mejnun for piety and intercede to detach him from his ruinous obsession with Leyla.

The marginality of Bedouin culture after Islam. Although Fuzuli adds to his version elements that reflect the conditions of sixteenth-century Iraq, *Leyla and Mejnun* hearkens to a lost Bedouin past, when the nomads of Arabia ruled the desert. According to the Quran and the traditions of the Prophet, the Bedouin nomads of Arabia had played an ambiguous role in the initial Islamic expansion. They provided military recruits essential to the advancement of the first empire, but their desire to maintain tribal affiliations violated a central tenet of the Muslim faith. Many refused to surrender their tribal identities to become full-fledged members of the new community. In the story, the king's paramount concern for his son is for him to recover his senses so that he can take up his birthright, leadership of the tribe, upon his father's death. He persists in this desire even after he meets Mejnun in the desert for the last time and realizes that his son is on a virtuous spiritual journey.

Ironically, the Bedouins' contributions to the conquests of the great sedentary civilizations of Iran, Iraq, Syria, and Egypt, only curtailed their influence in the larger Muslim community. The notables of Mecca and Medina who led the conquests did not wish to alienate their new non-Muslim subject population, so they adopted administrative structures that they already found in the different areas in place. They also tried to curb the customary Bedouin raids against the northern borders of the Arabian Desert. After the Prophet Muhammad died, the Bedouins rebelled, whereupon Abu Bakr, the first caliph, or successor to the Prophet, refused to grant them tax concessions. The enmity ensued. In 633, Abu Bakr defeated the Bedouins in the Battle of al-Aqraba.

The first caliphs settled the Bedouin troops that fought in the north into quarters separate from the indigenous populations to preserve them as "an elite military caste" (Lapidus, p. 34). Nevertheless, a rift soon emerged between the newly settled Bedouins and those Arabs who continued to practice nomadism. The urbanizing Bedouins grew wealthy from booty and tax revenues, and adopted the cultural accoutrements of the civilizations under their control. Soon enough, the settled Arabs no longer needed the Bedouins as military advance troops. There were enough new converts to fill the ranks of the army. Under the rule of the Umayyad dynasty (661-750), the Bedouins witnessed the full subordination of their "ancient, pagan, and nomadic" culture to the values of the multi-ethnic, interregional Muslim community (Khan, p. 77).

In early versions of the Leyla and Mejnun story, one can detect nostalgia for a lost Bedouin way of life from the protagonists' struggles with the community. Kays's very membership in the Banu Amir tribe brings to mind the Quranic episode in which the Prophet Muhammad stipulates that a certain Banu Amir chieftain should not participate in the Muslim leadership after his death (Khan, p. 81). Kays's choice of the medium of poetry suggests an idyllic, heroic Bedouin past; ultimately he abandons his birth community and sheds what he perceives to be superficial, conformist, and alien values.

The Story in Focus

Plot summary. *Leyla and Mejnun* begins in the household of a great Arab chieftain. Although famous throughout Iraq for his boldness and virtue, the chieftain is unhappy, because none of his wives have given birth to a son (Fuzuli, *Leyla and Mejnun*, p. 152). He fears that his failure to produce an heir will lead to gossip that undermines his authority and tarnishes the family name, so he prays for deliverance. God answers his prayers, and the household welcomes a son, Kays, into the world. The infant quickly proves

to be a mixed blessing. He cries incessantly, and no one can comfort him. One day while walking in the street, his nurse meets an attractive young woman who opens her arms to the crying infant. Dazed by her beauty, Kays falls silent. The young woman becomes the child's caretaker.

As the years pass, Kays grows into a handsome youth. He meets Leyla at school and becomes enamored with her dark eyes, pearly teeth, and flushed cheeks. Kays flirts with Leyla and she reciprocates. Gradually the two fall in love:

> These two, tall, fair as jasmine, straight and slender as a dart
> Were bound and tied, the one to other, firmly fast by loving art.
> Drinking deep the wing of pleasure, drinking deeply of desire,
> Drowned in unity of sadness, all engulfed in passions fire.
>
> (*Leyla and Mejnun*, p. 158)

In the classroom, Kays disguises his attempts to get Leyla's attention. He leaves his notebook on his desk after class for Leyla to return to him and asks her to help him write out his lessons.

Despite this care, "wicked tongues" wag about the budding romance, and Leyla's mother rebukes her for being indiscreet and forward (*Leyla and Mejnun*, p. 160). She removes Leyla from school and sequesters her at home. Leyla denies her mother's allegations, but she cultivates her love for Kays in secret. Meanwhile, Kays is adversely affected by the separation. He becomes obsessed with the image of Leyla in his mind, loses interest in school, and falls into the "blackest discontent" (*Leyla and Mejnun*, p. 167).

Rumors spread that Kays is descending into madness. He takes the name Mejnun, or Madman, to confirm his devotion to Leyla. As in his infancy, the intervention of friends and family cannot dissuade Mejnun from his desire for beauty. He starts to wander the countryside aimlessly. He sings of his undying love for Leyla in plaintive verse and serenades the mountains, trees, and animals of the desert. The people who encounter him disseminate his fine verse, and his reputation as an accomplished poet begins to grow.

One day Mejnun happens upon Leyla's entourage as it picnics in the spring meadows. Mejnun approaches, picks up a lute (*saz*), and sings of his love for Leyla. So overcome are both he and Leyla that they slip into unconsciousness. When Mejnun wakes, he finds that Leyla's companions have taken her away. He rends his garments and cries tears of blood. From that point on, he vows to forsake all ties to humanity. He asks his human companions to leave him and to bring word to his father of his despair.

The chieftain is inconsolable at the news. He strikes out in search of Mejnun, finds him lying in the desert, and begs him to return to his senses. When Mejnun refuses, the chieftain has to deceive him into returning home. He lies and says that Leyla is staying as a guest with the family. Upon their return home, the chieftain attempts to relieve his son's affliction in several ways. First, he goes to Leyla's father to arrange a marriage. Leyla's father refuses on the grounds that he cannot marry his daughter to a man who is "bereft of sense" (*Leyla and Mejnun*, p. 188). Second, the chieftain consults "a thousand skilled physicians," who prescribe for his son elixirs (*sherbet*) and visits to saints' tombs, but to no avail (*Leyla and Mejnun*, p. 190). Third, he organizes a pilgrimage to Mecca (*hajj*) in the hope that God will "supplication grant" (*Leyla and Mejnun*, p. 191). But Mejnun prays only for God to strengthen his love for Leyla.

No remedy abates his ailment, so Mejnun retreats once more into the desert to keep company with the mountains and animals, and he composes verse to express his anguished love. In a familiar trope of Middle Eastern folklore, he rescues a gazelle from a hunter's snare. He sees in the animal's eyes his own plight and the face of his beloved. Next Mejnun frees a pigeon from a cage and offers its captor a pearl in compensation. The creatures become his devotees, and he gains extraordinary power to communicate with the natural world.

Meanwhile, Leyla continues to mourn her separation from Mejnun. She likewise sees reflections of her grief in the natural world. She identifies with the moth that cannot resist the candle's flame and falls to its death. The moon's phases represent to her the changing fortunes of love, and she bids the moon to find her sun. She begs the wind and the clouds to find Mejnun and tell him to return. They deliver the message, as well as Mejnun's reply. He "grieves a hundredfold more" than Leyla (*Leyla and Mejnun*, p. 214).

This answer torments Leyla. She covers herself with garments, anklets, and pearls to conceal her grief. Her heavy raiment arouses the curiosity of a young nobleman named Ibni Salam, who crosses her path while hunting with falcons. Attracted, Ibni Salam sends an old man to arrange a marriage. Her family agrees—the young nobleman is a good prospect; he offers "gems and money" (*Leyla and Mejnun*, p. 217).

Before Ibni Salam marries Leyla, Mejnun befriends another nobleman, who proposes to reunite him with Leyla by force. Nevfel, the noble, from a powerful Turkish tribe, learns of Mejnun's troubles after hearing a recitation of his verse. He searches for the love-struck poet, discovering him surrounded by the beasts of the desert, which Nevfel disperses with his sword. He writes a letter to Leyla's family, asking for compliance with his wish to wed her to Mejnun, but they refuse. So Nevfel gathers his tribesmen, and they besiege the camp of Leyla's clansmen. Mejnun recognizes that Nevfel's army is fighting on his behalf but nevertheless roots for Leyla's tribe because they fight for his beloved. When the battle turns against him, Nevfel heeds the calls of his soldiers to retreat for the day, knowing that "Mejnun was of God divinely favored" (*Leyla and Mejnun*, p. 224). However, Nevel's forces regroup and win the battle on the second day. When he learns of Ibni Salam's engagement to Leyla, he decides to respect the customs of the Arabs.

The battle brings Mejnun within sight of Leyla, but he cannot cross the battle lines to meet her without creating a stir. So, to move into her camp, he wraps himself in chains and disguises himself as a mendicant beggar. Leyla pities the beggar and relates several verses of lamentation. Mejnun responds by "snapping into fragments all his chains" and sallying away "again in lonely solitude" (*Leyla and Mejnun*, p. 232). Later, he finds another pretext to visit Leyla. He binds his eyes and masquerades as a blind man who begs for alms.

Although Leyla has no desire to marry Ibni Salam, she has little choice but to abide by her family's wishes. To quell the reproaches of her kinsmen and the gossip of the community, she adorns herself "with sweet embellishment and cunning art" worthy of the occasion (*Leyla and Mejnun*, p. 239). On the wedding night, Leyla informs Ibni Salam that she loves not him but Mejnun. Ibni Salam agrees to forestall the consummation of the marriage. He clings to the vain hope that Leyla in time will forget Mejnun and grow to love him.

Mejnun learns of the marriage from his friend Zayd. He immediately begins to question Leyla's fidelity, indifferent to the social pressures on her. At this point, he grows so disillusioned with Leyla that his desire for her is transformed. He no longer craves her as a corporeal being but desires instead the ideal of love that she has become to him. Years of isolation have distilled this image in his mind: "Now I, myself, with but an image left, / Can find contentment sweet in its regard" (*Leyla and Mejnun*, p. 246). In fact, he convinces himself that Ibni Salam has married but a shadow of the true Leyla.

No longer concerned with Leyla's body but her soul, Mejnun sends his friend Zayd to reprimand her. Zayd poses as a magician and insinuates himself into Ibni Salam's camp by proposing to cure Leyla of her love sickness. He offers a letter from Mejnun to Leyla as an amulet. Leyla reads the letter and writes a response in verse: "Thou knowest well that I am but the jewel / within the market, haggled for by all" (*Leyla and Mejnun*, p. 251). She swears that she has remained chaste and vows her steadfast devotion to Mejnun.

The chieftain seeks out his son in the wilderness one final time. At first, since Mejnun's every thought is fixated on the image of Leyla, he does not even recognize his father. Mejnun demands news of his beloved. The chieftain begs his son to assume his birthright and give up the passions of youth. Although Mejnun concedes the wisdom of his father's advice, he tells him that he is no longer the Kays of old in any way: "For, though we [Leyla and Mejnun] own two bodies, yet the soul / is one and jointly owned, between us now / Duality is merged in a single state: No soul is mine but hers, and hers is mine" (*Leyla and Mejnun*, p. 262). The chieftain realizes the futility of his efforts. His last request of his son is to mourn his father's passing. A hunter who witnesses the chieftain's lonely death in the desert chastises Mejnun for not mourning his father's demise. Afterwards Mejnun goes to his father's tomb and grieves.

As the years pass, Ibni Salam grows weak from his unrequited love for Leyla: "His longing sadness and bitter grief / Soon worked on Ibni Salam's cypress frame / Till bent like a rattan, thin and quickly bent, / he dwindled in despair" (*Leyla and Mejnun*, p. 282). His death gives Leyla a new reason to lament life's frustrations. Upon learning of Ibni Salam's death, Mejnun feels no satisfaction. He in fact identifies with Ibni Salam as another poor wretch who has loved an "idol pure" to no avail (*Leyla and Mejnun*, p. 284).

The death of Ibni Salam frees Leyla to find Mejnun, but she hesitates at the prospect of a reunion. She has lived a chaste life into old age and does not know whether the fires of passion burn within her any longer. As she ponders this question, she falls unconscious, and her camel wanders from her caravan. She wakens to find herself alone in the desert night. As she searches for her caravan, she strays into the lands where Mejnun roams and encounters her beloved.

Leyla fails to recognized Mejnun at first, so worn by age and exposure has he grown. To prove his identity, Mejnun recites his now famous verses to her. Just as Leyla does not recognize Mejnun, Mejnun does not recognize Leyla at first. Once the two identify each other, Leyla approaches Mejnun:

> My heart is vowed to union with thee
> While all my soul was ever thine in trust. . . .
> If deep in love thou art, know me thy love.
> Come, dwell with me in rapture of desire,
> And for a fleeting moment be my mate.
> (*Leyla and Mejnun*, p. 302)

Mejnun rejects the advance. His love for Leyla is now solely platonic: "Thy image only, pure without flaw, / Gives more and fiercer heat than may consume / My feebleness; yet may I not resume / My fiercely burning passion, but withstand / The guerdon of the sweetly proferred hand" (*Leyla and Mejnun*, p. 304). He asks Leyla to join him in separation from worldly desires. Leyla accepts the wisdom of Mejnun's words. In like manner, he has become her idol and image of perfect love. Their physical closeness is short-lived, however. The caravan driver returns to retrieve Leyla and the two lovers pass their final days apart. When Leyla dies, Mejnun comes to mourn at her tomb and perishes of grief. He is laid to rest beside her; only in death are the two finally reunited.

The story as an allegory of Sufi love. Sufism is the principal branch of Islamic mystical thought. Although its theosophy is complex, Sufism's basic contention is that signs of God's presence saturate the material world. All creatures are aware of this presence, but reason cannot fathom the meanings behind the signs, since God works in incomprehensible ways. While separation makes the believer anxious for reunion with the creator, only death can put an end to the lover's suffering. The believer's sole recourse to the paradox that happiness in life comes only with death is the denial of the world and of the senses. Sufis accomplish this through a variety of rituals and disciplines.

Sufism developed many metaphors to characterize the bond between the believer and God. One of the primary metaphors is love. God loves creation, creation loves God, and life is but a striving for a reunion between the two. In Fuzuli's *Leyla and Mejnun*, the suffering of the two lovers transforms their mutual adoration into a purely metaphysical bond. Although Leyla and Mejnun's first youthful impulses are for physical intimacy, their forced separation allows them to comprehend love as an emanation of the soul.

Fuzuli was not the first writer to portray the story of *Leyla and Mejnun* as an allegory of Sufi love between a mystic and the divine, but his work stands out as the masterpiece of the genre. Mejnun is the mystic who first witnesses beauty in the physical world through Leyla, but comes to understand that his love for her is only part of the greater beauty behind God's creation. The true object of his desire is God. His pursuit of union with Leyla is therefore his pursuit of re-union with God.

The text is replete with Sufi motifs that help convey the sense of a higher purpose. For example, Mejnun frequently terms Leyla "the moon." The moon was a Sufi symbol, because its light is a reflection of the sun. The moon is the beloved, and the sun represents the lover. Mejnun also refers to Leyla as his pearl, from which the Sufis extract a symbol for inner beauty. The pearl is a node of perfection within the viscera and shell of the clam. Moreover, Fuzuli uses narrative techniques that warm the reader to the transfigurations that follow. As Leyla and Mejnun reach new insights, Fuzuli retreats from the narrative and allows the characters to assert their realizations in their own words. In this way, the main characters can demonstrate their mastery of mystical concepts of love without interference from the narrator.

In effect, the Sufi dimension of the story ennobles Fuzuli's protagonists. There is a lofty purpose to their separation, which in the end Mejnun himself helps effect by rejecting the opportunity to make love with Leyla. Her initial instinct is to consummate her love for Mejnun physically, but Mejnun rejects this as gratuitous and unworthy of Leyla's virtue:

> Still seek no union with her, for the wife
> Divorced, and lover wed, brings strife.
> Abandon now this path nonsensical,
> Recall the name of God so mystical . . .
> Duality is merged in single state:
> No soul of mine but hers, and hers is mine . . .
> If she is glad, the gladness is my share;
> If she repines, the sorrow clouds my days.
> (*Leyla and Mejnun*, pp. 260-2)

In the end, the two perish miserable but triumphant, having rejected the world and all its pleasures in order to enter the afterlife chaste and unadulterated.

Sources and literary context. The romance of *Leyla and Mejnun* is one of a corpus of Arabic Udhri love stories, stories in verse whose poets frequently came from the Banu Udhrah tribe. The stories typically involve transgression of the tribal code about contact between the sexes by a lover's making public his passion for his beloved, offending both the tribe and the beloved's family. The result is a ban on future contact with his beloved that turns him into a tormented, obsessed shadow of a man and her into an ideal. In Arabic letters, the most renowned example is the story of Leyla and Mejnun (in Arabic, *Layla* and *Majnun*), as told by Qays ibn al-Mulawwah (d. 688). The source of the story itself is of uncertain provenance. Some hold that Kays Ibn Mullawah, the young man who becomes Mejnun, was a real member of the Banu Amir Tribe. Other sources suggest that an anonymous young Umayyad, who loved a woman he could not marry, created Kays as a semi autobiographical character. Still others argue that Kays is a wholly invented character.

POETS, MUSIC, AND THE *SAZ*

~

Many Muslim poets intended their verse not only to be read, but also to be set to music. Fictional poet-heroes frequently propagated their verse through songs as well. As they journeyed through the countryside or wilderness to fulfill their quests, they wrote and sang poetry to mark their experiences. One of the most common instruments that itinerant minstrels took up was the lute-type *saz*. With a pear-shaped resonator and a long neck, the *saz* has between six and twelve strings distributed over three parallel ridges or fret courses (Picken, p. 217). When Mejnun encounters Leyla as she picnics with her entourage, he picks up a *saz* and begins to sing a mournful melody: "Two strings on a single *saz*, they played a moaning melody" (*Leyla and Mejnun*, p. 173). Of course the two strings that "played a moaning melody" are Leyla and Mejnun.

Once *Leyla and Mejnun* passed into lore, its transmitters added, expunged, and altered verse as they saw fit. When Abu al-Faraj al-Isfahani (d. 967) included the story in his tenth-century compilation of the Udhri corpus, the *Kitab al-aghani* (*Book of Songs*), he acknowledged that the original Udhri story had been lost. Recording all the discrepancies he found in oral traditions, he evaluated each interpretation (Khan, pp. 1-13). The transmission of oral and written texts was subject to a constant process of deviation, omission, addition, and revision. Therefore, each retelling entailed a revision that reflected the inclinations of the compiler.

By Fuzuli's day, in the early sixteenth century, the story had already passed into legend as the quintessential Bedouin romance. Many other literary masters, including the great twelfth-century Persian poet Nizami, had already produced masterful renditions of this and other Arabic love stories (see Nizami's **Khusraw and Shirin,** also in *WLAIT 6: Middle Eastern Literatures and Their Times*). Neither Fuzuli's decision to write in Turkish nor his efforts to portray Mejnun's life as an allegory of Sufi love were entirely new; his rendition, however, attained a unique blend of eloquence and levity. He employs a vocabulary heavy in Persian and Arabic loan words, but appends Turkish suffixes to them when it suits the meter (*hizaj*) and uses many words of Turkish origin. As Bombaci points out, Fuzuli's use of a heavily Persianized and Arabicized vocabulary conforms to an Ottoman Turkish literary convention that ensured his works broad dissemination "in Anatolia, in Azerbaijan, and in Central Asia," all predominantly Turkish-speaking areas (Bombaci, p. 86). Modern Anatolian Turkish is quite different from classical Ottoman Turkish in this regard.

Events in History at the Time the Story Was Written

Süleyman the Great and the Ottoman conquest of Iraq. A powerful Turkish tribe figures into Fuzuli's rendition of Leyla and Mejnun. The reconfiguration of Nevfel as a noble Turkish warrior is clearly an innovation because the earlier versions of Leyla and Mejnun antedate by several centuries any significant Turkish presence in the Middle East. Fuzuli most likely added this Turkish element as part of his bid to ingratiate himself with the new Ottoman authorities in Baghdad. Fuzuli hoped that his *Leyla and Mejnun* would be a tour de force that would impress the Ottomans into becoming his patrons. Therefore, the writing of Fuzuli's version of the story cannot be separated from the Ottoman conquest of Iraq.

Süleyman I's (1494-1566) involvement in Iraq stemmed from events during the reign of his father, Sultan Selim I (ruled 1512-20). Selim, during his days as a royal prince, served as governor for the eastern Black Sea port and Silk Route entrepot of Trabzon. His position made him well aware of the threat the nascent Shiite Safavid Empire of Persia posed to the Ottoman eastern frontier. The Safavid shahs fomented resistance to the Ottoman Empire's taxes and "the expropriation of pious bequests" among the heterodox populations of eastern Anatolia (Clot, p. 87). Selim defeated the Safavids at the Battle of Chaldiran on August 23, 1514, then concentrated the rest of his reign on subjugating Egypt under Mamluk rule. His son Süleyman became the next Ottoman sultan.

The pretext for the Ottomans to invade Iraq in 1533 was the "treasonable behaviour" of the Lord of Bitlis Sherif Khan and the assassination of the Safavid governor of Baghdad, who had switched allegiance to the sultan (Clot, p. 90). The Ottomans had directed their initial campaign against the Persian heartland, but bad weather, insufficient provisioning, and the light cavalry of Shah Tahmasp forced the army to cross the Zagros Mountains into Iraq. There the Ottomans met little resistance, and Süleyman marched triumphantly into Baghdad on December 4, 1534.

The conquest of Baghdad was a milestone for the Ottoman regime for a number of reasons. Until the Mongol sack of the city in 1258, the city had been the residence of the Abbasid caliphs since its foundation by al-Mansur in 762. With its capture, the Ottomans extended their dominion over all the historical seats of the caliphate in the central Islamic lands. The addition of Iraq stabilized the border with the Safavids. The Ottomans would control the region for the next 400 years. Highly sensitive to the turmoil and sectarian strife of the previous decades, Süleyman rebuilt the infrastructure of Iraq and installed a new provincial administrative regime.

Reception and impact. During his lifetime, Fuzuli's poetic accomplishments appear not to have provided him with opportunities to attain wealth or advance his career, but his verse reached a wide audience nonetheless, from the palaces of Istanbul to the villages of Iraq and Anatolia (Tanpinar, p. 160). In the centuries following his death, *Leyla and Mejnun* was "admired and imitated" for the style of his writing and the philosophical considerations behind his metaphoric language of love (Bombaci, p. 11). Fuzuli's works in general proved that Turkish could be treated as a literary language. Also he significantly influenced later Turkish writers, who emulated his Turkish usages and adopted his attitude toward the story. Individuals ranging from near contemporaries such as Baki (1526-1600) and Nabi (1642-1712) to Abdülhak Hamid (1852-1937), a major Ottoman writer of the *Tanzimat* (a period of Ottoman modernization in the nineteenth century), found inspiration in Fuzuli's work. Later his ideas resurfaced in the modern Republic of Turkey. Throughout the ages his *Leyla and Mejnun* has remained a prime example of how popular and mystical Islamic concepts of love intersected in Muslim literature.

—John K. Bragg

For More Information

Bombaci, Alessio. Introduction to *Leyla and Mejnun*, by Muhammad ibn Suleyman Fuzali. Trans. Elizabeth Davies. London: Allen and Unwin, 1970.

Clot, Andre. *Suleiman the Magnificent: the Man, the Life, His Epoch.* London: Saki Books, 1992.

Denny, Frederick M. *An Introduction to Islam.* New York: Macmillan, 1994.

Dols, Michael W. *Majnun: The Madman in Medieval Islamic Society.* Oxford: Clarendon Press, 1992.

Fuzuli, Muhammad ibn Suleyman. *Leyla and Mejnun.* Trans. Sofi Huri. London: Allen and Unwin, 1970.

Haywood, J. A. "Madjnun Layla." *Encyclopedia of Islam CD-ROM Edition,* version 1.1. Leiden: Koninklijke Brill NV, 2001.

Karahan, Abdalkadir. "Fuduli." *Encyclopedia of Islam CD-ROM Edition,* version 1.1. Leiden: Koninklijke Brill NV, 2001.

Khan, Ruqayya Yasmine. "Sexuality and Secrecy in the Medieval Romance of Madjnun Layla." Ph.D. diss., University of Pennsylvania, 1997.

Lapidus, Ira M. *A History of the Islamic Peoples.* Cambridge, U.K.: Cambridge University Press, 2002.

Nizami Ganjavi. *The Story of Layla and Majnun.* Trans. R. Gelpke. Oxford: Cassirer, 1966.

Nomanul Haq, S. "Islam and Ecology: Toward Retrieval and Reconstruction." *Daedalus* 130, no. 4 (fall 2001): 141-77.

Peters, F. E. *The Hajj: The Muslim Pilgrimage to Mecca and the Holy Places.* Princeton, N.J.: Princeton University Press, 1994.

Picken, Laurence. *Folk Musical Instruments of Turkey.* London: Oxford University Press, 1975.

Tanpinar, Ahmet Hamdi. *Edebiyat üzerine makaleler.* Istanbul: Dergah Yayinlari, 1977.

Maqamat

by
al-Hamadhani

In a literature renowned primarily for its poetry, Badi` al-Zaman al-Hamadhani (967-1007) achieved fame as a prose writer. Al-Hamadhani is best known for his collection of anecdotal short narratives in Arabic, called the *maqamat* (singular: *maqamah*). Comic as well as serious, they deal with some of the most controversial religious and ethical questions of the time, often in a lighthearted or ironic way. Al-Hamadhani's stature as one of the greatest writers of Arabic is paradoxical because of his Persian origins. As his name indicates, al-Hamadhani was born in Hamadhan, a city in northwestern Persia (modern-day Iran). In the early 990s, after living in the cities of Ray and Jurjan, he moved to Nishapur. Robbed by bandits during the journey, he arrived there destitute and had to contend with a formidable competitor in Nishapur, one of the great rhetoricians and prose writers of the time, Abu Bakr al-Khuwarizmi. After al-Khuwarizmi's death in 993 al-Hamadhani became the leading literary figure of his time. He moved from Nishapur to Herat, where he married into a rich family and remained until his death. Al-Hamadhani corresponded throughout his life with important rulers and literary figures. His letters, together with his collected poetry and *maqamat* have survived to the present day. Al-Hamadhani's most important contribution to Arabic literature was his supposed "invention" of the *maqamah* genre—a mixed form of prose and passages of poetry. The prose sections of the *maqamat* are remarkable in that they, like the poetry, have end rhymes. Yet the sections are considered prose, because they lack the other necessary feature of Arabic poetry—

THE LITERARY WORK

Three of 51 or 52 tales set in multiple locations throughout the Middle East and Central Asia from the late tenth to the early eleventh centuries; written sometime before 1007; published in Arabic in 1888-89, in English in 1915.

SYNOPSIS

A rogue manages to outwit some unsuspecting victims in the "Maqamah of Wine" and the "Maqamah of Baghdad," but is outwitted by a boastful merchant in the "Maqamah of the Madirah."

meter. Al-Hamadhani's innovation and originality in creating the then new *maqamah* genre earned him the epithet "Wonder of the Age" (Arabic: "*Badi` al-Zaman*"). In a subtle, comic, and non-judgmental manner, his fictional *maqamat* invite readers to come to their own moral and ethical conclusions on the behavior of the characters, in contrast to the preaching and sententious style so common in religious texts of his day.

Events in History at the Time of the Tales

Expansion of Islam and the Abbasid age. The essence of Islam is the prophecy of the religious and political leader Muhammad (d. 632), as expressed in the Muslim holy text, the **Quran** (also in *WLAIT 6: Middle Eastern Literatures and Their Times*). After Muhammad's death, the mix of religious and political leadership passed to the first four caliphs or successors, who became known collectively as the *Rashidun* (Rightly-guided) (632-661). These caliphs were followed, in turn, by the Umayyad dynasty (661-749) whose rulers governed from Damascus, Syria. During the periods of the Rashidun and the Umayyads, Islam expanded enormously from its origins on the Middle East's Arabian Peninsula eastward to Central and South Asia, through North Africa and westward as far as the Iberian Peninsula (Spain and Portugal). In the Middle East and Central Asia, the authority of the Umayyad dynasty gave way to the Abbasid dynasty (750-1258), whose rulers governed from Baghdad, Iraq. By 945, shortly before the birth of al-Hamadhani, the Abbasid Empire had disintegrated to the point that a group led by the Buwayhid clan took control of Baghdad. The Buwayhids did not formally replace the Abbasid government; they allowed its caliphs to continue as figurehead rulers. But the decline of a strong Abbasid central government led to severe economic and social problems. In its place came the dominance of large landowners and military warlords, under whom the general economy suffered greatly. Poverty prevailed among the intelligentsia as well as the masses. This poverty and the accompanying scarcity of even basic necessities partly explain the emphasis in many of the era's literary works on food and hospitality. Political instability resulting from the decline of the Abbasid Empire necessarily disrupted the traditional employment for writers, whose trade involved composing praise poems for powerful rulers. Since writers would no longer be rewarded for composing these praise poems, they turned their efforts to other genres. In al-Hamadhani's case, this was the completely new genre of the *maqamah*.

Divergent responses to Arabic dominance. The spread of Islam and its accompanying political authority to vast areas, whose native languages were not versions of the Arabic language, created many problems. In some areas, Arabic replaced the original local languages. In other places, especially Persia where al-Hamadhani was born, local languages and customs survived and flourished side-by-side with the Quranic Arabic used for religious purposes. During the eighth through the tenth centuries, Persians excelled at writing Arabic and translating manuals of conduct, protocol,

and *belles lettres,* or serious literature, into Arabic. The most famous of these translators from Persian to Arabic was Ibn al-Muqaffa` (d. 757 C.E.), translator of the fables *Kalilah wa Dimnah* into Arabic. Some of these works reflect a sense of superiority over and resentment against Arabs and Arabic on the part of the Persians. Persians willingly embraced Arabic, the language of the Quran and Arab governmental administration, when they adopted Islam. At the same time, the relegating of their native language and culture to a second-class status could only bring about ethnic resentment toward the Arabs. This resentment existed even when there were no active attempts by the Arabs to eradicate the native Persian language and culture. Even though al-Hamadhani's works do not directly reflect anti-Arab sentiment, the time and places he lived would have exposed him to such resentment. Al-Hamadhani's *maqamat* therefore can be seen in certain respects as an exercise in outperforming the Arabs in their own language.

During al-Hamadhani's lifetime, the forces of this Persian/Arabic bilingualism and biculturalism gave rise to a new variety of Persian literature that was written in Persian, but with Arabic script. Arabic script began to replace the Pahlavi characters for the writing of Persian in the ninth century. As with other languages that came into contact with Arabic (e.g., Ottoman Turkish and Mozarabic Spanish), Arabic script was used to transliterate the sounds of the native language. The native language remained unchanged: the form of written representation was the only foreign element. Literature originally written in Persian was recomposed in Arabic script. A contemporary of al-Hamadhani, Abu al-Qasim Firdawsi (c. 940-1025), recomposed the Persian masterpiece **Shahnamah,** an epic poem about the early history of Persia (also in *WLAIT 6: Middle Eastern Literatures and Their Times*). The composition, in a "new" Persian, influenced by Arabic vocabulary and syntax, contributed to the revival of Persian history and culture. The two writers, Firdawsi and al-Hamadhani, achieved their fame in divergent branches of the same hybrid culture. Al-Hamadhani devoted himself to the newer, imposed language and culture, Arabic; Firdawsi, to an Arabized version of the traditional language and culture, Persian.

**The Shi`ite/Sunni division.** The division between the Shi`ite and Sunni sects of Islam has its origins in disagreement over successors to the Prophet Muhammad. Members of the Shi`ite sect believe that religious authority is transmitted through individuals called "imams." This line of imams, or imamate, began with descendants of the Prophet Muhammad through his daughter Fatimah and her husband Ali. The martyrdom of Ali's second son, Husayn, in 680 in Karbala, Iraq, contributed to the unity of believers in the imamate, whose name emanates from the father. They were called partisans of Ali (Arabic: *shi`at Ali*), hence the name Shi`ite. In contrast, Sunni Muslims take their name from the *sunna*, the legally binding precedents based on the actions and sayings of the Prophet Muhammad. Disagreement over succession to Muhammad and doctrinal differences would lead to other sectarian divisions. On the general Shi`ite-Sunni level, the Shi`ites did not consider the Umayyads or Abbasids legitimate imams and opposed their political and religious authority.

By al-Hamadhani's time, Shi`ites were the predominant group in the areas where he was born, lived, and traveled. Nevertheless, al-Hamadhani's own sectarian affiliation is unclear. Although he claimed to have been a Sunni Muslim, his collected letters indicate allegiances with Shi`ism. Aside from the importance of al-Hamadhani's sect to his biography, his affiliation with either Sunni or Shi`ite carries significance for his *maqamat*. If, as some authorities believe, al-Hamadhani was a Shi`ite most of his life, one ought to read the *maqamat* in the context of free-will Shi`ite doctrine. The governing belief would be that the rogue protagonist and other characters perform unethical, damaging actions of their own free will. In keeping with this doctrine of free will, it can be assumed that characters are adversely judged by God for their misdeeds. However, if the determinism commonly associated with Sunni doctrine were applied to the *maqamat*, the characters and their actions become merely a part of a predetermined grand design. Since the characters' salvation also has been predetermined, they bear no real doctrinal responsibility for their actions.

Quran. The most important religious text for all Muslims is the Quran. In Islam, the Quran expresses the revelations of God to the Prophet Muhammad. Like the Old and New Testaments of the Bible, the Quran contains a vast variety of material, from accounts of individuals important to Judaism, Christianity, and Islam (the Jewish Patriarchs, Jesus, Mary, the Prophet Muhammad's Companions, etc.) to descriptions of correct personal and social conduct. The Quran does not, however, articulate specific doctrine on many questions—What are the attributes of God? Is an individual's salvation after this life predetermined by God and by fate, or earned through good conduct? Can a last-minute repentance before death "save" the individual? What are the attributes of the Quran itself: was it created by God, or has it always existed, like God? Differing opinions on these and many other such issues have given rise to a wide range of beliefs within Islam. Not only did these differences lead to the establishment of Sunni and Shi`ite sects. They led as well to the formation of various subgroups including the Mu`tazilites, the Sufis, and many others. Divergent doctrines also gave rise to six (today four) legal "schools" or differing approaches to interpreting questions of religious law. As in Judaism and Christianity, the explanation and interpretation of the faith's holy text became the object of an entire process of exegesis. Theologians from the beginning of Islam to the present era have devoted whole lifetimes to writing interpretations of the Quran's subtleties. The need for and differences of opinion on the Quran's interpretation have a parallel in the *maqamat*. Because the language of the *maqamat* is so rich and complex, the *maqamat*, like the Quran, often require a commentary to clarify the meaning. This explanation is usually printed in the margin of the page, next to the text it explains. Islamic theologians from a wide range of doctrinal groups use a similar method to explain the complexities of the Quran.

Authority of the text. Arabic texts during al-Hamadhani's time almost always carried with them a chain of transmission. Showing who had transmitted (usually orally) the text to whom, the chain was expressed as, "X said that Y said, that Z said" and so forth. There could be any number of transmitters in a chain, called an *isnad*. The purpose of the *isnad* was to ensure the authenticity of the text. If all the transmitters in the chain were reliable and honest, the text was assumed to be authentic and genuine. On the other hand, if one or more of the transmitters were unreliable or a liar, the text would be dismissed as a fabrication. This process was used for all kinds of texts, including news events, history, and most importantly, religious accounts of the lives of the Prophet and his followers (called *hadith*). Since the lives and sayings of the Prophet Muhammad and the first leaders of the Muslim community were so important for later periods, an entire science was developed by theologians to separate authentic from bogus accounts about these early Muslims. As with other aspects of the religion, there was disagreement between groups and individual theologians over the authenticity of certain accounts. Throughout al-Hamadhani's time, debate remained vigorous in this regard.

Al-Hamadhani's *maqamat* are similar to *hadith* in that the *maqamat* stories also have an *isnad*. The *isnad* of every *maqamah* by al-Hamadhani begins, "Isa ibn Hisham told us. . . ." Thus, the process for authenticating real texts is used to construct a fictional text, starting with a fictionalized narrator—Isa ibn Hisham. Al-Hamadhani's use of the fictionalized narrator was one of his innovations in Arabic literature. If we judge the text of the *maqamat* by the standards applied to a nonfictional text, the fact that the narrator is fictionalized should lead us to dismiss the text he transmits as inauthentic. Also, in many *maqamat*, the narrator's accounts are inconsistent, unreliable, or even bold-faced lies. By asking the reader to accept a fictional *isnad* and transparently false information, while at the same time maintaining the pretense of an authenticated text, al-Hamadhani creates irony in the *maqamat*. Al-Hamadhani's fictional narrator and transparently bogus *isnad* may also be an indirect criticism of the methods used to authenticate religious texts.

The *maqamat*'s use of the *isnad* furthermore places responsibility for interpreting and evaluating their moral content on the reader. Is the reader supposed to reject an entire *maqamah* and any possible ethical benefit from it, simply because the *isnad* has been fictionalized? Or, given that the text conveyed by the *isnad* is often ironic, is the reader expected to be so gullible as to accept an ironic text at face value? The *isnad* is obviously not valid, so perhaps the *maqamah* is to be understood simply as the model for transgressive behavior. Or, is the reader supposed to consider the invalid *isnad* part of the fictional aspect of *maqamat* written purely for entertainment value? Al-Hamadhani provides no answers for any of these questions in either his *maqamat* or other writings. The audience most capable of dealing with al-Hamadhani's irony and ambiguity would have been the literary elite of his day. The largely illiterate masses were probably unaware that the *maqamah* genre even existed, much less would they have read a *maqamah*.

The Tales in Focus

Contents overview. Al-Hamadhani's *maqamat* are a collection of 51 (in some manuscripts and editions, 52) anecdotes that share a common rogue protagonist (Iskandari) and narrator (Isa ibn Hisham). Beyond these features, there is

little to connect the stories, one to the other. The fact that the protagonist does not develop or change over time from one story to the next is a major difference between the *maqamat* and a modern novel. There is also no chronological ordering of the stories, as is often the case in the modern novel. In one *maqamah*, the protagonist may appear as an old man, while in the next he may be a young person. The ordering of the stories within the collection differs according to the manuscript(s) used by the editor. Another variable factor is the settings. Some *maqamat* take place in real locations, which have led modern editors to group certain tales together as the "Maqamah of Armenia," the "Maqamah of Shiraz," and so forth. Many of these real-life settings are places that al-Hamadhani either lived in or visited (Hamadhan, Nishapur, Jurjan). Other real-life settings are major cities of the time—Baghdad, Mosul, Kufah, and Shiraz, to name a few. Even when the settings are so specific, though, there are few, if any, "local color" descriptions of anything particular to the locations. There is, on the other hand, commonality in the style of the tales. Most individual *maqamat* adhere to a set framework that varies little from story to story. After the introductory *isnad*, which identifies the narrator, Isa ibn Hisham, as the source of the account, the *maqamah*'s plot generally follows this pattern:

1. Travel and arrival of the narrator (Isa ibn Hisham) to the *maqamah*'s setting.
2. Narrator's encounter with an unnamed preacher or orator who will later be unmasked as the rogue protagonist (Iskandari).
3. Sermon or speech by the rogue protagonist (variant: trickery by the protagonist of unsuspecting victim[s]).
4. Rogue's success at obtaining goods or money (variant: outright theft).
5. Rogue's attempt to flee.
6. Narrator's recognition of rogue.
7. Farewell and departure, as narrator and rogue protagonist go their separate ways.
   (Young, p. 76)

These major features, common to nearly every *maqamah*, are usually presented in passages of rhymed prose. The rogue protagonist's observations on the events, together with his observations on religion and philosophy, often appear in sections of poetry interspersed within the passages of rhymed prose.

Plot summaries—"Maqamah of Wine." In the "Maqamah of Wine," some drinking companions encounter a scoundrel who masquerades as both a religious leader and a tavern entertainer. The *maqamah* lampoons the hypocrisy of the drinkers and the scoundrel for indulging in this un-Islamic vice. In fact, of all al-Hamadhani's *maqamat*, the one that comes closest to approaching the comedy of Western "slapstick" is the "Maqamah of Wine." As is the case at the beginning of every *maqamah*, the writer attributes the account to Isa ibn Hisham, who does not give the *maqamah* a specific setting but does say that it occurred during his youth. In contrast to many young people, his has been a youth characterized by "temperance" and "moderation"—terms whose irony will become patently obvious (al-Hamadhani, "Maqamah of Wine," in *Maqamat of Badi` az-Zaman al-Hamadhani,* p. 178).

One evening, Isa ibn Hisham joins his drinking companions for a night of carousing. The group begins by consuming the wine on hand, exhausts this supply, and then resorts to tapping the wine storage jars. By early morning, even these containers are empty, so the companions go to a tavern for more wine drinking. But before they reach the tavern, dawn breaks. Throughout the Muslim world, this is the time when the *muezzin* gives the call to dawn prayers (*fajr*) in the mosque. The drinkers face two equally unpleasant alternatives. On the one hand, they can continue to the tavern, ignore the call to prayer, and risk the ostracizing contempt of their fellow Muslims for having missed the prayers. On the other hand, the drinkers can fulfill their duties by attending the prayer service, even though their inebriated state will invalidate their prayers, defile the mosque, and make them the object of scorn and ridicule by the other worshippers. They opt for the second choice. Temporarily putting aside their drinking to make an appearance at the prayer service, the drinkers take their place behind the leader of the prayers, the imam. His slow, deliberate motions prolong their discomfort, aggravating their impatience to leave and resume their drinking. At the conclusion of the service, the imam turns, faces the congregation, knowingly sniffs the air, and begins to chastise the drunkards present. He chides the wrongdoers, saying they should have stayed home instead of forcing the congregation to endure their polluted breath. Sullied is this breath, he continues, from flagrant indulgence in the "mother of enormities," wine drinking ("Maqamah of Wine," p. 179). The imam then incites the congregation against the drinkers by pointing them out, fully expecting the pious, abstinent congregation to react as violently as they

do. Physically attacking the drinkers, the rest of the congregation beats the wrongdoers and tears their clothes. The drinkers escape. Curious about the identity of the imam whose inflammatory speech caused the attack, they ask his name. A group of children reveal him to be Iskandari (also known as Abu al-Fath), the rogue and antihero of nearly every other *maqamah*. Learning the imam's name evokes a puzzled reaction on the part of the drinkers, since they are aware of Iskandari's reputation as a scoundrel and rogue himself. However, the group is not troubled by this paradox for long.

Intent on resuming their drinking, the drinkers continue their journey to the tavern, where they are met by a woman who kisses them warmly at the door. (The proprietress of the tavern and her employees are assumed to be Christian because Muslims would have been forbidden to sell wine.) After the proprietress extols, in the rhetoric of classical Arabic wine poetry, the quality of her wine, the drinkers inquire as to who provides entertainment in the tavern. The woman then describes an old, fatherly man whom she met one Sunday at a Christian convent. She was so taken with him that they began a romantic relationship and the old man came to stay with her in the tavern. When the drinkers are introduced to the old man, lo and behold, he turns out to be Iskandari, rogue and erstwhile imam. In the concluding lines of poetry, Iskandari not only expresses no remorse, he vows to continue his flagrant drinking in violation of Islamic law, justifying his hypocrisy with "everyone behaves this way" ("Maqamah of Wine," p. 182). Shocked by Iskandari's duplicity, the narrator and his companions nevertheless remain in the tavern with the rogue for a week of drinking and carousing. As in all the other *maqamat* in al-Hamadhani's collection, this one makes no clearcut moral or ethical statement. Is the beating at the hands of the congregation sufficient punishment for Muslims drinking wine? If so, it certainly does not dissuade the drinkers from continuing their indulgence in the vice. Should the reader accept at face value the rogue's explanation of "everybody does this" as a valid excuse for forbidden behavior? Or, is the *maqamah* merely a comic anecdote that actually endorses, contrary to Islamic law, consumption of alcoholic beverages? One wonders too about the moral status of the Christians in the story. Wine is not forbidden in their religion, and they make a profit "corrupting" Muslims by providing the beverage. What this suggests about Muslim-Christian dynamics is as open to debate as the rest of the details.

"Maqamah of Baghdad." In the "Maqamah of Baghdad," the narrator bests a country bumpkin by taking advantage of his greed. This *maqamah* is unusual in that the narrator, Isa ibn Hisham, rather than the rogue Iskandari, performs the trickery. Isa ibn Hisham introduces the *maqamah* by describing his poverty. In spite of his lack of money, Isa develops a sudden hunger for a rare, expensive variety of date. Isa makes his way to the market area of Baghdad, where he finds a naive, rustic, "country bumpkin," whom he has never met before. To initiate his scam, Isa addresses the rustic with the random name "Abu Zayd," all the while greeting him effusively as if he were a long lost friend. When the bumpkin corrects his name to "Abu Ubayd," Isa apologizes and faults himself for his forgetfulness yet continues to use the incorrect name. Isa attempts to establish his familiarity with the man by inquiring about his father. The rustic informs Isa that his father died some time earlier, for which Isa offers mock sympathy and condolences. In order to celebrate the unexpected meeting of the two supposedly long-lost friends, Isa suggests that they get something to eat. They can, says Isa, either go to his house (which he does not have) or eat in the market. Then Isa extends false hospitality by inviting the rustic to eat in Isa's home, but he forestalls acceptance of the invitation by mentioning in the same breath that the restaurants in the market are closer and offer better food. His duplicity is matched by the rustic's expectation of being treated to a free meal by his supposed friend. The pair begins by consuming the delicacies of the meat vendor. Their gluttony continues with the eating of pastries (probably of the non-sweet meat variety) and finally desserts. Isa instructs each food vendor to serve his friend (and himself) the best and most expensive variety of dishes available. At the end of the meal, Isa suggests to Abu Ubayd that he must be thirsty. Under the pretext of finding a water vendor, Isa disappears to a spot where he cannot be seen but can himself see the food vendors' location. When Isa does not return as promised, Abu Ubayd starts approaching his donkey to leave. But he is stopped by the meat vendor, who demands a large payment for the consumed meat. Abu Ubayd protests that he was invited to eat as a guest of Isa, who should be responsible for the bill. The meat vendor, of course, refuses to accept this excuse and beats Abu Ubayd into paying the bill. At the *maqamah*'s conclusion, Abu Ubayd laments the loss of the large sum of money for the food and the fact that Isa repeatedly mistook him for someone by the name of Abu Zayd. Isa offers his own cynical summation in verse: an individual has the right to do anything to earn a living. Whereas this self-serving justification applies to his own trickery, it could apply equally well to Abu Ubayd's greed when he thought he was eating at Isa's expense.

"Maqamah of Madirah." In the "Maqamah of the Madirah," the rogue's attempt to take advantage of a boastful merchant's hospitality backfires when the merchant outwits him. The narrator, Isa ibn Hisham, and the rogue, Iskandari, together attend a dinner at a merchant's house in Basra. The guests are served a delicacy known as a *madirah*, a dish made by stewing meat in milk and yogurt. Whereas the other guests are impressed by the lavish dish, the rogue, Iskandari, stands up, curses the dish, its cook, those who eat it, and the host. Those present misinterpret Iskandari's rage as a joke. When Iskandari leaves the room in a fury, those present reluctantly order the delicious dish removed. They then join Iskandari and inquire as to what provoked his violent reaction to the dish. This provides the framework for Iskandari to relate the story-within-a-story of his experiences at another dinner party in Baghdad.

Iskandari recounts that a Baghdad merchant had extended a dinner invitation to him in such an insistent, aggressive manner as to be rude. The attraction to accepting the invitation was the main dish, the *madirah*. As Iskandari accompanied the merchant to his home for dinner, the host began an endless harangue of bragging and boorishness. He started by praising his wife for her beauty, honesty, and domesticity. When the merchant and Iskandari reached the merchant's neighborhood, the bragging took the form of the merchant's asking Iskandari to guess the value of the houses in the area. Once the two arrived at the merchant's house, the boasting focused on details of the house—the teakwood door, the price of the brass doorknocker, and the staircase. The merchant took a break from his bragging to explain to his guest how he acquired the house. The previous occupant had been a wealthy man with a reckless, extravagant son. Upon the father's death, the merchant sensed the opportunity to acquire the house by giving the son small loans, for which the house was pledged as collateral. When the son inevitably defaulted on the loans, the merchant took advantage of the son's plight by foreclosing on the house and taking possession. The merchant's bragging continued. Among other boasts, he claimed to have made a fortune by buying, at unreasonably low prices, possessions from individuals in poor straits, then selling the goods at a high profit.

Iskandari mistakenly believed that mealtime was near when the merchant summoned the slave to bring a ewer, basin, and water for hand washing. However, this merely served as a pretext to extol the value of the slave, the workmanship of the ewer and basin, and the purity of the water. The next focus of boasting was the embroidered napkin, which, the merchant assured his guest, was so valuable and well guarded that no common Arabs had defiled it with their hands. After the merchant extolled the many advantages of the table, Iskandari interrupted his host to anticipate what might be the next object of bragging. Iskandari himself took up the line of bragging: he praised the kitchen utensils, the bread, its wheat, its baker, the vegetables, their cultivation, and the *madirah* and its preparation, mocking the merchant all the while. Still the vaunting continued. When Iskandari got up to go to the bathroom, the merchant could not resist the opportunity to brag about the room—the bath supposedly outdid that of a prince, with walls so highly polished that an ant would slip. The "last straw" for Iskandari was the merchant's bragging that the bathroom was so luxurious that guests want to eat there. At this point, Iskandari left the house; he was pursued by the merchant protesting that his guest would not get to enjoy the promised *madirah*.

In his attempt to get Iskandari to return, the merchant called out his guest's name along with the word *madirah*. So insistent and repetitious was his calling that some boys in the street believed that *madirah* was Iskandari's title. They proceeded to taunt Iskandari, calling him "Madirah." Enraged, Iskandari threw a stone at one of them, missed, and seriously injured an adult man. Retaliating, a crowd chased and beat Iskandari, who was apprehended and forced to spend two years in prison. The narrator concludes the story-within-a-story and the *maqamah* by saying that he and the other guests excuse Iskandari for not partaking of the *madirah*.

The reader is again left with the responsibility for determining what lesson, if any, is to be derived from the story. Is the *maqamah* simply a humorous anecdote about a boorish host and hapless guest? Does the guest's greediness in accepting the invitation put him in a position of being forced to tolerate the host's boorishness? Does the way the host acquired his wealth and the house generate moral questions? The

individual punished is the unlucky guest, not the host. Does this mean that the host's boorish bragging and predatory acquisition of material goods are acceptable or even praiseworthy? Again the *maqamah* raises ethical questions without supplying definitive answers.

Mu'tazilites. An important aspect of religious belief established before and during al-Hamadhani's life was the doctrine of rational theology. This doctrine held that the basic truths of Islam could be explained by reason rather than simply by faith. The many, mostly Shi'ite, supporters of this rational theology came to be known as

---

COMMANDING RIGHT AND FORBIDDING WRONG

Let there arise out of you
A band of people
Inviting to all that is good,
Enjoining what is right,
And forbidding what is wrong:
They are the ones to attain felicity.

(Quran 3:104 in Yusuf Ali, pp. 149-50)

This and other passages in the Quran emphasize the importance of advising and directing one's fellow humans to do what is right and avoid what is wrong. For a devout Muslim, providing such guidance has come to be considered an obligation, not a mere option. The actions and beliefs of many of the characters in al-Hamadhani's *maqamat* are clearly wrong by most standards of Islamic conduct—they drink, lie, cheat, and exhibit hypocrisy and greed. To what extent is al-Hamadhani encouraging these transparently wrong actions through their representation in his *maqamat*? On the other hand, do al-Hamadhani's stories serve as a negative example and fulfill his duty as a Muslim to encourage what is right and forbid what is wrong?—an overarching question, this one subsumes all the specific ones raised by his individual *maqamat*.

Mu'tazilites. Shortly before al-Hamadhani's time, Mu'tazilite doctrine enjoyed the official favor of the Abbasid caliphs. Even after Mu'tazilite belief ceased being the official doctrine of the caliphs, the Mu'tazilites remained numerous in the areas where al-Hamadhani lived.

An aspect of Mu'tazilite doctrine closely related to rational theology concerns the interpretation of the Quran itself. Because the language of the Quran is so complex, the text may have a superficial, literal meaning along with one or more secondary meanings. Therefore, the text of the Quran can be subjected to either literal or allegorical/figurative interpretations. The Mu'tazilites generally favored a non-literal, allegorical interpretation, whereas an adherence to a more literal interpretation was advocated by many Sunni groups.

The *maqamat* bear a similarity to the Quran in that many words in both are rare and frequently have multiple layers of meaning. Also like the Quran, the *maqamat* can be the object of a literal or figurative interpretation. The very "invention" of the *maqamat* by al-Hamadhani, given its need for interpretation, may connect al-Hamadhani with groups such as the Mu'tazilites, who advocated a non-literal interpretation of the Quran. Commentaries on al-Hamadhani's *maqamat* and other works of linguistic and rhetorical complexity in Arabic literature provide a model for this non-literal interpretation. These commentaries give a near line-by-line explanation of the meaning of each *maqamah* through a paraphrasing of content and definition of words with uncommon or multiple meanings. The explanation is usually printed in the *maqamah*'s margin, side-by-side with the text it explains, in the same way that Quranic exegesis is presented. An example of literal versus non-literal interpretation of Quranic text, as it relates to the central theme of the "Maqamah of Wine," is found in Quran 2 (al-Baqarah): 219-20: "They ask thee concerning wine and gambling. Say: 'In them is great sin, and some profit, for men.'" The Arabic word for wine, *khamr*, is interpreted literally as "fermented grape juice" (Yusuf Ali, n. 240, p. 86). An excessively literalist interpretation of the Quran would mean that wine consumption alone is prohibited. What about whiskey, gin, beer, sake, and vodka? All these beverages also contain alcohol yet are not mentioned in the Quranic prohibition. The universal agreement among Islamic religious authorities is that the prohibition on *khamr* applies by analogy to all beverages containing alcohol. An interpretation of the Quran based on an excessively literal meaning of *khamr* alone could conceivably ignore the application of the prohibition to alcoholic beverages other than wine. Again, the non-literal interpretation based on analogy extends the ban to all alcoholic beverages. Both the Quran and the *maqamat* are furthermore sprinkled with words and phrases open to multiple meanings, which compounds many times over the possible interpretations for the passages that contain them. Just as we have no definite proof as to whether al-Hamadhani was Shi'ite or Sunni, we have no proof for his being a Mu'tazilite, the group that championed a non-literal interpretation of the Quran. Nevertheless, since the Mu'tazilites were still such a highly influential force during his lifetime, their doctrine's effect cannot be ignored in reading the *maqamat*.

Sources and literary context. In spite of al-Hamadhani's reputation for novelty and innovation, his *maqamat* still reflect earlier and contemporary literary currents. As described above, al-Hamadhani appropriates the method for authenticating secular and religious texts to create a fictional work. Another formal characteristic of the *maqamah*, its rhymed prose (called *saj*), in many ways resembles large passages in the Quran. Even though al-Hamadhani may not have intended to imitate the Quran, the similarities between the *maqamah*'s rhymed prose and Quranic discourse are so striking as to call into question the doctrine of the Quran's inimitability. Al-Hamadhani also makes use of the pre-existing genre of poetry, to give an ironic cast to his *maqamat*. Fine poetry had been held in the highest esteem since pre-Islamic times. However, the passages of poetry in al-Hamadhani's *maqamat* are usually of such inferior quality that they poke fun at the commonly held idea that poetry is superior to prose. This idea is likewise lampooned in the characterization of the rogue, Iskandari, who is supposedly a brilliant, master poet, yet one capable of producing only mediocre poetry. Iskandari's "highly inspired poetry" is in many instances merely a combination of proverbs strung together in rhyme to give the appearance of poetry. In this way, al-Hamadhani's *maqamat* make frequent use of the pre-existing genre of proverbs. The tales rely too on the genre of the sermon. Their rogue protagonist, Iskandari, steps often ironically into the role of an itinerant preacher who delivers "fire-and-brimstone" sermons to gullible yet pious congregations.

The *maqamah* reworks the content of another pre-existing genre, the humorous anecdote. This genre had been practiced by a number of al-Hamadhani's predecessors, the most famous of whom was a writer better known by his nickname of "al-Jahiz" ("the one with the bulging eyes"), whose real name was Amr ibn Bahr (c. 776-869 B.C.E.). The butt of al-Jahiz's comic stories were groups of individuals, such as misers and possessors of slave singing-girls. Even though these anecdotes share the *maqamah*'s humor and irony, they differ in that they contain less rhymed prose than the *maqamah*. The anecdotes also differ in their focus on groups or "types" rather than on the individual rogue featured in the *maqamah*. Finally the humorous anecdote deploys a strategy other than the *isnad* for the supposed authenticating of the text. Al-Jahiz makes the tales appear to be sections of a learned treatise (*Kitab al-bukhala* [*Book of Misers*]) or of letters (*Risalat al-qiyan* [*Epistle of the Singing-Girls*]). Another predecessor, closer in time to al-Hamadhani, was al-Muhassin ibn Ali al-Tanukhi (938-57 C.E.), whose anecdotes are more similar to al-Hamadhani's tales. Like the *maqamat*, al-Tanukhi's collection of anecdotes, *al-Faraj ba`d al-shiddah* (Relief After Hardship), focuses on a rogue protagonist. This earlier collection, however, lacks al-Hamadhani's extensive and virtuosic use of rhymed prose.

There are no specific sources for al-Hamadhani's *maqamat* of "Wine," "Baghdad," and "Madirah." However, al-Hamadhani does exploit both past and contemporary literary and social traditions. For nearly all readers during al-Hamadhani's time, the "Maqamah of Wine" would recall the tradition of wine poetry. Abu Nuwas (d. 965), the best known practitioner of this type of poetry, glorifies the consumption and intoxicating qualities of wine. Given Islam's total prohibition on wine and other alcoholic beverages, wine poetry was rarely taken literally. It was more often an aesthetic exercise or perhaps a metaphor for a religious experience. The genre therefore was not seen as being particularly subversive or anti-Islamic. Al-Hamadhani's focus on the drinkers' riotous desecration of a prayer service and lack of self-control borrows from and makes literal, in a comic manner, the metaphors of wine poetry. The idealized, metaphoric intoxication of traditional wine poetry becomes in al-Hamadhani's *maqamat* the literal reality of drunkenness. References to the Christian hostess, to Muslims using Christian monasteries as taverns where they could drink, to the aging of the wine, and to the entertainment accompanying wine-drinking all hark back to the tradition of wine poetry.

Both the *maqamat* of "Baghdad" and "Madirah" deal with food and its consumption. In spite of their lack of a definite source, both *maqamat* reflect social conventions and economic conditions of the time. Hospitality as an all-important social norm in Arab-Islamic society provides the background for the two "invitations"—one to the unwitting country bumpkin in "Baghdad," the other to the rogue protagonist in "Madirah." In both *maqamat*, the guests are victimized as the result of their own greediness to exploit the social convention of hospitality. This focus on the exploitation and withholding of hospitality had already been the focus of al-Jahiz's *Book of Misers*.

Impact. The paradox of al-Hamadhani's being called "Wonder of the Age" is that his successors upstaged him. The model established by al-Hamadhani for the *maqamah* was taken up by Abu Muhammad al-Qasim al-Hariri (d. 1122 C.E.), who contributed his own mainly stylistic transformations to the genre. Al-Hariri made the *maqamah*'s rhyme schemes far more elaborate and performed virtuosic rhetorical feats such as alternating the dotted and undotted letters of the Arabic script. Beyond these stylistic innovations, he did little to offer new themes and situations over and above those already presented in

IMPORTANT DATES FOR COMPOSITION OF THE *MAQAMAT*

622 Migration (*hijra*) of Prophet Muhammad from Mecca to Medina, which marks the advent of Islam

757 Ibn al-Muqaffa`, translator of *Kalilah and Dimnah*, dies

869 al-Jahiz, prose writer of *Book of Misers* and *Epistle of the Singing Girl*, dies

c. 1000 Firdawsi, al-Hamadhani's contemporary, writes Persian epic the *Shahnamah*; al-Hamadhani develops the *maqamah* genre

1122 Death of al-Hamadhani's successor, al-Hariri, virtuoso writer of *maqamat*

al-Hamadhani's *maqamat*. But al-Hariri's stylistic feats were so impressive that his reputation eclipsed that of his predecessor and the originator of the *maqamah* genre, al-Hamadhani. When the *maqamah* is mentioned in the Arabic-speaking world today, the most common association is with the stylistic embellishments added by al-Hariri, rather than with the origins of the genre by al-Hamadhani. This reverence for al-Hariri at the expense of al-Hamadhani was the case with most writers of *maqamat* from al-Hariri's time onward. The best-known *maqamah* writer on the Iberian Peninsula when a good portion of it spoke Arabic was Ibn al-Ashtarquni, also called al-Saraqusti (d. 1143). Ibn al-Ashtarquni expressed great admiration for al-Hariri, yet barely mentioned al-Hamadhani. Later practitioners of the *maqamah* were the Iraqi writer Ibn al-Sayqal al-Jazari (d. 1273) and the Egyptian writer al-Suyuti (d. 1505). During the "Arab Renaissance" (the period of cultural revival and imitation of the West) of the nineteenth century, the writing of *maqamat* continued to a very limited extent, primarily in Middle Eastern Arabic-speaking countries. In 1988 the Egyptian fiction writer Najib Mahfuz (b. 1911) became Nobel Laureate in Literature for his adaptation of the Western novel into Arabic. Had the *maqamah* maintained its position as the foremost fictional prose form in Arabic, Mahfuz's well-deserved honor might have been bestowed for excellence in that genre. Instead, as with so many aspects of classical Arabic culture, the *maqamah* had long since been relegated to the status of a literary artifact. As a concession to modernity and what many erroneously perceived as the superiority of westernization, the *maqamah* genre faded into disuse. By the time of Mahfuz's Nobel victory, it had been replaced by the Arabic adaptation of the European novel.

—Douglas C. Young

For More Information

Allen, Roger. *An Introduction to Arabic Literature.* Cambridge, England: Cambridge University Press, 2000.

Cook, Michael A. *Commanding Right and Forbidding Wrong in Islamic Thought.* New York: Cambridge University Press, 2000.

al-Hamadhani, Badi` az-Zaman. *Maqamat of Badi` az-Zaman al-Hamadhani.* Trans. W. J. Prendergast. London: Luzac, 1915.

al-Hariri, Abu Muhamad. *The Assemblies of al-Hariri.* 2 vols. Trans. Thomas Chenery (Vol. 1); F. Steingass (Vol. 2). Westmead, England: Gregg International, 1969.

Hourani, Albert. *A History of the Arab Peoples.* Cambridge, Massachusetts: Harvard University Press, 1991.

Lapidus, Ira M. *A History of Islamic Societies.* New York: Cambridge University Press, 1988.

Margoliouth, D. S. "Hamadhani." In *The Encyclopaedia of Islam.* Ed. E. J. van Donzel. New York: E. J. Brill, 1993.

Monroe, James T. *The Art of Badi` az-Zaman al-Hamadhani as Picaresque Narrative.* Beirut: American University of Beirut, 1983.

————. *The Shu`ubiyya in al-Andalus.* Berkeley: University of California Press, 1970.

al-Saraqusti, Abu al-Tahir Muhammad ibn Yusuf. *al-Maqamat al-luzumiyah.* Trans. James T. Monroe. Leiden: E. J. Brill, 2002.

Young, Douglas C. Review of *Las sesiones del Zaragocí: relatos picarescos (maqamat) del siglo XII.* Trans. Ignacio Ferrando. *Journal of Arabic Literature* 32, no. 1 (2001): 74-83.

Yusuf Ali, Abdullah, ed. and trans. *The Holy Qur'an: Text, Translation, and Commentary.* Beirut: Dar al-Arabiya, 1968.

"Mechanical Doll" and Other Poems

by

Furugh Farrukhzad

Furugh Farrukhzad (also spelled Forugh Farrokhzad) was born on January 5, 1935, to a middle-class family in Tehran, Iran. Her father, a colonel in the army, was a stern and often distant head of the family, who, nevertheless, provided Farrukhzad and her siblings with the leisure to browse the family's well-stocked library of Persian literature. Farrukhzad's literary interests blossomed early. By 13 she was experimenting with the classical poetic form known as the *ruba`i* (quatrain). Between the ages of 16 and 19, like many women from the urban Iranian middle classes, Farrukhzad completed middle school and then entered an arts school, where she studied sewing and painting. Her formal education ended in 1951 when she married Parviz Shapur, a man 15 years her senior. A year later their son, Kamyar, was born. In 1954 her life took a drastic turn from the customary path. She divorced and thereby not only became estranged from her own family and her husband but, as was customary in Iran at the time, lost all rights to her son. Although she agonized over these events, she proceeded to write. Farrrukhzad published three volumes of her most candid poetry: *Asir* (1955, The Captive), *Divar* (1956, The Wall), and *I[u]syan* (1957, The Rebellion). "Sinning," the first poem discussed in this entry, is from *Divar*, though the poem was probably written some two years before this collection of poems was published (Katouzian, p. 286). Farrukhzad's rebirth required that she find ways to support herself. After a series of menial jobs, in 1958 she became a clerk-typist at the Gulistan (also Golestan) Film Studios (named for

THE LITERARY WORK

Three poems set in mid-twentieth-century Iran; published in Persian (as "Gunah," "Ay marz-i pur guhar," and "Arusak-i kuki") in 1955 and 1964, in English in newspapers and magazines as early as the mid 1960s.

SYNOPSIS

"Sinning" is an expression of sexual desire that violates strict standards of female modesty and decorum in Iran; "O Realm Bejewelled" and "Mechanical Doll" satirize the regimentation of society and suppression of political freedoms in Iran under Shah Mohammed Reza Pahlavi.

its founder Ibrahim Gulistan, b. 1922). The film company provided Farrukhzad with apprenticeship and travel opportunities; on two occasions (1958 and 1961) she visited Europe to study filmmaking. Becoming a filmmaker in her own right, Farrukhzad proceeded to collaborate with the studio on *Khanah siyah ast* (The House Is Black), which concerns a leper colony, and was selected best documentary at the 1963 Oberhausen Film Festival. Farrukhzad's career was unconventional for a women in 1960s Iran. Before she was 30, not only was she considered among the finest modern poets in her own country, she was known as a talented filmmaker in Europe. In 1964 the groundbreaking collection of poems for which

Farrukhzad is best known, *Tavalludi-i digar* (1964; *Another Birth*, 1981), appeared. Containing a couple of the poems covered here, the volume marks the emergence of a mature writer, whose outspokenness about sexuality has given way to a critical—even cynical—view of Iranian society.

Events in History at the Time of the Poems

National identity crisis. On August 19, 1953, the United States Central Intelligence Agency, in cooperation with British intelligence, orchestrated the overthrow of Prime Minister Dr. Mohammad Mosaddeq (1882-1967, known also as Musaddiq

---

FROM REZA SHAH PAHLAVI TO THE ISLAMIC REVOLUTION

1925 Qajar dynasty ends; an army general, Reza Khan, becomes His Majesty Reza Shah Pahlavi, ruler of Iran.

1941 Reza Shah abdicates in favor of his son Mohammed Reza Pahlavi.

1951-53 Mohammad Mosaddeq becomes Prime Minister of Iran; the shah, Mohammed Reza Pahlavi, lives in exile.

1953 Central Intelligence Agency-backed coup d'état removes Mosaddeq from power; restores Shah to the throne.

1960-63 Under pressure from the U.S. government, the Shah sponsors land reform, literacy and health corps, and the vote for women; riots erupt against the shah's dictatorship.

1964 The shah abandons reformist impetus in the wake of assassination of U.S. President John F. Kennedy; exiled from Iran, Ayatollah Khomeini ends up in Iraq.

1969-70 Leftist guerrilla movement forms in forests of northern Iran, poses new threat to monarchy.

1979 Islamic Revolution; Ayatollah Khomeini replaces the shah as head of the country.

---

al-Saltanah) and restored Mohammed Reza Pahlavi (ruled 1941-51; 1953-79) to the throne. To many Iranians this event was merely the latest in a series of humiliating defeats that began early in the nineteenth century when foreign powers became involved in Persian affairs. Iran was once again enmeshed in the geopolitical aims of two great powers. The Soviet Union needed access to the warm waters of the Persian Gulf, while the United States, post-World War II successor to Great Britain in the area, became responsible for denying the Soviets that access. As the largest

link in the Islamic belt that girds the southern border of the former Soviet Union, the country was vital to the American policy of containing Communism after World War II. In addition to its strategic importance, Iran had and still has infinitely more gas and oil than the other links in the belt: Turkey and Afghanistan. It was thus inevitable that the superpowers would meddle in the politics of the country.

The Mosaddeq affair was such an obvious demonstration of Iran's lack of autonomy that it demoralized many of its intellectuals, writers, poets, and members of the clergy (Langarudi, vol. 2, p. 15). Not only did it end in the removal of a democratically elected government; it meant that a great deal of Iran's wealth would remain in foreign hands. Many likened Mosaddeq's downfall to the shameful defeats of the past: the Arab invasion of Iran in the seventh century; the onslaughts of the Mongols in twelfth-century Iran; and the two territory-ceding treaties that Iran was forced to sign with Tsarist Russia in the nineteenth century. When the reinstalled shah adopted a policy of westernization, financed the education of thousands of young Iranians at American universities, and entered into strategic alliances with the United States, he confirmed the dissidents' (both secular and religious) suspicions about the threat his regime posed to the preservation of the national identity.

In 1967 one of the most alienated of the anti-Pahlavi critics, Jalal Al-i Ahmad wrote a polemic called *Gharbzadigi* (**Plagued by the West**, also in *WLAIT 6: Middle Eastern Literatures and Their Times*). Though the government immediately banned the work, it circulated widely underground and eventually surfaced as one of the seminal texts of the Islamic Revolution of 1979. Al-i Ahmad diagnosed Iranians' aping of Western culture as a disease he called "Westitis" (also known as "Westoxication"), which was ravaging an "authentic" Persian identity. If no cure for this disease were found, then there would be little to distinguish the millions of westernized Iranians from Americans.

Opponents of the shah's government could certainly point to aspects of urban nightlife in Iran as symptoms of advanced Westitis. At certain restaurants, clubs, and casinos, people openly engaged in forbidden activities like dancing, drinking alcohol, and gambling. (Indeed these activities were part of Persian society before westernization, but people engaged in them covertly then, on the margins of urban areas.) Television and cinema flooded the culture with images of attractive people dressed in the suggestive fashions of the 1960s. These highly visible signs of foreign influence encouraged two views that were antithetical but equally simplistic: on one hand, that the West was uniformly materialistic and depraved, and, on the other, that to be modern one merely had to act like cardboard Westerners. Prior to this time, most women wore chadors, or body veils; some men dressed in varieties of traditional clothing (baggy pants, felt hats or woven or cloth skullcaps, and open-toed sandals), others in conservative Western suits, ties, and fedoras. Women's skirts shortened and men's sideburns lengthened as modernization was reduced to tasteless imitations of American and European dress and grooming. These perceived affronts to public morality incensed the clerics and their followers, who still resented the mandatory unveiling of women the shah's father Reza Pahlavi (ruled 1921-41) had ordered in 1936. Traditional families insisted that female members preserve their *ismat* ("modesty, innocence") at all costs. At the other end of the spectrum, the leftists saw the indiscriminate embrace of Western culture on the part of the secular nouveaux riches and middle classes as proof that the Pahlavis were nothing but puppets dancing to the tune of their American masters.

Caught in the crossfire—the status of women. Farrukhzad's short life coincided with remarkable changes in the lives of Iranian women. In January 1936, a year after she was born, Reza Shah outlawed the veil, which meant that a majority of Iranian women, who had always kept their hair hidden from all but their closest relatives, now had to appear in public in Western hats or bareheaded. The practice of veiling became politicized. Religious authorities described unveiling as a perilous step toward secularism, while supporters of the shah saw it as necessary for modernization. The effect of unveiling was primarily felt in the cities. In Tehran a noblewoman like Sattareh Farman Farmaian's mother wept "with rage and humiliation" at the thought of allowing strange men to see her hair (Farman Farmaian, p. 95). In the rural areas, where women worked alongside men in the fields and often did not don the veil, the change was less apparent. Being unveiled was their foray into public education for young women under Reza Shah, for the veil connoted behaviors, such as seclusion from public forums, that began to be discarded with it; women found themselves taking classes from men to whom they were not related. Reza Shah's successor accelerated his father's westernizing and secularizing policies. Under the

provision of the Town Council Act (1962), women and members of recognized religious minorities (Christians, Jews, and Zoroastrians) gained the right to vote and, if elected to office, the right to swear allegiance to the holy book of their own confession. This act inflamed the religious opposition to the shah and eventually led to violent demonstrations. Women meanwhile gained the right to vote, which would be revoked a few months later under pressure from clerical leaders. The process of westernization continued, aspects of which greatly upset Farrukhzad. In her view, cosmetic changes were beginning to turn Iranian women into doll-like creatures with westernized appearances but empty minds. A small but growing number of women went abroad and returned to become active professionally as teachers, lawyers, or doctors. Some, like Farrukhzad, pursued careers in the arts. A divisive force, the movement of some women away from the traditional roles of daughter, wife, mother, widow, widened the gap between opponents of the shah (both clerical and secular) and his supporters. The veil became a convenient way of expressing one's political views. Many women began to wear the veil as a sign of protest against rampant westernization. At the state-sponsored universities even women who came from non-observant homes began to veil in open disobedience to the official prohibition of the chador on campus.

The Poems in Focus

Contents summary—"Sinning." "Sinning" depicts a man and a woman in the throes of sexual relations. At the outset, the woman portrays herself as being in a submissive position, but in the course of the poem the dynamic changes so that by the end, she becomes the dominant partner.

> In arms burning and hot I sinned
> a sin that utterly pleased me
> I sinned in his arms, and burning
> ironstrong and avenging was he
> In that dark and silent meeting
> the eyes I saw were full of mysteries
> My heart in my breast shook, anxious
> to answer his hungry eyes' pleas
> In that dark and silent meeting
> I rested in his arms, undone
> From his lips desire poured out on mine
> and my wild heart's gloom was gone
>   (Farrukhzad, "Sinning," *Bride of
>   Acacias*, p. 127)

In the next stanza, the speaker chants in her lover's ear words of desire. A shocking feature of

"Sinning" is the vivid depiction of lovemaking in the fifth stanza:

> Passion struck a flame in his eyes
> In the cup the wine danced red
> Against his breast my own body
> shivered drunk in the yielding bed
> I sinned a sin that pleased me utterly
> in arms that trembled with ecstasy
> In that dark and silent meeting
> O God, whatever happened to me?
> ("Sinning," p. 127)

The realism comes about partly through the use of prepositions. The entire poem, an account of foreplay, intercourse, and post-coital shudder and stupor, contains nearly all the common ways of indicating position in Persian. Literally paraphrased, the episode reads as follows: the poet is held *between* her lover's arms; her heart beats *in* her breast *out of* patience *from* (because of) the lust *of* her lover's eyes; his lips pour passion *onto* hers; she tells a story *down into* his ear; she lies *upon* him, *in the midst* of a soft bed, *beside* some wine dancing *in* a cup as a spark ignites *in* his eyes (Sprachman, p. 171).

"O Realm Bejewelled." "Sinning" exemplifies Farrukhzad's early voice, introspective yet rebellious. In contrast, "O Realm Bejewelled" issues from the mature poet, more politically engaged than her younger self. The title alludes to an unofficial national anthem, "O, Iran," in which the country is described as the "wellspring of the arts," whose "desert sands are better than gold."

The putative occasion of "O Realm Bejewelled" is the issuing of the speaker's identity card (in real life, parents obtain such an identity card for an Iranian child at birth). Rather than being a cause for celebration in the poem, the official recognition is greeted with nothing but sarcasm. The opening stanza decries the way the state equates enumeration and personal identity (the paraphrase of Descartes famous dictum, in dark print below, is a product of translation):

> I came out a winner
> Got myself registered
> Dressed up in an ID Card
> **I'm numbered, therefore I am**
> Long live 678 stamped at Precinct 5 Tehran resident
> Now all my worries are over
> At the loving breast of my motherland
> Glorious history trickling warmly down
> Crooning culture and civilization
> Rattlerattle [sic] goes its law

> Oooo
> My worries are all over now
> ("O Realm Bejewelled," *Bride of Acacias*, p. 82)

The rest of the poem looks unmercifully at some of the contradictions of modern Iran. The scenes recall the speaker's new identity as the number 678 recurs like a refrain in almost every stanza. Just after obtaining the card, the speaker "fervidly" gulps "six hundred seventyeight [sic] times, lungfuls [sic] of air, shitdusted [sic] and treated with essence of piss and garbage" ("O Realm Bejewelled," p. 82). In addition to being the exact number of elected officials in the assembly and local councils at the time (Hillmann, p. 54), the consecutive nature of the digits 678 suggests the mechanical inevitability of enumeration. The speaker's attention next turns to the hack poets who, sometimes for as little as the price of a good meal, sang the praises of the Pahlavis:

> What do I see here
> with my first registered glimpse through the blinds but six hundred seventy eight poets
> every one of them with the mug of some exotic bum
> scrounging in the dump for rhymes and meters . . .
> ("O Realm Bejewelled," p. 83)

"O Realm Bejewelled" also satirizes the penchant for "faithful" imitations of nature, such as plastic roses, on the part of the nouveaux riches. Low-maintenance and inexpensive plastic flowers and birds, many of them kitsch products of imported Western manufacturing processes, were becoming popular at the time. The idea that one could preserve and even beautify nature by molding it in plastic and plaster tormented artists such as Farrukhzad. Even roses (along with the nightingale, an image long associated with the theme of love in Persian poetry) are artificial in the bejewelled realm:

> And my first registered inhalation
> comes soaked with the scent of six hundred seventyeight neoprene roses
> distilled at the giant PLASCO factory
> ("O Realm Bejewelled," p. 83)

The speaker's disdain for other co-opted members of the thinking classes is no less than her contempt for paid panegyrists. She blames mercenary intellectuals for giving the Pahlavi regime an air of legitimacy:

> And as for our Persian intelligentsia
> whenever they put in an appearance at the senior citizen classes

IRANIAN TRADEMARKS—THE NIGHTINGALE AND THE ROSE

"Rose" (*gul*) and "nightingale" (*bulbul*) not only rhyme in Persian, they are definitive elements of every romantic garden in classical literature. The nightingale's fierce attraction to the rose has come to symbolize the infatuation of the lover with a beloved in lyric poetry. In the ***Divan of Hafiz*** (also in *WLAIT 6: Middle Eastern Literatures and Their Times*), the corpus of the most renowned fourteenth-century lyric poet, appears the following illustration:

I walked within a garden fair
At dawn, to gather roses there;
When suddenly sounded in the dale
The singing of the nightingale.
Alas, he loved a rose, like me,
And he, too, loved in agony;
Tumbling upon the mead he sent
The cataract of his lament.
With sad and meditative pace
I wandered in that flowery place,
And thought upon the tragic tale
Of love, and rose, and nightingale.
(Hafiz, p. 127)

In modern times, the phrase "country of roses and nightingales" has been used sarcastically to allude to all that is wrong in Iran, from frequent power failures, to rampant official corruption and poorly manufactured domestic products. The familiar expression when faced with one of these ills is "What do you expect? This is the country of roses and nightingales."

their chests are bedecked with six hundred
seventyeight electric kebab griddles
left wrists and right wrists braceleted with
six hundred seventyeight Timex watches, and
they know
in their hearts the empty pocket makes you
    weak,
and not the empty head
                    ("O Realm Bejewelled," p. 83)

The suggestion here is that the shah bought the support of intellectuals with prosperity. In return for their comfortable lives in the cities, various writers, filmmakers, and musicians praised the efforts of the shah to apply a veneer of Western civilization to Iran.

"The Mechanical Doll." The parallels between the loss of personal identity and freedom and the national dispossession of the Pahlavi period are also evident in "Mechanical Doll." Though this poem, like Farrukhzad's early work, highlights the perspective of women, the poem is far less

personal. Instead of the provocative assertion of sexual license in "Sinning," "Mechanical Doll" conveys a sophisticated picture of alienation in modern Iran. Two subjects found in much of the prose and poetry of the time surface in the poem: first, society's devaluation of women and, second, the death of nature.

"Mechanical Doll" opens with a woman, a solitary smoker, looking out a window. The smoker and everything around her are drained of life. Her fingers are *khushk*, "desiccated, stiff." Even the floral design in the Persian carpet on the floor, itself a traditional reproduction of nature that would normally animate the scene, is *bi-rang*, "colorless, void":

You can stare at cigarette smoke
hours at a time
staring frozenly into a cup
at a blank flower in the rug
the invisible line on the wall
You can draw the drapes open

with stiff fingers to find
it's pouring in the street
("Mechanical Doll," *Bride of Acacias*, p. 44)

The scene then shifts to the bedroom where nothing is natural. The speaker in the poem is not merely lifeless but *biganah*, "alien." Her body is denatured and objectified. The lover's embrace, described redundantly but feelingly in "Sinning" as "burning and hot," here is *chirah*, "ruling, sovereign":

> You can cry with a voice
> utterly false, utterly strange
> "I love you"
> In some man's overwhelming embrace
> you're a beautiful healthy woman
> a leather tablecloth for body
> with a pair of big, tough tits
> You can foul love's chastity
> in the bed of a drunk, a maniac, a bum
> ("Mechanical Doll," pp. 44-45)

The poem's view of the outside world is as bleak as that found in "O Bejewelled Realm." The "leather" woman of "Mechanical Doll" is a human analogue of the artificial rose in the former poem. Both suggest a kind of phoney, unnatural sort of beauty. The plastic flower remains eternally crimson without needing irrigation or pesticides. Similarly, one can feast on the "leather tablecloth" of a woman's body without the bother of having to engage her as a person.

The next two stanzas describe activities that serve to channel women's intellect and creativity into culturally acceptable pathways. They can "solve crosswords" or spend their lives praying at the cold tombs of Shi`ite saints. Or they can encrypt their physical beauty, becoming like dolls with unseeing, glass eyes.

The mechanical doll of the title, *arusak-i kuki* (literally, "the little wind-up bride"), does not appear until the last stanza of the poem:

> You can be like mechanical dolls
> gazing at your world with glassy eyes
> Your strawstuffed [sic] form
> can sleep through the years in its velvet case
> dressed up with sequined voile
> To the pressure of any passing hand
> you can squeak inanely
> "Oh, how happy I am!"
> ("Mechanical Doll," p. 45)

The doll is yet another image of superficiality, symbolic of Iran's westernization. It speaks of a connection with surface features only and a kind of physical contact devoid of substantive interaction. The doll's outside is shiny, dressed in a sheer, artificial fiber, and her voice is unfeelingly positive. Her empty insides give the lie to her programmed voice.

A poetic scapegoat. Though by modern Western standards, "Sinning" might strike one as a poem of passionate innocence, when released in Iran, it seemed almost seditious for its deliberate undermining of traditional values. The poem elicited outrage, as revealed in an introduction to a 1954 collection of Farrukhzad's poetry. Sayyid Hadi Ha'iri pointed out that the poets of the classical period had spoken of "rebellion and sin" without being sinful themselves (Ha'iri in Langarudi, p. 176). But now a woman was violating one of the basic conventions of femininity in Persian culture: namely that women are *za`ifah*, or "fragile and ruled by almost ungovernable passions" (Milani, p. 139). It is for this reason that families insisted their female members preserve their *ismat* or "modesty, innocence" at all costs. As noted, about two decades before the poem's appearance, Reza Shah had outlawed the veil, thereby removing the physical emblem of modesty, or *ismat*. To some, this was a "day of shame"; to others, it signaled emancipation (Milani, p. 34). By making her intimate emotions part of public discourse, Farrukhzad went much further, taking the unveiling beyond the physical to the emotional realm. The great popularity of the poem intimates that it resonated for many women of Iran, who at the time suffered repression in private as well as civil life.

The outrage against the poem was telling as well. "Sinning" was released at a particularly crucial time in contemporary Iranian history. The legitimacy of the regime was in question, and pressures to increase popular participation in government were mounting. Released into this environment in 1955, the poem exposed the naïve strategy of Pahlavi reform, which assumed rapid social, political, and cultural changes could be imposed from above without incurring a backlash from below. The backlash incurred by the poem reflected a reaction against change in general that was occurring in pockets of the population. To be sure, many conservative or traditional families were adamant in their opposition to the form of modernization that called on women to become individuals in the Western sense of the word. These opponents surfaced in large numbers among the rural and urban poor and middle classes and among the merchants in the bazaars. The anti-regime feelings would manifest themselves in symbolic acts of defiance: graffiti insulting to the royal family; the smashing of windowpanes at universities; and deliberate re-veiling by women who were not devout. That some quite progressive Iranians had objections to west-ernization becomes clear, as noted, in Farrukhzad's "Mechanical Doll," a poem that reacts not against women's becoming individuals, but against their trading one type of anonymity for another.

Sources and literary context. While Farrukhzad's poetry is indebted to the great au-thors of the past, such as Rumi (d. 1273), Sa`di (d. 1292), and Hafiz (d. 1389 or 1390), her po-ems would have been impossible without the groundbreaking verse of Nima Yushij (1897-1960). Nima departed from more than a millen-nium of classical conventions to create modernist Persian poetry. Breaking with the traditional strict rhyme and metrical schemes, he innovated in ways that gave rise to new schools of modern verse, known collectively as "Nima-i" or "Ni-maic." His innovations also led to translations of nineteenth- and twentieth-century European and American poetry. Poems by France's Paul Valéry, Paul Eluard, and Louis Aragon, Russia's Anna Akhmatova, Spain's Federico Garcia Lorca, and the English-speaking T. S. Eliot and Ezra Pound were translated into Persian in the 1950s and 1960s. Their styles and content influenced mod-ernist Persian poets, Farrukhzad among them. There are unmistakable parallels between her death-of-nature poetry and Eliot's "The Waste Land," as shown by these lines from her "Earth's Word": "The sun was cold / and the plenteous-ness went from the land / And grass withered on the fields" (Farrukhzad, "Earth's Word," *Bride of Acacias*, p. 57).

The poems covered here show an evolution in Farrukhzad's focus, from the type of intensely personal preoccupation of "Sinning" to the social issues of "O Realm Bejewelled" and "Mechanical Doll." In her first phase, Farrukhzad "typifie[d] the intellectual Iranian woman caught in the cross-tides of a strict, traditional society and the ever-increasing onslaught of Western ideas and modes of life" (Javadi and Sallée, p. 2). Next her poetry grew even bolder, challenging the world as created according to scripture, focusing espe-cially on the plight of women. From her socially oriented poems, she would progress, in the final stage, to a haunting preoccupation with the cos-mos, fixing on loneliness, death, and a not un-relieved darkness, in which lurks the promise of rebirth. (Specifically, she moved from poems such as "Sinning" and "Dreaming," to "Mechan-ical Doll" and "Green Delusion," to "I'll Be Greet-ing the Sun Again," "Let Us Believe in the

Oncoming Season of Cold," and "The Voice Alone Is Left.") This is how one critic character-izes her final compositions:

> Gone is the youthful voice of the lonely rebel recalling the sense of sin in the midst of a most pleasurable experience. Gone also is the paradoxical longing for, and loud protestations against, a prince riding a white horse, a housewife's apron, washed linen waving in the wind. Gone, finally, are snapshots of sweet elders surrounding childhood confusion, mechanical dolls lying in luxurious, coffin-like boxes, and the ever-present lonely woman in an enclosed space pleading for a window. In their place, we witness a deep human desire to engage the rich texts of an essentially mysterious universe, to hold communion with the unknown, to converse with utter solitude.
>
> (Karimi-Hakkak, pp. xxv-xxvi)

AN ANTHEM THAT RINGS HOLLOW

The title of "O Realm Bejewelled" is taken from Iran's un-official national anthem. Used ironically, it alludes to the rosy view of the anthem, which clashed with the dark realities of late 1950s and early 1960s Iran. By the time Farrukhzad wrote this poem, the Pahlavi promise that the country would soon become an advanced industrial nation seemed hollow, even cynical, to critics of the government. The regime cen-sored or imprisoned and tortured dissidents (both leftist and clerical) for expressing their views, while it rewarded medioc-rities and sycophants. In addition, rapidly proliferating exam-ples of bad taste in, for example, architecture grieved artists, who saw what they thought of as the "real" Iran disappear be-hind mansions better suited to the American community of North Hollywood than to North Tehran.

Reception. A great deal of the Persian criticism of Farrukhzad's early work, especially "Sinning," attacked the poet rather than evaluated the poem on its own terms. It is difficult to overstate how shocking "Sinning" was to readers in mid-1950s Iran. Critics, who were predominantly "subjec-tive and moralistic" at the time, condemned the poem on two counts: its technical immaturity (e.g., the redundancy of "burning" and "hot" in the first line) and its explicit sexual imagery (Langarudi, p. 25). In retrospect, a point would be made about the language of this early poem: that on one hand, the speaker delights in flaunting her sin but on the other hand, she uses the condemnatory language of patriarchy—most obviously, the value-laden term "sinned." Farrukhzad had yet to show the full lexical freedom that would surface in her later poems. In any case, the poem was initially taken as an unrepentant confession of sin; so often was it understood this way that it became necessary to defend Farrukhzad against charges of indecency. A traditional poet of her day, Ibrahim Sahba, satirized Farrukhzad's verse for the literary "lapses"—a clear reference to "Sinning." (Hillmann, p. 53). Although she claimed not to heed such criticism, there is some evidence to suggest that Farrukhzad got her revenge on Sahba in "O Realm Bejewelled." In a stanza not found in the Banani-Kessler translation, the speaker predicts that she will "hurl herself madly down into the affectionate bosom of the motherland" (Hillmann, p. 53). After this literary suicide, the poet conjures up the same Ibrahim Sahba to compose the dead speaker's elegy, which will rhyme in drivel (in Persian, *kashk*—literally, "whey"). Critically, "O Realm Bejewlled" won appreciation from at least some Iranian intellectuals for its innovative elements, among them, the equation of the self in the poem with Iranian society rather than with a sighing or grief-stricken speaker.

The responses to "Mechanical Doll" were affected by the fact that when it first appeared, critics in Iran were still reading Farrukhzad's poetry mostly as obscene and as protest against inequality between the sexes. Social change has since encouraged newer views with regard to this type of Farrukhzad poem. A Canadian edition of her poems conveys one such view:

> In these poems . . . we see the poet contemplating the condition of women in her society. Characteristically, she does so through her own experiences rather than through any general preconceptions. Being "a healthy beautiful female" in "a man's domineering arms" while viewing one's world "with eyes of glass" is indeed an apt depiction of the lifestyle imposed on a whole generation of Iranian women growing up in the 1950s and 60s.
> (Karimi-Hakkak, pp. xxi-xxii)

The poet's life ended tragically on February 14, 1967, when the jeep she was driving crashed into a wall to avoid a school bus. After this, the practice of eulogizing the poet on the anniversary of her death became a ritual among Iranian intellectuals and opposition groups. Admirers collected unpublished or rare scraps of her writing and rushed them into print to satisfy the brisk market in memorializing. With each generation, another version of the poet is reborn, and her poetry is recompiled to suit particular times and places. Under the Islamic Republic, Farrukhzad's *divan* (corpus of collected works) has been republished without certain poems deemed to exceed the moral standards of discourse in Iran (Farrukhzad, *Divan*, p. 8). These poems have been restored in collections published outside of Iran.

—Paul Sprachman

For More Information

Farman-Farmaian, Sattareh. *Daughter of Persia: A Woman's Journey from Her Father's Harem through the Islamic Revolution.* New York: Anchor, 1992.

Farrukhzad, Furugh. *Another Birth.* Trans. Hasan Javadi and Susan Sallée. Emeryville, Calif.: Albany Press, 1981.

———. *Bride of Acacias: Selected Poems of Forugh Farrokhzad.* Trans. Jascha Kessler with Amin Banani. Delmar, New York: Caravan, 1982.

———. *Divan-i ash`ar-i Furugh-i Farrukhzad.* Tehran: Murvarid, 1992.

Hafiz. *Fifty Poems of Hafiz.* Ed. Arthur J. Arberry. Cambridge, U.K.: Cambridge University Press, 1962.

Hillmann, Michael C. *A Lonely Woman: Forugh Farrokhzad and Her Poetry.* Washington, D.C.: Three Continents and Mage, 1987.

Karimi-Hakkak, Ahmad. *Remembering the Flight: Twenty Poems by Forugh Farrokhzad.* Vancouver: Nik, 1997.

Katouzian, Homa. "Of the Sins of Forough Farrokhzad." *Iranshinasi* 12, no. 2 (summer 2000): 264-87.

Langarudi, Shams. *Tarikh-i tahlili-i shi`r-i naw.* Vol. 2. Tehran: Nashr-i Markaz, 1991.

Milani, Farzaneh. *Veils and Words: The Emerging Voices of Iranian Women Writers.* Syracuse, N.Y.: Syracuse University Press, 1992.

Muradi-Kuchi, Shahnaz. *Shinakht-i Furugh Farrukhzad.* Tehran: Qatra, 2000.

Sprachman, Paul. *Language and Culture in Persian.* Costa Mesa, Calif.: Mazda, 2002.

Taj al-Saltanah. *Crowing Anguish: Memoirs of a Persian Princess from the Harem to Modernization.* Ed. Abbas Amanat. Washington, D.C.: Mage, 1993.

Memed,
My Hawk

by

Yaşar Kemal

Yaşar Kemal was born Sadik Kemal Gökçeli in 1923 in Hemite, a village in the Çukurova region (Adana province) of southern Turkey. As a child he was trained in the tradition of the wandering bards of Anatolia, who traveled throughout the region singing traditional folk songs and epics from a rich oral tradition. At age nine, Kemal attended school to learn to read and write, becoming one of the first literate members of his village. Kemal graduated from high school, but partly owing to poverty, never completed a university degree. Interested in the folklore and ethnology of Anatolia, he continued his studies through the *Halk Evleri* or "People's Houses," institutions established in 1932 by the new Republic of Turkey under its first president, Atatürk, to educate Turks in the cities and towns of Anatolia. Kemal's first literary endeavor was a collection of *agitlar,* or traditional laments, sung spontaneously by Anatolian women over the loss of a loved one. During the same period, Kemal worked as a professional letter writer in the nearby town of Kadirli. As a result of his socialist politics (for which he was eventually arrested, imprisoned, and tortured), he was hounded out of every job until he changed his name to Yaşar Kemal and moved to Istanbul, where he worked as a reporter for the premier newspaper, *Cumhuriyet;* most of his articles concerned the common people of Anatolia. Meanwhile, Kemal wrote short stories about Anatolian life and engaged in the formidable task of creating his own literary style, by drawing on traditional storytelling themes and motifs and by appropriating

> ## THE LITERARY WORK
>
> A novel set in the Çukurova plain of southern Anatolia during the 1920s and early 1930s, with flashbacks to the 1860s, and World War I (1914-18) and the Turkish War of Independence (1918-1923); published in Turkish (as *Ince Memed* [Slim Memed]) in 1955, in English in 1962.
>
> ## SYNOPSIS
>
> Cruelly oppressed by his overlord, a young peasant turns outlaw and tries to bring justice to his oppressed fellow villagers.

to some extent village idiom. He eventually forged a style that blended the language of the Istanbul literary establishment with the colloquial dialect of southeastern Anatolia. Kemal progressed from short tales to a longer story of Anatolian life, which was published serially in *Cumhuriyet* and became an instant success. This was *Memed, My Hawk,* Kemal's first novel, which won an important literary prize in Turkey and was published worldwide in nearly two dozen languages. The novel grew into a four-part saga, whose second part, *They Burn the Thistles* (1973), has also been translated into English. *Memed, My Hawk,* the progenitor of the saga, meanwhile gained distinction for its portrayal of Turkish village life and of a mountain brigand's harrowing yet in some ways socially salutary career.

Events in History at the Time the Novel Takes Place

Turkish village life. Much of Kemal's novel takes place in the Anatolian countryside, especially in the peasant villages of the Çukurova plain and the Taurus Mountains. In the early twentieth century Turkey experienced dramatic political changes, culminating in the abolition of the sultanate and the establishment of a republic in 1923. But while the new central government set about implementing various reforms, the remote, poverty-stricken villages of Anatolia—considered the Turkish homeland—were the last to feel the effects of these reforms.

Recognized as the smallest political entity in Turkey, a village could nonetheless choose its own headman and council of elders; the headman deferred in turn to the urban-bred district officer who was his immediate superior. Relations between town and country were uneasy, however; most villagers distrusted the central government on general principle, associating government officials with such hated practices as the collection of taxes or interference with cherished traditions and customs.

Thus, village life remained fundamentally untouched by the new regime, mainly because, as anthropologist Paul Stirling writes, "People [in the villages] did not know, or did not understand, or did not care what the central government was doing" (Stirling, p. 13). Moreover, the country's mountainous terrain and harsh climate—hot, dry summers and intensely cold winters—isolated most of Anatolia's estimated 35,000 villages not only from the cities but from each other as well. There were few roads, mostly only tracks in the dust, and villages were often 10 to 15 miles apart. Historian Richard D. Robinson, who spent several years in Anatolia, describes a typical village during the mid-twentieth century:

> The ordinary community—containing between 800 and 2,000 persons—consisted of a tight, compact cluster of homes, very frequently immediately adjoining one another. There were virtually no isolated dwellings, for villagers did not reside on their fields. Homes were constructed of rough-hewn stone or, more typically, sun-dried brick—an adobe type construction.
>
> (Robinson, p. 39)

While the inhabitants of any one village lived in close proximity to one another, individual villages inevitably became intimate, even insular. Stirling writes, "People belong to their village in a way they belong to no other social group. . . . The village is a community—a social group with many functions, not all of them explicit, and to which people are committed by birth or marriage, and bound by many ties" (Stirling, p. 29). Family households, invariably patriarchal in nature, formed the building blocks of each village.

Most villagers made their living by farming, planting subsistence crops of wheat and rye. Poor soil and capricious weather, however, could take their toll upon crop yields and villagers often feared that their stores of food would not last to the next harvest. Living conditions in nearly all villages were primitive and crude; the adobe houses contained little in the way of furnishings, so most families sat or slept on the floor. Since few could afford to burn wood for fuel, cakes of dried dung were used instead, and during the coldest winter days, the livestock—usually cows and bullocks—were brought into the house to help warm the air. There were no radios and no postal service in the village, and the villagers themselves were largely illiterate; consequently, word of mouth remained the most effective means of communication.

In *Memed, My Hawk*, Kemal vividly depicts the difficulties of Turkish village life. Memed and his neighbors struggle each year through broiling summers and freezing winters to eke out a living from the arid, thistle-ridden soil of the foothill plateaus of the Taurus Mountains. Their task is made even more difficult by the oppression of their parasitical *agha* ("overlord"; literally, "master" or "older person"). He claims most of their crop, leaving the peasants to survive on only a third of their harvest.

Atatürk and the new republic. The son of lower middle-class parents, Mustafa Kemal Atatürk (1881-1938) had been an ardent Turkish nationalist since his youth as a cadet in military school. During the First World War, he distinguished himself in battle, rising to the rank of brigadier general in the Turkish Army. He likewise proved to be an indomitable leader in the Turkish War of Independence, eventually assuming personal command of the nationalist forces and defeating the Greek army invasion of 1922. The following year, the Treaty of Lausanne consolidated peace between Turkey and the Allied nations of World War I and formally recognized Turkey as an independent nation, the Republic of Turkey. Mustafa Kemal served as its first president (he was granted the family surname Atatürk—"Father Turk"—by Parliament in 1934). During the 1920s and 1930s Mustafa Kemal and the Republican

Memed, My Hawk takes place near the Taurus Mountains, shown here in Köprülü Canyon National Park.

People's Party implemented major reforms, most of them aimed at secularizing Turkish public life and bringing the country more in line with the nations of the Western world. In 1924 the reformers abolished the office of caliph (Islamic ruler). In 1925 the republic passed a law requiring men to wear hats and outlawing the fez—a tasseled flat-crowned cap adopted by Ottoman Muslims in the nineteenth century—as a sign of their allegiance to Islam. The fez was ridiculed as "the headwear of a barbarous backward people" (Howard, p. 97). Also it became permissible for women to abandon the veil and appear in public with their heads and faces uncovered. In 1926 the Turkish parliament repealed Islamic Holy Law and adopted a new civil code, influenced by the codes of Italy and Germany. The legal status of women improved—they were granted the right to initiate divorce proceedings; meanwhile, polygamy and a man's right to divorce his wife by renunciation were both outlawed. And in 1928 the republic instituted perhaps the most dramatic change of all, abandoning the Arabic script in favor of the Roman, and introducing a new Turkish alphabet based upon phonetics. Although the rural villages were generally the last to feel the impact of Mustafa Kemal's changes, some laws had consequences even in the remote Anatolian countryside. Aware that the fez had been outlawed, brigands

intentionally wore one. As the hero of *Memed, My Hawk* explains, "Each brigand was wearing a red fez, as is the custom in the mountains, where the red fez is the badge of brigandage. A brigand wearing a cap or hat, as men now do in the villages and the cities has never yet been seen. . . . everyone who took to the mountains wore a fez too" (Yaşar Kemal, *Memed, My Hawk*, p. 102).

Land reform and the *aghas*. During the late nineteenth and early twentieth century, most of the land in Turkey was owned by the state, in this case the crumbling Ottoman Empire. Parcels of land were leased to farmers under secure tenure arrangements that resembled medieval feudalism: farmers cultivated the land and gave over part of their harvests in exchange for military and other services. Although the Ottoman Empire had restricted the growth of the landowning class in its earlier years, this trend was later reversed owing to the reinstitution of Islamic inheritance practices, the sale of state lands for increased revenue, and authorized land transfers. Thus, large landowners, along with landless peasants, predominated in many parts of rural Anatolia.

After the First World War and the establishment of the Turkish Republic, the new government attempted to implement land reforms by abolishing what remained of the feudal landlords' powers. However, changes had already begun to take place with the arrival of a new social element: the *aghas,* newly rich peasants, including some who made their fortunes profiteering in the post-World War I era. The *aghas,* who were eager to obtain as much fertile land as possible, either through purchase or less ethical means, soon came to dominate much of the countryside. In some areas, the *aghas* became the intermediary between the peasants and the government; the peasants had to work through the *aghas* if they wanted something from the government, while the government used the *aghas* to obtain votes or taxes from the peasants. Theoretically, the feudal landlords' power had dissolved, so peasants could own land, and especially since it had risen in value, they were determined to hang on to the little they had. But the *aghas* were equally determined to gain control of as much as possible for themselves. As Kemal explains it, the brigands had a hand in their gaining it: "The landholdings of the rich steadily increased when they also began to make use of brigands as a means of pressure on the poor who were fighting to defend their rights in a life-and-death struggle for the land" (*Memed, My Hawk,* p. 232).

As a child growing up in a rural Turkish villages, Kemal encountered many *aghas* in everyday life and had little good to say of them:

> Often the ag[h]as were without pity. They starved the people, seized their few belongings, and treated them like slaves. . . . They were completely deceitful, dishonest, and recognized no human values. They certainly knew how to give orders to everyone, and they exploited without pity the tenants who showed any strength or independence. . . . The ag[h]as were petty tyrants. Their power and wealth came not from tradition and family, but from land and cattle.
>
> (Yaşar Kemal, *Yaşar Kemal on His Life and Art,* p. 137)

In *Memed, My Hawk,* Kemal creates several characters in this tyrannical mold, the abusive Abdi Agha who beats and starves Memed as a child and the even more monstrous Ali Safa Bey who makes use of mountain brigands to increase his landholdings and keep the peasants frightened and under his control.

A tradition of brigandage. The phenomenon of banditry in Turkey is historically ancient, dating at least as far back as the Hittites, warrior invaders who swept into Anatolia late in the third millennium B.C.E. Indeed, in his memoirs, Kemal describes inscriptions on Hittite bas-reliefs and stele in his village, in which a Hittite sovereign boasts of subduing the bandits of the area (*Yaşar Kemal on His Art and Life,* p. 31). Brigands and bandits were also prevalent in the days of the Ottoman Empire (1395-1923), especially during the seventeenth century when the Ottoman state was becoming more centralized. To some extent, the bandits were themselves creations of the state, born of the mercenary troops hired by central authorities to enforce their own power over certain sectors of society, rather like a private army. Once their campaigns were concluded, these mercenaries found themselves decommissioned and unemployed. Consequently many roamed the countryside in armed gangs, offering their fighting skills for hire and engaging in theft and pillaging.

Besides former mercenaries, the brigand gangs of earlier eras included "vagrant peasants, rebellious religious students, unruly members of official retinues, and defiant or mutinous soldiers. Each of these groups turned to banditry in response to state action and resulting transformations in rural life" (Barkey, p. 141). Such disaffected social elements, along with fugitives from the law such as novel's Memed, could be found among the brigands of his day as well.

During the final years of World War I, the number of brigands in the country increased, thanks in part to deserters from the Ottoman army, which was fighting on the side of Germany. On the other hand, many brigands united with their countrymen to fight the Turkish War of Independence (1919-22). Turkish nationalists, led by Atatürk, squared off against the Greek army, which invaded western Anatolia with the intent of detaching it from Turkish rule. Also they squared off against the Allies (Italy, France, and Great Britain), whose leaders were attempting to partition the former Ottoman Empire into zones of influence to be governed by them.

In *Memed, My Hawk,* one of the characters, Big Ismail, describes this period with unabashed enthusiasm: "The French Occupation Forces then came to the Çukurova and the brigands, the deserters, the irregulars, the thieves, those who were good-for-nothing and the honest men, the young and the old, all the people of the Çukurova joined in the fight to throw the enemy out of the plain. They drove the French out and the whole country was thus liberated. A new government was set up and a new era began" (*Memed, My Hawk,* pp. 231-32). Historians Stanford J. Shaw and Ezel Kural Shaw present a more objective view, revealing that brigands and irregulars actually fought on *both* sides in the post-World War I conflict, some allying themselves with the French in the Çukurova region, others fighting on the side of the Turkish nationalist forces. The latter eventually succeeded in driving the French out of southeastern Turkish lands, and the Greeks, supported by the British, out of the west. After the new government was established, most of the brigands returned to the mountains and their former lifestyles, fighting each other and helping the newly rich class of *aghas* protect their holdings and control their tenants. Kemal's novel acknowledges that reality as well: "Nearly every Agha supplied some band of brigands on the mountains and protected them from the Government. . . . But the conflicting interests of the Aghas in the plains began to lead to fights among their brigand supporters in the mountains. The brigands on the mountains were continually fighting among themselves and oppressing the poor, while the estates of the Aghas grew steadily on the plains" (*Memed, My Hawk*, p. 232).

The Novel in Focus

Plot summary. After a short chapter describing the coastal region of Çukurova and the highland plateaus of the Taurus Mountains in southern Turkey, the novel depicts the child Memed fleeing from his home village of Deyirmenoluk and its feudal lord, Abdi Agha. The feudal lord owns all the land in and around the five villages on the Dikenli plateau, or Plain of Thistles. Cruel and abusive, he has singled out Memed and his widowed mother for persecution: Abdi Agha makes the boy plow barefoot in the frost and thistles, beats him constantly, and once tied him to a tree and left him to be devoured by wolves and birds of prey.

Unable to bear these torments any longer, Memed abandons his mother, Deuneh, and flees over the next mountain ridge to Kesme village. One villager, Süleyman, takes Memed in, adopts him, and makes him his goatherd. Memed thrives in this comfortable and loving environment, but he cannot help worrying about his mother, whom he left behind. One day, despite warnings from Süleyman, Memed takes the goats too close to Deyirmenoluk and encounters another resident, "Beetroot Hüsük," who recognizes and speaks to him. News of the encounter spreads to the other villagers, and an enraged Abdi, whose rule extends to Süleyman's Kesme village, forces Memed to return home.

After Memed and his mother finish harvesting the wheat, Abdi Agha takes his share of the crop. Normally, Abdi takes two-thirds, but this year he takes three-fourths as punishment for Memed's running away. Reduced to starvation during the winter, Memed and his mother give up their only cow and its yearling bull calf to Abdi in exchange for food. The calf is Memed's only hope for eventual independence; in taking the animals, Abdi kills Memed's hope for a better life.

At this point the story leaps forward to Memed as an undersized 18-year-old youth, still oppressed by Abdi Agha, but determined to make his first trip to town. On the journey, Memed and his friend Mustafa meet an old man, the famous mountain brigand Big Ahmet, who led an outlaw's life for 16 years, inspiring love and fear in the peasants, then retired after being pardoned in an amnesty.

While in town, the two boys meet Corporal Hasan, who describes town life and gives them a vision of new possibilities. Memed's view of the world is transformed in a moment: "He had grown in his own eyes and began to consider himself a man. . . . 'Abdi Agha's only human; so are we'. . . . The market of yesterday, the town of yesterday, the world of yesterday, seemed completely different to Memed's eyes today. All the bonds restraining his feet and his heart were now broken" (*Memed, My Hawk*, pp. 66-67). By the time Memed returns to his village, he has decided to run away to the Çukurova with his 15-year-old girlfriend, Hatche, to start a new life, free of the *agha*'s tyranny. Hatche, however, has just been betrothed against her will to Abdi's nephew, Veli. She and Memed flee at night, bound for the Çukurova. Caught in a downpour, they take shelter and consummate their love in a cave.

Discovering that the lovers have fled, Abdi Agha, in a rage, tramples the life out of Memed's mother. He then sets out with seven villagers, the jilted bridegroom, and the famed tracker Lame Ali to recapture Memed and Hatche. Although Lame Ali sympathizes with the lovers, he cannot resist the challenge of tracking them, and the posse catches up with the fugitives in the forest. Drawing his revolver, Memed kills Veli and wounds Abdi. Memed then sends Hatche back to Deyirmenoluk, promising to fetch her later. Now even more of a wanted man, Memed takes refuge in Kesme. His former foster-father, Süleyman, rescues him once again, this time taking him into the mountains to Mad Durdu's band of brigands.

In the following months, Memed learns the skills of brigandage but quickly becomes disenchanted with Mad Durdu as a leader. Not only is Mad Durdu capricious and cruel, like Abdi, but reckless as well. He is notorious for humiliating those whom he robs, stealing not only their money but their underclothing as well. After Durdu attempts to rob and shame Kerimoglu, a proud nomad chieftain who had earlier aided and tended Durdu's men after a skirmish with the police, Memed and two companions, Jabbar and Sergeant Rejep, break with the brigand leader and strike out on their own.

As the leader of the trio, Memed becomes an honorable brigand who fights oppression while protecting the poor—in the tradition of Big Ahmet, Reşit the Kurd, and other bandits who are remembered in folksongs sung by Anatolian bards of oral lore. At one point, Memed sets out to rob Ali and Hasan, two peasants returning to their mountain villages, but when he learns that they would rather die than return to their villages empty-handed after working for years in the Çukurova to make a better life for themselves, he frees them and returns their money, realizing that to rob them of their money would be to rob them of their dreams: "Who knows with what hopes they toiled!" (*Memed, My Hawk*, p. 191).

Soon after this incident, Memed visits Deyirmenoluk and learns that he did not in fact kill Abdi Agha; he also hears that his mother died of the injuries Abdi inflicted when he trampled on her and that Hatche has been falsely imprisoned for shooting Veli. Determined to exact his revenge, Memed goes to Abdi's home but finds him gone and only his wives and children present. Jabbar stabs one of the wives, but Memed stops Sergeant Rejep from killing Abdi's children and earns the respect of the villagers for his mercy.

Memed enlists Lame Ali in finding Abdi; eager to make amends to Memed for his earlier betrayal, the tracker soon discovers that the *agha* is hiding in a kinsman's home in a Çukurova village. Attempting to smoke out Abdi, Memed and his companions set fire to the *agha*'s hiding place and end up burning down the whole village. Pursued by angry villagers, the trio are forced to flee to the mountains. Sergeant Rejep dies from complications of a recent wound.

Believing that Abdi Agha died in the fire, Memed returns to Deyirmenoluk to distribute the fields that were once controlled by Abdi. The villagers rejoice at the news of the *agha*'s defeat, hail Memed as a liberator, and set fire to the thistle fields in celebration. When it is discovered that Abdi is still alive, however, nearly half the villagers turn on Memed, condemning him as a presumptuous upstart. Disillusioned by the villagers' cowardice, Memed and Jabbar return to the mountains for their own safety.

Meanwhile, having escaped from the burned-down house, Abdi seeks refuge in the village of Vayvay with a villainous but powerful *agha*, Ali Safa Bey, who hires a mountain brigand band to terrorize the peasants and steal their land. Ali Safa Bey and his henchman, the brigand Kalayji, set a trap to kill Memed, but Memed avoids the trap and kills Kalayji instead. Subsequently, Memed's fame spreads throughout the Çukurova and the Taurus Mountains; he assumes "legendary proportions," becoming a hero especially to the villagers of Vayvay, whom Ali Safa Bey oppresses the most. The villagers supply Big [Old] Osman with a large sum of money and send him as an emissary to Memed in the mountains. Delighted by the young brigand's prowess, Big Osman, himself a peasant, takes to calling Memed "My Hawk," a sobriquet that is taken up by the people.

Meanwhile, Hatche has been languishing in jail and is about to be transferred from the prison in town to another prison at Kozan, where a harsh final sentence will be passed against her. Parting company from Jabbar, who disapproves of this venture, Memed rescues Hatche from the police in broad daylight, along with her female fellow prisoner Iraz. All three escape to the mountains, establishing a hideout in a cave on Mount Alidagi. After several seasons of searching, the police find their refuge. Unable to flee because Hatche has gone into labor with their son, Memed surrenders to police sergeant Asim, but on discovering the true circumstances, Asim relents and lets the new father and his family escape.

Abdi Agha's fear of Memed mounts with each escape and he writes countless letters to the government, all to no effect. Pursuit of Memed soon resumes, however, under the command of Captain Faruk. During a shootout in Alayar, Hatche is killed by a stray bullet. Memed employs his wits as well as gunfire and grenades to drive away the police, and transports Hatche's corpse down to the nearest village for proper burial. At Iraz's request, Memed sends his child off with her to be raised in safety elsewhere, then returns to the mountains alone.

During a national holiday in the autumn, the Turkish government declares one of its periodic amnesties to pardon criminals in jail and brigands in the mountains. When Memed enters Deyirmenoluk one day, Big Osman is there with

THE IMMORTAL OUTLAW

The songs of wandering minstrels provide one window into the world of Anatolian nomads. "Ag[h]as, the Day of Judgement has arrived," warns one song, and later, "there is no justice in the government . . . we have no one to turn to" (Gould, p. 210). For hundreds of years, colorful figures—brigands, warriors, tribal chieftains—were immortalized in song and story. The historical personages who inspired the songs seemed to expect and accept such immortality as a compliment. In trying to persuade another bandit to join forces, the seventeenth-century outlaw Kalenderoglu remarked, "If we win over Kuyucu [the grand vizier], then we will have the Ottomans give up everything east of Scutari [i.e., will give up Anatolia], if we do not win we will be content being the heroes of folk songs!" (Kalenderoglu in Barkey, p. 208). Centuries later, Yaşar Kemal tried his hand at immortalizing in song a modern outlaw. The man was his father's former bodyguard, whom everybody called "Zala's Son." Kemal writes in his memoirs, "After my father's death, Zala's Son became one of the more famous outlaws in the Toros [the Taurus Mountains]. Some nights he would visit us and bring me presents. . . . One day the police trapped Zala's Son and killed him along with his five companions. When I heard the news, I composed a long elegy for him and sang it to my mother. For the first time she told me that she loved my work, and she made no other comment. I had won her over" (Yaşar Kemal, *Yaşar Kemal on His Life and Work*, p. 9).

an Arabian horse and the promise of 100 acres and a house in Vayvay village for the outlaw. This does not sit well with the villagers of Deyirmenoluk, however. They are disappointed in Memed because they know Abdi will return to oppress them anew. Mother Huru confronts Memed on behalf of Deyirmenoluk and charges him with cowardice. Stung, Memed again recruits Lame Ali to find Abdi Agha, which the tracker is eager to do.

Mounted on the Arabian horse, Memed travels to the town where Abdi is hiding, breaks into his enemy's house, and kills him. Escaping back to Deyirmenoluk, Memed tells the villagers they have no more claim on him. He then rides off on the Arabian horse and is never seen again, but every year before plowing time the peasants burn the thistle fields in remembrance of Memed, and a supernatural light appears on Alidagi so that "for three nights the mountain is white, as bright as day" (*Memed, My Hawk*, p. 371).

The outlaw as folk hero. In *Memed, My Hawk* the protagonist undergoes an almost mythical transformation from ordinary peasant to folk hero. Oppressed by poverty and Abdi Agha's abuse, Memed grows up short and stunted: "A thousand and one misfortunes prevented him from ever growing to his full height. His shoulders no longer developed, his arms and legs were like dry branches. Hollow cheeks, dark face, charred by the sun. . . . His appearance was that of an oak, short and gnarled" (*Memed, My Hawk*, pp. 51-52).

Once Memed becomes a brigand, however, his reputation and image undergo a miraculous change in the minds of the peasants. After he refrains from robbing two farm laborers, spares the children of his enemy Abdi Agha, and defeats the cruel bandit Kalayji, he becomes equally renowned for his mercy and his wiliness. Like the legendary bandit Big Ahmet, who roamed the mountains a generation earlier, Memed inspires love and fear. The common people listen raptly to his exploits and embellish them almost beyond recognition:

In the Chukurova and on the Taurus mountains Memed's adventures were repeated, much exaggerated, from mouth to mouth, everyone supporting Memed's cause. . . . At last the village had found a champion. They were elated and all began inventing tall stories about Slim Memed, who soon assumed legendary proportions in their eyes. They told of so many heroic deeds and fights that the lives of ten men would not have sufficed to perform them all.

(*Memed, My Hawk*, p. 274)

Big Osman of Vayvay, the villager who dubs Memed "My Hawk," a nickname suggesting the young man's resemblance to a bird of prey, comes to idolize him. When Memed is briefly presumed dead after a shootout with police, Big Osman weeps in lamentation, "What a gallant man was [M]y [H]awk! Such large eyes, such brows, such slim fingers! And so tall, like a cypress!" (*Memed, My Hawk*, p. 338). When it turns out that Memed is alive, Big Osman rejoices, claiming that his Hawk will defeat anyone the *aghas* send against him.

The fictional Memed's transformation into a Robin Hood-like figure is not unprecedented. Indeed, several historians have explored the conception of social banditry—in which brigandage may be viewed as a protest against poverty and oppression—in various cultures. Eric Hobsbawm writes,

> The point about social bandits is that they are peasant outlaws whom the lord and state regard as criminals, but who remain within peasant society, and are considered by their people as heroes, as champions, avengers, fighters for justice, perhaps leaders of liberation, and in any case as men to be admired, helped, and supported. This . . . distinguishes [social banditry] from two other kinds of rural crime: from the activity of gangs drawn from the professional "underworld" or of mere freebooters ("common robbers"), and from communities for whom raiding is part of the normal way of life, such as for instance the Bedouin.
>
> (Hobsbawm in Barkey, p. 178)

Brigandage boasts a long, "honorable" history in Turkish lands. During the sixteenth and seventeenth centuries, several social bandits acquired the status of folk heroes in Ottoman Anatolia, including Pir Sultan Abdal, Köroglu, and Dadaloglu. All three opposed the policies of the state and fought against local leaders who were oppressing the peasants.

Of the three, the late-sixteenth-century bandit Köroglu most resembled a Turkish Robin Hood. With a band of approximately 200 men—consisting of demilitarized mercenaries and vagrant peasants—Köroglu set up camp in the mountains, from which he launched periodic attacks upon local officials. The peasants themselves were not entirely exempt from his crimes, notes historian Karen Barkey: "Some documents of the period show that Köroglu attacked both judges and other local officials with reputations for tyranny[,] and innocent villagers"; but "other documents testify to his social consciousness, indicating that unlike other bandits he and his men never trampled village fields, even at the cost of their own security" (Barkey, pp. 181-82). Throughout the region of Bolu, he was associated with a famous call to arms: "I am Köroglu; I shatter the rocks, / I am the people's sword; I search for justice, / I hold the Sultan responsible, / Those who wake up join me!" (Köroglu in Barkey, p. 181).

Raised on the songs and legends of the Anatolian bards, Kemal was familiar with the figure of Köroglu. However, he also had a more personal source of inspiration for *Memed, My Hawk*: "On my mother's side, her father and brothers—all the men in her lineage—were outlaws. . . . My maternal uncle was Mahiro, the most famous outlaw in eastern Anatolia, Iran, and the Caucasus. . . . Several years after his death, many epic songs celebrated him as a hero" (*Yaşar Kemal on His Life and Art*, p. 5). As a child, Kemal often heard of his uncle's exploits. According to the family legend, Mahiro and his band were captured by the police and thrown into the Van Prison. During their imprisonment, the outlaws dug a tunnel and one night, after the tunnel was finished, Mahiro made his escape. His comrades were afraid to follow him, however; risking his newfound freedom, Mahiro returned time and again through the tunnel to persuade his band to escape as well, but to no avail. Finally he was spotted by a guard, who wounded Mahiro. The injured outlaw disarmed his assailant and held the police at bay for several hours before being recaptured and executed. He was 25 years old.

Sources and literary context. Perhaps most influential in Kemal's writing of this novel were the injustices he witnessed during his childhood in the Çukurova, and during his adult career as a newspaper correspondent. Another influence was a Turkish literary movement toward realism during the late 1940s and 1950s. Out of this movement emerged Mahmut Makal's *Bizim Köy* (1950), translated into English as *A Village in Anatolia* (1954). There are important social and ideological differences between Makal and Kemal, which help explain the different kinds of literature they produced. Makal was a teacher who went to Anatolia to educate the ignorant peasants. His naturalistic descriptions reveal the harsh realities of village life in Anatolia. Kemal, however, was a man of the people who understood the peasant mentality, and had suffered deprivation and social oppression in Anatolia himself.

Kemal avidly collected folklore and read literature from both the East and West. As a child, while trained in the ways of bardic declamation, he also absorbed his people's folk traditions. These he combined with received traditions of written literary style to produce his own voice, which reflected, to writers in these traditions at least, a highly poetic, even transcendent view of art and life. As an example, the thistles, which are described in detail at the beginning of the book and which appear as a *leit motiv* throughout, are both real thistles and a symbol of how harsh, painful experiences lead to greater understanding of life and appreciation for its beauty despite pain and suffering.

In *Memed, My Hawk*, Kemal transforms details from personal experience into art: Memed thinks of changing his name when he first runs away to Süleyman in Kesme village, just as Kemal changed his name to escape oppression when he 'ran away' from the Çukurova to Istanbul; Kemal also models characters on real-life acquaintances. Big Ahmet has features of his maternal uncle Mahiro, who, as noted, was a famous brigand. The elderly Big Ismail is based on the real-life Ismail Agha from Kemal's village. Horali, a watchman of a melon garden on an island in the Savrun River, is a throwback to Kemal's youth when he himself worked as a watchman of a melon garden on an island in the Ceyhan River. Such appropriation is not unusual for any writer.

Kemal is, however, original in the way he appropriates authentic folk material and incorporates it into his story, structurally and thematically. Not only does he frequently refer to folk motifs in woven stockings and authentic designs on woven materials from nomadic life, but Memed, in one of his most daring episodes is inspired by the folk tale of Köroglu, in which a famous bandit witnesses a little dog vanquish three huge dogs through his courage alone. The tale inspires Memed before he snatches Hatche from the police in broad daylight; after his successful exploit, his deeds are sung by the peasants and bards who hear of them, so that Memed's story becomes larger than life and inspires others to rebel against oppression. Thus the novel becomes a kind of modern folk tale with potential political overtones.

Events in History at the
Time the Novel Was Written

Politics and peasants in the 1950s. Although Atatürk's republic wrought many changes and brought reforms throughout the country, peasants and townsmen alike continued to distrust the new government. Many felt that the republic was too secular in its aims, to the point of being irreligious, even godless. They resented the abolishment of the fez, the replacement of the Arabic with the Turkish alphabet, and, above all, the lack of land redistribution and reform, which was what the peasants wanted most.

During the late 1940s, however, Turkey evolved from a one-party (Republican People's Party) to a multi-party state in which the strongest opposition was the Democratic Party. That party dominated the political scene for the next decade—from 1950, when Adnan Menderes was elected Prime Minister and Celal Bayar was elected President, until the military coup of 1960, which resulted in Menderes's being hanged along with two of his associates (Lewis, pp. 150-52). Unlike the previous regime, the Democratic Party pandered more consciously to the peasants, turning away from Atatürk's secular reforms. Religious education in public schools—restored on a voluntary basis in 1949—became compulsory in the primary grades under the Menderes government, which pleased the peasantry even as it alarmed the educated elite, many of whom had adopted Western values.

Despite their satisfaction with the new regime, the peasantry still struggled to survive. Between 1948 and 1953 the Turkish economy experienced an average annual growth rate that exceeded 12 percent. The greatest expansion occurred in the agricultural sector, due in large part to the importation of tractors and other more sophisticated farming equipment, which increased the amount of land under cultivation and resulted in greater harvests. Industrialization was to prove a mixed blessing for the rural poor, however; as mechanized agriculture became more prevalent in such regions as the Çukurova plain, agrarian laborers found themselves displaced by machines. Seeking employment, many relocated to the cities, which were ill-prepared to receive them. Makeshift shelters—called *gecekondu,* meaning "built in the night"—were erected on city outskirts to house the newcomers.

While the novel portrays the villains of his youth, Kemal wrote at a time when the sources of oppression, though different, resulted in equally degrading circumstances. As a correspondent for *Cumhuriyet,* he often wrote about the impact of mechanization on agriculture, which forced small farmers to sell their land to larger land owners, "a trend in cotton-growing areas like the Çukurova plain in the south" (Howard, p. 122). When the peasants in *Memed, My Hawk* burn the thistle fields to make the land easier to farm and to celebrate the downfall of their corrupt village *agha*, they, of course, do not anticipate that they might one day face another adversary: the two-edged sword of progress.

Reception. Turkish reaction to Kemal's novels was at first mixed. When the novel was published serially in Cumhuriyet, it was extremely popular; but when a leading publisher, Varlik, awarded *Memed, My Hawk* a prize for the best Turkish novel of the year, the novel was greeted with a "surprising critical silence" (Hickman, p. 55). In view of the overwhelming popularity of the novel when it was published serially, the critical silence may reflect a fear of recognizing a novel that portrays rebellion against social, political, and economic injustice in a society that during the 1950s was repressive not only of socialist ideas, but of any ideas that were remotely liberal or progressive. The novel, despite the critical silence, has remained continuously in print to this day, a testament to its ongoing popularity.

In England and the United States, the reception was generally positive, although sometimes mixed. Not every reviewer evinced understanding of Kemal's unique blend of oral and written traditions, so most of the negative comments may have been judging Kemal for not writing in the modern realist tradition. *The New Yorker,* for example, complained that "the workmanship is thin, so that in the end we feel that we have been given a very diluted fairy tale," while the *Times* of London found "his descriptions full of throwaway detail." *Bookmark*, however, called the novel "fascinating," and the *New York Herald Tribune* described it as having an "epic sweep and a pleasing flavor all its own" (all from Davison, pp. 746-47). More recently, Kemal's fiction has been compared to that of American novelist William Faulkner. Like Faulkner, Kemal portrays timeless features of the human condition in a context of social and historical transformation.

—Barry Tharaud and Pamela S. Loy

For More Information

Barkey, Karen. *Bandits and Bureaucrats*. Ithaca: Cornell University Press, 1994.

Davison, Dorothy P., ed. *Book Review Digest.* Vol. 57. New York: H. W. Wilson, 1962.

Gould, Andrew Gordon. *Pashas and Brigands*. Ph.D. diss., University of California at Los Angles, 1973.

Hickman, William. "Traditional Themes in the Work of Yaşar Kemal: *Ince Memed.*" *Edebiyat* 5, no. 1: 55-68.

Howard, Douglas A. *The History of Turkey*. Westport, Conn.: Greenwood Press, 2001.

Lewis, Geoffrey. *Turkey*. New York: Frederick A. Praeger, 1965.

Makal, Mahmut. *A Village in Anatolia*. Trans. Sir Wyndham Deedes. Ed. Paul Stirling. London: Valentine, Mitchell, 1965.

Öztürk, Gülsüm. "Folklore Elements and Idiomatic Expressions in Anatolia: A Study of Yaşar Kemal's Novels." Master's thesis, San Diego State University, 2001.

Robinson, Richard D. *The First Turkish Republic*. Cambridge: Harvard University Press, 1963.

Shaw, Stanford J., and Ezel Kural Shaw. *Reform, Revolution, and Republic; The Rise of Modern Turkey, 1808-1975*. Vol. 2 of *History of the Ottoman Empire and Modern Turkey*. Cambridge, U.K.: Cambridge University Press, 1977.

Stirling, Paul. *Turkish Village*. New York: John Wiley & Sons, 1965.

Yaşar Kemal. *Memed, My Hawk*. Trans. Edouard Roditi. New York: Pantheon Books, 1961.

———. *Yaşar Kemal on His Life and Art*. Trans. Eugene Lyons Hébert and Barry Tharaud. Ed. Barry Tharaud. Syracuse: Syracuse University Press, 1999.

Men in the Sun

by

Ghassan Kanafani

Ghassan Kanafani was born in Acre on the northern Mediterranean coast of Palestine in 1936. After his family moved to Jaffa, Kanafani attended a French Catholic school. His father, a lawyer and anti-British Mandate activist, was expelled to Acre at the start of the 1936 Palestinian revolt. In 1948, when Kanafani was 12 years old, his family fled Acre empty-handed to a small village in southern Lebanon, near the border, hoping to return home after the fighting ended. Overnight life changed drastically, with the family's plummeting from an upper to an under class. In 1952, Kanafani's father moved the family to Damascus, Syria, where Kanafani worked during the day and continued his studies at night. He earned his high-school certificate, then enrolled in Damascus University. Attracted to journalism, Kanafani contributed to a number of periodicals, including *al-Ra'y* (The Opinion), organ of the Arab Nationalist Movement (ANM).

In 1955 Kanafani traveled to Kuwait to teach art and sports in a government school for six years. There he was devastated to learn he had a severe form of diabetes that entailed daily insulin injections, which he self-administered until the end of his life, an ordeal he compared to his uprooting from Palestine: "When I was twelve, just as I began to perceive the meaning of life and nature around me, I was hurled down and exiled from my own country. And now, now, just as I have begun to perceive my path . . . along comes "Mr. Diabetes" who wants, in all simplicity and arrogance, to kill me" (Kanafani, *Palestine's*

THE LITERARY WORK

A novella set in Iraq and Kuwait in 1958; published in Arabic (as *Rijal fi al-shams*) in 1963, in English in 1978.

SYNOPSIS

Three Palestinian refugees who seek security and a future outside their homeland meet a grim fate without achieving their goal.

Children, p. 5). In 1960 George Habash, founder of the Popular Front for the Liberation of Palestine (PFLP), convinced Kanafani to leave Kuwait for Beirut, Lebanon, to work on *al-Hurriyah* (The Freedom). Here the writer met and married the Danish teacher Ann Hoover, and the couple had a son and daughter. Kanafani worked for several more newspapers, becoming editor-in-chief of the daily *al-Muharrir* (The Liberator), publishing the weekly *Filastin* (Palestine), and serving on the editorial board of the daily *al-Anwar* (The Lights) and as editor-in-chief of its weekly magazine. In 1969 Kanafani left the security of his job at al-Anwar to publish the weekly, *al-Hadaf* (The Goal), organ of the PFLP. He stepped into the job of official spokesman for the PFLP in 1970. Kanafani was assassinated by a car bomb on July 8, 1972. From his perspective, his political interests were always directly tied to his literary career. "Insofar as I am concerned, politics and the novel are an indivisible case" (Kanafani in Wild,

Ghassan Kanafani

p. 13). His novella remains a biting illustration
of this indivisibility, and of the Palestinian au-
thor-activist's point of view.

Events in History at the Time of the Novella

The Palestinians in Jordan. When the British
realized in 1947 that they would be unable to
strike a compromise between the Arabs and the
Jews in Palestine, they turned the whole matter
over to the United Nations, whose members
voted to partition Palestine between the two peoples. On May 14, 1948, the Jews declared statehood on the territory allotted to them. This declaration of the State of Israel led to military
confrontation between the Arabs and Jews,
which drove more than 700,000 Palestinians
from their homes and homeland. Moving outside
the newly established Jewish State, they became
a dispersed people—scattered among Lebanon,
Syria, Egypt, and Jordan. A great number of
Palestinians fled to the West Bank of the Jordan
River, which fell under the control of the Jordanian Arab Legion, and to Gaza Strip, controlled
by the Egyptian administration.

The population of Jordan skyrocketed as some
900,000 Palestinians joined the 400,000 Jordanians already there. Both groups were Arab peoples, but their backgrounds differed and the in-

flux posed a threat to the Jordanian status quo.
Jordan's King Abdullah acted to protect his people's holdings and identity. In 1950 the king issued a decree forbidding the word *Palestine* in
Jordanian documents. He labeled the Palestinian
area annexed to Jordan the "West Bank." ("East
Bank" came into use as another name for his
state, known then as the "Emirate of Transjordan.") Jordan granted citizenship to all its Palestinian population. Having taken the necessary
precautions, Abdullah was pleased to see his
population more than double and his kingdom
expanded by the addition of the West Bank.
Thereafter, many of the Palestinians sought their
fortune in the East Bank, which offered more economic opportunities. The move helped dissolve
barriers between the earlier Jordanians and newcomers. In the East Bank, the transported Palestinians engaged in agricultural and trade occupations. They remained politically conscious of
their separate identity, having undergone a long
struggle against the British Mandate and the
Zionists. Meanwhile, the earlier Jordanians, formerly nomadic Bedouins who moved between
the Arabian Peninsula and the Fertile Crescent,
continued to adjust to farming and settlement in
towns and villages.

On July 20, 1951, a Palestinian in East
Jerusalem assassinated Abdullah as he was entering the Mosque of Omar for the Friday prayer.
Abdullah's son Talal assumed the kingship for a
short while before being dethroned. His successor, King Hussein, demonstrated a remarkable
maneuverability by striking a balance between
concession and imposition of his will, especially
with Palestinian opponents. The dismissal of
General John Bagot Glubb and 36 senior British
officers from the Arab Legion on March 1, 1956,
is but one example of how his regime made concessions to the opposition in its sphere. An election in 1956 brought the opposition parties to
power in Jordan, leading to the appointment of
Sulayman al-Nabulusi, head of the National Socialists, as Prime Minister. In 1957 the king dismissed this cabinet, in the belief that his authority might easily be undermined by the
pan-Arab tendency of its members.

Politically speaking, Palestinians in Jordan
embraced the ideal of Arab unity given the fact
that since 1948 the Palestinian problem had been
treated as a general Arab cause. A number of political parties emerged among the Palestinians in
Jordan. Most of these parties—for example, the
*al-Ba`th* (Ba`th Party) and the *al-Qawmiyun al-
Arab* (Arab Nationalist Movement, ANM)—had

a strong pan-Arab ideology. Greatly impacting the political scene in Jordan were dramatic developments in the Arab world—the rise of Egypt's Gamal Abdel Nasser as a popular Arab leader (especially after the 1956 Suez War), the birth of the United Arab Republic (UAR, temporary union of Egypt and Syria) in 1958, and the coup d'état that toppled the pro-Western royal regime in Iraq that same year. Though economically they were adjusting to their new environs, many of the transported Palestinians remained emotionally tied to their homeland and showed a political restlessness about renewing their control of it. They followed events in the wider Arab world closely and weighed them against their national objective, the liberation of Palestine from Jewish control. The Jordanian establishment, a pro-Western group, whose policy was to cooperate with the United Nations, felt it necessary to crack down on dissidents. When it came to sharing official power in Jordan, the Palestinians remained at a disadvantage; appointments usually relegated Palestinian cabinet members to economic rather than political posts (Mishal, p. 42).

King Hussein struggled to gain popularity among the Palestinians of Jordan, intensifying his efforts in the late 1950s. During the fall of 1959, the king made several visits to West Bank cities trying to project the image of a caring leader. In another attempt to solidify his popularity in the Palestinian sector, the king announced on January 16, 1960, that East Jerusalem, under his control at the time, would be a second capital of Jordan and that the cabinet and parliament would meet there from time to time. The act was part of a campaign to emphasize the unity of the two banks, and it dovetailed with an Iraqi and Egyptian campaign to promote the concept of Palestinian identity.

This concerted effort to revive the Palestinian identity in the early 1960s was, in part, a response to the faltering drive to achieve Arab unity for the sake of resolving the Palestine question. A pan-Arabic alliance between Egypt and Syria fell apart, when on September 28, 1961, Syria seceded from its partnership with Egypt in the United Arab Republic. Two years later, negotiations to unify Egypt, Syria, and Iraq proved futile. The next year, 1964, saw the formation of the Palestine Liberation Organization (PLO), which held its first congress in Arab-controlled East Jerusalem. King Hussein agreed to recognize the PLO only after its chairman, Ahmad al-Shuqayri, promised not to threaten the integrity of Jordan. In 1966, when the PLO threatened the

king's authority over the Palestinians in his land, he closed its offices.

After the Arab-Israeli war of 1967, the West Bank passed into the hands of the Israelis and became subject to their occupation. At first, there was confusion regarding who held the reins of authority. To maintain its influence on the West Bank, the Jordanian government distributed payments to Palestinians who showed loyalty to the Jordanian authorities (Mishal, p. 118). In September 1970, battles broke out between the Jordanian army and the Palestinian Resistance Movement (PRM), a movement headquartered in Jordan and engaged in guerrilla warfare against the Israeli forces. Often called Black September or the Jordanian civil war, the fighting drove the armed Palestinians out of Jordan. The West Bankers' loyalty to the Jordanian throne was shaken by the conflict, giving rise to a political current that sought to secede from Jordan and establish a Palestinian entity in the occupied territories. This minority trend developed into a mainstream, majority position after 1973, when the idea of an independent West Bank state became an established part of PLO strategy. At a summit of the Arab League Council in October 1974, all the members of this pan-Arab Organization finally recognized the PLO as the sole legitimate representative of the Palestinians. The 1976 municipal elections in the West Bank, sponsored by the Israelis, proved beyond a doubt that the inhabitants there saw the PLO, not Jordan, as the object of their loyalty.

The Palestinians in Kuwait. In the field of education, the Palestinian contribution to Kuwait stems back to 1936. That year the Council of Education in Kuwait asked Amin al-Husayni, mufti (Palestine's highest Islamic religious authority) of Jerusalem and president of the Arab Higher Committee, to bring four Palestinian teachers to Kuwait. (The Arab Higher Committee [AHC] was formed to spearhead the Palestinian uprising against the British and the Zionists.) The four teachers, paid by the AHC, arrived in Kuwait on September 5, 1936 (Abu Bakr, p. 6). They were followed by two Palestinian siblings, sisters, who had been asked to start the first modern girls' school in Kuwait.

This Kuwaiti-Palestinian connection was renewed after the 1948 war, now in the economic rather than the educational realm. Most of the Palestinian pioneers to Kuwait, who hailed mainly from Jordan, came from lower- or middle-class origins. Almost everyone in this first wave had a high-school or college degree and

An early photo of the refugee camps in Beirut, Lebanon.

some working experience. A second wave of Palestinians in search of work came to Kuwait in the 1950s; unlike the first wave, this group consisted mostly of peasants, who struggled hard to adapt to city life (Ghabra, p. 63). Abu Qais in Kanafani's *Men in the Sun* is a representative of this second group.

At first, the peasantry had no means to reach Kuwait except via an underground railroad. Kuwait was still a British Protectorate at the time, and it was almost impossible for members of the second wave to obtain work visas from the British consulates in Jerusalem or Baghdad. So its members resorted to illegal tactics. Literally above ground, like the "underground railroad" used by slaves in antebellum America, this clandestine network of travel took the Palestinians on a long arduous route from Amman, Jordan, to Basra, Iraq, through Syria. Once in Basra, the "passengers" had to find a smuggler who would take them across the desert to Kuwait. Those men and boys who could make the proper arrangements were smuggled into the border area, then crossed on foot the 80-mile desert strip from Basra to Jahra (located 20 miles from Kuwait City). The trip was dangerous, for the group had to evade Kuwaiti as well as Iraqi patrols, which often meant walking up to 120 miles. Scores of people died on the desert trek. In many cases the

smuggler abandoned them (Ghabra, p. 67). Hundreds of Palestinians were captured after being smuggled into Syria, Iraq, or Kuwait, or while trying to enter these territories. By the mid-1950s, when Jordanian-Iraqi relations improved, the underground trail no longer had to pass through Syria; the Palestinians could travel directly to Baghdad and from there to Basra. Modified thus, the underground route remained operative throughout the decade.

Palestinians in Kuwait never received the refugee status attained in some other Arab countries. Kuwait did not grant them citizenship or travel documents (with a few exceptions), nor did it offer them the prospect of permanent residence. However, the size of the Palestinian community in Kuwait and the high positions it held in the bureaucracy made it an influential group. Furthermore, Palestinians were allowed to form their own unions. It was in Kuwait that the first central committee of Fath (or Fatah, the Movement for the Liberation of Palestine) was formed by Yasir Arafat, Khalid al-Hasan, Khalil al-Wazir, and Salim Za`nun, all of whom were residing in Kuwait at the time. Fath's headquarters would remain in Kuwait until 1966. The Palestinians formed a significant part of the population in Kuwait. A 1975 survey conducted by the United Nations Economic and Social Commission for

West Asia found that the Palestinians "constituted 28 percent of all [Kuwait's] engineers, 34 percent of surveyors and draftsmen, 27 of all doctors and pharmacists, 25 percent of all nursing staff, 38 percent of all economists and accountants, [and] 30 percent of the teaching staff" (Peretz, p. 22).

The harmony between Kuwait and its Palestinian community was neither absolute nor permanent, however, as shown by events that transpired between the publication of the novella in Arabic in the 1960s and its translation into English in the late 1970s. The first sign of tension emerged in 1970 during bloody clashes in Kuwait between Palestinian guerillas and the Jordanian army. In 1976, after the initial phase of the Lebanese civil war, the Kuwaiti authorities, fearing the effect of the strife on their land, closed the separate PLO schools in Kuwait and admitted Palestinian children to Kuwaiti government schools. Tensions would continue to manifest themselves in the next decade too. After the 1991 Gulf War around 350,000 Palestinians, long-time residents in the region, were expelled or forced to flee from Iraq, Kuwait, Saudi Arabia, and other Gulf countries (Farsoun and Zacharia, p. 152).

The Novella in Focus

Plot summary. *Men in the Sun* is about three uprooted Palestinians who leave Jordan for Kuwait without visas in 1958. The three are in search of work. They make arrangements in Basra, Iraq, to be smuggled over the border into Kuwait.

At the start of the story, the three Palestinians reach Basra at the same time but separately. Each one hunts for a smuggler to help him cross the border into Kuwait, the Promised Land, where their financial problems will be solved by finding work. The three men try to hire an Iraqi smuggler to help them reach Kuwait, but he turns out to be a fat, greedy man who refuses to lower the fees. He even beats up one of the three who threatens to inform the Iraqi police of the price gouger's illegal activities. When they fail to convince this professional smuggler, the three turn to Abul Khaizuran, who offers to get the job done at a discount. He will shuttle them into Kuwait in his empty water-tank truck, hiding them in the closed water tank while the officials at the checkpoints approve the driver's paperwork so he can cross the border. This plan succeeds at the Iraqi checkpoint, where the driver spends only six minutes. At the Kuwaiti crossing, however, things go awry. The bored Kuwaiti officials, in air-conditioned offices, detain Abul Khaizuran, gossiping about some juicy rumors that during his stay in Basra he was involved in a sexual encounter with a loose woman. The officials insist on getting details about this sexual encounter (ironically Abul Khaizuran is impotent). The director of the office, Abu Baqir, another fat man, refuses to clear the papers. All these interruptions delay the crossing until the three men in the airtight water tank suffocate to death. Finally cleared, Abul Khaizuran drives his truck to a Kuwaiti garbage dump and disposes of the three bodies, but only after removing their valuables and money. Before returning to his truck, he agonizes over his involvement in this senseless waste of life. "Why didn't they bang on the walls of the truck? Why?" he shouts, unable to contain himself (Kanafani, *Men in the Sun*, p. 56).

The action in the novella unfolds through a succession of flashbacks that provide background for each character. A separate section devoted to each of the adventurers (Abu Qais, Assad, and Marwan) acquaints the reader with his past and his plans for the future, starting with Abu Qais, the oldest.

Abu Qais hopes to earn enough money in Kuwait to secure the future of his family. He plans to provide his children with an education, to buy a small house, perhaps even to purchase one or two olive shoots. On his way to Kuwait, he reminisces about life in Palestine (he is the only one of the three old enough to harbor pre-1948 memories). He recalls Ustaz Selim, the new teacher from Jaffa who came to his village in Palestine. This teacher was different from his predecessors; instead of mastery over how to pray, he knew how to use arms.

> The mercy of God be upon you, Ustaz Selim, the mercy of God be upon you. God was certainly good to you when he made you die one night before the wretched village fell into the hands of the Jews. One night only. O God, is there any divine favour greater than that? You saved yourself humiliation and wretchedness, and you preserved your old age from shame.
> (*Men in the Sun*, p. 11)

Abu Qais represents the second wave of Palestinians, the peasants who traveled to Kuwait in the 1950s without any particular skill. As a peasant, he has an intimate relationship with the land: "Every time he breathed the scent of the earth, as he lay on it, he imagined that he was sniffing his wife's hair when she had just walked out of the bathroom, after washing with cold water. The very smell, the smell of a woman who had washed with cold water and covered his face with her hair while it was still damp. The same throbbing, like carrying a small bird in your hand" (*Men in the Sun*, p. 9). Abu Qais is the least adventurous among the three, perhaps because he is the oldest and is married.

For the younger Assad, Kuwait means freedom: freedom from his uncle who wants his daughter and Assad to marry. The young man hides from the authorities in Jordan because he is politically active. The smuggler who promises to help Assad reach Baghdad knows the young man's father (they fought together in Palestine in 1948). Now the smuggler, Abu-Abd, reminds young Assad of the danger of being a wanted man: "Do you think you'll spend your life here hiding? Tomorrow they'll arrest you" (*Men in the Sun*, p. 17). To avoid being caught by the border guards with a fugitive from the Jordanian regime, Abu-Abd sends the young man on a detour and promises to meet up with him beyond the checkpoint. But when Assad reaches the highway, he waits in vain for his father's friend and finally hitches a ride from a tourist. A determined Assad reaches Basra. There he negotiates with the smuggler Abul Khaizuran, not only for himself but also for his two companions. He gets Abul Khaizuran to admit that his job is not really transporting water but smuggling goods for Haj Rida, a Kuwaiti merchant. Smuggling people is just a sideline that brings in extra money. Certainly this sideline is risky, but in need of the money, he takes the risk.

Marwan, the youngest of the three, had to leave school at an early age to provide for his family. His brother is already working in Kuwait, but not for the family. He abandoned his financial responsibility toward them when he married. Marwan's father has also abandoned the family. He left his wife and four children to marry a one-legged woman who owns a three-room house, hoping to gain some financial security by renting out two of the three rooms.

Although he is a pivotal character, the driver, Abul Khaizuran, is not given his own section in the novella. He fought in the 1948 war in Palestine and paid dearly when he was wounded in battle and "lost his manhood." Since then, the impotent driver keeps repeating to himself the following refrain: "He had lost his manhood and his country, and damn everything in this bloody world" (*Men in the Sun*, p. 38).

Pan-Arabism. Behind the scenes of this novella is the specter of a great ideological and actual tension between pan-Arabism and the predilection to align oneself with a specific Arabic state such as Jordan, Palestine, or Kuwait. The fate of the novella's three victims can be read as a critique of specific nationalism, a force contrary to the drive for pan-Arabism, whose own roots are in the medieval era. In 1258 the Mongols conquered Baghdad, capital of the Abbasid Empire. Arabs lost their political independence and after that were ruled, in one form or another, by foreign powers until the end of World War II. In the second half of the nineteenth century, the Arabs began to identify themselves as a unit in a larger sphere; for them, as for other peoples, the era gave birth to a nationalistic impulse.

Among the pioneers of Arab nationalism—although his ideas were charged with religious overtones—was Abd al-Rahman al-Kawakibi (1849-1903). He harshly criticized the Ottoman sultan Abdülhamid for his despotism. Al-Kawakibi advocated granting the Arabs, rather than the Turks, the political power to rule the Muslims. Meanwhile, some Christian Arabs started contemplating the notion of Arabs' uniting to become one nation with a distinctive cultural identity. These intellectuals expressed their views through different platforms. In the last quarter of the nineteenth century, Butrus al-Bustani (1819-83) used his periodical *al-Jinan* (The Gardens) to foster a bond among the Arabs while maintaining Ottoman loyalty. A number of secret societies were formed in greater Syria calling for unity and autonomy, mostly by graduates of European and American missionary schools that had been set up in the Middle East in the 1860s. These schools, which emphasized the Arabic language and its literature in contrast to Turkish culture, helped raise a national consciousness among their students.

The political aspect of Arab nationalism manifested itself in the works and activities of a pioneering generation of intellectuals who resisted all attempts to assimilate the Arabs into larger Turkish society. One of these theorists, Negib Azoury (d. 1916), Lebanese by birth and French by education, set out to articulate his political views on Arab nationalism. He founded a political party (*Ligue de la Patrie arabe*—League of Arab Party) and published a monthly periodical (*L'Indépendence arabe*—Arab Independence). But most importantly, he published a book (1905, *Le Reveil de la nation arabe*—The Dream of the Arab Nation) that advocates the existence of one Arab nation that resides in Asia and includes both Muslims and Christians. This nation would be entitled to political independence from the Turks.

In addition to writings that promoted it, the idea of nationhood began to manifest itself in politics as early as the second decade of the twentieth century. In 1913 a group of individuals organized an Arab congress in Paris. Some 25 persons attended the congress; roughly half were Muslims and half Christians. The participants demanded the Ottoman Empire grant the Arabs certain rights. In the sphere of culture, they demanded Arabic be recognized as an official language in parliament as well as in local government (Hourani, p. 484).

After World War I, Qustantin Zurayq, an Orthodox Christian from Damascus, Syria, and a professor of history at the American University of Beirut, devoted himself to articulating the concept of Arab nationalism. In 1939 he published *al-Wa`y al-Qawmi* (The National Consciousness), a volume of essays on national identity. Zurayq analyzes the situation of the modern Arabs; they are in need, he concludes, of the sense of collective responsibility related to nationalism, which in their case draws its inspiration and principles from a religion. For Arabs, this religion can only be Islam, a surprising conclusion perhaps from a Christian, though Zurayq goes on to distinguish "the religious spirit" (*al-ruh al-diniyah*) from "sectarian solidarity" (*al-asabiyah al-ta'ifiyah*).

Another major Arab theorist, Sati al-Husri (1881-1968), rejects the British and French schools of thought that say a nation is any group that wants to be a nation. A nation to him is something that truly exists: a man is or is not an Arab whether or not he wants to be. One of the most important components of nationalism is a common language. The Arab nation, he argues, consists of all who speak Arabic as their mother tongue, no more, no less. Second to language comes history; a common history is important but only secondary.

Events as well as individuals contributed to the development of pan-Arabism. The Arab defeat in Palestine in 1948 was followed by intense soul-searching in the Arab world. The fragmentation of the Arab peoples was singled out as a major cause for the loss of Palestine. It followed that achieving Arab unity became a prerequisite for liberating Palestine. The intellectuals of the day, inspired by the earlier Arab thinkers named above, responded positively to this call. Zurayq's political views were particularly influential among a group of Arab students at the American University of Beirut. In 1951-52, led by two

Palestinian medical students there—George Habash, (b. 1925?) and Wadi Haddad (1927-1978)—they founded a political movement. It took the name *Harakat al-Qawmiyin al-Arab* (Arab Nationalist Movement, ANM), and its main objectives were fighting political fragmentation, imperialism, and Israel. "To Habash," writes Walid Kazziha, "the loss of Palestine was not only a national disaster, but also a painful personal experience. His feelings were shared equally by his close friend Haddad and by a number of their colleagues from different parts of the Arab world" (Kazziha, p. 18). In 1954 Habash started the weekly *al-Ra'y* (The Opinion) in Amman, Jordan, as an organ for the ANM. When it became critical of the pro-Western Arab governments in the Middle East, the Jordanian authorities ordered its closure. A few months later, the same weekly reappeared in Damascus, Syria, then was replaced

AN ALLEGORICAL TRUCK DRIVER?

Some scholars speak of *Men in the Sun* as a political allegory in which Abul Khaizuran plays a key part: "Abul Khaizuran, the truck driver, represents the Palestinian leadership at the time, emasculated and impotent, having 'lost his manhood' in 1948 in the first Arab-Israeli war . . . He bargains over rates with the three Palestinians . . . once they are dead [he] avails himself of their wristwatches" (Harlow, pp. 48-49).

by *al-Hurriyah* (The Freedom), published in Beirut. As noted, Kanafani worked on both periodicals.

Soon the ANM established branches outside Lebanon in Jordan, Syria, Iraq, and Kuwait. With the rise of the Egyptian popular leader Gamal Abdel Nasser in the 1950s, especially after he forged the Egyptian-Syrian union that became the United Arab Republic in 1958, the line between the ANM and Nasserism became hard to draw. The dissolution of the united republic in 1961 touched off a shift in the Arab Nationalist Movement. Its members turned to Marxism-Leninism, adopting it as the way to achieve "real" national unity, forged among the masses rather than regimes. The Arab defeat in the 1967 War would only deepen the movement's commitment to socialist policy. In keeping with its pan-Arabism, the doctrine of popular resistance against the Israeli occupation, rather than traditional military confrontation by the forces of separate regimes, became an attractive one.

The dissolution of the union between Egypt and Syria disheartened Kanafani, along with other pan-Arabists. The evaporation of the Arab dream to unite for the liberation of Palestine contributed to the rise of a separate Palestinian consciousness. This consciousness would find concrete expression in the formation of the PLO a year after the release of *Men in the Sun*. In fact, the novella itself can be seen as one of the first manifestations of the quest for Palestinian identity. It can also be seen as an indictment against larger Arabic society, including the Palestinians, for their homelessness. In Kanafani's story, both the price-gouging Iraqi smuggler and the Kuwaiti border officials contribute to the demise of the three passengers. The truck driver, a Palestinian

---

MEN IN THE SUN ON FILM

~

In 1972 the Egyptian director Tawfiq Salih adapted *Men in the Sun* as a black-and-white feature film called al-*Makhdu`un* (*The Dupes*). The film was banned in some Arab countries because of its perceived criticism of Arab regimes. A striking difference between the novella and the film lies in the ending. In the novella, the three men inside the water tank suffocate silently under the blazing sun. The driver, as noted, asks "Why didn't you knock on the sides of the tank?" In the film, however, the victims knock continuously on the sides of the tank, crying, "We are here, we are dying, let us out, let us free." Kanafani, who viewed the film several times before his death, did not disapprove of the altered ending (Harlow, pp. 53).

---

leader of sorts (after all, he promises to shuttle them safely to Kuwait), fails to deliver.

Sources and literary context. While Kanafani's stay in Kuwait can be seen as his formative years, his period in Lebanon (1960-72) was productive in terms of literary as well as journalistic writings. He began publishing his fiction in the early 1960s, with two collections of short stories—*Mawt sarir raqm 12* (Death of Bed No. 12) in 1961 and *Ard al-burtuqal al-hazin* (Land of Sad Oranges) in 1963. This same year saw the publication of his first novella—*Men in the Sun*. Kanafani's own car trip from Kuwait to Damascus in 1959,

coupled with other information regarding smuggling Palestinians from Amman to Kuwait, helped inspire the story.

Influential on Kanafani's writing was an array of literary works. While still in Syria, Kanafani began reading, most probably in Arabic translation, Western literature, including works by Charles Dickens, Honoré de Balzac, and Fyodor Dostoyevsky. He is known to have read Soviet literature during his stay in Kuwait (1955-60), particularly the works of Maksim Gorky. "I admired and still do the Soviet writers," Kanafani stated, "my admiration was absolute" (Kanafani in Abd al-Hadi, p. 17).

Kanafani sets his plot in 1958, ten years after the refugees left Palestine, a long enough interval to discourage them from making their way homeward. In fact, they are heading in the opposite direction, a reality that reduces the degree of sentimentality in *Men in the Sun*. Other novels of the decade (George Hanna's *Laji'ah* [1952; A Woman Refugee], or Isa al-Na`uri's *Bayt wara'a al-hudud* [1959; A House Beyond Borders]) were charged with heavy doses of sentimentality, so Kanafani's work stood in contradistinction to other Arabic fiction depicting the Palestinian dilemma at the time.

Composition and reception. *Men in the Sun* was written in January 1962, during a month in which Kanafani remained hidden at home in Beirut because he had no legal documentation. Prior to its publication, poetry was the genre through which the Palestinian ordeal was depicted. This poetry, in general, tended to highlight the suffering of the uprooted Palestinians caused by the *other*, whether that other was a Zionist or a European power. Kanafani's novella charged Palestinians with aiding and abetting their own victimization, and the revelation shocked the average reader (the novel's Assad is tricked by his father's Palestinian friend; the Palestinian driver does nothing to save his three passengers, then disposes of their corpses in a garbage dump after stealing their valuables). "At the time when the book was published," writes Hilary Kilpatrick, "many readers took the ending literally and Kanafani was accused by enraged compatriots of 'throwing Palestinians on the garbage heap'" (Kilpatrick in Kanafani, p. 3). Most critics, though, hailed *Men in the Sun* as an accomplished literary work, and the Palestinian critic F. Mansur applauded it as the first serious attempt to highlight the refugees' plight (Mansur, p. 211). The Egyptian literary historian Hamdi al-Sakkut goes further and endorses the idea that *Men in the Sun* is the first Palestinian novel in the full sense of what defines the genre. Al-Sakkut applauds Kanafani's courage in describing the Palestinian's plight in an innovative manner: "The author is to be commended for openly proclaiming through his novel an opinion on which the overwhelming majority of Palestinians and Jordanians generally disagree" (Sakkut, p. 78). The brave, unpopular opinion referred to here is that Arabs, including Palestinians, are complicit in the Palestinians' plight.

—Joseph Zeidan

For More Information

Abd al-Hadi, Fayh. *Wa`d al-ghad: dirasa fi adab Ghassan Kanafani.* Amman: Dar al-Karmal li-al-Nashr wa-al-Tawzi, 1987.

Abu Bakr, Tawfiq. *al-Filastiniyun fi al-Kuwayt 1936-1990 wa-azmat al-Khalij, 1936 M-1990 M.* Amman: Markaz Janin lil-Dirasat al-Istiratijiyah, 2000.

Farsoun, Samih K., and Christina E. Zacharia. *Palestine and the Palestinians.* Boulder: Westview Press, 1997.

Ghabra, Shafeeq N. *Palestinians in Kuwait: The Family and the Politics of Survival.* Boulder: Westview Press, 1987.

Harlow, Barbara. *After Lives: Legacies of Revolutionary Writing.* London: Verso, 1996.

Hourani, Albert. *Arabic Thought in the Liberal Age 1798-1939.* London: Oxford University Press, 1970.

Kanafani, Ghassan. *Men in the Sun.* Trans. Hilary Kilpatrick. Washington D.C.: Three Continents Press, 1978.

———. *Palestine's Children: Returning to Haifa and Other Stories.* Trans. Barbara Harlow and Karen E. Riley. Boulder: Lynne Reinner, 2000.

Kazziha, Walid W. *Revolutionary Transformation in the Arab World: Habash and His Comrades from Nationalism to Marxism.* London: Charles Knight, 1975.

al-Mansur, F. "Ghassan Kanafani fi kutubihi al-ahad ashar." *Shu'un Filastiniyah* 13 (September 1972): 205-21.

Mishal, Shaul. *West Bank/East Bank: The Palestinian in Jordan 1949-1967.* New Haven: Yale University Press, 1978.

Peretz, D. *Israel and the Palestinian Arabs.* Washington, D.C.: Middle East Institute, 1958.

Sakkut, Hamdi. *The Arabic Novel: Bibliography and Critical Introduction (1865-1995).* Vol. 1. Cairo: The American University in Cairo Press, 2000.

Wild, Stefan. *Ghassan Kanafani: The Life of a Palestinian.* Wiesbaden: Otto Harrassowitz, 1975.

Miramar

by
Najib Mahfuz

Born December 11, 1911, in the al-Gamaliyah neighborhood of Cairo, Egypt, Najib Mahfuz (also spelled Naguib Mahfouz) is the most renowned figure in Arabic literature today. He has gained this distinction not only because he is the only Arab writer to date to have won the Nobel Prize for Literature (1988) but also because his fiction evinces a profound understanding of human nature at large and of the Egyptian consciousness in particular. To read Mahfuz's literature is to encounter Egypt and Egyptians in a deeply reflective way. Mahfuz is often described as the writer of Cairo's middle class because his fiction deals with transformations that have affected it throughout the twentieth century. He is a novelist, short-story writer, and playwright. Mahfuz's fiction has frequently been divided into four categories: novels that center on history (1939-44); realistic/naturalistic novels (1945-52); symbolic, metaphysical, and existentialist narratives (1960s); and, from the 1970s until today, novels inspired by local sources, folktales, and Sufism. In 1952 Mahfuz completed *The Trilogy*, his *magnum opus*, the story of a middle-class family of Cairo before and during the 1919 revolution. He abstained from writing for the next few years, meanwhile studying the new revolutionary regime, and absorbing the sensibilities of the new period. After this silence, he produced another major work, *Awlad haratina* (1959; *Children of Gebelawi*, 1981), an allegorical novel about the descendants of a common ancestor. Next came *Liss wa-al-kilab* (1961; *The Thief and the Dogs*, 1984) and then novels that broke completely from his earlier techniques

THE LITERARY WORK

A novel set in Alexandria, Egypt, in 1967; published in Arabic in 1967, in English in 1978.

SYNOPSIS

The lives of seven strangers, five men and two women, intersect at an Alexandrian pension called Miramar.

and portrayals. *Miramar,* the last novel Mahfuz wrote in the 1960s, belongs to this phase of experimentation. The novel focuses on the clash between the old and new regimes, exploring the emotional trauma related to the loss of recently espoused nationalist ideals, as well as the coercive reality of Egypt in the 1960s.

Events in History at the Time of the Novel

Revolutionary overview. *Miramar* takes place during the 1960s in the city of Alexandria. However, a number of its characters are vestiges of an earlier period of Egyptian society. Egypt underwent some major political and social changes in the late nineteenth and early twentieth centuries, from occupation by the British, to local uprisings against the occupation, to the birth of an uncompromising nationalist movement. Resistance to the occupation persisted, leading to the Egyptian Revolution of 1952 (which abolished the monar-

Najib Mahfuz

was introduced, limiting landownership to 200 *feddans* per person or 300 per family (a *feddan* being somewhat larger than an acre). A blow to the wealthy landowners, the reform made the fledgling regime wildly popular with the peasants, obviously less so with the dispossessed landowners. In 1953 Egypt terminated its monarchy and declared itself a republic. A struggle for power ensued, leading to military purges, press crackdowns, pro-democracy demonstrations, and waves of arrests. The regime had begun to take repressive measures.

From pre- to post-revolutionary Egypt. *Miramar* peeks into the psyche of a few characters who together comprise a sample of Egyptians trying to adjust to the new social order. There is no attempt to glorify the old regime or to side with the new one. The novel simply explores the tensions that arise when supporters of pre-revolutionary Egypt encounter proponents of the post-revolutionary regime.

Pre-revolutionary Egypt was subject to 70 years of occupation by the British. They first arrived in 1882, intending to capitalize on Egypt's resources and maintain control over British trade routes to India. Almost immediately some Egyptians, led by Colonel Ahmad Urabi, mounted an army revolt against the occupiers, and other revolts followed. In 1919, for example, there was another revolt that saw Egyptian men and, for the first time, women marching down the streets, demanding independence. Prompting the revolt was a British decision to deport Sa`d Zaghlul, whose Wafd Party led the drive for national independence. By the mid-twentieth century, Egypt had experienced the rise of this and other political groups as well as increasing civil unrest against the British occupation. All this activism was in some measure a response to the weakness of Egypt's own monarch, King Faruq, and to the growing gap between large landowners and pauperized peasants as well as the rest of the land's rich and poor. Egypt was ripe for fundamental change.

On July 23, 1952, a group of army officers, the Free Officers, seized power, and forced King Faruq to abdicate. On July 24, Faruq sailed into exile and with this the 150-year-old monarchy (1805-1952) came to an end. The Free Officers established themselves as an army regime and the creators of a new order, distinct from the previous regime and its factions (such as the Wafd and the Muslim Brotherhood). Seeking independent legitimacy, the officers promoted a moderate brand of Islam and secular rule. Nasser emerged as the undisputed leader of the new order, thanks

chy and established Egypt as a republic), followed by Britain's evacuation in 1956. Emerging as leader of the Revolution, Gamal Abdel Nasser introduced an idealistic program of economic plans and political changes that aimed to forever alter the face of Egyptian society. The program promised to move Egypt away from the old feudal system to a new socialist regime that would redistribute wealth equally among its citizens. Pre-revolutionary Egypt has often been described as the "half-percent society," meaning only half a percent of the population (the ruling elites and upper class) was rich; everyone else belonged to the lower-middle and poorer classes. There was no upper-middle class to speak of, but this promised to change with the success of the Revolution. The revolutionaries espoused six principles: to end 1) imperialism, 2) the inequitable land system, and 3) capitalist monopolies, and to establish 4) social justice, 5) a strong military, and 6) true democratic rule. As it turned out, some people (for example, the newly established army bureaucracy and landless peasant) would benefit greatly from the transformations that did take place; others (such as politicians, businessmen, and the anti-reformist pre-revolutionary landowners) would suffer huge losses.

The 1950s saw some early reforms aimed at realizing the ideals. In 1952 a sweeping land reform to his ability to marshal mass support. Stepping into the presidency in 1956, he placed high on his agenda some sweeping objectives: to eliminate colonialism across the Arab world, to unify all Arabs, and to prepare for the struggle against Israel. These objectives amounted to the core of Nasser's ideology, which won him great popularity in the Arab world. He came to be regarded as a latter-day Arab hero.

In 1961 Nasser introduced some later reforms—a program of decrees characterized as social justice in contrast to the pre-revolutionary capitalism and feudalism. New laws were created to further dispossess the upper class and large landowners. The regime nationalized banks and insurance companies, as well as some heavy industrial and shipping companies. Other companies, textile manufacturers, for example, became partially state-owned. Justifying itself, the regime said the newly dispossessed were foreigners and Egyptian monopoly holders who ought not to be in charge of these important national assets. In 1962 Nasser issued a document, the Socialist Charter, which outlined a new ideology that his regime adopted. The document was based on the idea that a socialist transformation was inevitable, indeed imperative, for the much needed radical changes to transpire. His charter was followed by the formation of a huge political enterprise, The Arab Socialist Union (ASU), an untraditional alliance of peasants, workers, the army, and the intelligentsia. The ASU aimed to guide the masses and protect their rights. Throughout the 1960s, it influenced education, production, aesthetics, prices, and even sports, ultimately turning into a force that coerced society to conform to its policies. Arab socialism made progress on another front too—that of women—committing itself to social and economic egalitarianism across gender lines. The Charter "proclaimed that women and men should be considered equal working partners," and it took on the responsibility of representing both. As a national coalition that represented popular authority, the ASU would continue to stand at the center of power past the time of the novel, until it was liquidated by President Anwar al-Sadat in 1971.

Education. An element that figures in *Miramar's* storyline, education was one of the major reform initiatives of the Revolution. Nasser's Socialist Charter called for free schooling and medical facilities for all. The principles of socialism, Arabism, national consciousness, and freedom were furthermore to be infused into the educational curricula. As the regime became increasingly authoritarian, however, the gap between this lip service to the promotion of freedom and the reality of repression became increasingly clear. There was also a practical problem when it came to providing free education for all. The numbers of students at all educational levels increased to an alarming degree, taxing the existing resources. The result was an inevitable deterioration in the quality of education. No wonder, in view of their own frustrating conditions, that many students went on to become political activists and attach themselves to communist parties and radical religious societies, among other groups, in their search for better solutions. It should be noted here that Nasser always had a tense relationship with the communist elements inside and outside Egypt. He regarded them as a threat to his leadership and worked on rooting them out. One of the characters in *Miramar* is a young communist.

The turbulent sixties. The 1960s saw Nasser enter into a period of great popularity with the Arab world, in which he was viewed as a hero for his Arab nationalist fervor. His attention during this period was diverted from Egypt to "an inter-Arab international role" (Hopwood, p. 58). To solidify his pan-Arab leadership he unified Egypt with Syria in February 1958. Tension developed between Nasser and rulers across the Arab world, who saw this merger as a latent opportunity for Nasser to centralize Arab rule in Egypt. Some of those tensions escalated into open conflicts. By the mid-sixties, "the Arab world was more divided than ever. Syria was quarrelling with Egypt and Iraq; in Yemen, Egypt and Saudi Arabia, and to some extent Jordan, were fighting on opposing sides, and there were other inter-Arab disputes" (Hopwood, p. 67). Egypt intervened on the side of the anti-monarchical rebels in Yemen's civil war, and the cost turned out to be enormous. To fund the tens of thousands of Egyptian troops sent into Yemen, the Egyptian regime had to drain its coffers of funds needed to address problems at home—in education, for instance, as detailed above. Consequently the line between those who benefited from the 1952 Revolution and those who lost out because of it became more blurred. Now the newly endowed were losing out too. Those who profited from the changes moved closer to those who felt cheated by them.

When the Syro-Egyptian unity dissolved in 1961, the failure weakened Nasser's position in the Arab world. The next year Nasser acted to restore his leadership of Arab nationalism by issuing the National Charter. This charter outlined the path of Egyptian development by way of Arab socialism (as detailed above) and committed Egypt to exporting its revolution to all Arab states. It was with this commitment in mind that Nasser involved Egypt in the Yemeni Civil War, which pitted a reactionary theocracy against a dissenting faction that called for reforming Yemen into a republic. As with the United States in the Vietnam War, the outside powers who sent troops into Yemen found themselves entangled far longer than anticipated. The soaring costs of Egypt's involvement (1962-67) threw its whole economy out of balance. Not only did the financial drain cripple its ability to meet domestic needs, it compromised Egypt's international strength as well. Some of its finest troops were in Yemen when conflict with Israel broke out in 1967 (Hopwood, p. 65).

By then the drive for Arab unity, which Nasser had spearheaded for years, had backfired. The Arab world was more divided than ever and domestic disharmony plagued Egypt too. The Arab Socialist Union (ASU), which considered itself the "guardian and repository of the regime's ideology," failed to educate its activists, who were steadily increasing in numbers and forming a wide and unproductive bureaucracy (Baker, p. 113). This, along with the nationalization schemes of 1961 and 1962 (which did indeed lead to state ownership of all large-scale enterprises and resources) bred this inflated bureaucracy, whose members were too ill trained to administer efficiently. Privileges were abused, and the organization developed into a personal power base for its leader, Ali Sabri, among others. The impression spread that the ASU had formed a "spy-system designed to infiltrate the various hierarchies of the state and to report deviations" (Baker, p. 111).

Meanwhile, the Egyptian population increased substantially throughout the sixties, and people recognized the lower quality of education and fewer employment opportunities in the countryside as opposed to the cities. As a result, massive migration ensued from rural to urban centers such as Cairo, Alexandria, and Port Said, leading to overcrowding and various economic stresses on these centers.

Ironically, amidst all this unrest, the position of women improved. The number of female students increased steadily, and women entered most areas of white-collar and professional work; indeed, "the only positions they have not occupied are judge and head of state. . . . By 1957 two women had been elected to the national as-sembly, and by 1962 a woman, Dr. Hikmat Abu Zayd, had been appointed minister of social affairs by Nasser" (Ahmed, pp. 209, 210). Moreover, the 1950s-70s were active decades on the feminist front; women started to openly discuss traditionally taboo subjects such as contraception and to call for reform of the Personal Status Code, a body of law on issues of direct importance to women (divorce, polygamy, child custody, and so forth).

Alexandria. The northern coastline of Alexandria, the second largest city in Egypt, abuts the Mediterranean Sea. In climate and character, the city appears to be more Mediterranean than Middle Eastern. Alexandria's charm and historical aura have attracted poets, historians, and tourists since Alexander the Great founded the city in 332 B.C.E. It quickly became a pivotal trading port and a crossroads of many cultures. The city contains ruins and monuments of almost all the ancient civilizations, from pagan Egyptian, to Greek and Roman, to Jewish, Christian, and Islamic. For centuries, its population was a fusion of Greeks, Italians, Armenians, Maltese, and Lebanese, as well as Egyptians. The lifestyles and businesses of the foreign communities lent the city a cosmopolitan air. After the Revolution, this foreign population gradually left the city, making way for a more thoroughly Egyptian population. The emigration eroded much of the city's cosmopolitan verve. Over the last 40 years, the foreign community has dwindled to a tiny percentage, made up mostly of elderly people without the energy or strength to revive the past Mediterranean society. Still the city retains a distinct image in Egyptian society.

Alexandria is Egypt's most celebrated beach city; Egyptians themselves call it the bride (*arus*) of the Mediterranean. In their consciousness, Alexandria represents freedom from the restraints of serious concerns, and in keeping with its relaxing effect on guests, the city has come to represent a contrast to the stressful hustle and bustle of Cairo. Escaping the summer heat, which sweeps most of the Egyptian heartland, vacationers invade Alexandria in June to August in droves, seeking out its Mediterranean beaches and cool evening breezes. In the fall and winter months, the weather is frequently cold, windy, and rainy. During these seasons, the city often attracts people searching for solitude or for a hiding place. It is this aspect of the city that Najib Mahfuz weaves into the fabric of his novel. His choice of winter, as opposed to summer (the popular season), evokes an atmosphere conducive to hiding.

Alexandria, Egypt, in the 1960s.

The Novel in Focus

Plot summary. Unlike many of Mahfuz's novels, which are set in Cairo and tell the story of middle-class families, *Miramar* takes place in Alexandria and tells of a brief encounter among strangers. The lives of five men and two women intersect when they encounter one another at an Alexandrian *pension* (bed-and-breakfast) called Miramar. The five guests are

- **Amer Wagdi** An elderly retired political journalist in his 80s. Wagdi is a former activist in the nationalist Wafd Party; he participated in its 1919 revolt against the British.
- **Tulba Marzuq** Now elderly, Marzuq once served the king as a retainer; a former enemy of the Wafd and large landowner, he has been stripped of his holdings by Nasser's agrarian reforms.
- **Sarhan el-Behayri** About 30, el-Behayri is a member of the Arab Socialist Union and an opportunist who has profited from the Revolution.
- **Hosni Allam** A young uneducated landowner and playboy, Allam despises the new regime for elevating education above inherited landownership.
- **Mansur Bahi** This 25-year-old intellectual and communist believes in noble causes but does not back up his beliefs with action; Bahi betrays his fellow communists and fails to honor his promises to the woman he loves.

These five people, although unrelated to one another, connect spatially and emotionally. Aside from sharing the hospitality of Pension Miramar, they are all attracted to its beautiful maid, Zohra (a corruption of the word *zahra*, "flower"). She has fled her village to escape an arranged marriage to a much older man. The pension's owner knew Zohra's late father. The owner, Mariana, is an elderly Greek woman, who has been married twice. Her first husband, an English officer, was killed in the revolt of 1919, and her second, a rich grocer, went bankrupt and committed suicide. Thereafter she became the mistress of a number of wealthy men. Mariana knows the first two guests—Amer Wagdi and Tulba Marzuq—from the distant past (she sometimes refers to Tulba Marzuq as an old flame). A third guest, Mansur Bahi, has a brother she knows (a police detective) as well, but she has had no previous contact with Bahi himself. Nor has she ever met her two other guests—Sarhan el-Behayri and Hosni Allam—before now.

Amer Wagdi arrives at Pension Miramar first, followed by the rest of the lodgers. The story is told from the viewpoints of four of the male guests, beginning with Wagdi and moving on to Allam, Bahi, and finally el-Behayri. The fifth guest, Tulba, is not given a narrative voice. Each of the first four sections tells the same story, but from the perspective of the guest who narrates that section, starting with the guest's arrival at the pension and ending with the death of Sarhan el-Behayri. The same guest, Amer Wagdi, begins and ends the novel, unifying it. In his final section, the mystery of el-Behayri's death is unraveled and the maid Zohra leaves the pension for good.

With the exception of the owner, Mariana, every character in the pension is there to escape personal problems. As a group, they represent different generations, social classes, and levels of education and are all suspicious of one another. El-Behayri's arrival marks a shift in the pace and rhythm of the narrative, however. Both professionally secure and seemingly successful, he appears to be the model post-revolutionary citizen. This wins him no friends among the guests at the pension. Since almost everyone in the guesthouse has been scorched by the new regime, they all unite in despising him, except for Zohra, who falls in love with him. By this time, she has become the object of desire (or at the very least interest) of all the guests at the pension, and their hatred for el-Behayri only increases when she prefers him over all of them. According to the ideals of the new socialist society, a match between Zohra and Sarhan el-Behayri would be perfect, given that one of the major principles of the Revolution is to wipe out the old class system. But, idealism aside, el-Behayri hardly thinks an alliance with a maid will improve his social standing. In his stream-of-consciousness narration, he admits that he loves Zohra but cannot bring himself to marry her.

> Some inner voice tells me that I have been taking the girl's feelings too lightly and that God will not look kindly on me. But I can't come to terms with the idea of marrying her. Love is only an emotion and you can cope with it one way or another, but marriage is an institution, a corporation not unlike the company I work for, with its own accepted laws and regulations. What's the good of going into it, if it doesn't give me a push up the social ladder? And if the bride has no career, how can we compete in that rat race, socially or otherwise?
>
> (Mahfuz, *Miramar*, p. 112)

Realizing what might be going on in his mind, Zohra, who is an illiterate peasant, decides to get an education. She seeks out a schoolteacher and neighbor, Aleya, to educate her.

Aleya, another product of the Revolution, represents the new career-oriented and secular middle-class woman. She impresses el-Behayri as a woman who can contribute to his upward social mobility, so he proposes to her and hides this fact from Zohra. When she finds out, the jilted maid goes straight to Aleya's parents and tells them of his romantic advances and promises to her. They immediately break off their daughter's engagement, and Mariana makes him leave the pension. She also asks Zohra to leave. Meanwhile, el-Behayri's own corrupt and shady dealings are revealed; the authorities unearth his plot to embezzle funds and shipments from his company and, desperate and ashamed, he commits suicide. The fact that he dies by his own hand remains unknown until the end of the novel; for a while it seems that any of the other four pension guests may have murdered him, since each has an encounter with him the day he is found dead in a narrow, deserted alleyway. In fact, Mansur Bahi talks himself into believing that he has killed el-Behayri in defense of Zohra's honor and turns himself in to the police. At the end of his narration (the third account of the events), Mansur Bahi follows el-Behayri into a bar and then into a narrow alleyway with the intention of killing him. There he springs himself on el-Behayri, who we later discover has a razor in his pocket with which to cut his own arteries, which he does. However, before el-Behayri kills himself, Bahi hits him hard. Reeling from the blow, el-Behayri falls down in a near faint so Bahi believes that he has killed the man.

By the time the truth about el-Behayri's suicide comes out, Hosni Allam has already made up his mind to leave the pension. He purchases a nightclub from a foreigner who is seeking to liquidate his business in Egypt. Bahi is given a short prison sentence, presumably for attempted murder, and Zohra leaves. Although heartbroken over her episode with el-Behayri, she tells Amer Wagdi, who has been a good friend to her, that she will persevere and improve her life. Two guests remain in the pension, Wagdi and Marzuq, along with Mariana. The novel ends with Amer Wagdi reciting a passage from the Quran. He reads an excerpt from the Surah of the Beneficent.

Narrative voice and gender. Every chapter in *Miramar* is the inner voice of one of four guests at the Pension Miramar. These inner voices complement one another, each one commenting on the other characters and on external events in the novel from a subjective point of view. The buildup of the four personal accounts creates two levels of reality: an outer social reality shared by all characters, and an inner, more personal one related by individual voices. The shift from one narrative voice to another affects the way readers come to view the world of the novel; with every fresh voice, a new layer is added to the outer reality. The narrative technique creates a sense of alienation and detachment, depicting the characters as enclosed within their own private world/voice and, therefore, not totally in touch with their outer surroundings. Their separate narrative voices underscore the fact that humans can live under the same circumstances and share the same public space but experience a common event differently. In fact, the narrative mode undermines the contrived social rapport among the characters who happen to find themselves residing together at the Pension Miramar. If one takes society at the pension as a microcosm of the Egyptian nation in the late 1960s, then the suggestion is that any semblance of cohesion among the factions of society in this era is contrived. Hosni Allam comments on the insincere camaraderie among the lodgers:

> The whiskey draws us together in a sort of familiarity, but I know it won't last, that there will never be any real friendship between me and Sarhan [el-Behayri] and Mansour [Bahi], at most a transitory intimacy that will soon evaporate.
>
> (*Miramar*, p. 62)

The more their inner monologues reveal the extent of their intolerance for one another, the more affected and tense the external reality seems.

Again the suggestion is that Nasser's Egypt after the mid-1960s was afflicted with the same uneasiness. *Miramar* brings into focus this uneasiness. The novel depicts society as split between remnants of an old regime (Wagdi, Allam, Marianna, and Marzuq) and builders of a new one (el-Behayri, Zohra, Bahi, and Aleya). It furthermore exposes divisions among members within the new order, such as the one between the educated (Aleya) and illiterate (Zohra).

If there was divisiveness though, there was also progress in some respects. The novel illustrates this in relation to women. Since the four voices

---

A DECADE OF CONFUSION

"The sixties was indeed a decade of confusion, a decade of numerous huge projects and the abolition of almost all political activities; massive industrialization and the absolute absence of freedom; the construction of the High Dam and the destruction of the spirit of opposition; the reclamation of thousands of acres and the catastrophic detachment of the Sinai peninsula from Egyptian territory in the defeat of 1967; severe censorship and the emergence of evasive jargon among the intellectuals; deformation of social values and the students' and workers' upheavals; the enlargement of the public sector and the pervasive growth of corruption. During this decade, there was no public activity not subject to official control, everywhere one encountered not living but official beings concealing their individual personalities beneath a carapace of conformity, people who acted out social roles and repeated, automatically, slogans that were often contrary to their real hidden opinions."

(Hafez in Boullata, p. 171)

---

that relate the action in the novel are all men, and it is their stream of consciousness that is conveyed to the reader, the novel could be construed as a male narrative. Neither Zohra nor Mariana, both central characters, is given a narrative voice. Their actions and points-of-view are narrated by way of the subjective expression and thoughts of the four males. In spite of this seeming gender imbalance, Zohra and Mariana, as well as the neighbor Aleya, are the only characters who possess real and enduring power. Zohra, who represents the land and peasantry (in many interpretations of the novel, she stands for Egypt herself), endures because of her moral fiber, physical strength, and ability to rise after a fall. The ending of the story is another beginning for Zohra. Mariana, on the other hand, is the only constant in the novel. A shrewd charlatan, she is able to adapt to the new order with seeming ease, although she has had many grievances with the Revolution herself. Her calculated adaptability and entrepreneurial mind have kept her financially independent for years and she wields a measure of power over the guests of her small domain. Aleya represents a positive outcome of the Revolution; her education and career prospects indicate the continuing commitment of the regime to promoting women's rights at least. Aleya's professional growth has gained a momentum of its own by the time she meets el-Behayri, so probably she will not be derailed by her episode with him. The circumstances bode well for Zohra's future too. Meanwhile, Mariana continues to exude stability and command over her small corner of the country. So while the novel confers the narrative voice (nominal power) on the male characters, its gives the women the power to endure (real power). On the symbolic level, *Miramar* ends by laying the burden on women to continue where men seem to have failed.

Sources and literary context. *Miramar* is the last of six "novels of psychological development" written by Mahfuz in the 1960s. The first five works—which likewise deal with the inner turmoil of characters and their inability to connect with external reality—are

- *al-Liss wa-al-kilab* (1961; *The Thief and the Dogs,* 1984)
- *al-Summan wa-al-kharif* (1962; *Autumn Quail,* 1985)
- *al-Tariq* (1964; *The Search,* 1987)
- *al-Shahhadh* (1965; *The Beggar,* 1986), and
- *Thartharah fawq al-Nil* (1966; *Adrift on the Nile,* 1993)

Mahfuz's writing underwent drastic change in the sextet, compared to what it had been in the fifties. He no longer portrayed realistic characters impassioned with feelings of patriotism, and actively involved in achieving the ideals of independence and sociopolitical change. On the contrary, throughout the 1960s his novels express a general rift between human beings and their immediate surroundings. These novels feature "a new blend of realism, mysticism, and existentialism, mixed with social criticism and contemplative and analytical elements" (Hafez in Boullata, p. 176).

The widespread dissatisfaction and lack of clarity that pervaded the sociopolitical atmosphere of the 1960s is repeatedly commented on

by Mahfuz in this set of works. Their characters, living in the confusion of the sixties themselves, are portrayed as trying to find meaning in a world full of deficiencies, where ambiguity is the order of the day. Themes of alienation, disharmony between the individual and society, and withdrawal into the self as an escape from an incomprehensible external reality are a leitmotif. Intersecting those bleak narratives are subtexts and images of hope presented in some of Mahfuz's portrayals of the female characters, whose fortitude and resilience, in contrast to their male counterparts, enable them to rise above oppressive realities and reinvent themselves alone.

To depict the individual's isolation, Mahfuz uses inner monologues and stream of consciousness as the major stylistic modes. While in the early novels of the sextet, action is channeled through the consciousness of one central character, by the time of *Miramar*, it unfolds through four characters.

Mahfuz was not the only author of his day to infuse existential themes and new narrative forms into his fiction. Other contemporary novelists (such as Fathi Ghanim, Yusuf Idris, and Abd al-Rahman al-Sharqawi) experimented with similar ideas and writing techniques. Their literary output shows variations on the themes of loss, rejection of life, alienation, even nihilism. For instance, Ghanim's *al-Rajul alladhi faqada zillah* (1962; The Man who Has Lost His Shadow) features a main character who feels alienated, paranoid, and discontented with his sociopolitical milieu. Successful himself, he wrestles with guilt over sacrificing his morals to his desire to be integrated into society and live harmoniously in the established order. He shares with Mahfuz's Sarhan el-Behayri in *Miramar* qualities attributed by implication to those in power under Nasser. Nearly all of the 1960s narratives imply that to align oneself with the predominant ideology is to be self-serving and an enemy of the people.

Publication and reception. The six novels of psychological development that Mahfuz produced in the sixties took critics and readers by surprise. (They needed some time to understand and evaluate the new trend in his writing.) By the publication of the sixth novel, *Miramar*, it was clear that this stage in Mahfuz's career was indeed a gloomy one, capturing a mood of impending doom. In this light, his literary production of the sixties in general, and *Miramar* in particular, appears to be prophetic in predicting the direction Egypt and the Arab world at large would take. Sasson Somekh compares *Miramar* to Mahfuz's prior novels:

A MODERN-DAY ALLEGORY

It is from the perspective of allegory that the novel becomes social commentary, the pension representing Egypt, the guests symbolizing a cross-section of its population. A number of works of criticism on *Miramar* have expressed the opinion that Zohra may be a symbol of Egypt; her beauty represents the attraction colonial powers had towards Egypt and their desire to possess it. Zohra's resistance to exploitation, according to this same view, represents the unbreakable spirit of the Egyptian individual.

Another allegorical view holds that, with its faded beauty and dying society, the pension itself stands for pre-revolutionary Egypt. Outside is the new republic, full of potential and mystery. Inside, the lodgers of the guesthouse continue to be pigeonholed by their social classes and their backgrounds; it is only when they leave the confines of the pension that they can reinvent themselves for the better or worse.

The presence of the older characters in the pension—Wagdi, Mariana, and Mansur—turns the novel into a spy game of sorts, in which the older generation observes the younger one with wonder, and at times envy. But the older generation cannot understand the ways or morals of the younger one, while the younger generation has no interest in the older one. This makeshift community is, in essence, a failed one, in that it does not include a channel for communication.

This is a depressing book, which surpasses in its gloom any of the novels of the sixties in that its suffocating atmosphere is not mitigated by the intermittent humorous situations which are to be found in Mahfuz's earlier works. Treachery, malice and avarice have the upper hand, and violence is ever-present. Its verdict on the Egyptian sociopolitical scene of the mid-sixties is unprecedented in its harshness. Many Egyptian and Arabic critics have detected in *Miramar* . . . a prophetic voice warning Egypt, on the eve of the Six Day War, of the catastrophe that was in the offing.

(Somekh, p. 191)

Another, Syrian reviewer seems baffled and disappointed by the extent of murkiness in *Miramar*; Riyad Ismat praises the structure and character portrayal in *Miramar*, but censures Mahfuz for his excessive negativity. Whereas Mahfuz's earlier works, this reviewer says, always included characters and situations that represented hope for the future of Egypt, in *Miramar*, all characters are, "lost or deceptive; nostalgic or impotent. . . . Where then is the revolutionary Egyptian? Where are the elements that have constituted the new socialist Egypt? Sarhan has double standards; Mansur Bahi is a believer in the system, but is weak and unable to sacrifice anything for his beliefs. As a result of those portrayals we can only see the dark side" (Ismat, p. 60). Mahfuz himself concurs. According to him, *Miramar* is indeed a severe social and political critique of the sixties in Egypt, and its pessimistic views are intentional. Mahfuz furthermore reveals the difficulty that he and all similarly critical writers experienced with censorship in the sixties:

In *Miramar*, I blatantly dealt with ills of the Arab Socialist Union as well as the class conflict that existed at the time. I also tackled the subject of dictatorship and criticized it vehemently. In spite of this, some critics at the time . . . accused me of hypocrisy. Those voices had no idea what I went through; that upon writing a novel in those days, I was in perpetual fear of imprisonment. What more did they expect from me after I had so openly attacked authority, and after I had exposed the grave mistakes of the regime [in this novel]. Would I have written such condemnations if I were indeed a hypocrite.

(Mahfuz in al-Naqqash, p. 249; trans. D. Amin)

—Dina Amin

For More Information

Ahmed, Leila. *Women and Gender in Islam: Historical Roots of a Modern Debate*. Egypt: American University in Cairo Press, 1993.

Allen, Roger. *The Arabic Novel: An Historical and Critical Introduction.* Syracuse, N.Y.: Syracuse University Press, 1982.

Ansari, Hamied. *Egypt: The Stalled Society.* Albany: State University of New York Press, 1986.

Baker, Raymond William. *Egypt's Uncertain Revolution Under Nasser and Sadat.* Cambridge, Mass.: Harvard University Press, 1978.

Boullata, Issa J., ed. *Critical Perspectives on Modern Arabic Literature.* Washington D.C.: Three Continents Press, 1980.

Enani, M. M., ed. *Naguib Mahfouz Nobel 1988, Egyptian Perspectives: A Collection of Critical Essays.* Cairo: General Egyptian Book Organization, 1989.

Hopwood, Derek. *Egypt: Politics and Society 1945-1981.* London: George Allen & Unwin, 1982.

Ismat, Riyad. "Miramar." *al-Adab* (September 1967): 56-60.

Mahfuz, Najib (Mahfouz, Naguib). *Miramar.* Trans. Fatma Moussa Mahmoud. Cairo: American University in Cairo, 1978.

Mehrez, Samia. *Egyptian Writers between History and Fiction: Essays on Naguib Mahfouz, Sonallah Ibrahim, and Gamal al-Ghitani.* Cairo: American University in Cairo, 1994.

al-Naqqash, Raja. *Najib Mahfuz: safahat min mudhakkiratihi wa-adwa jadidah ala adabihi wa-hayatihi.* Cairo, Egypt: Markaz al-Ahram lil-Tarjamah wa-al-Nashr, 1998.

Rodenbeck, John. "Alexandria in Cavafy, Durrell, and Tsirkas." *Alif: Journal of Comparative Poetics* (2001): 141.

Somekh, Sasson. *The Changing Rhythm: A Study on Najib Mahfouz's Novels.* Netherlands: E. J. Brill, 1973.

Swerdlow, Joel L. "Tale of Three Cities: Alexandria, Cordoba, and New York." *National Geographic* 196, no. 2 (August 1999): 34-62.

Zayid, Mahmud Y. *Egypt's Struggle for Independence.* Beirut: Khayats, 1965.

Mr. Mani

by

A. B. Yehoshua

A. B. Yehoshua, one of Israel's leading writers, was born in Jerusalem in 1936. Unlike most prominent Israeli cultural figures, he was born into a Sephardi, rather than an Ashkenazi, Jewish family. His father's family has lived in Jerusalem for five generations; his mother came from a wealthy Francophone Moroccan family whose members immigrated to Palestine in 1932. Yehoshua attended a secular "Hebrew" gymnasium, rather than a traditional Sephardi school, then studied Hebrew literature and philosophy at Hebrew University in Jerusalem. He currently lives in Haifa and since 1972 has taught literature at Haifa University. Yehoshua published his first short-story collection (*Death of the Old Man*) in 1962 and his first novel (*The Lover*) in 1977. The novel is the genre for which he would become best known, though Yehoshua has also written numerous essays and plays. His fourth novel, the complex *Mr. Mani*, purports to be a Sephardi counternarrative to mainstream Jewish history. Showing an affinity with the experiments in perspective and narrative in works by the American novelist William Faulkner, *Mr. Mani* revisits key moments in recent Jewish history, refracting them through the specific viewpoints of a diverse ensemble of narrators.

Events in History at the Time of the Novel

Historically significant times and places. *Mr. Mani* is broken up into five sections, each comprised of a conversation between two (in the

THE LITERARY WORK

A novel in five parts, set in various times (1848, 1897, 1918, 1944, and 1982) and places (Jerusalem, Beirut, Athens, Poland, and Crete); published in Hebrew (as *Mar Mani*) in 1990, in English in 1992.

SYNOPSIS

Five separate narrators describe their encounters with six generations of the Mani family, whose personal history intertwines with key moments in Jewish history.

last section three) characters. However, in each section, only one character's speech is presented, while that of the other character or characters is "missing." Presented in reverse chronological order, each of the conversations occurs during a year of great importance in the history of Israel, Zionism, and modern nationalism in general:

- 1982 (Lebanon War)
- 1944 (World War II and the Holocaust)
- 1918 (end of World War I; period soon after the Balfour Declaration promises British support for the creation of a Jewish national home in Palestine)
- 1897 (First Zionist Congress)
- 1848 (eruption of nationalist movements in Europe)

Though Jerusalem stands at the geographic and metaphoric center of the novel, numerous other locations, including Beirut, Athens, Crete, and Poland, serve as the setting for either a conversation or the action it reports. In all these places, the conversations center on the same family of Sephardi Jews, a branch of Jewry usually neglected in accounts of modern Jewish history.

Sephardi and Ashkenazi Jewry. *Sephardi* and *Ashkenazi* are the two basic ethnic categories of world Jewry. In light of each term's historical origin, their modern application is at best only partially accurate. Members of the Sephardi (literally, "Spanish") branch are descendants of Jews who lived in Spain or Portugal prior to the expulsion of 1492. After the expulsion, these Jews scattered throughout North Africa, southeastern Europe (from modern-day Italy to Turkey), and the Levant, or eastern shores of the Mediterranean Sea. The term *Sephardi* is often used erroneously for all Jews of non-Ashkenazi origin, including Mizrachi (literally, "Eastern") Jews, who inhabited the areas of Iraq, Syria, and Yemen for hundreds, and in some cases thousands, of years.

References to *Ashkenazi* Jewry as the name for Jews living in Germany with distinct, non-Sephardi customs first emerged in the fourteenth century, though the term harks back to Noah's great-grandson, the biblical figure known as Ashkenaz (Genesis 10:3). Over time *Ashkenazi* has come to denote all Jews living in or descended from Jews in northwestern and eastern Europe (e.g. France, Germany, Poland, Lithuania, Russia, etc.). The Sephardim and Ashkenazim agree on the basic tenets of Judaism, but differ in customs and interpretation of matters ranging from the layout of synagogues to dietary rules during the Passover holiday.

At least 80,000 Jews lived in Spain at the end of the medieval era (c. 1000 to 1492). A remarkably vigorous culture, they produced such important figures as the poet Judah Halevi and the philosopher Moses Maimonides (see the ***Diwan of Judah Halevi***, also in *WLAIT 6: Middle Eastern Literatures and Their Times*). Their significance began to decrease in the seventeenth century, however, as the population of Ashkenazi Jewry grew. Prior to the Holocaust, the Ashkenazim represented 90 percent of the more than 16 million Jews worldwide. There has since been a shift in proportions. Today Sephardi Jewry numbers 2 million, or about 15 percent of the over 14 million Jews.

Sephardim and Ashkenazim in Israel. The modern Zionist project—that is, the modern project to re-establish a homeland for the Jews in Palestine—was an overwhelmingly Ashkenazi

A. B. Yehoshua

enterprise. Its first ideologues (Theodor Herzl, Ahad Ha`am, and others) and pre-state leadership (David Ben-Gurion, Chaim Weizmann), not to mention the thousands who immigrated to the Jewish settlements in Palestine, were predominately Ashkenazi Jews. Indeed, modern Zionism emerged as a solution to the particular problems (anti-Semitism, above all) plaguing Ashkenazi Jewry. The Sephardim of North Africa and the Eastern Mediterranean suffered instances of discrimination and persecution too. But there, among Muslim societies, the Jews lived as a relatively protected, if second-class, community. The rise of Arab nationalism in the Middle East, in part a response to Zionism's success in Palestine, and the establishment of Israel in 1948, made Jewish life in Arab and Muslim countries untenable.

In the years immediately following 1948, hundreds of thousands of Jews from Arab countries were resettled in the new state of Israel. While many of these Jews were indeed Sephardim, a large portion were neither Ashkenazi nor Sephardi, but rather Mizrachi Jews from Iraq, Syria, Yemen, and other nearby countries. These new Sephardi and Mizrachi immigrants (a distinction largely ignored) were socialized in an ideology and view of Jewish history largely foreign to them, which included a wholesale rejection of Jewish life in the diaspora. All governmental institutions were controlled by Ashkenazi Jews, a circumstance that, in combination with the limited state resources available for absorbing these immigrants, led to the creation of a large Sephardi underclass in Israel.

The Lebanon War. On June 6, 1982, the Israeli army invaded Lebanon. For years the Israel-Lebanon border had played host to skirmishes and attacks from both directions. Lebanon's devastating civil war in the mid-1970s worked to the advantage of the Palestine Liberation Organization (PLO), self-designated representative of dispossessed Palestinian Arabs wherever they might live. The war allowed the PLO to strengthen and expand its control of Palestinian refugee camps and other regions in southern Lebanon. Israel's government, led by Prime Minister Menachem Begin and Defense Minister Ariel Sharon, characterized the invasion as "Peace for the Galilee [Northern Israel]." But the Israeli offensive continued well beyond the border zone, all the way to the Lebanese capital of Beirut, the power base of the PLO leadership. Sharon planned to destroy the PLO as a force in Lebanon and to help establish a Lebanese government to Israel's liking. Ultimately the PLO leadership left Lebanon for Tunisia. Thus, the Israeli invasion may have achieved its immediate purpose, but it was costly on multiple counts. Israel's occupation of Southern Lebanon would last nearly 20 years, prompting some to call this "Israel's Vietnam" and leading to significant Israeli casualties. Civilian casualties in Lebanon were considerable too, highlighted by the infamous massacres in the Sabra and Shatila refugee camps—perpetrated by Israel's Phalangist allies with Israeli knowledge and noninterference (Sachar, p. 914). The 1982 war, in stark contrast to the Israeli view of prior wars, was an optional, offensive action rather than a mandatory, defensive one. In these ways, it has come to mark a turning point in Israeli history, one paralleled by ideological malaise throughout much of the country.

Germans in Crete during World War II. Located 60 miles off the coast of Greece, the island of Crete, where part of *Mr. Mani* takes place, has played host to some key moments in human history. Germany's Nazi army conquered Crete in May 1941, then proceeded to occupy the island until late 1944. Near the end of the war, when its defeat appeared imminent, Germany intensified its efforts to liquidate all Jews under its control, however few in number and far from Germany. In keeping with this policy of genocide, in June 1944, 260 Jews were deported by boat from Crete to the European mainland to be sent to the death camps. But they met their end before this plan could be executed. All aboard were killed when the boat was sunk by an unknowing British warplane.

The Jews had been deported from an island occupied by renowned societies. In ancient times, the Minoans (3000-1100 B.C.E.), whose civilization predates that of ancient Greece, dominated the region, thanks in large measure to their knowledge of metals (copper and then bronze). Theirs was the first so-called high civilization in the area, distinguished for its sophisticated cities and palaces, its extensive trade networks, and its artistic achievements. After the Minoans came the Mycenaeans (c. 1580-1120 B.C.E.), whose ruins still stand and whose history forms the basis of the Greek epics attributed to Homer. *Mr. Mani* treats Crete, perceived through the eyes of the German officer Egon Brunner, as the cradle of European culture. By setting part of his novel here, Yehoshua reaches before even the Greeks, who are typically invoked as the origin of European culture, to pre-classical times.

During the nineteenth century, European romantic and nationalist myths—including the German ideology of *Volk*——drew heavily on ancient cultures to "provide a foundation for the emergence of European culture" (Golomb Hoffman, p. 250). In fact, various national mythologies positioned the modern nation as the "true" inheritor of a particular ancient culture. These national ideologies simultaneously drew upon new forms of (pseudo)scientific thinking in order to make claims about racial purity and immutable, essential national identities, placing great importance on the discovery of archaeological ruins from ancient civilizations—such as the remnants of Minoan-Mycenaean palaces uncovered by Arthur Evans at the turn of the twentieth century.

Yehoshua debunks such claims to purity in *Mr. Mani*, a point of particular poignancy in light of the Sephardi heritage featured in the novel. As noted, Sephardi society emanated from medieval Spain, whose larger population was preoccupied with *limpieza de sangre* ("purity of blood"), a concern that many of the Sephardim seem to have imbibed. "In a variety of ways," observes literary scholar Arnold Band, "the novel is . . . a devastating critique of the notion of Sephardic family purity," which serves as an example of "destructive modern nationalism" (Band, p. 241).

The Balfour Declaration and Palestine at the end of World War I. The land that includes modern-day Israel and the Palestinian territories was controlled by the Ottoman Empire for four centuries prior to World War I. During this war, most of the empire's vast territorial holdings were lost to other colonial powers, primarily to the French and British. The British army conquered Palestine in 1917. Contact had already been established by the two colonial powers with Arab leaders throughout the Middle East, who sought promises and pledges in support of their autonomy. Simultaneously the Zionist leadership approached the British in hopes of getting their backing for its own national project in Palestine. Led by Chaim Weizmann, the Zionist movement scored an enormous diplomatic victory when it persuaded the British to issue the Balfour Declaration in November 1917. The declaration stated that the British government favors "the establishment in Palestine of a national home for the Jewish people" (Smith, p. 54). In 1922 the League of Nations awarded Britain a mandate to govern Palestine, which would remain in effect for the next 26 years.

At the outset, the League charged the British to "'Use their best endeavors to facilitate' Jewish immigration" in the interest of securing a national home here (Sachar, p. 128). While the ultimate future of British Mandate Palestine would remain uncertain up to and through the United Nation's vote to partition it between the Arabs and the Jews in 1947, for Western nations, the Balfour Declaration granted the Zionist project a new degree of legitimacy. The political value of this legitimacy was only reinforced when Britain was awarded the mandate in 1922, providing the Zionists with diplomatic leverage throughout the interwar period. From the point of view of the Arabs in Palestine, however, the British government had no right to determine its fate. They saw the Balfour Declaration (and for that matter British rule in their region) as an imposition of European imperial power on the indigenous population and thus as illegitimate.

Jewish nationalism, in the form of modern political Zionism, would clash directly with Arab nationalism in general and Palestinian nationalism in particular. Before the end of World War I, a pan-Arab nationalism had surfaced, one with hopes of independence for the Arab peoples throughout the Middle East, including Palestine. There were nearly 700,000 Arab inhabitants in Palestine by the end of the war, scattered through numerous villages and a few cities, such as Jaffa, Haifa, and Jerusalem. In contrast, there were approximately 60,000 Jews. It is therefore hardly surprising that the Balfour Declaration of 1917

Sir Edmund Allenby, commander of the British forces in Palestine, riding into the newly captured city of Jerusalem in December 1917.

met with Arab nationalist opposition. Initially much of this opposition came from Arab leaders outside Palestine, in particular from Sharif Husayn of Mecca, the main figure in the emerging pan-Arab nationalist movement. The years 1917 to 1922, however, saw strong opposition from journalists, lawyers, and other Palestinian Arabs too. Eventually the distinct nationalist movements tied to the Arab peoples of today (Syrians, Iraqis, Palestinians) would grow out of this larger pan-Arab nationalism. At the end of World War I, however, Palestinian nationalism was not yet a mass movement. A distinct Palestinian identity was still taking shape.

The First Zionist Congress. Theodor Herzl, the founder of modern political Zionism, created the institution of the Zionist Congress in order to fashion a coherent political movement. This first congress was held in Basel, Switzerland, in 1897. Delegates from 15 countries attended the congress; a landmark convocation, it produced the "Basel Program," which officially declared it the goal of Zionism to establish a "home" for the Jewish people in the land of Palestine (Morris, p. 23). To this end, the congress encouraged the resettlement of Jewish workers and artisans there and founded the World Zionist Organization. This first convocation was viewed as highly significant for non-Jews as well as Jews. Held the next year, in 1898, also in Basel, a Second Zionist Congress resolved through colonization and industrialization to improve the condition of the Yishuv—the Jewish community in Palestine. The next year, 1899, saw the convocation of a Third Zionist Congress, yet again in Basel. Herzl, despite setbacks, remained fixed on attaining a charter for a Jewish settlement in Palestine from its then Turkish overlords. At this time actual Zionist settlement in Palestine was just beginning. By 1903, the end of the first *aliyah,* or wave of Jewish immigration, the new *Yishuv* (the collection of Zionist communities in Palestine) contained 10,000 Jews, living mostly in recently founded settlements on 90,000 acres (purchased by the Jewish National Fund, which the Zionists had established to buy land in Palestine). The effort to revive Hebrew as a spoken language was underway at the time too. By the eve of World War I, despite economic stagnation, which set in soon after the turn of the century, the Jewish population in Palestine had risen more than five-fold, with comparable growth of the settlements.

Spring of Nations. Yehoshua ends his novel in 1848, a pivotal year that saw one nationalist movement after another erupt in Europe. A revolution in Paris in early 1848 led to the proclamation of a republican government in France, which sparked uprisings throughout Europe—in Berlin, in Milan, in Vienna, and in other parts of the Austrian Empire. The continent was reordering itself along popular national rather than imperial and religious lines. Middle-class doctors and lawyers called for greater political rights, industrial workers demanded a political voice, and peasants agitated for the abolition of feudal-style relationships with landowners. In France, the bourgeoisie, whose members patched together a provisional post-revolutionary government, committed itself to a bold new approach in European government—universal manhood suffrage. Responding in droves, peasants and villagers, who made up a large share of the 9.5 million new voters, for the first time cast their ballots, in the end to little short-term avail. This particular French republic would in four brief years fail, as would the revolutions mounted elsewhere in Europe. In the long run, however, they prompted irrevocable change. From 1848 onward, "the modern phenomena of mass politics began to emerge" (Wright, p. 129). The rash of 1848 revolutions drew mass populations into the governing of a nation, or, in cases like Germany, led to their unification into a newly

created nation. Lumping together the upheavals, history dubs them the "Spring of Nations," designating 1848 to be the year modern nationalism first emerged in earnest across Europe.

In *Mr. Mani,* Yehoshua retraces the emergence of modern nationalism, in particular Zionism, and its effect on the Middle East and the Jerusalem Sephardim. His choice of 1848 as the temporal point of departure is apt in view of the year's nationalist revolutions. At its foundation, *Mr. Mani* appears to question the role of nationalism in the formation of Israel and even the modern Middle East.

The Novel in Focus

Plot summary. *Mr. Mani* consists of five sections or "conversations." In each conversation a new speaker describes his or her encounter with a different member of the Mani family (in the fifth section a Mani himself takes on the role of speaker). The responses of the speaker's conversational partner are omitted, but his or her identity is known to the reader and clearly influences how the speaker communicates. In essence, every section contains two intertwined stories: the story related by the speaker (the "dialogue" is in fact closer to a monologue) and the interaction of speaker and addressee during the telling of the story. Information about both participants is provided in biographical content that bounds the conversation. An otherwise absent editor supplies the information in a neutral, authoritative tone.

The first conversation takes place in 1982 in Kibbutz Masha'abei Sadeh in Israel. The participants are Hagar Shiloh and her mother, Yael. Hagar describes her three-day-long encounter with Judge Gavriel Mani, the father of her boyfriend, Efrayim Mani, a soldier stationed in Lebanon. Convinced that she is pregnant with Efrayim's baby, Hagar travels from Tel Aviv to Jerusalem in order to deliver a message from Efrayim to his father: Efrayim will not be able to attend his paternal grandmother's unveiling. In Gavriel's Jerusalem apartment she discovers a noose and concludes that he is planning to commit suicide. Hagar resolutely remains in Jerusalem, despite Gavriel's efforts to send her back to Tel Aviv, in order to "save" him from himself.

Over the next few days, Hagar travels around Jerusalem, partially in pursuit of Gavriel, from his courthouse, to a Sephardi cemetery, to an old hospital. On the third day, when it appears to Hagar that Gavriel is no longer a threat to himself, she leaves Jerusalem and on a whim travels to her mother's kibbutz rather than returning directly to Tel Aviv. There ensues this first conversation. Throughout her telling, Hagar must resist her mother's psychological theorizing, in particular Yael's conviction that Hagar was attracted to Gavriel as a surrogate father-figure, her own father having been killed in the 1967 Six-Day War between Israel and the Arab nations. In the "biographical supplement" that follows the conversation, the reader learns that Hagar was indeed

MOVING BACKWARD IN TIME

The reverse chronological order or construction of Yehoshua's novel suggests two alternate models for understanding the past: archaeology and psychoanalysis. The reverse chronology of the narrative mirrors the perception of time in the two fields. In both, time is not viewed linearly from the past to the present. Rather it is viewed from the present to the past, with an emphasis on the simultaneity of the past in the present. In archaeology, this is manifested in ruins; in psychoanalysis, by a host of present memories and even neurotic symptoms based on past experience. Yehoshua additionally encourages the reader to consider the relevance of archaeological and psychoanalytic models in ways other than the novel's backward progression: by including an extended treatment of archaeology in the second conversation; by constructing each conversation as a lopsided exchange between two figures, much like a psychoanalytic session; by finally revealing or unearthing in the confession of the final conversation a possible original cause for the family's problems—a father's murder of his son. Though deeply historical, *Mr. Mani* might in these ways, and in its focus on the Sephardi experience, which falls outside traditional Jewish historiography, be considered an "antihistorical" novel (Band, p. 236).

not pregnant at the time, though she became so soon after Efrayim's return from Lebanon. He and Hagar do not marry, and he for the most part avoids his paternal responsibilities. In contrast, Gavriel develops a close relationship with his grandson, and through him with Hagar's mother. This section ends some five years later, with a description of Gavriel's car being struck by a rock as he drives through the Palestinian city of Hebron on the way to Yael's kibbutz.

The second conversation takes place in German-occupied Crete in 1944 between a German soldier, Egon Brunner, and his non-biological grandmother, Andrea Sauchon. Beginning with a description of the German aerial invasion of Crete in 1941, Egon relates his experiences on the island. He encounters Yosef Mani and his son, Efrayim, and comes into contact with ancient Minoan ruins. In his narration to "Grandmother," Egon has fused the Manis and the Minoan into an elaborate theory that, he believes, offers a solution to the imminent disaster facing Germany. For Egon, this ancient civilization offers Germany a way out, a purifying return to origins capable of redeeming the nation from its present barbarism. In Efrayim Mani, Egon finds his theory oddly substantiated. Egon discovers that the Manis are Jews, but when confronted, Efrayim responds, "I was Jewish, but I am not anymore . . . I've canceled it" (Yehoshua, *Mr. Mani*, p. 123). From this, Egon happily concludes, "if that stubborn, beastly essence of Jewishness can cancel its own self, then there's hope for us too" (*Mr. Mani*, p. 125). Egon spends much of the next two years closely monitoring Mani, in order to confirm that he has not cancelled the cancellation (*Mr. Mani*, p. 129). As the war turns against the Germans, the Jews of Crete are rounded up for deportation. Egon elects not to arrest the self-cancelled, once-Jewish Mani, only to arrest him later for helping other Jews (that is, his wife and son) escape. Mani dies aboard a ship destined for the death camps as it sinks into the Mediterranean.

The third conversation is set in Jerusalem in 1918, soon after the British capture Palestine. The speaker is Ivor Horowitz, a British Jew and military advocate. The occasion for his narration is a report to Colonel Michael Woodhouse, who will be the presiding judge at the treason trial of a Yosef Mani, whom the reader encountered in the second conversation. Yosef, who is considered British since his parents were British subjects, is being tried for providing military plans to the enemy. Ivor will serve as prosecutor. In his report, he details Yosef's strange, multilayered identity: Yosef is a polyglot and self-pronounced "*homo politicus*," who shuttles effortlessly between and feels at home in the multiple cultures and languages of Jerusalem. When his language skills are discovered, Yosef is enlisted as an interpreter for the British army. He soon discovers Britain's Balfour Declaration, endorsing the Jewish nationalist project in Palestine, and is "bowled over" by it (*Mr. Mani*, p. 184). In response—and possibly out of concern for the Arab communities with which he once identified—Yosef repeatedly steals British war plans and delivers them to the enemy in order to have an audience with the local Arab population. Here he takes it upon himself to implore the Arabs to

> Get ye an identity . . . before it is too late! All over the world people now have identities, and we Jews are on our way, and you had better have an identity or else!
>
> (*Mr. Mani*, p. 190)

Eventually Yosef Mani gets caught, and this leads to his trial for treason. Throughout his part of the conversation, the Jewish military man, Ivor, is forced to demonstrate his allegiance with British (as opposed to Jewish) interests. He hopes at the same time to avoid asking for the death penalty, as the law dictates. In the end, Woodhouse suggests deporting Yosef to Crete, to which Ivor happily agrees.

The fourth conversation, between Dr. Efrayim Shapiro and his father, Sholom Shapiro, takes place late one night in 1897 in Jelleny-Szad, Poland (a few miles from what would become the Auschwitz concentration camp). Efrayim and his sister, Linka, have just returned from a trip to the Third Zionist Congress in Basel, Switzerland. At the congress, they encounter the Sephardi doctor Moshe Mani, a commanding, charismatic figure, who becomes enamored with Linka and convinces the brother and sister to return with him to Jerusalem. There he introduces them to Mani's birthing clinic, which treats women of all backgrounds and nationalities. Linka and Mani engage in a full-fledged affair, until Efrayim takes it upon himself to return to Poland with his sister. Mani, on his own initiative, accompanies the siblings on the first few legs of this long journey, all the way to a train station in Beirut, Lebanon. A moment after a reluctant farewell, Efrayim and Linka watch in horror as Mani throws himself in front of an oncoming train:

> Mani had reached the last car by now. He let his overcoat drop to the platform—the thought struck me that he did not want to bloody it— and then—with a gentle movement—lowered himself onto the tracks. A Turkish soldier started to shout at him. But Mani just turned away his face, which—in the reddish light that drifted in from the sea—looked hard and vanquished, and resumed walking along the tracks, wagging a reproving finger at the black locomotive that appeared around the bend as if it were a child home late from school. The locomotive tore him apart instantly, like a sword stroke.
>
> (*Mr. Mani*, pp. 284-285)

In the process of Efrayim's long narrative he searches for clues that might explain Mani's suicide, a trying task made more difficult by his belief that his own father is not listening and may even have fallen asleep. In the biographical supplement, the reader learns that Linka marries a Catholic and converts. Despite this, both she and her children, along with Efrayim, are killed by the Nazis during the Holocaust.

Set in Athens in 1848, the fifth conversation departs in many ways from the previous ones. Unlike the others, this conversation is narrated by a member of the Mani family, Avraham Mani. It furthermore has him address not just one but two conversation partners. Mani speaks to both his old teacher, Rabbi Shabbetai Hananiah Haddayah, and the rabbi's much younger wife, Flora Molkho-Haddayah. Having recently suffered a debilitating stroke and no longer able to speak, the rabbi requires the constant assistance of his wife. Avraham Mani has come to report to his one-time mentor the story of his journey to Jerusalem. In 1846 his son, Yosef, became the first Mani to travel to Jerusalem. This Yosef Mani (the grandfather of the Yosef Mani from the second and third conversations) goes to Jerusalem in order to escort his bride to Constantinople, but the two remain in Jerusalem. Unfortunately, they have no children. Avraham thus follows his son to Jerusalem, where he finds that his son spends his time among the local Arabs, who, Yosef is convinced, are simply "Jews who did not know that they were Jews" (*Mr. Mani*, p. 323). Avraham's narration and the novel as a whole climax in his nightmarish description of his son's moblike murder on the Temple Mount, in front of the Dome of the Rock. Avraham not only witnesses the murder, but may in fact have perpetrated it himself (the novel is famously ambiguous on this crucial point, though Yehoshua claims otherwise, as discussed below). Afterwards, Avraham stays in Jerusalem and sleeps with his daughter-in-law in order to continue the family line. Avraham has thus come to Athens to confess and seek judgment from his rabbi: can he take his own life as punishment for these acts? The rabbi, completely incapacitated, provides no answer.

The binding of Isaac. From among all the foundational moments in the Hebrew Bible, perhaps none has so preoccupied Jewish thought as the binding of Isaac or the *akedah* (Genesis 22). In this story, God commands Abraham to sacrifice his son, Isaac, as a test of Abraham's loyalty. Abraham follows God's command, and only at the last possible instant, when Abraham has the knife in his hand, does one of God's angels intervene and save Isaac. Abraham is rewarded by God for his loyalty, and is told: "because you have done this thing and have not held back your son, your only one, I will greatly bless you and will greatly multiply your seed, as the stars in the heavens and as the sand on the shore of the sea" (Genesis 22:16-17).

Though the Hebrew Bible is replete with scenes of violence, both potential and realized, few if any are so morally problematic. Simply put, what type of God orders his follower to murder his own son? The deeply troubling nature of this story is only compounded by its centrality to the biblical narrative. While the Hebrew Bible is the narrative of the Jews' early history, this episode is unique in that it forms part of the original covenant between God and Abraham. For these reasons, the *akedah* has been the focus of endless interpretation, elaboration, and, at times, justification in Jewish literature, both religious and secular. The figure of Isaac as sacrifice has often been invoked as a metaphor to explain and to justify Jewish suffering. Before the founding of Israel, Jews in the Diaspora often spoke of Isaac as a model or archetype when discussing martyrdom or *Kidush ha-Shem* (sanctification of the Divine Name). This occurred even in the Holocaust, the Nazi attempt to exterminate European Jewry (in fact, *holocaust* is Latin for "burnt offering" or "sacrifice" and appears in the Latin translation of the *akedah*). Though modern Zionism rejected traditional Jewish martyrdom, the figure of Isaac has remained central in Israel too, echoing the seemingly endless chain of "sons" sacrificed in its wars.

A. B. Yehoshua views *Mr. Mani* as a response to the binding of Isaac and the role it has played in the Jewish imagination throughout history. The novel itself climaxes with a not-so-subtle re-enactment of the biblical episode: a man named Abraham kills his son on the Temple Mount, or Mount Moriah, the site of the original *akedah*. But as this summary indicates, Yehoshua's version of the story differs from the original in one important way. In his own words, "that which in the bible story was merely a threatened sacrifice would be turned into an awesome reality" (Yehoshua, "*Mr. Mani* and the Akedah," p. 64). To his mind, the *akedah* is "an appalling story" that is "morally insupportable for the believer in the objective existence of God and his providential supervision of humankind" (Yehoshua, "*Mr. Mani* and the Akedah," pp. 61-62). He set out in his novel to respond forcefully to this episode once and for all: "I wanted to free myself from the myth by bringing it to full realization . . . I wanted to . . .

present it in a credible realistic situation . . . and at the actual biblical site (Yehoshua, "*Mr. Mani* and the Akedah," p. 61). Through a fulfillment of the threat of the *akedah*, he aimed to drain it of its appeal as a metaphor for the Jewish experience. He employed *Mr. Mani* as a corrective to the sort of blind loyalty at the center of the *akedah*, a type of loyalty that in the century and a half covered by the novel has "subjected humanity to its most horrendous atrocities" (Yehoshua, "*Mr. Mani* and the Akedah," p. 62).

Yehoshua, Faulkner, and the relationship between narrative and identity. In interviews concerning his work, Yehoshua has long been open about the influence of the American writer William Faulkner on his writing. In particular, Yehoshua notes an attraction to Faulkner's use of multiple narrating voices and interior monologues. Yehoshua comments:

> Reality here [in Israel] is so diverse and there is no controlled center anymore. And if I really wanted to reflect the diverse reality of Israel in my novel, I had to take into account that there are different points of view. And this is the reason why the technique of Faulkner was so helpful.
> (Yehoshua in Horn, p. 51)

Yehoshua's first two novels, *ha-Me'ahev* (1977; *The Lover*, 1977) and *Gerushim me'uharim* (1982; *A Late Divorce*, 1984), are constructed in this Faulknerian manner; an ensemble of characters within the story takes turns narrating the action to illuminate the "diverse" Israeli reality by conveying it through their varied perspectives. In *Mr. Mani* Yehoshua takes the strategy one step further, turning his attention toward the narrators themselves to demonstrate the interdependent relationship between their narration and identity.

The narrators in *Mr. Mani* are not only subjective, biased observers, but each uses his or her narration as an opportunity to refashion his or her identity, or at least represent it in a very particular light. The third conversation (the first Yehoshua was to write) demonstrates this clearly. Ivor Horowitz uses his narration to assert his own identity as first and foremost British. From the opening of the conversation the reader senses the constraints under which Ivor speaks:

> —Colonel, sir. Lieutenant Ivor Stephen Horowitz of the advocate-general's corps, attached to the adjutant's office of the 52nd division. I'm most grateful to you for finding the time to discuss with me this matter of—
> —Horowitz, Colonel, with two "o's."
> —British, of course. Born in Manchester, sir.
> —1897, sir.

—Yes, sir.
—My father, sir, did not have the good fortune to be born in the United Kingdom, although he arrived in it as a very young lad. My mother, on the other hand—
—From Russia, sir. But as a very young child. What deucedly foul weather!

(*Mr. Mani*, pp. 149-50)

Ivor senses, and indeed has reason to believe, that the reception of his narrative depends on his addressee's (i.e., Colonel Woodhouse's) opinion of Ivor, in particular his qualifications, military and genealogical. Ivor presents the colonel with a narrative of his origins that stresses his British identity, meanwhile dismissing those elements of his family's past that mark him as anything less than "purely" British. He repeats his mention of his father's early arrival to the United Kingdom, while looking for an opportunity to switch to his other parent and stress his mother's non-immigrant status. When the colonel remains interested in the non-British branches of Horowitz's family tree, Ivor tries to divert his attention to the weather.

While Ivor uses the narrative as an opportunity to present a very particular version of his identity, to "remember" certain aspects of it while "forgetting" others, it is difficult to understand his motive. Does Ivor wish to be seen as primarily British, or is this only a function of his suspicion that Woodhouse is an anti-Semite? Might Horowitz present a different identity were he speaking with a fellow Jew and not a fellow Englishman? Like each of the other speakers of the novel, Ivor speaks to a figure of greater authority (in the other conversations the narrators speak to a parent, grandparent, or teacher). The scene demonstrates that the situation of narration—which is rarely, if ever, neutral—often demands a particular type of narrative.

When Ivor introduces the figure of Yosef Mani, the relationship between narrative and identity grows only more complex. Yosef is a polyglot, educated in part in Beirut, and overall his identity is anything but fixed. This is seen most clearly in his layers of clothing. Yosef sheds one layer to reveal another—the removal of his peasant's cloak reveals a western suit and tie. Capitalizing on his skills, he serves as an adept translator for the British forces in the region—his mastery of numerous languages signifies his ability to shuttle between different identities. The Balfour Declaration, establishing the possibility of a partition of Palestine along religious or national lines, is a blow to the multiethnic, even multinational Yosef. Despite being a Jew, Yosef fears for the indigenous Arab population, since through a shared language he identifies with them as well. As such, he takes it upon himself to give away British military secrets in order to gain access to the local Arab communities. The Arabs are implored to "get ye an identity" so as not to be swept over by tide of nationalism flowing through the region (*Mr. Mani*, p. 190).

Not surprisingly, Ivor's narrative about Yosef tries to make sense of his treachery by identifying its origins. Ivor's earlier presentation of his own origins suggests his interest in the subject as a way of simplifying matters. Origins and beginnings become the first step in an arbitrary process of creating meaning through narrative, in which one part of the past is suppressed in order to present another aspect as solely representative. Ivor says

It's best to begin from the beginning. But just where is the beginning, sir, if you'll allow me to reflect for a moment? Suppose we say on the twenty-eight of February.

(*Mr. Mani*, p. 156)

Ivor's use of the conditional "suppose we say" betrays the arbitrary character of his narrative, a narrative that nevertheless comes to function as "reality," a stand-in for the otherwise inaccessible past. As Faulkner demonstrated in novels such as *The Sound and the Fury* and *Absalom, Absalom!*, the act of narration actively shapes the past, by forcing it to conform to an outside narrative framework constructed in the present. The "beginning" of Yosef Mani's story only exists, in other words, thanks to the beginning that Ivor creates through his narration.

Particularly remarkable in Yehoshua's treatment of these issues is the way his novel makes narrative central not just to individual identity, but to collective identity as well. Standing behind Ivor's obsession with the beginning of Mani's treachery is the larger matter of the origins of nationalism and national identity in the region. As a Jew born in Britain to an Englishwoman and a Russian immigrant, Ivor has a complicated identity that he tries to simplify by embracing his British and dismissing his Russian side. Likewise the absurdity of Yosef's command to the Arabs to "get ye an identity" suggests the inevitable arbitrariness of the national identity to be taken. Though Yosef is spared the death penalty, his degree of national hybridity cannot survive once the streamlining model of nationalism—with its arbitrary borders—enters the region. Ivor's use of narrative to shape his own mixed identity suggests that the national collective's effort to formulate its own identity may well involve a narrative of forgetting too. Indeed, Ernest Renan, one of the first scholars who attempted to clarify the elusive meaning of the modern nation and its reliance on history observed over a hundred years ago: "Forgetting . . . is a crucial factor in the creation of the nation" (Bhabha, p. 11).

Sources and literary context. Modern Hebrew fiction emerged among Askenazi Jewry in Europe in the late nineteenth century and over a hundred years later remains largely dominated by the more culturally prominent Ashkenazi in Israel. But a sizeable group of Sephardi and Mizrachi Hebrew writers have emerged in Israel as well. The best known among these—Sami Michael, Shimon Ballas, Eli Amir—have provided Israeli society with powerful counter-narratives to the standard Ashkenazi accounts of Israeli history and society. To some degree, *Mr. Mani* can be said to participate in this movement in Hebrew fiction. The novel, however, is perhaps best understood as a singular happening for several reasons. First, Yehoshua is not a recent immigrant but a sixth-generation Jerusalemite, who was already one of the best-known writers in Israel before the publication of *Mr. Mani*; also Yehoshua's turn toward his Sephardi heritage at this juncture appears related to personal events as much as to any developments in Israeli society at large.

The composition of *Mr. Mani* took place intermittently over the course of almost ten years. Yehoshua wrote the third section in 1984-1985, but then left the project for two years to write a different novel, *Five Seasons* (in Hebrew, *Molkho*). Though Yehoshua himself claims that this last novel was a deliberate effort on his part to avoid collective, political questions, the critical establishment saw it otherwise. *Five Seasons* has come to be viewed as Yehoshua's first "Sephardi" novel, one whose themes in many ways resemble those in *Mr. Mani*. In 1987 A. B. Yehoshua wrote an introduction to a posthumous collection of essays by his father, Yaakov Yehoshua. In contrast to the father's sentimental, nostalgic recreations of his Jerusalem childhood, in his introduction, the son investigates the complex, if often repressed, nature of his own Sephardi identity. There is in the introduction a fusion of three themes: "Yehoshua's relationship to his father, his attitude to his Sephardism, and the type of fiction he produces. . . . We . . . see in this essay of 1987 some of the same basic structures that shape *Mar Mani*, which was written about the same time" (Band, p. 235).

Reception. Portions of *Mr. Mani* were published in journals in 1986 and 1988, while a segment of one conversation was performed as a monologue in 1988. Thus primed for an unusual literary event, the critical establishment and general reading public made the novel a runaway bestseller and, in less than a year, the focus of no fewer than 30 scholarly articles. The best known of these articles, by the eminent literary scholar Dan Miron, explicitly echoed a sentiment found in much of the interpretive response to the novel: namely, that he was just scratching the surface of the novel's complexity.

In the United States, *Mr. Mani* received similarly enthusiastic reviews from writers as notable as Cynthia Ozick and Alfred Kazin. A portion of the third conversation was published in *The New Yorker* to great interest, and the novel was selected as a *New York Times* Notable Book of the Year. Struck by how ambitious and powerful a novel it is, the *Nation* acknowledged the work as a remarkable achievement; "The Nobel Prize," its reviewer observed, "has been given for less" (Solotaroff, p. 826).

—Todd Hasak-Lowy

For More Information

Band, Arnold. "*Mar Mani*: The Archaeology of Self-Deception." *Prooftexts* 12 (1992): 231-244.

Bhabha, Homi K., ed. *Nation and Narration*. London and New York: Routledge, 1990.

Golomb Hoffman, Anne. "The Womb of Culture: Fictions of Identity and Their Undoing in Yehoshua's *Mr. Mani*." *Prooftexts* 12 (1992): 245-263.

Horn, Bernard. *Facing the Fires: Conversations with A. B. Yehoshua*. Syracuse: Syracuse University Press, 1997.

Mintz, Alan. *Translating Israel*. Syracuse: Syracuse University Press, 2001.

Morris, Benny. *Righteous Victims: A History of the Zionist-Arab Conflict, 1881-2001*. New York: Vintage, 2001.

Ruiz, Teofilo F. *Spanish Society 1400-1600*. Harlow, England: Pearson Education, 2001.

Sachar, Howard M. *A History of Israel from the Rise of Zionism to Our Time*. New York: Alfred A. Knopf, 2000.

Smith, Charles D. *Palestine and the Arab-Israeli Conflict*. New York: St. Martin's, 1996.

Solotaroff, Ted. *Nation* 254, no. 23 (15 June 1992): 826-29.

Wright, Gordon. *France in Modern Times*. New York: W. W. Norton, 1987.

Yehoshua, A. B. *Mr. Mani*. Trans. Hillel Halkin. New York: Harcourt Brace, 1992.

———. "*Mr. Mani* and the *Akedah*." *Judaism* (winter 2001): 61-65.

Murder in Baghdad

by
Salah Abd al-Sabur

Salah Abd al-Sabur (1931-81), who dominated the Egyptian poetic scene from the end of World War II to his death, established himself as the foremost Egyptian representative of Arabic literary modernism of his era. His poetry was known for its simple, straightforward language and its concern with Egyptian village life, including the anecdotes, folktales, and epic stories that circulated among the common people. This early interest in promoting the language and point of view of ordinary people did not stop Abd al-Sabur from becoming a consummate administrator and government functionary in the latter half of his life. He held high government posts in cultural affairs and served as editor for a number of influential literary publications. Until his death in 1981, Abd al-Sabur also served as the managing director of the General Egyptian Book Organization (GEBO), the official government publishing house. He thus had a significant impact on Egyptian cultural policy during the final years of the presidency of Gamal Abd al-Nasser and the beginning of Anwar Sadat's term in office. His influence diminished, however, in the late 1970s. An ardent Arab nationalist and supporter of Nasser's political and social reforms, Abd al-Sabur disapproved of Sadat's increasingly repressive treatment of Egyptian intellectuals and refused to support Egypt's separate peace treaty with Israel in 1977. The writer's misgivings were confirmed when, in the wake of the treaty, other Arab nations broke ties with Egypt, the most populous Arab country, and it suddenly became a pariah, culturally and commercially isolated from its neighbors. Abd al-Sabur spent the final years of

THE LITERARY WORK

A verse play set in Baghdad in the early 900s, during the decline of the Abbasid dynasty; first performed in 1965; published in Arabic (as *Ma'sat al-Hallaj*) in 1964, in English in 1972.

SYNOPSIS

A tragedy in two acts, the play chronicles the arrest, trial, and execution of Mansur al-Hallaj—a real-life mystic, poet, populist preacher, and probable political agitator of the medieval Arab world.

his life out of favor with political power, focusing much of his attention on two journals he had helped found and still oversaw as chairman of the Board of the Directors of GEBO, which underwrote them financially. The first of these, *Fusul*, a journal of theoretical literary criticism, gave vent to his lifelong interest in making Egyptians more aware of the best and most innovative of Western writing about literature. The second journal, *al-Masrah* (The Theater), was devoted to the stage, both Egyptian and international, a personal interest of Abd al-Sabur. He showed an enduring fascination with drama during his life, composing five verse plays over his career. The first of these, *Ma'sat al-Hallaj* (literally "The Tragedy of al-Hallaj," translated as *Murder in Baghdad*) has had a lasting impact on modern Arabic drama, though somewhat limited audience appeal, largely because it attempts to take post-World War II innovations in Arabic poetry and transfer them to a dramatic framework. Its theme, the difficult choices intellectuals confront when they engage in political struggles, was timely when written and continues to resonate today in a world where those who choose the path of activism face harassment and even punishment, imprisonment, and death.

Events in History at the Time the Play Takes Place

The decline of the Abbasid caliphate. By the time Mansur al-Hallaj, the main character in *Murder in Baghdad*, was born (in 857 C.E.), the Abbasid dynasty had begun a long, slow decline that would culminate in a mass execution of its last pitiful representatives on the banks of the Tigris River outside Baghdad at the hands of the invading Mongols in 1250 C.E. Even before al-Hallaj's birth, there was debilitating conflict in the Arab/Muslim Empire. The sons (Amin and Ma'mun) of the Abbasid's most powerful caliph, Harun al-Rashid, had fought a long and bitter civil war over who was to succeed their father as ruler, a war that devastated the empire for over 20 years (809-833 C.E.). Eventually Ma'mun won, but so seriously did the war weaken the empire's infrastructure that he was never able to fully consolidate his power base. This set the stage for a slow disintegration of centralized rule that affected subsequent reigns, as strong provincial governors redirected their tax revenues to local purposes, refusing to send them to Baghdad. Though they paid formal allegiance to the reigning Abbasid dynasty, they were in practice independent rulers, with their own troops and cadres of administrators, loyal only to them. Such breakaway rulers were often described as "sultans," an Arabic term that means "the one who wields power," regardless of the legitimacy of his claim for exercising that power. There was trouble too in the territories under their immediate control, where the weakness of the later Abbasids was exacerbated by dissident religio-political movements and by rebellions instigated by oppressed subjects. Given this state of affairs, the caliphs in "power" at the time were sometimes termed by those they ruled as mere "sultans."

Due to the slow pace of conversion, it was only in the 800s, some 200 years after Islam first appeared, that most of the caliph's subjects could be characterized as Muslim, rather than the adherents of other religions. Ironically this greater religious unity gave rise to disharmony—the caliph's subjects made more demands on him for fair treatment and showed rising dissatisfaction with the ways the state sought to impose a consensus version of Islam on them. Competing interpretations of the religion flourished and sometimes clashed. There was a concomitant waning of central authority.

This decline in central authority did not necessarily signify the weakness of the Muslim commonwealth. "As they became converted, people in the various provinces demanded to be admitted to the political process as full members of the Muslim community. . . . They were good Muslims, but their loyalty to a caliph and centralized Muslim government, hundreds, even thousands of miles away in a land they had never seen, was naturally limited" (Kennedy, pp. 202-03). A product of these contentious times, al-Hallaj became caught up in the ensuing tensions between local and central control.

A self-made man. The son of a poor wool-carder (which is the meaning of his name), Mansur al-Hallaj was a self-made man whose own success shows how the Muslim polity was expanding to include a much greater spread of social, economic, and geographical backgrounds at the time. Al-Hallaj was born in the province of Fars and spent his earliest years in the city of Tustar, on the eastern side of the Tigris and Euphrates rivers in what is today Iran. According to the most reliable sources, his father was employed in the cloth-weaving industry there, so his family was part of the working lower class (Massignon, p. 21). Still, al-Hallaj could pursue his education to an advanced level since medieval Islamic society offered opportunities to ambitious youth.

At the time Tustar was a heavily Arabized city, home to detachments of Arabic-speaking Abbasid troops. Al-Hallaj actually traced his lineage to Persian roots, and his grandfather was a Zoroastrian. However, al-Hallaj received his education in the Iraqi cities of Basra and Wasit, wrote most of his extant works in Arabic, and probably by adulthood seldom used his Persian in formal contexts. He completed his education at age 16, then returned briefly to Tustar and affiliated himself with a Sunni mystic leader in the city. He went back to Basra soon after, continuing the studies in mysticism that would become his life's vocation. During this period, al-Hallaj made long trips to the Islamic holy city of Mecca on the Arabian peninsula and, even more ambitiously, turned eastward at least twice for extensive journeys through cities of the Iranian plateau and as far as western India.

Upon his return, he settled in Baghdad, the imperial capital of the Abbasids. Becoming an intimate of great figures at the Abbasid court, acting as their spiritual guide and mentor, he grew deeply involved in—and ultimately fell victim to—the various attempts to strengthen the caliphal hold on power. His visibility and forthrightness in expressing his opinions about religious and social reform made him a tempting target. He often went about the streets of Baghdad publicly preaching his ideas wherever he could gather a crowd. Thus, the enemies of his supporters could more easily attack him than his more circumspect and well-guarded patrons. Eventually he was accused of religious blasphemy and political agitation and, despite the efforts of his supporters to save him, was executed in 922 C.E.

During the Abbasid decline, periods of relative prosperity alternated with threatening times of disruption and uncertainty. Al-Hallaj experienced both types of times. During his youth, the caliph al-Mu`tamid (r. 870-92), in partnership with his brother al-Muwaffaq, maintained order and rebuilt the financial and territorial underpinnings of the state after a nine-year period of anarchy. For much of al-Mu`tamid's reign, al-Hallaj lived in Basra, where order was harder to maintain, however. Rebellion was rife there. Basra was the center of the most protracted revolt against the government, one with an element of "class struggle" to it and racial overtones as well. This was the revolt of the Zanj, the black slaves from sub-Saharan Africa, over labor and living conditions. The term *Zanj* (derived perhaps from the name of the island Zanzibar) was used at the time for the East African slaves whom the Arabs had imported over the preceding two centuries so they could reclaim the marshlands of southern Iraq for agricultural purposes. The Zanj suffered horrendous living conditions and a correspondingly high mortality rate, which was uncharacteristic of slavery in the Islamic world. "This seems to have been the only area in the Islamic world where this sort of large-scale agricultural slavery was practised, elsewhere farming was conducted by free peasants while slaves were used for domestic, administrative or military purposes" (Kennedy, p. 179). In their rebellion against these conditions, the Zanj employed terror tactics. Al-Hallaj, living in Basra and 15 years old at the time, would have witnessed one such tactic when the rebels sent the heads of hundreds of massacred victims floating downstream past the city in an attempt to break its resistance to their siege. The enmity between the supporters of the caliph and the slaveowners, on the one hand, and the Zanj and their allies in Basra, on the other, was expressed in religious terms, as a breach between the two subdivisions of Islam, the Shi`ite and the Sunni. The entrenched powers identified with the Sunnism of the caliph and his court, the rebels with the Shi`ites. Whatever his reaction to the floating heads, al-Hallaj allied himself in marriage to a family that supported the same Shi`ite sect as the Zanj leaders. So he probably viewed the revolt with some sympathy, though there is no other direct evidence of this.

Suppression of the Zanj revolt, along with other, largely class-based insurrections, became a major concern for Caliph al-Mu`tamid and his brother al-Muwaffaq, and for the latter's son, al-Mu`tadid, when he succeeded his uncle in 892 C.E., and for al-Mu`tadid's eldest son al-Muktafi, who died in 908 C.E. But the essential soundness of their rule, and health of the caliphate at that time can be seen in the fact that at the death of al-Muktafi "the treasury was full and the caliph left 15 million *dinars*" to his heirs (Kennedy, p. 187).

With the reign of al-Muktafi's younger brother, all of this changed. Al-Muqtadir was only 13 when he became caliph and, though he reigned for 25 years, during most of that time he was essentially a puppet, guided first by his mother, the Byzantine concubine Shaghab, and manipulated later by representatives of two competing factions of government ministers. The first faction was led by the family known as the Banu al-Furat, the second by the Banu al-Jarrah.

The Banu al-Furat (led by Ali ibn al-Furat, who would connive at al-Hallaj's trial to ensure his execution) were Shi`ites of Baghdad. This Shi`ite affiliation may have been significant in that the Shi`ites would not have felt the strongest loyalty to the Sunni Abbasid caliph, but even more importantly, Ali ibn al-Furat was a consummate opportunist. He would enrich himself and his clan in the short term, often at the expense of what would have been sound fiscal policy in the long term. The other faction, the Banu al-Jarrah, were staunch Sunni Muslims like the caliph. At the head of this clique was Ali ibn Isa, who was completely unlike his rival. Abrasive and impatient, Ali ibn Isa lacked the finesse and sophistication of the urbane Ali ibn al-Furat, yet "at the time of each of his [four] departures from office, Ibn Isa left a restored budget, with reserves left aside, whereas at the time of his three falls from power, . . . Ibn al-Furat left an unbalanced budget and no reserves" (Massignon, p. 413). Ibn Isa's faction, the Banu al-Jarrah, had as their allies the

Madhara'iyun family, who boasted extensive contacts in Syria and Egypt. It was this alliance of the Banu al-Jarrah and the Madhara'iyun family, along with the caliph Muqtadir's mother and her chamberlain, Nasr al-Qushuri, who were admirers of al-Hallaj and protected him at the time of his initial arrest in 912 C.E. As Act One, Scene Two of *Murder in Baghdad* suggests, al-Hallaj may have been involved in treasonable correspondence with the branch of the Madhara'iyun in Egypt and their protégé, the able and famous breakaway governor of Egypt, Ibn Tulun, who established an independent dynasty there (Massignon, pp. 414-15).

Upon his initial arrest, al-Hallaj was sentenced to a mild punishment, three days public exposure while bearing a placard labeling him a political agitator. After that, he lived in the royal palace, under house arrest and, at the interces-

---

THE "CRUCIFIXION" OF AL-HALLAJ

One of the earliest accounts of al-Hallaj's death refers to his being "crucified" (*maslub*) (Massignon, p. 16). In the medieval Islamic world, the term refers to a live prisoner's being hung from a gibbet, or t-shaped crossbar, also often used as a gallows for hanging, and exhibited to the surrounding crowd for public humiliation (Massignon, pp. 452-53).

---

sion of Nasr al-Qushuri, was even given his own private quarters there. Sometime during this period al-Hallaj wrote works on the political theory and duties of a vizier, the caliph's chief deputy, which he dedicated to Ali ibn Isa, among others (Massignon, p. 29).

In 919 a fiscal crisis weakened the position of Ali ibn Isa, and he came into conflict with another minister, Hamid (who had ties to the Banu al-Furat). The inquiry into al-Hallaj's activities was reopened at this time, probably to undermine the caliph's confidence in Ali ibn Isa and his ally, the chamberlain Nasr al-Qushuri. Although it may have been no more than a pretext, al-Hallaj was indicted and brought to trial for heresy, specifically for claiming to perform miracles, for asserting that divinity can be embodied in human form, and for denying "divine unity," the most basic Islamic doctrine that there is only one God

(Massignon, p. 291). In 922 he was condemned and executed on a related charge, "of daring to alter the legal rituals" by arguing that it was possible to carry out the obligation of performing the pilgrimage at home, without actually traveling to the holy city of Mecca (Massignon, p. 545). He was subjected to an extremely cruel form of execution. After being subjected to a thousand lashes, his hands and feet were cut off, he was strung up and exhibited on a gibbet, then cut down and decapitated the next morning. Once dead, his body was burned and the ashes scattered into the Tigris River from the top of the highest minaret in Baghdad.

The development of Sufism. More than just a political activist or a religious preacher, al-Hallaj was a mystic, or *sufi. Sufi* is the term for those Muslims who, in the historical development of Islam, exhibited a particular interest in cultivating a close spiritual relationship to God.

Most religions in some measure seek to incorporate a reciprocal balance between encouraging in their followers an individual awareness of the sacred, and the impetus to build a godly community with fellow believers. In Islam, which early in its history developed a very strong focus on the community, the more individualized spiritual orientation, known as Sufism, emerged slowly. But it grew quickly in sophistication and depth. By al-Hallaj's time, Sufism had penetrated all social levels and occupied an important niche in the fabric of all Muslim groups, whether Sunni or Shi`i.

Not until a century later, however, would Sufism develop a systematic doctrine and history. Only in the later 900s, after al-Hallaj's death, did Sufism become institutionalized. Before that, its practice was extremely variable. The lives of its founders, who served as models for those seeking a deeper understanding of Sufism, were very much the stuff of legend. It was later, in retrospect, that Sufis discerned in the founders recognizably consistent positions on various questions important to the discipline. The later Sufis delineated these positions in three important manuals of conduct—the *Kitab al-luma fi al-tasawwuf* (The Book of Illuminations Concerning Sufism) by Abu Nasr al-Sarraj, *al-Ta`arruf li-madhhab ahl al-tasawwuf* (The Doctrine of the Sufis) by Abu Bakr Muhammad al-Kalabadhi, and *Qut al-qulub* (The Food of Hearts) by Muhammad ibn Ali al-Makki, all probably composed after 950 C.E. All three included an account of Sufism that traced it back to the devotional practices of the Prophet Muhammad and his immediate successors.

There followed a set of early mystics who cultivated, say the accounts, a sense of awe, wonder, and even fear at the terrible might and majesty of God. Hasan al-Basri (d. 728), a noted leader of this group, expressed its basically ascetic and gloomy outlook in the utterance, "O son of Adam, you will die alone and enter the tomb alone and be resurrected alone, and it is with you alone that the reckoning will be made" (al-Basri in Schimmel, p. 30). "Known as 'those who constantly weep,'" the group lamented "the miserable state of the world," and "the meditation on their own shortcomings made them cry in hope of divine help and forgiveness" (Schimmel, p. 31).

But even as these attitudes of revulsion at worldly concerns and active withdrawal from life took hold, a counter-current began to emerge that emphasized the cultivation of the mystic's longing for union with God, a longing that found its closest analogue in the love of an enraptured lover for his (or her) beloved. The most striking early representative of this trend in Sufism was Rabi`ah (d. 801 C.E.), a poor freedwoman of Basra. Annemarie Schimmel's description of her captures the essence of her character, as portrayed by later Sufis, in a few well-chosen sentences: Her "love of God was absolute. . . . The world meant nothing to her. She would shut the windows in spring without looking at the flowers and become lost in the contemplation of Him who created flowers and springtime" (Schimmel, p. 39). The trend focused on perfecting one's love for God, as Rabi`ah did, on the one hand, and on affirming this world (or at least not showing hostility to this life) rather than denying it a place of import, on the other hand. It was this last form of piety that al-Hallaj would adopt over a century later.

When this variety of teaching is pursued to its highest degree, the human lover's identity becomes submerged in that of the Divine Beloved, and he or she experiences a radically disorienting sense of unity with God. Later on, Sufi teachers would call this experience *fana,* Arabic for "annihilation." By this, they meant a person's awareness of self, of his or her egotistical desires and pride, would be destroyed, and the person would attain a rush of spiritual intuition permeated by a sense of God's presence everywhere. In the opinion of many, the closest analogue was the emotional surge one felt upon getting drunk, a comparison made all the more poignant by the fact that, although drinking intoxicating beverages was normally forbidden to Muslims, a "spiritual drunkenness" of this sort was perfectly legitimate. Sufis would stay up for long hours, meditating on God until hunger and sleep deprivation heightened and distorted their senses; they would engage in group chanting and dancing that carried them beyond the ordinary limits of human consciousness.

Not all Muslims understood or welcomed such behaviors; in fact, to behave in these ways was to invite disapproval and even punishment. It was in such a spiritually intoxicated state that al-Hallaj uttered the famous phrase, "I am the Truth" (*ana al-haqq*). "Al-Haqq" (the Truth) was one of the honorific titles of God in Islamic liturgy, so, to contemporary observers, the statement was blasphemous. It was as if al-Hallaj had said, "I am God." The incident was later used in evidence at the trial where he was condemned, lending support to the charges of heresy laid against him.

The three Sufi manuals, when they appeared shortly thereafter, were careful to criticize al-Hallaj for such utterances, and to call attention to his rashness in expressing his feelings and intuitions so publicly, in front of ordinary people, ill-equipped to interpret them properly. In the opinion of these manuals, al-Hallaj had failed to marry the sense of *fana,* or annihilation, to *baqa*. Literally this last term means "persistence" or "maintenance," but they were using it to denote the state of consciousness that a mystic experiences as he or she emerges from spiritual "intoxication." In this emergent state, one experienced a sense of returning sobriety or equilibrium, imbued with a new, transcendent awareness of divine immanence, one that kept bathing the believer in a kind of holy light.

From the tenth century on, Sufism underwent a period of systematization. The systematizers tried to contain the experiences of the early mystics by formulating a disciplined framework of education and training, most often compared to a path down which the initiate would be guided by a "master" or teacher. Eventually these educational practices, and the religious devotional exercises surrounding them, became even more institutionalized through the formation of organized Sufi groups, known in Western sources as "brotherhoods" or "fraternities," or even, misleadingly, as "orders" (from Christian monasticism, which has little relevance to Islamic practice). The groups owned meeting places where like-minded Sufis would gather to learn or to practice rites and rituals that enabled them to perfect their spiritual discipline. Not suprisingly, these fraternities sometimes became centers for protest against what their members perceived as unjust political or social practices. This was particularly true of the poor and downtrodden, who often balked when the Islamic ideals of egalitarianism and justice were subverted in larger society and found in the Sufi group the only effective avenue for making their protests heard. Over time, this seemingly paradoxical aspect of Sufism—not as withdrawal but as a potential source of organized opposition to an unjust ruler—would become well established in the Islamic world.

THE REAL SHIBLI

The play's Shibli is based on a real-life mystic of the same name. The real Abu Bakr Shibli (861-946 C.E.) was born to a family of Turkish court officials. He received substantial land grants, which he forfeited on becoming a Sufi. Though a follower of al-Hallaj and his closest friend, Shibli became famous for betraying him in his hour of need. Mystical tradition has it that when al-Hallaj was led to his execution, Shibli followed at a distance. At the gibbet, people began throwing stones at al-Hallaj. He reacted not at all, but when Shibli threw a rose that struck him, al-Hallaj screamed in pain. Why, he was asked, did you react to the rose and not the stones? "They do not know what they do," he answered, "but he should have known it" (al-Hallaj in Schimmel, p. 68). Shibli was summoned to testify at al-Hallaj's trial (Massignon, p. 529). When presented with evidence that al-Hallaj claimed to have become united with God, Shibli reportedly advised the court that "if someone speaks in this way, he must be forbidden to do so" (Massignon, p. 529). The reply, though it stops short of calling for his execution, was nevertheless used by the court to support its verdict.

The Play in Focus

Plot summary—Act 1. A play in two acts, the beginning unfolds much like a detective mystery. A dead body (soon to be revealed as that of al-Hallaj) hangs in Baghdad's main public square. The body is discovered by a group of passing strangers, after which, in flashback style, the act lays the groundwork for al-Hallaj's apprehension and arrest.

The first three characters encountered in *Murder in Baghdad* are the three passers-by who dis-

cover al-Hallaj's body: a merchant, a peasant, and a preacher from the local mosque. Rather than being well-rounded individuals, they represent the three major social classes in the medieval Islamic world. Seeking to discover the identity of the dead man, the three approach a nearby crowd. Members of the crowd openly contend it was they who killed the old man and, moreover, they did it with words. From their statements it becomes clear that they were bribed by the caliph's agents to shout at al-Hallaj's trial that he was a heretic.

As the crowd wanders offstage, a group of Sufis approach. The original three passers-by, not truly understanding why the authorities would want to spend so much time and gold insuring the death of one apparently harmless old man, resolve to ask the Sufis for more information. But the Sufis are even less forthcoming than the crowd. They say only that the old man sought death and they obliged:

> Preacher: Were you frightened when the poor
>   people shouted?
> And did you then forsake him?
> Is this your guilt?
> Sufis: Frightened? No. No.
> Only the dead fear death
> We fulfilled his wish!
>   (Abd al-Sabur, *Murder in Baghdad*, p. 6)

"Only the dead fear death," say the Sufis, referring to ordinary people who do not use their consciousness to be aware of God's presence everywhere. A true Sufi is fortified by the thought of God's nearness after death and so does not fear it. Al-Hallaj wanted to die so he could "return to heaven" and be close to God, whom he loved as a beloved (*Murder in Baghdad*, p. 7). So theirs is just the guilt of omission. They failed to acknowledge that they shared his beliefs when the mob called for his execution as a heretic.

After the Sufis leave, an old man with a single flower steps out from behind a tree. The man is Shibli, leader of the mystics and a close friend of al-Hallaj. Shibli blames himself for his friend's death, because he failed to publicly defend the accused and risk becoming a martyr at his side. After Shibli's confession, the three passers-by depart, troubled that there seem to be too many candidates for the role of murderer in the death of al-Hallaj.

The second scene reverts to the recent past. Shibli and al-Hallaj are seated, discussing Shibli's argument that it is better to withdraw from the world and from contact with people in order to come closer to God. Al-Hallaj objects to this view; it abdicates their responsibility as good Muslims and good Sufis to oppose evil in this world and save their fellow humans from injustice. To this, Shibli replies:

Evil is old in the world
Evil is meant for those who are in this world
So that the Lord can know
who shall be saved and who shall perish.
Each man must find the road to his own
    salvation,
So if by chance you find that road, then take it.
(*Murder in Baghdad*, p. 15)

Al-Hallaj is reluctant to accept this justification for abandoning his commitment to social change. His impulse is rather to create a world that more truly reflects the commandments of God, to make the world a more nurturing environment for the kind of spiritual quest in which he is engaged. But before he can fully explain himself to Shibli, they are interrupted by Ibrahim, one of their followers.

Ibrahim has come to warn al-Hallaj that he is in imminent danger. The authorities surrounding the caliph have discovered that al-Hallaj has been corresponding with rebel leaders in the empire. Among his correspondents are the al-Madhara'i brothers, the financial controllers of Egypt under the government of Ibn Tulun, who will later attempt to found his own dynasty, independent of the Abbasids.

Al-Hallaj replies he has corresponded with these men only to guide them to become better rulers:

These men you name are leaders of the
    nation;
They are also my friends, and have my love.
They promised me that if they should come
    to power
They will live righteously and not do ill;
They will grant the people their rights,
And the people will render them theirs.
They are my prime hope in this world, my
    dear Ibrahim,
Therefore, I quench their thirst with thought,
Refresh them with gentle words.
(*Murder in Baghdad*, p. 16)

Taking the more cynical traditional Islamic view toward politics, Shibli objects that these men, should they come to power, will behave like so many other tyrants before them, succumbing to corruption when they wield absolute power, even committing murder. But al-Hallaj refuses to concede. If he fails now, he argues, his ideas will live on in his words; they will carry his message to future generations, to people in a better position to heed his counsel.

Throughout this speech, Ibrahim grows more and more agitated. He urges al-Hallaj to flee eastward to the province of Khurasan, at the border of the empire, far from the caliph's reach. Al-Hallaj refuses, declaring that there is no haven on earth that he would prefer to the company of his true friends, those who have already been martyred for their beliefs and worship God in heaven. He vows instead to preach to the people, speaking of God's will and urging them to be as just and loving as their Lord. To show his rejection of Shibli's more traditional Sufi withdrawal from the world, he casts off his patched cloak, which signifies his commitment to poverty and self-denial, and throws it to the ground.

In the third scene, the passers-by (merchant, preacher, and peasant) reappear, joined by three others from the crowd: a hunchback, a lame man, and a leper. The lot of them encounter three Sufis who are debating the wisdom of al-Hallaj's dramatic gesture at the end of the second scene. Showing cynicism and unworldliness, all three sets of characters reveal themselves to be unready for al-Hallaj's radically novel view of the world, in which politics, social justice, and ethics intertwine and reinforce one another.

Al-Hallaj himself comes onstage next, followed by three individuals, dressed alike and acting suspiciously. The crowd guesses them to be members of the *shurtah*, the caliph's police force charged with keeping order in the large cities. The suspicion is justified, as the group goads al-Hallaj into declaring publicly his private vision wherein he felt he had become united with God. Once the admission is made public, the officer tries to arrest al-Hallaj, particularly because the mystic leader linked his personal awareness of God's presence in the world around him to a condemnation of those who allow poverty and injustice to persist in this same world. God is perfect, he says, and desires to see that perfection reflected in the humans He has created to be His representatives on earth (*Murder in Baghdad,* p. 27). But this is not what He sees before Him on the streets of Baghdad:

Now, behind poverty, under its unfurled
    banner,
March poverty's soldiers, the legions of evil
    vengeance;
Those malformed creatures of fearful
    appearance
Who are led by the devil, Vizier of the
    kingdom of poverty.
Murder, demagoguery, theft,
Betrayal, flattery, anger,
Aggression, tyranny:

These are the citizens of poverty's realm, the
   battalions of Satan, its Vizier.
God, most high, disdains to see Himself in
   creatures like us
And He turns His face from us.
How then shall we purify our black hearts
So that they reflect God's image?
So that they reveal His beauty?
With prayer?
With reading the Koran?
With pilgrimage?
With fasting in Ramadan?
Yes! But, mind you, these are only the first
   steps toward God.
These are steps taken by the feet.
But the Lord seeks the heart,
And only love, which is of the heart, pleases
   Him.

(*Murder in Baghdad*, pp. 28-29)

JUDGING THE JUDGES

Abd al-Sabur's Ibn Surayj is modeled on a real-life jurist, who died before the events portrayed in the play. The real Ibn Surayj was involved not in al-Hallaj's second case but his first one, at the end of which he issued a legal opinion saying that judgement on the inner beliefs of someone in a state of inspiration like al-Hallaj lay outside the province of Islamic law, and should be left to God on the Day of Resurrection (Massignon, p. 370). His arguments fall into line with sayings by the Prophet Muhammad, such as, "anyone who accuses someone else of heresy (*kufr*) is equally deserving of that designation" (Wensinck, p. 40). In other words, for Muslims, charging someone with heresy means setting oneself on the same level as God. To claim the ability to look into people's hearts and know that their words are heretical assumes the accuser has powers equal to God's (a heretical thought). In Abbasid times, few Muslims were willing to behave so presumptuously and risk, according to the belief, eternal damnation (Massignon, p. 378).

Although al-Hallaj does not directly call for a revolt against the government here, his plea to reform society and eliminate injustice and poverty would have been viewed with great nervousness by corrupt authorities like the Banu al-Furat, who held the vizierate at the time.

The policemen try to hustle al-Hallaj offstage before he says anything more, but their exit is temporarily interrupted by a Sufi, who seeks to stir the crowd: "Think. Are they arresting him because of what he said about love? / No, because of what he said about poverty" (*Murder in Baghdad*, p. 31). But when the crowd tries to defend him, al-Hallaj refuses their help. He deserves any punishment he gets, says al-Hallaj, because he has dared to reveal the secrets of his heavenly Beloved. The first half of the play ends somewhat surprisingly. Al-Hallaj does not embrace political activism by getting the crowd to prevent his arrest but is willingly led off to the palace to await judgment for heresy.

Act 2: Death. The second act focuses on al-Hallaj's prison experience and trial. A brief scene in prison underscores his commitment to suffering and being punished to make up for what he perceives as his fault in revealing too many details about his union with God. Then comes the scene at court, where al-Hallaj is tried by a trio of *qadis*, or Muslim judges, for religious blasphemy.

The judges are a blend of fact and fiction. The chief judge, Abu Umar, was the presiding judge at al-Hallaj's historical trial, and his character in the play conforms to his real-life image as a cultivated man-of-the-world who was quick to bend to the prevailing political winds (Massignon, p. 438). In the play, the other two real-life judges, whose characters are rather bland and obscure, are replaced by two invented characters, who serve as foils to Abu Umar. These are Ibn Surayj and Ibn Sulayman. Ibn Sulayman illustrates how a weak-willed but essentially good-hearted individual can be subverted and dominated by a stronger personality. He begins the trial genuinely interested in determining al-Hallaj's innocence or guilt, but by the end, he acquiesces in Abu Umar's verdict of guilt.

The lone advocate for the ideals of justice on the tribunal is Ibn Surayj, who consistently argues that no man can judge another on the question of heresy. Only God can make this judgement. First, he reiterates the legal opinion that Islamic law cannot judge on "a matter between a man and his Creator" (*Murder in Baghdad*, p. 66). Next he argues that the only crime he and his colleagues can render a verdict on is whether al-Hallaj sought to incite the people to rebel against the caliph and his deputies. In the midst of an exchange between al-Hallaj and Abu Umar on this issue, the proceedings are suddenly interrupted by a messenger carrying a letter from the vizier. The letter pardons al-Hallaj for any acts of political revolt but directs the court to reopen the question of heresy, for "[t]he Sultan may grant amnesty for a crime committed against the

State / But God does not forgive one who sins against Him" (*Murder in Baghdad*, p. 71). This leads to a tense exchange between Ibn Surayj and Abu Umar.

> **Ibn Surayj:** [*to al-Hallaj*] Do you believe in God?
> **Hallaj:**   He is our creator, and to Him we return.
> **Ibn Surayj:**   This is sufficient statement of his belief in God.
> **Abu Umar:** Ibn Surayj,
> I am not investigating his belief in God,
> But the manner of his belief.
> **Ibn Surayj:** The manner of his belief?
> Do you mean to probe his soul?
> Is this one of the ruler's rights?
> Or is it God's right?
> **Abu Umar:** This is the right of the Ecclesiastical Courts.
> **Ibn Surayj:** No, it is God's right, and His alone,
> And I do not have the temerity to question a man's faith.
> If you will persist in committing this sinful
> . . .
> **Abu Umar:**   [*Interrupting.*] Yes, we will, Ibn Surayj.
> **Ibn Surayj:** Then I will resign from this Court.
> **Abu Umar:** That is your prerogative, Sir.
>   (*Murder in Baghdad*, p. 72)

Once Ibn Surayj has left the room in disgust, Abu Umar calls the witnesses to al-Hallaj's heresy, including Shibli. A terrified Shibli gets drawn into explaining how mystics seek oneness with God. When asked if this is a practice of all mystics, or only al-Hallaj, he abruptly takes refuge in silence, which is understood by the court to be an accusation against al-Hallaj. The other witnesses, all members of the crowd who have been paid to accuse al-Hallaj of heresy, now chant their accusations. Judgement is rendered, and to the accompaniment of the mob's jeers and taunts, al-Hallaj is led forth to his execution, which takes place offstage.

To be or not to be an activist?—the Sufi question.

In Act One, Ibrahim comes to warn al-Hallaj that he is a wanted man, only to find him and his disciple Shibli in the middle of a central debate about whether Sufis should withdraw from the world in order to concentrate more fully on union with God, or whether they should remain committed to the basic Islamic goal of building a truly godly community on earth.

Al-Hallaj constitutes one of the earliest examples of a major Sufi leader becoming involved in the political affairs of his time, through his public preaching and willingness to advise political leaders. Although he acted as an individual and not as the leader of a brotherhood, he tried directly to change the irresponsible behavior of some factions of the caliph's court through admonition, perhaps even lending his support to conspiratorial movements seeking to overthrow Abbasid power. In his verse play, Salah Abd al-Sabur exploits this perception of al-Hallaj as a social activist, joining it to recollections of the political role played by Sufism from the late Middle Ages right up to the early twentieth century.

The choice of al-Hallaj as hero is deliberate, because of his relevance to the dramatist's own times. The medieval martyr becomes a prototype for the modern, politically committed intellectual who finds it untenable to function in isolation from the surrounding world. As Abd al-Sabur himself said about his motives for writing the drama:

> The torment of al-Hallaj is an analogue for the torment of intellectuals in most modern societies and the confusion they experience in choosing between the sword and word. After having scorned the option of a purely personal salvation achieved by casting off the world and humanity from their shoulders, they have preferred instead to take the burden of humanity in its entirety upon their shoulders.
> (Abd al-Sabur, *Hayati fi al-shi'r* p. 120; trans. T. DeYoung)

Sources and literary context. The early-to-mid 1960s constituted a remarkable period of innovation and florescence in the Egyptian theater. Although drama was a new art form, imported into the Arab world, Egypt had folk traditions that incorporated dramatic elements and harked back to the ancient Egyptians. It had furthermore been exposed to European drama since the dawn of the nineteenth century. The mid-twentieth-century saw a liberalization of Egyptian cultural life in which dramatists such as Yusuf Idris, Salah Abd al-Sabur and Abd al-Rahman al-Sharqawi sought inspiration from the traditional folk spectacles and shadow plays of popular Egyptian culture as well as from the current experiments in European avant-garde theater.

In all five of his dramatic works, Abd al-Sabur chose to return to the formalized tradition of the verse play. His choice was probably influenced by the success of a number of plays in this form in the West, most notably *Murder in the Cathedral* (1935) by T. S. Eliot. It was probably also influenced by a desire to rework the artifice-filled, static verse plays of Ahmad Shawqi, written between 1926 and 1932, which had attracted some renewed attention (Jayyar, p. 8).

A serious student of the theater, Abd al-Sabur wrote numerous studies of the Egyptian theatrical tradition, including an article on Shawqi as a dramatic poet. He himself translated T. S. Eliot's *Murder in the Cathedral* into Arabic in 1964, which would not be published until after his death in 1981 (Budayr, p. 12). It should be noted that a considerable number of critics argue against the position that *Murder in the Cathedral* inspired *Murder in Baghdad,* including Salah Abd al-Sabur (see Boullata, p. 241). The author always emphasized that his inspiration was classical Greek tragedy and that, in al-Hallaj, he was seeking to create a hero in the Aristotelean sense, one with a tragic flaw that set the action in motion. His portrayal of al-Hallaj, by his own admission, was deeply influenced by his reading of Louis Massignon's biography of the hero and by other Western sources on the subject ("Nadwat," p. 5).

Events in History at the Time the Play Was Written

A thousand-year parallel—the not-so-distant past. *Murder in Baghdad* was published at the end of 1964, when Nasser's socialist government was enjoying success in its campaign to suppress indigenous religio-political movements like the Muslim Brotherhood in Egypt. At no time before or since would the orientation of Egyptian society be more resolutely secular. It is eerily prescient that Abd al-Sabur was able in the play to articulate issues that would come very much to the forefront by the mid-1970s, when Nasser's successor, Anwar al-Sadat, would rehabilitate the Islamists and seek their support in his struggles against opponents among the secular intellectuals. These opponents—including Abd al-Sabur—had enthusiastically embraced an interpretation of al-Hallaj as someone who joined religion as private inspiration to a public activism that does not emphasize religious conformity. In their view, Sadat was betraying the legacy of Arab socialism (a brand of socialism that does not reject religion out of hand as "the opiate of the masses") by letting capitalist speculators operate willy-nilly in the country without government oversight or control. Later the Islamists would turn on Sadat, and a violent faction among them would target him for assassination. But the increased popularity of Islamist groups and their ideology has meant that the regime of his successor, Husni Mubarak, has found it expedient to accommodate them wherever possible, at the expense not infrequently of the secular intelligentsia. In the early

1980s, the Muslim religious establishment was allowed to proceed with court cases seeking to ban writings deemed "anti-religious" or "obscene." Classic texts like **The Arabian Nights**, along with numerous modern works, were included in the tally (also in *WLAIT 6: Middle Eastern Literatures and Their Times*). Such an atmosphere of increasing intolerance for divergent points of view or lack of conformity to religious norms can surely be seen as an element in the assassination of journalist Faraj Fawda (also spelled Farag Foda) in 1992 and the attempted assassination of Nobel-prize-winning novelist Najib Mahfuz in 1994 (see Mahfuz's **Miramar**, also in *WLAIT 6: Middle Eastern Literatures and Their Times*). Thus, the contention that the play's al-Hallaj is a stand-in for the tortured figure of the modern intellectual has gained relevance since publication, in ways al-Sabur could not have foreseen. *Murder in Baghdad* underscores the dangers facing truth seekers in many modern societies that have shown an increasing proclivity to suppress individual freedoms, especially freedom of thought.

Performance and reviews. Because *Murder in Baghdad* was a verse play—and therefore the dialogue was in Modern Standard Arabic rather than Egyptian Colloquial—it experienced some initial difficulty in getting performed. The play was first presented in the autumn of 1965 on al-Birnamij al-Thani—the Egyptian equivalent of the National Public Radio—a mode that emphasized its poetic, rather than dramatic elements (Khashaba, p. 68). Its first successful staging for the public (in the summer of 1967) took place at the University of al-Azhar, a centuries-old center for Islamic studies in the Arab world. The play attracted the al-Azhar officials because of the religious focus and "lack of female roles" [female actors would have violated the restrictions on sexual segregation in force on the al-Azhar campus at that time] (Sharif, p. 72). Given the controversial hero and the play's bold treatment of a tension-filled relationship between religion and state, the willingness of the Sunni religious establishment to stage it at all bespeaks a tolerance and openness to multiple points of view characteristic of the best in Islamic tradition.

In 1966 *Murder in Baghdad* won the Egyptian State Encouragement Prize, the highest honor the government bestows on a single work. The play was also reviewed favorably, not once but twice (in 1966 and 1967) in the most prominent Arabic cultural periodical of the day, *Al-Adab*. The editors devoted one of their monthly "Roundtable" ("Nadwat al-adab") features to a discussion of the play, involving Abd al-Sabur and two of Egypt's foremost literary critics of the day, Abd al-Qadir al-Qitt and Izz al-Din Isma`il. Isma`il summed up the discussion, which centered on the use of the verse form:

[Al-Hallaj] is a mystic (Sufi), and it is not easy to speak about mystic emotions in the language of dry prose. . . . He is at the same time a man fighting for justice, which is also not an idea easily conveyed . . . without . . . something to make it soar. Here is the justification . . . to use poetry as a medium for expression.

(Isma`il in "Nadwat," p. 5)

—Terri DeYoung

For More Information

Abd al-Sabur, Salah. *Hayati fi al-shi`r.* Beirut: Dar al-Awdah, 1969.

———. *Murder in Baghdad.* Trans. Khalil Semaan. Leiden: E. J. Brill, 1972.

Badawi, Muhammad Mustafa. *Modern Arabic Drama in Egypt.* Cambridge: Cambridge University Press, 1987.

Boullata, Issa. Review of *Murder in Baghdad. The Muslim World* 63, no. 3 (July 1973): 241.

Budayr, Hilmi. Salah. *Abd al-Sabur: qira'at fi bibliyujrafiyah al-sha`ir.* Cairo: Dar al-Thaqafah, 1984.

Jayyar, Midhat. *Masrah Shawqi al-shi`ri.* Cairo: Dar al-Ma`arif, 1992.

Khashabah, Sami. "Al-Nashat al-thaqafi fi al-watan al-Arabi." *al-Adab* 13, no. 9 (September 1965): 66-68.

Kennedy, Hugh. *The Prophet and the Age of the Caliphates: The Islamic Near East from the Sixth to the Eleventh Century.* London: Longman, 1986.

Massignon, Louis. *The Passion of al-Hallaj: Mystic and Martyr of Islam.* Vol. 1. Trans. Herbert Mason. Princeton: Princeton University Press, 1982.

"Nadwat al-adab: Ma'sat al-Hallaj." *al-Adab* 14, no. 8 (August 1966): 3-7, 67.

Schimmel, Annemarie. *The Mystical Dimensions of Islam.* Durham: University of North Carolina Press, 1975.

Sharif, Ayida. "al-Nashat al-thaqafi fi al-watan al-Arabi." *al-Adab* 15, no. 10 (October 1967): 71-73.

Wensinck, Arendt Jan. *The Muslim Creed: Its Genesis and Historical Development.* Cambridge: Cambridge University Press, 1932.

My Michael

by

Amos Oz

Amos Oz (1938-) was born Amos Klausner in Jerusalem to Jewish parents of Eastern European and Central European origins. He lived on a kibbutz and in Jerusalem when it was a divided city, later using both as settings in his stories. Oz earned a Bachelor's degree in philosophy and literature at the Hebrew University of Jerusalem in 1963, then earned a Master's degree from Oxford University in England in 1970. In 1965, he published his first book, *Artzot ha-tan* (*Where the Jackals Howl,* 1981), a collection of short stories about life on a kibbutz. He followed this with his first novel, *Makom aher* (1966; Elsewhere Perhaps), and two years later with the novel that would catapult him to fame—*My Michael*. Oz's subsequent novels include *La-ga`at ba-mayim, la-ga`at ba-ruah* (1973; *Touch the Water, Touch the Wind,* 1974), *Kufsah shehorah* (1986; *Black Box,* 1988) and *Panter ba-martef* (1995; *Panther in the Basement,* 1997). As a rule, Oz's novels reach bestseller status in Israel and *My Michael*, the first of his books to be translated into English, was no exception. The novel uses 1950s Jerusalem as a metaphor for Israel itself, portraying the community as it then was—a mostly besieged enclave in an ever-threatening wilderness. Through its protagonist, the novel suggests the challenges of daily existence to one's mental and emotional fortitude, especially when these are already compromised by other factors within someone's life.

THE LITERARY WORK

A novel set in Jerusalem in the 1950s; first published (as *Mikha'el sheli*) in 1968, in English in 1972.

SYNOPSIS

A young Israeli woman's frustrations with her marriage contribute to her psychological breakdown.

Events in History at the Time the Novel Takes Place

The founding of Israel—hopes and fears. The establishment of a Jewish homeland in Palestine—a long-cherished dream and the objective of Jews active in the Zionist movement—was a process that took many years and encountered numerous obstacles, not the least of which was the bitter opposition of Palestinian Arabs. During the 1920s and 1930s, Great Britain, which had been granted control over the region by the League of Nations, adopted a seesaw policy, first backing the drive for an official Jewish homeland, then, in response to Arab agitation, limiting Jewish immigration to Palestine. The policy satisfied neither the Zionists nor the Arabs. In the 1930s the Arabs expressed their

Amos Oz

displeasure through a series of demonstrations and revolts aimed at both the British and Jews. The Arabs resented the British for behaving like a colonial ruler, the Jews for threatening to displace them. Though in the 1930s the Palestinian Arabs still outnumbered the Jews by more than two to one, they were well aware both of the rapidly rising Jewish presence and the persistent desire for a Jewish state in the land.

Britain made no significant change to its Palestinian policies during World War II. After 1945, however, the grim truths of the Holocaust—the extermination by Nazi Germany of nearly six million European Jews—became common knowledge, and the idea of a Jewish state took on heightened significance for Jews everywhere. Many believed that the founding of such a state was the only way to prevent this type of devastation from befalling their people again. Meanwhile, Western nations that were formerly opposed to the idea came overwhelmingly to support it, despite the continuing dissent of the Arab world. In 1947 the issue was turned over to the newly formed United Nations, which proposed partitioning the land into separate Jewish and Arab states. Both the Palestinian Arabs and the surrounding Arab states rejected this proposal.

War broke out in Palestine in November 1947. It would be prosecuted in two parts. The first part, which lasted until mid-May 1948, can be characterized as a guerrilla-style struggle between the Arabs and the Jews of Palestine. Arabs attacked Jews in several cities, including Haifa, Tel Aviv, and Jerusalem, while anti-Jewish riots raged in Beirut, Aleppo, Damascus, and Baghdad. Initially the Jews fought a defensive war but they switched to an offensive posture by the time this phase of the fighting ended. While the Arab troops achieved some success in the early months of this civil war, Jewish forces gained the ascendancy by April 1948. Hundreds of thousands of Palestinian Arab civilians fled or were driven from their homes to neighboring lands in this part of the war, especially to Transjordan, the Arab state to the east of Israel (presently known as Jordan). The refugees headed for makeshift camps on the west bank of the Jordan River (which formed most of the Palestine-Transjordan border) and for the Gaza Strip (along the Mediterranean coast).

As the British Mandate of Palestine approached its expiration date of May 15, 1948, the Zionists assembled a provisional national council, which elected a 13-member provisional government, to be headed by David Ben-Gurion as prime minister and defense minister. On May 14, 1948, this council gathered in Tel Aviv and proclaimed the establishment of the independent State of Israel, bringing to fruition a dream that had been nearly three-quarters of a century in the making. The very next day the second part of this Arab-Israeli conflict began—a conventional war between Israel and the Palestinian Arabs, now joined by neighboring Arab armies. The armies invaded, in support of the Palestinians and to realize their own territorial ambitions (Sachar, pp. 315-16).

With the invasion, the conflict grew into a full-blown war of independence. Five surrounding countries—Egypt, Syria, Transjordan, Lebanon, and Iraq—declared war on Israel. Most of the Arab leaders in the campaign refused to recognize the new state's existence; they resolved to wrest away its land. The Israelis were no less determined to defend their new nation; by mid-July 1948, an Israeli force of 65,000 troops was facing Arab armies that together totaled 40,000 (Morris, p. 217). In the three phases of fighting that followed, the Israeli forces each time extended the territory under their control. "The first phase lasted for about a month and was followed by a short truce. The second . . . took place between July 8 and July 18. . . . A final round of fighting began in October and continued until the following January" (Tessler, p. 264).

A fierce battle for Jerusalem transpired before the first phase, intensifying when Transjordan invaded on May 19. Already the Arabs had attacked the Jewish quarters of the city. Also the Arabs had gained control of all three roads leading to the city and were using this control to besiege Jewish Jerusalem and to ambush relief columns that tried to get there. For an unnerving time, the Jews of Jerusalem faced the imminent danger of being overrun or starved out. "The Arabs controlled every height around the city and within it" (Sachar, p. 324). Finally, on June 9, relief reached the Jews via a newly cut road through the mountains. Although *My Michael* begins later, its protagonist would likely have lived in besieged Jerusalem since she was native to the city.

As the intermittent struggle proceeded, Israel defeated each of its Arab attackers—the Arabs did not mount a united offensive—and captured several territories that the United Nations had allocated to the Palestinian Arabs for the proposed Palestinian state. The fighting ended in early 1949. By July 1949 Israel had signed a series of armistice agreements with Egypt, Lebanon, Jordan, Iraq, and Syria.

Even after the armistices were signed, however, many Arab countries remained hostile—all the more so because they felt humiliated and frustrated by their multiple defeats at the hands of the Israeli forces. Israel likewise continued to be wary of its Arab neighbors. At various times following the end of the 1949 war, serious peace overtures were made on both sides, but these usually met with rebuffs from either the Arab leaders or Israel. A continuing atmosphere of tension and mutual suspicion ensued, aggravated by, among other factors, the occurrence of small-scale Palestinian infiltrations—supported by the Arab states—into Israeli territory. While the vast majority of the Palestinian infiltrators during the 1949-56 period came to see their old homes, retrieve property, harvest abandoned crops, or obtain food, some were terrorists. Operating from Arab states such as Jordan or from the refugee camps in the West Bank and Gaza Strip, the terrorists attacked Israelis and sabotaged Israeli targets. Around 200 Israeli civilians were killed in such armed raids. In retaliation, Israel adopted a "shoot on sight" defensive policy that resulted in the deaths of 2,700 to 5,000 mostly unarmed Palestinian infiltrators from 1949 to 1956; in addition, several hundred Palestinians were killed as a result of Israeli retaliatory raids (Morris, p. 274).

Not surprisingly, the raids and other infiltrations kept Israelis on a constant state of alert, preventing the new nation from achieving any sense of peaceful normality or security. This state of psychological tension informs the background of *My Michael*—set during the 1950s—and comprises a constant atmospheric presence that looms over the narrative, despite being alluded to only sparingly. Palestinian infiltration comes up directly only in passing. The novel refers to newspaper coverage of "gangs of infiltrators in the Negev," the desert in southern Israel whose arid land Israelis were striving to transform into agricultural fields at the time (Oz, *My Michael*, p. 102). More central to the novel are the protagonist's recurrent fantasies about two Arabs, twin boys with whom she grew up in a Jerusalem neighborhood in the late 1930s and early 1940s. In her fantasies she envisions them as grown men, Arab fighters festooned with weapons and dressed in combat fatigues, conducting mysterious guerrilla operations by night.

PALESTINIAN ARAB REFUGEES

In *My Michael*, Hannah Gonen is obsessed with two displaced Arab twin brothers with whom she played as a young girl. Part of a wealthy Arab family who lived nearby in Jerusalem, they have not crossed paths with her since childhood yet she fantasizes about the twins as adults: "I expect they live in a refugee camp now," she, in passing, tells the reader (*My Michael*, p. 251).

The Sinai-Suez War of 1956. Between 1949 and 1956 Israel and its Arab neighbors existed in a state of armed truce. Relations between Israel and Egypt, in particular, became increasingly strained during this period. The pattern of Palestinian infiltrations followed by harsh Israeli reprisals continued, and many Israelis came to believe that Egypt supported or at least condoned raids into their territory because of Egypt's control over the Gaza Strip from which hostile infiltrators launched most of their attacks. On February 28, 1955, Israeli forces retaliated by destroying military targets inside Gaza and ambushing an Egyptian convoy of reinforcements; the attack left 38 Egyptians dead and 62 wounded (Tessler, p. 345). In response, Egypt began to organize and equip squads of Palestinian commandos (fedayeen), which were sent across the border into Israel, where they often attacked civilian targets.

A vicious cycle of raids and reprisals ensued, exacerbating Israeli-Egyptian hostilities to the point where open warfare seemed imminent.

In addition to sponsoring fedayeen raids, Egypt imposed a blockade upon the Gulf of Aqaba, sealing the straits of Tiran and preventing ships from entering or leaving Israel's port of Eilat. Egypt also began to increase its military might by making arms agreements with Communist bloc countries. Then, on July 26, 1956, Egypt angered not only Israel but also Britain and France when Egyptian president Gamal Abdel Nasser nationalized the Suez Canal Company. (France had planned the building of the canal and Britain controlled it; it was scheduled to be turned over to Egypt, in whose territory it sat and whose people had labored mightily to construct it, in 1968.) British Prime Minister Anthony Eden wrote to President Eisenhower of the United States:

> The canal is an international asset and facility, which is vital to the free world. The maritime powers cannot afford to allow Egypt to expropriate it and to exploit it by using the revenues for her own internal purposes irrespective of the canal and the canal users. . . . My colleagues and I are convinced that we must be ready, in the last resort, to use force to bring Nasser to his senses.
>
> (Eden in Tessler, pp. 348-49)

In August 1956 the British and French began planning for an invasion of Egypt, even as they engaged in diplomatic efforts to find a nonviolent solution to the problem. In October, Britain and France agreed to combine forces with Israel, which had been denied access to the Suez Canal since Nasser's nationalization of the company. Representatives of all three nations met in Sèvres, France, to finalize their plans for an armed attack on Egypt. Additional factors motivated their strategy. A charismatic figure, Nasser was trying to achieve a pan-Arab unity. Also he supported Algeria's rebels in their fight against French rule, and, in defiance of the Western powers, he was receiving arms from the Soviets. All of this was perceived as a serious threat.

On October 29, 1956, Israeli forces entered the Sinai Peninsula and attacked positions of the Egyptian army; by November 5, Israel had occupied the Gaza Strip and captured several strategic locations throughout the Peninsula, including Sharm al-Sheikh. Meanwhile, France and Britain moved to occupy the canal zone, between the Sinai Peninsula and the rest of Egypt, and took control of Port Said, Egypt. With so much of its territory occupied by foreign troops, Egypt was forced to admit defeat and a cease-fire went into effect.

Facing strong condemnation from the U.N. Security Council, France and Britain agreed to withdraw their troops from the Canal Zone; evacuation of their forces was completed on December 22, 1956. Israel, however, maintained troops in Sharm al-Sheikh and the Gaza Strip, demanding an end to fedayeen raids and removal of all restrictions on Israel's use of the Suez Canal and the Gulf of Aqaba in exchange for its withdrawal from the region. The United Nations was not inclined to address those issues at the time and a stalemate ensued, broken by intervention from the United States, whose diplomats persuaded Israel to remove its forces without a guarantee of the conditions upon which it had earlier insisted. Israeli troops withdrew from Sinai in March 1957.

The Sinai-Suez War plays a pivotal role in *My Michael*; Michael Gonen—husband of Hannah, the protagonist—is called into military service for several weeks during the initial campaign in the Sinai Peninsula. Oz does not focus upon the events of the campaign itself, but rather upon the effect it has upon Israeli civilians. While Michael accepts the war and his part in it (as a wireless operator) with characteristic stoicism, the emotional Hannah broods—sometimes missing her husband, sometimes resenting him, and at other times taking refuge in various fantasies to escape from the mingled tension and tedium of her daily life. At one point during Michael's absence, she reflects upon the nature of their marriage and their fundamental differences by recalling his reaction to the Sinai Campaign:

> You knew in advance that you were being called up for a war, not for maneuvers. That the war would be in Egypt and not in the east. That the war would be a short one. All this you deduced with the aid of a well-balanced inner mechanism by means of which you continually produce thoroughly reasoned ideas. I have to present you with an equation on whose solution I depend in the way that a man standing on the edge of a precipice depends on the strength of the railing.
>
> (*My Michael*, pp. 219-20)

Jerusalem—the divided city. Arab-Israeli tensions in the 1950s were especially marked in Jerusalem, where the novel's Hannah Gonen grew up and still lives. Jerusalem was the British administrative capital throughout the Mandate period (1922-48). In a spiritual sense, the city was the site of the ancient Temple around which the religion was centered, and after its destruction and the dispersal of the Jews outside Palestine, remained the focal point of their longing for return. As the new Israeli government recognized, Jerusalem was Israel's heart and its branches moved their offices there at the beginning of 1950, declaring it to be the capital of the new state. Yet things were far from simple, for the city's experience has been (and remains) one of deep division. Because it contains leading religious sites for Jews, Christians, and Muslims, the ancient city of Jerusalem has been among the thorniest issues in Arab-Israeli negotiations. Its symbolic importance for people of all three faiths makes it perhaps the most revered and at the same time the most contested piece of real estate in the world.

Paradoxically, Jerusalem was considered a cultural backwater at the time of the novel. Indeed, during the first half of the twentieth century, Zionists neglected Jerusalem because it represented staid religious tradition and the home of the old Yishuv, or Jewish community in Palestine; instead, Zionists concentrated upon Tel Aviv, which was established as the first modern, Hebrew-speaking city in the region. Even after the founding of modern Israel, Jerusalem was marked by a provincial isolation that often put it outside the mainstream of Israeli life. Much of this isolation came simply from the city's physical location. Israel's other major cities (Haifa and Tel Aviv) lie along the Mediterranean coast, along with minor cities. Removed from these busy, vibrant ports, Jerusalem lies in the interior. In the 1950s, it was furthermore bordered to the north, south, and east by stretches of no-man's land and by Jordan, with its Palestinian Arab refugees. Only to the west was Jewish Jerusalem joined to the rest of Israel. It was, from the western coastal perspective, little more than an outpost at the end of an insecure territorial corridor that gave the otherwise closed-off town a pathway to the sea. During the 1948 war, Arab fighters had temporarily blocked the main road of this corridor, besieging Jewish Jerusalem for several months. Even with the corridor open, to some the otherwise hemmed-in town no doubt felt constricting.

Most of the plans for partitioning Palestine proposed by the United Nations during the Mandate period had included the establishment of Jerusalem as an international zone under a neutral (non-Arab, non-Zionist) administration. After the 1948 war, the international community continued to call for such an agreement. So, while recognizing Israel, other nations at first refused to recognize Jerusalem as Israel's capital. Instead, they established their embassies in the modern, Jewish-populated city of Tel Aviv, on the coast. However, both Israel and Jordan—the two states that ended up controlling Jerusalem—refused to turn the city over to international rule. Throughout the time of the novel, the city was effectively partitioned, reflecting the territories that Jews and Arabs had respectively come to occupy during the 1948 war. While Jordan administered Arab East Jerusalem, Israel controlled Jewish West Jerusalem, from which Palestinians had fled or been exiled during the war. Both parts of the divided city grew during the 1950s, with East Jerusalem increasing to 70,000 while West Jerusalem grew to 195,000 by 1966 (Gilbert, p. xi). In the novel, Hannah Gonen comments on the city's rapid growth after the 1948 war, although she remains deeply ambivalent about Jerusalem, still seeing it as a changeless backwater that imprisons its inhabitants.

> Jerusalem is spreading and developing. Roads. Modern sewers. Public buildings. There are even some spots which convey for an instant an impression of an ordinary city: straight, paved avenues punctuated with public benches. But the impression is fleeting. If you turn your head you can see in the midst of all the frantic building a rocky field. Olive trees. A barren wilderness. . . . And all around, the hills. The ruins. The wind in the pine trees. The inhabitants.
>
> (*My Michael*, pp. 269-70)

Life in West Jerusalem in the 1950s. Although many Palestinian Arabs had lived in the western part of Jerusalem before the emergence of Israel, most of them fled or were expelled during the war of independence; their abandoned dwellings were razed to the ground or were occupied by Jews. Consequently, there were few Arabs in West Jerusalem and likewise virtually no Jews in East Jerusalem during the 19 years that the city was divided (1948-67). Both the Palestinian Arabs and the Israeli Jews generally abided by the cease-fire line, but daily life grated on the nerves. On the Israeli side, residents lived under the perpetual threat of sniper fire. Hardly a month went by that "somebody was not killed or wounded on the frontier, or at least struck by a stone thrown from the wall" (Kollek in Gilbert, p. 268). Sniper fire took the lives of nine people in 1954 and wounded 54 more. In 1956 a Jordanian soldier opened fire on 199 civilians at an Israeli archaeological conference and killed four. The next day a Jordanian army patrol shot into a group of Israeli women olive pickers and killed one, and so on.

Meanwhile, the division of the city was patently visible. Where a street had previously run through both sides, there loomed a 15-to-20 foot concrete wall. Barbed wire fences, mines, and stretches of no-man's land divided the city into two as well. There was only one crossing point, the Mandelbaum Gate; not really a gate, the crossing was named after a Mr. Mandelbaum, who once owned a nearby house.

West Jerusalem, the Israeli side, continued as little more than a sleepy border town in the 1950s. To the north, totally cut off from the town but still held by the Jews, was an enclave on Mount Scopus, former site of the now hauntingly empty Hebrew University and Hadassah Hospital. Improvising, the university moved its center of operation to Jewish or New Jerusalem, for the time being, setting up shop in a one-time Christian site, the Franciscan Terra Sancta College, where the novel's Hannah meets her future husband, Michael.

Life in the Jewish sector was subdued. There were no sidewalk cafes and there was little nightlife. The downtown shopping center was a mixture of the old and the new: "Arab-looking men riding donkeys down the street; bearded men with long earlocks and large felt hats, driving horses and wagons filled with kerosene; women shoppers with string bags . . . bicycles, motorcycles, cars, horses, . . . beggars squatting on corners" (Clawson in Gilbert, p. 251). Shabbiness abounded. A hodgepodge of residential styles emerged. Large new housing projects, featuring boxlike blocks of apartments, sprung up around former Arab and Christian quarters that were transformed into Jewish living spaces. Many Jews from Arab lands resided in immigrant camps, or *maabarot*. The largest, Talpiot, housed close to 8,000 people in 1954. It had one water tap for every 20 families and no toilets, just walled off holes in the ground that emitted a nauseating smell. Sanity was a common casualty of camp life, reports Dr. Fanny Ribnowitz, who in three months treated five new cases of insanity at Talpiot alone (Gilbert, p. 260). These breakdowns bring to mind *My Michael*'s Hannah, victim to just some of the same stresses, since she is not a newcomer living in a camp.

Jerusalem in the 1950s had better residential districts too, with gardens and trees. But even in these districts, residents suffered daily uncertainties—about safety, food, money.

Workers' salaries were invariably late and one never knew exactly how late. Most people could not afford a telephone. For years after the 1948 war, daily staples—coffee, eggs, meat, and the like—were rationed, and there was the persistent pressure of living in a contested city. "Half the time you drove down a road or a side street, you ran into a sign reading "Stop! Danger! Frontier Ahead!" (Gilbert, p. 268). These are the everyday stresses with which people in general had to contend in 1950s Jerusalem, along with their more personal problems.

The Novel in Focus

Plot summary. *My Michael* is the private journal of 30-year-old Hannah Gonen, a Jerusalem housewife, mother, and part-time kindergarten teacher. Hannah opens the narrative with a declaration of a sense of disillusionment, and of the danger therein: "I am writing this because people I loved have died. I am writing this because when I was young I was full of the power of loving, and now that power of loving is dying. I do not want to die" (*My Michael*, p. 3).

Through her private journal, the older Hannah introduces readers to her 20-year-old self, a bright, imaginative student of literature at the Hebrew University in 1950. At the university Hannah meets Michael Gonen, the man she will soon marry. Describing him as "a geologist, a good-natured man" but "not a witty man," she recalls their first date (*My Michael*, pp. 3, 6). Michael talks about his father, Yehezkel Gonen, a widower whose own father had been a respected scientist in Poland before immigrating to Israel. Yehezkel Gonen has put most of his modest salary from his job at a municipal water department into Michael's education, cherishing the idea that Michael will carry on the family tradition of science. Hannah, in turn, tells Michael about her family. Her father, a quietly intellectual man who owned a small electronics shop, died in 1943. Since then, her mother, who knits and reads novels in her native Russian, has lived with Hannah's brother, Emanuel, and his family on a kibbutz.

The young Hannah abandons a possible profession in academia to marry the quiet, even-tempered Michael, who is in many respects her polar opposite. But she retains her love for literature—especially for the stories of Jules Verne—the source of some of her fantasies:

> When I was small I read and reread my brother's copy of Jules Verne's *Twenty Thousand Leagues*

Under the Sea. There are some rich nights when I discover a secret way through the watery depths and the darkness among green and clammy sea-creatures until I beat at the door of the warm cavern. That is my home. There a shadowy captain waits for me surrounded by books and pipes and charts. His beard is black, his eyes hold a hungry gleam. Like a savage he seizes me, and I soothe his raging hatred.

(*My Michael*, p. 22)

Hannah and Michael move into an old two-room apartment in a somewhat shoddy neighborhood. Three months after the wedding, she becomes pregnant and suffers a host of physical and psychological ailments, including "a permanent headache" and "tormented" dreams, from which she "would wake up screaming" (*My Michael*, p. 65). Their son, Yair, is born early the following year, in 1951. Owing to unspecified complications, the doctors keep Hannah in the hospital for ten days after she gives birth. When released, she is told "to stay in bed and avoid any form of strain" (*My Michael*, p. 84). Hannah remains ill all summer, and Michael cares for the baby while pursuing his studies in geology.

As Yair grows into a toddler and then a young boy, Michael establishes a positive, if somewhat wooden, relationship with him. Michael enjoys Yair's curiosity and his interest in clocks and other mechanical objects. To convey the importance of not interrupting, Michael teaches the boy to say "I have finished" when he is done speaking (*My Michael*, p. 116). Hannah, in contrast, finds her son mildly repugnant and intolerably insolent. She sometimes beats Yair. By the age of four or five, he has grown into "a strong, silent child," intelligent but with "a tendency towards extraordinary violence" (*My Michael*, p. 117).

Although Hannah's physical health seems to improve, she continues to have disturbing, violent dreams and fantasies. Many of them involve two Arab boys, twins named Halil and Aziz, with whom she played as a girl. In her dreams they "practice throwing hand grenades before dawn among the ravines of the Judean Desert," with "submachine guns on their shoulders" in "worn commando uniforms stained with grease" (*My Michael*, p. 105). She also fantasizes about a strong man of action named Michael Strogoff (taken from a novel of the same name by Jules Verne) and about vague military campaigns involving a British naval destroyer called H.M.S. *Dragon*. In many of her dreams and fantasies she is a warrior princess commanding armies and planning military strategy.

In the summer of 1955 the family spends a week with Michael's father, Yehezkel Gonen, now a retired municipal worker, staying at Yehezkel's apartment in Holon, near Tel Aviv. Yair and Grandpa Yehezkel become fast friends. Yehezkel's explanations of the town's water, power, and transportation systems fascinate Yair, as do the old man's accounts of guerrilla battles between Arabs and Zionists in the days before independence. Four days after the family returns to Jerusalem, they are saddened to receive word that Yehezkel has died suddenly, collapsing at a bus stop near his apartment. Shortly afterward, Hannah's impulsive spending—in a decade of austerity in Jerusalem and Israel at large—force the still grieving Michael to ask some friends for a loan.

That fall, rumors of impending war with the Arabs sweep through the city. "Housewives in

WHOSE MICHAEL?

In Oz's novel, Hannah fantasizes about the strong, mysterious hero of Jules Verne's *Michael Strogoff: A Courier of the Czar*, a novel published in Hebrew in 1940 that took its new readership by storm. Set in late-nineteenth-century Russia, Verne's novel features a handsome, solidly built, courageous hero, a man far more exciting and romantic than Hannah portrays her husband to be in *My Michael*. Verne's protagonist sets out on a 3,000-mile journey to warn the brother of the tsar about a rebellion in the Siberian provinces. Wounded, temporarily blinded, snared by his enemies, the resolute Michael Strogoff presses on through every obstacle to reach his goal.

the shops said that the Arab Legion was installing gun batteries around Jerusalem. Canned food, candles, and paraffin lamps vanished from the shops" (*My Michael*, p. 193). Soldiers, armed with machine guns, become a common sight on the city's streets as Israel responds to troop buildups in the surrounding Arab countries. One chilly morning Hannah comes down with a serious fever that leads to a state of near psychological collapse. She has barely begun recovering when Michael is called up for military service as Israeli tanks invade and occupy the Sinai Peninsula. He assures Hannah that he will be in no danger, since he is only a radio officer. Several weeks later Michael returns home, weakened and stricken with a digestive illness.

In the following months, small changes enter into their lives. Yair starts school, and several older acquaintances pass away. Hannah complains, as she has earlier to the reader, about "a sameness of the days and a sameness in me" (*My Michael*, p. 254). In an attempt to relieve her ennui, Hannah brings a revived enthusiasm to the couple's sex life. She finds the contact to be merely physical, however, and thinks that in arousing her husband sexually, she is only deceiving him "with his own body" (*My Michael*, p. 259). In the spring of 1959, Hannah takes a new job, and Michael finally completes his doctoral thesis. Anticipating his success in the academic world, they have already planned to move into a larger apartment in a new suburb of the city. Hannah is pregnant again. The pregnancy leaves her drained, and in her exhaustion she begins to suspect Michael of harboring an

---

THE MENTAL COST OF WAR

Hannah's most serious mental collapse comes just when the country is gearing up for war, as Michael is called up to serve in Israel's invasion of the Sinai Peninsula. This dramatic climax, the Israeli critic Gershon Shaked has observed, "corresponds to the [actual] Sinai Campaign, which was perceived as discharging tensions that had built up from years of 'living on the edge'" (Shaked, p. 190).

---

attraction to the pretty typist who is helping him with his thesis. But she finds herself not caring much one way or the other, or so she says in her diary. More real to her are her fantasies about the Arab twins Halil and Aziz. Ultimately Hannah acknowledges the end of her marriage with indifference and retreats into her fantasy world, dispatching the twins on a terrorist mission to destroy the water tower in Jerusalem, her city of birth but one in which she has never felt at home and has come to hate for "haunting" her (*My Michael*, p. 282). It is late at night when Hannah imagines sending the twins off on this final commando mission; lost in fantasy, she awaits their return as "quiet cold calm" heralds the pale light of dawn over Jerusalem (*My Michael*, p. 287).

Exotic dreams, mundane realities. Perhaps the most striking aspect of *My Michael* is Oz's choice of protagonist; the main character and narrator

is not the "Michael" of the title but Michael's troubled wife, Hannah. Intriguingly, Oz himself was reluctant to tackle her perspective, as he revealed in an interview about the novel's development:

> [Hannah] said to me; "Look, I am here, I will not let you go. You will write what I am telling you [to write], or you will have no peace." And I argued back, I excused myself; I told her: "Look, I cannot [do it], go to somebody else. Go to some woman author; I am not a woman; I cannot write you in the first person; leave me alone." But no, she did not give up.
>
> (Oz in Cohen, p. 143)

Whatever Oz's initial reservations, Hannah proves to be a memorable, if not always reliable, narrator. When the novel begins, she has already reached her current age of 30 and—the reader discovers—her current mental dissolution, which subtly undermines the accuracy of her recollections.

Significantly, most of Hannah's fantasies involve triumph over or escape from a humdrum or unsatisfying reality. As her marriage to Michael disintegrates under the strains of her ill health, their mutual incompatibility, and the daily stresses of life in 1950s Jerusalem, Hannah becomes ever more entangled in her fantasy world. Continually bemoaning "the dreary sameness of the days," she imagines herself in different incarnations: as Yvonne Azulai, an exotic Sephardic woman in search of adventure and sexual thrills, as a warrior princess of Danzig, and as the commander/lover of the now-grown Arab twins, whom she sends on missions involving espionage and sabotage (*My Michael*, p. 176). At one point, delirious with fever, Hannah suffers what appears to be a complete break with reality, all of her identities, yearnings, and fantasies merging in a confused, sexually charged, kaleidoscopic vision:

> Silently the twins clasped my arms to tie them behind my back. . . . Hands pressed my body. Kneaded. Pounded. Probed. I laughed and screamed with all my strength. Soundlessly. The soldiers thronged and closed round me in their mottled battle dress. A furious masculine smell exuded from them in waves. I was all theirs. I was Yvonne Azulai. Yvonne Azulai, the opposite of Hannah Gonen. . . . I am made of ice, my city is made of ice, and my subjects too shall be of ice. Every one. The Princess has spoken.
>
> (*My Michael*, pp. 197-98)

Many readers of *My Michael* have speculated on the cause of Hannah's descent into madness—whether it is attributable to her unsatisfactory marriage to a man whom she tries but fails to dominate, to her secret but deep-rooted hatred of Jerusalem, or to the stresses of daily life in Israel during its war-torn early years. Perhaps Hannah's breakdown could most reasonably be tied to a combination of causes rather than any one cause. It is, however, worth noting that the fantasies in which she seeks oblivion are as exciting and exotic as her real-life existence as a suburban housewife in 1950s Jerusalem is both mundane to the point of tedium and fraught with periods of unbearable tension and anxiety.

In the novel, a mentally unstable fictional character is continually confronted by a discrepancy between the ideal and the real. This same discrepancy confronted real-life Israeli society in her day. For half a century, Zionists had been driven by ideals. The founder of modern Zionism, Theodor Herzl, set the tone at the start of the twentieth century with his *Altneuland* (Old-New Land), an inspirational novel that envisioned Palestine's Jewish community developing into a consort of successful farmers, business leaders, and industrialists within 20 years. Women would enjoy equal rights with men, jobs would abound, and Arabs and Jews would co-exist peacefully. Next came the ideal of labor Zionism, trumpeted by Aaron David Gordon (1856-1922), who touted redemption by labor in the Holy Land and who himself tilled the soil, working shoulder-to-shoulder with other pioneers to realize his ideals until the end of his dedicated life. Another inspirational idealist, Joseph Trumpeldor (1880-1920) championed a Jewish labor battalion, advocating austerity and the collective, resolving to sow seeds "a handful at a time" and tackle every task from road-building to swamp drainage "until we conquer the Land of Israel" (Trumpeldor in Sachar, p. 145). Heeding the call, newcomers streamed in to join old-timers, bringing more ideals, such as the notion of collective farming so integral to the kibbutz.

Then came statehood—the realization of these long-held ideals—and the dreamers were left with just the hardships. Rapid progress had to be made, and indeed the achievements were remarkable. By the end of the 1950s, only 6 percent of the Jewish households in Israel lacked running water; only 19 percent had no access to electricity; almost all the *maabarot*, or immigrants' camps, had been dismantled. From Europe and the Arab Middle East, Jewish immigrants meanwhile poured into a country unprepared but determined to receive them. The swift progress and re-population exacted an emotional price. Hannah's collapse no doubt struck a chord in many an exhausted life. A fictional character, with her own peculiar problems, she nevertheless reflects a sense of disillusionment that was widespread in the 1950s:

> For several years, the influx of hundreds of thousands of semimendicants threatened to extinguish the idealism even of Israel's veteran European population. . . . The selfless and spontaneous emotional commitment of the pre-1948 era appeared increasingly out of date. The old idealism, then, was the most lamented casualty of Israel's postwar independence era.
> (Sachar, pp. 427-28)

Sources and literary context. Amos Oz's own experiences growing up in Jerusalem during the 1940s and part of the 1950s provided the most important overall source for the novel. "The Jerusalem of my youth was a city of sleepwalkers, awash with contradictory dreams," explains Oz (Oz in Balaban, p. 79). The image brings to mind *My Michael*'s Hannah and her penchant for losing herself in reverie. Like other Jewish boys, Oz attended "a Hebrew elementary school with strong religious and national tendencies, where they taught us to long for the glory of the ancient kingdoms of Israel and to aspire to restore them in blood and fire" (Oz in Balaban, p. 79). This same wording appears in *My Michael* in a Zionist slogan that fascinates Hannah: "Judaea fell in blood and fire, in blood and fire will Judaea rise," a refrain that echoes over and over in her mind (*My Michael*, p. 119).

Oz has suggested that during the 1950s, when *My Michael* takes place, many Jerusalemites felt a deep nostalgia for the city as it had existed under the British Mandate (before 1948). Some critics have seen the novel's evocative descriptions of the changes in Jerusalem in the 1950s as a reflection of this longing for the earlier period.

A similar sense of disquiet about national changes was expressed by various Israeli writers of Oz's generation after 1956. Gershon Shaked saw the Sinai Campaign as a turning point in how these younger writers viewed Zionism and its attendant mythology:

> For those born in the 1930s, the Sinai Campaign of 1956 was the experience that changed their relation to the Zionist metaplot [or master narrative]. Unlike the war of 1948, this seemed more a war of choice than a matter of survival. . . . The ambivalence engendered by the war brought about changes in the form as well as the content of the fiction. . . . Writers produced anti-establishment allegories that to some degree veiled their intentions.
> (Shaked, p. 189)

Shaked characterizes *My Michael* as one of several "anti-establishment" stories that spoke in veiled terms around this time. Others include Aharon Megged's *Fortunes of a Fool*, published in Hebrew in 1959, and A. B. Yehoshua's allegory "The Last Commander," published in Hebrew (in *The Death of an Old Man*) in 1962.

Reception. *My Michael* was completed on the eve of the 1967 Six-Day War, before the struggle itself was prosecuted and won. As one might expect, given the triumphant exuberance that characterized Israeli public life after the Six-Day War, the novel evoked a storm of controversy when published in 1968. An immediate bestseller, it roused both bitter condemnation and enthusiastic approval among Israelis. Hostile critics focused their attention on Hannah Gonen's sexual fantasies, accusing her of being "anti-Zionist" and an "Arab-lover" (Balaban, p. 175). Others praised the novel's penetrating treatment of the deep but often unacknowledged psychological connections between Israeli Jews and their Arab neighbors.

American reviewers took up this last theme after the English translation appeared in 1972. Writing in *The New York Times Book Review*, Paul Zweig noted that *My Michael* was "extremely disturbing to Israelis" when first released.

> At a time when their country had asserted control over its destiny as never before, Oz spoke of an interior life which Israel had not had time for, which it had paid no heed to, an interior life that contained a secret bond to the Asiatic world beyond its border.
>
> (Zweig, p. 5)

From the American critics, the novel received high praise for its literary strengths, especially the rich detail and suggestive imagery by which it traces Hannah's slow mental erosion.

—Colin Wells and Pamela S. Loy

For More Information

Asali, K.J. *Jerusalem in History*. New York: Olive Branch Press, 2000.

Balaban, Avraham. *Between God and Beast: An Examination of Amos Oz's Prose*. University Park, Penn.: Pennsylvania State University Press, 1993.

Cohen, Joseph. *Voices of Israel*. Albany: SUNY Press, 1990.

Gilbert, Martin. *Jerusalem in the Twentieth Century*. New York: John Wiley & Sons, 1996.

Morris, Benny. *Righteous Victims: A History of the Zionist-Arab Conflict, 1881-2001*. New York: Vintage, 2001.

Oz, Amos. *My Michael*. New York: Knopf, 1972.

Sachar, Howard M. *A History of Israel*. New York: Alfred A. Knopf, 2000.

Shaked, Gershon. *Modern Hebrew Fiction*. Trans. Yael Lotan. Bloomington: Indiana University Press, 2000.

Tessler, Mark. *A History of the Israeli-Palestinian Conflict*. Bloomington: Indiana University Press, 1994.

Torstrick, Rebecca L. *The Limits of Coexistence: Identity Politics in Israel*. Ann Arbor: University of Michigan Press, 2000.

Wasserstein, Bernard. *Divided Jerusalem: The Struggle for the Holy City*. New Haven: Yale University Press, 2001.

Zweig, Paul. Review of *My Michael*. *The New York Times Book Review*, 21 May 1972, 5.

My Name Is Red

by
Orhan Pamuk

One of the most well-known and controversial authors writing in Turkey today, Orhan Pamuk was born in Istanbul in 1952. He aspired to be a painter in his youth, characterizing himself as the artistic member of a family of engineers. His education shows a penchant for writing despite earlier aspirations; after attending an American preparatory school in Istanbul, Pamuk earned a diploma in journalism at Istanbul University. He turned seriously to the craft of writing in 1974. In 1982, after eight years of searching for a publisher, Pamuk released his first novel, *Cevdet Bey ve ogullari* (*Cevdet Bey and His Sons*), which won two prizes and launched him on a rapid rise to fame. His subsequent novel *Beyaz kale* (1985; *The White Castle*), translated into English in 1990, met with enthusiastic international acclaim. Later novels—*Kara kitap* (1990; *The Black Book,* 1994), *Yeni hayat* (1994; *The New Life,* 1997), *My Name Is Red* (1998), and *Kar* (2002; *Snow*)—have stirred up intense reactions in Turkey and earned him a reputation abroad as one of the world's major living writers. Although he continues to live and work in Istanbul, Pamuk spent several years in New York City, and often describes himself as a bridge between the East and the West. He writes in an experimental and playful manner that appeals to Western audiences, meanwhile drawing on Turkish life for his subjects and characters. All of his novels concern themselves with the struggle to merge Eastern and Western influences into a dual-souled identity that is uniquely Turkish. *My Name Is Red* directly considers these questions, as

> ## THE LITERARY WORK
>
> A novel set in Istanbul in 1591; published in Turkey (as *Benim adim kirmizi*) in 1998, in English in 2001.
>
> ## SYNOPSIS
>
> An illustrated book commissioned by the Ottoman sultan leads to the murder of a master gilder; while a young man works to both solve the mystery and win the heart of his beloved, the murderer roams the streets of medieval Istanbul.

artists trained in the miniature painting style of the Ottomans decide whether to assimilate or reject the new "Frankish" portrait painting.

Events in History at the Time the Novel Takes Place

Who were the Ottomans? One of the world's largest and longest lasting empires, the Ottoman Empire (1299-1923) ruled for 600 years and at its height stretched from the Caspian Sea to the Mediterranean coast and included much of the modern Middle East, North Africa, Southeastern Europe, and the Balkan Peninsula. It was a highly organized empire ruled by a family dynasty of sultans, with the help of an elite cadre of soldiers, bureaucrats, and religious functionaries, who

Orhan Pamuk

Arabic script. On the other hand, the Ottomans interacted with the West, engaging in diplomacy, cultural exchange, and trade, though there were hostilities as well. The empire was in frequent dialogue with the city-states and kingdoms of Europe, in the process gaining exposure to European ideas and technologies. Some sultans welcomed technological and cultural influences from the West, while others discouraged them: for example, Mehmed II (1429-81) had Venetian painter Giovanni Bellini (1430-1516) decorate the palace with frescos, while his son, Bayezid II (r. 1481-1512) had these frescos covered up. In the novel, Pamuk portrays the character Sultan Murad III (1567-1603) as being secretly interested in Italian Renaissance portraiture. Perhaps intending to prefigure the eventual breakup of the Ottoman Empire in 1923, Pamuk shows the stresses in the multifaceted Ottoman identity: the artists in Pamuk's novel struggle with a whirlwind of conflicting allegiances to the sultan, to religion, to tradition, to innovation, to ambition, and to themselves as creative artists.

Istanbul at the end of the sixteenth century. Istanbul is situated on seven hills above the Bosporus Strait, a natural channel which both divides and connects the European and Asian continents. Formerly called Constantinople, the city was the capital of the Christian Byzantine empire for a thousand years before becoming the capital of the Islamic Ottoman Empire for the next 600. Istanbul was home to Topkapi Palace, the residence of the sultans, serving as the seat of imperial power in the empire. Although very few had access to the palace, the city itself was a center of commerce and culture. Here the various peoples of the diverse empire met and mingled.

Set in 1591, *My Name Is Red* takes place just after the golden age of Süleyman. Having reached a high point of expansion, the Ottomans now became embroiled in conflicts of an increasingly defensive nature, in both the East and the West. Economic problems were the cause of much of the instability of the period. A currency devaluation caused by an influx of silver from the newly discovered Americas led to high inflation and skyrocketing prices all over Europe. The ensuing increase in counterfeiting, corruption, and bribery are alluded to in the novel, as is the increase in the population of Istanbul as migrants poured in from outlying areas to find work. *My Name Is Red* portrays the period as one of change and mobility, both upwards and downwards.

themselves were considered Ottoman. The name Ottoman (*Osmanli* in Turkish) derives from the accepted founder of the dynasty, Osman (d. 1326). Although he and his people descended from Turkic nomads originating in Central Asia, the Ottomans developed a separate language and identity, rejecting the designation "Turk" and applying it to the peasants. Cultural attributes rather than race determined whether one was Ottoman; ethnic origin had little to do with the matter. Being Ottoman meant being literate in the languages of Ottoman Turkish, Persian, and Arabic, mastering the culture of Islamic civilization, being a Muslim, serving the state in some capacity, and owing absolute allegiance to the sultan. It was possible for people from conquered territories to acquire these attributes and work their way up into high state positions, becoming part of the Ottoman elite. But not all subjects of the empire were considered Ottoman (e.g., Greeks, Armenians, Jews, and indeed most Arabs and Turks), since imperial policy was to allow local languages, religions and cultures to persist in its lands.

The Ottomans were aligned, on the one hand, to Islamic culture. They drew strongly on Persian and Arabic achievements in science, theology, poetry, and art. Ottoman Turkish, spoken only by the educated, absorbed many Persian and Arabic elements; it was even written in the

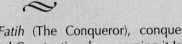
Not as richly supported by the state as in the golden age, the palace artists in the novel complain of having to sell costume books and erotic illustrations for extra money. The character Enishte, by contrast, has been able to build a two-story house in a new region of the rapidly expanding city.

In the late sixteenth century, economic hardship among the poor increased resentment of the Ottoman elite. This resentment was exploited by Islamic extremists who channeled it into attacks on what they claimed were decadent cultural institutions, such as wine-drinking establishments and coffeehouses. The novel's Nusret Hoca of Erzurum may be based on one of these real-life extremists—Mehmet of Birgi, a sixteenth-century cleric who preached against coffee, tobacco, wine, and music. However, fundamentalism was not the only religious force at the time. Sufi orders, which represented the mystical branch of Islam, were active too, and they were another target of the fundamentalists. Many of the great poets and philosophers of the Middle East were Sufis, a point acknowledged in Pamuk's novel. The novel makes a distinction between political Islam, seen as a destructive, anti-intellectual force, and mystical Islam, seen as the source of great cultural riches. Throughout Ottoman times, depending on the orientation of the sultan, Istanbul observed the dictates of Islam more or less strictly. Sometimes its administrators tolerated wine, sometimes not; the Istanbul coffeehouses were opened, closed, and opened again.

Istanbul under the Ottomans had thriving Greek, Armenian, Jewish, and Italian neighborhoods. Encouraging such diversity, Ottoman policy allowed all peoples with a "covenant" (meaning Jews and Christians as well as Muslims) to practice their religions freely. With certain restrictions they could build synagogues and churches, and establish their own courts of law. Indeed, from the end of the fifteenth century, many Jews fled to Istanbul from Europe to escape persecution. While some discrimination against non-Muslim minorities did exist, many of Istanbul's minority citizens became successful and prominent.

Women in the Ottoman Empire. Minorities in Istanbul were not expected to conform to Muslim traditions. In Pamuk's novel, Esther, a Jewish character, moves freely and unveiled throughout the city, carrying love letters for Ottoman ladies, who themselves were more restricted in their movements. History has conjured up a popular image of the sequestered Ottoman woman, con-

fined to the house and not allowed to go out unless heavily veiled. New scholarship is showing that the reality was more complex and that women's lives, although segregated from men's in the public sphere, were richer than once supposed. Ottoman women enjoyed property and inheritance rights unknown to European women in the sixteenth century, and those with money freely engaged in economic activities, investing in real estate, commercial ventures, and international trade. Prominent noblewomen of Istanbul initiated and sponsored the building of public ar-

---

SOME LANDMARK EVENTS IN OTTOMAN HISTORY PERTINENT TO *MY NAME IS RED*

1453 Mehmed II, or *Fatih* (The Conqueror), conquers the Christian Byzantine capital Constantinople, renaming it Istanbul and making it the capital of the Ottoman Empire.

1520-56 Süleyman I, or *Kanuni* (The Lawgiver), reigns over the golden age of the Ottoman Empire. A time of economic prosperity, his rule marks the height of geographic expansion and is traditionally considered the cultural zenith of the Ottoman arts, including poetry, ceramics, and miniature painting. Characters in *My Name Is Red* look back on this era with nostalgia.

1571 The Battle of Lepanto results in the Ottomans' defeat at sea against an alliance of Western powers. Although the Ottomans gain Cyprus, the loss of the battle shatters the image that they are an invincible empire and shakes Ottoman moral.

1574-95 Sultan Murad III reigns. A great patron of miniature painting, Murad III commissions many illuminated manuscripts from the palace workshop under the direction of Master Osman.

1578-90 The Ottoman Empire battles the Safavid Empire, which rules Persia from 1501-1736.

---

chitectural projects, such as fountains, mosques, and soup kitchens, while women of all classes frequented the courts. Court records show that women knew and defended their legal rights, even, in some cases, against their husbands. Not as sequestered as one might think, elite women in the Ottoman period socialized regularly with each other in a variety of accepted venues. Most elite women were literate, and a few exceptional Ottoman women, such as Mihri Hatun (d. 1506) became successful court poets. That being said, Ottoman society was very segregated, and women

An illustration by the real-life master painter Bihzad, who greatly influenced Ottoman miniaturists.

huge territory spanning Central Asia and Persia from the fourteenth until the sixteenth century), the Safavid Empire, the Ottoman Empire and the Moghul Empire (which ruled India from the fourteenth until the nineteenth century). Each of these schools had a distinct style, the result of a blend of Persian aesthetics, Turkish taste, and the influence of Chinese painting—which had been introduced earlier by the Mongol conquerors. Miniature painting flourished and matured in Timurid Herat (located in today's Afghanistan), home of the renowned painter Bihzad (1440-1514), whose dramatic colors, bold compositions, and focus on individual character had a huge influence on Ottoman painting. For subjects of miniature paintings, artists commonly looked to the classics of Persian poetry, such as Nizami's **Leyla and Mejnun** and **Khusraw and Shirin,** love stories written in the twelfth century that remained favorites throughout the Islamic world (also in *WLAIT 6: Middle Eastern Literatures and Their Times*). Firdawsi's **Shahnamah,** or **Book of Kings** (1010), a verse compilation of Persian myth and history, inspired illustrated versions for centuries (also in *WLAIT 6: Middle Eastern Literatures and Their Times*).

Illustrated manuscripts were considered royal treasures and many came to the Ottomans as spoils of conquest. The Ottoman painters were influenced by these works but developed a style of their own. Less inclined to illustrate poetry, Ottoman miniaturists tended to portray historical events in ways that would glorify the sultan. Although painted according to Persian aesthetic traditions, Ottoman miniatures were less ornamented and more realistic, and they incorporated meticulous real-life details. A great patron of miniature painting, Murad III commissioned a number of illustrated books from the palace workshop. The *Book of Festivities, Book of Victories,* and *Book of Skills,* produced in that workshop under the direction of a Master Osman, are now considered treasures of the Ottoman cultural heritage. This historical workshop inspired the one in the novel.

did not socialize with men. Society esteemed modest behavior in women, and Ottoman men considered it an obligation to protect their daughters and wives from unwanted attention by providing them with servants to do shopping and errands, which lower class women had to do for themselves. The higher a woman's class, the more her activities would be limited by custom and decorum.

Ottoman miniature painting. The Ottoman *Nakkashhane,* a workshop connected to the Topkapi Palace that created illustrated books for the sultan, was one of several schools of court artists attached to the Middle Eastern imperial courts. The creation of illustrated books was a courtly art that aimed to bring glory to the ruler. It involved an entire workshop of calligraphers, artists, and bookbinders, who labored together under the direction of a master. The manuscripts combined text with painted illustrations (the miniatures), which were composed of brilliant colors concocted from minerals. The bookmakers gilded a manuscript with gold leaf and bound it in finely tooled leather.

Different schools of miniature painting are associated with each of the great Islamic empires, in particular the Timurid Empire (descendents of the Mongol conqueror Tamerlane who ruled a

The Novel in Focus

Plot summary. *My Name Is Red* is a murder mystery told in a series of first-person monologues by 12 different narrators. The opening chapter is narrated by the corpse of Elegant Effendi, a master gilder of illuminated manuscripts, now dead at the bottom of a well in the outskirts of Istanbul. Elegant's corpse hints that he has been murdered by one of three master miniature painters from the palace workshop. He was working together with them on a secret project. Nicknamed Elegant, Stork, Butterfly, and Olive, these four labored at home under the direction of a man they called Enishte (a respectful title meaning "uncle-in-law" or "brother-in-law") to create an illuminated book for the Ottoman sultan Murad III. They had been doing so without the knowledge of Master Osman and the rest of the workshop, for the book was to be illustrated in the "Frankish" or "Venetian" painting style. It is a style that Master Osman detests and many consider sinful. "My death conceals an appalling conspiracy against our religion, our traditions, and the way we see the world," warns the corpse of Elegant, and the reader quickly surmises that this "conspiracy" is the group's working on the secret book (Pamuk, *My Name Is Red*, p. 5).

Meanwhile, a young man named Black has arrived in Istanbul, summoned by Enishte for assistance on the book. Enishte's former ward, Black had begun an apprenticeship at the palace workshop, but did not stay the course. Having left Istanbul in emotional torment after his love for Enishte's daughter Shekure was rejected, Black spent 12 years working for the Ottoman bureaucracy in the Arab and Persian territories of the Ottoman Empire. After Black's departure, Shekure married a cavalry officer, who set out to fight the Safavid Persians and has now been missing for four years. Left with her two sons, Shevket and Orhan, Shekure is in limbo—neither married nor divorced. She cannot marry again until there is proof of her husband's death. Having fled her husband's house because of unwanted attention from his brother Hasan, Shekure lives with her father. Seeing that Black has returned to Istanbul, she spies on him talking to her father and becomes intrigued. Glimpsing her face through a window as he leaves, Black is overcome with love for her.

Into the picture comes Esther, a clever but illiterate cloth seller who specializes in the risky business of arranging matches for Ottoman ladies. Esther has long been carrying secret love letters from Hasan to Shekure, letters that Shekure reads and saves, but does not answer. Shekure initiates a correspondence with Black, which Esther facilitates, though she stops at Hasan's on the way so he can read their letters too. As Hasan becomes inflamed with jealousy and anger, a suspicious Shekure uses her children as intermediaries to arrange a meeting with Black alone in secret.

Meanwhile, Elegant's body is found, and rumors fly that the murder is somehow connected to the secret book. Enishte, suspecting that the

murderer is one of the remaining three artists, sends Black out to investigate the crime. All equally arrogant, self-indulgent, and talented, each painter asserts his innocence. However, chapters told by the murderer reveal that he is indeed one of the painters. From the murderer, the reader learns that Elegant had fallen under the influence of the fundamentalist cleric Nusret Hoca of Erzurum and was preparing to denounce the secret book as sinful, especially the final page,

ISLAM AND FIGURATIVE PAINTING

The Western reader might be confused by the multiplicity of views on Islam and painting represented in *My Name Is Red*. Some characters assert that Islam forbids painting the human figure; others argue that miniature painting is acceptable but Western portrait painting is a sin, still others maintain that all painting is acceptable. Some are simply unsure and tormented by confusion. By raising this issue, Pamuk has added his voice to a debate that has gone on for centuries. The Quran does not expressly forbid figurative painting, although the creation of idols is strongly forbidden, as in the Old Testament. There is, however, an antipathy towards figurative painting by some legal schools of Islam, based on several of the *hadith*, or sayings attributed to the prophet Muhammad. In one *hadith*, painting is censored for being a distraction to contemplation of the divine. Another *hadith* condemns painters to damnation for attempting to rival God by creating life. However, the *hadiths* are not considered reliable by everyone, and are open to interpretation. These controversies did not repress Islamic art but channeled it in certain directions. Calligraphy and the decorative arts in particular flourished, achieving great heights of artistry. The history of Islamic art also includes many examples of figurative painting in murals, paintings, and manuscript illustrations.

intended to be a portrait of the sultan drawn in the "Frankish" style. The murderer initially claims that he killed Elegant because he was afraid that Nusret Hoca's mobs would kill them all for working on the heretical book. The murderer and the other miniaturists frequent a coffeehouse where a storyteller uses illustrations to spin tales that do double duty. Aside from entertaining the guests, the tales denounce Nusret Hoca, in the process adding the opinions of a dog, a tree, a horse, a gold coin, the color red, Satan, death, and the cross-dressing storyteller himself to the narrative.

Tormented with guilt and doubt, the murderer begins to wonder whether the final page of the secret book, which he has not yet seen, really is heretical. According to the murderer's ever more deranged logic, if the final page is sinful, then he should not have murdered Elegant and will go to hell. In that case, Enishte and his book are to blame for the murderer's crime. Arriving at Enishte's house exactly when Shekure and Black have met in secret to indulge their passion, the murderer engages Enishte in a discussion about the book. Becoming more and more agitated as Enishte defends the "Frankish" style, the murderer kills Enishte and absconds with the final page.

Finding her father murdered, a desperate Shekure orchestrates a quick divorce and marriage to Black before Hasan can claim that she should move back to her father-in-law's house, where he also lives. She, however, refuses to consummate the marriage until Black has found her father's murderer. Black himself falls under suspicion of the murder, and is called to the sultan's court at Topkapi Palace to testify. Under threat of torture, Black is compelled to prove his innocence by using clues from the paintings of the secret book to identify which of the painters is the murderer. He works with Master Osman to do so. Searching for the source of an unusual method of illustrating a horse that appears in a sketch found on the deceased Elegant, Black and Master Osman enter the palace treasury. An elderly master devoted to Near Eastern traditions of miniature painting, Master Osman is contemptuous of Western methods and of Enishte's attempts to copy them. While in the treasury, Master Osman finds the needle used by Bihzad, who reportedly blinded himself rather than be forced to change his style. As Master Osman blinds himself while gazing at a copy of *The Book of Kings*, Black finds the clue that could identify the murderer. The novel comes to a dramatic conclusion as the coffeehouse is raided by Nusret Hoca's mob, and Black, Stork, Butterfly, and Olive all confront each other in the murderer's hideaway. Black is wounded in the struggle while the murderer, whose identity is finally revealed, escapes, only to be beheaded by a crazed Hasan. Narrating the last chapter, Shekure relates how after the death of Murad III, miniature painting was abandoned, and reveals her own secret desire to have her portrait painted in the Western style.

Murder for art's sake. Elegant Effendi's murder is the catalytic event for the entire action of the novel, yet at the end it is still an open question as to why he was killed. The murderer, who is plainly concealing much, even from himself, first claims he committed the murder because he was afraid that Elegant would denounce them to Nusret Hoca's mobs. However, his motives turn out to be more complicated.

"I didn't kill him out of fear," he admits to Enishte. "You murdered him because you wanted to paint as you wished," Enishte retorts, indicating that the murderer had killed a representative of the forces who would repress his artistic freedom (*My Name Is Red,* p. 166). The murderer is deeply attached to the traditional style, but his attraction to the new Western style is so intense that the conflict literally splits him into two characters, one of whom speaks as a gifted miniature painter, the other as a fiendish murderer.

In order to understand the intensity of this conflict between styles, it is important to recognize that in Pamuk's view, not just painting, but an entire way of seeing the world was being threatened by the influence of Italian Renaissance portraiture. Using newly discovered techniques of perspective and shadowing, the Italians were able to create portraits that looked exactly like the person who was painted. In Europe, this development signaled the change from a medieval, God-centered world to a Renaissance, man-centered world. More than an attitude towards painting, this shift to the human perspective, with an emphasis on the individual, could be seen as a predilection for a democratic rather than the existing autocratic society.

The author considers Islamic painting an art meant not to glorify the individual painter, but to glorify the beauty of the world that God has created. "Painting," his fictional artists assert, "is the act of seeking out Allah's memories and seeing the world as He sees the world" (*My Name Is Red,* p. 79). The idea is to recreate the world as God sees it, from above, representing the essential, timeless beauty of a horse, a tree, a beautiful woman. Some paintings show a cross-section of a house with everything going on inside or an entire battle that could never be seen from one place, as if to indicate God's all-seeing view. In Renaissance art, on the other hand, shadows, clothing folds, and vanishing points all indicate unseen places—humanity's, not God's, perspective.

Individual style, so important to Western concepts of creativity and artistic genius, is seen as an artistic flaw by Pamuk's painters, who measure talent by the ability to paint in the style of the old masters of Herat. The history of miniature painting, where various stylistic innovations (such as those of Bihzad) were absorbed by different schools, is perceived not as innovation but as the discovery of new artistic laws, to be incorporated by all subsequent painters. The novel's Master Osman felt it was his job to merge the talents of all of his painters into a harmony that would be the style of the school. In fact, the typical palace illustration was painted by several artists, not just one. The painters in the novel recoil from the whole idea of individual "style," which the murderer equates with flawed art and with crime. "If I do have style and character, it's not only hidden in my artwork, but in my crime and in my words as well!" the murderer taunts the reader, "Yes, try to discover who I am from the color of my words!" (*My Name Is Red*, p. 98). And indeed, the attentive reader can use clues from the murderer's narratives to solve the crime long before it is solved in the book.

Individual "style," however, has an attraction for all of the painters. Even as they profess belief in their traditions, the artists push the boundaries of the aesthetic constraints that bind them, as if driven by the creative desire to expand. One of them, striving for greater and greater realism, had traveled to battlefields to paint the realities of war as no one had before him. And all of them have a simultaneous attraction and repulsion to the most sinful and alluring of "Frankish" innovations, the portrait.

In the novel, painting a portrait is compared to rivaling God's power to create life, and becoming the subject of a portrait is equated to becoming a god—perhaps suitable for a sultan, but not for an ordinary man. At one point, Enishte describes how after seeing a portrait in Venice, "it was as if I too wanted to feel extraordinary, different, and unique. . . . It's as if it were a sin of desire, like growing arrogant before God, like considering oneself of utmost importance, like situating oneself in the center of the world" (*My Name Is Red*, p. 109). Enishte struggles with this desire until he finds a solution that works for him—while he feels it would be a sin to put himself in the center of the painting, he can put the sultan in the center of a painting with a clear conscience. The murderer, however, is racked with doubt whether even this is acceptable after Elegant declares that the portrait of the sultan will bring damnation on them all. Shortly before murdering Enishte, the murderer challenges him and reveals his conflict:

In the last painting, you've supposedly rendered the face of a mortal using the Frankish techniques, so the observer has the impression not of a painting but of reality, to such a degree that this image has the power to entice men to bow down before it, as with icons in churches. . . . Your reliance on the methods of the Venetians as well as your mingling of our own established traditions with that of the infidels will strip us of our purity and reduce us to being their slaves.

(*My Name Is Red*, p. 160)

The murderer is intensely attracted to painting in the Western style and wishes to be free to do so, which is one reason why he murders Elegant. At the same time, he deeply believes in preserving the "purity" of Near Eastern tradition, even fearing for its survival, which is a reason he murders Enishte. Deeply conflicted, he works in two separate places, painting traditional paintings at home, and painting secret self-portraits in his hideaway. After having stolen the last page from the murdered Enishte, he commits the ultimate blasphemy by painting his own portrait on it, as if having overstepped his bounds by committing a murder, he feels emboldened to overstep the bounds in his art. "Am I an artist who would suppress the masterpieces I was capable of in order to fit the style of the workshop?" he asks (*My Name Is Red*, p. 279). But there is no masterpiece. His attempts to use the portrait style fail, and the head he seeks to immortalize in a portrait ends up severed from his body.

The conflict between the pull of tradition and the lure of the new has led the troubled painter to madness, a split personality that cannot harmonize its two halves. One half remains true to tradition, the other rejects tradition and tries to copy the new style. Merely imitating the West, the novel suggests, will produce nothing but bad copies, unless the new Western techniques are infused with Turkish cultural traditions. It is Enishte's attempts to fuse the two styles that emerge as the most positive step to take. Although Master Osman depicts the style of the secret book as "miserable painting that was neither Venetian nor Persian," Enishte's philosophy of art reflects the position the author himself has expressed in interviews (*My Name Is Red*, p. 250). Emphasizing that Bihzad himself combined Chinese and Islamic aesthetics to create the Persian style, Enishte tells the murderer that "Nothing is pure . . . whenever a masterpiece is made, whenever a splendid picture makes my eyes water out of joy and causes a chill to run down my spine, I can be sure of the following: Two styles heretofore never brought together have come together to create something new and wondrous. . . . To God Belongs the East and the West" (*My Name Is Red*, pp. 160-61). A quote from the Quran, "To God Belongs the East and the West" also appears on the front page of the novel, indicating the author's belief in the essential unity of these divided worlds. Arguing not for the inevitable conflict of civilizations, Pamuk is arguing for their creative contact, even suggesting that such contact is divinely sanctioned. Despite the fact that in his novel this contact leads to madness and murder, there is a hope that through the vehicle of art, which acts as both mirror and window, East and West can begin to glimpse their common, human affinity. Recalling a portrait of an Italian nobleman, Enishte muses:

> The image was of an individual, somebody like myself. It was an infidel, of course, not one of us. As I stared at him, though, I felt as if I resembled him. Yet he didn't resemble me at all. He had a full round face that seemed to lack cheekbones, and moreover, he had no trace of my marvelous chin. Though he didn't look anything like me, as I gazed upon the picture, for some reason, my heart fluttered as if it were my own portrait.
>
> (*My Name Is Red*, p. 26)

Although Enishte perishes because of his beliefs and the novel leaves the future of art in Istanbul unresolved, the great, positive example that Pamuk gives is the novel itself. In form, it seems to reflect the victory of the Renaissance style: not told from an omniscient, God-like perspective, each chapter is narrated in the first person from an individual viewpoint, placing the individual at the center of the canvas, so to speak. Pamuk's method eschews an omniscient narrator and allows each character to speak to the reader and try to impress, convince, deceive, amuse, and educate. However, the circuitous digressions, elaborate lists, ornamental language, and intricately constructed interrelationships of the characters reflect the Eastern style of ornamental design. Reminiscent of the intricate patterns designed to inspire concentration in Ottoman art, which in turn reflect pre-Islamic Turkic aesthetics of geometric design, Pamuk's style forms a kind of circle where the post-modern meets the pre-modern. The aesthetics blend so gracefully in Pamuk's novel that it is difficult to tell where one begins and another ends, as in an imaginative chapter narrated by the color red, who boasts:

> I embellished Ushak carpets, wall ornamentation, the combs of fighting cocks, pomegranates, the fruits of fabled lands, the mouth of Satan, the subtle accent lines within picture borders, the curled embroidery on tents, flowers barely visible to the naked eye made for the artist's own pleasure. . . . I love engaging in scenes of war where blood blooms like poppies. . . . I love illuminating the wings of angels, the lips of maidens, the death wounds of corpses and severed heads bespeckled with blood.
>
> (*My Name Is Red*, p. 186)

Sources and literary context. As a youth, Pamuk used to paint reproductions of Ottoman and Persian miniatures, and indeed, this novel is filled with his love for this lost art and for the legends and poems that inspired them. This Ottoman cultural heritage was almost swept away by the reforms of Kemal Atatürk (1881-1938), who formed the Turkish Republic out of the ruins of the Ottoman Empire in 1923. After abolishing the sultanate, Atatürk sought to westernize almost every aspect of life and break Turkey's connection with the Islamic past. He changed the alphabet from Arabic to Latin and purged the Turkish language of its Persian and Arabic elements. Espousing European education, dress, and art forms, Atatürk paradoxically attempted to create a Western-style secular democracy by autocratic decree. The Ottoman past, now seen as autocratic, decadent, backwards and Eastern, was maligned in favor of a new identity that was based on the pre-Islamic Turkic past and looked westward towards the future. Recently however, more sophisticated attempts to define Turkish identity have led to a new interest in the Ottoman period and the publication of several popular histories. Although meticulously researched, *My Name Is Red* gives a very personal and subjective view of the period. "I really love these paintings," Pamuk said in an interview, "and I wanted to glorify the little romantic beauties of these hidden little pictures. All these artists are dead now. Everyone forgot about them. So the book addresses that lost beauty" (Pamuk in Farnsworth). Anachronistically, Pamuk personalized these lost Ottoman times by inserting his own family into the narrative: Shekure, Shevket, and Orhan are the names of his mother, his brother, and himself, and he had an "Enishte" who was the editor of a progressive, Western-style literary magazine.

In the history of Turkish literature, Pamuk is in some ways an anomaly, and in others a product of its legacy. The attempt to forge a new national literature to fit the new Turkish Republic encouraged social realist novels, meant to expose social ills and promote modernization. Literature from the Ottoman past was maligned, and, because of the language reform, unreadable by anyone who was not a specialist. There was a huge push to school the educated classes in Western literary tradition, and to this day most higher education in Turkey is conducted in English. The ideas of Turkish writer Ahmet Hamdi Tanpinar (1901-62), who theorized on the divided identity emerging as Turks looked at themselves with the eyes of the West, had an important impact on Pamuk. However, somewhat like his miniaturists, he is the recipient of an imported aesthetic tradition, a student of such Western writers as Marcel Proust, Thomas Mann, and William Faulkner. Often making references to the works of Fyodor Dostoyevsky in his novels, he shares Dostoyevsky's love for passion and crime as well as his ambivalent relationship with the West. In addition, Pamuk cites as influences the postmodernist writers Jorge Luis Borges, Julio Cortazar, Italo Calvino, and Umberto Eco. Pamuk works in Istanbul, in an office from which he can see the bridge that connects the continents of Europe and Asia. In many ways, it is his ability to act as a bridge between Eastern and Western cultures that engages readers on both shores.

Events in History at the Time the Novel Was Written

From the 1590s to the 1990s—historical parallels. Pamuk composed *My Name Is Red* between the years 1990 and 1998, a decade that witnessed the fall of the Soviet Union and the ensuing realignment of the balance of power in the world. Like many countries, Turkey had been struggling to find its place in the new order, as many of the nations surrounding it fell into disarray. The breakup of Yugoslavia and the ensuing war in Bosnia led to a flow of refugees from the West, while the first Persian Gulf War caused an influx of refugees from Iraq in the East. Istanbul additionally experienced a massive influx of people moving in from rural areas to look for work because of extreme inflation and economic crisis, recalling the demographic upheaval in the Ottoman period about which Pamuk was writing.

Islamic political parties, which had been consistently repressed by a state committed to secularism, continued to gain popularity throughout the decade. More than once their candidates were democratically elected and then forced to step down. Ironically a female member of Parliament was prevented from wearing a headscarf into the Parliament building, demonstrating how the state, in its fear of fundamentalism, was repressing basic rights and freedoms. Turkey's external relations featured a continued policy of alliance with the West and a quest to increase economic and political integration with Europe. Western movies and music became increasingly popular with the young, while rising numbers of American fast food chains peppered the boulevards where the Ottomans used to walk. Issues about Western cultural influence strongly preoccupied Turkey's intellectuals in the 1990s, as did intense debates on the direction the country should take. *My Name Is Red* is a work that both reflected and added to this ongoing discussion.

> In a way, after Kemal Atatürk's occidentalist, secular reforms, Turkish culture was divided in two: the modern culture influenced by Europe and the Ottoman Islamic heritage. The founders of the republic naively thought that a shortcut to modernity, to Europe, would be to forget about the past, and they crudely suppressed Ottoman Islamic cultural history. They thought this would in itself make the country modern. But as Freud says, what is suppressed comes back. I sometimes make a joke and say I am what comes back.
>
> (Pamuk in Smith, p. 39)

Reviews. When *My Name Is Red* was first published in Turkey, its astonishing sales became a media event, precipitating a court case won by the publisher because a newspaper had doubted the reality of the sales figures. Both avant-garde and best-selling, the novel has received sharp criticism from Turkish reviewers in light of this very success. An outspoken critic of both political Islam and the Kemalist state, Pamuk has drawn fire from all sides. Some accuse Pamuk of writing an American-style commercial bestseller with elevated levels of sex and violence to increase sales. Others complain that Pamuk is an overly westernized outsider and is not in touch with the real Turkey. Still others complain that of a multiplicity of voices in Turkey, Pamuk's idiosyncratic view is the only one that gets any attention in the West. From Islamists *My Name Is Red* drew accusations of misinterpreting Islamic themes, such as the relationship between religion and art, in order to push forward his Western ideas. Other critics have complained that Pamuk's style is overly baroque and his Turkish unnatural. The writer also drew criticism for his unflattering depictions of his mother and brother. Despite the storm of criticism, Pamuk's quirky, intelligent, rebellious attitude and acute awareness of the ironies and paradoxes of Turkish life appeal to a large audience in his homeland. As one reviewer wrote, "Pamuk is very brave in confronting Islamists with his ideas about the Quran, and also very brave in confronting the secularists by mentioning God's name so many times. . . . It is quite irrelevant if Pamuk uses characters from his real life or not. Who cares! Being a writer in Turkey is not easy" (Sertabiboglu, p. 1; trans. S. O. Şenarslan).

DEBATES ON SEXUALITY IN THE OTTOMAN COURT

Pamuk depicts the Ottoman court milieu as being openly bisexual; even characters with wives are involved with a multitude of men and boys. Scholars are currently debating the extent of homosexuality and bisexuality in Ottoman culture, and the jury is still out. Centuries of Western travelers, intoxicated by stereotypes of the "lustful Turk," wrote imaginative and untrustworthy accounts of Ottoman sexuality that have had a great influence on opinions about the period. Clouded by Western obsessions with forbidden desires and Turkish discomfort with the subject, judgments on Ottoman sexuality are complicated by the fact that in Turkish the same word is used for "he" or "she," sometimes making it difficult to know whether the subject of a love poem is a man or a woman. Some scholars argue that since women were segregated and were supposedly considered intellectual inferiors, young men were a safer and more interesting outlet for romantic adventures. Based on their writings, the Ottomans seemed comfortable and tolerant with homosexuality and bisexuality among men, which was neither condemned nor persecuted in the court setting. However, some scholars have pointed out that much mystical poetry describing an intense passion for God is being mistakenly read as homoerotic, and there is much ambiguity in writings from the period that has yet to be decoded. Possibly influenced by Western daydreams of Oriental harems and bath houses, the image of the unbridled and unfettered sexual life of the Ottomans may well be exaggerated.

My Name Is Red was released in English in 2001, and was immediately hailed for being a window into the world of Islam. Seen as Pamuk's most interesting and accessible novel to date, it evokes praise for its foray into a history little known to critics before its appearance. Despite the dense complexity of the unfamiliar subject matter in this work, Western reviews have been overwhelmingly positive, seeming to expect such difficulties from a Middle Eastern writer. John Updike called the novel "a curious, sumptuous, protracted thriller," enjoying its dark and complex mood, and most reviewers have been delighted with Pamuk's stylistic innovations and playfulness (Updike, p. 93). American critics, however, tend to take his views on Ottoman history and Islamic thought at face value without realizing that his ideas are at the center of a storm of debate. Not completely accepted in his homeland, not completely understood abroad, Pamuk perhaps truly is like a bridge from Europe to Asia, "speaking to each shore without completely belonging to either" (Pamuk in Simons, p. 39).

> What is important is not a clash of parties, civilizations, cultures, East and West, whatever. But . . . that other peoples in other continents and civilizations are exactly like you and you can learn this through literature. Pay attention to good literature and novels, and do not believe in politicians.
>
> (Pamuk in Farnsworth)

—Anna Oldfield Şenarslan

For More Information

Atil, Esin, ed. *Turkish Art.* Washington: Smithsonian Institution Press, 1980.

Farnsworth, Elizabeth. "Bridging Two Worlds." *The MacNeil/Lehrer Newshour.* Public Broadcasting System, 20 November 2002.

Grabar, Oleg. *Mostly Miniatures: An Introduction to Persian Painting.* Trans. Terry Graber. Princeton: Princeton University Press, 2000.

Kinzer, Stephen. *Crescent and Star: Turkey Between Two Worlds.* New York: Farrar, Straus and Giroux, 2001.

Mansel, Phillip. *Constantinople: City of the World's Desire, 1453-1924.* New York: St. Martin's Griffin, 1998.

Pamuk, Orhan. *My Name Is Red.* Trans. Erdag Göknar. New York: Alfred A. Knopf, 2001.

———. "Turkey's Divided Character." *New Perspectives Quarterly* 17 (spring 2000): 20-23.

Seng, Yvonne. "Invisible Women: Residents of Early 16th Century Istanbul." In *Women in the Medieval Islamic World.* New York: St. Martin's, 1998.

Sertabiboglu, Süha. "Benim adim kirmizi." *Kitap gazetesi,* 6 October 2002, 1.

Simons, Char. "The Deadly Art of Portraits." *The Christian Science Monitor* 93, no. 222 (11 October 2001): 19.

Smith, Sarah. "A Private History." *The Guardian* (Manchester, U.K.), 7 December 2002, 39.

Updike, John. "Murder in Miniature." *The New Yorker,* 3 September 2001, 92-95.

Mystical Poetry of Yunus Emre

Although the poetry of Yunus Emre (c. 1240-c. 1320) is well-known throughout the Turkish-speaking world, little reliable information exists about the life of the poet. What can be ascertained comes from the probably apocryphal legends and scant autobiographical allusions in his poetry. According to a frequently repeated legend, one year when the harvest in his village was scant, Yunus Emre approached a local dervish lodge to solicit food. There he met Haci Bektaş Veli (1201-1271), founder of the Bektaşis, a mystical order that later had close ties to an elite Ottoman military guard known as the Janissary Corps. When Yunus Emre begged for wheat, Haci Bektaş offered him blessings instead. Three times Yunus refused this offering, and finally he received the wheat. On the way home, realizing his mistake, Yunus turned around and headed back to the dervish lodge for the blessing. But he had missed his chance, said Haci Bektaş, who referred Yunus to Taptuk Emre. Thus began 40 years of spiritual instruction with this teacher, during which Yunus Emre began to compose mystical poetry. From the verses themselves, it seems that he was fairly well educated; his poetry shows knowledge of the sciences of his day, and of some Persian and Arabic as well as the Turkish language. The poetry reveals more personal biographical details too—the poet was married, had children, and traveled throughout Anatolia and to Damascus. He appears to have devoted his life to putting his inspiration into poetic form in a manner that would be accessible to common people. Yunus Emre

THE LITERARY WORK

A collection of 415 poems set in northwestern Anatolia sometime between the late-thirteenth and early-fourteenth centuries; composed in Turkish (as *Divan-i Yunus Emre*) in the fourteenth century; published in part in English in 1972.

SYNOPSIS

In couplet form and a highly accessible Turkish, the poetry conveys Sufi, or Islamic mystical, ideas.

was one of the first to communicate such ideas in language close to the Turkish popularly used in Anatolia in his day.

Events in History at the Time of the Poems

Anatolia—from the Seljuks to the Ottomans. Yunus Emre was born in Anatolia, the peninsula that today forms the Asian part of Turkey. At the turn of the thirteenth century, before his time, Anatolia was already an international crossroads. It linked Persia and Central Asia to Byzantine Europe from east to west; from north to south, it linked the Russian steppes and Caucasus Mountains to the Arab world. Turkic nomads were already living on the peninsula by this time. They had in fact been emigrating from Central Asia to parts of the Middle East since the tenth century. After the victory of Sultan Alp Arslan, near Manzikert in 1071, a Turkic presence established itself in Anatolia under a branch of what was known as the Seljuk (also known as Seljukid) royal family. The Seljuks of Anatolia made Iconium (Konya) the capital of their domain—the sultanate of Rum. They fostered the growth of a materially rich, culturally vibrant civilization, complete with mosques, hospitals, and inn-like caravanserais. Many of these buildings, famous for their fine stonework and ceramic tiling, still stand today. In the medieval era, great intellectuals, such as the philosopher Ibn al-Arabi (1165-1240) and the Persian-born Sufi poet Jalal al-Din Rumi (1207-73) found patronage in the sultanate of Rum (see Rumi's *The Spiritual Couplets,* also in *WLAIT 6: Middle Eastern Literatures and Their Times).*

Destructive popular rebellions (1230-40), followed by the Mongol invasion of 1243, ended Seljuk dominance and radically altered the political landscape of Anatolia. Power devolved into a patchwork of minor Turkic principalities, such as the Chandaroglu, Karesi, and Danishmand. During Yunus Emre's lifetime, another leader, Osman (1258-1324), son of Ertugrul, appeared at the head of a border principality in northwest Anatolia. His followers emerged as the major Muslim rival of the declining (Christian) Byzantine Empire. Within a century under Osman and his successors, the Ottomans assumed control of most Byzantine territory in Anatolia. The Mongol conquerors meanwhile pursued one of two courses: they either exacted tribute and returned to Persia, or they remained in Anatolia and acculturated to Turkic society. By the time Yunus Emre began to compose his poetry, some parts of Anatolia had gained stability; emerging family dynasties, though still often involved in political competition, began to support the arts and to reestablish civic life. During the final days of Mongol overlordship (late thirteenth century), the Anatolian emirates entered an especially prosperous period. In essence, Yunus Emre was the product of a culturally sophisticated but often politically troubled environment.

The Sufis of Anatolia. The term *Seljuk* derives from the name of a Central Asian leader of a loose collection of Turkic tribes known as the Oghuz peoples. A grandson of Seljuk, named Tugril, directed the conquest of Persia and Iraq in 1055, and it was the line of successors who followed him that became known collectively as the Seljuks. While still in Central Asia, the group underwent a religious transformation, converting to Islam largely because of Sufi missionaries. Some authorities maintain that the Sufis succeeded so well with the Turkic population of Central Asia in part because they assumed the civic roles of the pre-Islamic spiritual leaders, or shamans. The belief is that these shamans held a prominent place in the nomadic societies, furnishing spiritual guidance about everyday problems, political advice to tribal leaders, and healthcare. Stepping into these roles themselves, the Sufis blended so smoothly into the Central Asian communities that it often became hard to distinguish them from shamans.

After 1071, when the Seljuk family consolidated authority in Anatolia, the Sufis moved there too. The Seljuks were powerful advocates of the Sunni subdivision of Islam (as opposed to the Shi`ite subdivision), in which there was a mystical or Sufi branch. It is thought that some of the Sufis filled the same civic roles in Anatolia as they had in Central Asia. When the Seljuk government in Konya weakened in the thirteenth century, Sufi organizations assumed political roles and performed such governmental and administrative services as the policing of towns and roads. The Sufis helped form trade guilds in the towns and introduced new technologies to agricultural areas, including peach cultivation to the region of Bursa, which remains famous for its peaches today.

Generally, Sufis organized themselves into groups, each of which recognized a primary "guide" or "mentor" (*shaykh, pir, murşid*) whose name became identified with that "order" (*tarikat*) henceforth. The guide or mentor possessed absolute discretion in the training of his disciples, exercising an authority that was considered essential to the well-being of the order. Disciples had to undergo the rigors of training and observe the order's guidelines, however challenging they might be. Sufi orders advocated broadly similar methods of enlightenment, but under the tutelage of successive leaders, they diversified into groups with distinct practices. Each order developed a set of rituals to aid instructors in the grooming of disciples and to set standards-of-conduct for them in everyday life. Some orders, such as the Mevlevis and Bektaşis, showed an appreciation for music and poetry. During their rituals, shaykhs and disciples recited Quranic or other verses. Sometimes these Sufis played musical instruments such as the *nay* (reed flute) and *saz* (a long-necked lute), which Yunus

Emre mentions when recalling his participation in a Mevlevi ritual. In contrast, other orders—the Naqshbandiyah, for example—prohibited music, dismissing it as non-Islamic. This order taught that Satan lurked in the making of music, whereas the poet Rumi, associated with the Mevlevis, compared music to the sound of the opening of the doors to Paradise.

On the whole, Sufis had no aversion to orthodox Islam. They were in fact full members of the Islamic community themselves. One of the most important forms of devotion for the Sufi and non-Sufi alike was the statutory prayer (*salat* in Arabic, *namaz* in Persian and Turkish) offered five times a day at specific hours. Sufis shared the common view that these were opportunities to reach out to God and surrender the soul to the Divine. They likewise accepted and adhered to the four other basic prescriptions of Islam—the fast from dawn to dusk during the holy month of Ramadan, the pilgrimage to Mecca, the distribution of alms, and the proclamation of faith in God (*shahadah*): "There is no god but God and Muhammad is His servant and messenger." Together with the obligatory daily prayers, these prescriptions formed the five pillars. Although a few Sufi orders diverged from the mainstream observance of these pillars, they did not question their importance.

Where Sufis differed from the larger community of Muslims was in their use of rituals to hone one's understanding of God as the central force. Sufi rituals were performed individually or in groups. Most importantly, they included a ritual for the recollection or remembrance of God (*dhikr*), either silently (*hafi, kalbi*) or aloud (*jahri*). The subject of the *dhikrs* could be verses of the Quran, prayers ascribed to the Prophet Muhammad (the *shahadah*), or religious poetry of the dervish lodges. The object was to focus attention on God.

Another significant ritual was "hearing" (*sema*). *Sema* took the form of a dance, or a series of rhythmic movements to the accompaniment of music, with the dancers frequently whirling around a director-shaykh. For Sufis, the symmetry and movement in the ritual symbolized the orderliness of the divinely guided cosmos. In many *sema*, the supplicant would lift one hand into the air with palm raised while the other hand faced downward toward the ground; the idea was to make the dancer an intermediary between heaven and earth. One hand reached up for knowledge from and the blessing of God; the other down toward the transitory and base material world. The *sema* of the Mevlevis has become world famous.

Among the Sufi orders of Anatolia, the Mevlevis and Bektaşis were known for their tolerance and inclusiveness. It is this sentiment that Yunus Emre expresses in the line *"we love the created beings because of the Creator"* (Yunus Emre in Gölpinarli, p. 56; trans. Z. Baskal). These Sufis facilitated interaction between different religious, ethnic, and linguistic groups. Rumi, for example, composed his poetry in three languages: Persian, Turkish, and Greek.

The tolerant attitudes and well-structured organizations of Sufi orders in Antolia during the

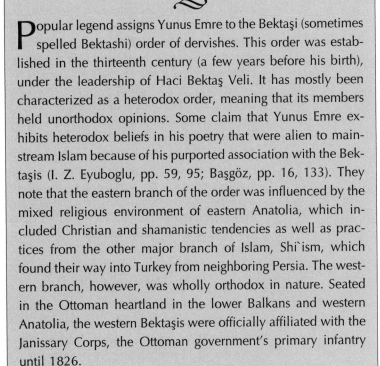

THE BEKTAŞI ORDER

Popular legend assigns Yunus Emre to the Bektaşi (sometimes spelled Bektashi) order of dervishes. This order was established in the thirteenth century (a few years before his birth), under the leadership of Haci Bektaş Veli. It has mostly been characterized as a heterodox order, meaning that its members held unorthodox opinions. Some claim that Yunus Emre exhibits heterodox beliefs in his poetry that were alien to mainstream Islam because of his purported association with the Bektaşis (I. Z. Eyuboglu, pp. 59, 95; Başgöz, pp. 16, 133). They note that the eastern branch of the order was influenced by the mixed religious environment of eastern Anatolia, which included Christian and shamanistic tendencies as well as practices from the other major branch of Islam, Shi`ism, which found their way into Turkey from neighboring Persia. The western branch, however, was wholly orthodox in nature. Seated in the Ottoman heartland in the lower Balkans and western Anatolia, the western Bektaşis were officially affiliated with the Janissary Corps, the Ottoman government's primary infantry until 1826.

Seljuk period survived the Mongol invasion and carried over into the early Ottoman period. In keeping with their practice in Seljuk society, many Sufis would assume roles within Ottoman society, helping to educate the masses, establish social tranquility, and preserve and enhance particular cultural traditions.

Sufi beliefs. At its philosophical core, Sufism proposes to explain the metaphysical meaning behind the universe. Sufis contend that all substances and forces that exist are physical manifestations of a divine plan—God created the world so others may appreciate His greatness and glory. Human beings hold a special place among all of existence because they alone possess the ability to reason and can therefore choose to love God of their own free will. In a well-known and often repeated saying, or *hadith,* of the Prophet Muhammad, God told him, "I was a Hidden Treasure and I desired (loved) to be known and I created the creatures so that I might be known" (Chittick, p. 250). It follows, say the Sufis, that the principal relationship between God and human beings is one of love, a reciprocal bond that exceeds all others. Sufis, who view the love of and for God as the central focus of their lives, try to reduce the material world to a realm of metaphor. To them, all things in the world are outward signs of God; yet to accept these things at face value or to idolize them is to be deceived, because the will of God cannot be comprehended through reason, intuition, or the senses, but only through love. The world is a transitory place of trials to attain the love of God. Love is both the cause and the goal of existence.

Accepting the religious worldview outlined above, the various orders and individuals elaborated on it in further ways. Yunus Emre's poetry, for example, shows that for him there are three degrees of Islam—belief (*iman*), application or rules (*islam*), and doing the beautiful (*ihsan*). Yunus Emre uses the word *Sufi* or *dervish* for someone who has already achieved the first two degrees and is searching for the third, living the beautiful, in mind, body, and soul.

The Poems in Focus

Contents summary. The oldest-known manuscripts of Yunus Emre's poetry date to the fifteenth century, although at least some of the poems must have circulated orally from their inception. As is typically the case, the poems are untitled and their arrangement in the manuscript collections is not thematic. The lack of an autograph manuscript or authoritative early version makes difficult the task of establishing decisively which poems are authentically Yunus's. Nevertheless, the work is unified by the overriding idea that one can overcome base human nature and aspire to spiritual perfection through union with God. The poems suggest that Sufism is the true way to attain spiritual perfection. They are replete with Sufi ideas and images, founded on a basic devotion to developing a greater awareness of God through careful contemplation of the universe and the self. Likewise the poems conform to the Sufi conception of God as omnipresent, just, and beneficent.

There are three didactic elements in the poetry: first, death is an absolute certainty so material existence is transitory; second, one must strive to understand the order and purpose of the universe and share this knowledge; third, the ultimate goal of the human soul is to love and to praise God in appreciation of creation and in hope of reunion.

Death, the absolute certainty. The inevitability of death is a major theme in Yunus Emre's poems. To stress the ephemeral nature of life, they portray death grotesquely as a way of warning readers (or listeners) not to form false attachments.

> [Death] takes away the young and old, burns
>   the mother's heart.
> It untangles the hair of blonde girls on
>   benches where corpses are washed.
> It takes away young lads in their prime.
> It mixes the henna of brides with dirt.
>   (Yunus Emre, *Yunus Emre Divani*, p. 211;
>   trans. Z. Baskal)

As in other poems, this one portrays steps in the process of death with great interest. First the angel of death takes the life out of a body. Then the corpse is carried to the graveyard. The verse goes on to describe the deceased's separation from loved ones and the burial. Finally, angels interrogate the deceased in the grave. The scene closes with the living quickly forgetting the dead (*Yunus Emre Divani*, p. 23).

In this macabre manner, the poetry reminds readers that they too must leave this world and that life is a brief sojourn. Even beautiful things will pass. Couplets such as the following attest to the world's sensual attractiveness: "This world is a bride dressed in green and red / One cannot get tired of looking at a new bride" (*Yunus Emre Divani*, p. 116; trans. Z. Baskal). Other couplets warn the reader not to be taken in by the world's outward beauty: "Worshipping the world is like savoring a poisonous meal / The one who cares about the end of life abandons the meal" (*Yunus Emre Divani*, p. 88; trans. Z. Baskal). The aim is to redirect the reader's focus from worldly things to the transitory nature of life.

Devotion to God becomes an alternative to fears of mortality: "The world is the enemy of people; the goal is the Soul (God) of the souls / One should know that the world passes, abandon the world, my dear" (*Yunus Emre Divani*, p. 170; trans. Z. Baskal). Contrasting earthly time with cosmic time, the poetry beckons readers to prepare for inevitable death. In one of the most masterful and harmonious couplets of Turkish literature, Yunus Emre holds out the eternal reward of salvation for the faithful: "Why are you afraid of death? / Don't be afraid! You will live forever" (*Yunus Emre Divani*, p. 49; trans. Z. Baskal). As a Sufi, Yunus Emre believes that all life is dedicated to God and all souls must return to God, which brings them an immortality that makes human mortality inconsequential.

Understanding and explaining the order of the universe. According to the Sufis, to direct one's heart to God requires a long mystical journey. Everyone is able to reveal the attributes of God in him or her self and to strive for perfection. An understanding of God's totality accrues by degrees (*maratib*) and involves contemplation of both the natural world and human nature. As noted, there is an obligation to share the understanding one attains with others, which Yunus Emre accomplishes through his poetry.

> The Beloved is with us all the time; He is not
>   different to each person.
> The length of the road depends on our selves,
>   I have found that the Friend is close, my
>   friend.
> Eventually, I got to know myself and I have
>   found the God I desired.
> I was fearful until I found Him, I was rescued
>   from fear, my friend.
>   (*Yunus Emre Divani*, p. 373; trans. Z. Baskal)

In other couplets, Yunus Emre shares what he himself has learned by striving to understand the natural world and human nature. Underlying his strategy in the following verse is the belief that God has two visible aspects (*sifat*) from which to begin the journey of enlightenment. On the microcosmic level, God is manifested in certain human features. A human being possesses attributes, such as rationality and free will, which mirror divine powers. On the macrocosmic level, the order and integrity of the universe demonstrates God's control. The human being is the more tangible aspect of God because of the accessibility and density of the representation. Yunus Emre speaks of gaining awareness of God through introspection about his own human nature.

> While I was searching my self, I came upon
>   the Astonishing Mystery.
> You should see in your self the Friend I saw
>   in me, the Friend.
> I have looked into my self and saw the One
>   who becomes me within my self in my self.
> I understood the One who becomes the soul
>   of my body, my friend.
>   (*Yunus Emre Divani*, p. 373; trans. Z. Baskal)

In this and other poems, "Friend" refers to God, whereas "friend" with a lower case "f" refers to the reader or listener. The reason why both God and the reader or listener have the same name is not only because God is a benevolent presence but also because aspects of God are evident within everyone.

The same poem alludes to Ibn Mansur al-Hallaj (857-922), a major Sufi figure. The poem later mentions al-Hallaj by name because the tenth-century mystic was a major exponent of the theory of the unity of being (*wahdah al-wujud*), which states that God is disclosed in all things. "I wanted and found Him, if He is me where am I? / I could not distinguish me from Him; once I became Him, friend!" (*Yunus Emre Divani*, p. 373; trans. Z. Baskal).

Both al-Hallaj and Yunus Emre maintain that humans and God are in fact one. In his well-known

---

ENLIGHTENMENT BY DEGREES

In Sufi thought, the degrees of development that an individual must undergo in the process of understanding God's totality are determined by his or her knowledge (*ma`rifah*). Although a master (*murşid*) can help a seeker (*murid*) tune the heart and mind to God, fulfillment ultimately depends on the seeker's devotion and eagerness to find the right path. In the words of Ibn al-Arabi, "Just as the one and the same light is variously colored as it passes through pieces of glass of various colors, the same Form of the Absolute is differently manifested in different men with different capacities" (Ibn al-Arabi in Izutsu, p. 139).

---

statement "I am God" (*Ana'l Haqq*), al-Hallaj argued that human identity is inextricably bound to its divine origin and nature. According to al-Hallaj, God's presence within the human essence obviates the need for identification with the self. Even to say "I" is a mistake since this implies a duality. Many Sufis supported al-Hallaj by pointing to the passage in the Quran that states, "To Allah belongs the east and the west: Whithersoever ye turn, there is the presence of God" (Quran, 2:115). Still, al-Hallaj's actions attracted the ill will of hostile authorities, who ultimately convicted and executed him (see **Murder in Baghdad**, also in *WLAIT 6: Middle Eastern Literatures and Their Times*). In death, he became a martyr for many Sufis, a revered symbol of a perfected human being who died for his enlightenment.

Mystical Poetry of Yunus Emre

In love and praise. Sufis contend that the mind's capacity to reason and to exercise free will links human beings to God, but the heart (*gönul*) is the dwelling place of the soul. The mind, they maintain, has its purposes but also its limits. Despite all the evidence of God in others and the natural world, a mind alone cannot fathom the essence of God. The heart, on the other hand, intuits the inherent truth of God: "My heart does not obey the one who says the human form is clay / I made the essence of this clay attain God, friend" (*Yunus Emre Divani*, p. 373; trans. Z. Baskal). To Sufis, one who depends solely on intelligence and

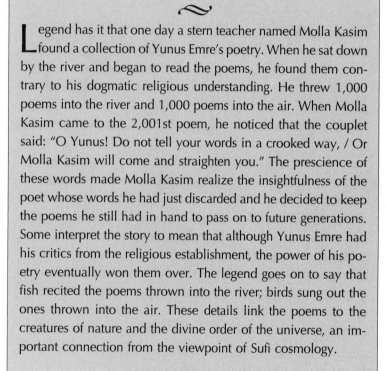

MOLLA KASIM, A CRITIC OF YUNUS EMRE

Legend has it that one day a stern teacher named Molla Kasim found a collection of Yunus Emre's poetry. When he sat down by the river and began to read the poems, he found them contrary to his dogmatic religious understanding. He threw 1,000 poems into the river and 1,000 poems into the air. When Molla Kasim came to the 2,001st poem, he noticed that the couplet said: "O Yunus! Do not tell your words in a crooked way, / Or Molla Kasim will come and straighten you." The prescience of these words made Molla Kasim realize the insightfulness of the poet whose words he had just discarded and he decided to keep the poems he still had in hand to pass on to future generations. Some interpret the story to mean that although Yunus Emre had his critics from the religious establishment, the power of his poetry eventually won them over. The legend goes on to say that fish recited the poems thrown into the river; birds sung out the ones thrown into the air. These details link the poems to the creatures of nature and the divine order of the universe, an important connection from the viewpoint of Sufi cosmology.

reason to judge the world sees the "form" but not the "essence" beyond the form. (In some Sufi texts, to be called intelligent or reasonable is more a criticism than a compliment.) As shown by the couplet above, Yunus Emre's poetry speaks of the heart's relative importance. In other verses, he asserts that to break someone's heart is to nullify all the good deeds performed over a lifetime. The overriding goal of the human soul is to love and to praise God in appreciation of creation and in hope of reunion. Love, the Sufis teach, has a transformational power that affects all human faculties and can bring one's heart closer to God. In the

following verses, the speaker is an impassioned lover who expresses devotion to his beloved—God. As the beloved, God has the power to negate the egoistic self: "It is Your love that has taken me from me / What I need is You, You / I have been burning [with love] day and night / What I need is You, You" (*Yunus Emre Divani*, p. 383; trans. Z. Baskal).

Fixing on God as the beloved helps Yunus Emre, along with other Sufis, to negate the ephemeral distractions of a passing world and to submerge himself into a higher consciousness. In the following couplet, he expresses his pleasure at being freed from materiality by love: "Neither do I become happy for wealth / Nor do I become sorry for poverty / I am consoled with Your love, / What I need is You, You" (*Yunus Emre Divani*, p. 383; trans. Z. Baskal). God reciprocates. In this sense, the lover becomes the beloved of God, who uses omnipotence to free the individual from worldly concerns:

> Your love kills lovers
> It makes the lovers dive into the ocean of love
> It fills them with manifestations
> What I need is You, You.
> (*Yunus Emre Divani*, p. 384; trans. Z. Baskal)

For the Sufi who has attained a high level of awareness of God, life becomes an interminable waiting period. Detaching from the world, a perfected Sufi "dies before dying" and awaits the afterlife, the soul's true destination—reunion with God.

Yunus Emre and the Turkish language. Yunus Emre's use of an accessible dialect of the Turkish language is one of the most important aspects of his poetry. Previously few poets wrote in the dialect that common people could speak or understand. The poetry became groundbreaking in part because Yunus Emre structured his poems around Turkish root words and an elementary Turkish grammar so that he could convey Sufi ideas to a broad audience, whether they were literate or non-literate. The comprehensible nature of his poetry was a major innovation, since other major poets of the day had been composing their verses in a Turkish that relied heavily on words and constructions of Arabic and Persian origins. Because of the political history of the region, these two languages long remained dominant in the literature, theology, and administration of the reigning Muslim kingdoms. One of Yunus's contemporaries, the Turkish poet Aşik Paşa (1271-1332) went so far as to say, "Nobody would look at the Turkish language [as a poetical tool]" (Aşik Paşa in Gibb, p. 182). After Yunus Emre, an increasing number of poets wrote in accessible Turkish. Yunus Emre demonstrated that everyday language was indeed suitable for the expression of didactic and aesthetic sentiments. In doing so, he straddled the lines of social stratification in Turkish society. It became common in the twentieth century for nationalist literary historians to consider Yunus Emre the first exponent of "pure Turkish" (öztürkçe, Turkish expunged of foreign loan words, grammatical forms, and syntax) and the progenitor of a genuine Turkish literature (Köprülü, p. 1). In his day, most Sufi orders used Arabic or Persian, predominantly in their poetry and their rituals. Whether Yunus Emre was aware of his role or not, his poetry led to wider use of Turkish in Sufi orders throughout Anatolia.

Sources and literary context. Arguing either that he was an inspired folk poet or that he was inspired directly by God, some critics have asserted that Yunus Emre was illiterate. Recent scholarship has proven that Yunus Emre was not only well educated but intimately familiar with the major religious and literary texts of his day. His poems draw on these texts, along with his real life experiences. The concerns expressed in his poetry surface surfaced earlier in the works of such figures as Ahmed Yesevi (d. 1166), Rumi (1207-1273), Fahr al-Din Iraqi (1213-c. 1289), and Ibn al-Arabi (1165-1240). Many of Yunus Emre's couplets are interpretations of Quranic verses and *hadiths* (sayings of the Prophet Muhammad).

Reception. The earliest references on record to the poetry of Yunus Emre appear in fifteenth-century sources. From these and subsequent writings, it is clear that his verses enjoyed widespread favor. A broad range of dervish brotherhoods used his poetry for devotional and training purposes. Other poets imitated his choice of style and subject matter, which led to some confusion over attribution. Even poems that did not belong to Yunus Emre's body of work were ascribed to him in later centuries.

General interest in Yunus Emre's poetry has grown over the years, especially since Fuad Köprülü's landmark study *Türk Edebiyatinda Ilk Mutasavviflar* (1918; The First Mystics in Turkish Literature). Yunus's writings have inspired hundreds of books, poems, and plays about him. His poetry has also been honored by the United Nations Educational, Scientific, and Cultural Organization (UNESCO), which proclaimed 1991 the International Yunus Emre Year, recognizing his poetry as a quintessential representation of humanistic values.

From his verse, scholars have tried to determine to which order Yunus Emre belonged, his degree of literacy and familiarity with Islamic and mystical literary traditions, the genuineness of his Sufi beliefs, and the extent to which pre-Islamic Anatolian and Turkic elements influenced him. Fuat Köprülü stresses Yunus Emre's intellectual ties to his Central Asian Turkic predecessor Ahmed Yesevi (Köprülü, p. 1). Burhan Toprak compares the use of Turkish in Yunus Emre's work to Dante's use of Italian in *The Divine Comedy* (Toprak, p. 19). Others portray Yunus Emre as an opponent of Islamic dogmatism, a missionary who brought the spirit of Islam to the Turks, or one of many dervish poets who played a role in the Islamization of Anatolia (Halman, *Yunus Emre,* pp. 2-3, 41-57; Karakoç, p. 44). One reviewer of a late-twentieth-century English edition of his poetry speaks of Yunus Emre as "probably the greatest folk mystic writing in the Turkish language. . . . his universalism, his humanitarian and ecumenical spirit, his quintessential lyrics, and hymns, his simple and straightforward style make his verses relevant to our age"; he might well be regarded, adds this reviewer, as the premier folk poet of the whole Islamic tradition (Halman, Review, p. 693).

—Zekeriya Baskal

For More Information

Başgöz, Ilhan. *Yunus Emre*. 3 vols. Istanbul: Cumhuriyet, 1999.

Chittick, William C. *Sufi Path of Knowledge.* New York: SUNY Press, 1989.

Eyuboglu, Ismet Zeki. *Yunus Emre*. Istanbul: Geçit, 1991.

Gibb, Elias John Wilkinson. *A History of Ottoman Poetry.* Vol. 1. London: Luzac, 1958.

Gölpinarli, Abdülbaki. *Yunus Emre ve Tasavvuf.* Istanbul: Remzi, 1961.

Halman, Talat S. Review of *The Drop That Became the Sea: Lyric Poems,* by Yunus Emre. *World Literature Today* 64, no. 4 (autumn 1990): 692-93.

———, ed. *Yunus Emre and His Mystical Poetry.* Indiana: Indian University Turkish Studies 2, 1981.

Izutsu, Toshihiko. *A Comparative Study of the Key Philosophical Concepts In Sufism and Taoism, Ibn Arabi and Lao Tzu, Chuang-Tzu.* Tokyo: Keio Institute of Cultural and Linguistic Studies, 1966.

Karakoç, Sezai. *Yunus Emre*. Istanbul: Diriliş, 1999.

Köprülü, Fuat. *Türk Edebiyatinda Ilk Mutasavviflar.* Ankara: Türk Tarih Kurumu, 1976.

Smith, Grace Martin. *The Poetry of Yunus Emre, A Turkish Sufi Poet.* Berkeley: University of California Press, 1993.

Toprak, Burhan. *Yunus Emre Divani.* Istanbul: Akşam, 1934.

Yunus Emre. *Yunus Emre Divani.* Ed. Mustafa Tatçi. Ankara: Milli Egitim Bakanligi, 1995.

"Ode on the Conquest of Amorium"

by
Abu Tammam

In 837 or 838 C.E. Abu Tammam went before the caliph, or Islamic ruler, al-Mu`tasim at Samarra and under his patronage became the most celebrated panegyric or praise poet of his age. By this time the center of power in the Islamic world had moved from Arabia to Syria and then to Iraq, where the Abbasid dynasty built its capital, first in Baghdad and then to the north of Baghdad in Samarra. It was there, in the year 838, that Abu Tammam presented his "Ode on the Conquest of Amorium" to the caliph. This was 34 years after the birth of the poet in 804 in the Syrian town of Jasim to a Christian named Thadus, keeper of a wine shop in nearby Damascus. At some point the poet added Arab tribal elements to his name and converted to Islam, so that he is known in the tradition as Abu Tammam Habib ibn Aws al-Ta'i. After spending his youth as a weaver's assistant in Damascus, he went to Egypt, where he studied poetry and earned his living as a water-carrier in a mosque. Upon his return to Syria in 830, Abu Tammam composed panegyric poems for the caliph al-Ma'mun (reigned 813-33), who was on his way back from campaigns against the largely Christian empire of the Byzantines. Events in the reign of the subsequent caliph, al-Mu`tasim (reigned 833-43), became occasions for the composition of some of Abu Tammam's major panegyric odes: about the capture and execution of the arch-heretic Babak the Khurramite (837-38), the conquest of Amorium (838), the rebellion of Maziyar in Tabaristan (838-39), and the execution of al-Mu`tasim's notorious Persian general-turned-traitor, al-Afshin (841). Over the course of his

THE LITERARY WORK

A classical Arabic panegyric ode set in 838, composed in Arabic (as "Al-sayfu asdaqu anba'an min al-kutubi") in 838; published in Arabic in 1951; in English in 1965.

SYNOPSIS

The poem celebrates the Muslim conquest of the Byzantine city of Amorium as the triumph of Islam.

career, Abu Tammam acquired other patrons of his poetry—the caliph al-Wathiq, generals, and leading men-of-state—and served in other capacities too. Shortly before his death (845), he was appointed postmaster of Mosul, and it is here that Abu Tammam lies buried. His fame rests on two major achievements: his own poetic *diwan* (collected poems), through which he emerged as the major proponent of the new *badi`* style of poetry, and second, his authoritative anthology of the early Arabic heroic and lyric tradition, *Diwan al-hamasah* (Anthology of Courage). His own "Ode on the Conquest of Amorium," a poetic tour de force in *badi`* style, celebrates the Islamic victory over the Byzantine city of Amorium.

Events in History at the Time of the Ode

The Abbasid caliphate: political and military context. The year 750 witnessed a revolution in

The city of Samarra, Iraq, where Abu Tammam first presented his ode.

the Islamic empire that ousted the Umayyad dynasty and ushered in Abbasid rule. With this ousting came a shift in the seat of the Islamic empire from Damascus in Syria to Baghdad in Iraq. Here in Baghdad a new cosmopolitan culture arose, inspired by the far-reaching influence of Persian officers and courtiers. The Persians, proud of the rich traditions of their own former Sasanian empire, tried to compete for prestige with the newly powerful Arabs through a literary cultural movement known as Shu'ubiyah, "which is often regarded as an argument" between Persians and Arabs "over the relative merits of their respective cultural heritages" (Allen, p. 37).

Meanwhile, at the head of government stood the caliph (means "successor [of the Prophet of God]"), whose rule was grounded in Islam and in Arabicity—that is, the preeminence of Arabs, over for example, Persian or Turkish followers of the Islamic faith. The Abbasids based the legitimacy of their rule on their descent from the Quraysh tribe of Mecca, which was the tribe of the Prophet Muhammad, and on their direct descent from the Prophet's uncle, al-Abbas. Controversy erupted over their right to rule, however. They faced threats from other Arab groups—the Alids, the Kharijites, and supporters of the toppled Umayyad caliphate—and from non-Arabic populations as well. There were stir-

rings for independence by Iranians and Turkish nationals in far-flung provinces of the empire. As if these challenges to power from within the Islamic *ummah* (community of believers) were not enough, the caliph faced an external menace. At the border of the empire, the Byzantine frontier posed an ongoing threat, becoming the site of almost annual military expeditions, a situation that would persist for centuries.

The reign of al-Mu'tasim and the Amorium campaign. In the early ninth century, during the rule of al-Mu'tasim, the Abbasids were plagued from within by the rebellion of the Khurramite heretical sect in Azerbaijan and from without by the recurrent border wars with the Byzantines. A key factor in the political-military history of the Abbasid caliphate, one that would lead to the demise of caliphal power over the coming century, was al-Mu'tasim's increased reliance on Turkish and North African slave troops instead of his own people for military might. In 836 he transferred his capital to Samarra, north of Baghdad, to distance himself and his troops from the discontent of the populace.

In the year 838 matters came to a head. Babak, the leader of the 20-year Khurramite rebellion, encouraged the Byzantine emperor Theophilos to make incursions into Abbasid territory. Theophilos set out from Constantinople (present-day Istanbul) with an army of 100,000 and crossed into Muslim territory in northern Mesopotamia, where he attacked and destroyed the Muslim city of Zibatrah and took its inhabitants captive. He then attacked the nearby Muslim city of Malatya, where, according to reports, Theophilos took more than 1,000 women captive and mutilated the men by putting out their eyes and cutting off their noses.

In his commentary on Abu Tammam's diwan, the eleventh-century scholar al-Tibrizi relates that on the day the Byzantines conquered Zibatrah, a Muslim woman who was taken captive cried out "Help, O Mu`tasim!" (waa Mu`tasimaah). Informed of this just as he was about to quaff a cup of wine, the caliph put it down and ordered that it be kept for him to drink when he returned from the conquest of the fortified Byzantine city of Amorium in central Asia Minor (present-day Turkey). The historical sources give a less dramatic version of the caliph's determination to retaliate against this outrage to the Islamic ummah. After he had vanquished the rebel Babak, al-Mu`tasim asked which Byzantine city was the most defended and best fortified. He was told, "Amorium—no Muslim has embarked against it since the appearance of Islam; it is the wellspring and root of Christianity, and more honored among them than Constantinople" (al-Tabari in Stetkevych, Abu Tammam, p. 198). Amorium was indeed an appropriate target for revenge: not only was it the native city of the ruling Byzantine dynasty, it was also a powerful fortress whose walls were fortified with 44 towers.

Al-Mu`tasim had under his command a renowned Persian general, al-Afshin, who had earlier routed the army of Byzantine emperor Theophilos at Damizon. In the face of such a formidable foe, Theophilos's courage faltered. He sent ambassadors to al-Mu`tasim to offer humiliating promises and explanations, but al-Mu`tasim would not be dissuaded. He conquered and devastated Ankara, Amorium's sister city, at which point Theophilos withdrew to Dorylium to await the fate of his natal city, Amorium. Unlike al-Mu`tasim, Theophilos would not participate personally in the Amorium campaign.

After three days of violent combat in which thousands perished on both sides, Amorium was virtually delivered into the hands of the Muslims by treason. A former Muslim resident of the city guided al-Mu`tasim's forces to a weakened place in the wall. Al-Mu`tasim directed his ballistas (engines of warfare that hurled heavy ammunition at a target) to make a breach in the wall at precisely this spot. After three more days of siege, the gap ever widening and the Byzantines suffering many more casualties, Wandu, a Byzantine commander of the section where the breach was, sought aid from his fellow commanders. When they refused, he went directly to al-Mu`tasim, pleading for mercy for the children and offering to surrender Amorium to him. The caliph ordered his troops to refrain from combat until his return from the negotiations, but during the parley with Wandu, the Muslim army, ignoring this order, stormed and conquered the city.

**Abbasid poetry—the badi` style begins.** During the first hundred years of Abbasid rule, a preeminent religious and intellectual movement known as the Mu`tazilism flourished. The Mu`tazilites were the "People of the Justice and Unity [of God]," their name referring to their two most fundamental principles. Members of the movement espoused certain beliefs about both the Muslim holy book, the Quran (the Word of God as revealed through the Prophet Muhammad), and the hadith (traditions of what Muhammad said and did). At the time, one point of controversy concerned the "uncreatedness" or "createdness" of the Quran (i.e., whether the Quran is eternal with God or part of His creation). In keeping with the principle of divine unity, the Mu`tazilites taught that the Quran (as a sacred Arabic text) was "created," that is, part of God's creation, since to believe it was eternal with God would compromise His unity. This belief led to freedom in theorizing about the Arabic language. The Mu`tazilites also believed that likening God to man compromised God's unity—His oneness and uniqueness. Hence, they considered anthropomorphic statements in the Quran and in the hadith to be figurative, not literal statements. Such statements demanded ta'wil ("interpretation"). Thus, to the Mu`tazilites, expressions such as "God's two hands" were taken to mean "God's grace"; "God's eye" to mean "His knowledge," and so forth.

The Mu`tazilite thinker al-Jahiz, the preeminent Arab man of letters of the ninth century (d. 868), takes an example from the hadith—"the razor of God is the sharpest and the fore-arm of God is the strongest" (al-Jahiz in Stetkevych, Abu Tammam, p. 6). From the Mu`tazilite point of view, this statement can only be read as a metaphor for God's might and power. The expression, according to al-Jahiz, serves as example of the new style of writing, badi`, which was based on precisely such a metaphorical mode of expression. In effect, for al-Jahiz, *badi* and *ta'wil* are two sides of the same explanatory coin: *badi* puts the abstract in concrete terms (using strategies such as personification and metaphor), whereas *ta'wil* interprets such expressions. This Mu'tazilite method of Quranic explanation became a habit of conceptual thinking, and it spread beyond studies of the Muslim holy book. The method was applied to poetry as well. For the *badi* poets, it became a means of literary expression.

The term *badi* was first used in the ninth century to describe a radically new style of poetry, the beginning of which has been attributed either to Bashshar ibn Burd (d. 783) or to Muslim ibn al-Walid (d. 823). Their near contemporary, the already mentioned al-Jahiz, observes that at the time "*Badi* [was] found only among the Arabs, and because of it their language excel[led] all others and exceed[ed] every other tongue" (al-Jahiz in Stetkevych, *Abu Tammam*, p. 6). Characterizing this new style of poetic expression were two inter-related features: 1) an intensified and self-conscious use of figures of speech and rhetorical devices and 2) conceits that are abstract, conceptual, and sometimes awkward and far-fetched.

Closely tied to the religious and intellectual movement of Mu'tazilism is the appearance of *kalam* (a type of theology whose purpose is to establish religious beliefs by producing proofs through argumentation). In essence *kalam* is a religious science. The Mutakallimun (practitioners of *kalam*), represented the views both of the various factions of Mu'tazilites and their opponents on issues such as the status of a believer who sins, the "uncreatedness" or "createdness" of the Quran, predestination versus free will, and so forth. In the literary realm, the term *al-madhhab al-kalami* (the manner of *kalam*, dialectical mannerism) was associated with the *badi* style. In poetry, the "manner of *kalam*" was far from being just a rhetorical device that imitated the jargon and speculative argumentation of the Mutakallimun. Rather it was a manner of abstract reasoning as demonstrated in the following passage (which was cited by al-Jahiz):

> The Mutakallimun select expressions for their concepts, deriving their terminology for things which the Arab language originally had no word. In doing so they have set the precedent in this for all those who came after them, and the model for all who followed. Thus . . . they use the terms "thisness" (*hadhiyah*), "identity" (*huwiyah*), and "quiddity" [or "essence"]

(*mahiyah*). . . . One of them preaching in the very heart of the caliph's palace once said, "God brought him out of the door of nonbeing (*laysiyah*) and made him enter the door of being (*aysiyah*)."

(al-Jahiz in Stetkevych, Abu Tammam,
pp. 16-17)

The *badi* style develops. Al-Jahiz and others of the first half of the ninth century belong to the first Mu'tazilite period, which celebrated the creative and innovative aspects of the Arabic language. In contrast, the following period gave rise to an "orthodox resurgence," whose proponents adopted the doctrine of the "uncreated Quran." Their belief that the Quran has existed from eternity with God and is not part of His creation produced a more guarded and conservative attitude toward language. By this time, however, the stylistic elements of *badi* had thoroughly penetrated Arabic poetry. It is from this period that the classical Arabic definition of *badi* was formulated by the poet and critic Ibn al-Mu'tazz (d. 908) in his *Kitab al-badi* (Book of the New). Unsurprisingly for a man of his period, Ibn al-Mu'tazz does not capture the innovative spirit of *badi*. Rather he provides a list of its technical requirements with the aim of legitimizing *badi* poetry in the eyes of his conservative contemporaries. Ibn al-Mu'tazz claims that the *badi* style is not really new at all; instead it more intensively uses rhetorical devices already in the most authentic Arabic linguistic sources, such as the Quran, the *hadith*, and ancient (pre-Islamic through Umayyad) poetry.

Ibn al-Mu'tazz describes five primary rhetorical devices, whose extensive use typifies the *badi* style.

1) **Metaphor** (*istiarah*, borrowing a word from something it is associated with for something it is not associated with). Example: assigning talons to fate in "When fate digs in her talons."
2) **Root-play** (*tajnis*, the use of different words of the same root). Example: the root *kh-l-j* in "A day when you dragged (*khalajta*) their souls on a rope (*khalij*)."
3) **Antithesis** (*mutabaqah*). Example: "[War] turned [the women's] black hair white, and their white faces black."
4) **End-repetition** (*radd al-ajuz ala al-sadr*). Example: "Let your cares <u>depart</u> . . . for everything . . . someday <u>departs</u>.
5) **The manner of *kalam*** (*al-madhhab al-kalami*, expressions that require "mental gymnastics" to figure out the intended meaning). Example: "Glory is not pleased that you are pleased / with your supplicants' pleasure, but only with God's pleasure."

A product of this cultural environment, Abu Tammam makes insistent use of the sorts of devices described above. The lines of his ode reflect the conceptualized thought, argumentative reasoning, and linguistic inventiveness of the Mu`tazilites and the Mutakallimun.

The Poem in Focus

The contents. The "Ode on the Conquest of Amorium" opens with "the sword," setting the tone for a *qasida* (Arabic ode) that is dominated by martial imagery. Eight sections follow, depicting various aspects of the Muslim victory and Byzantine defeat.

Section 1. In lines 1-10 the poet gloats that the caliph's sword is a truer determiner of events than the Byzantine astrologers' books (which predicted that the city could not be taken at that time).

> The sword is more veracious than the book,
> Its cutting edge splits earnestness from sport.
> The white of the blade, not the black of the page,
> Its broadsides clarify uncertainty and doubt.
> (Abu Tammam, "Ode on the Conquest of Amorium," lines 1-2, in *Diwan Abi Tammam bi-sharh al-Khatib al-Tibrizi;* trans. S. Stetkevych)

Section 2. Lines 11-14 celebrate the Islamic conquest through, on the one hand, fertility imagery of rainfall, lush flowering herbage, and abundant honeyed milk, and, on the other hand, through astrological terms that express Islamic victory and infidel (Byzantine Christian) defeat.

> A conquest for which the sky's gates opened
> And the earth appeared decked out in raiment new.
> O Battle-Day of Amorium! Desires went forth from you
> Yielding milk, abundant, honeyed.
> You left the fortune of the Sons of Islam ascendant
> And in decline the fortune of idolaters and their abode.
> ("Amorium," lines 12-14; trans. S. Stetkevych)

Section 3. A historical prologue to the conquest comprises lines 15-22; in this prologue the city is portrayed as both "mother" to the Byzantines and an "unaging virgin," imagery that recurs later in the rape of the conquered community.

> A virgin whom the hand of fate had not deflowered
> And to whom time's ambition could not aspire.
> From the age of Alexander or before, the locks of night
> Had hoaried, but she had not grown old.
> ("Amorium," lines 17-18; trans. S. Stetkevych)

Section 4. Lines 23-35 describe the battle proper, using images of blood, fire, and smoke. Yet another astrological image contrasts the Muslims' good fortune with the Byzantines' bad fortune.

> How many a heroic horseman lay between her walls
> His forelocks reddened by hot flowing blood!
> . . . .
> You left her in a black night bright as forenoon
> For in her midst a dawn of flame dispelled the dark.
> . . . .
> There was light from the fire while darkness still clung,
> And dark from the smoke in the ghastly noonday sun.
> ("Amorium," lines 23, 26, 28; trans. S. Stetkevych)

Sections 5 and 6. These two sections reiterate the pair of ideas underlying the poem. Lines 36-49 (Section 5) shower praise (*madih*) on the heroic and divinely appointed caliph al-Mu`tasim, who led his army in the conquest of Amorium; lines 50-58 (Section 6) level satire or invective (*hija*) against the cowardly and materialistic Emperor Theophilos, who fled the field, abandoning his companions to the Muslim sword. Al-Mu`tasim is described:

> Directed by one relying (Mu`tasim) on God, avenging for God,
> Striving and yearning toward God.
> . . . .
> You replied with the sword, penetrating—
> To reply without the sword would have been no reply.
> ("Amorium," lines 37, 48; trans. S. Stetkevych)

Theophilos is depicted quite differently:

> Theophilus turned his back, his tongue bridled by fear
> Of the Khatti spear, below his innards in uproar.
> He issued death to his intimates
> And spurred on flight, the fleetest of his steeds.
> ("Amorium," lines 35-36; trans. S. Stetkevych)

Section 7. In lines 59-66 the idea of the "fruits of conquest" and the revitalization of the Islamic *ummah* through the defeat of the enemy—the slaying of their men and rape of their women—provides the thematic and rhetorical climax of the poem.

> The lives of ninety thousand warriors, like Mount Shara's lions,
> Were ripe for plucking before the figs and grapes.
>
> . . . .
>
> How many a [maiden like a] beaming moon they took beneath war's lightning beam!
> How many a white-toothed maid beneath war's cloud!
>
> . . . .
>
> How many a maid, like a reed trembling on a sand-dune,
> Did the drawn and trembling Indian swords obtain!
>
> ("Amorium," lines 59, 63, 65; trans. S. Stetkevych)

Section 8. The ode closes with the poet blessing the caliph and affirming the ruler's legitimacy and divine appointment. In the last line is a final antithesis between the sickly pale faces of the defeated Byzantine infidel and the triumphant glow of the victorious Muslim Arabs.

> O Caliph of God, for your striving for the root of Religion
> Honor, and Islam, God reward you!
>
> . . . .
>
> Then the closest lineage connects the days of [the Battle of] Badr
> To your victorious days.
> They have left the faces of the Yellow [Byzantines] jaundiced,
> And the Arab's faces burnished with triumph.
> ("Amorium," lines 67, 70, 71; trans. S. Stetkevych)

From history to myth: The rhetoric of Islamic triumph. Reading Abu Tammam's "Ode on the Conquest of Amorium" in light of the Arab and Byzantine historical chronicles illuminates the role of the classical Arabic victory ode in mythmaking. The ode actually did double duty. First, in its immediate political setting, it showered public praise on the victorious caliph and, second, as a record of achievement it served as an enduring literary testament to Arab-Islamic dominion. Though grounded in the historical details of the event, the ode is not a narrative recounting of the military campaign. Rather, using the structure, diction, and imagery of the classical Arabic ode and the rhetorical elements of the *badi`* style, the poet transforms a fleeting political and martial event into a poem that constitutes a ritual of allegiance to Abbasid dominion and an enduring myth of Arab-Islamic triumph.

Lines 23-29 make especially intense use of antitheses—light and dark, day and night, fire and smoke—and of the "mental gymnastics" that characterize the method of *kalam*. Together these techniques create visual imagery that conveys the concept of the cosmic and mythic power of the divinely appointed caliph, who can overturn the celestial cycles of day and night:

> In Amorium you left a black night bright as forenoon,
> For in her midst a dawn of flame dispelled the dark.
>
> . . . .
>
> There was light from the fire while darkness still clung
> And dark from the smoke in the ghastly noonday sun.
> The sun was rising from one, when it had set
> And setting from the other, when it had not.
> ("Amorium," lines 26, 28, 29; trans. S. Stetkevych)

The transformation of the historical into the mythical through the poetic techniques of the *badi`* continues in the next three sections of the ode. In line 41 the poet subtly compares God's election of the caliph al-Mu`tasim to His election of the Prophet Muhammad by evoking Quranic phraseology. Abu Tammam's words "God hurled you against her two towers and (*He*) destroyed her," evoke the Quranic verse: "Then you did not kill them but God did, and you did not throw, when you threw, but God did" ("Amorium," line 41; Quran 8:17). This verse refers to a celebrated early Islamic victory, the Battle of Badr, in which the Prophet Muhammad and a small band of Muslims, though greatly outnumbered, defeated their adversaries from Mecca. The reference paves the way for the explicit comparison in line 70 between al-Mu`tasim's conquest of Amorium and this astounding victory of the Prophet Muhammad. Again the passage memorializes the Amorium campaign not by recounting the historical details, but rather by casting the campaign in mythic terms, such as divine agency and Islamic vengeance, and in metaphorical terms, such as razing the tent of polytheism. (From the Islamic point of view, the Christian doctrine of the Trinity violated the unity of God and thus constituted polytheism.)

> To the voice of the Zibatran woman you replied, pouring out

A cup of drowsiness and the sweet saliva of
   loving wives.
You replied baring the sword, penetrating—
To reply without the sword would have been
   no reply!
Till, undistracted by the tent-pegs and ropes,
You left Polytheism's tent-pole fallen in the dust.
                     ("Amorium," lines 46-49;
                              trans. S. Stetkevych)

In contrast to the abstract and lofty terms used
to describe the moral and spiritual motivation for
the caliph al-Mu`tasim's participation in the Amo-
rium campaign, in lines 50-59 the poet employs
crude bodily terms to depict the cowardly and
materialistic Byzantine emperor. Although the
historical sources tell us that the emperor
Theophilos withdrew a safe distance to Dorylium,
Abu Tammam depicts him as actually witnessing
the attack upon his native city, tongue-tied with
terror, his bowels churning from fear. He then
abandons his companions and flees.

The opposite relation holds between the historian's and poet's representations of the rape
of the Amorian women (lines 59-66). A narrative account by the twelfth-century Christian
chronicler Michael the Syrian provides a
graphic and emotive depiction designed to stir
the sympathy and horror of his Christian readers over the fate of the Christian populace of
Amorium:

> When the inhabitants saw that Bodin [the
> traitor Wandu] had let the Taiyaye [Arabs] enter
> the city, some fled to the church, crying *Kyrie
> eleison*, others into the houses, others into
> cisterns and still others into pits; the women
> covered their children, like mother hens, lest
> they be separated from them, whether by the
> sword or slavery. The sword of the Taiyaye
> began the massacre and amassed heaps of
> corpses; when their sword was drunk with
> blood, the order came not to massacre any
> more, but to take the population captive and
> conduct them outside. Then they pillaged the
> city. When [al-Mu`tasim] entered to see the city,
> he admired the beautiful structure of the
> temples and palaces. But when he received
> some news that disturbed him, he put the city
> to the torch and burned it. There were convents
> and monasteries of women so numerous that
> more than a thousand virgins were led into
> captivity, not counting those who had been
> massacred. They were given over to the Turkish
> and Moorish slaves and abandoned to their
> outrages: Glory to the incomprehensible
> decrees (of God)!
>   (Michael the Syrian in Stetkevych, *Poetics of
>   Islamic Legitimacy*, p. 155)

By contrast, Abu Tammam's poetic account
conceives of the conquest of Amorium and the
rape of its women as a rhetorical abstraction, a
metaphor for the victory of Islam. Using elements
like antithesis, root-play, and strategically chosen
diction, he relates the conquering Muslim (male)
troops to the conquered female Christians. There
is a poetic shock here as the Christian maidens
and elements of the heroic military action are
described in almost identical terms. The city's
"white-skinned damsels," reeds "trembling on a
sand dune," are brought into contact with a
"drawn and trembling sword [phallus]," "white
blades drawn from their sheaths" ("Amorium,"
lines 63, 65, 66). The intention of the Christian
chronicler's graphic depiction of the massacre of
men and rape of women at Amorium is to foreground the brutality of the Muslim armies and
hence the enormity of Christian suffering. On the
other hand, Abu Tammam's rhetorical stylization
of this same massacre and rape foregrounds
the symbolic significance: the dishonor of the
Byzantines and the concomitant restoration of
Arab Muslim honor, which had been besmirched
by the previous Byzantine conquest of Zibatrah.
Turnabout was fair play: at Zibatrah, Muslim men
had been slain and mutilated, Muslim women
defiled.

The poem achieves two feats in the final blessing and celebratory closure. The first is the
mythic parallel that the poem draws between
al-Mu`tasim's victory at Amorium and the mirac-
ulous and original Islamic victory, that of the
Prophet Muhammad and a small party of early
Muslims against the massive armies of Meccan
polytheists arrayed against them at the Battle of
Badr: "The closest lineage connects the days of
Badr to your victorious days" ("Amorium," line
70). By using the word *lineage,* the poet invokes
the Abbasids' genealogical claims to the caliphate
(rule over the Islamic *ummah*), and establishes
a "kinship" or "bond" between the reign of al-
Mu`tasim and the age of the Prophet Muhammad.
What is striking, in light of the historical sources
concerning the Amorium campaign, is how false
the poet's analogy is. Whereas the fledgling
Muslim army at the Battle of Badr is said to have
achieved an astounding victory through divine
aid (in the form of angels fighting on the
Muslim side), both Muslim and Christian historical chronicles agree that Amorium, after a
12-day siege, was ultimately taken by treachery.
In this section, and indeed throughout the entire
poem, the poet provides no hint of any treachery that would detract from the Muslim heroism

and military prowess in the conquest of Amorium. Moreover, as the poem presents it, the conquest of Amorium is not an isolated historical incident but one of a long series of divinely ordained Islamic victories, which, like the Abbasid house itself, has a lineage that extends back to the Prophet's time.

The Abbasids claimed that their dynasty was legitimate in part because of their Arab heritage, which they considered the requisite heritage for the ruler of the Islamic *ummah*. In keeping with this claim, the closing line (71) reduces the entire set of contrasts in the poem to a racial one: the triumphant bronze complexion of the Arabs versus the pale and blood-drained faces of the vanquished Byzantines. Historical accounts tell us that al-Mu`tasim's army—particularly those troops that took part in the Amorium campaign—was largely Turkish and North African, as opposed to Arab, and that al-Mu`tasim's gifted Persian general, al-Afshin, played a major and indispensable role. In fact, al-Mu`tasim's reign witnessed broad challenges to Arab racial and cultural rule throughout the Islamic *ummah* by the Turkish military and by a Persian movement (the Shu`ubiyah movement), which celebrated the superiority of Persian over Arab culture. The effect of Abu Tammam's closing line is to suppress the true racial makeup of the Islamic forces that took part in the Amorium campaign and indeed that of the Islamic *ummah* in general. His goal is to identify Islam with the Arabs, to reassert Arab dominion, and to promulgate the myth of Islam as the native Arab religion.

In the "Ode on the Conquest of Amorium," we witness the poetic transformation of history into myth. With a masterful manipulation of the conventions of poetic form, Abu Tammam exploits the rhetorical and conceptual possibilities of the *badi`* style to produce a poem that transforms a military victory into a declaration of Abbasid legitimacy, a vindication of Arab rule, and an enduring myth of Islamic triumph.

Literary context. Abu Tammam's master-poem takes its place in a long and venerable tradition of Arabic praise poems of the sort that can be called "victory odes." The tradition has its roots in such celebrated pre-Islamic masterpieces as Alqamah's "A Heart Turbulent with Passion," composed to memorialize the victory of the Ghassanid Arab king al-Harith ibn Jabalah when he defeated and slew his rival, the Lakhmid Arab king al-Mundhir ibn Ma al-Sama at the Battle of Ayn Ubagh (in 554). Precursors in Islamic times include "The Tribe Has Departed" by the Umayyad poet-laureate al-Akhtal,

which celebrates the God-given victory of the caliph Abd al-Malik ibn Marwan over supporters of his rival claimant to the caliphate, Abd Allah ibn al-Zubayr (ca. 691-92). Later in the Abbasid period the formative influence of Abu Tammam's distinctively modern *badi`* poetics will emerge in verse by the most celebrated and beloved of the classical Arab poets, al-Mutanabbi (d. 965), especially in his odes commemorating the military victories of the Arab emir of Aleppo, Sayf al-Dawlah, over the Byzantines. Throughout this tradition, military victories are transformed from fleeting historical events into a mythic-poetic form that legitimates the victorious ruler and simultaneously perpetuates the ideal of divinely sanctioned rule.

Reception. The literary reception of Abu Tammam's poetry is difficult to disentangle from that of the *badi`* style. As Ibn al-Mu`tazz, one of our earliest sources, puts it, "Then . . . Abu Tammam . . . became so infatuated with *badi`* that he mastered it, developed it, and used it profusely. In some cases he did well, in others poorly. The latter are the result of excess and the issue of immoderation" (Ibn al-Mu`tazz in Stetkevych, *Abu Tammam*, p. 21). The response to Abu Tammam's poetry sparked a literary debate that lasted for several centuries and took the form, primarily, of the dispute between the supporters of Abu Tammam and those of his student and rival, al-Buhturi. The major champion of Abu Tammam was the tenth-century literary scholar, Abu Bakr al-Suli (d. 946).

Though much influenced by his master's style, the poetry of al-Buhturi was considered more traditionally lyrical and less given to the excesses and artificialities that, according to some, flawed Abu Tammam's poetry. Someone once asked al-Buhturi, "Who is the better poet, you or Abu Tammam?" He replied, "His good poetry is better than my good poetry, and my poor poetry is better than his poor poetry" (al-Suli in Stetkevych, *Abu Tammam*, p. 48).

The controversy between the two poets reached its apex in the *Muwazanah* of al-Amidi (d. 981), the "weighing" of the poetry of Abu Tammam against that of al-Buhturi. A proponent of the conservative Arab taste of the tenth century, al-Amidi preferred the "ancient" poets to the "moderns" (early Abbasid on, especially the *badi`* poets). It is not surprising then that he inclines toward the conventional lyricism of al-Buhturi rather than the radically innovative *badi`* poetry of Abu Tammam. Nevertheless, al-Amidi is aware that, in the end, it is largely a matter of taste:

WEIGHING ONE POET AGAINST ANOTHER

In his magisterial work, *al-Muwazanah* (The Weighing), the tenth-century literary critic al-Amidi "weighs" the complex and innovative *badi`* poetry of Abu Tammam against the more lyrical and conventional poetry of his more conservative younger rival, al-Buhturi. In the example below, al-Amidi compares the two poets' use of the poetic convention of stopping at the ruins of the encampment where the poet and his beloved once dwelt. Abu Tammam compares this emotional experience to a religious one and concludes with a *badi`*-style play on "love" and "pledge" to transform the empty ruin into a metaphor for the poet's lovelorn heart.

> I stopped at a ruin
> and questioned it,
> Until its abode became almost
> a mosque to me.
> I kept on describing it
> and inquiring after its folk,
> And grief was my companion
> whether inquiring or describing.
> May rain fall on you where
> once love was pledged,
> But for that place my heart would not
> be pledged to love.
>> (Abu Tammam in Stetkevych,
>> *Abu Tammam*, pp. 86-87)

Al-Amidi prefers al-Buhturi's more elegantly lyrical passage:

> I knew your abode as
> the coy maidens' rendezvous,
> A place whose company departed,
> then wild beasts came.
> Stingy the eyelids that did not
> lend their tears;
> Harsh the heart that did not stay the night with you
> when you were stricken.
> The cooing of the dove did not
> disquieten me,
> Nor did it distract me from my passion
> when it sang.
>> (al-Buhturi in Stetkevych,
>> *Abu Tammam*, pp. 86-87)

Those who prefer al-Buhturi do so because of their predilection for sweetness of expression, beautiful transitions, proper placement of words, correctness of expression, ease of comprehension, and clarity of meaning that they attribute to him—these are the secretaries and the desert Arabs, the naturally gifted poets and the rhetoricians. Those who prefer Abu Tammam do so because of their predilection for the abstruseness and subtlety of meaning

THE LYRICISM OF THE DESERT

A bu Tammam's anthology of early Arabic poetry, *Diwan al-hamasah* ("Anthology of Courage" or "Zeal"), achieved a degree of influence and popularity unequalled by any other anthology of classical Arabic poetry. The collection consists mostly of short selections, largely from the ancient poets, ordered according to subject in 11 chapters, from the first of which it takes its name. Critics have long noted the disparity between the jarringly innovative *badî* style of Abu Tammam's own poetic production and the far simpler and more traditional aesthetics of the ancients whose selections he included in *al-Hamasah*. Typical of the traditional sensibility is a poem from the chapter on *nasib*, elegiac love poetry, by the Umayyad bedouin poet, al-Sammah ibn Abd Allah al-Qushayri:

> I say to my companion as the gray camels bear us swiftly
> Between the hill of al-Munifah and the valley of Dimar:
> "Delight in the scent of the ox-eye of Najd,
> For after this evening the ox-eye will be no more.
> How beloved are the zephyrs of Najd,
> The fragrance of its meadows after rainfall,
> And your people when the tribe alight in Najd,
> When you are not unhappy with your fate.
> When whole months elapse, and we notice
> Neither their midpoints nor their final nights!"
>
> (al-Qushayri in Stetkevych,
> *Abu Tammam*, p. 326)

that they attribute to him and the great amount of his work that requires elucidation, commentary, and deduction—these are the conceptualists, the poets of artifice, and those that tend toward subtlety and philosophical speech.

(al-Amidi in Stetkevych,
Abu Tammam, p. 50)

As for Abu Tammam's "Ode on the Conquest of Amorium," the Abbasid secretary al-Hasan ibn Wahb applauded its strengths, even though, like al-Amidi, he preferred ancient poetry to modern. He knew of no poem, he asserted, "more innovative in its meanings, more perfect in its praise, or more agreeable in its courtesy" than Abu Tammam's masterpiece (Ibn Wahb in al-Suli, pp. 109-13; trans. S. Stetkevych).

Whatever his poetic excesses, Abu Tammam created, in "Ode on the Conquest of Amorium" and his other *badi*-style poetry, a definitively "modern" poetics that influenced all the major poets that followed him and shaped the literary aesthetics of classical and post-classical Arabic lit-

erature. His poem remains a fundamental text in the classical Arabic literary canon.

—Suzanne Pinckney
Stetkevych

For More Information

Abu Tammam. *Diwan Abi Tammam bi-sharh al-Khatib al-Tibrizi*. Ed. Muhammad Abduh Azzam. 4 vols. Cairo: Dar al-Ma`arif, 1951.

Allen, Roger. *An Introduction to Arabic Literature*. Cambridge: Cambridge University Press, 2000.

Badawi, M. M. "The Function of Rhetoric in Medieval Arabic Poetry: Abu Tammam's 'Ode on Amorium.'" *Journal of Arabic Literature* 9 (1978): 43-56.

Sperl, Stefan. "Islamic Kingship and Arabic Panegyric Poetry in the Early 9th Century." *Journal of Arabic Literature* 8 (1977): 20-35.

Stetkevych, Suzanne Pinckney. *Abu Tammam and the Poetics of the Abbasid Age*. Leiden: E. J. Brill, 1991.

———. *The Poetics of Islamic Legitimacy: Myth, Gender, and Ceremony in the Classical Arabic Ode*. Indianapolis: Indiana University Press, 2002.

al-Suli, Abu Bakr Muhammad ibn Yahya. *Akhbar Abi Tammam*. Eds. Khalil Mahmud Asakir, Muhammad Abduh Azzam, and Nazir al-Islam al-Hindi. Beirut: al-Maktab al-Tijari, n.d.

al-Tabari, Abu Ja`far Muhammad ibn Jarir. *Storm and Stress along the Northern Frontiers of the Abbasid Caliphate*. Vol. 33 of *The History of al-Tabari*. Trans. C. E. Bosworth. Albany: State University of New York Press, 1991.

Vasiliev, A. A. *Byzance et les Arabes: Tome I: la dynastie d'Amorium*. Ed. H. Grégoire and M. Canard. Brussels: Editions de l'Institut de Philologie et d'Histoire Orientales, 1935.

"Ode on the Reconquest of al-Hadath"

by
al-Mutanabbi

Al-Mutanabbi is one of the most celebrated poets in the Arabic literary tradition. He was born Ahmad ibn al-Husayn in the city of Kufah, Iraq, in 915, then traveled around the Muslim world for most of his life. As a young boy, al-Mutanabbi spent time with the Bedouins of Samawa, a region between Kufah in Iraq and Palmyra in Syria. The Bedouins were believed to have spoken the purest form of Arabic, and al-Mutanabbi's sojourn with them helped him develop a firm command of the language, a skill that later in life filled him with great pride. At the end of 928, al-Mutanabbi moved to Baghdad, then to Syria in hopes of pursuing a career as a panegyrist, or writer who creates praise poetry for a patron. After spending some time wandering through Syria to no avail, a frustrated al-Mutanabbi organized a rebellion, which "must have been political as well as religious" (Blachère, p. 769). The poet allegedly became known as *al-Mutanabbi* (literally, "the person who claimed to be a prophet") after the rebellion. But in the end, al-Mutanabbi and his followers were defeated and the poet was jailed. Around 937, after two years in prison, al-Mutanabbi resumed his travels and his career as a panegyrist. He moved from one patron to another, slowly building his reputation but not attaining real fame until 948, when he associated himself with the emir (prince) of Aleppo, Sayf al-Dawlah (d. 967). Becoming Sayf al-Dawlah's foremost court poet, al-Mutanabbi composed some of his finest odes in praise of this emir and his military encounters with the Byzantines. After nine years in Sayf al-Dawlah's court, the poet left Aleppo, moving to

THE LITERARY WORK
A classical Arabic panegyric ode, composed and presented in Arabic (as *Ala qadri ahli al-azmi ta'ti al-aza'imu*) in 954; published in English in 1965.

SYNOPSIS:
The ode celebrates the victory of the prince of Aleppo, Sayf al-Dawlah al-Hamdani, over the Byzantine army, a feat that led to the reconquest of al-Hadath fortress.

Egypt, Iraq, and elsewhere in hopes of settling at the court of a new patron. His travels ended abruptly in 965 when he was killed under mysterious circumstances. Though his life was cut short, his poems have endured, especially those of his golden period at Sayf al-Dawlah's court. Among the most famous, "Ode on the Reconquest of al-Hadath" glorifies the emir's bravery and victory, and thereby confirms his legitimacy as the rightful Islamic ruler of Aleppo.

Events in History at the Time of the Poem

Arabs versus the Byzantines. The "Ode on the Reconquest of al-Hadath" describes one episode—the 954 battle of al-Hadath—that was part of a much larger history of conflict between the Arab Muslims and the Christian Byzantines. After the

A camel caravan tours past the market and mosque in the city of Aleppo, Syria, where the poet al-Mutanabbi lived.

Prophet Muhammad died in 632 and his trusted friend Abu Bakr (d. 634) became the Muslim leader, a period of challenges ensued. These challenges posed a threat to Muhammad's unification of the Arabian Peninsula. Rebelling after Muhammad's death, some tribes balked at the new leadership; Abu Bakr dealt firmly with the renegades, managing to subjugate all of Arabia within a year. He subsequently sent troops to Syria, which was then under the control of the Byzantines, and to Iraq, which was part of the Sasanid Empire. His successor, Umar (d. 644), continued the Muslim campaigns in Syria and Iraq, scoring a great victory in 636, completely destroying the Byzantine army in Syria in the great battle of Yarmuk. By 644 most of Syria and Egypt had been wrested from the Byzantines and incorporated into the newly emergent Islamic Empire.

Meanwhile, the Arab armies fought the Sasanid Empire for control of Iraq, securing a victory that led to the complete destruction of the Sasanid Empire. The Byzantine Empire, however, remained a threat. Bolstered by its richest and most densely inhabited provinces—Anatolia and the Balkans—the Byzantines engaged in nearly continuous border warfare with the Arabs, always threatening to wrest lost territories back from them. Arab victories over the Byzantines thus amounted to insecure triumphs. At the border of the Arab Empire, there was a frontier of contested lands; the Byzantines in effect constituted "a permanent barrier to [Arab] expansion" (Lapidus, p. 39). It was a rivalry that would continue until the Muslim Ottomans, led by Mehmet II, conquered the Byzantine capital of Constantinople in 1453 and the Byzantine Empire collapsed. (The fallen city of Constantinople, renamed Istanbul, would become the capital of the Ottoman Empire.) It is the period preceding the destruction of the Byzantine Empire, an era replete with attacks and counterattacks, that is the temporal context for the ode featured here; centering on the battle of al-Hadath, it highlights just one example of many such incidents on the Arab-Byzantine frontier.

The conflict between Arabs and other Muslims on one side and Byzantines on the other had been going on for centuries (roughly the seventh to the fifteenth century). During the Umayyad caliphate (661-750) and the first century of the Abbasid caliphate (750-861), the Arab armies were mostly on the offensive. They besieged Constantinople more than once, attacking Byzantine lands and conducting the famous campaign described by Abu Tammam in his "**Ode on the Conquest of Amorium**" (also in *WLAIT 6: Middle Eastern Literatures and Their Times*). Later the Abbasid caliphate grew weak and decentralized; although provincial governors declared allegiance to the Abbasid caliph, their deference was more symbolic than real. They exercised independent power within their provinces. The Byzantines, taking advantage of the decentralized nature of the domain, attacked the Arab frontiers, whereupon the provincial governors rallied their forces to combat the attackers. One such governor, Sayf al-Dawlah al-Hamdani, won wide renown for his military confrontations against the Byzantines, thanks largely to al-Mutanabbi's poetic accounts.

The Hamdanid state in northern Syria. In northwestern Syria, in the city of Aleppo and its environs, Sayf al-Dawlah al-Hamdani established an independent emirate known as the Hamdanid state. Sayf al-Dawlah founded the state in 944, when he entered Aleppo to defend its borders from Byzantine attacks. He himself would prove to be its pre-eminent ruler, his reputation intimately tied to his military prowess.

Overall Sayf al-Dawlah fought more than 40 battles against the Byzantines, with mixed results. Although he initiated some successful raids, his lack of resources forced him to adopt a generally defensive strategy. He reinforced the towns most vulnerable to assault and rebuilt those destroyed by the Byzantines. Given limited military and political power, his approach varied greatly from that of the earlier Umayyad and Abbasid caliphs, whose armies went on the offensive, even besieging the Byzantines in their capital.

There were two stages to Sayf al-Dawlah's conflict with the Byzantines. The first, from 947 to 957, was marked by his victories inside and outside his domain. But the second stage, from 961-2 to 967, saw him suffer military and personal setbacks. The Byzantines temporarily occupied his capital, he lost the region of Cilicia, internal rebellion plagued his domain, and paralysis struck one side of his body. His earlier victories endured, though, through the words of writers who had become part of his court circle.

According to historian Marius Canard, "The brilliance which [Sayf al-Dawlah] conferred on the emirate of Aleppo by his military victories and by his cultural influence, and through the poets and the prose-writers of what has been called the 'circle of Sayf al-Dawla,' has made him one of the most famous rulers of Islam" (Canard, p. 129). Other members of this circle, along with al-Mutanabbi, include the poet Abu Firas, the prose writer Abu Bakr al-Khuwarizmi, and the philosopher al-Farabi. It was indeed an illustrious court.

Al-Hadath fortress. Today the fortress and town of al-Hadath no longer exist, but they once sat in the province of Antioch, in a plain at the foot of the Taurus Mountains, near three lakes on the upper Aksu River in what is now southern Turkey. For many years, al-Hadath was the "center stage" for the conflict between the Arabs and the Byzantines because of its location on the frontier. The Arabs conquered it during the reign of the caliph Umar (634-44). Subsequently—under the first Umayyad caliph, Mu`awiyah—they used it as a base from which to invade Byzantine territory. The town was sacked and

"Ode on al-Hadath"

ARAB POETS AND THEIR PATRONS

Throughout the medieval period and up to the early twentieth century, Arab Muslim rulers prided themselves on the presence of court poets, who regularly praised the accomplishments of their patrons. The most famous poet/patron relationship in Islamic history is that of al-Mutanabbi and Sayf al-Dawlah. The poet admired the prince, accompanied and fought at his side in various battles, and wrote some of his finest verse in praise of the emir. It is said that he felt genuinely tied to his patron, "who was in his eyes the personification of the ideal Arab chief, brave, magnanimous, and generous" (Blachère, p. 770). In return, Sayf al-Dawlah, who recognized the importance of poetry, showered al-Mutanabbi with generous gifts. Over the years, however, court intrigues strained the relationship. No longer feeling safe, al-Mutanabbi fled to Damascus in 957, abruptly ending what was to become the most celebrated association between a poet and a patron in the history of Arabic literature.

---

burned by the Byzantines during the Abbasid caliphate, then rebuilt by the Arabs. Caliph Harun al-Rashid (d. 809), who rebuilt it, maintained a strong army there. Like their predecessors, the Abbasids used the town as a strategic base from which to attack Byzantine territory. In 950, a few years after Sayf al-Dawlah became the ruler of northern Syria, the Byzantine army seized al-Hadath and leveled its fortifications. Four years later Sayf al-Dawlah began his campaign to reconquer the town and rebuild the fortress.

The battle of al-Hadath. Four years after the Byzantines seized the fortress, Sayf al-Dawlah achieved a major victory that would lead to the reconquest of al-Hadath. Sayf al-Dawlah defeated a large Byzantine army, capturing and imprisoning many Byzantine generals, including the son of the Byzantine commander Bardas Phocas. In various editions of al-Mutanabbi's *diwan* (collected poems), the "Ode on the Reconquest of al-Hadath" is introduced by an anecdote that provides an account of the battle. (Compilers or commentators customarily included such anecdotes to introduce a major ode, particularly those on military encounters.) Translated here, the anecdote introducing al-Mutanabbi's ode relates the details of the battle from the Arab perspective.

> Sayf al-Dawlah went to the fortress of al-Hadath to [re]build it. . . . He reached it on [a] Wednesday, in the year [954]. He began building the foundation [of the fortress] and digging the base with his own hands. On Friday, Ibn al-Fuqqas [Bardas Phocas] took the field against [Sayf al-Dawlah] with about fifty thousand cavalry and infantry. The fighting took place on Monday . . . from morning until afternoon. Then Sayf al-Dawlah attacked him with five hundred of his army, winning the battle, killing three thousand Byzantine men, and taking many captives. He killed some of them and remained there until he had rebuilt al-Hadath fortress—placing the last stone with his own hand . . . . So, on the same day, [al-Mutanabbi] composed this ode to him in al-Hadath.
>
> (al-Yaziji, p. 202; trans. M. al-Mallah)

Sayf al-Dawlah's control of al-Hadath was short-lived, however. In 957, only three years after reconquering it, the Byzantines won it back, after which al-Hadath no longer figured as a key site in the military history of the region.

The Poem in Focus

The contents—Part 1. The first part of the ode (lines 1 to 6 below) defines its overall theme—that the high rank attained by Sayf al-Dawlah and his legitimacy as ruler are based on his bravery in battle. At the start the poem speaks of character traits that pertain to Sayf al-Dawlah's victory at al-Hadath. The first line implies that his military deeds are the essence of nobility and resolve; the second line indirectly describes the man whose high rank is at the heart of this poem—Sayf al-Dawlah. Part 1 goes on to praise the emir's courage and lofty aspirations as well as his high expectations for his army. It concludes with lines that depict Sayf al-Dawlah's power and ability to supply the eagles of the desert with fresh meat (enemy dead).

Ode on the Reconquest of al-Hadath—Part 1

1. Man's resolutions are in measure with his will; his noble deeds in measure with his noble heart.
2. Petty affairs appear grave in the eyes of the petty, while grave matters appear petty in the eyes of the great.
3. Sayf al-Dawlah [now] imposes his aspiration upon his army when before even vast armies could not bear [such aims]!
4. And he demands that his men be as [courageous] as he is, and that is more [courage] than even lions can claim.
5. Birds that live long, young and old desert eagles, offer [their lives] as ransom for his weaponry.
6. Had these birds been created without claws, it would not have harmed them, for the blades and hilts of his swords [provide carrion] for them.
   (al-Mutanabbi, "Ode on the Reconquest of al-Hadath," in *Diwan Abi al-Tayyib al-Mutanabbi bi-sharh Abi al-Baqa al-Ukbari*; trans. M. Al-Mallah)

Part 2. In its second part (lines 7-38 below), the ode depicts the battle in four sections. The first section (lines 7-15) centers on the rebuilding of al-Hadath; the second (lines 16-19) on the Byzantine army; the third (lines 20-32) on Sayf al-Dawlah's bravery in battle; and the fourth (lines 33-38) on the cowardice of the Byzantine general—the Domesticus (the title for Bardas Phocas). Initially this part announces Sayf al-Dawlah's feat—his recovery of al-Hadath from the Byzantines and his rebuilding of it. Blood becomes foundational for the rebuilding: "Does al-Hadath the Red know its color, and does she know which of the two that watered her are the clouds? / Before [Sayf al-Dawlah] came, lightening clouds watered her, but when he marched close by, she was watered with [the blood of] skulls" (lines 7-8). The second section depicts the vast army the Byzantines assembled to fight Sayf al-Dawlah. "Their five-part [army] advances east and west, creating a rumbling of the ear" (line 18). Then comes a section that praises Sayf al-Dawlah's bravery in battle, lauding him for distinguishing himself as a lion among men. The section describes the weapons and warriors, exploiting the fact that *Sayf* (the hero's name) means "sword." Not all men's resolve and nobility are equal, and, by the same token, not all "swords" (i.e., men) are the same in the midst of battle: "Swords that could not cut shields and spears were cut down" (line 21). The distinction here is between swords that break and warriors who flee when the real battle starts, on one hand, and the genuine warrior, the Sayf/sword who cannot be destroyed like ordinary swords and who stays in battle without fleeing, on the other hand. Byzantine soldiers run from the fray, but the emir stands fast. Sayf al-Dawlah challenges death and fights without fear or hesitation. In an attempt to depict the emir as someone who has mythic, larger-than-life powers, the poet declares that Sayf al-Dawlah knows the unknown (in other words, fate) and defeats the Byzantine army by himself. His weapon of choice—the sword—requires hand-to-hand combat, unlike the spear, which is thrown from a distance. The play on the emir's name continues—the key to victory is the sword, that is, Sayf al-Dawlah himself. The fourth section of Part 2 brings the battle scene to a close by describing how cowardly the Domesticus, the Byzantine leader, is. The image of him as faint-hearted emerges in one of the poem's most famous lines, which is based on the idea that receiving blows from the back means one is fleeing from the battle instead of facing the enemy: "On every day that the Domesticus advances [against Sayf al-Dawlah], his nape blames his face for advancing" (line 33 below).

Ode on the Reconquest of al-Hadath—Part 2

7. Does al-Hadath the Red know its color and does she know which of the two that watered her are clouds?

8. Before [Sayf al-Dawlah] came, lightening clouds watered her, but when he marched close by, she was watered with [the blood of] skulls.

9. He built her high while spears were clashing against each other, and the waves of death crashed around her.

10. It was as if she had gone mad, then became sane once more, after he hung [enemy] corpses [on her walls] like amulets.

11. She was fate's prey, but you returned her to the religion [of Islam] by spears—and fate was forced to accept.

12. All that you take from the nights you take [with impunity], while they pay the price for whatever they take from you!

13. If what you intend is a verb in the future, it is accomplished in the perfect, before it can be negated.

14. And how do the Byzantines and the Russians hope to demolish [al-Hadath] when the stabber [Sayf al-Dawlah] is her foundation and pillars?

15. They tried to impose their rule on her, but death [in battle] ruled over them; the oppressed did not perish and the oppressor did not live.

16. They came to you trailing chain mail as if they were riding horses with no legs.

17. When they flash like lightning, you cannot tell their swords from them, for their robes and turbans are made of iron.

18. Their five-part [army] advances east and west, creating a rumbling of the earth that reaches the ears of the Gemini.

19. In it is gathered every tongue and nation, so only the translators understand what is said.

20. By God, what a time! Its fire smelted away base metals, till only cutting weapons and [men] brave [as] lions remained.

21. Swords that could not cut shields and spears were cut down, and heroes who could not clash [in combat] fled.

22. You stood up knowing that those who stood would die, as if you were in the eyelid of death while it was sleeping.

23. Heroes pass by you—bleeding and defeated—while your face is shining and your mouth is smiling.

24. You went beyond the limits of bravery and reason till people said that you have knowledge of fate.

25. You gathered the army's two wings over the heart [of the enemy's army], killing both hidden and fore-feathers.

26. With striking of skulls when victory is [still] distant, then striking the throats once victory has arrived.

27. You despised the Rudayni spears and threw them away until it seemed that the sword reviled the spear.

28. He who seeks [the doors] of illustrious victory must use as keys swords that are light yet cutting.

29. You dispersed them on Mount Uhaydib like *dirhams* scattered over a bride.

30. Your horses tread the birds' nests on the mountaintop, increasing the food around the nests.

31. The eagle's nestlings think that you brought their mother to visit, but in fact you led noble and strong steeds.

32. If these horses slip [while going up the mount], you make them crawl on their bellies like snakes ascending elevated land.

33. On every day that the Domesticus advances [against Sayf al-Dawlah], his nape blames his face for advancing.

34. Does [the Domesticus] not recognize the scent of the lion until he can taste it—[don't] even cattle know the scent of the lion?

35. And the emir's devastating attacks left [the Domesticus] bereft of his son, his son-in-law, and his grandson.

36. He came to thank his friends for his escaping the swords' edges, for their skulls and wrists preoccupied the swords.

37. He understands the sound of Mashrafi swords when they strike his friends, even though swords speak a foreign language.

38. He is pleased with what he has given you—not out of ignorance, for a defeated man who escapes from you counts himself a winner.

("al-Hadath"; trans. M. Al-Mallah)

Part 3. The final part (lines 39-46) concludes the poem with a direct *madih* (panegyric) of the qualities that make the emir a legitimate leader. This part emphasizes Sayf al-Dawlah's victory and his defense of the community. The victory reinforces not just this leader's legitimacy but also that of his religion; as a protector of Islam, Sayf al-Dawlah has had the benefit of God's support, unlike the Byzantines, whose Christian beliefs, as the poet sees it, are wrong. Besides breathing new life into the polity through his victory, the emir has also inspired al-Mutanabbi's ode. The final few lines return to the subjects of war and victory while reaffirming the qualities that make Sayf al-Dawlah the community's legitimate leader. He is a sword always battling the enemy, never sheathed, forever leveling blows that hit their mark. Certainly, asserts the final line, God will always protect Sayf al-Dawlah, for his presence guarantees that strikes against the enemy will forever persist.

39. And you are not [merely] a king routing another king, but you are Islam defeating Polytheism.

40. All of Adnan, not only Rabi`ah, are honored because of him, and the whole world, not only the province of Antioch, is proud of him.

41. Yours is the praise in the pearls, mine is the utterance, for you provide the [pearls], and I string them together.

42. I ride into battle on the steed that you bestowed on me [and fight valiantly], so no blame falls on me, and you do not regret [your gift]—

43. A steed that runs swiftly when the battle-din reaches its ears.

44. O you, who are the sword that is never sheathed, your power is undoubted and nothing can ward off your blow.

45. Let the striking of heads, the glory and high rank and those who place their hope in you and Islam rejoice because you are safe!

46. And why wouldn't God protect your blades' two edges as long as He can, for with you, the splitting of the enemy's skulls will never cease!

("al-Hadath"; trans. M. Al-Mallah)

Echoing pre-Islamic poetry. Arabs and Byzantines engaged in numerous battles for control of al-Hadath fortress, one of the most famous, though not necessarily the most historically important, being the battle of al-Hadath during Sayf al-Dawlah's time. As noted, the victory had no long-term effect. Yet the poem made this battle one of the best-remembered of the Arab-Byzantine conflict.

Critics debate the function of odes that concern military conflict. Some contend that the writers "described heroism and horsemanship to create poetic documentation of war" (al-Mahasini, p. 230; trans. M. Al-Mallah). But while odes include battle descriptions, these may or may not coincide with historical realities and such poems have other functions as well. Beyond a simple declaration of facts, the ode renders a political interpretation of them in the pursuit of an ultimate goal—in this case, to claim legitimacy for Sayf al-Dawlah based on his military victory.

Instead of unfolding in a linear narrative that tells the "story" from beginning to end, al-Mutanabbi's ode invokes the theme of blood vengeance in pre-Islamic poetry. The three parts of his ode correspond to the three stages in sacrifice rites: "entry into the sacrifice; the sacrifice itself; and the rites of exit" (Stetkevych, *The Mute Immortals Speak,* p. 56). Part 1 marks the entry into the sacrifice through the image of an emir who habitually provides eagles with fresh meat. Part 2 depicts the battle, particularly the defeat of the Byzantines and thus the spilling of their blood (the sacrifice itself). Finally, in praising Sayf al-Dawlah for the victory, Part 3 provides an exit from the sacrifice.

In the tradition of pre-Islamic poetry, "Ode on the Reconquest of al-Hadath" invokes the theme of blood vengeance as well as sacrifice. On the literal level, the imagery of blood affirms the death and defeat of the enemy, an important achievement given the tense circumstances on the borders during the period. Victory meant life and a continued, if threatened, existence; defeat meant death and destruction. On the symbolic level, the themes of blood vengeance and sacrifice elevate Sayf al-Dawlah's achievement into the realm of myth. There was an ethic of blood vengeance in pre-Islamic Arabia that called upon a tribe to exact retribution for its dead by slaying a person of equal stature from the tribe of the aggressor. Poets of the avenging tribe used the motif of spilling the blood of the aggressor (or an equivalent) as a metaphor for the revival and immortality of their own tribe and their fallen warriors. In much the same way, al-Mutanabbi depicts Sayf al-Dawlah as possessing mythical powers that enable him to revive and sustain his community by defeating the enemy, expressed through the image of spilling the enemy's blood. The emir's feat—he preserved the polity—allows the poet to immortalize the emir by celebrating his victory in verse—"a remarkable reversion to the tribal function of the pre-Islamic poet" (Gibb, p. 85). By echoing the three stages, al-Mutanabbi moves away from a mere historical account and attempts to transform into myth the reconquest and rebuilding of al-Hadath. His ode mythicizes Sayf al-Dawlah's reconsecration of the fortress after it has been defiled by Byzantine rule and construes the victory as "proof" that the emir deserves to rule.

Sources and literary context. It is reported that al-Mutanabbi often accompanied Sayf al-Dawlah into battle and fought at his side, and that this first-hand experience contributed to his verses' vivid battle descriptions. Perhaps boosting his own status, al-Mutanabbi mentions his fighting alongside Sayf al-Dawlah in some of his odes. In "Ode on the Reconquest of al-Hadath," he implies that Sayf al-Dawlah and his victory have inspired him to compose fine poetry ("Yours is the praise in the pearls, mine is the utterance, for you provide the [pearls], and I string them together"—line 41). He also mentions his participation in battle on the steed Sayf al-Dawlah gave him ("I ride into battle on the steed that you bestowed on me [and fight valiantly]—line 42"). Though the poet does not say explicitly that he fought at al-Hadath, this poetic mention, coupled with the anecdote that precedes the ode, suggests that he probably witnessed the battle. According to the anecdote, al-Mutanabbi recited the ode at the site of the fortress and not back in Aleppo.

The poet mentions Sayf al-Dawlah several times throughout the poem, but just as there is no way to verify the poet's own presence at the battle, one cannot verify the accuracy of his descriptions of the emir's prowess during the fight. Sayf al-Dawlah's victory at the battle of al-Hadath is documented by many historians. However, other than the anecdote that introduces the poem, there is no detailed account of either the battle or of how Sayf al-Dawlah waged it.

"Ode on the Reconquest of al-Hadath" belongs to the genre of Arabic panegyric or praise poetry, known as *qasidat al-madh*. Considered the foundation of the entire Arabic literary tradition for more than 1,500 years, *qasidat al-madh* played a crucial role in sociopolitical and court culture up to the early twentieth century. Panegyrics bolstered the reputation of many Arab rulers. Odes in praise of military feats were common. "Ode on the Reconquest of al-Hadath" is one in a long list composed after a military encounter and one among many poems that al-Mutanabbi wrote after battles against the Byzantines. The subgenre, which dates back to pre-Islamic poetry, is sometimes referred to specifically as *shi`r al-harb* (war poetry).

A GLOBAL RITE

The second part of the poem, about the military encounter between Sayf al-Dawlah and the Byzantines, echoes the "sacrifice" stage of the blood vengeance ritual. Here blood is spilled, a sacrifice made. In fact, the practice of consecrating buildings by sprinkling water or blood, even sacrificing an animal or a human at the foundation for protection, is long-standing and widespread in the world at large. Below is a European example that testifies to the belief that sacrifice, especially of human blood, is beneficial, even necessary, for the stability of a building.

> A Scottish legend tells that, when St. Columba first attempted to build a cathedral on Iona, the walls fell down as they were erected; he then received supernatural information that they would never stand unless a human victim was buried alive, and, in consequence, his companion, Oran, was interred at the foundation of the structure.
>
> (Westermarck, p. 462)

Al-Mutanabbi is often compared to Abu Tammam (d. 846) and al-Buhturi (d. 897), two other celebrated poets in the Abbasid period. "Ode on the Reconquest of al-Hadath" is in fact a descendant of Abu Tammam's own tribute to Arab victory over the Byzantines—"Ode on the Conquest of Amorium." Al-Mutanabbi was especially influenced by Abu Tammam's conscious use of the highly rhetorical *badi* style and his departure from some poetic conventions. For instance, several times in his ode, al-Mutanabbi uses one of Abu Tammam's favorite *badi* rhetorical devices: *mutabaqah* (antithesis, indicated in dark print below).

> They tried to impose their will on her, but
>   death [in battle] ruled over them;
> The oppressed did not **perish** and the
>   oppressor did not **live**.
>
> . . . .
>
> Their five part army advances **east** and **west**,
> Creating a rumbling of the earth that reaches
>   the ears of the Gemeni.
>
> (lines 15 and 18, *al-Hadath*;
> trans. M. Al-Mallah)

Al-Mutanabbi is furthermore credited with "blending the Arabian tradition of Abu Tammam with the smoothness and technical ingenuity of the "Iraqi school'" (Gibb, p. 91).

Like Abu Tammam before him, al-Mutanabbi's poetry became the focus of intense debate. The fact that al-Mutanabbi, in the tradition of Abu Tammam, challenged many poetic conventions of his day created waves of both criticism and praise. Like his predecessor, al-Mutanabbi defied the literary status quo and so excelled in his craft that he provoked great controversy. Whatever the jealousies of his own day may have been, al-Mutanabbi has won renown for a more masterful blend of the pre-Islamic classical style and the later *badi*` Abbasid style than any predecessor or poet of his own age.

Reception and impact. There is no direct evidence to tell us how al-Mutanabbi's "Ode on the Reconquest of al-Hadath" was received in the court or by critics, though over time it would come to be regarded as one of his finest works. In early times, as already noted, al-Mutanabbi's odes touched off a fierce debate between his admirers and his critics. In modern times, many focused their criticism on his acceptance of generous rewards in exchange for his panegyric poetry. Others idealized al-Mutanabbi and his relationship with Sayf al-Dawlah as the best possible example of a connection between a poet and a patron, their conviction being that al-Mutanabbi was sincere in his admiration and praise of Sayf al-Dawlah. Recent scholarship suggests otherwise:

> The ideal poet-patron match is celebrated . . . above all in the relationship of Abu al-Tayyib al-Mutanabbi, considered the last and the greatest of the classical poets . . . and Sayf al-Dawlah, the Hamdanid prince of Aleppo. . . . Although these two have been molded into a romanticized Arab ideological construct . . . the traditional sources nevertheless reveal an ultimate incompatibility between the two. . . . The tradition seems to place the blame for this

primarily on the poet himself, accusing him of the sin of excessive pride . . . . But other anecdotes demonstrate Sayf al-Dawlah's failure to defend al-Mutanabbi in the viciously competitive literary and poetic circles of his court.

> (Stetkevych, *The Poetics of Islamic Legitimacy*, pp. 184-85)

Whatever debates may have raged over the poetry or practices of al-Mutanabbi, there has been no argument over his impact on later poets, who measured their talent against his. As the literary scholar Roger Allen notes, "al-Mutanabbi is certainly the strongest of the strong Arab poets, the anxiety of whose influence was felt by all those who came after him" (Allen, p. 90). After his death, it would become the highest compliment to call a poet "al-Mutanabbi" to signify that the person is following in the steps of the most esteemed Arab poet. His verse has won similar renown. Perhaps the most fitting tribute to "Ode on the Reconquest of al-Hadath" is that its first two lines have become "proverbial and as famous as their celebrated author" (Latham, p. 1).

—Majd Al-Mallah

For More Information

Allen, Roger. *Introduction to Arabic Literature.* Cambridge: Cambridge University Press, 2000.

Bianquis, Th. "Sayf Al-Dawla." In *Encyclopaedia of Islam.* New Edition. Vol. 9. Leiden: E. J. Brill, 1997.

Blachère, R. "Al-Mutanabbi." In *Encyclopaedia of Islam.* New Edition. Vol. 7. Leiden: E. J. Brill, 1993.

Canard, M. "Hamdanids." In *Encyclopaedia of Islam.* New Edition. Vol. 3. Leiden: E. J. Brill, 1986.

Gibb, H. A. R. *Arabic Literature: An Introduction.* 2d. ed. Oxford: Clarendon Press, 1963.

Hodgson, Marshall G. S. *The Venture of Islam.* Vol. 1. Chicago: University of Chicago Press, 1974.

Lapidus, Ira M. *A History of Islamic Societies.* Cambridge: Cambridge University Press, 1994.

Latham, J. Derek. "Towards a Better Understanding of al-Mutanabbi's Poem on the Battle of al-Hadath." *Journal of Arabic Literature* 10 (1979): 1-22.

al-Mahasini, Zaki. *Shi`r al-Harb fi al-Adab al-Arabi fi al-Asrayn al-Umawi wa al-Abbasi ila Ahd Sayf al-Dawlah.* Cairo: Dar al-Ma`arif, 1968.

al-Mutanabbi, Abu al-Tayyib. *Diwan Abi al-Tayyib al-Mutanabbi bi Sharh al-Ukbari.* Vol. 3. Beirut: Dar al Ma`rifah, n.d.

Stetkevych, Suzanne. *The Mute Immortals Speak: Pre-Islamic Poetry and the Poetics of Ritual.* Ithaca: Cornell University Press, 1993.

———. *The Poetics of Islamic Legitimacy*. Bloomington: Indiana University Press, 2002.

Westermarck, Edward. *The Origin and Development of the Moral Ideas*. Vol. 1. London: Macmillan, 1906.

al-Yaziji, Nasif. *Al-Arf al-Tayyib fi Sharh Diwan Abi al-Tayyib*. Vol. 2. Beirut: Dar Sadir, 1964.

Once Upon a Time

by

Muhammad Ali Jamalzadah

Muhammad Ali Jamalzadah (also spelled Jamalzadeh) was born January 13, 1892, in Isfahan, Iran, to a progressive father who was a Muslim clergyman. A talented orator, the father, Sayyid Jamal al-Din Isfahani, denounced corrupt religious practices and lambasted the injustices of rule under the Qajar dynasty (1779-1925). He was consequently poisoned to death in 1908. His son soon left Iran, ending up in Beirut, Lebanon, where he attended the Antoura Catholic secondary school. Jamalzadah went on to earn a law degree from the University of Dijon in France, returning briefly to Iran before settling in Berlin, Germany, in 1916. There he supervised Iranian students for the Iranian embassy and wrote for *Kavah,* a Persian newspaper opposed to foreign intervention, which had long plagued Iran. At the beginning of 1921, *Kavah* published Jamalzadah's short story "Persian Is Sugar," and later that year added five more stories to produce *Once Upon a Time.* Some decades later, Jamalzadah moved to Geneva, Switzerland, where he worked for the International Labor Organization and taught Persian at the University of Geneva. He meanwhile wrote prolifically, producing numerous fictional works, most notably *Rahab namah* (1940; The Book of the Water Channel), *Dar al-majanin* (1942; The Madhouse); *Qultashan divan* (1946; The Custodian of the Divan), and *Saru-tah-i yak karbas* (1955; *Isfahan Is Half the World: Memories of a Persian Boyhood,* 1989). In his fiction, he both satirically evaluated life in Iran and advanced the use of colloquial and idiomatic Persian in literature. Much of the humor springs

---

THE LITERARY WORK

A collection of short stories set in early-twentieth-century Iran; written in 1915-21, published in Persian (as *Yaki bud va yaki nabud*) in 1921, in English in 1985.

SYNOPSIS

The stories address Iranian concerns of the early twentieth century, from the challenges of a modernizing society, to official corruption, foreign influence, political instability, the status of women, and questions of national identity.

---

from his juxtaposing speakers of different variants of Persian—out of the clashes of diction and dialect come some hilarious scenes. A pioneering work, *Once Upon a Time* helped chart the direction of the short story in Persian letters. Among the issues the collection addresses is the struggle for Iranian identity in the face of westernization and the central role of the Persian language in that struggle.

Events in History at the Time of the Stories

The emergence of modern Iran. Throughout the Middle Ages, Islamic cultures, including that of Iran, saw themselves as superior or at least equal to those of Christendom. In their view, their culture was the latest one spoken to by the universal God through his Prophet Muhammad. This perception changed, however, in the wake of the Mongol and Tatar invasion of the thirteenth through fifteenth centuries. The change was gradual but steady, as one Islamic culture after another found itself dominated by increasingly aggressive European powers, armed with gunpowder, new sciences and technologies, and the will to dominate countries everywhere. Their success gave rise to a genuine soul-searching among Muslims; some blamed Islam for their backwardness and powerlessness, while others believed the domination came about because they had deviated from the true path of their religion. In Iran, these two beliefs eventually manifested themselves in the growth of secularism and religious reform on the one hand, and what is known now as Islamic fundamentalism on the other hand.

The conversion of Iranian society to Islam was a phenomenon that started in the seventh century. Already by then the religion had begun to give rise to a basic subdivision—that between the Shi`ite and Sunni sects. Members of the Shi`ite sect believe that authority is transmitted through an individual called an imam, a descendant of the Prophet Muhammad through his daughter Fatimah and her husband, Ali. Sunni Muslims, by contrast, base authority not in descent from the Prophet but on the sayings and actions of Muhammad. By the fifteenth century, an increasingly Shi`ite Iran saw itself flanked by two powerful Sunni adversaries, the Ottomans in the northwest and the Uzbeks in the northeast. In the early sixteenth century, the first of the Safavid kings declared Shi`ism the official religion of Iran. This enabled Iran to meet the challenge from its Sunni rivals, but the country ended up isolating itself from most of the rest of the Muslim world.

By the end of the eighteenth century two colonial powers had established themselves in the vicinity of Iran, the British in the Indian subcontinent and the Russians in the Caucasus Mountains and Central Asia. Iran's encounters with these two powers, particularly its devastating wars with Russia in the early nineteenth century left it with a government powerless in the face of foreign intrusions but despotic at home. The country's first efforts at modernization emerged in this climate, as the nation's leaders struggled to maintain its independence and separate identity. By the mid nineteenth century, Iran had begun to send students to Europe, particularly to France, a country with no apparent designs on Iran's integrity in contrast to Great Britain and Russia. Iran itself was about to adopt a European-style educational system, led by a technical school that came to be known as the Dar al-Funun. For the next century and a half, the country would try hard to balance the need to modernize against the need to remain connected to its native culture and the religious faith practiced by most of its citizens. In the process, it would experience periods of either half-hearted modernization or diverse efforts to return to its roots, both Islamic and pre-Islamic. It is this historical background that provides the context for Jamalzadah's stories in *Once Upon a Time*.

Foreign and domestic relations. The twentieth century began ominously for Iranian independence. There was at first a promising development. The Constitutional Revolution of 1905-11, in essence a movement against autocratic rule and its foreign supporters, raised hopes for the establishment of a modern, independent nation. However, soon afterwards, the Anglo-Russian Agreement of 1907 divided Iran into spheres of influence, with Russia in control of the north, Britain in control of the south and east, and the two in competition for favor in the neutral zone at the center. The Qajar monarch, Muzaffar al-Din Shah (1896-1907), a weak ruler, granted concessions to the European powers who sought control of his country's resources and squandered money from those powers on his travels. People began to demand limits on royal authority and on foreign influence and to demand rule by law rather than autocratic decree. Muzaffar al-Din Shah's failure to respond to these demands led to protests by merchants, the clergy, and others in 1906. Under duress, the shah agreed to a constitution, drawn up by an elected assembly that, in turn, elected a parliament (Majlis) to represent the people. On December 30, 1906, the shah signed the constitution and five days later, he died.

In June 1908, the next king, Muhammad Ali Shah, tried to crush the constitution by having his Russian-led Persian Cossack Brigade bomb the Majlis building, arrest many of the deputies, and close down the assembly. But pro-constitutional forces marched to Tehran, deposed the king, and re-established the constitution. All this turmoil and Muhammad Ali Shah's attempt to regain the throne with Russian support in 1910 threatened to dash Iranian hopes for independence. In the end, the Constitutional Revolution would fail, thanks to the interference of foreign powers

The Russian-led Persian Cossack Brigade advances on activists in the early 1900s constitutional movement in Iran.

and a campaign by tribal (Bakhtiari) chiefs against the Majlis. But the constitution itself would survive.

When World War I broke out, Iran declared neutrality but to little effect. The country became a battleground for Russian, Ottoman, and British troops, one that drew the Iranians themselves into the factional fighting. The Germans provoked the southern tribes of Iran against the British, who responded by creating an armed defense force, the South Persia Rifles. Then, as World War I drew to a close and Russia became preoccupied with revolutionary movements at home, the British seized the opportunity for greater control. They established the Anglo-Persian Agreement of 1919, which, in effect, turned Iran into a British protectorate. But the agreement fueled opposition, and failed to win approval in the new Iranian parliament. A coup d'état was in the offing.

In February 1921, Reza Khan, a Persian Cossack Brigade officer, in collaboration with Sayyid Ziya al-Din Tabataba'i, a prominent journalist of the day, marched into Tehran and seized power. Their coup d'état toppled the rule of the Qajar monarchs, inaugurating a new era, and ultimately a new dynasty in Iran.

A few years after the coup, Reza Khan began a movement to establish a republic. However, the

Muslim clergy objected, arguing that such a government would be contradictory to Islam. Reza Khan then worked towards changing the Qajar dynasty but retaining the monarchical form of government. Eventually, on December 12, 1926, he himself became monarch, and soon afterward crowned himself first king of the Pahlavi Dynasty. He assumed the name Reza Shah, *shah* being the term for a monarch or king. Full-scale modernization became an urgent issue under Reza Shah (ruled 1925-41). He promoted a Western lifestyle, an end to British and Russian occupation, Iranian control of banks and other financial institutions, the development of industry, and the creation of a modern educational system. At the same time, his government began gradually to limit the influence of the clergy, to foreground Iran's pre-Islamic history, and purify the Persian language of its Arabic components.

In making all these changes, Reza Shah's government was seizing on tendencies already at play during the time of the short stories. Ultimately his dynasty would affect almost every aspect of Iranian life, from politics and religion, to language, dress, and education. The contingent of Iranian students abroad contributed to the transformations too. His government continued to send students to Europe for an education and when they returned, they often did not revert to the national dress—a long robe such as clergymen wear for men and a head-to-toe black covering for women. Various Iranians abandoned turbans for all kinds of hats from Europe; shortly after the stories take place, the government would order civil servants to wear a shortened version of a Western hat, called the Pahlavi hat. In its effort to purify the language, at one point the government toyed with the idea of romanizing the Persian alphabet. Religious reformers like Jamalzadah's father, Sayyid Jamal al-Din Isfahani, pushed for expanding Islamic studies beyond the central texts (Boroujerdi, p. 95). Economically Jamalzadah's stories take place a few years before

---

THE COSSACK BRIGADE

In an attempt to increase security, the Qajars employed Russian officers to form the Persian "Cossack" Brigade in Iran in 1879. The Cossacks—Russian fighters, farmers, peasants, pioneers, and even outlaws—were viewed as tough, proud, uncouth backwoodsmen by many Iranians. At one point, Iran's Cossack-led forces won command of three semi-independent provinces previously governed by an elected council and a headman, and repeatedly the forces fought off other troops sent by Russian tsars, meanwhile looting caravans on their way across Iran. Although the Cossack officers inspired fear because of all the raiding, they were commonly regarded as rabble-rousing foreigners. Their forces nevertheless formed a dependable fighting unit. Commanded by Russian officers until 1917, the Persian Cossack Brigade afterwards came under Iranian control, and at the command of Reza Shah its members were integrated into the Iranian army.

---

the major push toward industrialization, which began in 1925. Also there were relatively few educators, craftspeople, clergymen, or administrators at the time. The population consisted mostly of agricultural laborers, not a monolithic group since it included people from diverse ethnic (e.g., Azeris, Kurds), religious (e.g., Shi`ites, Sunnis, Jews, Christians, Zoroastrians), and linguistic (e.g., Azeris, Arabs) backgrounds—although the Persian language predominated. The peasants endured a daily round of toil, anxious dependence on weather fluctuations, and the pleasures of life in a close community with a shared language and customs. When times were especially tough, young men would trek to nearby countries for

jobs and funnel earnings back home. Over the years, thousands of Iranians sought work in Russia and the Caucasus region, which resulted in friction with the laborers there, since the Iranians worked for less pay (meagre perhaps by Russian standards, but a substantial amount to send back to Iran from their point of view).

Politics and the literary community. Occupied by the Allied forces during World War I, Iranians suffered from the weakness of their own government, which was unable to protect them from abuse such as that suffered by a character in Jamalzadah's story "With Friends Like That" at the hands of a Cossack soldier.

Only at the end of Qajar rule did various movements spring up to push for changes in government, the status of women, and the like. Persian literature had reached a high level of excellence in the millennium before the Qajars, through the creation of epics, panegyrics, and *ghazals* (lyrical love poems) and through historical, mystical, and didactic writings. But under Qajar rule, it declined enormously. By and large, literary elites of the nineteenth century tended to be reactionary, to champion traditionalist Islam and to oppose modernity. They were, for the most part, hired hands of the Qajar dynasty, who imitated esteemed writers of the past and failed to address urgent issues of the present. By the end of the Qajar era, however, the literary elite had become a more complex mix of writers hired by the state and those who opposed one or another of its policies. Part of this elite stirred with new ideas stimulated by Western concepts and a liberal nationalist bent, pushing for modernism in all aspects of Iranian life, including literature.

Since the Constitutional Revolution (1905-1911), new writers had been campaigning against the artificiality and arbitrariness of traditional prose. Theses writers, stimulated by their contact with the West, promoted innovative styles and ideas in newly established journals. Encouraged by the new emphasis on modernization, their early grassroots activities evolved into a literary movement. With the publication of *New Poetry* by Nima Yushij and short stories by Jamalzadah and Sadiq Hidayat in the 1920s and 1930s, this literary movement became dominant (Karimi-Hakkak, pp. 3-5). The movement gave rise to new genres in Persian literature—the short story and the novel, and poetry that differed in meter and rhyme from classical verse. Fiction broke with the previously inflated, ornamental prose and began to adopt a simpler, more widely comprehensible language, closer in form and content to the way people spoke than in the past. And, in prose, as in poetry, writers stopped praising Muslim personalities. Literature, like the rest of life, became more secularized.

Tossing aside—or drastically modifying—traditional norms and forms, pioneering writers approached literature in a radically different way, as a conveyer of fresh ideas and precepts. The writers not only introduced new styles but also made revolutionary ideas intrinsic to their works, as Jamalzadah does in *Once Upon a Time*.

The Short Stories in Focus

Plot summary—"Persian Is Sugar." Altogether *Once Upon a Time* includes six short stories, of which three that deal with distinct issues of the day are treated here. The lead story in the collection, "Persian Is Sugar," features four men who have come together in a jail in the northern port of Anzali, Iran. The narrator, a middle-class Iranian back from Europe, is taken to the jail after he disembarks. His "crime" is that he looks like a foreigner but carries an Iranian passport. In the makeshift cell, our narrator encounters two other prisoners. One is an Iranian clergyman (*shaykh*), who speaks a mixed variety of Persian and Arabic; the other a westernized Iranian, who speaks Persian with a French accent. Soon a fourth person is thrown into the mix—a simple apprentice at the local coffeehouse, who speaks a plain, colloquial Persian. All four have been confined for different "official" reasons but in truth are there because of the continual shifting of authority in the city, a byproduct of national instability. The story highlights the problem of communication in an environment of severe linguistic flux, deriving much of its satirical power from the four interlocutors' attempts to overcome this barrier.

The story satirizes Islamic rituals and the religious establishment of the era through its description of the shaykh, quickly adopting a tone that remains irreverent thereafter.

> I heard a hissing sound coming from one of the corners of the jail. . . . Something that I first took for a shiny white cat curled up sleeping on a sack of charcoal caught my eye. It was actually a shaik [sheik] who had wrapped himself from ear to ear in his cloak and was sitting seminary-style: cross-legged, his arms hugging his knees. The shiny white cat was his rumpled turban, part of which had come loose . . . and assumed the shape of a cat's tail. The hissing sounds I heard turned out to be the salutations in his prayers.
>
> (*Once Upon A Time*, p. 34)

Like the narrator, the simple apprentice, Ramazan, does not know why the authorities have arrested him, so he appeals to the shaykh for guidance. The shaykh, with "perfect declamation and composure," utters: "Believer! Deliver ye not the reins of thy rebellious and weak soul to anger and rage for those who control their wrath and are forgiving toward mankind" (*Once Upon A Time*, p. 35). Ramazan is stunned by the shaykh's speech. He can follow the shaykh's voice but not the meaning of his words. Neither the heavily Arabicized Persian nor the religious terminology make sense to Ramazan, yet on rants

Once Upon a Time

WRITTEN AND SPOKEN PERSIAN

Like any other language, Persian has written (formal) and spoken (colloquial) styles of communication. The written form has changed far less over the centuries than the spoken form. "In our country," Jamalzadah observes in the original introduction to *Once Upon a Time*, "the literary elite, when holding the pen to write, writes for the literati and ignores others, even the people who can read and understand simple compositions." He continues, "our literary elite, when they write, ignore the ordinary people and writes an obscure composition absolutely incomprehensible to the ordinary, whereas, in all other civilized countries where progress has been achieved, simple and comprehensible writings predominate" (Jamalzadah, *Yaki bud va yaki nabud*, pp. 3, 5; trans. K. Talattof). Forging new ground in Persian letters, Jamalzadah insisted on writing the way people talk.

---

the shaykh: "Patience is the key to release. *Spero* that the object of our imprisonment shall become manifest *ex tempore*; but whatever the case, whether sooner or later, it most assuredly will reach our ears" (*Once Upon a Time*, p. 36).

Now sure that he will not receive any useful information from the shaykh, Ramazan turns to the westernized Iranian, only to receive another potent dose of linguistic confusion, this time from the other direction. He cannot understand the gentleman's Persian, which is peppered with French words and is spoken with a thick French accent. Describing his own encounter with this westernized Iranian, the narrator refers to him as one of those gentlemen "who will serve as monuments to coddling, idiocy, and illiteracy in Iran until the Resurrection" (*Once Upon A Time*, p. 34). The narrator himself has a decidedly westernized appearance, but he can speak the language of the common people, which Jamalzadah describes as the "true, sweet language" of Persian. He is able therefore to quell Ramazan's worst fear—that he has been thrown into the company of lunatics. The only one to fully understand the goings-on in this cell, the narrator emerges as the model to emulate. He adopts attributes of Western culture such as dress, which in Jamalzadah's view do not undermine Iranian identity, yet remains Iranian in his speech. At the end, a new passport officer takes power, and all four prisoners are released as frivolously as they were arrested, on a whim. Taking their leave together, they enjoy a hearty laugh at the official's expense when they see yet another new passport officer racing to replace him.

THE WESTERN-ORIENTED GENTLEMAN

"Persian is Sugar" features, along with its three other main characters, a Western-oriented gentleman, calling him a "Wog." The expression is adapted from an Italian context, where it was originally used for the many Italians who sojourned in the United States and returned too westernized for the taste of many. Jamalzadah's story speaks of a Frenchified Iranian as a Wog. He reads not a Persian but a French novel in the story, while another character, the shaykh, recites not Persian but Arabic holy verses. The story roundly satirizes both of them, thus conveying the author's disapproval.

"With Friends Like That." In the company of a few fellow travelers, the narrator rides a coach from the city of Malayer to Kermanshah during World War I in order to visit his mother. The coach must pass through the town of Kangavar, which is in control of the Russians, against whom the Iranian nationalists are fighting. One of the passengers, a young, friendly Iranian worker named Habibollah (also called Habib) is bound for Kangavar to take charge of the family of his brother, who has been killed in the war. On the way the coach comes across a wounded Russian Cossack left to die in the snow. Dismissing the protests of his fellow passengers, Habib rescues the Cossack and bribes the coach driver to let in the extra passenger. As he removes the coin

for the bribe, the genial Habib accidentally drops his purse, which ominously catches the Cossack's eye. When they reach Kangavar, the Cossack hails some comrades and together they beat up Habib as his fellow passengers look on without lifting a finger to save him. Hours after the Cossacks shoot the amicable fellow dead, the narrator witnesses a scene that makes his blood boil and brings the story to a sardonic close: the Cossack whom Habib rescued approaches his lifeless corpse, steals his purse, and walks away with total impunity.

"Molla Qorban Ali's Complaint." In the capital city of Tehran, a middle-aged man becomes a preacher, a reciter of the Quran and religious narratives. Illiterate, he learns his trade by memorizing the sermons he hears. He earns his living by reciting the passion of Hossein (in Arabic, *Husayn*), the third Shi`ite Imam, at various gatherings of the faithful. His neighbor Hajji Samad calls on him to perform a weekly recitation in his home because God has answered his prayer for the recovery of his only daughter, the young Gawhar. To make the blessing all the more effective, Hajji asks the young girl to give the coin to the preacher in person. In the third week, as the 16-year-old beauty is handing the coin to the preacher, her head-covering gets caught on a rosebush and slips to reveal her face and her long, flowing head of hair. Thus begins an obsession that the Molla (or *mullah*, a person versed in theology and Islamic law) cannot shake, despite hours of prayer, recitations, and tricks to distract himself. His obsession eventually keeps him from going out to work except to preach at the Hajji's home. His wife sickens and dies from the financial stress of it all. Soon after, the beautiful Gawhar falls ill again and dies too. At the story's end, Molla Qorban Ali finds himself drawn to the mosque where Gawhar's lifeless corpse awaits burial. Alone with the corpse, Molla works himself into a frenzy and begins to violate the dead girl. He is seen, beaten, and arrested in the act. The story is narrated retrospectively by him from prison, where he has remained silent for seven years. The reference to love, the beloved, and roses, as well as Jamalzadah's playful rendering of many expressions, reminds readers of the tradition of the love lyric in Persian. Jamalzadah, however, tells his story in a simple, comprehensible language accessible to all, remaining faithful to the goal of creating an idiom for modern Persian literature matching that in which the characters interact.

What constitutes Iranian-ness. In "With Friends Like That," the narrator describes his superior at work in sarcastic terms, using an element of traditional Islam to do so, debunking both the traditional element and the superior.

> The head of my office was a kind soul, a person of zest and enthusiasm, dervish-like with a mystic's manner and the disposition of a Sufi: at peace with everyone and put off by disputes, uninhibited, considerate, and benign. His only faults were that he knew the mysteries of chess better than matters of finance and that he was more familiar with a deck of cards than with the cards in a ledger file or the accounts of our office income and expenditures.
> (*Once Upon a Time*, pp. 65-66)

"Persian is Sugar" is equally ironic when it contrasts both the shaykh's unintelligible Persian ("contaminated" with Arab-Islamic terminology) and the Wog's Persian (equally "polluted" with half-digested French borrowings) to the narrator's ordinary yet beautiful and sweet language of the man-in-the-street. Finally, "Molla Qorban Ali's Complaint" shows a society victimized by tradition. The protagonist's making love to a corpse underscores the problem of interaction between males and females in a society where the two sexes are generally constrained to view each other from afar. The story suggests that such a situation needs to be reformed and that tradition itself may be viewed as a corpse that holds an obsessive and unhealthy attraction for modern Iranians. Also being suggested perhaps is the idea that the beautiful aspects of a once living culture continue to hold a morbid fascination for modern Iranians, keeping them from moving forward.

All these messages coincide with the views of the new literary movement inaugurated by Jamalzadah and his peers. Perhaps foremost among these views was their high regard for Persian. They endorsed the language, considering it the most admirable part of the Iranian heritage, and set out through their writings to expose the damage done by the seventh-century Islamic conquest of Persia. The literary movement had specific objectives:

- To denounce the use of Arabic terminology
- To purify Persian by not using such foreign vocabulary
- To promote a fictional language closer to common parlance than the conventional written style
- To link ancient Iran to the present, expunging centuries of Islamic dominance
- To introduce new literary forms

Although the movement's members believed that traditional literary elements—fables, the epic form, standard symbols, and Quranic metaphors—were inadequate to address contemporary social issues, they did not abandon these elements. Rather they infused them into the new genres, often in a satirical manner, as Jamalzadah does in "Persian Is Sugar," which features a shaykh saying prayers in an incomprehensible language and curled up like a cat. Such a preacher would no doubt fail miserably to communicate with the average Persian.

Interestingly, many scholars of Persian literature have categorized these innovative early-twentieth-century writers, including Jamalzadah, as "nationalists" (Yarshater, p. 34; Saad, p. 26). It is true that

---

A UNIVERSAL REMEDY

In "With Friends Like That," one of the passengers, an opium addict, counsels the narrator to escape grim reality by smoking opium himself. It will inure him to such gross but everyday injustices as that suffered by Habib and to the guilt of doing nothing to stop it. Certainly the man was not alone in seeing opium as a viable remedy to the travesties of daily life. Iranians had in fact long used opium as a medical remedy, as did the British, who imported much of Iran's opium. The nineteenth century had seen the supply of opium burgeon in Iran, and the populace showed a growing addiction to the drug. "By the turn of the [twentieth] century," explains one historian, "addiction to smoking was widespread, touching all strata of the society" (Poroy, p. 5).

---

nationalism influenced literary figures of the era, as shown by the anti-Russian tone in Jamalzadah's "With Friends Like That." In general, however, their writings did not acquire a specifically nationalistic character; the story just mentioned does not spare the Iranians, who passively accept a Cossack soldier's savage injustice to one of their own and are therefore complicit in it. Like Jamalzadah, other major writers of the period—Hidayat, for example—did not champion nationalism. They in fact left Iran to live in Europe. A few stayed in Iran and produced works with anti-state rhetoric, even challenging the notion of an Iranian culture, questioning how one defines national identity in such an ethnically diverse society. Abroad and at home, writers reflected on and criticized many national

HUSAYN, THE THIRD SHI`ITE IMAM

While Sunni Muslims subscribe to the belief that leadership of the Muslim community ought to be the result of consensus, the Shi`ite Muslims have historically advanced the notion of hereditary succession. After the Prophet Muhammad died, some argued that only someone as charismatic as he could succeed, both as a spiritual and worldly ruler. The Prophet's descendants were thought to be the most qualified candidates. Husayn, the third in the direct line of descendants from Muhammad and the man who had lost his life leading a revolt against the ruling caliph, was particularly revered and considered worthy of the title *Imam* (leader). His murder in the village of Karbala in modern Iraq in the year 680 c.e. became a watershed that deepened the Sunni-Shi`ite divide in Islam. Within the Shi`ite community, the narrative of Karbala became a source of recitations, the reservoir for a variety of themes and motifs on which preachers drew all year round.

In time, Husayn's saga began to be commemorated annually by Shi`ite Muslims in dramatic readings and passion plays that re-enact the circumstances of his death. To this day, during the Islamic month of Muharram, when Husayn was martyred, many ceremonies and activities take place. The climax of the holiday, on the day of Ashura (the actual day of the massacre of Karbala), is a mournful annual event. Incidentally, children take advantage of the occasion to play games such as hide-and-seek, and young adults to avail themselves of a dating opportunity, since on the crowded sidewalks one can get close to the opposite sex. Others invite a preacher into their home to deliver a sermon, believing that they will be rewarded for this by God. In his sermon, the preacher recites the events of Karbala and the martyrdom of Husayn, typically narrating some of the dialogue in Arabic and inducing the men and women to weep. Like younger people, the adults take advantage of the opportunity to socialize, exchanging news and possibly jokes.

characteristics as they wrestled with the question, meanwhile embracing language as an uncontestable element of Iranian-ness.

Sources and literary context. Jamalzadah wrote the lead story, "Persian is Sugar" in 1916, upon returning to Europe after a brief visit to Iran. He may well have experienced some administrative difficulties similar to the narrator's during this trip. Another brief trip to Iran during World War I could have provided the material for "With Friends Like That," since he spent a few months in Kermanshah at the time.

As noted, Jamalzadah was highly influenced by Western ideas. For the most part, his modernist and Western orientation is reflected in his choice of topics, his critical approach, and his questioning of tradition. He dealt with issues as diverse as the attitudes espoused by Western-educated Iranians, the injustices of the justice system, and the corruption that plagued the practice of Islam in his time. Again, he promoted the

short-story genre, which has its most immediate roots in Western literary tradition. Jamalzadah also drew on Persian literary tradition, specifically on the anecdotal narrative of the *maqamah* genre (see *The Maqamat*, also in *WLAIT 6: Middle Eastern Literatures and Their Times*). Modern prose writing first became popular in Iran at the beginning of the twentieth century, especially in the 1920s, when Muhammad Ali Jamalzadah and Sadiq Hidayat established the genre as the main means of literary expression, a position until then enjoyed by poetry. Along with Hidayat, Jamalzadah raised the short story to a position of prominence it would enjoy until the 1979 Revolution, after which the novel replaced it in popularity.

Reception and impact. As indicated, most of the stories in *Once Upon a Time* were originally published in Berlin in the Persian magazine *Kavah*. When published in Iran a year later as part of *Once Upon at Time*, they met with stiff resistance from clerical leaders and a wildly enthusiastic welcome from progressive Iranians, mainly because of the stories' innovative use of spoken Persian. The work especially caught the attention of the elites who were satirized. In a November 8, 1922, letter, Abd al-Rahim Khalkhali, a bookseller and scholar, informed Jamalzadah that *Once Upon a Time* has caused an uproar in Tehran: "Cries aimed against 'infidels' and shouts of 'woe to our religion' were raised like waving cudgels. . . . Because of your book, my bookstore was almost burned down and myself almost martyred" (Moayyad in Jamalzadah, p. 10). Despite the passage of time, the work remains offensive to some and immensely attractive to others.

Once Upon a Time had an undeniably democratizing effect on Iranian society with its use of spoken Persian, which attached the prestige of literature to everyday life, bringing these two spheres closer together than ever before. A few years after its release, scholars began to acknowledge it as *the* work that initiated Persian realism. At the beginning of the original Persian edition is an introduction by Jamalzadah that criticizes prevailing literary trends and calls for literary freedom. This introduction itself has gained distinction as the "manifesto that officially established the course of modern Persian fiction" (Yusufi, p. 105; trans. K. Talattof).

—Kamran Talattof

For More Information

Beard, Michael. *Hedayat's Blind Owl as a Western Novel.* Princeton, N.J.: Princeton University Press, 1990.

Boroujerdi, Mehrzad. *Iranian Intellectuals and the West: The Tormented Triumph of Nativism.* Syracuse, N.Y.: Syracuse University Press, 1996.

Chaqueri, Cosroe. *The Russo-Caucasian Origins of the Iranian Left: Social Democracy in Modern Iran.* Surrey, U.K.: Curzon Press, 2001.

Ghanoonparvar, M. R. *In a Persian Mirror: Images of the West and Westerners in Iranian Fiction.* Austin: University of Texas Press, 1993.

Humayuni, Sadiq. "Mardi ba Karavat-e Surkh." In *Dihbashi, Ali.* Ed. Yad-i Muhammad Ali Jamalzadah. Tehran: Sales, 1998.

Jamalzadah, M. A. *Once Upon a Time.* Trans. H. Moayyad and P. Sprachman. New York: Bibliotheca Persica, 1985.

———. *Yaki bud va yaki nabud.* Tehran: n.p., 1922.

Karimi-Hakkak, Ahmad. *Recasting Persian Poetry: Scenarios of Poetic Modernity in Iran.* Salt Lake City: University of Utah Press, 1995.

Poroy, Ibrahim I. *An Economic Model of Opium Consumption in Iran and Turkey during the Nineteenth Century.* San Diego: San Diego State University Center for Research in Economic Development, 1981.

Saad, Joya. *The Image of Arabs in Modern Persian Literature.* Lanham, Md.: University Press of America, 1996.

Talattof, Kamran. *The Politics of Writing in Iran: A History of Modern Persian Literature.* Syracuse: Syracuse University Press, 2000.

Yarshater, Ehsan. "The Development of Iranian Literatures." In *Persian Literature.* Ed. Ehsan Yarshater. Albany, N.Y.: Bibliotheca Persica, 1988.

Yusufi, G. H. "Bank-i Khurus-i Sahari." In *Yad-i Muhammad Ali Jamalzadah.* Ed. Ali Dihbashi. Tehran: Sales, 1998.

Only Yesterday

by
Shmuel Yosef Agnon

Shmuel Yosef Agnon (1887-1970) was born Shmuel Yosef Czaczkes in Buczacz, a small town in eastern Galicia (then part of the Austro-Hungarian Empire) to middle-class Jewish parents. His father, a furrier, belonged to a sect of pietistic Jews known as the Hasidim. From age three to ten, Agnon received a traditional Hebrew education at the elementary level, then studied with private teachers, learning **Talmud** (also in *WLAIT 6: Middle Eastern Literatures and Their Times*). He also read Jewish folklore and Hasidic literature. Agnon's mother, a devotee of German letters, helped expose the boy to a variety of languages, in which he read secular literature in translation. Along with German, Agnon learned Yiddish and Hebrew. In 1908, having become active in Zionist circles, Agnon immigrated to Palestine, where he settled in Jaffa and worked for Zionist organizations and a literary journal as an assistant editor. Agnon wrote his first stories in Yiddish, then turned to Hebrew. He quickly adopted the surname *Agnon*, taking it from the title of his first important story, "Agunot" (1908), the Hebrew word for wives abandoned but not divorced by their husbands and so forced to live in marital limbo. In 1912 Agnon left Palestine to study in Germany. Stranded there at the outbreak of World War I, he remained in Germany until 1924, passing some productive years mingling with the country's Jewish intellectuals and acquiring a patron—Salman Schocken—who became his publisher. He wrote short fiction in Germany and married Esther Marx, with whom

> ### THE LITERARY WORK
> A novel set in Palestine, especially in Jaffa and Jerusalem, from about 1908 to 1912; published in Hebrew (as *Temol shilshom*) in 1945, in English in 2000.
>
> ### SYNOPSIS
> A simple Galician Jew immigrates to Palestine hoping to work the land and, just when his personal problems seem to be solved, meets with an untimely death.

he would have two children. In 1924, after a fire destroyed their home and Agnon's collection of books and manuscripts, the family relocated permanently to Jerusalem. Agnon resumed the religious life he had abandoned during his first period in Palestine and continued to produce fiction. In 1931 he published a long novel, *The Bridal Canopy (Hakhnasat kalah)* about a Hasidic Jew's quest to find dowries and husbands for his three daughters. A few years later, in 1935, he published *In the Heart of the Seas (Bi-levav yamim)* and that same year *A Simple Story (Sipur pashut)*, closing out the decade with *A Guest for the Night (Oreah natah la-lun,* 1939). His impressions and experiences of the Second Aliyah (wave of Jews to Palestine) inspired his magnum opus, *Only Yesterday (Temol shilshom)* in 1945. Agnon would go on to win

Shmuel Yosef Agnon

the Nobel Prize for literature in 1966. Still considered his masterpiece by many, *Only Yesterday* intertwines social history with the comic grotesque to convey some hopes and realities of Jewish life in early-twentieth-century Palestine.

Events in History at the Time the Novel Takes Place

Zionism and the Second Aliyah. Year after year in the diaspora—the dispersal of Jews outside their ancient homeland—the exiles voiced their yearning to return. The term *Zionism,* coined in 1893 (by Nathan Birnbaum), came to signify both this ancient aspiration and the modern unrelenting movement for return. One of the main ideals of modern Zionism was the in-gathering of exiles from every part of the world, an aim that would be advanced by waves, or *aliyot,* of immigrants with distinctive characteristics:

First Aliyah (1882-1903)
20,000-30,000 immigrants

Reacting to pogroms (deadly attacks on Jewish communities) and to persistent anti-Semitism in Russia, most of these immigrants were well-educated residents of small towns and cities who knew little about agriculture. Some came from Galicia, Agnon's home territory.

Second Aliyah (1904-1914)
35,000 to 40,000 immigrants

Disappointed with the failures of the Russian Revolution of 1905, and driven out by a new wave of pogroms, most of these settlers came from Russia. Generally young, single, male, and socialist, they would establish the first kibbutz, the Histadrut labor union, and other important institutions.

Third Aliyah (1919-1923)
35,000 immigrants

Consisting mostly of men from the Soviet Union, Poland, and Romania, these immigrants were better prepared than previous waves. Many received Zionist agricultural training in Europe before their departure.

Fourth Aliyah (1924-1930)
88,000 immigrants

Largely Polish, middle class and urban, this wave faced high unemployment upon arrival.

Fifth Aliyah (1932-1938)
215,000 immigrants

In flight from the ever worsening pre-World War II conditions in Germany, Poland, and Austria, this wave assumed tidal proportions. Threatened by the numbers, because of the increasing viability of establishing a Jewish nation, the indigenous Arabs responded with violence and convinced the British to curb immigration.

World War II and Aliyah Bet—(1939-45)
82,000 immigrants

Known as immigration B (nonofficial immigration), the smuggling of Jewish war refugees into Palestine greatly boosted the number in this last wave before the appearance of Agnon's novel.

Only Yesterday is set during the Second Aliyah, which was distinctive, among other reasons, for the pivotal ideals that propelled the immigration. Back in Russia, the Jewish intelligentsia heeded criticism that they were not a nation because they had no peasant or identifiable working class. They had remained small traders in Europe, or storekeepers, peddlers, industrial workers, and craftsmen. They needed a fresh start, went the logic, a land in which they could enter every branch of the economy; once they became economically independent, political independence would follow naturally. With this in mind, young Zionist pioneers immigrated to Israel, not just to establish themselves as a nation, but having just been victimized by a particularly vicious onslaught of pogroms, to re-assert their manhood,

FIRST ALIYAH VERSUS SECOND ALIYAH

The First Aliyah showed animosity toward the Second, feeling threatened by the newcomers. These new pioneers, warned an orange growers' journal, "aren't just interested in work and food. . . . They want power, economic and social dictatorship over the agricultural domain and those who own it" (Bustenai in Sachar, p. 73). How did the experiences of the two differ? In 1882, idealistic Jews in the Russian empire—mostly university students—formed an emigration society known as "Bilu," (an acrostic "House of Jacob, let us go"). A small contingent of 19 Biluites immigrated to Palestine and set up a communal agricultural colony, enduring not only the harsh, unforgiving climate and the diseases but also the rigorous work schedule. Mikveh Israel, an agricultural training school founded more than a decade earlier, set them to work in the fields for 11 or 12 hours a day for a mere pittance. Even after the Biluites obtained their own tract of land—about 100 acres eight miles inland from Jaffa—they struggled economically and some left the new settlement, Rishon l'Zion ("first of Zion"), returning to Mikveh Israel or to Russia.

Meanwhile, other Jewish agricultural settlements struggled for survival too, including Petach Tikva in the Sharon Valley, Zamarin near Mount Carmel, and Rosh Pina in the Galilee. Unlike Rishon l'Zion, these farms were privately, not cooperatively, owned. In 1884 several of the settlements, including Rishon l'Zion, received financial aid from Baron Edmund de Rothschild—about $6 million spent on land, housing, machinery, and livestock for the settlers. Rothschild's money financed the construction of synagogues, dispensaries, and old-age homes too, but not without strings. In return, he expected control over the selection of crops to grow and administrators to employ. These were the administrators who first resorted to the hiring of cheap Arab labor (hence the drive by the idealists in the Second Aliyah to control their own finances and to promote the hiring of Jewish labor).

to remake themselves from the ground up through hard physical toil. They embedded their goal in the lyrics of a folk song, which Agnon echoes in first line of his novel:

"*Anu banu Artza, liv'not u'l'hibanot ba*" goes the song—"We've come to the Land of Israel to build, and to be rebuilt, here."

"Like all our brethren of the Second Aliya," says the novel, "the bearers of our Salvation, Isaac Kumer left his country and his homeland and his city and ascended to the Land of Israel to build it from its destruction and to be rebuilt by it."

(Sachar, p. 76; Agnon, *Only Yesterday*, p. 3)

In keeping with the ideal, this contingent of pioneers scorned material luxury, embraced hard work, and took comfort in the collective, embracing it as an ideology. It was the Second Aliya that founded the land's first kibbutz (Degania in 1909), whose members held property in common and met mutual needs together.

Many of these Second Aliyah immigrants embraced Labor Zionism, a synthesis of Zionist and socialist ideals propounded by Nachman Syrkin and Ber Borochov. Separately, Syrkin and Borochov argued for a Jewish society in Palestine that controlled its own finances and hired only Jewish laborers, in contrast to the prior Jewish settlements there. The older Zionists, already in Palestine, scoffed at these ideas but they attracted young Russian Jews already drawn to communism and socialism, and inspired the formation of a new political party, *ha-Po'el ha-tsa'ir* (The Young Worker).

Acting on its ideals, the Second Aliyah set out on a "conquest of labor," meaning they intended to replace Arab labor with Jewish labor in the existing Zionist agricultural settlements.

Organizations helped, providing subsidies to enterprises that hired Jewish labor. But times were trying for the Second Aliyah immigrants, and many of them despaired. Most flocked to the cities, especially to Jaffa. But be it Jaffa or Jerusalem, they found the community to be provincial, hot, dusty, and otherwise uninviting. There was no warm welcome from the Turkish authorities of the Ottoman empire, or from the Orthodox Jews and Jewish farmers of the First Aliya, who tended to be either more religious or more capitalistic than the Second Aliyah pioneers. Certainly there was no welcome from the Arabs, who now stood in greater danger of being displaced. Add to this cold reception a dearth of job opportunities plus rampant diseases like malaria, and the disillusionment that ensued is hardly surprising. In the face of all the obstacles, perhaps 80 percent of the Second Aliyah left Palestine within a few weeks or months, returning to Europe or pressing on to America. The remaining 20 percent, or 8,000, struggled stubbornly to be accepted and to forge a Jewish society in Palestine. Mostly young, single, and male, they endured a daily existence replete with a piercing loneliness; again, the antidote for many (though not for Agnon's protagonist) was the collective.

Mea Shearim—the ultra-Orthodox alternative. A popular religious movement thrived back in Russia and Central and Eastern Europe, wellspring of the immigrants who peopled the first two aliyot. Founded in the eighteenth century, the religious movement, Hasidism, was a pietistic type of Judaism that derived certain ideas from the faith's mystic tradition and differed in approach from the scholarly mainstream. Hasidism focused on the emotional component, stressing fellowship, charismatic leadership, and piety and intensity of prayer over strict observance and study of **Torah** (also in *WLAIT 6: Middle Eastern Literatures and Their Times*). Reaching out to the masses, the new movement soon spread into Galicia, original home to the novel's protagonist. The movement attracted an increasing number of adherents and underwent change. By the early 1800s, Hasidism had evolved into an ultraconservative movement that the community of Orthodox Jews accepted as a legitimate variation.

The Hasidic community organized itself into groups, each centered around a charismatic spiritual leader known as the *tsaddik* ("righteous one") or *rebbe* (a term of address for a teacher). This format would endure, as would an emphasis on the joy in worship. Praying actively, the Hasidim stimulated themselves into a religious fervor through song and dance, or more quietly through intense reflection on God and creation. The *rebbe,* the luminary around whom a group of Hasidic Jews clustered, differed from the mainstream rabbi, whose status derived from a command of Jewish law and rabbinic literature. A rebbe, Hasidism taught, embodies the Torah. He is a moral and practical advisor who can work wonders and who leads by virtue of his wisdom, piety, and luminous spirituality, which results from his ability to commune with God. Despite this distinction, Hasidism developed a new focus on the study of Torah in the nineteenth century, and it too endured.

Hasidic groups came to Palestine as early as the eighteenth century and many Hasidim immigrated in the aliyot. In Jerusalem they flocked to certain neighborhoods, among them, one that is frequented by the protagonist in *Only Yesterday.* The neighborhood is called Mea Shearim, after a verse from Genesis (26:12)—"And Isaac sowed in this land and he 'reaped hundredfold' [*mea shearim*]." Founded in the 1870s, a few decades before the novel takes place, the neighborhood is square and fort-like, enclosing houses of worship and an academy devoted to the study of Talmud. Its early-twentieth-century residents included various Hasidic groups, each organized in customary fashion around a rebbe. Distancing themselves from the modern world, the groups refused to participate in Zionist politics. A man was counseled to spend his free time studying the Torah. Marriage and family was the sole forum for interaction between men and women in Hasidic circles. Then, as now, the primary focus was on idealistic spiritual goals. If the Zionists of the Second Aliyah embraced one set of ideals, the Hasidim of Palestine embraced another, and the two sets clashed—severely.

The Hasidim, in fact, Orthodox Jewry in general, had long opposed the Zionists in Palestine. As they saw it, the return of the Jews to Jerusalem and Palestine must happen because of divine—not human—intervention. The Orthodox Jews organized in opposition to the Zionists as early as 1912, coordinating efforts in various countries through the formation of Agudat Israel (the Federation of Israel). Jews had to pray for return to Palestine, believed its members, but to hasten this return was a grievous sin. Zionism itself was part of a "Satanic conspiracy," a plot to forestall the coming of the Messiah, who alone could reestablish a Jewish state. Certainly it did not help matters that religion played no great part in the idealistic notions of the Second Aliyah. Zionism, railed the ultra-Orthodox Jews, "wanted to leave religion out of the national revival and as a result the nation would become an empty shell"; having suffered so greatly for two thousand years, was it "not madness now to aim at transforming the Jews into a nation like all others, to politicise them, to establish a state which was neutral towards religion" (Lacquer, p. 408). The ultra-Orthodox of Palestine, concentrated in Jerusalem, especially in Mea Shearim, and otherwise mostly retired from public life, found an ally for their own anti-Zionist stance in Agudat Israel.

The birth of modern Hebrew. The inhabitants of Mea Shearim mostly spoke Yiddish. Of course, the scripture they studied was in Hebrew and in Aramaic. But the Hebrew was a biblical form of the language. They had no use for the modern Hebrew being forged by some of the Zionists at the time. This was not an old language being revived but a new one being re-formulated and re-created for the twentieth-century environment. Clearly the ancient language was too stilted, too artificial to pertain to modern realities. Something new had to be formulated. A legendary figure often associated with this re-creation is Eliezer ben Yehuda (1858-1922), who published four volumes of a modern Hebrew dictionary, coining 200 new Hebrew words in the process. In fact, however, he had no direct influence on the revival of the language, which took root during the Second Aliyah. It was this group of pioneers that consciously promoted Hebrew and strove to use it in their social settings, which was no simple proposition. "It was, indeed, not easy to start speaking a new language that is not spoken in society, and has no established models to imitate" (Harshav, p. 114). The goal was one Hebrew pronunciation to replace the jargons that diverse immigrants spoke—from Yiddish, to Ladino, to a mix of other languages counterproductive to unification.

Before the efflorescence of modern Hebrew as a spoken tongue came a Hebrew literary renaissance (c. 1890-1920). This renaissance built on the work of Mendele Mokher Sefarim, who forged a synthetic literary Yiddish (which balanced Hebrew, Slavic, and German elements) and a similarly blended Hebrew (which balanced layers of Hebrew and Aramaic). Writers like U. N. Gnesin, Yosef Chaim Brenner, and *Only Yesterday*'s Agnon advanced the evolution of the modern language into its next phase, translating world literature into the synthetic Hebrew prose and using it to create new fiction as well. In this next phase, fragments from different layers of Hebrew (e.g., biblical, rabbinic, medieval, modern) might be intermingled in a sentence but were still detectable, could still be unwoven, so to speak.

The fusing of the layers into a seamless whole would occur later, after the Second Aliyah, thanks to the conversational Hebrew that its social groups introduced and to the journalistic endeavor—"it was primarily Hebrew journalism that boldly formulated the style of modern spoken Hebrew" (Harshav, p. 125). The Second Aliyah pioneers were the groundbreakers, though. They championed the use of Hebrew in schools and in their new city of Tel Aviv, founded in 1909 and sometimes touted as "the first Hebrew city." A few years earlier, in 1904, a teacher-training institute in Hebrew had opened in Jerusalem. In 1906 a secondary school in Jaffa began instruction in Hebrew, and other schools followed suit. By 1912, when *Only Yesterday* ends, there was a network of Hebrew schools in Palestine, teaching some 3,200 students. That same year the Hebrew Language Committee insisted that banks and other institutions speak Hebrew only. But it would take much longer for the language to become dominant in the *Yishuv*, the Jewish community of Palestine. In 1916, a minority of Jews—40 percent—declared Hebrew their main language. It remained for the Third Aliyah to introduce secular Hebrew as the uniform language for official meetings and writings in the *Yishuv*.

The Novel in Focus

Plot summary. *Only Yesterday* is divided into five parts—a prologue and four chapters, whose settings alternate between Jaffa and Jerusalem. The prologue, which begins in Galicia and ends in Jaffa, Palestine, relates the story of Isaac Kumer, an idealistic young Jew who desires nothing more than to immigrate to Palestine, where he hopes to work the land. In time Isaac's father, a poor shopkeeper, scrapes together enough money to help his son realize this dream. Isaac travels to Lemberg, the capital of Galicia, then on to Trieste, Italy, to be officially approved for passage into Palestine. He boards a ship bound for the Holy Land. On the voyage, the rather feckless Isaac is taken under the wing of the ship's cook, who feeds the young man because poor planning has left him with insufficient resources. Issac meets an elderly Jew, Moyshe Amram, and the two almost strike up a friendship but secular and religious differences interfere.

Isaac arrives in Jaffa to find himself quite alone at first, but eventually ends up at the home of Yedidya Rabinovitch, a fellow immigrant. Like Isaac, Rabinovitch and his housemates have come to Palestine to cultivate the land. Their efforts to find farmwork prove unsuccessful—Jewish settlers from previous generations are hiring Arabs over Jews—and all the new immigrants become discouraged. Isaac fortunately finds work as a house painter. A poor painter, he nevertheless earns enough to afford a room of his own; his painting improves thanks to a new acquaintance, the bohemian Leichtfuss (Sweet-foot)—so nicknamed because he was cured of snakebite by having his foot wrapped in halvah candy.

Meanwhile, Isaac's friend, Rabinovitch, finds work in a clothing store and becomes so successful in the trade that he leaves Palestine temporarily to establish himself as a successful merchant in Europe. After his departure, Isaac falls in love with Rabinovitch's cosmopolitan girlfriend, Sonya. For her part, the worldly Sonya becomes fond of Isaac for his innocence and simplicity, then tires of him and ends the relationship, deciding to concentrate on her new job as a teacher. Already feeling guilty over his supposed betrayal of Rabinovitch, Isaac is stung when she breaks up with him. Restless and dissatisfied, he neglects his own job, visits the agricultural colony of Petach Tikva, and decides to move to Jerusalem. Sonya sees him off at the train station.

Jerusalem proves more conservative than Jaffa and more given to social and religious divisions. But Isaac manages to adapt to his changed environment and to make new friends. He meets Bloykof, an artist who suffers from a fatal illness and, like Sweet-Foot before him, helps Isaac become a better painter. When Bloykof at last succumbs to the disease, a bereaved Isaac finds solace in religion, resuming rituals he neglected in Jaffa. He grows the long beard favored by Hasidic Jews and listens to the fiery sermons of Rabbi Grunam Yekum Purkan. Again Isaac encounters Moyshe Amram, who now lives in the ultra-Orthodox neighborhood of Mea Shearim, and this time the two strike up a friendship. Isaac meets Moyshe's shy granddaughter Shifra, the child of his daughter, Rebecca, and her fanatically Orthodox husband, Reb Fayesh. Although Fayesh disapproves of Isaac's Galician origins and his Zionist ideals, Isaac becomes attracted to Shifra.

During his stay in Jerusalem, Isaac performs an act that ultimately has fatal consequences. One day while working he encounters a stray dog and whimsically paints the words "Crazy Dog" on its skin. Jews who come across the dog—Balak is his name—construe the words as "Mad (Rabid) Dog" and run off or throw rocks at the stray to drive

it away. Reb Fayesh, encountering Balak one night, becomes so frightened that Fayesh suffers a paralyzing stroke from which he never recovers. While he is bedridden, Isaac visits the family and becomes increasingly drawn to Shifra, deciding at last to propose. The naïve Issac intends to clear up matters between him and Sonya in Jaffa first. Before leaving Jerusalem, he visits Reb Mohel, the ritual slaughterer who circumcised him as a baby and, on the anniversary of his mother's death, makes a pilgrimage to the Western (Wailing) Wall to pray for her soul.

Back in Jaffa, Isaac surprises Sonya with his changed appearance and demeanor; she treats their relationship as something well in the past, freeing him to return to Shifra without divided loyalties. But Isaac stays in Jaffa for a while. He attends a birthday party for a child born on the ship to Palestine and reconnects with some old friends, including Rabinovitch, returned from Europe as a successful businessman. Now happily married to a wealthy woman, he invites his friend to go into business with him, and Isaac considers the offer but finally opts to return to Jerusalem.

Isaac repeatedly berates himself for not working the land.

Meanwhile, the dog Balak has become the focus of newspaper stories; many Jerusalemites have seen him and nearly every sector of society—from the religious to the political—has a theory as to what his purpose might be. Some even blame the dog for the drought that has stricken the city. For his part, Balak senses that he is experiencing isolation and persecution, and the experiences cause him great confusion. In contrast to the realistic tone that pervades the rest of the novel, it slips here into a fantastic, modernist mode in which the dog's consciousness is represented at times through the use of interior monologue, with the dog even breaking into rhymed prose. He begins to go mad and exhibits symptoms of rabies.

Returning to Jerusalem, Isaac resumes his house painting and courts Shifra, despite gossip from the neighbors. He grows more religious than before, moving in with a pious family, studying Torah, and praying daily. On learning of Isaac's love for Shifra, Reb Alter and his wife intercede for the young man with Shifra's mother, Rebecca, who at last consents to the marriage. The wedding takes place, though many of Rebecca's neighbors refuse to attend because of the groom's background. However, a great rabbi saves the day. Hearing of the wedding, he calls upon the Fayesh household; his presence attracts many guests, filling Rebecca with joy and honor.

On the final day of the week-long festivities, tragedy strikes. Attending one of Rabbi Grunam Yekum Purkan's sermons, Isaac spots Balak approaching. The other attendees want to flee, but Isaac assures them the dog is not mad; he himself painted the words on Balak's skin. Recognizing the house painter as the cause of his troubles, the rabid dog bites him. A few weeks later, Isaac develops rabies and dies in agony, bound to a bed in a locked room. On the day of his burial, the drought ends and rain falls at last.

> The water flowed from above and from below, on the roofs of our houses and underneath our houses . . . and the whole Land was like a Garden of the Lord. . . . And you our brothers, the elite of our salvation . . . you went out to your work in the fields and the gardens, the work our comrade Isaac wasn't blessed with. . . . May all mourners mourn for that tortured man who died in a sorry affair. And we shall tell the deeds of our brothers and sisters, the children of the living God, the nation of the lord, who work the earth of Israel for a monument and fame and glory.
>
> (Only Yesterday, pp. 641-42)

Jaffa and Jerusalem. Isaac Kumer flits between Jaffa and Jerusalem in the novel, between Sonya in the first city and Shifra in the second. In contemplating his relationship to Sonya, he reveals himself to be an unreliable narrator. The reader cannot trust Isaac, not because he is dishonest, but because he is naïve. He misreads the affair with Sonya, blaming himself for not marrying her while she sees their interlude as a casual fling. He furthermore refers to masters of manipulation as "distinguished leaders" and to ordinary men as "mentors" (Halkin, p. 4). Thus, to understand the perceptions of the novel, the reader must rely on the interplay of its elements rather than on Issac Kumer's voice.

A key polarity emerges when Isaac flits from Jaffa to Jerusalem and back again. His entire experience in Palestine can be described as an aimless wandering between a nebulous present and a fossilized past in search of a purpose that never quite materializes. Thwarted in his dream to work the soil as a farmer and lacking the socialist zeal of many fellow immigrants, he becomes a house-painter who drifts between the new world (Jaffa) and the old (Jerusalem). He finds no noble place for himself in the new order and, though he returns to the old, is marginalized there too. His rootlessness surfaces also in his

off-again, on-again relationship with religious observance and in his private doubts. Although descended from a pious Jew, Reb Yudel Hasid, who "made aliyah" to the Holy Land after discovering a treasure that secured his family's prosperity, Isaac feels the age of miracles is past and no such good fortune will befall *him*. In this, he is correct, though whether his unremarkable days are due to the disillusioned time in which he lives or his own wavering faith remains am-

OF DOGS AND MEN

Dog imagery abounds in *Only Yesterday*: dogs appear as pets, mascots, decorations, symbols, and destructive forces. Isaac's friend Leichtfuss keeps a dog as a companion, while Rabinovitch alters his destiny for the better when he feeds chocolate to a lapdog and attracts its wealthy mistress, who later becomes his wife. Likewise, Isaac seals his own tragic fate by capriciously painting "Crazy Dog" on a stray in Jerusalem. The novel follows the painted dog, Balak, through his wanderings around Jerusalem; rejected and persecuted, the animal is ultimately driven mad. The dog has been the subject of much critical speculation. "Explications have ranged rather amusingly from the inevitable hypothesis that the dog symbolizes the Jewish people, to more ingenious exercises that characterize the dog as a detailed articulation" of the psyche of Issac Kumer (Band, *Nostalgia and Nightmare*, pp. 416-417). A symbol of different things in different places, the dog's significance is summed up by Rabbi Grunam Yekum Purkan in one of his fiery sermons. Condemning those, like the Zionists, who seek secular rather than religious solutions, he rants that "the face of the generation is like the face of a dog. And not just an ordinary dog, but a crazy dog" (*Only Yesterday*, p. 621).

biguous. In any case, torn between Jaffa and Jerusalem, without a firm foothold in either, he gravitates to the latter, the familiar Hasidic experience, but the novel will not let him find satisfaction in the old world either.

> While Jaffa is the new life of halutsim [pioneers], labor, national revival and Sonia [Isaac's worldly girlfriend], Jerusalem is the eternal city with its traditions, possibilities for return to religious behavior, and Shifra [Isaac's orthodox bride]. . . . The vectors of the plot and hence, [Isaac's] yearnings, oscillate: Jaffa,

JERUSALMEN AND JAFFA—THE LITERAL CONTRAST

Thousands of years old, Jerusalem, along with Hebron, Safed, and Tiberias, made up one of the four "holy cities" of Palestine, where Jewish communities had been established long before the influx of twentieth-century immigrants. These prior Jewish inhabitants were known collectively as the "Old Yishuv." On visiting their inland city of Jerusalem in 1898—which by then included Mea Shearim (est. 1874)—Theodor Herzl, founder of the World Zionist Organization, registered shock at "the musty deposits of two thousand years of inhumanity, intolerance, and foulness" and charged the Zionists with building "a glorious new Jerusalem," which would arise only after the Second Aliyah (Herzl in Armstrong, p. 366). In contrast, Jaffa, though also an ancient city, came then to represent change and progress. Its situation as a port city was a contributing factor. Merchants, many of them Jews of the First and Second Aliyot, opened an estimated 400 shops associated with "a heavy investment in private housing, public buildings, mosques, and commercial buildings" between 1880 and 1910 (Kimmerling and Migdal, p. 45). Wishing to avoid the more parochial atmosphere of Jerusalem, Zionists established Jewish cultural and administrative organizations, including Hebrew schools and the first workers' federations, in Jaffa. In 1909 the Zionists obtained financial backing for the construction of a new Jewish suburb, begun on the sand dunes just north of Jaffa; by the end of the Second Aliyah (1914), the suburb—Tel Aviv—contained 139 houses and 1,419 Jewish residents (Sachar, p. 88). In one of many digressions in the novel, *Only Yesterday* describes the building of Tel Aviv.

Jerusalem, Jaffa, Jerusalem. The novel is, in effect, a literary statement that redemption can be found in neither place, in neither way of life. Jaffa is unsatisfying; the satisfaction that Jerusalem offers is only a brief prelude to a brutal, meaningless death.

(Band, *Nostalgia and Nightmare,* p. 444)

It is a nihilistic vision, the perception of the author himself who lived in Palestine during the Second Aliyah and wrote as Orthodox Jewry of Russia and Eastern Europe was being annihilated by the Nazi perpetrators of the Holocaust.

Sources and literary context. Many of Agnon's own experiences influenced *Only Yesterday.* Like his protagonist, Isaac Kumer, the novelist was a native of Galicia, and he too immigrated to Palestine as part of the Second Aliyah. Also like Isaac, Agnon spent considerable time in Jaffa and Jerusalem. Hasidism was a factor in his upbringing, and he himself witnessed the decline of religious faith among the Jewish settlers of Palestine, which became an integral part of his novel. Finally, the novel is "studded with terms taken from pious texts" that were part of the novelist's background (Band, "Exile in Redemption," p. 5).

Agnon's earlier fiction echoes in *Only Yesterday.* In the course of the story, the reader learns that Isaac descends from Reb Yudel Hasid, the protagonist of *The Bridal Canopy.* Isaac is not based upon Agnon himself; the writer, Hemdat, whom Isaac befriends in Jaffa, comes closer to filling that role. The protagonist also encounters in Jaffa someone from real life, the novelist Yosef Chaim Brenner. His presence in the novel is fraught with unspoken meaning. Four decades before *Only Yesterday,* Brenner wrote a similarly despondent novel, *Breakdown and Bereavement* (1920), also about a Zionist pioneer. Agnon's work follows in the same tradition.

Because of its enormous scope and its painstaking recreation of the development of Palestine in the 1900s, *Only Yesterday* is often described as an epic novel of the Second Aliyah. According to literary scholar Arnold Band, it is "actually the opposite. It is a novel written a generation later" that "employs the deadly tensions between the ideals of the Second Aliyah and their impossible realization as a paradigm of the human tragedy involved in believing in powerful myths that one cannot realize in life situations" (Band, "Exile in Redemption," p. 7).

Some critics also believe Isaac Kumer's trajectory makes the work a *Bildungsroman*—"novel of growth"—of sorts, which charts its protagonist not so much from innocence to experience as from innocence to failure and pointless death. Many also compare the biblical Isaac to Agnon's hapless protagonist, noting that the sacrifice of the latter seems ultimately meaningless, unlike that of his biblical ancestor. The episodes concerning the dog Balak evoke comparisons with the comic-grotesque writings of Franz Kafka and other surrealists. Considering the novel as a whole, *Only Yesterday* emerges as "one of [Agnon's] most intricately textured books" and, despite the tragic fate of its protagonist, "marvelously comical . . . The novel abounds with hilarious satires of [Isaac's] naïveté, of Zionist bureaucrats, of religious fanatics like Reb Fayesh and Grunam Yekum Purkan, and the self-confident foibles of the modern settlers of Palestine" (Band, *Nostalgia and Nightmare*, p. 445). At the same time, the novel raises perplexing questions, like "what can we learn from this absurd and shocking ending about the meaning and value of Zionism and the pioneering enterprise?" (Miron, p. 10). So heavily did these questions weigh on Agnon himself that he ends his story with the promise of a future novel that picks up where this one leaves off: "Complete are the deeds of Isaac / The deeds of our other comrades . . . / Will come in the book *A Parcel of Land*." But it was never written (*Only Yesterday*, p. 642).

Events in History at the Time the Novel Was Written

Mandate period to World War II. *Only Yesterday* was composed from 1931-1942, with parts of it appearing in serial format throughout the 14-year stretch. Palestine had by the beginning of this stretch transferred hands, passing out of the control the now-defunct Ottoman Empire into the hands of Great Britain, as mandated by the League of Nations (in 1922). Through all these changes, the waves of Jewish immigration rolled on, first encouraged by the British, then stymied on the strength of Arab resistance.

Meanwhile, Palestine itself was undergoing vital development. Zionist land holdings mounted, new industries began operation, scientific agriculture came to model collective farms, and various cooperatives were founded. Public utilities and communications began operation as cities developed and suburbs arose. All the while there was Arab resistance, which mounted as the Jewish community grew, prompting the British government to issue the "White Paper" in 1939, calling for the establishment of an independent Palestinian state within ten years. Both the Jews and Arabs rejected the specifics of the proposal, each feeling betrayed by the British. In any case, before it could be put into effect, World War II broke out, effecting a temporary truce in Jewish-Arab hostilities. Although *Only Yesterday* makes no direct reference to the mandate or the resulting strife between Jews and Arabs, it does allude to the spread of madness—represented by the dog Balak—which it connects to world war. "Since [Balak] had tasted the taste of human flesh, he went biting. Many were injured by him and many mentioned him with horror. Until the troubles of the great war came and that trouble was forgotten" (*Only Yesterday*, p. 640). The reference here is to World War I. But given that most of the novel was written during the onset of World War II "when news of the meaningless slaughter of millions of Yitshaks in Europe reached Jerusalem, the correspondence between the central metaphor of the novel and the historical situation is too striking to be disregarded" (Band, *Nostalgia and Nightmare*, p. 447).

The Zionist and ultra-Orthodox controversy. The growing *Yishuv*, Arab anti-Jewish violence, the annihilation of Eastern European and Russian Jewry in World War II—all these realities prompted much of the Orthodox camp to modify its virulent anti-Zionist stance. This contingent did not accept Zionism, but it did begin to take a more active hand in settling the *Yishuv*. In the 1920s and '30s members of the once strenuously anti-Zionist Agudat Israel themselves moved to Palestine, establishing settlements and dropping their former resistance to the modern Hebrew language. They became part of a general proliferation of factions in Israel that belong to three basic currents—socialism and Labor Zionism, the religious parties, and right-wing Revisionists. The religious parties included Zionists as well as non-Zionists. From the beginning, the Zionists had included a religious faction, the Mizrahi Party. Modern Zionism, said party members, was not a secular movement but the first step in God's plan to carry out the promise of this land to the Jewish people. The ultra-Orthodox continued to disagree, but while some still refused to participate in Zionism, others, including Agudat Israel, started to involve themselves. The picture grew less bifurcated, more complex and factionalized.

Zionism itself became factionalized. In 1935 the General Zionists split into groups A and B. Group A was nonideological. Against socialism, group B championed private enterprise. A third group, the Revisionists, pushed for attaining maximum territory, political control, and military preparedness, dropping out of the cooperative Zionist movement in the 1930s to establish an underground paramilitary unit (Irgun Zvai Leumi, or National Military Organization). The year before Agnon's novel was published, this unit began conducting guerrilla warfare to achieve its ends. Released as a complete novel in 1945, *Only Yesterday* appeared in a world that domestically as well as globally could be seen as touched by confusion and madness.

Reviews. *Only Yesterday* was warmly received, indeed celebrated in the *Yishuv*, winning the Ussiskin Prize in 1946. Critical consensus saw this, along with earlier and later works by Agnon, as "the most comprehensive and important artistic endeavor produced during the development of the Hebrew novel, from . . . the 1850s until our own day"; more exactly, Baruch Kurzweil describes *Only Yesterday* as "the most important and successful experiment in the field of the social novel in [Israeli] modern literature" (Kurzweil in Miron, p. 3).

It would be a half century before the work was translated into English, only to again meet with an enthusiastic reception. Dan Jacobsen of the *New York Review of Books* called the translation "a labor of love" and praised the novel's epic scope, saying no other Israeli writer "conveys more vividly, in more gritty and humanly recognizable terms, the strangeness of the entire Zionist enterprise" (Jacobsen in Riviello, p. 18). Jonathan Rosen, in the *New York Times Book Review*, admired the way "[a]ncient religious longing, modern political aspirations, and personal dreams all intersect" (Rosen, p. 28).

Several critics commented on Agnon's unique use of religious and folkloric sources that made his work seem at once ancient and modern, and on his deft wielding of irony and satire. Hillel Halkin, writing for *New Republic*, remarked that "for a great writer [Agnon] flirts dangerously with parody all the time, his pseudo-rabbinic Hebrew being so exquisitely styled that it teeters constantly on the brink of self-mockery. He uses languages like a bull-fighter's cape, daring us to fume at it and charge, only to find the blade of his irony plunged into us up to the hilt" (Halkin in Riviello, p. 19). And Robert Alter summed up *Only Yesterday* as "a scathing vision of God and man, Zionism and Jewish history, desire and guilt, language and meaning. . . . A work of powerful, and eccentric originality" (Alter, p. 3).

—Pamela S. Loy and Nancy E. Berg

For More Information

Agnon, S.Y. *Only Yesterday.* Trans. Barbara Harshav. Princeton: Princeton University Press, 2000.

Alter, Robert. "My Life as a Dog." Review of *Only Yesterday. Los Angeles Times Book Review,* 7 May 2000, 3.

Armstrong, Karen. *Jerusalem: One City, Three Faiths.* New York: Alfred A. Knopf, 1996.

Band, Arnold J. "Exile in Redemption." Paper presented at the international conference The Poetics of Exile, the University of Auckland, Auckland, N.Z., 17-19 July 2003.

———. *Nostalgia and Nightmare: A Study in the Fiction of S. Y. Agnon.* Berkeley: University of California Press, 1968.

Halkin, Hillel. Review of *Only Yesterday,* by Shumel Yosef Agnon. *The New Republic,* 7 August 2000, 39.

Harshav, Benjamin. *Language in Time of Revolution.* Berkeley: University of California Press, 1993.

Kimmerling, Baruch, and Joel S. Migdal. *Palestinians: The Making of a People.* New York: The Free Press, 1993.

Laqueur, Walter. *A History of Zionism.* New York: Schocken, 1976.

Meijers, Daniel. *Ascetic Hasidism in Jerusalem.* Leiden: E. J. Brill, 1992.

Miron, Dan. "Domesticating a Foreign Genre: Agnon's Transactions with the Novel." *Prooftexts* 7 (1987), pp. 1-27.

Riviello, Barbara Jo, ed. *Book Review Digest.* New York: The H. W. Wilson Company, 2001.

Rosen, Jonathan. Review of *Only Yesterday. New York Times Book Review,* 24 September 2000, 28.

Sachar, Howard M. *A History of Israel: From the Rise of Zionism to Our Time.* New York: Alfred A. Knopf, 2000.

Ottoman Lyric Poetry: "Those Tulip-Cheeked Ones" and "Row by Row"

by
Necati and Baki

Necati was born in the first half of the fifteenth century, probably somewhere in Eastern Europe. Like many elite members of Ottoman society, he came into the empire as a slave. He was educated and freed, then made his way to Istanbul, where his talents attracted the attention of powerful patrons. In 1481, near the end of the reign of Sultan Mehmed II, called Mehmed the Conqueror (of Constantinople), his poetry won the admiration of the ruler and he received an appointment in the palace bureaucracy. Necati later served as a secretary in the retinue of two royal princes; he died in 1509 as one of the empire's most popular poets.

The most renowned poet of the latter half of the sixteenth century wrote under the pen name Baki ("the Eternal Enduring," pronounced "bah-key"). Originally named Mahmud Abdül-baki, he was born in 1526 to the Istanbul family of a humble *muezzin* (caller-to-prayer). In his youth, Baki was apprenticed either to a saddle-maker or a tender of mosque lanterns. These humble beginnings did not prevent him from receiving an education, which took him through theological school and gained him positions as a professor and prominent judge. His talents at poetry attracted the attention of Sultan Süleyman (the Magnificent and the Lawgiver; r. 1520-1566), after which he became a popular member of the sultan's inner circle of friends. Baki died in 1600. At the core of his poetry, as well as that of Necati, is a belief in the overwhelming power of love, as interpreted in fifteenth- and sixteenth-century Ottoman society.

THE LITERARY WORK

Two poems set in late fifteenth and sixteenth-century Turkey; published in manuscript in Ottoman Turkish (untitled) in the late fifteenth or early sixteenth century and in the mid-to-late sixteenth century; in English in 1997.

SYNOPSIS

Necati and Baki use the form of the sonnet-like *ghazal* to express a traditional ideal of love in ways that reflect Ottoman society and thought.

Events in History at the Time of the Poems

The rise of the Ottomans. In the middle of the eleventh century, a powerful confederation of nomadic Turkic clans from Central Asia known as the Oghuz invaded the heartland of the Islamic Middle East. The mainstream of this invasion seized territories that included present-day Afghanistan, Iran, and Iraq. Establishing themselves in Baghdad in Iraq, the conquerors founded the Muslim Turkic dynasty known as the Great Seljuks (1038-1157). In 1071 the Seljuks defeated a Byzantine Greek army near the town of Malazgirt (Manzikert) in eastern Anatolia (Asia Minor). Afterward, Oghuz clans began to settle in Asia Minor, driving the Byzantines back and establishing a satellite sultanate in the town of Konya, known as the Seljuks of Rum (Anatolia/Asia Minor). The Seljuks of Rum would outlast their Great Seljuk cousins in the East, surviving until just after the devastating Mongol invasions of the mid-thirteenth century.

The Mongol invasion left Asia Minor a shattered region, divided into petty Muslim Turkic princedoms. The westernmost of these princedoms was ruled by the clan of a man called Ertugrul, whose son, Osman, would give rise to the Osmanli dynasty, otherwise known as the "Ottomans." Initially the Ottoman Turks were a band of raiders; throughout the fourteenth century they expanded to the west, acquiring lands, booty, and subject peoples at the expense of nearby Christian

---

NO DISGRACE

Slaves came into the Ottoman Empire in various ways. The empire's military expansion into Eastern Europe brought in a flood of captives, mostly men. Wealthy Ottomans would often purchase them as slave servants, provide them with an education, and later free them to perform a good deed, as recommended by the Islamic faith. Other slaves came from the Ottoman practice of levying on the non-Muslims of the Balkans a tribute of young men in their early teens. These youths were educated, converted to Islam, then trained for service in the professional army (the Janissary corps) as well as the highest administrative offices in the land. It was no disgrace and often a real advantage to be a slave in Ottoman society during Necati's day.

Byzantine rivals. Adventuresome young men, drawn by the allure of Holy War for the spread of Islam and by the opportunity to acquire fame and fortune, swelled the Ottoman armies into a tide that flowed from Asia into Europe. By the first half of the fifteenth century, this tide had turned the Byzantine capital of Constantinople into an island in a sea of Muslim territories. Although disoriented by a 1402 defeat at the hands of the Byzantine leader Timur (or Tamburlaine), the Ottomans soon recovered and resumed their advance. In 1453, under the young Ottoman sultan Mehmed II, they besieged and finally conquered Constantinople.

With the acquisition of one of the world's great urban centers, Ottoman aspirations to empire

flourished. Mehmed rebuilt Constantinople (which the Ottomans called Istanbul), making it his own capital, and began to re-establish it as a hub of commerce and culture. From the mid-fifteenth through the sixteenth centuries, the Ottoman Empire underwent stunning expansion. Mehmed subdued the remaining post-Seljuk Muslim Turkish principalities of Asia Minor and made the Black Sea an Ottoman lake. His grandson Selim I (r. 1512-20) expanded Ottoman domination to Syria, Egypt, and the Hejaz (western Arab Peninsula, where the holy cities of Mecca and Medina are located). Under Mehmed's great-grandson Süleyman (r. 1520-66), the Ottomans conquered the remaining sovereign rulers of the Balkans and Hungary. Ottoman rule had by that time extended northwest to the gates of Vienna; the Ottomans held sway over much of the North African coast, and dominated the Mediterranean Sea. During the sixteenth century, there was even an official position in the palace bureaucracy for a poet who versified the conquests of the sultans.

The first flowering of Ottoman Turkish literature among the empire's elites occurred during what historians call "the long sixteenth century," which stretched from the last quarter of the fifteenth through the initial quarter of the seventeenth century. Poets abounded in all the major cities of the empire at the time, especially the capital.

Europe and the Middle East at the height of Ottoman rule. The long sixteenth century was a period of tumultuous artistic, intellectual, and social change in the Mediterranean world. In 1492 Christopher Columbus made his momentous "discovery" of the Americas and Spain carried out the final days of its *Reconquista* (the Christian reconquest of Muslim Spain). In these final days, the Catholic rulers of Spain began a series of expulsions of Jews and Muslims from their lands, exiling the remnant of a once vibrant Arab-Hebrew-Spanish culture. This series of expulsions was one of the first major steps in carving out ethnic national states, each with its own national language, from Europe's large multicultural, multiethnic empires. Along with the Islamic exiles, many of the Spanish Jewish refugees were welcomed into the Muslim Ottoman Empire, which remained multiethnic. These Jewish refugees established thriving communities and served as physicians, translators, financiers, and traders under Ottoman rule. Mehmed's son Bayezid II is said to have thanked the Spanish for some of his most valuable citizens.

Both Ottoman and European culture flourished in the fifteenth and sixteenth centuries. This was the late Renaissance period in Europe, which

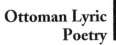

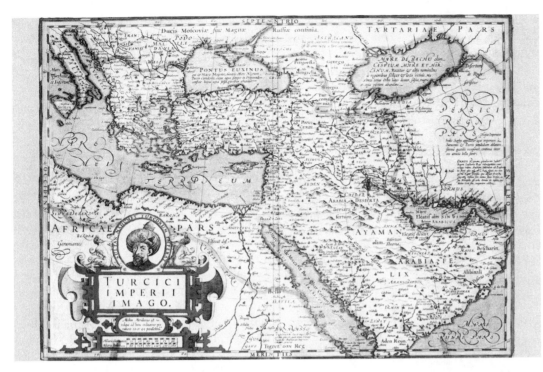

A European map of 1606 showing the Ottoman Empire.

began with a brilliant burgeoning of Italian art and literature produced by such artistic giants as Leonardo Da Vinci (1492-1519), Michelangelo (1475-1564), and Benvenuto Cellini (1500-71). Mehmed II had the celebrated Gentile Bellini (1429?-1507) brought to Istanbul to have a portrait of himself painted in the Italian style. Among other literary marvels of the age were the Petrarchan poets, the boldly satirical writer Aretino, and brilliant women writers, from Veronica Franco to Gaspara Stampa and Tullia d'Aragona. This was also a golden age of Ottoman poetry, the time of the master male poets Necati, Zati, Hayali, Yahya the Janissary, and Baki, as well as the famed female poets, Zeynep, Mihri, and Hubbi.

Religion too underwent innovation and transformation in such a fecund climate, both in Western Europe and Ottoman Eurasia. The spiritual hegemony of the Roman Catholic Church was broken in the early 1500s, when the reforms attempted by Martin Luther led to the founding of Protestant Christianity. Disgruntled Protestant peasants in Germany considered inviting Ottoman rule, thinking they would be treated fairly and allowed to worship as they wished under it. But the Muslim world was experiencing religious conflicts of its own. Early in the sixteenth century, Isma`il the Safavid, the heir of a

powerful Shi`ite family (see sidebar), began to take control of Iranian territories in the East and to challenge Ottoman power in Anatolia, where many inhabitants had sympathies with the Shi`ite faction of the Muslim religion.

Politically Europe saw the long reigns of young, powerful, ambitious rulers: Henry VIII of England (r. 1509-47), Francis I of France (r. 1515-47), Charles V of Spain and the Holy Roman Empire (r. 1516-56), and Süleyman, sultan of the Ottomans (r. 1520-66). The climate of change in which they ruled was widely perceived as the end of a familiar world and to many seemed to presage the end of time. Apocalyptic speculation was rampant. A variety of Christians and Muslims—the seers, astrologers, and geomancers—as well as Jewish kabbalists (practitioners of Jewish mysticism) predicted the coming of an invincible universal ruler. The belief was that he would unite the world under one religion, either as the Messiah (*mahdi* in Islamic lore) or a commander-in-chief who would prepare the world for the coming of the Messiah. Although there were several contenders for the role, most prognostications favored either the Holy Roman Emperor Charles or the Ottoman ruler Süleyman. Surprisingly, a number of European Christians were convinced that Süleyman would be the ultimate victor. By the same token, there were Muslims who believed that Jesus would be the long awaited Messiah.

In sum, in a period when the world seemed in flux, poised (as we know now) on the threshold of modernity, absolute monarchs dominated Europe and the Middle East. Their power, wealth, and glory made them seem God-like or like agents of God. It appeared that all benefits flowed from their good will, disaster from their anger. In such an age, for poets within the Ottoman sphere of influence, the expression of love, no matter how hot and physical it might seem, always implied love for the ruler, which implied the love of God. This is something to keep in mind when reading early-modern love poetry, be it Ottoman or European.

SUNNAH AND SHI`AH

The great ideological split between Sunnah and Shi`ah has its roots in a conflict about who was to be heir to the Prophet Muhammad's leadership of the Islamic community. Those who believed the mantle of leadership had passed to the Prophet's son-in-law Ali and his descendants called themselves the Party (Arabic *shi`ah*) of Ali and became known as Shi`ites. Those who believed in the legitimacy of the successors chosen by the Muslim community after Muhammad's death and in the supremacy of the sayings and practices (*sunnah* in Arabic) of the Prophet became known as Sunnis.

Poets and patrons. Scholars have recently made the observation, with regard to Renaissance England, that in early modern times the "supposedly "private" sphere of love can be imagined only through its similarities and dissimilarities to the public world of the court" (Jones and Stallybrass, p. 54). This was as true of the Ottoman court as of the English court under the Tudor monarchs. Even more than his European counterparts, the Ottoman sultan was the sole locus of power. There was no competing faction of hereditary nobility to challenge him; the Ottoman family was the only family that could rule legitimately. During the height of Ottoman power, a son who succeeded his father would have all his brothers and their offspring killed so that there would be no hereditary claimants to the throne except for his own sons. The most

powerful men among the sultan's administrators, underlings, and standing army were slaves.

For the Ottoman elites (both free and slave), power, position, preferment, wealth, and even life were controlled by the ruler and granted by his benevolence. The court-dependent elites were bound to the ruler and the ruler's surrogates by ties that went beyond simple loyalty. These were ties that were traditionally described in the language of love. Even the panegyric *kaside* (Arabic: *qasidah*), or poem of praise, seemed often to be an extended love poem.

Until the late sixteenth century, when Süleyman regularized the system of appointments to the educational system and bureaucracy, successful poets could count on lucrative jobs doled out by their patrons often as a reward for lavish poems of praise that not only extolled the patron's virtues but often asked for some specific gift or position. These Ottoman poets, whether of humble or better birth, identified with elite society. They frequented the salons of the powerful, relied on the gifts of their patrons, and often sought paying posts in the administrative or the military bureaucracy. In this climate, any poem of love could be understood as an appeal to the ruler or patron. The counterpart to praise was the threat of scathing lampoons or satires, in which a disappointed poet might hold a powerful figure up to public ridicule with the crudest insults couched in the most elegant poetic style. But the closer to power a poet was, the more precarious his position: a satirical verse at the wrong time might result in his execution; a paying position might be taken away at a patron's whim.

Being a master poet implied that a person could read and write and was skilled in polite conversation. These were qualities valued at court. The biographies of poets tell how Necati caught the eye of Sultan Mehmed II with a poem. It appears that the poet had a friend who was one of the sultan's companions. This man, likely an elite slave, was often summoned to play chess with the ruler. One day he went to his chess game armed with a *ghazal* by Necati written on a scrap of paper jutting from the folds of his turban. Spotting the paper, the sultan was intrigued and asked to read the poem, which greatly impressed him. He inquired after the poet's name, then awarded him a secretarial position at a wage of 17 silver pieces a day. In other words, attracting the attention of the royal beloved or wealthy patron had very practical benefits. Patrons liked taking into their service someone willing to suffer countless torments (emotional or other types) and endure hopeless longing for them.

There were other ways besides patronage to become a successful poet in Ottoman society. Zati, a contemporary of Baki, refused patronage positions and kept a fortuneteller's shop in the bazaar, ghostwriting love poems for would-be suitors and accepting the gifts of wealthy admirers. Another contemporary, Hayali, started out as a street urchin in the provinces, traveled to Istanbul with a group of wandering mystics, attracted the attention of powerful figures with his poetry, and ended up as a provincial governor.

Although Ottoman poets competed to attract the attention of the highest echelons of society, the subject matter of poems, indeed many poetic expressions and attitudes, seeped into wider urban society. Poets such as Necati and Baki frequented coffeehouses, millet beer halls, pudding shops, public baths, taverns, and merchants' stores, where they came in contact with many ordinary people. In fact, it was common for a beloved to be part of the non-elite population; poets courted attractive shop boys with elite, high-culture love poems. Lovers who were unable to write their own poetry even paid well-known poets to compose seductive verses to a beloved for them. Popular songs repeated lines of elite poetry and a class of urban folk poets appeared who moved easily between the styles and rhythms of folk poetry and simplified elite verse. In such ways, society as a whole shared some core themes of love, passionate faith, and entertainment, which echoed through Ottoman lands.

Ottoman society—urban entertainment culture. Throughout the early modern period, the central city of Istanbul was home to a lively entertainment culture that revolved around taverns, coffeehouses, country excursions, holiday festivals, the salons of courtiers, and the gardens of private homes. Just to the north of the central city, across the inlet of the Golden Horn, was the suburb of Galata, home to the European trading colonies. The villas of the wealthy dotted shores of these colonies, and many Muslim dervish lodges (communal dwellings of the mystical orders) were situated in them too. Although Islam forbade Muslims from drinking wine, in Galata, non-Muslims (Italian Christians and Jews) ran popular taverns that sold wine to roistering Muslim poets and their friends. Love relationships abounded, with the object of a man's affection not necessarily being a woman. During early modern times in the Ottoman Empire as well as in Europe, upper-class families protected their women from public ex-

A miniature from the seventeenth-century Ottoman manuscript *Turkish Memoirs,* which shows a meeting in the Council Chamber of the Topkapi Palace in Istanbul between the sultan—the ultimate earthly beloved of Ottoman poetry—and his most devoted advisors.

posure; consequently literary love among the cultural elites was often homoerotic and sexual relations between men and boys were common. So Ottoman poets sang the beauties of popular shop boys, dancing boys, tavern waiters, young Janissary soldiers, roguish street urchins, and, in some cases, "public" women such as non-Muslims, prostitutes, and gypsy dancers. At the time there was no category of thought corresponding to what we call "homosexuality"; in fact, there were no sexual categories. Attraction to boys or to women was considered a preference. The authorities, both religious and civil, might approve of a man's love for a boy when it was part of the mystical spirituality of elite culture, tolerate it when carried on privately, or condemn it when it offended the morality of the public, but they did not conceive of it as fundamentally different from other practices. It was even thought more "manly" among Ottoman elites to have a general preference for boys. In the end, however, the Turkish language does not indicate gender, so the beloved is always in some sense ambiguous. As any broad survey of Ottoman poems shows, the boundaries of love—between the desirable boy, the beloved friend, the adored patron, the mystical master—were always hazy and shifting.

There was in fact plenty of occasion for fraternizing with other men or with the public variety of women. Istanbul often saw gala public entertainments. During the great feasts, especially the Feast of Sacrifice (celebrating Abraham's willingness to sacrifice his beloved son Isaac) and the Fast-Breaking Feast after Ramadan (the month of fasting), the people frequented great carnivals, complete with rides such as a wooden Ferris wheel and swings, and performers such as acrobats, strongmen, musicians, jugglers, magicians, and puppeteers. The circumcision of a royal prince would be the occasion for weeks of celebration, including huge parades, fireworks, and pageants on the water. Any of these occasions gave lovers the opportunity to flirt with a beloved.

POPULAR POETRY

The poetry of the elites was by no means the only variety of Turkish poetry. Throughout Ottoman times there existed a large and lively tradition of popular poetry. Whereas the elite poetry used Persian forms and rhythms and a vocabulary full of Persian and Arabic words, the popular poetry invoked the Turkish of daily speech. The best-known group of popular poets, minstrels—generally called *aşiks,* or "lovers"—took the role of wanderers who moved from village to village, spreading love poetry throughout the world as they sought a beloved seen only in a dream. Some *aşiks* wrote in both the elite and popular forms, creating a bridge in their poetry over which language and ideas moved between the elites and the larger population.

Dervish groups in society. Common to the observance of Islam are everyday prayers, communal duties, and religious obligations derived from the Quran and the way in which the Prophet Muhammad practiced the faith. Parallel to the ordinary practice of religion were the beliefs and activities of Muslim mystics, known as "dervishes" or "Sufis." Mysticism, or Sufism, exerted a strong attraction among the general population, promising an immediate, intense, emotional experience of contact with the Divine. There existed in Ottoman times widespread and influential networks of dervish orders. They attracted both devotees who planned to dedicate their lives to mystical discipline and lay adherents from all walks of life. These lay adherents participated in dervish rituals and ceremonies but carried on ordinary lives outside the dervish lodges. The rituals performed by Sufis ranged from the sedate whirling dance of the Mevlevi dervishes, to the collective chanting, leaping, spinning, and purportedly painless self-mutilation practiced by more extreme groups. There were ritualistic, formalized wine-party-style ceremonies with a mystical master as the "beloved" and there were drunken orgies with beautiful boys. In larger Islamic society, dervish influences were felt everywhere. Each corps of the standing army had a resident dervish master, and craft or artistic guilds would attach themselves to dervish lodges. Given its reliance on direct, emotional experience of the Divine, dervish mysticism was an important bridge by which many of the conquered peoples converted to Islam.

The understanding of Islamic mysticism varied widely. One strain took a highly refined, philosophical approach that intersected in some respects with European neo-Platonism (the philosophy of Plato that considers ideal forms to be real and existing forms to be an imperfect, temporary reflection of reality). According to the members of this strain, the only true reality is on the ideal plane where all existence is essentially unified and subsumed in the being of God. Everything else is illusory, including the sense we have of a self that is individual and separate from the Divine Unity. The project of the mystic is to get beyond the illusion of the self and to be re-immersed in the primal Unity.

Another strain of Sufism was manifested in the personal morality of shaven, dirty, wandering dervishes, who rejected all the outward practices of Islam in favour of the truth of Divine Unity, to which only a select group was privy. Belief in this esoteric truth manifested itself in popular ecstatic rituals and in legends of holy dervishes who performed miracles of mastery over the physical world. Since a dervish master, thought many, could act on the ideal plane of Unity, he was not subject to the constraints of time and space that rule the physical (illusory) world. The master could be praying on his prayer rug in a dervish lodge in Turkey and at the same moment be seen in Mecca praying in the Holy Kaaba. Out of such reports came the popular legends of flying carpets.

By convention the Ottoman poet would routinely take on the persona of a mystic/Sufi. It follows that in the Ottoman poems by elite writers, passionate love of this world's beloved and drunkenness with this world's wine are no more than bridges to blessed intoxication with Divine Love.

The Poems in Focus

The contents—an overview. Ottoman elite poets collected and published their works in handwritten volumes called *divans*. Thus, Turkish literary historians refer to poets of the Ottoman elite tradition as "divan poets." A typical divan might contain panegyric (praise) poems—to God, to Muhammad, to the sultan, and to various other powerful people. Also in the divan could be a large number of *ghazals,* stanza poems, fragments, individual lines, and couplets. While some of the poems for special occasions have descriptive headings such as "In Praise of the Glorious Sultan," most poems are listed in alphabetic order by the last letter of the rhyme.

The number of poems in a typical divan could run from a few hundred to more than a thousand. Necati's established divan contains 650 *ghazals*; Baki's, 548. Some of the recurring elements of Ottoman love poetry are a beloved, a melancholy lover, a garden (or tavern), a party with wine, and close friends. It is important to keep in mind that every Ottoman poem is full of references that needed only to be hinted at in passing because Ottoman audiences knew them so well.

A ghazal by Necati. The full contents of Necati's "Those Tulip-Cheeked Ones" is rendered in English below, followed by a detailed explication.

> Those tulip-cheeked ones—what they dared
>   do in the garden
> Beside them, the cypress could not sway,
>   nor the rosebuds open
>
> They wouldn't let the wild tulip into the
>   conversation of the roses
> Saying it was a stranger from the distant
>   steppes
>
> The custom of the beautiful ones is tyranny
>   and torment
> But they've never ruined anyone the way
>   they've ruined me
>
> What about those brows like a bow,
>   those pointed glances
> They left arrows in my breast
>   wouldn't allow my heart to beat
>
> There are a thousand beauties
>   as lovely as Joseph
> But they are never sold,
>   never seen

> So praise God for our sakis, with their
>   life-giving wine
> They don't let us thirst for the water of life
>   nor for the rivers of paradise
>
> Hey Necati, have patience, what can you do?
> Who among the lovers has not learned
>   torment from the beauties?
>   (Necati in Andrews, Bates,
>   and Kalpakli, p. 41)

In Necati's poem, as in all such poems, the beloved and the garden come to represent each other. The first couplet makes the beloved's cheek into a tulip; the beloved's body is a cypress; the hair, a hyacinth; the mouth, a rosebud. When the beloved appears in the garden, the cypress tree is abashed at the sight of the more beautiful cypress that is the beloved's body; the tree dares not sway in competition with this body. Likewise, the rose dares not blossom in the presence of the beloved's mouth, which, by smiling, blossoms. The garden is the beloved; the beloved, the garden.

THE *GHAZAL*

Although other subjects may be addressed in a *ghazal,* it is primarily a poem of love, either interpersonal or spiritual. The length of a *ghazal* may vary, but most commonly it is a short poem of five to seven couplets, with the pen name of the poet worked into the final couplet. The *ghazal* is written in monorhyme; that is, it has the same rhyme throughout, on the pattern *aa ba ca da* and so forth.

In the second couplet, the garden is both the place where a party is held and an image of the party itself. The garden-party of Ottoman poems has slender cypress-like bodies; tulip cups of ruddy wine; beloved friends, inebriated and blossoming like roses; nightingale poets. Beloveds are likened to the shining face of the moon or a bright scented candle that draws lover-moths to their doom. In this couplet, the gathering of intimate friends rejects the "wild tulip," who is like a rustic Turkic tribesman from the hinterlands and not the kind of refined and elegant companion that an Ottoman gentleman (or garden) would prefer. For an Ottoman, the garden represents the ultimate in safety and security. In the privacy of a garden a man can put off the formal attire and manners of public life, relax, and be honestly himself amid the beauties of nature and close friends.

By the third couplet we have been introduced to the garden and the party of intimate friends. Now we jump to party conversation. The poet boasts to his friends of the torments he has suffered at the hands of beautiful beloveds.

The fourth couplet refers to a commonplace early-modern notion also seen in European poetry. Love is inflicted on the hapless lover as the beloved's glances pierce his heart. Thus, the beloved's eyebrows are depicted as bows, and from this an Ottoman reader would recognize that the eyelashes are arrows shot by a glance at the lover, who is always in great danger of being killed by love.

The fifth couplet mentions Joseph, the biblical character whose story is also told in the Quran. In Islamic lore, Joseph is the paragon of male beauty and male chastity. There is a play in this line on the word *sold*. It refers to the fact that Joseph was sold by his brothers into slavery but also refers (negatively) to a beloved who "sells" him or herself by being visible in public. The idea is that there are many beauties out there who are not public beauties.

Next we return to the party and the one beloved who brings a cure to the poet/speaker for the torments of love. This is the "saki" or wine server, who helps the partygoers pass from the intoxicating torment of love into the oblivion of drunkenness.

In the end, the poet comforts himself with a concluding bit of wisdom for the love-plagued: "Have patience; everyone suffers from love."

A *ghazal* by Baki. The full contents of Baki's "Row by Row" is rendered in English below, followed by a detailed explication.

Your rebellious glance lines up the cavalry
  of your lashes
Soldiers armed with lances, they wait for war,
  row by row

To watch you on the path of the rose garden
Swaying cypresses stand along each side,
  row by row

To combat the throngs of my tear-soldiers
The world sea sends forth its waves,
  row by row

Don't think it's a flock of cranes crying
  in the sky
It's the birds of my heart and soul returning
  to you, row by row

To see who prays with you knee to knee
  in the mosque
The tearful eye, like the water-seller,
  roves from row to row

The people of the heart are drowned
  in your blessings of grief and pain
At the table of your kindness guests await
  your gifts, row by row

If the reed pen sways like a banner
  while telling of your body
Then the books draw up their verses
  like soldiers, row by row

The lovers stand near you on every side
Like the columns of the Kaaba, row by row

Oh Baki, they will know your worth
  upon the funeral stone
And your friends will stand before you,
  hands clasped in reverence, row by row
                (Baki in Andrews, Bates,
                and Kalpakli, pp. 98-99)

Baki's poem has a peculiar rhyme element that the Ottoman poets loved. It is called *redif*, which in Arabic means the person who rides to battle on the back of another person's saddle. In poetry it means a word or phrase that repeats after the rhyme letter, in the above poem "*saf saf,*" meaning "row by row." This gives the poem a unifying theme, allowing the poet to jump from topic to topic as things in rows remind him of his beloved and his life as a lover.

Baki's first couplet references the eyelashes in somewhat the same context as Necati's poem, but here they are not arrows. They are the lances of the Ottoman feudal cavalry lined up in battle formation for an assault on the heart of the lover. This very military image would make an Ottoman audience suspect the beloved is the ruler or a patron.

In the second couplet the cypresses line up to watch the beloved in exactly the way that the various groups of dignitaries would line up in rows to greet the sultan on formal occasions.

Next the poet embarks on a series of exaggerated depictions of the depth of his passionate devotion. He pictures himself standing at the seashore weeping for his beloved, and he imagines the rows of waves pounding the shore as phalanxes of soldiers resisting the torrent of tears that pour from his eyes.

In the fourth couplet, the poet sees a flock of migrating cranes in the sky. Turkish folk mythology has it that cranes flying with mournful cries are really the souls of the dead ascending to paradise. So the poet points out to his beloved that these are not cranes at all but his heart and soul flying to the one he loves. This is the ultimate devotion, a devotion that mirrors the desire of the soul to return to its divine origin.

Even in the mosque, the lover is focused on his beloved. In a very down-to-earth image, like the water-seller who roams the ranks of worshippers, the tear-filled eye forsakes its devotions as it jealously wanders the rows to see with whom the beloved might be praying. Behind this seemingly very secular image lies the notion that the true, mystical worshipper turns from the mundane devotions of the mosque to a direct, emotional connection to the Divine-as-beloved. The audiences of Ottoman poetry understood that those who know the secret of mystical love are "people of the heart." And the secret is that the pain and suffering doled out by the beloved is the most wonderful of gifts—because it causes the lover to give up selfish desires, to die to this fragmented world and awaken to the world of Divine Unity.

The poem moves to images of the beloved's lovers. The guests at the sultan's table in the sixth couplet are his devoted lovers—the administrative, legal, and educational elite who gather in the palace courtyard on formal occasions.

In the seventh couplet, we turn to the work of a poet and another battle image. As the poet writes, the pen sways like the battle standards of troops, who fall into line like the lines of verse that arrange themselves on the page. Then the Holy Shrine of the Kaaba in Mecca is surrounded by a portico supported by columns, which stand like devoted (and respectful) lovers around the beloved.

Like every *ghazal*, the poem ends addressing the poet by name. The poet customarily praises his own abilities. Here Baki evokes the image of intimate friends standing row by row before his dead body as they recount his virtues.

From courtly love to Sufi love. The business of the Ottoman state was warfare. Each spring the army set out to expand the borders of Islam and drive non-Muslims further back into Europe. New lands, new fiefs, and new taxes fed the voracious appetite of the expanding empire. Given this state of affairs, armies and the panoply of war were never too far from the awareness of even the most refined poet or lover. Indeed the connection between a poem's beloved and the concerns of the Ottoman court is famously evident in Baki's *ghazal*, in which the beloved's lashes are compared to a cohort of the feudal cavalry. Other court connections surface in the poem too. Swaying cypresses line the beloved's path,

evoking not only the garden but also the slave pages of the palace, who serve the ruler and train for high administrative positions. The business of the writer is linked to the military effort in the image of the poet's madly scribbling reed pen as a battle standard waving in the heat of combat.

Ottoman poets and their audiences understood that love was of two types—real and metaphoric. To them, "metaphoric love" meant the love that is aroused by worldly objects: the sultan, a patron, a beautiful boy, a lovely woman, a beloved friend, a mystical master. These loves are "metaphoric" because people who really know about these things realize that the highest and best use of worldly love is as a bridge to "real love," which is love of the Divine.

In Sufism, actual love, love in the world, is seen as a metaphor for "real" love, longing for return to unity with the Divine. The lover, separated from the ultimate object of desire, seeks to cast off all ties to the self and the multiplicity of the world we perceive with our senses. The extreme melancholy, the torment, the weeping that we see in the poems are only "the blessings of grief and pain" that the beloved bestows as a lesson, in an attempt to convince the lover to die to the self and be reborn in Divine Unity.

The ruling metaphors of Sufism were those of love and intoxication. Like the extreme ecstasy of unfulfilled desire, the intoxication of the wine drinker is seen as a bridge to the joyous experience of spiritual reunion. The beautiful saki (wine server, a potential beloved) holds out a double remedy for attachment to this treacherous world: the intoxication to be derived from passion and from wine.

Sources and literary context. The Ottomans saw themselves as stewards of the Islamic community, politically, religiously, and culturally. This cultural tradition included, among many things, the Arabic and Persian literary traditions. Literary works included histories and chronicles in both prose and verse, popular stories and legends in the tradition of **The Arabian Nights** (also in WLAIT 6: *Middle Eastern Literatures and Their Times*). There were also saints' tales, travel accounts, and scientific, religious, and philosophical works. Most popular in all three societies, however, was the medium of poetry. The basic elements of Ottoman poetry—the beloved, the garden, the wine party, the group of friends, and the melancholy lover—hark back to a long tradition of Arabic and Persian love poetry.

Ghazal poetry descends directly from the Persian literary tradition. In fact, Ottoman poets

Ottoman Lyric Poetry

often wrote in Persian as well as Turkish. The Persian masters produced a vast corpus of not only love poems and poems of praise but also narrative poems about legendary lovers such as **Leyla and Mejnun**. Ottoman poets saw the Persian masters—Firdawsi (**The Shahnamah**), Jalal al-Din Rumi (**The Spiritual Couplets**), and Hafiz (**The Divan of Hafiz**)—as models and were sensitive to the literary fashions of the Persian-speaking world (all also in *WLAIT 6: Middle Eastern Literatures and Their Times*).

THE INVISIBLE FEMALE

Public life in the Ottoman Empire—and to only a slightly lesser extent in Europe—was predominantly male. Only lower-class women had any public presence. "Respectable" women went about heavily veiled and accompanied by protective retinues, if they went out at all. Even the powerful women in the sultan's harem, who had huge stipends and intrigued with high officials to promote the interests of their offspring, had to conduct their public business through male intermediaries. Literary production too was overwhelmingly male. Among the hundreds of noted fifteenth- and sixteenth-century Ottoman poets, less than a handful were women. The poet Mihri (d. 1512), for example, was educated by a doting father who had no sons to promote. She led a highly unusual public life, tied to the literary circles in the court of an Ottoman prince in her home town of Amasya. Her poetry—submitted to the court by male intermediaries—brought Mihri substantial cash rewards from the prince/sultan. But in most cases, women were invisible, their influence and talents unknown.

However, the Ottomans were closely attentive to the styles and fashions of their fellow Ottoman poets as well. By writing "parallel poems" (poems repeating the rhyme, rhythm, and themes of previous poems), they both competed with one another and reinforced the styles of popular master poets. A famed poet such as Baki, for example, would be imitated by numerous poets over hundreds of years, who thereby maintained his style as part of the perceived tradition. Given this concern for tradition and continuity, there were no radical changes in Ottoman poetry in more than 500 years. In fact, when radical literary change did occur in the nineteenth century, it meant abandonment of the Ottoman tradition and a turn toward a more Europeanized modern literature.

Impact. Beginning in the sixteenth century, the Ottomans developed their own version of a "biographies of poets" genre, which had precedents in Persian and Arabic letters. The authors of these accounts gave information about the poets' lives and often critiqued their poetry. It is clear from these biographies that the generation that followed Necati considered him the poet in whose work the use of Ottoman Turkish rose from the speech of rude tribesmen and nomads to a poetic language on a par with Arabic and Persian. The biographies also reveal that Baki attained the title "sultan of poets" and won wide renown during his lifetime.

Both Necati and Baki are foundational Ottoman poets. Turkish students today struggle through some of their poems, likely the very poems discussed above, much as students in Great Britain might struggle through Old or Middle English verse. Even Turkey's most modernist poets make gestures of respect to these ancient masters, as shown in the following translation of a quatrain by a well-known living poet:

> Oh master of glances, hero of hopes
> You described the indescribable in a rose.
> As we began to grieve, we were your
>   apprentices
> The *Divan of Baki* is the birds you put to
>   flight
>
> (Hilmi Yavuz in Silay, p. 510)

—Walter G. Andrews and Joyce Moss

For More Information

Andrews, Walter G. *Poetry's Voice, Society's Song*. Seattle: University of Washington Press, 1985.

Andrews, Walter G., Dana Bates, and Mehmet Kalpakli, eds. *Ottoman Lyric Poetry: An Anthology*. Austin: University of Texas Press, 1997.

Davison, Roderic H. *Turkey: A Short History*. Beverley: Eothen, 1981.

Gibb, E. J. W. *A History of Ottoman Poetry*. Vols. 1-6. London: Luzac, 1900-1906.

Holbrook, Victoria Rowe. *The Unreadable Shores of Love*. Austin: The University of Texas Press, 1994.

Jones, Ann Rosalind, and Peter Stallybrass. "The Politics of *Astrophel and Stella*." *Studies in English Literature, 1500-1900*, vol. 24, no. 1 (winter 1984): 53-68.

Silay, Kemal, ed. *An Anthology of Turkish Literature*. Bloomington, Indiana: Indiana University Turkish Studies, 1996.

Plagued by the West (Gharbzadigi)

by

Jalal Al-i Ahmad

Jalal Al-i Ahmad (1923-1969; also spelled Al-e Ahmad) spent his childhood in relative comfort. Many members of his family, including his father, older brother, and a brother-in-law, were all Muslim clerics. Early in the 1930s when the Ministry of Justice under Reza Pahlavi (also Reza Khan; ruled 1921-41) began to regulate the activities of the clergy, Al-i Ahmad's father went into voluntary retirement. His decision forced young Jalal Al-i Ahmad to leave school and work at various jobs in the market-place (such as watchmaking and selling leather goods). Despite his father's expressed wishes that his son become a clergyman and succeed him, Al-i Ahmad secretly attended a secular school at night and in 1943 obtained his diploma. In 1946 he received the equivalent of a Bachelor's degree and the next year began to teach literature in high school. Al-i Ahmad's break with his family's re-ligious traditions occurred when he was in high school, when he began to read the writings of secular reformer Ahmad Kasravi (assassinated in 1945) and of the Tudeh (Iranian Communist) Party. Al-i Ahmad joined the Tudeh Party in 1944 and in the space of four years evolved from a simple rank-and-file member to a member of its Tehran Central Committee. He also edited and contributed to a number of Party publications before he and a small group of influential thinkers dissolved their ties to it in 1947. Al-i Ahmad continued to work in politics for a time, then withdrew into a "period of silence," during which he translated the French works of André Gide, Jean-Paul Sartre, and Albert Camus into

THE LITERARY WORK

An essay set in Iran in the mid-twentieth century; published in Persian (as *Gharbzadigi*) in 1962; first published in English in 1982.

SYNOPSIS

The essay traces Iran's millennia-old relationship with the outside world to explain the abject state of the country in the early 1960s, blaming the country's ills on a generation that apes Western values and ways.

Persian (Al-i Ahmad 1964, p. 50). In 1949 he married translator and novelist Simin Danishvar (see **Savushun [A Persian Requiem]**, also in WLAIT 6: *Middle Eastern Literatures and Their Times*). When nationalization of Iranian oil became the issue of the day (1950-53), Al-i Ahmad once again entered politics as part of a group aligned with Prime Minister Mohammad Mosaddeq (also Musaddiq al-Saltanah, 1882-1967) but dropped out altogether when a coup d'état, engineered by the Western powers, top-pled Mosaddeq and restored Shah Mohammed Reza to the throne (1953). Al-i Ahmad then de-voted himself to traveling, teaching, and writing. Several journeys around Iran led him to conclude that the country had become, in his words, a "Tyrannyville" (*zulmabad*) or "Plunder City" (*gharatkadah*). This pessimism achieved its fullest expression in *Plagued by the West,* acclaimed as the first work to speak so openly, forcefully, and eloquently in Persian of the impact on Iran of its attitude toward the West.

Events in History at the Time of the Essay

The White Revolution. After his restoration to the throne in 1953, Shah Mohammed Reza Pahlavi sought to strengthen his hold on power. He derived internal backing from Iran's military and security services, Western-educated technocrats, and other professionals, and from the growing middle and upper classes, who benefited

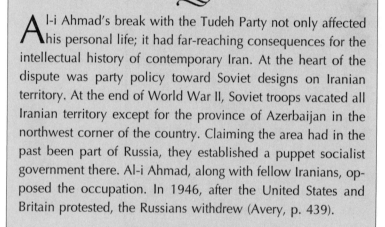

BREAKING (*INSHI`AB*) WITH THE IRANIAN COMMUNIST PARTY

Al-i Ahmad's break with the Tudeh Party not only affected his personal life; it had far-reaching consequences for the intellectual history of contemporary Iran. At the heart of the dispute was party policy toward Soviet designs on Iranian territory. At the end of World War II, Soviet troops vacated all Iranian territory except for the province of Azerbaijan in the northwest corner of the country. Claiming the area had in the past been part of Russia, they established a puppet socialist government there. Al-i Ahmad, along with fellow Iranians, opposed the occupation. In 1946, after the United States and Britain protested, the Russians withdrew (Avery, p. 439).

from modernization. The shah also relied heavily on advice and aid from foreign powers, principally the United States and Britain. In 1961 the administration of the new U.S. president, John F. Kennedy, declared that aid would depend on a program of internal reform. The shah was thus pressured to adopt at least the pretense of increased popular participation in the political and economic affairs of Iran in the early 1960s. In 1963, shortly after the release of *Plagued by the West* in Persian, the shah would announce a "White Revolution" aimed at instituting political and agrarian changes designed to distribute wealth more evenly among the population. The land-reform program "would do away with Iran's reliance on agriculture" (Behrooz, p. 35). On the one hand, this would decrease the power of the social strata of large landowners (the so-called

"one-thousand" families) and the clergy, who administered lands donated as religious endowments. On the other hand, it would promote the growth of industry and thereby increase the power of labor unions, presumably more democratic institutions than those of the feudal system. Though such reform never managed to equitably distribute land among the peasants, it did mechanize agriculture in Iran. The logic of using a resource (oil) that was plentiful to accelerate the production of a scarcity (food) in Iran was compelling. Change, however, did not come without social costs. Many displaced farmhands headed for the city and became part of a large urban underclass. *Plagued by the West* mentions the flood of foreign-made tractors that had been disfiguring the traditional countryside for some years (Al-i Ahmad, *Plagued by the West,* p. 41).

To inaugurate and demonstrate popular support for reform, in 1963 the shah submitted the following six principles to a plebiscite: 1) land reform; 2) sale of some state-owned factories to finance the land reform; 3) the enfranchisement of women; 4) nationalization of forests and pastures; 5) formation of a literacy corps, and 6) profit-sharing schemes for workers in industry (Arjomand, p. 72).

Though many boycotted the plebiscite, according to a revised edition of Al-i Ahmad's essay 5,598,711 people (Iran's population was approximately 30 million at the time) endorsed the six principles by voting for them (*Plagued,* p. 6).

Electoral reform. In 1962 the cabinet of Prime Minister Asadallah Alam (1919-77) decreed that localities throughout Iran were to elect their own representatives to regional and district councils. This seemingly innocuous law was groundbreaking for two reasons. First, it gave women the vote. Second, by stipulating that the representatives could swear their allegiance on any holy book, it allowed members of recognized minority faiths (Christianity, Judaism, Zoroastrianism) to swear by their own Holy Books rather than the Quran when they took local office. This measure aroused considerable opposition among the Muslim clergy. Ayatollah "Khomeini, joined by religious leaders elsewhere in the country, protested vigorously against" the measure "and it was ultimately repealed" (Khomeini, p. 16). *Plagued by the West* objects to the attempt to enfranchise women that the decree entailed. In Al-i Ahmad's view, it was a Western-inspired farce, for true elections did not exist in Iran. The opposition identified several plagues from the West: technicians and military personnel imported from

URBANIZATION AND CONSUMERISM

Iranian society of the late 1950s and early 1960s underwent a transformation associated with the mechanization of agriculture and the fostering of industry. Many people left the land and entered the cities in search of employment. Meanwhile, the shah's economic reforms abetted the growth of an urban middle class. State policy downplayed traditional Islamic ideals such as modesty and thrift, and encouraged a return to the ostentatious consumption of the Persian Empire. This is not to say that conspicuous consumption was something imported solely from the West. During his reign, the shah sought to put Iran's pre-Islamic past in the foreground, which meant touting aspects of the Achaemenian empire (700-331 B.C.E.)—especially its notion of divine kingship—and downplaying Islamic civilization. Courtiers encouraged the shah to restage the lavish life style of the Achaemenian court, while the clergy countered these displays with idealized notions of frugality and plainness. The appetite for Western consumer goods—such as cars, washing machines, and electric rice-cookers—was becoming insatiable during this period. Private capital went into concrete apartment blocks and Western-style villas that began to sprout madly from cities, stopping only when they reached natural barriers like rivers and mountains. The rapidity of the transformation of traditional Iranian landscapes led many thinkers to question the wisdom of the White Revolution. It also encouraged nostalgia for a hard-to-define authenticity, for the "real" Iran of the good old days.

Western countries to supplement the indigenous work force; capitulation to the West on the issue of their soldiers' being extradited back to the home country for trial if they broke Iranian laws; Western publications, films, restaurants, brothels, and bars in the large cities that catered to guest workers and Iranians who had returned from the West; and the beginnings of profligate spending on Western arms with which Iran was to police the Persian Gulf for America.

The fall of Mosaddeq. On August 19, 1953, the U.S. Central Intelligence Agency (CIA), in cooperation with British intelligence, orchestrated the overthrow of Prime Minister Dr. Mohammad Mosaddeq and restored Shah Mohammed Reza Pahlavi to the throne (Risen). To many Iranians this event was merely the latest in a series of humiliating defeats that began early in the nineteenth century when foreign powers became involved in Persian affairs. Iran was once again enmeshed in the geopolitical aims of two great powers. As the largest link in the Islamic belt that girded the southern border of the Soviet Empire, the country was vital to the U.S. policy of containing communism after World War II. In addition to its strategic importance, Iran had and still has infinitely more gas and oil than the other

links in the belt: Turkey and Afghanistan. Thus, it was inevitable that the superpowers would meddle in the politics of the country.

National identity crisis. The 1953 coup was such an obvious demonstration of Iran's lack of autonomy that it demoralized many of its intellectuals, writers, poets, clergy, and other members of society. Not only did it end in the removal of a popular politician, it meant that a great deal of Iran's wealth would effectively remain in foreign hands. Many likened Mosaddeq's downfall to the shameful defeats of the past: the Arab invasion of the seventh century; the onslaughts of the Mongols of the twelfth century; and the two territory-ceding treaties (Gulistan, 1813; Turkmanchay, 1828) that Iran was forced to sign with Tsarist Russia. When the reinstalled shah adopted Western models of modernization, financed the education of thousands of young Iranians at U.S. universities, and made strategic alliances with the United States, it confirmed the dissidents' (both secular and religious) suspicions about the deliberate eradication of their national heritage.

The Amini government, 1961-62. Though many intellectuals like Al-i Ahmad withdrew from political life after the Western-engineered coup of 1953, remnants of Mosaddeq's partisans (the National Front), along with some clergy, persisted in their active opposition to the shah's policies. They faulted him for the corruption and waste that came with rapid modernization and westernization. While internal opposition mounted, the presidential administration in the United States was pressuring Iran to move toward democracy. Complicating the situation was the poor condition of the Iranian economy, which forced the country to appeal to the West for immediate aid. In order to mute the internal opposition and meet the Kennedy administration's expectations of reform, the shah chose Ali Amini (b. 1905) as Prime Minister. Amini, himself a large landowner, was related to the previous royal line in Iran, the Qajars. He was also favored by the United States and had served as ambassador in Washington D.C. Amini was immediately able to secure a $33 million loan from the United States that temporarily allayed Iran's fiscal crisis.

A skilled politician, Amini recognized the need to placate the clergy of Iran. He traveled to the holy city of Qum and met with the leading religious authorities there. But Amini's growing popularity soon began to trouble the shah, who jealously guarded his position as "First Person of the State." In July 1962, when Amini tried to reduce the military budget, he lost favor with the monarch and resigned. Amini's resignation was a blow to true reform, for he was the last independent prime minister the shah appointed. After him, politics in Iran devolved into displays of competition between two government-created parties, aptly characterized as the "Yes" Party and the "Of course" Party.

The Essay in Focus

Contents summary. The first chapter of *Plagued by the West* describes an illness called *Gharbzadigi* (also *Gharbzadegi*, defined here as "Westitis"). Literally the term means "Weststrickenness"; so unwieldy and difficult is it to translate that there are at least three English renderings of the essay's title: "Plagued by the West," "Occidentosis," and "Weststruckness." None of these quite captures Al-i Ahmad's monolithic intent. To him "West" is not a place, but a state of surplus; "East" is a state of need. Thus, "most of the countries of Latin America are part of the East," while Japan is part of the West (*Plagued by the West*, p. 4). The West has machines, while the East lacks

them, which creates a dependency relationship between the two monoliths. The West has a surfeit of military power, money, education, food, and so on. With this surfeit, it dominates the East, whose sole function is to be the willing source of such raw materials as oil, coal, rubber, precious metals and stones, and of such human capital as doctors, engineers, and technicians. By this definition pre-industrial Iran with its large oil and gas deposits, its foreign-educated technocrats, and its poverty is clearly in the East. Its situation here makes Iran eminently prone to a disease Al-i Ahmad calls "Westitis."

The remainder of *Plagued by the West* explores the etiology, diagnosis, and prognosis of Westitis. Though the disease is not confined to any particular region of the world, its cause—at least in Iran—is in large part related to geography. Because they inhabited plains subject to repeated invasions from the northeast (Aryans, Parthians, Mongols) and from the west (Greeks, Arabs, Ottomans, English, Americans), Iranians had little opportunity to develop urban civilization. As soon as one aggressive wave receded, allowing time to build cities, for example, another would crash against the plains, destroying what had been built. The regular cycle of invasion and withdrawal engendered in Iranians an initiative-robbing fatalism, a "this-too-shall-pass" mentality. According to Al-i Ahmad, a sense of helplessness (*bi-charagi*) in the face of outside power eroded the people's self-confidence. They internalized the outside powers' perception of Iranians as inferior and accepted this justification for their exploitation by the West.

Plagued by the West then reviews Muslim history and finds it to be an unrelieved tale of schism and decline. From its height in the ninth and tenth centuries, says the essay, Islamic civilization (which is identified with Iran throughout the essay) continued to decay, becoming moribund by the nineteenth century. Wars, invasions, and treachery weakened the Islamic body politic so much that it was left with little immunity to Westitis.

When *Plagued by the West* turns to present-day Iran, its criticism becomes sharper. At the beginning of the twentieth century, impoverished Iranian governments signed agreements with both individuals and governments from the West. These agreements generally ceded the country's mineral wealth and customs revenues to opportunistic concessionaires. In 1941 the British deposed Reza Shah Pahlavi, who had ruled for 20 years, and replaced him with his Swiss-educated son. With the enthronement of

WESTERNIZATION AND THE CHADOR

Al-i Ahmad found the symptoms of Westitis mainly in urban areas and especially among Iranians who had lived abroad. He pinpointed Western-trained intellectuals as a group afflicted with advanced Westitis because of their strong commitment to secularism. Al-i Ahmad himself conceived of Iran as a nativist blend of Islam and Persian ethnicity. In contrast, the Pahlavi regimes promoted a traditionless Iran, which in their view constituted modernity. To this end, Shah Mohammed Reza attempted in subtle ways to persuade women to abandon the traditional body veil (chador), which covered the torso, the legs, and the hair, leaving only the face showing. His father had forbidden women from wearing the chador in public places, and he himself tried more subtly to move society in this same direction. Al-i Ahmad noticed that the strictly enforced prohibition coincided with the rise of the mini-skirt in 1960s Iran. To many conservatives, unveiled women (whether in mini-skirts or not) were naked and were violators of traditional norms of decency and modesty. Al-i Ahmad himself did not approve of the veil. His wife, Simin Danishvar, was not veiled under the shah, but, like many modern women, she re-veiled under the Islamic Republic.

Mohammed Reza Pahlavi, there was nothing to stop Westitis from infecting the entire country.

After a review of contemporary history, the essay rails against symptoms of the disease. Peasants, stunned by their first encounters with machines, suffer culture shock in the cities. Women are compelled to leave the home *chador*-less and live the shallow lives of those obsessively concerned with appearance. "Indigenous" media tout the latest Western achievements in science and technology, entertainment, and sports but are silent about Iran and Eastern culture.

Next the essay focuses on Westitis's most unmistakable symptom: the West-stricken man,

> who is a member of the ruling establishment of the country [and] has no place to stand. He is like a dust particle floating in space, or a straw floating on water. He has severed his ties with the essence of society, culture, and custom. He is not a bond between antiquity and modernity. He is not a dividing line between the old and the new. He is something unrelated to the past and someone with no understanding of the future.
>
> (*Plagued by the West*, p. 67)

To Al-i Ahmad this neither-here-nor-there man is the principal vector of Westitis. He has corrupted education in Iran by imposing his Western, secular model on traditional forms of learning. He also serves as a conduit for Westitis by bringing back foreign brides, thereby contributing to the dilution of "authentic" Iran.

Al-i Ahmad's prognosis for Westitis comes in the final chapter (11), whose heading, "The Hour of Resurrection Drew Near," alludes to the Quran (14:1). He takes comfort in the fact that prescient Westerners like Albert Camus, Eugene Ionesco, Jean-Paul Sartre, and Ingmar Bergman share his apocalyptic vision of the West. At the end of the book, Al-i Ahmad with characteristic hyperbole warns that if "the machine demon [is] not harnessed and put back into the bottle, [it] will place a hydrogen bomb at the end of the road for mankind" (*Plagued by the West*, p. 111).

Iranian essentialism. One of the most remarkable aspects of *Plagued by the West* was its immediate and unprecedented popularity. Before its publication, Al-i Ahmad was well-known in certain circles, particularly among leftist intellectuals, owing to his writing and editorial work. After the essay appeared, and especially after the government suppressed the work in Iran, he became a star of the first magnitude. He was in constant motion, speaking here, lecturing there, and representing dissident Iranian intellectuals everywhere.

Al-i Ahmad's simple anti-Westernism was especially responsive to the spiritual and psychological needs of the time (Sprachman, p. 303). Iranians, naturally distressed by the complexities of modernization, began to yearn for the "good old days" when life was thought to be uncomplicated. By positing a regional suffering from Westitis, he implied the existence of a noble Iranian, pure and confident of his/her own cultural and religious lineage. The diagnosis offered by *Plagued by the West* was comforting. If the distress brought by modernity were a disease, then like many other maladies it might be susceptible to treatment. This model also offered the soothing notion, however valid or invalid it might be, that there was such a thing as a "Persian essence." One merely had to regain one's essential Iranian-ness, to return to a Persian core, to become healthy once again.

The great irony of *Plagued by the West* is that its author, the most famous diagnostician of Westitis, was also a victim of the disease. It is quite evident from Al-i Ahmad's tone that his essay is a moral polemic. It relies on traditional polemist artillery: hyperbole, provocative inconsistencies and errors, jargon, and ready-made phrases to frame absolutist positions on Iranian history, education, and society.

- Today all "isms" and ideologies have become paths leading to the exalted throne of "machinism."
- The first thing a city-dweller thinks about is his stomach, and after that is satisfied, the region below his stomach.
- Women do not have it in them to be judges, give testimony. . . .
(*Plagued by the West,* pp. 5, 43, and 47, with changes)

The essay takes a simple bifurcated position that parallels that of some renowned Western, as well as Communist, personalities. For example, the simple identification of the West as the source of all problems echoes the black-and-white duality of Rudyard Kipling's famous line from "The Ballad of East and West": "Oh, East is East, and West is West / and never the twain shall meet." Regardless of the target of the essay's outrage (be it politics, history, or society), there is a constant set of ideological and cultural boundaries between East and West. Critics have noticed the similarities between *Plagued by the West*'s theory and the traditional Marxist analysis of colonialism, which demonizes imperialism as wholly exploitative. Indeed the essay's attitude is reminiscent of the unrelenting reaction against the West exhibited by the Soviet leader Vladimir Ilich Lenin (1870-1924). *Plagued by the West* identifies the French historian René Grousset, for example, as one of *their* historians, for his views on Eastern history are *their* views (*Plagued by the West,* p. 52). *The London Times* and *The New York Times* are *their* newspapers and therefore report the news as *they* want it reported (*Plagued by the West,*

p. 63). The spirit of the West haunts every corner of Al-i Ahmad's version of Iran's decline and even takes responsibility for the country's recovery after World War II. In this rendition of contemporary history, Iran is not even in command of its own welfare. The country has been robbed of all volition by the demon West.

Sources and literary context. Intellectuals first broached the issue of Persian essentialism in the early nineteenth century, and the debate about what constitutes true Iranian-ness went on for at least a century and half before the appearance of *Plagued by the West.* One of the first modern Persian texts to address the loss of Iranian identity because of contact with the West was *Taskhir-i tammadun-i farangi* ("The Appropriation of Western Culture"), written in 1947 by F. Shadman. This text castigates *fowkuls* (French *faux cols* or "false collars," a reference to the shirts of European-educated Iranians). Al-i Ahmad acknowledges his intellectual debt to this work in the essay, but judges Shadman's cure for loss of roots (intensive study of one's mother tongue), to be ineffective (*Plagued by the West,* pp. 33, 70).

Al-i Ahmad read the basic leftist and progressive texts of the 1940s. His references in *Plagued by the West* show how indebted he was to French-language (or translated into French) analyses of colonialism and neo-colonialism. Among the authors he mentions are Tibor Mende, Josue de Castro, André Gide, and André Malraux.

Certainly *Plagued by the West* was influenced by its author's life experiences. In fact, some view the essay as autobiography (Mohibbi, pp. 120-23). According to this school, although Al-i Ahmad left Islam at an early age and gravitated toward communism, in middle age he became disillusioned with secularism and began to gravitate back toward the comfort of his father's religion. His pilgrimage to Mecca and Medina is taken as one piece of evidence of the return to his roots. Another is *Plagued by the West,* which prescribes a heavy dose of traditional belief as an antidote to Westitis.

Publication and reception. *Plagued by the West* was first prepared as a report for two sessions (29 November 1961 and 17 January 1962) of Iran's Council on Educational Goals (Al-i Ahmad, *Gharbzadigi,* 1963, p. 15). Finding the book inflammatory, Pahlavi government censors suppressed all copies of the first (1962) and the second (revised) edition (1963), but the book circulated underground in Iran and was published in various formats abroad. The suppression greatly impacted the author. He grew despondent when the government suppressed his essay along with a journal, *Kayhan-i mah* ("*Kayhan* Monthly"), he edited, taking solace in trips abroad, to Western Europe (1962), the Soviet Union (1964), on a pilgrimage to Mecca and Medina (1964), and to the United States (1965). Despite or perhaps because of Al-i Ahmad's stature among thinking people in and out of Iran, the government continued to harass him. When he participated in the founding of the Iranian Writers Union (Kanun-i Nivisandigan-i Iran) in 1968, agents of the security police (SAVAK) intensified the harassment (Musavi-Bujnurdi, p. 557). Contrary to the many rumors that circulated at the time about his suffering an untimely end because of foul play, Jalal Al-i Ahmad died naturally on September 9, 1969. His writing would remain enormously popular and influential. Despite or, perhaps, because of official suppression, it greatly impacted the generation that participated in the 1979 Islamic Revolution.

The book's phenomenal popularity when it first appeared was not merely a product of its suppression, though. It conveyed ideas in very plain language that prior works had only implied. This bluntness was stunning. Unlike contemporary critiques of Iranian society and culture, which were couched in appeals to classical literature, high-sounding academic phrases, and allusions, *Plagued by the West* is refreshingly direct. One is never in doubt about Al-i Ahmad's intent. This candor along with the use of colloquial language in what was masquerading as an "academic" study endeared the book to young people (Mohibbi, p. 132). On the other hand, the same candor incensed the authorities. Not only did his outspokenness incur the wrath of the censors, it was criticized harshly by professional historians. Al-i Ahmad never claimed to be documenting verifiable facts. Indeed he plainly states, "I am not writing history, I am extrapolating from it. You [the reader] will have to look up the actual events in the history books yourself" (*Plagued by the West*, p. 37). Nevertheless, one critic hunted down the errors in the essay (Aghdashlu, pp. 374-96). The historian Faridun Adamiyat went further. He saw Al-i Ahmad's work as symptomatic of the general "decline in historiography in Iran" (Adamiyat, p. 538; trans. P. Sprachman). *Plagued by the West*, according to Adamiyat, was like "a silo filled with straw in which a few kernels of wheat can be found—the kernels consisting of snippets translated from [W]estern critics (especially Fanon and Memmi)" (Adamiyat, p. 548; trans. P. Sprachman). Such criticism

ignores the openly polemical nature of the work, which is perhaps not so surprising since much of the writing in Iran was polemical at the time and readers were generally accepting of this fact.

The essay's hyperbole and distortions of the historical record notwithstanding, the frankness displayed by *Plagued by the West* made it otherwise different from most writing of the time. No matter what their political or religious affiliations, writers of the day usually couched their views in opaque academic language and adorned—some would say clouded—plain speech with allusions to classical literature, especially to master poets of the classical period (eleventh-fifteenth century). The strategy afforded writers some protection from charges of anti-shahism, blasphemy, or breaking with the party line. Not concerning himself with such self-protection, Al-i Ahmad broke new ground by speaking his mind in plain language that could be widely understood and, though censored for his daring, nonetheless exerted an enormous impact. As one Persian reader observed, whether a person agrees with *Plagued by the West* or not, its purpose is to provoke, to stimulate discussion, and at this it succeeds; one cannot remain indifferent to the work (Ashuri, p. 251).

—Paul Sprachman

For More Information

Adamiyat, Faridun. "Ashuftagi dar fikr-i tarikhi." In *Yadnamah-'i Jalal Al-i Ahmad.* Tehran: Pasargad, 1985.

Aghdashlu, Aydin. "Nigahi dubarah bih tarikh." In *Yadnamah-'i Jalal Al-i Ahmad.* Tehran: Pasargad, 1985.

Al-i Ahmad, Jalal. *Gharbzadigi.* 2nd ed. Tehran: Rivaq, 1963.

———. *Plagued by the West.* Trans. Paul Sprachman. Delmar, N.Y.: Caravan, 1982.

———. *The School Principal.* Trans. John K. Newton. With an introduction by Michael C. Hillman. Minneapolis: Bibliotheca Islamica, 1974.

———. *Weststruckness.* Trans. John Green and Ahmad Alizadeh. Costa Mesa, Calif.: Mazda, 1982.

Arjomand, Said Amir. *The Turban for the Crown: The Islamic Revolution in Iran.* New York: Oxford University Press, 1988.

Ashuri, Daryush. "Jalal Al-i Ahmad." In *Yadnamah-'i Jalal Al-i Ahmad.* Tehran: Pasargad, 1985.

Avery, Peter, Gavin Hambly, and Charles Melville, eds. *Cambridge History of Iran.* Vol. 7. Cambridge, U.K.: Cambridge University Press, 1991.

Behrooz, Maziar. *Rebels with a Cause: The Failure of the Left in Iran.* London: Taurus, 1999.

Khomeini (also Khumayni), Ruhollah. *Islam and Revolution*. Trans. Hamid Algar. Berkeley, Calif.: Mizan, 1981.

Mohibbi, Sa'id. "Jalal nivisandah-i kih nasli-ra bih khud mashghul kard." In *Yadman-i Jalal Al-i Ahmad*. Tehran: Mu'assasah-i Farhangi-i Gustarish-i Hunar, 1988.

Musavi-Bujnurdi, Kazim, ed. "Al-i Ahmad, Jalal" *Da'irat al-ma'arif-i buzurg-i Islami*. Vol. I. Tehran: Markaz-i Da'irat al-Ma'arif-i Buzurg-i Islami, 1990.

Risen, James. "Secrets of History: The C.I.A. in Iran." *The New York Times,* 16 April 2000. In *The Iranian.* www.iranian.com/History/2000/April/CIA (5 July 2003).

Shadman, Fakhr al-Din. *Taskhir-i tamaddun-i farangi*. Tehran: Majlis, 1947.

Sprachman, Paul. "Hajji Baba Meets the Westomaniac." In *Persian Studies in North America: Studies in Honor of Mohammad Ali Jazayery*. Ed. Mehdi Marashi. Bethesda, Md.: Iranbooks, 1994.

The Quran (Koran)

From traditional accounts, we hear that Muhammad (c. 570-632 C.E.) was born under the shadow of an uncertain future in the city of Mecca in today's Saudi Arabia. His father died before he was born; his mother, when he was only six; and his first guardian, his grandfather, shortly thereafter. As detailed in our earliest major source, the biography *The Life of Muhammad* by Ibn Ishaq (d. 767 C.E.), the young orphan was finally taken in by a kindly paternal uncle, Abu Talib. He grew into an adult who, explains the biography, had a reputation for honesty and fairness. His early life was uneventful. A young Muhammad began to work as a merchant in northward-bound trading caravans headed for ports of the eastern Mediterranean coast in his teens and twenties. When he was 25, he married Khadijah, a wealthy widow about 40 years of age, who had previously been his employer and who would, during her lifetime, be his only wife. The couple had three daughters and as many as three sons. While the boys all died in infancy, the daughters lived to maturity. But only one of the daughters, Fatimah (who married Muhammad's cousin Ali, the son of Abu Talib), had children of her own. About 610 C.E., when Muhammad was around 40 years old, reports the biography, he received his initial summons from God to be a prophet and began to experience the revelations that would eventually be compiled into the Islamic scripture known as the Quran. Despite the universal applicability of its message, valid for all times and audiences, the Quran remains in many ways an intensely per-

THE LITERARY WORK

The sacred book of the Islamic religion; said to have been revealed orally to the Prophet Muhammad in Mecca and Medina during c. 610-32; compiled in Arabic by 656; first translated into English in 1649.

SYNOPSIS

According to Islamic tradition, the Quran is a verbatim record of all the revelations from God received by Muhammad during his lifetime. Its 114 chapters (or surahs) not only delineate the nature of God and the role of the Prophet Muhammad; they also address individual spiritual questions as well as social and legal matters.

sonal document, a moving record of Muhammad's individual encounter with the divine, marked especially in the early chapters, or surahs, by intensely spiritual language. These surahs document Muhammad's divine summons to preach to his fellow townsmen a message of both uncompromising monotheism and their need to accept individual personal responsibility for their actions before God. When in 622 C.E. he led his followers to the more northerly Arabian city of Medina to found an Islamic fellowship that could for the first time worship freely, God's revelations to Muhammad, as recorded in the Quran, changed markedly in nature. Their focus shifted to the needs of a growing community trying to live according to the ideals of their new religious beliefs, addressing questions such as marriage regulations, inheritance laws, and the Muslim's duty to help the poor and unfortunate.

Events in History at the Time of the Quran

The Bedouins: beyond the desert. Like other biblical prophets before him, Muhammad grew up in obscurity in a corner of the Mediterranean world that was regarded as marginal by such imperial capitals of the day as Constantinople or Ctesiphon. His distant ancestors came from a background of nomadic camel herders, called Bedouins, who lived in small tribal groupings deep in the desert for about 2,500 years, their subsistence lifestyle differing greatly from that of their neighbors in the great empires to the north. Many of these Bedouins retained their ancient pagan religions, worshipping multiple gods long after the majority of inhabitants in the Mediterranean empires had converted to monotheistic religions.

But over the centuries some Bedouin tribes moved away from nomadic desert life. By the time Muhammad was born, in the sixth century C.E., his tribe, the Quraysh, had been settled for several generations in the city of Mecca, about midway up the western (Red Sea) coast of the Arabian Peninsula, where they worked as merchants and pursued some modest agricultural activities, such as the cultivation of date palms. They also acted informally as custodians for the idols, many of which belonged to the surrounding tribes and were placed in the city's religious shrine for safekeeping.

Recent research indicates that the Bedouins were better integrated into the larger Mediterranean world than previously thought. Relatively few passed their entire lives as lone Bedouins grazing camels in the high deserts. Many, like Muhammad himself, frequently visited surrounding territories in the course of their work in merchant caravans. Others became mercenary soldiers in the royal armies of neighboring empires. Even those who remained on the Peninsula hosted Christians who came to proselytize and minister to tribes that they had already converted. Muhammad and his neighbors were, in view of this interaction, most likely familiar with Christianity and Judaism, the two earlier monotheistic traditions. Indeed, a preoccupation with them marks many passages in the Quran.

Muhammad, like many earlier prophets, including Moses, was not an eloquent orator. So when the revelations from the Quran began to roll off his tongue in measured, highly polished, and moving language, the development struck many as miraculous. Indeed they referred to the Quran as Muhammad's chief (and even only) miracle. His listeners were likewise struck by the fact that the words of the Quranic revelations were in their own Arabic language, unlike the biblical texts of the Christians and Jews, which were available only in Hebrew, Greek, or Syriac, all foreign tongues that were at best only vaguely familiar to them.

Despite these advantages to the Quranic expressions, Muhammad's message of an uncompromising belief in one God (implicitly rejecting the Christian belief in the Trinity), in angels, and in the essential truth of revelations from previous prophets in the monotheistic traditions of Judaism and Christianity, was not welcomed immediately or wholeheartedly by his fellow Meccans. Many members of the most prominent families in his own tribe bitterly opposed Muhammad, and continued to do so for many years. They felt particularly threatened because, along with all its other tenets, the new faith emphasized social responsibility, that is, care and concern for those less fortunate members of the community, backed up with vivid images of a final judgment day when all would be called to account for the consequences of their deeds in this world. The wealthy Meccans seem to have been very much aware that adopting such a religion would require them to embrace new ethical principles and radically reorder their society.

Later, when Muhammad encountered groups of Arab Bedouins who had converted to Christianity and Judaism, he found them equally unreceptive to the Quran's message. The biography implies that this was because they had distorted the teachings of the founders in their own two traditions and so balked at Muhammad's attempt to bring monotheism back to its origin; also, they felt threatened by the new religion (Ibn Ishaq, pp. 260-77). How much these nearby versions of Christianity and Judaism had actually distorted their traditions in Muhammad's day is unclear; but a distinctive feature in early Islamic teachings, including the Quran, is an emphasis on the need to reform the preceding monotheistic traditions, at least as they existed at the time.

Impact of the Byzantines. Muhammad is thought to have been born just five years after the end of the reign of Justinian (d. 565), the greatest of the

Byzantine emperors in late antiquity. In those days the Arabian Peninsula was a contested area, a border zone over which the Byzantine (Greek-speaking) and Sasanian (Pahlavi/Old Persian-speaking) empires frequently did battle. Justinian's rule and that of his immediate predecessors was marked by a series of protracted, inconclusive wars with the Sasanians that disrupted normal life, especially trade, on the eastern Mediterranean Sea. The hostilities forced merchants to take alternate routes, including one across the Arabian Peninsula (Simon, pp. 32-39; Bell and Watt, pp. 2-4). These merchants, increasingly recruited from the local Arabs, brought new prosperity to the tribes who controlled the routes and small cities along the way, such as Muhammad's hometown of Mecca, where the caravans stopped to refresh themselves. Emerging from this environment are central messages of the Quran—one condemns the hoarding of wealth; another warns against exploiting the weak for economic gain (Quran 4:2-10; 63:9-10). The scripture requires adherents to abide by the principles of egalitarianism and to treat one another with equal respect no matter what their status, prescriptions that would have direct relevance to a society exposed to new opportunities for material gain (Quran 3:110-117; 49:9-12). Later generations would in fact see these injunctions as evidence that Meccan society in Muhammad's day had become badly split by inequalities in class and wealth that threatened to tear it apart.

In October 610 (about the time the Quranic revelations began), General Heraclius was crowned emperor of the Byzantine Empire. Heraclius had just deposed Phocas, a junior army officer who ruled the empire for eight years after murdering his predecessor, Maurice. Maurice had ordered the Byzantine army to wage war throughout the bitterly cold winter months, whereupon the army revolted, bringing about the downfall of a rule that had in some ways been advantageous (Whittow, p. 69). While emperor, Maurice had extended timely aid to a young Sasanian ruler, Khosrow II, who reclaimed the Persian throne and then contracted peace with the Byzantines. It was a peace that would end, however, with Maurice's life. When Khosrow heard that his benefactor had been killed, he invaded Byzantine territory to topple first Phocas and then his replacement, Heraclius. Khosrow attacked the cities of Byzantine Mesopotamia and western Syria with success. By 614 he had occupied Damascus, Jerusalem, and the surrounding territories after destroying the most sacred church in

Christendom, the Church of the Holy Sepulchre in Jerusalem.

Meanwhile, the Christian church was experiencing bitter internal dissension, largely because of Byzantine state policy toward those who did not conform to the doctrines of Chalcedonian Christianity (named for a church council of 451 in the Anatolian town of Chalcedon). By the middle of the sixth century, the majority of Christians had accepted the tenets adopted at the Council of Chalcedon, which decreed that Christ was a single being in whom two natures, human and divine, were inextricably mingled and thus inseparable. A minority group in the East, the Monophysites, argued that Christ had a single, not a double nature. Some of them believed this single nature entirely divine while others held that it combined the divine and human, somehow without mingling the two together (Frend, pp. 118-19, 365, 367-68). A third group, the Nestorians, emphasized Jesus's human nature. Declared heretics by the council, this last group fled into the Sasanian territories and farther East, where the group flourished under moderately tolerant non-Christian rulers (Herrin, pp. 107-09).

In the fifth and sixth centuries, the Monophysites gained strength in Egypt, Syria, and the other non-Anatolian provinces of the Byzantine Empire. The Monophysites, though not labeled outright heretics, had suffered persecution under emperors after Justinian. This was brought home to the Arabs during the reign of Maurice, who had banished from his realm a ruler by the name of Mundhir, who was a Monophysite and the head of an Arab dynasty. The Byzantines, unhappy about his religious divergence, tried to break his dynasty's power over its local area (Frend, pp. 329-30; Shahid, pp. 453-64). In short, the Arabs of Muhammad's day were very much aware of the dangerous consequences of Christian doctrinal disputes. They were also aware of how intolerant one Byzantine emperor, Heraclius, was of the Jews. In 634 Heraclius ordered all Jews within the empire to either convert or be executed (Lamoreaux, p. 12). There is speculation that all this Byzantine persecution contributed to disaffection on the part of the local populations on the eastern shore of the Mediterranean. The thinking is that these populations therefore lent support to the Arab invaders, helping them defeat the Byzantines. How much religious persecution contributed to disloyalty in Byzantium is debatable. But a rejection of Christian sectarianism is clearly implied in the Quran's emphasis on tolerance for all those who accept a belief in one God, both within and without Islam.

The Quran stresses the continuity of its message with prior revelations ascribed to the Jews and Christians (Quran 46:12; 57:25-27; 87:18-19) and implies in some passages that the adherents of these other monotheistic creeds, called in the Quran "People of the Book," will have a heavenly reward (Quran 2:62; 5:69) and should be treated with kindness and respect (Quran 60:79) as long as they do not fight against Muslims. These statements must be read in conjunction with others that register disappointment, even irritation, with the obstinacy of Jews and Christians who refuse to recognize the validity of the message of Islam and who seek to ridicule or actively oppose it (Quran 5:72-81). Clearly the Quran does not convey a consistent message in this regard. It is, however, important to recognize that on the basis of the Quran and Muhammad's pronouncements (called the *hadith*, or "traditions"), the early Muslims articulated a policy of tolerance toward People of the Book. Christians and Jews, especially, are singled out as monotheists who should be free "to practice their faith—to worship and be governed by their own religious leaders and laws in such areas as marriage, divorce, and inheritance" (Esposito, p. 36). In return they had to pay a poll tax (*jizya*) that bought them Muslim protection from invaders and exemption from serving in the military. This liberal policy contrasted sharply with that of the Byzantine Empire toward many of its subjects in the years just prior to the Muslim conquests.

Wars—holy and unholy. The strife prevalent during Muhammad's lifetime may have also influenced the Quran with respect to its focus on *jihad*, or "struggle." The concept of jihad pertains to both an external struggle against hostility and injustice, and an internal struggle, within one's self, against the soul's tendency to evil. In modern times a great many Muslim intellectuals emphasize the inner struggle in their writings on *jihad*. But against the backdrop of constant warfare between the Christian Byzantines and the Persians, and among various Bedouin tribes of Muhammad's day, the Quran's pronouncements would have originally been understood to refer to actual fighting, not to an individual internal contest between good and evil.

Probably most influential on the Quran's policy with respect to jihad was a series of confrontations between the Muslims and the Quraysh, the leading tribe of Mecca, after the Muslims relocated to the city of Medina.

Although some branches of the tribe opposed Muhammad's preaching from the beginning, his own clan generally protected him and championed his right to speak freely. But with the death of the clan leader, his uncle Abu Talib, in 619 C.E., Muhammad's personal safety became increasingly uncertain. From this time on, his opponents formally shunned Muhammad and his followers, refusing to buy and sell from them or to deal with them in any way, and subjecting them to increasingly severe persecution, harassing and tormenting the more vulnerable Muslims but stopping short of actually killing anyone. Over a period of about a year, parties of Muslims made their way north to Medina, until only Muhammad and a few followers were left in Mecca. When Muhammad finally left the city, the situation had so deteriorated that he felt compelled to depart secretly, taking along only one companion (the faithful Abu Bakr). Even so, a group of Quraysh set out after him, intending but failing to kill him when he was alone and far from help.

Tensions further escalated following Muhammad's establishment of his new community in Medina. He and his followers fought three battles with the Quraysh over the next five years. In the first battle, at the wells of Badr in March 624 C.E., a small party of Muslims scored an unexpected victory over a much larger force of Meccans, killing over 70 of them in the fray, some of whom had been important opponents of Muhammad. All of Surat Anfal (The Spoils), the eighth chapter of the Quran, describes this event.

By contrast, the second engagement, almost exactly a year later at a small mountain outside Medina called Uhud, resulted in an unexpected disaster. Muhammad barely escaped with his life. The last 60 verses of the third surah of the Quran, Al Imran (The Family of Imran), are said to have been revealed to Muhammad after this battle. In them, God comforts Muhammad, explaining that the Muslims' inability to prevail was designed to test them in adversity and expose followers who had committed themselves to the new religion not because of true belief, but rather because of its worldly successes in previously defeating the Meccans, interfering with their caravan trade, and making many new converts among the Medinans. God promises in these verses that those who died in the battle did not die in vain but will be received immediately into heaven.

The third battle, called "The Battle of the Trench" (*khandaq*), was much closer to a pitched engagement. Employing the strategy of digging a trench that would impede the mounted Meccans' entry into Medina, the Muslims triumphed. Most of the early part of Surah 33, al-Ahzab (The Confederates), concerns the battle and its aftermath. This final encounter broke the power of the Meccans to wage armed battle against Muhammad. Eventually they concluded a peace treaty with him. Relations became such that at the end of his life he was able to return to Mecca in triumph for a farewell pilgrimage. Some tribal groups outside the cities, however, remained restless and were not entirely reconciled to Islamic rule. They intermittently rebelled, and refused to continue their allegiance to Islam after Muhammad's death. Abu Bakr, for instance, who became Muhammad's successor (the Arabic term for "successor" in this context is *khalifah*, usually Anglicized to "caliph") spent most of his short rule (632-34) subduing these rebellious Bedouin and persuading or compelling them to return to the Islamic fold.

Notable in the Quranic pronouncements on the legitimacy of fighting are two verses related to the final period of Muhammad's relationship with the Meccans and allied tribes. These so-called "Sword Verses" (Quran 2:216; 9:5) deal with instances when various tribal groups reneged on alliances they had made with the Muslims. At first glance, the verses seem quite bloodthirsty: "But when these months when fighting may not take place are completed, then kill the polytheists wherever you may find them, surround them and take them prisoner, sit in wait for them at every place they might congregate" (Quran 9:5; trans. T. DeYoung). But there are two key points to remember. First, the term translated as "polytheist" (sometimes as "idolater" or "infidel") does not refer to non-Muslims in general. It refers only to those who—like the pagan Meccans that opposed Muhammad most fiercely—worship many gods and put them on the same level as the one God of all the monotheistic People of the Book. So the command is not a general one to make war upon non-Muslims, for it excludes other monotheists—the Jews and Christians. Second, the command in the context of the rest of the verse is not to make war on all polytheists no matter who they are but only on those polytheists who have broken non-aggression pacts with the Muslims. In fact, line 7 of the text specifically states: "If they act honorably to you, then do the same to them, for God loves those who act mercifully" (Quran 9:7; trans. T. DeYoung). If this is the behavior prescribed toward non-Muslim Arabs who have fulfilled their treaty obligations, then Muhammad is obviously ordering his followers to hunt those who are still fighting in violation of such pacts.

Ethical themes of the Quran. Probably the most frequently repeated obligation prescribed for every Muslim is "to command the good and forbid the evil" (Quran 3:104; trans. T. DeYoung). This injunction imposes on individuals the responsibility to combat evil in the society around them. They may do so through verbal rather than physical means, through persuasion rather than compulsion—as the instruction "to command" implies—but they cannot permit evil to pass unremarked. This emphasis in Islam on the believer's activist social involvement takes on greater salience when one considers there was an increasing stress in Christian writings and practice in late antiquity on the necessity of distancing oneself from society to live the godly life. As Peter Brown, a foremost authority on life in the late Roman and Byzantine Empire, has said,

> The central problem of late Roman religious history is to explain why men came to act out their inner life through suddenly coagulating into new groups, and why they needed to find a new focus in the solidarities and sharp boundaries of the sect, the monastery, the orthodox Empire. The sudden flooding of the inner life into social forms: this is what distinguishes the Late Antique period, of the third century onwards, from the classical world.
>
> (Brown, p. 13)

While this trend invigorated the minority who peopled monastic establishments and nurtured spiritual commitment among individual Christians, some contemporaries saw it as having an adverse effect on the community. At one point the Quran condemns this Christian practice, singling out monasticism as the aspect of the religion most seriously distorted: "But [the Christians] created monasticism, which had not been prescribed for them by Us [refers to God], except for seeking the pleasure of God; yet they did not observe it [that is, monasticism] as it should have been rightly observed" (Quran 57:27; trans. T. DeYoung). The suggestion here is that Muhammad's audience would have responded positively to the idea that Islam had been revealed to reform and sweep away this and other practices in Christianity at the time. Certainly it anticipates by many centuries the historian Edward Gibbon in *The Decline and Fall of the Roman Empire*, who saw in "the success of monasticism . . . the signal emblem of the superstition that sapped the civic spirit of the Roman Empire" (Leyser, p. 583).

For early Muslims, the individual had a personal responsibility to ensure that religious precepts were followed by society at large as well as in private observance. This notion was reinforced by a strong emphasis on a Judgment Day, when everyone is called to account for his or her deeds, including those in relation to others, in this world. To counter any tendency toward fanaticism based on this injunction toward social activism, the Quran also advocates the search for a balanced life, "an hour for your heart, an hour for your Lord" as the Arabic proverb puts it. The Quran consistently condemns extremes of behavior such as miserliness or, on the other hand, excessive generosity, which in the pre-Islamic period often resulted in one's dependents being reduced to

---

HOW THE QURAN SOUNDS

The uniqueness of the Quran's rhythmic style should not be underestimated, since for most, if not all, Muslims, a large part of the scripture's power is its sound. Appreciation of the distinctive "Quranic voice" is developed early in life, by young children through recitation and memorization in schools called *kuttab*s. Part of Islamic education for centuries, *kuttab*s, though never incorporated into modern publicly financed educational systems, remain popular throughout the Islamic world. Part of the reason, suggests one scholar, may be that when the students in these schools begin to memorize the *ayahs* from the Quran, "they are not simply learning something by rote, but rather interiorizing the inner rhythms, sound patterns, and textual dynamics—taking it to heart in the deepest manner" (Sells, p. 11).

---

beggars. At the end of Surah 25, the surah that describes the ideal Muslim, the Quran articulates the sanctioned alternatives to these extremes.

64 Those who spend their nights either in prostration or standing before their Lord;

65 Who say: "O our Lord, turn away from us the torment of Hell; its punishment would be a grave penalty.

66 It would indeed be an evil place to halt and an evil abode;"

67 Who are neither prodigal nor miserly in their spending but follow a middle path;

68 Who do not invoke any god apart from God; who do not take a life which God has forbidden except for a cause which is just,

and do not fornicate—and anyone who does so will be punished for the crime. (Quran 25:64-68; trans. T. DeYoung)

Few places in the Quran so neatly encapsulate the essence of the new Islamic message to Muhammad's followers. Inherent in the lines are a practical simplicity, social commitment, and an openness to spiritual searching that would ensure a flood of converts to the new religion in the years after Muhammad's death from a sudden and unexpected illness in 632 C.E.

The Quran in Focus

The contents of the Quran. Like the Bible, the Quran is divided into sections. Each is called a *surah*, an otherwise uncommon word in Arabic, translated variously as "step or gradation of a structure," "chapter," or perhaps most aptly "book," since each surah is a self-contained unit. Often the surah includes an assortment of subsections with revelations from different occasions in Muhammad's prophetic career.

Each surah is formally divided into *ayahs*, a feature that corresponds to the verses found in the Bible. (*Ayah* also means "miracle," a sense reinforced by the belief that Muhammad's key miracle was his revelation of the surahs of the Quran to his followers.) Within an *ayah* and between *ayahs*, there are incidents of parallelism and a kind of rhyme based mostly on assonance. But the *ayahs* in a group are of unequal lengths, and they do not have a regular rhythm like verses of poetry. It would thus be incorrect to consider them either poetry or unadorned prose.

Altogether the Quran consists of 114 surahs. They are ordered by length, the longest first and the shortest last. Because the shortest surahs also contain the earliest portions of the revelations to Muhammad, the effect on the reader moving from the beginning of the Quran to the end is to assimilate the impact of the divine message to his prophet roughly in reverse chronological order. In other words, the material revealed after the Muslims left Mecca for Medina, dealing with outward adherence to the practice of the religion (how Islam regulates communal and devotional behavior) as well as the Muslims' polemical encounters with people opposed to their beliefs, is introduced first. Then, as the reader develops a greater psychological receptivity to the inner spiritual demands Islam makes upon its adherents, he or she enters more deeply into the highly sacral world Muhammad encountered at the beginning of his own prophetic experience.

Crowds of Muslims make a pilgrimage to Mecca, Saudia Arabia, to fulfill an obligation of Islam.

The major exception to the rule of "longest (latest) first, shortest (earliest) last" is the first surah, "The Opener" (al-Fatihah), which was probably given its special place because it is used constantly by Muslims in a number of liturgical contexts. It also expresses some basic Muslim beliefs in compact form, such as the power and omnipotence of the one God, his beneficence and mercy to human beings, the human need for divine guidance and for awareness that a judgment day will come. Surat al-Fatihah (the normally silent final "h" in *surah* is pronounced "t" when followed by a possessive phrase, such as "*of* the Opener") is succeeded by a group of 11 very long surahs (each is over 100 verses) that mix together a number of heterogeneous topics. Surat al-Baqarah, the second surah, is a good model for how they are structured. It begins with a section dealing primarily with the rejection or hypocritical acceptance of Muhammad's message by his fellow Arabs and the inhospitable reception to it from the other two monotheistic groups as well. Included are admonitions and exhortations addressed first and foremost to the Jews, since the Jewish tribes of Medina were the first large concentration of People of the Book encountered by Muhammad after his migration to that city in 622. In its second half, this surah incorporates a wealth of regulations for the new Muslim community, from rules about fasting and the direction of prayer and pilgrimage, to rules concerning marriage, debts, and the regulation of the Islamic calendar. Throughout, it interpolates some stories about earlier prophets, only briefly alluding to particular events from the narrative of their lives. These earlier prophets would have been familiar to anyone raised in the other monotheistic traditions. Extensive passages, for example, deal with the story of Adam and his fall from Paradise (Quran 2:30-39), the experiences of Moses and his people in the wilderness after the exodus from Egypt (Quran 2:53-61, 2:67-71, 2:92-93), and Abraham's witness to the omnipotence of God (Quran 2:258-260). The stories serve as proof texts, or evidence, of God's mercy to those who believe in him and are grateful for his bounties; also the stories illustrate how the faithful must always contend with opposition and disbelief.

It is very characteristic of all the surahs in the Quran to include incidents from the stories of familiar Jewish and Christian prophets (often with details different from the models) to illustrate the main theme in the passage of the relevant surah. The exception to this pattern of using illustrative examples from the stories of the prophets, rather than narrating the tale of a particular prophet in its entirety, occurs in Surah 12 ("Joseph"). This surah relates the entire story of the biblical patriarch Joseph. In some respects, it differs from the tale of Joseph in the Hebrew Bible; in other respects the two versions complement each other.

Because of its comprehensiveness, Surat al-Baqarah is sometimes referred to as "a Quran in miniature." Its structural similarities to the surahs that come after it can be seen below:

Surah 2 al-Baqarah (The Cow)

286 verses, revealed in Medina:

vv. 1-29: The Quran as a guide to those who believe; characteristics of believers and hypocrites defined.

vv. 30-39: The fall of Adam from Paradise.

vv. 40-152: Exhortation to the Jews, calling upon them to cease hostility to Islam—includes references to exodus of Moses and Israelites from Egypt, change in the direction of prayer, Abraham's commitment to one God.

vv. 153-57: How believers should deal with misfortune.

vv. 158-79: How believers should deal with non-believers.

vv. 180-286: Regulations for the community, including pronouncements on inheritance and wills, fasting, jihad, and pilgrimage.

Surah 3 Al Imran (Family of Imran)

200 verses, revealed in Medina:

vv. 1-32: The omnipotence of God and the guidance He gives believers through scripture, defining the difference between those who believe and those who do not.

vv. 33-63: Incidents from the story of Mary and Jesus.

vv. 64-101: Appeal to the People of the Book not to spread lies about the relationship between their religions and Islam.

vv. 102-200: Material related to the Battle of Uhud, including sermons delivered before and after the battle, explanations of the defeat, and reassurance of the Muslims.

Surah 4 al-Nisa (The Women)

176 verses, revealed in Medina:

vv. 1-39: Regulations regarding the treatment of those who are dependent on others: orphans, women, the poor and needy.

vv. 40-148: The justice of God; the dangers of people who are hypocritical.

vv. 149-177: The dangers of causing dissension, which is illustrated by the behavior of the People of the Book toward the Muslims.

Surah 5 al-Ma'idah (The Table)

120 verses, revealed in Medina:

vv. 1-7: The obligations incumbent on Muslims in their behavior toward others and regulations about food and cleanliness.

vv. 8-32: A promise that justice will prevail and there will be rewards for doing good, contrasted with behavior of People of the Book who distort the truth, behave hypocritically, and break agreements; example of Cain and Abel.

vv. 33-50: Punishments decreed for crimes like murder and theft.

vv. 51-120: Relations of Muslims to their opponents and to those who are sympathetic to them among the People of the Book.

Surah 6 al-Anam (The Cattle)

165 verses, revealed in Mecca:

vv. 1-3: God is the Creator.

vv. 4-73: Despite the evidence of God's power, many people will not worship Him.

vv. 74-82: Abraham's message of God's omnipotence rejected by his people.

vv. 83-94: Description of some prophets sent to mankind before Muhammad and how they were rejected.

vv. 95-165: The signs that God exists, including the order of the natural world, angels sent as messengers, miracles granted to prophets, and the Quran.

Surah 7 al-Araf (The Battlements)

206 verses, revealed in Mecca:

vv. 1-10: The Quran is a warning to mankind, showing how earlier peoples have been punished by God for disobedience.

vv. 11-53: The fall of Adam from Paradise; the lesson his punishment should teach to mankind.

vv. 54-58: The blessings God bestows upon those who revere him.

vv. 59-64: The punishment of Noah's people for their disobedience.

vv. 65-72: The punishment of the ancient Arabian people of Ad for disbelieving their prophet Hud.

vv. 73-84: The punishment of the ancient Arabian people of Thamud for disbelieving their prophet Salih.

vv. 85-93: The punishment of the people of Midian for disbelieving Shuayb.

vv. 94-102: Many peoples have been disobedient to God and have been punished.

vv. 103-41: The punishment of Pharaoh and the people of Egypt for persecuting Moses and the Israelites.

vv. 142-47: Moses receives the Tablets of the Law on Mt. Sinai.

vv. 148-57: The punishment of the Israelites for worshipping the golden calf.

Highly illuminated pages from a sixteenth-century Egyptian Quran, featuring Surat al-Fatihah (The Opener) and Surat al-Baqarah (The Cow).

vv. 158-206: Instructions to Muhammad on how to convey his message to his people, prediction that some of them will be disobedient.

Surah 8 al-Anfal (The Spoils of War)

75 verses, revealed in Medina:

vv. 1-4: The distribution of spoils of war; definition of who is a true believer.

vv. 5-75: Description of the preparations for the Battle of Badr and the aftermath.

Surah 9 al-Tawbah (Repentance)

129 verses, revealed in Medina:

vv. 1-23: A declaration of the abrogation of any treaties between Muslims and polytheists.

vv. 24-89: Condemnation of hypocrites and hostile People of the Book.

vv. 90-99: The Bedouin Arabs described.

vv. 100-129: Distinguishing between hypocrites and upright individuals.

Like "The Cow," all these surahs contain very diverse material arranged in sections that are freestanding, juxtaposed like the parts of a mosaic. Nevertheless some general observations about these surahs can be made. Almost all the surahs are labeled as being revealed, either wholly or for the most part, in Medina. This means they are associated with the late phase of Muhammad's prophetic career and are thus as-sociated with him in his role as guide and law-giver for the community and not as individual seeker after religious truth. The exceptions to this are the sixth and seventh surahs, "Cattle" and "The Battlements." "Cattle" conveys a relatively unified depiction of Islamic doctrine concerning death, judgment, and resurrection. "The Battlements" expands upon this subject by depicting a series of incidents drawn from the lives of the monotheistic prophets before Muhammad; known in modern religious studies as "punishment stories," these depictions illustrate the ingratitude of men in the face of God's bounty and favors. These were all issues of great relevance to the formative phase of doctrinal development in Islam.

Also there are several extensive passages in these surahs that deal with events surrounding the major battles and political developments of the Medinan period. "The Spoils," for example, concerns events associated with the Battle of Badr; "The Family of Imran" includes a long section about the Battle of Uhud; and "Repentance" constitutes a response to the growing tensions between the Islamic community and its opponents in the last years of Muhammad's life, when he was under pressure to reconsider his practice of making non-aggression pacts with non-Muslim tribes.

At the other end of the Quran, we encounter a very different kind of surah. These are much shorter and tend to be much more unified in their presentation, with a given surah incorporating at most two or three separate brief sections. Some have only a single, dramatic focus, like the 112th Surah, al-Ikhlas ("The Sincere Religion"):

1 Say: He is God, One
2 God the everlasting
3 He was not born of anyone, nor will He beget children.
4 There has never been anyone equal to Him.
    (Quran, 112:1-4; trans. T. DeYoung)

Here, the reader's attention is directed unwaveringly to one of the central tenets of Islam, the indivisible unity of God.

Of particular interest in the last two-thirds of the Quran are the surahs believed to contain the earliest material to have been revealed. In the era they were first collected, the surahs were known by their titles and soon after were assigned numbers according to their order in the Quran. The table below lists them not in this order, but rather in the most commonly accepted order in which they were revealed to Muhammad. For each surah, the early material is in dark (boldface) print.

Surah 96 al-Alaq (The Blood Clot)
    19 verses, revealed in Mecca:
    vv. 1-5: First verses to be revealed, emphasizing God's role as a creator and his beneficence to mankind.
    vv. 6-19: Criticism of Muhammad's opponent Abu Jahl.

Surah 74 al-Muddaththir (The Shrouded)
    56 verses, revealed in Mecca:
    vv. 1-10: Muhammad is commanded to warn his people of the imminent Day of Judgment.
    vv. 11-26: One of Muhammad's Meccan opponents is threatened with Divine retribution for rejecting Muhammad's teaching.
    vv.27-48: Description of Hell.
    vv. 49-56: The opposition to Muhammad is described as wanting to become prophets themselves.

Surah 73 al-Muzzammil (The Enwrapped)
    20 verses, revealed in Mecca:
    vv. 1-9: Muhammad is commanded to prepare himself for his coming mission.
    vv. 10-19: Muhammad is comforted and his opponents are promised punishment on the Judgment Day.
    v. 20: Abrogation of night-vigils.

Surah 81 al-Takwir (The Coiling)
    28 verses, revealed in Mecca:
    vv. 1-14: A description, in detail, of the Day of Judgment.
    vv. 15-28: The truth of Muhammad's prophetic powers is supported.

Surah 93 al-Duha (The Forenoon)
    11 verses, revealed in Mecca:
    vv. 1-11: Muhammad is comforted and warned not to forget the needy and orphans.

Surah 94 al-Inshirah (The Easing)
    8 verses, revealed in Mecca:
    vv. 1-8: God reminds Muhammad that He has given him comfort and hope.

Of these surahs, 96, "The Blood Clot," is the most noteworthy. It is the first revelation, and unlike the other surahs referenced above, it can be connected to a first-person narrative purported to come directly from Muhammad himself. Located at the beginning of the surah, the narrative contains all the background details about this first occasion of revelation.

The rest of Surat al-Alaq comes from much later in Muhammad's prophetic career. A prominent citizen of Mecca, about the same age as Muhammad and nicknamed Abu Jahl, or "Father of Ignorance," became an unrelenting enemy of the new religion. He harassed Muhammad and tormented his followers at every opportunity; one of his favorite devices was to interfere with Muhammad while he prayed. Once when Abu Jahl tried to do this, lines 6-19 of this surah were revealed as a rebuke to him and a warning of the punishment awaiting him in the afterlife. Though addressed to him, not Muhammad, the dramatic immediacy of these lines ties them rhetorically to the earlier lines, which may have dictated their placement in the same surah with the earlier address to Muhammad himself.

Strategic writing, strategic reading. The beginning of Surat al-Alaq is very unlike the beginning of Genesis from the Hebrew Bible.

From the Quran:
1 Read! In the name of your Lord who created,
2 Created a human being from a [mere] blood clot,
3 Read! And your Lord is most generous
4 Who taught by the pen
5 Taught a human being what he knew not.
    (Quran, 96:1-5; trans. T. DeYoung)

From the Hebrew Bible:

1 In the beginning God created the heaven and the earth
2 And the earth was without form, and void; and darkness was upon the face of the deep. And the Spirit of God moved upon the face of the waters.
3 And God said, Let there be light: and there was light.

(Genesis 1:3)

In the Hebrew Bible, all the material necessary for making connections between the various actions is supplied, including a time ("the beginning"), a place ("the earth"), and a main character ("the spirit of God"), who sets the whole tableau in motion by speaking ("Let there be light"). Everything is rendered from an external third-person perspective. Surat al-Alaq, in contrast, uses an almost diametrically opposed strategy. The reader must, even before approaching the Quranic surah, take the initiative to discover the details of the story from another source, either from the biography by Ibn Ishaq or one of the commentaries on the Quran. According to the biography, the Prophet's first revelation came about during one of his retreats into the mountains around Mecca to withdraw from the world and meditate on religious matters for one month a year (Ibn Ishaq, p. 106).

One year (probably 610 C.E.), while on his retreat, Muhammad enters a cave deep within the mountains and has a pivotal experience. While in this cave—called Hira—Muhammad receives a visit from a strange figure (later identified as the angel Gabriel), carrying "a coverlet of brocade" inscribed with "some writing." The figure commands Muhammad to "Read!" (the verb can also be translated as "Recite!"), whereupon Muhammad asks in surprise—either because he cannot see the writing in the angel's hand or is unable to read—"What should I read?" The angel, dissatisfied with Muhammad's words, grabs him by the throat and presses down upon his chest, ordering him again to read. Muhammad, frightened, hurt, and confused, repeats his initial response. The sequence is repeated twice more, whereupon Muhammad says emphatically and unambiguously, "*What* should I read?" At this point the angel utters out loud the words upon the brocade, which are the first five lines of Surat al-Alaq: "Read! In the name of your Lord who created, / created a human being from a [mere] blood clot. . . ." Afterwards the angel leaves as suddenly as he appeared. Except for the angel's final words, all the foregoing and following in-

formation is left out of the Quran and must be retrieved from other sources.

When Muhammad returns to his senses, his reaction is not relief or excitement. Rather, like so many of the earlier prophets of the Bible, he rejects the summons, believing it indicates that he has gone mad. He even resolves upon suicide. As he says in his own words: "I thought, Woe is me [I am a] poet or possessed—Never shall Quraysh say this of me! I will go to the top of the mountain and throw myself down that I may kill myself and gain rest" (Muhammad in Ibn Ishaq, p. 106). But when he tries to carry out his resolution, the angel Gabriel reappears, announces to Muhammad that he is a prophet, and places him back upon the path. He finally returns down the mountain to the waiting arms of his wife, Khadijah, who comforts him and tries to persuade him that he has not lost his reason.

The repeated commands to "Read!" seem to throw into contrast God's omnipotence and the individual's inadequacy before that overwhelming power, yet they also emphasize God's willingness to teach and help, concepts that become manifest through the narrative we have about the first revelation from Muhammad's own lips. This willingness is infused into the Quran by the very style it employs, its strategy of addressing the reader directly and drawing him or her into the learning experience in the process of relating Muhammad's revelation.

The reply to Muhammad's question "What should I read?" which initiates the dialogue with Gabriel, is "Read in the name of your Lord who created / Created a person from a [mere] blood clot." The repetition—and verse division—between the first mention of the verb "created" and the second allows for a pause where one could plausibly insert the question "What did the Lord create?" Then the second verse ("a human being") becomes the smoothly flowing response to that question. A parallel gap for question-response occurs after "and your Lord is most generous," allowing for the thought "How is He so generous?" which is then answered with "[because] He taught a human being what he knew not." While the Quran incorporates into its lexicon many rhetorical strategies from diverse religious texts—including the conventional linear narrative of the Bible, dialogue between characters, the sermon, the prayer, and other kinds of exhortation—it repeatedly invokes direct address. In fact, this kind of direct address to the reader—insistently inviting a response that encourages the reader to enter into an almost dialogic relationship with the text—is probably the Quran's most characteristic feature.

Sources and literary context. The Quran speaks of itself in a number of places (for example, Quran 4:105 and 6:92) as a "book" (*kitab*), by which it is understood to mean a "scripture," like the Hebrew Bible and the New Testament, which document divine messages to other prophets, principally Moses and Jesus (2:87, 3:48). Thus, the Quran is placed securely in the monotheistic tradition, which gives great reverence to the written record of God's words as evidence for the presence of the Divine in the world. Also regarded as proof for a Supreme Being in articulations of biblical thought are the seemingly divine principles of order that animate the natural world, the so-called "Book of Nature"; in a number of places the Quran too appeals to this evidence for God's existence, most notably at the beginning of Surah 55 ("The Merciful")

> 5 The sun and moon move to an
>   arithmetical equation,
> 6 The stars and the trees prostrate
>   themselves in adoration,
> 7 The heavens He raised and placed there a
>   scale.
> 8 Beware not to overbalance that scale!
> 9 Measure out with equity and do not short
>   the scale.
> 10 The earth He put in place for all creatures
> 11 Containing fruits and date palms with
>   clusters sheathed,
> 12 Grain in the husk, and aromatic herbs.
> 13 So which of your Lord's favors will you
>   deny?
>
> (Quran 55:5-13; trans. T. DeYoung)

Here, God is depicted as pointing with pride to the beauty and bounty of the world He has created, and calling upon His creatures to bear witness to His existence by acknowledging their debt to Him for these natural riches.

Though the Quran falls into line with the scriptural tradition begun by the Bible, it has clear differences from its model, most notably in its lack of adherence to a strict chronological, and thus historical, progression in its presentation. Unlike the original bible (written in Hebrew) and the New Testament (written mostly in Greek), the Quran was revealed in Arabic, a language whose status was marginal before the seventh century C.E. The only proof of its use as a subtle vehicle for complex ideas comes from pre-Islamic poetry such as **Stop and We Will Weep** by Imru al-Qays (also in *WLAIT 6: Middle Eastern Literatures and Their Times*). Such pre-Islamic

poems were passed on orally and only written down about 100 years after the codification of the Quran in written form. Since they may have undergone substantial alterations in the interim, they do not provide incontrovertible evidence for the ideas and customs circulating among the Bedouin Arabs prior to the rise of Islam. If the poems do represent, however, the pre-Islamic ethos, it was a worldview almost diametrically opposed to the "balanced life" upheld in the Quran itself. That pre-Islamic poetry continued to command high esteem after the rise of Islam suggests that the two worldviews must have coexisted in a kind of dynamic tension similar to the complementary roles played by the Greco-Latin classics and the Bible in Western culture. This dialectic helped give rise to, for example, John Milton's *Paradise Lost*, which employs the conventions of the Greek classical epic to tell the biblical story of Adam and Eve's fall from the Garden of Eden. A similarly productive engagement would eventually take place in the relationship between pre-Islamic poetry and the Quran.

Compilation and composition. Muhammad's revelations are generally held to have been passed on to new converts in oral form until they were collected and written down in a definitive version about a quarter century after his death under the supervision of the third caliph, Uthman.

From the time he began to receive revelations in 610 C.E. until his death in 632, Muhammad had been communicating the contents of the Quran orally to his followers. Some traditional accounts tell us that he had begun to supervise the transcription of the Quran as a written text before his death. Most accounts from Muslim sources, however, place the beginning of this process of collection shortly after he died, during the rule of his close friend and first successor, Abu Bakr. According to this story, Abu Bakr, at the urging of Umar, a fellow disciple of Muhammad and the man who would shortly follow Abu Bakr as the second caliph, was persuaded to gather together and commit to writing all the memorized text of the Quran, so that it would not be "lost and forgotten" (Tabari, p. 25). Abu Bakr entrusted the task to Zayd ibn Thabit, who had been Muhammad's chief scribe during his lifetime. Zayd wrote the revelations on "page-size pieces of hide, small pieces of scapula [bones] and palm leaves" (Tabari, p. 25). During Umar's rule these were all transferred to a single scroll, which, upon Umar's death, was placed in the

INIMITABILITY OF THE QURAN

~

Muslim attitudes toward the Quran as a text eventually crystallized around the notion that its rhetorical structure could not be imitated. In the early centuries of Islam, although many tried, no one was able to compose an imitation that was accepted by contemporaries as equal to the Quran in persuasive power—believers saw this failure as proof of the text's peerlessness, or inimitability (Boullata, p. 141). The belief gave great impetus to the study of rhetoric in Arabic literature, as many scholars sought to categorize and describe the means that the Quran used to construct its inimitable language and to compare these to the stylistic devices/strategies used in the secular literary tradition. This reverence for the Quran as a literary model has persisted into modern times as indicated by the words of such prominent writers as Najib Mahfuz (see *Miramar*, also in *WLAIT 6: Middle Eastern Literatures and Their Times*). Egypt's foremost contemporary novelist and winner of the Nobel Prize for literature, Mahfuz was attacked for having devoted himself to a literary genre (the novel) imported from the West without roots in indigenous Arabic literature, whereupon he objected: "The Quran contains some of the most beautiful stories imaginable and the narrative techniques employed by Quranic stories are some of the sweetest and freshest possible," employing "features of modern style in the art of narrative from the standpoint of images, style and language" (Mahfuz in Naqqash, p. 144). His words testify to the fact that the Quran has, among its other vital functions, remained a potent force in the development of the Arabic literary heritage.

keeping of his daughter Hafsah, who had been one of Muhammad's wives.

There may be some reason to doubt elements of this story, since the different versions of it do not agree on their details (Bell and Watt, pp. 40-42). But the account of what subsequently happened has much greater authority. Some time during the caliphate of Uthman (644-56 C.E.), between 18 and 24 years after the death of Muhammad, it became clear that divergences were appearing in the way different groups of Muslims in the now far-flung empire were reciting the texts of the revelations from the Quran. So Uthman appointed Zayd and several other highly regarded early Muslims to form a commission to write down the entire text and come to an agreement about disputed passages. This they did, and after three revisions, they compared and collated it with the original text in Hafsah's safekeeping (Tabari, p. 26). Uthman then sent copies of this final version to the three Muslim provincial capitals of Kufah, Basrah, and Damascus. One copy was kept in Medina, and all other versions were ordered burned.

Impact. Although the Islamic worldview and ideas drawn from the pre-Islamic heritage would

become intertwined strands in Arabic literature, the initial effect of the revelation of the Quran was to suppress secular poetic activity for around a half century after Muhammad's death. This resulted in part from the fact that the Quran specifically condemns poets (at the end of Surah 26): "And the poets—[only] those who are misled follow them / Haven't you seen them in every valley, wandering distracted? / And indeed they say what they do not do" (Quran 26:224-26; trans. T. DeYoung). These verses were welcomed by Muhammad's followers as a conclusive refutation to his opponents who accused him of being a poet. Such an accusation could not be left unanswered in pre-Islamic Arabia, since it was believed poets were madmen. The poet, as pre-Islamic Arabs saw him, was possessed by evil spirits that gave him a power over words and this power made him dangerous to the harmonious workings of society, since the seductive beauty of his verses could persuade people to believe lies. (Here the Quran espouses ideas very similar to the Greek philosopher Plato's reasons for banishing poets from his ideal republic [*The Republic*, Book X]). But despite the danger ascribed to poets, the Quran relents somewhat in the next lines of the surah. Having condemned some poets in the previous line, it now says there may be others who to a degree behave more acceptably: "Except those who believe and do good and mention God frequently and seek to defend themselves only when they have been wronged" (Quran 26:227; trans. T. DeYoung). The reference at the end of the line is to the practice of using poetic satires to defame the reputation of someone the poet considers an enemy. The Quran stipulates that such a path can be followed only in self-defense, not, as some poets did, to incite violence against the Muslim community. Thus the Quran leaves the door open to a reconciliation between secular literature and its own sacred vision, which occurs especially in the writings of the later Islamic mystics (like al-Hallaj and al-Niffari), who express the paradoxes of their religious experience in language borrowed extensively from metaphors and images first made popular in non-religious verse.

—Terri DeYoung

For More Information

Bell, Richard, and W. Montgomery Watt. *Bell's Introduction to the Qur'an*. Edinburgh: Edinburgh University Press, 1970.

Boullata, Issa J. "The Rhetorical Interpretation of the Quran: i`jaz and Related Topics." In *Approaches to the History of the Interpretation of the Quran*. Ed. Andrew Rippin. Oxford: Clarendon Press, 1988.

Brown, Peter. *Religion and Society in the Age of Saint Augustine*. London: Faber and Faber, 1972.

Esposito, John. *Islam: The Straight Path: Expanded Edition*. Oxford: Oxford University Press, 1988.

Frend, W. H. C. *The Rise of the Monophysite Movement*. Cambridge: Cambridge University Press, 1972.

Herrin, Judith. *The Formation of Christendom*. Princeton: Princeton University Press, 1987.

Ibn Ishaq, *The Life of Muhammad*. Trans. Alfred Guillaum. Oxford: Oxford University Press, 1955.

Lamoreaux, John. "Early Christian Responses to Islam." In *Medieval Christian Perceptions of Islam*. Ed. John Victor Tolan. New York: Garland, 1996.

Leyser, Conrad. "Monasticism." In *Late Antiquity: A Guide to the Postclassical World*. Ed. G. W. Bowersock, Peter Brown, and Oleg Grabar. Cambridge: Harvard University Press, 1999.

Naqqash, Raja. *Najib Mahfuz: safahat min mudhakkiratih*. Cairo: Markaz al-Ahram, 1998.

Sells, Michael. *Approaching the Quran: The Early Revelations*. Ashland, Ore.: White Cloud, 1999.

Shahid, Irfan. *Byzantium and the Arabs in the Sixth Century*, Washington D.C.: Dumbarton Oaks, 1994.

Simon, Robert. *Meccan Trade and the Rise of Islam*. Budapest: Akademiai Kiado, 1989.

Tabari, Abu Jafar Muhammad ibn Jarir. *The Commentary on the Quran*. Trans. John Cooper. Oxford: Oxford University Press, 1987.

USC Muslim Students Association, ed. *The Quran*. 1996. http://www.usc.edu/dept/MSA/quran (30 March 2003).

Whittow, Mark. *The Making of Byzantium: 600-1025*. Berkeley: University of California Press, 1996.

Ruba`iyat of Omar Khayyam

Authorship of the *Ruba`iyat* (commonly spelled *Rubaiyat*) is attributed to the Persian scientist and poet Omar Khayyam. Khayyam (c. 1048-1122) was born Ghiyas al-Din Abulfath Omar bin Ibrahim Khayyam in Nishapur (also spelled Naishapur, Naishabur, or Nayshabur), a city located in Khurasan, the northeastern province of Persia. His family had lived there for several generations, engaged perhaps in the trade of "tent-making," as the surname *Khayyam* suggests. Khayyam attained his early education in Nishapur and Balkh, another Khurasan city, studying mathematics, geometry, and astronomy, subjects that would preoccupy him throughout life. Legend tells of a pact of lifelong friendship he formed in childhood with two renowned personages: Nizam al-Mulk, who later became a powerful vizier, and Hasan Sabbah, the leader of the Isma`ili Muslims, a variant of the Shi`ite branch of Islam and later of the radical groups known as the Assassins. After completing his education, Khayyam traveled to Samarqand, where he wrote a treatise on algebra and worked for the chief magistrate, Abu Tahir, and Tahir's master, Shams al-Mulk Nasr, the ruler of Bukhara. Later, Khayyam entered the service of the Seljuk sultan Malikshah (r. 1072-1092) and his famous vizier Nizam al-Mulk (possibly Khayyam's childhood friend) as one of several distinguished astronomers. In that capacity he was appointed in 1074 to a team of mathematicians, astronomers, and other scholars commissioned to reform the inexact solar calendar that Iran had relied upon since the early centuries of

> ## THE LITERARY WORK
> Quatrains set in Persia (Iran) at an unspecified time; written in the eleventh century; found in Persian manuscripts dating from 1207-08; published in English in 1859.
>
> ## SYNOPSIS
> A philosopher-poet contemplates such issues as the beauties of nature, the essence of love, the mysteries of existence, the limits of private life, the joys of wine, and the necessity of seizing the day.

Islam. The reformed calendar, one of the most precise in the world, is still used in Iran today. Khayyam's contribution to this scientific endeavor earned him the respect of his patron and spread his fame through the vast empire. After Malikshah's death and Nizam al-Mulk's murder at the hands of the Assassins in 1092, Khayyam may have fallen from favor, for he retired from the royal court, returning to his hometown, Nishapur. There he lived the rest of his life in relative obscurity, restricting his circle of acquaintances.

Khayyam probably composed the *ruba`i*'s, or quatrains, upon which his poetic reputation rests throughout his adult life. None of the verses attributed to him appear to have been set down or collected in manuscript until after his death, leading some scholars to reject him as the

Omar Khayyam, an imaginative rendering.

Ruba`iyat's author. However, most are of the opinion that enough evidence exists to credit him with authorship of at least some portion of the existing canon. Like so many other works authored in pre-Mongol Iran, the earliest manuscripts have been lost to posterity. Groups of quatrains by Khayyam appear as part of larger works from the early thirteenth century, and manuscripts of the *Ruba`iyat* date from the fourteenth century. However, it was not until the nineteenth century that the verses became widely known, through the English translation of the writer Edward FitzGerald. While FitzGerald took his share of liberties, his translation of the *Rubaiyat* has been praised for its fidelity to the spirit of the original and as a work of beauty in its own right. Its timeless themes resonated for English readers, as they had to a degree in the Middle East, and still do for people worldwide today.

Events in History at the Time of the Poems

The Seljuk sultanate. During Omar Khayyam's lifetime, a Turkish tribe, known as the Seljuks, ruled over an empire that spread from Persia, to Mesopotamia, Palestine, Syria, and parts of Central Asia up to the Aral Sea. Their rise to power had begun about 970 C.E., when a group of Oghuz Turks from Central Asia entered the eastern outskirts of Muslim territory under the leadership of Seljuk himself. A Turkish chieftain, Seljuk had recently converted to Islam and became the progenitor of the people who later took his name.

It was during the first half of the eleventh century that the Seljuks, led by their chieftain's grandson, Tugrul Beg, embarked on a series of military expeditions into Persia. In 1040, a few years before Khayyam was born, the Seljuks occupied Khurasan, defeating the forces of another group of Turkish nomads, the Ghaznavids, and extending their control over Persia and Mesopotamia. Pushing his conquest south and east, Tugrul Beg reached Baghdad in 1055 and received a cordial welcome from the Abbasid caliph al-Qua'im, who awarded him the crowns of Persia and Arabia in recognition of lands that he had already conquered. In addition to awarding him the crowns, the caliph bestowed a title on Tugrul Beg—al-Sultan ("he with authority").

The power of the Seljuks increased throughout the reigns of Tugrul Beg, his nephew Alp Arslan, and Alp's son Malikshah. During Malikshah's sultanate the dynasty reached its zenith: new roads were opened; mosques, constructed; religious schools, founded; and canals, dug. For his chief minister, or vizier, Malikshah selected the highly competent Persian administrator Nizam al-Mulk. Nizam reorganized the realm's economy from a purely monetary to a modified feudal system by distributing land to deserving military officers in exchange for their loyalty to the Crown. He made significant contributions to Persian culture as well, helping to establish the Nizamiyah, one of the first institutions of higher learning in Islam, and enlisting several astronomers, including Omar Khayyam, to reform the calendar.

Religious orthodoxy was a salient characteristic of the Seljuks' regime. Recognized by the caliph as "King of the East and West" and "Reviver of Islam," Tugrul Beg ruled as a devout Sunni Muslim, as did his successors, so "Khayyam and his contemporaries found themselves living under a renewed if not unprecedentedly forceful application of the principles of Islamic law" (Avery and Heath-Stubbs, p. 12). Heterodox views were strongly discouraged, despite the various factions within Islam itself and the numerous other religions practiced within the Islamic empire, including Judaism, Christianity, and Zoroastrianism. In such a context, it is not surprising that many of the verses in *The Ruba`iyat of Omar Khayyam* seem to advocate retirement from public into private life, where one can keep one's own counsel and avoid persecution for one's beliefs:

"Some for the Glories of This World; and some / Sigh for the Prophet's Paradise to come; / Ah, take the Cash and let the Credit go, / Nor heed the rumble of a distant Drum!" (FitzGerald, *The Ruba'iyat of Omar Khayyam*, lines 49-52).

Conflicting philosophies. The Seljuks' ascendancy in Persia heralded intellectual as well as political changes. For many centuries, Persia had operated as an ideological "crossroads between East and West"—Greek, Asian, and Indian, as well as Islamic ideas all found adherents there (Avery and Heath-Stubbs, p. 14). In twelfth-century Persia, the Islamic ideas gave rise to Sufism or Islamic mysticism, which promulgated a closer and more intimate relationship between worshipper and deity. Piety, asceticism, and the elevation of spiritual love over reason and philosophy were some of Sufism's salient traits.

As one might imagine in the religiously orthodox environment of Khayyam's day, unconventional philosophical views met with disapproval. Greek philosophy, in particular, fell into disfavor among Persian intellectuals who felt that Hellenic thinking represented a threat to the Islamic faith. One of the key figures whose views came under attack was the Persian philosopher and scientist Ibn Sina (also known as Avicenna; 980-1037), who had attempted to reconcile Greek ideas—mostly Aristotelian and neo-Platonic—with Islamic beliefs. The philosopher al-Ghazzali, who had facilitated the acceptance of Sufism by bringing its practices in line with Islam became a key critic. Al-Ghazzali attempted to discredit Ibn Sina and the Greek school as guides for Muslim philosophy. In his treatise *Tahafut al falasifa* (c. 1090; Incoherence of the Philosophers), al-Ghazzali refuted Ibn Sina on no less than 20 points, arguing that reason—and by extension, philosophy—could not fathom the absolute and the infinite and should therefore limit itself to the finite and relative. Only the inner knowledge derived from true religious faith was capable of attaining absolute truth according to al-Ghazzali.

As a mathematician in the service of the Seljuk sultanate, Khayyam said little out loud that would cast doubt on his own orthodoxy. However, he subscribed to the teachings of Ibn Sina, calling him "my spiritual master," and elevated reason above speculation and intuition (Khayyam in Dashti, p. 72). In the introduction to his treatise on algebra, Khayyam uncharacteristically complained,

We are the victims of an age when men of science are discredited, and only a few remain who are capable of engaging in scientific research. Our philosophers spend all their time in mixing true with false and are interested in nothing but outward show; such little learning as they have they expend on material ends. When they see a man sincere and unremitting in his search for the truth, one who will have nothing to do with falsehood and pretence, they mock and despise him.

(Khayyam in Dashti, p. 78)

Khayyam's devotion to the sciences had a disorienting effect on him, robbing him of the certitudes that characterized so many of the devout around him. As one scholar saw it, "in all matters he sought for rational proof, whereas the existence of the Creator cannot be subjected to such proof. There was nothing left for Khayyam but doubt" (Dashti, p. 88). Khayyam's doubts, as well as his adherence to Ibn Sina's ideas, certainly did not endear him to the increasing population of Sufis in Persian society. According to biographer

---

THE SCIENTIST-POET

Rejecting the opinion that Khayyam did not write any of these short four-line poems, the prominent literary historian Jan Rypka states, "Such an opinion certainly went too far, for it overlooked the circumstances that in medieval Iran science and poetry went as it were hand in hand and that Iranian scholars in no way scorned the writing of verse" (Rypka, p. 191).

Ali ibn Zaid, Khayyam and al-Ghazali had a brief, hostile meeting at which the latter expressed disdain for the former's opinions on astronomy. Later, after Khayyam's death, the Sufi poet Farid al-Din Attar composed a poem envisioning

Khayyam in the afterlife, ashamed and confused on being rejected at God's threshold. There his 'knowledge' availed him nothing, having only made him deficient in those spiritual qualities without which no one can be blessed by God's acceptance.

(Attar in Avery and Heath-Stubbs, p. 17)

Significantly, the *Ruba'iyat of Omar Khayyam* echoes the doubts of its author, especially regarding such unknowable mysteries as existence, death, the afterlife, and the very nature of the universe. In one quatrain, the speaker observes, "Into the Universe, and *Why* not knowing / Nor *Whence*, like Water willy-nilly flowing; / And out of it, as Wind along the Waste, / I know not

Whither, willy-nilly blowing" (*Ruba`iyat*, lines 113-116). Such doubts certainly did not conform to orthodox Islamic beliefs, which held that on the day of creation God had put into motion a grand design for the universe and that human beings were fulfilling His will.

**The importance of the *ruba`iyat*.** *Ruba`iyat* is the Persian plural for *ruba`i*, a two-couplet stanza of poetry. A *ruba`i* consists of four metric units, resulting from the division of each couplet, or stich, into two hemistichs (or lines, in terms of English poetry). Each hemistich contains no more than 13 syllables, forming a self-contained quatrain, with the rhyme scheme *aaba* or, sometimes, *aaaa*.

Considered a purely Persian innovation, the *ruba`i* was especially popular in northeastern Persia in the eleventh and twelfth centuries, during which Omar Khayyam lived. It is speculated that poets of that period wearied of adhering to the Arabic model of writing long, courtly,

monorhymed poems. In any case, the *ruba`i*'s very simplicity heightened its appeal. The form gave poets increased freedom in contrast to their prior confinement to a pattern that called for numerous lines ending in the same rhyming letter. The force of this less rigorous form reveals itself in the short, telling statement of any given *ruba`i*. In essence, it is an epigrammatic stanza with a descriptive or reflective opening, whose moral is driven home in the last line, which "thrusts the finger nail into the heart" (Sa'ib in Avery and Heath-Stubbs, p. 7). For example, the following *ruba`i*, attributed to Khayyam, mounts a vehement, even vitriolic, attack upon religious zealots: "And those who vaunt their prayer-rugs are but mules— / Mere hypocrites who use those rugs as tools; / Behind the veil of zealotry they trade / The Faith! Ah, worse than heathen are those fools" (Saidi, p. 104).

The *ruba`i* became a convenient means for poets to express their innermost thoughts, feelings, and doubts. Some of the quatrains, circulated anonymously, even expressed criticisms of certain rulers, regimes, and, as shown, established dogmas. So pithy and expressive was the *ruba`i* format that it appealed not only to jaded court poets but to the poor and uneducated as well, its very brevity making it easy to compose and memorize. Not surprisingly, intellectuals, nonconformists, and free-thinkers of Khayyam's time were quick to embrace the *ruba`i* as a genre and, also unsurprisingly, some attributed their own lines to him. At the time, this was a common practice for works resembling that of a known author, and here it served to disguise the true identity of writers who thought it imprudent to attach their own names to unpopular or irreverent beliefs.

In any event, Edward FitzGerald accepted Khayyam as author of the quatrains that he received and retained the *ruba`i* form, focusing on the task of translating the content into English. His rendition would capture various facets of Khayyam's thought, as the following quatrain demonstrates: "Ah, make the most of what we yet may spend, / Before we too into the Dust descend; / Dust into Dust, and under Dust to lie, / Sans Wine, sans Song, sans Singer, and—sans End!" (*Ruba`iyat*, lines 93-96). As the *ruba`i* indicates, there was a positive side to the doubtful quatrains, an energetic focus on living in and for the moment, which was as novel to mainstream perceptions as the doubts themselves.

The Poems in Focus

Plot summary. Among the many translations into English of the *Ruba`iyat of Omar Khayyam*, the ones by Edward FitzGerald are probably the best known to modern readers. Originally each *ruba`i* was composed as a separate entity that may not have anything to do with the verse that preceded or followed it in manuscript collections. FitzGerald imposed an order of sorts on the lot that he translated, arranging them as stanzas in a larger narrative poem that chronicles a day in the life of the narrator.

The poem begins at morning, on New Year's Day in Iran, which is the first day of spring. The speaker, identified in FitzGerald's first edition as "old Khayyam" but left nameless in subsequent editions, exhorts his companion to wake and accompany him into the garden. He tells his companion (an addressee whose gender remains undetermined since Persian pronouns are not distinguished by gender) that just before dawn he thought he heard a voice within the tavern. The voice chided those who tarried outside while others clamored impatiently to be admitted, because "You know how little while we have to stay, / "And once departed, may return no more" (*Ruba`iyat*, lines 6, 11-12). For the speaker, the tavern becomes a metaphor for the outside world, while the wine so eagerly sought by the customers represents the very essence of life, which must inevitably drain away, drop by drop.

In the garden with his companion, the speaker reflects upon the beauty of nature and the glory of the past, arriving at the melancholy conclusion that everything is transitory: the rose may bloom again each spring, but mortals, whether humble or exalted, once dead, cannot return. Therefore, the speaker counsels his companion to live for today, consigning yesterday to the past and dismissing tomorrow as something yet unborn, a day when he may no longer exist: "Ah, my Beloved, fill the Cup that clears / TO-DAY of past Regret and future Fears: / *To-morrow!*—Why, To-morrow I may be / Myself with Yesterday's Sev'n thousand Years" (*Ruba`iyat*, lines 81-84).

The speaker goes on to argue that, as worldly ambition and grandeur prove impotent in the face of mortality, so do learning and wisdom. In his youth the poet eagerly sought knowledge from masters in every field, but, despite his efforts, he now finds himself unable to unravel "the Master-Knot of Human Fate" (*Ruba`iyat*, line 124). The deepest mysteries of the universe, of existence and death, remain unsolved, and wine—a symbol of life itself—remains the best palliative the world has to offer against confusion, frustration, and the anguish of not knowing *more*. The speaker renounces all intellectual pursuits and reiterates the importance of enjoying oneself in the moment, rather than reaching futilely after answers that remain elusive or after earthly rewards that prove hollow: "Waste not your Hour, nor in the vain pursuit / Of This and That endeavor and dispute; / Better be jocund with the fruitful Grape / Than sadden after none, or bitter, Fruit" (*Ruba`iyat*, lines 213-216). Nor should one perplex oneself about what happens after death, for those who have gone before cannot return to speak of what they have seen: "Oh threat of Hell and Hopes of Paradise! / One thing at least is certain—*This* Life flies / One thing is certain and the rest is Lies— / the Flower that once has blown forever dies" (*Ruba`iyat*, lines 249-252). It was this sort of lyrical outburst that eventually got Khayyam into trouble with the religious authorities. They saw in his sentiments

A POETRY OF POTTERY

Iran's ancient civilization and desert culture have given rise to a rich imagery of pottery and pots in Persian poetry. Pottery was widespread on the Iranian plateau as early as 6,000 B.C.E., when production techniques already included painting and burnishing. The potter's wheel, known to have existed in Greece since 2000 B.C.E., was in existence in the Iranian village of Sialk far earlier, by 3500 B.C.E. At first pottery was purely a functional craft, pots being used to store water for a short time. Designs on pots at first imitated basket-weaving patterns, drawing from the only art older than pottery making, but over time the designs grew ever more sophisticated. Meanwhile, pots became commoner and more diverse as large vats and smaller jugs were produced and used to ferment or store wine, and a variety of other vessels and utensils were made for everyday use. Pottery makers discovered that the best clay for their craft came from graveyards, possibly because decomposing human bodies made the earth around corpses oilier and therefore more malleable. This discovery led to an analogy in the minds of people such as Khayyam, who personifies pots as humans of long ago, still eager to be filled with wine and its forgetfulness-inducing properties. As pottery shops flourished in cities along the desert, such as Nishapur, a wealth of images arose from the contemplation of them, adding to the already rich stock of imagery in Persian poetry. At the same time, winemaking grew as an industry. The two arts—that of winemaking and that of pottery—intersected on the pages of Persian Sufi poetry, as the idea of fermentation came to serve as a metaphor for the human capacity to attain union with God. If simple sweet grapes could be turned into potent intoxicating wine, wouldn't it be possible for humans to be merged into union with God. Both Sufi poets and poets like Khayyam used these complex sets of images for their own different purposes. In the *Ruba`iyat*, the pot is most often seen as a thing of beauty caught in the hands of a whimsical potter who keeps making and breaking his own beautiful creations.

not just a threat to the certainties they preached; in their eyes, a man of science was accusing them of preaching falsehoods altogether.

Nor does the speaker of these quatrains spare God, who is portrayed as a whimsical puppet-master or a calculating chess player utterly heedless of the human lot. To him, human beings are merely "helpless pieces of the Game He plays / Upon this Chequer-board of Nights and Days" (*Ruba`iyat*, lines 272, 273-274). The Creator's very omnipotence, the speaker contends, renders the idea of a predestined fate unlikely. As imperfect models of clay formed by an all-knowing Deity, humans can only do the best they can with what they have been given. They cannot repay the Creator in "pure Gold for what he lent [them] dross-allayed" and should therefore not be punished for their imperfections: "O Thou, who didst with pitfall and with gin / Beset the Road I was to wander in, / Thou wilt not with Predestined Evil round / Enmesh, and then impute my Fall

to Sin!" (*Ruba`iyat*, lines 314, 317-320). This may well be Khayyam's way of highlighting the much-debated question of whether individuals are predestined for heaven or hell.

Such reflections lead the speaker of the *Ruba`iyat* to recall a dream or fantasy, set in a potter's house among numerous clay vessels of different shapes and sizes. Several vessels speak among themselves, pondering the same concerns as humans: the nature and purpose of their existence, their particular forms, and the identity of the potter who made them. All the pots are made to hold wine, and as the moon arises, all eagerly anticipate being filled with the beverage of forgetfulness, sweet balm in an incomprehensible world.

Watching pots as they take shape or break up, as they are filled with wine or emptied of it, the speaker of the *Ruba`iyat* contemplates the human condition. He recalls how his new devotion to wine has tarnished his scholarly reputation and how he previously resolved to repent of his excesses but abandoned repentance with the return of spring. Once again, he laments "that Spring should vanish with the Rose! / That Youth's sweet-scented manuscript should close!" (Ruba'iyat, lines 381-382). He wishes he had the power to rewrite what fate has ordained, that he and his companion could transform "this sorry Scheme of Things entire" into something "nearer to the Heart's Desire"—a better world, perhaps, a less fleeting life, eternal love (Ruba'iyat, 394, 396). But the passage of time is inevitable and one night, the moon will return to the garden and find him gone from the company of "the Guests Star-Scattered on the Grass," with only a downturned wine glass to mark the spot where he once was (Ruba'iyat, line 402).

Khayyam and his translators. Although we may never know in any satisfactory way how many ruba'i's Omar Khayyam really composed, we know that the canon of ruba'i's credited to him grew in time, as many writers attributed to Khayyam quatrains they did not wish to claim as their own for fear of the consequences. The current canon that bears his name has, in short, been used as a repository of diverse unorthodox ideas of an agnostic or atheistic nature about God and man, this world and the next, and individual doubts that question widely accepted dogmas. This is why, given the highly orthodox nature of religion in Persia over the ages, the growing canon continued to occupy a marginal space within the constellation of Persian poetry. Only after news of the Ruba'iyat's success in the Western world reached the shores of the poet's native land, in successive waves, did the Iranians begin to take note of Khayyam as a poet.

In the West, the Ruba'iyat achieved wide recognition through the efforts of two scholars in Victorian England—Edward Cowell and Edward FitzGerald. While working in the Bodleian Library at Oxford University in 1856, Cowell, a scholar who taught himself to read Persian at an early age, discovered a fourteenth-century manuscript of the verses in the Ouseley collection and made a copy for his own use. Cowell showed the verses to his friend, FitzGerald, whom he had been teaching Persian for several years, and that summer the two men spent their time reading and discussing Khayyam's works and philosophy. FitzGerald was much taken with the Ruba'iyat, writing to another friend, the poet Alfred Tennyson,

> I have been the last Fortnight with the Cowells.
> We read some curious Infidel and Epicurean
> Tetrastichs by a Persian of the Eleventh Century
> . . . mostly of Epicurean Pathos of this kind—

> "Drink—for the Moon will often come round
> to look for us in this Garden and find us not."
> (FitzGerald in Jewett, p. 73)

Although Cowell left England in August 1856 to teach at Presidency College in Calcutta, India, he gave FitzGerald a second copy of the verses and corresponded frequently with him about the latter's progress in Persian studies. FitzGerald, who had entered into a difficult and ultimately unsuccessful marriage that year, delved eagerly into the Ruba'iyat of Omar Khayyam as a means of distraction, and the work continued to fascinate him. Again he wrote Tennyson about his new enthusiasm:

> [Khayyam] writes in little Quatrains, and has scarce any of the iteration and conceits to which his People are given. One of the last things I remember of him is that—"God gave me this turn for Drink, perhaps God was drunk when he made me"—which is not strictly pious. But he is very tender about his Roses and Wine, and making the most of this poor little Life.
> (FitzGerald in Martin, p. 203)

In early 1857 FitzGerald set out to collate the verses from the Ouseley manuscript with another copy of the Ruba'iyat, perhaps to be found in Paris libraries. He wrote the French scholar Garcin de Tassy, enclosing a transcript of the quatrains already in his possession. Although De Tassy had not heard of Khayyam before, he was enchanted by the verses, writing a paper "Note sur les ruba'iyat de Omar Khaiyam" (Note on the Ruba'iyat of Omar Khayyam) that appeared in the Journal Asiatique of 1857.

Meanwhile, Cowell had discovered another manuscript of the Ruba'iyat in Calcutta, this one containing about 516 quatrains in contrast to the Ouseley manuscript's 158. Once more Cowell made a copy of the verses he found and showed them to FitzGerald. Receiving the transcript in June 1857, FitzGerald collated the new material with the Ouseley verses, made annotations as he worked, and began to consider publishing a translation of the quatrains. In August 1857 he wrote to Cowell to say that the quatrains could be shaped into a "very pretty" eclogue, or pastoral poem, but he suspected Cowell would disapprove of its moral (FitzGerald in Jewett, p. 79).

His misgivings about Cowell's reception of his interpretation of Khayyam's poems were well-founded. A man of strong Christian scruples, Cowell published a scholarly article "Omar Khayyam, the Astronomer Poet of Persia" in the Calcutta Review of March 1858, in which he

VARIATIONS ON A THEME

While subject matter and imagery remain constant, each translator of the *Rubaiyat of Omar Khayyam* brings his particular phrasing to the poems. Below are four translations of the same quatrain, ranging from the most literal to the "freest."

> We are the pawns, and Heaven is the player;
> This is plain truth, and not a mode of speech.
> We move about the chessboard of the world,
> Then drop into the casket of the void.
>
> (Dashti, p. 191)

> We are the puppets and the firmament is the puppet master,
> In actual fact and not as a metaphor;
> For a time we acted on this stage,
> We went back one by one into the box of oblivion.
>
> (Avery and Heath-Stubs, p. 52)

> But helpless pieces of the Game He plays
> Upon this Chequer-board of Nights and Days;
> Hither and thither moves, and checks, and slays,
> And one by one back in the Closet lays.
>
> (FitzGerald, p. 105)

> We are but chessmen Player to amuse
> (In fact and not in metaphor I muse),
> On board of life we play, then one by one
> In nihility chest we're laid to snooze.
>
> (Saidi, p. 129)

expressed disapproval of what he saw as Khayyam's worldliness and impiety. Although Cowell did not favor Persian mysticism for its own sake, he felt Khayyam would have fared better had he been a mystic:

> The mysticism, in which the better spirits of Persia loved to lose themselves, was a higher thing, after all, than his keen worldliness, because this was of the earth, and bounded by the earth's narrow span, while that, albeit an error, was a groping after the divine. . . . Omar Khayyam builds no system,—he contents himself with doubts and conjectures,—he loves to balance antitheses of belief, and settle himself in the equipoise of the sceptic.
>
> (Cowell in Jewett, p. 81)

By contrast, FitzGerald embraced the very elements in Khayyam of which Cowell disapproved. Although he raised no opposition to

his friend's article, he made it clear that he intended to progress with his own plans for the *Ruba`iyat*:

> Well: don't be surprised (*vext*, you won't be) if I solicit Fraser [the editor of *Fraser's Magazine*] for a few Quatrains in English Verse, however—with only such an Introduction as you and Sprenger give me—very short—so as to leave you to say all that is Scholarly if you will. I hope this is not very Cavalier of me. But in truth I take old Omar rather more as my property than yours; he and I are more akin, are we not? You see all his Beauty, but you don't feel *with* him in some respects as I do.
>
> (FitzGerald, p. xxxi)

FitzGerald thus continued with his "Epicurean Eclogue in a Persian Garden," which was first published anonymously in 1859 by the antiquarian bookseller Bernard Quaritch (FitzGerald,

p. xxxi). In producing the rendition, FitzGerald arranged and transposed existing quatrains, omitted others that detracted from his chosen themes of religious doubt and the importance of life lived in the moment, and even added images and phrases of his own to give the work unity. His intent had never been to create a literal translation; rather, he was striving for fidelity to the *spirit* of Omar Khayyam. After completing his rendition of the poem, FitzGerald wrote, "I suppose very few People have ever taken such pains in Translation as I have, though certainly not to be literal. But at all Cost, a Thing must *live*: with a transfusion of one's own worse Life if one can't retain the Original's better. Better a live Sparrow than a stuffed Eagle" (FitzGerald in Martin, p. 204). And despite FitzGerald's liberties with the text, few would deny that his translation not only *lives*, but also admirably introduces the *Ruba`iyat of Omar Khayyam* to an English-speaking audience.

**The cult of the *Ruba`iyat*.** In a sense, Victorian England and early-twentieth-century America were thirsting for the ideas expressed in the *Ruba`iyat*. The famous story about the work's making the circles among the English poets of the time best illustrates the immediate success of the poems. It is said that after the journalist Whitley Stokes (1830-1909) showed a copy of FizGerald's 1859 edition to the poet Dante Gabriel Rossetti, and he, in turn, showed it to the poet Algernon Charles Swinburne and others, London bookshops were raided for copies of the work. Thus began a cult of Khayyam worship in England and America that lasted well into the twentieth century and went far beyond literary circles to involve all manner of philosophers, religious thinkers, and other intellectuals of the age. This same enthusiasm gave rise to numerous other works that emulated or justified, modified or refuted the ideas their authors saw enshrined in the work. Both FitzGerald and Cowell tried to distance themselves from the blasphemy that had come to be associated with Omar Khayyam's poetry, the former through his later translation of other Persian mystical poets such as Attar and Jami, the latter most famously in a letter after FitzGerald's death:

> I unwittingly incurred a grave responsibility when I introduced his [Khayyam's] poems to my old friend in 1856. I admire Omar as I admire Lucretius, but I cannot take him as a *guide*. In these grave matters I prefer to go to Nazareth, not to Naishapur.
>
> (Yohannan, p. 171)

1909 illustration by Gilbert James portraying a quatrain from the *Ruba`iyat*.

The Khayyam bandwagon had become unstoppable, though. By the dawn of the twentieth century, the appeal of the quatrains had grown overpowering. While some devoted readers resolved to save Khayyam from the end to which his agnostic, irreverent genius seemed to have doomed him, others were bent on keeping him just as blasphemous as FitzGerald's version made him appear. Thus, in 1907, Louis C. Alexander composed a long poem entitled *Testament of Omar Khayyam* (1907), proclaiming him to be "a man of lofty yet humble piety" (Alexander in Yohannan, p. 207). In response, another Khayyam devotee by the name of H. Justus Williams published 63 quatrains, which he claimed Khayyam had written toward the end of his life. Called *The Last Ruba`iyat of Omar Khayyam*, it was designed to prove that rumors of the poet's repentance had been exaggerated. In America, the *Ruba`iyat* was the rage of literary circles throughout the first half of the twentieth century. It seems that an eleventh-century Persian poet managed to mirror conceptions of the human condition held by many in Victorian England and modern America, and to elicit the emotions that these conceptions evoked in them.

Sources and literary context. Although no manuscripts of the *Ruba`iyat* have apparently survived from Khayyam's lifetime, there is sufficient evidence to suggest that he had indeed composed poetry. According to Ali Dashti, the earliest reference to Khayyam's verses appears in an Arabic book some 55 years after Khayyam's death. Between the thirteenth and fifteenth centuries allusions to Khayyam's poetry appear in numerous written works.

Selections from the *Ruba`iyat* were furthermore printed in several Persian anthologies, where the expansion of the collection suggests a growing number of verses. All told, the estimated number of quatrains attributed to Khayyam is a startling 2,213, although various scholars contend that Khayyam composed only about 200 *ruba`i*'s. As was typical of the genre, the quatrains ranged over a variety of moods, from light-heartedness to melancholy, ventured in directions that orthodox Islam might have considered heretical, and ended with an epigrammatic sting in the tail. Literary scholar Iran B. Hassani Jewett writes,

> Persian scholars regard [Omar Khayyam] as a liberal agnostic in the tradition of Avicenna and as a forerunner of [Hafiz] in whose poetry Omar's earthly wine assumes a mystical significance. Omar's place in the hierarchy of poets is expressed best in a statement attributed to the Moghul Emperor of India, Akbar, who said that each of Hafez's *ghazals* ("lyrics") should be accompanied by a *rubai* from Omar Khayyam, for reading Hafez without Omar was like wine without relish.
>
> (Jewett, p. 100)

Reception. Individuals, whatever their era or country of origin, have approached Khayyam and the *Ruba`iyat* variously. The Victorian scholar Cowell, as has been shown, considered him a heathen, while the more worldly FitzGerald embraced him as a kindred spirit who appreciated all present pleasures. Still others analyzed the *Ruba`iyat* in terms of Sufism, assigning a mystical meaning to the repeated motifs of wine (spiritual love, or forbidden fruit, since wine was forbidden to Muslims), the beloved companion (the Deity) and the tavern (the world, or Sufi lodge). The vigor and variety of interpretations attests to the work's enduring appeal through the centuries.

Within a few years of its anonymous publication in England, FitzGerald's *Ruba`iyat of Omar Khayyam* attracted much admiration. Rossetti, who was a painter as well as a poet, became an immediate enthusiast and recommended the work to many of his friends. The Pre-Raphaelite Brotherhood—upstarts in art who protested convention (and included not only Swinburne but also Edward Burne-Jones and William Morris), eagerly bought up what copies they could find,

some priced as low as a penny. So impressed was the influential critic John Ruskin that he wrote a note to the translator of the *Ruba`iyat,* to be delivered when his identity should become known: "I do not know in the least who you are, but I do with all my soul pray you to find and translate some more of Omar Khayyam for us: I never did—till this day—read anything so glorious, to my mind, as this poem . . . and this is all I can say about it—and that I am ever gratefully and respectfully yours" (Ruskin in Yohannan, p. 161). The note would not be delivered until 1872, when FitzGerald released a third edition.

The increased demand for the *Ruba`iyat* had prompted FitzGerald's publisher to ask for a second edition. Initially reluctant, FitzGerald was at last persuaded to oblige, polishing the original translation and adding new stanzas, increasing the number of quatrains from 75 to 110; this was later cut back to 101 stanzas in the 1872 and 1879 editions. Published anonymously again, the poems of the second edition appeared in 1868. Meanwhile, the *Ruba`iyat* had attracted praise and a following in America; Charles Eliot Norton, writing for the *North American Review*, called the *Ruba`iyat* not just a translation but as a masterpiece in its own right:

> He is to be called translator only in default of a better word, one which should express the poetic transfusion of a poetic spirit from one language to another, and the re-presentation of the ideas and images of the original in a form not altogether diverse from their own, but perfectly adapted to the new conditions of time, place, custom, and habit of mind in which they reappear. In the whole of our literature there is hardly to be found a more admirable example of the most skilful poetic rendering of remote foreign poetry. . . . It has all the merit of a remarkable original production, and its excellence is the highest testimony that could be given, to the essential impressiveness and worth of the Persian poet. It is . . . not a translation, but the redelivery of a poetic inspiration.
>
> (Norton in Jewett, pp. 89-90)

In 1870 an unsigned review by Thomas W. Hinchcliff in *Fraser's Magazine* praised "the excellence and elegance of [the translator's work]" and noted the timeless appeal of Khayyam's poetry: "We must be content to admire his verse[s] for their intrinsic beauty. The vigor of his thought and expression, and their harmony with much that is now going on around us, inspire us with a strange feeling of sympathy for him who in the darkest ages of Europe filled himself with all knowledge accessible to him before he went to his last sleep under the roses of Naishapur" (Hinchliff in Jewett, p. 91).

Inevitably Khayyam and FitzGerald were to become inextricably linked in the minds of critics, with some reviewers even seeing the later as a reincarnation of the former. In 1897 John Hay, a lecturer for the Omar Khayyam Club, related how he came across a "literal translation of the *Ruba`iyat*, and I saw that not the least remarkable quality of Fitz-Gerald's poem was its fidelity to the original. In short, Omar was an earlier Fitz-Gerald, or Fitz-Gerald was a reincarnation of Omar" (Hay in Harris and Tennyson, p. 268). Critics also defended FitzGerald's translation from Persian scholars who complained of the liberties taken with the original. Commenting upon FitzGerald's principles of translation, essayist Arthur Platt observed,

> The unhappy translator is always being impaled on the horns of a dilemma. If he translates literally he produces stuff no mortal can read. . . . If, on the other hand, he makes a good and readable thing of it, then arise all people who know the original, and begin to peck at it like a domestic fowl. If one steers a middle course, one pleases nobody. . . . [FitzGerald] omits whole passages, puts in bits of his own, modifies and arranges everything, and makes—a poem.
>
> (Platt in Harris and Tennyson, p. 267)

—Ahmad Karimi-Hakkak and Pamela S. Loy

For More Information

Avery, Peter, and John Heath-Stubbs. *The Ruba`iyat of Omar Khayyam*. London: Allen Lane, 1979.

Dashti, Ali. *In Search of Omar Khayyam*. Trans. L. P. Elwell-Sutton. London: George Allen & Unwin, 1971.

FitzGerald, Edward, trans. *The Ruba`iyat of Omar Khayyam: A Critical Edition*. Charlottesville: University Press of Virginia, 1997.

Goldschmidt, Arthur. *A Concise History of the Middle East*. Boulder: Westview Press, 1988.

Harris, Laurie Lanzen, and Emily B. Tennyson, eds. *Nineteenth-Century Literary Criticism*. Vol. 9. Detroit: Gale Research, 1985.

Hourani, Albert. *A History of the Arab Peoples*. New York: Warner, 1991.

Jewett, Iran Hassani. *Edward FitzGerald*. Boston: Twayne, 1977.

Keddie, Nikki R., and Rudi Matthee, eds. *Iran and the Surrounding World*. Seattle: University of Washington Press, 2002.

Landau, Rom. *Islam and the Arabs*. New York: The Macmillan Company, 1959.

Martin, Robert Bernard. *With Friends Possessed: A Life of Edward FitzGerald*. London: Faber and Faber, 1985.

Rypka, Jan, et al. *History of Iranian Literature*. Dordrecht, Holland: D. Reidel, 1968.

Saidi, Ahmad, trans. *Ruba`iyat of Omar Khayyam*. Berkeley: Asian Humanities Press, 1991.

Yohannan, John D. *Persian Poetry in England and America: A 200-Year History*. Delmar, New York: 1977.

Savushun
(A Persian Requiem)

by

Simin Danishvar

S imin Danishvar, one of Iran's best-known pioneers of women's writing, was born in Shiraz, Iran, in 1921. She attended missionary schools in Shiraz, and in 1948 moved to the capital of Tehran to study Persian literature at Tehran University, from which Danishvar (also spelled Daneshvar) would receive her doctorate. At the university, she met and later married Jalal Al-i Ahmad (1923-1969), a prominent socially engaged writer who later in life composed a strong critique of westernization in Iran under Reza Shah Pahlavi entitled *Gharbzadigi* (**Plagued by the West**, also in *WLAIT 6: Middle Eastern Literatures and Their Times*). Danishvar traveled to the United States in 1952 on a Fulbright Fellowship to study creative writing at Stanford University in California. Becoming a teacher, she later joined the faculty at Tehran University. Danishvar's earliest works include the collection of short stories *Atash-i khamush* (1948; Fire Quenched). Her subsequent works, including the short-story collection *Shahri chun bihisht* (1961; A City Like Paradise), show a longstanding commitment to prose fiction. In addition to her own writing, Danishvar has translated landmark fiction and drama into Persian (Anton Chekhov's *The Cherry Orchard*, Nathaniel Hawthorne's *The Scarlet Letter*, Alan Paton's *Cry the Beloved Country*, William Saroyan's *Human Comedy*, Arthur Schnitzler's *Beatrice*, and George Bernard Shaw's *Arms and the Man*). She is best known for her novel *Savushun (A Persian Requiem)*, which was published only a few months before her husband's premature death. While she has released a number of later works, including *Bih*

THE LITERARY WORK

A novel set in the ancient city of Shiraz during World War II-occupied Iran; published in Iran (as *Savushun*) in 1969, in English in 1990.

SYNOPSIS

When the Allied forces occupy Iran, a husband refuses to sell them crops and his wife struggles to exercise her will in support of her husband's refusal.

---

ki salam kunam? (1980; Whom Should I Salute?), *Ghurub-i Jalal* (1981; Jalal's Sunset), and *Jazirah-i sargardani* (1998; The Wandering Island), none has surpassed *Savushun* in popularity. Portraying the turmoil of 1940s Iran, its plot brings to the fore two contemporary social issues that intersect by the close of the novel.

Events in History at the Time the Novel Takes Place

Modernization and its failings. A historical underpinning central to *Savushun* is the memory of the occupation of Iran by outside political powers during the Second World War. This occupation represented just one more incident in a series of events that had long characterized Iran's tenuous relationship to the major Western powers in the region: Britain and the Soviet Union. Because of its strategic location, throughout the eighteenth and nineteenth centuries Iran faced numerous attempts by outsiders (mainly Great Britain but also Tsarist Russia) to exert control over its lands. While much of Asia and Africa fell under foreign control throughout the nineteenth and twentieth centuries, Iran and Afghanistan retained some independence. In the case of Iran, this independence was largely due to the dynamics of Russian and British imperial expansion rather than to any formidable military resistance. Iran lay in a crucial position from the points-of-view of both these powers, so for either to gain a dominant share of control was to risk a major war.

Russian interests in Iran differed from those of the British. For the Russians, who by the middle of the nineteenth century had gained control through military force of Baku, Georgia, Daghestan, Armenia, and much of eastern Transcaucasia, the motivation for expansion into Iran was the historical drive for a warm-water outlet. For the British, at least prior to the discovery of oil, the overwhelming interest in Iran was its proximity to India. The British and Russian empires were thus engaged in a perpetual rivalry based on economic control and domination of Iran. Both empires vied for economic concessions from Iran, each gaining an advantage over Iran's merchants in the process. Not all Iranians suffered from this economic competition. However harmful it may have been to Iranians who labored to sell their products at a fair price, other Iranians profited, particularly at the royal court. The Iranian monarchy derived great financial reward by playing the two powers against each other, and the strategy meanwhile insured the survival of Iran as a country. The end result, however, was devastating to Iran: An ever higher percentage of its resources fell under outside control as more foreign concessions were granted, it grew more indebted to outside powers because of additional loans from them, and corruption in the Iranian government increased. Meanwhile, the local population grew impoverished while harvests were allocated to foreign armies. If British soldiers wanted grain, they would approach the open silos. In the event of Iranian resistance, the soldiers often destroyed the silos and took what they needed for themselves.

In the early 1930s, the autocratic ruler Reza Shah initiated a vigorous program to modernize Iran on the model of European countries, minus their political systems. The price for some of his most important economic policies, however, was stifling dictatorship until his abdication in 1941 during World War II in favor of his son

Tribal nomads—such tribes mounted resistance when British and Soviet troops took control of Iran during World War II.

(Mohammad Reza Pahlavi). The country, though advancing economically, remained stagnant politically. By incorporating Western technology and bureaucracy and by attempting to curtail the power of clerical leaders, Reza Shah tried to foster modernization. But his regime did not embrace other aspects of Western society; it refused to allow political parties, free elections, or a free press. In lieu of political parties and political participation, Reza Shah invoked Iran's pre-Islamic past as the ideological foundation for the mission of modernizing the nation. Ultimately this ideology would fail; instead of becoming a great and independent nation-state, Iran would find its fate bound up yet again with the more powerful and modern states of Britain, the Soviet Union, and later, the United States.

An authoritative style. Unsurprisingly the shah's reforms led to the expansion of the bureaucracy and the Iranian army, which served primarily to heighten governmental authority over peasants, tribes, and organized urban opposition. As Reza Shah set out to unify the nation and establish the mechanisms for a strong nation-state, he emphasized the need for a strong military. A drive for national unification ensued, gaining impetus from the efforts to erase the legacy of foreign control of

Iran and to "Persianize" the country by discouraging minority languages, tribal allegiances, and religious affiliations.

As part of his agenda of westernization, Reza Shah ordered the mass unveiling of women in 1936. The state saw the drive to emancipate women and elevate their status as a necessary element in creating a modern nation and countering the omnipotence of the mosque. In forcing women to abandon the veil, Reza Shah hoped to create a symbol of modernization and westernization for the nation. There was a backlash, however, and not only from conservative groups. At first a number of women's organizations—established before the 1930s and dedicated to expanding women's rights in education, the workplace, and politics (women's gaining the vote)—had supported the shah's reforms. But as his policies became concerned more with state control, these women's groups became devoid of any real political power. Instead of helping them effect substantive change, the shah's government initiated token measures. The forced unveiling was not wholeheartedly supported by these women's groups; some objected that it was too harsh and abrupt a change, and that it was unaccompanied by any program of education or real reform.

The net result of the shah's modernizing policies, combined with his authoritative style, was to produce significant opposition. Although social reforms and modernization programs—such as the development of the railroads and the centralization of government—created the basis for Iran's emergence as a "modern" nation-state, by 1941 the social and political position of most Iranians had not changed and, in some cases, had worsened. For women, although the mandatory unveiling law took effect, true liberation was not fully realized due to the persistence of a fundamentally patriarchal view of them in government. Women were still subject to Islamic jurisprudence in marriage, divorce, child custody, and inheritance, which "discriminated against women's equality in the family" (Moghissi, p. 38). It was this mix of countervailing forces that brought about the kind of display of character in *Savushun*, which features a woman who ends up asserting her individuality while at the same time remaining loyal to her husband.

European-Iranian relations. For all his talk of independence, the fact remained that Iran under Reza Shah was still affected by the Western powers. The Iranian government sought relationships with both Germany and Britain, the latter of which continued to be the major power in Iran.

British capital investment in the oil fields during the 1930s overshadowed all Iranian investment in trade and industry. The British held one of the most lucrative oil concessions in Iranian history, and although Reza Shah temporarily cancelled the Anglo-Persian oil concession in 1932, it was quickly revised and restored. The chief interest of the British was to foster a pro-British regime that would act as a buffer to Russian expansionism and protect the western flank of the Indian empire. Thanks to the discovery of oil in Iran early in the twentieth century and to the creation of the Anglo-Persian Oil Company (APOC) in 1909, the British continued to play a key role in Iran's domestic political scene, often supporting political groups and tribal factions that would promote British interests. Throughout Reza Shah's reign, the British sought to manipulate Iranian politics, including its *Majlis* (parliament), in the service of oil concessions that favored Britain at the expense of Iran's own wealth.

By 1941 Germany had become the leading country in Iranian foreign relations and had figured significantly in helping to establish the Iranian industrial base, by, among other things, completing the Trans-Iranian Railroad. Germany's influence was not limited to the economic realm. Because of the large numbers of Iranians who had been educated in Germany prior to the war, Iran was viewed as a breeding ground for pro-German and even Nazi sentiment. The Germans went so far as to declare Iran a pure "Aryan" country, a slogan that suited Reza Shah's dictatorial and nationalistic inclinations. The presence of German agents and the sympathies of the shah towards Germany were the two principal reasons given for the invasion and occupation by British and Soviet troops in 1941, though there were others: opening a new corridor to Russia, safeguarding oil installations (which had principally benefited Britain), and pre-empting any pro-Axis officers who might have been tempted to oust the unpopular shah and install a pro-German regime.

Allied pressure forced Reza Shah to abdicate in favor of his son in September 1941, and he was deported and died in 1944. After his deportation, Iran was divided into three zones by the British and Russians. Soviet troops occupied the north; British troops, the south; and Tehran, along with some other important areas, remained unoccupied. In January 1942, Great Britain, Iran, and the Soviet Union signed an alliance. The Allies guaranteed to safeguard Iran's economy from the negative effects of war and to withdraw their troops within six months after the war's end.

On the home front. After Reza Shah abdicated and his son, Mohammad Reza Pahlavi, was installed as monarch, a greater openness dawned in society. By 1942, a number of organizations and political groups had re-established themselves and had begun to make demands on the government. Trade unions, most of them Marxist, reappeared. The revival of a free press led to the flourishing of newspapers, which were often advocates of political and economic change. For women, the removal of Reza Shah from power had contradictory effects. On the one hand, the anti-religious atmosphere cultivated by Reza Shah's government dissolved, so clerics gained a stronger voice. Many women found themselves re-veiling out of social pressure or, alternatively, personal preference, now that they did not have to abide by Reza Shah's dictates. Some women, however, refused to reassume the veil and fought to get women's issues on the agendas of political parties. A number of publications dedicated to women's issues began to be distributed at this time, and several women's associations, which had been quashed during the 1930s, reemerged.

Although there was greater openness, the occupation had detrimental effects on the population as well. Bread riots erupted in Tehran in the winter of 1942 because of an acute grain shortage, which was aggravated by hoarding and speculation and the diversion of food supplies to the occupying armies. The result was widespread famine in many areas. The occupation, Reza Shah's abdication, and wartime economic and social problems gave rise to growing unrest. In the north, encouraged by the Russians, minority peoples—the Azerbaijanis and Kurds—agitated for the right to use their own languages. New political parties, such as the *Tudeh* (Communist Party), and leftist trade unions sprung up in other areas. The South saw tribal leaders, landlords, and religious leaders raise their voices, with British encouragement. By 1942 and 1943, American advisers had come to Iran to assist in the transport of war supplies via the Trans-Iranian Railroad. All three of the Allied forces tried to influence internal Iranian affairs, due to postwar as well as wartime concerns connected to Iran's close proximity to the Soviet Union, and a desire for control over Iranian oil resources.

The occupation, which eventually resulted in Iran's support of the Allies, left deep scars on the political, economic, and cultural life of the Iranian people. The desire for independence and a self-sufficient economy grew in the postwar years, but as the reality of global politics and the U.S.-Soviet competition for world leadership known as the Cold War pressed in on Iran, it became increasingly vulnerable to those interests. By 1951, Iranians were anxious for greater independence and the ability to exercise control over their own oil resources. Under the leadership of Mohammad Mosaddeq, Iran ended its relationship with Britain over its oil resources and called for the nationalization of the oil industry.

The ultimate blow to Iranian independence came in 1953 when a CIA-directed coup toppled the popularly elected government of Mohammad Mosaddeq and reinstalled Mohammed Reza Pahlavi, the son of Reza Shah, to power. The coup signaled the beginning of a brutal military dictatorship, wiping away the opportunities for independence and democratic reform. The coup was not an isolated event, however; rather it was an extension of the pre- and post-war designs of the superpowers. While Britain's influence decreased considerably, the United States stepped into the void. For many Iranians, the coup just repeated history; once again foreign invaders and collaborating Iranians would deny the people and nation the right to control their own destiny.

The Novel in Focus

Plot summary. *Savushun* unfolds through the heroine Zari's thoughts and musings, as well as through events and incidents that advance the socio-historic dimension of the story. The novel opens during World War II, at the height of the British occupation of the south, and centers on the landowning class of Shiraz, who are attending the wedding of the governor's daughter, Gilantaj. At the wedding are the novel's hero and its more understated heroine—the married couple Yusof and Zari. They mingle with other members of the Shirazi elite and some foreign officers of armies that have occupied Iran for four years during the war. There is small talk about politics. While Yusof takes a stand against the occupation, his older brother, Khan Kaka, hopes to influence members of the British army so they will help him land an appointment to the parliament.

In the novel, Shiraz is portrayed as a city robbed of its classical greatness and physically compromised by the effects of occupation. Yusof comments during the wedding reception to MacMahon, an Irish war correspondent whom Yusof befriends, that "the people of this city are born poets, but you (the British) have stifled their poetry" (Danishvar, *Savushun*, p. 34). Although

Iran has not experienced direct European colonialism, the novel alludes to a number of typically colonial institutions that have penetrated Iranian life, such as the missionary school that Zari attends and the missionary hospital in which her children were born.

Among the more notable European characters at the party is a Sergeant Zinger, who, says Zari, came to Iran 17 years earlier to sell Singer sewing machines to Iranian women. At the time the novel takes place, however, Zinger is a military officer in British uniform.

A benevolent and well-respected landowner, Yusof refuses to sell his crops to the occupying armies. He does not want to see the peasants who lease land from him and the people of Shiraz starve at the expense of British and Russian soldiers. Spotting a way to make some money off the occupation, his brother, Khan Kaka, suggests that Yusof sell his harvest to the army men or they will "take it by force" (*Savushun*, p. 32). Yusof's statement at the beginning of the novel presages his ultimate martyrdom:

> "There is nothing surprising and new about the foreigners coming here uninvited, Khan Kaka," Yusof replied. "What I despise is the feeling of inferiority which has been instilled in all of you. In the blink of an eye, they make you all their dealers, errand boys, and interpreters. At least let one person stand up to them so they think to themselves, 'Well, at last, we've found one real man.'"
>
> (*Savushun*, p. 32)

Yusof's peers consider him an idealist. Living up to the image, he takes his rations of sugar and food coupons from the government and distributes them among the poor peasants in the villages.

Yusof's wife, Zari, emerges as a quiet, unconventional heroine. Much of the novel is narrated from her point of view. Zari's primary concern remains her family. She is preoccupied with her three children (a boy and twin girls) and is expecting a fourth. Yet she begins to question her own limited position as a woman in this patriarchal culture of hers. As Yusof leads and organizes a resistance against the foreign occupiers, she quietly does the work of women: mothering, providing charity to the less fortunate, and serving and supporting her husband. All the while she harbors an increasing number of questions about the suppression of women in the face of male domination. She begins to view this gender-based suppression as parallel to Iranians living under the yoke of foreign domination. Her questioning of male dominance, however, occurs largely in private. Through Zari's internal dialogue with herself, the reader becomes privy to the psychological entrapment she feels because of the limited opportunities available to women in her society.

Zari's charitable work in the poor neighborhoods of Shiraz is one of the few ways she can contribute beyond her isolated household roles of devoted wife and mother. And even this is belittled by her husband, who dismisses her religious and social devotion as "useless" and "rotten to the core" (*Savushun*, p. 149). Unlike Yusof, who is preoccupied with dramatic political and historical events of the day—that is, with plotting his dangerous resistance movement to the foreign occupation—Zari quietly submits. When she isn't tending her husband and children, she spends her days ministering to the poor, the sick, and the insane. She understands that unlike the men, "the only brave thing that she could do was to not keep the others from being brave and let them—with their free hands and thoughts, with their tool of tools—do something" (*Savushun*, p. 248).

Zari's quiet resignation to her female role and her own limitations are shaken near the end of the novel when the repeated nightmares she has about her husband's death become real. The last time Yusof heads out to the pastures to give food to the peasants rather than to the British army, he does not come home alive. Allegedly his killer is one of the peasants who has worked for him, but there is suspicion that the British officer Sergeant Zinger is behind Yusof's death. In her sorrow, Zari retreats into angry, violent thoughts and teeters on the edge of madness. Then, instead of becoming a silent, mournful widow, she emerges as an outspoken supporter of her husband and the cause for which he fought. She goes about telling others that he died because he wanted to keep the contents of the silos for his own farmhands. This marks Zari as a woman who, while remaining faithful to the family structure, far exceeds the role it ascribes to a woman. While her husband lives, she shies away from bold defiance, but after he's been killed, she embraces it. She had wanted to raise her children "with love in a peaceful environment," proclaims Zari, but instead will "raise them in hatred" (*Savushun*, p. 317). She vows to put a gun in her son Khorow's hands.

An Iranian woman's political awakening. Zari's anger serves as a catalyst for her political awakening and initiates her movement from a private into a public realm. By participating in her husband's funeral procession and demanding that he be properly honored as a martyr for the cause of

Iranian independence, Zari undergoes an inner transformation that imbues her with a new self-confidence and courage. She does this by speaking up in protest against those who would keep her husband's death a private event.

The day of the funeral for Yusof, friends and mourners flood the house and yard. There is disagreement among the mourners about where to parade Yusof's body in the occupied city. "With the foreign army in the city . . . there'll be a riot," says Khan Kaka (*Savushun*, p. 363). Zari, increasingly incensed at her brother-in-law's lack of respect, insists on the public procession: "They killed my husband unjustly. The least that can be done is to mourn him. Mourning is not forbidden, you know. During his life, we were always afraid and tried to make him afraid. Now that he is dead, what are we afraid of anymore? I, for one, have gone beyond all" (*Savushun*, p. 363). Emboldened, she claims her voice and challenges her brother-in-law Khan Kaka, whom she finds hypocritical and self-interested. By the end of the novel, Zari understands the story of Siyavash, an ancient Iranian hero, who like Yusof, becomes a martyr (see **Shahnamah, or Book of Kings**, also in *WLAIT 6: Middle Eastern Literatures and Their Times*). From the blood of Siyavash's dying body, goes the legend, a tree issued forth. His legendary story is relayed by a peasant woman, who explains the meaning of the day and evening that commemorate the martyr's death. Zari relates her own husband's death to the harvest ritual on this day of commemoration and collective mourning for a fallen hero, and the connection encourages her to challenge those who are complicit in her husband's death. Participating in the funeral procession that leads her husband's coffin down the streets of Shiraz, which are full of chaos and rioting, Zari becomes an activist of sorts. She quotes her husband, saying, "A city must not be completely without men" (*Savushun*, p. 376). Ironically Zari herself becomes the sort of heroic figure that both her husband and the story of Siyavash envision, though in both these cases the ideal is a male. At the end of the novel, her fate is uncertain, but in understanding Siyavash, she celebrates a part of her culture that eluded her at the British-run schools in which she studied Christian heroes and memorized Western poets such as John Milton (Cook, p. 197). The suggestion is that finding her identity as a woman requires drawing on her national heritage and is furthermore related to finding her identity as an Iranian. Zari's self-awareness grows as she makes the connection between her own limited opportunities as a female in Iran and those of her countrymen under the yoke of Western occupation.

Zari's dawning awareness reflects a growing consciousness among her real-life counterparts in Iran. By the early 1960s Mohammed Reza Pahlavi had initiated the so-called "White Revolution," which promoted modest reforms throughout society. Included in these reforms were an expansion of women's educational opportunities and the granting of suffrage to women. Some of the changes had an impact on women's lives, but as late as 1969 Mohammed Reza Pahlavi showed a contradictory stance toward the position of women in Iranian society, as revealed in the following interview with Italian journalist Oriana Fallaci in 1976.

> Look, let's put it this way. I don't underrate them (women); they've profited more than anyone else from my White Revolution. I've fought strenuously so that they'd have equal rights and responsibilities. I've even put them in the army, where they get military training for six months and are then sent to the villages to fight the battle against illiteracy. And let's not forget I'm the son of the man who took away women's veils in Iran. But I wouldn't be sincere if I stated I'd been influenced by a single one of them. Nobody can influence me, nobody. Still less a woman. Women are important in a man's life only if they're beautiful and charming and keep their femininity. . . . This business of feminism, for instance. What do these feminists want? What do you want? You say equality. Oh! I don't want to seem rude, but. . . . You're equal in the eyes of the law but not, excuse my saying so, in ability.
>
> (Mohammad Reza Shah in Fallaci, p. 62)

Such contradictory attitudes toward women were widely held in Iranian society. On the surface, women gained a semblance of equality when they gained the vote, but when they tried to redefine the parameters of their preconceived roles, they often met with ambivalent or hostile attitudes.

The final lines of the novel, a note of condolence to Zari from MacMahon, articulate a sentiment about the struggle for Iranian independence throughout history that can likewise be applied to the struggle for women's rights: "Do not weep, sister. In your home, a tree shall grow, and others in your city, and many more throughout your country. And the wind shall carry the message from tree to tree and the trees shall ask the wind, 'Did you see the dawn on your way?'" (*Savushun*, p. 378). These lines suggest that Yusof's death was not in vain. MacMahon, an Irishman who is familiar with the effects of occupation and colonization because of his own country's experience with the British, offers a hopeful way to understand Zari's loss: her husband's death can be seen as an act of martyrdom and the beginning of a movement that will eventually liberate Iran. Additionally his words can be understood as a hopeful sign that women such as Zari could and would play a role in the life of Iran's modern history.

Sources and literary context. By the middle of the twentieth century, some modernist female poets had broken new ground in Iran by interjecting a female voice into an almost exclusively male poetic tradition. But there were few women who had begun to experiment in the newer field of prose fiction. Actually because there was no long-standing fictional tradition in Iran, at least in the modern sense of the genre, the emergence of a female voice in the novel and short story was far less threatening than in poetry. Simin Danishvar is usually credited as the first female author to publish a work of fiction, namely her 1947 collection of short stories *Atash-i khamush* (Fire Quenched). The collection received very little attention and, although she continued to write, not until the publication of *Savushun* in 1969 did she gain respect as a serious author. Even then, she did not receive as much attention as male writers.

> [Danishvar] belonged to an age when unwritten laws had developed to communicate to every artist the expectations of the avant-garde intellectual community. A corpus of literary strictures insisted that only certain kinds of experiences, certain kinds of characters, and certain views of society were worthy of serious consideration. Those authors who violated these notions of socio-political engagement or proper thematic concern faced social stigmatization, slight, or neglect.   (Milani, "Power, Prudence and Print," p. 331)

As suggested, *Savushun* can be understood as a reflection of women's growing awareness and public participation in twentieth-century Iran. Danishvar was one of the first to portray such a reality in the character of a female protagonist who speaks in her own voice. Whereas earlier works written by men had depicted women as the *object* of change rather than as *agents* of change, *Savushun* gives voice to a female perspective and a female's voice.

Events in History at the
Time the Novel Was Written

Writers as social critics. Throughout twentieth-century Iranian history, the country's poets and prose writers dealt with turbulent social and political developments. During the 1960s and 1970s the Iranian intelligentsia saw itself as the articulate vanguard of social criticism and opposition to both the tyranny of the shah and the anti-reformist stance of the clergy. Poetry and prose fiction became the principal vehicles for expressing discontent with the Iranian political system and its effects on society. Writing provided Iranian intellectuals and artists with the possibility of communicating these concerns through a complex scheme of literary metaphors that could survive the scrutiny of powerful government censors. The modern intellectual class, *rushanfikr* (literally, "enlightened thinkers"), as well as foreign observers, evaluated much of Iranian literature based on whether or not it was politically engaged and registered political and social criticism. Of course, the corpus of this modern literature was largely the product of male authors; it was in essence the "public" discourse of a male-centered intellectual world. *Savushun* is a much more understated and less political novel. While it does of course deal with events of national history, it is a much subtler political critique and includes a critique of Iranian patriarchal culture as well.

In a country where segregating the sexes and upholding a feminine ideal are facts of life, Iranian women writers had difficulty overcoming obstacles to writing and publishing. Not only were there external barriers to overcome, but there was their own internal hesitancy born of years of suppression. Yet some women, such as Danishvar, managed to penetrate, transform, and go beyond this largely male literary world. Readers were moved, for example, sometimes shocked, by the poetry of Furugh Farrukhzad (see **"Sinning" and Other Poems,** also in *WLAIT 6: Middle Eastern Literature and Their Times*), which encompassed social commentary and expressed a woman's search for autonomy, growth, and love, including erotic love. Other works by women were criticized for being overly sentimental or were ignored altogether. Danishvar's own success can in part be attributed to the fact that she focused on the interior thoughts and feelings of her protagonist, a private, not a public space. Also the infusion of modern Iranian history and the events of World War II into the story gave it an element that resonated for a wide readership.

Reception. Hushang Gulshiri, himself a famous writer, offered the first serious critical treatment of Danishvar's complete works in an Iranian literary journal, *Naqd-i Agah*, in 1984. Gulshiri mentions the novel's enormous popularity. It gained renown for becoming the most sold book in the country in the twentieth century. One of the reviews, by M. R. Ghanoonparvar, attributes the popularity of the novel to "its unpretentious narrative. In other words, in this novel, Danishvar tells her story simply, in a way that does not alienate the average reader" (Ghanoonparvar, p. 78).

Because of the enormous flourishing of women's writing after the 1979 revolution, Danishvar has undergone a re-evaluation of sorts by a younger generation of authors who recognize her achievements in both the literary and feminist contexts. By writing against the grain of socially acceptable forms of prose fiction and revealing the inner thoughts and feelings of her protagonist, she created a precedent, opening up a whole new landscape of characters and literary models for younger writers. Her focus, moreover, on a young woman caught up in the events of an era suggests that women have not been absent from Iran's sociopolitical history, that their participation has perhaps been understated and undervalued. The socially engaged novel *Savushun* is itself an example of such participation. In questioning the role of women in Iran, the novel has promoted change to a degree that the programs and policies of the monarchical state did not.

—Persis M. Karim

For More Information

Abrahamian, Ervand. *Iran Between Two Revolutions*. Princeton: Princeton University Press, 1982.

Al-i Ahmad, Jalal. *Plagued by the West (Garbzadegi)*. Trans. Paul Sprachman. Delmar, N.Y.: Caravan, 1982.

Cook, Michaela. "The Muslim Woman as Hero in Daneshvar's *Savushun: A Novel about Modern Iran*." In *Violence, Silence, and Anger: Women's Writing as Transgression*. Ed. Deidre Lashgari. Charlottesville: University Press of Virginia, 1995.

Danishvar, Simin. *Savushun*. Trans. M. R. Ghanoonparvar. Washington, D.C.: Mage, 1990.

Fallaci, Oriana. *Interview with History*. Trans. John Shepley. New York: Liveright, 1976.

Ghanoonparvar, M. R. "On *Savushun* and Simin Daneshvar's Contribution to Persian Fiction." *Iranshinasi* 3, no. 4 (winter 1992): 77-98.

———. *Prophets of Doom: Literature as a Socio-Political Phenomenon in Modern Iran*. Lanham, Md.: University Press of America, 1984.

Hillmann, Michael C. "Persian Prose Fiction: An Iranian Mirror and Conscience." In *Persian Literature*. Ed. Ehsan Yarshater. Albany, N.Y.: Biblioteca Persica, 1988.

Keddie, Nikki. *Roots of Revolution*. New York: Yale University Press, 1981.

Milani, Farzaneh. "Power, Prudence and Print: Censorship and Simin Daneshvar." In *Journal of Iranian Studies* 18, nos. 2-4 (spring-autumn 1985): 325-48.

———. *Veils and Words: The Emerging Voices of Iranian Women Writers*. Syracuse: Syracuse University Press, 1992.

———. "What Can a Heroine Do? Or Why Can't Women Write?" In *Images of Women in Fictions: Feminist Perspectives*. Ed. Susan Koppelman Cornillon. Bowling Green, Ohio: Bowling Green University Popular Press, 1972.

Moghissi, Haideh. *Populism and Feminism in Iran: Women's Struggle in a Male-Defined Revolutionary Movement*. New York: St. Martin's Press, 1994.

The Secret Life of Saeed the Ill-fated Pessoptimist

by

Emile Habiby

THE LITERARY WORK

A novel set in Israel from 1948 to c.1972; published in Arabic (as *al-Waqa'i al-gharibah fi ikhtifa Sa`id Abi al-Nahs al-Mutasha'il*) in 1974, in English in 1982.

SYNOPSIS

In a seriocomic novel, a Palestinian refugee-turned-informer recounts his experiences from the inception of Israel to his escape into outer space.

Emile Habiby (also spelled Imil Habibi) belonged to a Christian Arab family that traces its origins to the town of Shafa Amr in northern Palestine. Habiby himself was born August 29, 1921, in Haifa, a central coastal city in Palestine. He attended elementary school in Haifa and secondary school in Acre, a city across the bay. Habiby's early maturity was scarred by tragedy; the young woman whom he hoped to marry was among the 91 British, Arab, and Jewish victims killed in Jerusalem on July 22, 1946, when the extremist Zionist group Irgun Tsevai Leumi bombed the King David Hotel, part of which was being used as British governmental and military offices. Habiby himself was in the hotel lobby at the time, waiting for his sweetheart to take a lunch break from her secretarial duties upstairs. He would later marry Nada Abd Allah Jubran (1922-2000), who worked with him in the Communist Party secretariat.

In 1956 Habiby moved to Nazareth, his chief place of residence for the rest of his life. He died there on May 2, 1996, but was buried in Haifa, a city close to his heart. On his tombstone is an epitaph coined by the writer himself—"He who remains in Haifa." During his lifetime, Habiby's Arabic-speaking homeland was from his point of view under occupation, first by the British, then by the Israelis. Under the British, Habiby worked from 1941-43 for the Palestine Broadcasting Service they had set up, serving as an announcer and as cultural director of its Arabic section. He left to help establish Palestine's Communist Party, the only political party that would address Palestinian grievances under Israeli rule. Habiby served as a Communist Party deputy in the Israeli parliament from 1951-59 and 1961-72, and also edited the Arabic-language Communist Party journal *al-Ittihad*. In 1989 ideological and tactical differences with the party leadership resulted in his resigning from these responsibilities. Two years later he resigned from the party itself, though he remained a devoted communist all his life.

In his early career Habiby published short stories in Arabic that appeared in journals in Palestine, Lebanon, Iraq, and Egypt. He later wrote several quasi-autobiographical novels, including three not yet available in English: *Sudasiyat al-ayyam al-sittah* (1967; Six-part Tale of the Six Days [War]), *Ikhtiyah* (1985), and *Saraya bint al-ghul* (1991; Saraya, Daughter of the Ghoul). All illustrate and comment upon aspects of the experiences of Arabs living in Israel, as does

The Secret Life of Saeed the Ill-fated Pessoptimist. A slender yet searing and wide-sweeping novel with sardonic humor, it conveys the plight of Israeli Arabs from the inception of the state to the pivotal early 1970s.

Events in History at the Time of the Novel

Establishment of the State of Israel. Ever since the destruction of their second Temple in Jerusalem by the Romans and their enforced dispersal from Palestine for the second time in 70 C.E., many Jews have, regardless of their places of domicile in the Diaspora, looked forward to the possibility of "returning" to live in the area. They point to its designation in the Old Testament of the Bible as their homeland, though some have viewed it as a God-given duty to live forever outside the Holy Land and provide an example for how humankind should live and worship.

Some 13 centuries passed with only minimal Jewish presence in Palestine before Zionism, a secular movement supporting the emigration of Jews to Palestine, gained practical momentum. In the late nineteenth century, with the help of financial backing from well-to-do European Jewish families, dozens of agricultural settlements were established in Palestine for Jewish immigrants largely from central and Eastern Europe. During the final years of World War I émigrés of East European Jewish extraction in London, led by Chaim Weizmann, a lecturer in chemistry at Manchester University, vigorously advanced the cause of Zionism. Following a trip to the United States by a fellow Zionist, Nahum Sokolow, to consult with President Woodrow Wilson and Supreme Court Justice Louis Brandeis, Chairman of the Provisional Executive Committee for General Zionist Affairs, Weizmann persuaded the British government to lend support to Jewish immigration to Palestine. Motivated in part by the expectation that a large Jewish population in Palestine would ensure safe passage for the British through the Suez Canal, Britain's foreign secretary Arthur Balfour wrote the following landmark letter in 1917 to Lord Rothschild, a prominent Jewish leader and financier in Britain:

> I have much pleasure in conveying to you, on behalf of His Majesty's Government, the following declaration of sympathy with Jewish Zionist aspirations which has been submitted to, and approved by, the Cabinet.
> "His Majesty's Government view with favour the establishment in Palestine of a national

Emile Habiby

> home for the Jewish people, and will use their best endeavours to facilitate the achievement of this object, it being clearly understood that nothing shall be done which may prejudice the civil and religious rights of existing non-Jewish communities in Palestine, or the rights and political status enjoyed by Jews in any other country."
>
> (Balfour in Laqueur, p. 312)

Emerging victorious from World War I, Britain awarded itself control over Palestine and Iraq, and won approval for its mandate over Palestine from the League of Nations on July 24, 1922. Thereafter, the British government appointed a Jewish governor over Palestine, Sir Herbert Samuel, who facilitated unlimited Jewish immigration to the area. In consequence, its Jewish population climbed from 108,000 in 1925 to 300,000 in 1930 and 720,000 in 1948. Most of these immigrants came from Eastern Europe, especially Poland.

Throughout this formative period, coincident with Habiby's upbringing, the Arab communities of Palestine vigorously resisted the Zionist immigration policy, using every means open to them, from argumentation and agitation to street protests and strikes, to violence against both Jewish settlers and the British civil and military authorities. In a variety of "White Papers" from the 1920s-40s, the British government acknowledged the reasons for the continuing disorder and adjusted their policies by attempting to limit Jewish immigration, efforts that were countered by those of Zionist groups both within and outside Palestine.

Post-World War II developments. From Turkish overlords under the Ottoman Empire, which held sway before the First World War, to British overlords, to the imminent possibility of Jewish overlords, Palestine's Arab population balked at outside control. Once the Second World War ended, however, circumstances and the tide of global sentiment conspired against them and their protests were largely disregarded by those who held power in the area. As a result of the persecution and mass murder of European Jews by the Nazi regime, worldwide support for Zionism and for unlimited immigration of Jews into Palestine grew, despite the bitter opposition of the Arab and Muslim worlds. Examination of the issue by the United Nations resulted in a U.N. General Assembly Resolution (November 29, 1947) recommending the partition of Palestine into Jewish and Arab states, which would still, however, function together as an economic union; Jerusalem was to be placed under international control. According to U.S. Undersecretary of State Sumner Welles, it took great effort for the resolution to pass: "By direct order of the White House, every form of pressure . . . was brought to bear by American officials upon those countries outside the Muslim world that were known to be either uncertain or opposed to partition" (Welles, p. 63).

While the Jews of Palestine and Zionist organizations abroad accepted the proposal, Palestine's Arabic-speaking population and the surrounding Arab and Muslim countries rejected it. At the time, Palestine's inhabitants included 1.3 million Arabs and 650,000 Jews (Morris, p. 192). Under the partition proposal, the Jewish portion would encompass 55 percent of the country, even though Arabs held much of the land in this sector. The sector, consisting in large part of the sparsely inhabited Negev Desert, was to be Jewish, but its initial population would consist of almost as many Arabs as Jews.

The British government, frustrated by its failure to find a solution and lacking support at home for further involvement in Palestine, made it clear in September 1947 that it would end its mandate on May 15, 1948, the date established by the League of Nations. Acting accordingly, the British withdrew their administrative and military presence, which left the country in the control of the dominant local administrations and terrorist organizations, whether Arab or Jewish. Conflict between these remaining parties intensified.

In December 1947 the Arab League sanctioned the formation of an army of 3,000 volunteers to oppose any Jewish rule in Palestine. The initial advances made in the north by these troops early the next year led to no solid gains for the Arabs. There began a large-scale emigration of Arab refugees from Palestine, totaling several hundred thousand persons. This mass exodus gained impetus from violence on the part of Jewish extremist paramilitary groups, most notably the Irgun and Stern organizations, that attacked Arab villages and towns. On May 14, 1948, as promised, the last British High Commissioner left Palestine. That same day David Ben-Gurion (born David Green in Poland), now leader of the Jewish Agency, proclaimed the creation of Israel as a Jewish state on the part of Palestine the Jews had been apportioned under the U.N. partition proposal. Again, this amounted to far more land than they actually held at the time. In the spring of 1948, Jews held 5.67 percent of Palestine's land; Arabs, 47.79 percent; state lands comprised 46 percent, and other residents held the remainder.

Immediately after the proclamation, regular units of the armed forces of Egypt, Iraq, Syria, and Transjordan, entered into the violent conflict between the area's Arabs and Jews. The total Arab force in Palestine grew to 45,000 by the end of the first week in July 1948; the Jewish force to 60,000 (Sachar, pp. 328, 330). Combat was fierce and widespread but inconclusive, and successive cease-fires arranged by the United Nations were disregarded by all sides. Not until January 1949 would the fighting cease, by which time only 21 percent of Palestine remained under Arab control. Israel now held nearly 80 percent instead of the 55 percent allotted to Israel by the U.N. partition. A U.N. commission proposed that Arab refugees be allowed a choice between return to their properties or compensation for their loss, but the proposal was rejected by Israel. Its counteroffer to take back 100,000 refugees was rejected by the Arab states as inadequate, and negotiations foundered. As Prime Minister Ben Gurion declared to the first American ambassador to his state, "What Israel has won on the battlefield, it is determined not to yield at the council table" (Ben Gurion in McDonald, p. 79).

A displaced people. Some 900,000 Palestinians lived in the areas occupied by Israel in 1947-48; in a matter of weeks, the vast majority was

The Arab-Israeli dispute over Palestine forced many Palestinians Arabs out of their homes and into refugee camps.

abruptly uprooted. Altogether more than 700,000 Palestinians became refugees while between 100,000 and 180,000 stayed in Israel. The protagonist of *The Secret Life of Saeed the Ill-fated Pessoptimist* opts to stay, first fleeing to Lebanon, then slipping back into Israel, as Habiby did in real life. Of the vast number who became refugees, some 100,000 fled to Lebanon; another 80,000 escaped to Syria, and 5,000 to 10,000 to Iraq. By far the largest groups took refuge in eastern Palestine; in the Gaza Strip (115-150,000), controlled by Egypt; and in the West Bank (250-325,000), adjacent to what was then Transjordan (Farsoun, p. 123).

The Palestinians named the 1948 fight and its consequences *al-Nakbah* ("the catastrophe"). Victims of war, they had evacuated their properties and towns in the heat or expectation of battle, fully intending to return for their possessions, if not for residence. In the end, there was little to return to; some 400 Palestinian villages were ultimately demolished; just 100 remained. Arab lands were freely appropriated by the Israelis for security and other reasons; Arab homes were razed or occupied by new immigrants from abroad. Meanwhile, thousands of Jews, afraid of or subjected to retaliatory violence, were encouraged by the Israeli government to leave Jewish communities that had existed in Arab countries

for centuries. Some 400,000 Arabized Jews moved to Israel from 1948-53 (Sachar, p. 438). Roughly 121,000 Jews were airlifted into Israel from Iraq alone. Meanwhile, the only option for most Palestinians was to move in desperation to hastily established refugee camps. If Israel's formative years were full of challenges laced with hope for Jewish immigrants from other lands, they were "dark with tragedy for Arab refugees" (McDonald, p. vii).

> The camp was talking about an Arab businessman from Haifa. The day before he had taken his two sons from behind the tent, shot them through the head, and turned the gun on himself. . . . He was penniless and couldn't stand watching his children's bellies bloat. . . . The tent camp at Ramallah was even worse. . . . [There was a widow whose] husband, a Ramle carpenter, had been killed in the war. . . . Agonized, she asked me what happened to her home. I could have told her it was probably occupied by a family from Bulgaria or Poland, but I stalled with a don't know answer.
>
> (Bilby in Sachar, p. 436)

Israeli Arabs. The relative handful of Arab Palestinians, Emile Habiby among them, who remained in Israel after its inception included merchants, shopkeepers, restaurant owners, teachers, and civil servants, as well as peasants and small landowners. They occupied some 90 villages and parts of five mixed-population towns—Acre, Haifa, Jaffa, Ramlah, and Jerusalem. For nearly 20 years, the villages were governed by military rule, which kept them under strict surveillance. Villagers needed passes to travel outside their regions of residence. In 1966 these restrictions were partially lifted; two years later they were completely lifted. The restrictions had empowered the military administrators to use all force necessary to ensure security. Police and military personnel could search any home or business suspected of activity that threatened public safety. They could detain or search people, limit their movement, enact curfews, suspend mail, and deport people. The wide latitude troubled some Israelis, who called their compatriots to account, pointing to the discrepancy between reality and democratic claims of equality and justice for all Israelis. In the 20 years of military administration, only the regulation restricting the movement of Arabs between towns and villages was applied continuously. The other regulations were invoked or not as the years passed, and Israel's Supreme Court often stepped into the act and reversed deportations.

Public opinion had little effect. The world at large mostly ignored the plight of the Israeli Arabs, those Palestinians who remained in Israel, its indifference rendering "a whole nation so utterly and completely forgotten" that Habiby felt compelled to write his novel to jar awake not only his Israeli compatriots but also non-Israeli Arabs (Habiby, *The Secret Life of Saeed the Ill-fated Pessoptimist*, pp. 16, 81).

Arab-Israeli wars and the Israeli Arabs. Over the past half century the Arab-Israeli dispute over Palestine has persisted, bringing death, displacement and despair to many on both sides. The 1956 crisis over Egypt's nationalization of the Suez Canal Company resulted in the so-called Tripartite Aggression, in which Britain and France encouraged Israel to overrun Egyptian forces in the Sinai Peninsula in hopes of returning the canal to international control. Following the withdrawal of the three aggressors from the Canal Zone, it took Egypt ten years to once again become a potential military threat to Israel. In 1967 full-scale war erupted once more following a pre-emptive strike by the latter's forces against Egypt and Syria after Arab "boast[s] that Israel was facing national liquidation" (Sachar, p. 638); Jordan was also drawn into the conflict. Israel's victory enabled it to occupy the Sinai Desert, annex Jerusalem, control the entire West bank of the Jordan river, and occupy the Golan Heights region of Syria. Habiby wrote his novel several years after this cataclysmic event but prior to the Arab-Israeli war of 1973. In this "Yom Kippur War," the Arabs would regain some footing when the Egyptian army dislodged the entrenched Israeli forces in Sinai.

The treatment of Israeli Arabs by Israel's Jewish authorities shifted somewhat over this volatile time span. From the start, there was discrimination in society at large. Arab workers in Jewish businesses labored at the more difficult, less well-paid jobs; landlords showed a reluctance to rent to Arabs, and they were relegated to distinct neighborhoods. In Haifa, where the protagonist lives, a few-thousand-strong Arab minority was first congregated into two areas— the downtown Wadi Nisnas neighborhood and along Abbas Street. With the onset of statehood came the development of an Israeli secret service charged, among other tasks, with subjecting the Arab population to close scrutiny. There was perennial fear of armed rebellion on the part of the Arabs, which escalated with world events like Algeria's war of liberation (1954-62), in which Frantz Fanon counseled the downtrodden to use violence in *Les damnés de la terre* (1961; *The Wretched of the Earth*, 1963).

Arab Palestinians raise their voices. As noted, 700,000 Arab refugees left the Israeli portion of Palestine in 1948. In 1949, to provide them with education, health relief, and social services, the U.N. established the United Nations Relief and Welfare Agency (UNRWA), which draws funding from both governments and individuals. Under its auspices, camps were set up for the refugees in the West Bank and in the Gaza Strip. After the 1967 war, in which these areas were lost to Israel, many residents of the West Bank moved over to the East Bank into Jordan. Those currently under UNRWA care represent four generations of registered Palestinian refugees and total roughly 4 million. Another unspecified number have left the area altogether and settled throughout the world. Meanwhile, the relative handful of Arab Palestinians, Habiby among them, who remained in Israel after its inception, would rise to about 300,000 by the 1967 war and then to 900,000, or 19 percent of the population today. They form a distinct minority, separate from the Jewish majority of Israel and from those Palestinians who live in exile today.

From 1948 to 1967 the Arab Palestinians endured physical and spiritual hardships borne not only of the discrimination they suffered in employment and housing but also of emotional isolation. In *al-Nakbah,* the catastrophe, family members were often separated and children lost. Some fragmentation came from a conscious choice by men who sent their loved ones out of harm's way or found desperately needed jobs and settled apart from their families in towns like Haifa. "Cut off from home for long periods, they lacked an adequate social or recreational life. The results were especially painful for un-married men," such as the novel's Saeed (Sachar, p. 534).

The trials and tribulations of being Arab in Palestine began to surface in Arab Israeli litera-

---

ISRAELI SECRET SERVICE

Shin Bet (otherwise known as the General Security Services), is the branch of the Israeli Intelligence Services devoted to domestic security. The branch has long prized Jewish immigrants from the Middle East as useful field men for dealing with Arab affairs. In the novel, Saeed the informer has a field supervisor who is a Mizrachi or Oriental Jew—a Jew born in the Middle East (this group is often subsumed under the category of Sephardim, which strictly speaking refers to Jews from Spain). These men at first occupied lower-level, nonexecutive posts, themselves experiencing discrimination. The top positions were filled by Ashkenazim, Jews from northern and eastern Europe. Israel's Shin Bet operatives were charged with ferreting out for-eign spies and domestic subversives, with combing the Arab mi-nority in Israel for infiltrators. In 1951 the Israeli government established the Mossad (equivalent to the U.S. Central Intelli-gence Agency) to concentrate and coordinate Israel's various intelligence and security services, including Shin Bet.

---

ture in the 1960s. Already in the 1950s young Arabs, frustrated by the ongoing inequities and prevailed upon by outside foes, escaped across the border, often attempting to return to Israel as spies. The outcome of the 1967 Six-Day War between Arab states (mainly Egypt, Jordan, and Syria) and Israel radicalized many Palestinians. Guerrilla attacks by Palestinian rebels against the Israelis had already begun, progressing from thefts and sabotage to arson and murder. Taking their cue from the Vietnam War as well as Frantz Fanon, the rebels saw popular armed struggle as an answer to recapturing their homeland. Instead

of conventional war, the Palestine Liberation Organization (PLO) opted for a slow, incipient people's war, resolving after the 1967 defeat to renew the fight. The PLO grew more radical, influenced in part by another, secret society, al-Fatah ("Victory"), whose members planted re-sistance cells in the West Bank and later, when this strategy failed, in nearby Jordan. Conflict mounted on the Israeli-Jordanian border, esca-lating from 97 incidents in 1967 to 916 in 1968 to 2,432 in 1969 (Farsoun, p. 182).

For many Arabs, the loss of the 1967 war by the Arab powers tipped the balance in favor of the *fida'iyin* (self-sacrificers), the guerrilla fight-ers. An Israeli punitive attack upon al-Karamah, a refugee camp and key guerrilla base inside Jordan, won them further credibility. Here, in March 1968, the *fida'iyin* fought with such brave determination that they were joined by regular Jordanian soldiers until the Israelis retreated to their own turf. The battle was pivotal:

> The inspiring battle of al-Karameh . . . allowed the radical, revolutionary guerrilla organizations to move aboveground, take off politically, and redefine the nature and tactics of the Palestinian-Israeli conflict. Tens of thousands of Palestinian and Arab volunteers joined the ranks of the feda´iyyin [or *fida'iyin*] in the next few months. The new ideology of national liberation—people's war and guerrilla tactics—spread like wildfire.
>
> (Farsoun, p. 182)

Israel dealt severely with this turn of the tide. Its secret service, Shin Bet, took charge of law and order in the West Bank and Gaza Strip. Residents suspected of aiding and abetting the guerrillas had their homes demolished, and many were exiled: "From the early weeks of running what Israel called 'the administered territories,' Arab resi-dents believed to have ties with PLO terrorists were escorted across the bridges into Jordan" (Raviv and Melman, p. 169).

Meanwhile, in the heart of Israel, a few bold Arab-Israeli voices confronted the authorities and the public at large with injustices long inflicted upon Arabs in the state. Israel made attempts to address the injustices. A 1953 Land Acquisition Law mandated compensation to the dispossessed Palestinians for property coopted, but progress has been agonizingly slow. The issue of lands lost in the 1947-48 war—villages razed, towns left (Acre, Ramlah, Jaffa), fields appropriated—remains unresolved. The communists, says Habiby's novel, came up with an ironic new name for the Custodian of Abandoned Properties—"the

Custodian of Looted Properties" (*The Secret Life*, p. 45). Yet, in the 1970s, when Habiby's novel appeared, the Israeli Arabs could practice their religion and traditions freely. They voted without restriction and, as always, a small contingent sat in the Knesset, Israel's parliament. Arabic was the primary language of instruction in the Arab schools of Israel and its universities were open to Israeli Arabs. Some restrictions existed—service in the Israeli armed forces, for example, was limited to Jews or the Druze (a distinct religious community that broke with Islam in the eleventh century). Even so, notes one Arab Israeli, the picture was not altogether grim: "The refugees in Lebanon say Israel is a criminal state. But I am here. The police will not arrest me unless I have done something wrong. I am living in my homeland. It is true that the Israelis took my land, but I can see it" (Abu Amer in La Guardia, p. 184). The novel's Saeed seems, to some extent, to be of like mind, though this optimistic attitude is countered by a series of demoralizing experiences that fill him with pessimism as well and result ultimately in his debilitating case of angst.

The Novel in Focus

Plot overview. *The Secret Life of Saeed the Ill-fated Pessoptimist* presents the consequence of real-life events in Israel from 1948-70s, using satire to convey the viewpoint of the Arab population of Palestine. Its central figure is the antithesis of the ideal hero. Saeed, whose name ironically means "happy," is a gullible, amoral, self-engrossed, cowardly, but far-from-happy fool. As the reader witnesses his inevitable progression towards madness, it becomes clear that the issues he faces are so complex and his experience so excruciatingly painful that it would be unreasonable to expect anyone to respond more effectively. Saeed is in no sense extraordinary; rather he is the Palestinian "everyman": "Those like me are everywhere—towns, villages, bars, everywhere. I am 'the rest.'" (*The Secret Life*, p. 7). While usually identified as a novel, the text combines qualities associated with a variety of genres, including autobiography and social commentary. The plot follows the progression of events in the life of the protagonist-narrator, Saeed, which are divided into three "books" of extremely brief and fragmentary "chapters." In the novel's first line, an unidentified speaker introduces a framing tale: what follows is a letter from someone who calls himself "Saeed The Pessoptimist." Each of the three "books" is Saeed's separate message to an unidentified journalist. These messages, quoted verbatim, form the body of the novel.

Plot summary—"Book 1." In the first part of the novel, or "Book 1," Saeed describes his curious present circumstances and his early life. Currently he is floating in outer space at the invitation of some unidentified extraterrestrial beings. This information leads the reader to question Saeed's sanity hereafter. In the first chapters, Saeed reveals his confused sense of his ethnic origins, recounting the history of his family and of the Palestinian nation in a barbed manner. Through comments such as "The Pessoptimist family is truly noble and long established in our land," as well as a variety of absurd tales stressing the ethnic purity of Saeed's extended family, the novel ridicules the emphasis on ethnicity and genealogy in Arab culture and also implicitly calls into question Jewish claims to a historical right to Palestine (*The Secret Life*, p. 8).

A series of short, comical scenes recounts Saeed's flight to Lebanon at the outbreak of the summer of the 1948 war between the newly declared state of Israel and the Arab states, and his surreptitious return months later once the conflict has subsided. His father, ironically killed by Israelis in crossfire, had been an agent and informer for the Zionists in Palestine, a role Saeed is eager now to emulate. In becoming an informer, he is motivated purely by financial and career considerations; he appears to experience no moral dilemma in working for the Israeli security services.

After witnessing Israeli maltreatment of Palestinian villagers, scenes he represses to maintain his sanity, Saeed ingratiates himself with the Israeli authorities. He uses his late father's contacts to gain employment as an informer for the so-called Union of Palestinian Workers in Israel. The union is supposedly antagonistic to the Israeli Communist Party (to which many real-life Arabs in Israel belonged). It is the communists on whom Saeed will be informing. Since he learns Israeli Hebrew quickly and easily, Saeed soon feels superior to many Jewish immigrants, who are often limited to their birth languages. (The narration makes occasional ironic comments about discrimination by the Ashkenazi Jews against the Sephardic and Oriental Jews, who come largely from Iraq, Yemen, and North Africa.) His awareness of the language difficulties they are having convinces Saeed that he should also ingratiate himself with the remaining members of the ostensibly nationalist Arab elite of Israel, in case the new state should fail to establish itself firmly. However, his meetings with his chief Arab contact, a self-serving, hypocritical lawyer, are unproductive. Moreover, his new associations come to the attention, through the sophisticated surveillance to which he is subjected, of his Israeli boss and mentor, Jacob, an Oriental Jew who demeans and slaps him. Saeed now realizes that he must be an "ass" no more and act with greater circumspection (*The Secret Life*, p. 52). At this point, dated as December 11, 1948, Yuaad (whose name means "again" or "will be brought back"), a girl Saeed loved as a schoolboy, enters the story. In defiance of Israeli restrictions on travel for Palestinians, she sneaks into Haifa to tell her sister that their father has been jailed based on an informant's testimony. The young woman accuses Saeed of being this informer but ultimately accepts his protestations of innocence. With nowhere else to stay, Yuaad takes refuge with him in his flat. In a hilarious scene Saeed spends a sleepless night paralyzed with fear at the prospect of making romantic advances toward Yuaad, despite her welcoming demeanor. As dawn breaks, he finally plucks up enough courage to enter her bedroom, but it is too late: Israeli soldiers force their way in and seize Yuaad as an illegal infiltrator. She resists arrest with great courage but is forcibly removed, shouting to Saeed that she will return. "Book 1" ends with Saeed's receiving a pathetic note from Yuaad, who refers to herself as his wife and promises fidelity; he spends years thereafter hoping for contact with her but lacking the courage to discover her whereabouts (presumably she lives in exile as a refugee in Jordan). Though always hoping that Jacob, his Israeli boss, will fulfill a secret promise he has made to effect Yuaad's return in exchange for Saeed's total cooperation, he eventually marries a different woman, Baqiyya ("the girl who stayed"). She is a Palestinian from a small seaside village, and her marriage has been facilitated by Jacob as a reward for her role in ensuring that the elections in her area would result in only a tiny vote for the Communist Party.

"Book 2." Another epistle from Saeed to the journalist relays the circumstances of his marriage. Presently Saeed is taking refuge, along with one of his "friends from outer space," in an ancient cave complex in Acre. The two go fishing, and we learn from their dialogue that the June 1967 war between Israel on one side and Egypt, Syria, and Jordan on the other has come and gone, as have Saeed's wife and son. What follows describes his life in Israel over the 19 years that have passed since early Israeli statehood, the period covered in "Book 1." The two friends discuss the impact of

the publication of "Book 1" by Saeed's journalist contact. The critics have likened the book's bitter vision of the world and the gullibility of its narrator, Saeed, to the naiveté of Voltaire's narrator Candide, who witnesses the bestiality of his eighteenth-century European world in the novel of the same name. The discussion alludes to specific instances of brutality and humiliation subjected on Palestinians while Israel was being established.

Further chapters detail Saeed's meeting of and marriage to Baqiyya, whose seaside village of Tanturah has been demolished, a fate shared by many Palestinian villages, some of which are named in the text. Baqiyya, who personifies the stoic determination of the Arabs in Israel to persist and resist, reveals to Saeed the secret whereabouts of a family "treasure," a chest which symbolizes Palestinian solidarity. Buried in an undersea cave near her village, the chest contains weapons. Knowledge of this "treasure" weighs heavily upon Saeed, who suspects that if his Israeli bosses learn of its existence they will seize it and declare it to be property of the state, since its authorities have seized private property owned by Palestinians before. Saeed tries to transmit his own heightened sense of insecurity to his son, Walaa. But Walaa rejects his father's timidity and devotes himself to the Palestinian resistance as a guerrilla fighter, concealing his activities from his parents.

Saeed and Baqiyya are therefore dumbfounded when, in the autumn of 1966, they are informed by Israeli security forces that their son, a guerrilla, is trapped and under fire in a defensive position on the beach where he has taken refuge. Now under suspicion of complicity in anti-Israeli activities, they are asked by the security forces to persuade Walaa to surrender. At this point, the novel's longest chapter features a moving dialogue between Baqiyya and her son in which she argues that he should surrender, choosing life over certain death. He responds persuasively that death is preferable to the fear and subservience endured by his parents. When his mother asserts that she and Saeed are committed to a search for freedom, despite their apparent collusion and compliance with the authorities, Walaa asks how, and the following dialogue ensues:

> "As nature seeks its freedom. Dawn rises only after night has completed its term. The lily buds only when its bulb is ripe. Nature is averse to abortion, my son. And the people aren't ready to face what you are about to do."
> "I shall bear the burden for them until they are ready."

"My son! My son! Oh, let me hug you close to me!"

Silence again. Then I heard him moan: "Mother, mother, how long must we wait for the lilies to bud?"

(*The Secret Life*, pp. 110-11)

The scene ends with Baqiyya's racing to join Walaa, and their joint disappearance in the sea, where they presumably die or take refuge in the cave with the "family treasure," the chest filled with weapons. While this unfolds, Saeed remains immobilized by fear, as always; the disappearance of his family leaves him grief-stricken. "Book 2" ends with a reference to the start of the Israeli-Arab war of June 1967.

"**Book 3.**" The final part of the novel opens with Saeed's realization that being an Arab living in Israel is akin to sitting atop a flat-surfaced pole, unable to descend. His dilemma is briefly resolved by his meeting with a second woman named Yuaad as he is released from jail. He was imprisoned because, at the outbreak of the 1967 war, he offended his bosses by displaying a white sheet above the roof of his house in Haifa, deep within Israel, when a radio broadcast had asked Palestinians on the West Bank to display a flag of surrender. Saeed reflects on his time in jail, recounting the brutality he suffered in the Israeli prison with an inspiring resistance fighter, a guerrilla who bears the same name, Saeed. Overwhelmed by hero-worship for his cellmate, the protagonist pretends that he too has been jailed for his activism. Ultimately released, Saeed hitchhikes a ride from a passing car and discovers that its occupants, a young man and a woman named Yuaad, have been visiting their relative, his own cellmate, in jail. His mind in utter confusion, Saeed somehow thinks that this Yuaad is the very same one he loved but lost so many years ago. In his delirious joy he opens the door of the moving car, still gripping the girl's hand, and they fall out by the roadside. People from a nearby Palestinian village, inside Israel, who assume that he and Yuaad are father and daughter, nurse him to recovery from injuries suffered in the fall. The villagers believe that Saeed and Yuaad are both visitors from Arab lands and communists, the allies of a political party the villagers support, so the two guests are feted accordingly. The villagers speak of the cordon frequently placed around their village and describe the constant surveillance they suffer, as well as the random searches and imprisonment. Hearing of their stoic silence, Saeed suddenly realizes he has never been able to inform on anyone who remained silent, so

he determines henceforth to embrace silence himself.

Saeed and Yuaad leave the village and proceed towards Haifa. On the way, Yuaad tries to explain to the still confused Saeed that it was her own mother who had been the first Yuaad, the object of his affections. Returning his love, she has named her children by another man after Saeed and herself. Strangely, Saeed is unable to accept this and hopes that when he takes Yuaad to his old apartment in Haifa she will recall their night there prior to her arrest. As they sit in his apartment, they know that history will repeat itself, that Yuaad will be seized and evicted. Saeed suggests that she hide until the guerrillas succeed; she asks sarcastically whether the guerrillas, when successful, will "donate freedom to those who hide" and argues that their lives will be wasted as they wait (*The Secret Life*, p. 154). In her view, only a new beginning based on fundamentally different attitudes can restore their freedom. As expected, the soldiers arrive. They inform Yuaad that her entry permit has been cancelled, but treat her with far more respect than they had shown her mother.

In the final chapter we learn that once Yuaad left, Saeed, depressed and confused, returned to his old ways, too indecisive and afraid to participate, despite the pleas of all those he has known, who, he imagines, visit him. Finally he sees a strange, floating apparition whom he recognizes as the leader in outer space. Accepting his offer of refuge, Saeed mounts his back and they fly off. His former acquaintances celebrate his departure. From Yuaad, the daughter, comes the comment, "When this cloud passes, the sun will shine once more" (*The Secret Life*, p. 160).

The work ends with an epilogue in which the journalist recounts his search for the author of these letters. He discovers references to a man of similar name who recently died in a mental hospital in Acre and had been visited by a "daughter" from Beirut. But the identification is tentative, and his account concludes that all should search for Saeed, though none are likely to find him, except by chance.

Self-recrimination. "Brutus is no big deal now, no subject worth writing about," says Saeed in an ironic statement that refers to his role as an informer and turncoat (*The Secret Life*, p. 4). In fact, the novel is consumed with a self-scrutiny borne of accusations that the Palestinians who remained in their homeland when it became Israel were cowardly and treacherous. Saeed's shame at submitting passively to his status as a second-class citizen in his own homeland surfaces in jail when he meets the guerrilla prisoner, also named Saeed: "Should I tell him I was a mere 'sheep,' one who had stayed on in the country, or should I confess that it was through crawling [not bold defiance] that I entered his court [of resistance]" (*The Secret Life*, p. 132). The main character struggles with the terrifying reality that defiance could easily cost him his life. Early in the novel, he fortifies himself with lines from the ancient poet Imru al-Qays about a time that called for no less courage, when his road ahead led to a fearsome Byzantine foe. In the ancient poem, a speaker em-

---

THE PALESTINIAN QUESTION—OPPOSITE ENDS OF THE SPECTRUM

Abba Eban, Israeli ambassador to the United Nations, 1950, on whether Palestinian refugees should return or settle in other Arab lands: "[Israel is] the object of an official proclaimed state of war and the target of a monstrous rearmament campaign. . . . Can the mind conceive anything more fantastic than the idea that we can add to these perils by the influx from hostile territory . . . of people steeped in the hatred of our very statehood?"

(Eban in Sachar, p. 440)

Salah Ta`mari, Palestinian refugee, after the Arabs lost the last vestiges of Palestine in 1967: "Our world was turned upside down. . . . I dropped out of Cairo University in my final year and picked up a gun. I became a full-timer in al-Asifah, the military wing of Fatah. . . . I wanted to become a teacher, a writer maybe. Most of us who picked up a gun were more an intelligentsia in khaki than primitive people who did not know any better."

(Salah Ta`mari in La Guardia, p. 139)

---

boldens a friend: "Allow not your eyes to weep, for we / Our kingdom back must get or die and pardoned be" (*The Secret Life*, p. 36). A few pages later Saeed is confronted by a savior who lobs back to him an appeal for help: "Is any one of you lacking a life he can offer?" (*The Secret Life*, p. 39). Embedded in Habiby's fiction are responses to the challenge. In one of his later stories, "Rubabikiyah," a saleswoman of second-hand goods lives, like Saeed, in Haifa, tending to her people's needs in vital if less patently visible

ways than a militant refugee. *The Secret Life* comes to the defense of the Israeli Arabs by making much the same point: "Who erected the buildings, paved the roads, dug and planted the earth of Israel, other than the Arabs who remained there? Yet those Arabs who stayed, stoically, in land occupied by our state received never so much as a mention in . . . Ahmad Shuqayri's [first leader of the PLO] ringing speeches" (*The Secret Life*, p. 81). Unsparingly, the text chastises Israeli society, larger Palestinian and Arab society, and the author himself.

If there are multiple views about how to solve the problem of the displaced Palestinians, there is also blame enough for everyone to share in relation to their plight. The surrounding Arab countries gave only qualified welcome, at best, to the refugees from Palestine. As McDonald notes, "The Arab refugees pouring into Lebanon—whose population is delicately balanced between Christians and Moslems—threatened to upset that balance because the majority of the refugees were Moslem. Consequently, the Lebanese Government was openly hostile to them in the hope they would move on to neighbouring Syria" (McDonald, p. 93). Likewise, the novel records the unwelcome reception accorded the Palestinian refugees by Jordanian soldiers, who "met them with curses, and they are still swearing at them today" (*The Secret Life*, p. 63). By the early 1970s, violence in the Arab host countries had surged to deathly heights. In Jordan, in September 1970, thousands died when King Hussein's regular Jordanian troops attacked the newly self-assertive and armed refugee camps to suppress the guerrillas and regain control in and around the capital of Amman. The Palestinians remember it as "Black September," a fitting name for an incident in which so many died (*The Secret Life*, p. 94). Such incidents heightened the insecurity of the exiled Palestinians, infusing many of them with "a constant angst," that left them in a condition similar to that of Saeed, the Palestinian who stayed (Farsoun, p. 159).

Habiby also satirizes the leadership class of pre-1948 Arab Palestine. One day Saeed's path takes him past "the villas that had belonged to the Arab officials of Haifa. They had built these before moving to Lebanon to build other villas, only to leave them too" (*The Secret Life*, p. 48). In fact, the Arab refugees "fled from Jewish-controlled Palestine as the result of a mass panic when the wealthy Arabs, almost to a man, began running away in November, 1947, after the U.N. voted partition" (McDonald, pp. 159-60).

Finally the novel satirizes the hypocrisy of the Arab nationalist lawyer in Israel who

> recognized neither the state nor its newspapers and adamantly refused to meet any but foreign journalists. His declarations therefore appeared only in the two *Times*, that of London and that of New York, as well as in the major newspapers in the Arab world. As for us, leaders in the Union of Palestine Workers, we whistled in amazement, our lips pursed, at his patriotic impudence when we heard he had refused to educate his son at the Hebrew University in Jerusalem. But when he sent him to Cambridge—Cambridge, no less—we whistled in even greater astonishment.
> (*The Secret Life*, pp. 50-51)

Sources and literary context. Habiby's novel intends, in part, to redress the standard version of history that has depicted the creation of Israel and the treatment of the Palestinians as benign. He was not the first Arab Israeli novelist to do so. Already in the 1960s, Atallah Mansour, writing in Hebrew, had produced *In a New Light* (1966), a tale of an Arab seeking membership in a kibbutz that sits on the ruins of an Arab village. Mansour was part of a larger group of Israeli Arab writers whose works began to convey "hostility toward the state" (Sachar, p. 582). In protest poetry, Mahmud Darwish, Michel Haddad and others also preoccupied themselves with issues particular to the Israeli Arabs (displacement, discrimination, identity crisis). Habiby produced a novel that stood at the crest of this protest poetry and fiction, capturing the attention and acclaim of the larger Arab world as well as that of the Israelis.

In interviews filmed shortly before his death, Habiby revealed that many of the scenes depicted in the novel closely reflect his own personal experiences. Along with these firsthand experiences are a host of literary works on which he drew. Habiby and others have identified sources as diverse as the **Maqamat** of medieval Arabic literature (also in *WLAIT 6: Middle Eastern Literatures and Their Times*), the fluent yet concise style of the Egyptian writer Taha Husayn, and the witty texts and commentaries of Marun Abbud. Non-Arabic influences include Voltaire's novel *Candide* (1759) and Czech writer Jaroslav Hašek's *Good Soldier Schweik* (1931), whose protagonist shares many personal traits with Saeed.

Writing in Arabic, not Hebrew, Habiby is said to have inserted a "consciousness" of the existence of a Palestinian or Arab Israeli strand of literature into the general Israeli literary culture. His novel

jarred the majority culture by confronting it with an incriminating version of its history, shattering "the idealized version" so many Israelis "had taken for granted" (Brenner, pp. 91, 96). Meanwhile, in Arabic letters, Saeed distinguished himself as "the epitome of the anti-hero, perhaps the most finely drawn in modern Arabic literature, complex to the point of inconsistency (and therefore very human)" (LeGassick, p. 220).

Reception. *The Secret Life of Saeed the Ill-fated Pessoptimist* was well-received by Arab and Jewish critics alike. Jewish critics lauded the irony, the compassion, and the humor. Habiby was celebrated as a first-rate artist, commendable above

---

A CONTROVERSIAL VICTORY

In 1992 Habiby's works won him the foremost Israeli literary honor—the Israeli Prize. (Two years earlier he had been awarded the State of Palestine Certificate of Merit and the Medal of Jerusalem for Culture, Literature, and Art by Yasir Arafat.) His acceptance of the Israeli award ignited heated controversy in the Arab world. Some intellectuals declared him a traitor to the Palestinian cause, protesting that he should have demanded the release of jailed Palestinian writers in Israel or refused the award (Brenner, p. 92). In a London daily (*al-Hayat*), 25 Arab scholars demanded he give it back. He retained it, but donated the accompanying money to the Red Crescent, the Arab equivalent of the International Red Cross.

---

all for his literary strategies, "so that the book is funny and irresistible and the 'message' gets in through the back door" (Sasson Somekh in Brenner, p. 93). In the late 1980s the novel was adapted into a one-man play for the Israeli stage, performed by Muhammad Bakri. Audience reactions showed a split reaction to the story that drives both the novel and the play. "No doubt," says Hava Novak, "we witness true and real events, and it does not help me that I know *the other truth* [the Jewish point of view]. . . . These facts do not ease the awakening sense of guilt" (Novak in Brenner, p. 96). Novak predicted correctly that some would walk away from the work full of resentment and protest, others deeply troubled. But many applauded it, comparing the Palestinian under Israeli rule to a Jew surviving by his wits in a gentile-dominated world. By fixing their gaze on universals, concludes one

Israeli scholar, they averted their eyes from the unmasking of and attack on the power relationship between the oppressive Jewish majority and the oppressed Arab minority in Israel (Hever, p. 164). The picture the novel draws of the past and present experience of the Palestinian Arabs in Israel is not a pretty one. "And the outlook, Habibi suggests, does not bode well," a prediction tragically borne out by recent history (LeGassick, p. 223).

—Trevor LeGassick

For More Information

Boulatta, Issa J. "Symbol and Reality in the Writings of Emile Habibi." *Islamic Culture: An English Quarterly* 62, nos. 2-3 (April-July 1988): 9-21.

Brenner, Rachel Feldhay. "'Hidden Transcripts' Made Public: Israeli Arab Fiction and Its Reception." *Critical Inquiry* 26, no. 1 (autumn 1999): 85-108.

Farsoun, Samah K., and Christina E. Zacharia. *Palestine and the Palestinians.* Boulder, Colo.: Westview, 1997.

Habiby, Emile. "The Odds and Ends Woman." Trans. Roger Allen and Christopher Tingley. In *An Anthology of Modern Palestinian Literature.* New York: Columbia University Press, 1992.

———. *The Secret Life of Saeed the Pessoptimist.* Trans. S. K. Jayyusi and T. LeGassick. New York: Interlink, 2002.

Hever, Hannan. "Emile Habiby: A Palestinian Writer in the Context of Israeli Culture." *Palestine-Israel Journal of Politics, Economics and Culture* 3, nos. 3/4 (summer/autumn 1996): 167-69.

Jayyusi, Salma Khadra. Introduction to *The Secret Life of Saeed the Pessoptimist,* by Emile Habiby. New York: Interlink, 2002.

La Guardia, Anton. *War without End: Israelis, Palestinians and the Struggle for a Promised Land.* New York: St. Martin's, 2001.

Laqueur, Walter. *A History of Zionism.* New York: Holt, Rinehart, and Winston, 1972.

LeGassick, Trevor. "The Luckless Palestinian." *The Middle East Journal* 34, no. 2 (spring 1980): 215-23.

McDonald, James G. *My Mission in Israel 1948-1951.* London: Gollancz, 1951.

Morris, Benny. *Righteous Victims: A History of Zionist-Arab Conflict, 1881-2001.* New York: Vintage, 2001.

Raviv, Dan, and Yossi Melman. *Every Spy a Prince: The Complete History of Israel's Intelligence Community.* Boston: Houghton Mifflin, 1990.

Sachar, Howard M. *A History of Israel from the Rise of Zionism to Our Time.* New York: Alfred A. Knopf, 2000.

Welles, Sumner. *We Need Not Fail.* Boston, Mass.: Houghton Mifflin, 1948.

"The Secret Shrine" *and* "The Frog Prayer"

by
Ömer Seyfettin

Ömer Seyfettin was born in Gönen (now in Turkey) in 1884. He was educated at the Ottoman Military Academy and served two separate terms of duty in the military. The first was in 1909, when he was part of the army that suppressed the *Irtica*, a rebellion by religious groups against the newly reinstated constitutional order. The second was at the start of the Balkan War, during which he spent approximately one year (1912-13) as a prisoner of war in Greece. In 1914 Seyfettin accepted a position teaching literature at a high school in Istanbul; he died of diabetes only a few years later in 1920 at the early age of 36. By this time, he had written a number of works, including a novel and more than a dozen short stories, although not all were published by the time of his death. When Seyfettin resigned his first military post in 1911, he devoted his time to writing. Along with Ziya Gökalp and Ali Canip Yöntem, Seyfettin began publishing "Young Pens" (*Genç Kalemler*), a journal that is generally credited with starting the movement toward a Turkish national literature. Authors who considered themselves members of this movement, which flourished between 1911 and 1923, wrote about topics significant to Muslim Turks and their national values. They tended to favor a simpler, more concise form of Turkish than their predecessors, with fewer Persian and Arabic words and grammatical constructions. These new authors were credited with fostering an awareness and appreciation of Turkish language and culture among Turkish citizens, a theme that is critical in several of Seyfettin's works. He became a transitional writer, combining Turkish themes with

THE LITERARY WORK

Two short stories, the first set in an Istanbul suburb and the second in a small town not far from Istanbul, both in the 1910s; published in Turkish (as "Gizli Mabet" and "Boş inançlar: kurbada duasy") in 1919 and 1920, in English in 1978.

SYNOPSIS

In both stories, one's preconceptions and prejudices result in strange and humorous misperceptions. In "The Secret Shrine," the misperceptions arise from a foreigner's prejudices about Turkey; in "The Frog Prayer," from a misplaced belief in a teacher's spell.

the realist short-story method of the West to create some of the first modern Turkish short stories. In "The Secret Shrine" and "The Frog Prayer," Seyfettin examines such issues as Turkey's attempts to westernize and modernize, and the appropriate role of religion in Turkish society.

Events in History at the Time the Short Stories Take Place

The Young Turks. In the summer of 1908, officers of the Ottoman Second and Third Armies revolted against the authoritarian rule of Sultan Abdülhamid, and demanded that the Constitution of 1876 be reinstated. Known as The Young

Turks, these revolutionaries were all members of a political group called the Committee of Union and Progress (CUP; Ittihat ve Terakki Cemiyeti). Formed in 1889 in France by Ottoman émigrés, the group opposed the sultan's despotic tendencies, which included the dismissal of parliament and the suspension of the Ottoman constitution. Although the CUP decided to allow the sultan to remain in power, it was clear that behind the scenes, the Young Turks exercised the true political power. In addition to the reinstatement of the constitution, elections were ordered, and a myriad of other reforms undertaken. These included the reform of the educational system and the elimination of censorship of the media. As Feroz Ahmad describes the change, "A society which had been closed to the outside was suddenly thrown open, at least in cities and towns. . . . The Young Turks experimented with virtually every sphere of life; hardly anything was left untouched. They not only changed the political system but they also attempted to refashion society by borrowing more freely from the West than ever before" (Ahmad, p. 31).

It was the issue of "borrowing" from the West in order to modernize that caused one of the biggest rifts not only within the CUP itself, but also in society at large. The question of westernization was a burning issue during the period after the revolution, as the Turkish people had come to what one scholar called "a crisis of culture," and even "a crisis of civilization" (Lewis, p. 234). The two general positions found in Turkish literature during the Young Turk period were the "Islamists and the Westernizers, with a wide range of compromise and confusion between them" (Lewis, p. 234). Basically, Islamists were those who felt that the future of the Ottoman Empire depended upon strengthening the place of religion in society. In addition to fundamentalist sects, there were also moderate Islamists who argued that the Islamic religion could benefit from some reform. What all Islamists had in common, however, was the view that there was nothing to be gained from looking to the West for direction in social, political, legal, and economic matters.

Opposing this view were those who favored using the West's achievements as a yardstick of Ottoman success. A moderate sect within this camp argued that only certain (i.e., technical) aspects of Western achievements be imported. Intransigents argued against this piecemeal copying of the West, calling it superficial, and proclaiming that European culture had to be adopted in its entirety. Several years after the revolution, Abdullah Cevdet, an eminent and politically influential Turkish intellectual, wrote that "there is no other civilization: Civilization means European civilization, and it must be imported with its roses and thorns" (Cevdet in Halman, p. 24).

Seyfettin deals with the issue of westernization in his writing. In a short story called "The First White Hair," Seyfettin sketches the outlines of Turkish nationalism as the solution to Turkey's crisis of culture. According to Seyfettin, Turks share a common language and heritage, in addition to a common religion; as such, they "have a distinct and separate personality in every branch of culture. They can progress when they discover this personality" (Seyfettin in Paksoy, p. 113). However, Seyfettin was not anti-westernization—in fact, he was part of a pro-westernization movement that included the sociologist Ziya Gökalp and the first president of the Turkish Republic, Kemal Atatürk. Like them, Seyfettin felt that European ideas of democracy, technology, and progress were salutary. However, he felt Turks should promote and appreciate their own culture instead of merely copying the West. In the story "Fon Sadristein's Wife," he pokes fun at a Turkish man who marries a German wife, and at the man's subsequent inability to become German. Similarly in "The Secret Shrine," he makes fun of Westerners who are attracted to the so-called Oriental elements of Turkish culture.

"The Secret Shrine" tackles the issue of westernization more directly; the story vehemently attacks the European perspective as personified by a young Frenchman from the Sorbonne who is visiting Turkey. The protagonist, a native Turk who is charged with showing this young student around, criticizes the naiveté of "these Westerners who don't venture beyond the limits of their 'fixed ideas'" (Seyfettin, "Secret Shrine," p. 45). When the French student is confronted with the error of his ridiculous assumptions regarding a Turkish "temple," he lashes out, saying that it is the Turks who are "blind" to their own culture. The Turkish protagonist's response concludes the story, and shows how little he values European insights into Turkish culture:

> But in no way did he say what this thing was that only he saw and we could not see. Indeed, it is known that Turks are very courteous in their judgments. The response came right to the tip of my tongue: 'If we're blind, then it's you who are mute!'. But I remained silent. I didn't utter a sound.
>
> ("Secret Shrine," p. 51)

SEYFETTIN'S DIARIES

Seyfettin kept a diary during his military service, which included a detailed account of his own observations during the *Irtica* of 1909. As a firsthand account of an educated and intelligent observer and participant, Seyfettin's journals are considered invaluable. Seyfettin recorded verbatim the speeches of various officials, such as the army's Commanding General and the Postmaster. He also preserved private conversations that occurred in such places as the local club and army headquarters. His journals describe what is going on in the streets, giving us a taste of public reaction at the time. The diaries furthermore provide the reader with a glimpse into a young officer's preparations, as Seyfettin is about to be deployed into battle:

> Dated April 3: Volunteers are arriving. The reserve Battalion is mobilizing. There is unprecedented activity. . . . I collected my books and papers and placed them in the big strongbox. I kept out a change of underwear and clothes for the suitcase . . . I am completely ready.
>
> (Seyfettin in Alangu, p. 139)

Seyfettin movingly describes his diary, and the important role it plays in his life:

> However, my poor notebook, I found and dragged you from under my books. You were idle for the past six months. Possibly, more important events will occur that I will commit to you. I entrust to your neutral white pages those thoughts of mine which I cannot confide to even the youngest and most progressive friends for fear of being "misunderstood." Hundreds of your pages are filled. I read you in order to prompt myself into action. As long as I live, you are going to be my companion.
>
> (Seyfettin in Alangu, p. 135)

The counterrevolution of 1909. Many religious extremists deeply resented the various reforms and secular policies of the Young Turks. In the fall of 1908, during the month of Ramadan (the Muslim month of fasting), conservative religious groups began staging public protests and demonstrations calling for closing bars and censoring other forms of public entertainment, and urging restrictions on women's freedom of movement consistent with Islamic principles. The *Irtica* ("Reaction") was instigated by members of the Unified Mohammedan Party, who included mainly students of the *madrasah* (theological school) and some rank and file officers. Ultimately they took some army officers hostage, and demanded a return to Islamic law, which they felt the constitution had usurped.

Within days, The CUP had assembled an "action army" (*Hareket Ordusu*) to counter the rebellion. Ottoman troops stationed in Macedonia, of which Seyfettin was a member, were called to Istanbul to quell the *Irtica* rebellion. They traveled by train to Istanbul, where they occupied the city and suppressed the rebellion. Many of the rebels were tried, convicted, and executed under the auspices of the two courts-martial that had been established.

Seyfettin's loyalties were clearly against the rebels, whom he calls "that disgusting crowd spilling blood in Istanbul" (Seyfettin in Alangu, p. 134). He saw the religious revolutionaries as usurpers of the rightful constitutional order.

Seyfettin's negative opinion of religious fervor recurs in his literary works. In Seyfettin's "The First White Hair," the protagonist, an engineer who was educated in France and then returns to Istanbul, reflects on Turkey's nationalism, and the relationship between religion and nationality. His conclusion is that Turkey has unfortunately neglected its nationality in favor of fostering the *umma*, or religious community. The Turks, therefore, have neglected the bond with their fellow countrymen, and have focused instead on their bond with other Muslims. The protagonist muses that this pan-Islamism, wherein Turks attempt to resemble Persians and Syrians, has proven detrimental to Turkish nationalism. In the story "Savior," Seyfettin explores the distinction between being a Muslim and being a Turk. One of the protagonists argues that Turkey will be "saved" not by the lone promised savior of the Muslims, but by various "real" individuals who will all act as guides to revolution and freedom from oppression.

In "The Frog Prayer," considered here, Seyfettin is also critical of religion, and its effects on progress. The short story is set at a school in a province outside of Istanbul. The religion teacher is portrayed as a staunch conservative who believes that "the duty of teachers is to insist on good old-fashioned training for the children," and that "life, not the school, is the place for social revolution" (Seyfettin, "The Frog Prayer," p. 53). During the course of the

---

"LOTI'S TURKEY"

Pierre Loti is the pseudonym of French novelist Julien Viaud. Born in 1850, Viaud wrote, among other things, accounts of his travels to such destinations as Constantinople, Tahiti, China, and British India. He chronicled his visit to the Holy Land in three different volumes, "Le Desert," "Jerusalem," and "La Galilée" (1895-96). Though Viaud was known for taking blatant liberties with the facts, and demonstrating a flagrant misunderstanding of the local inhabitants he met during his journey, his accounts—part autobiography, part romance, and part adventure story—were fascinating to his readers.

---

story, the teacher dupes the villagers, and cruelly allows them to believe that he performed a "miracle." He defends his actions and requests the protagonist's complicity by saying that "one shouldn't destroy the beliefs of simple people. They have no need for scientific truths" ("The Frog Prayer," p. 57).

The Short Stories in Focus

Plot summaries—"The Secret Shrine." "The Secret Shrine" is the wry tale of a young Frenchman's impressions and expectations during a visit to Turkey. Described by the protagonist as a "fanatical Orient-lover," the young man complains that the authentic, historical Turkey of Loti, the Turkey that he has come in search of, no longer exists. The Frenchman insists that

Turks, in some misguided impulse to imitate everything Western, have "Europeanized" their manners, their customs, their clothing, and even "their minds, their very way of thinking" ("Secret Shrine," p. 45).

During a stroll with the Frenchman, the protagonist is amused to note the former's reactions to their surroundings. What the Turks view as examples of "our poverty, our brutality, our ignorance," the Frenchman pronounces "Marvelous" ("Secret Shrine," p. 46). The young student from the Sorbonne is also utterly bewildered that the Turks feel no "esthetic stirring" in the presence of what the protagonist refers to as "those endless dunghills and owl-topped ruins" ("Secret Shrine," p. 46). Finally, he begs to be taken to an "unwesternized" Turkish home, and the protagonist agrees to take him along on a visit to his foster mother's house ("Secret Shrine," p. 46).

As it turns out, the foster mother is a widow, an "extremely devout, extremely stoical, and extremely conservative" old woman, who would probably not permit a Christian into her home ("Secret Shrine," p. 46). The Frenchman and his host must stop to buy the visitor a fez, and the European is instructed to pretend that he is a Circassian (a Sunni Muslim from the Caucasas) come to Istanbul before he goes to Mecca to make the pilgrimage. Rather than be insulted by the need for the ruse, the Frenchman actually enjoys this "bit of intrigue" ("Secret Shrine," p. 46). Once in the house, he is in raptures over everything from the latticework and the Persian carpets to the Ottoman books and the silver tray on which the meal is served. The two men bid each other good night before retiring to their assigned guest rooms for the rest of the evening.

In the morning, the two leave the widow's house and the protagonist suggests to the Frenchman that they go to a coffeehouse near a shrine to smoke a water pipe, "in order to submerge him all the more in the quaintness of the Orient" ("Secret Shrine," p. 48). When asking the Frenchman his opinion of the majestic shrine opposite their table, which is one of Istanbul's most famous monuments, the protagonist is quite surprised at the indifferent reaction he receives. Why, he wonders, should the student be so unaffected by this impressive Turkish site when just yesterday he had been "aflutter . . . like a madman, in the presence of fallen-down fountains and twisted walls" ("Secret Shrine," p. 48).

When pressed a bit, the Frenchman declares this monument to be "nothing," because he has seen Turkey's secret shrine, "a mystery unknown to any other European" the previous night in the widow's house ("Secret Shrine," p. 49). When the protagonist denies that any such thing exists, the Frenchman ignores him, and solemnly promises not to reveal this "secret shrine that you've been hiding from the Europeans for centuries" when he returns to Paris ("Secret Shrine," p. 49). The Frenchman proceeds to read from his notebook a description of what he witnessed, a melodramatic account of his entry into a room in which there were wondrous religious inscriptions and carvings hanging on the walls, gold embellished vessels filled with holy water, and iron-bound caskets containing the bodies of Turkey's venerable dead. He also describes in detail the complex patterns portrayed on the walls by the hanging of lengths of cord, and dangling from the cords, what he presumes to be relics of the deceased. The Frenchman dares to taste the holy water, which he assumes is from Mecca or Medina, and feels "an incomprehensible exhilaration," and he departs "with the excitement of a blasphemer, a deceiver, an infidel who has penetrated a forbidden shrine" ("Secret Shrine," p. 50).

Upon hearing this description of the secret shrine, the Turkish protagonist begins to roar with laughter. He informs the Frenchman that the room he happened into was not a shrine, but his foster mother's storeroom. Still laughing, he tells the French student that the inscriptions hanging on the walls are samples of his foster father's calligraphy, which the widow keeps for sentimental reasons. The vessels of holy water are jugs intended to catch rain-water, because the roof over the storeroom leaks. The caskets are clothing chests, boxes designed to hold clothing that the Turkish people use instead of dressers with drawers and mirrors. And the fascinating geometric patterns and relics hanging from them are simply clotheslines used to dry the laundry when it rains. The protagonist muses that the Frenchman has made mistaken assumptions similar to those of Pierre Loti,

> his famous compatriot who thought the *mashallah* inscriptions over our houses were the billboards of a national insurance company, and that the amulet slippers that swing on our eaves were shoes left stuck there by thieves fleeing from roof to roof.
>
> ("Secret Shrine," p. 51)

Even when confronted with the truth, and the ridiculous nature of his assumptions, the European clings to his assertion that though it was only a storeroom, he was able to experience "an incomprehensible, such an impalpable, such a religious quality" therein ("Secret Shrine," p. 51). In fact, the Frenchman goes so far as to say that he is sensitive enough to appreciate this quality, while the Turks themselves are "blind" to it. The story ends with the protagonist, out of courtesy, biting back his sharp reply that if it is the Turks who are blind, then it is the European who is mute.

"The Frog Prayer." The events in this tale take place at a secondary school in one of the provinces outside Istanbul. The protagonist is one of the teachers, and the story begins as the teachers decide, at the invitation of the town doctor, to attend a festive party at the Bektashi dervish lodge. The promised attractions include "roast lamb, music, and wine," and with a bit of reluctance, the teachers all decide to attend ("Frog Prayer," p. 54). The religion teacher, Bahir Hoja, only agrees on the condition that he can bring his water pipe, which he smokes at least ten times a day.

At the lodge, on a Friday, the men are having a grand time, listening to music in a place that "was like a vision of paradise still fresh from some blissful bygone days," and that overlooked a large pool "sleeping in emerald shadows" ("Frog Prayer," p. 54). As the music starts to play, and the wine is brought around, all the teachers are laughing and enjoying themselves. But their enjoyment is hampered by the "incessant, hellish uproar" caused by about a million frogs "screaming at the top of their voices" ("Frog Prayer," p. 55). The buzzing becomes unbearable, and prevents the company of friends from hearing themselves talk. One after the other, the doctor and the various teachers attempt to stop the noise by throwing stones, dirt, even flaming newspapers at the frogs, in order to scare them away. The staff at the lodge warns them that "no matter what you do, you won't be able to silence them" ("Frog Prayer," p. 55).

Just as the party has decided to give up and leave the lodge, the religion teacher, Bahir Hoja, announces that he has a solution: "If I want, I'll silence them in a second . . . I'll cast a spell, they'll be quiet instantly" ("Frog Prayer," p. 55). The doctor expresses doubts, and Hoja begins "swinging his fist with zeal" and "swearing" at his friends' skepticism. He vows that if the frogs do not quiet down as a result of his spell, everyone can spit in his face. Hoja proceeds to go to the edge of the pond, turn his back to the company, and blow on the surface of the water. Within a minute, "the frogs suddenly became quiet. Not even a peep came from the pond. We were amazed" ("Frog Prayer," p. 55).

About half an hour later, the frogs begin their noisemaking again, but Bahir Hoja quiets them once more with his spell. This continues throughout the evening. Curiously whenever Bahir Hoja goes to the pond to cast his spell, he never leaves his water pipe behind at the table, claiming that his colleagues are drunk so they might break it.

Everyone is amazed by the teacher's feat. The fiddler, the local officials, the staff at the lodge, all seem astonished at this accomplished spell-casting. Apparently the doctor is the only one present who does not believe it, "but he didn't have the nerve to deny the result that he saw with his own eyes" ("Frog Prayer," p. 56).

All week the protagonist is distracted and confounded by what he witnessed at the lake. After giving the matter a lot of thought, he decides to lay "a clever, scientific trap" for the religion teacher. He engages him in a discussion on spiritual matters, in which Bahir Hoja is very interested. During the course of their exchange, he gets Hoja to admit that animals have no souls and "live outside the spiritual dimension of creation" ("Frog Prayer," pp. 56-57). The protagonist points out that this cannot be so if Hoja cast a spell on the frogs. Hoja knits his brows, and the protagonist gloats that he has "pushed him into a corner. . . . He was either going to admit his ignorance or tell the truth" ("Frog Prayer," p. 57). Hoja finally admits that he did not cast a spell, but rather dangled the tube of his water pipe at the lake's edge. This quieted the frogs because they thought the tube was a snake, and escaped to the bottom of the pond.

Hoja swears the protagonist to secrecy, saying that the "beliefs of simple people" shouldn't be destroyed ("Frog Prayer," p. 57). Since the ability to keep secrets is a feature of provincial life, the protagonist remains silent, and the rest of the town is allowed to continue believing that Bahir Hoja cast a spell. The story's concluding paragraph tells of the consequences of this hoax, which have overpowered even the rational skeptic represented by the doctor.

> The whole town heard about the hoja's miracle. The Bektashis themselves had witnessed it, and even the doctor's doubts gradually melted away. Whenever the subject of the miracle arose, the poor doctor would always shrug his shoulders and say, 'How many unknown things there are in this world, and our knowledge isn't equal to one-billionth of them!' And he no longer laughed his usual jolly laugh.
>
> ("Frog Prayer," p. 57)

Orientalism. In his highly influential work *Orientalism*, Edward W. Said explores the theoretical construct of "Orientalism," an intellectual tradition and ideal created and propagated by Europeans. Said uses Michael Foucault's notion of discourse to explore the ways in which "European culture was able to manage—and even produce—the Orient politically, sociologically, militarily, ideologically, scientifically, and imaginatively during the post-Enlightenment period" (Said, p. 3). According to Said, it is impossible to understand or view the Orient without referring to, or being influenced by, this theoretical construct that has less to do with actual fact than with the expectations, beliefs, and prejudices of Europeans regarding what the Orient means to them. The Orient has always been viewed by the West as mysterious and exotic, but ultimately, inferior.

Seyfettin touched upon similar themes approximately half a century prior to the publication of Said's analysis. In "The Secret Shrine," the European protagonist is chagrined not to find the Turkey that Pierre Loti described in his evocative essays. In fact, he refers to "Loti's Turkey" several times during the story and is constantly measuring what he sees against the vivid descriptions in Loti's accounts of his travels. The protagonist remarks that this naïve European continually looks at examples of wretched poverty and decay with glee! The Frenchman hardly seems to realize that these conditions might not be the most beneficial for the Turks themselves to be living under; all that matters is that his experience of Turkey mesh with his preconceived notions or "fixed ideas" ("Secret Shrine," p. 45). Consider the following passage from the introduction of Said's book, which echoes many of Seyfettin's ideas as expressed in "The Secret Shrine":

> On a visit to Beirut during the terrible civil war of 1975-1976, a French journalist wrote regretfully of the gutted downtown area that "it had once seemed to belong to . . . the Orient of Chateaubriand and Nerval." He was right about the place, of course, especially so far as a European was concerned. The Orient was almost a European invention, and had been since antiquity a place of romance, exotic beings, haunting memories and landscapes, remarkable experiences. Now it was disappearing; in a sense it had happened, its time was over. Perhaps it seemed irrelevant that Orientals themselves had something at stake in the process . . . that now it was they who were suffering; the main thing for the European visitor was a European representation of the Orient and its contemporary

THE OTTOMAN EMPIRE

The first Turks were tribally organized seminomadic peoples who began to settle in Anatolia in the mid-eleventh century and won a great victory over the Byzantine army shortly thereafter, at the Battle of Manzikert in 1071. The Turkish migration and settlement of Anatolia continued at the expense of the Byzantine Empire, as one by one, the Greek and Armenian states of Byzantium were defeated and conquered by the Turks. In 1301 Osman I declared himself Sultan of the Turks, and with Mehmed II's capture of Constantinople in 1453, the Ottoman Empire was established. By the sixteenth century, the conquests of Sultan Selim (1467-1520) had resulted in an empire that included all of Anatolia and the Balkans, as well as portions of northeastern Africa and southwestern Asia. In addition to ruling over such notable port cities as Cairo, the Ottoman Empire now controlled the holy cities of Mecca, Medina, and Jerusalem. The empire would endure for several centuries longer, until its defeat in World War I. In 1923 the sultanate was officially abolished and Turkey was declared a republic, after much internal strife and a national struggle led by General Mustafa Kemal, also known as Atatürk, who became the Republic's first president. Seyfettin, unfortunately, did not live to see the creation of a Turkish nation-state and the Turkish Grand National Assembly, an outcome that his literary efforts are said to have influenced and helped effect.

fate, both of which had a privileged communal significance for the journalist and his French readers.

(Said, p. 1)

Ottomanism and education. In his short story "The Frog Prayer," Seyfettin is relentlessly critical of particular aspects of the educational system. For example, the protagonist tells us that the principals, administrators, teachers, and students "had come from the most distant corners of that vast empire of ours," individuals of "every race and every type, not Turkicized in anything other than their language" ("Frog Prayer," p. 52). The French teacher is Jewish, and does not even understand the language well. During evening study hall he writes down questions the students ask him in Latin in his notebook, and he asks the protagonist their meaning the next day. One evening the children ask about the meaning of "divine rapture," and the confused instructor is at a complete loss as to why they were asking about "the divine coffeepot" ("Frog Prayer," p. 53).

These humorous observations constitute a critique of the notion of "Ottomanism" as manifest in the context of education. The Ottoman Empire existed for half a millennium, until its defeat in World War I. Historically, the empire, which was composed of various ethnic and religious groups, was organized into villages shared by these diverse groups. Each group, however, had its own internal administrative structure based on both religion and ethnicity; so the Orthodox Greeks, for example, remained distinct from the Jews of the empire. More often than not, rights and privileges were not conferred equally: there was a great deal of favoritism towards Muslims and Turks, which resulted in the granting of special prerogatives.

With the revolution of 1908, the notion of Ottomanism was significantly revised. Now every individual living in the Ottoman Empire, regardless of nationality or religion, was to be considered a full and equal citizen. Seyfettin, the Turkish nationalist, was fiercely critical of this notion, calling it an "illusion, a fantasy":

> It was not possible to constitute a "composite" nationality from the sum total of individuals who have separate religions, languages, moralities, histories, cultures and grounds for pride. Was "Ottomanism" in actuality anything more than the name of our government. . . . Those of us who speak Turkish, were a nation with a history of five thousand years.
>
> (Seyfettin in Paksoy, p. 115)

The Young Turks, among their many other reforms, undertook an improvement of the cumbersome Ottoman educational system. One of the most far-reaching reforms was that schools would now be allowed to open their doors to women. The reformers looked to Europe for models, and the result was the creation of various teachers' training colleges and specialized institutes, with the University of Istanbul theoretically at the apex.

Seyfettin is also critical of the school's structure and personnel in "The Frog Prayer." The protagonist criticizes the principal as an incompetent "law and order fanatic," who never socializes with anyone he feels is beneath him ("Frog Prayer," p. 53). While the principal is preoccupied with acting "like a Greek god," he fails to adequately oversee the business of running a school whose teachers consist of "twenty different men—old, young, intelligent, stupid, talkative, quiet—formed by four or five schools whose programs and aims were all contrary to each other" ("Frog Prayer," pp. 52-53). Seyfettin, well-known for his satire and wit, wryly observes that despite all this, a "convivial harmony" existed among the staff, as "religious fanatics, reactionaries, liberals, and finally those with no profession or special character lived together as brothers" ("Frog Prayer," p. 52).

Sources and literary context. Seyfettin is considered the founder of the short-story tradition in Turkish literature, as well as one of its best exemplars. By the 1960s, with the publication of the 144th edition of his books, Ömer Seyfettin became the most widely read author in Turkey. Like other members of the National Literature Movement, Seyfettin treated themes that include an examination of national values and Turkey's domestic and political problems.

The Nationalist Literature Movement, or *milli edebiyat*, is said to have begun with the publication of the journal *Young Pens*, which was started by Ömer Seyfettin, Ali Canip Yöntem, and sociologist Ziya Gölkap, who is sometimes referred to as "the theoretician of Turkish Nationalism" (Iz in Seyfettin, p. 20). Authors who represented the short story and novel in this movement include Yakup Kadri Karaosmanoglu and Halide Edip Adivar. Poetry was represented by various authors with very different approaches and perspectives, including that of Mehmet Akif Aksoy, the lyricist of the Turkish national anthem, who wrote realistically about national social issues. Seyfettin, like other nationalist authors, wrote in a much more colloquial style than most of his

The Balkan War, a conflict in which Seyfettin participated.

predecessors, often set his stories in locations other than Istanbul, and favored realism rather than romanticism in his works. He is widely known as a writer of short stories aimed at ordinary people, and for the wit and humor he brought to the genre. How effective his approach was can be seen from the fact that his "style of writing had a tremendous influence on the younger generation" (Prusek, p. 169).

Seyfettin participated in a tumultuous period in Turkey's history, having taken part both in the Balkan War and the suppression of the *Irtica* of 1909. The writer kept a journal throughout his years of service in the military and apparently drew on this journal when writing some of his short stories. Along with personal experience, events and ideas of his era greatly influenced his tales. In sum, says one scholar, they were "inspired by [Seyfettin's] experiences as an officer in the Balkans, by the conflicting ideologies of his time, and by episodes of Turkish history" (Iz in Seyfettin, p. 21).

Seyfettin was an original writer who nonetheless remained attached to certain cultural traditions, especially Turkish folklore. Seyfettin recorded that during an illness, Ali Canip Yöntem's mother told him folktales, themes from which he used in his stories (Tuncer, p. 300). In addition, Seyfettin was well versed in classics of the West and was strongly influenced by the French realists Guy de Maupassant and Emile Zola, citing that their works "help people to develop their skills for thinking and seeing reality" (Seyfettin in Kurdakul, p. 269; trans. S. O. Şenarslan). Indeed Seyfettin's stories have been compared to Maupassant's, as well as to Anton Chekov's.

Reception. Seyfettin's short and intense writing career has had a large impact in his native country. "The Secret Shrine" and "The Frog Prayer" were both published in newspapers during Seyfettin's lifetime. "The Secret Shrine" was republished in a collection by the same name in 1926, and beginning in 1935, Ali Canip Yöntem published a complete collection of his friend's works.

Although now considered classics, at the time of their release, Seyfettin's stories sharply challenged the traditional literary establishment. The critic Halit Ziya Uşakligil implied that Seyfettin was not a true artist, when he argued that "lacking innate ability, Seyfettin used everyday language in a satirical way to achieve success" (Uşakligil in Boratav p. 333). Quoted by Pertev Boratav in 1942, this last literary scholar countered with praise for Seyfettin's pioneering spirit, asserting that "what makes him great is his courage in breaking taboos" (Boratav, p. 334).

Ömer Seyfettin's stories are still widely beloved in Turkey, where "The Secret Shrine" has been republished in countless anthologies. Perhaps the enduring popularity of this story indicates that Turks are still dealing with issues of Orientalism even as they struggle to enter into the European Union. "The Frog Prayer" has received less attention in Turkey, related no doubt to the fact that Seyfettin's (and Atatürk's) strong anti-clerical stance has been continuously challenged here, now seeming to many to be extreme.

However, Seyfettin's intelligent humor and his promotion of clear, graceful Turkish, which he called "natural language—national language," has been cited over and over by critics as an enduring gift to the Turkish people (Seyfettin in Kudret, p. 22; trans. S. O. Şenarslan).

—Despina Korovessis

For More Information

Ahmad, Feroz. *The Making of Modern Turkey.* New York: Routledge, 1993.

Alangu, Tahir. *Ömer Seyfettin: ülkücü bir yazarin romani.* Trans. H. B. Paksoy. Istanbul: May Yayinlari, 1968.

Boratav, Pertev. "Folklor ve edebiyat." Istanbul: Adam Yayincilik, 1982.

Halman, Talat Sait, ed. *Contemporary Turkish Literature: Fiction and Poetry.* New Jersey: Associated University Presses, 1982.

Kudret, Cevdet. *Türk edebiyatinda hikaye ve roman, 1859-1959.* Ankara: Bilgi Yayinevi, 1967.

Kurdakul, Şükran. *Çaddaş Türk edebiyati: meşrutiyet dönemi.* Istanbul: May Yayinlari, 1976.

Lewis, Bernard. *The Emergence of Modern Turkey.* Oxford: Oxford University Press, 2002.

Paksoy, H. B. "Koprulu/Veles (Yugoslavia) Ottoman Garrison's Response to the 1909 Recidivist Uprising in Istanbul." *Turkistan Newsletter.* Vol. 97-1: 18a, 2 July 1997, 3-16.

Průšek, Jaroslav, ed. *Dictionary of Oriental Literatures.* Vol. 3. Ed. Jiří Bečka. New York: Basic Books, 1974.

Said, Edward W. *Orientalism.* New York: Random House, 1979.

Seyfettin, Ömer. "The Secret Shrine" and "The Frog Prayer." In *An Anthology of Modern Turkish Short Stories.* Ed. Fair Iz. Chicago: Bibliotheca Islamica, 1978.

Tuncer, Hüseyin. *Meşrutiyet devri Türk edebiyati.* Izmir: Akademi Yayinevi, 1994.

Zurcher, Erik J. *Turkey: A Modern History.* London: I. B. Tauris, 1993.

See Under: Love

by

David Grossman

David Grossman, one of contemporary Israel's leading writers, was born in Jerusalem in 1954. His family immigrated to Palestine from Poland in the 1930s, before the Second World War, so he is neither a Holocaust survivor nor a child of survivors. Grossman studied philosophy and theater at the Hebrew University in Jerusalem and embarked on a writing career. Beginning in the early 1980s, he published six novels, a short-story collection, two nonfiction books, and numerous children's books. His articles and editorials on current events in Israel regularly appear in the Hebrew press. His *ha-Zeman ha-tsahov* (1987; *The Yellow Wind*, 1988), a nonfiction book on Israeli-Palestinian relations, encouraged Israel to confront the moral cost of its occupation of the West Bank and Gaza Strip, territories that it had conquered in the 1967 Six-Day War. His second novel, *See Under: Love* is an intensely creative treatment of the Holocaust and its aftermath. Some have criticized the degree of experimentation in the novel, given its grave subject matter. Nevertheless, the novel's deeply compassionate evocation of the lives of survivors and their children, combined with its bold innovations in language and form, make *See Under: Love* a central achievement of modern Hebrew literature.

Events in History at the Time of the Novel

Multiple, overlapping settings. *See Under: Love* is divided into four sections: "Momik," "Bruno,"

THE LITERARY WORK

A novel set primarily in Israel in the late 1950s and early 1980s, as well as in a Nazi death camp during World War II; published in Hebrew (as *Ayen erekh: ahavah*) in 1986, in English in 1989.

SYNOPSIS

An Israeli child of Holocaust survivors tries to understand and tame the "Nazi Beast" in the hopes of protecting his parents; 20 years later, he attempts a series of ambitious and imaginative literary responses to the Holocaust.

"Wasserman," and "The Complete Encyclopedia of Kazik's Life." With the exception of "Momik," which is set solely in 1959 Jerusalem, each section is set in numerous times and places: Israel in the early 1980s, a Nazi death camp, the port city of Danzig during World War II, and the depths of the ocean, among others. In the last two sections of the novel, characters from different times and places encounter one another. For instance, the narrator (and implied author) Shlomo Neuman, writing in 1980s Israel, interacts with his protagonist, Anshel Wasserman, during Wasserman's time in a Nazi death camp during World War II. A great portion of the last two sections consists of a story related by Wasserman, whose characters at times interact with figures from the camps and

David Grossman

even with Neuman himself. Thus, while Grossman's novel engages concrete historical events, the text's crossing of normally impermeable temporal and spatial boundaries distinguishes *See Under: Love* from the conventional historical novel. In contrast to most other contemporary Israeli novels, it proceeds with little direct reference to setting, focusing at the start on a community of Holocaust survivors who are almost completely detached from the larger Israeli society.

Surviving the Holocaust. With the rise to power of Adolf Hitler and the Nazi party in 1933, anti-Semitism worsened in German society. Throughout the 1930s the government introduced increasingly severe anti-Semitic policies and general persecution of the Jews mounted. During World War II, Nazi Germany instituted the Final Solution, a program of genocide targeted against the Jews of Europe. Investing massive resources and relying on the most efficient technology, the Nazis relocated Jews from all over Europe to concentration camps, where millions were gassed to death. The end of the war prevented the completion of the program, but not before 6 million Jews and thousands from other persecuted groups (homosexuals, Gypsies, etc.) had been murdered.

Many of the concentration camps were essentially death factories; in the extermination camps, Jews were efficiently unloaded from trains, briefly inspected, and then sent directly to the gas chambers. A very small percentage of the imprisoned Jews were kept alive to operate the death camps. Among other tasks, these prisoners were forced to remove corpses from the gas chambers and bring them to the crematoria. A comparatively small number of Jews survived the Holocaust in this way, witnessing and being forced to participate in its horrors day after day for months or years at a time. Others survived because they were selected for work duty as slave labor rather than for immediate death.

After the war, which wiped out their Jewish communities in Europe, survivors were faced with the challenge of integrating into new societies. In addition to coming to terms with their wartime experiences, whether they had lived in the camps or in hiding, survivors had to figure out how to resume "normal" lives. After employing the most extreme strategies of survival for years, after witnessing brutality of a sort and on a scale previously unimaginable, these Jews were now expected to function as members of civil society. Many survivors experienced post-traumatic symptoms, including chronic anxiety, recurring nightmares, and even guilt for having survived at all when so many of their relatives had perished. The children of survivors were marked by the burden of the trauma too, as they tried to comprehend their parents' experiences, experiences often cloaked in silence.

Israeli attitudes to the Holocaust. Over a quarter million Holocaust survivors immigrated to Israel during the early years of the state. Founded in 1948, only a few years after the end of World War II, and conceived of as a safe haven for persecuted Jews everywhere, the state of Israel has had a complicated relationship with the survivors of the Holocaust. To a certain extent, the Holocaust came to be viewed in early Israeli culture as the logical culmination of the widespread and constant anti-Semitism and persecution that marked the Jewish experience in the diaspora. This approach to the Holocaust reflected Zionism's longstanding rejection of Jewish life in the diaspora community, which, according to many Zionists, had been passive in the face of persecution during 2,000 years of exile.

The general rejection of the diasporic experience left the state ill-equipped to address and at times even acknowledge the horrors endured by the massive number of Holocaust survivors that it absorbed after the war. Instead, until the

Allied Supreme Commander Dwight D. Eisenhower and military officials view the German concentration camp at Gotha, Germany, after liberation.

early 1960s, the Israeli response to the Holocaust consisted largely of silence and (less markedly) of explicit disdain for the survivors, whom some saw as representative of the passive diasporic Jew. In sum, the survivors were expected to integrate into a society that repudiated their experiences and viewed those murdered by the Nazis as having gone "like sheep to the slaughter."

The 1961 trial of Nazi war criminal Adolph Eichmann sparked a shift in Israeli attitudes toward the Holocaust. For the first time in Israel, survivors' testimonies were made public, forcing the general population to confront these experiences. Subsequent wars in Israel sensitized the citizenry to their collective vulnerability. Especially shocking was the 1973 Yom Kippur War, when Israel was attacked on the Jewish Day of Atonement and suffered massive casualties before overwhelming the Egyptian and Syrian armies. These experiences, along with factors such as the gradual waning of Zionist ideology and its anti-diaspora attitudes, led to a new empathy with Holocaust victims and survivors. Among the other factors was the maturation of the post-Holocaust generation, including children who sought to understand their parents' experience as much as possible.

The life and death of Bruno Schulz. The real-life Polish Jewish writer Bruno Schulz (1892-1942), to whom the chapter "Bruno" in Grossman's novel refers, was born in Drohobycz (then a Polish town, today in the Ukraine). Trained in lithography and drawing, Schulz taught for a number of years in Drohobycz as an art teacher. He started writing in his thirties and authored a small body of highly regarded, deeply imaginative, often phantasmagoric fiction, published in English as *The Street of Crocodiles* (1995) and *Sanatorium Under the Sign of the Hourglass* (1977). An unfinished novel, *The Messiah*, in which Schulz had invested some four years, disappeared during the war, and Schulz himself was murdered. Years later he would find a champion in Grossman, whose own enthusiasm sparked increased interest in Schulz's works in Israel and abroad.

Schulz's writing was marked by unbridled fantasy and the search for an innovative, truly personal language. In his *The Street of Crocodiles,* the narrator's reflections on a giant city map, which his father once owned, blossom into an intricate tour of a section of the city known as the Street of Crocodiles. The remarkable detail in the narrator's conjectural ruminations on the area creates an unmistakable tension with the colorlessness of the place itself. Ultimately the reader's hypothetical

THE PRECURSOR TO EARLY ISRAELI ATTITUDES TOWARD SURVIVORS—ZIONISM AND THE DIASPORA

Modern Zionism, the movement that set in motion the creation of a Jewish nation-state in the historic land of Israel, emerged in Europe during the last decades of the 1800s, a half century before the Holocaust of World War II. European anti-Semitism was already widespread at the time; indeed it functioned as one of the primary factors in the early Zionist leadership's rejection of Jewish life in the diaspora. Spearheading this rejection was Theodor Herzl, a Viennese Jewish journalist and the father of modern Zionism. While Herzl and other Zionist figures denounced European anti-Semitism, they also internalized a host of anti-Semitic Jewish stereotypes, reflected in their criticism of the standard roles that the Jew had taken on in European society (e.g., moneylender, member of the bourgeoisie) and of the characteristics or personality attributed to the Jew. The European intelligentsia during this era tended to link biology to cultural characteristics, and the European Jewish intelligentsia was no exception. Common among Zionist thinkers was a subtle self-hatred that viewed the Jew as weak, passive, and even diseased. This condition, argued the Zionists, could be remedied by the creation of a Jewish society in Palestine. Jews would be forced to fill various positions in such a society; in particular, they would benefit from a return to physical labor. The Zionist settlements in Palestine before 1948 (known collectively as the *Yishuv*) to a large extent realized this program of creating an alternative Jewish society. Many of the Zionist settlers rejected the diaspora Jews (Jews living outside Palestine) in favor of the new native "Hebrews" (Jews born in Palestine), who were celebrated as active, strong, and healthy. Throughout the 1920s and 1930s, Zionist rejection of the diaspora grew more pronounced, as the *Yishuv* came to view the nearly 2,000-year-long Jewish exile since the destruction of the Second Temple in 70 C.E. as an essentially monolithic experience of persecution and national degeneration.

experience of the Street of Crocodiles, an experience entirely mediated by the narrator, seems more authentic than the actual place and recalls another representation of the Street of Crocodiles—the elaborate map of the city from the story's opening. Here, as in many other stories by Schulz, fantasy and representation—the products of an unrestrained play of language—eventually overwhelm and displace reality.

Bruno Schulz was shot and killed by a Nazi officer in the ghetto of Drohobycz, Poland, in November 1942. A story surrounding his death, partially reproduced in *See Under: Love,* claims that Schulz was protected during the war by a German officer and that he was killed by this officer's rival. When Schulz's protector later encountered this rival (who had a similar relationship with a different Jewish man), the rival declared, "I killed your Jew"; in response Schulz's protector declared, "O.K., now I will kill your Jew."

Grossman has expressed deep admiration for Schulz's writing, and in fact claims that the "Bruno" section of *See Under: Love* is the center of the novel and his attempt to redeem Schulz from the unspeakable logic tied to his death. As he relates in an interview, Grossman felt shocked when he first heard the particulars of Schulz's death; he was stunned by the ability of language to formulate so coldly the type of "My Jew/Your Jew" equivalency cited below (Grossman in Kashtan, p. 17). In essence, observes one critic, Grossman's novel asks a question of universal significance:

Can art . . . create an explosive new, revelatory, "messianic" language, as the historical Bruno Schulz dreamed, or is all human speech doomed to obscenity once it has made it possible for one Nazi officer to say in German to another in the Drohobych ghetto, "You killed my Jew, now I'm going to kill your Jew"?

(Alter, p. 100)

The Novel in Focus

Plot summary. *See Under: Love* is divided into four sections, loosely tied together by the shifting figure of Shlomo Efraim Neuman (nicknamed Momik and Shleimeleh), who appears as the young protagonist of the first section and as the older author/narrator/editor protagonist of the remaining sections.

The first section, "Momik," takes place in 1959 and begins with the delivery of Anshel Wasserman, Momik's grandfather (actually great-uncle) who was presumed killed in Auschwitz, from an Israeli insane asylum to the boy's Jerusalem neighborhood. Before Anshel's arrival, Momik had known of him only through the adventure stories about the Children of the Heart that Anshel wrote before the war. Momik safeguards a fragment of one of Anshel's stories, a sacred text and priceless treasure Momik naively views as the source of all literature. Unfortunately the real Anshel now only mutters incoherently parts of what Momik believes to be another story. The nine-and-a-half-year-old Momik is precocious but isolated, virtually the only child in an insular community of Holocaust survivors, who refuse to explain to the curious boy the nature of their experiences in what is simply referred to as the "Over There." Thirsting for an understanding of the past world of the adults in his community, Momik latches on to the figurative phrase "the Nazi Beast," which he is told "could come out of any kind of animal if it got the right care and nourishment" (Grossman, *See: Under Love,* p. 13). Interpreting these words literally, Momik captures a variety of animals; in the family cellar, he proceeds to mistreat them in various ways in an attempt to draw out the Nazi Beast in order to tame it. Momik's repeated failures drive him to ever more extreme methods, until he concludes that what the Nazi Beast likes most is Jews. He therefore brings Anshel, along with the other deranged survivors from the neighborhood, down into the cellar. Momik's project ends in failure: unable to lure the Nazi Beast out of its hiding place, Momik finds himself consumed by hatred and contempt for the very Jews he sought to save. During the climax in the cellar, the Israeli boy, naïvely confident in the possibility of undoing the Holocaust, stops identifying with the survivors and instead assumes, however briefly, the role of a full-fledged German anti-Semite:

> Grandfather Anshel started telling his story from the beginning again, and Momik squeezed his head because he didn't think he could stand it anymore, he wanted to vomit everything, everything he'd eaten for lunch and everything he'd learned about lately, including himself, and now these stinky Jews here too, the kind the goyim called Jude, before he thought that was just an insult, but now he saw it suited them perfectly, and he whispered, Jude, and felt a warm thrill in his stomach and felt his muscles filling out all over, and he said it again out loud, Jude, and it made him feel strong, and he shook himself and stood over Grandfather Wasserman, sneering, Shut up already, enough already. . . .
> (*See Under: Love,* pp. 84-85)

The novel's second and most experimental section, "Bruno," takes places 20 years later, when the now grown-up Shlomo Neuman (alias Momik) has become a writer, like his grandfather Anshel before him. The phantasmagoric section revolves around Neuman's effort to re-imagine the death of a real-life Polish-Jewish writer, Bruno Schulz. Neuman imagines that, instead of being shot by a Nazi officer, Schulz escapes into the sea, where he gradually transforms into a salmon. This section alternates between the story of Schulz's transformation, Neuman's effort to write about the Holocaust in general, and the sea's own encounter with Schulz, told from the sea's feminine perspective. The section ends with a surreal encounter between Bruno Schulz and Neuman in Schulz's lost novel *The Messiah,* set during the emergence of the Messianic era, when the world would be free from war and want. Featuring unbridled, individual creative forces, the surreal scene ultimately proves too chaotic to be tenable. As Bruno Schulz disappears, Neuman asks him about the story his grandfather "Anshel Wasserman told the German called Neigel" (*See Under: Love,* p. 181). Schulz encourages Neuman to retell the story, to remember it, although, paradoxically, Neuman has never heard it before.

The "Wasserman" section is Neuman's magical realist retelling of the experiences of his grandfather, Anshel Wasserman, in a Nazi death camp. Unable to be killed by any means—gas does nothing to him, a gunshot merely buzzes through his skull—Wasserman is brought to the camp commander, Herr Neigel. The German officer eventually discovers Wasserman to be the author of the young people's adventure stories, Children of the Heart, which he adored as a boy (readers have encountered a fragment of these stories in the novel's first section). The two men strike a deal, inverting the frame-story of Shahrazad from **The Arabian Nights** (also in *WLAIT 6: Middle Eastern Literatures and Their*

Times). In the original *The Arabian Nights*, Shahrazad tells a story each night to postpone being killed by the king; in *See Under Love*, the indestructible Wasserman becomes a storyteller for the opposite reason. He will tell Neigel part of a new Children of the Heart adventure story each night, and in exchange Neigel will try to kill the Jew. Wasserman watched as his only daughter was murdered and now his strongest desire is to die himself.

Wasserman uses his storytelling as an opportunity to "infect" the Nazi with some humanity. The storyteller reintroduces the original Children of the Heart as aging adults, now accompanied by the band of deranged but (thanks to Wasserman's inventiveness) newly heroic survivors from Momik's neighborhood. Eventually a baby, Kazik, is discovered among them; he suffers from a strange condition that will cause him to live his full life in only 24 hours. Neigel, who becomes deeply attached to the characters, particularly the baby, protests vehemently, but Wasserman refuses to change the story, which spills over into the fourth section.

"The Complete Encyclopedia of Kazik's Life" consists of a series of entries, arranged alphabetically (according to the Hebrew alphabet), about the 24-hour-long life of the baby, who is not actually a baby for more than a few hours. The novel's title, *See Under: Love*, comes from a reference in this fourth and final section. Throughout the encyclopedia, the narrative boundaries separating Neuman (the editor) from Wasserman (the storyteller) and Wasserman from the Children of the Heart characters are regularly and boldly crossed. In the entry entitled "Kazik, the Death of," contact between Wasserman and his fictional creations, commented on by Neuman, the editor, creates a particularly potent effect:

> He [Kazik] could no longer bear his life. He asked Otto to help him see the world in which he had lived. The untasted life beyond the fence. At a nod from Otto, Harotian tore an opening in the cage bars. Instead of the zoo, the opening revealed a view of Neigel's camp. [*Editorial comment: no wonder. The camp had always been waiting there.*] Kazik saw the high, gloomy watchtowers and the electrified barbed-wire fences, and the train station which leads to nowhere but to death. And he smelled the smell of human flesh burned by human beings, heard the screaming and snorting of a prisoner hanged all night long by his feet, and the tortured groans of one Obersturmbannführer Neigel, who was imprisoned with him. Wasserman told him—his voice utterly monotonous—how in

his first days at work cremating bodies in the camp, his overseers had found that women burn best, especially fat women, so they instructed the gravediggers to put fat women at the bottom of the pile. This saves a lot of fuel, Wasserman explained. Kazik's eyes grew wide. A tear burst through so fiercely that it made his eye bleed.
> (*See Under: Love*, p. 428)

In addition to the numerous episodes from Kazik's life and the Children of the Heart's new adventure, the reader also encounters the resolution of the Wasserman-Neigel/Jewish inmate-Nazi camp commander story. The Nazi becomes deeply invested in the creation of the narrative, through which he encounters his own humanity. This recognition seems irreconcilable with the massive destruction for which he is responsible. In response, Neigel commits suicide.

Reclaiming language. While on the most general level *See Under: Love* is about the Holocaust, the novel repeatedly focuses on texts and storytelling as well. It sustains a central storytelling motif, progressing from the fragment of Anshel's early Children of the Heart serial treasured by young Momik, to Bruno Schulz's lost and reimagined novel *The Messiah*, to Neuman's agonized efforts to write about the Holocaust in a mythical "White Room," to a children's encyclopedia of the Holocaust that Neuman hopes to create, to Wasserman's story told for and with Neigel, and finally to the encyclopedia of Kazik's life. Indeed, direct representations of the camps and of the historical period as a whole are relatively scant throughout the novel, and at times seem to appear as background for the more central task of storytelling and writing. In turn, this motif is tied to the larger theme of creation; together they constitute the central thrust of *See Under: Love*'s imaginative and affirming response to the Holocaust.

In the "Bruno" section of the novel, Neuman describes his first encounter with Bruno Schulz's writing:

> It was the first time I ever began to reread a book as soon as I finished it. And I've read it a good many times since. For months it was the only book I needed. It was the Book for me in the sense Bruno had yearned for *that great tome, sighing, a stormy Bible, its pages fluttering in the wind like an overblown rose.*
> (*See Under: Love*, p. 99)

Neuman goes on to explain that he began transcribing sections of Schulz's writing, much like he had done with Grandfather Anshel's writings 20 years earlier. Here in the narrative Neuman reveals that he began, almost involuntarily, writing like Schulz at the moment he came to realize (or imagine) that Schulz had "escaped." In other words, Schulz's transformation into a salmon coincides with Neuman's sudden ability to write like Bruno Schulz, to channel the dead writer's creative voice.

In a 1986 interview David Grossman described his impetus for writing the "Bruno" section and later the novel as a whole:

> I decided, yes, childishly, I will write a book that will avenge his death, that will pull him out of his biography . . . a book that will redeem Schulz. I wanted to create a book that would be alive, bursting with life, a book that would be like a person, a book that would tremble on the shelf.
>
> (Grossman in Kashtan, p. 17)

Grossman's comments reveal his belief—a belief that he admits is naïve—in the power of language. In real life Grossman came to write the "Bruno" section by endlessly rereading, like his protagonist Neuman, Schulz's work until their voices began to overlap. In this regard, Grossman's fascination with writing and the power of language turns the act of writing into a redemptive rearticulation of another writer's voice.

Along these lines, the second section, "Bruno," climaxes with a surreal encounter between Schulz and Neuman that can be viewed as a re-imagining of Schulz's lost manuscript, *The Messiah*. In the episode, based partly on Schulz's short story "The Age of Genius," Neuman becomes one of the story's characters—Shloma, son of Tobias. Schulz's town of Drohobycz is suddenly redeemed by the arrival of the Messianic era. The era is marked by unmitigated individual expression, the sort Schulz sought in his own writing and that Neuman (and Grossman) aspired to through Schulz. The realization of this aim proves too much, but as the scene spins out of control and as the section draws to an end, Schulz encourages Shloma (alias Neuman) to retell the story his grandfather Wasserman told the German Neigel. By doing so, Neuman marks the following third and fourth sections of the novel as rearticulations. Wasserman's creation, his story, will not only be his opportunity to vanquish the Nazi but will include the redemption of the group of deranged adults from Momik's childhood, who now reappear as central members of the Children of the Heart. In this light, Grossman's project is less about the impossible goal of undoing the Holocaust than of reclaiming writers, literature, and even language from a world in which things like "you killed my Jew" can be said.

Storytelling and creative responses to the Holocaust. Grossman's investigation of the limits of language's creative force is not the novel's only encounter with the concept of creation. By setting much of the second section in the depths of the ocean and by casting a feminized sea as a character in his kaleidoscopic plot, Grossman, while narrating in Schulz's voice, simultaneously describes his return to the primordial and mythic creative forces of the sea. "Bruno" is undeniably difficult to navigate, but reading it against early Canaanite and Mesopotamian creation myths and epics (e.g., The Mythic Cycle of Ba'l and 'Anat, the Mesopotamian Epic of Creation), which are subtly alluded to throughout the section, can provide a helpful framework. In these ancient mythic narratives, the sea is represented as the unruly, chaotic, original site of creation, where all life began. The story of Bruno's transformation into a salmon, which sounds almost comically arbitrary at first, likewise resonates with the theme of creation. In the Bruno section, the reader follows the school of salmon as it travels tirelessly around the globe. The salmon continue, at times suicidally, to return upstream to spawn, obeying an instinct to procreate their species. Set against the Holocaust, when Nazi Germany attempted to destroy the Jewish people, Grossman's focus on the salmon collective—whose ultimate goal is to recreate—suggests itself as a potent counter-narrative. In contrast to the Nazis' elaborate but single-minded devotion to the destruction of life, Grossman provides an alternate collective entirely devoted to creating life.

These subjects of language, life, and creation surface throughout the third and fourth sections of the novel. Like Bruno Schulz before him, Wasserman struggles with all the life-affirming possibilities of artistic creation in the third section. It is, however, in the encyclopedia of the final section that all these creative strands are intertwined, that love, artistry, and sex are brought together as a vital response to the destructive power of the Holocaust. An entry near the end of the encyclopedia, "Zeitren, Hannah," is named for one of the survivors from Momik's Jerusalem neighborhood, a woman whose madness finds her, in the first section of the novel, running stark naked through the streets at night, calling for God. Here in this final section she is an "Artist of love," a person redeemed, conquering murderous Nazis (who have killed her two children and husband) through her magical reproductive system (*See Under: Love*, p. 409). She and her second husband, Barkov, respond to death with life in the most literal way possible:

We gave birth to my son Dolek, and my Rochka, and then Nechemia, and Ben-Zion, and Abigail. And our last child. And Bartov lay with me again and again. And we scratched and bit each other till we bled. . . . And my womb was a giant funnel, cornucopia. Seas and mountains and forests and land. And children flowed out of Barkov and me and filled the streets, and the ghetto, and all of Warsaw. And our passion knew no bounds. And our children were murdered outside. And we made new children.

THE LAYERED QUALITY OF MODERN HEBREW

Though often referred to as "dead" until its "resurrection" as a spoken language around the turn of the twentieth century, the Hebrew language had in fact been in continuous, if limited, use throughout the time of the Jewish exile. Not only did Hebrew regularly surface in a variety of religious settings, but it was intermittently the medium of literary and secular texts, ranging from poetry to travel books. As a result, Hebrew is not merely an old language, but a deeply layered language, with the most pronounced layerings being biblical, Talmudic, and modern Hebrew, each of which has its distinct vocabulary and grammar. Modern Hebrew literature, predating by a few decades the revival of Hebrew as a spoken language, called on these earlier layers in bold and original ways in order to forge a language capable of describing the modern world. And though it is much less evident in the English translation, *See Under: Love* reveals itself to be an inclusive document of modern Hebrew's range and flexibility, as the reader encounters technical, colloquial, poetic, childish, and standard instances of modern Hebrew, in addition to Wasserman's European or *Haskalah* (Enlightenment) Hebrew, with its sprinklings of biblical and Talmudic locutions.

And then we heard shots outside again. So we made more children. And toward dawn we knew we could never stop. And then we felt everything move with us, the bed and the room and the house and the street. Everything rose and fell and writhed and sweated and groaned. And when dawn broke, all the world was with us, all the world was dancing our dance.
                                                    (*See Under: Love*, p. 411)

Not only does *See Under: Love* end with an act of creation, but throughout the novel, characters confront the urgency of creating, whether the product is a story or another human being.

Grossman himself repeatedly confronts this urgency in his writing of the varied sections, encouraging the reader to view the entire novel as a step in the recovery and regeneration that, almost a half century after the Holocaust, had not yet been achieved or even adequately addressed.

Sources and literary context. Like the rest of Israeli culture and society during the first decade after the founding of Israel in 1948, Israeli literature—in particular its fiction—mostly avoided an engagement with the Holocaust. This avoidance can be seen as more than a mere reflection of the larger cultural climate. From the beginnings of modern Zionism in the nineteenth century, Hebrew literature has occupied a formative place in Zionist and later in Israeli culture. Hebrew works regularly gave voice, often for the first time, to Zionist ideals and aspirations. Since 1948 this trend has continued, with Hebrew literature reflecting and at times visibly influencing the country's political climate and ongoing questions about Israeli and even Jewish identity. In this light, the literature's early reticence in relation to the Holocaust is significant; it not only mirrored but also reinforced Israel's failure to confront the Holocaust.

Once Israeli writers began to deal with this topic in earnest, they focused less on realistically recreating Europe during the war than on the post-Holocaust experience of survivors, their children, and even Israelis with no direct link to the events themselves. Such is the case in Yehuda Amichai's *Lo me-akhshav, lo mi-kan* (1963; *Not of This Time, Not of This Place*, 1968), Hanoch Bartov's *Pits'e bagrut* (1965; *The Brigade*, 1969), Yoram Kaniuk's *Adam ben kelev* (1969; *Adam Resurrected*, 1971), and Aharon Appelfeld's *Bartfus ben ha-almavet* (1988, *The Immortal Bartfuss*, 1988). Amichai's and Kaniuk's novels are boldly experimental in their treatment of time, place, and even causality. Not until the mid-1980s would this approach be popular again in Hebrew fiction, beginning with Grossman's novel.

See Under: Love is generally viewed as unique in scope and ambition, having less in common with antecedents in Hebrew literature than with certain post-World War II landmarks in world literature, such as Günter Grass's *The Tin Drum* (1959), Gabriel García Márquez's *One Hundred Years of Solitude* (1967), and Salman Rushdie's *Midnight's Children* (1981). The commonality is that these works rely on magic realism and other postmodernist devices to invoke the unprecedented upheavals of the twentieth century; in the words of one critic, such texts suggest "that the laws of nature may have to be abrogated by the novelist in order to body forth in fiction the appalling murderousness of twentieth-century reality" (Alter, p. 102).

While Grossman drew inspiration from other imaginative works—Bruno Schulz's fiction, creation myths, and *The Arabian Nights*—he also turned to documentary evidence in his construction of *See Under: Love*. Grossman conducted extensive historical research on Nazism and the Holocaust throughout his writing of the novel.

Reviews. Though Grossman's second novel was immediately recognized in Israel as a work of great importance—and marked Grossman as a major figure in Hebrew literature—*See Under: Love* was not uniformly praised. Many critics questioned the liberties that Grossman took in his treatment of such a sacred subject, particularly in the "Bruno" section, where Grossman's dense, extended, nearly stream-of-consciousness passages on the sea are at once difficult to navigate and, at least at first glance, apparently unrelated to the Holocaust. Other reviewers challenged Grossman's right to treat the Holocaust at such length, since he is neither a survivor nor the child of a survivor. Yet, despite these objections, many recognized the novel's brilliance, and there was unanimous praise for the opening "Momik" section. Readers considered it to be the most poignant portrait of a child of survivors yet to appear in Holocaust literature.

The English translation of *See Under: Love* was not published until 1989, after Grossman's later, much discussed nonfiction book on Palestinians in Israel, *The Yellow Wind*, had appeared in translation and Grossman already had a significant reputation in the United States. A few years later a translation of his less-successful first novel, *The Smile of the Lamb*, was released. Thus, Grossman the novelist was introduced to the English-speaking world at the height of his abilities. His *See Under: Love* met with a generally positive critical reception in the United States, where a seemingly insatiable thirst for material

on the Holocaust was already evident, though some American reviewers voiced reservations about the final three sections of the novel. One reviewer remarks that "In depicting Neigel as redeemable, Momik-Grossman risks trivializing . . . what he along with countless others during the past half century has been consumed by: the Holocaust itself" (Motola, p. 41). Yet this critic concludes that the virtues of the novel outweigh its shortcomings; in his view, *See Under: Love* "is so stunning that even its flaws are eclipsed by its ultimate brilliance" (Motola, p. 37).

—Todd Hasak-Lowy

For More Information

Alter, Robert. *Hebrew and Modernity*. Bloomington: Indiana University Press, 1994.

Grossman, David. *See Under: Love*. Trans. Betsy Rosenberg. New York: Washington Square Press, 1989.

Harshav, Benjamin. *Language in Time of Revolution*. Berkeley: University of California Press, 1994.

Kashtan, Rivka. "Perpetual Redemption: David Grossman's *See Under: Love*." *The Jewish Quarterly* 38, no. 2 (spring 1990): 16-23.

———. *Translating Israel*. Syracuse: Syracuse University Press, 2001.

Morahg, Gilead. "Israel's New Literature of the Holocaust: The Case of David Grossman's *See Under: Love*." *Modern Fiction Studies* 45, no. 2 (summer 1999): 457-79.

Motola, Gabriel. "Love and the Holocaust." *Midstream* 35, no. 4 (Winter 1989): 37-43.

Schulz, Bruno. *The Street of Crocodiles*. Trans. Celina Wieniewski. New York: Viking Press, 1995.

Shaked, Gershon. "The Children of the Heart and the Monster: David Grossman: *See Under: Love*: A Review Essay." *Modern Judaism* 9, no. 3 (October 1989): 311-24.

Sokoloff, Naomi. "The Holocaust and the Discourse of Childhood: David Grossman's *See Under: Love*." *Hebrew Annual Review* 11 (1987): 387-406.

Zerubavel, Yael. *Recovered Roots: Collective Memory and the Making of Israeli National Tradition*. Chicago: University of Chicago Press, 1995.

Shahnamah, or Book of Kings

by

Abu al-Qasim Firdawsi

THE LITERARY WORK

An epic in verse, set in the kingdom of Persia from the earliest times to about 650 C.E.; completed in Persian about 1010 C.E.; published in English in 1832.

SYNOPSIS

Recounting the lives of Persia's renowned kings and heroes, the epic combines history and myth to describe how they shaped events up to the Arab conquest of Persia.

Abu al-Qasim Firdawsi (940-1025; also spelled Abu'l Qasem Ferdowsi) lived during a time of political change in the Persian-speaking world. The "golden age" of Islam had passed some time before, and in places like his native city, far from the capital city of Baghdad, various dynasties and sects were emerging and coming into conflict with each other. While the Arabic language was the official language of Islam and of Islam's central government, languages very different from Arabic, such as Persian and Turkish, remained important to people and their poets, who started to use them as a vehicle for writing down local traditions and expressing national and regional identities. Firdawsi, a Muslim himself, was one such poet. The little that is known about his life provides hints about his career and personality, but much remains a mystery. Even his given name has not been established: "Abu al-Qasim" means "father of Qasim," and "Firdawsi," meaning "from paradise," was the name by which he was known. What is certain is that he came from a family of landowners—well-off but not nobility—and that he spent most of his life in the city of Tus, now Mashhad, in northeastern Iran. In his day, the city was linked to major trade routes that traversed Asia from China to Persia and the Byzantine Empire. Just over a hundred years before Firdawsi's birth, Tus had become a pilgrimage center for Shi'ite Muslims, the subdivision to which Firdawsi almost certainly belonged. The Shahnamah (pronounced "Shah-na-MEH"; also spelled Shahnama, Shah-nama, or Shahname), his masterpiece, is his only work to survive. More

than 50,000 verses long, the epic appears to have taken him some 30 years to complete. Though there are many gaps in information about Firdawsi's life, aspects of his personality can be gleaned from the Shahnamah. Embedded in the epic are his anxieties about aging and his grief over the death of his son. On a national level, the epic allowed Firdawsi to convey traditions that he and people of his social class valued in Iran under Arab rule. But the effort seems also to have been part of a deeper project—to work out what it meant to be a non-Arab Muslim and human in a time of great change.

Events in History at the Time the Epic Takes Place

Scope of the epic. The Shahnamah describes the lives of some 50 kings, in a line going back to the first man, Gayumars—a Persian Adam. The episodes concerning the earliest kings—Gayumars and several of his successors—derive from ancient Persian myths, set on the Iranian plateau. Each of the kings in this section contributes something to the march of civilization. Arts and crafts, writing, and social institutions—including, first and foremost, that of kingship itself—are credited to the rulers of this mythical period.

The vision of civilization is ambivalent, however. Although there is a steady progression toward more complex and hierarchical ways of life, for every positive accomplishment there are negative implications. Kingship, established by Gayumars, is an example. Whereas he used his power to benefit people, the career of a later king, Jamshid, shows how power can blind a leader to his human limitations. It is ultimately from this negative aspect of power that evil emerges as a force distinct from, and destructive of, good.

After this mythic period comes a series of legendary kings, many of whom are connected with historical figures, although not identical to them

Zoroaster, founder of the pre-Islamic faith of Persia.

in every detail. This is the section of the *Shahnamah* that is most truly epic. Here, Firdawsi integrates two different traditions—the legends of a dynasty called Kayanians (Persian kings who dwelled in what is now northeastern Iran and just beyond into Central Asia) and a powerful group to the south, in Sistan, now in eastern Iran and southwestern Afghanistan. Some of the Sistanians were kings, but more important than the kings for the *Shahnamah* are the Sistanian heroes: strong

champions who could fight in the service of a king.

The last section of the *Shahnamah* moves from legendary to recognizably historical material concerning the kings of the Parthian (c. 248 B.C.E.-226 C.E.) and Sasanian (c. 226-651 C.E.) dynasties. Firdawsi's account stops when Islam emerges as a force in Persia and the rest of the world.

Persia—historical vs. mythical origins. The Persian people, distant relatives of many European peoples, did not always live in the region of Iran. Scholars believe that the Persians were at one time united with the "Aryans," who would invade India around 2000 B.C.E. (The name "Iran" comes from the same root as "Aryan.") The original Indo-Iranian community made its first known appearance in Mesopotamia, then moved far to the northeast, to Central Asia. The Aryans probably came down to the Iranian heartland along both sides of the Caspian Sea, although some people believe that migration was northward from the Indian subcontinent. Arriving in Iran, the migrants mixed with the people already settled there. From this mix, the Persians arose. Their language belongs to the family of Indo-European languages (which includes Greek, Latin, Russian, Spanish, French, German, and English); Arabic belongs to an altogether different language family known as "Semitic."

The Persians came to view their country as the heart of the world, not just politically but

PERSIA'S ORIGINAL FAITH

Although Firdawsi was a Muslim, a significant amount of the material he incorporated into the *Shanamah* derived from texts and traditions of the pre-Islamic faith of Persia: Zoroastrianism. The faith is named for its founder Zoroaster (or Zarathustra), who probably lived around 1000 B.C.E. In the *Shahnamah,* Zoroaster is linked to the king, Isfandiyar, an association that has *not* been established in history. Zoroaster integrated ancient Persian beliefs and principles into a coherent religious system of moral teachings and ritual practices. It is in Zoroastrianism that the first expression appears of certain beliefs that are important for Judaism, Christianity, and Islam: angels, the judgment of the soul for good and evil deeds, and the conceptions of Heaven and Hell.

Zoroastrian communities remained fairly strong in Iran through the ninth century C.E., when they began to suffer increasing persecution by Muslim rulers. In response, many but not all Zoroastrian communities migrated to India, where communities of the remaining 200,000 followers live today. Their most popular festival is the Spring Equinox, or Nawruz ("new day," falls about March 21). The festival spread to non-Zoroastrians, and the Persians turned it into a national holiday, which was later Islamicized.

In the background of Persian mythology is a cosmic struggle between good and evil, light and darkness, purity and impurity characteristic of Zoroastrianism. The world is the product of a good creator-god, Ahura Mazda, who does constant battle with Ahriman, a principle of evil and the source of corruption and impurity. Human beings, part of the good creation, must fight on the side of good, even if the victory does not take place in their lifetime. In practical terms, Zoroastrianism lays great stress on upholding contracts and speaking the truth. The saying "Hear no evil; see no evil; speak no evil" is Zoroastrian.

Important material in the *Shahnamah* corresponds to Zoroastrian scripture—the Hymns (*Yashts*) and the *Bundahishn*—and the epic speaks explicitly of Zoroastrian priests (*mobads*); Ahriman, the Evil Principle; and the themes of Nawruz day.

cosmically too. They put their homeland at the center of concentric rings of countries surrounded by a vast global-ocean, with a heaven above and an underworld, or hell, below. This view contrasted in significant ways with that of the ancient Greeks, who regarded their rugged peninsulas and islands as a small part of a world that might be useful to explore.

Several factors about Persia's actual geography probably served to reinforce the ancient view. From the earliest times of their settlement in the region, probably before 1000 C.E., Persians were outstanding gardeners, developing skills in irrigation and in the cultivation of crops, especially fruit trees, that created lush gardens in a dry land. The people developed an existence that contrasted sharply with the nomadic ways of various neighbors. Fear of attack from these neighbors—nomads and settled tribal peoples to the east and northeast—was strong. The oldest

Zoroastrian texts speak of the terror brought on by *maryas,* roving bands of young men who plagued settled people and carried off their cattle. In the *Shahnamah* this conflict is apparent in the long-standing struggle between the good Persian kings and the Turanians in the north and east. There is a sense too of tension with lands to Persia's southwest, in the Arabian Peninsula. The evil king Zahhak who comes to rule Iran is described as coming from Arabia.

The *Shahnamah* relates ancient tradition concerning the way Iran, presumably once the entire settled world, was broken into competing parts. King Faridun, a descendant of Gayumars, the first king, had three sons: Salm, Tur, and Iraj. Faridun bequeathed to Salm the lands to the west, including Rum (Rome/Byzantine Empire); to Tur he bequeathed the lands to the east and north, which thus became known as Turan. (By Firdawsi's time, people associated this name from legend with

"Turk," for the Turkish-speaking people who had moved in there, but that was not the original referent.) Finally, to Iraj, the youngest son, he bequeathed the finest land, Iran. The two older brothers grew jealous and killed Iraj. Faridun, distraught, bided his time until Iraj's grandson, Manuchihr, matured and took power, which returned control of the land to a legitimate king. But thereafter the realm remained perpetually insecure. Subsequent kings had to rely on the hero Rustam, a powerful champion from a different family line, to safeguard the kingdom from enemies.

While the documented history of Persian monarchy does not correlate precisely with the *Shahnamah*, there is enough correspondence to indicate real historical awareness. Historically the first dynasty was that of the Achaemenid kings, which began in the sixth century B.C.E. and whose first monarch, Cyrus, was in many ways the most distinguished. Cambyses, Xerxes, and Ardashir (also called Artaxerxes) followed. In 331 B.C.E. Darius III fell in battle against the Macedonian conqueror Alexander the Great, marking the end of Achaemenid rule. Alexander, who in fact had no blood relationship to the Persians, established a short-lived line of governors in Persia, called the Seleucids. After them, for over four centuries, the Parthians ruled. Beginning around 226 C.E., with King Ardashir, the Sasanian dynasty continued until Muslim (mainly Arab) forces finally conquered Persia in 651.

The Sasanians, who were often at war with the Byzantine Empire, ruled a population that was quite diverse, especially in cosmopolitan areas. Syriac and other Christians, as well as Jews, settled in Sasanian domains, where some went on to become distinguished translators and physicians as well as artisans and traders. There were also Manichaeans (followers of Mani, who preached a body-spirit dualism). Officially, Zoroastrianism continued to be the royally endorsed religion. By then it had developed into a tradition dominated by priests who performed elaborate rituals of purification and sacrifice and remained closely tied to the kings. The last Sasanian king was Yazdagird III. By his death in 651, Yazdagird's power had fallen so low that he was killed by a miller with whom he had taken refuge. It is with this event that the *Shahnamah* concludes. It refrains from entering into Islamic history in relation to Iran, though an introductory passage showers formal praise on the Prophet Muhammad, as was expected of any literary composition.

Arabizing Persia. The *Shahnamah* may appear to slight Islam by dwelling on the pre-Islamic Persian past and by concluding before that faith's emergence as a belief system and force in world civilization. Nevertheless, there are many passages praising God, and Firdawsi himself was evidently a reasonably devoted Shi`ite Muslim. From a historical perspective, the ease with which Arabs conquered Persia—and Islam took hold among its people—suggests the existence of negative cultural and social conditions under Sasanian rule, and probably under previous Persian dynasties as well. Arab culture provided a writing system that was well adapted to the Persian language, and a faith (Islam) that was easy to learn and relatively egalitarian. Instead of priests and complicated rituals, the new Islamic faith stressed the welfare of the community and the individual's responsibility to God. Rigid Zoroastrian purity laws had resulted in the exclusion of groups of people from the rest of society. Anyone, for example, who worked as a cleaner or a tanner or cared for the dead had been designated as permanently impure. Under Sasanian rule, the priests and kings had towered over a strictly stratified society that relegated the common people to the bottom of the hierarchy. Evidently commoners were ready to throw off this rigid hierarchy at the first opportunity, which Islam provided. At the same time, there was enough in their earlier experience to make it worth remembering fondly. The fact that after the advent of Islam, just before Firdawsi's time, the Persian language experienced a renaissance testifies to the vitality of Persian culture in the pre-Islamic period.

The Epic in Focus

Plot summary. The *Shahnamah* begins with a summary of God's creation of the good elements—fire, the planets, plants and animals, and human beings—without reference to evil.

> Going beyond these creatures [plants and
>   animals], man appeared,
> To become the key to all these close-linked
>   things.
> His head was raised up like the cypress,
> He was endowed with good speech and
>   applied reason to use.
>   (Firdawsi, *The Epic of Kings:*
>   *Shah-nama*, p. 2)

Further on in the Persian original, the epic discusses its own sourcebook, from which it drew the stories for the *Shahnamah:*

> There was a book [*nama*] from ancient times
> In which there was an abundance of stories.

It was dispersed into the hands of every
    mobad [Zoroastrian priest; wise Man]
Every wise one [of the *mobads*] possessed a
    portion of it.
                (*Shahnamah* in Davidson, p. 49)

Subsequent verses describe this "book" as containing the history of the kings of the world, of when and how they reigned in the earliest ages. To date, no one has been able to determine exactly what "source" or sources lie behind the narratives of the *Shahnamah*. We do not know if this was a single book or many books, or even orally transmitted. It may have been one or several, written or spoken. If it was written, it is not clear whether Firdawsi himself was able to read its language or indeed whether he ever saw it.

The *Shahnamah*'s account of the kings of the world begins with Gayumars. At first he and his courtiers live in complete harmony with one another and with all the animals. But Ahriman, "the evil principle," disrupts this peaceful existence by sending his son, the Black Demon, and a host of lesser demons to invade Iran. This wicked band kills Gayumars's son Siyamak in battle. With the assistance of helpful angels, lions, and tigers, Gayumars's grandson Hushang avenges the death, killing the Black Demon in single combat.

During his reign, Hushang teaches people the skills of mining metal. Since metal is forged by heat, it is altogether fitting that he also discovers fire, which he teaches them to worship as a heavenly gift. Hushang's son Tahmures instructs the people in other useful arts: spinning and weaving, breeding horses for battle, and raising cheetahs and falcons for hunting. A group of demons that he has taken captive offers to teach him yet another art, writing, in return for their freedom. He learns the skill but does not release the demons and so becomes known as *Div-Band*, "Demon-Binder."

The next ruler, Jamshid, son of Tahmures, is the King Solomon of Persian tradition, renowned for his wisdom and furthering of civilization. At first his reign proves to be a golden age of unparalleled wealth and luxury; he teaches his people the manufacture of both armor and fine cloth, such as silk and brocade. But attachment to riches and self-love become his undoing. Jamshid has a band of demons lift him, on his jeweled throne, high into the air to proclaim the Spring Festival (Nawruz), which many Iranians still celebrate. In the end, his arrogant belief in his own magnificence causes God to withdraw his *farr*, a

divine blessing that is understood as conferring the right to rule.

Zahhak was originally an Arab prince and a good but somewhat naïve man. Iblis (the Arabic word for Satan, the counterpart of Ahriman in Zoroastrianism) entered the king's service by persuading the king to take him on as a cook. Preparing delicious dishes of meat—which people had rarely eaten until that time—he tantalized Zahhak to the point that the king offered Iblis any reward he wished. Iblis said that all he wanted was to kiss the king's shoulders. When he did, two black snakes emerged from the spots he kissed. Each of the snakes, Iblis informed Zahhak, requires the brain of a youth for food every day. Thus, Zahhak began putting the best of his own subjects to death on a regular basis.

Back in Jamshid's kingdom, his subjects grow restive. So dissatisfied are they with their egocentric king that some of the Persian nobles ask Zahhak, horrible as he has become, to take over the rule of their land. Zahhak complies, imposing his own cruel regime on Iran. Terrified, its people cower in silence until the brave blacksmith Kava arises. Kava, who has lost all but one of his

18 sons to Zahhak's slaughter, openly denounces the tyrant. Waving his leather blacksmith's apron as a banner, he marshals the people to search for a leader who will end the tyranny:

> Noble worshippers of God, let all who side with [the rebel] Faridun liberate their heads from the yoke of Zahhak! Let us go to Faridun and find refuge in the shelter of his *Farr* [royal glory]. Let us proclaim that this present king is Ahriman [the Maker of Evil], who is at heart the enemy of the Creator. By the means of that leather [Kava's apron], worth nothing and costing nothing, the voice of the enemy was distinguished from the voice of the friend.
>
> (*Shah-namah*, p. 20)

After long battles, aided by Kava and his forces, the virtuous Faridun drives Zahhak inside Mount Damavand, Iran's highest mountain. Faridun plans to slaughter Zahhak, but an angel convinces the hero to leave the evil ruler alive, bound in chains under the mountain. Faridun divides his realm among his three sons, Salm, Tur, and Iraj, giving the choicest portion to Iraj, who is then killed by his jealous brothers. Years pass and Faridun is very old when the grandson of Iraj—Manuchihr—avenges the wrong, killing both Salm and Tur in battle before taking the throne himself.

Meanwhile, to the east, another family emerges into history: the heroic Sistanians, named after their home province of Sistan, in what is now southeastern Iran and southwestern Afghanistan. The first of these heroes, Sam, has a son named Zal. The child is a strong healthy lad, but his hair is completely white. Alarmed by this abnormality, then regarded as a sign of demonic parentage, Sam abandons Zal at the foot of Mount Damavand, north of what is now Tehran. A great, magical bird, the Simurgh, saves the infant from death and raises him in a nest with her own chicks. Zal grows up to be so mighty that a passing caravan spreads rumors about him throughout the kingdom. Hearing these rumors, Sam realizes the mighty figure must be his son and searches for him. As a parting gift, the Simurgh gives Zal a feather. If in dire need, he can burn it, and she will come to his aid with her supernatural powers.

Zal eventually travels to a court farther to the east, where he falls in love with a princess named Rudabah. The two love each other deeply, but there is a problem: Rudabah is a descendant of the wicked Zahhak. In order to marry her, Zal must get his father, Sam, as well as the Iranian king, Manuchihr, to agree. Rudabah's father, Mihrab, himself becomes apprehensive about the match and at one point threatens to solve everything by killing his own daughter. In the end, Rudabah's loyal and wise mother, Sindukht, saves the day by traveling to Sam's court with gifts to plead for the marriage. Despite all the worries, the marriage works out well. Both husband and wife live very long lives, with Rudabah surviving even their son Rustam, greatest champion of all, who defends Iran's kingship for hundreds of years.

Rustam is a deeply human figure, despite the supernatural strength and size that earns him the name *Pil-tan*, meaning "Elephant-bodied." Totally devoted, his deepest loyalty is to upholding the "throne and crown" of Iran. But when the kings do not deserve that loyalty, the hero feels conflicted. Rustam's deepest affection appears to be reserved for his fabulous horse, Rakhsh. One day on a ride in remote lands, the horse is stolen from camp. Frantic, Rustam ends up at the foreign court of a nobleman whose beautiful daughter, Tahminah, has become captivated with Rustam from stories of his exploits. Promising to find his horse (which she does), Tahminah draws him to her bed and the two conceive a child.

For this adventure, Rustam eventually pays a heavy price. Having never met his son, Suhrab, he fails to recognize him in battle years later and kills him. Too late, the father identifies him as his son by an amulet Rustam once gave Tahminah to bind on the boy's arm.

After the reign of Kaykubad, a Persian king whom Rustam fetches out of hiding to place on the throne, the subsequent kings and princes all have weaknesses. Kaybubad's son, Kay Kavus, is forceful but self-centered. One of the most tragic figures in the *Shahnamah*, Siyavush, Kay Kavus's son, is almost too pure for his own good. He forges a peace treaty with the Turanian king, Afrasiyab.

While the Persian kings have their faults, the rival king shows virtues. Afrasiyab approaches the association with good intentions toward the young Persian prince. But a bad dream fills Afrasiyab with premonitions that things will not turn out well: "Afrasiyab cried out, as if / He were a man who spilled his secrets while / Delirious, and trembled in his bed" (Firdawsi, *The Legend of Seyavash*, p. 39). The king's brother, Garsivaz, who will turn Afrasiyab against Siyavush, runs to his side and asks what is wrong. "The king replie[s], 'Don't ask, don't speak to me. / Give me a moment till my mind has cleared. / And hold me tightly for a little while'" (*The Legend of Seyavash*, p. 39).

In the end, Siyavush's death at Turanian hands is all the more poignant because of the

The epic hero Rustam, born by caesarian section.

rival king's affection for him. Afrasiyab had earlier provided him not only with a palace but also with one of his own daughters to wed. After Siyavush dies, his wife Farangis bears his son, Kay Khusraw, who goes on to become one of Iran's great kings. Siyavush's death is not forgotten. His martyred blood lends him almost mythic stature, suggesting godlike qualities that even the earliest kings of legends do not have:

From the dust that drank /
the blood of Seyavash a tree rose up /
To touch the clouds; each leaf displayed his
    likeness.

. . . .

Those who mourned for Seyavash
Would gather and bewail his death and
    worship.

(*Shah-nama*, p. 131)

The line of the great Kayanian kings comes to an end with Prince Isfandiyar's death at Rustam's hands. Shortly thereafter, Rustam is killed by his own half-brother, Shaghad. Born of Zal and a slave-woman, Shaghad is jealous of Rustam. He schemes with his father-in-law, the king of Afghanistan, to lure Rustam to his death in a pit.

The *Shahnamah*'s stories about the Sasanian kings, while numerous and varied, are less vivid than the earlier ones in the narrative. Memorable characters in the Sasanian section include Bahram Gur and Bahram Chubin. The epic

portrays Nushirvan (Khusraw I) as one of the greatest Persian kings— historians portray him similarly. Another great Sasanian king is Khusraw Parviz. The story of his love for the Armenian princess, Shirin, takes on a life of its own in subsequent literature, with several complete romances devoted to the subject (see **Khusraw and Shirin**, also in WLAIT 6: *Middle Eastern Literatures and Their Times*).

Women in the *Shahnamah*. The visibility of women in the *Shahnamah* is likely to strike the modern reader as a positive statement about women's rights, as though Firdawsi either lived in a world where women were particularly active or wished to propose that they should be. But given what were probably very restricted roles for women in Firdawsi's own time, the idea may have been that women may figure prominently in stories, and only there.

In much of the *Shahnamah*, there is a rather harsh view of women. Rustam, detecting the hand of Afrasiyab's daughter in the betrayal of the good Prince Siyavush, remarks bitterly, "Fortunate is the woman whose mother never bears her" (*Shanama* in Motlagh, p. 115). In other places where women play a major role, misfortune results. One of the strongest examples is Sudabah, the favored wife of King Kay Kavus and Siyavush's stepmother. Sudabah falls in love with her stepson and calls him to her in the harem. He resists going to see her at first, wanting nothing to do with women, but gives in at her insistence. Then, virtuously, the stepson rejects her outright. An enraged Sudabah turns to a confidante—presumably a servant—who is pregnant with twins. Sudabah convinces the expectant mother to concoct a magic potion to abort the children, then claims that they were Sudabah's own children by the king and that Siyavush raped her, causing a miscarriage. King Kavus decides to test his son by fire, whereupon Siyavush proves his innocence by passing through the flames unharmed. The king prepares to execute the devious Sudabah by hanging, but the ever-good Siyavush intervenes to spare her life.

In the story of Sindukht and Rudabah, the *Shahnamah* presents another, rarer face of womanhood: loyal, intelligent, and courageous. Here one would expect disastrous results, since mother and daughter descend from the evil Zahhak. But both prove to be positive characters. Rudabah endures a horrendous pregnancy and a Caesarean section to give birth to the great Rustam, and in the end she outlives him, and even her grandson Suhrab. Certainly her fate is contrary to all expectations.

In real life, the Zoroastrians spoke of women's ritual impurity. They seem to have believed that diabolical forces could more easily sway women than men toward the practice of evil magic, as Sudabah is swayed in her passion for Siyavush. That negative images of women persisted into Firdawsi's time is evident in his own readiness to envision the earth as a cruel mother who might seize and swallow up her children at any moment. Reflecting on Siyavush's death, he writes,

> Such is the way this ancient crone we call
> The earth will act . . . .
> . . . when the heart
> Has learnt to love the world she drags the head
> Down—suddenly—into the dust.
>
> (Shah-nama, p. 131)

RUSTAM THE UNROYAL

Rustam's presence in the *Shahnamah* sets up a tension between two prominent types, the king and the hero, represented by Rustam. This division is similar to those of the legendary British king Arthur and his knights. The king is responsible to his realm, while the knights or heroes are bound to undertake all sorts of challenges and adventures in his defense. Although the roles are complementary, the possibility of conflict is ever present. In the *Shahnamah,* tragedy ultimately comes to pass, as Rustam kills the Persian prince Isfandiyar in a battle forced on both of them.

Historically women were repressed in both pre-Islamic times and Firdawsi's own. Some Muslims attribute the conception of *purdah,* sequestering of women, as well as full veiling, to Sasanian traditions that were wrongly incorporated into Islam. There is evidence that the wives of Sasanian kings were indeed concealed from public view. In both pre-Islamic and Islamic times, working women had considerably more freedom but little social status.

Sources and literary context. After Islam was established in Arabia in the lifetime of the Prophet Muhammad (570-632 C.E.), the faith quickly spread to Syria, Egypt, and Persia. The Arabic language spread rapidly as well—to Egypt and Syria at least. While the Persians converted to Islam with remarkable speed, they chose not to adopt Arabic, continuing instead to speak the Persian language. They passed on to their children as well an account of their Persian heritage dating back to the kings of the sixth century B.C.E. Also sustained was a reverence for the pre-Islamic faith of Zoroastrianism. Firdawsi, though a Muslim, recorded and so helped them sustain the components of the legacy. We do not know how he learned the traditions he recorded, with one exception. Early in the *Shahnamah,* Firdawsi states that he has incorporated some 1,000 lines from a *Shahnamah* written by a somewhat older poet named Daqiqi.

There were two principal ways that Persian Muslims were reminded of their pre-Islamic heritage. First, monuments honored their historic kings from the Achaemenid and Sasanian dynasties. With occasional inscriptions, monuments like the palace and tombs of Persepolis testified to the impressive reigns of shahs (kings) like Xerxes, Cyrus, and Darius. The other way that pre-Islamic Persian history endured was through the practices and scriptures of Zoroastrians who did not convert to Islam. But the details of Zoroastrian texts are so different from the *Shahnamah* that these could not have been direct sources for Firdawsi.

All too little remains from Sasanian literature, in its difficult script, called Pahlavi, and, of course, even less evidence can be gleaned from the unwritten arts of storytelling, dance, or music. But the scant evidence that does exist suggests that in the Sasanian courts and probably among the common people too, there was a rich artistic tradition, from which Firdawsi must have drawn. The *Shahnamah* itself provides some of this evidence, as in the episode of Barbad, a singer-storyteller who hides himself in a cypress tree in the garden of the Sasanian king Khusraw Parviz, to enchant him with music and song. The lively imagination at work in the *Shahnamah,* with its fairies, witches, demons, monsters, and fantastic adventures, is almost certainly not Firdawsi's alone, but an aspect of Persian heritage.

There appear to be three main strands of material woven into the fabric of the *Shahnamah*: Zoroastrian myths, history of the period after Alexander's invasion, and a loosely connected narrative from the house of Rustam. Finally the *Shahnamah's* episode of Alexander the Great has an independent source: a Greek Alexander "romance" that inspired stories of the conqueror throughout Europe and Asia, from ancient times through the Middle Ages. The *Shahnamah's* account of Alexander took on something of a life of its own, inspiring separate narratives in Persian called Iskandarnamahs, or Alexander Books. One of the few romantic episodes in these Iskandarnamahs also appears in the *Shahnamah*: Alexander's visit to Queen Qaydafa, a strong, attractive, mature woman reminiscent of the Queen of Sheba. In some versions Alexander defeats her, but Firdawsi has the two leaders part in friendship.

Events in History at the Time the Epic Was Written

Persian resurgence. During the tenth and eleventh centuries, during which Firdawsi lived, the strong center of the Islamic world was disintegrating and the vast territories of Asia, including Persia, were experiencing gradual fragmentation. Since the seventh century, Muslims had been governed by an administration called the "caliphate," similar to the Holy Roman Empire in Europe somewhat later. The first caliphate, that of the Umayyads, lasted from 661 to 750 and had its capital in Damascus, Syria. This dynasty of Muslim leaders succeeded in conquering most of the territory that Islam was to hold, except for India and Indonesia. The Umayyads were replaced by another dynasty, the Abbasids, who moved the capital to Baghdad. The Abbasids ruled from 750 until 1258, during the time in which the *Shahnamah* was written.

Rather than conquest, the first Abbasid caliphs concentrated their resources on culture: architecture, literature, science, and philosophy. The early Abbasid era, from about 750 to 850, came to be considered the "Golden Age" of Islam, a time of relative peace and prosperity, when trade by land and sea brought great wealth into Islam's domains. By contrast, Europeans were living in a period that, if not actually dark, was unstable and primitive.

In the 800s, however, a series of weak caliphs and external threats brought about a decline in the Abbasids' power. In Persia, particularly, the survival of local identity—due largely to an independent language and continuing leadership traditions—led to the rise of local dynasties such as the Buwayhids, Safarids, and Samanids. Meanwhile, to the north and east of the regions under Abbasid control, various Turkish-speaking people were gaining sufficient strength to entertain political ambitions. Whereas the Persian speakers were mostly urban dwellers or farmers, the Turkish speakers were generally nomadic herders, horse-breeders, and caravan traders. United in

their resentment of Arab Muslims, who regarded both the Persian and Turkish speakers as inferior, the two groups clashed with each other as well: their different ways of life fueled the conflict.

Reception. There is some evidence that Firdawsi first began to compose his epic for a Persian ruler, the Samanid governor Abu Mansur. When the Samanids fell to the Turkish ruler Mahmud of Ghazni, Firdawsi either had to forego the project or write for the new ruler, and he chose the latter course.

Like many other ambitious Turkish-speaking rulers of his era, Mahmud of Ghazni knew Persian well and admired Persian literature. He would have had plenty of reason to approve of the *Shahnamah*. As a language of literature and culture, Persian was second only to Arabic in the Islamic world. If a local ruler wished to establish a dynasty with some independence from the Arab-dominated caliphate, it was in his interest to become fluent in the Persian language and assimilate into the culture, regardless of his ethnicity. For a Turkish ruler, identifying with the Persian heritage was a great help in establishing his authority. Mahmud's slighting of Firdawsi by paying him poorly probably has more to do with personal than ethnic differences.

It was a Turkish and Mongolian dynasty (the two groups being closely related) that secured the *Shahnamah*'s reputation a few centuries after Firdawsi composed it. The Ilkhanids (1256-1353), descendents of Genghis Khan, ruled Persia at the time. Their courts produced some of the finest manuscripts to come out of Persia, including the first known illustrated versions of the *Shahnamah*, beginning around 1300.

For several centuries after its composition, the *Shahnamah* gave rise to sequels, some by poets who recorded their names, and others by anonymous poets who recited their sequels orally in popular circles. The sequels themselves often concerned secondary characters in the original: Alexander, for example, or the hero Garshasp. Firdawsi's accomplishment was such that no one attempted anything of the *Shahnamah*'s scope or seriousness after him. To this day, many Iranians, especially men, are named after characters in the *Shahnamah*: Faridun, Manuchihr, and Isfandiyar, for example. And many people memorize verses, which they drop into everyday conversations or simply recite for pleasure. The style of composition, nearly a thousand years old, is considered a model of Persian language, being relatively free of Arabic words and written in a simple and free manner that is nevertheless

MATTHEW ARNOLD'S "SOHRAB AND RUSTAM"

The nineteenth-century English writer Matthew Arnold (1822-1888) evidently did not have access to the text of Firdawsi's *Shahnamah*, even in translation, and he never traveled to Persia. Yet drawing on summaries, he created a moving composition that is remarkably faithful to the original.

Sohrab is Rustam's son by the Turanian noblewoman Tahminah. With the consent of Tahminah's father, Rustam spends the night with her. Before leaving, Rustam gives Tahminah a seal to tie in the hair of their future child, if a girl, or to bind on the arm if a boy. In Arnold's account, Tahminah sends word to Rustam that the child is a girl, which is why Rustam later fails to identify Sohrab as his son.

In service to the Turanian king, Sohrab has two ambitions: to prove himself in battle against the Persians and to meet his father, whom he knows to be Rustam. At the outset of the episode, Persians and Turanians are encamped by the Oxus River, ready to do battle. Sohrab makes it known that he wishes to fight the best of the Persians, one-on-one. When Rustam takes up the challenge, both of Sohrab's ambitions are conflated in a single event and tragedy ensues.

The two champions, father and son, are well matched both in power and in underlying generosity and tenderheartedness. Indeed, it is the son who seems to have the edge in terms of strength and fighting skill. Early on, Sohrab suspects Rustam's identity. At one point, he explicitly asks if his opponent is not Rustam: "Oh, by thy father's head! By thine own soul! / Art thou not Rustam? Speak! Art thou not he?" (Arnold, lines 342-343). But an unsuspecting Rustam lies about his own identity, reasoning that whoever this young opponent is, he will flee the fight if his foe be known, as past experience shows. Sohrab gets Rustam down but spares him, urging a truce. Rustam refuses. Then once again Sohrab finds himself in position to wield a deadly blow, but that instant Rustam cries out his own name, which so unnerves Sohrab that he fails to fend off the fatal thrust:

> But that beloved name unnerved my arm—
> That name, and something, I confess, in thee,
> Which troubles all my heart, and made my shield
> Fall; and thy spear transfixed an unarmed foe.
> (Arnold, lines 547-550)

profound. At the same time, its tales remain vibrant and enduring. The *Shahnamah* draws on ancient traditions, but its human truths have not grown old.

Although several *Shahnamah* manuscripts were brought to Europe in earlier times, Europeans only began to take its contents seriously when the British started colonizing India in the eighteenth century. In the nineteenth century, a scholar named Jules Mohl produced a French translation in prose. Between 1906 and 1925, two brothers, George and Edmund Warner, completed an English translation in blank verse. Based on summaries he had read in French and English, the British poet Matthew Arnold composed his verse "Sohrab and Rostam" around the year 1852.

—Caroline Sawyer

For More Information

Arnold, Matthew. *The Poems of Matthew Arnold.* Ed. Kenneth Allott. New York: Barnes and Noble, 1965.

Banani, Amin. "Ferdowsi and the Art of Tragic Epic." In *Persian Literature*. Ed. Ehsan Yarshater. Columbia Lectures on Iranian Studies. New York: Persian Heritage Foundation, 1983.

Christensen, Arthur. *L'Iran sous les Sassanides* [Iran under the Sasanians]. Copenhagen: Munksgaard, 1944.

Curtis, Vesta Sarkhosh. *The Legendary Past: Persian Myths*. Austin: University of Texas Press, 1998.

Davidson, Olga M. *Poet and Hero in the Persian Book of Kings*. Ithaca: Cornell University Press, 1994.

Firdawsi. *The Epic of Kings: Shah-nama, the National Epic of Persia by Ferdowsi*. Trans. Reuben Levy. London: Routledge and Kegan Paul, 1967.

———. *The Legend of Seyavash*. Trans. Dick Davis. New York: Penguin, 1992.

———. *The Tragedy of Sohráb and Rustam*. Trans. Jerome W. Clinton. Publications on the Near East 3. Seattle: University of Washington Press, 1987.

Hillenbrand, Robert. "The Arts of the Book in Ilkhanid Iran." In *Legacy of Genghis Khan: Courtly Art and Culture in Western Asia, 1256-1353*. Ed. Linda Komaroff and Stefano Carboni. New York: Metropolitan Museum of Art, 2002.

Motlagh, Djalal Khaleghi. *Die Frauen im Schahname* [Women in the *Shahnama*]. Islam kundliche Untersuchungen. Bd. 12. Freiburg i. Br.: Klaus Schwarz, 1971.

———. "Ferdowsi." *Encyclopaedia Iranica*. Vol. 9. New York: Bibliotheca Persica Press, 1999.

Robinson, B. W. *The Persian Book of Kings: An Epitome of the Shahnama of Firdawsi*. New York: Routledge Curzon, 2002.

Schulthesis, Rob. "The Enduring Splendors of, Yes, Afghanistan." *Smithsonian,* February 2003, 32-40.

Songs of the Land of Zion, Jerusalem

by

Yehuda Amichai

Yehuda Amichai was born in 1924 in Würzburg, Bavaria, to a family of Orthodox Jews and was educated at Orthodox schools. As a result of the rise to power of the Nazis, the family migrated to Palestine in 1935, settling first in Petach Tikva and then in Jerusalem, where Amichai continued his religious education. During World War II, Amichai joined the Jewish Brigade of the British Army and served in Egypt. Later, as part of the *Palmah*, the elite force of the pre-state army, he smuggled arms and Jewish immigrants into Palestine. During his adolescence Amichai abandoned formal religious practice, but he would continue to draw on biblical and liturgical texts in his poetry. Amichai's first book of poems, *Akhshav uva-yamim ha-aherim* (Now and in Other Days), appeared in 1955. It was followed in 1958 by *Be-merhak shete tikvot* (Two Hopes Apart), which introduced the themes that would characterize the remainder of Amichai's work: love, war (he served in the War of Independence and the Six-Day War), time, memory, his father, and his own sense of guilt. Proving his skill as a prose writer as well, in 1961 Amichai published the short-story collection *Ba-ruah ha-nora'ah ha-zot* (In This Terrible Wind), and in 1963 both the novel *Lo me-akhshav, lo mi-kan* (Not of This Time, Not of This Place) and the radio play *Pa'amonim ve-rakavot* (Bells and Trains). He published another eight volumes of poetry as well, culminating with *Patuah sagur patuah* (Open Closed, Open) in 1998, a collection of long poems and cycles that suggest he was re-evaluating the

THE LITERARY WORK

A cycle of 39 poems set in Israel in 1974; published in Hebrew (as *Shire Erets Tsiyon, Yerushalayim*) in 1974, in English (as *Patriotic Songs*) in 1978.

SYNOPSIS

The cycle begins with poems relating to the Yom Kippur War in Israel, then reflects on aspects of Israeli history and culminates with a contemplation of the city of Jerusalem.

religion he had abandoned in his youth. He died in September 2000, leaving behind poetry that discusses with particular sensitivity all aspects of human life and response to events. The experience of nation and individual involved in almost constant warfare is one of Amichai's dominant themes. His poetry on war is generally regarded as the most profound and moving in all of modern Hebrew literature.

Events in History at the Time of the Poems

Zionism and the establishment of the State of Israel. *Songs of the Land of Zion, Jerusalem* was published soon after the October War in Israel (known also as the Yom Kippur War). Fought in 1973, the conflict was the climax of several key events associated with the Zionist impulse. It was

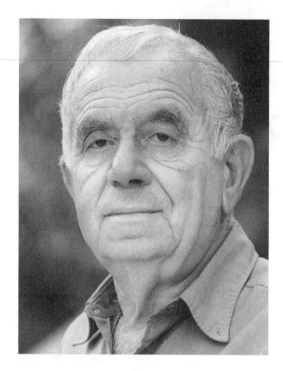

Yehuda Amichai

the ideology of modern Zionism that had led to the establishment of the State of Israel just 25 years before the war. Zionism held that it was the right of the Jewish people to end their dispersal in the diaspora and re-establish a national homeland in Palestine. Formally launched in the 1890s, Zionism had by the time of the First World War become a major political force, despite serious divisions within the Zionist movement and with Jews who did not support it. The British government, which was granted mandatory control of Palestine by the League of Nations in 1920, had earlier proclaimed sympathy for the establishment of a Jewish national home in the Balfour Declaration in November 1917. This declaration won the endorsement of the European powers and the United States but met with ferocious Arab opposition, as the Arabs were fiercely against a Jewish state's being established in Palestine. Later, in the interwar 1930s, Jewish immigration continued to be the central issue. The decade brought in more than 200,000 Jewish newcomers, despite the introduction of severe restrictions by the British after the Arab Rebellion of 1936-39. With the rise of Nazism in Germany, freedom of immigration became crucial for Jewish survival, and Article 6 of the Mandate actually obliged Britain to facilitate Jewish immigration to Palestine under suitable circumstances. But, given the persistent violent opposition of the

Arabs in the Middle East, the British restrictions continued. Immigration was at times severely limited or stopped altogether.

Eventually the British government referred the problem to the United Nations (U.N.), which, in November 1947, recommended the division of Palestine into independent Arab and Jewish states. Jerusalem was to be "internationalized," that is, run by the United Nations itself, but the plan never went into effect. It was scotched by subsequent events. The British withdrew from Palestine at the termination of the Mandate on May 15, 1948, and war broke out the next day. Five Arab armies, supported by the Arab states, simultaneously invaded the Jewish settlement in Palestine (called the *yishuv*). This led to the War of Independence, during which Jerusalem would be divided between Israel (controlled West Jerusalem, the new city) and Jordan (controlled East Jerusalem, including the walled Old City). In the end, the war secured the Jewish state for the Jews, but at an enormous cost given the scale of human casualties on both sides. About 750,000 Arabs fled or were driven from their homes to settle as best they could in refugee camps in Egypt, Lebanon, Syria, and Jordan. A small proportion of Palestinian Arabs remained in Israel, becoming citizens of the state. In 1949 Israel signed cease-fire agreements with the Arab states.

The Six-Day War, Jerusalem reunified. Securing the state did not secure peace. Arab attacks continued, with Israeli retaliation. Egyptian forces moved into the Sinai Peninsula, secured the withdrawal of United Nations forces there, and closed the Straits of Tiran to Israeli shipping. Seeing this as a cause of war, Israel launched a pre-emptive strike against Egypt on June 5, 1967, and the so-called Six-Day War began in earnest. Within a few days Syria and Jordan had entered the fray, to little avail. All three Arab states were quickly and overwhelmingly defeated, and a much larger Israel emerged. The Israelis gained control over Jordanian territory on the western bank of the Jordan River (the "West Bank"), including East Jerusalem. Also they gained the Gaza Strip and Sinai Peninsula (both of which had been ruled by Egypt) and the Golan Heights (conquered from Syria). As a result, Jerusalem was unified under Israeli control. Israel subsequently offered to withdraw from the Sinai Peninsula and the Golan Heights, and did return the Sinai to Egypt. But divisiveness among the Israelis, as well as Arab intransigence, led Israel to harden its position—there would be no return to pre-war borders. Indeed, to prevent this, Israel began to establish Jewish settlements in the newly won Golan Heights, West Bank, and Gaza, even though these last two areas were already densely populated with Palestinian Arabs.

Along with the territories, Israel acquired their angry residents. About a million Palestinian Arabs in the West Bank and Gaza came under Israeli military rule, further stimulating the growth of Palestinian nationalism, which had been unmitigatedly hostile to Israel from the start. As intimated, the Arabs as a whole had for years refused to accept Israel's *de facto* existence or recognize the right of Jews to a state of their own. Positions hardened as a result of the Six-Day War, a turning point in Arab-Israeli relations, first because Israel conquered territories in which the Palestinians lived and second because the Arab nations saw Israel as a permanent threat to their existence. Their foreign policy became directed towards war against Israel, which prompted it to wage war each time the new state perceived a real or potential threat to its existence.

Victory in the Six-Day War bolstered Israeli esteem and brought great self-assurance, but led also to problems. While Zionism's aim had been to establish a *Jewish* state in Palestine, after 1967 the state found itself in the role of the conqueror and ruler of a large non-Jewish population. Another concern was the rise of militant Jewish religious-nationalist groups, whose members settled in the disputed territories. In the eyes of these militants, and various others, the areas that had been gained in the 1967 war were the inalienable possession of the Jewish people, not to be ceded back to the Palestinians; settlement, legal or illegal, ought to occur in the areas to restore for the nation the entire Land of Israel (*Erets Yisrael*, "Greater Israel"), in accordance with such biblical promises as, "unto thy seed I give the land, from the river of Egypt unto the great river, the River Euphrates" (Genesis 15:18). The whole situation ultimately reinforced the growth of a Palestinian national consciousness. Advocating the right to reclaim the territories in which they had once lived, the Palestinians resolved to divest themselves of Israeli rule as well as the humiliation of living under the occupation.

The October War. This was the status of Arab-Israeli relations at the outbreak of the next major Arab-Israeli confrontation—the October or Yom Kippur War (called the Ramadan War by the Arabs). Fought in 1973 between Egypt and Syria on one side and Israel on the other, the war broke out for various reasons. Both Israel and the international community had underestimated the sense of humiliation among the Arabs after their rapid defeat in the Six-Day War, and it was only aggravated by Israel's own postwar euphoria. Also the territorial dispute had not been resolved. Israel refused to withdraw to the pre-1967 lines; in its view, relinquishing conquered territory would not bring lasting peace and the new territories offered security by creating buffer zones in the north, south, and west. Moreover, Israel did not take Egypt's president, Anwar Sadat, seriously when he threatened war.

The surprise attack by the Arabs occurred on Yom Kippur, the Day of Atonement, the holiest day of the year for the Jewish people. Syria attacked in the north, on the Golan front, while Egypt struck across the Suez Canal. The Soviet Union and the United States joined the battle, with the Soviet Union assisting the Arabs and the United States supporting Israel, both through airlifts of arms and supplies. The situation was potentially so dangerous that Henry Kissinger, the U.S. secretary of state, traveled to the Soviet Union to negotiate a cease-fire. By war's end, Israeli forces had rallied and held the strategic heights of Mount Hermon, which dominated the entire region between the battlefield and the Syrian capital, Damascus. They also held positions further east, which placed the outskirts of Damascus within range of Israel's artillery. On the Egyptian front, Israeli forces mounted a successful counterattack by land and air. Eventually the Israelis secured military victory on both fronts, but the Arabs managed to cause high casualties and to do serious damage to the Israeli army before the fighting stopped.

The Yom Kippur War differed from the other wars in that the attack took the Israelis by surprise. It emerged after the war that Israel's commanders were unprepared for the October attack because they misinterpreted the build-up of armed forces and new Egyptian fortifications along the Suez Canal as military exercises instead of preparation for war. A postwar Israeli judicial inquiry indicted many leading officers for their failure to provide adequate command. Confidence in the political leadership, particularly in Prime Minister Golda Meir and Defense Minister Moshe Dayan, was seriously eroded. There had been a refusal in Israel to take intelligence reports seriously enough to prepare for war. Behind this refusal were mistaken beliefs that Israel's devastating victory in 1967 and its control of vast stretches of Arab territory intimidated the Arabs,

The Yom Kippur War

and that the Arab armies were in no condition to conduct an attack. Egypt and Syria had set out to regain their lost territories and do damage to the strength of the Israel Defense Forces. In this second aim, they had met with some success.

The episode brought confidence and optimism to Egypt and Syria, and dealt a serious blow to Israel's self-confidence.

The cost to Israel in lives was greater than in any conflict since 1948—close to 2,300 dead and 5,500 wounded (Morris, p. 431). Israelis emerged from the war shocked by their casualties and frightened by their early military setbacks, despite their army's quick recovery of the upper hand. The Yom Kippur War reawakened society to the possibility of the annihilation of Israel and the Jewish people. In the eyes of most Israelis, the Arabs' goal was to destroy Israel rather than merely to regain the territories lost in 1967. A profound lack of confidence replaced their post-1967 pride, or perhaps even hubris. Aside from the physical cost, the war took a heavy moral toll. Continued occupation of the territories undermined Israel's international image (and perception of itself) as a valiant small power confronting large massed armies, David fighting Goliath. Furthermore, it did damage to the society's definition of itself as a democracy and

heralded the onset of serious internal dissension. A poll shortly after the war found that three-quarters of urban Israelis were prepared to give up all or nearly all the land occupied in both wars in exchange for peace. They realized, as one bereaved father told a *Newsweek* reporter, "we have been living in a fool's paradise since the Six-Day War. We couldn't afford all that boasting and self-confidence. If we have to give up some occupied territory, and then come to our senses in other ways, some good may yet come of all this" (Insight Team, p. 234). The consensus on the means to national survival disintegrated, and there arose a profound division in society about the shape of Israel's future. The internal friction, combined with the blow to national morale and the realization of its vulnerability, led Israel into a national trauma. An integral part of this trauma was what some regarded as the transformation of Zionism, a liberal nationalist movement, into a militant vision of control over the entire Land of Israel. Along with a relatively small group of religious extremists, some Labor Party members and secular intellectuals were devoted to securing this control.

Jerusalem. Jerusalem has been inhabited since 1800 B.C.E. and is one of the principal holy places of the three major monotheistic faiths—Judaism, Christianity, and Islam. The Jewish presence in the city began with King David's conquest (c. 1000 B.C.E.) of Jerusalem and its transformation into the capital of a united Israelite kingdom under his rule. For Jews, the city has been the focus of Jewish nationhood since their ancient dispersal from the Land of Israel. For Christians, Jerusalem is the location of the ministry and sufferings of Jesus in the period following the Last Supper and including the Crucifixion. For Muslims, the city contains the site from which the Prophet Muhammad is believed to have ascended to heaven.

After the War of Independence, Jerusalem was divided between Israel and Jordan by a cease-fire border, which ran roughly from the north to the south of the city. A modern road carrying traffic from north Jerusalem to the center of the city followed the line that served as a no-man's-land between Israeli and Jordanian Jerusalem. On both sides, the border was guarded. Israel, as noted, controlled West Jerusalem, which became the country's capital in 1950. The Jordanians controlled East Jerusalem, which contained the Old City, center of Jewish as well as other holy sites. Among the Jewish sites were the Western Wall (also known as the Wailing Wall, remnant of the ancient Second Temple), an ancient cemetery on Mount of Olives, and the Tomb of King David. These sites remained inaccessible to the Jews for 19 years (1948-67), until the Six-Day War.

In early June 1967, Israeli forces broke through the Lions' Gate to the Old City and captured it. The two parts of the city were officially united under Israeli control on June 28, 1967. For the first time in nearly two decades, inhabitants from one side could visit the other side. After 1967, Jews, Christians, and Muslims would reside both outside the Old City's walls, in modern Jerusalem, and within the Old City itself. But despite religious freedom under Israeli rule, Jerusalem continues to be a city of tensions, primarily between Arabs and Jews, but also between Christian sects, with many incidents of violence.

Particularly since the start of the first Intifada (Palestinian Arab uprising) in 1987, the city has been divided almost as severely as before 1967, with little social contact between Jews and Arabs. The Arab population lives primarily in East Jerusalem while the majority of Jews reside in the western parts of the city. In 1980 the Knesset (Israeli parliament) declared that "reunited" Jerusalem is the official capital of Israel, which stirred considerable international controversy, particularly in the context of discussion about Jerusalem's possibly becoming an international city or a city divided between Arabs and Jews. Recognition of Jerusalem as the capital was withheld by numerous countries. In the following years, the encroachment of Jewish housing on traditionally Arab areas would remain a point of international contention; nevertheless, beyond the Old City, Jerusalem would become a thriving modern city with many new commercial and residential developments—sports facilities, cafes, hotels, discos, concert halls, a large shopping mall, and galleries. Meanwhile, within its walls, the Old City has continued to exude spirituality through its Jewish, Christian, and Arab Quarters, and its synagogues, churches, and mosques.

The Poem in Focus

Contents overview. The first 16 poems of the cycle (the poems are all numbered) deal with the Yom Kippur War and aspects of Israel's early history. Although the poems do not give the military or political details of the war, some are set in October, identifying it to be this war. In Poem 2 the speaker tell us that "The war broke out in the autumn" (Amichai, Poem 2, *Shire Erets Tsiyon Yerushalayim*, p. 7; trans. G. Abramson). This first part of the cycle is not so much about the progress of the war itself, though Amichai refers to soldiers and death on the battlefield, but rather about Israel, the Israelis, and the immediate postwar mood. The poetic cycle clearly reflects the confusion and the substantive questions that emerged in the society after the war. Its poems do not enlighten readers about the progress of historical events; they reflect on the results of these events within a society deeply affected by them. In the second section of the cycle (Poems 17-39), the speaker reflects on Jerusalem after 1967. There is no obvious link in the cycle between the war and Jerusalem other than the city's strong association with Zion, the locus of spiritual longing. In fact, it is the title of the cycle, *Songs of the Land of Zion, Jerusalem*, that makes the direct connection between the two entities. Clearly the poet sees Jerusalem as a component of, or symbolic focus for, the territorial wars fought by the state from the beginning of its existence.

Section 1: War and Zionism. The poems in Section 1 (Poems 1-16) are related in subject matter, though each can stand alone. Two central topics bind the poems together: the war and the ideology of Zionism. Whether or not the poet refers explicitly to Zionism, it is central to his discussion of the war, the establishment of the Jewish homeland, and his response to it.

The cycle begins with the statement that the war broke out just as the speaker's child was being weaned (Poem 1). This means the end of innocence, the fundamental connection of the child with the mother. Certainly the October War signaled the end of Israel's political innocence as that autumn young soldiers, with their heavy army kits, left their families behind but carried a memory of their loved ones in their knapsacks (Poem 2). The short distance between adulthood in war and childhood innocence is conveyed in a moving image: "A soldier fills sandbags with soft sand / He once played in," from which the poem moves to "The October sun warms our dead, / Sadness is a heavy wooden board, / And

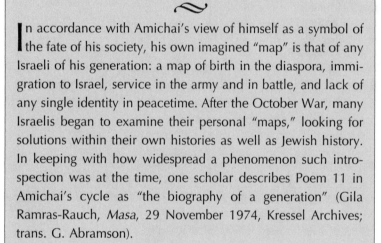

A GENERATION'S MAPMAKER

In accordance with Amichai's view of himself as a symbol of the fate of his society, his own imagined "map" is that of any Israeli of his generation: a map of birth in the diaspora, immigration to Israel, service in the army and in battle, and lack of any single identity in peacetime. After the October War, many Israelis began to examine their personal "maps," looking for solutions within their own histories as well as Jewish history. In keeping with how widespread a phenomenon such introspection was at the time, one scholar describes Poem 11 in Amichai's cycle as "the biography of a generation" (Gila Ramras-Rauch, *Masa*, 29 November 1974, Kressel Archives; trans. G. Abramson).

tears are the nails" (Poem 3, *Shire Erets Tsiyon*, p. 8; trans. G. Abramson). These last images allude to sacrifice when they liken sadness to a wooden board whose nails are made of tears. The word "board" may refer either to the board placed above Jesus' head (which was nailed to the cross) or to the lid of a coffin. In October the sun, which is not strong, warms the dead and this in itself is the sadness: the weak October sun is unable to revive them (Poem 3).

From the start, Zionism was conceived of as an ideology in which the collective transcended and expressed the individual. Consistent with this ideology, the poems in the cycle intertwine the personal and the national so that each

becomes a symbol of the other, undivided and indivisible. In the sixth poem this idea is joined to the main topics of war and Zionism: the conception of the mystic unity of the individual and the land emerges clearly in an image of a bullet wounding the soil after passing through a soldier's body. In a collective, ideological society such as Israel's, the pain of war is felt both by the wounded soldier and the land. Amichai writes that when the question is asked, "Where was he wounded?" one doesn't know whether this means a place on the soldier's body or on the earth. In a similar vein, the speaker comments wryly that because there is no peace in his heart, there is war outside (Poem 9).

There is another kind of fusion in this part of the cycle: as in many of Amichai's poems, the experience of the individual reflects certain aspects of Jewish history. The speaker recalls all the places identified with his past that have been wiped out by wars (Poem 11). The city of his birth was destroyed in the Second World War. The same war sank the ship on which he immigrated to Israel, and subsequent wars erased every other landmark of his life. Amichai's speaker imagines that there is a map of his life that has been destroyed, which, in fact, is the map of his memory. All that stands between him and nothingness is memory, for he is the only creator of himself and his past. Nothing objective remains. He is, he says, with a note of whimsy, not reliable as a lover or a son or as a lodger or neighbor, implying that he is reliable only as a poet, because in his poetry, his "map," or memory, is preserved.

Israel's pioneers, who were generally not Orthodox Jews, saw the land, rather than the Messiah, as the fulfillment of the ancient dream of redemption for the Jewish people. The speaker first seems to uphold but then questions this form of messianism, which proposes the unity of individual and land. Again he takes the Zionist idea of pioneering and joins it to war. The land will fulfill messianic expectations only through the massive sacrifice of young people in war. In Israel those who die in war are like the precious metals deep in the ground that constitute a country's natural wealth. Instead of referring to the country's material wealth, the speaker refers to the *spiritual* wealth stored in the earth: "This is a country whose dead are in the earth / In place of coal and gold and iron / They are the fuel for the coming of messiahs" (Poem 12, *Shire Erets Tsiyon*, p. 12; trans. G. Abramson). This would be an idealistic conclusion, and a comforting one in the face of almost perpetual warfare, but for the word "messiahs." Amichai gives no idea of who these messiahs are, whether the plural indicates an ironic reference to modern leadership, or whether the messiahs will redeem Israel or be as false as some of the "messiahs" in Jewish history. This twelfth poem is one of the most powerful of the cycle in its questioning of the very purpose of sacrifice for the nation:

> Like bumble bees in crazy buds
> We built the new homeland
> On Trumpeldor's last words,
> "It is good to die for our country."
> Even if these were not the words
> Or he didn't say them, or
> They were said and then vanished,
> Their space remains,
> Arched like a cave. Concrete
> Became harder than stone.
> (Poem 12, *Shire Erets Tsiyon*,
> p. 12; trans. G. Abramson)

Poem 13 is directly linked to the cycle's title even though it departs from the topic of the war. The poem begins with a reference to Naftali Hertz Imber, the poet responsible for the lyric of the Zionist and later Israeli national anthem, "Hatikvah" (set to music by Samuel Cohen). The title of Amichai's cycle borrows a phrase from "Hatikva": "To be a free people in our land, the land of Zion, Jerusalem." Poem 13 is a love poem, suggesting the separation of lovers and the regret, even despair, it occasions on the part of the reader. He has thoughts of acting in a violent way to stop the separation, of blowing up an airport, for example, but then realizes the futility of this— there would always be another way for his lover to leave. The poem moves away from war in theme only, not in language. Words such as "the last battle," "destroy," and "severely wounded" still point to battle—only this time it is the battle of love. The poem uses Imber and his lyric as a metaphor for the *loss* of hope in love. Through many untranslatable puns and plays on the title "Hatikvah" ("the hope"), Amichai explores the idea of hope and hopelessness in love. At the same time, the strong link between Imber (who, the speaker tells us, "died without hope") and the cycle's title brings the reader back to the overall topics linked together in the cycle: nation, Zionism, and war. Within the context of a cycle on war, even a love poem must use the terminology of war, so that war can never be far from the reader's mind.

Amichai takes the idealistic imagery of pioneering out of its historical context (as an outcome of Zionist ideology) and applies this imagery metaphorically to his speaker. "My holding back the tears / hardened the foundations. And my feet treading / in despairing joy were like ploughs / and pavers of roads" (Poem 14, *Shire Erets Tsiyon*, p. 13; trans. G. Abramson). He personalizes the national endeavour by using the locations and activities of the *halutzim,* or pioneers, as symbols of himself, imagining that his own deeply felt emotions provide the power for strengthening or building the foundations of the country. He laments that he was too late for draining the marshes or for A. D. Gordon, a Zionist ideologue, but the poet contributes in other ways: his sadness serves to harden the country's foundations and his tempered joy ploughs the fields (Poem 14).

Thoughts about the war continue throughout Section 1 of the cycle, which ends with the

---

PIONEERS

Afirst contingent of Jewish immigrants came to Palestine in the early 1880s after a wave of pogroms in Russia. Later, after 1897, in response to the Zionist movement, thousands of idealistic young Jews from Eastern Europe went to live in Palestine as pioneers (*halutzim*). Many who took part in the early-twentieth-century revolutionary struggle in Russia immigrated and laid the foundation for the Israeli labor movement. Beginning as hired laborers, they went on to establish collective farms (kibbutzim), build roads, drain marshlands, and generally transform the countryside.

---

speaker's wry comment that his entire life seems to have been defined by war: "Even my love affairs are measured by times of war, / I say that this happened after the Second World War,/ or we met one day before the Six-Day War" (Poem 16, *Shire Erets Tsiyon*, p. 14; trans. G. Abramson).

Section 2: Jerusalem. The second, longer, section of the cycle (Poems 17-39) contains poems about Jerusalem. There is an implicit political element in any mention of modern Jerusalem, and when it appears in a cycle concerned with the theme of war, this is certainly the case. In the cycle the speaker gives us a factual statement about the city's 19-year division between Israel and Jordan. He regrets the unification, not for political reasons but because of a certain romance lent to life by the division of the city:

> For nineteen years the city was divided,
> The lifetime of a young man

Who perhaps died in the war.
I long for the tranquillity and the yearning.
Crazy people would cross the dividing fence,
Enemies would breach it,
Lovers would go and check it . . .
> (Poem 23, *Shire Erets Tsiyon*, p. 18; trans.
> G. Abramson)

For Amichai's speaker, paradoxically the longing for Jerusalem was more satisfying than the acquisition of the entire city. Perhaps the longing for Zion, always represented by Jerusalem, is more desirable than the achievement of it, a possibility confirmed in the poem in, "I long for the *tranquillity*" and "the areas of no-man's-land were like *calm* bays [italics added]," indicating the comparative peace *before* Jerusalem was restored to the Jews (Poem 23, *Shire Erets Tsiyon*, p. 18; trans. G. Abramson). In the subsequent poem (Poem 24), the speaker gives reasons for feeling this way. He contrasts the dignified, quiet of divided Jerusalem with the entity he now calls a noisy, fat woman wearing gold and copper, whom, he says explicitly, he does not love. In the modern, brash city, crowded with tourists, the speaker has lost the sense of spirituality invested in Jerusalem by historical and religious loss and longing.

Elsewhere the speaker asks implicitly what Jerusalem is for and gives the answer in one of his startling similes: it is like a ship in a bottle that does nothing but stand for the real ship on the sea (Poem 19). Jerusalem represents the ideal holy city, one that does not exist but could exist. The idea behind this poem is that there is a real Jerusalem known to God but he has given us nothing but a representation, preserved and unchanging, merely an object to be admired or a memory of true holiness. Both in Poem 19 and later in Poem 23 the fantasy satisfies more than the reality. The speaker indicates that the actual Jerusalem is a city built on death with gravestones as foundations (Poem 18), or a dead city whose citizens are earthworms (Poem 35).

Nevertheless the inner beauty of Jerusalem is there for those who seek it, not at the commercial Western Wall but at David's tomb (Poem 26), an interior space, sensed but unseen. To a certain extent, this hidden element sustains modern Jerusalem: King David's tomb, which the poet describes in elevated images, and four buried synagogues (buried to protect them from "God's bombing") are its spiritual subsoil (Poem 31, *Shire Erets Tsiyon*, p. 23; trans. G. Abramson). In truth, the gains and despoilings of Jerusalem's past can never be wholly excised from the speaker's awareness. But, despite his deep affection for the city, there is a sense of fatigue that stems from the need to remember and the constant guilt of forgetting, which defines Amichai's writing. What is the nature of his obligation to remember? His answer is that whatever it is, religious tradition, national aspirations, Zionism, or the wars, he finds it tiring to be so active and constant a component of history, as if the remembering ensures the nation's existence. For the Israelis, the historical and political past is a living part of their present and the very weight of active memory is burdensome. "Let everyone remember," the speaker says, "so that I can rest" (Poem 34, *Shire Erets Tsiyon*, p. 26; trans. G. Abramson).

While the speaker, tired of the burden of memory, may want to relegate the keeping of the spiritual and historical heritage to official institutions (Poem 34), he is constrained to remember a single individual who fell in Jerusalem "at the gate of Gethsemane," whose body is "an added gate in the wall" and of whose death "all of Jerusalem is a meaning" (Poem 38, *Shire Erets Tsiyon*, p. 29; trans. G. Abramson). The speaker may be referring to a soldier in this instance. But the scholar Hillel Barzel takes "Gethsemane" (where Jesus went to pray and was arrested after the Last Supper) to indicate Jesus, who represents all those slain for the sake or in the name of Jerusalem. "Gethsemane" may point not to the fallen soldier or the *person* of Jesus, but rather to their quality as victims, the archetypes of all who have fallen in war for Jerusalem's sake. The idea of dead soldiers being fuel for the coming of messiahs (Poem 12) is linked to this poem (Poem 38) about martyrdom; the word "messiahs," to the oblique reference to Jesus. In any case, the true nature of Amichai's earthly Jerusalem (the ship in the bottle) asserts itself: it is a place of death, introduced in this cycle by images of blood and war, culminating in the strangely glorious figure of the slain one, a soldier or Christ, who ascends to heaven (Poem 38).

The "Jerusalem" part of the cycle is more abstract than the previous section, yet reminders of Jerusalem's troubled history are embedded throughout. The lurking reality of the Yom Kippur War and other wars are directly recalled in Poem 35, which mentions "jihad and war" bursting out "like figs"; in the previous poem, national flags are the "coloured shrouds of history," and other images of the homeland are coupled with pain, death, and memory (Poems 35, 34, *Shire Erets Tsiyon*, p. 26; trans. G. Abramson).

WILFRED OWEN AND JOSEPH TRUMPELDOR

Wilfred Owen, an English soldier-poet, wrote bitter verses about the death of soldiers in World War I. His poem "Dulce et Decorum Est" ends ironically with the Latin poet Horace's words, "Dulce et decorum est pro patria mori"; that is, "It is sweet and decorous to die for one's country" (Owen in Parsons, p. 64). Similar words have been attributed to the Israeli pioneer Joseph Trumpeldor. Trumpeldor (1880-1920) was a Russian-born Jewish hero who fought first in the Russo-Japanese War (1904), in which he lost an arm, and then in World War I, distinguishing himself for bravery in the British offensive at Gallipoli (1915). Later Trumpeldor devoted himself to organizing pioneer groups to settle in Palestine. In 1920 he was killed in the Arab riots at Tel Hai in the north of Israel, which he was helping to fortify. It is reported that his last words were, *"En davar, tov la-mut be-`ad artsenu"* ("Never mind; it is good to die for our country"). Whether or not he really said these words is debatable, but in any case, his life and death became a symbol to pioneer youth from all parts of the diaspora. Songs, poems, and stories were written about Trumpeldor. His courage, idealism, and personal appeal made him an icon for pioneering socialist movements and right-wing groups alike. Poem 12 in Amichai's cycle ends with an image of dead soldiers as fuel for the coming of messiahs, which, taken with the original Latin slogan and Trumpeldor's supposed last words, makes the poem as unequivocally bitter as Owen's.

Yet two verses before the end (Poem 37), Amichai creates a metaphor of great beauty, that of Jerusalem as a launching pad for the next world, the hollows of its valleys having been filled in with all its history, and its artifacts, good and bad, to make a level, smooth runway "for my sweet aircraft / which will come to take me up there" (Poem 37, *Shire Erets Tsiyon*, p. 28; trans. G. Abramson). In similar fashion, the final verse is a simple, sentimental affirmation of hope. The first poem in the cycle told of a child being weaned; the last expresses the hope of another birth: in holy Jerusalem "two people are lying together / on the bed / to make a new and happy person (Poem 39, *Shire Erets Tsiyon*, pp. 29-30; trans. G. Abramson).

Poetic protest. Poem 12 features the line *Dulce et decorum est pro patria mori*. With its idea of the supreme sacrifice—one's life for one's country—the motto has long been a watchword of war. In the poem, the slogan is linked not explicitly to war, but to building the homeland, a dangerous endeavor because of its association with war. After 1967 and to an even greater extent after 1973, the phrase began to ring hollow in Israel and Israelis started to question the sacrifice of the nation's youth. This poem of Amichai's echoes that questioning, a questioning that makes the emphasis on sacrifice in *Songs of the Land of Zion, Jerusalem* so representative. The poet's apparent denigration of this slogan, supposedly recited by the Zionist pioneer Joseph Trumpeldor, can be seen as a denigration of the kind of Zionism that Trumpeldor represented. Yet, the poem suggests, so entrenched are these words in the national consciousness that they can never be erased and will continue to motivate sacrifice in war. Later, with Amichai's permission, this poem would be printed in an anthology of poetry that protested the Lebanon War of 1982. Including Poem 12 in a volume devoted to criticizing the Lebanon campaign ensured that it was read as a political statement.

Central to the whole cycle of poems is Amichai's bitterness about the wars that Israel has fought and in which he served. In a country where everyone serves in the army—esteemed as a force for good, the source of security, and the backbone of nationhood—the constant denunciation of war could be read as a subversive statement. However, the poet does not blame Zionism for the wars: his attitude is more radical than that.

In Poem 4, the poet claims to "have nothing to say about the war. / I have nothing to add, I'm ashamed" (Poem 4, *Shire Erets Tsiyon*, p. 8; trans. G. Abramson). Of course, the poet may not be "ashamed" of the *war*, but of his inability to say anything about it. In fact, he goes on in the poem to say a great deal. He makes two absurd observations, each followed by the word "yes": that the sun revolves around the earth and that the earth is flat. These are followed by a third observation—"there is a God in heaven, yes" (Poem 4, *Shire Erets Tsiyon*, p. 8; trans. G. Abramson). Taken together, the lines build to an irony that reveals what the poet thinks about God's place in the scheme of war: his poetry indicts God as either the maker of war or an indifferent onlooker. In this regard, Amichai differs from other poets of his generation: his poetry invariably implicates God in Israel's wars.

Literary context. Members of the first literary generation of the State of Israel, to which chronologically Amichai belonged, were either born in Israel or, like Amichai, came to Israel at an early age and learned Hebrew. Many of them distinguished themselves in the War of Independence and all saw Israel proclaim itself a state while they were still in their teens or early twenties. This was the first generation to speak Hebrew as their mother tongue or as a vernacular. Almost all these writers had something profound to say about war; the war poetry of certain writers— Haim Guri (b. 1922), for example—became hymns for the fighters. More than any one of these writers, Amichai seemed to distill the war experience of his generation, expressing, without bravado or sentimentality, the reality of being a soldier and the terrible sadness of war.

Songs of the Land of Zion, Jerusalem takes a view of war that differs from that of other contemporary Israeli poets. The cycle does not talk explicitly about the battlefield, but hints at the reasons for the war and gives readers insight into the post-1973 mood. There is an equally unique attitude to Jerusalem in the cycle: it does not portray the city with any kind of reverence, but depicts it ambiguously, as mysteriously attractive, aloof, and dangerous. The equation of Zion and Jerusalem with war in general and the October War in particular shows clearly that Amichai's view of Jerusalem was less than wholly positive, and by no means conventional.

Reception. Amichai received many prestigious prizes, among them the Bialik Prize (1976) and the Israel Prize (1981), and in 1986 he became a foreign member of the American Academy of Arts and Letters. Overall, the reception accorded to *Songs of the Land of Zion, Jerusalem* at the time of its publication (in *Behind All This a Great Happiness Is Hiding*) was positive. The cycle

aroused no great controversy, perhaps because Amichai had already written a very much stronger Jerusalem cycle after the war in 1967 (Jerusalem 1967), which severely criticized Jerusalem and suggested that it was not worth all the sacrifices made for it. *Songs of the Land of Zion, Jerusalem* is gentler and more elegiac and while it hints at Jerusalem's heart of darkness, which Amichai had explored in detail in the earlier Jerusalem cycle, it also indicates some affection for its spiritual beauty. Literary scholars praised the lyricism of the cycle and, above all, its ability to express the collective experience. One noted critic wrote of "the beauty of sensual and ironic poetry whose effect has not lessened to this day" (Blat, *ha-Tsofeh*, p. 4; trans. G. Abramson).

Some members of the younger generation have faulted Amichai, along with other writers, for the content and tone of his poetry and fiction. The political scientist Yoram Hazony accuses several Israeli writers of "a pronounced difficulty in relating in a constructive fashion to the Jewish state" and singles out Amichai for conjuring "deeply ambivalent" images about the Jewish political restoration, citing as evidence *Songs of the Land of Zion, Jerusalem* (Hazony, p. 29). Such criticism is a part of a debate raging about Jewish nationalism, Zionism, and the disputed territories, not only in Israel but throughout the diaspora. In the eyes of some, Amichai's poetic meditations are a denial of the value of the Jewish state; others find fault with his admiration for the heroes of the *Palmah*, going so far as to say that his writing glorifies the values of military might and warfare (Dalia Karpel, *Ha'ir*, 3 November 1989, in Kressel Archives). Most writers and artists meanwhile consider it their task to constitute a voice of opposition or to puncture any vainglorious or hubristic sense within the nation, an objective that *Songs of Zion, Jerusalem* certainly achieves.

—Glenda Abramson

For More Information

Abramson, Glenda. *The Writing of Yehuda Amichai: A Thematic Approach.* Albany: State University of New York Press, 1989.

Amichai, Yehuda. "Patriotic Songs." In *Amen.* Trans. Yehuda Amichai and Ted Hughes. Oxford University Press, 1978.

———. *Shire Erets Tsiyon, Yerushalayim* (Songs of Zion, Jerusalem). In *Me-ahore kol zeh mistater osher gadol* (Behind All This Lies a Great Happiness). Jerusalem: Schocken, 1974.

Barzel, Hillel. "ha-Kinot ha-metukot shel Yehudah Amihai" (The Sweet Lamentations of Yehuda Amichai). *Me'asef le-sifrut tarbut ve-omanut, Yediot Aharonot,* 25 October 1974, 2.

Blat, Avraham. "Meshorer ha-akhzavut" (Poet of Disappointment). *Ha-Tsofeh,* 27 December 1974, 4.

Cohen, Joseph. *Voices of Israel: Essays on Interviews with Yehuda Amichai, A. B. Yehoshua, T. Carmi, Aharon Appelfeld and Amos Oz.* New York: State University of New York Press, 1990.

Finkelstein, Norman G. *Image and Reality of the Israel-Palestine Conflict,* London: Verso, 1995.

Hazony, Yoram. *The Jewish State: the Struggle for Israel's Soul,* New York: Basic Books, 2000.

Insight Team of the Sunday Times. *Insight on the Middle East War.* London: Andre Deutsch, 1974.

Kressel Archives. Leopold Muller Library. Oxford Center for Hebrew and Jewish Studies. Oxford, United Kingdom.

Kronfeld, Hana. *On the Margins of Modernism.* Berkeley: University of California Press, 1996.

Morris, Benny. *Righteous Victims.* New York: Vintage, 2001.

Parsons, I. M., ed. *Men Who March Away.* New York: Viking, 1965.

Yudkin, Leon. *Escape Into Siege.* London: Routledge and Kegan Paul, 1974.

The Spiritual Couplets

by

Jalal al-Din Muhammad Balkhi Rumi

J alal al-Din Muhammad Balkhi Rumi (1207-73) was born near the ancient city of Balkh and died in the Anatolian city of Konya. His father, Baha al-Din, was a leading Islamic cleric and a Sufi who taught at a madrasah, or religious school. It was in such religious schools, as well as from his father's circle of friends, that Rumi gained a basic knowledge of Islam and its mystical trend known as Sufism. Rumi was also an avid reader, not just of the **Quran** (also in *WLAIT 6: Middle Eastern Literatures and Their Times*) but also of his father's writings, which were later compiled into a book known as *Ma`arif* (Teachings). Around 1215, Rumi's family left Balkh and emigrated westward. The family eventually settled in Konya, capital of the young Seljuk dynasty of Anatolia, in modern-day Turkey. After his father died in 1232, Rumi succeeded him as the leader of the Konya Muslims. He had taken to writing poetry by then, mostly short lyrics of 5-15 lines known as *ghazals*. The remainder of Rumi's life and work would subsequently be shaped by some telling encounters.

In 1244 Rumi met Shams-i Tabrizi, a dervish, that is, an itinerant follower of Sufism. The friendship lasted for some three years, during which Rumi is said to have spun *ghazals* day and night, producing some of the most passionate love lyrics in Persian poetry. Late in 1247 or early 1248 Shams disappeared as mysteriously as he had appeared. Rumi had already begun to use Shams's name as his own pen-name, as if he had become Shams. He would proceed to call his collected book of *ghazals* "The Divan of Shams," as if Shams, and not he, had authored the colossal

---

THE LITERARY WORK

A compendium of didactic stories and parables interspersed with diverse comments and told in rhyming couplets, set in the Persian Empire in the mid-to-late thirteenth century; composed in Persian (as *Masnavi-i ma`navi*) 1258 to 1273; published in English between 1925 and 1934.

SYNOPSIS

The collection of stories, some derived from the Quran and prophetic traditions in Islam, others based on animal fables or street jokes, instructs the reader in the philosophy and lives of the Sufis.

---

work. Rumi next selected the goldsmith Salah al-Din Zarkub as his closest associate. Legend has it that Rumi was walking in the bazaar one day when, upon hearing the rhythmic tapping of a goldsmith's hammer, he began to move his body in a quickening dance. So absorbed was the goldsmith in Rumi's movement that he kept up the beat, even when the blows began to ruin the precious gold he was shaping to a customer's order. Seeing how easily the goldsmith transcended his interest in material possession, Rumi walked over, led him out of his shop by the hand, and appointed him as his new friend and master.

In 1258 Salah al-Din passed away, and Rumi turned to a longtime associate, Husam al-Din, as his final closest companion. He is the one credited with recommending that Rumi compose *The Spiritual Couplets*. Begun in 1258 and finished just a few months before Rumi's death, the collection conveys what many describe as the most wide-ranging series of stories ever submitted to allegorical interpretation for the purpose of communicating the principles of Islamic mysticism to the initiate and lay reader alike.

Events in History at the Time of the Poems

Institutionalized Sufism. As a way of conceptualizing and practicing Islam, Sufism experienced a gradual rise in importance among Muslims. In fact, the tradition had gained so much esteem by the thirteenth century that kings made a show of periodically receiving blessings from Sufi masters, noblemen sought to enhance their nobility by attaching themselves to great Sufi guides, and rich merchants donated large sums to the Sufi order, fraternity, or lodge of their choice. In this formative era, fundamental Sufi doctrine, based on the Quran and the traditions of the Prophet Muhammad, remained relatively stable. The early Sufis shared some foundational views, including such all-inclusive definitions of God as "the first and the last and the outwardly manifest and the inwardly hidden" (Quran 57:3). Another common view, arising in part from the categorical observation that "Wherever you turn, there is the face of God," concerned the relationship between the human and the divine, which differed from orthodox views in that the Sufis saw it as centered more on love, less on fear (Quran 2:115). Such basic doctrine would endure; however, Sufism soon came to be interpreted in different, sometimes conflicting ways. For example, individual expressions of mutual affection between God and humans gradually gave way to established norms for imagining God as the un-needing beloved and human beings as the supplicant lover that formed a central theme in the Persian love lyric. Similarly, the practice of constantly repeating the many names of God as an act of reminding oneself and others of His presence, which was part of the ascetic lifestyle of the early Sufi saints, turned into ritual group dances such as the Sama practiced and propagated by Rumi himself and the Mevleviyeh order he founded. As such, the pietistic and ascetic Sufism of the early Islamic mystics underwent drastic changes. The early Sufis wore a coarse woolen robe, known in Arabic as *suf* (a word that has given its name to the whole movement).

A post-fourteenth-century rendition of a legendary scene outside a goldsmith shop, showing Rumi in the foreground and the goldsmith in the background.

Their belief was that in constantly scratching the skin, the coarse cloth served as a reminder that personal comfort and the pleasures of the body should be shunned or at least kept in check. Moreover, the coarseness symbolized pious renunciation by the virtuous of the many luxuries to which other Muslims had succumbed after Islam came into contact with the Mesopotamian and Persian civilizations—luxuries like the silk and satin robes that the Persians' Arabic overlords in the Abbasid dynasty had begun to wear as a sign of social distinction.

By Rumi's time, Sufism itself had given way to the lure of wealth. Monetary endowments supported competing Sufi orders, each of which grew accustomed to enriching itself and outdoing the others. As the Muslim community, or *ummah*, grew more diverse, with the proliferation of various sects and tendencies, Sufism became practically synonymous with tolerance. People conceived of the mystical tradition as a variant that viewed the relationship between the human and the divine—as well as the human bond among followers of all faiths—as governed more by love than by anything else.

At the height of the Sufi movement, in the twelfth and thirteenth centuries, what distinguished the Sufi movement from Muslim orthodoxy was the former's reliance on experiencing religion individually and from within. While more orthodox Muslims sought to learn the shari`ah, or canon of Islamic laws from established religious leaders, the Sufis, who called themselves men of the tariqah, the path, aspired to go their own ways. They set out to experience the spiritual dimensions of Islam personally and existentially.

In time, Sufism divided into various orders and brotherhoods, each with its own founder and version of beliefs, its own set of customs and followers, and its own sphere of influence. By the thirteenth century, Baghdad had become home to the Suhrawardi order, named after the Persian philosopher Shihab al-Din Suhrawardi (d. 1191); India to the Chishtiyah order, consisting of the followers of Mu`in al-Din Chishti (d. 1236); and Khwarazam to the Kubrawi order, named after its founder Najm al-Din Kubra (1158-1221), to which Rumi's father is said to have belonged. In short, there was a great deal of effort to institutionalize Sufism through the establishment of monasteries, hospices, lodges, and other Sufi institutions during Rumi's lifetime. Shortly before his death, Rumi himself founded the Mevleviyeh order, which is still a strong force today, especially in Turkey. Most medieval Sufis believed that the path they walked could only be traversed in the company of a guiding shaykh (sheik), one who knows the way and can lead the wayfarer on the right course. Rumi himself was certainly of this mind.

Sufis also believed that Adam's transgression against God caused him to be exiled to the earth, an event that is known in Islamic philosophy as "the cosmic descent." Although Islam is explicit about God's forgiveness (which is why the concept of original sin does not exist in Islam), the challenge remains for human beings to find their way back to God. Sufis taught that this feat could be achieved if Muslims begin to purify their souls. They posited the concept of "the perfect man," human beings like Jesus and Muhammad who achieved perfection by purifying their souls of all that was earthly. They could then ascend to the presence of God after death; and what is more, they could have glimpses of their ascent even while living.

Balkh and Konya—imperial outposts. Both of the cities with which Rumi is associated were large urban areas with ethnically and religiously diverse populations. The ancient city of Balkh, known as "mother of all cities," lay at the crossing of major trade routes from the Roman

Empire to China. In Islamic times, the city had attained a commercial and economic prosperity that put it on par with the largest of the urban areas in Asia. This allowed the city to nurture the development of many scientists, scholars, and Sufi saints, such as Rumi's father. That Buddhists, Hindus, and others lived alongside the rising Muslim population in Balkh, and that their temples, though in ruins, were still visible when Rumi was growing up, provided contemporary and historical reminders of coexistence. These reminders were no doubt absorbed by him as he roamed the city.

A LEGENDARY DEATH

Legend relates the event of Rumi's death in this way: in the fall of 1273 an earthquake shook the city of Konya. When the frightened citizens questioned Rumi about its meaning, he told them not to worry. "The earth," he said, "is opening its mouth because it is ready to swallow a big morsel." He died a few months later, on December 17, 1273.

Rumi's next hometown, Konya, had an ancient history too. Its name, derived from eikon or "image," refers to the legend of the gorgon's head, used by the Greek hero Perseus to vanquish the local populace and found the city as a Greek community two centuries before Christ. After the Greek civilization was overtaken by the Roman, Konya became part of the Roman province of Galatia, and later formed the headquarters of the Eastern Roman or Byzantine Empire. As both the Persian Empire and the Byzantine Empire in turn fell to the Muslim Arabs in the seventh and eighth centuries, Konya lost much of its significance as a cultural center. However, in the late eleventh century, after the Seljuks of Anatolia—an ethnically Turkic people who had converted to Islam— conquered it and made it the capital of their sultanate of Rum, Konya thrived once again. The Seljuk palace still stands on the city's acropolis mound. Near this important site are both a mosque that contains the Tomb of Ala al-Din, the Muslim ruler who rebuilt this Seljuk city on the model of Islamic urban architecture, and the monastery that houses the Sufi order Rumi founded. Clearly the diversity of the population played a part in the spirit of tolerance and the acceptance of different ways of worship

RUMI ON THE IMPORTANCE OF A SUFI MASTER

The following *ghazal* from Rumi's *Divan of Shams* reads like a space journey, at least on the surface.

A luminous vessel appeared at dawn in the sky;
it descended from the sky and looked upon me,
then like a falcon picking up a bird in the hunt
that vessel picked me up and sped across the sky.
As I looked inward at me I did not see my self
inside the vessel my body turned tender as the soul
and as I traveled through my soul I saw nothing but the vessel
until the mystery of the pre-eternal epiphany was revealed to me.
When the nine heavenly firmaments sank into the vessel
the whole ship of my being hid beneath an ocean
and as the ocean's waves heaved, reason reared its head
roaring about how things were and what things became.
And when the ocean's waves made foam, each piece
made manifest a likeness of this thing, a body of that man,
thus every foamy particle that took in a glimpse of the ocean
melted at once, flowed, and became one with the ocean.
Without the fortune of serving the true Sun of Tabriz
you can neither see that luminary vessel nor be one with the ocean.
   (Rumi, *Kulliyat-i Shams ya divan-i kabir*, vol. 2, pp. 65-66; trans.
   Ahmad Karimi-Hakkak)

The poem depicts a spaceship snatching up the speaker and taking him to the depths of the ocean-like sky. The speaker tells of a grand meltdown where all apparently separate things become one flowing mass. The closing line mentions Rumi's friend Shams, proclaiming that such an experience is possible only if one has the good fortune to select him for a master. Clearly, the whole journey is a metaphor for the ascent and transformation that becomes possible when a novice commits himself to the care of a Sufi master. The poem is also an example of the Persian *ghazal*, an important genre in Persian poetry.

that the Sufis espoused and that is ever-present in Rumi's poetry.

In the Middle Ages, in the Islamic world as in Christendom, people were identified with cities rather than countries. Just as Dante is forever linked with Florence, many Muslim saints, scientists, and poets are known by the name of the city where they were born or where they made their careers. This is why Persian writers such as Firdawsi and Attar are associated with the cities of Tus and Nishapur—both in modern Iran—and Nizami is identified as Nizami of Ganja—today in the Republic of Azerbaijan. (See Firdawsi's **Shahnamah**, Attar's **The Conference of the Birds**, and Nizami's **Khusraw and Shirin**, all also in

WLAIT 6: *Middle Eastern Literatures and Their Times.*) In the case of Rumi, the Persians link him to Balkh while the Turks connect him to the region of Rum, or Anatolia, where the city of Konya is located.

The Poems in Focus

Contents overview. Although *Spiritual Couplets* is a compendium of 25,000 rhyming couplets with no overall plot, the work opens with a flute reed that laments its separation from the reed-bed. The image reflects the sense of exile from the presence of God that frames and permeates the whole work. The work takes an episodic, digressionary approach. It is, in effect, a rambling philosophical discourse, with parables and anecdotes that unfold according to the free association of ideas and are anchored by diverse moral observations. Instead of aiming for overall coherence, Rumi clarifies his philosophical or moral argument through parables and anecdotes. At times, a new purpose emerges from a tangential aspect of a story, creating the impression that, momentarily at least, the central theme has been lost. Thus scholars have turned to Rumi's other works for his precise philosophical views, while this one provides access to Rumi as a teacher of Islamic mysticism. The 25,000 couplets are divided into six parts, of almost equal length. After the *nay-namah* (song of the reed-flute) come the various tales, each usually followed by a commentary, aimed at expounding the inner meaning of things from a Sufi perspective.

"The Reed Flute's Song." The opening poem alludes to a story told by the reed flute; lamenting that it has been separated from the reed bed, the flute relates its past experiences and its longing for home. If the book of couplets can be said to have a governing structure, it is hidden in this initial tale, whose first half follows:

> Listen to the story told by the reed,
> of being separated.
>
> "Since I was cut from the reedbed,
> I have made this crying sound.
>
> Anyone apart from someone he loves
> understands what I say.
>
> Anyone pulled from a source
> longs to go back.
>
> At any gathering I am there,
> mingling in the laughing and grieving,
>
> a friend to each, but few
> will hear the secrets hidden
>
> within the notes. No ears for that.
> Body flowing out of spirit,
>
> spirit up from body: no concealing
> that mixing. But it's not given us
>
> to see the soul. The reed flute
> is fire, not wind. Be that empty."
> (Rumi, "The Reed Flute's Song,"
> *The Essential Rumi*, pp. 17-18)

The crying sound that the reed says it has made since separation can be interpreted as every human being's recollection, in language, of the memory of an original state of existence in oneness with God and the desire to return to that state. This is the theme in a great many stories that follow, whether of a lover king suffering for the sake of his beloved slave girl, or an Indian parrot in captivity recalling the freedom of the forests (Rumi, *Masnawi*, bk. 1. vol. 1, pp. 6-8, 95-96).

The poem moves on to the difficulty of communicating this condition. The people who hear my song, says the reed flute, cannot grasp the secret hidden in the notes. Sufis in general found language both inescapable and an impediment, a subject of many stories in *The Spiritual Couplets*. One of these describes an Arab, a Turk, and an Indian, each of whom craves a particular fruit (Rumi, *Masnawi*, bk. 2, vol. 1, pp. 454-56). If they only knew each other's language, they would realize, the speaker concludes, that they all were asking for the same thing: grapes.

Sufi masters and teachers were also intent on pointing out the flaws and shortcomings in the way we perceive the world. That "few will hear the secrets hidden within the notes" of the reed flute—that many important aspects of life remain hidden from us—may be a commonplace, but a true Sufi would never give up his quest to discover them. It is the mark of the true Sufi to acknowledge the presence of things in the invisible world of the spirit, even though "it's not given us to *see* the soul." For the Sufi, the world is not confined to those things that can be seen or heard or touched. That the human mind, being finite, is incapable of grasping the infinite is a basic belief in Sufism. Scores of stories in *The Spiritual Couplets* illustrate the foregoing cluster of points. Finally, Sufis are encouraged to empty themselves of habitual ways of seeing the world and of being in it; they can and should become as empty (i.e., receptive) as the reed flute to gain the ability to turn the wind that blows through them into the fire of desire for oneness with God.

In its second half, "The Reed Flute's Song" elaborates the conditions that may be obtained through higher states of consciousness. Because it has the fire of love in its notes, the reed flute can be a true friend to all those who wish to tear asunder the veil that prevents them from seeing the human body, the world, and life as they are in truth: a thing, a place, and a state of existence where opposites have temporarily come together. As a true seeker on the path of union with God, the Sufi must cherish and nurture the desire for that ultimate union to such an extent that its force would propel the Sufi forever and with increasing speed on this path. And what if someone does not wish to tread on the path at all?

Then, Rumi counsels, the true Sufi must "cut the conversation, say good-bye, and leave."

> Hear the love fire tangled
> in the reed notes, as bewilderment
>
> melts into wine. The reed is a friend
> to all who want the fabric torn
>
> and drawn away. The reed is hurt
> and salve combining. Intimacy
>
> and longing for intimacy, one
> song. A disastrous surrender
>
> and a fine love, together. The one
> who secretly hears this is senseless.
>
> A tongue has one customer, the ear.
> A sugarcane flute has such effect
>
> because it was able to make sugar
> in the reedbed. The sound it makes
>
> is for everyone. Days full of wanting,
> let them go by without worrying
>
> that they do. Stay where you are
> inside such a pure, hollow note.
>
> Every thirst gets satisfied except
> that of these fish, the mystics,
>
> who swim a vast ocean of grace
> still somehow longing for it!
>
> No one lives in that without
> being nourished every day.
>
> But if someone doesn't want to hear
> The song of the reed flute,
>
> It's best to cut conversation
> Short, say good-bye, and leave.
> ("The Reed Flute's Song,"
> *The Essential Rumi*, p. 18)

As a metaphor for the great changes such a journey could lead to, winemaking was fascinating to the Sufi poets, particularly because of the imperfectly understood transformation it involved. What turns grape juice into wine was thought to be analogous to the imperceptible transformation that turned certain human beings into prophets, mystics, or poets. "Love" was the name given to that elixir that facilitated the transformation. Thus, the theme of love dominates the work. Another passage extols love through a series of seemingly disparate binary opposites, which are finally reconciled through love. Love, says this poetic passage, is the substance that can turn bitter things into sweet ones, copper into gold, lees and dregs into pure ruby wine, pain into remedy, and the dead corpse into a living

and breathing creature (Rumi, *Masnawi*, bk. 2, vol. 1, pp. 330-31).

And what of those, motivated by love, who do set out to know the self and God, the ones who listen to the reed flute? Rumi suggests that they find themselves more and more fired by desire, more eager for greater and greater degrees of self-knowledge, which is key to knowing God. The idea is then concretized in the image of the Sufis as resembling the thirsty fish who, even in the midst of water, move their lips as if they are forever thirsty. This image is important to the Sufi poets because it establishes a relationship between the quest and the object, the path and the destination. Since Sufis believed that the path to a higher and truer understanding of God passes through self-knowledge, they posited the quest as internal, the effort to polish the mirror of the human soul.

One crucial story in the collection pits two teams of painters against each other (Rumi, *Masnawi*, bk. 1, vol. 1, pp. 213-15). While one group paints the most colorful mural on one wall, the other simply polishes the opposite wall for the most perfect reflection. Between the two teams is a divider. When the divider is removed and the patron king stands in the middle to declare a winner, not the wall with the mural but the polished wall that reflects it is judged more artistically accomplished because it invites a deeper glance. In the passage above, the fish move their mouths as if to drink the water all around them, and, though nourished by it every day, are not wholly satisfied. Theirs, like that of the mystics, is an internal thirst.

"Moses and the Shepherd." One of the most significant lines of separation between Muslim orthodoxy and Sufism lies between strict adherence to Islamic "law" and the "path" the Sufis of Rumi's day took in their quest to reach God. Those who obeyed the canon of the laws (*shari`ah*) believed that the observance of established religious prescriptions and prohibitions was the only road to salvation. In contrast, the Sufis advocated an individual approach to salvation. In *The Spiritual Couplets* the story of "Moses and the Shepherd" addresses that basic dichotomy (Rumi, *Masnawi*, bk. 2, vol. 1, pp. 341-46). A shepherd speaks words that sound blasphemous to Moses and, reproached severely, the shepherd flees the scene, as if to escape his former self. The exchange between the two might be paraphrased as follows:

"Where are you, God, O my God? Show your face to me, and I will do anything you command me to. I will sacrifice my sheep and goats, nay, my whole house and household, to you. I long to crawl to your bedchamber at night and make your bed, O God, carrying the best of my fresh milk for your nourishment. I will kiss your hands and rub your lovely feet, and then put your moccasins before you. And I will serve you most sincerely, O God, in every way you command."

Enraged, Moses questions the shepherd and chides him. The words that ensue may be paraphrased thus: "Whom are you speaking to, man?" Moses demands to know. "Why God, of course!" responds the shepherd, to which Moses replies in the sonorous voice of ultimate authority: "You wretch of an errant creature, you! Cease your nonsense this instant, before a huge calamity engulfs us all. That's not how you address the creator of the earth and the high firmaments, for heaven's sake. Do you imagine God as like your uncle or something? Do you suppose him in need of milk or other nourishment? And what is this nonsense about his bed and his moccasins? Quick, man, supplicate yourself in abject repentance or else!"

At his wit's end, the shepherd throws dust in his mouth, tears up his clothes, and runs aimlessly, trying to get away from his errant self. At this point God intervenes to tell Moses that he, and not the shepherd, is the one who has erred, by thinking that God listens to people's speech rather than directly to their hearts:

> You have separated me
> from one of my own. Did you come as a Prophet
> to unite, or to sever?
> I have given each being a separate and unique
>   way
> of seeing and knowing and saying that knowledge.
>
> What seems wrong to you is right for him.
> What is poison to one is honey to someone else.
>
> Purity and impurity, sloth and diligence in worship,
> these mean nothing to me.
> I am apart from all that.
> Ways of worshipping are not to be ranked as better
> or worse than one another.
> Hindus do Hindu things.
> The Dravidian Muslims in India do what they do.
> It's all praise, and it's all right.
>
> It's not me that's glorified in acts of worship.
> It's the worshippers! I don't hear the words
> they say. I look inside at the humility.
>   (Rumi, "Moses and the Shepherd," The
>   Essential Rumi, p. 166)

God also reveals such secrets to his prophet that, in Rumi's words, "simply cannot be put into words." When Moses hears God's reprimand and is made privy to new and higher secrets and mysteries, he runs after the shepherd for hours to give him the good news. After many hours of following the erratic traces of the shepherd's footsteps, Moses finds him, but in a new mental state. In answer to the good tidings that God has accepted his worship just as he had articulated it, the shepherd speaks words, paraphrased here, that bring the story—and its moral—to a close: "Moses, I am now beyond all that. Colored with my heart's blood, I have moved hundreds of thousands of years beyond all describable conditions. I now live an existence that cannot be reduced to words." In short, the shepherd has risen to a state of understanding far higher and more immediate than even Moses can comprehend: he now sees the relationship between himself and God in ways incomprehensible to him an hour earlier. The story's moral, initially, that it is the condition of the heart and not the speech of the tongue that matters, now points to a wordless understanding far higher than anything language can express.

"The Merchant and His Pet Parrot." When a rich merchant is about to embark on a commercial journey to India, he asks every member of his household what souvenir they covet: fine silk fabrics? gold necklaces? rare and much desired Indian spices? Each member names something he or she would like to have. When it is time for the pet parrot to speak, he says he wants only a message to be delivered to the parrots of India. "And what would that message be?" the merchant asks, in effect. "When you see them flying freely from one tall branch to an even higher one, say that here in my cage I am thinking of them" (Rumi, Masnavi-i, bk. 1, vol. 1, p. 96; trans. A. Karimi-Hakkak).

Although baffled by the unusual request, the merchant promises to deliver the message. As his trip concludes, he finds himself passing by a lush forest, where flocks of parrots freely sing and play. Remembering his pet parrot's request, he stops and delivers the message verbatim to a nearby flock of parrots. Upon hearing the words of his caged kin, one parrot faints and falls from the tree branch, dead. The merchant regrets having caused the bird's death. "Was this bird perchance my parrot's relative?" he wonders. Alas, there's nothing he can do (Rumi, Masnavi-i, bk. 1, vol. 1, p. 98; trans. A. Karimi-Hakkak).

Back home, having distributed all the material souvenirs, the merchant is questioned by his parrot about his message. "O do not ask," comes the merchant's reply, summarized here, "for it is a sad tale indeed."

"Still, you must tell me," the parrot retorts, "for you have promised."

The merchant reluctantly relates what transpired at the edge of that lush forest back in India, falling silent in sadness as he recounts the death that his message caused. On hearing the account, the merchant's pet parrot also falls dead on the cage floor, as if undone by the tragic tale. "What is the meaning of all this?" the twice remorseful merchant wonders. And he ponders the meaning of the two deaths long and hard. Yet what has been done cannot be undone. In utter sorrow, he opens the cage door and removes the lifeless bird, laying it down to prepare it for proper burial. It is at this point that the pet parrot flies toward the uppermost branch in the tallest tree nearby.

Dazzled, the merchant questions the parrot about the trick, and is told that both his message and the Indian parrot's response were encoded communiqués. What the free parrot conveyed through his message was the fact that the caged parrot would not be liberated until he was perceived as dead, as no longer able to entertain and charm his master with his pleasing acrobatics and sweet speech. The parrot's final speech, summarized here, goes thus: "He taught me that I must die to free myself from the bondage of your cage—adieu" (*Masnavi-i*, bk. 1, vol. 1, pp. 111-12; trans. A. Karimi-Hakkak).

The narrative makes its moral fairly clear. The Sufis conceptualized the human body, as a contradiction in terms, a temporary gathering of the discordant elements of mortal flesh and eternal soul. When death comes and the various elements fall apart, the soul is left free to return to its place of origin, for which it longs and labors through life. For the Sufi, death brings deliverance from the earthly cage of the body, a chance for the soul to soar upward all the way to the presence of its creator, there to be united with its essence once again. Whether the song of a reed-flute or the sweet words of a parrot, things related to our earthly existence are ephemeral and incomplete. They entrap us and only death frees us.

A poetry of dialogue. In *The Spiritual Couplets*, as in other poems by Rumi, dialogue is a common means of expression. The stories of "Moses and the Shepherd" and "The Merchant and His Pet Parrot" are but examples of the way Rumi relies on dialogue to move the reader to ever higher planes of argument. In many cases, the storyline simply presents vignettes in which two individuals, often a master and a disciple, are placed in conversation, or one, often the disciple, is addressing the other or recalling an encounter with him. This rhetorical situation seems particularly to suit the Sufi quest to seek his individual God, free from all the stereotypes in religious textbooks or preachy injunctions from the pulpit. This technique of using dialogue in Sufi verse upset orthodox Muslims. While the orthodox might find little objectionable in a Sufi poem when it came to doctrine or theology, clerics often protested depictions that humanized God more than they would have liked. As custodians of Islam, they thought such portrayals might have a deleterious moral effect on less sophisticated members of the Muslim community. Most importantly, because Sufi poets conveyed the notion that God was directly and immediately accessible to everybody, they appeared to undermine the authority of the clergy as intercessors between God and human being or interpreters of God's words to lay people. Finally, the orthodox leaders argued that if people cease to fear God's wrath and punishment, they would be less inclined to shun evil and do good.

As demonstrated by Rumi's three central friendships (with Shams al-Din, Salah al-Din, and Husam al-Din), dialogue occupied a central place in his daily existence as well as his poems. The poet's mind and spirit sought human company, or, more exactly, companionship in which dialogue played a major role. Rumi showed an ever-present need for an interlocutor, someone he could address, typically a Sufi teacher like himself. His desire for responsive understanding finds its fulfillment in his use of dialogue in his poems, be it with man or God or some real or imaginary, absent or present disciple or master. It was through his addressees, more than through any other means, that Rumi strove to gain union with the divine.

Sources and literary context. The stories Rumi tells in *The Spiritual Couplets* have their roots in his discourses as a Sufi leader and guide, and as a teacher of Islamic mysticism. His discourses may have provided opportunities for stories or anecdotes that could then be related to the topic at hand through commentary. For a long time, works by Sana'i and Attar formed the staple of the curriculum in Sufi madrasahs, or religious schools (see Attar's **The Conference of the Birds**, also in WLAIT 6: *Middle Eastern Literatures and Their Times*). But these works had been written in a different environment, a century or two earlier. It

RUMI AND SHAMS—THE ARCH COMPANION

Legend has it that one day in October or November 1244, as Rumi was making his way back home from his daily prayer, a wandering dervish questioned him about the relative importance in the eye of God of the Prophet Muhammad versus a particular Sufi saint. On the face of it, this was clearly blasphemous, even though it had been put in the form of a question. Nonetheless, Rumi must have sensed a deeper purpose in the question. He invited the dervish to his home and sat in private conversation with him for forty days and forty nights. Understandably, Rumi's associates and disciples felt uneasy as nobody knew who this dervish was, under whom he had studied, or what ideas he held. Thus began a period of momentous changes in Rumi's life and art, in which he accepted Shams-i Tabrizi (The Sun of Tabriz) as his master and guide and spoke of him not just in reverential terms but as his beloved, calling him the sun that illuminated the darkest recesses of his soul. Everyone, Shams taught Rumi, must look into his or her own heart and develop a language of worship that suits it. Commonplace as this idea may seem, it was revolutionary for its time, since it followed that no religious orthodoxy could claim sole access to the truth. Unsurprisingly, the idea was vehemently opposed by orthodox Muslims.

was important, in light of new developments in mystical philosophy and in Persian poetry, to update the foundational texts of Sufism. Far more people now trod the path of Sufism, so many more madrasahs needed materials for their curriculum. Also Rumi and his circle of Anatolian Sufis may have found the language of Sana'i and Attar quaint, as many changes had occurred in the Persian language and in Persian poetry. In any case, many Sufi masters and teachers believed that an updating of the Sufi curricula was in order, and Rumi's closest associates thought that they needed a fresh compendium of Sufi lore and legend.

The ideas Rumi expounds in *The Spiritual Couplets* were the result of intense introspection, dialogue (largely with the Sufi masters who became his closest associates), and assorted readings. Rumi's first wife, Gawhar Khatun, recalled how in his youth her husband would stand under a tall lamp, reading his father's writings all night long. Beyond his father's works, Rumi familiarized himself with Plato and Aristotle, and perhaps also with leading Islamic philosophers such as Ayn al-Qudah, Suhrawardi, and Ibn Sina (Avicenna). No doubt, Rumi knew of the most famous living Sufi Muslim, Ibn al-Arabi (1165-1240) and of his philosophical system Wahdat al-Wujud (Unity of Being). Some scholars believe Rumi may even have studied with this master, who lived and taught for several

decades in Aleppo, just a hundred miles south of Konya.

All this provided material for *The Spiritual Couplets*. Many of its stories are retellings of previous Sufi tales; some were well-known stories, which Rumi interpreted mystically. More than any single work, it was Attar's *Ilahi-Namah* (Book of the Divine) that can be called the model for *The Spiritual Couplets*. In basing his masterpiece on that model, Rumi in effect "donned Attar's mantle as the leading exponent of narrative Sufi poetry" (Lewis, p. 65).

Impact. Rumi's poetry contributed immensely to the institutionalization of Sufism, particularly in Anatolia and Iran. It not only gave rise to a new Sufi order but provided ways for expanding mystical ideas and expressing them in poetry. In so doing, *The Spiritual Couplets* affected the course of Islamic mysticism more than any other single work.

Toward the end of his life, Rumi himself may have paved the way for the formation, shortly after his death, of the Mevleviyeh order, which takes its name from Rumi's honorific name, Mawlana, meaning "our master." It was left to his son Sultan Valad, Rumi's friend Husam al-Din, and other followers to complete the institutionalization of the order, which they did rather successfully; the order has flourished through the centuries, at times under adverse circumstances, such as strong modernization projects in the Muslim world. At the dawn of the twenty-first century, the order, and the poetry that forms its most central text, are beginning once again to find tremendous popular appeal, not just in Iran and Turkey but in the Western world as well.

In the larger Iranian world, Rumi's fortunes have waxed and waned and waxed again with the tides of religious belief and the progress of more modern and tolerant versions of Islam. Abd al-Rahman Jami (1414-92), the last great medieval poet of Iran, was an adept adapter of Rumi's mystical ideas while Muhammad Ali Sa'ib Tabrizi (1601-77) modeled much of his poetic divan on Rumi's *ghazals*. In the sixteenth century when the Safavid kings made Shi`ism the official religion of Iran, restrictions were gradually placed on Rumi's explicitly Sunni stance and his acceptance of religious differences were criticized. In the same period, however, Rumi's poetry found large and devoted audiences in Afghanistan, in Persian–speaking Central Asia, and in the Indian subcontinent. In the late nineteenth century, a modernizing Iran began to rediscover Rumi. Iranian modernists recognized him, along with other poets such as Firdawsi and Hafiz (see the **Shahnamah** and **The Divan of Hafiz,** also in *WLAIT 6: Middle Eastern Literatures and Their Times*), as fundamental to Iran's national identity. Rumi's works were incorporated into the creation of a modern nation-state from the remnants of a once thriving Persian-speaking culture.

In recent decades, efforts made by American poets such as Coleman Barks to produce modern versions of Rumi's poetry in English have created an upsurge in his popularity in the United States. Himself a notable poet, Barks used existing translations of Rumi to create *The Essential Rumi* (1995), which contains his own renditions of episodes from *The Spiritual Couplets* and Rumi's *Divan.* Barks's renditions bring the essence of the Persian mystic's thinking to modern readers. *Lambda Book Report* praises them as "crystalline, sensual, and utterly compelling. . . . Open [the book] anywhere, and you will lose yourself in moments. The freshness of the images is startling" (Lambda, p. 29).

—Ahmad Karimi-Hakkak

For More Information

DeBruijn, J. T. P. *Persian Sufi Poetry: An Introduction to the Mystical Use of Classical Poems.* Surrey: Curzon Press, 1997.

Karamustafa, Ahmet T. *God's Unruly Friends: Dervish Groups in Islamic Later Middle Period, 1200-1550.* Salt Lake City: University of Utah Press, 1994.

Karimi-Hakkak, Ahmad. "Beyond Translation: Interactions between English and Persian Poetry." In *Iran and the Surrounding World, 1500-2000.* Ed. Nikki Keddie and Rudolph Matthee. Seattle: University of Washington Press, 2001.

Lewis, Franklin D. *Rumi, Past and Present, East and West: The Life, Teaching and Poetry of Jalal al-Din Rumi.* Oxford, U.K.: Oneworld Publications, 2000.

Review of *The Essential Rumi,* by Coleman Barks. *Lambda Book Report* 5, no. 11 (May 1997): 29.

Rumi, Jalal al-Din Muhammad. *The Essential Rumi.* Trans. Coleman Barks. New York: HarperCollins, 1995.

———. *Kulliyat-i Shams ya divan-i kabir.* 10 vols. Ed. Badi` al-Zaman Furuzanfar. Tehran: Danishgah-i Tihran, 1958.

———. *Masnavi-i ma`nawi.* Ed. Reynold A. Nicholson. 4 vols. Tehran: Amir-i Kabir, 1984.

———. *The Mathnawi of Jalalu'ddin Rumi.* 4 vols. Ed. and trans. Reynold A. Nicholson. Cambridge, U.K.: Cambridge University Press, 1977.

Schimmel, Annemarie. *I Am Wind, You Are Fire: The Life and Works of Rumi.* Boston: Shambhala, 1992.

"Stop and We Will Weep: The Mu`allaqah"

by

Imru al-Qays

I mru al-Qays ibn Hujr (d. circa 550 C.E.) was one of the most renowned poets of pre-Islamic Arabia. His biography, like that of most of the classical pre-Islamic poets, straddles legend and history. According to the most common account of his life, he was the youngest son of Hujr, the last great chieftain of the southern Arabian tribal group Kindah and king over the unruly tribes of the Banu Asad and Banu Ghatafan. The young Imru al-Qays's devotion to poetry, especially erotic poetry, led to his banishment from his father's house. His father instructed his servant Rabi`ah to put his son to death and bring back his eyes as evidence that he had carried out the order. Taking pity on the boy, Rabi`ah killed an antelope and brought back its eyes instead. Hujr later repented, and Imru al-Qays returned to his father's house. But later banished once again, he took up the life of a profligate, wandering the desert with a band of companions, devoting himself to the hunt, wine, gambling, and slave-girls. Such was his state when news reached him of the regicide of his father, Hujr, at the hands of the rebellious Banu Asad. Exclaiming "wine today, business tomorrow!" Imru al-Qays caroused for one more day, then swore off his debauchery to devote himself to avenging his father: "Wine and women are forbidden to me until I have killed a hundred of the Banu Asad and cut the forelocks of a hundred more!" (Stetkevych, *Mute Immortals*, p. 245). With help from other tribes, he proceeded to inflict heavy casualties on the Banu Asad. Still not satisfied, he spent the rest of his days seeking further vengeance for his slain father. His search for allies led him to the Jewish

THE LITERARY WORK

One of seven celebrated *Mu`allaqat* (Suspended Odes; sing. *Mu`allaqah*) set in pre-Islamic Arabia; orally composed in Arabic (as *Kifa nabki min dhikra habibin wa-manzili*) around the mid-sixth century C.E.; compiled in written form in the eighth to ninth centuries; published in English in 1782.

SYNOPSIS

A melancholy poet stops with his two companions at a ruined abode and mourns his lost beloved who once dwelt there. After reminiscing about a series of erotic escapades, he spends a troubled night of inner turmoil. Day breaks to reveal the heroic poet and his steed on an oryx hunt, and the poem closes with a description of a destructive yet purifying desert storm.

prince of Tayma, al-Samaw'al, to whom Imru al-Qays entrusted his ancestral coats of armor before making his way to the court of the Byzantine emperor Justinian. At first Justinian lent Imru al-Qays an army with which to avenge his father's murder and regain his throne, but rumors that he had seduced Justinian's daughter prompted the emperor to send the poet a poisoned robe. When Imru al-Qays donned the garment, his body broke out in sores, earning him the nickname "the man covered with sores." The condition proved fatal; the poet supposedly lies buried near Ankara, where he received the poisoned gift. Whatever truth there is in the legends, his "Stop and We Will Weep," more commonly known as "The Mu'allaqah of Imru al-Qays," became the most renowned work of pre-Islamic Arabic poetry and provided later Arab Islamic society with a dramatic portrait of its pagan tribal past.

Events in History at the Time of the Poem

The pre-Islamic age. The Muslims termed their pagan past the Jahiliyah (Age of Ignorance) and considered it to have come to an end with the advent of Islam (dated from Prophet Muhammad's emigration from Mecca to Medina in 622 C.E.— year number one of the Islamic Hijrah calendar). *Jahiliyah* therefore refers to the period from about the fifth to early seventh centuries C.E., in the Arabian Peninsula and the Arabized regions of Syria and Iraq.

The culture of the Jahiliyah was orally preserved in poetry and lore inherited and compiled in written form during the early Islamic centuries. The Arabs of this period were primarily Bedouin, pastoralist tribes who migrated seasonally in search of pasturage for their herds of camels, sheep, and goats. A martial ethos developed among the warrior class of the tribal elites, who defended the tribe, its herds, grazing lands, and water holes from the incursions of competitors, and raided them for plunder. This pastoral economy depended primarily on the camel: wealth was measured by the size of one's herds; major obligations such as the blood-price and bride-price were paid in camels. In addition to meat, milk, and camel-hair, the camel provided transportation through the stark desert climes of Arabia, so that a major component of the Bedouin economy was providing a supply of camels to caravan merchants. By contrast, the greatly prized and pampered Arabian horse was reserved for the use of the warrior aristocracy in battle and the hunt.

The tribal society of pre-Islamic Arabia flourished at the margins of the great dominions of its day, the Christian Byzantine Empire with its capital at Constantinople (modern Istanbul, Turkey) and the Persian Sasanian Empire with its capital at Ctesiphon (southeast of present-day Baghdad, Iraq). Subject to these two empires were Arab kingdoms, the Ghassanids of Syria, who were vassals of the Byzantines, and the Lakhmids, who were vassals of the Sasanians. To the south, in what is now Yemen, was the South Arabian kingdom of the Himyarites. Thus,

besides their own indigenous Arab Semitic culture, with its ritual and mercantile center at Mecca, the Arabs of the Jahiliyah were heirs to a dynamic mix of influences—the Ancient Near Eastern, Hellenistic, Byzantine, Persian, and South Arabian cultures, and the religious traditions of Christianity, Judaism, and Zoroastrianism.

In addition to the Arab kingdoms of the Ghassanids and Lakhmids, the pre-Islamic period witnessed the continual formation and dissolution of a variety of tribal federations in which a powerful chieftain or overlord ruled almost like a king. Examples of tribal chieftains who accrued such power are Hujr, the father of Imru al-Qays, and, perhaps most renowned in the lore of pre-Islamic Arabia, Kulayb Wa'il, the instigator of the infamous War of al-Basus.

***Muruwwah* and the warrior aristocracy.** A full male member (*hurr*, "free man") of the tribe's warrior elite was expected to behave according to a system of moral values that can be subsumed under the term *muruwwah* (virtue, manliness). Chief among them was "nobility" or "generosity" (*karam*), coupled with might and valor. A man so endowed would be willing to sacrifice his life in battle to avenge a slain kinsman or in the hunt to provide sustenance for his people. He prided himself on giving of his wealth—slaughtering his finest camels to serve the guest or stranger, or sustaining the indigent and those under his protection when in need, or supplying comrades with wine in times of celebration. He was expected to speak eloquently and authoritatively at tribal councils on behalf of tribal rights and customs. A man of noble character exercised the virtue of *hilm* (forbearance), acting with restraint and clemency, as opposed to its antonym, the vice of *jahl* (recklessness), losing self-control and acting out of passion.

***Jahl*, blood-vengeance, and the War of al-Basus.** Central to the moral and political economy of the Jahiliyah was the law of blood-vengeance. This stipulated that if a kinsman was killed by an enemy, his blood was to be avenged by slaying a man of equal rank from the enemy tribe. If a man was slain by one of his own kin, presumably by accident, then, rather than engaging in hostilities that would be divisive and destructive to the kin-group, the blood-price (normally 100 she-camels) was paid. The law of blood-vengeance thus served as a deterrent to violence, on the one hand, and a limitation to it on the other. Failure to observe this law could prove disastrous: a tribe that failed to avenge its slain would soon be marked as weak and conquered by a stronger tribe; a tribe that wreaked

HEROIC VALUES

The heroic values of the Jahiliyah are summed up in the term *muruwwah*, meaning "manliness" or "virtue." Poetry was the main vehicle for the expression and celebration of these values, as shown in a renowned poem attributed to al-Samaw'al, a Jewish Arab poet of the Jahiliyah:

> When a man's honor is not stained by iniquity,
> Then every robe he dons becomes him.
> When a man's soul cannot bear the burden of injustice,
> He will find the road to honest praise cut off.
> [Our clanswoman] reviles us for being few in number,
> "The noble," I reply, "are always few."
>
> . . . .
>
> No lord of ours dies quietly in bed,
> And none of us, once slain, lies unavenged.
> Our souls flow out from us on sword-blades,
> And save for on the sword, they don't flow out.
> Limpid is our lineage; we are not muddied.
> Our root was kept pure by dams who bore us well
> and well-bred stallions.
>
> . . . .
>
> For we are as pure as the storm-cloud's water:
> There is no blunt blade in our grip and no miser among us.
>
> . . . .
>
> When a chief among us passes on, another chief stands in his stead,
> Eloquent in the speech of noble men, forceful in deeds.
> (al-Samaw'al ibn Adiya in Stetkevych, *Abu Tammam*,
> pp. 291-93, with changes)

excessive vengeance would unleash uncontrollable and devastating violence. The quest for vengeance in excess of what the law of retaliation required was an instance of *jahl*, of reckless impetuosity. Imru al-Qays's unquenchable thirst for vengeance for his slain royal father, al-Hujr, is clearly such a case. So, too, is the infamous blood-feud of the Jahiliyah, the War of al-Basus.

This 40-year conflict was ignited when the overbearing tribal chieftain Kulayb Wa'il killed the she-camel of al-Basus, a kinswoman by marriage, who was under his protection. Her kinsman al-Jassas impetuously retaliated by slaying his brother-in-law Kulayb Wa'il, setting off an inexorable chain of vengeance and counter-vengeance between the kindred clans of the Banu Bakr (al-Jassas's clan) and the Banu Taghlib (the clan of Kulayb). The chief protagonist and leading poet of the War of al-Basus was Kulayb's younger brother Muhalhil.

Arabic literary lore depicts Muhalhil, before the death of his brother Kulayb, as a feckless, self-indulgent, and resentful adolescent. While alive, Kulayb chastises his younger brother for being a dandy who spends his time flirting with women, gambling, and drinking wine. However, when Kulayb is slain, Muhalhil abandons his debauchery and swears an oath to avenge his brother. So exaggerated is his estimation of his brother's worth that he refuses the Banu Bakr's offer of 1,000 she-camels—ten times the standard blood-price of 100 she-camels. Instead, Muhalhil slays Bujayr, whose death was generally esteemed to even the score, exclaiming famously "Die in retaliation for Kulayb's sandal-strap!" (al-Nuwayri in Stetkevych, *Mute Immortals*, p. 224). As intimated by this line, many would die on both sides and the kindred clans of Bakr and Taghlib would be forever split asunder before the thirst for vengeance would be slaked.

The War of al-Basus provides a literary, cultural, and historical backdrop to the life, legend, and poetry of Imru al-Qays. The law of blood-vengeance and the tragic consequences of defying its limits, the existence of an Oedipal resentment between Kulayb and Muhalhil and later Hujr and Imru al-Qays, the dramatic shift from self-indulgence and familial resentment to extravagant blood-lust: all of these dramatic elements are shared by these two episodes of the Jahiliyah. It should come as no surprise then that Muhalhil is said to be Imru al-Qays's maternal uncle—a genealogy that may in truth be more literary than historical.

Women in the Jahiliyah. A primary point of honor for the tribal elite was that its female kin—mothers, wives, sisters, and daughters—live in chaste and guarded luxury. A girl's virginity was jealously guarded until marriage, and after marriage, only her husband had sexual rights to her. As the Arab poet's beloved is from this social stratum, many poems provide an idealized picture of such a "free woman" (hurrah): confined largely to the women's tents, they traveled in large how-dahs—tentlike structures borne by bulky male camels. Their skin is described as delicate and pale. Attended by servant- and slave-girls, these "free women" need not work so their bodies grow plump, their hands are smooth and uncallused. The poetry speaks of their having the soft dark eyes of the gazelle or oryx-doe, lush locks of black hair, and a taste for luxury goods such as silks and rare perfumes. Well protected, they appear in public only in times of crisis: during the ritual lamentation for a slain kinsman, the equally ritual incitement of their menfolk to vengeance and battle, or when taken captive by a raiding tribe.

The pampered life of the "free women" of the tribal elite is in direct contrast to that of servant- and slave-girls or women of indigent subject tribes, who serve their mistresses, and, together with the boys and men of the lower orders, undertake the domestic chores of the Bedouin encampment and tend the herds. Likewise, chastity is not the slave-girl's lot, rather, she is "defiled / By every hand" (Hind bint Hudhayfah in Stetkevych, *Mute Immortals*, p. 198)

The structure and themes of the qasidah. The lore and poetry that have come down to us from the Jahiliyah, or Age of Ignorance, were, for the most part, orally composed and preserved by the warrior aristocracy of tribal Arabia. At the courts of the Lakhmids and Ghassanids, poets competed in offering poems of praise, and tribes, too, had their tribal poets and poetic traditions. The pre-eminent poetic form was the ode, or *qasidah*, that encoded and celebrated the values of the warrior aristocracy and became, in Islamic times, the literary and cultural foundation for Islamic concepts of heroism and nobility of character. Although by no means uniform, the *qasidah* had many conventional features. It might range in length from about 15 to 80 lines, each composed of two half lines, but always maintained the same meter and rhyme throughout.

Literary scholars of the Islamic period recognized three main structural units of the *qasidah*: 1) the *nasib*, an elegiac and amorous introductory section whose major themes are the ruined encampment where the poet's beloved once dwelt, and the poet's reminiscence of his lost beloved; 2) the *rahil*, a journey, in which the solitary poet completes a perilous desert crossing mounted on his trusty she-camel, which is often described at length; 3) the "goal" of the poem, most often either *fakhr*, the poet's boastful celebration of himself and his tribe, or *madih*, the praise of a patron to whom the poet comes as supplicant. This final section is characterized by the triumphal description and celebration of the heroic virtues of the warrior aristocracy: raids and battles, blood-vengeance, the hunt, slaughtering prized she-camels to feed the indigent, speaking with eloquence and authority in tribal councils.

It is important to note in examining the structure of the classical *qasidah* that the emotional trajectory of the thematic sections describes a psycho-social rite of passage from the immature and impassioned adolescent self-involvement, through the solitary quest for self-knowledge, to the integration of the poet into the mature, heroic warrior aristocracy of his tribe.

The Poem in Focus

Contents overview. The "Mu`allaqah of Imru al-Qays" conforms to the mood-and-theme sequence of the *qasidah* form, except that it exhibits a two-part, rather than three-part, structure. The first section of the poem is the lyric-elegiac prelude (*nasib*), in which a melancholy poet expresses his nostalgia over the irretrievable past. To convey this, Imru al-Qays invokes the traditional images of the poet weeping over an abandoned Bedouin encampment and the poet's reminiscence of his former mistress, or, in Imru al-Qays's case, former mistresses. The *nasib* concludes with a despondent and troubling night scene, which, inasmuch as it effects a psychological transition in the poet, serves a structural function similar to that of the traditional desert journey (rahil). The second section of the poem is the martial heroic boast (fakhr), in which the poet celebrates his manly virtue (muruwwah) as a member of the tribal warrior aristocracy. The poet and his steed appear in an early morning oryx hunt that leads into a description of the horse. Then the poem closes with a dramatic depiction of a desert storm.

Nasib. "The Mu`allaqah" opens with the convention of the poet asking his two companions to stop awhile so that he might weep at the ruins of the encampment where his beloved once dwelt. He evokes place-names of the Bedouin desert, situating in both geography and memory the locus of his lost love:

> Halt, two friends, and we will weep
>   for the memory of one beloved
> And an abode at Siqt al-Liwa
>   between al-Dakhul, then Hawmal,
> Then Tudih, then Miqrat, whose trace
>   was not effaced
> By the two winds weaving over it
>   from south and north.
> You see the droppings
>   of white antelope
> Scattered on its outer grounds and lowlands
>   like peppercorns.
>   (Imru al-Qays, "The Mu`allaqah of Imru al-
>   Qays," lines 1-3, in Stetkevych, *Mute
>   Immortals*, pp. 249-50)

The poet's memory of his beloved unleashes an uncontrollable flood of tears that, in turn, unleashes a flood of memories of other amorous encounters. This unexpectedly long description of his erotic escapades diverges from typical *qasidah* proportions. Imru al-Qays's *nasib* section extends to over 40 lines, whereas normally a *nasib* for an ode of this length would continue for about 15 lines. This in itself suggests the poet's excessive attachment to romantic involvements and failure to move on to the more manly pursuits of the *fakhr* section. His adventures include affairs with two married women, Umm al-Huwayrith and her neighbor Umm al-Rabab (lines 7-8); the day he slew his mount for a group of virgins at Darat Juljul (lines 10-12); his escapade in the camel-litter with the coquettish Unayzah (lines 13-15); his scandalous lovemaking with a woman who is both pregnant and nursing (lines 16-17); and his rocky relationship with Fatimah, whose love slew his heart (lines 19-22). A final extended erotic description is devoted to a woman he refers to as "the 'egg' of the curtained quarters," meaning a beautiful protected virgin whose formidable

kinsmen stand guard over her to ward off any would-be seducers. From the description of her life of guarded luxury, one surmises that she is the pampered and protected daughter of the tribal aristocracy:

> Many an "egg" of the curtained quarters,
>   whose tent none dares seek,
> I took my pleasure with her,
>   unhurried.
> I stole past guards
>   to get to her, past clansmen
> Eager, could they conceal it,
>   to slay me.
> . . . .
> I came when she, before the tent curtain,
>   had shed her clothes for sleep,
> And was clad in nothing but
>   an untied shift.
> . . . .
> I led her forth from her tent,
>   walking as she trailed
> Over our tracks the train
>   of her gown of figured silk.
> . . . .
> I drew her temples toward me, and she
>   leaned over me
> With a hollow waist, but plump the place
>   that anklets ring.
> . . . .
> In the forenoon crumbs of musk
>   still deck her bed,
> And she, late morning sleeper, still is clad
>   in sleeping-gown, ungirded.
>   ("The Mu`allaqah,"
>   lines 23, 24, 26, 28, 30, 37)

Imru al-Qays concludes this last extended amorous description by declaring that his paramour is so irresistible that even the staid mature man cannot help but be moved to passion by her beauty, much less the disconsolate poet.

At this point, the poet's despondency, which was sparked by the scene of the abandoned encampment and the reminiscences of failed love affairs that it engendered, deepens. We find the solitary poet overwhelmed by the sorrows of a seemingly endless night, what might be termed the poet's "dark night of the soul":

> Many a night like the billowing sea
>   let down its veils over me
> With all kinds of cares
>   to test me.
> . . . .
> Then, oh, what a night you are!
>   as if its stars
> Were bound by tight-twisted ropes
>   to Mount Yadhbul,
> As if the Pleiades were

in midcourse suspended
By flaxen cords
from obdurate rock.
("The Mu'allaqah," lines 44, 47, 48)

Thus, the *nasib* ends with the poet in a state of spiritual crisis in the suspended animation of the endless night. The poem does not say what has set off this crisis, but from the flood of cares that overwhelms him and the motionlessness of the stars, one can deduce a sense of spiritual paralysis. The poet's emotional life is stalled and, as the series of fruitless erotic escapades suggests, rather than maturing, the poet suffers from arrested development. Nevertheless, as the ensuing *fakhr* section establishes, the "dark night of the soul" also serves as a period of incubation, self-realization, and maturation.

Fakhr. The shift from the melancholy despondency of the night scene that ends the *nasib* to the heroic celebratory boast that characterizes the *fakhr* section is signaled by the temporal change from night to early morning and by a change in subject to the poet's steed. As a mount, the horse was reserved for the heroic pursuits of the hunt and the battle, and it is therefore fitting that it makes its appearance in the *fakhr* section. It is understood by association that the might, prowess, and muscular beauty of his steed are ultimately the poet's own:

I would ride forth early,
    the birds still in their nests,
On a steed sleek and swift,
    a shackle for wild game, huge.
Now wheeling, now charging, advancing,
        retreating,
    all at once,
Like a mighty boulder the torrent has washed
    down from the heights.
("The Mu'allaqah," lines 53-54)

The description of the steed's speed, strength, and prowess leads into a depiction of its skill in the hunt, and the ensuing feast:

There appeared before us an oryx herd
    as if its cows were virgins
Circling round a sacred stone
    in long-trained gowns.
. . . .
One after the other, [the steed] hit
    a bull and cow,
And yet was not awash
    with sweat.
("The Mu'allaqah," lines 64, 67)

The horse passage concludes by telling us how precious the poet's steed is, how dazzling to the eye, how carefully tended:

And our glance, in the evening,
    almost failed before him,
To whatever spot the eye was raised,
    dazzled, it dropped.
All night he remained, his saddle and bridle
    upon him,
All night he stood beneath my gaze, not
    loosed to graze.
("The Mu'allaqah," lines 69, 70)

The most unusual feature of Imru al-Qays's "Mu'allaqah" is its concluding passage, the magnificent storm scene. While the other thematic passages of his ode are conventional, the description of a desert storm is far less common. It occurs in precisely that place where the conventions of the genre would lead us to expect a battle scene, or some other description of the military or political might of the poet's tribe, or of its wealth and generosity.

The storm scene opens with the poet and his companion observing the storm from afar and trying to predict its course from the clouds and lightning:

O friend, do you see the lightning?
    There is its flash—
Like two hands shining in a high-crowned
    cumulus!
. . . .
Over Mount Qatan, as I read the signs,
    the right flank of its downpour falls,
Over Mount al-Sitar, then Mount Yadhbul,
    falls the left.
("The Mu'allaqah," lines 72, 74)

Imru al-Qays depicts the two-fold might of storm, both its destructive (overturning trees and buildings) and life-giving (often in terms of robes and fabric) aspects:

Then in the forenoon it was pouring
    its water down around Kutayfah,
Overturning the lofty *kanahbal* trees
    upon their beards.
. . . .
In Tayma it did not leave
    a single palm trunk standing,
Or a single castle but
    those built of stone.
As if Mount Thabir in the foremost
    of its rains
Were a tribal chieftain wrapped
    in a striped cloak.
. . . .
It deposited its load on
    the low-lying desert
Like a Yemeni [merchant] alighting with
    his [fabric]-laden bags.
("The Mu'allaqah,"
lines 75, 77, 78, 80)

The poem closes with a sublime couplet that evokes all the ancient Near Eastern mythic and symbolic associations of the flood: death and rebirth, pollution and purification, the corruption of the flesh versus the immaculateness of the spirit. Beginning with the intoxicated birds of the purified spirit, the couplet contrasts them to the dross corpses of the flesh:

> As if, early in the morning,
>   the songbirds of the valley
> Had drunk a morning draught
>   of fine spiced wine.
> As if the wild beasts drowned at evening
>   in its remotest stretches
> Were wild onions'
>   plucked-out bulbs.
>   ("The Mu`allaqah," lines 81, 82)

Instead of the expected celebration of tribal glory, the ode ends with mythic-symbolic imagery of universal significance.

The main sections of Imru al-Qays's "Mu`allaqah"—the lyric-elegiac nasib, with its ruined encampment, reminiscences of amorous escapades, and the care-filled night, followed by the virile celebratory fakhr with its monumental horse passage and formidable storm scene—fulfill the expectations of mood and subject for a qasidah, or ode, but with this final twist.

The tragic-heroic pattern. The pre-Islamic Arabic ode depicts the ethos of the Bedouin warrior aristocracy, much as the Homeric epic does for archaic Greece. We can detect in the Greek hero Achilles' behavior a pattern of immature and adolescent self-indulgence and arrested development (his mother disguises him in women's clothes so he won't have to serve in the Trojan War; he seems to pout endlessly over Agamemnon's taking away his slave-girl Briseis; he long refuses to go into battle). In a dramatic transformation Achilles grows enraged and goes to battle sworn to extravagant vengeance for the death of his friend Patroclus. The tragic-heroic transformation of the petulant adolescent into the impetuous avenger appears in the Arabic tradition as well, where both Muhalhil, the poet-protagonist of the War of al-Basus, and later his sister's son, Imru al-Qays, fit the mold. They both exhibit Oedipal resentment and irresponsible adolescent behavior—womanizing, wine-drinking, and gambling. Likewise, both cast aside their profligate ways to fulfill an oath of vengeance that far exceeds tribal standards of just vengeance.

Although Imru al-Qays's profligate youth as depicted in the literary lore of his life resonates with the extensive erotic escapades that fill the long nasib of his "Mu`allaqah," the ode is by no means merely a rhymed and metered rendition of the poet's biographical lore. Still, it is possible to detect in the way the poet uses the structurally determined moods and themes of the qasidah genre the same tragic-heroic pattern that informs the lore of his life. The poetic details of the nasib—stopping at the ruined abode, the poet's tears, the unduly long series of amorous escapades, and the endless care-filled night—can be understood as expressions of prolonged adolescence and arrested psychological development on the part of the poet. In the larger tribal scheme of things, immaturity is characterized by self-indulgence, whereas maturity, which we can equate with muruwwah (manliness, virtue), consists above all of shouldering the obligations of the warrior elite: to risk one's life to avenge a dead kinsman, to take part in the hunt, to provide camels for slaughter to feed the tribe, its guests, and its hangers-on.

The first indicator of the poet's immaturity is his excessive weeping. In the tribal ethos, women and children shed tears, whereas men shed blood—either in battle or the hunt. The poem opens with weeping, and the poet intensifies the motif into a major theme: lines 4-6 describe his shedding copious tears, until his comrades bid him, "Don't perish out of grief, / control yourself!" to which the poet replies, "Surely my cure is tears / poured forth" ("The Mu`allaqah," lines 5-6). More than 30 lines later, the poet remains disconsolate and is quite explicit about how, unlike other men, he has failed to outgrow the passions of youth:

> [Grown] men find consolation from
>   the follies of their youth
> But my heart refuses solace for
>   its love for you.
>   ("The Mu`allaqah," line 42)

The sheer number of the poet's amorous encounters suggests his inability to settle down and grow up, especially if we keep in mind that the traditional nasib features a poet reminiscing about one lost love only. The details of this poet's escapades only reinforce the idea of relationships that are immature, unstable, illicit, and without (at least legitimate) issue. Indeed, they are diametrically opposed to sanctioned marriage (the hallmark of mature and responsible sexuality) and an outrage to the jealously guarded chastity of the women of the tribal elite.

The first two affairs involve married women, Umm ("mother of") al-Huwayrith and Umm al-Rabab ("The Mu`allaqah," line 7), thus compounding fornication with adultery. By contrast, the poet's escapade at Darat Juljul is an adolescent frolic, in which the image of the virgins playing with the fringes of camel-fat, rather than cooking and eating the meat, suggests immature amorous play rather than consummated mature sexuality. Next, the comic "instability" of the poet's exploits is highlighted in his fumbling attempt to seduce Unayzah as she rides in her enclosed camel litter. In what one is tempted to read as sexual double-entendre, she cries that the speaker has crippled her camel with his extra weight and commands him to get down, to which he replies that she should take it easy ("The Mu`allaqah," lines 14-15).

The following episode contains what the classical Arab critics considered some of the most obscene lines of the Arabic poetic tradition. Here the poet is having sex with a married woman who is both pregnant and nursing—thus not only betraying her husband, but neglecting both the newborn and unborn:

> Then many a woman like you, pregnant and
>   nursing,
>   have I visited by night
> And distracted from her amuleted
>   one-year-old.
> When he cried from behind her, she turned
>   her upper half toward him,
> But the half that was beneath me
>   did not budge.
>   ("The Mu`allaqah," lines 16, 17)

The last affair in the poem, that of the "'egg' of the curtained quarters," again emphasizes the illicit nature of the relationship, as the determined poet steals by guards to get to his paramour, risking his life at the hands of her murderously protective kinsmen. Quite contrary to licit marital relations within a tribal enclosure, he leads her out into the desert:

> I led her forth from her tent,
> . . . .
> Then, when we had crossed
>   the clan's enclosure
> And made our way to a sandy hollow
>   surrounded by long winding dunes,
> I drew her temples toward me. . . .
>   ("The Mu`allaqah," lines 28, 29, 30)

A restless night follows, in which the ode conveys the same failure of maturation, this time not through amorous exploits but through a sense of psychological paralysis, which seems to grip the poet in his seemingly endless, care-ridden night. The poet's impatient plea, "Alas, long night, will you not dispel," points to his own arrested

development, while "The Pleiades . . . / in mid-course suspended" is above all a metaphor for the poet's own psychological stagnation ("The Mu`allaqah," lines 46, 48). At the same time, the psychological interiority of the night scene suggests that it is an incubation period, a period in which, through self-examination and realization of his immaturity, the poet experiences a profound inner growth that allows him to suddenly "emerge" in the heroic hunt scene that ensues. In this respect, although on the surface the night scene differs in subject matter from the conventional *rahil* (journey section), in "The Mu`allaqah," it effects the same self-discovery. The psychological growth is parallel to that achieved by a solitary poet braving the hardships and terrors of the desert crossing on his trusty she-camel.

The *fakhr* (boast) section is signaled by a dramatic shift from the motionless despondency of the night scene to the stirring exuberance of the early morning hunt. As if to highlight this contrast, the opening lines of the *fakhr* section abound in images and diction of dynamic movement: "a steed sleek and swift," "Pouring forth his gallop" ("The Mu`allaqah," lines 53, 57). Above all, there is the tremendous energy and momentum of line 54: "Now wheeling, now charging, advancing, retreating, all at once, / Like a mighty boulder the torrent has washed down from the heights" ("The Mu`allaqah," line 54). The descriptions of the steed convey energy and motion, and, in the comparisons to boulders and a rain-driven torrent, suggest fertility and virility, associated with the horse and the hunt. This imagery subtly prepares the ground for the final storm scene as well.

Other symbolically important elements of the horse and hunt scene are the many allusions to licit tribal life. Here we should keep in mind that the heroic hunt on horseback is a chief responsibility, as well as the exclusive right, of the mature male member of the warrior aristocracy of tribal Arabia. In the Darat Juljul escapade of the *nasib* the virgins are described as childishly frolicking, but, as noted, there is no cooking or eating of the poet's camel's flesh ("The Mu`allaqah," lines 10-12). By contrast, in the *fakhr* section the horse's gallop is compared to "a cauldron's boil"; the oryx are compared to virgins, but when their blood is shed, the meat is cooked and fed to the members of the tribe ("The Mu`allaqah," lines 56, 64, 68). Cultural imagery appears in a series of comparisons: of the steed's rump to "a stone / A bride pounds perfumes with"; of the oryx's blood

An oryx, object of the hunt in "The Mu`allaqah of Imru al-Qays."

on the steed's throat to henna on an old man's hair; of the oryx cows to "virgins / Circling round a sacred stone / in long-trained gowns" ("The Mu`allaqah," lines 62, 63, 64). Perhaps the most telling metaphor for natural power tamed to serve society, in other words, of the mature male who subordinates his personal desires to the needs of the tribe, is the image that closes the horse passage: that of the steed kept all night tethered before the poet's eye, in his saddle and bridle, not free to graze ("The Mu`allaqah," line 70).

At the point where both the poetics of the *qasidah* structure and the biographical lore about Imru al-Qays might have led us to expect a blood-vengeance battle scene, the poet surprises us with the majestic storm scene. This might not be as divergent from conventional expectations as it seems at first glance. If we keep in mind that in the tribal ethos of pre-Islamic Arabia, blood shed in vengeance for a slain kinsman was understood to revitalize the kin group, we can detect in the imagery of the destructive yet revitalizing might of the desert storm a metaphorically identical pattern of pollution and purification, death and rebirth. The overturning of trees "upon their beards" and the knocking down of palm trunks and all but the strongest buildings suggest acts of war as well as forces of nature ("The Mu`al-laqah," lines 75, 76).

The reconstitution of the social fabric, that is, the revitalization of the polity through the achievement of blood vengeance, is likewise hinted at in the metaphors that describe the rain-ravaged mountains—"a tribal chieftain wrapped / in a striped cloak"—and in the similes that describe the herbs that spring up on the low-lying desert "Like a Yemeni [merchant] alighting with / his [fabric]-laden bags" ("The Mu`allaqah," lines 78-80). Further, the pre-Islamic ritual of drinking wine to celebrate the achievement of blood vengeance lurks eerily below the surface of the otherwise idyllic closing couplet: the early morning warbling of songbirds drunk on spiced wine is contrasted with the evening scene of bulb-like bloated bodies of beasts drowned in the torrent's flood.

The beauty and genius of the closing passage lie precisely in Imru al-Qays's substitution of the anticipated blood-vengeance battle with the destructive yet revitalizing desert rainstorm. In the tribal ethos of pre-Islamic Bedouin Arabia, this substitution suggests metaphorical equivalence—blood-vengeance in the tribal ethos is a form of destruction that renews and revitalizes the kin-group, just as the mighty and devastating desert storm revives the desert, turning its barren tracts into lush pasturage. Thus, however grounded "The Mu`allaqah of Imru al-Qays" may be in the local tribal feuds of the Jahiliyah, through his employ of the tragic-heroic pattern and the image of the purifying flood, Imru al-Qays has created a poem of broad, indeed universal, appeal, in which the cultures and religions of the ancient Near East still resonate.

Sources and literary context. Given the historical uncertainties in the oral transmission of both pre-Islamic poetry and poetic lore from the mid-sixth century C.E. until the time these materials were compiled into writing during the ninth and tenth centuries, any attempt to pinpoint the precise circumstances behind the writing of Imru al-Qays's "Mu`allaqah" can be nothing more than a speculative literary exercise. This said, we can suggest that, inasmuch as the biographical lore of Imru al-Qays is dominated by the regicide of his father and his excessive search for blood vengeance, this same theme may motivate and inform the greatest poem attributed to him. If we further consider the mythic significance of the killing of a king as creating a "wasteland," then to avenge that death is to restore life and fertility to that wasteland—precisely the image of a desert storm. Pursuing this line of reasoning, we could tie Imru al-Qays's "Mu`allaqah" to his great

THE ARABIC ODE

The ode, or *qasidah*, was the pre-eminent Arabic literary form from pre-Islamic times until the early twentieth century. A few lines from "The Mu`allaqah" of the pre-Islamic poet Labid provide a sense of the Arabic *qasidah*'s sequence of themes and moods: the nostalgic self-involvement of the *nasib* (elegiac introduction); the solitary quest on camelback of the *rahil* (desert journey); and the celebratory self-confidence of the *fakhr* (tribal boast).

[*nasib*]
Effaced are the abodes,
   brief encampments and long-settled ones
At Mina the wilderness has claimed
   Mount Ghawl and Mount Rijam

. . . .

Stripped bare, where once a folk had dwelled,
   then one day departed.
Abandoned lay the trench that ran around the tents,
  the thumam grass that plugged their holes.
The clanswomen departing stirred your longing
   when they loaded up their gear,
Then climbed inside their howdah frames
   with squeaking tents.

. . . .

What then do you remember of Nawar
   when she has gone far off,
And her bonds, both firm and frayed,
   are cut asunder?
[*rahil*]
Cut off your love from him
   whose bond is not secure . . . .
With a camel-mare jaded by journeys
   that have reduced her to a remnant,
Till she is emaciate
   of loins and hump.

. . . .

Yet she is as nimble in the reins
   as if she were a rose-hued cloud,
Rain-emptied, running with the south wind,
   sprightly.
[*fakhr*]
And many a bitter morn of wind and cold
   I curbed,
When its reins were in the hand
   of the north wind.
I defended the tribe, my battle-gear borne
   by a winning courser,
Her reins my sash when I
   rode forth at dawn.

. . . .

> When tribal councils gather
> there is always one of us
> Who contends in grave affairs
> and shoulders them.
>
> . . . .
>
> Out of superior might: a man munificent,
> who with his bounty succors,
> Openhanded: a winner and plunderer of all
> that he desires.
>
> . . . .
>
> Their honor is not sullied, their deeds
> not without issue,
> For their judgment is not swayed
> by passion's flights.
>
> . . . .
>
> They are a springtime
> to those that seek refuge
> And to indigent women, their food-stores exhausted,
> when the year stretches long.
>
> ("The Mu`allaqah of Labid" in Stetkevych,
> *Mute Immortals*, pp. 9-17, with changes)

and bloody victory over the Banu Asad—either to the one he first achieved with the aid of the Banu Bakr and the Banu Taghlib, or the one he hoped to achieve before the poisoned Byzantine robe claimed his life.

Concerning the place of this ode in Arab-Islamic literature, the pre-Islamic *qasidah* has traditionally been regarded as one of its twin foundations, together with the Quran. Early in the spread of Islam, scholars deemed the Quranic text as the word of God, to be inimitable (see **The Quran**, also in *WLAIT 6: Middle Eastern Literatures and Their Times*). So, too, did they consider the poetry of the Jahiliyah, or pre-Islamic poets, to be of a beauty and originality unattainable by poets of the Islamic period. The poetics of the pre-Islamic *qasidah*—its meters, its length (usually between 15 and 80 lines of two half-lines each), its monorhyme, its two- or three-part structure of motifs and images, its diction, many of its similes and metaphors—dominated Arabic poetic production from its inception until the early twentieth century. Of all these poems, the most celebrated is "The Mu`allaqah of Imru al-Qays."

Impact. The pride of place that "The Mu`allaqah of Imru al-Qays" enjoys in the Arabic poetic tradition is indicated first and foremost by the fact that in all recensions of the *Mu`allaqat*, it occupies the opening position. No record exists of the poem's initial reception. Indeed, the earliest recorded source for both the diwan (collected poems) of Imru al-Qays and of the *Mu`allaqat* is a certain Hammad al-Rawiyah ("the transmitter") (d. 772), an extremely knowledgeable connoisseur of poetry, but also a renowned forger. The high esteem accorded the *Mu`allaqat*, seven long odes, each by a different pre-Islamic poet, is indicated by the traditional explanation of their title, "The Suspended Odes." It refers, goes the explanation, to a pre-Islamic custom whereby the winning poems in a poetry competition at the fair of Ukaz were written in gold letters on fine linen and suspended from the Kaaba in Mecca, the shrine believed to have been built by Adam, then rebuilt by Abraham and Ishmael. The complex attitude of Islamic culture toward the Jahiliyah is one that combines aesthetic admiration with moral condemnation. It is perhaps most succinctly and powerfully expressed in the Prophet Muhammad's estimation of the most celebrated poet of the pagan age: that Imru al-Qays was the best of all the poets, and their leader into Hellfire.

—Suzanne Pinckney Stetkevych

For More Information

Abu-Deeb, Kemal. "Toward a Structuralist Analysis of Pre-Islamic Poetry (II): The Eros Vision." *Edebiyat* 1 (1976): 3-69.

Arberry, A. J. *The Seven Odes: The First Chapter in Arabic Literature*. New York: Macmillan, 1957.

Boustany, S. "Imru' al-Kays B. Hudjr." In *Encyclopaedia of Islam*. Vol. 3. Leiden: E. J. Brill, 1971.

Haydar, Adnan. "*The Mu`allaqa of Imru' al-Qays*: Its Structure and Meaning." Part I: *Edebiyat* 2 (1977): 227-61; Part II: *Edebiyat* 3 (1978): 51-82.

Imru al-Qays. "The Mu`allaqah of Imru' al-Qays." In *The Mute Immortals Speak: Pre-Islamic Poetry and the Poetics of Ritual*. Ithaca, New York: Cornell University Press, 1993.

Stetkevych, Suzanne Pinckney. *Abu Tammam and the Poetics of the Abbasid Age*. Leiden: E. J. Brill, 1991.

————. *The Mute Immortals Speak: Pre-Islamic Poetry and the Poetics of Ritual*. Ithaca, New York: Cornell University Press, 1993.

————. *The Poetics of Islamic Legitimacy: Myth, Gender and Ceremony in the Classical Arabic Ode*. Bloomington: Indiana University Press, 2002.

The Story of Zahra

by
Hanan al-Shaykh

THE LITERARY WORK

A novel set in Beirut during the first five years of the Lebanese civil war (1975-1990); published in Arabic (as *Hikayat Zahrah*) in 1980, in English in 1986.

SYNOPSIS

War suspends social norms in the Lebanese capital and allows for the empowerment of an unattractive, middle-aged woman whose newly acquired taste for adventure leads to her murder.

Hanan al-Shaykh, one of the best-known Arab writers in the English-speaking world, was born in Beirut, Lebanon, in 1945. Growing up in Ras al-Naba, a conservative and predominantly Shi`ite Muslim neighborhood in the Lebanese capital, she experienced many restrictions both at home and in the Amiliah Muslim girls' primary school. After transferring to the progressive Ahliyah School, she made friends with several girls who later also rose to prominence. In 1963 al-Shaykh traveled to Egypt, where she studied for three years at the American College for Girls in Cairo. During her stay in the Egyptian capital, she met with the popular novelist Ihsan Abd al-Qaddus, who encouraged her to write her first novel, *Suicide of a Dead Man*, which was published in 1967. Upon her return to Beirut, al-Shaykh became a full-time journalist, working first for *al-Hasna*, a women's magazine, and then for the Lebanese daily, *al-Nahar*. She left Lebanon in 1976 for a six-year stay on the Arabian Peninsula, then moved to London in 1982, where she now lives. Al-Shaykh has published six novels, several short stories, and most recently plays. Her writings focus on women's social roles in times of peace and war. Her third novel, *The Story of Zahra*, written in the Arabian Peninsula, reflects the conditions of violence she experienced during the first two years of the civil war. The bildungsroman, or novel of development, traces the stages in the life of a lonely, abused Shi`ite girl who flourishes in war. Because no publisher in Lebanon accepted the novel, al-Shaykh first published it at her own expense in 1980. Its translation into French in 1985 and then into English the following year gained al-Shaykh an international reputation. Her next novel, *Misk al-ghazal* (1988; *Women of Sand and Myrrh*, 1989), is likewise situated in the Arab world, but the following couple of novels, *Barid Bayrut* (1992; *Beirut Blues*, 1995) and *Innaha Landan ya azizi* (2000; *Only in London*), concern Arabs on exile soil. While the latter two works deal with fabulously wealthy as well as impoverished exiles, the *Story of Zahra* focuses on a middle-class Lebanese woman and her curious sense of empowerment in wartime society.

Events in History at the Time of the Novel

According to the 1932 census. Lebanon, a predominantly Christian country in an overwhelmingly Muslim region, has a tradition of friendship with Catholic France that dates back to the sixteenth century. This relationship was not restricted to Lebanon's various Christian groups but also included its Druze—the self-governing religious group that broke from Islam in the eleventh century. Unlike other Arabs, therefore, the Lebanese were much less suspicious of the French *mission civilisatrice* (civilizing mission) of the nineteenth century, which tried to subdue the Muslim populations of Algeria, Tunisia, Morocco, and Greater Syria. After World War I, the Versailles convention parceled out the countries of the southern and eastern Mediterranean regions among the French, British, and Italians. Lebanon fell under French Mandate rule in 1920.

In 1932 the French conducted a census that still determines the political structure of the country today. The diversity of the population in terms of religion made it the decisive identity marker. Census figures indicated that the largest community was Maronite Christian, the next was Sunnite Muslim, and the third was Shi`ite Muslim. These three religious groups, along with 14 others (the least numerous of which is the "Protestant"), were allocated political office according to the numbers of their community in the 1932 census. Proportional representation of the different religious communities, or confessions, would continue thereafter. "Confessionalism," as it was referred to, became the organizing principle for the Lebanese political structure. The confessional system was legitimized by the national pact of 1943, which allocated political offices according to sect. Up to the present, the 1932 census dictates that the president of the country is a Maronite Christian; the prime minister, a Sunni Muslim; and the speaker of the house, a Shi`ite Muslim (al-Shaykh's religious affiliation).

Religiously the Maronites regard the Pope in Rome as their highest authority but differ from Roman Catholicism in their practices. The Shi`ites (from *Shi`at Ali*—"the Party of Ali") see legitimate authority as stemming from the Prophet Muhammad through his son-in-law Ali and Ali's descendants. Sunnis look to the Quran and the Prophet's "habitual behaviors" (*sunna*) for such authority.

While Shi`ites formed the majority in Mount Lebanon during various periods of history, they were mostly found in the rural areas. Migrations to the suburbs of Beirut during the twentieth century "intensified sectarian loyalty at the expense of family allegiance, because Shi`a replaced family as the channel for participating in local politics" (Fawaz, p. 109). Although they were not as numerous as the Maronites and the Sunnis in 1932, their numbers grew so swiftly that by the 1950s they had outstripped the other two religious groups. Since 1932 no new census has been officially taken, perhaps because it would substantiate the Shi`ite claim that they have long been the most numerous religious group. Under such circumstances the distribution of power would have to be radically changed, and the Shi`ites would be entitled to the leadership of the country and to all posts that are allocated to the major religious sect. The main character of the novel is Shi`ite and thus part of Lebanon's demographically dominant but politically suppressed religious community. Zahra's brother joins a militia that is "anxious to draw attention to the demands of the repressed Shi`ite minority [and] . . . to destroy imperialism" (al-Shaykh, *The Story of Zahra*, p. 121).

Civil war. Lebanon gained full independence from France in 1945, the year of al-Shaykh's birth. Within ten years, the political structure of the country did not match the demographic distribution. The first civil war broke out in 1958, in part over demands for a correct census to reallocate official positions in a proportionally representative manner. Power had continued to rest primarily in the hands of the Maronites, despite the fact that they were now outnumbered by the Shi`ites.

Lebanese officials asked the U.S. Marines to quell the unrest. Within six months, the war was "over," and the status quo secured. However, dissatisfaction continued to simmer below the surface, and the number of Shi`ites in Lebanon grew. The rising numbers of Palestinians only exacerbated tensions. In 1970, the Palestinian leadership was expelled from neighboring Jordan, and the Palestine Liberation Organization established a new military base in the Lebanese capital. The Maronites, particularly the Phalangists, the militia belonging to the Jumayyil clan, were the most adamantly opposed to the Palestinians, and in April 1975 the occasional confrontations between these two groups exploded into another civil war. Other groups were drawn into the fighting, which began with three main participants—the Phalangists became the driving force in a Christian confederation (the Lebanese Front); mostly Muslim parties formed a second confederation (the Lebanese National Movement); and the Palestinian resistance comprised the third force. The two confederations formed militias, as did other groups. In the first few months, for example, the war gave rise to the radical Shi`ite militia Amal (means "hope"), which opposed the traditional Shi`ite leadership in Lebanon.

Lebanese women before the civil war. A traditionally patriarchal, feudal society, Lebanon in the present day has shown itself to be more open to education for women and to other modernizing influences than many Arab countries. Marriage within ethnic and sectarian communities may be preferred, but it is no longer the incontrovertible norm, as it was before the Second World War. The postwar period saw formerly rigid traditions begin to give way to some extent, especially in urban areas. City women enjoyed more rights in Lebanon than women in many other Arab countries. Although no woman held high political office, some upper-middle and middle-class women became active in the public domain—in education, media, and medicine. This was not generally true of rural and tribal women before the mid-1970s civil war. There were considerable differences among the lots of the urban, rural, and tribal women in Lebanon in this prewar period. Overall, though, few women worked and most of those who did were poor and single. Working-class women tended to engage in paid labor that could be performed at home. In the villages and in the Biqa Valley, peasant and pastoralist women's work, though labor intensive, was rarely paid. With modernization came general changes in labor options. Reduced needs for physical human labor drove men into entrepreneurship and women into market-oriented production. During the 1960s, village women, especially Shi`ites from the south, started to migrate into the cities in their search for education and employment.

Lebanese women during the civil war. The 16 years of war, which claimed 150,000 lives or 6 percent of the resident population and displaced some 500,000 people, changed relationships between men and women. Many men left Lebanon; some were caught up in the fighting, some emigrated. Overwhelmingly it was men who left, because although the war did not make mass exodus necessary, it did prevent men from earning a living. Life in Lebanon was not unliveable, however. Indeed the incidents of violence were so scattered, sporadic, and long confined to specific areas in Beirut that civilians could spend years without witnessing an act of war. So women often remained in Lebanon to take care of family matters, while men left to find

jobs and then sent home money. The number of female heads of household therefore rose exponentially. According to one scholar, during the war, "women's major achievement was to hold together the collapsing structures of Lebanese society" (Shehadeh, p. 50).

THE NATURE OF LEBANESE POLITICS

Strains of sectarianism and feudalism have long dominated Lebanese politics. Historically the most powerful families have been members of the Druze and the Maronite communities. But tensions arise even within confessional communities, particularly when political office is at stake. There are three prominent Maronite clans: Jumayyil, Chamoun, and Frangieh. Each has competed for the presidency of the country, sometimes by resorting to extreme violence. Although in the twentieth century the less populous Druze have not wielded as much power as the Maronites, in the past there was heavy competition for control of Lebanon, particularly between two Druze families, the Jumblatts and the Takieddines. More recently, Sunnis and Shi`ites have likewise relied on strong families, such as the Hariris (Sunni) and the Berris (Shi`ite). Rivalry for political power in Lebanon has thus been both inter- and intra-confessional.

The Novel in Focus

Plot summary. The novel revolves around a Shi`ite family living in Beirut. The relationships between parents and children and among young people in the city are examined before and after the outbreak of hostilities in Beirut. The story operates on many levels and uses several different voices, but in the center is a bewildered and directionless young woman, Zahra, who finds in the Lebanese civil war an opportunity to escape oppression and assert a measure of control over her life.

The first part of the novel, narrated by three voices, establishes Zahra as a physically unappealing woman. Plagued with acne, Zahra constantly picks at her scab-encrusted pimples. She escapes male predators by fleeing to the bathroom. There she can pick and squeeze her lesions at leisure.

Zahra is the quintessentially abused woman. In the first half of the novel, narrated alternately by Zahra, her uncle Hashim, and her husband

Beirut in May 1976, during the civil war in Lebanon.

Majid, she totters from one abusive situation to another. Zahra is raped by peers, molested by the men in her family, and traumatized from bearing witness to her mother's lascivious affair. Again, her only solution when in crisis is to escape to the nearest bathroom and lock the door.

At the invitation of her uncle Hashim, Zahra travels to Africa where Hashim has lived since the early 1960s. He was involved in a failed coup d'état and cannot return to Lebanon for fear of arrest. Zahra takes on a symbolic significance for her uncle, reminding him of Lebanon, becoming a Lebanon he can finally possess. Meanwhile, Hashim's incestuousness reminds Zahra of another relative's unhealthy interest in her body.

Wherever Zahra turns, she seems to be at the mercy of those who would use her body for their own needs and pleasures.

To escape her uncle, Zahra marries Majid, another needy exile. She quickly realizes that once again she has been turned into a vehicle: this time she represents a middle-class Lebanon that the working-class Majid could not have aspired to in Lebanon. At the moment, however, that Majid feels most confident of possessing a socially respectable wife, he loses her. She flees back to Beirut, where war has just broken out. For the first time, Zahra imagines how to retain control of her body and destiny. She feels more in command of her own life than ever before, attributing this newfound sense of power to the war: "It begins to occur to me that the war, with its miseries and destructiveness, has been necessary for me to start to return to being normal and human" (*The Story of Zahra*, p. 138). There is a physical improvement too—Zahra begins to lose her unsightly pimples.

In the second part of the novel, Zahra takes over the narration. Her female voice virtually erases the male voices that dominate the first part. Zahra does what was unimaginable before the war. She volunteers to work with a hospital that is handling war casualties; no longer does she focus solely on herself. Her relationship with her mother changes. Formerly utterly dependent on her mother, Zahra now sees through her mother's deceit. She understands the consequences of having to silently witness her mother's trysts and suffer her mother's mockery. Not only did Zahra's mother fail to love her; the child was also made to pay for her need for maternal affection. During the war, however, the situation changes. The normally fearless, egocentric mother is suddenly full of fear whereas the daughter is no longer afraid.

Zahra's new self-confidence extends beyond the home and relationships with known individuals. She ventures into a domain typically thought of as male—that of armed struggle. Stepping up to danger, Zahra dares to do what no other woman, or even man, has thought to do, by going out to meet a sniper who holds sway over an entire neighborhood. Not only does she create a lull in his shooting; she also initiates a sexual relationship with him. For the first time, the formerly exploited woman experiences sexual pleasure.

Zahra returns regularly to the sniper's perch on the roof. Over time the impersonality and violence of the first encounter, when all she wanted was to stop the shooting, are replaced by a measure of tenderness and friendship. He provides a sheet for their lovemaking, for example. The sniper also discloses some information about his past, although he never does reveal his political affiliations to her. Only when Zahra insists does the sniper tell her his name—Sami. Finding herself pregnant with their child, she asks his name so he can assume another identity in her eyes: that of her baby's father. She starts to dream of marriage with him. In her eyes the sniper Sami becomes a family man, not the emblem of the war's senseless savagery that he in fact is. So Zahra refuses to abort the fetus. She initiated the affair with little personal interest in the sniper, but given time and the pregnancy, her thoughts turn to the possibility of a normal life outside the logic of the war. Sami wants no part of the dream, though. Pretending to acquiesce in her decision to keep the baby, he lets Zahra go. But once she is back in the street, he shoots her.

The novel ends with Zahra speaking beyond her death: "He kills me with the bullets that lay at his elbow as he made love to me. He kills me, and the white sheets which covered me a little while ago are still crumpled from my presence. . . . Although I try, I can hear no sound from my own voice" (al-Shaykh, *The Story of Zahra*, p. 183). Her narration slips into that of the author, who articulates her death. Her lover, the sniper, has killed her.

War and feminine empowerment. Zahra's empowerment seems destined to end when it does. The conclusion of her story suggests that the Lebanese civil war did not promote conditions for healthy survival or lasting empowerment on the part of women. In Lebanese postwar society, as in many other postwar societies, women experienced a return to their prewar status quo in most respects. But Zahra's case is also atypical. She ventures onto fighting ground to stop a sniper, in itself unusual, and her imagination transforms him into something he is not. She does gain personal strength by standing up

to the fear-inducing sniper, but only temporarily. In fact, her particular tragedy indicates that sexual exploitation of a woman can occur even when the woman initiates the abusive relationship.

Zahra initiates this relationship by trespassing into a place where only men, in fact militarized men, usually go. Her trespassing is itself significant. It structures a counter-narrative to the standard "war story" of the pre-twentieth and twentieth centuries, a story that usually focuses on the experience of men and that firmly distinguishes between the places of men and women. In most historical writings, women are excluded from the armed conflict part of a battleground, which has long been thought of as male space. *The Story of Zahra* suggests how incomplete the conventional war story is, how much truth it erases when told in standard fashion. Recent revisionist accounts

---

CIVIL WAR AND SOCIAL CHANGE

Wartime Lebanon saw women's roles in society change. Jocelyn Khweir narrates her real-life experience as a leader in the Lebanon war, insisting on the "role military training and combat fighting play in a girl's self-confidence and sense of accomplishment" (Khweir in Shehadeh, p. 221). The war relaxed some of the more stringent patriarchal norms that restricted women's access to public space in peacetime Lebanon, a reality that is reflected by the developments in *The Story of Zahra*. At the same time, the war created a new moneyed elite in real-life Lebanese society, less defined by old-time feudal associations between notable personages and their separate cadres of followers than in the past. This moneyed elite was defined instead by its accumulation of war capital. Meanwhile, the lines separating social classes were becoming more permeable than ever before, a development likewise reflected in the novel.

---

of war, whether historical or literary, indicate that the binary of men at the front and women on the home front is, and probably always has been, a fiction: in the Lebanese civil war, some 5 to 10 percent of the fighting corps consisted of women (Shehadeh, p. 150). More than 100 militias participated in the struggle and it is known that women played some role in a few of them. Unsurprisingly they often took on tasks that were extensions of those performed at home—preparing food, providing medical care, serving

THE LEBANESE IN WEST AFRICA

Along with the United States and Brazil, West Africa has been a key destination for Lebanese laborers abroad. The Lebanese are in fact the major Arab population in West Africa. In *The Story of Zahra*, the protagonist's uncle, Hashim, has been living in Africa since the early 1960s. Emigrants from Lebanon had by 1962 formed sizeable communities in various African countries, from the North (Egypt), to the South (South Africa), to the West (Ivory Coast, Senegal, Nigeria, Guinea Conakry, Sierra Leone, and more).

1962 Population Dispersal of Lebanese in Africa

Ivory Coast	80,000
South Africa	60,020
Egypt	33,008
Senegal	10,070
Nigeria	6,150
Guinea Conakry	3,008
Sierra Leone	2,900
Liberia	2,697
Ghana	2,200
Sudan	1,600
Guinea Bissau	1,050

(Adapted from Rais, p. 4)

Certainly individuals emigrated from Lebanon but the main pattern has been for whole families or communities to emigrate from a specific part of the home country to the same location, especially in West Africa. In the mid-to-late twentieth century, for example, most Lebanese in Senegal came from the Lebanese town of Tyre.

Overall the emigrants and their descendants have gravitated to two occupations: retail sales*men* (in the late twentieth century, trade was overwhelmingly male; the Lebanese women were housewives) or middlemen. The middlemen might purchase produce from African farmers, then sell it to European firms, or they might purchase goods from the Europeans for retail sales to the Africans. In West Africa, the exact nature of the economic experience depended to some degree on the country. Not only did the Lebanese predominate in the general merchandise trade in Sierra Leone, for example, they also gained a large measure of control in the diamond trade. In Senegal, the Lebanese specialized in retail sales of cloth. It was common in late-twentieth-century West Africa for the Lebanese cloth shops to be clustered onto one or two streets of a town, suggesting an insular tendency that was borne out in the group's social life. In contrast to the earlier waves of immigrants to the Americas, who assimilated into the larger population, the Lebanese in West Africa remained tenaciously separate from it. Almost always, the men and women married not only other Lebanese, but other Shi`ite, Sunni, Maronite, or Druze Lebanese.

as clerks. Usually the sexes were segregated in the militia, which organized for women a separate Women's Affairs Department. A few women actually served as fighters, training alongside men in the use of light arms.

Just as there have always been men away from the battlefield so there have always been women in the killing fields. The undermining of this gendered separation of space, in Lebanon, as in the rest of the world, has become important, not only for accuracy's sake but also for the ramifications generated by setting the record straight.

Literary context. The Lebanese civil war was a time of accelerated literary activity, especially among women. During the first seven years of the war, before the Israeli invasion of 1982, a school of women writers called the Beirut Decentrists published novels, short stories, and poetry about the war. Al-Shaykh belonged to this school, along with various contemporaries. Emily Nasrallah's *Iqla aks al-zaman* (1980; *Flight Against Time,* 1987), Etel Adnan's *Sitt Marie Rose* (1978; *Sitt Marie Rose,* 1982), Ghada Samman's *Kawabis Bayrut* (1979; *Beirut Nightmares,* 1997), and Claire Gebeyli's many poems in newspapers all address the senseless violence. A number of these poems focus on women's attempts to exert some control over the "unruly boys," or male fighters, and describe the alarm of the women once they realize these boys are no innocents but intensely dangerous. Adnan lyrically details the slaughter of a woman teacher called Sitt Marie Rose. The Christian militiamen who perform the execution in front of a class of deaf and dumb children cannot tolerate the relationship between a fellow Christian and a Palestinian who is neither of their faith nor of their nation. The writing of the Beirut Decentrists calls for an expanded sense of commitment to their country, a humanist nationalism that insists on the need to stay on the land and nurture it as one would a child. Their writings contrast with those of male authors, like Ilyas Khoury, who describe the war as a revolution, a justifiable explosion on behalf of a worthwhile cause. Among all the female characters in this literature, Zahra stands out as the one who is the most transformed by her encounter with violence.

Reviews. A number of Arab critics expressed dislike for *The Story of Zahra* because of what they considered its pornographic bent. According to Elise Manganaro, al-Shaykh is unpopular in her native Lebanon because she "does not fulfill a folkloric criterion deemed suitable for the government educational curriculum, nor has she been able to claim a voice from within the larger public" (Manganaro in Shehadeh, p. 122). But critics in the West reacted differently. Here the novel was received as a powerful portrayal of the tragedy of war, particularly in the Lebanese civil war: "It is Hanan al-Shaykh's . . . *The Story of Zahrah* . . . that . . . using a Shi`i girl as its focus, reveals in most graphic and accomplished detail the full scale of the insane destruction that the armies of the various political and religious subgroups rained upon each other" (Allen, p. 189). A testament to its evocative power, the praise points to the novel's effectiveness as a war novel despite its unconventional war story.

—miriam cooke

For More Information

Accad, Evelyne. *Sexuality and War.* New York: New York University Press, 1990.

Adnan, Etel. *Sitt Marie Rose.* Trans. Georgina Kleege. Sausalito, Calif.: Post-Apollo Press, 1980.

Allen, Roger. *An Introduction to Arabic Literature.* Cambridge, U.K.: Cambridge University Press, 2000.

cooke, miriam. *War's Other Voices: Women Writers on the Lebanese Civil War.* New York: Cambridge University Press, 1988.

———. *Women and the War Story.* Berkeley: California University Press, 1997.

Fawaz, Leila. *Merchants and Migrants in Nineteenth-Century Beirut.* Cambridge, Mass.: Harvard University Press, 1983.

Ghandour, Sabah. "Hanan al-Shaykh's *Hikayat Zahra.*" In *Gender, Nation, and Community in Arab Women's Novels.* Ed. Lisa Suhair Majaj, Paula W. Sunderman, and Therese Saliba. Syracuse: Syracuse Universe Press, 2002.

Hiro, Dilip. *Lebanon: Fire and Embers: A History of the Lebanese Civil War.* New York: St. Martin's Press, 1992.

Nasrallah, Emily. *Flight Against Time.* Trans. Issa J. Boullata. Austin: Center for Middle Eastern Studies, University of Texas at Austin, 1997.

Rais, Marina. *The Lebanese of West Africa: An Example of a Trading Diaspora.* Berlin: Das Arabische Buch, 1988.

Samman, Ghada. *Beirut Nightmares.* Trans. Nancy N. Roberts. London: Quartet, 1997.

al-Shaykh, Hanan. *The Story of Zahra.* Trans. Peter Ford. London: Quartet, 1986.

Shehadeh, Lamia Rustum, ed. *Women and War in Lebanon.* Gainesville: University Press of Florida, 1999.

The Talmud

The image of the sea is often used to depict the vastness of the Talmud, a work of law and commentary on that law, that is one of the highest literary achievements of the Jewish tradition. A cornerstone of Halakhah (Jewish law), the Talmud extends beyond the confines of legal matters to include narrative discourse. There are in fact two Talmuds—the Palestinian Talmud (PT), or *Talmud Yerushalmi*, which was produced in Israel in the late fourth or early fifth century C.E., and the Babylonian Talmud (BT), or the *Talmud Bavli*, editorially completed in Babylonia in the sixth century or seventh century. When the term "Talmud" (from the Hebrew *limed*, "to teach") is used alone, it refers to the Babylonian Talmud. Less than half the size of the Babylonian Talmud, the Palestinian Talmud is written mostly in a dialect of Western Aramaic, and was produced in the Galilean academies of Sepphoris, Tiberias, and Caesarea. Like the Palestinian Talmud, the Babylonian Talmud includes Mishnaic and post-Mishnaic Hebrew but was written in an Aramaic that is akin to Syriac, the eastern Aramaic dialect then prevalent in Babylonia. Replete with legend and moral teachings as well as law, the Talmud has remained one of the major documents by which Judaism is understood. Much more than a static compilation of dictates, it is a dynamic corpus of legal disputes and disquisitions, an ongoing record and learned reconstruction of the proceedings of the early rabbinic study houses, and a treasure trove of stories, sage advice, and musings. Over time the Babylonian Talmud has exercised greater authority than its Palestinian

---

THE LITERARY WORK

A multivolume work of legal discourse, narratives, moral dicta, and scriptural exegesis spanning the first through sixth centuries C.E.; generated in Israel and Babylonia, primarily in Aramaic, probably in the fifth and seventh centuries; complete English edition published in 1935-52.

SYNOPSIS

Produced by learned Jewish men, the Talmud is a compendium of sage advice and religious laws pertaining to even the most trivial aspects of Jewish daily life.

---

counterpart, helping to sustain life in the diaspora (outside Israel) for well over a thousand years.

Events in History at the Time of the Discourse

Emergence of Rabbinic Judaism. The Second Temple, the spiritual and national center of the Jewish people, was completed in Jerusalem in 515 B.C.E., 19 years after Cyrus the Great, king of Persia, defeated the Babylonians and invited the Jews to return to Judea and rebuild the First Temple, which the Babylonians under King Nebuchadnezzar had destroyed in 586 B.C.E. Like the First Temple, the Second Temple became the center of Jewish social, cultural, and religious life. A main aspect of the religious life was an elaborate sacrificial system, involving animal offerings to God (of bulls, goats, and lambs), and meal offerings of flour and first fruits, to ensure the spiritual stability of the Jewish people. Priests made these offerings on behalf of individuals as well as the community at large. Performed daily, the sacrifices served as the vehicle used to gain access to the entity the Jews identified as the one God, to insure God's favor, and, when followers erred, to appease God. The belief was that if they strayed from God's ways, he could unleash his wrath and bring about the cultural and political subjugation that had befallen past generations.

When the second wave of Israelites returned to Judah from Babylonian exile in the mid-fifth century B.C.E. (a first wave had arrived nearly a century earlier), the priest and scribe Ezra assembled the Jewish people in Jerusalem for a public reading of the **Torah** of Moses (also in *WLAIT 6: Middle Eastern Literatures and Their Times*)—the books of law and narrative that trace the history of the Jews from the Garden of Eden to their arrival at the border of the Promised Land, which, according to the Torah, God pledged to Abraham's descendants for all eternity (Genesis 17:7ff). A dedication ceremony, which reaffirmed the commitment of the Jewish people to their covenant with God, followed Ezra's public reading, signifying their devotion to God's teaching as written in the Torah. The Torah began to play a newly important role in the religious life of the Jews. Ezra, and in turn the priests, exerted both religious and, along with the Persian-appointed governor, political authority over the Jewish community. While the Temple, which operated under the priests, was the physical locus of this power, the Torah as interpreted by the priests and scribes provided the spiritual blueprint to guide the Jewish people. Gradually the practice of reading the Torah in public developed.

In 332 B.C.E., Alexander the Great conquered Judea, and from the late fourth century until the victory of Islam in the seventh century C.E., except for a brief period of self-rule in Palestine (141 B.C.E.-63 B.C.E.), the Jews lived within the cultural, political, and social spheres of Greco-Roman civilization. In general, local Jewish institutions were afforded a great deal of autonomy under Roman rule. Relations between the Jews and Romans gradually deteriorated, however, and in 66 C.E. for various socioeconomic reasons, the Jews revolted. The Roman destruction of the Second Temple in 70 C.E. and the defeat of the rebels four years later

had serious consequences for the Jews in Palestine. Both the high priesthood and the Sanhedrin, the judicial body of the Jewish community chaired by a high priest, lost power and ceased to exist. The Temple had been snuffed out.

The Jews who lived outside the Holy Land, in the diaspora, were affected by the Temple's destruction too, for it had bound the diasporic communities to those in Palestine.

> The half shekel contributed annually by diaspora Jews and the pilgrimages undertaken for the festivals bound together the entire Jewish community. . . . The ideology of the temple also served as a binding force: it represented monism and exclusivity. Only one place was suitable for God's home on earth, and that place was the temple mount in Jerusalem.
>
> (Cohen, p. 106)

How then were the Jews to mend the broken axis?

From the rubble and ruins, rabbinic Judaism eventually emerged as a transformation of the sacrificial cult. Some time after the destruction of the Temple, the rabbis, who replaced the priests as figures of authority, drew on many aspects of the Second Temple period (515 B.C.E.-70 C.E.) to configure a conceptually new "temple"—that is, a new mode by which Jewish religious life could thrive in the absence of a physical spiritual center. For the rabbis, the study of the Torah and initially the less important development of functions at the synagogue, became central aspects of a more democratized system of worship than before. In time, personal and communal prayer replaced Temple sacrifices as a means of remaining connected to the Divine. Prayer attained the fixity of sacrificial services; the obligatory prayers, by and large, correspond to prayers once recited by the priests who made the daily sacrifices at the Temple. While prayer was available to Jews of all social strata, Torah study, which the rabbis espoused as tantamount to Temple sacrifice, was available only to a limited group of men with sufficient time to pursue it. The importance of Torah study then and now is captured in the Talmud:

> The study of Torah is more beloved by God than burnt offerings, for if a man studies Torah he comes to know the will of God, as it is said [in Scripture], "Then thou shall understand the fear of the Lord, and find the will of God" (Proverbs 2:5). Hence, when a sage sits and expounds [S]cripture to the congregation, Scripture accounts it to him as if he had offered up fat and blood on the altar.
>
> (Rabbi Nathan in Goldin, p. 32)

Stepping into the breach, the rabbis developed a system not only of daily prayers but also of rituals performed at the synagogue to replace the sacrificial temple services. They furthermore exalted Torah learning, as illustrated above; the evolution of the Talmud, which is committed to elucidating all aspects of the Torah, epitomizes this devotion.

The rabbis. The term *rabbi* (means "master") was first applied to a member of a group of learned men. Teachers rather than priests (although some of the rabbis were also priests), they produced major texts on Jewish law, religion, and culture between the first and seventh centuries C.E. The rabbis were likely the philosophical and theological descendants of the Pharisees, one of the sectarian groups to emerge during the Second Temple period. The Pharisees accepted the authority of "the tradition of the fathers," extrabiblical teachings transmitted orally through the generations, and were the only sectarian group to weather the destruction of the Temple. Most scholars consider them proto-rabbis.

The transition from priestly leadership to the rabbis is depicted in a famous legend about one of the leading rabbis, Yohanan ben Zakkai, who escaped Jerusalem during the Roman siege of the city. As a ploy to leave the city so he could make contact with the Roman general, Vespasian, ben Zakkai asked his disciples to hide him in a coffin, since the Romans permitted the Jews to bury their dead outside the city. Once beyond the walls of Jerusalem, he was led to Vespasian, who was impressed by Rabbi Yohanan's audacity, wisdom, and peace-loving stance. He was furthermore charmed by the rabbi's prediction that Vespasian would be the next Roman emperor, which indeed came true in 69 C.E. Having ingratiated himself, ben Zakkai received permission to establish a center of Jewish learning in the coastal town of Yavneh, 25 miles west of Jerusalem.

According to legend, the destruction of the Temple for a second time made it clear to Rabbi Yohanan ben Zakkai and his colleagues that no building could be relied on to preserve Jewish spiritual stability. The only way to guarantee the continuity of tradition was to promote the centrality of the Torah. With this in mind, they developed ordinances to relocate ritual practices from the Temple to the home and synagogue. The festival of Sukkot, for example, commemorates the peregrinations of the Israelites in the wilderness for 40 years, and also celebrates the Israelite fall harvest. Originally the festival called for the *lulav* (a ceremonial bundle of branches) to be carried inside the Temple for seven days and in the countryside for just one day. After the Temple was destroyed, ben Zakkai ordained that the *lulav* be taken into the country for seven days. He modified the existing regulations to accommodate the absence of the Temple.

The tannaim, the first generation of rabbis, flourished roughly from the destruction of the Second Temple to the compilation in 200 C.E. of the Mishnah—the first section of the Talmud, a collection of originally oral interpretations of the scriptures. As well as the Mishnah, this generation produced the Tosefta (supplements to the Mishnah), and the earliest collection of rabbinic biblical interpretation of Exodus, Leviticus, and Deuteronomy, known as Halakhic Midrashim. The death in 220 C.E. of Judah Ha Nasi, official high priest of the Palestinian Jews, ushered in a new series of sages, the Amoraim, who produced the Gemara (the second part of the Talmud, consisting of commentary on the Mishnah) for both Talmuds.

Rabbinic tradition states that God gave Moses the Oral as well as the Written Torah at Mount Sinai, a concept promoted to consolidate authority within the Jewish community. As it says in the opening lines of Pirke Avot ("The Sayings of the Fathers"), a collection of moral and religious pronouncements in the Mishnah: "Moses received Torah from Sinai and passed it on to Joshua; Joshua to the Elders; the Elders to the Prophets; the Prophets to the men of the Great Assembly [body of scholars who interpreted the Torah and its precepts from c. 539 B.C.E. to 332 B.C.E.]" (Babylonian Talmud, Pirke Avot 1:1). The chain of transmission ends with the earliest rabbis, the tannaim. The Oral Torah, the teachings of the rabbis, was eventually compiled in the form of the Mishnah, and between 200 and 600 C.E., the rabbis of the Palestinian and Babylonian Talmuds engaged in interpretation of the Written and Oral Torahs. Their interpretations comprise the Gemara. By the mid-second century C.E., a revived Sanhedrin had been installed in Galilee, the center of Jewry in the land of Palestine. At the apex of the Sanhedrin was the high priest, by now an official appointee called the Patriarch (leader of the Fatherland) or Ethnarch (leader of the ethnos, people). Over time, the office of Patriarch gained both official Roman recognition and the support of the Jewish populace. By the mid-fourth century, the Patriarch would be granted senatorial rank and authority to collect taxes from all Jews who lived within the ambit of the Roman Empire. During the

GLOSSARY OF TALMUDIC TERMS

Torah The first five books of the Hebrew scriptures (Genesis, Exodus, Leviticus, Numbers and Deuteronomy); also known as the Pentateuch.

Mishnah The originally oral law that forms the basis of the Talmud; according to tradition, this oral law was given to Moses by God at Sinai along with the Ten Commandments, which were written on tablets; the oral law was codified c. 200 C.E. by Judah Ha Nasi (Judah the Prince).

Gemara The second part of the Talmud, consisting of commentary on the Mishnah. Unless otherwise noted, the Gemara refers to the commentary in the Babylonian Talmud. Censors also used the term as a substitute for *Talmud,* which was deemed offensive to Christians.

Tosefta ("supplement") A collection of early rabbinic teachings contemporaneous with the Mishnah.

Rashi The medieval comments of Rabbi Solomon ben Isaac on the Talmud, printed, in general, in a distinctive semicursive script on the part of the page closest to the binding.

Tosafot Medieval glosses on the Talmud, of predominantly French and German origin, generally printed opposite Rashi's comments, on the outer margin of the Talmudic page.

Baraita (plural, *baraitot*) Any teaching of the early rabbinic period not included in the Mishnah, but discussed elsewhere in the Talmud.

Halakhah Jewish law; designates all legal discussions.

Haggadah Non-legal material and rabbinic narrative.

Midrash Rabbinic biblical interpretation that explains legal points or teaches lessons through word play, parables, stories and legends. Some compilations of Midrash are verse-by-verse interpretations of books of scripture such as Genesis Rabbah, and others are arranged as collections of sermons such as Leviticus Rabbah and Pesikta de Rav Kahana.

Tannaim From the Hebrew *tanna,* "repeater" or "reciter"; rabbis of the first, second, and third centuries C.E. who taught the oral law as recorded in the Mishnah and in Baraitot.

Amoraim From the Hebrew *amora,* "speaker," "interpreter"; rabbis of the third, fourth, and fifth centuries C.E. who produced the *gemara,* or commentary, of both Talmuds as well as the Haggadic Midrashim.

Synagogue From the Greek *synagoge,* literally "congregation" or "assembly"; some time after the destruction of the Temple, it emerged as the central institution of Jewish communal worship and study, and remains so to this day.

centuries of the Patriarchate (late first century to 425 C.E.), the Exilarchate, a parallel institution in Babylonia under the late Parthian and Sasanian empires, emerged.

Both Palestine and Babylonia boasted thriving rabbinic communities with rival academies. The rabbis of Babylonia furthered the Palestinian rabbinic tradition of learning by developing their own interpretations and spawning their own eminent sages. Abbaye (c. 278-338), a fourth generation *amora*, who was head of the Babylonian study house at Pumbedita, and Rava (c. 299-352), a teacher at Pumbedita and then at Mahoza (also in Babylonia), are two of many examples. The myriad disputations between these illustrious sages are found throughout the Talmud and their subtle arguments are models of the dialectic method of Halakhic discourse.

The Collection in Focus

Contents overview. The Talmud contains many sources, authors, and redactors from different eras. Its sheer volume (37 tractates, or treatises) is impressive. One can in fact appreciate just how monumental the work is by examining a single page. Every page has two sides, A and B, on each side of which are four main components: Mishnah (the oral law), Gemara (commentary on the Mishnah), Rashi (commentary on the Mishnah and Gemara by Rabbi Solomon ben Isaac), and the Tosafot (commentaries, often on Rashi).

The Mishnah is divided into six broad categories, called *Seders* (Orders): Zeraim ("Seeds"), about agricultural laws; Moed ("Festivals"), about Sabbath and festival laws; Nashim ("Women"), about family law, inheritance, and marriage and divorce; Nezikin ("Damages"), about penalties, punishment, civil and criminal law, and torts; Kodashim ("Holy Things"), about cultic ritual in the Jerusalem Temple; and Tohorot ("Purity"), on rules governing ritual purity. Each seder contains a number of tractates, whose names are derived from the prevalent theme of the work (for example, the tractate "Sabbath" deals with laws governing the Sabbath). These tractates are further divided into chapters. The Mishnah in fact has 63 tractates, but the Gemara comments on only 37 of these tractates, probably because many of the topics covered were not considered relevant enough to diasporic Jews to warrant further attention. For example, the agricultural laws discussed in Seder Zeraim apply only to land actually within historical Israel itself. Interestingly, there is commentary for Seder Kodashim (regarding the Jerusalem Temple); why the rabbis preserved and proliferated teachings about a destroyed temple vexes scholars of rabbinics. Perhaps it reflects the hope that the Temple might be rebuilt again, making a detailed account of cultic concerns valuable for posterity; perhaps the study of cultic regulations was a way of maintaining the Temple in spirit, if not in fact.

The very structure of a Talmudic page, with commentaries from different generations, that is, a mix of multiple voices from several eras, reflects the Talmud's most distinctive feature. At the center of a page of the Talmud is a passage of Mishnah followed by *gemara,* Talmudic commentary in which several rabbis explain a specific law by referring to scriptural proof-texts and engaging in logical argumentation. More often than not, the sages of the Talmud raise other issues and discuss other rabbinic texts when discussing a law in the Mishnah. The *gemara* might also refer to topics raised in a *baraita,* writing contemporary with but not collected in the Mishnah. The discussion can include advice on mundane topics (how to deal with bad dreams, how to tie one's shoes, or how to cure a sore throat), as well as ruminations on important theological questions (why evil exists in the world).

Scattered through the pages of the Talmud are case precedent, scriptural interpretation, philosophical reflections, and historical and legendary stories of grand and simple proportions. For example, the Mishnah states that there are "40 minus one" principal types of work that a person must avoid during the Sabbath. In an effort to define more clearly the scriptural prohibition against working on the Sabbath, the rabbis of the Mishnah list 39 activities that fit the category "work." The rabbis of the Talmud, however, pose the question, "To what do the 40 minus one principal kinds of works refer?" (Babylonian Talmud, Shabbat 49b), debate the reference to "40 minus one," and then discuss each activity—such as ploughing, reaping, threshing, sifting, kneading,

HILLEL

According to tradition, the famous and influential sage, Hillel (c. 70 B.C.E.-c. 10 C.E.), developed his own methods for interpreting Torah. These methods would serve as the basis for much of the Talmudic analysis that followed. A great teacher of Torah, Hillel exhorted his students to study it for its own sake, and gained a reputation for ethical conduct that is integral to his being described as one of the greatest teachers who ever lived. Once a non-Jew sought Hillel's counsel, promising that he would convert, "on condition that you [Hillel] teach me the whole Torah while I stand on one foot." "What is hateful to you, do not to your neighbor," replied Hillel. "That is the whole Torah, while the rest is commentary; go and learn it."

(Hillel in Babylonian Talmud, Shabbat 31a)

and building—individually. In the process of highlighting different lines of thought, disputes between different rabbis often remain unresolved. The lines of thought, however, bring to the fore perennial concerns of as much relevance to life today as to the ancient and medieval past.

To take another example, Mishnah Berakhot, Chapter One, discusses when and how to say the Shema (the central confession of Jewish faith proclaiming the oneness of God, which is recited twice daily): "From what time may a person recite the morning Shema? From the time that one is able to distinguish between blue and white.

First page of commentary on the Pentateuch, written by the eleventh-century Talmud scholar Rashi.

R. Eliezer says, Between blue and green. And he must finish it by sunrise. R. Joshua says, [The person must finish it] within three hours of sunrise" (Babylonian Talmud, M. Berakhot 1:2). Cited are differing opinions of when the morning Shema may be recited, but no resolution is offered—none of the opinions is declared definitive. The sages of the Talmud thus resume the thread of discourse, but generally do not resolve disputes among the rabbis.

Halakhic statements in the Mishnah are subject to the scrutiny of rigorous rational argumentation. The most prosaic matters are debated with the same intensity as matters of life and death. Understanding divine law as it manifests itself in daily life is of utmost importance to the rabbis, who see the activity of providing detailed, logically sound arguments in support of a law as a form of religious devotion. As the scholar Jacob Neusner explains, "Reason and logic . . . carry Torah—revealed teaching—from heaven down to earth, and conversely . . . make the profane sacred. They are modes of religious expression" (Neusner, p. xvii).

Because the Talmud is not easily comprehensible to the uninitiated, a tradition of commentary upon it developed in the medieval period. Rashi (Rabbi Solomon ben Isaac, 1040-1105) composed the most influential of these

commentaries, and in all editions of the Talmud beginning with the Bologna (Italy) version of 1482, his commentary, written in the distinctive printer's convention of semi-cursive "Rashi script," is found closest to the binding, and in a sense at the heart of Talmudic study. Typically, Rashi's explanation of a Talmudic passage is terse and precise, anticipating a student's queries in attempting to make sense of an obscure comment, a vague reference, or a complex legal argument.

Later authorities wrote commentaries on Rashi, the most important of which is the Tosafot, located on the outer margin, opposite Rashi's commentary. The first of these commentators were Rashi's grandsons and sons-in-law, the most famous of whom are Rabbi Shmuel ben Meir (Rashbam), and Rabbi Yaakov ben Meir (Rabbenu Tam).

Religious law. Written in Hebrew and Aramaic, the Talmud has a unique style that initially makes it difficult to study, an adventure further complicated by many technical legal terms and obscure references. Furthermore, the laws in the Talmud are not expressed casuistically; they rarely tell the reader specifically what to do or not do. Rather, the laws describe how one behaves or does not behave, and interpreters glean the dictate from these descriptions. The language of Halakhah is therefore different from contemporary legal language. Laws are recorded, but more importantly the reader is made privy to careful argumentation among a community of scholars dedicated to clarifying every ramification of the law. One gains insight into their private deliberations, as well as the very process of argumentation.

The Talmud's distinctive style is illustrated in the following excerpt from tractate Sukkah 49b-50a, which tackles the question of what is greater, performing sacrifices, acts of charity, or acts of loving-kindness:

> Rabbi Eleazar said, "Greater is the one who performs charity (*tzedakah*) than [the one who offers] all the sacrifices, as Scripture says, "Doing charity and justice is more acceptable to the Lord than offering sacrifices," (Proverbs 21:3). Rabbi Eleazar stated, "Acts of loving-kindness (*Gemilut Hasidim*) is [sic] greater than charity, for Scripture says, 'Sow for yourselves charity and reap according to loving-kindness (*hesed*),' (Hosea 10:12). If a person sows, it is doubtful whether or not he will eat [the harvest], but when a man reaps, surely he will eat. . . ." Our rabbis taught [in a baraita]: In three respects is performing acts of loving-kindness (*Gemilut Hasidim*) superior to charity: 1. Charity can be done with one's money,

whereas acts of loving-kindness can be done with both one's person and one's money; 2. Charity can be given only to the poor, but deeds of loving-kindness can be performed for both the rich and the poor; 3. Whereas charity can only be given to the living, deeds of loving-kindness can be done both to the living and to the dead [i.e., attending to their funeral and burial]. . . . Rabbi Hama ben Papa stated, "Every person bestowed with loving-kindness is undoubtedly a God-fearing person, for it is said in Scripture, 'But the loving-kindness of the Lord is from everlasting to everlasting,'" (Psalm 103:17). R. Eleazar continued, "What is the meaning of the scriptural verse, 'She opened her mouth with wisdom and the Torah of loving-kindness (hesed) is on her tongue,' (Proverbs 31:26)? Is there then a Torah of loving-kindness and a Torah, which is not of loving-kindness? Rather Torah, which is studied for its own sake is the Torah of loving-kindness and Torah, which is studied for ulterior purposes is a Torah not of loving-kindness. There are some who say that Torah studied in order to teach is Torah of loving-kindness, but Torah which is not studied for pedagogical purposes is not of loving-kindness."

(Babylonian Talmud, Sukkah 49b-50a; adapted by C. Bakhos)

The placement of this particular passage within the Talmud points to another of the work's difficulties: its organization. Although this debate would more obviously fit in tractate Baba Batra 7b-11a, a general discussion about the collection and distribution of charity, the rabbis placed it in tractate Sukkah, a treatise on the Feast of Tabernacles (Sukkot). Specifically, it follows a Mishnah outlining how the water libation ceremony was performed during the festival of Sukkot during Temple times. The rationale is as follows: In ancient Israel, rain was considered a bountiful gift from God. Since the rainy season succeeds the fall festival of Sukkot, the holiday was a time for prayers and supplication having to do with rainfall. The ritual act of pouring water and wine in the Temple therefore symbolized the rain that God would pour forth on the land. In the above passage, scriptural verses are explained in detail and simultaneously used to support a position. Rabbi Eleazar uses scripture to explain why charity outranks sacrifices and why, in turn, acts of loving-kindness outrank charity. Secondly, positions are not merely stated, but rather the reader is exposed to each building block of thought. Instead of just stating Rabbi Eleazar's position that acts of loving-kindness outrank sacrifices and charity, the Talmud takes the reader through each step and illustrates the progression of thought. Later, the

introduction of a verse from the Torah appears to lead into a new topic. When the passage segues into Proverbs 31:26, "She opened her mouth with wisdom and the Torah of loving-kindness (hesed) is on her tongue," the discussion appears to veer in a seemingly different direction—to the study of Torah. But the "digression" turns out to be a consistent argument on the importance of intention. That is to say, the passage in part argues that actions must arise from good intentions. Acts of loving-kindness are greater when selfless. Some

RASHI

Born in 1040 in Troyes, France, Rabbi Solomon ben Isaac, or Rashi, as he is popularly known, wrote the most influential of the medieval commentaries on the Bible and Talmud. He studied in Worms and Mainz, Germany, then returned home, where he opened a school in 1070. His stand-alone commentary on the Pentateuch (the first five books of the Hebrew Bible) was printed in Reggio, Italy, in 1475, the first dated Hebrew book to be printed. In 1482 his commentary was included as marginalia in the Bologna edition of the Pentateuch. The first edition of the entire Talmud with Rashi's commentary was published in Venice in 1520-22.

Rashi supported himself not only as a rabbi but also as a wine merchant; his connection to the "real world" is evident in his writings, which are filled with folklore and homilies that convey a charming wit. His influence spread beyond northern France and southern Germany, to reach Jewish communities in Spain, in Provence, and in eastern regions. His painstaking scriptural analysis also influenced Christian theologians, including Martin Luther (who, ironically, wrote virulently against the Jews), by way of Nicholas of Lyre's "Postillae Perpetuae," which draws heavily from Rashi's work. Rashi died in Troyes in 1105.

rabbis would argue that Torah studied for the purpose of edifying others, in addition to improving oneself, is an act of loving-kindness, for the intention, albeit ulterior, is nonetheless good. The passage includes a baraita, a teaching from an earlier generation, which principally agrees that acts of loving-kindness are greater than acts of charity. Lastly the passage illustrates how the Talmud makes obsolete practices of the past relevant to the present. Its debate about loving-kindness forms part of a larger discussion on the water libation ritual during the Sukkot holiday when the Temple was still standing. Like God, who gives us rain out of loving-kindness, we are called to do the same. What at first seems a peculiar digression is indeed related to the issue at hand—performing acts of loving-kindness in imitation of God, who gives all people, the underprivileged and privileged alike, rain.

First and foremost, the Talmud is concerned with legal matters, but in the course of its explanations, it tells folktales about the common dimensions of human experience and stories about prominent rabbis and the house of study (*beit midrash*) in both Israel and Babylonia. The values espoused in these rabbinic stories are the same as those that underpin legal statements. The famous story of the "Oven of Akhnai," found in tractate Baba Metsia 59a-59b, affirms that the majority has authority over the minority in making legal decisions, going so far as to boldly assert the authority of the rabbinic majority over God. At the start of the story, R. Eliezer is debating with other rabbis about whether an oven made of tiles separated by sand is clean or unclean. There is a rabbinic law that says once a clay vessel becomes impure (unclean), it cannot be made pure unless it is broken. The law does not apply, argues R. Eliezer. The oven is made of separate ("broken") tiles; therefore, it is not a single entity and so is not liable to uncleanness. The other rabbis counter that the outer coating of mortar unifies the oven and makes it a single entity, so it is liable to uncleanness. R. Eliezer brings forward every rational argument possible, but the rabbis remain unconvinced, at which point he resorts to another form of persuasion—miraculous works. He says to them, "If the law is as I say, let the carob tree prove it," and instantly a nearby carob tree is uprooted (Babylonian Talmud, Baba Metsia 59a-59b). The other rabbis, unperturbed, reply that a moving carob tree cannot prove or disprove a legal position, nor can any other miraculous event. Not even the voice of God himself coming from the heavens in support of Eliezer can sway the other rabbis from their position. "Since the Torah was already given at Mount Sinai," retorts R. Yirmiyah, "we do not listen to a Heavenly Voice, and in it [the Torah] is written, 'Incline after the majority' (Exodus 23:2)" (Babylonian Talmud, Baba Metsia 59a-59b). In other words, once given to Moses, the Torah is no longer in God's hands but in the hands of the generations of scholars who interpret it. Law, asserts the passage with a reference to scripture, must follow the majority opinion, to which even God is subject. So says the Talmud, and its story continues. Rabbi Natan meets Rabbi Elijah, the biblical prophet (who was a living presence for the rabbis of the Talmud) and asks, "What was the Holy One doing at that time?" whereupon Elijah answers, "He laughed and smiled and replied, 'My sons have defeated me, my sons have defeated me'" (Babylonian Talmud, Baba Metsia 59a-59b).

The Law Codes. The centrality of the Talmud as the foundation of Jewish law in the medieval period led to the growth of another type of literature, the Jewish Law Codes. The codifiers, great rabbinic scholars, culled the Talmud for all arguments relevant to a specific issue and compiled only the outcome. Most often these scholars applied standards and rules of codification that were foreign to the writers of the Talmud. The scholars aimed not to transmit the legal tradition, but rather to state the law. Moses Maimonides' *Mishneh Torah* (The Second Law) is generally acknowledged as the foremost of the codifications. Written in Hebrew and compiled in 1180, his 14-book *Mishneh Torah*, organized topically, became the first work to classify all of the Written and Oral Laws. As his sources Maimonides used both the Babylonian and the Palestinian Talmuds as well as other early rabbinic works, namely the Halakhic Midrashim—the Sifra, (the Halakhic Midrash to the book of Leviticus), Sifrei (the Halakhic Midrash to the Book of Numbers and Deuteronomy), and Mekilta (the Halakhic Midrash to the book of Exodus). He also incorporated principles of Aristotelian science and metaphysics and other non-Jewish works into his own. Almost as soon as the *Mishneh Torah* appeared so did its vehement critics, who disapproved of the fact that Maimonides did not cite any of his sources, did not write in Aramaic, and had imposed his own order on the books of the Talmud. Nonetheless, the *Mishneh Torah* won widespread approval and, ironically, this work that aimed always to be brief became the subject of intense scrutiny, generating reams of interpretive literature.

Another famous law code is the *Shulhan Arukh* (The Set Table) of Rabbi Joseph Caro (1488-1575). Like Maimonides, Caro tended to ignore earlier sources or opinions, but unlike his predecessor, Caro omitted discussion of laws, such as those pertaining to the Temple, that had no contemporary relevance. Completed probably in 1555 and first published in Venice ten years later, the *Shulhan Arukh* spawned a massive protest (having mostly to do with the rival traditions of different groups of European Jews) and many critical commentaries, which, ironically, served to cement its position as one of the most influential works on law in Jewish life; in time, it became the de facto standard by which Jewish communities around the world viewed Jewish law as found in the Talmud. More recently, it has become associated with Orthodox Judaism.

Despite the relative economy of the law codes, the Talmud remains paramount in Jewish tradition, for it is not merely a book of law. To be sure, its raison d'être is the elaboration and articulation of law, as noted, but as shown too, it far exceeds legal discourse, serving also as a text of historical, literary, rhetorical, and ethical import.

Sources and literary context. The Talmud, it has been suggested, draws on an assortment of sources, from the Hebrew Scriptures to the Mishnah, the Baraitot, and the Midrashic literature of the rabbis. It further abounds in legends about the rabbis themselves. One of its venerable sages, Rabbi Akiba, who lived in the first through mid-second century C.E., is said to have been a shepherd of modest means who worked for an affluent Jerusalemite, Kalba Sevua. A pious man with an exceptional character, Akiba attracted the attention of the Jerusalemite's daughter, who promised to marry him if he would give up tending cattle and study Torah, which he did for 24 years, and in the process acquired 24,000 students. The Jerusalemite meanwhile disinherited his daughter, forcing the couple to live in squalor. Later, seeing how Akiba earned universal respect and attained unprecedented stature for his acumen, Kalba Sevua prostrated himself at his son-in-law's feet, kissed them, and bequeathed half his fortune to Akiba.

It is Akiba who is credited with laying the foundation for the compilation of the Mishnah, or Oral Torah. The tractate Avot de Rabbi Nathan (Chapter 18) likens him to a worker who went out with his basket and collected wheat, barley, spelt, beans, and lentils. When he arrived home, he sorted each item individually. So, too, Akiba systematized Halakhah, Jewish law. He became known as well for evolving a novel method of interpreting Torah, his assumption being that every jot of scripture possesses special significance. Even the smallest word, such as "if" or "and" has meaning. If something appears superfluous and inconsequential, this is only because a person's limited intelligence cannot comprehend its meaning. Even "and" or "*et*," a signifier in Hebrew that indicates which word is the direct object, has interpretive value. Take, for example, Rabbi Akiba's explication of "And you shall fear the Lord your God." In the Hebrew this verse includes an *et*, which, according to Rabbi Akiba, indicates that not only God is to be feared but also God's Torah. On another occasion, Akiba explained the verse as referring to both God and scholars. In both instances, he uses the direct object marker, *et* ("You shall fear *et* the Lord your God."), as the basis of his exegesis, thus deriving meaning on the premise that the study of God's word must break free of the strictures of literal interpretation.

Impact. The redaction of the Talmud spanned several generations, beginning with the Amoraim and ending with the early Saboraim, the

---

MAIMONIDES

Also known as Rambam (Rabbi Moses ben Maimon), Maimonides (1138-1204) was born in Cordoba, Spain, spent his adolescence wandering in northern Africa after his family chose exile from Spain over embracing Islam as decreed by the Almohads dynasty, and lived his adult life in Cairo, an important Jewish center. Not only a Talmudist, he eventually became personal physician to the Egyptian viceroy, and wrote reputed works in Arabic on such diverse scientific subjects as astronomy, haemorrhoids, sexual intercourse, and hygiene. His fame, however, is based primarily on two works, the *Mishneh Torah* and the *Moreh Nevukhim* (Guide for the Perplexed, completed in 1187). The former was written in Hebrew and was the first systematized code of Mosaic and rabbinical law; the latter, written in Arabic, reconciles classical philosophy with rabbinical literature and indeed with the Scriptures themselves. The *Moreh Nevukhim* became hugely influential across religious boundaries, influencing the medieval Jewish philosopher Baruch Spinoza, as well as such important Christian theologians as Albertus Magnus and Duns Scotus.

---

scholars who are believed to have finalized the internal form of the Gemara in the sixth or seventh century C.E. During the Middle Ages, due in large measure to the role of the Geonim (singular, *Gaon*), the heads of the Palestinian and Babylonian academies, rabbinic teaching gained authority in an unprecedented way, and the teaching found in the Talmud became the basis of all Jewish religious life and has remained so for traditional Jews to the present. Because Jews from all over looked to the heads of the Babylonian academies for guidance on religious legal matters related to divorce, inheritance, and communal affairs, the rabbis of the medieval period needed to clarify Talmudic law so that it could be applied to sundry new situations. The challenge facing the religious Jewish leaders was finding ways in which the Talmud, the basis of religious authority, could be made viable to a generation of Jews living in a time different from that of the final redactors of the Talmud. Answers to specific questions by rabbis of various local communities addressed to the heads of the communities are called *responsa*. The *responsa* were distributed beyond the academies of Palestine and Babylonia, and the law codes of Maimonides and then Caro followed. One might think that law codes would make the study of Talmud obsolete, but the sixteenth century certainly was not the end of Talmudic study.

The reception of the Talmud has not always been favorable. In an effort to undermine Judaism in the thirteenth century, Jewish converts to Christianity brought the Talmud, which contains disparaging passages about Jesus and Christianity, to the attention of Christians in positions of power and influence. In 1233, Pope Gregory IX officially condemned the Talmud and in 1242 ordered the burning of copies of the Talmud in Paris, a practice Pope Gregory IX's successors maintained throughout Western Europe in the thirteenth century. The Talmud was also opposed by Jews who placed greater importance on mystical means to commune with the Divine.

Study of the Talmud has endured nonetheless. Today scholars pore over the work, using it as a portal into the world of the ancient rabbis of Palestine and Babylonia and a means to intimate knowledge of what is understood as God's laws. The structure of the Talmud, from the ordering of a single page, to the ordering of each tractate, to the ordering of the voluminous corpus of 37 tractates, remains unparalleled in world literature. Also unique is the fact that the Talmud preserves lengthy deliberations based on laws, theological truths, and ethical teachings, as well as lengthy speculations about the derivation of these truths. Other compilations preserve the final conclusions without all the argumentation.

—Carol Bakhos

For More Information

Abrams, Judith Z. *The Babylonian Talmud: A Topical Guide*. Lanham, Md.: University Press of America, 2002.

Cohen, Shaye J. D. *From the Maccabees to the Mishnah*. Philadelphia: Westminster Press, 1987.

Goldenberg, Robert. "The Talmud." In *Back to the Sources*. Ed. Barry Holtz. New York: Touchstone, 1984.

Goldin, Judah, trans. *The Fathers According to Rabbi Nathan*. New Haven: Yale University Press, 1955.

Hebrew-English Edition of The Babylonian Talmud. 30 vols. Trans. Maurice Simon. Ed. I. Epstein. London: Soncino Press, 1965-94.

Neusner, Jacob. *Invitation to the Talmud*. New York: Harper and Row, 1973.

Rubenstein, Jeffrey. *Rabbinic Stories*. New York: Paulist Press, 2002.

Strack, Herman Leberecht, and Günter Stemberger. *Introduction to the Talmud and Midrash*. Minneapolis: Fortress Press, 1992.

The Torah

The five books that comprise the Torah, the first section of the Hebrew Bible, are Genesis, Exodus, Leviticus, Numbers, and Deuteronomy. Also called the Humash, "the Five-fold," (in Greek, "Pentateuch"), they are viewed by Jews as the holiest and most authoritative of the three parts of the Hebrew Bible—the "Torah," "Prophets," and "Writings" (the Hebrew acronym is *Tanakh*). In the Torah a framework of narrative encapsulates a great body of legislation, believed to have been divinely revealed, reflecting a covenant, or treaty, between God and the community of Israelite slaves newly escaped from Egypt. There are also a few passages of poetry, a section of speeches in the Book of Deuteronomy, genealogies, and a scattering of other literary genres. Read on a yearly cycle in synagogues as part of the liturgy, the Torah has been the basis of Jewish life for 2,500 years. The composition of the Torah spanned at least 500 years before the probable date of its completion, in the mid-fifth century B.C.E.

According to the religious tradition of Jews and Christians, the Torah was written 3,500 years ago by Moses (hence the common appellation "Five Books of Moses") at the direct dictation of God. Intense scholarly study has resulted in a consensus opinion that views the Torah differently. According to this scholarly opinion, the Torah, or "Book of the Law of Moses," was brought by Ezra, a Jewish scribe and an official of the Persian government, from Babylon to the Jewish community of Jerusalem, newly returned from exile, about 450 B.C.E. The work was

> **THE LITERARY WORK**
>
> Five books that constitute the first section of the Hebrew Bible, set in the ancient Near East from c. 2000-1400 B.C.E. (according to the biblical chronology); completed and probably published in Hebrew by the fifth century B.C.E., in English in the fifteenth century C.E.
>
> **SYNOPSIS**
>
> A work of religious concepts and laws as well as narrative, the Torah recounts the development of the Israelites from Creation to the arrival of their 12 tribes at the border of the "Promised Land" of Canaan (later known as Palestine).

part of the attempt by authorities, both Jewish and Persian, to normalize and stabilize the religious and social life of the Jews. So successful was the attempt that the work has since remained the constitution of Judaism. Ezra's book is thought by scholars to be the final form of the Pentateuch, expanded during the exile with a great mass of priestly cultic and ritual legislation. In essence, the work is the product of several centuries of historical turmoil of war, exile, and renewal. It is therefore unsurprising that scholars also see the Pentateuch as the product of centuries of literary growth, in its final form an accretion of a number of sources joined to and superimposed on each other. The earliest complete manuscripts of the Torah are no more than

1,000 years old, though substantial sections have been found among *The Dead Sea Scrolls*, which are more than 2,000 years old (also in *WLAIT 6: Middle Eastern Literatures and Their Times*). Overall, for a religious work, there is surprisingly little theological speculation in the Torah. The Five Books are predominantly a historical-legal work, in which religious ideas must be deduced from a mass of concrete detail. They form an altogether astounding amalgam of historiography and religion, one of whose most perplexing conundrums is whether or not to regard the narrative element as fact.

Events in History at the Time the Torah Takes Place

A matter of fact? Jewish religious tradition regards the Pentateuch as a work written down in the fifteenth century B.C.E. As noted, modern scholarship understands its present form to be a product of the fifth century B.C.E. The problem is how to deal with the intervening millennium. Many scholars consider it safest to treat the narrative as a work of fiction, or, at best, legend, and to focus on the religious and literary values the Torah contains. They view its claim to history as an aspect of historiography only, a claim unsubstantiated by historical and archaeological evidence.

Archaeology has indeed shed much light on c. 2000-1400 B.C.E., the period of events described in the Torah from Abraham to Moses. In fact, the dates of this period are in contention; most modern scholars place the end date closer to 1250 B.C.E. But either way, the time spans various recorded events, depending on one's environs. In Syria-Palestine the period covers the Middle and part of the Late Bronze Age, an era of city-states that toward the end became subject to Egyptian control. In Egypt, this same period covers the end of the chaotic First Intermediate Period, the peaceful Middle Kingdom, the Hyksos incursion, and the founding of the war-like New Kingdom. In Mesopotamia the time-span encompasses the end of the Sumerian revival in the Third Dynasty of Ur and the Isin-Larsa Period, the invasion of the West-Semitic Amorites and the establishment of the Old Babylonian kingdoms (most famously the one ruled by Hammurabi), and the occupation of Mesopotamia by Kassites. In Anatolia the Hittite state rose to prominence, and in the region of the upper Euphrates and Tigris, the kingdoms of Assyria and Mitanni.

Of all this, there is no direct mention in any part of the Torah's narrative. Nothing of what modern historical and archaeological study has discovered corroborates any specific event or person named in the work. However, some scholars maintain that much circumstantial and background information has been discovered about the historical facets recounted in the work, although the significance of much of this information is open to debate.

The Torah, for example, speaks of the patriarch Abraham as coming from the Sumerian city of Ur in southern Mesopotamia, a city that was indeed at the height of its prosperity around 2000 B.C.E.; it also, however, enjoyed a revival in the mid-first millennium B.C.E. and so could have been known to authors writing a thousand or more years after the supposed patriarchal age. Similarly, the ancestors of Israel are associated with the city of Haran in northern Mesopotamia and with a people called the Arameans. Both the city and the people, however, are also associated with the later period. Likewise, the patriarchal type of religion, which centers on the intimate connection between a protective deity and a clan, is attested to in antiquity, but again in connection with periods both contemporary with the patriarchs and from much later.

In truth, it would be safest to view the stories of the patriarchs as compounded of bits of traditional legends of the ethnic groups that were to form historical Israel and Judah after 1100 B.C.E. Much the same point can be made about the events of the exodus and wandering in the desert. The pharaoh who welcomed Jacob and his family in Egypt may have been one of the Semitic Hyksos who ruled Egypt in the sixteenth century B.C.E. Appearing in Egyptian records are slaves of the same Hebrew background as the ancestors of Israel, and there is much local Egyptian background in the Joseph and Moses narratives. As in the other cases, scholars debate whether these incidental details best fit the second millennium B.C.E., and so are authentic historical memories, or only fit the first millennium B.C.E., after the Torah purports to take place, in which case they would most appropriately be viewed as literary color.

The Torah in Focus

Contents summary—Genesis. The Pentateuch consists of narrative and laws. It is from the laws that it receives its traditional name *Torah* (Hebrew for "Instruction"). Spread over the five books that comprise the work, beginning with Genesis, the narrative plot line extends from creation to the arrival of the 12 Israelite tribes at the border of the Promised Land of Canaan.

The primeval history (in the first 11 chapters of Genesis) recounts the creation of the world from chaos by divine command (Genesis 1-2:4). God plants a garden in Eden, creates the first man and woman (Adam and Eve), and places them there to tend the garden, forbidding them to eat fruit from the trees of knowledge and eternal life. Adam and Eve are physically naked, and both are ingenuous. Tempted by the serpent, Eve eats the forbidden fruit of knowledge and shares it with Adam. They become aware of their nakedness and attempt to hide from God. As punishment, God expels them from the garden and places them under a curse: Eve will produce children with great pain; Adam must work the land with the sweat of his brow.

The pair have two sons, Cain, a farmer, and Abel, a shepherd. Both offer sacrifices to God, but Cain's is rejected. Out of jealousy, Cain murders Abel; then, under a divine curse, Cain is ordered to wander the earth restlessly. Adam and Eve produce another son, Seth, and humankind multiplies for ten (in other biblical traditions, seven) generations. Over these generations, people become corrupt, engaging in acts of depredation and violence. God resolves to wipe out humanity in a great flood but spares righteous Noah and his family. Noah is told to build a large boat and fill it with pairs of animals of all species. The boat and its occupants survive the year while the flood rages, destroying all humanity except those in the vessel. After the flood subsides, Noah offers sacrifices to God, who promises never to destroy humankind again and establishes the rainbow as a sign of the promise. God also concedes that people have an unredeemably evil urge and allows them to kill animals for food (earlier generations had been vegetarian). On dry land now, Noah plants a vineyard, gets drunk, and exposes himself. His pious sons, Shem and Japheth, rush to his aid by covering their father's nakedness. Noah's other son, Ham, has a son of his own, named Canaan, who looks on Noah's nakedness, is cursed, and condemned to servitude. This is a foreshadowing of Israel's later conquest of the land of Canaan.

People multiply and attempt a communal endeavor, the building of a great tower (the tower of Babel) that aims to reach heaven. God frustrates their plan by confusing their language so that they cannot understand one another.

Humanity scatters over the earth and develops into 70 nations, which are listed in Genesis 10.

Next come the patriarchal narratives, which form the remainder of Genesis. From Genesis 11, the Pentateuch focuses on a single nation, Israel. Genesis 11-50 tell the stories of the ancestors of Israel—Abraham, Isaac, and Jacob, their wives and their concubines, and their children. The single largest segment describes the career of Jacob's son, Joseph.

The family of Terah, one of the descendants of Noah's pious son Shem, migrates from Ur in southern Mesopotamia to Harran, in the far north of that region. A son of Terah's, Abram, is commanded by God to leave Harran and travel to Canaan—land that God promises to give to Abram's descendents. Abram travels to Canaan with his wife Sarai, and his nephew, Lot, and builds an altar for God at the city of Shechem. Suffering a famine, the family makes their way to Egypt for sustenance. There, to save his own life, Abram passes Sarai off as his sister. When Pharaoh takes her into his harem, God intervenes by smiting Pharaoh's household, and Abram and Sarai return to Canaan. A less fortunate Lot is captured by a coalition of foreign kings. The captive nephew is rescued by Abram, who afterwards receives a blessing from Melchisedek, king of Salem (Jerusalem).

Abram has a dream or vision of God passing between pieces of dismembered sacrificial animals (Genesis 15:17; in ancient times, people would customarily slice an animal in half and walk through the halves to seal a contract). He receives a divine promise of the land of Canaan for his descendants, which is later confirmed. Abram's name is expanded to Abraham, explained as "father of a multitude of peoples," and Sarai become Sarah ("princess"). On God's order, Abraham now undergoes the rite of circumcision as a sign of the covenant. It is to be performed on all his male descendants.

Sarah is old and childless and offers Abraham her slave Hagar. But when Hagar becomes pregnant, she treats Sarah disrespectfully, so Sarah persuades Abraham to drive Hagar out. In the desert an angel rescues Hagar and tells her to return. She gives birth to Ishmael.

The story now turns to the fate of Abraham's nephew, Lot, who has settled in Sodom, a town that, along with its neighbor Gomorrah, is infamous for its wickedness. God determines to destroy both places. Back at Abraham's abode, three men (actually, angels) appear. Abraham treats them with great hospitality, and the guests predict that Sarah (now 90 years old!) will give birth to a son. Sarah laughs. When one of the men reveals himself to be God and declares the coming immolation of the two towns, Abraham argues with him, pleading that the wicked cities be spared if as few as ten righteous men can be found. But in Sodom the inhabitants surround Lot's house and demand that he deliver his guests to them for the sin of sodomy. Lot is commanded to flee with his family and not look back as fire and brimstone from heaven consume the cities. Defying the command, his wife does look back and is turned into a pillar of salt.

As predicted, the elderly Sarah gives birth to a son, whom she names Isaac (means "Laughs"). A few years later Sarah sees Ishmael, Hagar's son, "sporting" with Isaac and persuades Abraham to again expel Hagar, this time with her son. They are rescued in the desert by an angel, who promises a prosperous, if somewhat unruly, career for Ishmael. God decides to test Abraham's faith by commanding him to sacrifice his remaining son, Isaac. Ready to comply, Abraham binds Isaac on an altar to perform the sacrifice, but an angel stays his hand. Abraham instead sacrifices a ram he finds entangled in a bush. God promises that Abraham's descendents will make offerings on the site of the binding of Isaac, later identified with the Temple Mount in Jerusalem.

After Sarah dies, Abraham purchases the cave of Machpelah in Hebron as a burial place. He then arranges for a wife for Isaac by sending his trusted steward, Eliezer, back to Abraham's family in Harran. There Eliezer encounters Rebecca, sister of the wily Laban, and she agrees to marry Isaac. She gives birth to twins, wild, hairy Esau and smooth, sly Jacob (means "Tricks"). Rebecca persuades Jacob to deceive old, blind Isaac by stealing the parental blessing that will confirm the transfer of heirship from the older Esau to the younger Jacob (Esau, ravenous with hunger, had already sold his birthright to Jacob for a bowl of soup). To escape Esau's wrath, Jacob flees to Harran. On the way, at Bethel, he has a vision of angels ascending and descending the ramp ("ladder") to the heavenly abode of God. He prays for divine protection to bring him back home safely. In Harran he falls in love with Rachel, Laban's younger daughter, and agrees to work seven years for her. But on the wedding night, his crafty uncle substitutes Leah, the elder and hitherto unmarriageable daughter. In order to marry Rachel too, Jacob works for Laban another seven years. Afterwards Jacob returns to

Canaan and is reconciled with a generously forgiving Esau. It is at this point that Jacob becomes the recipient of the divine promise originally made to Abraham. After a nocturnal struggle with a mysterious stranger, who is either an angel or God himself, Jacob wins, though he is lamed in the process. He receives the additional name of Israel ("Wrestles with God" or "Divine Wrestler"). By now, Jacob's family has grown to the 12 sons who will become the ancestors of the Israelite tribes. Two of them, Simeon and Levi, massacre the people of the city of Shechem after its leader's son rapes their sister, Dinah.

When Jacob grows old, he is putty in the hands of his vain son, Joseph, the issue of his favorite wife, Rachel. The more Jacob favors him, the more his brothers hate him. Finally they ambush him and sell him into slavery in Egypt. There he rises in the service of Potiphar, one of Pharoah's chief officers, until he resists the advances of his master's wife. She accuses him of dalliance, whereupon Joseph is thrown into prison. A jailed Joseph correctly interprets the dreams of two of Pharaoh's officials, and when the matter is brought to the attention of Pharaoh, he asks Joseph to interpret his royal dreams. Joseph predicts coming prosperity followed by severe famine. At this point, Pharaoh makes Joseph the head official, or vizier, a role that enables him to gather provisions and administer the land.

The predicted famine descends on Egypt. When it spreads to Canaan, Joseph's brothers journey to Egypt for food. They tremble before a remote, haughty Egyptian whom they do not recognize as their wronged brother. For a while, Joseph toys with them, accusing them of being spies. But when he sees how truly remorseful they are, he is overcome with pity for them and longing for his father, and reveals himself to them. He invites Jacob and his whole clan of 70 to move to Goshen, a fertile province of the Nile Delta.

Genesis ends with the death of Jacob and Joseph.

Exodus. Exodus opens with a description of the spiraling increase in the descendants of Jacob, who soon evolve into the people of Israel. A new Pharaoh enslaves them in an attempt to control them, but when they continue to swarm, he orders that all males born to the Hebrews be thrown into the Nile River. To save her son, a "Hebrew" woman (used as a synonym for Israelite) sends him down the Nile in a little reed boat. He is rescued by Pharaoh's daughter, who draws him from the waters, naming him Moses (means

COVENANT

∾

The Torah views the relationship between God and Israel as a covenant, or treaty, formed at Sinai (Horeb) with the ex-slaves from Egypt, in which Moses served as mediator. The main Hebrew words for covenant are *berit* and *edut.* While *edut* means "witnessing" or "testimony" (hence "testament," as in Old and New Testaments), *berit* has as yet no definite Hebrew etymology. The likeliest explanation is that it is related to Akkadian *birit,* "between." A covenant is literally a "betweenness," a relationship between two parties. The terms of the covenant between God and Israel are found in a number of places, such as Deuteronomy 26:16-19: Yahweh promises to be Israel's God and to give it the land of Canaan; Israel promises to obey the terms of the covenant (i.e., the commandments) and to be loyal to Yahweh alone, worshipping no other god.

There are two types of covenants in the Hebrew Bible:

1. **A promissory covenant,** modeled on the ancient covenant of grant in which an overlord makes a free gift to a loyal vassal. Such is the covenantal promise of descendants and land made to the patriarchs Abraham, Isaac, and Jacob, in Genesis. There are no obligations on the recipient other than the rite of circumcision, which is viewed as a "sign" of the covenant (Genesis 17). Another such covenant later in the Hebrew Bible is the divine covenant with the House of David, granting it eternal kingship over Israel (and, eventually, through the Davidic messiah, over the world).

2. **A conditional covenant,** in which both parties have obligations: Israel, to keep the commandments; God, to fulfill the promises of land made to the patriarchs. This kind of covenant contains curses expressing the penalty Israel will pay for breach of the covenant (Leviticus 26, Deuteronomy 28). The Sinai covenant is of this type. Later in the Hebrew Bible King Josiah of Judea is portrayed as renewing this covenant in 621 B.C.E. (2 Kings 22-23). Its final renewal in the Bible is the agreement made between Ezra and the returned exile community in Judah, around 450 B.C.E., in which the official text of the covenant was probably a form of the Pentateuch, at least its legal parts.

The form of the covenant is modeled on ancient treaties and contracts, especially suzerainty treaties between an overlord and his vassals. Such treaties often consisted of a historical prologue, summarizing the benefits the vassal had received from his lord in the past; a list of terms and stipulations; a list of blessings for maintaining the treaty and of curses for violating it; a requirement that the treaty be written on an upright stone, or stele, and placed at a shrine; a covenant ritual involving an oath; and a list of witnesses. Parts of this treaty pattern are discernible in the Pentateuch, especially in Exodus 20-23, Leviticus 26, and the Book of Deuteronomy as a whole. But elsewhere covenants involve only human partners; only biblical religion took the treaty model as the expression of a national relationship to its God. Despite the fact that the covenant has been the object of intense scholarly debate involving questions of historicity and date, it is clear that biblical religion took a legal form to express its basic religious intuitions. The boldness of making humans the covenantal partners of a deity can be understood as an affirmation of man's dignity. Since the covenant is presented in the Torah as having been agreed to willingly by Israel, it may also be viewed as an expression of the primacy of free will.

"drawn," or in Egyptian "child"). He grows up as an Egyptian prince but is aware of his Hebrew background enough to murder an Egyptian he sees beating some Hebrew slaves (the slaves, characteristically, are quite ungrateful). Now a fugitive, Moses flees to the desert of Midian, where he marries a daughter of the local priest, Jethro, and becomes a shepherd. One day he is in the midst of leading his flock, when he receives a divine revelation at the "Mountain of God." God appears as a flaming but unconsumable desert bush and, with some difficulty, commissions the tongue-tied Moses to shepherd people instead of sheep. With the help of his fluent brother, Aaron, Moses should return to Egypt and lead the Israelites out to a certain mountain—the mountain of the revelation. God reveals himself to be Yahweh, a name of uncertain etymology that, in the context of the narrative, is defined as "He Will Be With (Moses and Israel)."

When Pharaoh refuses to heed the divine command to let the Israelites go, ten plagues beset the Egyptians, culminating in the death of all the first born of Egypt. The Israelites daub the blood of a slaughtered lamb on their doorposts, a sign to the "Destroyer" to "pass over" their houses and spare their first born. The detailed laws of the later festival of Passover, or Unleavened Bread, are here inserted. After 400 years of slavery (in other biblical traditions, four generations), the Israelites go forth ("exodus") from Egypt, taking along the mummy of Joseph and a not inconsiderable amount of booty. Soon, however, Pharaoh repents of having freed the Israelites. He pursues them and is drowned with his army when the Reed Sea, which has miraculously split so the Israelites can pass dry-shod, sweeps suddenly back to its banks.

In the desert, the Israelites begin their long tradition of grumbling. God provides water and food in the form of manna, a white crust that, according to later tradition, tasted like whatever one wanted. Later, the people tire of eternal vegetarianism and demand meat, so miraculous flocks of quails arrive to satiate them to the point of disgust. Jethro, Moses's father-in-law appears in the Israelite encampment, sees that Moses is overworked, and advises that he share the burden of power. But his sage advice is immediately overshadowed by the great revelation at the "Mountain of God," named Sinai (in other biblical traditions, Horeb). This is the mountain of the revelation (Exodus 19 and 20).

From Chapter 19 of Exodus through the remainder of that book, all of Leviticus, and the first ten chapters of Numbers, the narrative recounts the Sinai revelation. Most of this text consists of detailed laws, civil and cultic. In the armor of a swirling storm, God descends on Sinai and the people hear the thundering Ten Commandments. Terrified, they demand Moses to henceforth act as mediator and alone receive the direct divine revelation. He ascends the mountain, receives a code of laws, returns, and reads them to the people, who accept them and agree to make a covenant, or contract, with their God. Ascending the mountain once again, Moses receives a detailed blueprint for the erection of a tabernacle, a shrine for the divine Presence in the midst of the people. It consists of an elaborate but portable tent, with all its ritual paraphernalia. Moses spends 40 days receiving this cultic revelation on two stone tablets of the covenant.

In the meantime, the people, fearful and restless, induce Aaron to smelt the Egyptian booty into a golden image of a calf, which they proclaim to be the God who led them from Egypt. Moses returns, and, enraged, shatters the tablets of the covenant. He goes on to punish the apostates, intercede for the remainder of the people with an infuriated God, and trudge back up the mountain for a recreation of the covenantal tablets (which will eventually be placed in the holiest part of the tabernacle—the ark, a sacred box). The divinely instructed tabernacle is built and the Presence (called the "Glory") of God descends on the completed shrine. So ends Exodus.

Leviticus and Numbers. Leviticus and much of Numbers deal with elaborate divine instructions for the sacrificial cult and other ritual matters. The tabernacle is dedicated, Aaron and his sons are appointed hereditary priests (two of them are incinerated by fire from heaven for a cultic lapse), and after a year's stay, Israel leaves Sinai/Horeb to travel to the land of Canaan, promised long ago to the patriarchs. From a desert encampment, they send spies, who weaken the people's resolve by bringing back news about the impregnability of the cities and the gigantic stature of the inhabitants. God grows angry again. To punish the Israelites, he proclaims that their entrance will be delayed 40 years, until the generation of the exodus is consumed by wandering in the desert. Most of this interim actually seems to be spent at a single place, the lush desert oasis of Kadesh. The most notable events here are the jealous charges brought by Moses's brother and sister, Aaron and Miriam, against Moses because of his marriage to a Cushite woman (perhaps Zipporah, Jethro's Midianite

An 1866 illustration by Gustave Dore depicting Moses shattering the tablets of the covenant.

daughter). This is only a pretext; the two want to share power with Moses. God rebukes them, punishing Miriam temporarily with leprosy. A further challenge to Moses by a cabal of elders, led by a man named Korah, results in the miscreants being swallowed alive by the underworld.

When the journey to Canaan resumes, the Israelites must do battle with the inhabitants of Transjordan, who attempt to block their transit. Balak, king of Moab, hires the seer Bileam to curse Israel's progress, but God turns his curse into a blessing.

In an enigmatic incident, Moses and Aaron are denied entrance into the Promised Land through their failure to properly sanctify God. The incident transpired when the people demanded water; apparently Moses and Aaron struck a great rock with Moses's miracle-working staff and took credit for the resulting flow. Aaron soon dies, and Moses's days are also numbered. The Israelites are now in Moab, across the Jordan River from Canaan. Here they engage in cultic sexual rites with the Moabite women, ritually "yoking" themselves to the pagan god Baal. After the inevitable divine punishment, and a ferocious holy war against the Midianites (Moses's relatives!), the Israelites are at the point of crossing the river into Canaan. All that remains is for Moses to die.

Deuteronomy. Moses's death, however, is delayed to the last chapter of the next book, Deuteronomy ("Repetition of the Law"). The final book of the Pentateuch, Deuteronomy unfolds as Moses's lengthy farewell speech. It consists of a retrospective view on the wandering in the desert; a set of admonishing sermons on the meaning of the Sinai (here called Horeb) covenant, which are major statements of biblical theology (two of the passages are the text of the Shema, the central prayer of Judaism); and a repetition and elaboration (involving change and contradiction) of the earlier Pentateuchal laws. Finally, Moses ascends Mt. Nebo, views the Promised Land, dies at the age of 120, with undiminished vigor, and is buried in an unmarked grave in Moab. That he is the central hero of the Pentateuch is proven by the fact that the work ends with his death, though the main plot line remains incomplete. It is only in the following book, Joshua, that the conquest of Canaan fulfills the promise made to Abraham, Isaac, and Jacob. In terms of plot one must therefore speak of a Hexateuch rather than a Pentateuch.

Pentateuch as law. The Greek translation of Torah was "The Law" (*nomos*), which has led many to view it primarily as a legal document, a kind of constitution for the religious community. But in fact the laws are embedded in narratives and cannot be considered laws in any modern sense. They fall into two categories. Apodictic laws consist of simple *dos* and *don'ts*, and so are really commands or, in some cases, advice. These laws are intended as statements of principle, like the Bill of Rights in the United States. They tend to form lists, of which the Ten Commandments (the Decalogue) in Exodus 20 and Deuteronomy 5 is the most famous but not the only example. Along with these apodictic laws, there are casuistic laws. This type of law contains two clauses, a case and its penalty. "Do not kill" is apodictic; "Whoever kills someone shall be put to death" is casuistic. Casuistic law grows out of the legal tradition of the ancient world, particularly Mesopotamia. The parallels between these and the famous laws of the ancient Babylonian ruler Hammurabi (1792-50 B.C.E.) are especially striking. But Hammurabi's laws are also not laws as understood in Western culture. They are model decisions intended to demonstrate, less to his people than to the gods, that he was a just and therefore legitimate ruler. In other words, they had a religious and a political function. So, too, with the three main law "codes" of the Pentateuch—the "Covenant Code" of Exodus 21-23, the priestly "Holiness Code" of

THE SHEMA AND MONOTHEISM

The Jewish confession of faith is the Shema, named after its opening word, "Hear (*shema*), Israel, the Lord our God, the Lord is one." The text is Deuteronomy 6:4. Together with the following text (Deuteronomy 6:5-9, plus Deuteronomy 11:13-21 and Numbers 15:37-41), it comprises a set of passages collectively referred to as the Shema, which forms a central part of the Jewish liturgy. The first sentence, quoted above, is often taken as an affirmation of divine unity, in opposition to Christian trinitarianism. In addition, the reference to God's "oneness" is usually understood as a declaration of monotheism, that is, of the existence of only one deity. But the Shema dates from at least seven centuries before the rise of Christianity; and absolute monotheism, as a philosophical doctrine, was not part of the cultural and intellectual equipment of the ancient Near Eastern world in which the Hebrew Bible arose. The concept of monotheism, which denies even the possibility of the existence of other than one deity, seems to have originated later, with the pre-Socratic philosophers, in the sixth to fifth centuries B.C.E. Most scholars view biblical religion as henotheistic (focusing on one deity) or monolatrous (allowing the worship of one deity). Comparable religious developments occurred in ancient Mesopotamian and Egyptian religions, most famously in the Aten cult sponsored by the heretic Egyptian pharaoh Akhenaten in the fourteenth century B.C.E. However, the henotheistic or monolatrous movements elsewhere were marginal and short-lived compared with biblical religion. In fact, the statement that "the Lord is one" is most naturally taken in Hebrew as a statement of emotional rather than numerical singularity, as the following words in Deuteronomy 6:5 show: "You shall love the Lord, your God, with all your heart and with all your life, with all your strength." In other words, God is declared to be Israel's "one and only" in terms of love and devotion to him, on the analogy of human love. The Shema is therefore a statement not of an abstract doctrine, but of an intense relationship.

Leviticus 17-26, and the "Deuteronomic Code" of Deuteronomy 12-26. These are not like later law codes, but are mixtures of casuistic and apodictic laws intended to express religious principles. As the terms of a covenant—meaning a contract or treaty—they express loyalty to that covenant and so, ultimately, faith in God. From this standpoint, all the laws are religious, even those that are not narrowly cultic.

In many cases the laws express attempts at religious reform or a revision of an earlier view. So, for example, the later Deuteronomic Code aims at rejecting the principle of collective punishment for crime, which appears in earlier documents such as the Ten Commandments (God is said to punish sinners down to the fourth generation of their descendants); instead, Deuteronomy says, no one can be put to death for the crime of another. Deuteronomy also clearly elevates the status of women by separating them from household property and slaves.

The law of circumcision reflects priestly viewpoints in the Holiness Code about the need for physical separation between Israelites and non-Israelites. In relation to social hierarchy, the Holiness Code tries to express notions of equality through such utopian edicts as that of the jubilee, which required that all land return to its original owners after 50 years, an injunction as noble as it is impractical. The priests associated with this code furthermore viewed the Sabbath, or day of rest, as a quasi-mystical institution linked to creation, with human respite modeled on the divine "rest" on the seventh day. In the later Deuteronomic Code, the Sabbath is primarily a social and historical institution memorializing the exodus from Egyptian bondage. The laws of Passover in the three codes are especially linked to religious reform movements of the time when the codes were composed. The famous *lex talionis* ("an eye for an eye"), a principle already set forth, and in some cases literally practiced, in the laws of Hammurabi, appears in the earliest biblical code. Even here, however, it has evolved into a principle, a "law" of monetary compensation and social equality: there is to be one standard of recompense for personal injury.

Pentateuch as religion. As suggested, the Pentateuch is a work of historical narrative and laws, both embedded in religion, but it is not a work of theology; that is, it contains no speculation or theoretical discussion on the nature of God, divine omnipotence, omniscience, or similar topics. Indeed, the ancient Near East appears to have had no linguistic or philosophical tools to even discuss such matters before the advent of the Greeks. Biblical religion is expressed in concrete imagery and institutions, from which religious ideas must be extrapolated. For example, the religion of the Pentateuch is certainly monotheistic, maintaining that there is only one God for the Israelites. But the only way it can express the abstract, quasi-philosophical concept of monotheism is through the cult, through the insistence that God may be worshipped only in one place, the central shrine—one God, one temple. It is important to recognize this concrete way of expressing religious ideas, because on the surface the Pentateuch, with its mixture of narratives and laws, hardly seems like a religious book at all, especially when one considers the almost chaotic combination of contradictory traditions from different periods. The monotheism in the Torah is an implicit, not an explicit, concept.

The Pentateuch is dominated by two religious viewpoints, the priestly and the Deuteronomic, which often conflict in theology and practice. The priestly texts, represented by Leviticus and parts of Exodus and Numbers, view God as immanent, present (however mystically) in the sanctum of the temple. Deuteronomy holds that the Deity is transcendent, represented on earth only by the "name" He has placed on the shrine. As noted, many laws in the Torah are contradictory. For example, Exodus 12 (a priestly text) describes Passover as a festival meal of roasted lamb eaten by families at home. Deuteronomy 16 presents it as a meal of boiled beef or mutton consumed by pilgrims at the temple. When such contradictions and inconsistencies are added to the complications involved in superimposing both of these views on the mass of older legends, poetry, and law in the Pentateuch, the result is a work of astounding and often bewildering, if not mystifying, complexity.

Biblical religion is often said to have broken with ancient mythology by substituting "history" for myth. But the term here does not mean academic history. Rather it means the record of divine acts of intervention to rescue Israel, what scholars call "salvation-history." The basic principle that guides biblical religion is the primacy of relationship. Nothing is abstract or static; all is dynamic, held in tension to other things. For example, the very covenant itself is between a human and divine partner, the Israelites and God—a relationship between equals who are yet unequals. Indeed, the covenant may be viewed as a concretization of the principle of relationship itself. The Pentateuch, like the rest of the Bible, is the record of the tortured relationship between the Israelites and their God. God himself is described in human terms. The anthropomorphism of biblical religion goes beyond mere metaphors; they are essential to it. In the Torah, God has a real personality: he can be petty, peevish, vain, as well as exalted, incomprehensible, holy.

The Israelite nation also has a personality, in its frequent querulousness and inability to rise to the heights demanded of it. Likewise, the great figures of the Pentateuch—Abraham, Jacob, Esau, Moses—are real personalities. The richness of personality is perhaps best compared to that of Shakespeare, who also revels in the concrete and human. In sum, religion in the Pentateuch, without ceasing to be God-centered, is a religion of and for humans.

Sources and literary context. The following survey represents the consensus of scholars who take a positive view of the possible historicity of at least some of the Pentateuch. First, the Garden of Eden story draws on ancient iconography on many points, such as the tree of life in the divine garden and the guardian cherubim. Primeval history of Genesis 1-11 must, of course, be viewed as essentially myth, although it contains much ancient Near Eastern, especially Mesopotamian and Canaanite myth and legend reworked (sometimes only slightly) from a monotheistic point of view. The flood story, for example, has direct Babylonian parallels. The Atrahasis epic (c. 1600 B.C.e) recounts the flood brought by the gods to counter human overpopulation. A later treatment, in the *Gilgamesh* epic (also in *WLAIT 6: Middle Eastern Literatures and Their Times*), tells of a wise hero named Utanapishtim, who was commanded by his patron deity, Ea, to build a boat and save his family. Many details are strikingly close to the biblical account, including the sending out of birds to determine if the earth had dried out, and the offering of a sacrifice after the emergence from the boat. Next comes the tower of Babel, which seems to reflect the great ziggurat, or temple tower, of Babylon, the top of which is said to have "reached heaven." The patriarchal narratives may reflect West Semitic tribal movements of the second millennium B.C.E. Many details of the semi-nomadic way of life described in Genesis, as well as the type of names and specific societal customs, have been confirmed, at least as possibilities, by archaeology for the putative patriarchal period (c. 1800-1200 B.C.E.). They particularly fit the context of the Amurru (biblical Amorite) expansion of the early second millennium from the western desert into the settled regions of Mesopotamia and Canaan. However, it must also be admitted that most of these details pertain as well to life a millennium later, and that the patriarchal stories contain many anachronisms, such as the presence of camels as domesticated beasts, something attested to only after c. 1200 B.C.E.

Many of the legendary materials on which the stories of the patriarchs are probably based seem to have been passed down at ancient local shrines, then collected sometime after c. 900 B.C.E. They were expanded, perhaps with historical romance, totally revised according to later religious viewpoints, and probably put into their present form in the Babylonian Exile of the sixth century B.C.E. It was their final adaptation to the main storyline of the completed Pentateuch that occurred 100 years later, in the fifth century B.C.E.

Probably the present narratives that describe the events of the exodus from Egypt preserve shreds of the legendary traditions of at least some proto-Israelites (especially the tribe known as the Levites, some of whom, like Moses, Miriam, Phinehas, and Hor, possess authentic Egyptian names). The name of the city of Ramses, built by the Hebrew slaves, also seems to be authentic. The exodus tradition early became embedded in the historical consciousness of all Israel, probably no later than the ninth or eighth centuries B.C.E., since the prophets of that period already speak of it as a cherished, and ancient, sign of divine intervention. Details like the manna and clouds of quail that fed the Israelites in the desert, as well as the name of their encampments on the way to Canaan, reflect authentic details of desert life, but are undateable, and might reflect only later vivid storytelling. Scholars generally agree that the great account of the Sinai revelation and covenant are *not* well embedded in Israelite traditions older than the Pentateuch. The covenant

spoken of here does reflect ancient treaty-making practices to some extent, but there is no definite information to link it to a historical era. The closest approximation of the treaty genre is the Book of Deuteronomy, which seems to reflect only later Assyrian practices of the first millennium B.C.E.; on the other hand, however, it may only be bringing an authentically old tradition up to date.

The classic theory about the origin and growth of the Torah is the "Documentary Hypothesis." It posits that the earliest source is a southern composition—known by the rubric J or Y, for "Yahwistic source"— from the ninth or even tenth centuries B.C.E. According to the hypothesis, Y compiled and interpreted older, probably oral traditions, and became the first to give the Pentateuch its narrative shape. About a century later Y was augmented by material from a northern source, E, for "Elohistic source." In 621 B.C.E. a "Book of the Instruction" was reported to have been found in the temple in Jerusalem. The book is known to have served as the basis of a great religious reform instigated by Josiah, the King of Judea, and scholars have identified it with Deuteronomy, now added to the proto-Pentateuch. Lastly P, for "Priestly source," was joined to the others in the fifth century B.C.E. P gave the Pentateuch its chronological framework and added the great body of ritual and cultic law that forms a third of the final redaction. Though criticized and revised in the past century, the Documentary Hypothesis continues to form the basis for scholarly discussion of the Pentateuch. Conservative religious circles reject such a historical reconstruction, preferring to treat the Pentateuch as an object of faith.

Events in History at the Time the Torah Was Written

War, exile, and renewal. It is difficult to describe the historical context of so massive a work as the Torah, composed over so long a period, and so much the object of scholarly debate and factual uncertainty. Much of the narrative of the Pentateuch may hark back to traditions of the time it claims to represent, but it is more likely that the basic pattern and most of the actual text comes from the first millennium B.C.E., probably from the late eighth through the fifth centuries B.C.E. This was a chaotic and tragic time in the history of the states of Israel and Judah. The former was wiped out by the Assyrians in 722 B.C.E. The latter, Judah, survived, and became the site in which the Torah probably began to take shape. But Judah was also destroyed, by the Neo-Babylonians in 586 B.C.E., and its leading classes were deported to southern Mesopotamia. There, after getting adjusted to the shock of uprooting, the exiles seem to have prospered. But many of them longed for restoration and renewal. The Babylonian exile was a time of intense literary activity, as old traditions were revised, expanded, and composed into large works, such as the historical books of the Former Prophets (Joshua, Judges, Samuel, and Kings) and, presumably, also an early form of the Pentateuch. Some of the exiles returned when the Persians conquered Babylon, but the restored community struggled with extinction and assimilation, until the middle of the fifth century B.C.E., when the activity of Nehemiah and Ezra put them on firmer political, legal, and communal ground. As described, Ezra is credited with bringing the "Book of the Law of Moses" back from Babylonia; he is also credited with instigating major religious reforms on its authority.

A Persian subculture. As a completed work, the Torah must be viewed in the context of the interaction between the Judean elite and the Persian government in the mid-fifth century B.C.E. It was Persian imperial policy to encourage subject peoples to live by their own laws, provided they remained loyal to the empire. The struggling Jewish community of returnees around Jerusalem occupied an important geographic position on the border of Egypt, a province the Persians had much difficulty in controlling. Having the state of Judah as a strong and loyal vassal was highly desirable to them. Coincidentally imperial policy coincided with the attempt by the Jewish intellectual and religious elite in Babylonia to restore a purified temple cult in Jerusalem and to restore the authority of law as presented in the venerable tradition of Moses. Ezra, not only a priest and a scribe but also the "minister for Jewish affairs" in the Persian government, was given orders to return to Judah and impose strict Jewish law on the lax community of returned exiles. The final form of the Torah reflects this historical situation.

We do not know how the work achieved its present shape in the final redaction. It has been suggested that it was the result of a compromise between competing religious traditions, achieved by what in effect was a committee. Nevertheless, it seems clear that the final form of the Pentateuch was meant to address the situation of the Jews, both those still in Babylon and those who had already returned to Jerusalem. The fact

that the Torah is incomplete in terms of narrative, breaking off with Moses's death, before Israel enters the Promised Land, is supposed to correspond, in a kind of typology, to the position of the Jews on the threshold of restoration to that land upon their return as a result of Persian largesse in the mid-fifth century B.C.E. Their movement from Mesopotamia back to Judah was supposed to have been anticipated a thousand and more years earlier by the journey of their patriarch Abraham from Ur to Canaan. The implication is that if the Judean community remains strictly loyal to the covenant of Moses, it will relive the spiritual pattern of journey and renewal represented by their ancestors, the patriarchs and the Israelites of Moses's age.

The Axial Age. The Torah must also be viewed within the larger cultural context of the eighth through fifth centuries B.C.E., a period known as the "Axial Age." This was the beginning of the succession of world empires with totalitarian claims to exclusive power. The chain runs from the Assyrians to the Neo-Babylonians, Persians, Greeks, and Romans. For small states such as Israel and Judah, the rise of these master empires threatened extinction, physical or cultural. A feeling of insecurity afflicted the masters too, because the very innovation of empire, as opposed to the older looser system of competing smaller states, brought peoples in contact with each other in new ways that shook and challenged cultural certainties. It gave rise to a cultural atmosphere that was, on the one hand, fraught with danger, but, on the other hand, invigorated with new opportunities. The older cultures responded by trying to return to their classical roots, reviving more ancient cultural forms and traditions. The classic type of literary document of the age was the "fraus pia," the pious fraud, claiming to be composed in antiquity, but actually contemporary. Deuteronomy is the famous biblical example, purportedly written by the ancient prophet Moses, but actually a product of the late seventh century B.C.E. The Pentateuch as a whole must be viewed in this context, as an attempt by members of a troubled and threatened community to provide an authoritative ancient document for themselves. Whether the authors went about their task conscious of the implicit historical irony of addressing conditions in the present by reconstructing the past can only be a matter for speculation. In any case, the result was something quite new, a book-based religion that formed the basis of all of the major Western religious traditions that followed.

BEYOND TYPOLOGY

Traditional Jewish and Christian exegesis recognizes a strongly prescient aspect to many narratives. Actions ascribed to individuals such as the patriarchs are often intended to foreshadow events that will occur to their descendents (a principle the rabbis formulated as "the deeds of the fathers are symbolic of what will happen to their children"). For example, Abraham descends to Egypt. His endangerment there and rescue by divine intervention clearly foreshadow the later enslavement and exodus of Israel. The patriarchal dealings with their Canaanite neighbors, especially the destruction of the city of Shechem by Simeon and Levi (Genesis 34), anticipates the later conquest of Canaan under Joshua. The rest of the Bible continues these chains of foreshadowing, or typology. The paradigm of slavery-redemption foreshadows the exile of the Jews from Canaan to Babylonia and the promised return to Jerusalem. God's promise to Abraham uses language that foreshadows the monarchy of King David, even as the latter becomes the typological pattern for messianism.

Recent study by Meir Sternberg and many others has uncovered the sophisticated literary techniques that underlie the seemingly ingenuous narratives. In addition to typology, for example, there are

- Patterns of chiasm (inverted phrases, such as "Heaven and Earth . . . Earth and Heaven" in Genesis 2:4)
- Envelope structure (beginning and ending a section with the same phrase)
- Artful juxtaposition of themes and narratives
- The prevalence of ambiguity and paradox (whom exactly did Jacob wrestle with? man, angel, or God?)

Biblical narrative style is sparse and often laconic. Verbs are plentiful; adjectives, rare. Significant details are often left to the imagination, inviting personal interpretation. What did Abraham think when God commanded him to sacrifice his precious son Isaac? Did he accept the cruel demand with the blind faith of an automaton, or was he tormented by inner anguish and doubt? It is these silences that make the biblical stories so "'fraught with background'" (Auerbach, p. 9).

Reception. A confluence of political, social, and religious motives among the Israelites of the fifth century B.C.E. caused the frequent logical incoherence of the Torah to fall into the background. In the mid-fifth century B.C.E., a large wave of Israelites returned to Judah from Babylonian exile. Ezra, a Jewish priest and Persian official, assembled the returned exiles in Jerusalem for a public reading of the Torah. The reading, authorized by the Persian Empire, aimed to establish a foundation of law and order in the province; no doubt even sages of the age could not have foreseen the tenacious role the Torah would play. It was at this point that the Torah

began to take a central role in the religious life of the Jews. Afterwards, in the post-biblical period, religions like later Judaism and to some extent Christianity mistakenly viewed the Torah as a working legal system, and problems resulted from the inevitable gaps and internal contradictions. Readers of the *Talmud* (also in WLAIT 6: *Middle Eastern Literatures and Their Times*) are familiar with the legal-linguistic dexterity required by later commentators.

The stories of the Torah have embedded themselves deeply into Western religious, artistic, and literary culture (see *The Gospel According to Matthew* and *The Quran*, also in WLAIT 6: Mid-

dle Eastern Literatures and Their Times). While traditional religion views the particulars of the stories simply as historical fact, others take a more literary approach, seeing in them powerful reflections of human emotions and universal needs. The narrative structure and devices of the Pentateuch have been much analyzed in recent years using various approaches, from psychoanalytical, to anthropological, symbolic, feminist, and deconstructionist (focuses on inherent internal contradictions). Along with the laws, the stories have given rise to a vigorous body of interpretations (*Midrashim*) over the ages, which serves as a continuing source of sermons and homilies. Interpretation of the Torah has been and continues to be the central process of traditional Judaism.

—Stephen Geller

For More Information

Auerbach, Erich. *Mimesis: The Representation of Reality in Western Literature.* Trans. Willard R. Trask. Garden City, N.Y.: Doubleday Anchor, 1957.

Hayes, John H. *An Introduction to Old Testament Study.* Nashville: Abingdon, 1979.

JPS Hebrew-English Tanakh. Philadelphia: Jewish Publication Society, 1999.

Scheindlin, Raymond P. *A Short History of the Jewish People: From Legendary Times to Modern Statehood.* New York: Oxford University Press, 1998.

Shanks, Hershel. *Ancient Israel from Abraham to the Roman Destruction of the Temple.* Washington, D.C.: Biblical Archaeology Society, 1999.

Sternberg, Meir. *The Poetics of Biblical Narrative.* Bloomington: Indiana University Press, 1985.

Index

NOTE: In view of the potential for variants in personal names, the *Middle Eastern Literatures and Their Times* index has provided an aid to the reader's further research by giving the full Library of Congress (LC) form of a name. Where common usage differs from the LC form, the index uses the common form followed by the full LC form in parenthesis, e.g. Gemayel, Bashir (LC: Jumayyil, Bashir). Names beginning with the prefix *al-* (meaning "the") are alphabetized under the letter following the prefix (e.g., for al-Jahiz, look under Jahiz).

A

Abbasid caliphate (750–1258) (*entries in chronological order*)
    Abu al-Abbas and Abbasid rise to power 14–15, 222, 356
    ruthless elimination of remaining Umayyad family members 222–223
    capital moved to Baghdad, courtly culture, and patronage of arts 58, 132–134, 356, 489
    badi' style of poetry developed 357–359
    competition between Persian and Arabs at court 356
    civil war over succession 316
    growing independence of provincial governors 316
    conflict with Byzantines, reign of al-Mu'tasim and Amorium campaign 356–357, 367–368
    rival dynasties segmenting empire 58, 211, 369, 489
    further decline, reliance on Turkish slave army and bodyguards 22
    economic and social problems, dominance of large landowners and warlords 258
    mass execution of remaining family at hands of Mongol invaders 316
Abd al-Mu'min (Caliph of the Almohades) 178

Abd al-Nasir, Jamal. *See* Nasser, Gamel Abdel
Abd al-Sabur, Salah, *Murder in Baghdad* 179, 315–325, 351
Abdel (or Abdul) Nasser, Gamal. *See* Nasser, Gamel Abdel
Abdülhamid II, Sultan of the Turks 66
Abdullah, King of Jordan 286
Abraham (Biblical patriarch) (Abram) 168, 546
Abu al-Abbas, al-Saffah (the Bloodshedder), first Abbasid caliph 15, 222
Abu Bakr, Caliph (first caliph after Muhammad) 210, 419
Abu Nidal (Palestinian group) 87
Abu Nuwas (*also* al-Hasan ibn Hani Abu Nuwas), *Diwan of Abu Nuwas, The* 131–140, 265
Abu Tammam (LC: Abu Tammam Habib ibn Aws al-Ta'i), "Ode on the Conquest of Amorium" 138 (*sidebar*), 355–365, 368, 373–374
Achilles 521
Adunis, "Introduction to the History of the Petty Kings" 209–220
Africa, Lebanese in 532 (*sidebar*)
Agaoglu, Adalet, *Curfew* 101–110
Agnon, Shmuel Yosef, *Only Yesterday* 387–396
Agriculture
    of ancient Iran, predation by nomads 484
    of ancient Mesopotamia 154–155
    Islamic viticulture 133 (*sidebar*)

Agriculture (continued)
kibbutzim, collectives and settlements in British mandate of Palestine   *389–390*
mechanized in 1950s Turkey   *283*
Agudat Israel movement of Orthodox Jews   *390, 391, 395*
Akiba, Rabbi   *543*
Akkadian language   *154 (sidebar), 160*
"al-" (*prefix meaning "the," which is ignored for sorting of names; e.g. for al-Jahiz, look under* Jahiz.)
Alcohol/wine consumption   *49, 53–54, 133 (sidebar), 134–136, 401, 433, 435*
Aleppo, Syria   *368 (illus.)*
Alexander the Great   *112, 484, 488–489*
Alexander II, Emperor of Russia   *198*
Alexandria, Egypt   *298, 299 (illus.)*
Al-i Ahmad, Jalal (LC: Al Ahmad, Jalal), *Plagued by the West (Gharbzadigi)*   *268, 407–414, 441*
"Aliyot" (waves, of immigration to Palestine/Israel)   *34, 388, 389 (sidebar)*
Allegory, interpretations of text as
animal fables in *Kalilah and Dimnah,*   *226-228*
Conference of the Birds,   *95*
Hayy ibn Yaqzan,   *178, 183, 184*
Leyla and Mejnun,   *252-253*
Men in the Sun,   *291 (sidebar)*
Miramar,   *303 (sidebar)*
Secret Life of Saeed the Ill-fated Pessoptimist,   *455*
Sufist interpretation of Quran,   *95–96, 99–100*
Allenby, Sir Edmund   *308 (illus.)*
Almohads   *58, 143, 149*
Almoravids   *143, 177–178*
Amichai, Yehuda, *Songs of the Land of Zion, Jerusalem*   *493–503*
al-Amidi (LC: al-Amidi, al-Hasan ibn Bishr)   *362–364, 363 (sidebar)*
al-Amin (Caliph)   *134*
Amini, Ali   *409–410*
"Amm Mutwalli" and "Hagg Shalabi" (Mahmud Taymur)   *1–11*
Amorium ("Ode on the Conquest of")   *355–365, 368, 373–374*
Amphora (large clay jugs)   *133 (sidebar)*
Anatolia, Turkey (Asia Minor)   *276, 277 (sidebar)*
al-Andalus (*entries in chronological order*)
conquest for Islam (711)   *142*
independence from central Islamic Empire (756)   *142, 211*
Islamic ascendancy, independence from central Islamic empire (750–1300)   *141, 211*
Umayyad Dynasty, economic and cultural flourishing (756–1000)   *58, 142*
flourishing of Jewish aristocracy   *141, 149–150*
breakup into warring miniature states and encroachment of Christianity (11th century)   *142–143*
Almoravid victories over Christian Castilians and numerous *taifa* kingdoms (1086–1091)   *143, 177–178*

Almohad invasion and hegemony (1146–1147)   *58, 143, 178*
Almohad repression of monotheistic minorities (Jews)   *143, 149*
Christian "Reconquest," expulsion or forced conversion of non-Christians (1492)   *211*
(*See also* Islamic world; Spain)
Animal fables
Brer Rabbit   *227 (sidebar)*
Kalilah and Dimnah   *221–228*
Anti-clericalism
Hafiz's criticism of hypocrisy   *126, 128*
Maronite   *69–70*
Anti-Semitism
blood libel   *200*
in early-20th-century Vienna   *26*
exacerbated by success of Austrian Jewry   *27 (sidebar), 29*
in Hitlerite Germany   *472*
Holocaust *Hiwis (Hilfswillige* or "willing helpers") found among local populace   *27–28*
incitement and virulence of Russian pogroms   *200–203, 205 (sidebar)*
Jesus' rhetoric and anti-Judaism   *173 (sidebar)*
Kishinev pogrom   *200–202*
Kristallnacht ("Night of the Broken Glass")   *29*
masses of Muslims in medieval Baghdad   *58*
outraged world reactions to Russian pogroms   *202, 205 (sidebar)*
in Tsarist Russia   *198–199, 388*
Appelfeld, Aharon (LC: Appelfeld, Aron), *Badenheim 1939*   *25–35*
Arabian Nights, The (Husain Haddawy, translator)   *2, 13–23, 161, 242, 242 (sidebar), 475–476*
Arab Israelis   *453–454, 457–459*
(*See also* Palestinians)
Arab-Israeli wars, works related to
"Clockwork Doll, The" and Other Poems (Dalia Ravikovitch) (1982 Lebanon War)   *85–91*
"Introduction to the History of the Petty Kings" (Adunis) (1967 Six-Day War)   *209–220*
Men in the Sun (Ghassan Kanafani) (1948 War of Independence)   *244, 285–293*
Mr. Mani (A.B. Yehoshua) (1982 Lebanon War)   *305–314*
My Michael (Amos Oz) (Sinai-Suez War of 1956)   *327–336*
Secret Life of Saeed the Ill-fated Pessoptimist, The (Emile Habiby) (1948 War of Independence, Sinai-Suez War of 1956, 1967 Six-Day War)   *449–460*
Songs of the Land of Zion, Jerusalem (Yehuda Amichai) (1973 October War/Yom Kippur War)   *493–503*
Arab Nationalist Movement (ANM) (LC: Harakat al-Qawmiyin al-Arab)   *291*
Arab Socialist Union (ASU)   *297*
Arab world: works set in
Arabian Peninsula
Quran (Koran), The   *415–428*

"Stop and We Will Weep: The Mu'allaqah" (Imru al-Qays)   426, 515–526

Egypt

"Amm Mutwalli" and "Hagg Shalabi" (Mahmud Taymur)   1–11

"Introduction to the History of the Petty Kings" (Adunis)   209–220

King Is the King, The (Sa'dallah Wannus)   237–246

Miramar (Najib Mahfuz)   295–304

Iraq and Kuwait, *Men in the Sun* (Ghassan Kanafani)   244, 285–293

Islamic caliphates

Arabian Nights, The (Husain Haddawy, translator)   2, 13–23, 161, 242, 242 (*sidebar*), 475–476

Book of Tahkemoni, The (Hebrew Maqamat) (Judah al-Harizi)   57–64

Diwan of Abu Nuwas, The (Abu Nuwas)   131–140, 265

Hayy ibn Yaqzan (Ibn Tufayl)   177–185

Maqamat (al-Hamadhani)   61, 257–266

Murder in Baghdad (Salah Abd al-Sabur)   179, 315–325, 351

"Ode on the Conquest of Amorium" (Abu Tammam)   355–365, 368, 373–374

"Ode on the Reconquest of al-Hadath" (al-Mutanabbi)   362, 367–375

Lebanon

Broken Wings, The (Kahlil Gibran)   65–73

Story of Zahra, The (Hanan al-Shaykh)   71, 527–533

Saudi Arabia, *Cities of Salt* (Abd al-Rahman Munif)   75–84

(*See also Secret Life of Saeed the Ill-fated Pessoptimist, The*)

Arafat, Yasir   288

Aramaic language   154 (*sidebar*)

Aramco (Arabian American Oil Company)   77

Ardashir I, King of Iran   14, 484

Argov, Shlomo   87

Aristotle   144, 178, 432 (*sidebar*)

Arnold, Matthew   490, 490 (*sidebar*)

Artists and intellectuals

al-Naksah ("the disaster"), effect of   244

Arab poets and patrons   369 (*sidebar*), 400–401

attempt at East-West rapprochement through art   344

Egyptian in early 20th century   1, 9–10

experimentation for Iranians of 1930s   380–381

founding of modern Arabic drama   242

ghostwriters of love poems   401

golden age of Ottoman poetry   399

Iranian in 19th century   37

Iranian writers as social critics in 1960s and 1970s   447

Islam and figurative painting   341 (*sidebar*)

liberal tradition of late 19th century Vienna   25–26

Nahdah (Awakening) (19th century)   2–5

Ottoman miniature painting   340

Palestinian and Arab Israeli   285, 292, 459

persecution in Iran under Reza Shah Pahlavi   38

Persian literary movement   383–384

Persian scientist-poets   431 (*sidebar*)

potters   434 (*sidebar*)

Quran on poets as dangerous   427–428

role of poets as spokesmen and intermediaries   218, 219 (*sidebar*)

social classes, focus on middle and lower classes   8–9, 238–242, 295

Turkish movement toward national literature   461

Wogs (Western-oriented gentlemen) satirized in Iran   382 (*sidebar*)

women writers' group "Beirut Decentrists"   533

(*See also* Censorship and banning of literary works)

Asceticism

in Judaism   146 (*sidebar*)

in Sufism   506

al-Ash'ari, Abu al-Hasan Ali   128

Ash'arites   128 (*sidebar*)

Ashkenazim (Eastern European Jews)   306, 454 (*sidebar*)

Assad, Hafez (LC: al-Assad, Hafez)   87, 238–239

Assassins, Order of   122

Assyrian language   154 (*sidebar*)

Astrology   60

Atatürk, Kemal   102, 189, 276–277, 344, 462, 467 (*sidebar*)

Atrahasis epic and flood story   553

Attar, Farid al-Din, *Conference of the Birds, The*   93–100

Austria: works set in, *Badenheim 1939* (Aharon Appelfeld)   25–35

Avempace (Ibn Bajjah)   178

Averroes (Ibn Rushd)   178

Avicenna. *See* Ibn Sina

Ayatollah Khomeini (LC: Khomeini, Ruhollah)   268 (*sidebar*), 408

Azerbaijan   47, 48, 408 (*sidebar*), 444

Azoury, Negib   290

B

Babel, tower of   547, 554

Babylonian language   154 (*sidebar*)

Babylon, Mesopotamia   58, 168, 535, 536, 554

Badenheim 1939 (Aharon Appelfeld)   25–35

Badi' style of poetry   355, 357–359, 364

Baghdad, Iraq   15, 131–132

Baki, Ottoman Lyric Poetry: "Row by Row"   397–406

Balfour Declaration   308, 450, 494

Bedouins

adjustment to farming, villages and towns of Jordan   286

code of blood vengeance   516–518, 521, 523

Bedouins (continued)
    loyalty to house of Sa'ud secured by settlement
      and education, *76–77, 78*
      martial ethos, warrior class, camels, horses *516*
      Muhammad's distant ancestors *416*
      Muruwwah (virtue, manliness) and warrior
        aristocracy *516–518, 517 (sidebar), 521, 523*
      rich mix of influences, shifting tribal federations
        516
      small tribal groupings, ancient pagan religions,
        subsistence lifestyle *416, 516–518*
      speaking purest form of Arabic *367*
      women's lives *518*
      workers unwillingly sucked into oil economy
        78
Begin, Menachem *87*
Beirut, Lebanon *87, 288 (illus.), 530 (illus.)*
Ben-Gurion, David *306*
Ben-Yehuda, Eliezer *391*
Bialik, Hayyim Nahman (*also* Bialik, Chaim
    Nachman), "In the City of Slaughter" *197–207*
Bible. *See* Scripture, religious texts and
    commentaries, holy works
Bidpai (Indian philosopher) *225*
"Black September" *287, 458*
Blind Owl, The (Sadiq Hidayat) *37–46*
Blood libel *200*
Blood vengeance and sacrifice *372–373, 373
    (sidebar), 516–518, 517 (sidebar), 521, 523*
Book of Dede Korkut, The *47–55*
Book of Tahkemoni, The (Hebrew Maqamat) (Judah
    al-Harizi) *57–64*
Bosnia *345*
Brecht, Bertold (LC: Brecht, Bertolt) *242, 243*
Brer Rabbit *227 (sidebar)*
Brigandage
    maryas in ancient Persia *483*
    outlaw as folk hero *281–282, 281 (sidebar)*
    in Turkey *278–279*
Britain. *See* Colonization and colonialism, British;
    Great Britain
Broken Wings, The (Kahlil Gibran) *65–73*
Byzantium
    Constantinople as capital *338*
    continuous border warfare *14, 15, 20, 22, 229,
      230, 231, 356, 368, 489*
    Heraclius, Emperor of the East *417*
    Justinian (LC: Justinian I, Emperor of the East)
      416–417, 515
    Maurice, Emperor of the East *417*

C

Cairo, Egypt *5 (illus.)*
Calcedonian Christians *417*
Calendars
    Islamic lunar or Hijrah *39 (sidebar), 516*
    Islamic solar *39 (sidebar)*
    reform attributed partly to Omar Khayyam
      429

"Caliph" (successor of Muhammad) *14, 142*
Cambyses II, King of Persia *484*
Camels *516, 554*
Canaan *547, 550, 554*
Caro, Rabbi Joseph (LC: Karo, Joseph ben Ephraim)
    542
Censorship and banning of literary works
    Al-i Ahmad and *Plagued by the West* *411,
      412–413*
    in Egypt, Iraq, Morocco after 1967 *245*
    in Egypt under Nasser *218, 301 (sidebar), 303,
      304*
    in Iran under Reza Shah Pahlavi *38*
    in Persian Gulf countries, Munif's novels
      83–84
    Talmud, burning by Catholic Church *544*
    in Turkey, Hikmet's poetry *187, 194*
    in Turkey by military government *105*
    Wannus's strategy for avoiding *243*
Central Asia: works set in, *Book of Dede Korkut, The*
    47–55
Chador (body veil) *269, 277, 411 (sidebar), 443*
Cheetahs *139 (sidebar)*
"Christ" ("Messiah," anointed, chosen for rule or
    priesthood) *168*
Christianity
    Calcedonians, Monophysites, and Nestorians
      417
    conquests in Islamic dominions (1099–1492)
      143, 149
    encroachment upon al-Andalus *142–143*
    First Crusade, capture of Jerusalem *22, 58, 142
      (illus.), 211 (sidebar)*
    Gibbon on monasticism as sapping civic spirit
      419
    importance of Jerusalem *497*
    Jewish elements *120*
    Maronites *67–68, 528*
    monasteries and wine drinking *137*
    Nestorian *132*
    Quran's emphasis on tolerance for all
      monotheists ("People of the Book") *417–418*
Circumcision *547, 549 (sidebar), 552*
Cities of Salt (Abd al-Rahman Munif) *75–84*
Class consciousness and social stratification
    in ancient Sasanian Persia *14, 230, 484*
    Egyptian intellectuals against masses and popular
      culture *4*
    Hellenized versus traditional Jews *112*
    limpieza de sangre ("purity of blood") *307*
    Meccan society in 7th century *417*
    middle classes as focus in Mahfuz's works *295*
    in Mount Lebanon *68*
    Sephardi, Ashkenazi, and Mizrachi in Israel
      306–307, 454 (sidebar)
    Wannus's attack on *244 (sidebar)*
    (*See also* Poverty, income gap between haves and
      have-nots)
"Clockwork Doll, The" and Other Poems (Dalia
    Ravikovitch) *85–91*

Cold War
    competition between superpowers (1945–1989)
        190
    strategic importance of Iran   268
Colonization and colonialism
    French in Egypt   3
    superpowers in Iran   409
Colonization and colonialism, British in
    Arabian peninsula   77
    Egypt, Red Sea routes to India, and Suez Canal
        3, 3 (*sidebar*), 4 (*sidebar*)
    Iran in 18th and 19th centuries   441–442
    Sudan   6
Color symbolism in Arabic   215 (*sidebar*)
Communism: actions and reactions
    Habiby's support of   449
    imprisonment of Hikmet   187
    Nasser in Egypt   297
    repression of 1953 Aramco strike   79
    Tudeh (Iranian Communist) Party   407, 444
    (*See also* Marxism-Leninism)
Community Rule, The (from Dead Sea Scrolls)
    114–116
Conference of the Birds, The (Farid al-Din Attar)
    93–100
Constantinople (present-day Istanbul), capital of
    Byzantine Empire   338
Consumerism   81, 409 (*sidebar*)
Corruption of governments/elites
    aghas, newly rich Turkish peasants   278–279
    Egypt of 1960s   301 (*sidebar*)
    Iranian government of 1800s   442
    Palestinians   307–308
Covenant of God with Jewish people
    reaffirmed with public reading of Torah   536
    as relationship and treaty   549 (*sidebar*)
Cowell, Edward (translator of *Ruba'iyat of Omar
    Khayyam*)   435–436, 437, 438
Creation story
    in *Gilgamesh*   158
    in Hafiz's vision   125
    in Torah   546–548
Crime. *See* Brigandage
Crusades   22, 58, 142 (illus.), 211 (*sidebar*)
Ctesiphon   132, 229–230, 516
Culture clashes
    Iran versus "Westitis"   268–269
    materialism and consumerism versus proud aus-
        terity, poverty, and independence of Arabs   81
    Orientalism   464 (*sidebar*), 466
    pull of tradition versus lure of new Western
        techniques   343
    racism and prejudice against Egyptians on part of
        British   4 (*sidebar*)
    support of Persian instead of Arabic literature by
        Persian speakers   489
    Western concept of legal liability versus Arabian
        custom of payment of blood money   80
    White Revolution questioned in Iran   409
        (*sidebar*)

    (*See also* Arab-Israeli wars; Palestinians; Racism;
        Westernization)
Cuneiform writing and literacy   155, 160, 162
    (*sidebar*)
Curfew (Adalet Agaoglu)   101–110
Cyprus   105, 339 (*sidebar*)
Cyrus, King of Persia   484, 535

D

Dabshalim (Indian king)   225 (*sidebar*)
Dance. *See* Music and dance; Popular culture and
    values
Danishvar, Simin, *Savushun (A Persian Requiem)*
    441–449
Darwinism/Social Darwinism, impact on Egyptian
    Nahdah   3
David, King of Israel   168
Dayan, Moshe   495
Dayf, Ahmad   9
Dead Sea Scrolls from Qumram, The   111–120,
    546
Dede Korkut (legendary figure)   50 (*sidebar*)
    (*See also Book of Dede Korkut, The*)
Demirel, Süleyman   104–105
Dervishes (itinerant followers of Sufism)   96, 349
    (*sidebar*), 402–403, 505
    (*See also* Sufism)
Deuteronomy, book of   551, 553, 554, 555
Dharan, Saudi Arabia   78 (*sidebar*)
Diaspora (dispersal of Jews out of ancient homeland)
    114, 167, 173, 174, 388, 450, 472
Diseases. *See* Health issues
Divan of Hafiz, The (Hafiz)   121–129, 271 (*sidebar*),
    406, 514
"*Divans*" (collections of Turkish or Persian poems)
    121, 403
Divorce
    Egyptian   4, 5
    in Israel   86
    reform in Turkey   277
Diwan of Abu Nuwas, The (Abu Nuwas)   131–140,
    265
Diwan of Judah Halevi, The (Judah Halevi)
    141–151, 306
"*Diwans*" (collections of Arabic poems)   134, 135
"Documentary Hypothesis" for origin and growth of
    Torah   554
Dog symbolism in *Only Yesterday*   393 (*sidebar*)
Drug/substance use and abuse, opium   383
    (*sidebar*)
Druze   68, 455, 528, 529 (*sidebar*)

E

Eban, Abba (LC: Eban, Abba Solomon)   458
    (*sidebar*)
Economic issues
    Abbasid caliphate's severe problems, dominance
        of large landowners and warlords   258

Economic issues (continued)
    cost of Egypt's involvement in war in Yemen   298
    cost of Egypt's program of free education   297
    oil wealth, inflation, and inequities   78
    transformation of 8th century Baghdad   15
    Turkey's capitalist approach and adverse
        developments   103
    Turkish workers to Europe   104–105
    (*See also* Land tenure/reform issues;
        Modernization; Nationalization of
        industries/services; Urbanization)
Education and literacy rates
    cuneiform writing   155, 160, 162 (sidebar)
    Institute of Egypt   3 (sidebar)
    in modern Turkey   345
Education, of men
    in Abbasid times   21
    in Egypt of 1960s   297
    Jewish *yeshivot* (academies) in Babylonia   58
    Jews in al-Andalus   143
    madrasahs (Islamic colleges)   58, 235, 236
    Madrasat al-Hikmah in Lebanon   66–67
    in medieval Baghdad   131
    Nizamiyah, Persian educational institution   430
    Ottomanism and Seyfettin's education   467–468
    Sasanid period of ancient Persia   20
Education, of women
    in Abbasid times   21
    in Egypt of 1960s   297
    in Egypt of early 1900s   5, 9
    Iranian middle classes   267
    Sasanid period of ancient Persia   20
Egypt: works set in
    "Amm Mutwalli" and "Hagg Shalabi" (Mahmud
        Taymur)   1–11
    Miramar (Najib Mahfuz)   295–304
Egypt (*entries in chronological order*)
    exodus of Hebrew slaves (c. 1000 B.C.E.)   554
    Fatimid dynasty in North Africa and Levant (late
        9th century)   211
    Ayyubid dynasty and Saladin (1138–1193)   58
    Mamluks (slave dynasty)   20 (sidebar), 22, 122
    social and economic ferment (18th century)   2
    Napoleonic conquest and occupation
        (1798–1801)   2
    Muhammad Ali reign (1804–49)   2
    Khedive Ismail and financial crisis of late 1800s
        2, 3
    Mahdist Revolt in Sudan (1881–98)   5–6
    occupation by British, revolts (1882–1952)
        6–7, 296
    Wafd Party and revolution (1919)   6–7
    limited independence (1922)   7
    Wafd Party in power (1924–1936)   7
    influx of Palestinian refugees from new state of
        Israel (1948)   494
    Egyptian Revolution abolishing monarchy,
        establishing republic (1952)   212, 295–296
    Nasser nationalization of Suez Company (1956)
        330, 453

    Sinai-Suez War, Tripartite Aggression, Gaza Strip
        (1956)   329–330, 453
    creation and dissolution of United Arab Republic
        (pan-Arab alliance with Syria) (1956–1961)
        287, 291, 292
    Nasser presidency, socialism, discontent,
        repression (1956–1970)   212, 296,
        297–298
    nationalization of industries/services, land reform
        (1961)   296–297
    repression, massive industrialization, censorship
        (1960s)   301 (sidebar), 302
    Nasser's suppression of Muslim Brotherhood
        (1964)   324
    involvement in war in Yemen (1962–1967)
        213, 298
    defeat by Israel, loss of Gaza Strip and Sinai
        (1967)   213, 238, 301 (sidebar)
    death and eulogization of Nasser (1970)   212,
        212 (illus.), 217–218, 218 (illus.)
    Sadat's rehabilitation of Islamists   324
    Alexandria's loss of foreign communities and
        cosmopolitanism   298
    Mubarak's accommodation of Islamist groups,
        censorship, assassinations (1980s)   324
    (*See also* Islamic world)
Egyptian *Nahdah* (Awakening)   2–5
Eichmann, Adolf   29, 473
Eitan, Raphael   87
Eliot, T. S.   273, 323, 324
Elites
    intellectuals of Egyptian *Nahdah*   3–4
    Iranian in 19th century   37
    Jewish priests' taxation of peasants in support of
        Temple   167
    Lebanese moneyed profiteers from civil war
        531 (sidebar)
    in medieval Baghdad   132–134
    pre-Islamic tribal/warrior aristocracy   516–518,
        517 (sidebar), 521, 523
    resistance to Muhammad's new ethical principles
        416
    Roman alliances with locals   166
    Roman and Jewish rulers' extravagance
        166–167, 167 (sidebar)
    (*See also* Corruption of governments/elites)
Emigration. *See* Immigration
Emmanuel ("God with us")   168
England. *See* Great Britain
Enlightenment, Arab attraction to secular rationalism
    2
Epic of Gilgamesh, The   153–163, 553
Epic poetry
    Epic of Gilgamesh, The   153–163, 553
    Shahnamah, or *The Book of Kings* (Abu al-Qasim
        Firdawsi)   233 (sidebar), 258, 406, 446,
        481–491, 514
Erikson, Erik H.   182 (sidebar)
Essenes   111–112, 113, 114–116, 117–118, 117
    (sidebar)

Ethnic and cultural conflicts and social stratification
    Israeli Arabs in Israel   453
    Sephardim and *limpieza de sangre* ("purity of blood")   307
    support of Persian instead of Arabic literature by Persian- or Turkish-speakers   489
Exodus, book of   548, 550, 553, 554
Exports
    dates   76
    oil   75, 77–78, 79 (illus.), 443
Ezra (biblical figure)   536, 545, 555, 556

F

Fanon, Frantz   453, 454
"*Farr*" (halo, "royal glory," right to rule)   485, 485 (sidebar)
Farrukhzad, Furugh (*also* Farrokhzad, Forough), "Mechanical Doll" and Other Poems   267–274
Faruq (LC: Faruk I), King of Egypt   296
al-Fatah (Movement for the Liberation of Palestine)   288
Fatimah (Muhammad's daughter)   415
Fatimid dynasty   211
Faulkner, William   312, 313
Fedayeen (*Fida'iyin*)   214, 454
Feminism. *See* Women's rights movement (and feminism)
Ferdowsi. *See* Firdawsi, Abu al-Qasim
Feudalism, in Ottoman rule of Lebanon   66
Fida'iyin   214, 454
Firdawsi, Abu al-Qasim, *Shahnamah* or *Book of Kings*   233 (sidebar), 258, 406, 446, 481–491, 514
Fitzgerald, Edward (translator of *Ruba'iyat of Omar Khayyam*)   430, 433, 435, 436–437, 438, 439
Flood story   157–159, 161–162, 547, 553
Flying carpets, Sufis and popular legends   402
Frame narratives
    Arabian Nights, The (Husain Haddawy, translator)   2, 13–23, 161, 242, 242 (sidebar), 475–476
    technique used by playwright Wannus   243
"Fraus pia" (pious fraud) literary documents   555
Freud, Sigmund   44 (sidebar)
"Frog Prayer, The" (Ömer Seyfettin)   461–469
Fuzuli, *Leyla and Mejnun*   48, 217 (sidebar), 247–255

G

Garden of Eden narrative   553
Gaza Strip   286, 328, 329–330, 452, 453, 494
Gemayel, Bashir (LC: Jumayyil, Bashir)   87
Genesis, book of   546–548, 554
Genghis Khan   22
Geographical considerations, Iranian plains subject to repeated invasions   410
Germany (*entries in chronological order*)
    economic crisis fueling rise of Hitler and Naziism   188, 472
    Anschluss (annexation) of Austria (1938)   26–27, 30 (illus.)
    Kristallnacht ("Night of the Broken Glass") (1938)   29
    invasion of Poland (1939)   190
    open persecution of Jews (1939)   27, 472
    perpetration of genocide: "Final Solution" in Holocaust   472
"*Ghazals*" (sonnet-like poems)   121, 403, 403 (sidebar), 405–406
al-Ghazzali   144, 431
Gibbon, Edward   419
Gibran, Kahlil, *Broken Wings, The*   65–73
God
    as anthropomorphically described in Torah   553
    indivisible unity of   424
    nature of divine revelations to Muhammad   415–416
    role of, Gospel of Matthew   168
    Sufism and desire for intense relationship, spiritual union with   93, 95, 248, 252–253, 350, 402, 506, 510
Golan Heights, Syria   238, 494
Gordon, David Aaron   335
Gospel According to Matthew, The   165–175
Governance issues
    absolute monarchs dominating Europe and Middle East of 1500s   400
    "confessionalism" in Lebanon for allocation of political offices   528
    Egypt's financial crisis of late 1800s   2, 3
    foreign powers in Iran   409
    in Judea, priests and Persian-appointed governor   536
    Mesopotamian origins of civilization, writing, government, and laws, (4000–3000 B.C.E.)   155, 160, 162
    Oghuz nomadic warriors   48
    pre-Islamic tribal/warrior aristocracy   516–518, 517 (sidebar), 521, 523
    Roman warfare, intimidation, ruthlessness, alliances with local elites   166
    Shah's jealousy of Amini, Amini's resignation a blow to reform   410
    Turkey's military's interventions   102
    viziers   236
    (*See also* Corruption of governments/elites; legal codes, systems, and courts)
Great Britain
    Balfour Declaration   308, 450, 494
    strategic interests in Iran and rivalry with Tsarist Russia/Soviet Union   441–442
    WWI Allies' breakup of Ottoman Empire into five mandates   213
    (*See also* Colonization and colonialism)
Grossman, David, *See Under: Love*   471–479

H

Habash, George   291
Habiby, Emile (LC: Habibi, Imil), *Secret Life of Saeed the Ill-fated Pessoptimist, The*   449–460

Habukkuk, Commentary on (from Dead Sea Scrolls) 116–117

Haci Bektaş Veli   347, 349 *(sidebar)*

Haddad, Wadi   291

Hadiths (accounts of life of Muhammad as examples) 21, 259

Hafiz, *Divan of Hafiz, The*   121–129, 271 *(sidebar)*, 406, 514

Haganah (Jewish defense organization)   86

Halevi, Judah (LC: Judah ha-Levi)
   Diwan of Judah Halevi, The   141–151, 306
   Kuzari   145 *(sidebar)*

al-Hallaj, al-Husayn ibn Mansur   316–317, 351

Halo from *farr* ("royal glory," right to rule)   485, 485 *(sidebar)*

"*Halutsot*" (Jewish women pioneers in Palestine) 85

"*Halutzim*" (Jewish pioneers in Palestine)   499

al-Hamadhani (LC: Badi' al-Zaman al-Hamadhani), *Maqamat*   257–266

Hammurabi, King of Babylonia   551

al-Hariri (LC: al-Hariri, Abu Muhammad al-Qasim) 265

al-Harizi, Judah (LC: al-Harizi, Judah ben Solomon), *Book of Tahkemoni, The* (Hebrew Maqamat) 57–64

Harun al-Rashid, Caliph   15–16, 316

Hasan al-Basri   319

Hasidim and Hasidism   112, 390

Hasmoneans   112, 113, 118

Hayy ibn Yaqzan (Ibn Tufayl)   177–185

Health issues
   circumcision   547, 549 *(sidebar)*, 552
   love sickness   248
   opium use   40 *(sidebar)*
   psychosomatic illness following loss of independence and traditional way of life   82

Hedayat, Sadegh. *See* Hidayat, Sadiq

Heraclius, Emperor of the East, Byzantine Empire 417

heresy, Muhammad on   322 *(sidebar)*

Herod Antipas (Tetrarch of Galilee)   166, 169

Herod the Great (LC: Herod I, King of Judea) 114, 166

Heroic epics
   Book of Dede Korkut, The   47–55
   characteristics   54
   Epic of Gilgamesh, The   153–163, 553
   Shahnamah, or *The Book of Kings* (Abu al-Qasim Firdawsi)   233 *(sidebar)*, 258, 406, 446, 481–491, 514

Herzl, Theodor   199, 306, 308, 335, 394 *(sidebar)*, 474 *(sidebar)*

Hidayat, Sadiq, *Blind Owl, The*   37–46

Hikmet, Nazim, *Human Landscapes from My Country* 187–195

Hillel   539 *(sidebar)*

Hindustan   99

Hitler, Adolf   26

Hittites   278

"Hiwis" (*Hilfswillige* or "willing helpers")   27–28

Holocaust
   anti-Semitic *Hiwis* (*Hilfswillige* or "willing helpers") found among local populace   27–28
   Appelfeld's experience of   25, 33
   avoidance of discussion in early years of Israeli statehood   33
   concentration camp at Gotha, Germany   473 *(illus.)*
   genocide as "Final Solution"   472
   German camp system   28 *(sidebar)*
   inconceivable horror of   32
   meaning "burnt offering" or sacrifice in Latin 312
   survivors suffering post-traumatic symptoms and guilt   472

Holy works. *See* Scripture, religious texts and commentaries; holy works

Homosexuality
   Abu Nuwas   131, 134, 136
   king's affection for slave boy in *Conference of the Birds*   96
   in medieval Baghdad   134
   in medieval Muslim world   136 *(sidebar)*
   Ottoman acceptance of love for both sexes 401–402
   and Sufi homoeroticism   136 *(sidebar)*, 140, 402

Hoopoe bird   98 *(illus.)*

Horses
   in nomadic, martial life   516, 520
   in Persian civilization   233 *(sidebar)*

Hujr   515, 516

Hulagu Khan (Hulegu)   22, 122

Human Landscapes from My Country (Nazim Hikmet) 187–195

"Humash" (the Five-fold, The Torah)   545

Hunting poems   139 *(sidebar)*

Husayn (LC: Husayn ibn Ali)   384 *(sidebar)*

al-Husri, Sati   291

Hussein, King of Jordan   286, 287

I

Ibn al-Muqaffa', Abd Allah (translator of *Kalilah and Dimnah*)   221, 223

Ibn Bajjah (LC: Avempace)   178

Ibn Ezra, Abraham (LC: Ibn Ezra, Abraham ben Meïr)   59 *(sidebar)*

Ibn Rushd (LC: Averroes)   178

Ibn Sina (LC: Avicenna)   178, 179 *(illus.)*, 180 *(sidebar)*, 184, 431, 432 *(sidebar)*

Ibn Tufayl (LC: Ibn Tufayl, Muhammad ibn Abd al-Malik), *Hayy ibn Yaqzan*   177–185

Ibn Tumart, Muhammad   178

Iliad, The   161, 521

Imams as intermediaries to the Divine   94

Immigration
   to America from Israel in early 1900s   390
   Iranian laborers in Russia   380
   to Israel in *aliyot* (waves)   34, 388, 389 *(sidebar)*

Lebanese to West Africa   532 (sidebar)
Turkish workers to Europe   104–105
Imperialism. See Colonization and colonialism
Imru al-Qays, "Stop and We Will Weep: The
    Mu'allaqah"   426, 515–526
"In the City of Slaughter" (Hayyim Nahman Bialik)
    91, 197–207
India (entries in chronological order)
    Aryan migration to Mesopotamia, then to Central
        Asia (c. 1000 B.C.E.)   482
    destruction of temple at Somnath by Mahmud of
        Ghazni (1025)   99
    (See also Arabian Nights, The)
Industrialization, in Iran of 1950s and 1960s   409
    (sidebar)
Inflation   338
"Introduction to the History of the Petty Kings"
    (Adunis)   209–220
Iran (entries in chronological order)
    historical versus mythical origins   482–484
    Aryan migration from India to Mesopotamia to
        Central Asia (c. 1000 B.C.E.)   482
    Kings Gaymars, Faridun, and Manuchihr, and
        hero Rustam   483–484
    Achaemenid kings Cyrus, Cambyses, Xerxes, and
        Darius (c. 500 B.C.E.)   484, 535
    irrigation systems, gardens, crops, predation by
        nomads (c. 500 B.C.E.)   483
    Seleucid governors after conquest by Alexander
        the Great (331 B.C.E.)   484
    Parthian period (250 B.C.E. to 226 C.E.)   14
    Sasanian empire, King Ardashir, cultural
        advances, caste system and resentment
        (226–651)   14, 19–20, 230, 368, 417, 484,
        488
    intermittent wars with Byzantines (500s–600s)
        229, 230, 231, 368
    Muslim Arab conquest of Persia, welcome from
        estranged populace (640–650s)   14, 230, 231
    adoption of Islam but not Arabic language, pride
        in Persian past   488
    rule from Damascus by Umayyid caliphate
        (661–750)   489
    rule from Baghdad by Abbasid caliphate
        (750–1258)   131–132, 489
    Abbasid decline, rise of local dynasties of
        Buwayhids, Safarids, Samanids (800s)   489
    revolt of the Zanj (East African slaves) (c. 871)
        317
    feuding between factions of elites, Shi'ite versus
        Sunni (early 900s)   317–318
    Seljuk rule over Persia, advancement,
        enforcement of Sunnism, (1055–1157)   235,
        430–431
    Mongol invasion of Persia (1256–1258)   122,
        235
    establishment of Il-Khanate (1258)   122, 235,
        236
    dynamic literary activity (late 1300s)   123

rival local princely houses, sociopolitical
    confusion, disorder, and tyranny (late 1300s)
    122
austere rule of Muzaffarid leader Mubariz al-Din
    123
Turcoman White Sheep Empire (1378–1508)
    47, 48
conquest by Timur   123, 398
Safavid kings, Shi'ism official religion, isolation
    from most of Muslim world (15th century)
    378
domination by European powers, soul-searching,
    backwardness and powerlessness (18th century)
    378
pressure from British and Russians (18th and
    19th centuries)   378, 441–442
Qajar monarchy, half-hearted modernization,
    concessions to European powers (1796–1925)
    38, 378
start and ultimate failure of Constitutional
    Revolution (1905–1911)   38, 378–379
Anglo-Russian Agreement dividing Iran into
    spheres of influence (1907)   378
WWI battleground for Russian, Ottoman, and
    British troops   379
British protectorate leading to coup (1919)
    379
dissolution of Qajar monarchy, attempts at
    republic (1920s)   379
Reza Shah Pahlavi dictatorship, modernization,
    Persianization (1921–1941)   38, 268 (sidebar),
    379–380, 442–444, 446
adoption of Islamic calendars (1925)   39
    (sidebar)
occidentalist foreign policy, oil concessions (early
    1900s)   443
veiling of women outlawed (1936)   269, 272,
    411 (sidebar), 443
German interests and influence (1941)   443
occupation by British and Soviets (1941)   443
Reza Shah abdication in favor of son,
    Mohammed Reza Pahlavi (1941)   268
    (sidebar), 409, 410–411, 442, 444
Marxist trade unionism, activist clerics, and press
    (1942)   444
political unrest, bread riots, and famine
    (1942–1943)   444
Soviet invasion, eventual withdrawal (mid-1940s)
    408 (sidebar)
Cold War pressure and West's attempts at
    control (1950s)   444
Mosaddeq plans nationalization of oil industry
    (1951)   444
CIA-backed coup restores shah, ousts Mosaddeq
    (1951–1953)   268, 268 (sidebar), 408, 409,
    444
U.S. as new "invader" (1953)   444
national identity crisis, demoralization (1953)
    268, 409, 444

Iran (*entries in chronological order*) (continued)
reforms, riots against shah's dictatorship
(1960–1963)   *268 (sidebar), 269–273, 408–409*

resignation of Amini as blow to reform
(1961–1963)   *409–410*

suffrage to women, later revoked (1962)   *269,
408*

debates over Persian/Iranian essentialism (1800s
to present)   *411–412*

White Revolution, land redistribution, urban
underclass of displaced farm hands   *408, 446*

reforms abandoned, shah exiled (1964)   *268
(sidebar)*

leftist guerrilla movement (1969–1970)   *268
(sidebar)*

Islamic Revolution, Ayatollah Khomeini replaces
shah (1979)   *268 (sidebar)*

(*See also* Islamic world)

Iran/Persian Empire: works set in
Blind Owl, The (Sadiq Hidayat)   *37–46*

Conference of the Birds, The (Farid al-Din Attar)
93–100

Divan of Hafiz, The (Hafiz)   *121–129, 271
(sidebar), 406, 514*

"Khusraw and Shirin" (Nizami of Ganja)
229–236, 254

"Mechanical Doll" and Other Poems (Furugh
Farrukhzad)   *267–274*

Once Upon a Time (Muhammad Ali Jamalzadah)
44, 377–385

Plagued by the West (*Gharbzadigi*) (Jalal Al-i
Ahmad)   *268, 407–414, 441*

Ruba'iyat of Omar Khayyam (Omar Khayyam)
39, 127, 429–439

Savushun (*A Persian Requiem*) (Simin Danishvar)
441–449

Shahnamah, or *The Book of Kings* (Abu al-Qasim
Firdawsi)   *233 (sidebar), 258, 406, 446,
481–491, 514*

Spiritual Couplets, The (Jalal al-Din Muhammad
Balkhi Rumi)   *39, 100, 348, 406, 505–514*

Iraq: works set in
Diwan of Abu Nuwas, The (Abu Nuwas)
131–140, 265

Men in the Sun (Ghassan Kanafani)   *244, 285–293*

Iraq (*entries in chronological order*)
adaptation to sedentary cultures, eventual
subordination of Bedouin nomadic culture
(660–750)   *250*

Abbasid caliphate (750–1258)   *14–16, 22, 58,
131–132*

Abbasid courtly culture, patronage of arts,
Shu'ubiyah   *132–134, 138, 258, 356*

Persian/Arabic bilingualism and biculturalism
(800s)   *258*

civil war between al-Amin and al-Ma'mun (813)
134

reign of al-Mu'tasim, slave armies, and Amorium
campaign against Byzantines (838)   *356–357*

pressure from Byzantine Empire (840s)   *356*

Buwayhid clan takes control of Baghdad (945)
258

Jews in successful and stable community
(1000s–1200s)   *58*

Oghuz invasion, Great Seljuk Turkish dynasty
(1038–1157)   *397–398, 430–431*

Oghuz federation, Turcoman White Sheep
(*Ak-koyunlu*) Empire (1378–1508)   *47, 48*

Ottoman conquest of Baghdad by Süleyman the
Great (1534)   *254*

arrival of Palestinian refugees (1948–1949)
451–452

expulsion of Palestinians after Gulf War (1991)
289

(*See also* Islamic world; Mesopotamia)

Irgun Tsevai Leumi (National Military Organization
of Zionists)   *396, 449, 451*

Isaac (biblical patriarch)   *311–312*

Iskandar (Alexander the Great)   *112, 484, 488–489*

Islam
Arab-Persian relations   *138 (sidebar)*

Ash'arites   *128 (sidebar)*

figurative painting   *341 (sidebar)*

heresy, Muhammad on   *322 (sidebar)*

Ibn Tufayl's critique of   *183–184*

imams as intermediaries to the Divine   *94*

importance of Jerusalem   *497*

medieval views of nature, God, and universe
178–183

music+ condemned by orthodox   *96*

Mutakallimun   *358*

Mu'tazilites and doctrine of rational theology,
allegorical/figurative interpretation of Quran
128 (sidebar), 263–264, 357–359

al-muwahhidun (the Unitarians)   *76*

purdah (sequestering of women) as Sasanian
tradition wrongly incorporated into Islam   *488*

"Renaissance of Islam"   *132*

Shi'ites (*also* Shi'ah)   *210, 222, 400 (sidebar)*

Shi'ite-Sunni religious schism   *94, 222,
258–259, 378, 400 (sidebar)*

Wahhabism (*also* Wahhabiyah)   *76*

(*See also* Muhammad, Prophet; Quran (Koran);
Sufism)

Islamic world (*entries in chronological order*)
life of Prophet Muhammad   *415–419, 425*

death of Muhammad, crisis of succession (632
C.E.)   *210, 258, 497*

Abu Bakr, Umar, Uthman, Ali as successive
"rightly-guided" caliphs (*Rashidun*) (632–661)
210, 221, 258, 368

Sunni-Shi'ite split (beginning 632)   *94,
258–259, 378*

continuous border warfare with Byzantine
Empire (600s–1453)   *368*

wresting of Syria, Iraq, and Egypt from
Byzantines (634–644)   *368*

Ali as caliph (656–661), assassination by
Mu'awiyah, Shi'ite-Sunni religious schism   *94,
222, 258–259, 400 (sidebar)*

death of Husayn, Ali's last living son, massacre at Karbala, enmity of Shi'ites (680)   *210, 222, 259, 384 (sidebar)*

Umayyad dynasty, Mu'awiyah ruling Iran, Iraq, and Syria (661–749)   *15, 210, 221–222, 258*

extension of Islamic dominion to Spain (al-Andalus) (711–1492)   *58*

Abbasid movement promising era of justice and piety (720s–740s)   *222*

Umayyads replaced by Abbasids, decentralization and growing ineffectualness (750-1250)   *211, 222, 258, 316, 355–356, 368–369*

rise and fall of petty kings (750–c. 1500)   *211–212*

caliphate of Harun al-Rashid (786–809)   *15–16, 316*

civil war over succession (809–813)   *316*

failure by al-Ma'mun to establish standardized version of Islam, growing independence of provincial governors (813-833)   *316*

Hamdanid state in northern Syria (944)   *369*

conquest (954) and loss (957) of Al-Hadath fortress   *369–370*

Oghuz/Seljuk invasions, Great Seljuk dynasty (970–1157)   *397–398, 430–431*

reign of Mahmud, sultan of Ghazni (998–1030)   *97, 99, 482 (sidebar), 489*

Seljuk defeat of Ghaznavids by Tugrul Beg (1040)   *430*

Seljuk rule over Persia, advancement, enforcement of Sunnism, (1055–1157)   *235, 430–431*

disintegration of authority in Holy Land, Muslim marauders as excuse for First Crusade   *211 (sidebar)*

first Crusade, capture of Jerusalem, establishment of small Christian principalities (1096–1200)   *22, 58, 142 (illus.), 211 (sidebar)*

Christian pressure in Mediterranean, gradual conquests (1099–1492)   *143, 149*

Saladin and retaking of Jerusalem, reconquest (1170s)   *211 (sidebar)*

Mongol invasions (1221 and 1258)   *22*

Mamluks' seizure of power in Egypt (1250)   *22*

Ottoman Empire as one of world's largest and longest lasting empires (1299–1923)   *337–338, 467 (sidebar)*

Ottoman Turkish conquests (beginning c. 1300)   *22, 212, 398*

Abbasid weakness, Christian encroachments and danger of Arab/Muslim disunity   *211–212, 316, 398*

Ottoman demand for tribute of slaves, some sent into Janissary Corps   *347, 398 (sidebar)*

conquest of Constantinople by Mehmed II (1453)   *339 (sidebar), 368, 398*

Christian "Reconquista" of Muslim Spain, expulsion of non-Christians, many to Ottoman Empire (1492)   *398*

immigration of Jews expelled from Spain (1492)   *398*

Selim I's defeat of Safavids (1514)   *254*

reign of Süleyman I, golden age, height of geographic extension of empire (1520–1556)   *339 (sidebar)*

Süleyman I and Ottoman conquest of Baghdad (1533)   *254*

loss of Battle of Lepanto against Western powers, gain of Cyprus (1571)   *339 (sidebar)*

battles with Safavid Empire of Persia (1578–1590)   *339 (sidebar)*

political Islam versus mystical Islam   *339*

WWI Allies' breakup of Ottoman Empire into five mandates (1920)   *213*

(See also al-Andalus; Egypt; Iran; Iraq; *Jahiliyah* (Age of Ignorance) or pre-Islamic age; Jordan; Lebanon; Palestine; Saudi Arabia; Syria; Turkey)

Isma'ilis (Order of the Assassins)   *122*

Israel: works set in

"Clockwork Doll, The" and Other Poems (Dalia Ravikovitch)   *85–91*

Mr. Mani (A.B. Yehoshua)   *305–314*

My Michael (Amos Oz)   *327–336*

Secret Life of Saeed the Ill-fated Pessoptimist, The (Emile Habiby)   *449–460*

See Under: Love (David Grossman)   *471–479*

Songs of the Land of Zion, Jerusalem (Yehuda Amichai)   *493–503*

(See also Palestine: works set in)

Israel (*entries in chronological order*)

conquest by King David (c. 1000 B.C.E.)   *496–497*

Assyrian conquest (722 B.C.E.)   *554–555*

destruction of First Temple in Jerusalem by Nebuchadnezzar, Babylonian exile (586 B.C.E.)   *535, 536, 554, 555*

Jews return to Judea, complete Second Temple in Jerusalem (515 B.C.E.)   *535, 536*

Judeans as Persian subculture after Babylonian exile (c. 450 B.C.E.)   *555, 556*

Greek conquest by Alexander the Great, Hellenization (300–100 B.C.E.)   *112, 113, 536*

Maccabean revolt, religious persecution (164 B.C.E.)   *112, 113*

Maccabean/Hasmonean rule, Hellenized elites, and sectarianism 152–63 B.C.E.)   *112–113*

sectarian competition among Maccabees, Hasidim, Sadducees, and Essenes (134–76 B.C.E.)   *112–113*

Roman conquest and rule of Judea (63–37 B.C.E.)   *113–114, 118, 165*

Herod the Great's ruthless rule of Judea (37–4 B.C.E.)   *114, 166*

rule by Archelaus (4 B.C.E.– 6 C.E.)   *166*

Roman and Jewish elites, peasants' opposition to, *166–167, 167 (sidebar)*

Herod Antipas's rule, hardship in Galilee (6–39 C.E.)   *166, 169*

Pontius Pilate as Roman governor (26–36 C.E.)   *166*

Israel (*entries in chronological order*) (continued)
  Jesus' confrontation with temple elite, crucifixion (30 C.E.)   *166, 167, 168, 171 (sidebar), 173 (sidebar)*
  First Jewish Revolt for independence from Rome (66 C.E.)   *114, 536*
  destruction of Second Temple and Jerusalem, dispersal, diaspora of Jews (70 C.E.)   *114, 167, 173, 536*
  emergence of rabbinic Judaism, religious law, law codes   *535–538*
  Roman celebration of domination over Judea and Jews within Empire (71 C.E.)   *174*
  Old Yishuv of ancient "holy cities"   *309, 394 (sidebar), 395, 474 (sidebar)*
  First Aliyah (1882–1903)   *388, 499 (sidebar)*
  New Yishuv of Zionist communities in Palestine (1903)   *309, 474 (sidebar)*
  Second Aliyah (1904–1914)   *388, 389 (sidebar)*
  animosity of First Aliyah to Second   *389 (sidebar)*
  Agudat Israel movement of Orthodox community (1912)   *390, 391, 395*
  Third Aliyah (1919–1923)   *388*
  Britain's seesaw policy encouraging, then discouraging Jewish immigration   *327–328*
  Fourth Aliyah (1924–1930)   *388*
  post-WWI British control, Jewish immigration, violence between Jews and Arabs (1918–1948)   *327–328, 395, 450–451*
  Fifth Aliyah (1932–1938)   *388*
  Aliyah Bet (1939–1945)   *388*
  British "White Paper" calling for independent Palestinian state (1939)   *395*
  immigration by Europe's war refugees, (late 1940s)   *34*
  discovery of Dead Sea Scrolls (1946)   *119*
  Irgun bombing of King David Hotel in Jerusalem (1946)   *449*
  Post-WWII British proposal for dual states (1947–1948)   *451*
  British withdrawal, violence between Arabs and Jews (1948)   *329, 331, 451*
  creation of Sephardi/Mizrachi underclass   *307, 454 (sidebar)*
  partition of Palestine, war, and mass exodus of Arabs (1948)   *213, 451, 494*
  declaration of statehood and War of Independence (1948–1949)   *86, 328–329, 451–452, 452 (illus.), 494*
  Israeli Arabs under strict surveillance (1948–1968)   *452–453*
  terrorism by Palestinian infiltrators, harsh reprisals (1949–1956)   *329*
  complicated attitudes toward Holocaust   *33, 472–473, 478*
  influx of Arabized Jews (1948–1953)   *452*
  Jerusalem as divided city (1949–1967)   *330–332, 497*
  establishment of Mossad (1951)   *454 (sidebar)*
  attempts to address injustices done Israeli Arabs (1953)   *454–455*
  occupation of, then withdrawal from Gaza Strip (1956–1957)   *330*
  Sinai-Suez War (1956)   *329–330*
  rapid progress, re-population, and disillusionment (late 1950s)   *334 (sidebar), 335*
  trial of war criminal Eichmann (1961)   *473*
  punitive attack on al-Karamah camp and guerrilla base, bravery of *fida'iyin* (1968)   *454*
  Six-Day War: pre-emptive strike against Egypt (1967)   *453, 454, 494–495, 497*
  Israeli rule in occupied territories (1968)   *454, 454 (sidebar), 495*
  settlements in newly won territories   *495*
  Arab and PLO escalation of guerrilla tactics   *453–454*
  Yom Kippur War and loss of some occupied territories and confidence (1973)   *453, 473, 493, 495–496, 496 (illus.)*
  continued occupation, profound divisions, heavy moral toll , damage to democracy (1970s)   *496*
  attacks on PLO bases in southern Lebanon (1981, 1982)   *87*
  invasion and occupation of southern Lebanon (1982–2000)   *307*
  massacres by Phalangist allies in Sabra and Shatila camps (1982)   *87–88, 88 (sidebar), 89 (sidebar), 307*
  raging debate over Jewish nationalism, Zionism, and disputed territories   *502*
  (*See also* Palestine)
Israel ("Wrestles with God"), additional name of Jacob, biblical patriarch   *548*
Istanbul, Turkey   *191 (illus.), 338–339*

J

Ja'far al-Barmaki (*also* Ja'far ibn Yayha al-Barmaki)   *16*
Jaffa, Israel   *213, 214, 217, 394 (sidebar)*
Jahiliyah (Age of Ignorance) or pre-Islamic age
  code of blood vengeance   *516–518, 521, 523*
  Muruwwah (virtue, manliness) and warrior aristocracy   *516–518, 517 (sidebar), 521, 523*
  rich mix of influences, shifting tribal federations   *516*
  slave trade from early days   *6, 20 (sidebar)*
  tribal society of Bedouin Arabia   *516–518*
  women's lives   *518*
al-Jahiz   *138 (sidebar), 264–265*
Jalal al-Din Rumi (LC: Jalal al-Din Rumi, Maulana), *Spiritual Couplets, The*   *39, 100, 348, 406, 505–514*
Jamalzadah, Muhammad Ali, *Once Upon a Time*   *44, 377–385*
Janissary Corps   *347, 398 (sidebar)*
Jerusalem
  to Amichai and his poetic speaker   *500, 502*

as ancient site and holy place of monotheistic faiths 496–497

Arab siege of 1948 329, 331

as divided, provincial, isolated, 330–331

Hasidim in Mea Shearim neighborhood 390

as holy city of Old Yishuv, Herzl's hope of Zionist glorious new city 394 (sidebar)

as locus of Jewish spiritual longing 497

in 1950s 332

reunification, U.N. recommendation for international control 451, 494

Jesus of Nazareth (Jesus Christ)

derivation of name from Joshua ("God saves") 168

and Pharisees 112–113, 118, 166

some Muslims believing in messianic mission 400

story as told in Gospel According to Matthew 165–175

Jews

in Austro-Hungarian Empire 25–26

Babylonian exile 536

in Christian Spain 58

condemnation of passivity, formation of defense groups 203–204, 206

Kishinev pogrom 200–202

occupations in al-Andalus 143

Ostjuden 27 (sidebar)

persecution under Visigoths in Spain 143

Quran's emphasis on tolerance for all monotheists ("People of the Book") 417–418

rabbinical academies in medieval Baghdad 132

Russian repression and waves of anti-Semitism 198–199

Sephardi, Ashkenazi, and Mizrachi 306–307, 454 (sidebar)

threatened with execution by Byzantine Emperor Heraclius 417

Zionism, response to Russian pogroms 199–200, 199 (sidebar)

(See also Anti-Semitism; Israel; Judaism)

Jiddah, Saudi Arabia 76

John the Baptist 166, 169, 170

Jordan (entries in chronological order)

creation by WWI Allies of Transjordan mandate (1920) 213

discovery of Dead Sea Scrolls (1946) 119

influx of Palestinian refugees from new state of Israel (1948) 213, 286, 328, 451–452, 494

King Abdullah and West Bank 286

King Hussein's attempts to gain popularity with Palestinians (1950s) 286–287

formation of PLO (1964) 287, 292

influx of more Palestinian refugees after 1967 Arab-Israeli War 213

loss of West Bank (1967) 287

expulsion of PLO, civil war and Black September (1966 and 1970) 214, 287, 458

(See also Islamic world)

Joseph (son of Jacob in Genesis) 168, 404

Josephus (Jewish historian; Josephus, Flavius) 167 (sidebar)

Judaism

biblical, patriarchal period 554

conversion of Khazar king 145 (sidebar)

democratized system of worship, personal and communal prayer 536

Essenes 111–112, 113, 114–116, 117–118, 117 (sidebar)

festival of Sukkot 537

Halevi and asceticism 146 (sidebar)

Hasidim and Hasidism 112, 390

Hasmoneans 112, 113, 118

holy text, The Talmud 535–544

importance of Jerusalem 496–497

importance of Torah study 536

Levites 115, 146

observance of Sabbath 552

Orthodox opposition to Zionists in Palestine, reliance on Messiah 390

Passover 550, 552, 553

Pharisees 112–113, 118, 166, 537

rabbinic 120, 535–536

role of early priests and elaborate sacrificial rituals 536

Sadducees 113

Shema as central prayer 551, 552 (sidebar)

synagogue dispute, writing of Matthew's gospel 173

wrestling with meaning of destruction of Temple and Jerusalem, exile into diaspora 146, 174, 472, 536

yearning for return to Israel 141, 147–149

Judicial issues. See legal codes, systems, and courts

Justinian (LC: Justinian I, Emperor of the East, Byzantine Empire) 416–417, 515

K

"kalam" (theology by proofs through argument) 358

Kalilah and Dimnah (LC: Kalilah wa-Dimnah) (Abd Allah Ibn al-Muqaffa', translator) 221–228

Kanafani, Ghassan, Men in the Sun 244, 285–293

Karbala, Iraq 210, 222, 259, 384 (sidebar)

Kasravi, Ahmad 407

Kawakibi, Abd al-Rahman 290

Kazakhstan 48

Kemal, Yaşr, Memed, My Hawk 54, 275–284

Khayyam, Omar, Ruba'iyat of Omar Khayyam 39, 127, 429–439

Khazars 145 (sidebar)

Khedive Ismail (LC: Ismail, Khedive of Egypt) 2, 3

Khomeini, Ayatollah (LC: Khomeini, Ruhollah) 408

Khosrow II, King of Persia (also Khusraw) 231, 417, 488

"Khusraw and Shirin" (Nizami of Ganja) 229–236, 254

Kibbutzim (collective farms in Israel)   499 *(sidebar)*

King Is the King, The (Sa'dallah Wannus)   237–246

Kishinev, Russia, pogrom   200–202

Kissinger, Henry   495

Konya, Turkey   507–508

Koran. *See* Quran (Koran)

Köroglu (Turkish Robin Hood)   282

"*Kunya*" method of naming in Arabic   245 *(sidebar)*

Kurds   444

Kuwait *(entries in chronological order)*

    Palestinian connection and refugees (1936–1976)   287

    expulsion of Palestinians after Gulf War (1991)   289

Kuzari (Judah Halevi)   145 *(sidebar)*

L

Labor Zionism   389

Land tenure/reform issues, in Turkey of 1920s and 1930s   278–279

Language issues. *See* Linguistic considerations

Lebanon: works set in

    Broken Wings, The (Kahlil Gibran)   65–73

    "Clockwork Doll, The" and Other Poems (Dalia Ravikovitch)   85–91

    Story of Zahra, The (Hanan al-Shaykh)   71, 527–533

Lebanon *(entries in chronological order)*

    association with Catholic France (from 16th century)   528

    denominational strife, French intervention, autonomy for Mt. Lebanon (1860s)   68, 68 *(sidebar)*

    Ottoman rule, feudalism (1876–1909)   66

    under French mandate rule   528

    political office allocation based on "confessional" census (1932)   528

    independence from France (1945)   528

    influx of Palestinian refugees (1948–1949)   451–452, 494

    Shi'ite majority since 1950s, politically suppressed   528

    civil war over demand for correct census (1958)   528

    population dispersal of Lebanese in Africa (1962)   532 *(sidebar)*

    Palestinians establish military base, civil war with Phalangists (1970)   528–529, 530 *(illus.)*

    civil/sectarian war (1975–1990)   86, 238

    PLO establishment of base of operations (late 1970s)   86–87

    Israeli attacks on PLO bases in south (1978, 1981, 1982)   87

    family-, clan-, and confessional-based factions (1980s)   529 *(sidebar)*

    Sabra-Shatila massacres (1982)   87–88, 88 *(sidebar)*, 89 *(sidebar)*, 307

    (*See also* Islamic world)

legal codes, systems, and courts

absence of, in tribal nomadic *Jahiliyah*, law of blood vengeance   516–518, 517 *(sidebar)*, 521, 523

covenant of God with Jewish people   549 *(sidebar)*, 552, 553, 554

Deuteronomic code of Torah rejecting principle of collective punishment   552

Jewish Law Codes as distillation of Talmud   535, 542–543

lex talionis ("an eye for an eye")   552–553

Pentateuch as law   551–553

Quran as law   422–423

Talmud as religious law   540–542

Lenin, Vladimir Ilich   188, 412

Lepanto, Battle of   339 *(sidebar)*

Levites   115, 146

Leviticus, book of   550–551, 553

Lex talionis ("an eye for an eye")   552–553

Leyla and Mejnun (Fuzuli)   48, 217 *(sidebar)*, 247–255

Limpieza de sangre ("purity of blood")   307

Linguistic considerations

    Akkadian   154 *(sidebar)*

    Arabic

        Bedouins speaking purest form of   367

        lore about alphabet   216 *(sidebar)*

        Modern Standard versus Egyptian Colloquial   324

        Taymur's ironic playing with names   9 *(sidebar)*

        utilitarian approach   2

        versus Persian or Turkish   383, 489

    Aramaic   154 *(sidebar)*

    Azerbaijani, agitation for right to use   444

    Babylonian   154 *(sidebar)*

    Gilgamesh, languages of composition and translations   154 *(sidebar)*

    Hebrew

        birth of modern   59, 64, 197, 199, 309, 391, 478 *(sidebar)*

        al-Harizi's use for Arabic-style *maqamah* short story   57

    Kurdish, agitation for right to use   444

    Persian

        confusing genderless usage of "he" and "she"   346 *(sidebar)*, 433

        endorsement of   383–384

        Jamalzadah's idiomatic and colloquial diction, clashes with dialect   377, 385

        literary movement to endorse Iranian Persian heritage   383

        replacement of Pahlavi characters with Arabic script   258, 338

        second-class status in Islamic world   258, 488, 489

        versus Arabic and Turkish   489

        written and spoken   381 *(sidebar)*

    Semitic languages   160

    Sumerian   154 *(sidebar)*

    Turkish

adoption of Latin alphabet   *102*

confusing genderless usage of "he" and "she"   *346 (sidebar)*, *433*

dialect as literary language   *275*, *352–353*

Persianized and Arabicized vocabulary   *254*

versus Arabic or Persian   *383*, *489*

Yiddish   *205*, *391*

(*See also* Translation issues)

Linguistic considerations: etymological

"*aliyot*" (waves, of immigration to Palestine/Israel)   *34*, *388*, *389 (sidebar)*

"caliph" (successor of Muhammad)   *14*, *142*

"Christ" ("Messiah," anointed, chosen for Divine role)   *168*

"*divans*" (collections of Turkish or Persian poems)   *121*, *403*

"*diwans*" (collections of Arabic poems)   *135*

"*farr*" (halo, "royal glory," right to rule)   *485*, *485 (sidebar)*

"*ghazals*" (sonnet-like poems)   *121*, *403*, *403 (sidebar)*, *405–406*

"*halutsot*" (women pioneers) in Palestine   *85*

"*halutzim*" (Jewish pioneers in Palestine)   *499*

"Hiwis" (*Hilfswillige* or "willing helpers")   *27–28*

"*Humash*" (the Five-fold, The Torah)   *545*

"*kalam*" (theology by proofs through argument)   *358*

"*kibbutzim*" (collective farms in Israel)   *499 (sidebar)*

"*kunya*" method of naming in Arabic   *245 (sidebar)*

"*maqamah*" (short tales, largely rhymed narrative prose)   *2*, *57*

"*Muruwwah*" (virtue, manliness) of pre-Islamic tribal/warrior aristocracy   *516–518*, *517 (sidebar)*, *521*, *523*

"*purdah*" (sequestering of women)   *488*

"*qasidah*" (odes)   *2*, *360–362*, *372–373*, *518*, *524–525*, *525 (sidebar)*

"*saz*" (lute-type musical instrument)   *253 (sidebar)*

"*sultan*" (one who wields power)   *316*

"*taifa*" (kingdoms, miniature states of al-Andalus)   *142*, *178*

"*vizier*" (minister)   *14*

"Westitis" or "Westoxication"   *268*

"Wogs" (Western-oriented gentlemen)   *382 (sidebar)*

Literacy. *See* Education and literacy rates

Literary experimentation and categories

Agnon's use of religious and folkloric sources   *396*

Al-i Ahmad's polemics and bluntness   *413*

Arabic of mid-19th century   *2*

Arabic Udhri love stories   *253*

Arab innovations after events of 1967   *245*

Badi' style of poetry   *355*, *357–359*, *364*

bildungsroman (novel of development)   *527*

Egyptian search for national identity and character   *9–10*

foreshadowing of "future" events   *556 (sidebar)*

"fraus pia" (pious fraud)   *555*

"*Ghazals*" (sonnet-like poems)   *121*, *403*, *403 (sidebar)*, *405–406*

Gibranesque poetic prose and prose poetry   *71*

Gilgamesh as adaptable ancient text   *160*

al-Hamadhani's humorous anecdotes   *264*

al-Hamadhani's innovation and originality   *257*

al-Hamadhani's ironic use of fictionalized narrator   *260*

Hebrew literary renaissance   *391*

Iranian, fresh ideas, precepts, styles   *381*

magic realism   *478–479*

maqamah as short tales, largely rhymed narrative prose   *57*

Munif's alternative historiography   *82*

outlaw as folk hero   *281–282*, *281 (sidebar)*

Pamuk's playful, experimental manner   *337*, *344*, *345*

Persian divine wordplay   *94 (sidebar)*

"Persian" melancholic skepticism and stoicism   *39*

Persian realism and literary freedom   *385*

qasidah (odes)   *2*, *360–362*, *372–373*, *518*, *524–525*, *525 (sidebar)*

roman à clef (fictionalized account of real events)   *75*

satire   *455*

secular literature of advice with entertainment   *227–228*

sophisticated techniques underlying Biblical stories   *556 (sidebar)*

"textuality" as adaptations of ancient texts   *160*

Turkish realism   *282*

(*See also* Allegory, interpretations of text as; Oral tradition and storytellers; Plays: experimentation with; Poetry: experimentation with)

Locke, John   *185*

Loti, Pierre (pseudonym of Julien Viaud)   *464 (sidebar)*

Love

courtly, metaphoric, and "real" in Sufism   *405*

Hafiz's vision of *ishq* in Sufi doctrine   *125–126*

love triangle   *234*

madness resulting from excess   *248*

Quran on relationships   *247–248*

for ruler implying love of God   *400*, *401 (illus.)*

as Sufi metaphor for bond between believer and God   *248*, *252–253*, *350*

Love stories (traditional)

"Khusraw and Shirin" (Nizami of Ganja)   *229–236*, *254*

Leyla and Mejnun (Fuzuli)   *48*, *217 (sidebar)*, *247–255*

Lute-type musical instrument: *saz*   *253 (sidebar)*

Maccabean revolt   *112, 113*

Maccabee, Judah (LC: Judas, Maccabeus)   *112, 113*

Madrasahs (Islamic colleges)   *58, 235, 236*

Magi   *168*

Mahdi, The (Divinely or Rightly Guided One) (LC: Ibn Tumart, Muhammad) (12th-century spiritual leader)   *178*

Mahdi, The (Divinely or Rightly Guided One) (LC: Mahdi, Muhammad Ahmad) and Mahdist Revolt in Sudan (1881–1898)   *5–6*

Mahfuz, Najib (*also* Mahfouz, Naguib), *Miramar*   *295–304, 427 (sidebar)*

Mahmud, Sultan of Ghazni (*also* Mahmoud)   *97, 99, 482 (sidebar), 489*

Maimonides (LC: Maimonides, Moses)   *144, 181, 542, 543 (sidebar)*

Malikshah (LC: Malik-Shah, Sultan of the Seljuks)   *430*

Mamluks (slave dynasty)   *20 (sidebar), 22, 122*

Manichaeism   *484*

Mani, founder of Manichaeism   *484*

al-Mansur, Abu Jafar (Caliph)   *131, 132*

Mansur al-Hallaj. *See* al-Hallaj, al-Husayn ibn Mansur

Maqamah (short tales, largely rhymed narrative prose)

   Book of Tahkemoni, The (Hebrew Maqamat) (Judah al-Harizi)   *57–64*

   Maqamat (al-Hamadhani)   *61, 257–266*

   seen as vulgar and debased   *2*

Maqamat (al-Hamadhani)   *61, 257–266*

Mark, gospel of   *172*

Maronite Christians   *67–68, 528*

Marrash, Fransis of Aleppo   *67 (sidebar)*

Marriage

   arranged in Maronite communities of Mount Lebanon   *68*

   polygyny/polygamy   *4, 5, 277*

   (*See also* Sexual dimension of life; Women in relation to society, politics, and men)

Marxism-Leninism

   in Iran   *412*

   Nazim Hikmet's exposure to   *187*

   in United Arab Republic   *291*

Maurice, Emperor of the East, Byzantine Empire   *417*

Mea Shearim neighborhood of Jerusalem   *390*

Mecca, Saudi Arabia   *76, 416, 417, 421 (illus.), 525*

"Mechanical Doll" and Other Poems (Furugh Farrukhzad)   *267–274*

Medicine. *See* Health issues

Medina, Saudi Arabia   *76, 415*

Mehmed II, *Fatih* (The Conqueror), Sultan of the Turks   *339 (sidebar), 398*

Meir, Golda   *85–86, 495*

Memed, My Hawk (Yaşr Kemal)   *54, 275–284*

Menderes, Adnan   *102, 103, 104, 283*

Men in the Sun (Ghassan Kanafani)   *244, 285–293*

Mesopotamia: works set in

   Epic of Gilgamesh, The   *153–163, 553*

   Talmud, The   *535–544, 556*

Mesopotamia (*entries in chronological order*)

   abundant harvests and growing populations (c. 5000 B.C.E.)   *154*

   Great Flood (c. 5000 or 2000 B.C.E.)   *159, 161–162*

   growth of cities, markets, palaces, temples, and ziggurats (4000–3000 B.C.E.)   *155*

   origins of civilization, writing, government, and laws, (4000–3000 B.C.E.)   *155, 160, 162*

   transformation, territorial disputes and fortifications (2700 B.C.E.)   *155, 156 (illus.)*

   absorption of Sumerians into Akkadian culture   *160–161*

   conquests of Sargon (c. 2300 B.C.E.)   *160*

   final flowering of Sumerian culture (c. 2100 B.C.E.)   *161*

   conquest by Ur (c. 2100 B.C.E.)   *161*

   empires of Babylonians and Assyrians (c. 1800–600 B.C.E.)   *161*

   destruction of First Temple in Jerusalem by Nebuchadnezzar, Babylonian exile of Jews (586 B.C.E.)   *535, 536, 554, 555*

   Jewish *yeshivot* (academies) in Babylonia   *58*

   invasion by Persians (539 B.C.E.)   *161*

   (*See also* Iraq)

"Messiah" (anointed, chosen for Divine role)   *168*

Mevleviyeh order of Sufism   *507, 513*

Middle class

   in Mahfuz's novels on Egypt   *295*

   in modern Turkey   *103, 104*

   Saudi Arabian discontent   *83*

Mihri (female poet of 1500s)   *406 (sidebar)*

Miniature painting by Ottoman artists   *340*

Minoans   *307*

Minstrels   *47*

Miramar (Najib Mahfuz)   *295–304*

Mizrachim (eastern Jews)   *306–307, 454 (sidebar)*

Modernization

   Egypt, British and French influences   *3–5, 3 (sidebar)*

   Iran of 1930s and 1940s, culture shock   *38, 43, 379–380, 411–412, 442–443*

   Iran, industrialization in 1950s and 1960s   *409 (sidebar)*

   Jerusalem in 1950s   *332*

   Saudi Arabia, Wahhabi Bedouin communities' suspicion of technology   *77*

   Turkey, Hikmet's enthusiasm   *189 (sidebar)*

   Turkey under Menderes   *102–104*

   (*See also* Economic issues; Urbanization)

Mohammed Reza Pahlavi, Shah of Iran (*also* Mohammed Reza Shah)   *268 (sidebar), 408, 409, 411 (sidebar), 446*

Molla Kasim   *352 (sidebar)*

Mongol invasions (1221, 1243, and 1258)   *22, 122, 235, 316, 348*

Monophysite Christians   *417*

Monotheism   552, 552 (sidebar), 553

Mosaddeq, Mohammad   409

Moses   550

Moses ben Maimon. *See* Maimonides

Mount Bisutun, Iran   234

Mr. Mani (A.B. Yehoshua)   305–314

Mu'awiyah ibn Abi Sufyan, Caliph (first Umayyad caliph)   210, 221–222

Mubarak, Husni (LC: Mubarak, Muhammad Husni)   324

Muhammad Ahmad (The Mahdi) (LC: al-Mahdi, Muhammad Ahmad)   6

Muhammad Ali (LC: Muhammad Ali Basha) (Governor of Egypt)   2, 5

Muhammad Ali Shah, Shah of Iran   378

Muhammad ibn Abd al-Wahhab, founder of the Wahhabi version of Islam   76

Muhammad ibn Sa'ud, Prince of Nejd   76

Muhammad, Prophet (*entries in chronological order*)
    birth in Mecca to Quraysh clan (570)   415
    orphaned in 578, raised by uncle   415
    work as caravan merchant   415
    marriage, children, daughter Fatimah and grandchildren   415
    divine summons and revelations (c. 610)   415
    first revelation in cave from angel Gabriel (610)   425
    Quraysh clan harassment (c. 619)   418
    move to Medina (622)   415–416, 418
    first battle with Quraysh (624)   418
    second battle with Quraysh, Muhammad nearly killed (625)   418
    third battle with Quraysh (627)   418–419
    return to Mecca in triumph (630)   419
    rebellions by Bedouin tribes   419
    death and succession by Abu Bakr (632)   419
    ascension into heaven from Jerusalem, as believed by devout   497
    (*See also* Islam; Islamic world)

Munif, Abd al-Rahman, *Cities of Salt* 75–84

al-Muqtadir, Caliph   317

Murder in Baghdad (Salah Abd al-Sabur)   179, 315–325, 351

"*Muruwwah*" (virtue, manliness) of pre-Islamic tribal/warrior aristocracy   516–518, 517 (sidebar), 521, 523

Music and dance
    condemned in orthodox Islam   96
    lute-type *saz*   253 (sidebar)
    Turkic minstrels   47, 275, 281 (sidebar)
    as viewed by Sufis   349
    (*See also* Popular culture and values)

Muslim Brotherhood   324

Mustafa Kemal. *See* Atatürk, Kemal

Mutakallimun   358

al-Mu'tamid, Caliph   317

al-Mutanabbi (LC: al-Mutanabbi, Abu al-Tayyib Ahmad ibn al-Husayn), "Ode on the Reconquest of al-Hadath"   362, 367–375

al-Mu'tasim, Caliph   355, 356–357

Mu'tazilites   128 (sidebar), 263–264, 357–359

Muzaffar al-Din Shah, Shah of Iran   378

Mycenaeans   307

My Michael (Amos Oz)   327–336

My Name Is Red (Orhan Pamuk)   337–346

Mystical Poetry of Yunus Emre, The (Yunus Emre)   347–353

Myths
    flood story   157–159, 161–162, 547, 553
    Garden of Eden story   553

N

Nahdah (Awakening) (19th century)   2–5

Naimy, Mikhail (LC: Nu'aymah, Mikha'il)   71–72

al-Nakbah ("the catastrophe") (1948)   452

al-Naksah ("the disaster") (1967)   238, 244

Napoleon   2, 3 (sidebar)

al-Naqqash, Marun, *The Cheapskate*   242–243

Nasser, Gamel Abdel (*also* Abd al-Nasir, Jamal or Gamal), President of Egypt, President of United Arab Republic   209, 212, 212 (illus.), 217–218, 218 (illus.), 291, 296, 297, 330

Nationalism and search for national identity
    Egyptian anticolonialism   6–7
    Egyptian *Nahdah* (Awakening) (19th century)   2–5
    Iran of 1950s and 1960s   268, 410–411
    Iran and religion in 20th century   43
    modern Jewish   199, 204
    movements all over Europe, emergence of modern phenomena of mass politics   309
    pan-Arabism   78, 79, 211, 212, 213, 287, 290–292
    Sudan   6
    Turkey of 1910s and 1920s   54, 463–464
    (*See also* Zionism)

Nationalization of industries/services, by Nasser in Egypt of 1960s   213, 297

NATO (North Atlantic Treaty Organization)   102, 105

Nature
    conflicting views in Islamic teaching   248–249
    medieval Islamic views of   178–183
    in Ottoman poetry   403–404

Naziism   26, 28–29, 188

Nazim Hikmet, *Human Landscapes from My Country*   187–195

Nebuchadnezzar II, King of Babylonia   535, 536

Necati (LC: Necati Bey), Ottoman Lyric Poetry: "Those Tulip-Cheeked Ones"   397–406

Nestorian Christianity   132, 417

"New" poetry (*mudath*) with rhetorical embellishment and metaphor   138

Nicholas I, Emperor of Russia   198

"Nightingale" and "rose" as symbols in Iran   271 (sidebar)

Nizam al-Mulk   234–235, 430

Nizami of Ganja (Nizami Ganjavi), "Khusraw and Shirin"   229–236, 254

Noah's flood story *157–159, 161–162, 547, 553*
Nomads
   Iranian *442 (illus.)*
   Oghuz Turks *48*
   (*See also* Bedouins)
Novels and novellas: experimentation with
   Agaoglu's provincial settings and future-as-present narrative style *108–109*
   Agnon's alternating settings and dog symbolism *393, 393 (sidebar), 394*
   Grossman's crossing of temporal and spatial boundaries *472*
   Grossman's innovations in language and form *471, 477*
   Hidayat's linguistic style, vocabularies, and repeated passages *44–45*
   Kemal's blend of literary language with colloquial dialect *275, 283*
   Mahfuz's blend of realism, mysticism, existentialism *302*
   Mahfuz's layered narrative technique *301, 302*
   Yehoshua's diverse ensemble of narrators in reverse chronological order *305, 309, 310 (sidebar), 312–314*
   (*See also* Linguistic considerations)
Novels and novellas
   Badenheim 1939 (Aharon Appelfeld) *25–35*
   Blind Owl, The (Sadiq Hidayat) *37–46*
   Broken Wings, The (Kahlil Gibran) *65–73*
   Cities of Salt (Abd al-Rahman Munif) *75–84*
   Curfew (Adalet Agaoglu) *101–110*
   Memed, My Hawk (Yaşr Kemal) *54, 275–284*
   Men in the Sun (Ghassan Kanafani) *244, 285–293*
   Miramar (Najib Mahfuz) *295–304*
   Mr. Mani (A.B. Yehoshua) *305–314*
   My Michael (Amos Oz) *327–336*
   My Name Is Red (Orhan Pamuk) *337–346*
   Only Yesterday (Shmuel Yosef Agnon) *387–396*
   Savushun (A Persian Requiem) (Simin Danishvar) *441–449*
   Secret Life of Saeed the Ill-fated Pessoptimist, The (Emile Habiby) *449–460*
   See Under: Love (David Grossman) *471–479*
   Story of Zahra, The (Hanan al-Shaykh) *71, 527–533*
Nu'aymah, Mikha'il *71–72*
Numbers, book of *550–551, 553*

O

Occupations and trades
   in 13th century Persia *93*
   Iran of 1920s *380*
   Jews in al-Andalus *143*
   Jews in Europe of early 1900s *388*
   Lebanese immigrants in Africa *532 (sidebar)*
   in medieval Persia *236*
   modern Egyptian bureaucrats *295*
   Saudi oil workers *78, 78 (sidebar), 84 (sidebar)*

   scribes or accountants in ancient times *162 (sidebar)*
   Turkish business class *103, 104*
   Turkish villagers' subsistence farming *276*
   (*See also* Artists and intellectuals)
October War (Yom Kippur War) *453, 473, 493, 495–496, 496 (illus.)*
"Ode on the Conquest of Amorium" (Abu Tammam) *355–365, 368, 373–374*
"Ode on the Reconquest of al-Hadath" (al-Mutanabbi) *362, 367–375*
Odyssey, The *161*
Oghuz Turks *47, 53–54, 397–398, 430*
Oil *75, 77–78, 79 (illus.), 443*
Ömer Seyfettin, "Secret Shrine, The" and "Frog Prayer, The" *461–469*
Once Upon a Time (Muhammad Ali Jamalzadah) *44, 377–385*
Only Yesterday (Shmuel Yosef Agnon) *387–396*
Opium *40 (sidebar), 383 (sidebar)*
Oral tradition and storytellers
   Anatolia's wandering bards *275, 281 (sidebar)*
   continuation in Turkic world *54*
   Oghuz integrating past and present, emphasizing adaptation and forgiveness *53*
   tales evolving over time *13, 21, 153, 227*
   Turkic, combined verse and prose *47*
Oryx *523 (illus.)*
Osman I, Sultan of the Turks, and Osmanli Turks *48, 348, 467 (sidebar)*
Ostjuden *27 (sidebar)*
Ottoman Empire (1299–1923)
   far-flung empire enduring until defeat in WWI *337–338, 467 (sidebar)*
   map showing extent in year 1606 *399 (illus.)*
   (*See also* Islamic world; Turkey)
Ottoman Lyric Poetry: "Those Tulip-Cheeked Ones" and "Row by Row" (Necati and Baki) *397–406*
Owen, Wilfred *501 (sidebar)*
Oz, Amos, *My Michael* *327–336*

P

Pahlavi. *See* Mohammed Reza Pahlavi; Reza Shah
Palestine: works set in
   Mr. Mani (A.B. Yehoshua) *305–314*
   Only Yesterday (Shmuel Yosef Agnon) *387–396*
   Talmud, The *535–544, 556*
Palestine (*entries in chronological order*)
   Jewish kibbutzim, agricultural collectives and settlements (late 1800s) *389–390*
   Zionism and immigration of disapora Jews (late 1800s) *199, 308–309, 388, 390–391, 395–396, 450*
   Palestinian resistance to immigrants *450–451*
   British conquest and Balfour Declaration (1917) *308, 450, 494*
   populations of Arabs and Jews (1917) *308*
   British "White Paper" calling for independent Palestinian state (1939) *395*

British withdrawal, violence between Arabs and Jews (1948)   329, 331, 451

Israel's declaration of statehood and War of Independence (1948–1949)   86, 328–329, 451–452, 452 (illus.), 494

partition, war, and mass exodus of Arabs (1948)   213, 451

(*See also* Israel)

Palestinian Resistance Movement (PRM)   287

Palestinians: works concerning

Men in the Sun (Ghassan Kanafani)   244, 285–293

Secret Life of Saeed the Ill-fated Pessoptimist, The (Emile Habiby)   449–460

Palestinians (*entries in chronological order*)

Kuwaiti connection and refugees (1936–1976)   287

refugees flee to Gaza Strip and Transjordan's West Bank (1948)   286–287, 328, 451–452

some returning to Israel   452

anger and growth of Palestinian national consciousness   495

expulsion of PLO from Jordan, civil war and Black September (1966 and 1970)   214, 287, 458

Sabra and Shatila refugee camp massacres in Lebanon (1982)   87–88, 88 (sidebar), 89 (sidebar), 307

expulsion from Gulf region after Gulf War (1991)   289

four generations of refugees still in camps (2004)   453

Palmah (elite force of pre-state Israel)   493

Pamuk, Orhan, *My Name Is Red*   337–346

Pan-Arabism   78, 79, 183, 211, 212, 213, 287, 290–292

Panegyric or praise poetry   373

Passover   550, 552, 553

Pentateuch, The (The Torah)   536, 545–557

"People of the Book"   417–418

Persian Cossack Brigade   379 (illus.), 380 (sidebar)

Persian Empire. *See* Iran

Phalangists   87

Pharisees   112–113, 118, 166, 537

Philosophy

Andalusian intellectuals and anti-philosophical trend   178

Greek rationalism and logic as threat to religious and communal distinctness   144

Islamic world view in 12th century   178–183

Mu'tazilites and Ash'arites   128 (sidebar), 263–264, 357–359

predestination and free will   126–127, 259, 434

Quran, Plato, and poets   406

rationalism versus fatalism   128 (sidebar)

"rindi" as honorable scoundrel in Hafiz   127 (sidebar)

Sufi attempts to limit role of reason   431–432

Sufism, free will, reason and choice to love God   350

Pilgrimages (hajj)

Halevi's hope for   141, 147–149

to Mecca, Medina, Najaf, Mashhad and Karbala   94, 249, 384 (sidebar)

by Sufis   94–95

Plagued by the West (*Gharbzadigi*) (Jalal Al-i Ahmad)   268, 407–414, 441

Plato   178, 402, 428

Plays: experimentation with

Wannus's breaking down of traditional barriers between stage and audience   237, 243

Wannus's infusing drama with *turath*, Arab heritage   237, 242, 243

Wannus's theater of politicization, spurring audience into action   237, 245

Plays

King Is the King, The (Sa'dallah Wannus)   237–246

Murder in Baghdad (Salah Abd al-Sabur)   179, 315–325, 351

PLO (Palestine Liberation Organization)   86–87, 214, 287, 292, 307, 454, 528

Poe, Edgar Allan   41, 45 (sidebar)

Poetry: experimentation with

Abu Nuwas's innovations   134, 135

Abu Nuwas's wine poems   135–137, 265

Abu Tammam and *badi'* style   355, 357–359, 364

Adunis's use of cultural syncretism amd symbology   214, 219

Arabic protest poetry   137

Bialik's use of personal voice and persona of prophet   205

freedom from rigid rules of traditional Arabic versification   219

free-verse style (*al-shi'r al-hurr*)   219

Hebrew poets adapting Arabic poetic elements   141, 150

Human Landscapes resisting categorization   190, 193–194, 195

imitation and concern for tradition and continuity   406

Israeli protest poetry   91

mujun genre and offensive sexual explicitness   138 (sidebar)

al-Mutanabbi's blend of pre-Islamic, classical, and *badi'* style   374

"New" poetry (*mudath*) with rhetorical embellishment and metaphor   138

by Nima Yushij   273

Nizami's egalitarian story of love defying social status   234

Nizami's style   235 (sidebar), 236

as political tool and entertainment   143–144

rhetorical embellishment and metaphorical sophistication   138

ruba'i as Persian innovation   432–433

scatalogical compositions   137

secular Hebrew, Arabized, Jewish disapproval of   144, 145 (sidebar)

Poetry: experimentation with (continued)
   set to music   253 (sidebar)
   Yunus Emre's use of Turkish popular dialect
      347, 352–353
Poetry: types
   ghazals (sonnet-like poems)   121, 403, 403
      (sidebar), 405–406
   hunting poems   139 (sidebar)
   imitation and concern for tradition and
      continuity   406
   panegyric or praise poetry   373
   poetry as protest   91, 137
   poets and patrons   369 (sidebar), 400–401
   "qasidah" (odes)   2, 360–362, 372–373, 518,
      524–525, 525 (sidebar)
   sexual   135, 136 (sidebar), 272
   Turkish love poems of wandering minstrels
      402 (sidebar)
Poetry
   "Clockwork Doll, The" and Other Poems (Dalia
      Ravikovitch)   85–91
   Conference of the Birds, The (Farid al-Din Attar)
      93–100
   Divan of Hafiz, The (Hafiz)   121–129, 271
      (sidebar), 406, 514
   Diwan of Abu Nuwas, The (Abu Nuwas)
      131–140, 265
   Diwan of Judah Halevi, The (Judah Halevi)
      141–151, 306
   epic
      Epic of Gilgamesh, The   153–163, 553
      Shahnamah, or The Book of Kings (Abu al-Qasim
         Firdawsi)   233 (sidebar), 258, 406, 446,
         481–491, 514
   Human Landscapes from My Country (Nazim
      Hikmet)   187–195
   "In the City of Slaughter" (Hayyim Nahman
      Bialik)   91, 197–207
   "Introduction to the History of the Petty Kings"
      (Adunis)   209–220
   "Khusraw and Shirin" (Nizami of Ganja)
      229–236, 254
   Leyla and Mejnun (Fuzuli)   48, 217 (sidebar),
      247–255
   "Mechanical Doll" and Other Poems (Furugh
      Farrukhzad)   267–274
   Mystical Poetry of Yunus Emre, The (Yunus
      Emre)   347–353
   "Ode on the Conquest of Amorium" (Abu
      Tammam)   355–365, 368, 373–374
   "Ode on the Reconquest of al-Hadath" (al-
      Mutanabbi)   362, 367–375
   Ottoman Lyric Poetry: "Those Tulip-Cheeked
      Ones" and "Row by Row" (Necati and Baki)
      397–406
   Ruba'iyat of Omar Khayyam (Omar Khayyam)
      39, 127, 429–439
   Shahnamah, or The Book of Kings (Abu al-Qasim
      Firdawsi)   233 (sidebar), 258, 406, 446,
      481–491, 514

Songs of the Land of Zion, Jerusalem (Yehuda
   Amichai)   493–503
Spiritual Couplets, The (Jalal al-Din Muhammad
   Balkhi Rumi)   348, 406, 505–514
"Stop and We Will Weep: The Mu'allaqah" (Imru
   al-Qays)   426, 515–526
"Those Tulip-Cheeked Ones" and "Row by Row"
   (Necati and Baki)   397–406
Poland   190
Political activism
   and execution of Mansur al-Hallaj   317, 318,
      318 (sidebar), 351
   in Israel over 1982 invasion of Lebanon and
      Sabra-Shatila massacres   87–88, 88 (sidebar),
      89 (sidebar), 307
   by Kemal   275
   Labor Zionism   389
   proliferation of parties in Israel   395–396
   in Saudi Arabia, oil workers, indigenous Arabs,
      and pan-Arabist and socialist ideologies   78,
      79
   Sufi fraternities   320, 323
   in Turkey, political parties, economic stresses,
      and modernization   102
   Zionism   199
   (See also Pan-Arabism)
Polygyny/polygamy
   Egyptian   4, 5
   outlawed in Turkey   277
Popular culture and values
   Egyptian intellectuals' ambivalence toward masses
      4
   Oghuz Turks   48, 52–53
   Ottoman society, urban entertainment culture
      401–402
   Turkish love poems of wandering minstrels
      402 (sidebar)
   (See also Music and dance)
Pottery   434 (sidebar)
Poverty, income gap between haves and have-nots
   American versus Arab oil workers   80–81
   in Beirut at 20th century   66
   in Egypt of 1960s   296
   Meccan society in 7th century   417
   in Syria of 1970s   238
   (See also Class consciousness and social
      stratification)
Prose
   Arabian Nights, The (Husain Haddawy,
      translator)   2, 13–23, 161, 242, 242 (sidebar),
      475–476
   Book of Dede Korkut, The   47–55
   Book of Tahkemoni, The (Hebrew Maqamat)
      (Judah al-Harizi)   57–64
   Hayy ibn Yaqzan (Ibn Tufayl)   177–185
   Kalilah and Dimnah   221–228
   Maqamat (al-Hamadhani)   61, 257–266
   Plagued by the West (Gharbzadigi) (Jalal Al-i
      Ahmad)   268, 407–414, 441
   Talmud, The   535–544, 556

(*See also* Novels and novellas; Plays; Scripture, religious texts and commentaries, holy works; Short stories and short story collections)

Psychoanalysis, Iranians' interest in   44 (*sidebar*)

"*Purdah*" (sequestering of women)   488

Pursuit of knowledge
    in 8th century Baghdad   15
    astrology   60
    decline under Ottoman Turks   22
    importance of study of Torah   536
    introduction of European sciences and humanities   2
    Jewish *yeshivot* (academies) in Babylonia   58
    maturity, self-indulgent adolescents growing into   519, 521
    in Persia   14
    reason/intellect versus love   125
    "Renaissance of Islam"   132
    represented by Talmud   535, 542, 544
    Sufi attempts to limit role of reason   431–432
    Sufi master and disciple   96, 319, 512
    (*See also* Philosophy)

Q

"*Qasidah*" (odes)   2, 360–362, 372–373, 518, 524–525, 525 (*sidebar*)

Qasim, Amin   4–5, 70

Qumran caves (Dead Sea Scrolls)   111, 114 (*illus.*)

Quran (Koran), The   415–428
    allegorical interpretation by Sufism   95–96, 99–100
    ambiguity of statements on equality of women   21
    compilation and composition   426–427
    condemnation of extremes of behavior   420
    controversy of "createdness" or "uncreatedness"   357
    dialogic relationship with text   425–426
    emphasis on activist social involvement versus retreat into inner life or monasticism   419–420
    emphasis on Judgment Day   420
    emphasis on tolerance for all monotheists ("People of the Book")   58, 417–418
    enjoining right and forbidding wrong   263 (*sidebar*)
    as essence of Islam   257–258
    example of highly illustrated pages   423 (*illus.*)
    hadith (accounts of life of Muhammad as examples)   259
    inimitability   427 (*sidebar*), 525
    Mahfuz's praise for   427 (*sidebar*)
    on male-female relationships   247–248
    message of uncompromising monotheism and individual personal responsibility   415, 416
    Mu'tazilites and doctrine of rational theology, allegorical/figurative interpretation   263–264
    need to reform preceding monotheistic traditions   416

poets as dangerous to society   427–428
    powerful, rhythmic style, distinctive Quranic voice   416, 420 (*sidebar*)
    practical simplicity, social commitment, spiritual searching   420
    protection of Jews in   58
    scope, doctrinal questions and interpretation   259
    sequence, structure, and content, surahs (books or chapters) and ayahs (miracles)   420–424
    strategic writing, strategic reading   425–426
    stressing egalitarianism and respect for one another   417
    on when to make war, *jihad* (struggle), holy and unholy   418–419

al-Qushayri, al-Sammah ibn Abd Allah   364 (*sidebar*)

R

Rabi'ah (LC: Rabi'ah al-Adawiyah)   319

Rabikovitch, Dalia. *See* Ravikovitch, Dalia

Racism and prejudice
    against Egyptians on part of British   4 (*sidebar*)
    against *Ostjuden*   27 (*sidebar*)
    against Palestinians   289
    in Israel   306, 452–453
    in Lebanon   87, 528–529
    toward country bumpkins   262
    (*See also* anti-Semitism)

Rambam. *See* Maimonides

Rank, Otto   44 (*sidebar*)

Rashi (acronym of Rabbi Solomon ben Isaac)   541 (*sidebar*)

Ravikovitch, Dalia (*also* Ravikovitch, Dahlia), "Clockwork Doll, The" and Other Poems   85–91

Religion, spirituality, and folklore
    anti-clericalism   69–70, 126, 128
    dervishes (itinerant followers of Sufism)   96, 349 (*sidebar*), 402–403, 505
    Egyptian reformist attack on popular practice   4, 8–9
    Greek rationalism and logic as threat to   144
    innovation, transformation, expectation of messiah or *mahdi* in Europe and Middle East   399–400
    Manichaeism   484
    monotheism   552, 552 (*sidebar*), 553
    Oghuz shamanism   48–49
    pilgrimages (hajj) to Mecca, Medina, Najaf, Mashhad and Karbala   94, 249, 384 (*sidebar*)
    role of Satan   137, 169
    Sunni-Shi'ia religious schism   94, 222, 258–259, 378, 400 (*sidebar*)
    theology arising to counter Greek logic and rationalism   144, 145 (*sidebar*), 147
    Zoroastrianism   14, 132, 482 (*illus.*), 483 (*sidebar*), 484
    (*See also* Christianity; Islam; Judaism; Sufism)

Religious texts. *See* Scripture, religious texts and commentaries, holy works

"Renaissance of Islam"   132

Resistance movements of 20th century
   fedayeen (*fida'iyin*)   214, 454
   Iran, leftist guerrilla movement   268 (*sidebar*)
   Iran, Marxist trade unionism, activist clerics and press   444
   oil workers' strike at Aramco   75, 78–79
   Palestinian Mandate, Irgun Tsevai Leumi (National Military Organization)   396, 449, 451
   Palestinian Mandate, *Palmah* (elite force of pre-state Israel)   493
   Palestinian Resistance Movement (PRM)   287
   PLO (Palestine Liberation Organization)   86–87, 214, 287, 292, 307, 454, 528
   Saudi Arabia, uprising in Mecca by fundamentalists   83
   Syria, internal attacks on Assad regime, crushed uprisings   239
   Turkey, anti-imperialist War of Independence   189
   Turkey, extreme leftists and fascistic right-wing nationalists   105

Revolutions of 20th century
   Egypt, abolishing monarchy, establishing republic (1952)   295–296
   Egypt, Wafd Party and revolution (1919)   6–7
   Iran, Islamic Revolution, Ayatollah Khomeini replaces shah (1979)   268 (*sidebar*)
   Iran, start and ultimate failure of Constitutional revolution (1905–1911)   38, 378–379
   Iran, White Revolution, land redistribution, urban underclass of displaced farm hands (1963)   408, 446
   Israeli declaration of statehood and War of Independence (1948–1949)   86, 328–329, 451–452, 494
   Palestinians, popular movement   291
   Russia, October (Bolshevik) Revolution (1917)   188
   Turkey, Islamist counterrevolution *Irtica* ("Reaction") suppressed (1909)   463
   Turkey, social revolution   102

Reza Shah (LC: Reza Shah Pahlavi, Shah of Iran; *also* Reza Khan)   38, 268 (*sidebar*), 379–380, 410–411, 442–444

Roman à clef (fictionalized account of real events)   75

Roman Empire
   occupation of Judea   113–114, 118, 165
   warfare, intimidation, taxation, ruthlessness, alliances with local elites   166

"Rose" and "nightingale" as symbols in Iran   271 (*sidebar*)

Rothschild, Edmond, baron de   389 (*sidebar*)

"Row by Row" (Baki)   397–406

Ruba'iyat of Omar Khayyam (Omar Khayyam)   39, 127, 429–439

Rumi, Jalal al-Din Muhammad Balkhi (LC: Jalal al-Din Rumi, Maulana), *Spiritual Couplets, The*   39, 100, 348, 406, 505–514

Russia: works set in, "In the City of Slaughter" (Hayyim Nahman Bialik)   91, 197–207

Russia (also Soviet Union) (*entries in chronological order*)
   wave of pogroms (1881–1906)   199–202, 388
   October Revolution (1917)   188
   totalitarian bureaucracy, terror-ridden decades of Stalin's rule (1930s–1950s)   188
   invasion of Iran and Azerbaijan, withdrawal in 1946   408 (*sidebar*)

S

Sabbath observance   552

Sabra-Shatila massacres (1982)   87–88, 88 (*sidebar*), 89 (*sidebar*), 307

Sadat, Anwar (LC: al-Sadat, Anwar)   324, 495

Sadducees   113

Safavid Empire of Persia   254, 339 (*sidebar*)

Said, Ali Ahmad. *See* Adunis

Said, Edward W.   466

Saladin (LC: Salah al-Din Ibn Ayyub), Sultan of Egypt and Syria   58, 211 (*sidebar*), 213

Samarra, Iraq   356 (*illus.*)

Sargon   160

Sasanid dynasty (Persian) (226–651)   14, 19–20, 229, 368, 417, 484, 488

Satan
   in Islam, seen as tempter of man into sin   137
   in Persian cosmology   485
   as tempter of Jesus in Matthew's Gospel   169

Satire   455

Saudi Arabia: works set in, *Cities of Salt* (Abd al-Rahman Munif)   75–84

Saudi Arabia (*entries in chronological order*)
   Bedouins' small tribal groupings, ancient pagan religions, subsistence lifestyle   416
   Bedouins' martial ethos, warrior class, camels, horses   516
   role of Bedouins in initial Islamic expansion (700s)   249–250
   complex relationship of Bedouin and various princes   76
   conquests of Muhammad ibn Sa'ud (1744)   76
   extension of conquests by Sa'ud ibn Abd al-Aziz   76
   Saudi retreat to refuge in Kuwait (1889)   76
   reassertion of power by Abd al-Aziz ibn Sa'ud   76
   consolidation of control as Kingdom of Saudi Arabia (1925–1953)   77
   punishment and reward of Wahhabi Bedouin communities   77
   discovery of oil (1930)   75
   oil wealth, social change, and Saudi power   77–78
   founding of Dharan   78 (*sidebar*)

rule by successive Saudi princes, (1953–) 77, 79

workers' strike at Aramco and repression (1953) 75, 78–79

Western influence, recession, discontent (1960–1980) 82

uprising in Mecca by fundamentalists (1979) 83

urbanization and population shifts 84 (sidebar)

expulsion of Palestinians after Gulf War (1991) 289

(See also Islamic world)

Sa'ud ibn Abd al-Aziz (ruled c. 1911; grandson of Muhammad ibn Saud) 76

Savushun (A Persian Requiem) (Simin Danishvar) 441–449

Sayf al-Dawlah al-Hamdani, Ali ibn Abd Allah 369–370, 369 (sidebar), 373

Saz (lute-type musical instrument) 253 (sidebar)

Schools (madrasahs) 58

Schulz, Bruno 473–474

Scripture, religious texts and commentaries, holy works

Dead Sea Scrolls from Qumram 111–120, 546

echoes from Gilgamesh in Bible, Iliad, Odyssey, and Arabian Nights 2, 13–23, 161–162, 242, 242 (sidebar), 475–476, 553

extrabiblical and sectarian texts 114

flood narrative 157–159, 161–162, 547, 553

Gospel According to Matthew 165–175

hadiths (accounts of life of Muhammad as examples) 21, 259

Quran (Koran) 415–428

Talmud 535–544, 556

Torah 536, 545–557

of Zoroastrianism 483 (sidebar)

(See also Conference of the Birds; Mystical Poetry of Yunus Emre; Quran (Koran); Spiritual Couplets)

Secret Life of Saeed the Ill-fated Pessoptimist, The (Emile Habiby) 449–460

"Secret Shrine, The" and "The Frog Prayer" (Ömer Seyfettin) 461–469

Secular rationalism 2

See Under: Love (David Grossman) 471–479

Seljuk (also Seljuq) Turks 22, 48, 234, 235, 397–398, 430–431

Semitic languages 160

Sephardim ("Spanish" Jews) 306–307, 454 (sidebar)

Sermon on the Mount 169

Sexual dimension of life

debates on sexuality in Ottoman court 346 (sidebar)

gender blurring in Sufism 97

(See also Homosexuality)

Shahnamah, or Book of Kings (Abu al-Qasim Firdawsi) 233 (sidebar), 258, 406, 446, 481–491, 514

Shamanism of Oghuz 48–49

Sharon, Ariel 87, 88, 307

al-Shaykh, Hanan, Story of Zahra, The 71, 527–533

Shema as central prayer of Judaism 551, 552 (sidebar)

Shi'ah. See Shi'ites

Shibli (LC: al-Shibli, Abu Bakr) 320 (sidebar)

Shi'ites (Shi'ah) 14–15, 210, 222, 400 (sidebar)

Shi'ite-Sunni religious schism 94, 222, 258–259, 378, 400 (sidebar)

Shin Bet, Israeli General Security Services 454, 454 (sidebar)

Short stories: experimentation with

Egyptian realism 9

Jamalzadah and Hidayat in Iran 380–381

Seyfettin's combination of Turkish themes with Western realistic short-story method 461, 468

Taymur's focus on lower classes 1–2

Short stories and short-story collections

"Amm Mutwalli" and "Hagg Shalabi" (Mahmud Taymur) 1–11

Arabian Nights, The (Husain Haddawy, translator) 2, 13–23, 161, 242, 242 (sidebar), 475–476

Book of Dede Korkut, The 47–55

Book of Tahkemoni, The (Hebrew Maqamat) (Judah al-Harizi) 57–64

Maqamat (al-Hamadhani) 61, 257–266

Once Upon a Time (Muhammad Ali Jamalzadah) 44, 377–385

"Secret Shrine, The" and "The Frog Prayer" (Ömer Seyfettin) 461–469

Shu'ubiyah (9th-century movement, Persians seeking equality with Arabs) 132, 138, 356, 362

Silver, influx from New World and resulting inflation 338

Sinai Peninsula 213, 238, 301 (sidebar), 494

Sinai-Suez War (1956) 329–330, 453

"Sinning" and Other Poems (Furugh Farrukhzad) 267–274

Six-Day War (1967) 453, 454, 494–495, 497

Slavery

king's affection for slave boy in Conference of the Birds 96

Ottoman practice of levying tribute of Balkan teenage boys 398 (sidebar)

Ottoman slaves rising to education, army service, prominence 397, 398 (sidebar), 400

poet Necati as slave 397

in pre-Islamic Arabia 518

Zanj (East African slaves) in Iran 317

Slave trade

by Arabs 20 (sidebar), 398 (sidebar)

by Sudanese tribes 6

Social Darwinism, of Egyptian Nahdah 3

Socialism

Egypt 296, 297

Kibbutzim (collective farms in Israel) 499 (sidebar)

Labor Zionism 389

Socialism (continued)
United Arab Republic   291
Yaşr Kemal   275
"Sohrab and Rustum" (Matthew Arnold)   490, 490
(sidebar)
Soiree for the 5th of June   237, 243, 245, 246
Solomon   95–96
Solon (Greek poet)   182 (sidebar)
Songs of the Land of Zion, Jerusalem (Yehuda Amichai)
493–503
Soviet Union. See Russia
Spain (entries in chronological order)
Visigoth control, persecution of Jews (400–700)
143
Islamic conquests and rule (711–1492)   58
Almoravid victories over Christian Castilians
(1086–1091)   143, 177–178
Almohad invasion and hegemony (1146–1147)
58, 143
Christian "Reconquista" of Muslim areas,
expulsion of non-Christians, many to Ottoman
Empire (1492)   398
influx of silver from New World, currency
devaluation, high inflation across Europe   338
(See also al-Andalus)
Spiritual Couplets, The (Jalal al-Din Muhammad
Balkhi Rumi)   39, 100, 348, 406, 505–514
Spirituality. See Religion, spirituality, and folklore
"Stop and We Will Weep: The Mu'allaqah" (Imru al-
Qays)   426, 515–526
Story of Zahra, The (Hanan al-Shaykh)   71, 527–533
Sudan
Egyptian/Ottoman conquest   5–6
Mahdist Revolt   5–6
rule by Britain   6
slave trade   6
Suez Canal   3
Suffrage
for Egyptian women   5
to Iranian women, later revoked   269
Sufism
Adam's transgression as "cosmic descent" causing
need for purification of soul   507
affinity of Ruba'iyat   438
allegorical interpretation of the Quran   95–96,
99–100
Bektaşi order   349 (sidebar)
death, theories of   350–351, 512
dervishes (itinerant followers of Sufism)   96,
349 (sidebar), 402–403, 505
developmental influences and spread   123–124,
318–320
enlightenment by degrees   351 (sidebar)
ennobling power of love, intense relationship
between believer and God   248, 252–253,
350, 402, 506, 510
as explanation of metaphysical meaning of
universe   349–350
fermentation of wine as metaphor for union with
God   434 (sidebar), 510

free will, reason and choice to love God   350
God's presence saturating material world, need to
deny world and senses   252, 506, 512
Hafiz's relationship to   124
in Hayy ibn Yaqzan (Ibn Tufayl)   177–185
homoeroticism   136 (sidebar), 140, 402
inclusiveness and tolerant attitudes   349
intoxication as bridge to joy and spiritual union
with Divine   402, 403, 405
as intuitive revelation   123
language as inescapable and impediment   509,
511
love as metaphor for bond between believer and
God   248, 252–253, 350
manuals of conduct   318
Mevleviyeh order   507, 513
millenarianism   6, 8
mind's capacity to reason versus heart as
dwelling place of soul   352
mystical use of history   98–99
need for guiding master or shaykh   507, 508
(sidebar)
orders, lodges, monasteries centering on guiding
shaykh   348–349, 507
orthodox clergy's fear of being undermined by
individual worship   512, 513 (sidebar)
pilgrimages   94–95
quest for higher states of consciousness, oneness
with God   509
relationship to orthodox Islam   349
reliance on individual experience of God, versus
orthodox emphasis on laws and leaders   507,
510
rising esteem and monetary endowments   506
rituals and ritual group dances   349, 506
in Seljuk Anatolia   348
seven stages toward enlightenment   95 (sidebar)
in Sudan   5–6
suf as coarse woolen robe of early, pious ascetics
506
symbology of moon, pearl   253
synonymous with tolerance   506
union with God, mysticism, penance, and
poverty   93, 95
(See also Conference of the Birds; Islam; Mystical
Poetry of Yunus Emre; Spiritual Couplets)
Suicide, of Hidayat   37, 45
Süleyman the Great, Süleyman the Magnificent (LC:
Süleyman I, Sultan of the Turks), 241, 323
(sidebar)   254, 399–400
"Sultan" (one who wields power)   316
Sumer   154, 160
Sumerian language   154 (sidebar)
Sunni-Shi'ite religious schism   94, 222, 258–259,
378, 400 (sidebar)
Syria (entries in chronological order)
synagogue dispute in Antioch at writing of
Matthew's gospel (c. 70 C.E.)   173–174
Mu'awiyah and Umayyad dynasty ruling Iran, Iraq,
and Syria (661–749)   15, 210, 221–222, 258

Hamdanid state in north (944)   *369*

influx of Palestinians refugees (1948–1949)
451–452, 494

creation and dissolution of United Arab Republic
(pan-Arab alliance with Egypt) (1956–1961)
287, 291, 292

loss of Golan Heights to Israel (1967)   *238, 494*

Assad and Alawites to power, boom times and
rich/poor gap (1970s)   *238–239*

involvement in Lebanon's civil war (1970s)
238

internal attacks on Assad regime, crushed
uprisings (1970s, 1982)   *239*

(*See also* Islamic world)

T

"*Taifa*" (kingdoms, miniature states of al-Andalus)
142, 178

Talmud, The   *535–544, 556*

Ta'mari, Salah   *458 (sidebar)*

Tamerlane. *See* Timur

Taq-i Bustan ("Arch of the Grove"), Iran   *234*

Taurus Mountains, Turkey   *276, 277 (sidebar)*

Taymur, Mahmud, "Amm Mutwalli" and "Hagg
Shalabi"   *1–11*

Tel Aviv, Israel   *331, 394 (sidebar)*

Television, flooding Arab culture with Western
influences   *268–269*

Ten Commandments   *551*

Theophilos, Emperor of Constantinople   *356–357*

"Those Tulip-Cheeked Ones" (Necati)   *397–406*

Timur   *123, 398*

Torah, The   *536, 545–557*

Trade and traders
camels   *516, 554*
caravans taking routes around frequent wars
417
Muhammad as caravan merchant   *415*

Translation issues
American and European 19th and 20th century
works into Persian   *273*
Arabian Nights into French and English   *13*
Christian Bible into Arabic   *66*
Gilgamesh from Akkadian to Persian to European
languages   *154 (sidebar), 162*
great works in Arabic into Latin for Christians
58
Ibn Sina's (Avicenna's) works into Latin and
other European languages   *180 (sidebar), 185*
"In the City of Slaughter" from Hebrew into
Russian and Yiddish   *205*
Kalilah and Dimnah from Sanskrit to multiple
languages   *221, 228*
Leyla and Mejnun from Arabic to multiple
languages   *253–254*
Ruba'iyat of Omar Khayyam into landmark
English version   *435–437, 436 (sidebar)*
sensitivity to original *Arabian Nights*   *23*
(*See also* Linguistic considerations)

Transportation, camels   *516, 554*

Trumpeldor, Joseph   *335, 501 (sidebar)*

Tugrul Bey (LC: Tugrul, Sultan of the Seljuks)
430

Turcoman Turks   *48*

Turkey (*entries in chronological order*)
Hittite invasions (c. 3000 B.C.E.)   *278*
seminomadic peoples overcoming Byzantines
(1000s)   *467 (sidebar)*
Oghuz/Seljuks in Anatolia, rich vibrant
civilization, sultanate of Rum (c. 1038–1157)
347–348, 397–398
Sufis as shamans, Seljuks converting to Sufism
348
popular rebellions (1230–1240)   *348*
Mongol invasion (1243)   *348*
Osman and successor Ottomans assuming
control (1258–1324)   *348, 467 (sidebar)*
debates on sexuality in Ottoman court   *346
(sidebar)*
Ottoman Turkish conquests, unchanging
institutions (beginning c. 1300)   *22, 212, 398,
405, 467 (sidebar)*
Ottoman slaves rising to education, army service,
prominence   *397, 398 (sidebar), 400*
conquest of Constantinople, renamed Istanbul by
Mehmed II (1453)   *339 (sidebar), 398, 467*
Ottoman society as urban entertainment culture
401–402
Young Turks' reinstatement of Constitution,
elections (1908)   *462*
crisis of culture, Islamists versus Westernizers (c.
1910)   *462*
suppression of Islamist counterrevolution *Irtica*
("Reaction") (1909)   *463*
Ottoman Empire enduring until defeat in WWI
398, 405, 467 (sidebar)
nationalism and emerging republic (1920s)   *54*
WWI Allies' breakup of Ottoman Empire into
five mandates (1920)   *189, 213*
anti-imperialist War of Independence
(1919–1923)   *102, 189, 276–277, 344, 462,
467 (sidebar)*
modernization, Kemal Atatürk (1919–1923)
102, 189, 276–277, 344, 462, 467 (sidebar)
war against Greeks and Allies (1919–1922)   *278*
abolition of sultanate (1923)   *467 (sidebar)*
isolated village life untouched by reforms   *276*
outlawing of fez and veil (1925)   *277*
secular government, repeal of Islamic Holy Law
(1926)   *277*
Turkish alphabet, Roman script instead of Arabic
277
distrust of secular government and reforms
(1930s)   *283*
land reform, *aghas*, and brigandage (1930s)
278–279
presidency of Ismet Inönü (1938)   *102, 104*
pragmatic foreign policy during WWII
(1941–1945)   *190*

Turkey (*entries in chronological order*) (continued)
  development of political parties, public education
    (1950s)   *283*
  Menderes presidency (1950–1960)   *102, 103,
    104, 283*
  pro-Western regime, capitalism and adverse
    effects, repression (1950s)   *102–103, 104, 190*
  mechanized agriculture and urbanization of farm
    laborers (1950s)   *283*
  use of wealthy business class   *103–104*
  Demirel prime ministries, repression,
    industrialization, unrest (1965–1993)   *104–105*
  military coup, new constitution, and repression
    (1967)   *104*
  another military coup, violence, repression
    (1971)   *105*
  Ecevit prime ministry (1973)   *105*
  invasion of Cyprus (1974)   *105*
  terrorism by fascist Grey Wolves, economic
    restrictions (1978)   *105*
  resumption of military control (1980)   *105*
  secularism, Western cultural influence,
    occidentalist foreign policy, politicized Islam
    (1990s)   *345*
  influx of refugees from Iraq and Bosnia (1990s)
    345
  (*See also* Islamic world)
Turkey/Anatolia: works set in
  Book of Dede Korkut, The   *47–55*
  Curfew (Adalet Agaoglu)   *101–110*
  Human Landscapes from My Country (Nazim
    Hikmet)   *187–195*
  Memed, My Hawk (Yaşr Kemal)   *54, 275–284*
  My Name Is Red (Orhan Pamuk)   *337–346*
  Mystical Poetry of Yunus Emre, The (Yunus
    Emre)   *347–353*
  Ottoman Lyric Poetry: "Those Tulip-Cheeked
    Ones" and "Row by Row" (Necati and Baki)
    397–406
  "Secret Shrine, The" and "The Frog Prayer"
    (Ömer Seyfettin)   *461–469*
Turkmenistan   *48*

U

Ubayd, Isa   *10*
Umar ibn al-Khattab, Caliph (second caliph after
  Muhammad)   *210, 368*
Umayyad caliphate (661–750)   *15, 489*
United Arab Republic (UAR, pan-Arab alliance of
  Syria and Egypt) (1956–1961)   *287, 291, 292,
  297–298*
United States
  CIA-backed coup in Iran restores shah
    (1951–1953)   *268, 268 (sidebar), 408, 409, 444*
  interest in Cold War, Iran, and oil (1948–1987)
    409
  Iranian reforms under pressure, riots against
    shah's dictatorship (1960–1963)   *268
    (sidebar), 269–273*

as new "invader" of Iran (1953)   *444*
WWI Allies' breakup of Ottoman Empire into
  five mandates (1923)   *213*
Urbanization
  founding of Tel Aviv (1909)   *391*
  industrialization Egypt of 1960s   *298*
  in Iran of 1950s and 1960s   *409 (sidebar)*
  population shifts in Saudi Arabia   *84 (sidebar)*
  of Turkish farm laborers   *283*
Uruk (biblical Erech) in ancient Mesopotamia
  155, 156 (illus.)
Uthman ibn Affan, Caliph (third caliph after
  Muhammad)   *210, 221*
Uzbekistan   *48*

V

Veiling, with *chador* (body veil)   *269, 277, 411
  (sidebar), 443*
Verne, Jules   *333 (sidebar)*
Viaud, Julien (pen name Pierre Loti)   *464 (sidebar)*
Vienna, Austria   *25–26*
Visigoths   *143*
Viticulture   *133 (sidebar)*
"*Vizier*" (minister)   *14, 236*

W

Wahhabism (*Wahhabiyah*)   *76*
Wannus, Sa'dallah (LC: Wannus, Sa'd Allah), *King Is
  the King, The*   *237–246*
War of al-Basus   *516–518, 517 (sidebar), 521, 523*
Warfare
  Abbasid caliphate's reliance on Turkish slave
    army   *22*
  ballistas   *357*
  battle horses   *233 (sidebar), 516, 520*
  blood vengeance and sacrifice   *372–373, 373
    (sidebar)*
  decommissioned soldiers and mercenaries
    turning to brigandage   *278*
  mental cost of   *334 (sidebar)*
  Ottoman Janissary Corps   *347, 398 (sidebar)*
  Ottoman slaves rising to army service and
    prominence   *397, 398 (sidebar), 400*
  Palestinian strategy of popular uprising   *454*
  women active as participants in military units
    531–533
  (*See also* Arab-Israeli wars, works related to)
Weizmann, Chaim   *306, 450*
Westernization
  culture clashes, pull of tradition versus lure of
    Western new   *343*
  in Iran   *269, 379, 408*
  opposition in Turkey   *102, 278, 345, 462*
  in Saudi Arabia   *77–78*
  (*See also* Culture clashes)
"Westitis" or "Westoxication"   *268*
Wine drinking   *49, 53–54, 133 (sidebar), 134–136,
  401, 433, 435*

Wine poems   *134–136, 265*
"Wogs" (Western-oriented gentlemen)   *382 (sidebar)*
Women, literary works concerning
    "Amm Mutwalli" and "Hagg Shalabi" (Mahmud
      Taymur)   *1–11*
    Arabian Nights, The (Husain Haddawy, translator)
      2, 13–23, 161, 242, 242 (sidebar), 475–476
    Broken Wings, The (Kahlil Gibran)   *65–73*
    "Clockwork Doll, The" and Other Poems (Dalia
      Ravikovitch)   *85–91*
    Curfew (Adalet Agaoglu)   *101–110*
    "Mechanical Doll" and Other Poems (Furugh
      Farrukhzad)   *267–274*
    My Michael (Amos Oz)   *327–336*
    Savushun (A Persian Requiem) (Simin Danishvar)
      441–449
    Story of Zahra, The (Hanan al-Shaykh)   *71,
      527–533*
Women in relation to society, politics, and men
    in Abbasid times   *21*
    belief in ritual impurity   *488*
    in Deuteronomy   *552*
    in Egypt of 1960s   *297, 298, 302*
    famous Sufi, Rabi'ah (LC: Rabi'ah al-Adawiyah)
      319
    inferiority in Mediterranean Basin cultures   *19*
    "invisibility" in Ottoman Empire   *406 (sidebar)*
    Iran   *269, 272, 411 (sidebar), 443–444, 445, 446*
    in Israel   *85–86, 90*
    Lebanese   *68–69, 70–71, 529, 531 (sidebar)*
    medieval Islamic societies   *97 (sidebar)*
    Oghuz   *49, 53–54*
    in Ottoman Empire of 16th century   *339–340*
    as participants in military units   *531–533*
    in pre-Islamic Arabia   *518*
    purdah as Sasanian tradition incorporated into
      Islam   *488*
    Quran's ambiguous statements on equality of
      women   *21*
    in *Shahnamah's* view of women   *487*
    in *The Arabian Nights*   *19–21*
    Turkish   *107–108*
    (*See also* Divorce; Marriage; Sexual dimension of
      life)
Women's employment issues, in Israel   *90*
Women's rights movement (and feminism)
    Egyptian of 1950s–1970s   *298*
    Egyptian of early 1900s   *4–5*
    Iran of 1930s   *443–444*
    in Israel   *90*
    in modern Turkey   *103 (sidebar)*
World War I
    Allies' breakup of Ottoman Empire into five
      mandates   *213*
    British negotiations with Arab peninsular leaders
      77

causes in Great Power rivalries   *188*
    postwar treaties changing maps of Europe and
      Middle East   *188*
World War II
    Allied victory, long-lasting economic troubles,
      anti-imperialism   *190*
    Germans in Crete   *307*
    occupation of Iran by Britain and Soviet Union
      441–442

X

Xerxes I, King of Persia   *484*

Y

Yaşar Kemal, *Memed, My Hawk*   *54, 275–284*
Yehoshua, A. B., *Mr. Mani*   *305–314*
Yemeni Civil War   *298*
Yiddish language   *205, 391*
Yishuv   *309, 394 (sidebar), 395, 474 (sidebar)*
Yohanan ben Zakkai   *537*
Yom Kippur War (October War)   *453, 473, 493,
    495–496, 496 (illus.)*
Young Turks (popular name for Committee of
    Union and Progress)   *462*
Yunus Emre, Mystical Poetry of Yunus Emre, The
    347–353

Z

Zanj (East African slaves)   *317*
Zarathustra. *See* Zoroaster and Zoroastrianism
Zionism
    as ancient yearning and modern secular
      movement   *388*
    Arab opposition, British waffling   *308, 395,
      450–451, 494*
    Congresses, purposes, and Herzl   *199,
      308–309, 474 (sidebar)*
    disdain for diaspora Jews   *472, 473 (sidebar)*
    as major political force by World War I   *494*
    opposition from Orthodox Judaism   *391–392,
      395*
    as response to Russian pogroms   *199*
    split into factions   *396, 494*
    support from Britain, Balfour Declaration   *308,
      450, 494*
    supporting immigration of diaspora Jews into
      Palestine   *450*
    transformation from liberal nationalism into
      militant vision of control   *496*
Zoroaster and Zoroastrianism   *14, 132, 482 (illus.),
    483 (sidebar), 484*
Zurayq, Qustantin   *290*